r. Salomon Fritz Forkel
ד״ר שלמה פריץ פורקל

קינות מסורת הרב • נוסח אשכנז

The Koren Mesorat HaRav Kinot • Nusaḥ Ashkenaz

קינות מסורת הרב
THE KOREN MESORAT HARAV KINOT
THE LOOKSTEIN EDITION
TEFILLA FOR TISHA B'AV · KINOT · EIKHA

WITH COMMENTARY ON THE KINOT
BASED UPON THE TEACHINGS OF

Rabbi Joseph B. Soloveitchik

EDITED BY SIMON POSNER
TRANSLATION OF THE KINOT BY TZVI HERSH WEINREB

Commentary based on Jacob J. Schacter's compilation and redaction
of transcripts of the Rav's Tisha B'Av learning sessions

•

OU PRESS
KOREN PUBLISHERS JERUSALEM

The Koren Mesorat HaRav Kinot
Second Hebrew/English Edition, 2011

Koren Publishers Jerusalem Ltd.
POB 4044, Jerusalem 91040, ISRAEL
POB 8531, New Milford, CT 06776, USA
POB 2455, London W1A 6YW, ENGLAND

www.korenpub.com

OU PRESS, an imprint of the Orthodox Union (hereafter "OU")
11 Broadway, New York, NY 10004
www.oupress.org

Considerable research and expense have gone into the creation of this publication. Unauthorized copying may be considered *geneiva, hasagat gevul*, and breach of copyright law. No part of this publication (content or design, including use of the Koren fonts) may be reproduced, stored in a retrieval system or transmitted in any form or by any means electronic, mechanical, photocopying or otherwise, without the prior written permission of the publisher, except in the case of brief quotations embedded in critical articles or reviews.

Hebrew Texts
Eikha text © Koren Publishers Jerusalem Ltd. ("Koren"), 1962, 2010
Siddur text © Koren, 1981, 2010
Kinot text © Koren, 2010, with these exceptions:
　　Hebrew text of "Elegy on the Ḥurban" © Rabbi Shimon Schwab (date unknown)
　　Used with the kind permission of the Schwab family
　　Hebrew text of "Kina in Memory of the Martyrs of the European Ḥurban"
　　© Rabbi Shlomo Halberstam (date unknown)
　　Hebrew text of "Eli, Eli" ("Lament, Lament") © Y.L. Bialer (date unknown)
　　Hebrew text of "Kina in Memory of Our Six Million Martyrs Who Perished during 1939–1945"
　　© Rabbi Abraham Rosenfeld, 1965. Text used with permission of Davka Corporation

English Translations
English translation of Eikha by Harold Fisch © Koren, 1962, 2010
English Siddur translation © Jonathan Sacks, 2006, 2010
English translation of Kinot by Rabbi Tzvi Hersh Weinreb © OU, 2010, except:
　　English translation of "Elegy on the Ḥurban" by Rabbi Shimon Schwab is the translation traditionally
　　used by K'hal Adath Jeshurun, New York City
　　English translation of "Kina in Memory of the Martyrs of the European Ḥurban" by Rabbi Shlomo
　　Halberstam, by Naomi Kahn © OU, 2010
　　English translation of "Eli, Eli" ("Lament, Lament") by Y.L. Bialer, by Naomi Kahn © OU, 2010
　　English translation of "Kina in Memory of Our Six Million Martyrs Who Perished during 1939–1945"
　　by Rabbi Abraham Rosenfeld, by B. Shalom © Koren 2010

Commentaries & Digests
The Commentary of Rabbi Joseph B. Soloveitchik was edited by Rabbi Simon Posner © OU
The Digest of Tisha B'Av Laws was compiled by Rabbi Gil Student © OU
The Reshimot of Rabbi Joseph B. Soloveitchik were edited by Rabbi Menachem Genack © OU

Fonts
Koren Tanakh Font © Koren Publishers Jerusalem Ltd. 1962, 2010
Koren Siddur Font and text design, © Koren Publishers Jerusalem Ltd. 1981, 2010

The Publisher has sought to acquire permissions where available; in some cases, the copyright owners have not been found. We will be pleased to correct such information in future editions.

Standard Size, Hardcover, ISBN 978 965 301 249 3

Printed in Israel

In Dedication to
RABBI HASKEL LOOKSTEIN

כָּל הַמִּתְאַבֵּל עַל יְרוּשָׁלַיִם
זוֹכֶה וְרוֹאֶה בְּשִׂמְחָתָהּ

תענית ל:

*All who mourn the destruction of Jerusalem
will yet celebrate its joy.*

Ta'anit, 30b

For fifty years, as the lights dim at the onset of the 9th of Av, Rabbi Haskel Lookstein has invoked this Talmudic promise to his community at Congregation Kehilath Jeshurun.

And for fifty years Rabbi Lookstein has guided us on the path toward this future joy. He epitomizes the responsibility of every Jew in the rebuilding of Jerusalem through his commitment to *Ahavat Yisrael*, the love of all Jews. He has taught us that if any Jew in the world is in need, spiritual or material, it is the task of each of us to extend our hand.

Rabbi Lookstein is a beloved and loyal student of the Rav and a passionate believer in the central significance of Tisha B'Av. We are grateful for the opportunity to recognize his unflagging leadership, at home and around the world, on behalf of the Jewish people.

With love and respect,
The Kehilath Jeshurun Community

Anita and Jordan Abowitz
Diane and Hon. Robert Abrams
Dr. Nicole Schreiber and Raanan Agus
Jonathan Art
Marisa and Michael Bevilacqua
Deborah and Richard Born
Elana and Aryeh Bourkoff
Lauren and Keith Breslauer
Norma and Dr. Howard Bruckner
Doina and Dr. Larry Bryskin
Sherry and Neil Cohen
Rachel and Barry Cooper

Vivian and Lawrence Creizman
Sharon Dane
The Davenport Family
Rita and Fred Distenfeld
Suzanne and Jacob Doft
Shlomit and Chaim Edelstein
Suzanne and Samuel Eisenstat
Miriam and Eric Feldstein
Florence and Dr. Philip Felig
Anne and Natalio Fridman
Helen and Sidney Friedman
Ronalee and Russell Galbut

Jane and Ishaia Gol
Hadassah, Samuel and Ori Goldring
Dr. Tamar and Eric Goldstein
Rebecca and Laurence Grafstein
Judith and Dr. Martin Grumet
Gilda Guttman
Esther and Alan Haddad
Dr. Fanya Gottesfeld Heller
Hedwig and Dr. Joseph Heller
Ronnie Heyman
Mildred Hostyk
Wendy and Sidney Ingber
Judith and Dr. Hirshel Kahn
Dr. Jennifer and Michael Kaplan
Dr. Karin and Joel Katz
Judith and Gerald S. Kaufman
Carol and Jeffrey Kaufman
Ruth and Dr. Gerald Kestenbaum
Dr. Barbara Braffman and
   Benjamin Klapper
The Kobrin Family
Bertha and Dr. Henry Kressel
Wilma and Stephen Kule
Seryl and Charles Kushner
Sheila Levine
Jean and Armand Lindenbaum
Leora and Richard Linhart
Janice and Saul Linzer
Judy and David S. Lobel
Hannah and Edward Low
Jay Lunzer
Rochelle and Eugene Major
Dr. Vivian, David and Ian Mark
Caroline and Morris Massel
Paula & Dr. David Menche, Alexa,
   and Julia; and Livia, Elias,
   and Ezra Marcovici –
   In memory of Moshe Pniewski
Sheera and Michael Moffson

Jessica and Jason Muss
Helen Nash
Judith and Joseph Packin
Elisa and Alan Pines
Lauren and Mitchell Presser
The Propp Family
Amory Propp
Gabrielle Propp
Diana and Ira Riklis
Susan and Irwin Robins
Pamela and George Rohr
Marian and William Rosner
Susan and Martin Sanders
Sheira and Steven Schacter
Lynn and Wolf Scheck
Dr. Arlene Steinberg and Dr.
   Michael Schulder
Janie and Dr. Robert Schwalbe
Debbie and Daniel Schwartz
Erica and Robert Schwartz
Ruth and Irwin Shapiro
Judith and Isaac Sherman
Deena and Adam Shiff
Lisa and Lee Snow
Dr. Phyllis and Mark Speiser
Lili Stawski
Dr. Meg Rosenblatt and David Stein
Melvin Stein
Surie and Robert Sugarman
Randi and David Sultan
Judith Tanz
Adele and Ronald Tauber
Frances Trainin
Phyllis and Jonathan Wagner
Diane Wassner
Judith and Dr. Philip Wilner
Barbara Zimet
Gail Suchman and Jerald Zimmerman

In Loving Memory of Our Parents

Joseph and Gwendolyn Straus

יוסף שמואל בן בנימין
גינדל בת משה יעקב

Dedicated by
Moshael and Zahava Straus
Daniel and Joyce Straus

⇁⇀

In Honor of the Bar Mitzva of Our Grandson

Andrew Jeremy Katz

יצחק צבי כ״ץ

March 13, 2010
שבת פרשת ויקהל-פקודי תש״ע

Dedicated by
Mordecai D. and Dr. Monique C. Katz

⇁⇀

In Tribute to

Rabbi J.J. Schacter, Rabbi Ari Berman and Rabbi Yossie Levine

who have continued in the Rav's *derekh* with the full-time study on Tisha B'Av of the insights and gleanings of the Rav on the *Kinot*.

Dedicated by
Jonah and Fran Kupietzky

In Loving Memory of Our Sister

Adina Fishel

עדינה בת חיים

Dedicated by
David and Cookie Fishel

In Loving Memory of Our Dear Mother

Ruth Skydell

רחל לאה בת ר' חיים צבי

Devoted daughter of the legendary
Harry & Etta Herskowitz

She was a role model of generosity and integrity who, together with our dear father, Rabbi Adrian Skydell, שליט״א, perpetuated a legacy of devotion to Torah study as well as a profound and abiding concern for the welfare of others through their innumerable acts of *tzedaka vaḥesed*. May her deeds be an inspiration to us all.

Dedicated by
Myron and Laurie Goldberg and family
Bernard Skydell and family
Harry and Rachel Skydell and family

In Loving Memory of Our Father

Manfred Raphael Lehmann
משה רפאל בן החבר חיים ופייגה

An *Ish Eshkolot* who inspired us with his absolute faith in God, and in *hashgaḥa pratit* as revealed in history. In all that he did, he dedicated himself to the people of Israel.

And in Loving Memory of
His Beloved Son, Our Brother

James Harald Lehmann
חיים מנחם בן מנשה רפאל ושרה

An *Ish Eshkolot* – a loving, joyful, gentle, brilliant soul. The legacy of our father was enriched by the soul of his beloved son.

Dedicated by
Yitzchok and Barbie Lehmann Siegel and family

⊱⊰

In Loving Memory of Our Parents

Jack and Rochel Bodner
יעקב בן אלחנן
שרה רחל בת צבי

Joseph and Mary Keilson
יוסף בן אברהם שמריהו
מרים בת יוסף

Dedicated by
Lloyd and Harriet Keilson

In Loving Memory of Our Husband and Father

Rabbi Yitzchok Singer
הרב יצחק אהרן בן הרב אליהו

Rabbi of the Bialystoker Synagogue and a renowned תלמיד חכם

In Loving Memory of Our Brother-in-Law and Uncle

Rabbi Dovid Singer
הרב דוד בן הרב אליהו

Rabbi of First Congregation Anshe Sfard
and a scholar of great erudition

Dedicated by
Rebbetzin Bluma Singer
Baruch and Susan Singer   Eli and Rivki Singer
Nussie and Ruchy Singer   Yossi and Suri Singer   Sruly and Leah Singer

―――

In Loving Memory of Our Wife, Mother,
Grandmother, Great-Grandmother

Hadassah Friedman
אטל הדסה בת ר' הלל

She is missed by the family that is her legacy

Dedicated by
Nasan Friedman
Charles and Rachie Moche
Ilana, Gadi, Moshe and Hadassa Chesner   Avi and Jordana Moche
Eleora, Benjy, Raziel, Hadassa and Aderet Epstein
Uri, Tamar and Victor Moche
Shira Friedman (Avigzer)
Esther, Yotam, Naomi, Rina, Hillel and Yair Ehrlich
Meir, Limor, Eliad, Yishai and Inbal Avigzer
Itzik, Efrat, Amitai, Noa and Yonatan Avigzer   Naava Avigzer

CONTENTS

מפתח ענײנים לשורות הראשונות של הקינות	xii	Index of First Lines of Kinot
מבוא	xv	Preface
הקדמת המתרגם	xxii	Translator's Preface
הקדמה	xxiii	Foreword
מבוא המוציא לאור	xxvi	Publisher's Preface
נזכרים בשיעורו של הרב על תשעה באב	xxviii	Recollection of a Tisha B'Av Shiur Given by the Rav
פתיחה	xxxiii	Introduction
מעריב	1	Ma'ariv
מגילת איכה	33	Megillat Eikha
קינות לערב	49	Kinot for the Night
שחרית	73	Shaḥarit
קינות ליום	193	Kinot and Commentary for the Day
קינות על קדושי השואה	621	Kinot in Commemoration of the Holocaust
מנחה	651	Minḥa
מעריב למוצאי תשעה באב	709	Ma'ariv for Motza'ei Tisha B'Av
רשימות	755	Reshimot
הלכות	783	Halakha Guide

ALPHABETICAL INDEX OF KINOT

אַאַדֶּה עַד חוּג שָׁמַיִם	237
אֲבָל אֲעוֹרֵר	533
אׇהֳלִי אֲשֶׁר תָּאַבְתָּ עַד לֹא בְרֵאשִׁית, עִם כִּסֵּא כָבוֹד לְצָרְפוֹ	301
אָז בַּהֲלךְ יִרְמְיָהוּ אֶל קִבְרֵי אָבוֹת	469
אָז בִּמְלֹאת סֵפֶק, יָפָה כְּתִרְצָה	479
אֵי כֹּה אָמַר, כֹּרֵת לְאָב בְּפֶצַע	315
אֵיכָה אַצְתָּ בְּאַפְּךָ, לְאַבֵּד בְּיַד אֲדוֹמִים אֱמוּנֶיךָ	217
אֵיכָה אַשְׁפַּתּוֹ פָּתוּחַ כְּקֶבֶר	347
אֵיכָה אֵת אֲשֶׁר כְּבָר עָשׂוּהוּ	329
אֵיכָה יָשְׁבָה חֲבַצֶּלֶת הַשָּׁרוֹן	269
אֵיכָה תִּפְאַרְתִּי מֵרָאשׁוֹתַי הִשְׁלִיכוּ	255
אֵיכָה תִּפְאַרְתֵּנוּ מֵרָאשֵׁינוּ הֻשְׁלָכֶת	635
אֵיךְ מִפִּי בֵן וּבַת	55
אֵיךְ תְּנַחֲמוּנִי הֶבֶל	489
אֵלִי, אֵלִי, נַפְשִׁי, בְכִי	629
אֱלִי צִיּוֹן וְעָרֶיהָ	611
אִם תֹּאכַלְנָה נָשִׁים פִּרְיָם, עֹלְלֵי טִפֻּחִים	375
אָמַרְתִּי שְׁעוּ מֶנִּי, בַּבְּכִי אֲמָרֵר	497
אֶצְבְּעוֹתַי שָׁפְלוּ	525
אַרְזֵי הַלְּבָנוֹן, אַדִּירֵי הַתּוֹרָה	415
אֵשׁ תּוּקַד בְּקִרְבִּי	515
בְּלֵיל זֶה יִבְכָּיוּן וְיֵילִילוּ בָנַי	57
הַזּוֹכֵר מַזְכִּירָיו	621
הֶחֱרִישׁוּ מִמֶּנִּי וַאֲדַבֵּרָה, וְיַעֲבׇר עָלַי מָה	425
הַטֵּה אֱלֹהַי אׇזְנְךָ, לִתְפִלַּת מְנֹאֶצֶת, מִי לִי בַשָּׁמַיִם	407
וְאֶת נָוִי, חָטָאתִי הַשְׁמִימָה	439

383	וְאַתָּה אָמַרְתָּ, הֵיטֵב אֵיטִיב עִמָּךְ
289	וַיְקוֹנֵן יִרְמְיָהוּ עַל־יֹאשִׁיָּהוּ
361	זְכֹר אֵת אֲשֶׁר עָשָׂה צַר בִּפְנִים
51	זְכֹר יהוה מֶה־הָיָה לָנוּ
627	זִכְרוּ נָא וְקוֹנְנוּ כָּל יִשְׂרָאֵל
541	יוֹם אַכְפִּי הִכְבַּדְתִּי, וַיִּכְפְּלוּ עֲוֹנִי
393	לְךָ יהוה הַצְּדָקָה, בְּאוֹתוֹת אֲשֶׁר הִפְלֵאתָ, מֵאָז וְעַד עַתָּה
455	מִי יִתֵּן רֹאשִׁי מַיִם, וְעֵינִי מְקוֹר נוֹזְלִי
509	מְעוֹנֵי שָׁמַיִם, שְׁחָקִים יְזַבְּלוּךְ
61	עַד אָנָה בְּכִיָּה בְצִיּוֹן, וּמִסְפֵּד בִּירוּשָׁלַיִם
447	עַל־אֵלֶּה אֲנִי בוֹכִיָּה, עֵינִי עֵינִי יֹרְדָה מַּיִם
603	צִיּוֹן בְּמִשְׁפָּט לְכִי לָךְ עַם מְעוֹנֵךְ
607	צִיּוֹן, גְּבֶרֶת לְמַמְלָכוֹת מִצְרָיִךְ
555	צִיּוֹן, הֲלֹא תִשְׁאֲלִי לִשְׁלוֹם אֲסִירָיִךְ
587	צִיּוֹן, יְדִידוּת יְדִיד צָעִיר לִשְׂרִיד
577	צִיּוֹן עֲטֶרֶת צְבִי, שִׂמְחַת הֲמוֹנֵךְ
599	צִיּוֹן צְפִירַת פְּאֵר, חֶדְוַת אֲגוּדַיִךְ
571	צִיּוֹן, קְחִי כָּל צֳרִי גִּלְעָד לִיצִירָיִךְ
583	צִיּוֹן תְּקוֹנְנִי עֲלֵי בֵיתֵךְ אֲשֶׁר נִשְׂרָף
591	שַׁאֲלִי, שְׂרוּפָה בָאֵשׁ, לִשְׁלוֹם אֲבֵלָיִךְ
195	שַׁבָּת, סוּרוּ מֶנִּי שִׁמְעוּנִי עוֹכְרִי
59	שׁוֹמְרוֹן קוֹל תִּתֵּן, מְצָאוּנִי עֲווֹנִי
617	שׁוֹמְרוֹן קוֹל תִּתֵּן, מְצָאוּנִי עֲווֹנִי
549	שִׁכֹּרַת וְלֹא מִיַּיִן, הַשְׁלִיכִי תֻפֵּךְ

PREFACE

The *Koren Mesorat HaRav Kinot* consists of a compilation of insights and commentary on the Tisha B'Av *kinot* by Rabbi Joseph B. Soloveitchik, *zt"l*, the towering rabbinic thinker of the twentieth century. For "the Rav," as Rabbi Soloveitchik was known, Tisha B'Av was the occasion for an emotional, religious, and intellectual experience, and it was his practice for many years to spend virtually the entire day in the synagogue engrossed in the recitation and study of the *kinot*. After the conclusion of Shaḥarit, the Rav would commence the reading of *kinot*, which would occupy the better part of the day. While reciting the *kinot*, the Rav would pause often to explain and comment, sometimes briefly and sometimes more extensively. As one might expect, there was an element of repetition in the Rav's comments from one year to the next, but he often presented new interpretations or varied his prior interpretations. The commentary on *kinot* contained in this edition is based upon a composite transcript prepared by Rabbi Jacob J. Schacter of audio tapes of the Rav's Tisha B'Av learning sessions from the years 1970, 1973–1980, and 1982–1984. In his introduction to the Rav's *The Lord Is Righteous in All His Ways: Reflections on the Tish'ah be-Av Kinot* (KTAV Publishing House, 2006), which Rabbi Schacter edited and which is part of the Toras HoRav Foundation's MeOtzar HoRav Series, he describes the challenges he encountered in analyzing the tapes and preparing the transcript. The tapes for the years 1971–1972 and 1981 could not be found. As for the extant tapes, none of which was professionally prepared, the sound was often unclear and there were often gaps due to late arrival or early departure by the person making the tape, or other interruptions in the taping process. Nonetheless, it is clear that Rabbi Schacter did a masterful job in preparing the composite transcript, editing it to eliminate the repetitions from year to year while retaining the Rav's authentic "voice." The transcript surely represents an accurate rendition of the Rav's Tisha B'Av learning sessions over the years.

In addition to the commentary on the *kinot*, this edition includes a section of *Reshimot*, reconstructions of *shiurim* the Rav gave on other matters related to Tisha B'Av, prepared under the supervision of Rabbi Menachem Genack. Also included is a section of Halakhot, a digest of

laws and practices applicable to Tisha B'Av. This section is not meant to be an exhaustive treatment or a scholarly analysis, but rather a useful reference guide for the most common issues that arise on Tisha B'Av.

The commentary of *kinot* that the reader will find in this volume is not a verbatim rendering of Rabbi Schacter's composite transcript of the Rav's Tisha B'Av learning sessions. To have included the entire transcript would have resulted in a volume (or set of volumes) of such size that it would not be practical for use in the synagogue during the Tisha B'Av service. The goal of the OU Press was to offer a Tisha B'Av volume to the Jewish community that would contain the entire Tisha B'Av service and would be convenient for practical use, not a research tool for reference purposes only. In addition, the transcript of tapes represents the Rav's oral delivery, and the spoken word is different from the written word. The speaker will often repeat for purposes of emphasis, to attract the audience's attention and make sure they understand; or perhaps for purposes of clarity, as the speaker, in the course of impromptu delivery, searches for the perfect word or phrase to express a thought. In addition, many of the Rav's comments consist of straightforward and simple translations of non-controversial words and phrases in the *kinot*, a natural part of the Rav's teaching style, but not essential to be included as part of the Rav's commentary in view of the excellent English translation of the *kinot* which is included in this volume. Consequently, the Rav's commentary in this volume should be seen as a distillation of the transcript of the Rav's Tisha B'Av learning sessions. While I endeavored to retain the Rav's language and remain faithful to his unique style wherever possible, the commentary is abridged to make the size of the volume manageable, and edited to make the language flow smoothly and, hopefully, seamlessly. It does, of course, retain the Rav's major themes and conceptual profundity. It certainly retains the Rav's comments on definitions of words or phrases in the *kinot* where the definitions are conceptually significant or vary from the conventional approach.

The reader will notice that there is no commentary from the Rav for the *kinot* that are recited on the night of Tisha B'Av. As the Rav's *kinot* learning sessions took place only during the day, we do not have any record of a line-by-line commentary from the Rav for the *kinot* recited at night. There is one exception, and that is the *kina*, "*Shomron Kol Titen*,"

which is recited on Tisha B'Av night and also, according to some traditions, at the end of the daytime *kinot*. The Rav's commentary on this *kina* is found in *The Lord Is Righteous in All His Ways*, not in the composite transcript, and this commentary is included, in edited form, where "*Shomron Kol Titen*" is found at the end of the daytime *kinot*.

In his learning sessions, the Rav was particularly expansive in his analysis and discussion of the initial *kinot*. This expansiveness by the Rav was, in many cases, not necessarily related to the text of the specific *kina*, but rather was a discursive exposition of general themes of the *kinot* and Tisha B'Av. Where it did not affect the understanding of a specific *kina*, I took the liberty of moving some of this general thematic commentary from the initial *kinot* to later *kinot* in order to balance the distribution of commentary somewhat, and to make the volume easier for the reader to use.

With respect to sources for the Rav's statements in the commentary, the sources cited are those cited by Rabbi Schacter in the composite transcript. For those statements which did not have a source cited in the transcript, Rabbi Reuven Ziegler of the Yeshivat Har Etzion Virtual Beit Midrash and researchers working under him supplied the sources.

The English translation of the *kinot* by Rabbi Dr. Tzvi Hersh Weinreb, Executive Vice President Emeritus of the Orthodox Union, was commissioned especially for this edition of *kinot*. I was delighted that Rabbi Weinreb accepted the challenging task of composing the *kinot* translation, and the Jewish community is indebted to him for a lucid, literate and inspiring rendering of the *kinot* in English. Over the years, Rabbi Weinreb's Tisha B'Av *kinot* learning sessions, and more recently his Tisha B'Av webcasts, have been an inspiration to the Jewish community worldwide. It is most fitting that the translation of *kinot* for this edition was undertaken by Rabbi Weinreb, who has made the annual Tisha B'Av presentations one of his signature educational efforts. A word about the approach to the translation – it is not "the Rav's translation of *kinot*." By this, I mean that where the Rav's understanding of a word or phrase deviates from the conventional view, Rabbi Weinreb's translation follows the conventional approach which has the imprimatur of established precedent, and does not use the Rav's view of the translation. In these cases, the commentary, of course, notes the Rav's view of the meaning of the text and indicates

that it varies from the more standard approach. The brief introductions to each *kina* explaining its structure and background were prepared by Rabbi David Fuchs of Koren Publishers Jerusalem.

The order and text of the *kinot* in this edition follow the standard practice in Ashkenazic communities. Some variations in the order and the text of the *kinot* have arisen over the years, but the Rav did not seem to favor any particular version, as he was wont to use whatever edition happened to be available in the synagogue and often used the old paperback editions of *Kinot* that were in common use at that time. This edition follows the version researched by Koren Publishing Jerusalem under the direction of Rabbi David Fuchs, prepared specifically for this publication. Rabbi Fuchs and his team of scholars conducted extensive analysis and research of prior editions and manuscripts of the *kinot*, and the masterful Hebrew text of the *kinot* prepared by them is a model of scholarly accuracy.

A word about the *kinot* for the Holocaust is in order. The Rav was not in favor of reciting *kinot* that were composed to commemorate the Holocaust. His view was that the traditional Tisha B'Av *kinot* expressed mourning for all Jewish tragedies, and no new *kinot* were appropriate. Nonetheless, the practice has arisen in many communities to recite *kinot* for the Holocaust, and we have included several, consistent with our view that this edition should be of practical use for the general Jewish community and not a reflection of the Rav's personal practices.

The siddur portion of this volume and *Megillat Eikha* are from other publications of Koren Publishers Jerusalem. The Hebrew text and English translation of the prayers are from the recently published *Koren Sacks Siddur, American Edition*, and we are proud that the monumental translation of the prayers by Chief Rabbi Jonathan Sacks, a watershed event of our time, graces this edition. The text of *Megillat Eikha*, and its English translation by Dr. Harold M. Fisch, are from the *Koren Jerusalem Bible*. As with the translation of *kinot*, the siddur portion of this edition is not "the Rav's siddur." It follows the standard Ashkenazic practice and does not reflect the Rav's personal practices and *minhagim*. The goal was to make this edition functional and usable by the broad spectrum of the Jewish community, not to serve as a historical record of what the Rav's personal practices were.

In his published works, the Rav referred to biblical personalities and

books of the Bible by their common English names. In his *shiurim*, he would often use the Hebrew terms. The former is adopted as the unified style for this work. The Rav always used the term "Red Sea" to refer to the *Yam Suf*, while Koren uniformly uses "Sea of Reeds," or "Reed Sea" in its publications. Accordingly, "Red Sea" is used in the commentary to remain faithful to the Rav's style, while "Sea of Reeds" is used in the translations of the *kinot* and *tefillot* to maintain consistency with the Koren style. The transliteration conventions for this edition follow the transliteration style of the *Koren Sacks Siddur, American Edition*.

In working on this edition, I received assistance from a variety of sources, and it is my pleasant task to acknowledge them. First and foremost, it is hard to overstate the contribution of Rabbi Jacob J. Schacter. His painstaking efforts in preparing the composite transcript of the years of the Rav's Tisha B'Av learning sessions truly paved the way for my editing of the commentary for this edition. In the course of my working on this edition, I was often asked what the difference is between *The Lord Is Righteous in All His Ways*, edited by Rabbi Schacter and based on the transcripts of the Rav's Tisha B'Av learning sessions, and the commentary included in this new edition of *kinot*, which is based on the same transcripts. My response was always that the two works should be seen as complementary. In *The Lord Is Righteous in All His Ways*, Rabbi Schacter analyzed the Rav's line-by-line commentary of the *kinot*, edited and organized the material, and presented it thematically and conceptually. If, however, one wants to have the benefit of the Rav's commentary for each individual *kina*, this edition will satisfy that need.

Rabbi Schacter prepared the composite transcript of the Rav's Tisha B'Av learning sessions under the auspices of the Toras HoRav Foundation whose mission is the preservation and dissemination of the Rav's intellectual legacy.

My friend, mentor, and colleague at the Orthodox Union, Rabbi Menachem Genack, General Editor of the OU Press, was involved in every aspect of the preparation of this edition and was a source of constant encouragement and enthusiasm. Aside from guiding the overall direction of the project, he was involved in numerous details on a daily basis, including review of the entire draft of the commentary, participation in the preparation and review of the siddur portion of the edition,

and providing the material for the *Reshimot*. Without his erudition and ability, this project could not have been brought to fruition.

My good friend of many years Dr. Joel Wolowelsky was involved in this project from its earliest stages and was instrumental in moving it forward. He reviewed the entire manuscript of the commentary and made numerous editorial suggestions and improvements. In addition, he was a source of sage counsel and perceptive insight from the inception of this project through its culmination.

Mr. David Olivestone, my colleague at the Orthodox Union, assisted in the design features of this edition, and we are indebted to him for his efforts in working together with Koren Publishers and presenting the Jewish community with this volume of striking aesthetic quality.

Rabbi Gil Student, my colleague at the Orthodox Union, was most helpful in assisting with the Halakhot section. In addition, he reviewed sections of the manuscript and provided invaluable assistance in many other aspects of the publication process.

Rabbi Hershel Schachter provided important substantive suggestions in connection with the siddur portion of this edition and the Halakhot section. Rabbi Reuven Ziegler, in addition to his help in identifying sources cited by the Rav, as noted above, kindly assisted in the early stages of this project by providing working copies of the Hebrew text of the *kinot* in electronic form. Mrs. Yocheved Goldberg, our administrative assistant *par excellence*, provided outstanding assistance in preparation and refinement of the commentary and the English translations of the *kinot*. Chaim Yitzchak Genack coordinated the preparation of the *Reshimot*, and he was assisted by Rabbis Boruch Danzger, Eli Gersten, David Hellman, Daniel Lauchheimer, Ephraim Meth, David Nachbar, Gavriel Price, Isaac Rice, Jacob Sasson, Benjamin Samuels, Ethan Schnall, David Shabtai, Mordechai Shichtman, and Mordechai Shiffman.

The OU Press is indeed fortunate to have Koren Publishers as its publishing partner for this edition. I extend grateful appreciation to Matthew Miller, Raphaël Freeman, Rabbi David Fuchs and the entire Koren group for their professionalism and cooperation in coordinating this transcontinental project. Special thanks go to Rachel Meghnagi, Chaya Mendelson and the other members of the skilled Koren team for their superb work in the areas of editing, design and typesetting and for treating every aspect

of the production of this edition with the care and attention to detail that have become the hallmark of Koren's publications.

The Orthodox Union is an organization that holds the Rav's legacy in high esteem, and I express appreciation to Mr. Stephen Savitsky, President of the Orthodox Union, Dr. Simcha Katz, Chairman of the Orthodox Union Kashrut Commission, Mr. Julius Berman, Chairman of the OU Press Commission, and Rabbi Steven Weil, Executive Vice President of the Orthodox Union for their enthusiastic and unflagging support. I know that the leadership of the Orthodox Union and the editors of the OU Press are gratified that the OU Press is making the Rav's thoughts on *kinot* available to a wider audience.

Aḥarona, aḥarona ḥaviva – The debt of gratitude that I owe my wife, Bleema, who supported and encouraged my efforts every step of the way, is far greater than can possibly be expressed in a few short lines. She was my constant sounding board for issues of style and language in the commentary, as well as more general questions of approach and philosophy for the overall project. She reviewed the entire draft of the commentary and made numerous editorial suggestions and refinements, as she and I would spend hours together struggling to find just the right word or phrase to capture what we thought was the Rav's intent. Every aspect of my work in this edition is suffused with her wisdom, skill, and literary grace.

Simon Posner

TRANSLATOR'S PREFACE

The difficulties of translation are insurmountable. Therefore, a translator's goals must be modest.

My goal in this translation is to help the reader of English to experience the emotions expressed in these poems of lament. To capture all the scholarly nuance contained in them is not possible; to empathize with the poet's heartbreak is.

For me, the process of translation evoked many dark and painful feelings. But it also made me grateful: to the Creator for allowing me to live in an era closer to redemption than the ones described in the *kinot*, but also to the many colleagues who were of such great assistance throughout the project.

If only one of them can be mentioned in this brief introduction, then it must be Mrs. Yocheved Goldberg, whose insight, devotion, and diligence are all exemplary.

Tzvi Hersh Weinreb

FOREWORD

The OU Press, in conjunction with Koren Publishers Jerusalem Ltd., is proud to present this edition of the Tisha B'Av *Kinot* with a commentary by the *gadol haTorah* of the previous generation, Rabbi Joseph B. Soloveitchik, a giant whose status is best exemplified by the fact that he is simply referred to as The Rav – rabbi *par excellence*.

The Rav was a profound philosopher and Talmudist, but he often said that he saw himself as a "simple *melamed*," a teacher whose job it was it help his students understand the messages and beauty of halakhic Judaism. He was a *Rosh Yeshiva* at the Rabbi Isaac Elchanan Theological Seminary, but also a communal rabbi, the chief rabbinic figure in Boston and the head of the Maimonides School and Synagogue in Boston. In these *kinot* commentaries, we see him as the superb communal teacher he was.

In most synagogues, *kinot* – the liturgical poems recited on the major day of fasting and mourning for the destruction of the Temples – are read through quickly with little understanding. The Rav perceived that to understand the message of Judaism, one had to understand its language. Rather than rush through the *kinot*, the Rav established a custom – now adopted by many communal religious leaders – to spend the day at Maimonides explaining the *kinot* to all who would come to listen. Sometimes, the Rav would simply explain the words to those who could not appreciate the nuances of the language. Sometimes he would draw on his vast knowledge of Jewish sources to explain the references that went unnoticed. Always would he explain the connection of the text to the Jewish experience of his audience. Over the years, thousands of laymen and scholars would come to sit on the mourning floor with him and listen as he explicated the meaning of the liturgy.

I was one of those privileged to hear the Rav's recitation and elucidation of the *kinot*. The *mesora* – the Jewish tradition – permeated his very being, and simply by being in his presence and listening to him read the *kinot* one was drawn into the *mesora* and experience of Jewish history. Time and again, he made the text come alive, helping his students appreciate the meaning of the day – and the meaning of the days it commemorated. Through exposure to his intense feelings of faith, one also felt that

the *mesora* is not limited to the heritage of a glorious past. Those present sensed, by their encounter with the Rav, that the *mesora* speaks as well to the future, as it endows Jewish existence with noble destiny. Reading *kinot* with the Rav helped us focus not only on all the past tragedies of Jewish history but also on the messianic hopes that transcend them. We could not help but feel that the Rav himself personified this temporal dialectic of *mesora*. Having lived through the era of the *ḥurban* of the wellsprings of *mesora* in Europe during the Holocaust, and the destruction of our illustrious past, the Rav, in whose very persona the *mesora* was enshrined, laid the foundation for the rebuilding of our heritage and forged a new beginning for the transmission of *mesora* into the limitless future.

The mourning on Tisha B'Av reaches the apex of *avelut* where no solace and comfort is possible or appropriate. It is a day designated only for *kinot*, tears and profound mourning. Yet, remarkably, on this, the saddest day of the Jewish calendar, we do not recite *Taḥanun*. The reason given is that Tisha B'Av is called a *mo'ed*, a holiday. This semi-festive quality is due, the Midrash tells us, to the fact that the Messiah was born on the day of the destruction of the Temple. The paradox of not reciting *Taḥanun* on this day is critical to the Tisha B'Av experience. It is a statement of hope in the future and absolute faith in our destiny. Even within the midst of our ashes and despair, lie the seeds of our ultimate redemption. Phoenix-like, the Jewish nation will arise again.

The Talmud (*Makkot* 24b) tells us that Rabbi Akiva and some of his colleagues were walking near the destroyed Temple. His colleagues, upon seeing a fox traverse the Holy of Holies, began to cry at the sight of the desolation of the *Mikdash*. Rabbi Akiva, however, began to laugh. When asked by his colleagues why he was laughing, Rabbi Akiva answered that now that Uriah's prophecy of the destruction was fulfilled, so will Zechariah's prophecy of the redemption of the city, when the young and old will again fill Jerusalem's streets, be fulfilled. Though on Tisha B'Av, in our mind's eye our gaze is riveted on all the horror and pain that has befallen our people, we must also, like Rabbi Akiva, retain the vision of salvation and peace that will some day surely follow.

Alas, the Rav is no longer with us, but his teachings remain. Through this volume we can still learn with him, giving further meaning to our mourning experience.

For those of us who knew the Rav, the publication of this edition has been a labor of love. We have been ably assisted in our endeavors by our publishing partner, Koren Publishers Jerusalem. Matthew Miller, Raphaël Freeman, Rabbi David Fuchs, and the entire Koren team embraced the *Mesorat HaRav Kinot* project with enthusiasm. With their professionalism, we have, collectively, succeeded in presenting the Jewish community with a volume of rare value and beauty.

This edition is graced by Rabbi Dr. Tzvi Hersh Weinreb's translation of the *kinot*. When we were confronted with the need to compose an English translation of the *kinot*, Rabbi Weinreb accepted the challenging task, and he has provided us with a monumental literary opus. Faithful to the original, consistent with scholarly precedent, and yet sensitive to the emotional outpouring of the *paytan*, his translation conveys the feeling as well as the meaning of the *kinot*. Rabbi Julius Berman, Chairman of the OU Press Commission, was a prize student of the Rav, and this edition is a testament to his mission of disseminating the Rav's writings and teachings.

It is a special pleasure for me to thank my long-time friend Rabbi Simon Posner for his work as editor of this volume. From the very beginning, he infused this endeavor with his extraordinary talents, intelligence, and literary skill, never losing sight of the whole picture while overseeing every aspect of the project, no matter how minute. If not for his diligence, dedication to the Rav's legacy, and devotion to detail, we would not be able to sit low and yet be raised spiritually by reading the *Kinot* with the Rav's insights.

This Lookstein Edition of the *Kinot Mesorat HaRav* has been dedicated in honor of Rabbi Haskel Lookstein. Beloved by his congregation and esteemed by colleagues and lay people alike, Rabbi Lookstein has always been inspired by the Rav's *kinot*, and this edition is a fitting tribute to Rabbi Lookstein's lifetime of service to the Jewish community.

We are grateful for the generous assistance provided for the publication of this volume by Rabbi Lookstein's many friends and members of Kehilath Jeshurun, as well as by the Fishel, Friedman, Katz, Keilson, Kupietzky, Siegel, Singer, Skydell, and Straus families.

Menachem Genack
General Editor
OU Press

PUBLISHER'S PREFACE

Kinot are nothing less than the most profound response to Jewish tragedy; they combine our efforts of religious, emotional, and intellectual understanding, with a tragic beauty. Through *Kinot*, we seek to understand our relationship to God at the nadir of our physical and national existence, through the medium of poetry – a medium which is more difficult yet more emotionally pure.

We have attempted to present an especially ambitious edition of *Kinot* with the *Tefillot* for Tisha B'Av for the modern, English-speaking, thoughtful reader. We offer, together with our publishing partner, the OU Press, the profound intellectual reflection and analysis of The Rav – HaRav Joseph B. Soloveitchik – the Torah giant of the last century whose intellectual and practical influence on our generation is incalculable; the translation of *Kinot* by Rabbi Tzvi Hersh Weinreb, one of this generation's most literate and original writers; the eloquent translation of *Tefilla* by Rabbi Lord Jonathan Sacks; and an entirely new, critically revised edition of *Kinot* in Hebrew.

The creation of this volume has been a complicated yet happy collaboration between the OU Press and Koren Publishers Jerusalem. Consummate professionals from many disciplines and languages were involved, and I am gratified that we have achieved such a successful combination of their critical contributions.

Rabbi Simon Posner of the OU was the editor of the volume, having the immensely difficult task of distilling the transcript of HaRav Soloveitchik's learning sessions into this commentary; Rabbi Tzvi Hersh Weinreb of the OU translated the *Kinot* with rare beauty and profound insight; Rabbi Jonathan Sacks of the United Synagogue in Great Britain contributed his translation of the Siddur, for the *Tefillot* of Tisha B'Av. Rabbi Menachem Genack of the OU was the driving force behind the *Kinot*; Rabbi Gil Student, also of the OU, assisted in numerous aspects of the edition; Rabbi Julius Berman, Chairman of the OU Press Commission, was deeply committed to the project. Rachel Meghnagi of Koren copyedited the texts of the various contributors.

Editor Raphaël Freeman led the very professional team at Koren, including Rabbi David Fuchs, who prepared the new edition of the

traditional Hebrew *Kinot* assisted by Efrat Gross. The volume was typeset by Chaya Mendelson.

It has been both an honor and a real pleasure for us to collaborate together. Yet we pray this volume should become but a repository of memories of tragedies past, and that we see the *Beit HaMikdash* rebuilt speedily, in our days.

Matthew Miller, Publisher
Jerusalem 5770 (2010)

RECOLLECTION OF A TISHA B'AV SHIUR GIVEN BY THE RAV

It is an exceptional honor and pleasure for me to be associated with the publication of the *Kinot* commentaries of my revered *rebbe*, the Rav, Rabbi Joseph B. Soloveitchik, of blessed memory. Reading through them brought back memories of when my wife, Audrey, and I traveled to Israel in August of 1967 in order to see for ourselves the incredible results of the Six Day War, to feel the miraculous salvation of the people and State of Israel, and to see the devastation of the Arab armies which attacked Israel from all sides in June of 1967 and threatened the extinction of the State and its citizens.

We arrived in Tel Aviv on Erev Tisha B'Av, August 14, 1967, just in time to eat a meal before the fast and go to Rabbi Shlomo Goren's synagogue for the Tisha B'Av night service. The mood in Israel was anything but Tisha B'Av-like. There was simply no feeling of mourning or sadness. On the contrary, there was a feeling of exhilaration, confidence, excitement and redemption. It was clear that Israelis were in no mood to observe or even to feel the sadness and mourning of Tisha B'Av.

The service proceeded rather routinely, Rabbi Goren read *Eikha* and then the congregation began the first of the Lamentations. They got through about half of the stanzas and then they stopped, and everyone proceeded to leave *shul*. The mood of the country was one of liberation and redemption with people feeling that they had been saved from, God forbid, a second Holocaust and with the sensation that not only were we saved, but that the State of Israel had expanded its territory perhaps threefold and its holiest sites were back in our hands; all of this because of the hatred and mistakes of intractable foes. How could one feel depressed and mournful on that Tisha B'Av?

And yet, Audrey and I were very disturbed. It was, after all, Tisha B'Av, the saddest day of the year. Something inside of me said that this reaction, although understandable, was not appropriate. Ten months later, June 26, 1968, the Rav gave expression to our feelings in one of the most memorable *shiurim* I ever heard from him.

The Rav asked: How can one mourn for events that occurred 2,000 and 2,500 years ago? Tisha B'Av marks the destruction of the First and

Second Temples in Jerusalem in 586 BCE and 70 CE. They are historic events, long gone from memory. How are we able to sit *shiva* on Tisha B'Av, night and morning, for events that occurred twenty centuries ago? If a close relative of ours had died and we didn't learn about it until after thirty days, there would be no formal *shiva*. We would sit *shiva* symbolically for an hour and then get up and go about our business. How then, can we sit down on the ground for an event that happened two millennia ago?

The Rav gave three answers to that question, answers which were not only relevant to a halakhic analysis of our behavior on Tisha B'Av, but which also shed light on why our Israeli brethren, as well as we, should have been more conscious of the need for Tisha B'Av even in the aftermath of the dramatic victory of the Six Day War.

I

The first answer to the question of how we can observe the rules of *shiva* – sitting on the ground, not washing ourselves nor anointing our bodies – for an event that happened so long ago, is that in our Jewish consciousness the event did not happen in the past. It is not ancient history; it is a contemporary experience. This is the approach of the Jew to all of our history and its recollection in all of our festivals.

On the Seder night we proclaim: "*Bekhol dor*, in every generation, each person must feel as if he (himself) emerged (just now) from Egypt." The parenthetical additions are from Maimonides' quotation of the Mishna in his Code of Law. The exodus from Egypt is to be seen as a contemporary experience. On the Seder night, we feel that we have *just now* experienced slavery and liberation. That's why we recline, drink four cups of wine, recite Hallel and celebrate as if it all just happened. This is fundamental to the whole experience of Pesaḥ.

The same is true of Shavuot. We stand during the reading of the Ten Commandments in a synagogue that is decorated with greenery and flowers as if we were standing at Mount Sinai and receiving the Ten Commandments today, not 3,300 years ago. On Sukkot, we dwell in thatched-roof booths as if we were experiencing the desert travels of our people *today*.

So it is with Tisha B'Av. We sit down on the ground as if the Temple was burning now and Jerusalem was lying in ruins now and Jews were

being slaughtered now. The Jerusalem Talmud records that the rabbis experienced Tisha B'Av night "כְּאִישׁ אֲשֶׁר מֵתוֹ מוּטָל לְפָנָיו, Like someone whose relative's dead body lay before him."

The Rav then concluded his first answer by reminding us that in the Jerusalem Talmud there is a parallel for Tisha B'Av in the *"bekhol dor,* in every generation..." of Pesaḥ. "כָּל דּוֹר שֶׁלֹּא נִבְנָה בֵּית הַמִּקְדָּשׁ בְּיָמָיו, כְּאִלּוּ נֶחֱרַב בְּיָמָיו, Every generation in which the Temple has not been rebuilt is like the generation in which it was destroyed." This is not mourning for something that happened millennia ago; it is mourning for what happened just now.

II

The second answer to the question of why we observe Tisha B'Av in so dramatic a fashion when the event we remember occurred so long ago, rests on another question. What did the Jewish people do during the period of the Second Temple, from the end of the sixth century BCE until 70 CE? Was Tisha B'Av observed or not? The Rav went into a long analysis of the Talmudic discussion of this question and Maimonides' conclusion in his Code of Law which, as understood by the Rav, indicated that Tisha B'Av was actually observed during the period of the Second Temple. The Rav then asked the obvious question: How could they mourn for the First Temple when the Second Temple stood in all its glory? How could the Kohanim bring the daily sacrifice and then sit down on the ground to recite *kinot*? Are not the two experiences mutually exclusive?

He then gave an unforgettable answer to his question. He said that, of course, the Kohanim and the Levi'im could not have celebrated all of the daily rituals in the Second Temple on Tisha B'Av and then mourned for the destruction of the First Temple. That would have been absurd. *If they observed Tisha B'Av during the days of the Second Temple it was observed not in mourning, but in prayer; that what happened once should not happen again.* During the weeks preceding Tisha B'Av, the Rav said (I believe I am quoting him verbatim), "The ghost of the Ḥurban stalked the land." The people were terrified that history would repeat itself and that the destruction that came 600 years before would happen again. And, tragically, it did happen again. He didn't have to add the obvious: that Jews today, even after the Six Day War, need to observe Tisha B'Av not only

in mourning for what happened twice in our history but in prayer that, God forbid, it shouldn't happen a third time. During the intervening years since 1968 that feeling has haunted me, not just on Tisha B'Av. I imagine it has haunted others as well.

III

Finally, the Rav offered a third answer to why Tisha B'Av is mandatory and meaningful today. He pointed out that Tisha B'Av has been understood throughout our history as a day devoted not only to our mourning the destruction of two Temples, but also to our historic recollection of all the tragedies that have befallen our people over the centuries, from the destruction of the First and Second Temples, through Beitar, the Crusades, the Spanish Inquisition, the expulsions of Jews from many lands, the pogroms of eastern Europe and, finally, in the Holocaust. Our history has been one long experience of *Eikha*? How come? How could it be? Why is our people constantly persecuted? Why is our history punctuated by so many periods of despair and tragedy? The Rav said that *Eikha* is not the expression of Jeremiah alone, but of all of Jewish history as we ask the obvious question of God: Why us? Why have we suffered so? He said that, ultimately, when the Messiah comes, we will understand the entire course of Jewish history. At that point *Eikha* will have a period after it and not a question mark. As long as *Eikha* still has a question mark the Jewish people must observe Tisha B'Av.

Why Tisha B'Av today? The Rav, responding to the euphoric questioning of the relevance of Tisha B'Av after the Six Day War, offered three compelling reasons. First, we mourn not for something that happened millennia ago, but for tragedies that, in our unique historical consciousness, we relive today. Second, we observe Tisha B'Av not only in mourning, but also in prayer that what happened twice before should not, God forbid, happen again. And third, we observe this saddest day of the year because we cannot understand why our people continues to suffer so much tragedy. "*Eikha yasheva vadad*?" Why are Jerusalem and the Jewish people so alone? "*Ha'ir rabati am*?" A city and a people that was populous and prosperous? "*Hayeta ke'almana*?" Why is she – and why are we – bereft as a widow?

Until we can answer those questions, Tisha B'Av will be a day of mourning and *kinot* for us. And with this publication of the Rav's profound commentary, the *kinot* speak to us ever more clearly, directly, and powerfully.

Haskel Lookstein

INTRODUCTION

The *kinot* recited during the Shaḥarit service of Tisha B'Av constitute the largest uninterrupted block of *piyut*, that vast repository of Jewish liturgical poetry, recited in a single service in the entire Jewish liturgy. In his incomparable commentary on the *kinot* presented in this edition, the Rav, Rabbi Joseph B. Soloveitchik, *zt"l*, has unlocked the wealth of beauty and meaning in the *kinot*. The Rav has given us the opportunity to understand and appreciate these *piyutim* for what they are, profound statements of Jewish philosophy, strikingly original interpretations of Scripture and Midrash, keen observations on the Jewish condition, and powerful expressions of emotional intensity.

Piyut, on the whole, has not fared well in contemporary Ashkenazic worship. Most of the *piyutim* included in the siddur for recitation on special Shabbatot or included in the *maḥzor* for the Yom Tov service (known commonly, although inaccurately, as *"yotzrot"*) are often omitted in the synagogue service. A similar fate has befallen many of the *piyutim* included in the High Holiday *maḥzor*. Those *piyutim* which are recited, such as *Tefillat Tal* and *Geshem* and the *piyutim* which remain included in the High Holiday service, are either sung to melodies that usually bear little relationship to their meaning or are *"davened"* as quickly as possible. On occasions when the congregation confronts a significant body of *piyutim* as the main focus of the service, such as the *kinot* on Tisha B'Av, there is a variety of reactions: there are those who inquire as to what can be skipped; those who dispatch the recitation of the *piyutim* as expeditiously as they can; and those, often in a distinct minority, who recite them with obvious emotion. With the discovery of the Cairo Geniza and the continuing research which began over the last century into the thousands of documents and fragments that were deposited there, we have begun to perceive the integral role that *piyutim* once played in the *tefilla*, a role which the contemporary Jewish world scarcely appreciates.

The reasons for this benign neglect of *piyut* are not hard to identify. First and foremost, the language of many of the *piyutim* is complex and convoluted, with numerous abstruse allusions to Midrashim and verses of the Tanakh. These *piyutim* can be understood only if the reader is familiar with, or takes the time to explore, the verses and Midrashim to

which the *piyut* is alluding, and many people do not have the patience or the tools of scholarship to discern the meaning hidden in the *piyutim*, a problem compounded by the unfortunate dearth of readable English commentaries and translations. Second, the trend in modern synagogues has been to streamline the service and lay by the wayside those parts deemed "non-essential." The motive for this trend is often entirely noble, as synagogue leaders struggle to attract the unaffiliated and endeavor to keep regular worshipers, especially the young people, from becoming bored and alienated. In any event, the *piyutim*, difficult to understand and often lengthy and time-consuming to recite, have been easy targets for those whose goal it is to shorten the service. Finally, as a matter of halakha, some authorities (most notably Maimonides), are of the view that *piyutim* are an impermissible interruption in the service and should not be recited.

The *kinot* have not escaped the fate that has befallen *piyut* in general. With their tightly woven tapestry of obscure references and arcane language, many of the *kinot* are ignored or rushed through. A careful study of the *kinot*, however, reveals the immense richness contained within them. The Rav, the masterful teacher, unravels the complexities of these *piyutim*, explains their language, and brings their themes into clear focus. In so doing, the Rav immeasurably heightens the experience of Tisha B'Av. To give but a few summary examples of the Rav's insights: in the *kina*, "*Az Bahalokh Yirmiyahu*," as well as in other *kinot*, the Rav highlights the recurring bold and thought-provoking theme that God Himself went into exile with the Jewish people and will be redeemed with them. The Rav asserts that God's exile is, in fact, the firmest guaranty of Israel's redemption – just as it is inevitable that God will liberate Himself from captivity, so too, He will surely liberate the Jewish people. The *kina*, "*Az Bimlot Sefek*," describes the dramatic encounter between the prophet Jeremiah and a mysterious disheveled woman, symbolizing the Jewish people. The Rav distills the concept that an outer appearance of sin, ugliness, and corruption is caused by the travails of the Jewish people, but these travails can never extinguish the eternal inner purity, innocence and beauty of the Jewish soul, and he further posits the principle that this underlying purity serves as the philosophical basis for the possibility of *teshuva*, repentance. In his line-by-line analysis of the *kina*, "*Tziyon Halo Tishali LiShlom*

Asirayikh," the Rav shows how the *kina* is a restatement of Rabbi Yehuda HaLevi's philosophy, as set forth in the *Kuzari*, of the superiority of the land of Israel, that spirituality and closeness to God permeate the actual existence in the land of Israel the same way that sunshine and rainfall exist in other lands. A recurring theme which the Rav emphasizes is that the national calamity of the destruction of the Temple and Jerusalem should not obscure the individual tragedies of men and women swept up in the catastrophe. The Rav perceptively notes that the *kina*, "*Ve'et Navi Ḥatati Hishmima*," which laments the fate of the son and daughter of Rabbi Yishmael who are sold into slavery, is strategically placed amidst the other *kinot* that mourn the enormity of the national tragedy, precisely to emphasize the fundamental Jewish dialectic of the importance of the individual as well as the community. Another theme, woven through several *kinot*, is the concept that the physical structure of the *Beit HaMikdash* served as collateral for the Jewish people. Even though *Knesset Yisrael* deserved to be destroyed for its sins, God, in His infinite mercy, accepted the collateral, the destruction of the *Beit HaMikdash*, and spared the people. Paradoxically, once the destruction of the physical structure commenced on Tisha B'Av afternoon, consolation could begin, as God's decision to permit the survival of the Jewish people became apparent. This view of God's compassion is reflected in the halakhic principle that the degree of *avelut*, the observance of the practices of mourning, is lessened in the afternoon of Tisha B'Av. As the Rav said, "Tisha B'Av is a day of limitless despair and boundless hope and faith."

These few brief examples are representative of the nuance, sensitivity, and depth of the Rav's commentary that one will find in this edition. Surely, a revitalization of interest in the liturgy of Tisha B'Av and an enhanced understanding of the *kinot* and their sublime message will render us more sensitive to the emotional and religious impact of Tisha B'Av and all Jewish tragedy. May it be God's will that this edition of *kinot* with the majestic commentary of the Rav, serve as a consolation to *Knesset Yisrael* and help bring us closer to the fulfillment of the ultimate consolation, the rebuilding of God's dwelling place in Jerusalem, the *Beit Tefilla*, His House of Prayer for all.

Simon Posner

ליל תשעה באב

**SERVICE FOR
THE NIGHT
OF TISHA B'AV**

Ma'ariv for Tisha B'Av

On Motza'ei Shabbat, the Leader says the following:
Blessed is He who separates beween the sacred and the secular.
The Leader then removes his shoes.

וְהוּא רַחוּם He is compassionate. *Ps. 78*
He forgives iniquity and does not destroy.
Repeatedly He suppresses His anger, not rousing His full wrath.
Lord, save! May the King answer us on the day we call. *Ps. 20*

BLESSINGS OF THE SHEMA

The Leader says the following, bowing at "Bless," standing straight at "the Lord"; the congregation, followed by the Leader, responds, bowing at "Bless," standing straight at "the Lord":

Leader: # BLESS
the Lord, the blessed One.

Congregation: Bless the Lord, the blessed One,
for ever and all time.

Leader: Bless the Lord, the blessed One,
for ever and all time.

On Motza'ei Shabbat, the congregants remove their shoes.

בָּרוּךְ Blessed are You, Lord our God,
King of the Universe,
who by His word brings on evenings,
by His wisdom opens the gates of heaven,
with understanding makes time change
and the seasons rotate,
and by His will orders the stars in their constellations in the sky.

מעריב לתשעה באב

On מוצאי שבת, the שליח ציבור says the following:

בָּרוּךְ הַמַּבְדִּיל בֵּין קֹדֶשׁ לְחוֹל

The שליח ציבור then removes his shoes.

תהלים עח

וְהוּא רַחוּם, יְכַפֵּר עָוֹן וְלֹא־יַשְׁחִית
וְהִרְבָּה לְהָשִׁיב אַפּוֹ, וְלֹא־יָעִיר כָּל־חֲמָתוֹ:

תהלים כ

יהוה הוֹשִׁיעָה, הַמֶּלֶךְ יַעֲנֵנוּ בְיוֹם־קָרְאֵנוּ:

קריאת שמע וברכותיה

The שליח ציבור says the following, bowing at בָּרְכוּ, standing straight at ה׳; the קהל, followed by the שליח ציבור, responds, bowing at בָּרוּךְ, standing straight at ה׳:

ש״ץ:

אֶת יהוה הַמְבֹרָךְ.

קהל: בָּרוּךְ יהוה הַמְבֹרָךְ לְעוֹלָם וָעֶד.

ש״ץ: בָּרוּךְ יהוה הַמְבֹרָךְ לְעוֹלָם וָעֶד.

On מוצאי שבת, the קהל remove their shoes.

בָּרוּךְ אַתָּה יהוה אֱלֹהֵינוּ מֶלֶךְ הָעוֹלָם
אֲשֶׁר בִּדְבָרוֹ מַעֲרִיב עֲרָבִים
בְּחָכְמָה פּוֹתֵחַ שְׁעָרִים
וּבִתְבוּנָה מְשַׁנֶּה עִתִּים וּמַחֲלִיף אֶת הַזְּמַנִּים
וּמְסַדֵּר אֶת הַכּוֹכָבִים בְּמִשְׁמְרוֹתֵיהֶם בָּרָקִיעַ כִּרְצוֹנוֹ.

He creates day and night, rolling away the light before the darkness,
and darkness before the light.
▸ He makes the day pass and brings on night,
distinguishing day from night:
the Lord of hosts is His name.
May the living and forever enduring God rule over us for all time.
Blessed are You, Lord, who brings on evenings.

אַהֲבַת עוֹלָם With everlasting love
have You loved Your people, the house of Israel.
You have taught us Torah and commandments,
decrees and laws of justice.
Therefore, Lord our God, when we lie down and when we rise up
we will speak of Your decrees, rejoicing in the words of Your Torah
and Your commandments for ever.
▸ For they are our life and the length of our days;
on them will we meditate day and night.
May You never take away Your love from us.
Blessed are You, Lord, who loves His people Israel.

The Shema must be said with intense concentration.
When not with a minyan, say:
God, faithful King!

The following verse should be said aloud, while covering the eyes with the right hand:

Listen, Israel: the Lord is our God, the Lord is One.

Deut. 6

Quietly: Blessed be the name of His glorious kingdom for ever and ever.

וְאָהַבְתָּ Love the Lord your God with all your heart, with all your *Deut. 6* soul, and with all your might. These words which I command you today shall be on your heart. Teach them repeatedly to your children, speaking of them when you sit at home and when you travel on the way, when you lie down and when you rise. Bind them as a sign on your hand, and they shall be an emblem between your eyes. Write them on the doorposts of your house and gates.

בּוֹרֵא יוֹם וָלָיְלָה, גּוֹלֵל אוֹר מִפְּנֵי חֹשֶׁךְ וְחֹשֶׁךְ מִפְּנֵי אוֹר
וּמַעֲבִיר יוֹם וּמֵבִיא לָיְלָה
וּמַבְדִּיל בֵּין יוֹם וּבֵין לָיְלָה
יהוה צְבָאוֹת שְׁמוֹ.
אֵל חַי וְקַיָּם תָּמִיד, יִמְלֹךְ עָלֵינוּ לְעוֹלָם וָעֶד.
בָּרוּךְ אַתָּה יהוה, הַמַּעֲרִיב עֲרָבִים.

אַהֲבַת עוֹלָם בֵּית יִשְׂרָאֵל עַמְּךָ אָהָבְתָּ,
תּוֹרָה וּמִצְוֹת, חֻקִּים וּמִשְׁפָּטִים, אוֹתָנוּ לִמַּדְתָּ.
עַל כֵּן יהוה אֱלֹהֵינוּ בְּשָׁכְבֵנוּ וּבְקוּמֵנוּ נָשִׂיחַ בְּחֻקֶּיךָ
וְנִשְׂמַח בְּדִבְרֵי תוֹרָתֶךָ וּבְמִצְוֹתֶיךָ לְעוֹלָם וָעֶד
כִּי הֵם חַיֵּינוּ וְאֹרֶךְ יָמֵינוּ, וּבָהֶם נֶהְגֶּה יוֹמָם וָלָיְלָה.
וְאַהֲבָתְךָ אַל תָּסִיר מִמֶּנּוּ לְעוֹלָמִים.
בָּרוּךְ אַתָּה יהוה, אוֹהֵב עַמּוֹ יִשְׂרָאֵל.

The שמע must be said with intense concentration.
When not with a מנין, say:

אֵל מֶלֶךְ נֶאֱמָן

The following verse should be said aloud, while covering the eyes with the right hand:

שְׁמַע יִשְׂרָאֵל, יהוה אֱלֹהֵינוּ, יהוה ׀ אֶחָד

דברים ו

Quietly בָּרוּךְ שֵׁם כְּבוֹד מַלְכוּתוֹ לְעוֹלָם וָעֶד.

וְאָהַבְתָּ אֵת יהוה אֱלֹהֶיךָ, בְּכָל־לְבָבְךָ וּבְכָל־נַפְשְׁךָ וּבְכָל־מְאֹדֶךָ: וְהָיוּ הַדְּבָרִים הָאֵלֶּה, אֲשֶׁר אָנֹכִי מְצַוְּךָ הַיּוֹם, עַל־לְבָבֶךָ: וְשִׁנַּנְתָּם לְבָנֶיךָ וְדִבַּרְתָּ בָּם, בְּשִׁבְתְּךָ בְּבֵיתֶךָ וּבְלֶכְתְּךָ בַדֶּרֶךְ, וּבְשָׁכְבְּךָ וּבְקוּמֶךָ: וּקְשַׁרְתָּם לְאוֹת עַל־יָדֶךָ וְהָיוּ לְטֹטָפֹת בֵּין עֵינֶיךָ: וּכְתַבְתָּם עַל־מְזֻזוֹת בֵּיתֶךָ וּבִשְׁעָרֶיךָ:

דברים ו

וְהָיָה If you indeed heed My commandments with which I charge *Deut. 11* you today, to love the Lord your God and worship Him with all your heart and with all your soul, I will give rain in your land in its season, the early and late rain; and you shall gather in your grain, wine and oil. I will give grass in your field for your cattle, and you shall eat and be satisfied. Be careful lest your heart be tempted and you go astray and worship other gods, bowing down to them. Then the Lord's anger will flare against you and He will close the heavens so that there will be no rain. The land will not yield its crops, and you will perish swiftly from the good land that the Lord is giving you. Therefore, set these, My words, on your heart and soul. Bind them as a sign on your hand, and they shall be an emblem between your eyes. Teach them to your children, speaking of them when you sit at home and when you travel on the way, when you lie down and when you rise. Write them on the doorposts of your house and gates, so that you and your children may live long in the land that the Lord swore to your ancestors to give them, for as long as the heavens are above the earth.

וַיֹּאמֶר The Lord spoke to Moses, saying: Speak to the Israelites *Num. 15* and tell them to make tassels on the corners of their garments for all generations. They shall attach to the tassel at each corner a thread of blue. This shall be your tassel, and you shall see it and remember all of the Lord's commandments and keep them, not straying after your heart and after your eyes, following your own sinful desires. Thus you will be reminded to keep all My commandments, and be holy to your God. I am the Lord your God, who brought you out of the land of Egypt to be your God. I am the Lord your God.

True –

The Leader repeats:

▸ The Lord your God is true –

דברים יא

וְהָיָה אִם־שָׁמֹעַ תִּשְׁמְעוּ אֶל־מִצְוֺתַי אֲשֶׁר אָנֹכִי מְצַוֶּה אֶתְכֶם הַיּוֹם, לְאַהֲבָה אֶת־יהוה אֱלֹהֵיכֶם וּלְעָבְדוֹ, בְּכָל־לְבַבְכֶם וּבְכָל־נַפְשְׁכֶם: וְנָתַתִּי מְטַר־אַרְצְכֶם בְּעִתּוֹ, יוֹרֶה וּמַלְקוֹשׁ, וְאָסַפְתָּ דְגָנֶךָ וְתִירֹשְׁךָ וְיִצְהָרֶךָ: וְנָתַתִּי עֵשֶׂב בְּשָׂדְךָ לִבְהֶמְתֶּךָ, וְאָכַלְתָּ וְשָׂבָעְתָּ: הִשָּׁמְרוּ לָכֶם פֶּן־יִפְתֶּה לְבַבְכֶם, וְסַרְתֶּם וַעֲבַדְתֶּם אֱלֹהִים אֲחֵרִים וְהִשְׁתַּחֲוִיתֶם לָהֶם: וְחָרָה אַף־יהוה בָּכֶם, וְעָצַר אֶת־הַשָּׁמַיִם וְלֹא־יִהְיֶה מָטָר, וְהָאֲדָמָה לֹא תִתֵּן אֶת־יְבוּלָהּ, וַאֲבַדְתֶּם מְהֵרָה מֵעַל הָאָרֶץ הַטֹּבָה אֲשֶׁר יהוה נֹתֵן לָכֶם: וְשַׂמְתֶּם אֶת־דְּבָרַי אֵלֶּה עַל־לְבַבְכֶם וְעַל־נַפְשְׁכֶם, וּקְשַׁרְתֶּם אֹתָם לְאוֹת עַל־יֶדְכֶם, וְהָיוּ לְטוֹטָפֹת בֵּין עֵינֵיכֶם: וְלִמַּדְתֶּם אֹתָם אֶת־בְּנֵיכֶם לְדַבֵּר בָּם, בְּשִׁבְתְּךָ בְּבֵיתֶךָ, וּבְלֶכְתְּךָ בַדֶּרֶךְ וּבְשָׁכְבְּךָ וּבְקוּמֶךָ: וּכְתַבְתָּם עַל־מְזוּזוֹת בֵּיתֶךָ וּבִשְׁעָרֶיךָ: לְמַעַן יִרְבּוּ יְמֵיכֶם וִימֵי בְנֵיכֶם עַל הָאֲדָמָה אֲשֶׁר נִשְׁבַּע יהוה לַאֲבֹתֵיכֶם לָתֵת לָהֶם, כִּימֵי הַשָּׁמַיִם עַל־הָאָרֶץ:

במדבר טו

וַיֹּאמֶר יהוה אֶל־מֹשֶׁה לֵּאמֹר: דַּבֵּר אֶל־בְּנֵי יִשְׂרָאֵל וְאָמַרְתָּ אֲלֵהֶם, וְעָשׂוּ לָהֶם צִיצִת עַל־כַּנְפֵי בִגְדֵיהֶם לְדֹרֹתָם, וְנָתְנוּ עַל־צִיצִת הַכָּנָף פְּתִיל תְּכֵלֶת: וְהָיָה לָכֶם לְצִיצִת, וּרְאִיתֶם אֹתוֹ, וּזְכַרְתֶּם אֶת־כָּל־מִצְוֺת יהוה וַעֲשִׂיתֶם אֹתָם, וְלֹא תָתוּרוּ אַחֲרֵי לְבַבְכֶם וְאַחֲרֵי עֵינֵיכֶם, אֲשֶׁר־אַתֶּם זֹנִים אַחֲרֵיהֶם: לְמַעַן תִּזְכְּרוּ וַעֲשִׂיתֶם אֶת־כָּל־מִצְוֺתָי, וִהְיִיתֶם קְדֹשִׁים לֵאלֹהֵיכֶם: אֲנִי יהוה אֱלֹהֵיכֶם, אֲשֶׁר הוֹצֵאתִי אֶתְכֶם מֵאֶרֶץ מִצְרַיִם, לִהְיוֹת לָכֶם לֵאלֹהִים, אֲנִי יהוה אֱלֹהֵיכֶם:

אֱמֶת

The שליח ציבור repeats:

◂ יהוה אֱלֹהֵיכֶם אֱמֶת

וֶאֱמוּנָה – and faithful is all this,
and firmly established for us
that He is the Lord our God,
and there is none beside Him,
and that we, Israel, are His people.
He is our King, who redeems us from the hand of kings
and delivers us from the grasp of all tyrants.
He is our God,
who on our behalf repays our foes
and brings just retribution on our mortal enemies;
who performs great deeds beyond understanding
and wonders beyond number;
who kept us alive, not letting our foot slip;
who led us on the high places of our enemies,
raising our pride above all our foes;
who did miracles for us
and brought vengeance against Pharaoh;
who performed signs and wonders
in the land of Ham's children;
who smote in His wrath all the firstborn of Egypt,
and brought out His people Israel from their midst
into everlasting freedom;
who led His children through the divided Reed Sea,
plunging their pursuers and enemies into the depths.
When His children saw His might,
they gave praise and thanks to His name,
▸ and willingly accepted His Sovereignty.
Moses and the children of Israel
then sang a song to You with great joy,
and they all exclaimed:

> מִי־כָמֹכָה "Who is like You, Lord, among the mighty? *Ex. 15*
> Who is like You, majestic in holiness,
> awesome in praises, doing wonders?"

וֶאֱמוּנָה כָּל זֹאת וְקַיָּם עָלֵינוּ
כִּי הוּא יהוה אֱלֹהֵינוּ וְאֵין זוּלָתוֹ
וַאֲנַחְנוּ יִשְׂרָאֵל עַמּוֹ.
הַפּוֹדֵנוּ מִיַּד מְלָכִים
מַלְכֵּנוּ הַגּוֹאֲלֵנוּ מִכַּף כָּל הֶעָרִיצִים.
הָאֵל הַנִּפְרָע לָנוּ מִצָּרֵינוּ
וְהַמְשַׁלֵּם גְּמוּל לְכָל אוֹיְבֵי נַפְשֵׁנוּ.
הָעוֹשֶׂה גְדוֹלוֹת עַד אֵין חֵקֶר, וְנִפְלָאוֹת עַד אֵין מִסְפָּר
הַשָּׂם נַפְשֵׁנוּ בַּחַיִּים, וְלֹא נָתַן לַמּוֹט רַגְלֵנוּ
הַמַּדְרִיכֵנוּ עַל בָּמוֹת אוֹיְבֵינוּ
וַיָּרֶם קַרְנֵנוּ עַל כָּל שׂוֹנְאֵינוּ.
הָעוֹשֶׂה לָּנוּ נִסִּים וּנְקָמָה בְּפַרְעֹה
אוֹתוֹת וּמוֹפְתִים בְּאַדְמַת בְּנֵי חָם.
הַמַּכֶּה בְעֶבְרָתוֹ כָּל בְּכוֹרֵי מִצְרָיִם
וַיּוֹצֵא אֶת עַמּוֹ יִשְׂרָאֵל מִתּוֹכָם לְחֵרוּת עוֹלָם.
הַמַּעֲבִיר בָּנָיו בֵּין גִּזְרֵי יַם סוּף
אֶת רוֹדְפֵיהֶם וְאֶת שׂוֹנְאֵיהֶם בִּתְהוֹמוֹת טִבַּע
וְרָאוּ בָנָיו גְּבוּרָתוֹ, שִׁבְּחוּ וְהוֹדוּ לִשְׁמוֹ
‹ וּמַלְכוּתוֹ בְּרָצוֹן קִבְּלוּ עֲלֵיהֶם.
מֹשֶׁה וּבְנֵי יִשְׂרָאֵל, לְךָ עָנוּ שִׁירָה בְּשִׂמְחָה רַבָּה
וְאָמְרוּ כֻלָּם

מִי־כָמֹכָה בָּאֵלִם יהוה
מִי כָּמֹכָה נֶאְדָּר בַּקֹּדֶשׁ
נוֹרָא תְהִלֹּת עֹשֵׂה פֶלֶא:

שמות טו

MA'ARIV FOR TISHA B'AV

▸ Your children beheld Your majesty
as You parted the sea before Moses.
"This is my God!" they responded, and then said:

"The Lord shall reign for ever and ever." *Ex. 15*

▸ And it is said, "For the Lord has redeemed Jacob *Jer. 31*
and rescued him from a power stronger than his own."
Blessed are You, Lord, who redeemed Israel.

הַשְׁכִּיבֵנוּ Help us lie down, O Lord our God, in peace,
and rise up, O our King, to life.
Spread over us Your canopy of peace.
Direct us with Your good counsel,
and save us for the sake of Your name.
Shield us and remove from us every enemy,
plague, sword, famine and sorrow.
Remove the adversary from before and behind us.
Shelter us in the shadow of Your wings,
for You, God, are our Guardian and Deliverer;
You, God, are a gracious and compassionate King.
▸ Guard our going out and our coming in,
for life and peace, from now and for ever.
Blessed are You, Lord, who guards His people Israel for ever.

In Israel the service continues with Half Kaddish on page 14.

בָּרוּךְ Blessed be the Lord for ever. Amen and Amen. *Ps. 89*
Blessed from Zion be the Lord *Ps. 135*
who dwells in Jerusalem. Halleluya.
Blessed be the Lord, God of Israel, *Ps. 72*
who alone does wondrous things.
Blessed be His glorious name for ever,
and may the whole earth be filled with His glory. Amen and Amen.
May the glory of the Lord endure for ever; *Ps. 104*
may the Lord rejoice in His works.

• מַלְכוּתְךָ רָאוּ בָנֶיךָ, בּוֹקֵעַ יָם לִפְנֵי מֹשֶׁה
זֶה אֵלִי עָנוּ, וְאָמְרוּ

שמות טו

יהוה יִמְלֹךְ לְעֹלָם וָעֶד:

• וְנֶאֱמַר
כִּי־פָדָה יהוה אֶת־יַעֲקֹב, וּגְאָלוֹ מִיַּד חָזָק מִמֶּנּוּ:

ירמיהו לא

בָּרוּךְ אַתָּה יהוה, גָּאַל יִשְׂרָאֵל.

הַשְׁכִּיבֵנוּ יהוה אֱלֹהֵינוּ לְשָׁלוֹם
וְהַעֲמִידֵנוּ מַלְכֵּנוּ לְחַיִּים
וּפְרֹשׂ עָלֵינוּ סֻכַּת שְׁלוֹמֶךָ, וְתַקְּנֵנוּ בְּעֵצָה טוֹבָה מִלְּפָנֶיךָ
וְהוֹשִׁיעֵנוּ לְמַעַן שְׁמֶךָ.
וְהָגֵן בַּעֲדֵנוּ, וְהָסֵר מֵעָלֵינוּ אוֹיֵב, דֶּבֶר וְחֶרֶב וְרָעָב וְיָגוֹן
וְהָסֵר שָׂטָן מִלְּפָנֵינוּ וּמֵאַחֲרֵינוּ, וּבְצֵל כְּנָפֶיךָ תַּסְתִּירֵנוּ
כִּי אֵל שׁוֹמְרֵנוּ וּמַצִּילֵנוּ אָתָּה
כִּי אֵל מֶלֶךְ חַנּוּן וְרַחוּם אָתָּה.
• וּשְׁמֹר צֵאתֵנוּ וּבוֹאֵנוּ לְחַיִּים וּלְשָׁלוֹם מֵעַתָּה וְעַד עוֹלָם.
בָּרוּךְ אַתָּה יהוה, שׁוֹמֵר עַמּוֹ יִשְׂרָאֵל לָעַד.

In ארץ ישראל *the service continues with* חצי קדיש *on page 15.*

תהלים פט

בָּרוּךְ יהוה לְעוֹלָם, אָמֵן וְאָמֵן:

תהלים קלה

בָּרוּךְ יהוה מִצִּיּוֹן, שֹׁכֵן יְרוּשָׁלָיִם, הַלְלוּיָהּ:

תהלים עב

בָּרוּךְ יהוה אֱלֹהִים אֱלֹהֵי יִשְׂרָאֵל, עֹשֵׂה נִפְלָאוֹת לְבַדּוֹ:
וּבָרוּךְ שֵׁם כְּבוֹדוֹ לְעוֹלָם
וְיִמָּלֵא כְבוֹדוֹ אֶת־כָּל־הָאָרֶץ, אָמֵן וְאָמֵן:

תהלים קד

יְהִי כְבוֹד יהוה לְעוֹלָם, יִשְׂמַח יהוה בְּמַעֲשָׂיו:

MA'ARIV FOR TISHA B'AV

May the name of the Lord be blessed now and for all time. *Ps. 113*
For the sake of His great name *1 Sam. 12*
the Lord will not abandon His people,
for the Lord vowed to make you a people of His own.
When all the people saw [God's wonders] they fell on their faces *1 Kings 18*
and said: "The Lord, He is God; the Lord, He is God."
Then the Lord shall be King over all the earth; *Zech. 14*
on that day the Lord shall be One and His name One.
May Your love, Lord, be upon us, as we have put our hope in You. *Ps. 33*

הוֹשִׁיעֵנוּ Save us, Lord our God, gather us *Ps. 106*
and deliver us from the nations,
to thank Your holy name, and glory in Your praise.
All the nations You made shall come and bow before You, *Ps. 86*
Lord, and pay honor to Your name,
for You are great and You perform wonders:
You alone are God.
We, Your people, the flock of Your pasture, will praise You for ever. *Ps. 79*
For all generations we will relate Your praise.

בָּרוּךְ Blessed is the Lord by day, blessed is the Lord by night.
Blessed is the Lord when we lie down;
blessed is the Lord when we rise.
For in Your hand are the souls of the living and the dead,
[as it is written:] "In His hand is every living soul, *Job 12*
and the breath of all mankind."
Into Your hand I entrust my spirit: *Ps. 31*
You redeemed me, Lord, God of truth.
Our God in heaven, bring unity to Your name,
establish Your kingdom constantly,
and reign over us for ever and all time.

תהלים קיג	יְהִי שֵׁם יהוה מְבֹרָךְ מֵעַתָּה וְעַד־עוֹלָם:
שמואל א, יב	כִּי לֹא־יִטֹּשׁ יהוה אֶת־עַמּוֹ בַּעֲבוּר שְׁמוֹ הַגָּדוֹל
	כִּי הוֹאִיל יהוה לַעֲשׂוֹת אֶתְכֶם לוֹ לְעָם:
מלכים א, יח	וַיַּרְא כָּל־הָעָם וַיִּפְּלוּ עַל־פְּנֵיהֶם
	וַיֹּאמְרוּ, יהוה הוּא הָאֱלֹהִים, יהוה הוּא הָאֱלֹהִים:
זכריה יד	וְהָיָה יהוה לְמֶלֶךְ עַל־כָּל־הָאָרֶץ
	בַּיּוֹם הַהוּא יִהְיֶה יהוה אֶחָד וּשְׁמוֹ אֶחָד:
תהלים לג	יְהִי־חַסְדְּךָ יהוה עָלֵינוּ, כַּאֲשֶׁר יִחַלְנוּ לָךְ:

תהלים קו	הוֹשִׁיעֵנוּ יהוה אֱלֹהֵינוּ, וְקַבְּצֵנוּ מִן־הַגּוֹיִם
	לְהוֹדוֹת לְשֵׁם קָדְשֶׁךָ, לְהִשְׁתַּבֵּחַ בִּתְהִלָּתֶךָ:
תהלים פו	כָּל־גּוֹיִם אֲשֶׁר עָשִׂיתָ, יָבוֹאוּ וְיִשְׁתַּחֲווּ לְפָנֶיךָ, אֲדֹנָי וִיכַבְּדוּ לִשְׁמֶךָ:
	כִּי־גָדוֹל אַתָּה וְעֹשֵׂה נִפְלָאוֹת, אַתָּה אֱלֹהִים לְבַדֶּךָ:
תהלים עט	וַאֲנַחְנוּ עַמְּךָ וְצֹאן מַרְעִיתֶךָ, נוֹדֶה לְךָ לְעוֹלָם
	לְדוֹר וָדֹר נְסַפֵּר תְּהִלָּתֶךָ:

	בָּרוּךְ יהוה בַּיּוֹם, בָּרוּךְ יהוה בַּלַּיְלָה
	בָּרוּךְ יהוה בְּשָׁכְבֵנוּ, בָּרוּךְ יהוה בְּקוּמֵנוּ.
	כִּי בְיָדְךָ נַפְשׁוֹת הַחַיִּים וְהַמֵּתִים.
איוב יב	אֲשֶׁר בְּיָדוֹ נֶפֶשׁ כָּל־חָי, וְרוּחַ כָּל־בְּשַׂר־אִישׁ:
תהלים לא	בְּיָדְךָ אַפְקִיד רוּחִי, פָּדִיתָה אוֹתִי יהוה אֵל אֱמֶת:
	אֱלֹהֵינוּ שֶׁבַּשָּׁמַיִם, יַחֵד שִׁמְךָ וְקַיֵּם מַלְכוּתְךָ תָּמִיד
	וּמְלֹךְ עָלֵינוּ לְעוֹלָם וָעֶד.

יִרְאוּ May our eyes see, our hearts rejoice,
and our souls be glad in Your true salvation,
when Zion is told, "Your God reigns."
The Lord is King, the Lord was King,
the Lord will be King for ever and all time.
▸ For sovereignty is Yours,
and to all eternity You will reign in glory,
for we have no king but You.
Blessed are You, Lord,
the King who in His constant glory will reign over us
and all His creation for ever and all time.

HALF KADDISH

Leader: יִתְגַּדַּל Magnified and sanctified
may His great name be,
in the world He created by His will.
May He establish His kingdom
in your lifetime and in your days,
and in the lifetime of all the house of Israel,
swiftly and soon – and say: Amen.

All: May His great name be blessed for ever and all time.

Leader: Blessed and praised, glorified and exalted,
raised and honored,
uplifted and lauded
be the name of the Holy One,
blessed be He,
beyond any blessing,
song, praise and consolation
uttered in the world –
and say: Amen.

יִרְאוּ עֵינֵינוּ וְיִשְׂמַח לִבֵּנוּ
וְתָגֵל נַפְשֵׁנוּ בִּישׁוּעָתְךָ בֶּאֱמֶת
בֶּאֱמֹר לְצִיּוֹן מָלַךְ אֱלֹהָיִךְ.
יהוה מֶלֶךְ, יהוה מָלָךְ, יהוה יִמְלֹךְ לְעֹלָם וָעֶד.
כִּי הַמַּלְכוּת שֶׁלְּךָ הִיא, וּלְעוֹלְמֵי עַד תִּמְלֹךְ בְּכָבוֹד
כִּי אֵין לָנוּ מֶלֶךְ אֶלָּא אָתָּה.
בָּרוּךְ אַתָּה יהוה
הַמֶּלֶךְ בִּכְבוֹדוֹ תָּמִיד, יִמְלֹךְ עָלֵינוּ לְעוֹלָם וָעֶד
וְעַל כָּל מַעֲשָׂיו.

חצי קדיש

ש״ץ: יִתְגַּדַּל וְיִתְקַדַּשׁ שְׁמֵהּ רַבָּא (קהל: אָמֵן)
בְּעָלְמָא דִּי בְרָא כִרְעוּתֵהּ, וְיַמְלִיךְ מַלְכוּתֵהּ
בְּחַיֵּיכוֹן וּבְיוֹמֵיכוֹן וּבְחַיֵּי דְכָל בֵּית יִשְׂרָאֵל
בַּעֲגָלָא וּבִזְמַן קָרִיב, וְאִמְרוּ אָמֵן. (קהל: אָמֵן)

קהל ויש״ץ: יְהֵא שְׁמֵהּ רַבָּא מְבָרַךְ לְעָלַם וּלְעָלְמֵי עָלְמַיָּא.

ש״ץ: יִתְבָּרַךְ וְיִשְׁתַּבַּח וְיִתְפָּאַר וְיִתְרוֹמַם וְיִתְנַשֵּׂא
וְיִתְהַדָּר וְיִתְעַלֶּה וְיִתְהַלָּל
שְׁמֵהּ דְּקֻדְשָׁא בְּרִיךְ הוּא (קהל: בְּרִיךְ הוּא)
לְעֵלָּא מִן כָּל בִּרְכָתָא וְשִׁירָתָא
תֻּשְׁבְּחָתָא וְנֶחֱמָתָא, דַּאֲמִירָן בְּעָלְמָא
וְאִמְרוּ אָמֵן. (קהל: אָמֵן)

THE AMIDA

The following prayer, until "in former years," on page 30, is said silently, standing with feet together. Take three steps forward and at the points indicated by ˇ, bend the knees at the first word, bow at the second, and stand straight before saying God's name.

O Lord, open my lips,   *Ps. 51*
so that my mouth may declare Your praise.

PATRIARCHS

ˇבָּרוּךְ Blessed are You, Lord our God and God of our fathers,
God of Abraham, God of Isaac and God of Jacob;
the great, mighty and awesome God, God Most High,
who bestows acts of loving-kindness and creates all,
who remembers the loving-kindness of the fathers
and will bring a Redeemer to their children's children
for the sake of His name, in love.
King, Helper, Savior, Shield:
ˇBlessed are You,
Lord, Shield of Abraham.

DIVINE MIGHT

אַתָּה גִבּוֹר You are eternally mighty, Lord.
You give life to the dead
and have great power to save.

> *In Israel:* He causes the dew to fall.

He sustains the living with loving-kindness,
and with great compassion revives the dead.
He supports the fallen,
heals the sick,
sets captives free,
and keeps His faith with those who sleep in the dust.

עמידה

The following prayer, until קַדְמֹנִיּוֹת, *on page 31, is said silently, standing with feet together. Take three steps forward and at the points indicated by ʾ, bend the knees at the first word, bow at the second, and stand straight before saying God's name.*

תהלים נא

אֲדֹנָי, שְׂפָתַי תִּפְתָּח, וּפִי יַגִּיד תְּהִלָּתֶךָ:

אבות

ʾבָּרוּךְ אַתָּה יהוה, אֱלֹהֵינוּ וֵאלֹהֵי אֲבוֹתֵינוּ
אֱלֹהֵי אַבְרָהָם, אֱלֹהֵי יִצְחָק, וֵאלֹהֵי יַעֲקֹב
הָאֵל הַגָּדוֹל הַגִּבּוֹר וְהַנּוֹרָא, אֵל עֶלְיוֹן
גּוֹמֵל חֲסָדִים טוֹבִים, וְקוֹנֵה הַכֹּל
וְזוֹכֵר חַסְדֵי אָבוֹת
וּמֵבִיא גוֹאֵל לִבְנֵי בְנֵיהֶם, לְמַעַן שְׁמוֹ בְּאַהֲבָה.
מֶלֶךְ עוֹזֵר וּמוֹשִׁיעַ וּמָגֵן.
ʾבָּרוּךְ אַתָּה יהוה, מָגֵן אַבְרָהָם.

גבורות

אַתָּה גִּבּוֹר לְעוֹלָם, אֲדֹנָי
מְחַיֵּה מֵתִים אַתָּה, רַב לְהוֹשִׁיעַ

בארץ ישראל: מוֹרִיד הַטָּל

מְכַלְכֵּל חַיִּים בְּחֶסֶד
מְחַיֵּה מֵתִים בְּרַחֲמִים רַבִּים
סוֹמֵךְ נוֹפְלִים, וְרוֹפֵא חוֹלִים, וּמַתִּיר אֲסוּרִים
וּמְקַיֵּם אֱמוּנָתוֹ לִישֵׁנֵי עָפָר.

MA'ARIV FOR TISHA B'AV

Who is like You, Master of might,
and to whom can You be compared,
O King who brings death and gives life,
and makes salvation grow?
Faithful are You to revive the dead.
Blessed are You, Lord, who revives the dead.

HOLINESS

אַתָּה קָדוֹשׁ You are holy and Your name is holy,
and holy ones praise You daily, Selah!
Blessed are You, Lord, the holy God.

KNOWLEDGE

אַתָּה חוֹנֵן You grace humanity with knowledge
and teach mortals understanding.

> *On Motza'ei Shabbat say:*
>
> אַתָּה חוֹנַנְתָּנוּ You have graced us with the knowledge of Your Torah, and taught us to perform the statutes of Your will. You have distinguished, Lord our God, between sacred and profane, light and darkness, Israel and the nations, and between the seventh day and the six days of work. Our Father, our King, may the days approaching us bring peace; may we be free from all sin, cleansed from all iniquity, holding fast to our reverence of You. And

Grace us with the knowledge, understanding
and discernment that come from You.
Blessed are You, Lord, who graciously grants knowledge.

REPENTANCE

הֲשִׁיבֵנוּ Bring us back, our Father, to Your Torah.
Draw us near, our King, to Your service.
Lead us back to You in perfect repentance.
Blessed are You, Lord, who desires repentance.

מִי כָמוֹךָ, בַּעַל גְּבוּרוֹת
וּמִי דּוֹמֶה לָּךְ
מֶלֶךְ, מֵמִית וּמְחַיֶּה וּמַצְמִיחַ יְשׁוּעָה.
וְנֶאֱמָן אַתָּה לְהַחֲיוֹת מֵתִים.
בָּרוּךְ אַתָּה יהוה, מְחַיֵּה הַמֵּתִים.

קדושת השם
אַתָּה קָדוֹשׁ וְשִׁמְךָ קָדוֹשׁ
וּקְדוֹשִׁים בְּכָל יוֹם יְהַלְלוּךָ סֶּלָה.
בָּרוּךְ אַתָּה יהוה, הָאֵל הַקָּדוֹשׁ.

דעת
אַתָּה חוֹנֵן לְאָדָם דַּעַת, וּמְלַמֵּד לֶאֱנוֹשׁ בִּינָה.

On מוצאי שבת *say:*

אַתָּה חוֹנַנְתָּנוּ לְמַדַּע תּוֹרָתֶךָ, וַתְּלַמְּדֵנוּ לַעֲשׂוֹת חֻקֵּי רְצוֹנֶךָ, וַתַּבְדֵּל יהוה אֱלֹהֵינוּ בֵּין קֹדֶשׁ לְחֹל, בֵּין אוֹר לְחֹשֶׁךְ, בֵּין יִשְׂרָאֵל לָעַמִּים, בֵּין יוֹם הַשְּׁבִיעִי לְשֵׁשֶׁת יְמֵי הַמַּעֲשֶׂה. אָבִינוּ מַלְכֵּנוּ, הָחֵל עָלֵינוּ הַיָּמִים הַבָּאִים לִקְרָאתֵנוּ לְשָׁלוֹם, חֲשׂוּכִים מִכָּל חֵטְא וּמְנֻקִּים מִכָּל עָוֹן וּמְדֻבָּקִים בְּיִרְאָתֶךָ. וְ

חָנֵּנוּ מֵאִתְּךָ דֵּעָה בִּינָה וְהַשְׂכֵּל.
בָּרוּךְ אַתָּה יהוה, חוֹנֵן הַדָּעַת.

תשובה
הֲשִׁיבֵנוּ אָבִינוּ לְתוֹרָתֶךָ
וְקָרְבֵנוּ מַלְכֵּנוּ לַעֲבוֹדָתֶךָ
וְהַחֲזִירֵנוּ בִּתְשׁוּבָה שְׁלֵמָה לְפָנֶיךָ.
בָּרוּךְ אַתָּה יהוה, הָרוֹצֶה בִּתְשׁוּבָה.

FORGIVENESS

Strike the left side of the chest at °.

סְלַח לָנוּ Forgive us, our Father,
for we have °sinned.
Pardon us, our King,
for we have °transgressed;
for You pardon and forgive.
Blessed are You, LORD,
the gracious One who repeatedly forgives.

REDEMPTION

רְאֵה Look on our affliction,
plead our cause,
and redeem us soon for Your name's sake,
for You are a powerful Redeemer.
Blessed are You, LORD,
the Redeemer of Israel.

HEALING

רְפָאֵנוּ Heal us, LORD, and we shall be healed.
Save us and we shall be saved,
for You are our praise.
Bring complete recovery for all our ailments,

> *The following prayer for a sick person may be said here:*
> May it be Your will, O LORD my God and God of my ancestors, that You speedily send a complete recovery from heaven, a healing of both soul and body, to the patient (*name*), son/daughter of (*mother's name*) among the other afflicted of Israel.

---

for You, God, King, are a faithful and compassionate Healer.
Blessed are You, LORD,
Healer of the sick of His people Israel.

סליחה

Strike the left side of the chest at °.

סְלַח לָנוּ אָבִינוּ כִּי °חָטָאנוּ
מְחַל לָנוּ מַלְכֵּנוּ כִּי °פָשָׁעְנוּ
כִּי מוֹחֵל וְסוֹלֵחַ אָתָּה.
בָּרוּךְ אַתָּה יהוה
חַנּוּן הַמַּרְבֶּה לִסְלֹחַ.

גאולה

רְאֵה בְעָנְיֵנוּ, וְרִיבָה רִיבֵנוּ
וּגְאָלֵנוּ מְהֵרָה לְמַעַן שְׁמֶךָ
כִּי גּוֹאֵל חָזָק אָתָּה.
בָּרוּךְ אַתָּה יהוה
גּוֹאֵל יִשְׂרָאֵל.

רפואה

רְפָאֵנוּ יהוה וְנֵרָפֵא
הוֹשִׁיעֵנוּ וְנִוָּשֵׁעָה, כִּי תְהִלָּתֵנוּ אָתָּה
וְהַעֲלֵה רְפוּאָה שְׁלֵמָה לְכָל מַכּוֹתֵינוּ

The following prayer for a sick person may be said here:

יְהִי רָצוֹן מִלְּפָנֶיךָ יהוה אֱלֹהַי וֵאלֹהֵי אֲבוֹתַי, שֶׁתִּשְׁלַח מְהֵרָה רְפוּאָה שְׁלֵמָה
מִן הַשָּׁמַיִם רְפוּאַת הַנֶּפֶשׁ וּרְפוּאַת הַגּוּף לַחוֹלֶה/לַחוֹלָה *name of patient*
בֶּן/בַּת *mother's name* בְּתוֹךְ שְׁאָר חוֹלֵי יִשְׂרָאֵל.

כִּי אֵל מֶלֶךְ רוֹפֵא נֶאֱמָן וְרַחֲמָן אָתָּה.
בָּרוּךְ אַתָּה יהוה
רוֹפֵא חוֹלֵי עַמּוֹ יִשְׂרָאֵל.

PROSPERITY

בָּרֵךְ Bless this year for us, Lord our God,
and all its types of produce for good.
Grant blessing on the face of the earth,
and from its goodness satisfy us,
blessing our year as the best of years.
Blessed are You, Lord, who blesses the years.

INGATHERING OF EXILES

תְּקַע Sound the great shofar for our freedom,
raise high the banner to gather our exiles,
and gather us together
from the four quarters of the earth.
Blessed are You, Lord,
who gathers the dispersed of His people Israel.

JUSTICE

הָשִׁיבָה Restore our judges as at first
and our counselors as at the beginning,
and remove from us sorrow and sighing.
May You alone, Lord,
reign over us with loving-kindness and compassion,
and vindicate us in justice.
Blessed are You, Lord,
the King who loves righteousness and justice.

AGAINST INFORMERS

וְלַמַּלְשִׁינִים For the slanderers let there be no hope,
and may all wickedness perish in an instant.
May all Your people's enemies swiftly be cut down.
May You swiftly uproot, crush, cast down
and humble the arrogant swiftly in our days.
Blessed are You, Lord,
who destroys enemies and humbles the arrogant.

ברכת השנים
בָּרֵךְ עָלֵינוּ יהוה אֱלֹהֵינוּ אֶת הַשָּׁנָה הַזֹּאת
וְאֶת כָּל מִינֵי תְבוּאָתָהּ, לְטוֹבָה
וְתֵן בְּרָכָה עַל פְּנֵי הָאֲדָמָה, וְשַׂבְּעֵנוּ מִטּוּבָהּ
וּבָרֵךְ שְׁנָתֵנוּ כַּשָּׁנִים הַטּוֹבוֹת.
בָּרוּךְ אַתָּה יהוה, מְבָרֵךְ הַשָּׁנִים.

קיבוץ גלויות
תְּקַע בְּשׁוֹפָר גָּדוֹל לְחֵרוּתֵנוּ
וְשָׂא נֵס לְקַבֵּץ גָּלֻיּוֹתֵינוּ
וְקַבְּצֵנוּ יַחַד מֵאַרְבַּע כַּנְפוֹת הָאָרֶץ.
בָּרוּךְ אַתָּה יהוה, מְקַבֵּץ נִדְחֵי עַמּוֹ יִשְׂרָאֵל.

השבת המשפט
הָשִׁיבָה שׁוֹפְטֵינוּ כְּבָרִאשׁוֹנָה
וְיוֹעֲצֵינוּ כְּבַתְּחִלָּה
וְהָסֵר מִמֶּנּוּ יָגוֹן וַאֲנָחָה
וּמְלֹךְ עָלֵינוּ אַתָּה יהוה לְבַדְּךָ בְּחֶסֶד וּבְרַחֲמִים
וְצַדְּקֵנוּ בַּמִּשְׁפָּט.
בָּרוּךְ אַתָּה יהוה, מֶלֶךְ אוֹהֵב צְדָקָה וּמִשְׁפָּט.

ברכת המינים
וְלַמַּלְשִׁינִים אַל תְּהִי תִקְוָה
וְכָל הָרִשְׁעָה כְּרֶגַע תֹּאבֵד
וְכָל אוֹיְבֵי עַמְּךָ מְהֵרָה יִכָּרֵתוּ
וְהַזֵּדִים מְהֵרָה תְעַקֵּר וּתְשַׁבֵּר וּתְמַגֵּר וְתַכְנִיעַ בִּמְהֵרָה בְיָמֵינוּ.
בָּרוּךְ אַתָּה יהוה, שׁוֹבֵר אוֹיְבִים וּמַכְנִיעַ זֵדִים.

THE RIGHTEOUS

עַל הַצַדִּיקִים To the righteous, the pious,
the elders of Your people the house of Israel,
the remnant of their scholars,
the righteous converts, and to us,
may Your compassion be aroused,
Lord our God.
Grant a good reward to all
who sincerely trust in Your name.
Set our lot with them,
so that we may never be ashamed,
for in You we trust
Blessed are You, Lord,
who is the support and trust of the righteous.

REBUILDING JERUSALEM

וְלִירוּשָׁלַיִם To Jerusalem, Your city,
may You return in compassion,
and may You dwell in it as You promised.
May You rebuild it rapidly in our days
as an everlasting structure,
and install within it soon the throne of David.
Blessed are You, Lord,
who builds Jerusalem.

KINGDOM OF DAVID

אֶת צֶמַח May the offshoot of Your servant David soon flower,
and may his pride be raised high by Your salvation,
for we wait for Your salvation all day.
Blessed are You, Lord,
who makes the glory of salvation flourish.

על הצדיקים
עַל הַצַּדִּיקִים וְעַל הַחֲסִידִים
וְעַל זִקְנֵי עַמְּךָ בֵּית יִשְׂרָאֵל
וְעַל פְּלֵיטַת סוֹפְרֵיהֶם
וְעַל גֵּרֵי הַצֶּדֶק, וְעָלֵינוּ
יֶהֱמוּ רַחֲמֶיךָ יהוה אֱלֹהֵינוּ
וְתֵן שָׂכָר טוֹב לְכָל הַבּוֹטְחִים בְּשִׁמְךָ בֶּאֱמֶת
וְשִׂים חֶלְקֵנוּ עִמָּהֶם
וּלְעוֹלָם לֹא נֵבוֹשׁ כִּי בְךָ בָּטָחְנוּ.
בָּרוּךְ אַתָּה יהוה
מִשְׁעָן וּמִבְטָח לַצַּדִּיקִים.

בניין ירושלים
וְלִירוּשָׁלַיִם עִירְךָ בְּרַחֲמִים תָּשׁוּב
וְתִשְׁכֹּן בְּתוֹכָהּ כַּאֲשֶׁר דִּבַּרְתָּ
וּבְנֵה אוֹתָהּ בְּקָרוֹב בְּיָמֵינוּ בִּנְיַן עוֹלָם
וְכִסֵּא דָוִד מְהֵרָה לְתוֹכָהּ תָּכִין.
בָּרוּךְ אַתָּה יהוה
בּוֹנֵה יְרוּשָׁלָיִם.

משיח בן דוד
אֶת צֶמַח דָּוִד עַבְדְּךָ מְהֵרָה תַצְמִיחַ
וְקַרְנוֹ תָּרוּם בִּישׁוּעָתֶךָ
כִּי לִישׁוּעָתְךָ קִוִּינוּ כָּל הַיּוֹם.
בָּרוּךְ אַתָּה יהוה
מַצְמִיחַ קֶרֶן יְשׁוּעָה.

RESPONSE TO PRAYER

שְׁמַע קוֹלֵנוּ Listen to our voice, LORD our God.
Spare us and have compassion on us,
and in compassion and favor accept our prayer,
for You, God, listen to prayers and pleas.
Do not turn us away, O our King,
empty-handed from Your presence,
for You listen with compassion to the prayer of Your people Israel.
Blessed are You, LORD, who listens to prayer.

TEMPLE SERVICE

רְצֵה Find favor, LORD our God, in Your people Israel and their prayer.
Restore the service to Your most holy House,
and accept in love and favor,
the fire-offerings of Israel and their prayer.
May the service of Your people Israel always find favor with You.
And may our eyes witness Your return to Zion in compassion.
Blessed are You, LORD, who restores His Presence to Zion.

THANKSGIVING

Bow at the first nine words.

מוֹדִים We give thanks to You,
for You are the LORD our God and God of our ancestors
for ever and all time.
You are the Rock of our lives,
Shield of our salvation from generation to generation.
We will thank You and declare Your praise for our lives,
which are entrusted into Your hand;
for our souls, which are placed in Your charge;
for Your miracles which are with us every day;
and for Your wonders and favors at all times,
evening, morning and midday.
You are good – for Your compassion never fails.
You are compassionate – for Your loving-kindnesses never cease.
We have always placed our hope in You.

שומע תפילה
שְׁמַע קוֹלֵנוּ יהוה אֱלֹהֵינוּ
חוּס וְרַחֵם עָלֵינוּ, וְקַבֵּל בְּרַחֲמִים וּבְרָצוֹן אֶת תְּפִלָּתֵנוּ
כִּי אֵל שׁוֹמֵעַ תְּפִלּוֹת וְתַחֲנוּנִים אָתָּה
וּמִלְּפָנֶיךָ מַלְכֵּנוּ רֵיקָם אַל תְּשִׁיבֵנוּ
כִּי אַתָּה שׁוֹמֵעַ תְּפִלַּת עַמְּךָ יִשְׂרָאֵל בְּרַחֲמִים.
בָּרוּךְ אַתָּה יהוה, שׁוֹמֵעַ תְּפִלָּה.

עבודה
רְצֵה יהוה אֱלֹהֵינוּ בְּעַמְּךָ יִשְׂרָאֵל, וּבִתְפִלָּתָם
וְהָשֵׁב אֶת הָעֲבוֹדָה לִדְבִיר בֵּיתֶךָ
וְאִשֵּׁי יִשְׂרָאֵל וּתְפִלָּתָם בְּאַהֲבָה תְקַבֵּל בְּרָצוֹן
וּתְהִי לְרָצוֹן תָּמִיד עֲבוֹדַת יִשְׂרָאֵל עַמֶּךָ.
וְתֶחֱזֶינָה עֵינֵינוּ בְּשׁוּבְךָ לְצִיּוֹן בְּרַחֲמִים.
בָּרוּךְ אַתָּה יהוה, הַמַּחֲזִיר שְׁכִינָתוֹ לְצִיּוֹן.

הודאה

Bow at the first five words.

מוֹדִים אֲנַחְנוּ לָךְ
שָׁאַתָּה הוּא יהוה אֱלֹהֵינוּ וֵאלֹהֵי אֲבוֹתֵינוּ לְעוֹלָם וָעֶד.
צוּר חַיֵּינוּ, מָגֵן יִשְׁעֵנוּ אַתָּה הוּא לְדוֹר וָדוֹר.
נוֹדֶה לְּךָ וּנְסַפֵּר תְּהִלָּתֶךָ, עַל חַיֵּינוּ הַמְּסוּרִים בְּיָדֶךָ
וְעַל נִשְׁמוֹתֵינוּ הַפְּקוּדוֹת לָךְ, וְעַל נִסֶּיךָ שֶׁבְּכָל יוֹם עִמָּנוּ
וְעַל נִפְלְאוֹתֶיךָ וְטוֹבוֹתֶיךָ שֶׁבְּכָל עֵת, עֶרֶב וָבֹקֶר וְצָהֳרָיִם.
הַטּוֹב, כִּי לֹא כָלוּ רַחֲמֶיךָ, וְהַמְרַחֵם, כִּי לֹא תַמּוּ חֲסָדֶיךָ
מֵעוֹלָם קִוִּינוּ לָךְ.

For all these things may Your name be blessed and exalted,
our King, continually, for ever and all time.
Let all that lives thank You, Selah! and praise Your name in truth,
God, our Savior and Help, Selah!
▸Blessed are You, Lord, whose name is "the Good"
and to whom thanks are due.

PEACE

שָׁלוֹם רָב Grant great peace to Your people Israel for ever,
for You are the sovereign Lord of all peace;
and may it be good in Your eyes
to bless Your people Israel
at every time, at every hour, with Your peace.
Blessed are You, Lord, who blesses His people Israel with peace.

Some say the following verse:
May the words of my mouth and the meditation of my heart *Ps. 19*
find favor before You, Lord, my Rock and Redeemer.

אֱלֹהַי My God, *Berakhot 17a*
guard my tongue from evil and my lips from deceitful speech.
To those who curse me, let my soul be silent;
may my soul be to all like the dust.
Open my heart to Your Torah
and let my soul pursue Your commandments.
As for all who plan evil against me,
swiftly thwart their counsel and frustrate their plans.
    Act for the sake of Your name; act for the sake of Your right hand;
    act for the sake of Your holiness; act for the sake of Your Torah.
That Your beloved ones may be delivered, *Ps. 60*
save with Your right hand and answer me.
May the words of my mouth *Ps. 19*
and the meditation of my heart find favor before You,
Lord, my Rock and Redeemer.

Bow, take three steps back, then bow, first left, then right, then center, while saying:
May He who makes peace in His high places,
make peace for us and all Israel – and say: Amen.

וְעַל כֻּלָּם יִתְבָּרַךְ וְיִתְרוֹמַם שִׁמְךָ מַלְכֵּנוּ תָּמִיד לְעוֹלָם וָעֶד.
וְכֹל הַחַיִּים יוֹדוּךָ סֶּלָה, וִיהַלְלוּ אֶת שִׁמְךָ בֶּאֱמֶת
הָאֵל יְשׁוּעָתֵנוּ וְעֶזְרָתֵנוּ סֶלָה.
בָּרוּךְ אַתָּה יהוה, הַטּוֹב שִׁמְךָ וּלְךָ נָאֶה לְהוֹדוֹת.

ברכת שלום

שָׁלוֹם רָב עַל יִשְׂרָאֵל עַמְּךָ תָּשִׂים לְעוֹלָם
כִּי אַתָּה הוּא מֶלֶךְ אָדוֹן לְכָל הַשָּׁלוֹם.
וְטוֹב בְּעֵינֶיךָ לְבָרֵךְ אֶת עַמְּךָ יִשְׂרָאֵל
בְּכָל עֵת וּבְכָל שָׁעָה בִּשְׁלוֹמֶךָ.
בָּרוּךְ אַתָּה יהוה, הַמְבָרֵךְ אֶת עַמּוֹ יִשְׂרָאֵל בַּשָּׁלוֹם.

Some say the following verse:

תהלים יט

יִהְיוּ לְרָצוֹן אִמְרֵי־פִי וְהֶגְיוֹן לִבִּי לְפָנֶיךָ, יהוה צוּרִי וְגֹאֲלִי:

ברכות יז

אֱלֹהַי
נְצֹר לְשׁוֹנִי מֵרָע וּשְׂפָתַי מִדַּבֵּר מִרְמָה
וְלִמְקַלְלַי נַפְשִׁי תִדֹּם, וְנַפְשִׁי כֶּעָפָר לַכֹּל תִּהְיֶה.
פְּתַח לִבִּי בְּתוֹרָתֶךָ, וּבְמִצְוֹתֶיךָ תִּרְדּוֹף נַפְשִׁי.
וְכָל הַחוֹשְׁבִים עָלַי רָעָה
מְהֵרָה הָפֵר עֲצָתָם וְקַלְקֵל מַחֲשַׁבְתָּם.
עֲשֵׂה לְמַעַן שְׁמֶךָ, עֲשֵׂה לְמַעַן יְמִינֶךָ
עֲשֵׂה לְמַעַן קְדֻשָּׁתֶךָ, עֲשֵׂה לְמַעַן תּוֹרָתֶךָ.

תהלים ס
תהלים יט

לְמַעַן יֵחָלְצוּן יְדִידֶיךָ, הוֹשִׁיעָה יְמִינְךָ וַעֲנֵנִי:
יִהְיוּ לְרָצוֹן אִמְרֵי־פִי וְהֶגְיוֹן לִבִּי לְפָנֶיךָ, יהוה צוּרִי וְגֹאֲלִי:

Bow, take three steps back, then bow, first left, then right, then center, while saying:

עֹשֶׂה שָׁלוֹם בִּמְרוֹמָיו
הוּא יַעֲשֶׂה שָׁלוֹם עָלֵינוּ וְעַל כָּל יִשְׂרָאֵל, וְאִמְרוּ אָמֵן.

MA'ARIV FOR TISHA B'AV

יְהִי רָצוֹן May it be Your will, LORD our God and God of our ancestors,
that the Temple be rebuilt speedily in our days, and grant us a share in Your Torah.
And there we will serve You with reverence,
as in the days of old and as in former years.
Then the offering of Judah and Jerusalem
will be pleasing to the LORD as in the days of old and as in former years.

Mal. 3

FULL KADDISH

Leader: יִתְגַּדֵּל Magnified and sanctified may His great name be,
in the world He created by His will.
May He establish His kingdom
in your lifetime and in your days,
and in the lifetime of all the house of Israel,
swiftly and soon – and say: Amen.

All: May His great name be blessed for ever and all time.

Leader: Blessed and praised, glorified and exalted,
raised and honored,
uplifted and lauded be the name of the Holy One,
blessed be He, beyond any blessing,
song, praise and consolation
uttered in the world – and say: Amen.

May the prayers and pleas of all Israel
be accepted by their Father in heaven – and say: Amen.

May there be great peace from heaven,
and life for us and all Israel – and say: Amen.

*Bow, take three steps back, as if taking leave of the Divine Presence,
then bow, first left, then right, then center, while saying:*

May He who makes peace in His high places,
make peace for us and all Israel – and say: Amen.

*On Motza'ei Shabbat, the following is recited,
and the fingers are held up to a multi-wicked flame:*

בָּרוּךְ Blessed are You, LORD our God, King of the Universe,
who creates the lights of fire.

The congregation sits on the floor, and the Leader chants Eikha.

יְהִי רָצוֹן מִלְּפָנֶיךָ יהוה אֱלֹהֵינוּ וֵאלֹהֵי אֲבוֹתֵינוּ שֶׁיִּבָּנֶה בֵּית הַמִּקְדָּשׁ בִּמְהֵרָה בְיָמֵינוּ, וְתֵן חֶלְקֵנוּ בְּתוֹרָתֶךָ וְשָׁם נַעֲבָדְךָ בְּיִרְאָה כִּימֵי עוֹלָם וּכְשָׁנִים קַדְמֹנִיּוֹת. וְעָרְבָה לַיהוה מִנְחַת יְהוּדָה וִירוּשָׁלָיִם כִּימֵי עוֹלָם וּכְשָׁנִים קַדְמֹנִיּוֹת: מלאכי ג

קדיש שלם

ש״ץ: יִתְגַּדַּל וְיִתְקַדַּשׁ שְׁמֵהּ רַבָּא (קהל: אָמֵן) בְּעָלְמָא דִּי בְרָא כִרְעוּתֵהּ, וְיַמְלִיךְ מַלְכוּתֵהּ בְּחַיֵּיכוֹן וּבְיוֹמֵיכוֹן וּבְחַיֵּי דְכָל בֵּית יִשְׂרָאֵל בַּעֲגָלָא וּבִזְמַן קָרִיב, וְאִמְרוּ אָמֵן. (קהל: אָמֵן)

קהל וש״ץ: יְהֵא שְׁמֵהּ רַבָּא מְבָרַךְ לְעָלַם וּלְעָלְמֵי עָלְמַיָּא.

ש״ץ: יִתְבָּרַךְ וְיִשְׁתַּבַּח וְיִתְפָּאַר וְיִתְרוֹמַם וְיִתְנַשֵּׂא וְיִתְהַדָּר וְיִתְעַלֶּה וְיִתְהַלָּל שְׁמֵהּ דְּקֻדְשָׁא בְּרִיךְ הוּא (קהל: בְּרִיךְ הוּא) לְעֵלָּא מִן כָּל בִּרְכָתָא וְשִׁירָתָא, תֻּשְׁבְּחָתָא וְנֶחֱמָתָא דַּאֲמִירָן בְּעָלְמָא, וְאִמְרוּ אָמֵן. (קהל: אָמֵן)

תִּתְקַבַּל צְלוֹתְהוֹן וּבָעוּתְהוֹן דְּכָל יִשְׂרָאֵל קֳדָם אֲבוּהוֹן דִּי בִשְׁמַיָּא, וְאִמְרוּ אָמֵן. (קהל: אָמֵן)

יְהֵא שְׁלָמָא רַבָּא מִן שְׁמַיָּא וְחַיִּים, עָלֵינוּ וְעַל כָּל יִשְׂרָאֵל, וְאִמְרוּ אָמֵן. (קהל: אָמֵן)

Bow, take three steps back, as if taking leave of the Divine Presence, then bow, first left, then right, then center, while saying:

עֹשֶׂה שָׁלוֹם בִּמְרוֹמָיו הוּא יַעֲשֶׂה שָׁלוֹם עָלֵינוּ וְעַל כָּל יִשְׂרָאֵל וְאִמְרוּ אָמֵן. (קהל: אָמֵן)

On מוצאי שבת *the following is recited, and the fingers are held up to a multi-wicked flame:*

בָּרוּךְ אַתָּה יהוה אֱלֹהֵינוּ מֶלֶךְ הָעוֹלָם, בּוֹרֵא מְאוֹרֵי הָאֵשׁ.

The קהל *sits on the floor, and the* שליח ציבור *chants* איכה.

מגילת איכה

MEGILLAT EIKHA

1 1 How does the city sit solitary, that was full of people! how is she become like a widow! she that was great among the nations, and princess among
2 the provinces, how is she become a vassal! She weeps sore in the night, and her tears are on her cheeks: among all her lovers she has none to comfort her: all her friends have dealt treacherously with her, they have
3 become her enemies. Judah is gone into exile because of affliction, and because of great servitude: she dwells among the nations, she finds no
4 rest: all her persecutors overtook her within the straits. The ways of Zion do mourn, because none come to the solemn assembly: all her gates are desolate: her priests sigh, her virgins are afflicted, and she is in bitterness.
5 Her adversaries have become the chief, her enemies prosper; for the Lord has afflicted her for the multitude of her transgressions: her infants are
6 gone into captivity before the enemy. And from the daughter of Zion all her splendor is departed: her princes are become like harts that find no
7 pasture, and they are gone without strength before the pursuer. Jerusalem remembers in the days of her affliction and of her miseries all her pleasant things that she had in the days of old, when her people fell into the hand of the enemy, and none did help her: the adversaries saw her, and gloated at
8 her destruction. Jerusalem has grievously sinned; therefore she is become loathsome: all that honored her despise her, because they have seen her
9 nakedness: she herself also sighs, and turns backward. Her filthiness was in her skirts; she took no thought of her last end; therefore she came down astonishingly: she has no comforter. O Lord, behold my affliction: for
10 the enemy has magnified himself. The adversary has spread out his hand upon all her pleasant things: for she has seen that heathen nations invade her sanctuary, those whom You did forbid to enter into Your congregation.
11 All her people sigh, they seek bread; they have given their pleasant things for food to relieve the soul: see, O Lord, and consider; how abject I am
12 become. Is it nothing to you, all you that pass by? behold, and see if there is any pain like my pain, which is done to me, with which the Lord has
13 afflicted me in the day of His fierce anger. From above He has sent fire into my bones, and it prevails against them: He has spread a net for my feet, He
14 has turned me back: He has made me desolate and faint all the day. The yoke of my transgressions is fastened on by His hand: they are knit together, and come up upon my neck: He has made my strength to fall, the Lord has delivered me into the hands of those against whom I am not able to rise up.
15 The Lord has spurned all my mighty men in the midst of me: He has called an assembly against me to crush my young men: the Lord has trodden

מגילת איכה

א א אֵיכָה ׀ יָשְׁבָה בָדָד הָעִיר רַבָּתִי עָם הָיְתָה כְּאַלְמָנָה רַבָּתִי בַגּוֹיִם
ב שָׂרָתִי בַּמְּדִינוֹת הָיְתָה לָמַס: בָּכוֹ תִבְכֶּה בַּלַּיְלָה וְדִמְעָתָהּ עַל
לֶחֱיָהּ אֵין־לָהּ מְנַחֵם מִכָּל־אֹהֲבֶיהָ כָּל־רֵעֶיהָ בָּגְדוּ בָהּ הָיוּ לָהּ
ג לְאֹיְבִים: גָּלְתָה יְהוּדָה מֵעֹנִי וּמֵרֹב עֲבֹדָה הִיא יָשְׁבָה בַגּוֹיִם לֹא
ד מָצְאָה מָנוֹחַ כָּל־רֹדְפֶיהָ הִשִּׂיגוּהָ בֵּין הַמְּצָרִים: דַּרְכֵי צִיּוֹן אֲבֵלוֹת
מִבְּלִי בָּאֵי מוֹעֵד כָּל־שְׁעָרֶיהָ שׁוֹמֵמִין כֹּהֲנֶיהָ נֶאֱנָחִים בְּתוּלֹתֶיהָ
ה נּוּגוֹת וְהִיא מַר־לָהּ: הָיוּ צָרֶיהָ לְרֹאשׁ אֹיְבֶיהָ שָׁלוּ כִּי־יְהוָה הוֹגָהּ
ו עַל־רֹב פְּשָׁעֶיהָ עוֹלָלֶיהָ הָלְכוּ שְׁבִי לִפְנֵי־צָר: וַיֵּצֵא מִן־בַּת־צִיּוֹן מִבַּת־
כָּל־הֲדָרָהּ הָיוּ שָׂרֶיהָ כְּאַיָּלִים לֹא־מָצְאוּ מִרְעֶה וַיֵּלְכוּ בְלֹא־כֹחַ
ז לִפְנֵי רוֹדֵף: זָכְרָה יְרוּשָׁלִַם יְמֵי עָנְיָהּ וּמְרוּדֶיהָ כֹּל מַחֲמֻדֶיהָ אֲשֶׁר
הָיוּ מִימֵי קֶדֶם בִּנְפֹל עַמָּהּ בְּיַד־צָר וְאֵין עוֹזֵר לָהּ רָאוּהָ צָרִים
ח שָׂחֲקוּ עַל מִשְׁבַּתֶּהָ: חֵטְא חָטְאָה יְרוּשָׁלִַם עַל־כֵּן לְנִידָה הָיָתָה
כָּל־מְכַבְּדֶיהָ הִזִּילוּהָ כִּי־רָאוּ עֶרְוָתָהּ גַּם־הִיא נֶאֶנְחָה וַתָּשָׁב
ט אָחוֹר: טֻמְאָתָהּ בְּשׁוּלֶיהָ לֹא זָכְרָה אַחֲרִיתָהּ וַתֵּרֶד פְּלָאִים
י אֵין מְנַחֵם לָהּ רְאֵה יְהוָה אֶת־עָנְיִי כִּי הִגְדִּיל אוֹיֵב: יָדוֹ פָּרַשׂ
צָר עַל כָּל־מַחֲמַדֶּיהָ כִּי־רָאֲתָה גוֹיִם בָּאוּ מִקְדָּשָׁהּ אֲשֶׁר צִוִּיתָה
יא לֹא־יָבֹאוּ בַקָּהָל לָךְ: כָּל־עַמָּהּ נֶאֱנָחִים מְבַקְּשִׁים לֶחֶם נָתְנוּ
מַחֲמוֹדֵיהֶם בְּאֹכֶל לְהָשִׁיב נָפֶשׁ רְאֵה יְהוָה וְהַבִּיטָה כִּי הָיִיתִי
יב זוֹלֵלָה: לוֹא אֲלֵיכֶם כָּל־עֹבְרֵי דֶרֶךְ הַבִּיטוּ וּרְאוּ אִם־יֵשׁ מַכְאוֹב
יג כְּמַכְאֹבִי אֲשֶׁר עוֹלַל לִי אֲשֶׁר הוֹגָה יְהוָה בְּיוֹם חֲרוֹן אַפּוֹ: מִמָּרוֹם
שָׁלַח־אֵשׁ בְּעַצְמֹתַי וַיִּרְדֶּנָּה פָּרַשׂ רֶשֶׁת לְרַגְלַי הֱשִׁיבַנִי אָחוֹר
יד נְתָנַנִי שֹׁמֵמָה כָּל־הַיּוֹם דָּוָה: נִשְׂקַד עֹל פְּשָׁעַי בְּיָדוֹ יִשְׂתָּרְגוּ
עָלוּ עַל־צַוָּארִי הִכְשִׁיל כֹּחִי נְתָנַנִי אֲדֹנָי בִּידֵי לֹא־אוּכַל קוּם:
טו סִלָּה כָל־אַבִּירַי ׀ אֲדֹנָי בְּקִרְבִּי קָרָא עָלַי מוֹעֵד לִשְׁבֹּר בַּחוּרָי גַּת

16 the virgin, the daughter of Judah, as in a winepress. For these things I weep; my eye, my eye runs down with water, because the Comforter that should relieve my soul is far from me: my children are desolate, because the enemy has prevailed.
17 Zion spreads out her hands, and there is none to comfort her: the Lord has commanded against Jacob, adversaries round about him: Jerusalem is like a menstruous woman among them.
18 The Lord is righteous; for I have rebelled against His word: hear, I pray you, all the peoples, and behold my pain: my virgins and my young men are gone into captivity.
19 I called for my lovers, but they deceived me: my priests and my elders perished in the city, while they sought food for themselves to relieve their souls.
20 Behold, O Lord; for I am in distress: my bowels are troubled; my heart is turned within me; for I have grievously rebelled: abroad the sword bereaves, at home it is like death.
21 They have heard that I sigh: there is none to comfort me: all my enemies have heard of my trouble; they are glad that You have done it: You will bring the day that You have called, and they shall be like me.
22 Let all their wickedness come before You; and do to them as You have done to me for all my transgressions: for my sighs are many, and my heart is faint.

2 1 How has the Lord covered the daughter of Zion with a cloud in His anger, and cast down from heaven to earth the beauty of Israel, and remembered not His footstool in the day of His anger!
2 The Lord has swallowed up without pity all the habitations of Jacob: He has thrown down in His wrath the strongholds of the daughter of Judah; He has brought them down to the ground: He has profaned the kingdom and its princes.
3 He has cut off in His fierce anger all the horn of Israel: He has drawn back His right hand from before the enemy, and He has burned against Jacob like a flaming fire, which devours round about.
4 He has bent His bow like an enemy: with His right hand set like an adversary, He has slain all that were pleasant to the eye: in the tent of the daughter of Zion, He has poured out His fury like fire.
5 The Lord was like an enemy: He has swallowed up Israel, He has swallowed up all her palaces: He has destroyed its strongholds, and has increased in the daughter of Judah mourning and lamentation.
6 And He has stripped His tabernacle, as if it were a garden: He has destroyed His place of assembly: the Lord has caused the appointed seasons and sabbaths to be forgotten in Zion, and has spurned in the indignation of His anger both king and priest.
7 The Lord has cast off His altar, He has abhorred His Sanctuary, He has given up into the hand of the enemy the walls of her palaces; they have made a noise in the house of the Lord, as in the day of a solemn assembly.
8 The Lord has purposed to destroy the wall of the daughter of Zion: He

מגילת איכה

טז דָּרַךְ אֲדֹנָי לִבְתוּלַת בַּת־יְהוּדָה: עַל־אֵלֶּה ׀ אֲנִי בוֹכִיָּה עֵינִי ׀ עֵינִי יֹרְדָה מַּיִם כִּי־רָחַק מִמֶּנִּי מְנַחֵם מֵשִׁיב נַפְשִׁי הָיוּ בָנַי שׁוֹמֵמִים כִּי

יז גָבַר אוֹיֵב: פֵּרְשָׂה צִיּוֹן בְּיָדֶיהָ אֵין מְנַחֵם לָהּ צִוָּה יְהוָה לְיַעֲקֹב סְבִיבָיו צָרָיו הָיְתָה יְרוּשָׁלַ͏ִם לְנִדָּה בֵּינֵיהֶם: צַדִּיק הוּא יְהוָה

יח כִּי פִיהוּ מָרִיתִי שִׁמְעוּ־נָא כָל־עַמִּים וּרְאוּ מַכְאֹבִי בְּתוּלֹתַי הָעַמִּים

יט וּבַחוּרַי הָלְכוּ בַשֶּׁבִי: קָרָאתִי לַמְאַהֲבַי הֵמָּה רִמּוּנִי כֹּהֲנַי וּזְקֵנַי

כ בָּעִיר גָּוָעוּ כִּי־בִקְשׁוּ אֹכֶל לָמוֹ וְיָשִׁיבוּ אֶת־נַפְשָׁם: רְאֵה יְהוָה כִּי־צַר־לִי מֵעַי חֳמַרְמָרוּ נֶהְפַּךְ לִבִּי בְּקִרְבִּי כִּי מָרוֹ מָרִיתִי מִחוּץ

כא שִׁכְּלָה־חֶרֶב בַּבַּיִת כַּמָּוֶת: שָׁמְעוּ כִּי נֶאֱנָחָה אָנִי אֵין מְנַחֵם לִי כָּל־אֹיְבַי שָׁמְעוּ רָעָתִי שָׂשׂוּ כִּי אַתָּה עָשִׂיתָ הֵבֵאתָ יוֹם־קָרָאתָ

כב וְיִהְיוּ כָמֹנִי: תָּבֹא כָל־רָעָתָם לְפָנֶיךָ וְעוֹלֵל לָמוֹ כַּאֲשֶׁר עוֹלַלְתָּ לִי עַל כָּל־פְּשָׁעָי כִּי־רַבּוֹת אַנְחֹתַי וְלִבִּי דַוָּי:

ב א אֵיכָה יָעִיב בְּאַפּוֹ ׀ אֲדֹנָי אֶת־בַּת־צִיּוֹן הִשְׁלִיךְ מִשָּׁמַיִם אֶרֶץ תִּפְאֶרֶת יִשְׂרָאֵל וְלֹא־זָכַר הֲדֹם־רַגְלָיו בְּיוֹם אַפּוֹ: בִּלַּע אֲדֹנָי

ב לֹא חָמַל אֵת כָּל־נְאוֹת יַעֲקֹב הָרַס בְּעֶבְרָתוֹ מִבְצְרֵי בַת־ וְלֹא

ג יְהוּדָה הִגִּיעַ לָאָרֶץ חִלֵּל מַמְלָכָה וְשָׂרֶיהָ: גָּדַע בָּחֳרִי־אַף כֹּל קֶרֶן יִשְׂרָאֵל הֵשִׁיב אָחוֹר יְמִינוֹ מִפְּנֵי אוֹיֵב וַיִּבְעַר בְּיַעֲקֹב כְּאֵשׁ

ד לֶהָבָה אָכְלָה סָבִיב: דָּרַךְ קַשְׁתּוֹ כְּאוֹיֵב נִצָּב יְמִינוֹ כְּצָר וַיַּהֲרֹג

ה כֹּל מַחֲמַדֵּי־עָיִן בְּאֹהֶל בַּת־צִיּוֹן שָׁפַךְ כָּאֵשׁ חֲמָתוֹ: הָיָה אֲדֹנָי ׀ כְּאוֹיֵב בִּלַּע יִשְׂרָאֵל בִּלַּע כָּל־אַרְמְנוֹתֶיהָ שִׁחֵת מִבְצָרָיו וַיֶּרֶב

ו בְּבַת־יְהוּדָה תַּאֲנִיָּה וַאֲנִיָּה: וַיַּחְמֹס כַּגַּן שֻׂכּוֹ שִׁחֵת מֹעֲדוֹ שִׁכַּח יְהוָה ׀ בְּצִיּוֹן מוֹעֵד וְשַׁבָּת וַיִּנְאַץ בְּזַעַם־אַפּוֹ מֶלֶךְ וְכֹהֵן: זָנַח

ז אֲדֹנָי ׀ מִזְבְּחוֹ נִאֵר מִקְדָּשׁוֹ הִסְגִּיר בְּיַד־אוֹיֵב חוֹמֹת אַרְמְנוֹתֶיהָ

ח קוֹל נָתְנוּ בְּבֵית־יְהוָה כְּיוֹם מוֹעֵד: חָשַׁב יְהוָה ׀ לְהַשְׁחִית חוֹמַת

has stretched out a line, He has not withdrawn His hand from destroying: therefore He made the rampart and the wall to lament; they languish
9 together. Her gates are sunk into the ground; He has destroyed and broken her bars: her king and her princes are among the nations: there is no Torah;
10 her prophets also find no vision from the LORD. The elders of the daughter of Zion sit upon the ground, and keep silence: they have cast up dust upon their heads; they have girded themselves with sackcloth: the virgins of
11 Jerusalem hang down their heads to the ground. My eyes fail with tears, my bowels are troubled, my liver is poured upon the earth, for the breach of the daughter of my people; because the children and the sucklings swoon in
12 the broad places of the city. They say to their mothers, Where is corn and wine? when they swoon like wounded men in the broad places of the city,
13 when their soul is poured out into their mothers' bosom. What shall I take to witness for you? what shall I liken to you, O daughter of Jerusalem? what shall I equal to you, that I may comfort you, O virgin daughter of Zion? for
14 your breach is great like the sea: who can heal you? Your prophets have seen for you vain and foolish visions: and they have not exposed your iniquity, to restore your captivity; but have prophesied for you burdens of falsehood
15 and deceit. All that pass by clap their hands at you; they hiss and wag their head at the daughter of Jerusalem, saying, Is this the city that men call The
16 perfection of beauty, The joy of the whole earth? All your enemies have opened their mouth against you: they hiss and gnash the teeth: they say, We have swallowed her up: certainly this is the day that we have looked for; we
17 have found it, we have seen it. The LORD has done that which He devised; He has fulfilled His word that He commanded in the days of old: He has thrown down without pity: and He has caused the enemy to rejoice over
18 you, He has raised up the horn of your adversaries. Their heart cried to the LORD. O wall of the daughter of Zion, let tears run down like a river day
19 and night: give yourself no rest; let not the apple of your eye cease. Arise, cry out in the night: in the beginning of the watches pour out your heart like water before the face of the LORD: lift up your hands toward Him for the life of your young children, that faint for hunger at the head of every
20 street. Behold, O LORD, and consider to whom You have done this. Shall the women eat their fruit, their cherished babes? shall priest and prophet
21 be slain in the Sanctuary of the LORD? Young and old lie on the ground in the streets: my virgins and my young men are fallen by the sword; You have
22 slain them in the day of Your anger; You have killed, and not pitied. You have called as in the day of a solemn assembly, my terrors round about, so

בַּת־צִיּוֹן נָטָה קָו לֹא־הֵשִׁיב יָדוֹ מִבַּלֵּעַ וַיַּאֲבֶל־חֵל וְחוֹמָה יַחְדָּו
אֻמְלָלוּ: טָבְעוּ בָאָרֶץ שְׁעָרֶיהָ אִבַּד וְשִׁבַּר בְּרִיחֶיהָ מַלְכָּהּ וְשָׂרֶיהָ ט
בַגּוֹיִם אֵין תּוֹרָה גַּם־נְבִיאֶיהָ לֹא־מָצְאוּ חָזוֹן מֵיְהוָה: יֵשְׁבוּ לָאָרֶץ י
יִדְּמוּ זִקְנֵי בַת־צִיּוֹן הֶעֱלוּ עָפָר עַל־רֹאשָׁם חָגְרוּ שַׂקִּים הוֹרִידוּ
לָאָרֶץ רֹאשָׁן בְּתוּלֹת יְרוּשָׁלָםִ: כָּלוּ בַדְּמָעוֹת עֵינַי חֳמַרְמְרוּ יא
מֵעַי נִשְׁפַּךְ לָאָרֶץ כְּבֵדִי עַל־שֶׁבֶר בַּת־עַמִּי בֵּעָטֵף עוֹלֵל וְיוֹנֵק
בִּרְחֹבוֹת קִרְיָה: לְאִמֹּתָם יֹאמְרוּ אַיֵּה דָּגָן וָיָיִן בְּהִתְעַטְּפָם כַּחָלָל יב
בִּרְחֹבוֹת עִיר בְּהִשְׁתַּפֵּךְ נַפְשָׁם אֶל־חֵיק אִמֹּתָם: מָה־אֲעִידֵךְ יג
מָה אֲדַמֶּה־לָּךְ הַבַּת יְרוּשָׁלַםִ מָה אַשְׁוֶה־לָּךְ וַאֲנַחֲמֵךְ בְּתוּלַת
בַּת־צִיּוֹן כִּי־גָדוֹל כַּיָּם שִׁבְרֵךְ מִי יִרְפָּא־לָךְ: נְבִיאַיִךְ חָזוּ לָךְ שָׁוְא יד
וְתָפֵל וְלֹא־גִלּוּ עַל־עֲוֺנֵךְ לְהָשִׁיב שְׁבוּתֵךְ וַיֶּחֱזוּ לָךְ מַשְׂאוֹת שָׁוְא
וּמַדּוּחִים: סָפְקוּ עָלַיִךְ כַּפַּיִם כָּל־עֹבְרֵי דֶרֶךְ שָׁרְקוּ וַיָּנִעוּ טו
רֹאשָׁם עַל־בַּת יְרוּשָׁלָםִ הֲזֹאת הָעִיר שֶׁיֹּאמְרוּ כְּלִילַת יֹפִי מָשׂוֹשׂ
לְכָל־הָאָרֶץ: פָּצוּ עָלַיִךְ פִּיהֶם כָּל־אוֹיְבַיִךְ שָׁרְקוּ וַיַּחַרְקוּ־שֵׁן טז
אָמְרוּ בִּלָּעְנוּ אַךְ זֶה הַיּוֹם שֶׁקִּוִּינֻהוּ מָצָאנוּ רָאִינוּ: עָשָׂה יְהוָה יז
אֲשֶׁר זָמָם בִּצַּע אֶמְרָתוֹ אֲשֶׁר צִוָּה מִימֵי־קֶדֶם הָרַס וְלֹא חָמָל
וַיְשַׂמַּח עָלַיִךְ אוֹיֵב הֵרִים קֶרֶן צָרָיִךְ: צָעַק לִבָּם אֶל־אֲדֹנָי חוֹמַת יח
בַּת־צִיּוֹן הוֹרִידִי כַנַּחַל דִּמְעָה יוֹמָם וָלַיְלָה אַל־תִּתְּנִי פוּגַת לָךְ
אַל־תִּדֹּם בַּת־עֵינֵךְ: קוּמִי ׀ רֹנִּי בַלַּיְלָה לְרֹאשׁ אַשְׁמֻרוֹת שִׁפְכִי יט
כַמַּיִם לִבֵּךְ נֹכַח פְּנֵי אֲדֹנָי שְׂאִי אֵלָיו כַּפַּיִךְ עַל־נֶפֶשׁ עוֹלָלַיִךְ
הָעֲטוּפִים בְּרָעָב בְּרֹאשׁ כָּל־חוּצוֹת: רְאֵה יְהוָה וְהַבִּיטָה לְמִי כ
עוֹלַלְתָּ כֹּה אִם־תֹּאכַלְנָה נָשִׁים פִּרְיָם עֹלֲלֵי טִפֻּחִים אִם־יֵהָרֵג
בְּמִקְדַּשׁ אֲדֹנָי כֹּהֵן וְנָבִיא: שָׁכְבוּ לָאָרֶץ חוּצוֹת נַעַר וְזָקֵן בְּתוּלֹתַי כא
וּבַחוּרַי נָפְלוּ בֶחָרֶב הָרַגְתָּ בְּיוֹם אַפֶּךָ טָבַחְתָּ לֹא חָמָלְתָּ: תִּקְרָא כב

that in the day of the Lord's anger none escaped or remained: those that I have cherished and brought up my enemy has consumed.

3 ¹ ² I am the man who has seen affliction by the rod of His wrath. He has led ³ me, and brought me into darkness, but not into light. Surely He is turned ⁴ against me; He turns His hand against me all the day. He has made my flesh ⁵ and my skin to waste away; He has broken my bones. He has built a mound ⁶ against me, and has beset me round about at head and hell. He has set me ⁷ in dark places, as those who are long ago dead. He has hedged me about, ⁸ so that I cannot get out: He has made my chain heavy. Even when I cry and ⁹ call for help, He stops up my prayer. He has enclosed my ways with hewn ¹⁰ stone, He has made my paths crooked. He is to me like a bear lying in wait, ¹¹ and like a lion in secret places. He has turned aside my ways, and pulled me ¹² in pieces: He has made me desolate. He has bent his bow, and set me as a ¹³ mark for the arrow. He has caused the arrows of his quiver to enter into my ¹⁴ reins. I am become a derision to all my people; and their song all the day. ¹⁵ ¹⁶ He has filled me with bitterness, He has sated me with wormwood. He has also broken my teeth with gravel stones, He has pressed me down into the ¹⁷ ¹⁸ ashes. My soul is far removed from peace: I have forgotten prosperity. And ¹⁹ I said, My strength and my hope are perished from the Lord. Remember ²⁰ my affliction and my misery, the wormwood and the gall. My soul has them ²¹ still in remembrance, and is bowed down within me. This I recall to my ²² mind, therefore I have hope: that the Lord's steadfast love has not ceased, ²³ and that His compassions do not fail. They are new every morning: great ²⁴ is Your faithfulness. The Lord is my portion, says my soul; therefore I will ²⁵ hope in Him. The Lord is good to those who wait for Him, to the soul ²⁶ that seeks Him. It is good that a man should quietly hope for the salvation ²⁷ ²⁸ of the Lord. It is good for a man that he bear the yoke in his youth. Let ²⁹ him sit alone and keep silence, because he has taken it upon him. Let him ³⁰ put his mouth in the dust; perhaps there may be hope. Let him offer his ³¹ cheek to him who strikes him; let him take his fill of insult. For the Lord ³² will not cast off for ever: but though He may cause grief, yet will He have ³³ compassion according to the abundance of His steadfast love. For He does ³⁴ not willingly afflict or grieve the children of men. To crush under foot all ³⁵ the prisoners of the earth, to turn aside the right of a man before the face ³⁶ of the Most High, to subvert a man in his cause, the Lord approves not. ³⁷ Who is he that says, and it comes to pass, when the Lord commands it ³⁸ not? Out of the mouth of the Most High do not both good and evil come?

מגילת איכה

כְּיוֹם מוֹעֵד֙ מִסָּבִ֔יב וְלֹ֥א הָיָ֛ה בְּי֥וֹם אַף־יְהוָ֖ה פָּלִ֣יט וְשָׂרִ֑יד
אֲשֶׁר־טִפַּ֥חְתִּי וְרִבִּ֖יתִי אֹיְבִ֥י כִלָּֽם׃

ג א אֲנִ֤י הַגֶּ֙בֶר֙ רָאָ֣ה עֳנִ֔י בְּשֵׁ֖בֶט עֶבְרָתֽוֹ׃ אוֹתִ֥י נָהַ֛ג וַיֹּלַ֖ךְ חֹ֥שֶׁךְ וְלֹא־
ג אֽוֹר׃ אַ֣ךְ בִּ֥י יָשֻׁ֛ב יַהֲפֹ֥ךְ יָד֖וֹ כָּל־הַיּֽוֹם׃ בִּלָּ֤ה בְשָׂרִי֙ וְעוֹרִ֔י שִׁבַּ֖ר
ה עַצְמוֹתָֽי׃ בָּנָ֤ה עָלַי֙ וַיַּקַּ֔ף רֹ֖אשׁ וּתְלָאָֽה׃ בְּמַחֲשַׁכִּ֥ים הוֹשִׁיבַ֖נִי
כְּמֵתֵ֥י עוֹלָֽם׃ גָּדַ֧ר בַּעֲדִ֛י וְלֹ֥א אֵצֵ֖א הִכְבִּ֥יד נְחָשְׁתִּֽי׃ גַּ֣ם כִּ֤י אֶזְעַק֙
ט וַאֲשַׁוֵּ֔עַ שָׂתַ֖ם תְּפִלָּתִֽי׃ גָּדַ֤ר דְּרָכַי֙ בְּגָזִ֔ית נְתִיבֹתַ֖י עִוָּֽה׃ דֹּ֣ב אֹרֵ֥ב
יא ה֥וּא לִ֛י אֲרִ֖י בְּמִסְתָּרִֽים׃ דְּרָכַ֥י סוֹרֵ֛ר וַֽיְפַשְּׁחֵ֖נִי שָׂמַ֥נִי שֹׁמֵֽם׃ אֲרִי
יב דָּרַ֤ךְ קַשְׁתּוֹ֙ וַיַּצִּיבֵ֔נִי כַּמַּטָּרָ֖א לַחֵֽץ׃ הֵבִיא֙ בְּכִלְיוֹתָ֔י בְּנֵ֖י אַשְׁפָּתֽוֹ׃
יד הָיִ֤יתִי שְּׂחֹק֙ לְכָל־עַמִּ֔י נְגִינָתָ֖ם כָּל־הַיּֽוֹם׃ הִשְׂבִּיעַ֥נִי בַמְּרוֹרִ֖ים
טז הִרְוַ֥נִי לַעֲנָֽה׃ וַיַּגְרֵ֤ס בֶּֽחָצָץ֙ שִׁנָּ֔י הִכְפִּישַׁ֖נִי בָּאֵֽפֶר׃ וַתִּזְנַ֧ח מִשָּׁל֛וֹם
נַפְשִׁ֖י נָשִׁ֥יתִי טוֹבָֽה׃ וָאֹמַר֙ אָבַ֣ד נִצְחִ֔י וְתוֹחַלְתִּ֖י מֵיְהוָֽה׃ זְכָר־
יט עָנְיִ֥י וּמְרוּדִ֖י לַעֲנָ֥ה וָרֹֽאשׁ׃ זָכ֣וֹר תִּזְכּ֔וֹר וְתָשִׁ֥יחַ עָלַ֖י נַפְשִֽׁי׃ זֹ֛את וְתָשׁוּב
כא אָשִׁ֣יב אֶל־לִבִּ֑י עַל־כֵּ֖ן אוֹחִֽיל׃ חַֽסְדֵ֤י יְהוָה֙ כִּ֣י לֹא־תָ֔מְנוּ כִּ֥י לֹא־
כג כָל֖וּ רַחֲמָֽיו׃ חֲדָשִׁים֙ לַבְּקָרִ֔ים רַבָּ֖ה אֱמֽוּנָתֶֽךָ׃ חֶלְקִ֤י יְהוָה֙ אָמְרָ֣ה
נַפְשִׁ֔י עַל־כֵּ֖ן אוֹחִ֥יל לֽוֹ׃ ט֤וֹב יְהוָה֙ לְקוָֹ֔ו לְנֶ֖פֶשׁ תִּדְרְשֶֽׁנּוּ׃ ט֤וֹב
וְיָחִיל֙ וְדוּמָ֔ם לִתְשׁוּעַ֖ת יְהוָֽה׃ ט֣וֹב לַגֶּ֔בֶר כִּֽי־יִשָּׂ֥א עֹ֖ל בִּנְעוּרָֽיו׃
כח יֵשֵׁ֤ב בָּדָד֙ וְיִדֹּ֔ם כִּ֥י נָטַ֖ל עָלָֽיו׃ יִתֵּ֤ן בֶּֽעָפָר֙ פִּ֔יהוּ אוּלַ֖י יֵ֥שׁ תִּקְוָֽה׃
ל יִתֵּ֧ן לְמַכֵּ֛הוּ לֶ֖חִי יִשְׂבַּ֥ע בְּחֶרְפָּֽה׃ כִּ֣י לֹ֥א יִזְנַ֛ח לְעוֹלָ֖ם אֲדֹנָֽי׃ כִּ֣י
אִם־הוֹגָ֔ה וְרִחַ֖ם כְּרֹ֥ב חֲסָדָֽיו׃ כִּ֣י לֹ֤א עִנָּה֙ מִלִּבּ֔וֹ וַיַּגֶּ֖ה בְּנֵי־אִֽישׁ׃
לְדַכֵּא֙ תַּ֣חַת רַגְלָ֔יו כֹּ֖ל אֲסִ֥ירֵי אָֽרֶץ׃ לְהַטּוֹת֙ מִשְׁפַּט־גָּ֔בֶר נֶ֖גֶד
פְּנֵ֣י עֶלְי֑וֹן׃ לְעַוֵּ֤ת אָדָם֙ בְּרִיב֔וֹ אֲדֹנָ֖י לֹ֥א רָאָֽה׃ מִ֣י זֶ֤ה אָמַר֙ וַתֶּ֔הִי
לט אֲדֹנָ֖י לֹ֥א צִוָּֽה׃ מִפִּ֤י עֶלְיוֹן֙ לֹ֣א תֵצֵ֔א הָרָע֖וֹת וְהַטּֽוֹב׃ מַה־יִּתְאוֹנֵן֙

39 Why then does a living man complain, a man for the punishment of his
40 sins? Let us search and try our ways, and turn back to the Lord. Let us lift
41
42 up our heart with our hands to God in the heavens. We have transgressed
43 and have rebelled: You have not pardoned. You have covered with anger,
44 and pursued us: You have slain, You have not pitied. You have covered
45 yourself with a cloud, so that prayer should not pass through. You have
46 made us offscouring and refuse in the midst of the people. All our enemies
47 have opened their mouths wide against us. Fear and the pit are come upon
48 us, desolation and destruction. My eye runs down with rivers of water for
49 the breach of the daughter of my people. My eye trickles down, and ceases
50 not, without any intermission, till the Lord shall look down, and behold
51 from heaven. My eye affects my soul because of all the daughters of my city.
52 They chased me sore, like a bird, those who hate me without cause. They
53
54 have cut off my life in the dungeon, and have cast stones upon me. Waters
55 flowed over my head; then I said, I am cut off. I called upon Your name, O
56 Lord, out of the nethermost pit. You have heard my voice: hide not Your
57 ear at my sighing, at my cry. You did draw near in the day that I called upon
58 You: You did say, Fear not. O Lord, You have pleaded the causes of my
59 soul; You have redeemed my life. O Lord, You have seen my wrong: judge
60 my cause. You have seen all their vengeance and all their devices against me.
61 You have heard their insult, O Lord, and all their devices against me; the
62
lips of those who rose up against me, and their muttering against me all the
63 day. Behold their sitting down, and their rising up; I am their song. Render
64
65 to them a recompense, O Lord, according to the work of their hands. Give
66 them sorrow of heart; Your curse be on them! Pursue them in anger and
destroy them from under the heavens of the Lord.

4 1 How is the gold become dim! how is the most fine gold changed! the hal-
2 lowed stones are poured out at the top of every street. The precious sons of
Zion, comparable to fine gold, how are they esteemed as earthen pitchers,
3 the work of the hands of the potter! Even the jackals draw out the breast,
they give suck to their young ones: the daughter of my people is become
4 cruel, like the ostriches in the wilderness. The tongue of the sucking child
cleaves to the roof of his mouth for thirst: the young children ask bread,
5 and no man gives it to them. They that did feed on dainties are desolate
6 in the streets: they that were brought up in scarlet embrace dunghills. For
the doom of the daughter of my people is greater than the sin of Sodom,

מגילת איכה

מ אָדָם חָי גֶּבֶר עַל־חֲטָאָו: נַחְפְּשָׂה דְרָכֵינוּ וְנַחְקֹרָה וְנָשׁוּבָה עַד־
מא יְהוָה: נִשָּׂא לְבָבֵנוּ אֶל־כַּפָּיִם אֶל־אֵל בַּשָּׁמָיִם: נַחְנוּ פָשַׁעְנוּ
מב
מג וּמָרִינוּ אַתָּה לֹא סָלָחְתָּ: סַכֹּתָה בָאַף וַתִּרְדְּפֵנוּ הָרַגְתָּ לֹא
מד חָמָלְתָּ: סַכּוֹתָה בֶעָנָן לָךְ מֵעֲבוֹר תְּפִלָּה: סְחִי וּמָאוֹס תְּשִׂימֵנוּ
מה
מו בְּקֶרֶב הָעַמִּים: פָּצוּ עָלֵינוּ פִּיהֶם כָּל־אֹיְבֵינוּ: פַּחַד וָפַחַת הָיָה
מז
מח לָנוּ הַשֵּׁאת וְהַשָּׁבֶר: פַּלְגֵי־מַיִם תֵּרַד עֵינִי עַל־שֶׁבֶר בַּת־עַמִּי:
מט עֵינִי נִגְּרָה וְלֹא תִדְמֶה מֵאֵין הֲפֻגוֹת: עַד־יַשְׁקִיף וְיֵרֶא יְהוָה
נ
נא מִשָּׁמָיִם: עֵינִי עוֹלְלָה לְנַפְשִׁי מִכֹּל בְּנוֹת עִירִי: צוֹד צָדוּנִי כַּצִּפּוֹר
נב
נג אֹיְבַי חִנָּם: צָמְתוּ בַבּוֹר חַיָּי וַיַּדּוּ־אֶבֶן בִּי: צָפוּ־מַיִם עַל־רֹאשִׁי
נד
נה אָמַרְתִּי נִגְזָרְתִּי: קָרָאתִי שִׁמְךָ יְהוָה מִבּוֹר תַּחְתִּיּוֹת: קוֹלִי שָׁמָעְתָּ
נו אַל־תַּעְלֵם אָזְנְךָ לְרַוְחָתִי לְשַׁוְעָתִי: קָרַבְתָּ בְּיוֹם אֶקְרָאֶךָּ אָמַרְתָּ
נז
נח אַל־תִּירָא: רַבְתָּ אֲדֹנָי רִיבֵי נַפְשִׁי גָּאַלְתָּ חַיָּי: רָאִיתָה יְהוָה
נט
ס עַוָּתָתִי שָׁפְטָה מִשְׁפָּטִי: רָאִיתָה כָּל־נִקְמָתָם כָּל־מַחְשְׁבֹתָם לִי:
סא שָׁמַעְתָּ חֶרְפָּתָם יְהוָה כָּל־מַחְשְׁבֹתָם עָלָי: שִׂפְתֵי קָמַי וְהֶגְיוֹנָם
סב
סג עָלַי כָּל־הַיּוֹם: שִׁבְתָּם וְקִימָתָם הַבִּיטָה אֲנִי מַנְגִּינָתָם: תָּשִׁיב
סד
סה לָהֶם גְּמוּל יְהוָה כְּמַעֲשֵׂה יְדֵיהֶם: תִּתֵּן לָהֶם מְגִנַּת־לֵב תַּאֲלָתְךָ
סו לָהֶם: תִּרְדֹּף בְּאַף וְתַשְׁמִידֵם מִתַּחַת שְׁמֵי יְהוָה:

ד א אֵיכָה יוּעַם זָהָב יִשְׁנֶא הַכֶּתֶם הַטּוֹב תִּשְׁתַּפֵּכְנָה אַבְנֵי־קֹדֶשׁ
ב בְּרֹאשׁ כָּל־חוּצוֹת: בְּנֵי צִיּוֹן הַיְקָרִים הַמְסֻלָּאִים בַּפָּז אֵיכָה
ג נֶחְשְׁבוּ לְנִבְלֵי־חֶרֶשׂ מַעֲשֵׂה יְדֵי יוֹצֵר: גַּם־תַּנִּין חָלְצוּ שַׁד הֵינִיקוּ תַּנִּים
ד גּוּרֵיהֶן בַּת־עַמִּי לְאַכְזָר כִּי עֵנִים בַּמִּדְבָּר: דָּבַק לְשׁוֹן יוֹנֵק אֶל־חִכּוֹ כַּיְעֵנִים
ה בַּצָּמָא עוֹלָלִים שָׁאֲלוּ לֶחֶם פֹּרֵשׂ אֵין לָהֶם: הָאֹכְלִים לְמַעֲדַנִּים
ו נָשַׁמּוּ בַּחוּצוֹת הָאֱמֻנִים עֲלֵי תוֹלָע חִבְּקוּ אַשְׁפַּתּוֹת: וַיִּגְדַּל עֲוֹן
בַּת־עַמִּי מֵחַטֹּאת סְדֹם הַהֲפוּכָה כְמוֹ־רָגַע וְלֹא־חָלוּ בָהּ יָדָיִם:

7 that was overthrown as in a moment, no hands being laid upon her. Her Nazirites were purer than snow, they were whiter than milk, they were
8 more ruddy in body than rubies, their polishing was as of sapphire: now their visage is blacker than coal; they are not known in the streets: their skin is shriveled upon their bones; it is withered, it is become like a stick.
9 Those slain with the sword are better than those slain with hunger: for when pierced through, the former do ooze with the produce of the fields.
10 Hands of compassionate women have boiled their own children: they
11 were their food in the destruction of the daughter of my people. The LORD has accomplished His fury; He has poured out His fierce anger, and has
12 kindled a fire in Zion and it has devoured its foundations. The kings of the earth, and all the inhabitants of the world, would not have believed that the
13 adversary and the enemy would enter the gates of Jerusalem. It was for the sins of her prophets, and the iniquities of her priests, who shed the blood
14 of the just in the midst of her. They wandered blind through the streets, pol-
15 luted with blood, so that none could touch their garments. Away! unclean! they cried at them; away! away! do not touch. So they fled, and wandered away: among the nations it was said, They shall no longer sojourn here.
16 The anger of the LORD has divided them; He will no more regard them: they respected not the persons of the priests, they were not gracious to the
17 elders. As for us, our eyes do yet fail for our vain help: in our watching we
18 have watched for a nation that could not save. They hunt our steps, that we cannot walk in our broad places: our end is near, our days are fulfilled; for
19 our end is come. Our pursuers were swifter than the vultures in the sky: they chased us upon the mountains, they lay in wait for us in the wilderness.
20 The breath of our nostrils, the anointed of the LORD, was taken in their pits, of whom we said, Under His shadow we shall live among the nations.
21 Rejoice and be glad, O daughter of Edom, that dwells in the land of Utz; the cup shall also pass over to you: you shall be drunken, and strip yourself
22 bare. The punishment of your iniquity is accomplished, O daughter of Zion; He will no more carry you away into exile: He will visit your iniquity, O daughter of Edom; He will uncover your sins.

5 1 Remember, O LORD, what is come upon us: consider, and behold our
2 insult. Our inheritance is turned over to strangers, our houses to aliens. We
3
4 are become orphans and fatherless, our mothers are like widows. We have
5 drunk our water for money; our own wood is sold to us. We are pursued
6 to our necks: we labor, and have no rest. We have given the hand to Egypt,

ז זַכּוּ נְזִירֶ֙יהָ֙ מִשֶּׁ֔לֶג צַח֖וּ מֵחָלָ֑ב אָ֤דְמוּ עֶ֙צֶם֙ מִפְּנִינִ֔ים סַפִּ֖יר גִּזְרָתָֽם:

ח חָשַׁ֤ךְ מִשְּׁחוֹר֙ תָּאֳרָ֔ם לֹ֥א נִכְּר֖וּ בַּחוּצ֑וֹת צָפַ֤ד עוֹרָם֙ עַל־עַצְמָ֔ם יָבֵ֖שׁ הָיָ֥ה כָעֵֽץ:

ט טוֹבִ֤ים הָיוּ֙ חַלְלֵי־חֶ֔רֶב מֵֽחַלְלֵ֖י רָעָ֑ב שֶׁ֣הֵ֤ם יָז֙וּבוּ֙ מְדֻקָּרִ֔ים מִתְּנוּבֹ֖ת שָׂדָֽי:

י יְדֵ֗י נָשִׁים֙ רַחֲמָ֣נִיּ֔וֹת בִּשְּׁל֖וּ יַלְדֵיהֶ֑ן הָי֤וּ לְבָרוֹת֙ לָ֔מוֹ בְּשֶׁ֖בֶר בַּת־עַמִּֽי:

יא כִּלָּ֤ה יְהוָה֙ אֶת־חֲמָת֔וֹ שָׁפַ֖ךְ חֲר֣וֹן אַפּ֑וֹ וַיַּצֶּת־אֵ֣שׁ בְּצִיּ֔וֹן וַתֹּ֖אכַל יְסֹדֹתֶֽיהָ:

יב לֹ֤א הֶאֱמִ֙ינוּ֙ מַלְכֵי־אֶ֔רֶץ כֹּ֖ל יֹשְׁבֵ֣י תֵבֵ֑ל כִּ֤י יָבֹא֙ צַ֣ר וְאוֹיֵ֔ב בְּשַׁעֲרֵ֖י יְרוּשָׁלִָֽם:

יג מֵחַטֹּ֣אות נְבִיאֶ֔יהָ עֲוֺנ֖וֹת כֹּהֲנֶ֑יהָ הַשֹּׁפְכִ֥ים בְּקִרְבָּ֖הּ דַּ֥ם צַדִּיקִֽים:

יד נָע֤וּ עִוְרִים֙ בַּֽחוּצ֔וֹת נְגֹֽאֲל֖וּ בַּדָּ֑ם בְּלֹ֣א יֽוּכְל֔וּ יִגְּע֖וּ בִּלְבֻשֵׁיהֶֽם:

טו ס֣וּרוּ טָמֵ֞א קָ֣רְאוּ לָ֗מוֹ ס֤וּרוּ סוּרוּ֙ אַל־תִּגָּ֔עוּ כִּ֥י נָצ֖וּ גַּם־נָ֑עוּ אָֽמְרוּ֙ בַּגּוֹיִ֔ם לֹ֥א יוֹסִ֖יפוּ לָגֽוּר:

טז פְּנֵ֤י יְהוָה֙ חִלְּקָ֔ם לֹ֥א יוֹסִ֖יף לְהַבִּיטָ֑ם פְּנֵ֤י כֹהֲנִים֙ לֹ֣א נָשָׂ֔אוּ וּזְקֵנִ֖ים לֹ֥א חָנָֽנוּ:

יז עוֹדֵ֙ינוּ֙ תִּכְלֶ֣ינָה עֵינֵ֔ינוּ אֶל־עֶזְרָתֵ֖נוּ הָ֑בֶל בְּצִפִּיָּתֵ֣נוּ צִפִּ֔ינוּ אֶל־גּ֖וֹי לֹ֥א יוֹשִֽׁעַ:

יח צָד֣וּ צְעָדֵ֔ינוּ מִלֶּ֖כֶת בִּרְחֹבֹתֵ֑ינוּ קָרַ֥ב קִצֵּ֛ינוּ מָלְא֥וּ יָמֵ֖ינוּ כִּי־בָ֥א קִצֵּֽנוּ:

יט קַלִּ֤ים הָיוּ֙ רֹדְפֵ֔ינוּ מִנִּשְׁרֵ֖י שָׁמָ֑יִם עַל־הֶהָרִ֣ים דְּלָקֻ֔נוּ בַּמִּדְבָּ֖ר אָ֥רְבוּ לָֽנוּ:

כ ר֤וּחַ אַפֵּ֙ינוּ֙ מְשִׁ֣יחַ יְהוָ֔ה נִלְכַּ֖ד בִּשְׁחִיתוֹתָ֑ם אֲשֶׁ֣ר אָמַ֔רְנוּ בְּצִלּ֖וֹ נִֽחְיֶ֥ה בַגּוֹיִֽם:

כא שִׂ֤ישִׂי וְשִׂמְחִי֙ בַּת־אֱד֔וֹם יוֹשַׁ֖בְתְּ בְּאֶ֣רֶץ ע֑וּץ גַּם־עָלַ֙יִךְ֙ תַּעֲבָר־כּ֔וֹס תִּשְׁכְּרִ֖י וְתִתְעָרִֽי:

כב תַּם־עֲוֺנֵךְ֙ בַּת־צִיּ֔וֹן לֹ֥א יוֹסִ֖יף לְהַגְלוֹתֵ֑ךְ פָּקַ֤ד עֲוֺנֵךְ֙ בַּת־אֱד֔וֹם גִּלָּ֖ה עַל־חַטֹּאתָֽיִךְ:

ה א זְכֹ֤ר יְהוָה֙ מֶֽה־הָ֣יָה לָ֔נוּ הַבִּ֖יטָה וּרְאֵ֥ה אֶת־חֶרְפָּתֵֽנוּ:

ב נַחֲלָתֵ֙נוּ֙ נֶהֶפְכָ֣ה לְזָרִ֔ים בָּתֵּ֖ינוּ לְנָכְרִֽים:

ג יְתוֹמִ֤ים הָיִ֙ינוּ֙ אֵ֣ין אָ֔ב אִמֹּתֵ֖ינוּ כְּאַלְמָנֽוֹת:

ד מֵימֵ֙ינוּ֙ בְּכֶ֣סֶף שָׁתִ֔ינוּ עֵצֵ֖ינוּ בִּמְחִ֥יר יָבֹֽאוּ:

ה עַ֤ל צַוָּארֵ֙נוּ֙ נִרְדָּ֔פְנוּ יָגַ֖עְנוּ וְלֹ֥א הֽוּנַֽח־לָֽנוּ:

ו מִצְרַ֙יִם֙ נָתַ֣נּוּ יָ֔ד אַשּׁ֖וּר לִשְׂבֹּ֥עַ לָֽחֶם: וְלֹא

7 and to Ashshur, to be satisfied with bread. Our fathers have sinned, and
8 are no more; but we bear their iniquities. Servants rule over us: there is
9 none to deliver us out of their hand. We get our bread with the peril of our
10 lives because of the sword of the wilderness. Our skin is hot like an oven
11 because of the burning famine. Women are ravished in Zion, and maidens
12 in the cities of Judah. Princes are hanged by their hand: the faces of elders
13 are not honored. Young men drag the millstone, and youths stumble under
14 the wood. The elders have ceased from the gate, the young men from their
15 music. The joy of our heart is ceased; our dance is turned into mourning.
16
17 The crown is fallen from our head: woe to us, that we have sinned! For this
18 our heart is faint; for these things our eyes are dim. Because of the mountain
19 of Zion, which is desolate, foxes prowl over it. You, O Lord, are enthroned
20 forever; Your throne is from generation to generation. Why do You forget
21 us forever, why do You so long forsake us? Turn us to You, O Lord, and we
22 shall be turned; renew our days as of old: unless You have utterly rejected
us; and are exceedingly angry against us.

> Turn us to You, O Lord, and we shall be turned;
> renew our days as of old.

ז אֲבֹתֵ֤ינוּ חָֽטְאוּ֙ אֵינָ֔ם אֲנַ֖חְנוּ עֲוֺנֹתֵיהֶ֥ם סָבָֽלְנוּ: עֲבָדִים֙ מָ֣שְׁלוּ וְאֵינָ֥ם וַאֲנַ֖חְנוּ
ח בָ֔נוּ פֹּרֵ֖ק אֵ֥ין מִיָּדָֽם: בְּנַפְשֵׁ֙נוּ֙ נָבִ֣יא לַחְמֵ֔נוּ מִפְּנֵ֖י חֶ֥רֶב הַמִּדְבָּֽר:
ט
י עוֹרֵ֙נוּ֙ כְּתַנּ֣וּר נִכְמָ֔רוּ מִפְּנֵ֖י זַלְעֲפ֥וֹת רָעָֽב: נָשִׁים֙ בְּצִיּ֣וֹן עִנּ֔וּ בְּתֻלֹ֖ת
יא
יב בְּעָרֵ֣י יְהוּדָֽה: שָׂרִים֙ בְּיָדָ֣ם נִתְל֔וּ פְּנֵ֥י זְקֵנִ֖ים לֹ֥א נֶהְדָּֽרוּ: בַּחוּרִים֙
יג
יד טְח֣וֹן נָשָׂ֔אוּ וּנְעָרִ֖ים בָּעֵ֥ץ כָּשָֽׁלוּ: זְקֵנִים֙ מִשַּׁ֣עַר שָׁבָ֔תוּ בַּחוּרִ֖ים
טו מִנְּגִינָתָֽם: שָׁבַת֙ מְשׂ֣וֹשׂ לִבֵּ֔נוּ נֶהְפַּ֥ךְ לְאֵ֖בֶל מְחֹלֵֽנוּ: נָֽפְלָה֙ עֲטֶ֣רֶת
טז
יז רֹאשֵׁ֔נוּ אֽוֹי־נָ֥א לָ֖נוּ כִּ֥י חָטָֽאנוּ: עַל־זֶ֗ה הָיָ֤ה דָוֶה֙ לִבֵּ֔נוּ עַל־אֵ֖לֶּה
יח חָשְׁכ֥וּ עֵינֵֽינוּ: עַ֤ל הַר־צִיּוֹן֙ שֶׁשָּׁמֵ֔ם שׁוּעָלִ֖ים הִלְּכוּ־בֽוֹ: אַתָּ֤ה יְהוָה֙
יט
כ לְעוֹלָ֣ם תֵּשֵׁ֔ב כִּסְאֲךָ֖ לְדֹ֣ר וָדֽוֹר: לָ֤מָּה לָנֶ֙צַח֙ תִּשְׁכָּחֵ֔נוּ תַּעַזְבֵ֖נוּ
כא לְאֹ֣רֶךְ יָמִֽים: הֲשִׁיבֵ֨נוּ יְהוָ֤ה ׀ אֵלֶ֙יךָ֙ וְֽנָשׁ֔וּבָה חַדֵּ֥שׁ יָמֵ֖ינוּ כְּקֶֽדֶם: כִּ֚י
כב
אִם־מָאֹ֣ס מְאַסְתָּ֔נוּ קָצַ֥פְתָּ עָלֵ֖ינוּ עַד־מְאֹֽד:

הֲשִׁיבֵ֨נוּ יְהוָ֤ה ׀ אֵלֶ֙יךָ֙ וְֽנָשׁ֔וּבָה חַדֵּ֥שׁ יָמֵ֖ינוּ כְּקֶֽדֶם:

קינות לערב

KINOT FOR THE NIGHT OF TISHA B'AV

1

expressed in that verse. Each stich ends with an expression of lament ("Oh!" or "Oh! What has become of us!"). The last four lines are the last four verses of the Megilla.

זְכֹר Remember, God, what has happened to us,   Oh!
See and take heed of our shame,
                   Oh! What has become of us!   *Lam. 5:1*

נַחֲלָתֵנוּ Our possessions have been turned over to foreigners,   Oh!
Our homes to strangers,
                   Oh! What has become of us!

יְתוֹמִים We have become orphans with no father,   Oh!
Our mothers lament in the month of Av,
                   Oh! What has become of us!

מֵימֵינוּ We were forced to purchase water,   Oh!
Because we dishonored the water libation,
                   Oh! What has become of us!

עַל We were hounded at our necks,   Oh!
Because we hounded others hatefully,
                   Oh! What has become of us!

מִצְרַיִם We extended our hands to Egypt for help,   Oh!
But Assyria grasped us as a hunter would his prey,
                   Oh! What has become of us!

אֲבֹתֵינוּ Our fathers sinned and are no longer,   Oh!
But we suffer for their sins,
                   Oh! What has become of us!

עֲבָדִים Slaves rule over us,   Oh!
Because we failed to free our slaves,
                   Oh! What has become of us!

בְּנַפְשֵׁנוּ We must risk our lives to obtain our bread,   Oh!
Because we prevented our hands from giving to the poor,
                   Oh! What has become of us!

עוֹרֵנוּ Our skin has shriveled as from an oven's heat,   Oh!
Because we exchanged His glory for scandal,
                   Oh! What has become of us!

1

The structure of this kina is based on the fifth chapter of Eikha. The first eighteen verses are rhyming couplets, corresponding to the first eighteen verses of the chapter. The first stich of each couplet is the opening phrase of the verse in Eikha, while the second expands the idea

זְכֹר יהוה מֶה־הָיָה לָנוּ,	אוֹי.
הַבִּיטָה וּרְאֵה אֶת־חֶרְפָּתֵנוּ.	אוֹי מֶה הָיָה לָנוּ.
נַחֲלָתֵנוּ נֶהֶפְכָה לְזָרִים,	אוֹי.
בָּתֵּינוּ לְנָכְרִים.	אוֹי מֶה הָיָה לָנוּ.
יְתוֹמִים הָיִינוּ וְאֵין אָב,	אוֹי.
וְאִמּוֹתֵינוּ מְקוֹנְנוֹת בְּחֹדֶשׁ אָב.	אוֹי מֶה הָיָה לָנוּ.
מֵימֵינוּ בְּכֶסֶף שָׁתִינוּ,	אוֹי.
כִּי נְסוּךְ הַמַּיִם בָּזִינוּ.	אוֹי מֶה הָיָה לָנוּ.
עַל צַוָּארֵנוּ נִרְדָּפְנוּ,	אוֹי.
כִּי שִׂנְאַת חִנָּם רְדָפָנוּ.	אוֹי מֶה הָיָה לָנוּ.
מִצְרַיִם נָתַנּוּ יָד,	אוֹי.
וְאַשּׁוּר צָדָנוּ כְּצַיָּד.	אוֹי מֶה הָיָה לָנוּ.
אֲבוֹתֵינוּ חָטְאוּ וְאֵינָם,	אוֹי.
וַאֲנַחְנוּ סוֹבְלִים אֶת עֲווֹנָם.	אוֹי מֶה הָיָה לָנוּ.
עֲבָדִים מָשְׁלוּ בָנוּ,	אוֹי.
כִּי שִׁלּוּחַ עֲבָדִים בִּטַּלְנוּ.	אוֹי מֶה הָיָה לָנוּ.
בְּנַפְשֵׁנוּ נָבִיא לַחְמֵנוּ,	אוֹי.
כִּי קִפְּצָנוּ מֵעֳנִי יָדֵנוּ.	אוֹי מֶה הָיָה לָנוּ.
עוֹרֵנוּ כְּתַנּוּר נִכְמָרוּ,	אוֹי.
כִּי כְבוֹדָם בְּקָלוֹן הֵמִירוּ.	אוֹי מֶה הָיָה לָנוּ.

איכה ה, א

נָשִׁים Our enemies violated women in Zion,   Oh!
Because we each defiled our neighbor's wife,
> Oh! What has become of us!

שָׂרִים Our princes were hung by their hands,   Oh!
Because they robbed and cheated the poor,
> Oh! What has become of us!

בַּחוּרִים Our young men were forced to carry millstones,   Oh!
Because they frequented the house of the harlot,
> Oh! What has become of us!

זְקֵנִים Our elders were dislodged from the gates of judgment,   Oh!
Because they perverted justice for the widow and orphan,
> Oh! What has become of us!

שָׁבַת Joy was dispelled from our heart,   Oh!
Because we abandoned our pilgrimages to Jerusalem,
> Oh! What has become of us!

נָפְלָה The crown has fallen from our heads,   Oh!
For our Holy Temple has been burnt,
> Oh! What has become of us!

עַל It is for this that our hearts are pained,   Oh!
For the honor of our cherished House is gone,
> Oh! What has become of us!

עַל Thus is Mount Zion desolate,   Oh!
For an abominable idol has been placed on it,
> Oh! What has become of us!

אַתָּה But You, O Lord, are enthroned forever,
Your throne endures through the ages.
Why have You forgotten us utterly, forsaken us for all time?
Take us back, O Lord, to Yourself, and let us come back;
renew our days as of old!
For truly, You have rejected us, bitterly raged against us.   *Lam. 5:19–22*
Take us back, O Lord, to Yourself, and let us come back;
renew our days as of old!   *Lam. 5:21*

אוֹי.	נָשִׁים בְּצִיּוֹן עִנּוּ,
אוֹי מֶה הָיָה לָנוּ.	כִּי אֵשֶׁת אִישׁ טִמְּאוּ וְזִנּוּ.
אוֹי.	שָׂרִים בְּיָדָם נִתְלוּ,
אוֹי מֶה הָיָה לָנוּ.	כִּי גְּזֵלַת הֶעָנִי חָמְסוּ וְגָזְלוּ.
אוֹי.	בַּחוּרִים טְחוֹן נָשָׂאוּ,
אוֹי מֶה הָיָה לָנוּ.	כִּי בְּבֵית זוֹנָה נִמְצָאוּ.
אוֹי.	זְקֵנִים מִשַּׁעַר שָׁבָתוּ,
אוֹי מֶה הָיָה לָנוּ.	כִּי מִשְׁפַּט יָתוֹם וְאַלְמָנָה עִוְּתוּ.
אוֹי.	שָׁבַת מְשׂוֹשׂ לִבֵּנוּ,
אוֹי מֶה הָיָה לָנוּ.	כִּי נִבְטְלוּ עוֹלֵי רְגָלֵינוּ.
אוֹי.	נָפְלָה עֲטֶרֶת רֹאשֵׁנוּ,
אוֹי מֶה הָיָה לָנוּ.	כִּי נִשְׂרַף בֵּית מִקְדָּשֵׁנוּ.
אוֹי.	עַל זֶה הָיָה דָוֶה לִבֵּנוּ,
אוֹי מֶה הָיָה לָנוּ.	כִּי נִטַּל כְּבוֹד בֵּית מַאֲוַיֵּינוּ.
אוֹי.	עַל הַר צִיּוֹן שֶׁשָּׁמֵם,
אוֹי מֶה הָיָה לָנוּ.	כִּי נָתַן עָלָיו שִׁקּוּץ מְשׁוֹמֵם.

אַתָּה יהוה לְעוֹלָם תֵּשֵׁב, כִּסְאֲךָ לְדוֹר וָדוֹר:
לָמָּה לָנֶצַח תִּשְׁכָּחֵנוּ, תַּעַזְבֵנוּ לְאֹרֶךְ יָמִים:
הֲשִׁיבֵנוּ יהוה אֵלֶיךָ וְנָשׁוּבָה, חַדֵּשׁ יָמֵינוּ כְּקֶדֶם:
כִּי אִם־מָאֹס מְאַסְתָּנוּ, קָצַפְתָּ עָלֵינוּ עַד־מְאֹד:
הֲשִׁיבֵנוּ יהוה אֵלֶיךָ וְנָשׁוּבָה, חַדֵּשׁ יָמֵינוּ כְּקֶדֶם:

איכה ה, יט-כב
איכה ה, כא

2

On Motza'ei Shabbat, the following kina is read.
On all other nights continue with Kina 3 on page 56.
If Tisha B'Av begins on Motza'ei Shabbat, the prayer "May the Pleasantness" and Psalm 91
(usually recited on Motza'ei Shabbat) are not said (Geonim, quoted in the Tur, O.Ḥ. 559).

איך How from the mouth of boys and girls,
much sadness is now voiced instead of gleeful songs.

> "May the Pleasantness" is omitted this Motza'ei Shabbat.

אוי Oh! The decree is decreed with such anger, even rage.
His wrath is kindled against us and burns with a fiery flame.

> "May the Pleasantness" is omitted this Motza'ei Shabbat.

אוי Oh! They have defaced our homes and have defiled our virgins.
Distorted are our faces; blackened like a scorched skillet.

> "May the Pleasantness" is omitted this Motza'ei Shabbat.

אוי Oh! The foe has so seized us that even our princes have fallen;
precious sons of Zion, cherished like the pupil of the eye. *Lam. 4:2*

> "May the Pleasantness" is omitted this Motza'ei Shabbat.

אוי Oh! The crown is fallen; His turned back has triumphed.
Beauty and glory are suspended;
the Divine Presence has recoiled from her beloved.

> "May the Pleasantness" is omitted this Motza'ei Shabbat.

אוי Oh! The Menora is taken,
together with the frankincense and the stone Sanhedrin chamber.
The land flowing with milk and honey now mourns.

> "May the Pleasantness" is omitted this Motza'ei Shabbat.

2

On מוצאי שבת, the following קינה is read.
On all other nights continue with קינה 3 on page 57.
If תשעה באב begins on מוצאי שבת, the prayer "ויהי נֹעַם" and תהלים צא (usually recited on מוצאי שבת) are not said (Geonim, quoted in the Tur, O.H. 559).

אֵיךְ מִפִּי בֶן וּבַת / הֶגוֹת קִינוֹת רַבַּת.
תָּמוּר שִׁירִים וַחֲדָוֹת:
וִיהִי נֹעַם נִשְׁבַּת. בְּמוֹצָאֵי שַׁבָּת:

אוֹי כִּי נִגְזְרָה גְזֵרָה / בָּחֳרִי אַף וְגַם בְּעֶבְרָה.
וְאַפּוֹ בָּנוּ חָרָה / וּבְעֶרָה חֲמָתוֹ כְּלַבַּת:
וִיהִי נֹעַם נִשְׁבַּת. בְּמוֹצָאֵי שַׁבָּת:

אוֹי כִּי בָתֵּינוּ שֻׁנּוּ / וּבְתוּלוֹתֵינוּ עֻנּוּ.
וּפָנֵינוּ נִשְׁתַּנּוּ / וְגַם הֻשְׁחֲרוּ כְּמַחֲבַת.
וִיהִי נֹעַם נִשְׁבַּת. בְּמוֹצָאֵי שַׁבָּת:

אוֹי כִּי שַׁדּוּנוּ צָרִים / וְגַם נָפְלוּ בִי שָׂרִים.
בְּנֵי צִיּוֹן הַיְקָרִים / הָיוּ נְצוּרִים כְּבָבַת: איכה ד, ב
וִיהִי נֹעַם נִשְׁבַּת. בְּמוֹצָאֵי שַׁבָּת:

אוֹי כִּי נָפְלָה עֲטֶרֶת / וְגָבְרָה כָּתֵף סוֹרֶרֶת.
וְחָדַל הוֹד וְתִפְאֶרֶת / צִמְצוּם שֹׁכֵן חִבַּת:
וִיהִי נֹעַם נִשְׁבַּת. בְּמוֹצָאֵי שַׁבָּת:

אוֹי כִּי נִטְּלָה מְנוֹרָה / וּקְטֹרֶת לְבוֹנָה הַטְּהוֹרָה.
וְנִבְזָה גְוִית מְיָקָרָה / אָבְלָה אֶרֶץ זָבַת:
וִיהִי נֹעַם נִשְׁבַּת. בְּמוֹצָאֵי שַׁבָּת:

3

Some have attributed it to Rabbi Elazar HaKalir, one of Israel's earliest and most prolific liturgical poets (paytanim). Others have pointed out that its form is heavily influenced by later Spanish-Jewish poetry.

בְּלֵיל Tonight, my children weep and wail.
Tonight, my Sanctuary was ruined and my palaces burned.
The entire house of Israel expresses my agony,
and cries for the fire God kindled.   *Lev. 10:6*
          Tonight, my children weep and wail.

בְּלֵיל Tonight, cry bitterly, O waif who has lost it all.
She lives alienated from her Father's home;
has left His home, the door shut behind her.
Gone into captivity, devoured by every mouth;
cast that day into a consuming flame,
a glowing ember lit by the Lord.
          Tonight, my children weep and wail.

בְּלֵיל Tonight, the wheel of fortune spun to doom,
my first and second Houses destroyed.
She is not to be pitied, this wayward woman,   *Jer. 31:21;*
drunk with toxic waters swelling her belly.   *49:4*
Cast out of her home, she has forgotten past happiness.
Hate had the upper hand over love.
She is like a living widow, a deserted woman.
"And Zion said, 'The Lord has forsaken me.'"   *Is. 49:14*
          Tonight, my children weep and wail.

בְּלֵיל Tonight, I am dejected, the lights dimmed.
My House destroyed, the priestly watches discontinued.
Tonight, woe surrounds me, winds about me.
He summoned an assembly of five harsh decrees.
Tears shed in vain set the pattern forever.
The Lord brought it all about as predestined.   *1 Kings 12:15*
          Tonight, my children weep and wail.

בְּלֵיל Tonight, five appalling tragedies occurred.
A decree against our ancestors, denying them the Land;
afflicting them with oppressing pain and worse,
a day destined for harm and hurt.
The enemy stood and shrieked horribly,
"Attack! For this is the day that God foretold!"
          Tonight, my children weep and wail.

3

This kina emphasizes the especial quality of mourning particular to the night of Tisha B'Av, based on the Talmud in Sanhedrin 104b, "Whoever weeps at night – his voice is heard."

בְּלֵיל זֶה יִבְכָּיוּן וִילִילוּ בָנַי / לֵיל חָרַב קָדְשִׁי וְנִשְׂרְפוּ אַרְמוֹנַי.
וְכָל בֵּית יִשְׂרָאֵל יִבְכּוּ אֶת הַשְּׂרֵפָה אֲשֶׁר שָׂרַף יהוה: ויקרא י, ו

בְּלֵיל זֶה יִבְכָּיוּן וִילִילוּ בָנַי:

בְּלֵיל זֶה תְּיֵלִיל מַר עֲנִיָּה נֶחְדֶּלֶת / וּמִבֵּית אָבִיהָ בַּחַיִּים מֻבְדֶּלֶת.
וְיָצְאָה מִבֵּיתוֹ וְנִסְגַּר הַדֶּלֶת / וְהָלְכָה בַשִּׁבְיָה, בְּכָל פֶּה נֶאֱכֶלֶת.
בַּיּוֹם שָׁלְחָה, בָּאֵשׁ בּוֹעֶרֶת וְאוֹכֶלֶת / וְאֵשׁ עִם גַּחֶלֶת יָצְאָה מֵאֵת יהוה:

בְּלֵיל זֶה יִבְכָּיוּן וִילִילוּ בָנַי:

בְּלֵיל זֶה הַגַּלְגַּל סָבַב הַחוֹבָה / רִאשׁוֹן גַּם שֵׁנִי, בֵּיתִי נֶחֱרָבָה.
וְעוֹד לֹא רִחֲמָה בַּת הַשּׁוֹבֵבָה / הִשְׁקְתָה מֵי רֹאשׁ, וְאֵת בִּטְנָהּ צָבָה. ירמיהו לא, כא; מט, ד
וְשָׁלְחָה מִבֵּיתוֹ, וְגַם נָשְׂתָה טוֹבָה / גְּדוֹלָה הַשִּׂנְאָה מֵאֵת אֲשֶׁר אֲהֵבָהּ.
וּבְאַלְמָנוּת חַיּוּת כְּאִשָּׁה עֲזוּבָה / וַתֹּאמֶר צִיּוֹן עֲזָבַנִי יהוה: ישעיה מט, יד

בְּלֵיל זֶה יִבְכָּיוּן וִילִילוּ בָנַי:

בְּלֵיל זֶה קָדַרְתִּי וְחָשְׁכוּ הַמְּאוֹרוֹת / לְחֻרְבַּן בֵּית קָדְשִׁי, וּבִטּוּל מִשְׁמָרוֹת.
בְּלֵיל זֶה סַבּוּנִי, אֲפָפוּנִי צָרוֹת / וְגַם קָרָא מוֹעֵד, בְּדִין חֲמַשׁ גְּזֵרוֹת.
בְּכִי חִנָּם בָּכוּ, וְנִקְבַּע לַדּוֹרוֹת / יַעַן כִּי הָיְתָה סִבָּה מֵאֵת יהוה: מלכים א יב, טו

בְּלֵיל זֶה יִבְכָּיוּן וִילִילוּ בָנַי:

בְּלֵיל זֶה, אֵרְעוּ בוֹ חָמֵשׁ מְאֹרָעוֹת / גְּזַר עַל אָבוֹת, בִּפְרֹעַ פְּרָעוֹת.
וְדָבְקוּ בוֹ צָרוֹת מְצֵרוֹת וְגַם רָעוֹת / יוֹם מוּכָן הָיָה, בְּפֶגַע פְּגָעוֹת.
וְהֶעֱמִיד הָאוֹיֵב, וְהֵרִים קוֹל זְוָעוֹת / קוּם, כִּי זֶה הַיּוֹם אֲשֶׁר אָמַר יהוה:

בְּלֵיל זֶה יִבְכָּיוּן וִילִילוּ בָנַי:

4

שׁוֹמְרוֹן Samaria [the ten tribes of Israel, "Ohola"] proclaimed,
"My sins have caught up with me! My children have left me for another land!"
    And Oholiva [Jerusalem, Judah] screamed in response,
        "My palaces are in flames!" And Zion said, "The Lord has forsaken me." *Is. 49:14*

לֹא [Samaria answered,] "You cannot equate your plight to mine!
Can your downfall compare to my collapse?
I, Ohola, acted with spite and treachery;
my betrayal opposed me, and my rebellion accused me.
In a few short days, I paid my debt, and the Assyrian king devoured my fruits.
He stripped me bare of my treasures and jewels,
and carried off my captives to Halah and Habor.
So be still, Oholiva, don't cry as I do;
your years endured, but my years did not!"
    And Oholiva screamed in response, "My palaces are in flames!"
    "The Lord has forsaken me."

מְשִׁיבָה Oholiva responded, "I, too, was perverse
and betrayed the Companion of my Youth just as you did.
So be still, Ohola, as I recall my anguish.
You wandered but once; while I, many times.
I was entrapped by Chaldean hands
and descended to Babylon as a destitute prisoner.
The Temple of which I was so proud was burned.
After seventy years in Babylon, I was remembered
and returned to Zion to found my Temple yet again.
But this time, too, I was not long entrenched
before Rome snatched me, and I was almost no more,
for my multitudes were scattered to distant lands."
    And Oholiva screamed in response, "My palaces are in flames!"
    And Zion said, "The Lord has forsaken me."

הַחוֹמֵל He who pities the poor, take pity on their plight!
See their desolation and lengthy exile.
Do not be implacably angry, but remember their lowliness.
Remember not their foolish iniquities forever.
Mend their fissures, soothe their grief, for You are their Hope and their Hero.
Renew our days like the days long gone,
as You have spoken, "The Lord rebuilds Jerusalem." *Ps. 147:2*

4

This kina was written by Rabbi Solomon ibn Gabirol (Spain, 1021–1058). In Ezekiel chapter 23, the kingdoms of Israel and Judea are depicted as two unfaithful wives, Ohola and Oholiva. This kina is written as a conversation between them, and concludes with a prayer to God to have mercy on them.

שׁוֹמְרוֹן קוֹל תִּתֵּן, מְצָאוּנִי עֲוֹנַי / לְאֶרֶץ אַחֶרֶת יְצָאוּנִי בָנַי.
וְאָהֳלִיבָה תִּזְעַק נִשְׂרְפוּ אַרְמוֹנַי / וַתֹּאמֶר צִיּוֹן עֲזָבַנִי יהוה:

ישעיה מט, יד

לֹא לָךְ אָהֳלִיבָה, חֲשׁוֹב עָנְיֵךְ כְּעָנְיִי / הֲתַמְשִׁילִי שִׁבְרֵךְ לְשִׁבְרִי וּלְחָלְיִי.
אֲנִי אָהֳלָה, סוּרָה בָגַדְתִּי בְקַשְׁיִי / וְקָם עָלַי כַּחֲשִׁי, וְעָנָה בִי מֶרְיִי.
וּלְמִקְצָת הַיָּמִים שְׁלַמְתִּי נִשְׁיִי / וְתִגְלַת פִּלְאֶסֶר אָכַל אֶת פִּרְיִי.
חֲמוּדוֹתַי הִפְשִׁיט, וְהִצִּיל אֶת עֶדְיִי / וְלַחְלָח וְחָבוֹר נָשָׂא אֶת שִׁבְיִי.
דְּמִי אָהֳלִיבָה, וְאַל תִּבְכִּי כְּבִכְיִי / שְׁנוֹתַיִךְ אָרְכוּ, וְלֹא אָרְכוּ שָׁנָי:
וְאָהֳלִיבָה תִּזְעַק נִשְׂרְפוּ אַרְמוֹנַי / וַתֹּאמֶר צִיּוֹן עֲזָבַנִי יהוה:

מְשִׁיבָה אָהֳלִיבָה, אֲנִי כֵן נֶעֱקַשְׁתִּי / וּבְאַלּוּף נְעוּרַי כְּאָהֳלָה בָגַדְתִּי.
דְּמִי אָהֳלָה, כִּי יְגוֹנִי זָכַרְתִּי / נָדַדְתִּי אֶת אַחַת, וְרַבּוֹת נְדַדְתִּי.
הִנֵּה בְיַד כַּשְׂדִּים פַּעֲמַיִם נִלְכַּדְתִּי / וּשְׁבִיָּה עֲנִיָּה לְבָבֶל יָרַדְתִּי.
וְנִשְׂרַף הַהֵיכָל אֲשֶׁר בּוֹ נִכְבַּדְתִּי / וּלְשִׁבְעִים שָׁנָה בְּבָבֶל נִפְקַדְתִּי.
וְשַׁבְתִּי לְצִיּוֹן עוֹד, וְהֵיכָל יִסַּדְתִּי / גַּם זֹאת הַפַּעַם, מְעַט לֹא עָמַדְתִּי.
עַד לְקָחַנִי אֱדוֹם, וְכִמְעַט אָבַדְתִּי / וְעַל כָּל הָאֲרָצוֹת נָפוֹצוּ הֲמוֹנַי:
וְאָהֳלִיבָה תִּזְעַק נִשְׂרְפוּ אַרְמוֹנַי / וַתֹּאמֶר צִיּוֹן עֲזָבַנִי יהוה:

הַחוֹמֵל עַל דַּל, חֲמוֹל עַל דַּלּוּתָם / וּרְאֵה שׁוֹמְמוֹתָם וְאֹרֶךְ גָּלוּתָם.
וְאַל תִּקְצֹף עַד מְאֹד, וּרְאֵה שִׁפְלוּתָם / וְאַל לָעַד תִּזְכֹּר עֲוֹנָם וְסִכְלוּתָם.
רְפָא נָא אֶת שִׁבְרָם, וְנַחֵם אֲבֵלוּתָם / כִּי אַתָּה סִבְרָם וְאַתָּה אֱיָלוּתָם.
חַדֵּשׁ יָמֵינוּ כִּימֵי קַדְמוֹנַי / כְּנֶאֱמַךְ: בּוֹנֵה יְרוּשָׁלַיִם יהוה:

תהלים קמז, ב

5

עַד How long must Zion cry and Jerusalem mourn?
    Pity Zion, rebuild the walls of Jerusalem!   *Ps. 102:14*

א Then, because of our sins, the Sanctuary was destroyed;
    because of our sins, the Temple was burned.
ב Jerusalem's heavenly counterpart arranged to mourn,
    while the stars in the sky lamented.
ג Jacob's tribes wept bitterly.
    The constellations dripped tears.
ד The banners of Jeshurun were shrouded.
    Pleiades and Orion dimmed their glow.
ה Forefathers pleaded, but God would not hear;
    children wailed, but Father did not respond.
ו Moses' protest was sounded on high,   *Song. 2:12*
    but the Faithful Shepherd turned a deaf ear.
ז The sacred seed [the Jews] wore sackcloth;
    the angels in heaven donned sackcloth too.
ח The sun darkened, the moon was dim,
    the stars and planets withheld their shine.
ט Aries [corresponding to Nisan], first in the constellations, wept bitterly,
    for her lambs were led to slaughter.
י Taurus [corresponding to Iyar] bellowed up above,
    for we were pursued from behind.
כ Gemini [corresponding to Sivan] seemed torn asunder,
    for the blood of brothers was spilled like water.
ל Cancer [corresponding to Tammuz] clambered to the shore
    while we were faint with thirst.
מ The heavens trembled at Leo's [corresponding to Av] roar,
    but our roaring prayers never reached those heavens.
נ Young virgins were killed and also young lads.
    No wonder that Virgo [corresponding to Elul] is darkened in gloom.
ס Libra [corresponding to Tishrei] tipped her scales, yet prayed
    for those who chose death over a life of woe.
ע Scorpio [corresponding to Ḥeshvan] was overcome with fear and shuddering,
    for the Protector Himself condemned us to sword and hunger.
פ Our eyes overflowed with streams of tears;
    the hope of Sagittarius' [corresponding to Kislev] rainbow was denied us.

5

This kina, which concludes the night kinot, is a very ancient one. It is framed by verses of pleading for the redemption and rebuilding of Jerusalem. Each of the twelve signs of the Zodiac is mentioned, based on the Talmud (Ḥagiga 5b) which describes how, after the destruction of the Temples, even the heavenly hosts joined in mourning with Israel.

עַד אָנָה בְּכִיָּה בְצִיּוֹן, וּמִסְפֵּד בִּירוּשָׁלָיִם.
תְּרַחֵם צִיּוֹן וְתִבְנֶה חוֹמוֹת יְרוּשָׁלָיִם:

תהלים
קב, יד

אָז בַּחֲטָאֵינוּ חָרַב מִקְדָּשׁ / וּבַעֲוֹנוֹתֵינוּ נִשְׂרַף הֵיכָל.
בְּאֶרֶץ חֶבְרָה לָּהּ, קָשְׁרָה מִסְפֵּד / וּצְבָא הַשָּׁמַיִם נָשְׂאוּ קִינָה.
גַּם בָּכוּ בְמֶרֶר שִׁבְטֵי יַעֲקֹב / וְאַף מַזָּלוֹת יִזְּלוּ דִמְעָה.
דִּגְלֵי יְשֻׁרוּן חָפוּ רֹאשָׁם / וְכִימָה וּכְסִיל קָדְרוּ פְּנֵיהֶם.
הֶעְתִּירוּ אָבוֹת, וְאֵל כְּלֹא שׁוֹמֵעַ / צָעֲקוּ בָנִים וְלֹא עָנָה אָב.
וְקוֹל הַתּוֹר נִשְׁמַע בַּמָּרוֹם / וְרוֹעֶה נֶאֱמָן לֹא הִטָּה אֹזֶן.

שיר השירים
ב, יב

זֶרַע קֹדֶשׁ לָבְשׁוּ שַׂקִּים / וּצְבָא הַשָּׁמַיִם גַּם הֵם, שַׂק הוּשַׂם כְּסוּתָם.
חָשַׁךְ הַשֶּׁמֶשׁ וְיָרֵחַ קָדַר / וְכוֹכָבִים וּמַזָּלוֹת אָסְפוּ נָגְהָם.
טָלֶה רִאשׁוֹן בָּכָה בְּמַר נֶפֶשׁ / עַל כִּי כְבָשָׂיו לַטֶּבַח הוּבָלוּ.
יִלְלָה הִשְׁמִיעַ שׁוֹר בַּמְּרוֹמִים / כִּי עַל צַוָּארֵנוּ נִרְדָּפְנוּ כֻלָּנוּ.
כּוֹכַב תְּאוֹמִים נִרְאֶה חָלוּק / כִּי דַם אַחִים נִשְׁפַּךְ כַּמָּיִם.
לָאָרֶץ בִּקֵּשׁ לִנְפּוֹל סַרְטָן / כִּי הִתְעַלַּפְנוּ מִפְּנֵי צָמָא.
מָרוֹם נִבְעַת מִקּוֹל אַרְיֵה / כִּי שַׁאֲגָתֵנוּ לֹא עָלְתָה לַמָּרוֹם.
נֶהֶרְגוּ בְתוּלוֹת וְגַם בַּחוּרִים / עַל כֵּן בְּתוּלָה קָדְרָה פָּנֶיהָ.
סָבַב מֹאזְנַיִם וּבִקֵּשׁ תְּחִנָּה / כִּי נִבְחַר לָמוֹ מָוֶת מֵחַיִּים.
עַקְרָב לָבַשׁ פַּחַד וּרְעָדָה / כִּי בְחֶרֶב וּבְרָעָב שְׁפָטָנוּ צוּרֵנוּ.
פַּלְגֵי מַיִם הוֹרִידוּ דִמְעָה כַּנַּחַל / כִּי אוֹת בַּקֶּשֶׁת לֹא נִתַּן לָנוּ.

KINA 5

צ Water flowed plentifully above our head,
but even Aquarius' [corresponding to Shevat] bucket left our palates dry.

ק The sacrifices we offered were not accepted;
under Capricorn [corresponding to Tevet],
the goats, the sin-offerings, ended.

ר When compassionate mothers cooked their own children,
Pisces [corresponding to Adar] averted her eyes.

ש We ignored the Sabbath with our wayward hearts,
so God ignored whatever merits we had.

ת You will one day again take up Zion's cause with zeal,
and once more illuminate the populous city
with the light of Your splendor.

The congregation stands and the Leader says the following:

תְּרַחֵם Pity Zion as You have spoken.
  Make her firm as You gave Your word.

תְּמַהֵר Hasten salvation, hurry redemption.
  And return to Jerusalem with great compassion.

כַּכָּתוּב As is written by the hand of Your prophet: "Therefore, thus says the LORD: I have returned to Jerusalem with mercies, My House shall be rebuilt in it, says the LORD of hosts, and a line shall be stretched forth over Jerusalem." And it is said: "Proclaim further, saying, Thus says the LORD of hosts: My cities shall again overflow with prosperity; and the LORD shall yet comfort Zion, and shall yet choose Jerusalem." And it is said: "For the LORD shall comfort Zion: He will comfort all her waste places; and He will make her wilderness like Eden, and her desert like the garden of the LORD; joy and gladness shall be found in it, thanksgiving, and the voice of melody."

Zech. 1:16–17

Is. 51:3

צָפוּ מַיִם עַל רֹאשֵׁנוּ / וּבְדָלְיִ מָלֵא חִכֵּנוּ יָבֵשׁ.
קָרְבָּנוּ קָרְבָּן וְלֹא נִתְקַבַּל / וּגְדִי פָּסַק שָׂעִיר חַטָּאתֵנוּ.
רַחֲמָנִיּוֹת בִּשְּׁלוּ יַלְדֵיהֶן / וּמַזָּל דָּגִים הֶעְלִים עֵינָיו.
שָׁכַחְנוּ שַׁבָּת בִּלְבוּשׁ שׁוֹבָבִים / שַׁדַּי שִׁכַּח כָּל צִדְקוֹתֵינוּ.
תְּקַנֵּא לְצִיּוֹן קִנְאָה גְדוֹלָה / וְתָאִיר לְרַבָּתִי עַם מָאוֹר נָגְהֶךָ.

The קהל stands and the שליח ציבור says the following:

תְּרַחֵם צִיּוֹן כַּאֲשֶׁר אָמַרְתָּ / וּתְכוֹנְנֶהָ כַּאֲשֶׁר דִּבַּרְתָּ /
תְּמַהֵר יְשׁוּעָה וְתָחִישׁ גְּאֻלָּה / וְתָשׁוּב לִירוּשָׁלַיִם בְּרַחֲמִים רַבִּים:

כַּכָּתוּב עַל יַד נְבִיאֶךָ: לָכֵן כֹּה־אָמַר יְהוָה, שַׁבְתִּי לִירוּשָׁלַם בְּרַחֲמִים, זכריה א, טז-יז
בֵּיתִי יִבָּנֶה בָּהּ, נְאֻם יְהוָה צְבָאוֹת, וְקָו יִנָּטֶה עַל־יְרוּשָׁלָ͏ִם: וְנֶאֱמַר: עוֹד
קְרָא לֵאמֹר, כֹּה אָמַר יְהוָה צְבָאוֹת, עוֹד תְּפוּצֶנָה עָרַי מִטּוֹב, וְנִחַם יְהוָה
עוֹד אֶת־צִיּוֹן, וּבָחַר עוֹד בִּירוּשָׁלָ͏ִם: וְנֶאֱמַר: כִּי־נִחַם יְהוָה צִיּוֹן, נִחַם ישעיה נא, ג
כָּל־חָרְבֹתֶיהָ, וַיָּשֶׂם מִדְבָּרָהּ כְּעֵדֶן, וְעַרְבָתָהּ כְּגַן־יְהוָה, שָׂשׂוֹן וְשִׂמְחָה
יִמָּצֵא בָהּ, תּוֹדָה וְקוֹל זִמְרָה:

The following, usually said only on Motza'ei Shabbat, is said on Tisha B'Av regardless of the day of the week. "May the pleasantness," usually said on Motza'ei Shabbat, is not said on Tisha B'Av.

▸ You are the Holy One, enthroned on the praises of Israel. *Ps. 22*
And [the angels] call to one another, saying, "Holy, holy, holy *Is. 6*
is the Lord of hosts. The whole earth is full of His glory."
And they receive permission from one another, saying: *Targum Yonatan Is. 6*
"Holy in the highest heavens, home of His Presence; holy on earth,
the work of His strength; holy for ever and all time is the Lord of hosts;
the whole earth is full of His radiant glory."

▸ Then a wind lifted me up and I heard behind me the sound of a great *Ezek. 3*
noise, saying, "Blessed is the Lord's glory from His place."
Then a wind lifted me up and I heard behind me *Targum Yonatan Ezek. 3*
the sound of a great tempest of those who uttered praise, saying:
"Blessed is the Lord's glory from the place of the home of His Presence."

The Lord shall reign for ever and all time. *Ex. 15*
The Lord's kingdom is established for ever and all time. *Targum Onkelos Ex. 15*

יהוה Lord, God of Abraham, Isaac and Yisrael, our ancestors, may *1 Chr. 29*
You keep this for ever so that it forms the thoughts in Your people's
heart, and directs their heart toward You. He is compassionate. He *Ps. 78*
forgives iniquity and does not destroy. Repeatedly He suppresses His
anger, not rousing His full wrath. For You, my Lord, are good and *Ps. 86*
forgiving, abundantly kind to all who call on You. Your righteousness *Ps. 119*
is eternally righteous, and Your Torah is truth. Grant truth to Jacob, *Mic. 7*
loving-kindness to Abraham, as You promised our ancestors in ancient
times. Blessed is my Lord for day after day He burdens us [with His *Ps. 68*
blessings]; God is our salvation, Selah! The Lord of hosts is with us; the *Ps. 46*
God of Jacob is our refuge, Selah! Lord of hosts, happy is the one who *Ps. 84*
trusts in You. Lord, save! May the King answer us on the day we call. *Ps. 20*

בָּרוּךְ Blessed is He, our God, who created us for His glory, separating
us from those who go astray; who gave us the Torah of truth, planting
within us eternal life. May He open our heart to His Torah, imbuing
our heart with the love and awe of Him, that we may do His will and
serve Him with a perfect heart, so that we neither toil in vain nor give
birth to confusion.

The following, usually said only on מוצאי שבת, *is said on* תשעה באב *regardless of the day of the week.* ויהי נעם, *usually said on* מוצאי שבת, *is not said on* תשעה באב.

תהלים כב	וְאַתָּה קָדוֹשׁ יוֹשֵׁב תְּהִלּוֹת יִשְׂרָאֵל: וְקָרָא זֶה אֶל־זֶה וְאָמַר
ישעיהו ו	קָדוֹשׁ, קָדוֹשׁ, קָדוֹשׁ, יהוה צְבָאוֹת, מְלֹא כָל־הָאָרֶץ כְּבוֹדוֹ:
תרגום יונתן ישעיהו ו	וּמְקַבְּלִין דֵּין מִן דֵּין וְאָמְרִין, קַדִּישׁ בִּשְׁמֵי מְרוֹמָא עִלָּאָה בֵּית שְׁכִינְתֵהּ קַדִּישׁ עַל אַרְעָא עוֹבַד גְּבוּרְתֵהּ, קַדִּישׁ לְעָלַם וּלְעָלְמֵי עָלְמַיָּא יהוה צְבָאוֹת, מַלְיָא כָל אַרְעָא זִיו יְקָרֵהּ.
יחזקאל ג	וַתִּשָּׂאֵנִי רוּחַ, וָאֶשְׁמַע אַחֲרַי קוֹל רַעַשׁ גָּדוֹל בָּרוּךְ כְּבוֹד־יהוה מִמְּקוֹמוֹ:
תרגום יונתן יחזקאל ג	וּנְטָלַתְנִי רוּחָא, וּשְׁמָעִית בַּתְרַי קָל זִיעַ סַגִּיא, דִּמְשַׁבְּחִין וְאָמְרִין בְּרִיךְ יְקָרָא דַיהוה מֵאֲתַר בֵּית שְׁכִינְתֵהּ.
שמות טו תרגום אונקלוס שמות טו	יהוה יִמְלֹךְ לְעֹלָם וָעֶד: יהוה מַלְכוּתֵהּ קָאֵם לְעָלַם וּלְעָלְמֵי עָלְמַיָּא.
דברי הימים א׳ כט	יהוה אֱלֹהֵי אַבְרָהָם יִצְחָק וְיִשְׂרָאֵל אֲבֹתֵינוּ, שָׁמְרָה־זֹּאת לְעוֹלָם
תהלים עח	לְיֵצֶר מַחְשְׁבוֹת לְבַב עַמֶּךָ, וְהָכֵן לְבָבָם אֵלֶיךָ: וְהוּא רַחוּם יְכַפֵּר
תהלים פו	עָוֹן וְלֹא־יַשְׁחִית, וְהִרְבָּה לְהָשִׁיב אַפּוֹ, וְלֹא־יָעִיר כָּל־חֲמָתוֹ: כִּי־
תהלים קיט	אַתָּה אֲדֹנָי טוֹב וְסַלָּח, וְרַב־חֶסֶד לְכָל־קֹרְאֶיךָ: צִדְקָתְךָ צֶדֶק לְעוֹלָם
מיכה ז	וְתוֹרָתְךָ אֱמֶת: תִּתֵּן אֱמֶת לְיַעֲקֹב, חֶסֶד לְאַבְרָהָם, אֲשֶׁר־נִשְׁבַּעְתָּ
תהלים סח	לַאֲבֹתֵינוּ מִימֵי קֶדֶם: בָּרוּךְ אֲדֹנָי יוֹם יוֹם יַעֲמָס־לָנוּ, הָאֵל יְשׁוּעָתֵנוּ
תהלים מו תהלים פד	סֶלָה: יהוה צְבָאוֹת עִמָּנוּ, מִשְׂגָּב־לָנוּ אֱלֹהֵי יַעֲקֹב סֶלָה: יהוה צְבָאוֹת,
תהלים כ	אַשְׁרֵי אָדָם בֹּטֵחַ בָּךְ: יהוה הוֹשִׁיעָה, הַמֶּלֶךְ יַעֲנֵנוּ בְיוֹם־קָרְאֵנוּ:

בָּרוּךְ הוּא אֱלֹהֵינוּ שֶׁבְּרָאָנוּ לִכְבוֹדוֹ, וְהִבְדִּילָנוּ מִן הַתּוֹעִים, וְנָתַן לָנוּ תּוֹרַת אֱמֶת, וְחַיֵּי עוֹלָם נָטַע בְּתוֹכֵנוּ. הוּא יִפְתַּח לִבֵּנוּ בְּתוֹרָתוֹ, וְיָשֵׂם בְּלִבֵּנוּ אַהֲבָתוֹ וְיִרְאָתוֹ וְלַעֲשׂוֹת רְצוֹנוֹ וּלְעָבְדוֹ בְּלֵבָב שָׁלֵם, לְמַעַן לֹא נִיגַע לָרִיק וְלֹא נֵלֵד לַבֶּהָלָה.

MA'ARIV FOR TISHA B'AV

יְהִי רָצוֹן May it be Your will, O Lord our God and God of our ancestors, that we keep Your laws in this world, and thus be worthy to live, see and inherit goodness and blessing in the Messianic Age and in the life of the World to Come. So that my soul may sing to You and not be silent. *Ps. 30* Lord, my God, for ever I will thank You. Blessed is the man who trusts *Jer. 17* in the Lord, whose trust is in the Lord alone. Trust in the Lord for *Is. 26* evermore, for God the Lord is an everlasting Rock. Those who know *Ps. 9* Your name trust in You, for You, Lord, do not forsake those who seek You. ‣ The Lord desired, for the sake of Israel's merit, to make the *Is. 42* Torah great and glorious.

FULL KADDISH

Leader: יִתְגַּדַּל Magnified and sanctified may His great name be,
in the world He created by His will.
May He establish His kingdom in your lifetime
and in your days, and in the lifetime of all the house of Israel,
swiftly and soon – and say: Amen.

All: May His great name be blessed for ever and all time.

Leader: Blessed and praised,
glorified and exalted,
raised and honored,
uplifted and lauded be
the name of the Holy One,
blessed be He, beyond any blessing,
song, praise and consolation uttered in the world –
and say: Amen.

The verse "May the prayers and pleas" is omitted.

May there be great peace from heaven,
and life for us and all Israel – and say: Amen.

Bow, take three steps back, as if taking leave of the Divine Presence, then bow, first left, then right, then center, while saying:

May He who makes peace in His high places,
make peace for us and all Israel – and say: Amen.

יְהִי רָצוֹן מִלְּפָנֶיךָ יהוה אֱלֹהֵינוּ וֵאלֹהֵי אֲבוֹתֵינוּ, שֶׁנִּשְׁמֹר חֻקֶּיךָ בָּעוֹלָם הַזֶּה, וְנִזְכֶּה וְנִחְיֶה וְנִרְאֶה וְנִירַשׁ טוֹבָה וּבְרָכָה, לִשְׁנֵי יְמוֹת הַמָּשִׁיחַ וּלְחַיֵּי הָעוֹלָם הַבָּא. לְמַעַן יְזַמֶּרְךָ כָבוֹד וְלֹא יִדֹּם, יהוה אֱלֹהַי, לְעוֹלָם אוֹדֶךָּ: בָּרוּךְ הַגֶּבֶר אֲשֶׁר יִבְטַח בַּיהוה, וְהָיָה יהוה מִבְטַחוֹ: בִּטְחוּ בַיהוה עֲדֵי־עַד, כִּי בְּיָהּ יהוה צוּר עוֹלָמִים: וְיִבְטְחוּ בְךָ יוֹדְעֵי שְׁמֶךָ, כִּי לֹא־עָזַבְתָּ דֹרְשֶׁיךָ, יהוה: יהוה חָפֵץ לְמַעַן צִדְקוֹ, יַגְדִּיל תּוֹרָה וְיַאְדִּיר:

תהלים ל
ירמיה יז
ישעיה כו
תהלים ט
ישעיה מב

קדיש שלם

ש״ץ: יִתְגַּדַּל וְיִתְקַדַּשׁ שְׁמֵהּ רַבָּא (קהל: אָמֵן)
בְּעָלְמָא דִּי בְרָא כִרְעוּתֵהּ, וְיַמְלִיךְ מַלְכוּתֵהּ
בְּחַיֵּיכוֹן וּבְיוֹמֵיכוֹן וּבְחַיֵּי דְכָל בֵּית יִשְׂרָאֵל
בַּעֲגָלָא וּבִזְמַן קָרִיב, וְאִמְרוּ אָמֵן. (קהל: אָמֵן)

קהל ושׁ״צ: יְהֵא שְׁמֵהּ רַבָּא מְבָרַךְ לְעָלַם וּלְעָלְמֵי עָלְמַיָּא.

ש״ץ: יִתְבָּרַךְ וְיִשְׁתַּבַּח וְיִתְפָּאַר
וְיִתְרוֹמַם וְיִתְנַשֵּׂא וְיִתְהַדָּר וְיִתְעַלֶּה וְיִתְהַלָּל
שְׁמֵהּ דְּקֻדְשָׁא בְּרִיךְ הוּא (קהל: בְּרִיךְ הוּא)
לְעֵלָּא מִן כָּל בִּרְכָתָא וְשִׁירָתָא, תֻּשְׁבְּחָתָא וְנֶחֱמָתָא
דַּאֲמִירָן בְּעָלְמָא, וְאִמְרוּ אָמֵן. (קהל: אָמֵן)

The verse תתקבל is omitted.

יְהֵא שְׁלָמָא רַבָּא מִן שְׁמַיָּא
וְחַיִּים, עָלֵינוּ וְעַל כָּל יִשְׂרָאֵל, וְאִמְרוּ אָמֵן. (קהל: אָמֵן)

Bow, take three steps back, as if taking leave of the Divine Presence, then bow, first left, then right, then center, while saying:

עֹשֶׂה שָׁלוֹם בִּמְרוֹמָיו
הוּא יַעֲשֶׂה שָׁלוֹם עָלֵינוּ וְעַל כָּל יִשְׂרָאֵל, וְאִמְרוּ אָמֵן. (קהל: אָמֵן)

Stand while saying Aleinu. Bow at ˒.

עָלֵֽינוּ It is our duty to praise the Master of all,
and ascribe greatness to the Author of creation,
who has not made us like the nations of the lands
nor placed us like the families of the earth;
who has not made our portion like theirs,
nor our destiny like all their multitudes.
(For they worship vanity and emptiness,
and pray to a god who cannot save.)
˒But we bow in worship
and thank the Supreme King of kings,
the Holy One, blessed be He,
who extends the heavens and establishes the earth,
whose throne of glory is in the heavens above,
and whose power's Presence is in the highest of heights.
He is our God; there is no other.
Truly He is our King, there is none else,
as it is written in His Torah: "You shall know and take to heart this day   *Deut. 4*
that the Lord is God,
in heaven above and on earth below. There is no other."

Therefore, we place our hope in You, Lord our God,
that we may soon see the glory of Your power,
when You will remove abominations from the earth,
and idols will be utterly destroyed,
when the world will be perfected
under the sovereignty of the Almighty,
when all humanity will call on Your name,
to turn all the earth's wicked toward You.
All the world's inhabitants will realize and know
that to You every knee must bow and every tongue swear loyalty.
Before You, Lord our God, they will kneel and bow down
and give honor to Your glorious name.
They will all accept the yoke of Your kingdom,
and You will reign over them soon and for ever.
For the kingdom is Yours, and to all eternity You will reign in glory,
as it is written in Your Torah: "The Lord will reign for ever and ever."   *Ex. 15*
▸ And it is said: "Then the Lord shall be King over all the earth;   *Zech. 14*
on that day the Lord shall be One and His name One."

Stand while saying עָלֵינוּ. *Bow at* ׳.

עָלֵינוּ לְשַׁבֵּחַ לַאֲדוֹן הַכֹּל, לָתֵת גְּדֻלָּה לְיוֹצֵר בְּרֵאשִׁית
שֶׁלֹּא עָשָׂנוּ כְּגוֹיֵי הָאֲרָצוֹת, וְלֹא שָׂמָנוּ כְּמִשְׁפְּחוֹת הָאֲדָמָה
שֶׁלֹּא שָׂם חֶלְקֵנוּ כָּהֶם וְגוֹרָלֵנוּ כְּכָל הֲמוֹנָם.
(שֶׁהֵם מִשְׁתַּחֲוִים לְהֶבֶל וָרִיק וּמִתְפַּלְלִים אֶל אֵל לֹא יוֹשִׁיעַ.)
׳וַאֲנַחְנוּ כּוֹרְעִים וּמִשְׁתַּחֲוִים וּמוֹדִים
לִפְנֵי מֶלֶךְ מַלְכֵי הַמְּלָכִים, הַקָּדוֹשׁ בָּרוּךְ הוּא
שֶׁהוּא נוֹטֶה שָׁמַיִם וְיוֹסֵד אָרֶץ
וּמוֹשַׁב יְקָרוֹ בַּשָּׁמַיִם מִמַּעַל
וּשְׁכִינַת עֻזּוֹ בְּגָבְהֵי מְרוֹמִים.
הוּא אֱלֹהֵינוּ, אֵין עוֹד.
אֱמֶת מַלְכֵּנוּ, אֶפֶס זוּלָתוֹ, כַּכָּתוּב בְּתוֹרָתוֹ

דברים ד

וְיָדַעְתָּ הַיּוֹם וַהֲשֵׁבֹתָ אֶל לְבָבֶךָ
כִּי יהוה הוּא הָאֱלֹהִים בַּשָּׁמַיִם מִמַּעַל וְעַל הָאָרֶץ מִתָּחַת, אֵין עוֹד:

עַל כֵּן נְקַוֶּה לְךָ יהוה אֱלֹהֵינוּ, לִרְאוֹת מְהֵרָה בְּתִפְאֶרֶת עֻזֶּךָ
לְהַעֲבִיר גִּלּוּלִים מִן הָאָרֶץ, וְהָאֱלִילִים כָּרוֹת יִכָּרֵתוּן
לְתַקֵּן עוֹלָם בְּמַלְכוּת שַׁדַּי.
וְכָל בְּנֵי בָשָׂר יִקְרְאוּ בִשְׁמֶךָ לְהַפְנוֹת אֵלֶיךָ כָּל רִשְׁעֵי אָרֶץ.
יַכִּירוּ וְיֵדְעוּ כָּל יוֹשְׁבֵי תֵבֵל
כִּי לְךָ תִּכְרַע כָּל בֶּרֶךְ, תִּשָּׁבַע כָּל לָשׁוֹן.
לְפָנֶיךָ יהוה אֱלֹהֵינוּ יִכְרְעוּ וְיִפֹּלוּ, וְלִכְבוֹד שִׁמְךָ יְקָר יִתֵּנוּ
וִיקַבְּלוּ כֻלָּם אֶת עֹל מַלְכוּתֶךָ
וְתִמְלֹךְ עֲלֵיהֶם מְהֵרָה לְעוֹלָם וָעֶד.
כִּי הַמַּלְכוּת שֶׁלְּךָ הִיא וּלְעוֹלְמֵי עַד תִּמְלֹךְ בְּכָבוֹד

שמות טו

כַּכָּתוּב בְּתוֹרָתֶךָ, יהוה יִמְלֹךְ לְעֹלָם וָעֶד:

זכריה יד

◄ וְנֶאֱמַר, וְהָיָה יהוה לְמֶלֶךְ עַל כָּל הָאָרֶץ
בַּיּוֹם הַהוּא יִהְיֶה יהוה אֶחָד וּשְׁמוֹ אֶחָד:

Some add:

Have no fear of sudden terror or of the ruin when it overtakes the wicked. *Prov. 3*
Devise your strategy, but it will be thwarted; propose your plan, *Is. 8*
but it will not stand, for God is with us. When you grow old, I will still be the same. *Is. 46*
When your hair turns gray, I will still carry you. I made you, I will bear you,
I will carry you, and I will rescue you.

MOURNER'S KADDISH

The following prayer requires the presence of a minyan.
A transliteration can be found on page 792.

Mourner: יִתְגַּדֵּל Magnified and sanctified may His great name be,
in the world He created by His will.
May He establish His kingdom
in your lifetime and in your days,
and in the lifetime of all the house of Israel,
swiftly and soon – and say: Amen.

All: May His great name be blessed for ever and all time.

Mourner: Blessed and praised, glorified and exalted,
raised and honored, uplifted and lauded
be the name of the Holy One,
blessed be He, beyond any blessing,
song, praise and consolation
uttered in the world –
and say: Amen.

May there be great peace from heaven,
and life for us and all Israel –
and say: Amen.

Bow, take three steps back, as if taking leave of the Divine Presence,
then bow, first left, then right, then center, while saying:

May He who makes peace in His high places,
make peace for us and all Israel –
and say: Amen.

Some add:

אַל־תִּירָא מִפַּחַד פִּתְאֹם וּמִשֹּׁאַת רְשָׁעִים כִּי תָבֹא: משלי ג
עֻצוּ עֵצָה וְתֻפָר, דַּבְּרוּ דָבָר וְלֹא יָקוּם, כִּי עִמָּנוּ אֵל: ישעיה ח
וְעַד־זִקְנָה אֲנִי הוּא, וְעַד־שֵׂיבָה אֲנִי אֶסְבֹּל, ישעיה מו
אֲנִי עָשִׂיתִי וַאֲנִי אֶשָּׂא וַאֲנִי אֶסְבֹּל וַאֲמַלֵּט:

קדיש יתום

The following prayer requires the presence of a מנין.
A transliteration can be found on page 792.

אבל: יִתְגַּדַּל וְיִתְקַדַּשׁ שְׁמֵהּ רַבָּא (קהל: אָמֵן)
בְּעָלְמָא דִּי בְרָא כִרְעוּתֵהּ, וְיַמְלִיךְ מַלְכוּתֵהּ
בְּחַיֵּיכוֹן וּבְיוֹמֵיכוֹן וּבְחַיֵּי דְכָל בֵּית יִשְׂרָאֵל
בַּעֲגָלָא וּבִזְמַן קָרִיב, וְאִמְרוּ אָמֵן. (קהל: אָמֵן)

קהל ואבל: יְהֵא שְׁמֵהּ רַבָּא מְבָרַךְ לְעָלַם וּלְעָלְמֵי עָלְמַיָּא.

אבל: יִתְבָּרַךְ וְיִשְׁתַּבַּח וְיִתְפָּאַר
וְיִתְרוֹמַם וְיִתְנַשֵּׂא וְיִתְהַדָּר וְיִתְעַלֶּה וְיִתְהַלָּל
שְׁמֵהּ דְּקֻדְשָׁא בְּרִיךְ הוּא (קהל: בְּרִיךְ הוּא)
לְעֵלָּא מִן כָּל בִּרְכָתָא
וְשִׁירָתָא, תֻּשְׁבְּחָתָא וְנֶחֱמָתָא
דַּאֲמִירָן בְּעָלְמָא, וְאִמְרוּ אָמֵן. (קהל: אָמֵן)

יְהֵא שְׁלָמָא רַבָּא מִן שְׁמַיָּא
וְחַיִּים, עָלֵינוּ וְעַל כָּל יִשְׂרָאֵל, וְאִמְרוּ אָמֵן. (קהל: אָמֵן)

Bow, take three steps back, as if taking leave of the Divine Presence,
then bow, first left, then right, then center, while saying:

עֹשֶׂה שָׁלוֹם בִּמְרוֹמָיו
הוּא יַעֲשֶׂה שָׁלוֹם עָלֵינוּ וְעַל כָּל יִשְׂרָאֵל, וְאִמְרוּ אָמֵן. (קהל: אָמֵן)

שחרית לתשעה באב

SHAHARIT FOR THE DAY OF TISHA B'AV

Shaḥarit for Tisha B'Av

The following order of prayers and blessings, which departs from that of most prayer books, is based on the consensus of recent halakhic authorities.

ON WAKING

On waking, our first thought should be that we are in the presence of God. Since we are forbidden to speak God's name until we have washed our hands, the following prayer is said, which, without mentioning God's name, acknowledges His presence and gives thanks for a new day and for the gift of life.

מוֹדֶה I thank You, living and eternal King,
for giving me back my soul in mercy.
Great is Your faithfulness.

Wash fingers up to the knuckles and say the following blessings.

בָּרוּךְ Blessed are You, LORD our God, King of the Universe,
who has made us holy through His commandments,
and has commanded us about washing hands.

בָּרוּךְ Blessed are You, LORD our God,
King of the Universe,
who formed man in wisdom
and created in him many orifices and cavities.
It is revealed and known
before the throne of Your glory
that were one of them to be ruptured or blocked,
it would be impossible to survive and stand before You.
Blessed are You, LORD,
Healer of all flesh who does wondrous deeds.

שחרית לתשעה באב

The following order of prayers and blessings, which departs from that of most prayer books, is based on the consensus of recent halakhic authorities.

השכמת הבוקר

On waking, our first thought should be that we are in the presence of God. Since we are forbidden to speak God's name until we have washed our hands, the following prayer is said, which, without mentioning God's name, acknowledges His presence and gives thanks for a new day and for the gift of life.

מוֹדֶה/ women /מוֹדָה/ אֲנִי לְפָנֶיךָ מֶלֶךְ חַי וְקַיָּם
שֶׁהֶחֱזַרְתָּ בִּי נִשְׁמָתִי בְּחֶמְלָה
רַבָּה אֱמוּנָתֶךָ.

Wash fingers up to the knuckles and say the following blessings.

בָּרוּךְ אַתָּה יהוה אֱלֹהֵינוּ מֶלֶךְ הָעוֹלָם
אֲשֶׁר קִדְּשָׁנוּ בְּמִצְוֹתָיו וְצִוָּנוּ עַל נְטִילַת יָדָיִם.

בָּרוּךְ אַתָּה יהוה אֱלֹהֵינוּ מֶלֶךְ הָעוֹלָם
אֲשֶׁר יָצַר אֶת הָאָדָם בְּחָכְמָה
וּבָרָא בוֹ נְקָבִים נְקָבִים, חֲלוּלִים חֲלוּלִים.
גָּלוּי וְיָדוּעַ לִפְנֵי כִסֵּא כְבוֹדֶךָ
שֶׁאִם יִפָּתֵחַ אֶחָד מֵהֶם אוֹ יִסָּתֵם אֶחָד מֵהֶם
אִי אֶפְשָׁר לְהִתְקַיֵּם וְלַעֲמֹד לְפָנֶיךָ.
בָּרוּךְ אַתָּה יהוה, רוֹפֵא כָל בָּשָׂר וּמַפְלִיא לַעֲשׂוֹת.

אֱלֹהַי My God,
the soul You placed within me is pure.
You created it, You formed it, You breathed it into me,
and You guard it while it is within me.
One day You will take it from me,
and restore it to me in the time to come.
As long as the soul is within me,
I will thank You, Lord my God and God of my ancestors,
Master of all works, Lord of all souls.
Blessed are You, Lord,
who restores souls to lifeless bodies.

TZITZIT

> *One should put on tzitzit, but, according to the opinion of most contemporary authorities, the blessing is not recited.*

BLESSINGS OVER THE TORAH

In Judaism, study is greater even than prayer. So, before beginning to pray, we engage in a miniature act of study, preceded by the appropriate blessings. The blessings are followed by brief selections from Scripture, Mishna and Gemara, the three foundational texts of Judaism.

בָּרוּךְ Blessed are You, Lord our God, King of the Universe,
who has made us holy through His commandments,
and has commanded us to engage in study
of the words of Torah.

וְהַעֲרֶב נָא Please, Lord our God, make the words of Your Torah
sweet in our mouths and in the mouths of Your people,
the house of Israel,
so that we, our descendants (and their descendants)
and the descendants of Your people,
the house of Israel,
may all know Your name and study Your Torah for its own sake.
Blessed are You, Lord,
who teaches Torah to His people Israel.

אֱלֹהַי
נְשָׁמָה שֶׁנָּתַתָּ בִּי טְהוֹרָה הִיא.
אַתָּה בְרָאתָהּ, אַתָּה יְצַרְתָּהּ, אַתָּה נְפַחְתָּהּ בִּי
וְאַתָּה מְשַׁמְּרָהּ בְּקִרְבִּי, וְאַתָּה עָתִיד לִטְּלָהּ מִמֶּנִּי
וּלְהַחֲזִירָהּ בִּי לֶעָתִיד לָבוֹא.
כָּל זְמַן שֶׁהַנְּשָׁמָה בְקִרְבִּי, מוֹדֶה/מוֹדָה women/ אֲנִי לְפָנֶיךָ
יהוה אֱלֹהַי וֵאלֹהֵי אֲבוֹתַי
רִבּוֹן כָּל הַמַּעֲשִׂים, אֲדוֹן כָּל הַנְּשָׁמוֹת.
בָּרוּךְ אַתָּה יהוה, הַמַּחֲזִיר נְשָׁמוֹת לִפְגָרִים מֵתִים.

לבישת ציצית

One should put on the טלית קטן, but, according to the opinion of most contemporary authorities, the blessing is not recited.

ברכות התורה

In Judaism, study is greater even than prayer. So, before beginning to pray, we engage in a miniature act of study, preceded by the appropriate blessings. The blessings are followed by brief selections from תנ״ך, משנה and גמרא, the three foundational texts of Judaism.

בָּרוּךְ אַתָּה יהוה אֱלֹהֵינוּ מֶלֶךְ הָעוֹלָם
אֲשֶׁר קִדְּשָׁנוּ בְּמִצְוֹתָיו
וְצִוָּנוּ לַעֲסֹק בְּדִבְרֵי תוֹרָה.

וְהַעֲרֶב נָא יהוה אֱלֹהֵינוּ אֶת דִּבְרֵי תוֹרָתְךָ
בְּפִינוּ וּבְפִי עַמְּךָ בֵּית יִשְׂרָאֵל
וְנִהְיֶה אֲנַחְנוּ וְצֶאֱצָאֵינוּ (וְצֶאֱצָאֵי צֶאֱצָאֵינוּ)
וְצֶאֱצָאֵי עַמְּךָ בֵּית יִשְׂרָאֵל
כֻּלָּנוּ יוֹדְעֵי שְׁמֶךָ וְלוֹמְדֵי תוֹרָתְךָ לִשְׁמָהּ.
בָּרוּךְ אַתָּה יהוה, הַמְלַמֵּד תּוֹרָה לְעַמּוֹ יִשְׂרָאֵל.

בָּרוּךְ Blessed are You, LORD our God, King of the Universe,
who has chosen us from all the peoples and given us His Torah.
Blessed are You, LORD, Giver of the Torah.

> יְבָרֶכְךָ May the LORD bless you and protect you. *Num. 6*
> May the LORD make His face shine on you
> and be gracious to you.
> May the LORD turn His face toward you
> and grant you peace.

> אֵלּוּ These are the things *Mishna Pe'ah 1:1*
> for which there is no fixed measure:
> the corner of the field, first-fruits,
> appearances before the LORD
> [on festivals, with offerings],
> acts of kindness and the study of Torah.

> אֵלּוּ These are the things *Shabbat 127a*
> whose fruits we eat in this world
> but whose full reward awaits us
> in the World to Come:
>
>> honoring parents; acts of kindness;
>> arriving early at the house of study
>> morning and evening;
>> hospitality to strangers; visiting the sick;
>> helping the needy bride; attending to the dead;
>> devotion in prayer;
>> and bringing peace between people –
>> but the study of Torah is equal to them all.

TALLIT AND TEFILLIN

The tallit and tefillin are put on at Minḥa, not Shaḥarit.

בָּרוּךְ אַתָּה יהוה אֱלֹהֵינוּ מֶלֶךְ הָעוֹלָם
אֲשֶׁר בָּחַר בָּנוּ מִכָּל הָעַמִּים
וְנָתַן לָנוּ אֶת תּוֹרָתוֹ.
בָּרוּךְ אַתָּה יהוה, נוֹתֵן הַתּוֹרָה.

במדבר ו

יְבָרֶכְךָ יהוה וְיִשְׁמְרֶךָ:
יָאֵר יהוה פָּנָיו אֵלֶיךָ וִיחֻנֶּךָּ:
יִשָּׂא יהוה פָּנָיו אֵלֶיךָ וְיָשֵׂם לְךָ שָׁלוֹם:

משנה פאה א:א

אֵלּוּ דְבָרִים שֶׁאֵין לָהֶם שִׁעוּר
הַפֵּאָה וְהַבִּכּוּרִים וְהָרֵאָיוֹן
וּגְמִילוּת חֲסָדִים וְתַלְמוּד תּוֹרָה.

שבת קכז.

אֵלּוּ דְבָרִים שֶׁאָדָם אוֹכֵל פֵּרוֹתֵיהֶם בָּעוֹלָם הַזֶּה
וְהַקֶּרֶן קַיֶּמֶת לוֹ לָעוֹלָם הַבָּא
וְאֵלּוּ הֵן
כִּבּוּד אָב וָאֵם, וּגְמִילוּת חֲסָדִים
וְהַשְׁכָּמַת בֵּית הַמִּדְרָשׁ שַׁחֲרִית וְעַרְבִית
וְהַכְנָסַת אוֹרְחִים, וּבִקּוּר חוֹלִים
וְהַכְנָסַת כַּלָּה, וּלְוָיַת הַמֵּת
וְעִיּוּן תְּפִלָּה
וַהֲבָאַת שָׁלוֹם בֵּין אָדָם לַחֲבֵרוֹ
וְתַלְמוּד תּוֹרָה כְּנֶגֶד כֻּלָּם.

עטיפת טלית והנחת תפילין

The טלית and תפילין are put on at מנחה, not שחרית.

PREPARATION FOR PRAYER

On entering the synagogue:

HOW GOODLY
Num. 24

are your tents, Jacob, your dwelling places, Israel.
As for me, *Ps. 5*
in Your great loving-kindness,
I will come into Your House.
I will bow down to Your holy Temple
in awe of You.
Lord, I love the habitation of Your House, *Ps. 26*
the place where Your glory dwells.

As for me,
I will bow in worship;

> I will bend the knee
> before the Lord my Maker.

As for me, *Ps. 69*
may my prayer come to You, Lord,

> at a time of favor.
> God, in Your great loving-kindness,
> answer me with Your faithful salvation.

הכנה לתפילה

On entering the בית כנסת:

מַה־טֹּבוּ

אֹהָלֶיךָ יַעֲקֹב, מִשְׁכְּנֹתֶיךָ יִשְׂרָאֵל:
וַאֲנִי בְּרֹב חַסְדְּךָ אָבוֹא בֵיתֶךָ
אֶשְׁתַּחֲוֶה אֶל־הֵיכַל־קָדְשְׁךָ
בְּיִרְאָתֶךָ:
יהוה אָהַבְתִּי מְעוֹן בֵּיתֶךָ
וּמְקוֹם מִשְׁכַּן כְּבוֹדֶךָ:

וַאֲנִי אֶשְׁתַּחֲוֶה

וְאֶכְרֳעָה
אֶבְרְכָה לִפְנֵי יהוה עֹשִׂי.

וַאֲנִי תְפִלָּתִי־לְךָ יהוה

עֵת רָצוֹן
אֱלֹהִים בְּרָב־חַסְדֶּךָ
עֲנֵנִי בֶּאֱמֶת יִשְׁעֶךָ:

(במדבר כד)

(תהלים ה)

(תהלים כו)

(תהלים סט)

The following poems, on this page and the next, both from the Middle Ages, are summary statements of Jewish faith, orienting us to the spiritual contours of the world that we actualize in the mind by the act of prayer.

Lord of the universe,
who reigned before the birth of any thing –

When by His will all things were made
then was His name proclaimed King.

And when all things shall cease to be
He alone will reign in awe.

He was, He is, and He shall be
glorious for evermore.

He is One, there is none else,
alone, unique, beyond compare;

Without beginning, without end,
His might, His rule are everywhere.

He is my God; my Redeemer lives.
He is the Rock on whom I rely –

My banner and my safe retreat,
my cup, my portion when I cry.

Into His hand my soul I place,
when I awake and when I sleep.

The Lord is with me, I shall not fear;
body and soul from harm will He keep.

The following poems, on this page and the next, both from the Middle Ages, are summary statements of Jewish faith, orienting us to the spiritual contours of the world that we actualize in the mind by the act of prayer.

אֲדוֹן עוֹלָם

אֲשֶׁר מָלַךְ בְּטֶרֶם כָּל־יְצִיר נִבְרָא.

לְעֵת נַעֲשָׂה בְחֶפְצוֹ כֹּל אֲזַי מֶלֶךְ שְׁמוֹ נִקְרָא.

וְאַחֲרֵי כִּכְלוֹת הַכֹּל לְבַדּוֹ יִמְלוֹךְ נוֹרָא.

וְהוּא הָיָה וְהוּא הֹוֶה וְהוּא יִהְיֶה בְּתִפְאָרָה.

וְהוּא אֶחָד וְאֵין שֵׁנִי לְהַמְשִׁיל לוֹ לְהַחְבִּירָה.

בְּלִי רֵאשִׁית בְּלִי תַכְלִית וְלוֹ הָעֹז וְהַמִּשְׂרָה.

וְהוּא אֵלִי וְחַי גּוֹאֲלִי וְצוּר חֶבְלִי בְּעֵת צָרָה.

וְהוּא נִסִּי וּמָנוֹס לִי מְנָת כּוֹסִי בְּיוֹם אֶקְרָא.

בְּיָדוֹ אַפְקִיד רוּחִי בְּעֵת אִישַׁן וְאָעִירָה.

וְעִם רוּחִי גְוִיָּתִי יְהוָה לִי וְלֹא אִירָא.

GREAT

is the living God and praised.
He exists, and His existence is beyond time.

He is One, and there is no unity like His.
Unfathomable, His Oneness is infinite.

He has neither bodily form nor substance;
His holiness is beyond compare.

He preceded all that was created.
He was first: there was no beginning to His beginning.

Behold He is Master of the Universe; and every creature
shows His greatness and majesty.

The rich flow of His prophecy He gave
to His treasured people in whom He gloried.

Never in Israel has there arisen another like Moses,
a prophet who beheld God's image.

God gave His people a Torah of truth
by the hand of His prophet, most faithful of His House.

God will not alter or change His law
for any other, for eternity.

He sees and knows our secret thoughts;
as soon as something is begun, He foresees its end.

He rewards people with loving-kindness according to their deeds;
He punishes the wicked according to his wickedness.

At the end of days He will send our Messiah
to redeem those who await His final salvation.

God will revive the dead in His great loving-kindness.
Blessed for evermore is His glorious name!

יִגְדַּל

אֱלֹהִים חַי וְיִשְׁתַּבַּח, נִמְצָא וְאֵין עֵת אֶל מְצִיאוּתוֹ.

אֶחָד וְאֵין יָחִיד כְּיִחוּדוֹ, נֶעְלָם וְגַם אֵין סוֹף לְאַחְדּוּתוֹ.

אֵין לוֹ דְּמוּת הַגּוּף וְאֵינוֹ גוּף, לֹא נַעֲרֹךְ אֵלָיו קְדֻשָּׁתוֹ.

קַדְמוֹן לְכָל דָּבָר אֲשֶׁר נִבְרָא, רִאשׁוֹן וְאֵין רֵאשִׁית לְרֵאשִׁיתוֹ.

הִנּוֹ אֲדוֹן עוֹלָם, וְכָל נוֹצָר יוֹרֶה גְדֻלָּתוֹ וּמַלְכוּתוֹ.

שֶׁפַע נְבוּאָתוֹ נְתָנוֹ אֶל־אַנְשֵׁי סְגֻלָּתוֹ וְתִפְאַרְתּוֹ.

לֹא קָם בְּיִשְׂרָאֵל כְּמֹשֶׁה עוֹד נָבִיא וּמַבִּיט אֶת תְּמוּנָתוֹ.

תּוֹרַת אֱמֶת נָתַן לְעַמּוֹ אֵל עַל יַד נְבִיאוֹ נֶאֱמַן בֵּיתוֹ.

לֹא יַחֲלִיף הָאֵל וְלֹא יָמִיר דָּתוֹ לְעוֹלָמִים לְזוּלָתוֹ.

צוֹפֶה וְיוֹדֵעַ סְתָרֵינוּ, מַבִּיט לְסוֹף דָּבָר בְּקַדְמָתוֹ.

גּוֹמֵל לְאִישׁ חֶסֶד כְּמִפְעָלוֹ, נוֹתֵן לְרָשָׁע רַע כְּרִשְׁעָתוֹ.

יִשְׁלַח לְקֵץ יָמִין מְשִׁיחֵנוּ לִפְדּוֹת מְחַכֵּי קֵץ יְשׁוּעָתוֹ.

מֵתִים יְחַיֶּה אֵל בְּרֹב חַסְדּוֹ, בָּרוּךְ עֲדֵי עַד שֵׁם תְּהִלָּתוֹ.

MORNING BLESSINGS

The following blessings are said aloud by the Leader, but each individual should say them quietly as well. It is our custom to say them standing.

בָּרוּךְ Blessed are You, Lord our God,
>King of the Universe,
>who gives the heart understanding
>to distinguish day from night.

Blessed are You, Lord our God,
>King of the Universe,
>who has not made me a heathen.

Blessed are You, Lord our God,
>King of the Universe,
>who has not made me a slave.

Blessed are You, Lord our God,
>King of the Universe,
>*men:* who has not made me a woman.
>*women:* who has made me according to His will.

Blessed are You, Lord our God,
>King of the Universe,
>who gives sight to the blind.

Blessed are You, Lord our God,
>King of the Universe,
>who clothes the naked.

Blessed are You, Lord our God,
>King of the Universe,
>who sets captives free.

Blessed are You, Lord our God,
>King of the Universe,
>who raises those bowed down.

Blessed are You, Lord our God,
>King of the Universe,
>who spreads the earth above the waters.

בּרכוֹת הַשַּׁחַר

The following blessings are said aloud by the שליח ציבור, but each individual should say them quietly as well. It is our custom to say them standing.

בָּרוּךְ אַתָּה יהוה אֱלֹהֵינוּ מֶלֶךְ הָעוֹלָם
אֲשֶׁר נָתַן לַשֶּׂכְוִי בִינָה
לְהַבְחִין בֵּין יוֹם וּבֵין לָיְלָה.

בָּרוּךְ אַתָּה יהוה אֱלֹהֵינוּ מֶלֶךְ הָעוֹלָם
שֶׁלֹּא עָשַׂנִי גּוֹי.

בָּרוּךְ אַתָּה יהוה אֱלֹהֵינוּ מֶלֶךְ הָעוֹלָם
שֶׁלֹּא עָשַׂנִי עָבֶד.

בָּרוּךְ אַתָּה יהוה אֱלֹהֵינוּ מֶלֶךְ הָעוֹלָם
men שֶׁלֹּא עָשַׂנִי אִשָּׁה. / women שֶׁעָשַׂנִי כִּרְצוֹנוֹ.

בָּרוּךְ אַתָּה יהוה אֱלֹהֵינוּ מֶלֶךְ הָעוֹלָם
פּוֹקֵחַ עִוְרִים.

בָּרוּךְ אַתָּה יהוה אֱלֹהֵינוּ מֶלֶךְ הָעוֹלָם
מַלְבִּישׁ עֲרֻמִּים.

בָּרוּךְ אַתָּה יהוה אֱלֹהֵינוּ מֶלֶךְ הָעוֹלָם
מַתִּיר אֲסוּרִים.

בָּרוּךְ אַתָּה יהוה אֱלֹהֵינוּ מֶלֶךְ הָעוֹלָם
זוֹקֵף כְּפוּפִים.

בָּרוּךְ אַתָּה יהוה אֱלֹהֵינוּ מֶלֶךְ הָעוֹלָם
רוֹקַע הָאָרֶץ עַל הַמָּיִם.

> *Some postpone the recital of this blessing until after the end of the fast when one puts on leather shoes.*

Blessed are You, Lord our God,
> King of the Universe,
> who has provided me with all I need.

Blessed are You, Lord our God,
> King of the Universe,
> who makes firm the steps of man.

Blessed are You, Lord our God,
> King of the Universe,
> who girds Israel with strength.

> *Some postpone the recital of this blessing until after they put on tefillin at Minḥa.*

Blessed are You, Lord our God,
> King of the Universe,
> who crowns Israel with glory.

Blessed are You, Lord our God,
> King of the Universe,
> who gives strength to the weary.

בָּרוּךְ Blessed are You, Lord our God, King of the Universe, who removes sleep from my eyes and slumber from my eyelids. And may it be Your will, Lord our God and God of our ancestors, to accustom us to Your Torah, and make us attached to Your commandments. Lead us not into error, transgression, iniquity, temptation or disgrace. Do not let the evil instinct dominate us. Keep us far from a bad man and a bad companion. Help us attach ourselves to the good instinct and to good deeds and bend our instincts to be subservient to You. Grant us, this day and every day, grace, loving-kindness and compassion in Your eyes and in the eyes of all who see us, and bestow loving-kindness upon us. Blessed are You, Lord, who bestows loving-kindness on His people Israel.

יְהִי רָצוֹן May it be Your will, Lord my God and God of my ancestors, to save me today and every day, from the arrogant and from arrogance itself, from a bad man, a bad friend, a bad neighbor, a bad mishap, a destructive adversary, a harsh trial and a harsh opponent, whether or not he is a son of the covenant.

Berakhot 16b

Some postpone the recital of this blessing until after the end of the fast when one puts on leather shoes.

בָּרוּךְ אַתָּה יהוה אֱלֹהֵינוּ מֶלֶךְ הָעוֹלָם
שֶׁעָשָׂה לִי כָּל צָרְכִּי.

בָּרוּךְ אַתָּה יהוה אֱלֹהֵינוּ מֶלֶךְ הָעוֹלָם
הַמֵּכִין מִצְעֲדֵי גָבֶר.

בָּרוּךְ אַתָּה יהוה אֱלֹהֵינוּ מֶלֶךְ הָעוֹלָם
אוֹזֵר יִשְׂרָאֵל בִּגְבוּרָה.

Some postpone the recital of this blessing until after they put on תפילין *at* מנחה.

בָּרוּךְ אַתָּה יהוה אֱלֹהֵינוּ מֶלֶךְ הָעוֹלָם
עוֹטֵר יִשְׂרָאֵל בְּתִפְאָרָה.

בָּרוּךְ אַתָּה יהוה אֱלֹהֵינוּ מֶלֶךְ הָעוֹלָם
הַנּוֹתֵן לַיָּעֵף כֹּחַ.

בָּרוּךְ אַתָּה יהוה אֱלֹהֵינוּ מֶלֶךְ הָעוֹלָם הַמַּעֲבִיר שֵׁנָה מֵעֵינַי וּתְנוּמָה מֵעַפְעַפָּי. וִיהִי רָצוֹן מִלְּפָנֶיךָ יהוה אֱלֹהֵינוּ וֵאלֹהֵי אֲבוֹתֵינוּ שֶׁתַּרְגִּילֵנוּ בְּתוֹרָתֶךָ וְדַבְּקֵנוּ בְּמִצְוֹתֶיךָ וְאַל תְּבִיאֵנוּ לֹא לִידֵי חֵטְא וְלֹא לִידֵי עֲבֵרָה וְעָוֹן וְלֹא לִידֵי נִסָּיוֹן וְלֹא לִידֵי בִזָּיוֹן וְאַל תַּשְׁלֶט בָּנוּ יֵצֶר הָרָע וְהַרְחִיקֵנוּ מֵאָדָם רָע וּמֵחָבֵר רָע וְדַבְּקֵנוּ בְּיֵצֶר הַטּוֹב וּבְמַעֲשִׂים טוֹבִים וְכֹף אֶת יִצְרֵנוּ לְהִשְׁתַּעְבֶּד לָךְ וּתְנֵנוּ הַיּוֹם וּבְכָל יוֹם לְחֵן וּלְחֶסֶד וּלְרַחֲמִים בְּעֵינֶיךָ, וּבְעֵינֵי כָל רוֹאֵינוּ וְתִגְמְלֵנוּ חֲסָדִים טוֹבִים. בָּרוּךְ אַתָּה יהוה, גּוֹמֵל חֲסָדִים טוֹבִים לְעַמּוֹ יִשְׂרָאֵל.

ברכות טז: יְהִי רָצוֹן מִלְּפָנֶיךָ יהוה אֱלֹהַי וֵאלֹהֵי אֲבוֹתַי, שֶׁתַּצִּילֵנִי הַיּוֹם וּבְכָל יוֹם מֵעַזֵּי פָנִים וּמֵעַזּוּת פָּנִים, מֵאָדָם רָע, וּמֵחָבֵר רָע, וּמִשָּׁכֵן רָע, וּמִפֶּגַע רָע, וּמִשָּׂטָן הַמַּשְׁחִית, מִדִּין קָשֶׁה, וּמִבַּעַל דִּין קָשֶׁה בֵּין שֶׁהוּא בֶן בְּרִית וּבֵין שֶׁאֵינוֹ בֶן בְּרִית.

THE BINDING OF ISAAC

On the basis of Jewish mystical tradition, some have the custom of saying daily the biblical passage recounting the Binding of Isaac, the supreme trial of faith in which Abraham demonstrated his love of God above all other loves.

Our God and God of our ancestors, remember us with a favorable memory, and recall us with a remembrance of salvation and compassion from the highest of high heavens. Remember, Lord our God, on our behalf, the love of the ancients, Abraham, Isaac and Yisrael Your servants; the covenant, the loving-kindness, and the oath You swore to Abraham our father on Mount Moriah, and the Binding, when he bound Isaac his son on the altar, as is written in Your Torah:

It happened after these things that God tested Abraham. He said to him, "Abraham!" "Here I am," he replied. He said, "Take your son, your only son, Isaac, whom you love, and go to the land of Moriah and offer him there as a burnt-offering on one of the mountains which I shall say to you." Early the next morning Abraham rose and saddled his donkey and took his two lads with him, and Isaac his son, and he cut wood for the burnt-offering, and he set out for the place of which God had told him. On the third day Abraham looked up and saw the place from afar. Abraham said to his lads, "Stay here with the donkey while I and the boy go on ahead. We will worship and we will return to you." Abraham took the wood for the burnt-offering and placed it on Isaac his son, and he took in his hand the fire and the knife, and the two of them went together. Isaac said to Abraham his father, "Father?" and he said "Here I am, my son." And he said, "Here are the fire and the wood, but where is the sheep for the burnt-offering?" Abraham said, "God will see to the sheep for the burnt-offering, my son." And the two of them went together. They came to the place God had told him about, and Abraham built there an altar and arranged the wood and bound Isaac his son and laid him on the altar on top of the wood. He reached out his hand and took the knife to slay his son. Then an angel of the Lord called out to him from heaven, "Abraham! Abraham!" He said, "Here I am." He said, "Do not reach out your hand against the boy; do not do anything to him, for now I know that you fear God, because you have not held back your son, your only son, from Me." Abraham looked up and there he saw a ram caught in a thicket by its horns, and Abraham went and took the ram and offered it as a burnt-offering instead of his son. Abraham called that place "The Lord will see," as is said to this day, "On the mountain of the Lord He will be seen." The angel of the Lord called to Abraham a second time from heaven, and said, "By Myself I swear, declares the Lord, that because you have done this and have not held back your son, your only son, I will greatly bless you and greatly multiply your descendants, as the stars of heaven and the sand of the seashore, and your descendants shall take possession of the gates of their enemies. Through your descendants, all the nations of the earth will be blessed, because you

Gen. 22

פרשת העקדה

On the basis of Jewish mystical tradition, some have the custom of saying daily the biblical passage recounting the Binding of Isaac, the supreme trial of faith in which Abraham demonstrated his love of God above all other loves.

אֱלֹהֵינוּ וֵאלֹהֵי אֲבוֹתֵינוּ, זָכְרֵנוּ בְּזִכְרוֹן טוֹב לְפָנֶיךָ, וּפָקְדֵנוּ בִּפְקֻדַּת יְשׁוּעָה וְרַחֲמִים מִשְּׁמֵי שְׁמֵי קֶדֶם, וּזְכָר לָנוּ יְהוָה אֱלֹהֵינוּ, אַהֲבַת הַקַּדְמוֹנִים אַבְרָהָם יִצְחָק וְיִשְׂרָאֵל עֲבָדֶיךָ, אֶת הַבְּרִית וְאֶת הַחֶסֶד וְאֶת הַשְּׁבוּעָה שֶׁנִּשְׁבַּעְתָּ לְאַבְרָהָם אָבִינוּ בְּהַר הַמּוֹרִיָּה, וְאֶת הָעֲקֵדָה שֶׁעָקַד אֶת יִצְחָק בְּנוֹ עַל גַּבֵּי הַמִּזְבֵּחַ, כַּכָּתוּב בְּתוֹרָתֶךָ:

בראשית כב

וַיְהִי אַחַר הַדְּבָרִים הָאֵלֶּה, וְהָאֱלֹהִים נִסָּה אֶת־אַבְרָהָם, וַיֹּאמֶר אֵלָיו אַבְרָהָם, וַיֹּאמֶר הִנֵּנִי: וַיֹּאמֶר קַח־נָא אֶת־בִּנְךָ אֶת־יְחִידְךָ אֲשֶׁר־אָהַבְתָּ, אֶת־יִצְחָק, וְלֶךְ־לְךָ אֶל־אֶרֶץ הַמֹּרִיָּה, וְהַעֲלֵהוּ שָׁם לְעֹלָה עַל אַחַד הֶהָרִים אֲשֶׁר אֹמַר אֵלֶיךָ: וַיַּשְׁכֵּם אַבְרָהָם בַּבֹּקֶר, וַיַּחֲבֹשׁ אֶת־חֲמֹרוֹ, וַיִּקַּח אֶת־שְׁנֵי נְעָרָיו אִתּוֹ וְאֵת יִצְחָק בְּנוֹ, וַיְבַקַּע עֲצֵי עֹלָה, וַיָּקָם וַיֵּלֶךְ אֶל־הַמָּקוֹם אֲשֶׁר־אָמַר־לוֹ הָאֱלֹהִים: בַּיּוֹם הַשְּׁלִישִׁי וַיִּשָּׂא אַבְרָהָם אֶת־עֵינָיו וַיַּרְא אֶת־הַמָּקוֹם מֵרָחֹק: וַיֹּאמֶר אַבְרָהָם אֶל־נְעָרָיו, שְׁבוּ־לָכֶם פֹּה עִם־הַחֲמוֹר, וַאֲנִי וְהַנַּעַר נֵלְכָה עַד־כֹּה, וְנִשְׁתַּחֲוֶה וְנָשׁוּבָה אֲלֵיכֶם: וַיִּקַּח אַבְרָהָם אֶת־עֲצֵי הָעֹלָה וַיָּשֶׂם עַל־יִצְחָק בְּנוֹ, וַיִּקַּח בְּיָדוֹ אֶת־הָאֵשׁ וְאֶת־הַמַּאֲכֶלֶת, וַיֵּלְכוּ שְׁנֵיהֶם יַחְדָּו: וַיֹּאמֶר יִצְחָק אֶל־אַבְרָהָם אָבִיו, וַיֹּאמֶר אָבִי, וַיֹּאמֶר הִנֶּנִּי בְנִי, וַיֹּאמֶר, הִנֵּה הָאֵשׁ וְהָעֵצִים, וְאַיֵּה הַשֶּׂה לְעֹלָה: וַיֹּאמֶר אַבְרָהָם, אֱלֹהִים יִרְאֶה־לּוֹ הַשֶּׂה לְעֹלָה, בְּנִי, וַיֵּלְכוּ שְׁנֵיהֶם יַחְדָּו: וַיָּבֹאוּ אֶל־הַמָּקוֹם אֲשֶׁר אָמַר־לוֹ הָאֱלֹהִים, וַיִּבֶן שָׁם אַבְרָהָם אֶת־הַמִּזְבֵּחַ וַיַּעֲרֹךְ אֶת־הָעֵצִים, וַיַּעֲקֹד אֶת־יִצְחָק בְּנוֹ, וַיָּשֶׂם אֹתוֹ עַל־הַמִּזְבֵּחַ מִמַּעַל לָעֵצִים: וַיִּשְׁלַח אַבְרָהָם אֶת־יָדוֹ, וַיִּקַּח אֶת־הַמַּאֲכֶלֶת, לִשְׁחֹט אֶת־בְּנוֹ: וַיִּקְרָא אֵלָיו מַלְאַךְ יְהוָה מִן־הַשָּׁמַיִם, וַיֹּאמֶר אַבְרָהָם אַבְרָהָם, וַיֹּאמֶר הִנֵּנִי: וַיֹּאמֶר אַל־תִּשְׁלַח יָדְךָ אֶל־הַנַּעַר, וְאַל־תַּעַשׂ לוֹ מְאוּמָה, כִּי עַתָּה יָדַעְתִּי כִּי־יְרֵא אֱלֹהִים אַתָּה, וְלֹא חָשַׂכְתָּ אֶת־בִּנְךָ אֶת־יְחִידְךָ מִמֶּנִּי: וַיִּשָּׂא אַבְרָהָם אֶת־עֵינָיו, וַיַּרְא וְהִנֵּה־אַיִל, אַחַר נֶאֱחַז בַּסְּבַךְ בְּקַרְנָיו, וַיֵּלֶךְ אַבְרָהָם וַיִּקַּח אֶת־הָאַיִל, וַיַּעֲלֵהוּ לְעֹלָה תַּחַת בְּנוֹ: וַיִּקְרָא אַבְרָהָם שֵׁם־הַמָּקוֹם הַהוּא יְהוָה יִרְאֶה, אֲשֶׁר יֵאָמֵר הַיּוֹם בְּהַר יְהוָה יֵרָאֶה: וַיִּקְרָא מַלְאַךְ יְהוָה אֶל־אַבְרָהָם שֵׁנִית מִן־הַשָּׁמָיִם: וַיֹּאמֶר, בִּי נִשְׁבַּעְתִּי נְאֻם־יְהוָה, כִּי יַעַן אֲשֶׁר עָשִׂיתָ אֶת־הַדָּבָר הַזֶּה, וְלֹא חָשַׂכְתָּ אֶת־בִּנְךָ אֶת־יְחִידֶךָ: כִּי־בָרֵךְ אֲבָרֶכְךָ, וְהַרְבָּה אַרְבֶּה אֶת־זַרְעֲךָ כְּכוֹכְבֵי הַשָּׁמַיִם, וְכַחוֹל אֲשֶׁר עַל־שְׂפַת הַיָּם, וְיִרַשׁ זַרְעֲךָ

have heeded My voice." Then Abraham returned to his lads, and they rose and went together to Beersheba, and Abraham stayed in Beersheba.

Master of the Universe, just as Abraham our father suppressed his compassion to do Your will wholeheartedly, so may Your compassion suppress Your anger from us and may Your compassion prevail over Your other attributes. Deal with us, Lord our God, with the attributes of loving-kindness and compassion, and in Your great goodness may Your anger be turned away from Your people, Your city, Your land and Your inheritance. Fulfill in us, Lord our God, the promise You made in Your Torah through the hand of Moses Your servant, as it is said: "I will remember My covenant with Jacob, and also My covenant with Isaac, and also My covenant with Abraham I will remember, and the land I will remember." *Lev. 26*

ACCEPTING THE SOVEREIGNTY OF HEAVEN

לְעוֹלָם A person should always be God-fearing, privately and publicly, acknowledging the truth and speaking it in his heart.
He should rise early and say:
>Master of all worlds,
>not because of our righteousness
>do we lay our pleas before You,
>but because of Your great compassion.

What are we? What are our lives?
What is our loving-kindness? What is our righteousness?
What is our salvation? What is our strength?
What is our might? What shall we say before You,
Lord our God and God of our ancestors?
Are not all the mighty like nothing before You,
the men of renown as if they had never been,
the wise as if they know nothing,
and the understanding as if they lack intelligence?
For their many works are in vain,
and the days of their lives like a fleeting breath before You.
The pre-eminence of man over the animals is nothing,
for all is but a fleeting breath.

אֶת שַׁעַר אֹיְבָיו: וְהִתְבָּרֲכוּ בְזַרְעֲךָ כֹּל גּוֹיֵי הָאָרֶץ, עֵקֶב אֲשֶׁר שָׁמַעְתָּ בְּקֹלִי: וַיָּשָׁב אַבְרָהָם אֶל־נְעָרָיו, וַיָּקֻמוּ וַיֵּלְכוּ יַחְדָּו אֶל־בְּאֵר שָׁבַע, וַיֵּשֶׁב אַבְרָהָם בִּבְאֵר שָׁבַע:

רִבּוֹנוֹ שֶׁל עוֹלָם, כְּמוֹ שֶׁכָּבַשׁ אַבְרָהָם אָבִינוּ אֶת רַחֲמָיו לַעֲשׂוֹת רְצוֹנְךָ בְּלֵבָב שָׁלֵם, כֵּן יִכְבְּשׁוּ רַחֲמֶיךָ אֶת כַּעַסְךָ מֵעָלֵינוּ וְיִגְלוּ רַחֲמֶיךָ עַל מִדּוֹתֶיךָ. וְתִתְנַהֵג עִמָּנוּ יהוה אֱלֹהֵינוּ בְּמִדַּת הַחֶסֶד וּבְמִדַּת הָרַחֲמִים, וּבְטוּבְךָ הַגָּדוֹל יָשׁוּב חֲרוֹן אַפְּךָ מֵעַמְּךָ וּמֵעִירְךָ וּמֵאַרְצְךָ וּמִנַּחֲלָתֶךָ. וְקַיֶּם לָנוּ יהוה אֱלֹהֵינוּ אֶת הַדָּבָר שֶׁהִבְטַחְתָּנוּ בְּתוֹרָתֶךָ עַל יְדֵי מֹשֶׁה עַבְדֶּךָ, כָּאָמוּר: וְזָכַרְתִּי אֶת־בְּרִיתִי יַעֲקוֹב וְאַף אֶת־בְּרִיתִי יִצְחָק, וְאַף אֶת־בְּרִיתִי אַבְרָהָם אֶזְכֹּר, וְהָאָרֶץ אֶזְכֹּר: ויקרא כו

קבלת עול מלכות שמים

לְעוֹלָם יְהֵא אָדָם יְרֵא שָׁמַיִם בַּסֵּתֶר וּבַגָּלוּי
וּמוֹדֶה עַל הָאֱמֶת, וְדוֹבֵר אֱמֶת בִּלְבָבוֹ
וְיַשְׁכֵּם וְיֹאמַר

רִבּוֹן כָּל הָעוֹלָמִים
לֹא עַל צִדְקוֹתֵינוּ אֲנַחְנוּ מַפִּילִים תַּחֲנוּנֵינוּ לְפָנֶיךָ
כִּי עַל רַחֲמֶיךָ הָרַבִּים.

מָה אָנוּ, מֶה חַיֵּינוּ, מֶה חַסְדֵּנוּ, מַה צִּדְקוֹתֵינוּ
מַה יְשׁוּעָתֵנוּ, מַה כֹּחֵנוּ, מַה גְּבוּרָתֵנוּ
מַה נֹּאמַר לְפָנֶיךָ, יהוה אֱלֹהֵינוּ וֵאלֹהֵי אֲבוֹתֵינוּ
הֲלֹא כָּל הַגִּבּוֹרִים כְּאַיִן לְפָנֶיךָ
וְאַנְשֵׁי הַשֵּׁם כְּלֹא הָיוּ
וַחֲכָמִים כִּבְלִי מַדָּע, וּנְבוֹנִים כִּבְלִי הַשְׂכֵּל
כִּי רֹב מַעֲשֵׂיהֶם תֹּהוּ, וִימֵי חַיֵּיהֶם הֶבֶל לְפָנֶיךָ
וּמוֹתַר הָאָדָם מִן הַבְּהֵמָה אָיִן
כִּי הַכֹּל הָבֶל.

אֲבָל Yet we are Your people, the children of Your covenant,
the children of Abraham, Your beloved,
to whom You made a promise on Mount Moriah;
the offspring of Isaac his only one who was bound on the altar;
the congregation of Jacob Your firstborn son
whom – because of the love with which You loved him
and the joy with which You rejoiced in him –
You called Yisrael and Yeshurun.

לְפִיכָךְ Therefore it is our duty
to thank You, and to praise, glorify, bless, sanctify
and give praise and thanks to Your name.
Happy are we, how good is our portion,
how lovely our fate, how beautiful our heritage.

▸ Happy are we who, early and late,
evening and morning,
say twice each day –

> Listen, Israel: the Lord is our God, the Lord is One. *Deut. 6*
>
> *Quietly:* Blessed be the name of His glorious kingdom for ever and all time.

Some congregations say the entire first paragraph of the Shema (below) at this point.
If there is a concern that the Shema will not be recited within the
prescribed time, then all three paragraphs should be said.

Love the Lord your God with all your heart, with all your soul, and with all your might. These words which I command you today shall be on your heart. Teach them repeatedly to your children, speaking of them when you sit at home and when you travel on the way, when you lie down and when you rise. Bind them as a sign on your hand, and they shall be an emblem between your eyes. Write them on the doorposts of your house and gates.

אַתָּה הוּא It was You who existed
before the world was created,
it is You now that the world has been created.
It is You in this world
and You in the World to Come.

שחרית לתשעה באב · קבלת עול מלכות שמים

אֲבָל אֲנַחְנוּ עַמְּךָ בְּנֵי בְרִיתֶךָ
בְּנֵי אַבְרָהָם אֹהַבְךָ שֶׁנִּשְׁבַּעְתָּ לּוֹ בְּהַר הַמּוֹרִיָּה
זֶרַע יִצְחָק יְחִידוֹ שֶׁנֶּעֱקַד עַל גַּבֵּי הַמִּזְבֵּחַ
עֲדַת יַעֲקֹב בִּנְךָ בְּכוֹרֶךָ
שֶׁמֵּאַהֲבָתְךָ שֶׁאָהַבְתָּ אוֹתוֹ, וּמִשִּׂמְחָתְךָ שֶׁשָּׂמַחְתָּ בּוֹ
קָרֵאתָ אֶת שְׁמוֹ יִשְׂרָאֵל וִישֻׁרוּן.

לְפִיכָךְ אֲנַחְנוּ חַיָּבִים לְהוֹדוֹת לָךְ וּלְשַׁבֵּחֲךָ וּלְפָאֶרְךָ
וּלְבָרֵךְ וּלְקַדֵּשׁ וְלָתֵת שֶׁבַח וְהוֹדָיָה לִשְׁמֶךָ.
אַשְׁרֵינוּ, מַה טּוֹב חֶלְקֵנוּ, וּמַה נָּעִים גּוֹרָלֵנוּ, וּמַה יָּפָה יְרֻשָּׁתֵנוּ.

‣ אַשְׁרֵינוּ, שֶׁאֲנַחְנוּ מַשְׁכִּימִים וּמַעֲרִיבִים עֶרֶב וָבֹקֶר
וְאוֹמְרִים פַּעֲמַיִם בְּכָל יוֹם

דברים ו

שְׁמַע יִשְׂרָאֵל, יהוה אֱלֹהֵינוּ, יהוה אֶחָד:

Quietly בָּרוּךְ שֵׁם כְּבוֹד מַלְכוּתוֹ לְעוֹלָם וָעֶד.

Some congregations say the entire first paragraph of the שמע (below) at this point.
If there is a concern that the שמע will not be recited within the
prescribed time, then all three paragraphs should be said.

וְאָהַבְתָּ אֵת יהוה אֱלֹהֶיךָ, בְּכָל־לְבָבְךָ, וּבְכָל־נַפְשְׁךָ, וּבְכָל־מְאֹדֶךָ: וְהָיוּ הַדְּבָרִים
הָאֵלֶּה, אֲשֶׁר אָנֹכִי מְצַוְּךָ הַיּוֹם, עַל־לְבָבֶךָ: וְשִׁנַּנְתָּם לְבָנֶיךָ, וְדִבַּרְתָּ בָּם, בְּשִׁבְתְּךָ
בְּבֵיתֶךָ, וּבְלֶכְתְּךָ בַדֶּרֶךְ, וּבְשָׁכְבְּךָ וּבְקוּמֶךָ: וּקְשַׁרְתָּם לְאוֹת עַל־יָדֶךָ וְהָיוּ לְטֹטָפֹת
בֵּין עֵינֶיךָ: וּכְתַבְתָּם עַל־מְזֻזוֹת בֵּיתֶךָ וּבִשְׁעָרֶיךָ:

אַתָּה הוּא עַד שֶׁלֹּא נִבְרָא הָעוֹלָם
אַתָּה הוּא מִשֶּׁנִּבְרָא הָעוֹלָם
אַתָּה הוּא בָּעוֹלָם הַזֶּה
וְאַתָּה הוּא לָעוֹלָם הַבָּא.

▸ Sanctify Your name
through those who sanctify Your name,
and sanctify Your name
throughout Your world.
By Your salvation may our pride be exalted;
raise high our pride.
Blessed are You, Lord, who sanctifies His name
among the multitudes.

אַתָּה הוּא You are the Lord our God in heaven and on earth,
and in the highest heaven of heavens.
Truly, You are the first and You are the last,
and besides You there is no god.
Gather those who hope in You
from the four quarters of the earth.
May all mankind recognize and know
that You alone are God over all the kingdoms on earth.

You made the heavens and the earth,
the sea and all they contain.
Who among all the works of Your hands, above and below,
can say to You,
"What are You doing?"

Heavenly Father,
deal kindly with us
for the sake of Your great name
by which we are called,
and fulfill for us,
Lord our God,
that which is written:
> "At that time I will bring you home, and at that time I will gather you, for I will give you renown and praise among all the peoples of the earth when I bring back your exiles before your eyes, says the Lord." *Zeph. 3*

• קַדֵּשׁ אֶת שִׁמְךָ עַל מַקְדִּישֵׁי שְׁמֶךָ
וְקַדֵּשׁ אֶת שִׁמְךָ בְּעוֹלָמֶךָ
וּבִישׁוּעָתְךָ תָּרוּם וְתַגְבִּיהַּ קַרְנֵנוּ.
בָּרוּךְ אַתָּה יהוה, הַמְקַדֵּשׁ אֶת שְׁמוֹ בָּרַבִּים.

אַתָּה הוּא יהוה אֱלֹהֵינוּ בַּשָּׁמַיִם וּבָאָרֶץ
וּבִשְׁמֵי הַשָּׁמַיִם הָעֶלְיוֹנִים.
אֱמֶת, אַתָּה הוּא רִאשׁוֹן וְאַתָּה הוּא אַחֲרוֹן
וּמִבַּלְעָדֶיךָ אֵין אֱלֹהִים.
קַבֵּץ קֹוֶיךָ מֵאַרְבַּע כַּנְפוֹת הָאָרֶץ.
יַכִּירוּ וְיֵדְעוּ כָּל בָּאֵי עוֹלָם
כִּי אַתָּה הוּא הָאֱלֹהִים לְבַדְּךָ לְכֹל מַמְלְכוֹת הָאָרֶץ.

אַתָּה עָשִׂיתָ אֶת הַשָּׁמַיִם וְאֶת הָאָרֶץ
אֶת הַיָּם וְאֶת כָּל אֲשֶׁר בָּם
וּמִי בְּכָל מַעֲשֵׂי יָדֶיךָ בָּעֶלְיוֹנִים אוֹ בַתַּחְתּוֹנִים
שֶׁיֹּאמַר לְךָ מַה תַּעֲשֶׂה.

אָבִינוּ שֶׁבַּשָּׁמַיִם
עֲשֵׂה עִמָּנוּ חֶסֶד
בַּעֲבוּר שִׁמְךָ הַגָּדוֹל שֶׁנִּקְרָא עָלֵינוּ
וְקַיֵּם לָנוּ יהוה אֱלֹהֵינוּ
מַה שֶּׁכָּתוּב:

צפניה ג

בָּעֵת הַהִיא אָבִיא אֶתְכֶם, וּבָעֵת קַבְּצִי אֶתְכֶם,
כִּי־אֶתֵּן אֶתְכֶם לְשֵׁם וְלִתְהִלָּה בְּכֹל עַמֵּי הָאָרֶץ,
בְּשׁוּבִי אֶת־שְׁבוּתֵיכֶם לְעֵינֵיכֶם, אָמַר יהוה:

OFFERINGS

The sages held that, in the absence of the Temple, studying the laws of sacrifices is the equivalent of offering them. Hence the following texts. In general, there are different customs as to how many passages are to be said, and one should follow the custom of one's congregation. The minimum requirement is to say the verses relating to The Daily Sacrifice below. Customs vary as to whether any of the following paragraphs, normally said here during the year, are omitted on Tisha B'Av, and one should follow the custom of one's congregation.

THE BASIN

The LORD spoke to Moses, saying: Make a bronze basin, with its bronze stand for washing, and place it between the Tent of Meeting and the altar, and put water in it. From it, Aaron and his sons are to wash their hands and feet. When they enter the Tent of Meeting, they shall wash with water so that they will not die; likewise when they approach the altar to minister, presenting a fire-offering to the LORD. They must wash their hands and feet so that they will not die. This shall be an everlasting ordinance for Aaron and his descendants throughout their generations. *Ex. 30*

TAKING OF THE ASHES

The LORD spoke to Moses, saying: Instruct Aaron and his sons, saying, This is the law of the burnt-offering. The burnt-offering shall remain on the altar hearth throughout the night until morning, and the altar fire shall be kept burning on it. The priest shall then put on his linen garments, and linen breeches next to his body, and shall remove the ashes of the burnt-offering that the fire has consumed on the altar and place them beside the altar. Then he shall take off these clothes and put on others, and carry the ashes outside the camp to a clean place. The fire on the altar must be kept burning; it must not go out. Each morning the priest shall burn wood on it, and prepare on it the burnt-offering and burn the fat of the peace-offerings. A perpetual fire must be kept burning on the altar; it must not go out. *Lev. 6*

May it be Your will, LORD our God and God of our ancestors, that You have compassion on us and pardon us all our sins, grant atonement for all our iniquities and forgive all our transgressions. May You rebuild the Temple swiftly in our days so that we may offer You the continual-offering that it may atone for us as You have prescribed for us in Your Torah through Moses Your servant, from the mouthpiece of Your glory, as it is said:

סדר הקרבנות

חז״ל held that, in the absence of the Temple, studying the laws of sacrifices is the equivalent of offering them. Hence the following texts. In general, there are different customs as to how many passages are to be said, and one should follow the custom of one's congregation. The minimum requirement is to say the verses relating to the קרבן תמיד below. Customs vary as to whether any of the following paragraphs, normally said here during the year, are omitted on תשעה באב, and one should follow the custom of one's congregation.

פרשת הכיור

שמות ל

וַיְדַבֵּר יהוה אֶל־מֹשֶׁה לֵּאמֹר: וְעָשִׂיתָ כִּיּוֹר נְחֹשֶׁת וְכַנּוֹ נְחֹשֶׁת לְרָחְצָה, וְנָתַתָּ אֹתוֹ בֵּין־אֹהֶל מוֹעֵד וּבֵין הַמִּזְבֵּחַ, וְנָתַתָּ שָׁמָּה מָיִם: וְרָחֲצוּ אַהֲרֹן וּבָנָיו מִמֶּנּוּ אֶת־יְדֵיהֶם וְאֶת־רַגְלֵיהֶם: בְּבֹאָם אֶל־אֹהֶל מוֹעֵד יִרְחֲצוּ־מַיִם, וְלֹא יָמֻתוּ, אוֹ בְגִשְׁתָּם אֶל־הַמִּזְבֵּחַ לְשָׁרֵת, לְהַקְטִיר אִשֶּׁה לַיהוה: וְרָחֲצוּ יְדֵיהֶם וְרַגְלֵיהֶם וְלֹא יָמֻתוּ, וְהָיְתָה לָהֶם חָק־עוֹלָם, לוֹ וּלְזַרְעוֹ לְדֹרֹתָם:

פרשת תרומת הדשן

ויקרא ו

וַיְדַבֵּר יהוה אֶל־מֹשֶׁה לֵּאמֹר: צַו אֶת־אַהֲרֹן וְאֶת־בָּנָיו לֵאמֹר, זֹאת תּוֹרַת הָעֹלָה, הִוא הָעֹלָה עַל מוֹקְדָה עַל־הַמִּזְבֵּחַ כָּל־הַלַּיְלָה עַד־הַבֹּקֶר, וְאֵשׁ הַמִּזְבֵּחַ תּוּקַד בּוֹ: וְלָבַשׁ הַכֹּהֵן מִדּוֹ בַד, וּמִכְנְסֵי־בַד יִלְבַּשׁ עַל־בְּשָׂרוֹ, וְהֵרִים אֶת־הַדֶּשֶׁן אֲשֶׁר תֹּאכַל הָאֵשׁ אֶת־הָעֹלָה, עַל־הַמִּזְבֵּחַ, וְשָׂמוֹ אֵצֶל הַמִּזְבֵּחַ: וּפָשַׁט אֶת־בְּגָדָיו, וְלָבַשׁ בְּגָדִים אֲחֵרִים, וְהוֹצִיא אֶת־הַדֶּשֶׁן אֶל־מִחוּץ לַמַּחֲנֶה, אֶל־מָקוֹם טָהוֹר: וְהָאֵשׁ עַל־הַמִּזְבֵּחַ תּוּקַד־בּוֹ, לֹא תִכְבֶּה, וּבִעֵר עָלֶיהָ הַכֹּהֵן עֵצִים בַּבֹּקֶר בַּבֹּקֶר, וְעָרַךְ עָלֶיהָ הָעֹלָה, וְהִקְטִיר עָלֶיהָ חֶלְבֵי הַשְּׁלָמִים: אֵשׁ, תָּמִיד תּוּקַד עַל־הַמִּזְבֵּחַ, לֹא תִכְבֶּה:

יְהִי רָצוֹן מִלְּפָנֶיךָ יהוה אֱלֹהֵינוּ וֵאלֹהֵי אֲבוֹתֵינוּ, שֶׁתְּרַחֵם עָלֵינוּ, וְתִמְחָל לָנוּ עַל כָּל חַטֹּאתֵינוּ וּתְכַפֶּר לָנוּ אֶת כָּל עֲוֹנוֹתֵינוּ וְתִסְלַח לָנוּ עַל כָּל פְּשָׁעֵינוּ, וְתִבְנֶה בֵּית הַמִּקְדָּשׁ בִּמְהֵרָה בְיָמֵינוּ, וְנַקְרִיב לְפָנֶיךָ קָרְבַּן הַתָּמִיד שֶׁיְּכַפֵּר בַּעֲדֵנוּ, כְּמוֹ שֶׁכָּתַבְתָּ עָלֵינוּ בְּתוֹרָתֶךָ עַל יְדֵי מֹשֶׁה עַבְדֶּךָ מִפִּי כְבוֹדֶךָ, כָּאָמוּר

SHAHARIT FOR TISHA B'AV

THE DAILY SACRIFICE

וַיְדַבֵּר The LORD said to Moses, "Command the Israelites and tell *Num. 28* them: 'Be careful to offer to Me at the appointed time My food-offering consumed by fire, as an aroma pleasing to Me.' Tell them: 'This is the fire-offering you shall offer to the LORD – two lambs a year old without blemish, as a regular burnt-offering each day. Prepare one lamb in the morning and the other toward evening, together with a meal-offering of a tenth of an ephah of fine flour mixed with a quarter of a hin of oil from pressed olives. This is the regular burnt-offering instituted at Mount Sinai as a pleasing aroma, a fire-offering made to the LORD. Its libation is to be a quarter of a hin [of wine] with each lamb, poured in the Sanctuary as a libation of strong drink to the LORD. Prepare the second lamb in the afternoon, along with the same meal-offering and libation as in the morning. This is a fire-offering, an aroma pleasing to the LORD.'"

וְשָׁחַט He shall slaughter it at the north side of the altar before the *Lev. 1* LORD, and Aaron's sons, the priests, shall sprinkle its blood against the altar on all sides.

May it be Your will, LORD our God and God of our ancestors, that this recitation be considered accepted and favored before You as if we had offered the daily sacrifice at its appointed time and place, according to its laws.

It is You, LORD our God, to whom our ancestors offered fragrant incense when the Temple stood, as You commanded them through Moses Your prophet, as is written in Your Torah:

THE INCENSE

The LORD said to Moses: Take fragrant spices – balsam, onycha, galbanum *Ex. 30* and pure frankincense, all in equal amounts – and make a fragrant blend of incense, the work of a perfumer, well mixed, pure and holy. Grind it very finely and place it in front of the [Ark of] Testimony in the Tent of Meeting, where I will meet with you. It shall be most holy to you.

And it is said:

Aaron shall burn fragrant incense on the altar every morning when he cleans the lamps. He shall burn incense again when he lights the lamps toward evening so that there will be incense before the LORD at all times, throughout your generations.

פרשת קרבן התמיד

במדבר כח

וַיְדַבֵּר יהוה אֶל־מֹשֶׁה לֵּאמֹר: צַו אֶת־בְּנֵי יִשְׂרָאֵל וְאָמַרְתָּ אֲלֵהֶם, אֶת־קָרְבָּנִי לַחְמִי לְאִשַּׁי, רֵיחַ נִיחֹחִי, תִּשְׁמְרוּ לְהַקְרִיב לִי בְּמוֹעֲדוֹ: וְאָמַרְתָּ לָהֶם, זֶה הָאִשֶּׁה אֲשֶׁר תַּקְרִיבוּ לַיהוה, כְּבָשִׂים בְּנֵי־שָׁנָה תְמִימִם שְׁנַיִם לַיּוֹם, עֹלָה תָמִיד: אֶת־הַכֶּבֶשׂ אֶחָד תַּעֲשֶׂה בַבֹּקֶר, וְאֵת הַכֶּבֶשׂ הַשֵּׁנִי תַּעֲשֶׂה בֵּין הָעַרְבָּיִם: וַעֲשִׂירִית הָאֵיפָה סֹלֶת לְמִנְחָה, בְּלוּלָה בְּשֶׁמֶן כָּתִית רְבִיעִת הַהִין: עֹלַת תָּמִיד, הָעֲשֻׂיָה בְּהַר סִינַי, לְרֵיחַ נִיחֹחַ אִשֶּׁה לַיהוה: וְנִסְכּוֹ רְבִיעִת הַהִין לַכֶּבֶשׂ הָאֶחָד, בַּקֹּדֶשׁ הַסֵּךְ נֶסֶךְ שֵׁכָר לַיהוה: וְאֵת הַכֶּבֶשׂ הַשֵּׁנִי תַּעֲשֶׂה בֵּין הָעַרְבָּיִם, כְּמִנְחַת הַבֹּקֶר וּכְנִסְכּוֹ תַּעֲשֶׂה, אִשֵּׁה רֵיחַ נִיחֹחַ לַיהוה:

ויקרא א

וְשָׁחַט אֹתוֹ עַל יֶרֶךְ הַמִּזְבֵּחַ צָפֹנָה לִפְנֵי יהוה, וְזָרְקוּ בְּנֵי אַהֲרֹן הַכֹּהֲנִים אֶת־דָּמוֹ עַל־הַמִּזְבֵּחַ, סָבִיב:

יְהִי רָצוֹן מִלְּפָנֶיךָ, יהוה אֱלֹהֵינוּ וֵאלֹהֵי אֲבוֹתֵינוּ, שֶׁתְּהֵא אֲמִירָה זוֹ חֲשׁוּבָה וּמְקֻבֶּלֶת וּמְרֻצָּה לְפָנֶיךָ, כְּאִלּוּ הִקְרַבְנוּ קָרְבַּן הַתָּמִיד בְּמוֹעֲדוֹ וּבִמְקוֹמוֹ וּכְהִלְכָתוֹ.

אַתָּה הוּא יהוה אֱלֹהֵינוּ שֶׁהִקְטִירוּ אֲבוֹתֵינוּ לְפָנֶיךָ אֶת קְטֹרֶת הַסַּמִּים בִּזְמַן שֶׁבֵּית הַמִּקְדָּשׁ הָיָה קַיָּם, כַּאֲשֶׁר צִוִּיתָ אוֹתָם עַל יְדֵי מֹשֶׁה נְבִיאֶךָ, כַּכָּתוּב בְּתוֹרָתֶךָ:

פרשת הקטורת

שמות ל

וַיֹּאמֶר יהוה אֶל־מֹשֶׁה, קַח־לְךָ סַמִּים נָטָף וּשְׁחֵלֶת וְחֶלְבְּנָה, סַמִּים וּלְבֹנָה זַכָּה, בַּד בְּבַד יִהְיֶה: וְעָשִׂיתָ אֹתָהּ קְטֹרֶת, רֹקַח מַעֲשֵׂה רוֹקֵחַ, מְמֻלָּח, טָהוֹר קֹדֶשׁ: וְשָׁחַקְתָּ מִמֶּנָּה הָדֵק, וְנָתַתָּה מִמֶּנָּה לִפְנֵי הָעֵדֻת בְּאֹהֶל מוֹעֵד אֲשֶׁר אִוָּעֵד לְךָ שָׁמָּה, קֹדֶשׁ קָדָשִׁים תִּהְיֶה לָכֶם:

וְנֶאֱמַר

וְהִקְטִיר עָלָיו אַהֲרֹן קְטֹרֶת סַמִּים, בַּבֹּקֶר בַּבֹּקֶר בְּהֵיטִיבוֹ אֶת־הַנֵּרֹת יַקְטִירֶנָּה: וּבְהַעֲלֹת אַהֲרֹן אֶת־הַנֵּרֹת בֵּין הָעַרְבַּיִם יַקְטִירֶנָּה, קְטֹרֶת תָּמִיד לִפְנֵי יהוה לְדֹרֹתֵיכֶם:

The rabbis taught: How was the incense prepared? It weighed 368 manehs, 365 — Keritot 6a
corresponding to the number of days in a solar year, a maneh for each day, half
to be offered in the morning and half in the afternoon, and three additional
manehs from which the High Priest took two handfuls on Yom Kippur. These
were put back into the mortar on the day before Yom Kippur and ground again
very thoroughly so as to be extremely fine. The incense contained eleven kinds
of spices: balsam, onycha, galbanum and frankincense, each weighing seventy
manehs; myrrh, cassia, spikenard and saffron, each weighing sixteen manehs;
twelve manehs of costus, three of aromatic bark; nine of cinnamon; nine kabs
of Carsina lye; three seahs and three kabs of Cyprus wine. If Cyprus wine was
not available, old white wine might be used. A quarter of a kab of Sodom salt,
and a minute amount of a smoke-raising herb. Rabbi Nathan the Babylonian
says: also a minute amount of Jordan amber. If one added honey to the mixture,
he rendered it unfit for sacred use. If he omitted any one of its ingredients, he is
guilty of a capital offence.

Rabban Simeon ben Gamliel says: "Balsam" refers to the sap that drips from the
balsam tree. The Carsina lye was used for bleaching the onycha to improve it.
The Cyprus wine was used to soak the onycha in it to make it pungent. Though
urine is suitable for this purpose, it is not brought into the Temple out of
respect.

It was taught, Rabbi Nathan says: While it was being ground, another would say,
"Grind well, well grind," because the [rhythmic] sound is good for spices. If it
was mixed in half-quantities, it is fit for use, but we have not heard whether this
applies to a third or a quarter. Rabbi Judah said: The general rule is that if it was
made in the correct proportions, it is fit for use even if made in half-quantity, but
if he omitted any one of its ingredients, he is guilty of a capital offence.

It was taught, Bar Kappara says: Once every sixty or seventy years, the accumu- — JT Yoma 4:5
lated surpluses amounted to half the yearly quantity. Bar Kappara also taught:
If a minute quantity of honey had been mixed into the incense, no one could
have resisted the scent. Why did they not put honey into it? Because the Torah
says, "For you are not to burn any leaven or honey in a fire-offering made to the — Lev. 2
Lord."

The following three verses are each said three times:

The Lord of hosts is with us; the God of Jacob is our stronghold, Selah. — Ps. 46
Lord of hosts, happy is the one who trusts in You. — Ps. 84
Lord, save! May the King answer us on the day we call. — Ps. 20

שחרית לתשעה באב • סדר הקרבנות

תָּנוּ רַבָּנָן: פִּטּוּם הַקְּטְרֶת כֵּיצַד, שְׁלֹשׁ מֵאוֹת וְשִׁשִּׁים וּשְׁמוֹנָה מָנִים הָיוּ בָהּ. כריתות ו.
שְׁלֹשׁ מֵאוֹת וְשִׁשִּׁים וַחֲמִשָּׁה כְּמִנְיַן יְמוֹת הַחַמָּה, מָנֶה לְכָל יוֹם, פְּרָס בְּשַׁחֲרִית
וּפְרָס בֵּין הָעַרְבַּיִם, וּשְׁלֹשָׁה מָנִים יְתֵרִים שֶׁמֵּהֶם מַכְנִיס כֹּהֵן גָּדוֹל מְלֹא חָפְנָיו
בְּיוֹם הַכִּפּוּרִים, וּמַחֲזִירָן לְמַכְתֶּשֶׁת בְּעֶרֶב יוֹם הַכִּפּוּרִים וְשׁוֹחֲקָן יָפֶה יָפֶה, כְּדֵי
שֶׁתְּהֵא דַקָּה מִן הַדַּקָּה. וְאֶחָד עָשָׂר סַמָּנִים הָיוּ בָהּ, וְאֵלּוּ הֵן: הַצֳּרִי, וְהַצִּפֹּרֶן,
וְהַחֶלְבְּנָה, וְהַלְּבוֹנָה, מִשְׁקַל שִׁבְעִים שִׁבְעִים מָנֶה, מוֹר, וּקְצִיעָה, שִׁבֹּלֶת נֵרְדְּ,
וְכַרְכֹּם מִשְׁקַל שִׁשָּׁה עָשָׂר שִׁשָּׁה עָשָׂר מָנֶה, הַקּשְׁטְ שְׁנֵים עָשָׂר, קִלּוּפָה שְׁלֹשָׁה,
קִנָּמוֹן תִּשְׁעָה, בֹּרִית כַּרְשִׁינָה תִּשְׁעָה קַבִּין, יֵין קַפְרִיסִין סְאִין תְּלָת וְקַבִּין תְּלָתָא,
וְאִם לֹא מָצָא יֵין קַפְרִיסִין, מֵבִיא חֲמַר חִוַּרְיָן עַתִּיק. מֶלַח סְדוֹמִית רֹבַע, מַעֲלֶה
עָשָׁן כָּל שֶׁהוּא. רַבִּי נָתָן הַבַּבְלִי אוֹמֵר: אַף כִּפַּת הַיַּרְדֵּן כָּל שֶׁהוּא, וְאִם נָתַן בָּהּ
דְּבַשׁ פְּסָלָהּ, וְאִם חִסַּר אֶחָד מִכָּל סַמָּנֶיהָ, חַיָּב מִיתָה.

רַבָּן שִׁמְעוֹן בֶּן גַּמְלִיאֵל אוֹמֵר: הַצֳּרִי אֵינוֹ אֶלָּא שְׂרָף הַנּוֹטֵף מֵעֲצֵי הַקְּטָף. בֹּרִית
כַּרְשִׁינָה שֶׁשָּׁפִין בָּהּ אֶת הַצִּפֹּרֶן כְּדֵי שֶׁתְּהֵא נָאָה, יֵין קַפְרִיסִין שֶׁשּׁוֹרִין בּוֹ אֶת
הַצִּפֹּרֶן כְּדֵי שֶׁתְּהֵא עַזָּה, וַהֲלֹא מֵי רַגְלַיִם יָפִין לָהּ, אֶלָּא שֶׁאֵין מַכְנִיסִין מֵי רַגְלַיִם
בַּמִּקְדָּשׁ מִפְּנֵי הַכָּבוֹד.

תַּנְיָא, רַבִּי נָתָן אוֹמֵר: כְּשֶׁהוּא שׁוֹחֵק אוֹמֵר, הָדֵק הֵיטֵב הֵיטֵב הָדֵק, מִפְּנֵי
שֶׁהַקּוֹל יָפֶה לַבְּשָׂמִים. פִּטְּמָהּ לַחֲצָאִין כְּשֵׁרָה, לִשְׁלִישׁ וְלִרְבִיעַ לֹא שָׁמָעְנוּ.
אָמַר רַבִּי יְהוּדָה: זֶה הַכְּלָל, אִם כְּמִדָּתָהּ כְּשֵׁרָה לַחֲצָאִין, וְאִם חִסַּר אֶחָד מִכָּל
סַמָּנֶיהָ חַיָּב מִיתָה.

תַּנְיָא, בַּר קַפָּרָא אוֹמֵר: אַחַת לְשִׁשִּׁים אוֹ לְשִׁבְעִים שָׁנָה הָיְתָה בָאָה שֶׁל שִׁירַיִם ירושלמי
לַחֲצָאִין. וְעוֹד תָּנֵי בַּר קַפָּרָא: אִלּוּ הָיָה נוֹתֵן בָּהּ קוֹרְטוֹב שֶׁל דְּבַשׁ אֵין אָדָם יומא ד,
יָכוֹל לַעֲמֹד מִפְּנֵי רֵיחָהּ, וְלָמָּה אֵין מְעָרְבִין בָּהּ דְּבַשׁ, מִפְּנֵי שֶׁהַתּוֹרָה אָמְרָה: כִּי ויקרא ב
כָל שְׂאֹר וְכָל דְּבַשׁ לֹא־תַקְטִירוּ מִמֶּנּוּ אִשֶּׁה לַיהוה:

The following three verses are each said three times:

יְהוה צְבָאוֹת עִמָּנוּ, מִשְׂגָּב לָנוּ אֱלֹהֵי יַעֲקֹב סֶלָה: תהלים מו

יְהוה צְבָאוֹת, אַשְׁרֵי אָדָם בֹּטֵחַ בָּךְ: תהלים פד

יְהוה הוֹשִׁיעָה, הַמֶּלֶךְ יַעֲנֵנוּ בְיוֹם־קָרְאֵנוּ: תהלים כ

You are my hiding place; You will protect me from distress and surround me with songs of salvation, Selah. *Ps. 32*

Then the offering of Judah and Jerusalem will be pleasing to the LORD as in the days of old and as in former years. *Mal. 3*

THE ORDER OF THE PRIESTLY FUNCTIONS

Abaye related the order of the daily priestly functions in the name of tradition and in accordance with Abba Shaul: The large pile [of wood] comes before the second pile for the incense; the second pile for the incense precedes the laying in order of the two logs of wood; the laying in order of the two logs of wood comes before the removing of ashes from the inner altar; the removing of ashes from the inner altar precedes the cleaning of the five lamps; the cleaning of the five lamps comes before the blood of the daily offering; the blood of the daily offering precedes the cleaning of the [other] two lamps; the cleaning of the two lamps comes before the incense-offering; the incense-offering precedes the burning of the limbs; the burning of the limbs comes before the meal-offering; the meal-offering precedes the pancakes; the pancakes come before the wine-libations; the wine-libations precede the additional offerings; the additional offerings come before the [frankincense] censers; the censers precede the daily afternoon offering; as it is said, "On it he shall arrange burnt-offerings, and on it he shall burn the fat of the peace-offerings" – "on it" [the daily offering] all the offerings were completed. *Yoma 33a*

Lev. 6

Please, by the power of Your great right hand, set the captive nation free.
Accept Your people's prayer. Strengthen us, purify us, You who are revered.
Please, mighty One, guard like the pupil of the eye those who seek Your unity.
Bless them, cleanse them, have compassion on them,
grant them Your righteousness always.
Mighty One, holy One, in Your great goodness guide Your congregation.
Only One, exalted One, turn to Your people, who proclaim Your holiness.
Accept our plea and heed our cry, You who know all secret thoughts.
Blessed be the name of His glorious kingdom for ever and all time.

Master of the Universe, You have commanded us to offer the daily sacrifice at its appointed time with the priests at their service, the Levites on their platform, and the Israelites at their post. Now, because of our sins, the Temple is destroyed and the daily sacrifice discontinued, and we have no priest at his service, no Levite on his platform, no Israelite at his post. But You said: "We will offer in place of bullocks [the prayer of] our lips." Therefore may it be Your will, LORD our God and God of our ancestors, that the prayer of our lips be considered, accepted and favored before You as if we had offered the daily sacrifice at its appointed time and place, according to its laws. *Hos. 14*

שחרית לתשעה באב • סדר הקרבנות

אַתָּה סֵתֶר לִי, מִצַּר תִּצְּרֵנִי, רָנֵּי פַלֵּט תְּסוֹבְבֵנִי סֶלָה: *תהלים לב*

וְעָרְבָה לַיהוה מִנְחַת יְהוּדָה וִירוּשָׁלָםִ כִּימֵי עוֹלָם וּכְשָׁנִים קַדְמוֹנִיּוֹת: *מלאכי ג*

סדר המערכה

אַבַּיֵי הֲוָה מְסַדֵּר סֵדֶר הַמַּעֲרָכָה מִשְּׁמָא דִגְמָרָא, וְאַלִּבָּא דְאַבָּא שָׁאוּל: *יומא לג*
מַעֲרָכָה גְדוֹלָה קוֹדֶמֶת לְמַעֲרָכָה שְׁנִיָּה שֶׁל קְטֹרֶת, וּמַעֲרָכָה שְׁנִיָּה שֶׁל קְטֹרֶת קוֹדֶמֶת לְסִדּוּר שְׁנֵי גִזְרֵי עֵצִים, וְסִדּוּר שְׁנֵי גִזְרֵי עֵצִים קוֹדֵם לְדִשּׁוּן מִזְבֵּחַ הַפְּנִימִי, וְדִשּׁוּן מִזְבֵּחַ הַפְּנִימִי קוֹדֵם לַהֲטָבַת חָמֵשׁ נֵרוֹת, וַהֲטָבַת חָמֵשׁ נֵרוֹת קוֹדֶמֶת לְדַם הַתָּמִיד, וְדַם הַתָּמִיד קוֹדֵם לַהֲטָבַת שְׁתֵּי נֵרוֹת, וַהֲטָבַת שְׁתֵּי נֵרוֹת קוֹדֶמֶת לִקְטֹרֶת, וּקְטֹרֶת קוֹדֶמֶת לְאֵבָרִים, וְאֵבָרִים לְמִנְחָה, וּמִנְחָה לַחֲבִתִּין, וַחֲבִתִּין לִנְסָכִין, וּנְסָכִין לְמוּסָפִין, וּמוּסָפִין לְבָזִיכִין, וּבָזִיכִין קוֹדְמִין לְתָמִיד שֶׁל בֵּין הָעַרְבָּיִם. שֶׁנֶּאֱמַר: וְעָרַךְ עָלֶיהָ *ויקרא* הָעֹלָה, וְהִקְטִיר עָלֶיהָ חֶלְבֵי הַשְּׁלָמִים: עָלֶיהָ הַשְׁלֵם כָּל הַקָּרְבָּנוֹת כֻּלָּם.

אָנָּא, בְּכֹחַ גְּדֻלַּת יְמִינְךָ, תַּתִּיר צְרוּרָה.
קַבֵּל רִנַּת עַמְּךָ, שַׂגְּבֵנוּ, טַהֲרֵנוּ, נוֹרָא.
נָא גִבּוֹר, דּוֹרְשֵׁי יִחוּדְךָ כְּבָבַת שָׁמְרֵם.
בָּרְכֵם, טַהֲרֵם, רַחֲמֵם, צִדְקָתְךָ תָּמִיד גָּמְלֵם.
חֲסִין קָדוֹשׁ, בְּרֹב טוּבְךָ נַהֵל עֲדָתֶךָ.
יָחִיד גֵּאֶה, לְעַמְּךָ פְּנֵה, זוֹכְרֵי קְדֻשָּׁתֶךָ.
שַׁוְעָתֵנוּ קַבֵּל וּשְׁמַע צַעֲקָתֵנוּ, יוֹדֵעַ תַּעֲלוּמוֹת.
בָּרוּךְ שֵׁם כְּבוֹד מַלְכוּתוֹ לְעוֹלָם וָעֶד.

רִבּוֹן הָעוֹלָמִים, אַתָּה צִוִּיתָנוּ לְהַקְרִיב קָרְבַּן הַתָּמִיד בְּמוֹעֲדוֹ וְלִהְיוֹת כֹּהֲנִים בַּעֲבוֹדָתָם וּלְוִיִּים בְּדוּכָנָם וְיִשְׂרָאֵל בְּמַעֲמָדָם, וְעַתָּה בַּעֲוֹנוֹתֵינוּ חָרַב בֵּית הַמִּקְדָּשׁ וּבֻטַּל הַתָּמִיד וְאֵין לָנוּ לֹא כֹהֵן בַּעֲבוֹדָתוֹ וְלֹא לֵוִי בְּדוּכָנוֹ וְלֹא יִשְׂרָאֵל בְּמַעֲמָדוֹ, וְאַתָּה אָמַרְתָּ: וּנְשַׁלְּמָה פָרִים שְׂפָתֵינוּ: *הושע יד*
לָכֵן יְהִי רָצוֹן מִלְּפָנֶיךָ יהוה אֱלֹהֵינוּ וֵאלֹהֵי אֲבוֹתֵינוּ, שֶׁיְּהֵא שִׂיחַ שִׂפְתוֹתֵינוּ חָשׁוּב וּמְקֻבָּל וּמְרֻצֶּה לְפָנֶיךָ, כְּאִלּוּ הִקְרַבְנוּ קָרְבַּן הַתָּמִיד בְּמוֹעֲדוֹ וּבִמְקוֹמוֹ וּכְהִלְכָתוֹ.

LAWS OF OFFERINGS, MISHNA ZEVAḤIM

אֵיזֶהוּ מְקוֹמָן What is the location for sacrifices? The holiest offerings were slaughtered on the north side. The bull and he-goat of Yom Kippur were slaughtered on the north side. Their blood was received in a sacred vessel on the north side, and had to be sprinkled between the poles [of the Ark], toward the veil [screening the Holy of Holies], and on the golden altar. [The omission of] one of these sprinklings invalidated [the atonement ceremony]. The leftover blood was to be poured onto the western base of the outer altar. If this was not done, however, the omission did not invalidate [the ceremony]. *Zevaḥim Ch. 5*

The bulls and he-goats that were completely burnt were slaughtered on the north side, their blood was received in a sacred vessel on the north side, and had to be sprinkled toward the veil and on the golden altar. [The omission of] one of these sprinklings invalidated [the ceremony]. The leftover blood was to be poured onto the western base of the outer altar. If this was not done, however, the omission did not invalidate [the ceremony]. All these offerings were burnt where the altar ashes were deposited.

The communal and individual sin-offerings – these are the communal sin-offerings: the he-goats offered on Rosh Ḥodesh and Festivals were slaughtered on the north side, their blood was received in a sacred vessel on the north side, and required four sprinklings, one on each of the four corners of the altar. How was this done? The priest ascended the ramp and turned [right] onto the surrounding ledge. He came to the southeast corner, then went to the northeast, then to the northwest, then to the southwest. The leftover blood he poured onto the southern base. [The meat of these offerings], prepared in any manner, was eaten within the [courtyard] curtains, by males of the priesthood, on that day and the following night, until midnight.

The burnt-offering was among the holiest of sacrifices. It was slaughtered on the north side, its blood was received in a sacred vessel on the north side, and required two sprinklings [at opposite corners of the altar], making four in all. The offering had to be flayed, dismembered and wholly consumed by fire.

דיני זבחים

איזהו מקומן של זבחים. קדשי קדשים שחיטתן בצפון. פר ושעיר של יום הכפורים, שחיטתן בצפון, וקבול דמן בכלי שרת בצפון, ודמן טעון הזיה על בין הבדים, ועל הפרכת, ועל מזבח הזהב. מתנה אחת מהן מעכבת. שירי הדם היה שופך על יסוד מערבי של מזבח החיצון, אם לא נתן לא עכב.

פרים הנשרפים ושעירים הנשרפים, שחיטתן בצפון, וקבול דמן בכלי שרת בצפון, ודמן טעון הזיה על הפרכת ועל מזבח הזהב. מתנה אחת מהן מעכבת. שירי הדם היה שופך על יסוד מערבי של מזבח החיצון, אם לא נתן לא עכב. אלו ואלו נשרפין בבית הדשן.

חטאת הצבור והיחיד. אלו הן חטאת הצבור: שעירי ראשי חדשים ושל מועדות. שחיטתן בצפון, וקבול דמן בכלי שרת בצפון, ודמן טעון ארבע מתנות על ארבע קרנות. כיצד, עלה בכבש, ופנה לסובב, ובא לו לקרן דרומית מזרחית, מזרחית צפונית, צפונית מערבית, מערבית דרומית. שירי הדם היה שופך על יסוד דרומי. ונאכלין לפנים מן הקלעים, לזכרי כהנה, בכל מאכל, ליום ולילה עד חצות.

העולה קדש קדשים. שחיטתה בצפון, וקבול דמה בכלי שרת בצפון, ודמה טעון שתי מתנות שהן ארבע, וטעונה הפשט ונתוח, וכליל לאשים.

זבחים
פרק ה

The communal peace-offerings and the guilt-offerings – these are the guilt-offerings: the guilt-offering for robbery; the guilt-offering for profane use of a sacred object; the guilt-offering [for violating] a betrothed maidservant; the guilt-offering of a Nazirite [who had become defiled by a corpse]; the guilt-offering of a leper [at his cleansing]; and the guilt-offering in case of doubt. All these were slaughtered on the north side, their blood was received in a sacred vessel on the north side, and required two sprinklings [at opposite corners of the altar], making four in all. [The meat of these offerings], prepared in any manner, was eaten within the [courtyard] curtains, by males of the priesthood, on that day and the following night, until midnight.

The thanksgiving-offering and the ram of a Nazirite were offerings of lesser holiness. They could be slaughtered anywhere in the Temple court, and their blood required two sprinklings [at opposite corners of the altar], making four in all. The meat of these offerings, prepared in any manner, was eaten anywhere within the city [Jerusalem], by anyone during that day and the following night until midnight. This also applied to the portion of these sacrifices [given to the priests], except that the priests' portion was only to be eaten by the priests, their wives, children and servants.

Peace-offerings were [also] of lesser holiness. They could be slaughtered anywhere in the Temple court, and their blood required two sprinklings [at opposite corners of the altar], making four in all. The meat of these offerings, prepared in any manner, was eaten anywhere within the city [Jerusalem], by anyone, for two days and one night. This also applied to the portion of these sacrifices [given to the priests], except that the priests' portion was only to be eaten by the priests, their wives, children and servants.

The firstborn and tithe of cattle and the Pesaḥ lamb were sacrifices of lesser holiness. They could be slaughtered anywhere in the Temple court, and their blood required only one sprinkling, which had to be done at the base of the altar. They differed in their consumption: the firstborn was eaten only by priests, while the tithe could be eaten by anyone. Both could be eaten anywhere within the city, prepared in any manner, during two days and one night. The Pesaḥ lamb had to be eaten that night until midnight. It could only be eaten by those who had been numbered for it, and eaten only roasted.

זִבְחֵי שַׁלְמֵי צִבּוּר וַאֲשָׁמוֹת. אֵלּוּ הֵן אֲשָׁמוֹת: אֲשַׁם גְּזֵלוֹת, אֲשַׁם מְעִילוֹת, אֲשַׁם שִׁפְחָה חֲרוּפָה, אֲשַׁם נָזִיר, אֲשַׁם מְצֹרָע, אָשָׁם תָּלוּי. שְׁחִיטָתָן בַּצָּפוֹן, וְקִבּוּל דָּמָן בִּכְלִי שָׁרֵת בַּצָּפוֹן, וְדָמָן טָעוּן שְׁתֵּי מַתָּנוֹת שֶׁהֵן אַרְבַּע. וְנֶאֱכָלִין לִפְנִים מִן הַקְּלָעִים, לְזִכְרֵי כְהֻנָּה, בְּכָל מַאֲכָל, לְיוֹם וָלַיְלָה עַד חֲצוֹת.

הַתּוֹדָה וְאֵיל נָזִיר קָדָשִׁים קַלִּים. שְׁחִיטָתָן בְּכָל מָקוֹם בָּעֲזָרָה, וְדָמָן טָעוּן שְׁתֵּי מַתָּנוֹת שֶׁהֵן אַרְבַּע, וְנֶאֱכָלִין בְּכָל הָעִיר, לְכָל אָדָם, בְּכָל מַאֲכָל, לְיוֹם וָלַיְלָה עַד חֲצוֹת. הַמּוּרָם מֵהֶם כַּיּוֹצֵא בָהֶם, אֶלָּא שֶׁהַמּוּרָם נֶאֱכָל לַכֹּהֲנִים, לִנְשֵׁיהֶם, וְלִבְנֵיהֶם וּלְעַבְדֵיהֶם.

שְׁלָמִים קָדָשִׁים קַלִּים. שְׁחִיטָתָן בְּכָל מָקוֹם בָּעֲזָרָה, וְדָמָן טָעוּן שְׁתֵּי מַתָּנוֹת שֶׁהֵן אַרְבַּע, וְנֶאֱכָלִין בְּכָל הָעִיר, לְכָל אָדָם, בְּכָל מַאֲכָל, לִשְׁנֵי יָמִים וְלַיְלָה אֶחָד. הַמּוּרָם מֵהֶם כַּיּוֹצֵא בָהֶם, אֶלָּא שֶׁהַמּוּרָם נֶאֱכָל לַכֹּהֲנִים, לִנְשֵׁיהֶם, וְלִבְנֵיהֶם וּלְעַבְדֵיהֶם.

הַבְּכוֹר וְהַמַּעֲשֵׂר וְהַפֶּסַח קָדָשִׁים קַלִּים. שְׁחִיטָתָן בְּכָל מָקוֹם בָּעֲזָרָה, וְדָמָן טָעוּן מַתָּנָה אַחַת, וּבִלְבַד שֶׁיִּתֵּן כְּנֶגֶד הַיְסוֹד. שִׁנָּה בַּאֲכִילָתָן, הַבְּכוֹר נֶאֱכָל לַכֹּהֲנִים וְהַמַּעֲשֵׂר לְכָל אָדָם, וְנֶאֱכָלִין בְּכָל הָעִיר, בְּכָל מַאֲכָל, לִשְׁנֵי יָמִים וְלַיְלָה אֶחָד. הַפֶּסַח אֵינוֹ נֶאֱכָל אֶלָּא בַלַּיְלָה, וְאֵינוֹ נֶאֱכָל אֶלָּא עַד חֲצוֹת, וְאֵינוֹ נֶאֱכָל אֶלָּא לִמְנוּיָיו, וְאֵינוֹ נֶאֱכָל אֶלָּא צָלִי.

SHAHARIT FOR TISHA B'AV

THE INTERPRETIVE PRINCIPLES OF RABBI YISHMA'EL

רַבִּי יִשְׁמָעֵאל Rabbi Yishma'el says:
The Torah is expounded by thirteen principles:

1. An inference from a lenient law to a strict one, and vice versa.
2. An inference drawn from identical words in two passages.
3. A general principle derived from one text or two related texts.
4. A general law followed by specific examples
   [where the law applies exclusively to those examples].
5. A specific example followed by a general law
   [where the law applies to everything implied in the general statement].
6. A general law followed by specific examples and concluding with a general law: here you may infer only cases similar to the examples.
7. When a general statement requires clarification by a specific example, or a specific example requires clarification by a general statement [then rules 4 and 5 do not apply].
8. When a particular case, already included in the general statement, is expressly mentioned to teach something new, that special provision applies to all other cases included in the general statement.
9. When a particular case, though included in the general statement, is expressly mentioned with a provision similar to the general law, such a case is singled out to lessen the severity of the law, not to increase it.
10. When a particular case, though included in the general statement, is explicitly mentioned with a provision differing from the general law, it is singled out to lessen in some respects, and in others to increase, the severity of the law.
11. When a particular case, though included in the general statement, is explicitly mentioned with a new provision, the terms of the general statement no longer apply to it, unless Scripture indicates explicitly that they do apply.
12. A matter elucidated from its context, or from the following passage.
▸ 13. Also, when two passages [seem to] contradict each other,
    [they are to be elucidated by] a third passage that reconciles them.

May it be Your will, LORD our God and God of our ancestors, that the Temple be speedily rebuilt in our days, and grant us our share in Your Torah. And may we serve You there in reverence, as in the days of old and as in former years.

ברייתא דרבי ישמעאל

רַבִּי יִשְׁמָעֵאל אוֹמֵר: בִּשְׁלֹשׁ עֶשְׂרֵה מִדּוֹת הַתּוֹרָה נִדְרֶשֶׁת

א מִקַּל וָחֹמֶר

ב וּמִגְּזֵרָה שָׁוָה

ג מִבִּנְיַן אָב מִכָּתוּב אֶחָד, וּמִבִּנְיַן אָב מִשְּׁנֵי כְתוּבִים

ד מִכְּלָל וּפְרָט

ה מִפְּרָט וּכְלָל

ו כְּלָל וּפְרָט וּכְלָל, אִי אַתָּה דָן אֶלָּא כְּעֵין הַפְּרָט

ז מִכְּלָל שֶׁהוּא צָרִיךְ לִפְרָט, וּמִפְּרָט שֶׁהוּא צָרִיךְ לִכְלָל

ח כָּל דָּבָר שֶׁהָיָה בִכְלָל, וְיָצָא מִן הַכְּלָל לְלַמֵּד לֹא לְלַמֵּד עַל עַצְמוֹ יָצָא, אֶלָּא לְלַמֵּד עַל הַכְּלָל כֻּלּוֹ יָצָא

ט כָּל דָּבָר שֶׁהָיָה בִכְלָל, וְיָצָא לִטְעוֹן טְעַן אֶחָד שֶׁהוּא כְעִנְיָנוֹ יָצָא לְהָקֵל וְלֹא לְהַחֲמִיר

י כָּל דָּבָר שֶׁהָיָה בִכְלָל, וְיָצָא לִטְעוֹן טְעַן אַחֵר שֶׁלֹּא כְעִנְיָנוֹ יָצָא לְהָקֵל וּלְהַחֲמִיר

יא כָּל דָּבָר שֶׁהָיָה בִכְלָל, וְיָצָא לִדּוֹן בַּדָּבָר הֶחָדָשׁ אִי אַתָּה יָכוֹל לְהַחֲזִירוֹ לִכְלָלוֹ עַד שֶׁיַּחֲזִירֶנּוּ הַכָּתוּב לִכְלָלוֹ בְּפֵרוּשׁ

יב דָּבָר הַלָּמֵד מֵעִנְיָנוֹ, וְדָבָר הַלָּמֵד מִסּוֹפוֹ

יג וְכֵן שְׁנֵי כְתוּבִים הַמַּכְחִישִׁים זֶה אֶת זֶה עַד שֶׁיָּבוֹא הַכָּתוּב הַשְּׁלִישִׁי וְיַכְרִיעַ בֵּינֵיהֶם.

יְהִי רָצוֹן מִלְּפָנֶיךָ, יהוה אֱלֹהֵינוּ וֵאלֹהֵי אֲבוֹתֵינוּ, שֶׁיִּבָּנֶה בֵּית הַמִּקְדָּשׁ בִּמְהֵרָה בְיָמֵינוּ, וְתֵן חֶלְקֵנוּ בְּתוֹרָתֶךָ, וְשָׁם נַעֲבָדְךָ בְּיִרְאָה כִּימֵי עוֹלָם וּכְשָׁנִים קַדְמוֹנִיּוֹת.

SHAḤARIT FOR TISHA B'AV

THE RABBIS' KADDISH

The following prayer requires the presence of a minyan.
A transliteration can be found on page 793.

Mourner: יִתְגַּדַּל Magnified and sanctified
may His great name be,
in the world He created by His will.
May He establish His kingdom in your lifetime
and in your days,
and in the lifetime of all the house of Israel,
swiftly and soon –
and say: Amen.

All: May His great name be blessed for ever and all time.

Mourner: Blessed and praised,
glorified and exalted,
raised and honored,
uplifted and lauded
be the name of the Holy One,
blessed be He,
beyond any blessing,
song, praise and consolation uttered in the world –
and say: Amen.

To Israel, to the teachers,
their disciples and their disciples' disciples,
and to all who engage in the study of Torah,
in this (*in Israel add:* holy) place or elsewhere,
may there come to them and you great peace,
grace, kindness and compassion,
long life, ample sustenance
and deliverance, from their Father in Heaven –
and say: Amen.

קדיש דרבנן

The following prayer requires the presence of a מנין.
A transliteration can be found on page 793.

אבל: **יִתְגַּדַּל וְיִתְקַדַּשׁ שְׁמֵהּ רַבָּא** (קהל: אָמֵן)
בְּעָלְמָא דִּי בְרָא כִרְעוּתֵהּ
וְיַמְלִיךְ מַלְכוּתֵהּ
בְּחַיֵּיכוֹן וּבְיוֹמֵיכוֹן וּבְחַיֵּי דְכָל בֵּית יִשְׂרָאֵל
בַּעֲגָלָא וּבִזְמַן קָרִיב
וְאִמְרוּ אָמֵן. (קהל: אָמֵן)

קהל
ואבל: **יְהֵא שְׁמֵהּ רַבָּא מְבָרַךְ לְעָלַם וּלְעָלְמֵי עָלְמַיָּא.**

אבל: יִתְבָּרַךְ וְיִשְׁתַּבַּח וְיִתְפָּאַר וְיִתְרוֹמַם וְיִתְנַשֵּׂא
וְיִתְהַדָּר וְיִתְעַלֶּה וְיִתְהַלָּל
שְׁמֵהּ דְּקֻדְשָׁא בְּרִיךְ הוּא (קהל: בְּרִיךְ הוּא)
לְעֵלָּא מִן כָּל בִּרְכָתָא וְשִׁירָתָא, תֻּשְׁבְּחָתָא וְנֶחֱמָתָא
דַּאֲמִירָן בְּעָלְמָא
וְאִמְרוּ אָמֵן. (קהל: אָמֵן)

עַל יִשְׂרָאֵל וְעַל רַבָּנָן
וְעַל תַּלְמִידֵיהוֹן וְעַל כָּל תַּלְמִידֵי תַלְמִידֵיהוֹן
וְעַל כָּל מָאן דְּעָסְקִין בְּאוֹרַיְתָא
דִּי בְאַתְרָא (בארץ ישראל: קַדִּישָׁא) הָדֵין, וְדִי בְּכָל אֲתַר וַאֲתַר
יְהֵא לְהוֹן וּלְכוֹן שְׁלָמָא רַבָּא
חִנָּא וְחִסְדָּא, וְרַחֲמֵי, וְחַיֵּי אֲרִיכֵי, וּמְזוֹנֵי רְוִיחֵי
וּפֻרְקָנָא מִן קֳדָם אֲבוּהוֹן דִּי בִשְׁמַיָּא
וְאִמְרוּ אָמֵן. (קהל: אָמֵן)

May there be great peace from heaven,
and (good) life for us and all Israel –
and say: Amen.

*Bow, take three steps back, as if taking leave of the Divine Presence,
then bow, first left, then right, then center, while saying:*

May He who makes peace in His high places,
in His compassion make peace for us and all Israel –
and say: Amen.

A PSALM BEFORE VERSES OF PRAISE

מִזְמוֹר שִׁיר A psalm of David. A song for the dedication of the House. *Ps. 30*
I will exalt You, Lord, for You have lifted me up,
and not let my enemies rejoice over me.
Lord, my God, I cried to You for help and You healed me.
Lord, You lifted my soul from the grave;
You spared me from going down to the pit.
Sing to the Lord, you His devoted ones,
and give thanks to His holy name.
For His anger is for a moment, but His favor for a lifetime.
At night there may be weeping, but in the morning there is joy.
When I felt secure, I said, "I shall never be shaken."
Lord, when You favored me, You made me stand firm as a mountain,
but when You hid Your face, I was terrified.
To You, Lord, I called; I pleaded with my Lord:
"What gain would there be if I died and went down to the grave?
Can dust thank You? Can it declare Your truth?
Hear, Lord, and be gracious to me; Lord, be my help."
▸ You have turned my sorrow into dancing.
You have removed my sackcloth and clothed me with joy,
so that my soul may sing to You and not be silent.
Lord my God, for ever will I thank You.

יְהֵא שְׁלָמָא רַבָּא מִן שְׁמַיָּא
וְחַיִּים (טוֹבִים) עָלֵינוּ וְעַל כָּל יִשְׂרָאֵל
וְאִמְרוּ אָמֵן. (קהל: אָמֵן)

*Bow, take three steps back, as if taking leave of the Divine Presence,
then bow, first left, then right, then center, while saying:*

עֹשֶׂה שָׁלוֹם בִּמְרוֹמָיו
הוּא יַעֲשֶׂה בְרַחֲמָיו שָׁלוֹם, עָלֵינוּ וְעַל כָּל יִשְׂרָאֵל
וְאִמְרוּ אָמֵן. (קהל: אָמֵן)

מזמור לפני פסוקי דזמרה

תהלים ל

מִזְמוֹר שִׁיר־חֲנֻכַּת הַבַּיִת לְדָוִד:
אֲרוֹמִמְךָ יהוה כִּי דִלִּיתָנִי, וְלֹא־שִׂמַּחְתָּ אֹיְבַי לִי:
יהוה אֱלֹהָי, שִׁוַּעְתִּי אֵלֶיךָ וַתִּרְפָּאֵנִי:
יהוה, הֶעֱלִיתָ מִן־שְׁאוֹל נַפְשִׁי, חִיִּיתַנִי מִיָּרְדִי־בוֹר:
זַמְּרוּ לַיהוה חֲסִידָיו, וְהוֹדוּ לְזֵכֶר קָדְשׁוֹ:
כִּי רֶגַע בְּאַפּוֹ, חַיִּים בִּרְצוֹנוֹ, בָּעֶרֶב יָלִין בֶּכִי וְלַבֹּקֶר רִנָּה:
וַאֲנִי אָמַרְתִּי בְשַׁלְוִי, בַּל־אֶמּוֹט לְעוֹלָם:
יהוה, בִּרְצוֹנְךָ הֶעֱמַדְתָּה לְהַרְרִי עֹז, הִסְתַּרְתָּ פָנֶיךָ הָיִיתִי נִבְהָל:
אֵלֶיךָ יהוה אֶקְרָא, וְאֶל־אֲדֹנָי אֶתְחַנָּן:
מַה־בֶּצַע בְּדָמִי, בְּרִדְתִּי אֶל שָׁחַת, הֲיוֹדְךָ עָפָר, הֲיַגִּיד אֲמִתֶּךָ:
שְׁמַע־יהוה וְחָנֵּנִי, יהוה הֱיֵה־עֹזֵר לִי:
◂ הָפַכְתָּ מִסְפְּדִי לְמָחוֹל לִי, פִּתַּחְתָּ שַׂקִּי, וַתְּאַזְּרֵנִי שִׂמְחָה:
לְמַעַן יְזַמֶּרְךָ כָבוֹד וְלֹא יִדֹּם, יהוה אֱלֹהַי, לְעוֹלָם אוֹדֶךָּ:

SHAḤARIT FOR TISHA B'AV

MOURNER'S KADDISH

The following prayer, said by mourners, requires the presence of a minyan.
A transliteration can be found on page 792.

Mourner: יִתְגַּדֵּל Magnified and sanctified
may His great name be,
in the world He created by His will.
May He establish His kingdom
in your lifetime and in your days,
and in the lifetime of all the house of Israel,
swiftly and soon –
and say: Amen.

All: May His great name be blessed for ever and all time.

Mourner: Blessed and praised, glorified and exalted,
raised and honored, uplifted and lauded
be the name of the Holy One,
blessed be He,
beyond any blessing,
song, praise and consolation
uttered in the world –
and say: Amen.

May there be great peace from heaven,
and life for us and all Israel –
and say: Amen.

Bow, take three steps back, as if taking leave of the Divine Presence,
then bow, first left, then right, then center, while saying:

May He who makes peace in His high places,
make peace for us and all Israel –
and say: Amen.

קדיש יתום

The following prayer, said by mourners, requires the presence of a מנין.
A transliteration can be found on page 792.

אבל: יִתְגַּדַּל וְיִתְקַדַּשׁ שְׁמֵהּ רַבָּא (קהל: אָמֵן)
בְּעָלְמָא דִּי בְרָא כִרְעוּתֵהּ, וְיַמְלִיךְ מַלְכוּתֵהּ
בְּחַיֵּיכוֹן וּבְיוֹמֵיכוֹן וּבְחַיֵּי דְכָל בֵּית יִשְׂרָאֵל
בַּעֲגָלָא וּבִזְמַן קָרִיב
וְאִמְרוּ אָמֵן. (קהל: אָמֵן)

קהל ואבל: יְהֵא שְׁמֵהּ רַבָּא מְבָרַךְ לְעָלַם וּלְעָלְמֵי עָלְמַיָּא.

אבל: יִתְבָּרַךְ וְיִשְׁתַּבַּח וְיִתְפָּאַר
וְיִתְרוֹמַם וְיִתְנַשֵּׂא וְיִתְהַדָּר וְיִתְעַלֶּה וְיִתְהַלָּל
שְׁמֵהּ דְּקֻדְשָׁא בְּרִיךְ הוּא (קהל: בְּרִיךְ הוּא)
לְעֵלָּא מִן כָּל בִּרְכָתָא וְשִׁירָתָא, תֻּשְׁבְּחָתָא וְנֶחֱמָתָא
דַּאֲמִירָן בְּעָלְמָא
וְאִמְרוּ אָמֵן. (קהל: אָמֵן)

יְהֵא שְׁלָמָא רַבָּא מִן שְׁמַיָּא
וְחַיִּים, עָלֵינוּ וְעַל כָּל יִשְׂרָאֵל
וְאִמְרוּ אָמֵן. (קהל: אָמֵן)

Bow, take three steps back, as if taking leave of the Divine Presence,
then bow, first left, then right, then center, while saying:

עֹשֶׂה שָׁלוֹם בִּמְרוֹמָיו
הוּא יַעֲשֶׂה שָׁלוֹם עָלֵינוּ וְעַל כָּל יִשְׂרָאֵל
וְאִמְרוּ אָמֵן. (קהל: אָמֵן)

PESUKEI DEZIMRA

The introductory blessing to the Pesukei DeZimra (Verses of Praise) is said standing. From the beginning of this prayer to the end of the Amida, conversation is forbidden.

Some say:

I hereby prepare my mouth to thank, praise and laud my Creator, for the sake of the unification of the Holy One, blessed be He, and His Divine Presence, through that which is hidden and concealed, in the name of all Israel.

BLESSED IS HE WHO SPOKE

and the world came into being, blessed is He.
> Blessed is He who creates the universe.
> Blessed is He who speaks and acts.
> Blessed is He who decrees and fulfills.
> Blessed is He who shows compassion to the earth.
> Blessed is He who shows compassion to all creatures.
> Blessed is He who gives a good reward
> > to those who fear Him.
>
> Blessed is He who lives for ever
> > and exists to eternity.
>
> Blessed is He who redeems and saves.
> Blessed is His name.

Blessed are You, Lord our God,
King of the Universe,
God, compassionate Father,
extolled by the mouth of His people,
praised and glorified
by the tongue of His devoted ones
and those who serve Him.
With the songs of Your servant David
we will praise You,
O Lord our God.

פסוקי דזמרה

The introductory blessing to the פסוקי דזמרה is said standing.
From the beginning of this prayer to the end of the עמידה, conversation is forbidden.

Some say:

הֲרֵינִי מְזַמֵּן אֶת פִּי לְהוֹדוֹת וּלְהַלֵּל וּלְשַׁבֵּחַ אֶת בּוֹרְאִי, לְשֵׁם יִחוּד קֻדְשָׁא בְּרִיךְ הוּא וּשְׁכִינְתֵּהּ עַל יְדֵי הַהוּא טָמִיר וְנֶעְלָם בְּשֵׁם כָּל יִשְׂרָאֵל.

בָּרוּךְ
שֶׁאָמַר

וְהָיָה הָעוֹלָם, בָּרוּךְ הוּא.
בָּרוּךְ עוֹשֶׂה בְרֵאשִׁית
בָּרוּךְ אוֹמֵר וְעוֹשֶׂה
בָּרוּךְ גּוֹזֵר וּמְקַיֵּם
בָּרוּךְ מְרַחֵם עַל הָאָרֶץ
בָּרוּךְ מְרַחֵם עַל הַבְּרִיּוֹת
בָּרוּךְ מְשַׁלֵּם שָׂכָר טוֹב לִירֵאָיו
בָּרוּךְ חַי לָעַד וְקַיָּם לָנֶצַח
בָּרוּךְ פּוֹדֶה וּמַצִּיל
בָּרוּךְ שְׁמוֹ
בָּרוּךְ אַתָּה יהוה אֱלֹהֵינוּ מֶלֶךְ הָעוֹלָם
הָאֵל הָאָב הָרַחֲמָן הַמְהֻלָּל בְּפִי עַמּוֹ
מְשֻׁבָּח וּמְפֹאָר בִּלְשׁוֹן חֲסִידָיו וַעֲבָדָיו
וּבְשִׁירֵי דָוִד עַבְדֶּךָ
נְהַלֶּלְךָ יהוה אֱלֹהֵינוּ.

With praises and psalms
we will magnify and praise You, glorify You,
Speak Your name and proclaim Your kingship,
our King, our God, ▸ the only One, Giver of life to the worlds,
the King whose great name is praised
and glorified to all eternity.
Blessed are You, LORD, the King extolled with songs of praise.

הוֹדוּ Thank the LORD, call on His name, make His acts known among the peoples. Sing to Him, make music to Him, tell of all His wonders. Glory in His holy name; let the hearts of those who seek the LORD rejoice. Search out the LORD and His strength; seek His presence at all times. Remember the wonders He has done, His miracles, and the judgments He pronounced. Descendants of Yisrael His servant, sons of Jacob His chosen ones: He is the LORD our God. His judgments are throughout the earth. Remember His covenant for ever, the word He commanded for a thousand generations. He made it with Abraham, vowed it to Isaac, and confirmed it to Jacob as a statute and to Israel as an everlasting covenant, saying, "To you I will give the land of Canaan as your allotted heritage." You were then small in number, few, strangers there, wandering from nation to nation, from one kingdom to another, but He let no man oppress them, and for their sake He rebuked kings: "Do not touch My anointed ones, and do My prophets no harm." Sing to the LORD, all the earth; proclaim His salvation daily. Declare His glory among the nations, His marvels among all the peoples. For great is the LORD and greatly to be praised; He is awesome beyond all heavenly powers. ▸ For all the gods of the peoples are mere idols; it was the LORD who made the heavens. *1 Chr. 16*

Before Him are majesty and splendor; there is strength and beauty in His holy place. Render to the LORD, families of the peoples, render to the LORD honor and might. Render to the LORD the glory due to His name; bring an offering and come before Him; bow down to the LORD in the splendor of holiness. Tremble before Him, all the

בִּשְׁבָחוֹת וּבִזְמִירוֹת
נְגַדֶּלְךָ וּנְשַׁבֵּחֲךָ וּנְפָאֶרְךָ
וְנַזְכִּיר שִׁמְךָ וְנַמְלִיכְךָ
מַלְכֵּנוּ אֱלֹהֵינוּ, ּ יָחִיד חֵי הָעוֹלָמִים
מֶלֶךְ, מְשֻׁבָּח וּמְפֹאָר עֲדֵי עַד שְׁמוֹ הַגָּדוֹל
בָּרוּךְ אַתָּה יהוה, מֶלֶךְ מְהֻלָּל בַּתִּשְׁבָּחוֹת.

הוֹדוּ לַיהוה קִרְאוּ בִשְׁמוֹ, הוֹדִיעוּ בָעַמִּים עֲלִילֹתָיו: שִׁירוּ לוֹ, זַמְּרוּ־לוֹ, שִׂיחוּ בְּכָל־נִפְלְאֹתָיו: הִתְהַלְלוּ בְּשֵׁם קָדְשׁוֹ, יִשְׂמַח לֵב מְבַקְשֵׁי יהוה: דִּרְשׁוּ יהוה וְעֻזּוֹ, בַּקְּשׁוּ פָנָיו תָּמִיד: זִכְרוּ נִפְלְאֹתָיו אֲשֶׁר עָשָׂה, מֹפְתָיו וּמִשְׁפְּטֵי־פִיהוּ: זֶרַע יִשְׂרָאֵל עַבְדּוֹ, בְּנֵי יַעֲקֹב בְּחִירָיו: הוּא יהוה אֱלֹהֵינוּ בְּכָל־הָאָרֶץ מִשְׁפָּטָיו: זִכְרוּ לְעוֹלָם בְּרִיתוֹ, דָּבָר צִוָּה לְאֶלֶף דּוֹר: אֲשֶׁר כָּרַת אֶת־אַבְרָהָם, וּשְׁבוּעָתוֹ לְיִצְחָק: וַיַּעֲמִידֶהָ לְיַעֲקֹב לְחֹק, לְיִשְׂרָאֵל בְּרִית עוֹלָם: לֵאמֹר, לְךָ אֶתֵּן אֶרֶץ־כְּנָעַן, חֶבֶל נַחֲלַתְכֶם: בִּהְיוֹתְכֶם מְתֵי מִסְפָּר, כִּמְעַט וְגָרִים בָּהּ: וַיִּתְהַלְּכוּ מִגּוֹי אֶל־גּוֹי, וּמִמַּמְלָכָה אֶל־עַם אַחֵר: לֹא־הִנִּיחַ לְאִישׁ לְעָשְׁקָם, וַיּוֹכַח עֲלֵיהֶם מְלָכִים: אַל־תִּגְּעוּ בִמְשִׁיחָי, וּבִנְבִיאַי אַל־תָּרֵעוּ: שִׁירוּ לַיהוה כָּל־הָאָרֶץ, בַּשְּׂרוּ מִיּוֹם־אֶל־יוֹם יְשׁוּעָתוֹ: סַפְּרוּ בַגּוֹיִם אֶת־כְּבוֹדוֹ, בְּכָל־הָעַמִּים נִפְלְאֹתָיו: כִּי גָדוֹל יהוה וּמְהֻלָּל מְאֹד, וְנוֹרָא הוּא עַל־כָּל־אֱלֹהִים: ּ כִּי כָּל־אֱלֹהֵי הָעַמִּים אֱלִילִים, וַיהוה שָׁמַיִם עָשָׂה:

הוֹד וְהָדָר לְפָנָיו, עֹז וְחֶדְוָה בִּמְקֹמוֹ: הָבוּ לַיהוה מִשְׁפְּחוֹת עַמִּים, הָבוּ לַיהוה כָּבוֹד וָעֹז: הָבוּ לַיהוה כְּבוֹד שְׁמוֹ, שְׂאוּ מִנְחָה וּבֹאוּ לְפָנָיו, הִשְׁתַּחֲווּ לַיהוה בְּהַדְרַת־קֹדֶשׁ: חִילוּ מִלְּפָנָיו כָּל־

דברי הימים א, טז

earth; the world stands firm, it will not be shaken. Let the heavens rejoice and the earth be glad; let them declare among the nations, "The LORD is King." Let the sea roar, and all that is in it; let the fields be jubilant, and all they contain. Then the trees of the forest will sing for joy before the LORD, for He is coming to judge the earth. Give thanks to the LORD, for He is good; His loving-kindness endures forever. Say: "Save us, God of our salvation; gather us and rescue us from the nations, to acknowledge Your holy name and glory in Your praise. Blessed is the LORD, God of Israel, from this world to eternity." And let all the people say "Amen" and "Praise the LORD."

▸ Exalt the LORD our God and bow before His footstool: He is holy. Exalt the LORD our God and bow at His holy mountain; for holy is the LORD our God. *Ps. 99*

He is compassionate. He forgives iniquity and does not destroy. *Ps. 78* Repeatedly He suppresses His anger, not rousing His full wrath. You, LORD: do not withhold Your compassion from me. May Your *Ps. 40* loving-kindness and truth always guard me. Remember, LORD, Your *Ps. 25* acts of compassion and love, for they have existed for ever. Ascribe *Ps. 68* power to God, whose majesty is over Israel and whose might is in the skies. You are awesome, God, in Your holy places. It is the God of Israel who gives might and strength to the people, may God be blessed. God of retribution, LORD, God of retribution, appear. *Ps. 94* Arise, Judge of the earth, to repay the arrogant their just deserts. Salvation belongs to the LORD; may Your blessing rest upon Your *Ps. 3* people, Selah! ▸ The LORD of hosts is with us, the God of Jacob is *Ps. 46* our stronghold, Selah! LORD of hosts, happy is the one who trusts *Ps. 84* in You. LORD, save! May the King answer us on the day we call. *Ps. 20*

Save Your people and bless Your heritage; tend them and carry *Ps. 28* them for ever. Our soul longs for the LORD; He is our Help and *Ps. 33* Shield. For in Him our hearts rejoice, for in His holy name we have trusted. May Your loving-kindness, LORD, be upon us, as we have put our hope in You. Show us, LORD, Your loving-kindness and *Ps. 85* grant us Your salvation. Arise, help us and redeem us for the sake of *Ps. 44*

הָאָרֶץ, אַף־תִּכּוֹן תֵּבֵל בַּל־תִּמּוֹט: יִשְׂמְחוּ הַשָּׁמַיִם וְתָגֵל הָאָרֶץ, וְיֹאמְרוּ בַגּוֹיִם יְהֹוָה מָלָךְ: יִרְעַם הַיָּם וּמְלֹאוֹ, יַעֲלֹץ הַשָּׂדֶה וְכָל־אֲשֶׁר־בּוֹ: אָז יְרַנְּנוּ עֲצֵי הַיָּעַר, מִלִּפְנֵי יְהֹוָה, כִּי־בָא לִשְׁפּוֹט אֶת־הָאָרֶץ: הוֹדוּ לַיהֹוָה כִּי טוֹב, כִּי לְעוֹלָם חַסְדּוֹ: וְאִמְרוּ, הוֹשִׁיעֵנוּ אֱלֹהֵי יִשְׁעֵנוּ, וְקַבְּצֵנוּ וְהַצִּילֵנוּ מִן־הַגּוֹיִם, לְהֹדוֹת לְשֵׁם קָדְשֶׁךָ, לְהִשְׁתַּבֵּחַ בִּתְהִלָּתֶךָ: בָּרוּךְ יְהֹוָה אֱלֹהֵי יִשְׂרָאֵל מִן־הָעוֹלָם וְעַד־הָעֹלָם, וַיֹּאמְרוּ כָל־הָעָם אָמֵן, וְהַלֵּל לַיהֹוָה:

תהלים צט ‹ רוֹמְמוּ יְהֹוָה אֱלֹהֵינוּ וְהִשְׁתַּחֲווּ לַהֲדֹם רַגְלָיו, קָדוֹשׁ הוּא: רוֹמְמוּ יְהֹוָה אֱלֹהֵינוּ וְהִשְׁתַּחֲווּ לְהַר קָדְשׁוֹ, כִּי־קָדוֹשׁ יְהֹוָה אֱלֹהֵינוּ:

תהלים עח וְהוּא רַחוּם, יְכַפֵּר עָוֹן וְלֹא־יַשְׁחִית, וְהִרְבָּה לְהָשִׁיב אַפּוֹ, וְלֹא־יָעִיר כָּל־חֲמָתוֹ: אַתָּה יְהֹוָה לֹא־תִכְלָא רַחֲמֶיךָ מִמֶּנִּי, חַסְדְּךָ תהלים מ
וַאֲמִתְּךָ תָּמִיד יִצְּרוּנִי: זְכֹר־רַחֲמֶיךָ יְהֹוָה וַחֲסָדֶיךָ, כִּי מֵעוֹלָם תהלים כה
הֵמָּה: תְּנוּ עֹז לֵאלֹהִים, עַל־יִשְׂרָאֵל גַּאֲוָתוֹ, וְעֻזּוֹ בַּשְּׁחָקִים: תהלים סח
נוֹרָא אֱלֹהִים מִמִּקְדָּשֶׁיךָ, אֵל יִשְׂרָאֵל הוּא נֹתֵן עֹז וְתַעֲצֻמוֹת לָעָם, בָּרוּךְ אֱלֹהִים: אֵל־נְקָמוֹת יְהֹוָה, אֵל נְקָמוֹת הוֹפִיעַ: הִנָּשֵׂא תהלים צד
שֹׁפֵט הָאָרֶץ, הָשֵׁב גְּמוּל עַל־גֵּאִים: לַיהֹוָה הַיְשׁוּעָה, עַל־עַמְּךָ תהלים ג
בִרְכָתֶךָ סֶּלָה: › יְהֹוָה צְבָאוֹת עִמָּנוּ, מִשְׂגָּב לָנוּ אֱלֹהֵי יַעֲקֹב תהלים מו
סֶלָה: יְהֹוָה צְבָאוֹת, אַשְׁרֵי אָדָם בֹּטֵחַ בָּךְ: יְהֹוָה הוֹשִׁיעָה, הַמֶּלֶךְ תהלים פד
תהלים כ
יַעֲנֵנוּ בְיוֹם־קָרְאֵנוּ:

הוֹשִׁיעָה אֶת־עַמֶּךָ, וּבָרֵךְ אֶת־נַחֲלָתֶךָ, וּרְעֵם וְנַשְּׂאֵם עַד־ תהלים כח
הָעוֹלָם: נַפְשֵׁנוּ חִכְּתָה לַיהֹוָה, עֶזְרֵנוּ וּמָגִנֵּנוּ הוּא: כִּי־בוֹ יִשְׂמַח תהלים לג
לִבֵּנוּ, כִּי בְשֵׁם קָדְשׁוֹ בָטָחְנוּ: יְהִי־חַסְדְּךָ יְהֹוָה עָלֵינוּ, כַּאֲשֶׁר
יִחַלְנוּ לָךְ: הַרְאֵנוּ יְהֹוָה חַסְדֶּךָ, וְיֶשְׁעֲךָ תִּתֶּן־לָנוּ: קוּמָה עֶזְרָתָה תהלים פה
תהלים מד

Your love. I am the Lord your God who brought you up from the land of Egypt: open your mouth wide and I will fill it. Happy is the people for whom this is so; happy is the people whose God is the Lord. ‣ As for me, I trust in Your loving-kindness; my heart rejoices in Your salvation. I will sing to the Lord for He has been good to me. *Ps. 81 / Ps. 144 / Ps. 13*

> *The following psalm recalls the thanksgiving-offering in Temple times.*
> *To emphasize its sacrificial nature, the custom is to say it standing.*

מִזְמוֹר A psalm of thanksgiving. Shout joyously to the Lord, all the earth. Serve the Lord with joy. Come before Him with jubilation. Know that the Lord is God. He made us and we are His. We are His people and the flock He tends. Enter His gates with thanksgiving, His courts with praise. Thank Him and bless His name. ‣ For the Lord is good, His loving-kindness is everlasting, and His faithfulness is for every generation. *Ps. 100*

יְהִי כְבוֹד May the Lord's glory be for ever; may the Lord rejoice in His works. May the Lord's name be blessed, now and for ever. From the rising of the sun to its setting, may the Lord's name be praised. The Lord is high above all nations; His glory is above the heavens. Lord, Your name is for ever. Your renown, Lord, is for all generations. The Lord has established His throne in heaven; His kingdom rules all. Let the heavens rejoice and the earth be glad. Let them say among the nations, "The Lord is King." The Lord is King, the Lord was King, the Lord will be King for ever and all time. The Lord is King for ever and all time; nations will perish from His land. The Lord foils the plans of nations; He frustrates the intentions of peoples. Many are the intentions in a person's mind, but the Lord's plan prevails. The Lord's plan shall stand for ever, His mind's intent for all generations. For He spoke and it was; He commanded and it stood firm. For the Lord has chosen Zion; He desired it for His dwelling. For the Lord has chosen Jacob as His own, Israel as His special treasure. For the Lord will not abandon His people; nor will He forsake His heritage. ‣ He is compassionate. He forgives iniquity and does not destroy. Repeatedly He suppresses His anger, not rousing His full wrath. Lord, save! May the King answer us on the day we call. *Ps. 104 / Ps. 113 / Ps. 135 / Ps. 103 / 1 Chr. 16 / Ps. 10 / Ps. 33 / Prov. 19 / Ps. 33 / Ps. 132 / Ps. 135 / Ps. 94 / Ps. 78 / Ps. 20*

תהלים פא	לָנוּ, וּפְדֵנוּ לְמַעַן חַסְדֶּךָ: אָנֹכִי יהוה אֱלֹהֶיךָ הַמַּעַלְךָ מֵאֶרֶץ
תהלים קמד	מִצְרָיִם, הַרְחֶב־פִּיךָ וַאֲמַלְאֵהוּ: אַשְׁרֵי הָעָם שֶׁכָּכָה לּוֹ, אַשְׁרֵי
תהלים יג	הָעָם שֶׁיהוה אֱלֹהָיו: ◂ וַאֲנִי בְּחַסְדְּךָ בָטַחְתִּי, יָגֵל לִבִּי בִּישׁוּעָתֶךָ, אָשִׁירָה לַיהוה, כִּי גָמַל עָלָי:

The following psalm recalls the קרבן תודה *in Temple times.*
To emphasize its sacrificial nature, the custom is to say it standing.

תהלים ק	מִזְמוֹר לְתוֹדָה, הָרִיעוּ לַיהוה כָּל־הָאָרֶץ: עִבְדוּ אֶת־יהוה בְּשִׂמְחָה, בֹּאוּ לְפָנָיו בִּרְנָנָה: דְּעוּ כִּי־יהוה הוּא אֱלֹהִים, הוּא עָשָׂנוּ וְלוֹ אֲנַחְנוּ, עַמּוֹ וְצֹאן מַרְעִיתוֹ: בֹּאוּ שְׁעָרָיו בְּתוֹדָה, חֲצֵרֹתָיו בִּתְהִלָּה, הוֹדוּ לוֹ, בָּרְכוּ שְׁמוֹ: ◂ כִּי־טוֹב יהוה, לְעוֹלָם חַסְדּוֹ, וְעַד־דֹּר וָדֹר אֱמוּנָתוֹ:
תהלים קד תהלים קיג	יְהִי כְבוֹד יהוה לְעוֹלָם, יִשְׂמַח יהוה בְּמַעֲשָׂיו: יְהִי שֵׁם יהוה מְבֹרָךְ, מֵעַתָּה וְעַד־עוֹלָם: מִמִּזְרַח־שֶׁמֶשׁ עַד־מְבוֹאוֹ, מְהֻלָּל
תהלים קלה	שֵׁם יהוה: רָם עַל־כָּל־גּוֹיִם יהוה, עַל הַשָּׁמַיִם כְּבוֹדוֹ: יהוה
תהלים קג	שִׁמְךָ לְעוֹלָם, יהוה זִכְרְךָ לְדֹר־וָדֹר: יהוה בַּשָּׁמַיִם הֵכִין כִּסְאוֹ,
דברי הימים א׳ טז	וּמַלְכוּתוֹ בַּכֹּל מָשָׁלָה: יִשְׂמְחוּ הַשָּׁמַיִם וְתָגֵל הָאָרֶץ, וְיֹאמְרוּ בַגּוֹיִם יהוה מָלָךְ: יהוה מֶלֶךְ, יהוה מָלָךְ, יהוה יִמְלֹךְ לְעוֹלָם
תהלים י תהלים לג	וָעֶד. יהוה מֶלֶךְ עוֹלָם וָעֶד, אָבְדוּ גוֹיִם מֵאַרְצוֹ: יהוה הֵפִיר
משלי יט	עֲצַת־גּוֹיִם, הֵנִיא מַחְשְׁבוֹת עַמִּים: רַבּוֹת מַחֲשָׁבוֹת בְּלֶב־אִישׁ,
תהלים לג	וַעֲצַת יהוה הִיא תָקוּם: עֲצַת יהוה לְעוֹלָם תַּעֲמֹד, מַחְשְׁבוֹת לִבּוֹ
תהלים קלב	לְדֹר וָדֹר: כִּי הוּא אָמַר וַיֶּהִי, הוּא־צִוָּה וַיַּעֲמֹד: כִּי־בָחַר יהוה
תהלים קלה	בְּצִיּוֹן, אִוָּהּ לְמוֹשָׁב לוֹ: כִּי־יַעֲקֹב בָּחַר לוֹ יָהּ, יִשְׂרָאֵל לִסְגֻלָּתוֹ:
תהלים צד תהלים עח	כִּי לֹא־יִטֹּשׁ יהוה עַמּוֹ, וְנַחֲלָתוֹ לֹא יַעֲזֹב: ◂ וְהוּא רַחוּם, יְכַפֵּר עָוֹן וְלֹא־יַשְׁחִית, וְהִרְבָּה לְהָשִׁיב אַפּוֹ, וְלֹא־יָעִיר כָּל־חֲמָתוֹ:
תהלים כ	יהוה הוֹשִׁיעָה, הַמֶּלֶךְ יַעֲנֵנוּ בְיוֹם־קָרְאֵנוּ:

> *The line beginning with "You open Your hand" should be said with special concentration, representing as it does the key idea of this psalm, and of Pesukei DeZimra as a whole, that God is the creator and sustainer of all.*

אַשְׁרֵי Happy are those who dwell in Your House; *Ps. 84*
they shall continue to praise You, Selah!
Happy are the people for whom this is so; *Ps. 144*
happy are the people whose God is the LORD.
A song of praise by David. *Ps. 145*
 I will exalt You, my God, the King, and bless Your name for ever and all time. Every day I will bless You, and praise Your name for ever and all time. God is great and greatly to be praised; His greatness is unfathomable. One generation will praise Your works to the next, and tell of Your mighty deeds. On the glorious splendor of Your majesty I will meditate, and on the acts of Your wonders. They shall talk of the power of Your awesome deeds, and I will tell of Your greatness. They shall recite the record of Your great goodness, and sing with joy of Your righteousness. The LORD is gracious and compassionate, slow to anger and great in loving-kindness. The LORD is good to all, and His compassion extends to all His works. All Your works shall thank You, LORD, and Your devoted ones shall bless You. They shall talk of the glory of Your kingship, and speak of Your might. To make known to mankind His mighty deeds and the glorious majesty of His kingship. Your kingdom is an everlasting kingdom, and Your reign is for all generations. The LORD supports all who fall, and raises all who are bowed down. All raise their eyes to You in hope, and You give them their food in due season. You open Your hand, and satisfy every living thing with Your favor. The LORD is righteous in all His ways, and kind in all He does. The LORD is close to all who call on Him, to all who call on Him in truth. He fulfills the will of those who revere Him; He hears their cry and saves them. The LORD guards all who love Him, but all the wicked He will destroy. ‣ My mouth shall speak the praise of the LORD, and all creatures shall bless His holy name for ever and all time.
We will bless the LORD now and for ever. Halleluya! *Ps. 115*

The line beginning with פּוֹתֵחַ אֶת יָדֶךָ *should be said with special concentration, representing as it does the key idea of this psalm, and of* פסוקי דזמרה *as a whole, that God is the creator and sustainer of all.*

תהלים פד
אַשְׁרֵי יוֹשְׁבֵי בֵיתֶךָ, עוֹד יְהַלְלוּךָ סֶּלָה:

תהלים קמד
אַשְׁרֵי הָעָם שֶׁכָּכָה לּוֹ, אַשְׁרֵי הָעָם שֶׁיהוה אֱלֹהָיו:

תהלים קמה
תְּהִלָּה לְדָוִד
אֲרוֹמִמְךָ אֱלוֹהַי הַמֶּלֶךְ, וַאֲבָרְכָה שִׁמְךָ לְעוֹלָם וָעֶד:
בְּכָל־יוֹם אֲבָרְכֶךָּ, וַאֲהַלְלָה שִׁמְךָ לְעוֹלָם וָעֶד:
גָּדוֹל יהוה וּמְהֻלָּל מְאֹד, וְלִגְדֻלָּתוֹ אֵין חֵקֶר:
דּוֹר לְדוֹר יְשַׁבַּח מַעֲשֶׂיךָ, וּגְבוּרֹתֶיךָ יַגִּידוּ:
הֲדַר כְּבוֹד הוֹדֶךָ, וְדִבְרֵי נִפְלְאֹתֶיךָ אָשִׂיחָה:
וֶעֱזוּז נוֹרְאֹתֶיךָ יֹאמֵרוּ, וּגְדוּלָּתְךָ אֲסַפְּרֶנָּה:
זֵכֶר רַב־טוּבְךָ יַבִּיעוּ, וְצִדְקָתְךָ יְרַנֵּנוּ:
חַנּוּן וְרַחוּם יהוה, אֶרֶךְ אַפַּיִם וּגְדָל־חָסֶד:
טוֹב־יהוה לַכֹּל, וְרַחֲמָיו עַל־כָּל־מַעֲשָׂיו:
יוֹדוּךָ יהוה כָּל־מַעֲשֶׂיךָ, וַחֲסִידֶיךָ יְבָרְכוּכָה:
כְּבוֹד מַלְכוּתְךָ יֹאמֵרוּ, וּגְבוּרָתְךָ יְדַבֵּרוּ:
לְהוֹדִיעַ לִבְנֵי הָאָדָם גְּבוּרֹתָיו, וּכְבוֹד הֲדַר מַלְכוּתוֹ:
מַלְכוּתְךָ מַלְכוּת כָּל־עֹלָמִים, וּמֶמְשַׁלְתְּךָ בְּכָל־דּוֹר וָדֹר:
סוֹמֵךְ יהוה לְכָל־הַנֹּפְלִים, וְזוֹקֵף לְכָל־הַכְּפוּפִים:
עֵינֵי־כֹל אֵלֶיךָ יְשַׂבֵּרוּ, וְאַתָּה נוֹתֵן־לָהֶם אֶת־אָכְלָם בְּעִתּוֹ:
פּוֹתֵחַ אֶת־יָדֶךָ, וּמַשְׂבִּיעַ לְכָל־חַי רָצוֹן:
צַדִּיק יהוה בְּכָל־דְּרָכָיו, וְחָסִיד בְּכָל־מַעֲשָׂיו:
קָרוֹב יהוה לְכָל־קֹרְאָיו, לְכֹל אֲשֶׁר יִקְרָאֻהוּ בֶאֱמֶת:
רְצוֹן־יְרֵאָיו יַעֲשֶׂה, וְאֶת־שַׁוְעָתָם יִשְׁמַע, וְיוֹשִׁיעֵם:
שׁוֹמֵר יהוה אֶת־כָּל־אֹהֲבָיו, וְאֵת כָּל־הָרְשָׁעִים יַשְׁמִיד:
‣ תְּהִלַּת יהוה יְדַבֶּר פִּי, וִיבָרֵךְ כָּל־בָּשָׂר שֵׁם קָדְשׁוֹ לְעוֹלָם וָעֶד:
וַאֲנַחְנוּ נְבָרֵךְ יָהּ מֵעַתָּה וְעַד־עוֹלָם, הַלְלוּיָהּ:

תהלים קטו

הַלְלוּיָהּ Halleluya! Praise the Lord, my soul. I will praise the Lord *Ps. 146* all my life; I will sing to my God as long as I live. Put not your trust in princes, or in mortal man who cannot save. His breath expires, he returns to the earth; on that day his plans come to an end. Happy is he whose help is the God of Jacob, whose hope is in the Lord his God who made heaven and earth, the sea and all they contain; He who keeps faith for ever. He secures justice for the oppressed. He gives food to the hungry. The Lord sets captives free. The Lord gives sight to the blind. The Lord raises those bowed down. The Lord loves the righteous. The Lord protects the stranger. He gives courage to the orphan and widow. He thwarts the way of the wicked. ‣ The Lord shall reign for ever. He is your God, Zion, for all generations. Halleluya!

הַלְלוּיָהּ Halleluya! How good it is to sing songs to our God; how *Ps. 147* pleasant and fitting to praise Him. The Lord rebuilds Jerusalem. He gathers the scattered exiles of Israel. He heals the brokenhearted and binds up their wounds. He counts the number of the stars, calling each by name. Great is our Lord and mighty in power; His understanding has no limit. The Lord gives courage to the humble, but casts the wicked to the ground. Sing to the Lord in thanks; make music to our God on the harp. He covers the sky with clouds. He provides the earth with rain and makes grass grow on the hills. He gives food to the cattle and to the ravens when they cry. He does not take delight in the strength of horses nor pleasure in the fleetness of man. The Lord takes pleasure in those who fear Him, who put their hope in His loving care. Praise the Lord, Jerusalem; sing to your God, Zion, for He has strengthened the bars of your gates and blessed your children in your midst. He has brought peace to your borders, and satisfied you with the finest wheat. He sends His commandment to earth; swiftly runs His word. He spreads snow like fleece, sprinkles frost like ashes, scatters hail like crumbs. Who can stand His cold? He sends His word and melts them; He makes the wind blow and the waters flow. ‣ He has declared His words to Jacob, His statutes and laws to Israel. He has done this for no other nation; such laws they do not know. Halleluya!

תהלים קמו

הַלְלוּיָהּ, הַלְלִי נַפְשִׁי אֶת־יהוה: אֲהַלְלָה יהוה בְּחַיָּי, אֲזַמְּרָה לֵאלֹהַי בְּעוֹדִי: אַל־תִּבְטְחוּ בִנְדִיבִים, בְּבֶן־אָדָם שֶׁאֵין לוֹ תְשׁוּעָה: תֵּצֵא רוּחוֹ, יָשֻׁב לְאַדְמָתוֹ, בַּיּוֹם הַהוּא אָבְדוּ עֶשְׁתֹּנוֹתָיו: אַשְׁרֵי שֶׁאֵל יַעֲקֹב בְּעֶזְרוֹ, שִׂבְרוֹ עַל־יהוה אֱלֹהָיו: עֹשֶׂה שָׁמַיִם וָאָרֶץ, אֶת־הַיָּם וְאֶת־כָּל־אֲשֶׁר־בָּם, הַשֹּׁמֵר אֱמֶת לְעוֹלָם: עֹשֶׂה מִשְׁפָּט לַעֲשׁוּקִים, נֹתֵן לֶחֶם לָרְעֵבִים, יהוה מַתִּיר אֲסוּרִים: יהוה פֹּקֵחַ עִוְרִים, יהוה זֹקֵף כְּפוּפִים, יהוה אֹהֵב צַדִּיקִים: יהוה שֹׁמֵר אֶת־גֵּרִים, יָתוֹם וְאַלְמָנָה יְעוֹדֵד, וְדֶרֶךְ רְשָׁעִים יְעַוֵּת: ›יִמְלֹךְ יהוה לְעוֹלָם, אֱלֹהַיִךְ צִיּוֹן לְדֹר וָדֹר, הַלְלוּיָהּ:

תהלים קמז

הַלְלוּיָהּ, כִּי־טוֹב זַמְּרָה אֱלֹהֵינוּ, כִּי־נָעִים נָאוָה תְהִלָּה: בּוֹנֵה יְרוּשָׁלַֽםִ יהוה, נִדְחֵי יִשְׂרָאֵל יְכַנֵּס: הָרֹפֵא לִשְׁבוּרֵי לֵב, וּמְחַבֵּשׁ לְעַצְּבוֹתָם: מוֹנֶה מִסְפָּר לַכּוֹכָבִים, לְכֻלָּם שֵׁמוֹת יִקְרָא: גָּדוֹל אֲדוֹנֵינוּ וְרַב־כֹּחַ, לִתְבוּנָתוֹ אֵין מִסְפָּר: מְעוֹדֵד עֲנָוִים יהוה, מַשְׁפִּיל רְשָׁעִים עֲדֵי־אָרֶץ: עֱנוּ לַיהוה בְּתוֹדָה, זַמְּרוּ לֵאלֹהֵינוּ בְכִנּוֹר: הַמְכַסֶּה שָׁמַיִם בְּעָבִים, הַמֵּכִין לָאָרֶץ מָטָר, הַמַּצְמִיחַ הָרִים חָצִיר: נוֹתֵן לִבְהֵמָה לַחְמָהּ, לִבְנֵי עֹרֵב אֲשֶׁר יִקְרָאוּ: לֹא בִגְבוּרַת הַסּוּס יֶחְפָּץ, לֹא־בְשׁוֹקֵי הָאִישׁ יִרְצֶה: רוֹצֶה יהוה אֶת־יְרֵאָיו, אֶת־הַמְיַחֲלִים לְחַסְדּוֹ: שַׁבְּחִי יְרוּשָׁלַֽםִ אֶת־יהוה, הַלְלִי אֱלֹהַיִךְ צִיּוֹן: כִּי־חִזַּק בְּרִיחֵי שְׁעָרָיִךְ, בֵּרַךְ בָּנַיִךְ בְּקִרְבֵּךְ: הַשָּׂם־גְּבוּלֵךְ שָׁלוֹם, חֵלֶב חִטִּים יַשְׂבִּיעֵךְ: הַשֹּׁלֵחַ אִמְרָתוֹ אָרֶץ, עַד־מְהֵרָה יָרוּץ דְּבָרוֹ: הַנֹּתֵן שֶׁלֶג כַּצָּמֶר, כְּפוֹר כָּאֵפֶר יְפַזֵּר: מַשְׁלִיךְ קַרְחוֹ כְפִתִּים, לִפְנֵי קָרָתוֹ מִי יַעֲמֹד: יִשְׁלַח דְּבָרוֹ וְיַמְסֵם, יַשֵּׁב רוּחוֹ יִזְּלוּ־מָיִם: ›מַגִּיד דְּבָרָיו לְיַעֲקֹב, חֻקָּיו וּמִשְׁפָּטָיו לְיִשְׂרָאֵל: לֹא עָשָׂה כֵן לְכָל־גּוֹי, וּמִשְׁפָּטִים בַּל־יְדָעוּם, הַלְלוּיָהּ:

הַלְלוּיָהּ Halleluya! Praise the LORD from the heavens, praise Him in the heights. Praise Him, all His angels; praise Him, all His hosts. Praise Him, sun and moon; praise Him, all shining stars. Praise Him, highest heavens and the waters above the heavens. Let them praise the name of the LORD, for He commanded and they were created. He established them for ever and all time, issuing a decree that will never change. Praise the LORD from the earth: sea monsters and all the deep seas; fire and hail, snow and mist, storm winds that obey His word; mountains and all hills, fruit trees and all cedars; wild animals and all cattle, creeping things and winged birds; kings of the earth and all nations, princes and all judges on earth; youths and maidens, old and young. ‣ Let them praise the name of the LORD, for His name alone is sublime; His majesty is above earth and heaven. He has raised the pride of His people, for the glory of all His devoted ones, the children of Israel, the people close to Him. Halleluya! *Ps. 148*

הַלְלוּיָהּ Halleluya! Sing to the LORD a new song, His praise in the assembly of the devoted. Let Israel rejoice in its Maker; let the children of Zion exult in their King. Let them praise His name with dancing; sing praises to Him with timbrel and harp. For the LORD delights in His people; He adorns the humble with salvation. Let the devoted revel in glory; let them sing for joy on their beds. Let high praises of God be in their throats, and a two-edged sword in their hand: to impose retribution on the nations, punishment on the peoples, ‣ binding their kings with chains, their nobles with iron fetters, carrying out the judgment written against them. This is the glory of all His devoted ones. Halleluya! *Ps. 149*

הַלְלוּיָהּ Halleluya! Praise God in His holy place; praise Him in the heavens of His power. Praise Him for His mighty deeds; praise Him for His surpassing greatness. Praise Him with blasts of the shofar; praise Him with the harp and lyre. Praise Him with timbrel and dance; praise Him with strings and flute. Praise Him with clashing cymbals; praise Him with resounding cymbals. ‣ Let all that breathes praise the LORD. Halleluya! Let all that breathes praise the LORD. Halleluya! *Ps. 150*

תהלים קמח

הַלְלוּיָהּ, הַלְלוּ אֶת־יהוה מִן־הַשָּׁמַיִם, הַלְלוּהוּ בַּמְּרוֹמִים: הַלְלוּהוּ כָל־מַלְאָכָיו, הַלְלוּהוּ כָּל־צְבָאָו: הַלְלוּהוּ שֶׁמֶשׁ וְיָרֵחַ, הַלְלוּהוּ כָּל־כּוֹכְבֵי אוֹר: הַלְלוּהוּ שְׁמֵי הַשָּׁמָיִם, וְהַמַּיִם אֲשֶׁר מֵעַל הַשָּׁמָיִם: יְהַלְלוּ אֶת־שֵׁם יהוה, כִּי הוּא צִוָּה וְנִבְרָאוּ: וַיַּעֲמִידֵם לָעַד לְעוֹלָם, חָק־נָתַן וְלֹא יַעֲבוֹר: הַלְלוּ אֶת־יהוה מִן־הָאָרֶץ, תַּנִּינִים וְכָל־תְּהֹמוֹת: אֵשׁ וּבָרָד שֶׁלֶג וְקִיטוֹר, רוּחַ סְעָרָה עֹשָׂה דְבָרוֹ: הֶהָרִים וְכָל־גְּבָעוֹת, עֵץ פְּרִי וְכָל־אֲרָזִים: הַחַיָּה וְכָל־בְּהֵמָה, רֶמֶשׂ וְצִפּוֹר כָּנָף: מַלְכֵי־אֶרֶץ וְכָל־לְאֻמִּים, שָׂרִים וְכָל־שֹׁפְטֵי אָרֶץ: בַּחוּרִים וְגַם־בְּתוּלוֹת, זְקֵנִים עִם־נְעָרִים: ‹ יְהַלְלוּ אֶת־שֵׁם יהוה, כִּי־נִשְׂגָּב שְׁמוֹ לְבַדּוֹ, הוֹדוֹ עַל־אֶרֶץ וְשָׁמָיִם: וַיָּרֶם קֶרֶן לְעַמּוֹ, תְּהִלָּה לְכָל־חֲסִידָיו, לִבְנֵי יִשְׂרָאֵל עַם קְרֹבוֹ, הַלְלוּיָהּ:

תהלים קמט

הַלְלוּיָהּ, שִׁירוּ לַיהוה שִׁיר חָדָשׁ, תְּהִלָּתוֹ בִּקְהַל חֲסִידִים: יִשְׂמַח יִשְׂרָאֵל בְּעֹשָׂיו, בְּנֵי־צִיּוֹן יָגִילוּ בְמַלְכָּם: יְהַלְלוּ שְׁמוֹ בְמָחוֹל, בְּתֹף וְכִנּוֹר יְזַמְּרוּ־לוֹ: כִּי־רוֹצֶה יהוה בְּעַמּוֹ, יְפָאֵר עֲנָוִים בִּישׁוּעָה: יַעְלְזוּ חֲסִידִים בְּכָבוֹד, יְרַנְּנוּ עַל־מִשְׁכְּבוֹתָם: רוֹמְמוֹת אֵל בִּגְרוֹנָם, וְחֶרֶב פִּיפִיּוֹת בְּיָדָם: לַעֲשׂוֹת נְקָמָה בַּגּוֹיִם, תּוֹכֵחוֹת בַּלְאֻמִּים: ‹ לֶאְסֹר מַלְכֵיהֶם בְּזִקִּים, וְנִכְבְּדֵיהֶם בְּכַבְלֵי בַרְזֶל: לַעֲשׂוֹת בָּהֶם מִשְׁפָּט כָּתוּב, הָדָר הוּא לְכָל־חֲסִידָיו, הַלְלוּיָהּ:

תהלים קנ

הַלְלוּיָהּ, הַלְלוּ־אֵל בְּקָדְשׁוֹ, הַלְלוּהוּ בִּרְקִיעַ עֻזּוֹ: הַלְלוּהוּ בִגְבוּרֹתָיו, הַלְלוּהוּ כְּרֹב גֻּדְלוֹ: הַלְלוּהוּ בְּתֵקַע שׁוֹפָר, הַלְלוּהוּ בְּנֵבֶל וְכִנּוֹר: הַלְלוּהוּ בְתֹף וּמָחוֹל, הַלְלוּהוּ בְּמִנִּים וְעֻגָב: הַלְלוּהוּ בְצִלְצְלֵי־שָׁמַע, הַלְלוּהוּ בְּצִלְצְלֵי תְרוּעָה: ‹ כֹּל הַנְּשָׁמָה תְּהַלֵּל יָהּ, הַלְלוּיָהּ: כֹּל הַנְּשָׁמָה תְּהַלֵּל יָהּ, הַלְלוּיָהּ:

SHAḤARIT FOR TISHA B'AV

בָּרוּךְ Blessed be the Lord for ever. Amen and Amen. *Ps. 89*
Blessed from Zion be the Lord *Ps. 135*
who dwells in Jerusalem. Halleluya!
Blessed be the Lord, God of Israel, who alone does wonders. *Ps. 72*
▸ Blessed be His glorious name for ever,
and may all the earth be filled with His glory.
Amen and Amen.

Stand until after "Bless the Lord" on page 140.

וַיְבָרֶךְ David blessed the Lord in front of the entire assembly. David *1 Chr. 29*
said, "Blessed are You, Lord, God of our father Yisrael, for ever
and ever. Yours, Lord, are the greatness and the power, the glory,
majesty and splendor, for everything in heaven and earth is Yours.
Yours, Lord, is the kingdom; You are exalted as head over all. Both
riches and honor are in Your gift and You reign over all things. In
Your hand are strength and might. It is in Your power to make great
and give strength to all. Therefore, our God, we thank You and
praise Your glorious name."   You alone are the Lord. You *Neh. 9*
made the heavens, even the highest heavens, and all their hosts,
the earth and all that is on it, the seas and all they contain. You give
life to them all, and the hosts of heaven worship You. ▸ You are the
Lord God who chose Abram and brought him out of Ur of the
Chaldees, changing his name to Abraham. You found his heart
faithful toward You, ◂ and You made a covenant with him to give
to his descendants the land of the Canaanites, Hittites, Amorites,
Perizzites, Jebusites and Girgashites. You fulfilled Your promise
for You are righteous. You saw the suffering of our ancestors in
Egypt. You heard their cry at the Sea of Reeds. You sent signs and
wonders against Pharaoh, all his servants and all the people of
his land, because You knew how arrogantly the Egyptians treated
them. You created for Yourself renown that remains to this day.
▸ You divided the sea before them, so that they passed through the
sea on dry land, but You cast their pursuers into the depths, like a
stone into mighty waters.

תהלים פט	בָּרוּךְ יהוה לְעוֹלָם, אָמֵן וְאָמֵן:
תהלים קלה	בָּרוּךְ יהוה מִצִּיּוֹן, שֹׁכֵן יְרוּשָׁלָֽםִ, הַלְלוּיָהּ:
תהלים עב	בָּרוּךְ יהוה אֱלֹהִים אֱלֹהֵי יִשְׂרָאֵל, עֹשֵׂה נִפְלָאוֹת לְבַדּוֹ:

‹ וּבָרוּךְ שֵׁם כְּבוֹדוֹ לְעוֹלָם
וְיִמָּלֵא כְבוֹדוֹ אֶת־כָּל־הָאָֽרֶץ
אָמֵן וְאָמֵן:

Stand until after בָּרְכוּ *on page 141.*

דברי הימים א, כט	וַיְבָֽרֶךְ דָּוִיד אֶת־יהוה לְעֵינֵי כָּל־הַקָּהָל, וַיֹּֽאמֶר דָּוִיד, בָּרוּךְ אַתָּה יהוה, אֱלֹהֵי יִשְׂרָאֵל אָבִֽינוּ, מֵעוֹלָם וְעַד־עוֹלָם: לְךָ יהוה הַגְּדֻלָּה וְהַגְּבוּרָה וְהַתִּפְאֶֽרֶת וְהַנֵּֽצַח וְהַהוֹד, כִּי־כֹל בַּשָּׁמַֽיִם וּבָאָֽרֶץ, לְךָ יהוה הַמַּמְלָכָה וְהַמִּתְנַשֵּׂא לְכֹל לְרֹאשׁ: וְהָעֹֽשֶׁר וְהַכָּבוֹד מִלְּפָנֶֽיךָ, וְאַתָּה מוֹשֵׁל בַּכֹּל, וּבְיָדְךָ כֹּֽחַ וּגְבוּרָה, וּבְיָדְךָ לְגַדֵּל וּלְחַזֵּק לַכֹּל: וְעַתָּה אֱלֹהֵֽינוּ מוֹדִים אֲנַֽחְנוּ לָךְ, וּמְהַלְלִים לְשֵׁם תִּפְאַרְתֶּֽךָ:
נחמיה ט	אַתָּה־הוּא יהוה לְבַדֶּֽךָ, אַתְּ עָשִֽׂיתָ אֶת־הַשָּׁמַֽיִם, שְׁמֵי הַשָּׁמַֽיִם וְכָל־צְבָאָם, הָאָֽרֶץ וְכָל־אֲשֶׁר עָלֶֽיהָ, הַיַּמִּים וְכָל־אֲשֶׁר בָּהֶם, וְאַתָּה מְחַיֶּה אֶת־כֻּלָּם, וּצְבָא הַשָּׁמַֽיִם לְךָ מִשְׁתַּחֲוִים: ‹ אַתָּה הוּא יהוה הָאֱלֹהִים אֲשֶׁר בָּחַֽרְתָּ בְּאַבְרָם, וְהוֹצֵאתוֹ מֵאוּר כַּשְׂדִּים, וְשַֽׂמְתָּ שְּׁמוֹ אַבְרָהָם: וּמָצָֽאתָ אֶת־לְבָבוֹ נֶאֱמָן לְפָנֶֽיךָ, ‹ וְכָרוֹת עִמּוֹ הַבְּרִית לָתֵת אֶת־אֶֽרֶץ הַכְּנַעֲנִי הַחִתִּי הָאֱמֹרִי וְהַפְּרִזִּי וְהַיְבוּסִי וְהַגִּרְגָּשִׁי, לָתֵת לְזַרְעוֹ, וַתָּֽקֶם אֶת־דְּבָרֶֽיךָ, כִּי צַדִּיק אָֽתָּה: וַתֵּֽרֶא אֶת־עֳנִי אֲבֹתֵֽינוּ בְּמִצְרָֽיִם, וְאֶת־זַעֲקָתָם שָׁמַֽעְתָּ עַל־יַם־סוּף: וַתִּתֵּן אֹתֹת וּמֹפְתִים בְּפַרְעֹה וּבְכָל־עֲבָדָיו וּבְכָל־עַם אַרְצוֹ, כִּי יָדַֽעְתָּ כִּי הֵזִֽידוּ עֲלֵיהֶם, וַתַּֽעַשׂ־לְךָ שֵׁם כְּהַיּוֹם הַזֶּה: ‹ וְהַיָּם בָּקַֽעְתָּ לִפְנֵיהֶם, וַיַּעַבְרוּ בְתוֹךְ־הַיָּם בַּיַּבָּשָׁה, וְאֶת־רֹדְפֵיהֶם הִשְׁלַֽכְתָּ בִמְצוֹלֹת כְּמוֹ־אֶֽבֶן, בְּמַֽיִם עַזִּים:

SHAḤARIT FOR TISHA B'AV

וַיּוֹשַׁע That day the LORD saved Israel from the hands of the Egyptians, and Israel saw the Egyptians lying dead on the seashore. ▸ When Israel saw the great power the LORD had displayed against the Egyptians, the people feared the LORD, and believed in the LORD and in His servant, Moses. *Ex. 14*

אָז יָשִׁיר־מֹשֶׁה Then Moses and the Israelites sang this song to the LORD, saying: *Ex. 15*
    I will sing to the LORD, for He has triumphed gloriously;
        horse and rider He has hurled into the sea.
The LORD is my strength and song; He has become my salvation.
    This is my God, and I will beautify Him,
        my father's God, and I will exalt Him.
The LORD is a Master of war; LORD is His name.
Pharaoh's chariots and army He cast into the sea;
    the best of his officers drowned in the Sea of Reeds.
The deep waters covered them;
    they went down to the depths like a stone.
Your right hand, LORD, is majestic in power.
    Your right hand, LORD, shatters the enemy.
In the greatness of Your majesty, You overthrew those who rose
    against You.
    You sent out Your fury; it consumed them like stubble.
By the blast of Your nostrils the waters piled up.
    The surging waters stood straight like a wall;
    the deeps congealed in the heart of the sea.
The enemy said, "I will pursue. I will overtake. I will divide the spoil.
    My desire shall have its fill of them.
    I will draw my sword. My hand will destroy them."
You blew with Your wind; the sea covered them.
    They sank in the mighty waters like lead.
Who is like You, LORD, among the mighty?
    Who is like You – majestic in holiness, awesome in glory,
    working wonders?

שחרית לתשעה באב • פסוקי דזמרה

שמות יד

וַיּוֹשַׁע יְהֹוָה בַּיּוֹם הַהוּא אֶת־יִשְׂרָאֵל מִיַּד מִצְרָיִם, וַיַּרְא יִשְׂרָאֵל אֶת־מִצְרַיִם מֵת עַל־שְׂפַת הַיָּם: וַיַּרְא יִשְׂרָאֵל אֶת־הַיָּד הַגְּדֹלָה אֲשֶׁר עָשָׂה יְהֹוָה בְּמִצְרַיִם, וַיִּירְאוּ הָעָם אֶת־יְהֹוָה, וַיַּאֲמִינוּ בַּיהֹוָה וּבְמֹשֶׁה עַבְדּוֹ:

שמות טו

אָז יָשִׁיר־מֹשֶׁה וּבְנֵי יִשְׂרָאֵל אֶת־הַשִּׁירָה הַזֹּאת לַיהֹוָה, וַיֹּאמְרוּ לֵאמֹר, אָשִׁירָה לַיהֹוָה כִּי־גָאֹה גָּאָה, סוּס וְרֹכְבוֹ רָמָה בַיָּם: עָזִּי וְזִמְרָת יָהּ וַיְהִי־לִי לִישׁוּעָה, זֶה אֵלִי וְאַנְוֵהוּ, אֱלֹהֵי אָבִי וַאֲרֹמְמֶנְהוּ: יְהֹוָה אִישׁ מִלְחָמָה, יְהֹוָה שְׁמוֹ: מַרְכְּבֹת פַּרְעֹה וְחֵילוֹ יָרָה בַיָּם, וּמִבְחַר שָׁלִשָׁיו טֻבְּעוּ בְיַם־סוּף: תְּהֹמֹת יְכַסְיֻמוּ, יָרְדוּ בִמְצוֹלֹת כְּמוֹ־אָבֶן: יְמִינְךָ יְהֹוָה נֶאְדָּרִי בַּכֹּחַ, יְמִינְךָ יְהֹוָה תִּרְעַץ אוֹיֵב: וּבְרֹב גְּאוֹנְךָ תַּהֲרֹס קָמֶיךָ, תְּשַׁלַּח חֲרֹנְךָ יֹאכְלֵמוֹ כַּקַּשׁ: וּבְרוּחַ אַפֶּיךָ נֶעֶרְמוּ מַיִם, נִצְּבוּ כְמוֹ־נֵד נֹזְלִים, קָפְאוּ תְהֹמֹת בְּלֶב־יָם: אָמַר אוֹיֵב אֶרְדֹּף אַשִּׂיג, אֲחַלֵּק שָׁלָל, תִּמְלָאֵמוֹ נַפְשִׁי, אָרִיק חַרְבִּי תּוֹרִישֵׁמוֹ יָדִי: נָשַׁפְתָּ בְרוּחֲךָ כִּסָּמוֹ יָם, צָלְלוּ כַּעוֹפֶרֶת בְּמַיִם אַדִּירִים: מִי־כָמֹכָה בָּאֵלִם יְהֹוָה, מִי כָּמֹכָה נֶאְדָּר בַּקֹּדֶשׁ, נוֹרָא תְהִלֹּת עֹשֵׂה פֶלֶא: נָטִיתָ יְמִינְךָ תִּבְלָעֵמוֹ אָרֶץ: נָחִיתָ בְחַסְדְּךָ עַם־זוּ גָּאָלְתָּ, נֵהַלְתָּ בְעָזְּךָ אֶל־נְוֵה

You stretched out Your right hand,
> the earth swallowed them.
In Your loving-kindness, You led the people You redeemed.
> In Your strength, You guided them to Your holy abode.
Nations heard and trembled;
> terror gripped Philistia's inhabitants.
The chiefs of Edom were dismayed,
> Moab's leaders were seized with trembling,
> the people of Canaan melted away.
Fear and dread fell upon them.
> By the power of Your arm, they were still as stone –
> until Your people crossed, Lord,
> until the people You acquired crossed over.
You will bring them and plant them
> on the mountain of Your heritage –
> the place, Lord, You made for Your dwelling,
> the Sanctuary, Lord, Your hands established.
> The Lord will reign for ever and all time.

The Lord will reign for ever and all time.
The Lord's kingship is established for ever and to all eternity.

When Pharaoh's horses, chariots and riders went into the sea,
> the Lord brought the waters of the sea back over them, but the Israelites walked on dry land through the sea.

> ▸ For kingship is the Lord's *Ps. 22*
> and He rules over the nations.
> Saviors shall go up to Mount Zion *Ob. 1*
> to judge Mount Esau,
> and the Lord's shall be the kingdom.
>
> Then the Lord shall be King over all the earth; *Zech. 14*
> on that day the Lord shall be One and His name One,
> (as it is written in Your Torah, saying:
> Listen, Israel: the Lord is our God, the Lord is One.) *Deut. 6*

שָׁמְעוּ עַמִּים יִרְגָּזוּן, חִיל קָדְשֶׁךָ:
אָחַז יֹשְׁבֵי פְּלָשֶׁת: אָז נִבְהֲלוּ אַלּוּפֵי
אֱדוֹם, אֵילֵי מוֹאָב יֹאחֲזֵמוֹ רָעַד, נָמֹגוּ
כֹּל יֹשְׁבֵי כְנָעַן: תִּפֹּל עֲלֵיהֶם אֵימָתָה
וָפַחַד, בִּגְדֹל זְרוֹעֲךָ יִדְּמוּ כָּאָבֶן, עַד־
יַעֲבֹר עַמְּךָ יהוה, עַד־יַעֲבֹר עַם־זוּ
קָנִיתָ: תְּבִאֵמוֹ וְתִטָּעֵמוֹ בְּהַר נַחֲלָתְךָ, מָכוֹן
לְשִׁבְתְּךָ פָּעַלְתָּ יהוה, מִקְּדָשׁ אֲדֹנָי כּוֹנְנוּ
יָדֶיךָ: יהוה יִמְלֹךְ לְעֹלָם וָעֶד:

יהוה יִמְלֹךְ לְעֹלָם וָעֶד.
יהוה מַלְכוּתֵהּ קָאֵם לְעָלַם וּלְעָלְמֵי עָלְמַיָּא.

כִּי
בָא סוּס פַּרְעֹה בְּרִכְבּוֹ וּבְפָרָשָׁיו בַּיָּם, וַיָּשֶׁב יהוה עֲלֵהֶם אֶת־מֵי
הַיָּם, וּבְנֵי יִשְׂרָאֵל הָלְכוּ בַיַּבָּשָׁה בְּתוֹךְ הַיָּם:

תהלים כב ‏כִּי לַיהוה הַמְּלוּכָה וּמֹשֵׁל בַּגּוֹיִם:
עובדיה א וְעָלוּ מוֹשִׁעִים בְּהַר צִיּוֹן לִשְׁפֹּט אֶת־הַר עֵשָׂו
וְהָיְתָה לַיהוה הַמְּלוּכָה:

זכריה יד וְהָיָה יהוה לְמֶלֶךְ עַל־כָּל־הָאָרֶץ
בַּיּוֹם הַהוּא יִהְיֶה יהוה אֶחָד וּשְׁמוֹ אֶחָד:

דברים ו (וּבְתוֹרָתְךָ כָּתוּב לֵאמֹר, שְׁמַע יִשְׂרָאֵל, יהוה אֱלֹהֵינוּ יהוה אֶחָד:)

SHAḤARIT FOR TISHA B'AV

יִשְׁתַּבַּח May Your name be praised for ever, our King,
the great and holy God, King in heaven and on earth.
For to You, LORD our God and God of our ancestors,
it is right to offer song and praise,
hymn and psalm,
strength and dominion,
eternity, greatness and power,
song of praise and glory,
holiness and kingship,
▸ blessings and thanks,
from now and for ever.
Blessed are You, LORD, God and King,
exalted in praises, God of thanksgivings,
Master of wonders,
who delights in hymns of song, King, God,
Giver of life to the worlds.

HALF KADDISH

Leader: יִתְגַּדַּל Magnified and sanctified
may His great name be,
in the world He created by His will.
May He establish His kingdom
in your lifetime and in your days,
and in the lifetime of all the house of Israel,
swiftly and soon – and say: Amen.

All: May His great name be blessed for ever and all time.

Leader: Blessed and praised, glorified and exalted,
raised and honored, uplifted and lauded
be the name of the Holy One, blessed be He,
beyond any blessing,
song, praise and consolation
uttered in the world – and say: Amen.

יִשְׁתַּבַּח
שִׁמְךָ לָעַד, מַלְכֵּנוּ
הָאֵל הַמֶּלֶךְ הַגָּדוֹל וְהַקָּדוֹשׁ בַּשָּׁמַיִם וּבָאָרֶץ
כִּי לְךָ נָאֶה, יהוה אֱלֹהֵינוּ וֵאלֹהֵי אֲבוֹתֵינוּ
שִׁיר וּשְׁבָחָה, הַלֵּל וְזִמְרָה
עֹז וּמֶמְשָׁלָה, נֶצַח, גְּדֻלָּה וּגְבוּרָה
תְּהִלָּה וְתִפְאֶרֶת, קְדֻשָּׁה וּמַלְכוּת
◂ בְּרָכוֹת וְהוֹדָאוֹת, מֵעַתָּה וְעַד עוֹלָם.
בָּרוּךְ אַתָּה יהוה, אֵל מֶלֶךְ גָּדוֹל בַּתִּשְׁבָּחוֹת
אֵל הַהוֹדָאוֹת, אֲדוֹן הַנִּפְלָאוֹת
הַבּוֹחֵר בְּשִׁירֵי זִמְרָה, מֶלֶךְ, אֵל, חֵי הָעוֹלָמִים.

חצי קדיש

ש״צ: יִתְגַּדַּל וְיִתְקַדַּשׁ שְׁמֵהּ רַבָּא (קהל: אָמֵן)
בְּעָלְמָא דִּי בְרָא כִרְעוּתֵהּ, וְיַמְלִיךְ מַלְכוּתֵהּ
בְּחַיֵּיכוֹן וּבְיוֹמֵיכוֹן וּבְחַיֵּי דְּכָל בֵּית יִשְׂרָאֵל
בַּעֲגָלָא וּבִזְמַן קָרִיב, וְאִמְרוּ אָמֵן. (קהל: אָמֵן)

קהל
ורש״צ: יְהֵא שְׁמֵהּ רַבָּא מְבָרַךְ לְעָלַם וּלְעָלְמֵי עָלְמַיָּא.

ש״צ: יִתְבָּרַךְ וְיִשְׁתַּבַּח וְיִתְפָּאַר וְיִתְרוֹמַם וְיִתְנַשֵּׂא
וְיִתְהַדָּר וְיִתְעַלֶּה וְיִתְהַלָּל
שְׁמֵהּ דְּקֻדְשָׁא בְּרִיךְ הוּא (קהל: בְּרִיךְ הוּא)
לְעֵלָּא מִן כָּל בִּרְכָתָא וְשִׁירָתָא, תֻּשְׁבְּחָתָא וְנֶחֱמָתָא
דַּאֲמִירָן בְּעָלְמָא
וְאִמְרוּ אָמֵן. (קהל: אָמֵן)

BLESSINGS OF THE SHEMA

The following blessing and response are said only in the presence of a minyan. They represent a formal summons to the congregation to engage in an act of collective prayer. The custom of bowing at this point is based on 1 Chronicles 29:20, "David said to the whole assembly, 'Now bless the L<small>ORD</small> your God.' All the assembly blessed the L<small>ORD</small> God of their fathers and bowed their heads low to the L<small>ORD</small> and the King." The Leader says the following, bowing at "Bless," standing straight at "the L<small>ORD</small>." The congregation, followed by the Leader, responds, bowing at "Bless," standing straight at "the L<small>ORD</small>."

Leader: # BLESS
the L<small>ORD</small>, the blessed One.

Congregation: Bless the L<small>ORD</small>, the blessed One,
for ever and all time.

Leader: Bless the L<small>ORD</small>, the blessed One,
for ever and all time.

The custom is to sit from this point until the Amida, since the predominant emotion of this section of the prayers is love rather than awe. Conversation is forbidden until after the Amida.

בָּרוּךְ Blessed are You, L<small>ORD</small> our God,
King of the Universe,
who forms light and creates darkness,
makes peace and creates all.

Is. 45

הַמֵּאִיר In compassion He gives light to the earth
and its inhabitants,
and in His goodness continually renews the work of creation,
day after day.
How numerous are Your works, O L<small>ORD</small>.

Ps. 104

You made them all in wisdom.
The earth is full of Your creations.
He is the King exalted alone since the beginning of time – praised, glorified and elevated since the world began.

קריאת שמע וברכותיה

The following blessing and response are said only in the presence of a מנין. They represent a formal summons to the קהל to engage in an act of collective prayer. The custom of bowing at this point is based on דברי הימים א' כט:כ, "David said to the whole assembly, 'Now bless the LORD your God.' All the assembly blessed the LORD God of their fathers and bowed their heads low to the LORD and the King." The שליח ציבור says the following, bowing at בָּרְכוּ, standing straight at 'ה. The קהל, followed by the שליח ציבור, responds, bowing at בָּרוּךְ, standing straight at 'ה.

ש״ץ: בָּרְכוּ

אֶת יהוה הַמְבֹרָךְ.

קהל: בָּרוּךְ יהוה הַמְבֹרָךְ לְעוֹלָם וָעֶד.

ש״ץ: בָּרוּךְ יהוה הַמְבֹרָךְ לְעוֹלָם וָעֶד.

The custom is to sit from this point until the עמידה, since the predominant emotion of this section of the prayers is love rather than awe. Conversation is forbidden until after the עמידה.

בָּרוּךְ אַתָּה יהוה אֱלֹהֵינוּ מֶלֶךְ הָעוֹלָם

ישעיה מה

יוֹצֵר אוֹר וּבוֹרֵא חֹשֶׁךְ

עֹשֶׂה שָׁלוֹם וּבוֹרֵא אֶת הַכֹּל.

הַמֵּאִיר לָאָרֶץ וְלַדָּרִים עָלֶיהָ בְּרַחֲמִים

וּבְטוּבוֹ מְחַדֵּשׁ בְּכָל יוֹם תָּמִיד מַעֲשֵׂה בְרֵאשִׁית.

תהלים קד

מָה־רַבּוּ מַעֲשֶׂיךָ יהוה, כֻּלָּם בְּחָכְמָה עָשִׂיתָ

מָלְאָה הָאָרֶץ קִנְיָנֶךָ:

הַמֶּלֶךְ הַמְרוֹמָם לְבַדּוֹ מֵאָז

הַמְשֻׁבָּח וְהַמְפֹאָר וְהַמִּתְנַשֵּׂא מִימוֹת עוֹלָם.

Eternal God,
> in Your great compassion,
> have compassion on us,
> Lord of our strength, Rock of our refuge,
> Shield of our salvation, You are our stronghold.

The blessed God, great in knowledge,
prepared and made the rays of the sun.
He who is good formed glory for His name,
surrounding His power with radiant stars.
The leaders of His hosts, the holy ones,
exalt the Almighty,
constantly proclaiming God's glory and holiness.
Be blessed, Lord our God,
for the magnificence of Your handiwork
and for the radiant lights You have made.
May they glorify You, Selah!

תִּתְבָּרַךְ May You be blessed,
our Rock, King and Redeemer, Creator of holy beings.
May Your name be praised for ever,
our King, Creator of the ministering angels,
all of whom stand in the universe's heights,
proclaiming together, in awe, aloud,
the words of the living God, the eternal King.
They are all beloved, all pure, all mighty,
and all perform in awe and reverence
the will of their Maker.
▸ All open their mouths in holiness and purity,
with song and psalm,
> and bless, praise, glorify,
> > revere, sanctify and declare the sovereignty of – ◂
The name of the great, mighty
and awesome God and King,
holy is He.

אֱלֹהֵי עוֹלָם
בְּרַחֲמֶיךָ הָרַבִּים רַחֵם עָלֵינוּ
אֲדוֹן עֻזֵּנוּ, צוּר מִשְׂגַּבֵּנוּ
מָגֵן יִשְׁעֵנוּ, מִשְׂגָּב בַּעֲדֵנוּ.

אֵל בָּרוּךְ גְּדוֹל דֵּעָה, הֵכִין וּפָעַל זָהֳרֵי חַמָּה
טוֹב יָצַר כָּבוֹד לִשְׁמוֹ, מְאוֹרוֹת נָתַן סְבִיבוֹת עֻזּוֹ
פִּנּוֹת צְבָאָיו קְדוֹשִׁים, רוֹמְמֵי שַׁדַּי
תָּמִיד מְסַפְּרִים כְּבוֹד אֵל וּקְדֻשָּׁתוֹ.
תִּתְבָּרַךְ יהוה אֱלֹהֵינוּ, עַל שֶׁבַח מַעֲשֵׂה יָדֶיךָ.
וְעַל מְאוֹרֵי אוֹר שֶׁעָשִׂיתָ, יְפָאֲרוּךָ סֶּלָה.

תִּתְבָּרַךְ
צוּרֵנוּ מַלְכֵּנוּ וְגוֹאֲלֵנוּ, בּוֹרֵא קְדוֹשִׁים
יִשְׁתַּבַּח שִׁמְךָ לָעַד
מַלְכֵּנוּ, יוֹצֵר מְשָׁרְתִים
וַאֲשֶׁר מְשָׁרְתָיו כֻּלָּם עוֹמְדִים בְּרוּם עוֹלָם
וּמַשְׁמִיעִים בְּיִרְאָה יַחַד בְּקוֹל
דִּבְרֵי אֱלֹהִים חַיִּים וּמֶלֶךְ עוֹלָם.
כֻּלָּם אֲהוּבִים, כֻּלָּם בְּרוּרִים, כֻּלָּם גִּבּוֹרִים
וְכֻלָּם עוֹשִׂים בְּאֵימָה וּבְיִרְאָה רְצוֹן קוֹנָם
◂ וְכֻלָּם פּוֹתְחִים אֶת פִּיהֶם בִּקְדֻשָּׁה וּבְטָהֳרָה
בְּשִׁירָה וּבְזִמְרָה
וּמְבָרְכִים וּמְשַׁבְּחִים וּמְפָאֲרִים
וּמַעֲרִיצִים וּמַקְדִּישִׁים וּמַמְלִיכִים ◂
אֶת שֵׁם הָאֵל הַמֶּלֶךְ הַגָּדוֹל, הַגִּבּוֹר וְהַנּוֹרָא
קָדוֹשׁ הוּא.

► All accept on themselves, one from another,
the yoke of the kingdom of heaven,
granting permission to one another
to sanctify the One who formed them,
in serene spirit,
pure speech and sweet melody.
All, as one, proclaim His holiness,
saying in awe:

All say aloud: Holy, holy, holy is the L<small>ORD</small> of hosts: *Is. 6*
the whole world is filled with His glory.

► Then the Ophanim and the Holy Ḥayyot,
with a roar of noise,
raise themselves toward the Seraphim and,
facing them, give praise, saying:

All say aloud: Blessed be the L<small>ORD</small>'s glory from His place.   *Ezek. 3*

לָאֵל To the blessed God they offer melodies.
To the King, living and eternal God,
they say psalms and proclaim praises.
> For it is He alone
> who does mighty deeds and creates new things,
> who is Master of battles, and sows righteousness,
> who makes salvation grow and creates cures,
> who is revered in praises,
> L<small>ORD</small> of wonders,

who in His goodness,
continually renews the work of creation, day after day,
as it is said,
> "[Praise] Him who made the great lights,   *Ps. 136*
> for His love endures for ever."

► May You make a new light shine over Zion,
and may we all soon be worthy of its light.
Blessed are You, L<small>ORD</small>, who forms the radiant lights.

‣ וְכֻלָּם מְקַבְּלִים עֲלֵיהֶם עֹל מַלְכוּת שָׁמַיִם זֶה מִזֶּה
וְנוֹתְנִים רְשׁוּת זֶה לָזֶה
לְהַקְדִּישׁ לְיוֹצְרָם בְּנַחַת רוּחַ
בְּשָׂפָה בְרוּרָה וּבִנְעִימָה
קְדֻשָּׁה כֻּלָּם כְּאֶחָד
עוֹנִים וְאוֹמְרִים בְּיִרְאָה

All say aloud קָדוֹשׁ, קָדוֹשׁ, קָדוֹשׁ יהוה צְבָאוֹת ישעיה ו
מְלֹא כָל־הָאָֽרֶץ כְּבוֹדוֹ:

‣ וְהָאוֹפַנִּים וְחַיּוֹת הַקֹּֽדֶשׁ
בְּרַֽעַשׁ גָּדוֹל מִתְנַשְּׂאִים לְעֻמַּת שְׂרָפִים
לְעֻמָּתָם מְשַׁבְּחִים וְאוֹמְרִים

All say aloud בָּרוּךְ כְּבוֹד־יהוה מִמְּקוֹמוֹ: יחזקאל ג

לָאֵל בָּרוּךְ נְעִימוֹת יִתֵּֽנוּ, לְמֶֽלֶךְ אֵל חַי וְקַיָּם
זְמִירוֹת יֹאמֵֽרוּ וְתִשְׁבָּחוֹת יַשְׁמִֽיעוּ
כִּי הוּא לְבַדּוֹ
פּוֹעֵל גְּבוּרוֹת, עֹשֶׂה חֲדָשׁוֹת
בַּֽעַל מִלְחָמוֹת, זוֹרֵֽעַ צְדָקוֹת
מַצְמִֽיחַ יְשׁוּעוֹת, בּוֹרֵא רְפוּאוֹת
נוֹרָא תְהִלּוֹת, אֲדוֹן הַנִּפְלָאוֹת
הַמְחַדֵּשׁ בְּטוּבוֹ בְּכָל יוֹם תָּמִיד מַעֲשֵׂה בְרֵאשִׁית
כָּאָמוּר
לְעֹשֵׂה אוֹרִים גְּדֹלִים, כִּי לְעוֹלָם חַסְדּוֹ: תהלים קלו
‣ אוֹר חָדָשׁ עַל צִיּוֹן תָּאִיר וְנִזְכֶּה כֻלָּֽנוּ מְהֵרָה לְאוֹרוֹ.
בָּרוּךְ אַתָּה יהוה, יוֹצֵר הַמְּאוֹרוֹת.

אַהֲבָה You have loved us with great love,
Lord our God,
and with surpassing compassion
have You had compassion on us.
Our Father, our King,
for the sake of our ancestors who trusted in You,
and to whom You taught the laws of life,
be gracious also to us and teach us.
Our Father, compassionate Father,
ever compassionate,
have compassion on us.
Instill in our hearts
the desire to understand and discern,
to listen, learn and teach,
to observe, perform and fulfill
all the teachings of Your Torah in love.
Enlighten our eyes in Your Torah
and let our hearts cling to Your commandments.
Unite our hearts to love and revere Your name,
so that we may never be ashamed.
And because we have trusted
in Your holy, great and revered name,
may we be glad and rejoice in Your salvation.
Bring us back in peace from the four quarters of the earth
and lead us upright to our land.
▸ For You are a God who performs acts of salvation,
and You chose us from all peoples and tongues,
bringing us close to Your great name for ever in truth,
that we may thank You
and proclaim Your Oneness in love.
Blessed are You, Lord,
who chooses His people Israel in love.

אַהֲבָה רַבָּה אֲהַבְתָּנוּ, יהוה אֱלֹהֵינוּ
חֶמְלָה גְדוֹלָה וִיתֵרָה חָמַלְתָּ עָלֵינוּ.
אָבִינוּ מַלְכֵּנוּ
בַּעֲבוּר אֲבוֹתֵינוּ שֶׁבָּטְחוּ בְךָ
וַתְּלַמְּדֵם חֻקֵּי חַיִּים
כֵּן תְּחָנֵּנוּ וּתְלַמְּדֵנוּ.
אָבִינוּ, הָאָב הָרַחֲמָן, הַמְרַחֵם
רַחֵם עָלֵינוּ
וְתֵן בְּלִבֵּנוּ לְהָבִין וּלְהַשְׂכִּיל
לִשְׁמֹעַ, לִלְמֹד וּלְלַמֵּד, לִשְׁמֹר וְלַעֲשׂוֹת, וּלְקַיֵּם
אֶת כָּל דִּבְרֵי תַלְמוּד תּוֹרָתֶךָ בְּאַהֲבָה.
וְהָאֵר עֵינֵינוּ בְּתוֹרָתֶךָ, וְדַבֵּק לִבֵּנוּ בְּמִצְוֹתֶיךָ
וְיַחֵד לְבָבֵנוּ לְאַהֲבָה וּלְיִרְאָה אֶת שְׁמֶךָ
וְלֹא נֵבוֹשׁ לְעוֹלָם וָעֶד.
כִּי בְשֵׁם קָדְשְׁךָ הַגָּדוֹל וְהַנּוֹרָא בָּטָחְנוּ
נָגִילָה וְנִשְׂמְחָה בִּישׁוּעָתֶךָ.
וַהֲבִיאֵנוּ לְשָׁלוֹם מֵאַרְבַּע כַּנְפוֹת הָאָרֶץ
וְתוֹלִיכֵנוּ קוֹמְמִיּוּת לְאַרְצֵנוּ.
כִּי אֵל פּוֹעֵל יְשׁוּעוֹת אָתָּה
וּבָנוּ בָחַרְתָּ מִכָּל עַם וְלָשׁוֹן
וְקֵרַבְתָּנוּ לְשִׁמְךָ הַגָּדוֹל סֶלָה, בֶּאֱמֶת
לְהוֹדוֹת לְךָ וּלְיַחֶדְךָ בְּאַהֲבָה.
בָּרוּךְ אַתָּה יהוה
הַבּוֹחֵר בְּעַמּוֹ יִשְׂרָאֵל בְּאַהֲבָה.

The Shema must be said with intense concentration. In the first paragraph one should accept, with love, the sovereignty of God; in the second, the mitzvot as the will of God. The end of the third paragraph constitutes fulfillment of the mitzva to remember, morning and evening, the exodus from Egypt.

When not praying with a minyan, say:
God, faithful King!

The following verse should be said aloud, while covering the eyes with the right hand:

Listen, Israel: the Lord is our God, the Lord is One.

Deut. 6

Quietly: Blessed be the name of His glorious kingdom
for ever and ever.

וְאָהַבְתָּ Love the Lord your God with all your heart, with all your soul, and with all your might. These words which I command you today shall be on your heart. Teach them repeatedly to your children, speaking of them when you sit at home and when you travel on the way, when you lie down and when you rise. Bind them as a sign on your hand, and they shall be an emblem between your eyes. Write them on the doorposts of your house and gates.

Deut. 6

וְהָיָה If you indeed heed My commandments with which I charge you today, to love the Lord your God and worship Him with all your heart and with all your soul, I will give rain in your land in its season, the early and late rain; and you shall gather in your grain, wine and oil. I will give grass in your field for your cattle, and you shall eat and be satisfied. Be careful lest your heart be tempted and you go astray and worship other gods, bowing down to them. Then the Lord's anger will flare against you and He will close the heavens so that there will be no rain. The land will not yield its crops, and you will perish swiftly from the good land that the Lord is giving you. Therefore, set these, My words, on your heart and soul.

Deut. 11

The שמע must be said with intense concentration. In the first paragraph one should accept, with love, the sovereignty of God; in the second, the מצוות as the will of God. The end of the third paragraph constitutes fulfillment of the מצוה to remember, morning and evening, the exodus from Egypt.

When not praying with a מנין, say:

אֵל מֶלֶךְ נֶאֱמָן

The following verse should be said aloud, while covering the eyes with the right hand:

שְׁמַע יִשְׂרָאֵל, יְהֹוָה אֱלֹהֵינוּ, יְהֹוָה ׀ אֶחָד׃ <small>דברים ו</small>

Quietly בָּרוּךְ שֵׁם כְּבוֹד מַלְכוּתוֹ לְעוֹלָם וָעֶד.

וְאָהַבְתָּ אֵת יְהֹוָה אֱלֹהֶיךָ, בְּכָל־לְבָבְךָ וּבְכָל־נַפְשְׁךָ וּבְכָל־ <small>דברים ו</small>
מְאֹדֶךָ׃ וְהָיוּ הַדְּבָרִים הָאֵלֶּה, אֲשֶׁר אָנֹכִי מְצַוְּךָ הַיּוֹם, עַל־לְבָבֶךָ׃
וְשִׁנַּנְתָּם לְבָנֶיךָ וְדִבַּרְתָּ בָּם, בְּשִׁבְתְּךָ בְּבֵיתֶךָ וּבְלֶכְתְּךָ בַדֶּרֶךְ,
וּבְשָׁכְבְּךָ וּבְקוּמֶךָ׃ וּקְשַׁרְתָּם לְאוֹת עַל־יָדֶךָ וְהָיוּ לְטֹטָפֹת בֵּין
עֵינֶיךָ׃ וּכְתַבְתָּם עַל־מְזֻזוֹת בֵּיתֶךָ וּבִשְׁעָרֶיךָ׃

וְהָיָה אִם־שָׁמֹעַ תִּשְׁמְעוּ אֶל־מִצְוֹתַי אֲשֶׁר אָנֹכִי מְצַוֶּה אֶתְכֶם <small>דברים יא</small>
הַיּוֹם, לְאַהֲבָה אֶת־יְהֹוָה אֱלֹהֵיכֶם וּלְעָבְדוֹ, בְּכָל־לְבַבְכֶם וּבְכָל־
נַפְשְׁכֶם׃ וְנָתַתִּי מְטַר־אַרְצְכֶם בְּעִתּוֹ, יוֹרֶה וּמַלְקוֹשׁ, וְאָסַפְתָּ
דְגָנֶךָ וְתִירֹשְׁךָ וְיִצְהָרֶךָ׃ וְנָתַתִּי עֵשֶׂב בְּשָׂדְךָ לִבְהֶמְתֶּךָ, וְאָכַלְתָּ
וְשָׂבָעְתָּ׃ הִשָּׁמְרוּ לָכֶם פֶּן־יִפְתֶּה לְבַבְכֶם, וְסַרְתֶּם וַעֲבַדְתֶּם
אֱלֹהִים אֲחֵרִים וְהִשְׁתַּחֲוִיתֶם לָהֶם׃ וְחָרָה אַף־יְהֹוָה בָּכֶם, וְעָצַר
אֶת־הַשָּׁמַיִם וְלֹא־יִהְיֶה מָטָר, וְהָאֲדָמָה לֹא תִתֵּן אֶת־יְבוּלָהּ,
וַאֲבַדְתֶּם מְהֵרָה מֵעַל הָאָרֶץ הַטֹּבָה אֲשֶׁר יְהֹוָה נֹתֵן לָכֶם׃
וְשַׂמְתֶּם אֶת־דְּבָרַי אֵלֶּה עַל־לְבַבְכֶם וְעַל־נַפְשְׁכֶם, וּקְשַׁרְתֶּם

Bind them as a sign on your hand, and they shall be an emblem between your eyes. Teach them to your children, speaking of them when you sit at home and when you travel on the way, when you lie down and when you rise. Write them on the doorposts of your house and gates, so that you and your children may live long in the land that the LORD swore to your ancestors to give them, for as long as the heavens are above the earth.

וַיֹּאמֶר The LORD spoke to Moses, saying: Speak to the Israelites *Num. 15* and tell them to make tassels on the corners of their garments for all generations. They shall attach to the tassel at each corner a thread of blue. This shall be your tassel, and you shall see it and remember all of the LORD's commandments and keep them, not straying after your heart and after your eyes, following your own sinful desires. Thus you will be reminded to keep all My commandments, and be holy to your God. I am the LORD your God, who brought you out of the land of Egypt to be your God. I am the LORD your God.

True –

The Leader repeats:
▸ The LORD your God is true –

וְיַצִּיב And firm, established and enduring,
right, faithful,
beloved, cherished, delightful, pleasant,
awesome, mighty, perfect, accepted,
good and beautiful
is this faith for us for ever.

אֹתָם לְאוֹת עַל־יֶדְכֶם, וְהָיוּ לְטוֹטָפֹת בֵּין עֵינֵיכֶם: וְלִמַּדְתֶּם אֹתָם אֶת־בְּנֵיכֶם לְדַבֵּר בָּם, בְּשִׁבְתְּךָ בְּבֵיתֶךָ, וּבְלֶכְתְּךָ בַדֶּרֶךְ וּבְשָׁכְבְּךָ וּבְקוּמֶךָ: וּכְתַבְתָּם עַל־מְזוּזוֹת בֵּיתֶךָ וּבִשְׁעָרֶיךָ: לְמַעַן יִרְבּוּ יְמֵיכֶם וִימֵי בְנֵיכֶם עַל הָאֲדָמָה אֲשֶׁר נִשְׁבַּע יהוה לַאֲבֹתֵיכֶם לָתֵת לָהֶם, כִּימֵי הַשָּׁמַיִם עַל־הָאָרֶץ:

במדבר טו

וַיֹּאמֶר יהוה אֶל־מֹשֶׁה לֵּאמֹר: דַּבֵּר אֶל־בְּנֵי יִשְׂרָאֵל וְאָמַרְתָּ אֲלֵהֶם, וְעָשׂוּ לָהֶם צִיצִת עַל־כַּנְפֵי בִגְדֵיהֶם לְדֹרֹתָם, וְנָתְנוּ עַל־צִיצִת הַכָּנָף פְּתִיל תְּכֵלֶת: וְהָיָה לָכֶם לְצִיצִת, וּרְאִיתֶם אֹתוֹ, וּזְכַרְתֶּם אֶת־כָּל־מִצְוֹת יהוה וַעֲשִׂיתֶם אֹתָם, וְלֹא תָתוּרוּ אַחֲרֵי לְבַבְכֶם וְאַחֲרֵי עֵינֵיכֶם, אֲשֶׁר־אַתֶּם זֹנִים אַחֲרֵיהֶם: לְמַעַן תִּזְכְּרוּ וַעֲשִׂיתֶם אֶת־כָּל־מִצְוֹתָי, וִהְיִיתֶם קְדֹשִׁים לֵאלֹהֵיכֶם: אֲנִי יהוה אֱלֹהֵיכֶם, אֲשֶׁר הוֹצֵאתִי אֶתְכֶם מֵאֶרֶץ מִצְרַיִם, לִהְיוֹת לָכֶם לֵאלֹהִים, אֲנִי יהוה אֱלֹהֵיכֶם:

אֱמֶת

The שליח ציבור repeats:

‣ יהוה אֱלֹהֵיכֶם אֱמֶת

וְיַצִּיב, וְנָכוֹן וְקַיָּם, וְיָשָׁר וְנֶאֱמָן
וְאָהוּב וְחָבִיב, וְנֶחְמָד וְנָעִים
וְנוֹרָא וְאַדִּיר, וּמְתֻקָּן וּמְקֻבָּל
וְטוֹב וְיָפֶה
הַדָּבָר הַזֶּה עָלֵינוּ לְעוֹלָם וָעֶד.

True is the eternal God, our King,
    Rock of Jacob,
    Shield of our salvation.
    He exists and His name exists
    through all generations.
    His throne is established,
    His kingship and faithfulness
    endure for ever.

    His words live and persist,
    faithful and desirable
    for ever and all time.
    ▸ So they were for our ancestors,
    so they are for us,
    and so they will be for our children
    and all our generations
    and for all future generations
    of the seed of Israel, Your servants. ◂

    For the early and the later generations
    this faith has proved good and enduring for ever –
True and faithful, an irrevocable law.

True You are the Lord:
    our God and God of our ancestors,
    ▸ our King and King of our ancestors,
    our Redeemer and Redeemer of our ancestors,
    our Maker,
    Rock of our salvation,
    our Deliverer and Rescuer:
    this has ever been Your name.
    There is no God but You.

אֱמֶת אֱלֹהֵי עוֹלָם מַלְכֵּנוּ
צוּר יַעֲקֹב מָגֵן יִשְׁעֵנוּ
לְדוֹר וָדוֹר הוּא קַיָּם וּשְׁמוֹ קַיָּם
וְכִסְאוֹ נָכוֹן
וּמַלְכוּתוֹ וֶאֱמוּנָתוֹ לָעַד קַיָּמֶת.

וּדְבָרָיו חָיִים וְקַיָּמִים
נֶאֱמָנִים וְנֶחֱמָדִים
לָעַד וּלְעוֹלְמֵי עוֹלָמִים
‹ עַל אֲבוֹתֵינוּ וְעָלֵינוּ
עַל בָּנֵינוּ וְעַל דּוֹרוֹתֵינוּ
וְעַל כָּל דּוֹרוֹת זֶרַע יִשְׂרָאֵל עֲבָדֶיךָ. ›

עַל הָרִאשׁוֹנִים וְעַל הָאַחֲרוֹנִים
דָּבָר טוֹב וְקַיָּם לְעוֹלָם וָעֶד
אֱמֶת וֶאֱמוּנָה, חֹק וְלֹא יַעֲבֹר.

אֱמֶת שָׁאַתָּה הוּא יהוה
אֱלֹהֵינוּ וֵאלֹהֵי אֲבוֹתֵינוּ
‹ מַלְכֵּנוּ מֶלֶךְ אֲבוֹתֵינוּ
גּוֹאֲלֵנוּ גּוֹאֵל אֲבוֹתֵינוּ
יוֹצְרֵנוּ צוּר יְשׁוּעָתֵנוּ
פּוֹדֵנוּ וּמַצִּילֵנוּ מֵעוֹלָם שְׁמֶךָ
אֵין אֱלֹהִים זוּלָתֶךָ.

עֶזְרַת You have always been the help of our ancestors,
Shield and Savior of their children after them
in every generation.
Your dwelling is in the heights of the universe,
and Your judgments and righteousness
reach to the ends of the earth.
Happy is the one who obeys Your commandments
and takes to heart
Your teaching and Your word.

True You are the Master of Your people
and a mighty King who pleads their cause.

True You are the first and You are the last.
Beside You, we have no king,
redeemer or savior.
From Egypt You redeemed us,
Lord our God,
and from the slave-house You delivered us.
All their firstborn You killed,
but Your firstborn You redeemed.
You split the Sea of Reeds
and drowned the arrogant.
You brought Your beloved ones across.
The water covered their foes;   Ps. 106
not one of them was left.

For this, the beloved ones praised and exalted God,
the cherished ones sang psalms, songs and praises,
blessings and thanksgivings to the King,
the living and enduring God.

עֶזְרַת אֲבוֹתֵינוּ אַתָּה הוּא מֵעוֹלָם
מָגֵן וּמוֹשִׁיעַ לִבְנֵיהֶם אַחֲרֵיהֶם בְּכָל דּוֹר וָדוֹר.
בְּרוּם עוֹלָם מוֹשָׁבֶךָ
וּמִשְׁפָּטֶיךָ וְצִדְקָתְךָ עַד אַפְסֵי אָרֶץ.
אַשְׁרֵי אִישׁ שֶׁיִּשְׁמַע לְמִצְוֹתֶיךָ
וְתוֹרָתְךָ וּדְבָרְךָ יָשִׂים עַל לִבּוֹ.

אֱמֶת אַתָּה הוּא אָדוֹן לְעַמֶּךָ
וּמֶלֶךְ גִּבּוֹר לָרִיב רִיבָם.

אֱמֶת אַתָּה הוּא רִאשׁוֹן וְאַתָּה הוּא אַחֲרוֹן
וּמִבַּלְעָדֶיךָ אֵין לָנוּ מֶלֶךְ גּוֹאֵל וּמוֹשִׁיעַ.
מִמִּצְרַיִם גְּאַלְתָּנוּ, יהוה אֱלֹהֵינוּ
וּמִבֵּית עֲבָדִים פְּדִיתָנוּ
כָּל בְּכוֹרֵיהֶם הָרָגְתָּ, וּבְכוֹרְךָ גָּאָלְתָּ
וְיַם סוּף בָּקַעְתָּ
וְזֵדִים טִבַּעְתָּ
וִידִידִים הֶעֱבַרְתָּ
וַיְכַסּוּ־מַיִם צָרֵיהֶם
אֶחָד מֵהֶם לֹא נוֹתָר:

עַל זֹאת שִׁבְּחוּ אֲהוּבִים, וְרוֹמְמוּ אֵל
וְנָתְנוּ יְדִידִים זְמִירוֹת, שִׁירוֹת וְתִשְׁבָּחוֹת
בְּרָכוֹת וְהוֹדָאוֹת לְמֶלֶךְ אֵל חַי וְקַיָּם

תהלים קמ

High and exalted, great and awesome,
He humbles the haughty and raises the lowly,
freeing captives
and redeeming those in need,
helping the poor
and answering His people
when they cry out to Him.

Stand in preparation for the Amida. Take three steps back before beginning the Amida.

▸ Praises to God Most High,
the Blessed One who is blessed.
Moses and the children of Israel
recited to You a song with great joy,
and they all exclaimed:
> "Who is like You, Lord, among the mighty?   *Ex. 15*
> Who is like You, majestic in holiness,
> awesome in praises, doing wonders?"

▸ With a new song, the redeemed people praised
Your name at the seashore.
Together they all gave thanks,
proclaimed Your kingship,
and declared:
> "The Lord shall reign for ever and ever."   *Ex. 15*

Congregants should end the following blessing together with the Leader so as to be able to move directly from the words "redeemed Israel" to the Amida, without the interruption of saying Amen.

▸ צוּר יִשְׂרָאֵל Rock of Israel! Arise to the help of Israel.
Deliver, as You promised, Judah and Israel.
> Our Redeemer, the Lord of hosts is His name,   *Is. 47*
> the Holy One of Israel.
Blessed are You, Lord, who redeemed Israel.

רָם וְנִשָּׂא, גָּדוֹל וְנוֹרָא
מַשְׁפִּיל גֵּאִים וּמַגְבִּיהַּ שְׁפָלִים
מוֹצִיא אֲסִירִים, וּפוֹדֶה עֲנָוִים וְעוֹזֵר דַּלִּים
וְעוֹנֶה לְעַמּוֹ בְּעֵת שַׁוְּעָם אֵלָיו.

Stand in preparation for the עמידה. *Take three steps back before beginning the* עמידה.

◂ תְּהִלּוֹת לְאֵל עֶלְיוֹן, בָּרוּךְ הוּא וּמְבֹרָךְ
מֹשֶׁה וּבְנֵי יִשְׂרָאֵל
לְךָ עָנוּ שִׁירָה בְּשִׂמְחָה רַבָּה
וְאָמְרוּ כֻלָּם

שמות טו

מִי־כָמֹכָה בָּאֵלִם, יהוה
מִי כָּמֹכָה נֶאְדָּר בַּקֹּדֶשׁ
נוֹרָא תְהִלֹּת, עֹשֵׂה פֶלֶא:

◂ שִׁירָה חֲדָשָׁה שִׁבְּחוּ גְאוּלִים
לְשִׁמְךָ עַל שְׂפַת הַיָּם
יַחַד כֻּלָּם הוֹדוּ וְהִמְלִיכוּ
וְאָמְרוּ

שמות טו

יהוה יִמְלֹךְ לְעֹלָם וָעֶד:

The קהל *should end the following blessing together with the* שליח ציבור *so as to be able to move directly from the words* גָּאַל יִשְׂרָאֵל *to the* עמידה, *without the interruption of saying* אמן.

◂ צוּר יִשְׂרָאֵל, קוּמָה בְּעֶזְרַת יִשְׂרָאֵל
וּפְדֵה כִנְאֻמֶךָ יְהוּדָה וְיִשְׂרָאֵל.

ישעיה מז

גֹּאֲלֵנוּ יהוה צְבָאוֹת שְׁמוֹ, קְדוֹשׁ יִשְׂרָאֵל:
בָּרוּךְ אַתָּה יהוה, גָּאַל יִשְׂרָאֵל.

THE AMIDA

The following prayer, until "in former years," on page 174, is said standing with feet together in imitation of the angels in Ezekiel's vision (Ezek. 1:7). The Amida is said silently, following the precedent of Hannah when she prayed for a child (1 Sam. 1:13). If there is a minyan, it is repeated aloud by the Leader. Take three steps forward, as if formally entering the place of the Divine Presence. At the points indicated by ˚, bend the knees at the first word, bow at the second, and stand straight before saying God's name.

O Lord, open my lips,   Ps. 51
so that my mouth may declare Your praise.

PATRIARCHS

˚בָּרוּךְ Blessed are You, Lord our God and God of our fathers,
God of Abraham, God of Isaac and God of Jacob;
the great, mighty and awesome God, God Most High,
who bestows acts of loving-kindness and creates all,
who remembers the loving-kindness of the fathers
and will bring a Redeemer to their children's children
for the sake of His name, in love.
King, Helper, Savior, Shield:
˚Blessed are You, Lord,
Shield of Abraham.

DIVINE MIGHT

אַתָּה גִּבּוֹר You are eternally mighty, Lord.
You give life to the dead and have great power to save.

In Israel: He causes the dew to fall.

He sustains the living with loving-kindness,
and with great compassion revives the dead.
He supports the fallen, heals the sick,
sets captives free,
and keeps His faith with those who sleep in the dust.

עמידה

The following prayer, until קְדֻשּׁוֹת, *on page 175, is said standing with feet together in imitation of the angels in Ezekiel's vision* (יחזקאל א:ז). *The* עמידה *is said silently, following the precedent of* חנה *when she prayed for a child* (שמואל א' א:יג). *If there is a* מנין, *it is repeated aloud by the* שליח ציבור. *Take three steps forward, as if formally entering the place of the Divine Presence. At the points indicated by* ՝, *bend the knees at the first word, bow at the second, and stand straight before saying God's name.*

תהלים נא

אֲדֹנָי, שְׂפָתַי תִּפְתָּח, וּפִי יַגִּיד תְּהִלָּתֶךָ:

אבות

՝בָּרוּךְ אַתָּה יהוה, אֱלֹהֵינוּ וֵאלֹהֵי אֲבוֹתֵינוּ
אֱלֹהֵי אַבְרָהָם, אֱלֹהֵי יִצְחָק, וֵאלֹהֵי יַעֲקֹב
הָאֵל הַגָּדוֹל הַגִּבּוֹר וְהַנּוֹרָא, אֵל עֶלְיוֹן
גּוֹמֵל חֲסָדִים טוֹבִים, וְקֹנֵה הַכֹּל
וְזוֹכֵר חַסְדֵי אָבוֹת
וּמֵבִיא גוֹאֵל לִבְנֵי בְנֵיהֶם, לְמַעַן שְׁמוֹ בְּאַהֲבָה.
מֶלֶךְ עוֹזֵר וּמוֹשִׁיעַ וּמָגֵן.
՝בָּרוּךְ אַתָּה יהוה, מָגֵן אַבְרָהָם.

גבורות

אַתָּה גִּבּוֹר לְעוֹלָם, אֲדֹנָי
מְחַיֵּה מֵתִים אַתָּה, רַב לְהוֹשִׁיעַ

בארץ ישראל: מוֹרִיד הַטָּל

מְכַלְכֵּל חַיִּים בְּחֶסֶד, מְחַיֵּה מֵתִים בְּרַחֲמִים רַבִּים
סוֹמֵךְ נוֹפְלִים, וְרוֹפֵא חוֹלִים, וּמַתִּיר אֲסוּרִים
וּמְקַיֵּם אֱמוּנָתוֹ לִישֵׁנֵי עָפָר.

Who is like You, Master of might,
and to whom can You be compared,
O King who brings death and gives life,
and makes salvation grow?
Faithful are You to revive the dead.
Blessed are You, Lord, who revives the dead.

> *When saying the Amida silently, continue with "You are holy" on the next page.*

KEDUSHA

> *During the Leader's repetition, the following is said standing
> with feet together, rising on the toes at the words indicated by* ▲.

Cong. then Leader:

נְקַדֵּשׁ We will sanctify Your name on earth,
as they sanctify it in the highest heavens,
as is written by Your prophet,
"And they [the angels] call to one another saying: *Is. 6*

Cong. then Leader:

▲Holy, ▲holy, ▲holy is the Lord of hosts
the whole world is filled with His glory."
Those facing them say "Blessed – "

Cong. then Leader:

"▲Blessed is the Lord's glory from His place."   *Ezek. 3*
And in Your Holy Writings it is written thus:

Cong. then Leader:

▲The Lord shall reign for ever. He is your God, Zion,   *Ps. 146*
from generation to generation, Halleluya!"

Leader:

From generation to generation we will declare Your greatness,
and we will proclaim Your holiness for evermore.
Your praise, our God, shall not leave our mouth forever,
for You, God, are a great and holy King. Blessed are You, Lord,
the holy God.

> *The Leader continues with "You grace humanity" on the next page.*

שחרית לתשעה באב • עמידה

מִי כָמְוֹךָ, בַּעַל גְּבוּרוֹת
וּמִי דּוֹמֶה לָּךְ
מֶלֶךְ, מֵמִית וּמְחַיֶּה וּמַצְמִיחַ יְשׁוּעָה.
וְנֶאֱמָן אַתָּה לְהַחֲיוֹת מֵתִים.
בָּרוּךְ אַתָּה יהוה, מְחַיֵּה הַמֵּתִים.

When saying the עמידה silently, continue with אַתָּה קָדוֹשׁ on the next page.

קדושה

During חזרת הש״ץ, the following is said standing
with feet together, rising on the toes at the words indicated by ᐊ.

שליח ציבור then קהל:

נְקַדֵּשׁ אֶת שִׁמְךָ בָּעוֹלָם, כְּשֵׁם שֶׁמַּקְדִּישִׁים אוֹתוֹ בִּשְׁמֵי מָרוֹם
כַּכָּתוּב עַל יַד נְבִיאֶךָ, וְקָרָא זֶה אֶל־זֶה וְאָמַר

ישעיה ו

שליח ציבור then קהל:

ᐊקָדוֹשׁ, ᐊקָדוֹשׁ, ᐊקָדוֹשׁ, יהוה צְבָאוֹת, מְלֹא כָל־הָאָרֶץ כְּבוֹדוֹ:
לְעֻמָּתָם בָּרוּךְ יֹאמֵרוּ

שליח ציבור then קהל:

ᐊבָּרוּךְ כְּבוֹד־יהוה מִמְּקוֹמוֹ:
וּבְדִבְרֵי קָדְשְׁךָ כָּתוּב לֵאמֹר

יחזקאל ג

שליח ציבור then קהל:

ᐊיִמְלֹךְ יהוה לְעוֹלָם, אֱלֹהַיִךְ צִיּוֹן לְדֹר וָדֹר, הַלְלוּיָהּ:

תהלים קמו

שליח ציבור:

לְדוֹר וָדוֹר נַגִּיד גָּדְלֶךָ, וּלְנֵצַח נְצָחִים קְדֻשָּׁתְךָ נַקְדִּישׁ
וְשִׁבְחֲךָ אֱלֹהֵינוּ מִפִּינוּ לֹא יָמוּשׁ לְעוֹלָם וָעֶד
כִּי אֵל מֶלֶךְ גָּדוֹל וְקָדוֹשׁ אָתָּה.
בָּרוּךְ אַתָּה יהוה, הָאֵל הַקָּדוֹשׁ.

The שליח ציבור continues with אַתָּה חוֹנֵן on the next page.

HOLINESS

אַתָּה קָדוֹשׁ You are holy and Your name is holy,
and holy ones praise You daily, Selah!
Blessed are You, Lord, the holy God.

KNOWLEDGE

אַתָּה חוֹנֵן You grace humanity with knowledge
and teach mortals understanding.
Grace us with the knowledge, understanding
and discernment that come from You.
Blessed are You, Lord, who graciously grants knowledge.

REPENTANCE

הֲשִׁיבֵנוּ Bring us back, our Father,
to Your Torah.
Draw us near, our King,
to Your service.
Lead us back to You in perfect repentance.
Blessed are You, Lord, who desires repentance.

FORGIVENESS

Strike the left side of the chest at °.

סְלַח לָנוּ Forgive us, our Father, for we have °sinned.
Pardon us, our King, for we have °transgressed;
for You pardon and forgive.
Blessed are You, Lord,
the gracious One who repeatedly forgives.

REDEMPTION

רְאֵה Look on our affliction, plead our cause,
and redeem us soon for Your name's sake,
for You are a powerful Redeemer.
Blessed are You, Lord, the Redeemer of Israel.

קדושת השם
אַתָּה קָדוֹשׁ וְשִׁמְךָ קָדוֹשׁ
וּקְדוֹשִׁים בְּכָל יוֹם יְהַלְלוּךָ סֶּלָה.
בָּרוּךְ אַתָּה יהוה, הָאֵל הַקָּדוֹשׁ.

דעת
אַתָּה חוֹנֵן לְאָדָם דַּעַת
וּמְלַמֵּד לֶאֱנוֹשׁ בִּינָה.
חָנֵּנוּ מֵאִתְּךָ דֵּעָה בִּינָה וְהַשְׂכֵּל.
בָּרוּךְ אַתָּה יהוה, חוֹנֵן הַדָּעַת.

תשובה
הֲשִׁיבֵנוּ אָבִינוּ לְתוֹרָתֶךָ
וְקָרְבֵנוּ מַלְכֵּנוּ לַעֲבוֹדָתֶךָ
וְהַחֲזִירֵנוּ בִּתְשׁוּבָה שְׁלֵמָה לְפָנֶיךָ.
בָּרוּךְ אַתָּה יהוה, הָרוֹצֶה בִּתְשׁוּבָה.

סליחה
Strike the left side of the chest at °.
סְלַח לָנוּ אָבִינוּ כִּי °חָטָאנוּ
מְחַל לָנוּ מַלְכֵּנוּ כִּי °פָשָׁעְנוּ
כִּי מוֹחֵל וְסוֹלֵחַ אָתָּה.
בָּרוּךְ אַתָּה יהוה, חַנּוּן הַמַּרְבֶּה לִסְלֹחַ.

גאולה
רְאֵה בְעָנְיֵנוּ, וְרִיבָה רִיבֵנוּ
וּגְאָלֵנוּ מְהֵרָה לְמַעַן שְׁמֶךָ
כִּי גּוֹאֵל חָזָק אָתָּה.
בָּרוּךְ אַתָּה יהוה, גּוֹאֵל יִשְׂרָאֵל.

SHAḤARIT FOR TISHA B'AV

The Leader adds:
עֲנֵנוּ Answer us, LORD, answer us on our Fast Day, for we are in great distress. Look not at our wickedness. Do not hide Your face from us and do not ignore our plea. Be near to our cry; please let Your loving-kindness comfort us. Even before we call to You, answer us, as is said, "Before they call, I will answer. While they are still speaking, I will hear." *Is. 65* For You, LORD, are the One who answers in time of distress, redeems and rescues in all times of trouble and anguish. Blessed are You, LORD, who answers in time of distress.

HEALING

רְפָאֵנוּ Heal us, LORD, and we shall be healed.
Save us and we shall be saved,
for You are our praise.
Bring complete recovery for all our ailments,

> *The following prayer for a sick person may be said here:*
> May it be Your will, O LORD my God and God of my ancestors, that You speedily send a complete recovery from heaven, a healing of both soul and body, to the patient (*name*), son/daughter of (*mother's name*) among the other afflicted of Israel.

for You, God, King, are a faithful and compassionate Healer.
Blessed are You, LORD, Healer of the sick of His people Israel.

PROSPERITY

בָּרֵךְ Bless this year for us, LORD our God,
and all its types of produce for good.
Grant blessing
on the face of the earth,
and from its goodness satisfy us,
blessing our year as the best of years.
Blessed are You, LORD,
who blesses the years.

adds: שליח ציבור *The*

עֲנֵנוּ יהוה עֲנֵנוּ בְּיוֹם צוֹם תַּעֲנִיתֵנוּ, כִּי בְצָרָה גְדוֹלָה אֲנָחְנוּ. אַל
תֵּפֶן אֶל רִשְׁעֵנוּ, וְאַל תַּסְתֵּר פָּנֶיךָ מִמֶּנּוּ, וְאַל תִּתְעַלַּם מִתְּחִנָּתֵנוּ.
הֱיֵה נָא קָרוֹב לְשַׁוְעָתֵנוּ, יְהִי נָא חַסְדְּךָ לְנַחֲמֵנוּ, טֶרֶם נִקְרָא אֵלֶיךָ
עֲנֵנוּ, כַּדָּבָר שֶׁנֶּאֱמַר: וְהָיָה טֶרֶם יִקְרָאוּ וַאֲנִי אֶעֱנֶה, עוֹד הֵם מְדַבְּרִים ישעיה סה
וַאֲנִי אֶשְׁמָע: כִּי אַתָּה יהוה הָעוֹנֶה בְּעֵת צָרָה, פּוֹדֶה וּמַצִּיל בְּכָל
עֵת צָרָה וְצוּקָה. בָּרוּךְ אַתָּה יהוה, הָעוֹנֶה בְּעֵת צָרָה.

רפואה
רְפָאֵנוּ יהוה וְנֵרָפֵא
הוֹשִׁיעֵנוּ וְנִוָּשֵׁעָה, כִּי תְהִלָּתֵנוּ אָתָּה
וְהַעֲלֵה רְפוּאָה שְׁלֵמָה לְכָל מַכּוֹתֵינוּ

The following prayer for a sick person may be said here:

יְהִי רָצוֹן מִלְּפָנֶיךָ יהוה אֱלֹהַי וֵאלֹהֵי אֲבוֹתַי, שֶׁתִּשְׁלַח מְהֵרָה רְפוּאָה שְׁלֵמָה
מִן הַשָּׁמַיִם רְפוּאַת הַנֶּפֶשׁ וּרְפוּאַת הַגּוּף לַחוֹלֶה/לַחוֹלָה *name of patient*
בֶּן/בַּת *mother's name* בְּתוֹךְ שְׁאָר חוֹלֵי יִשְׂרָאֵל.

כִּי אֵל מֶלֶךְ רוֹפֵא נֶאֱמָן וְרַחֲמָן אָתָּה.
בָּרוּךְ אַתָּה יהוה, רוֹפֵא חוֹלֵי עַמּוֹ יִשְׂרָאֵל.

ברכת השנים
בָּרֵךְ עָלֵינוּ יהוה אֱלֹהֵינוּ אֶת הַשָּׁנָה הַזֹּאת
וְאֶת כָּל מִינֵי תְבוּאָתָהּ, לְטוֹבָה
וְתֵן בְּרָכָה עַל פְּנֵי הָאֲדָמָה, וְשַׂבְּעֵנוּ מִטּוּבָהּ
וּבָרֵךְ שְׁנָתֵנוּ כַּשָּׁנִים הַטּוֹבוֹת.
בָּרוּךְ אַתָּה יהוה, מְבָרֵךְ הַשָּׁנִים.

INGATHERING OF EXILES

תְּקַע Sound the great shofar for our freedom,
raise high the banner to gather our exiles,
and gather us together from the four quarters of the earth.
Blessed are You, Lord,
who gathers the dispersed of His people Israel.

JUSTICE

הָשִׁיבָה Restore our judges as at first
and our counselors as at the beginning,
and remove from us sorrow and sighing.
May You alone, Lord,
reign over us with loving-kindness and compassion,
and vindicate us in justice.
Blessed are You, Lord,
the King who loves righteousness and justice.

AGAINST INFORMERS

וְלַמַּלְשִׁינִים For the slanderers let there be no hope,
and may all wickedness perish in an instant.
May all Your people's enemies swiftly be cut down.
May You swiftly uproot, crush, cast down
and humble the arrogant swiftly in our days.
Blessed are You, Lord,
who destroys enemies and humbles the arrogant.

THE RIGHTEOUS

עַל הַצַּדִּיקִים To the righteous, the pious,
the elders of Your people the house of Israel,
the remnant of their scholars,
the righteous converts, and to us,
may Your compassion be aroused, Lord our God.
Grant a good reward to all who sincerely trust in Your name.

קיבוץ גלויות
תְּקַע בְּשׁוֹפָר גָּדוֹל לְחֵרוּתֵנוּ
וְשָׂא נֵס לְקַבֵּץ גָּלֻיּוֹתֵינוּ
וְקַבְּצֵנוּ יַחַד מֵאַרְבַּע כַּנְפוֹת הָאָרֶץ.
בָּרוּךְ אַתָּה יהוה, מְקַבֵּץ נִדְחֵי עַמּוֹ יִשְׂרָאֵל.

משפט
הָשִׁיבָה שׁוֹפְטֵינוּ כְּבָרִאשׁוֹנָה וְיוֹעֲצֵינוּ כְּבַתְּחִלָּה
וְהָסֵר מִמֶּנּוּ יָגוֹן וַאֲנָחָה
וּמְלֹךְ עָלֵינוּ אַתָּה יהוה לְבַדְּךָ בְּחֶסֶד וּבְרַחֲמִים
וְצַדְּקֵנוּ בַּמִּשְׁפָּט.
בָּרוּךְ אַתָּה יהוה, מֶלֶךְ אוֹהֵב צְדָקָה וּמִשְׁפָּט.

ברכת המינים
וְלַמַּלְשִׁינִים אַל תְּהִי תִקְוָה
וְכָל הָרִשְׁעָה כְּרֶגַע תֹּאבֵד
וְכָל אוֹיְבֵי עַמְּךָ מְהֵרָה יִכָּרֵתוּ
וְהַזֵּדִים מְהֵרָה תְעַקֵּר וּתְשַׁבֵּר וּתְמַגֵּר וְתַכְנִיעַ בִּמְהֵרָה בְיָמֵינוּ.
בָּרוּךְ אַתָּה יהוה, שׁוֹבֵר אוֹיְבִים וּמַכְנִיעַ זֵדִים.

על הצדיקים
עַל הַצַּדִּיקִים וְעַל הַחֲסִידִים
וְעַל זִקְנֵי עַמְּךָ בֵּית יִשְׂרָאֵל
וְעַל פְּלֵיטַת סוֹפְרֵיהֶם
וְעַל גֵּרֵי הַצֶּדֶק, וְעָלֵינוּ
יֶהֱמוּ רַחֲמֶיךָ יהוה אֱלֹהֵינוּ
וְתֵן שָׂכָר טוֹב לְכָל הַבּוֹטְחִים בְּשִׁמְךָ בֶּאֱמֶת

Set our lot with them,
so that we may never be ashamed, for in You we trust.
Blessed are You, Lord,
who is the support and trust of the righteous.

REBUILDING JERUSALEM

וְלִירוּשָׁלַיִם To Jerusalem, Your city,
may You return in compassion,
and may You dwell in it as You promised.
May You rebuild it rapidly in our days
as an everlasting structure,
and install within it soon the throne of David.
Blessed are You, Lord,
who builds Jerusalem.

KINGDOM OF DAVID

אֶת צֶמַח May the offshoot of Your servant David soon flower,
and may his pride be raised high by Your salvation,
for we wait for Your salvation all day.
Blessed are You, Lord,
who makes the glory of salvation flourish.

RESPONSE TO PRAYER

שְׁמַע קוֹלֵנוּ Listen to our voice, Lord our God.
Spare us and have compassion on us,
and in compassion and favor accept our prayer,
for You, God, listen to prayers and pleas.
Do not turn us away, O our King,
empty-handed from Your presence,
for You listen with compassion
to the prayer of Your people Israel.
Blessed are You, Lord,
who listens to prayer.

וְשִׂים חֶלְקֵנוּ עִמָּהֶם
וּלְעוֹלָם לֹא נֵבוֹשׁ כִּי בְךָ בָּטָחְנוּ.
בָּרוּךְ אַתָּה יהוה, מִשְׁעָן וּמִבְטָח לַצַּדִּיקִים.

בניין ירושלים

וְלִירוּשָׁלַיִם עִירְךָ בְּרַחֲמִים תָּשׁוּב
וְתִשְׁכֹּן בְּתוֹכָהּ כַּאֲשֶׁר דִּבַּרְתָּ
וּבְנֵה אוֹתָהּ בְּקָרוֹב בְּיָמֵינוּ בִּנְיַן עוֹלָם
וְכִסֵּא דָוִד מְהֵרָה לְתוֹכָהּ תָּכִין.
בָּרוּךְ אַתָּה יהוה, בּוֹנֵה יְרוּשָׁלָיִם.

מלכות בית דוד

אֶת צֶמַח דָּוִד עַבְדְּךָ מְהֵרָה תַצְמִיחַ, וְקַרְנוֹ תָּרוּם בִּישׁוּעָתֶךָ
כִּי לִישׁוּעָתְךָ קִוִּינוּ כָּל הַיּוֹם.
בָּרוּךְ אַתָּה יהוה, מַצְמִיחַ קֶרֶן יְשׁוּעָה.

שומע תפילה

שְׁמַע קוֹלֵנוּ יהוה אֱלֹהֵינוּ
חוּס וְרַחֵם עָלֵינוּ
וְקַבֵּל בְּרַחֲמִים וּבְרָצוֹן אֶת תְּפִלָּתֵנוּ
כִּי אֵל שׁוֹמֵעַ תְּפִלּוֹת וְתַחֲנוּנִים אָתָּה
וּמִלְּפָנֶיךָ מַלְכֵּנוּ רֵיקָם אַל תְּשִׁיבֵנוּ
כִּי אַתָּה שׁוֹמֵעַ תְּפִלַּת עַמְּךָ יִשְׂרָאֵל בְּרַחֲמִים.
בָּרוּךְ אַתָּה יהוה, שׁוֹמֵעַ תְּפִלָּה.

TEMPLE SERVICE

רְצֵה Find favor, Lord our God, in Your people Israel and their prayer.
Restore the service to Your most holy House,
and accept in love and favor
the fire-offerings of Israel and their prayer.
May the service of Your people Israel always find favor with You.
And may our eyes witness Your return to Zion in compassion.
Blessed are You, Lord, who restores His Presence to Zion.

THANKSGIVING

Bow at the first nine words.

מוֹדִים We give thanks to You,
for You are the Lord our God
and God of our ancestors
for ever and all time.
You are the Rock of our lives,
Shield of our salvation
from generation to generation.
We will thank You and
declare Your praise for our lives,
which are entrusted into Your hand;
for our souls,
which are placed in Your charge;
for Your miracles
which are with us every day;
and for Your wonders and favors
at all times, evening,
morning and midday.
You are good –
for Your compassion never fails.
You are compassionate –
for Your loving-kindnesses never cease.
We have always
placed our hope in You.

During the Leader's repetition,
the congregation says quietly:

מוֹדִים We give thanks to You,
for You are the Lord
our God
and God of our ancestors,
God of all flesh,
who formed us
and formed the universe.
Blessings and thanks are due
to Your great and holy name
for giving us life
and sustaining us.
May You continue
to give us life and sustain us;
and may You gather our exiles
to Your holy courts,
to keep Your decrees,
do Your will and serve You
with a perfect heart,
for it is for us
to give You thanks.
Blessed be God
to whom
thanksgiving is due.

עבודה

רְצֵה יהוה אֱלֹהֵינוּ בְּעַמְּךָ יִשְׂרָאֵל, וּבִתְפִלָּתָם
וְהָשֵׁב אֶת הָעֲבוֹדָה לִדְבִיר בֵּיתֶךָ
וְאִשֵּׁי יִשְׂרָאֵל וּתְפִלָּתָם בְּאַהֲבָה תְקַבֵּל בְּרָצוֹן
וּתְהִי לְרָצוֹן תָּמִיד עֲבוֹדַת יִשְׂרָאֵל עַמֶּךָ.
וְתֶחֱזֶינָה עֵינֵינוּ בְּשׁוּבְךָ לְצִיּוֹן בְּרַחֲמִים.
בָּרוּךְ אַתָּה יהוה, הַמַּחֲזִיר שְׁכִינָתוֹ לְצִיּוֹן.

הודאה

Bow at the first five words.

מוֹדִים אֲנַחְנוּ לָךְ
שָׁאַתָּה הוּא יהוה אֱלֹהֵינוּ
וֵאלֹהֵי אֲבוֹתֵינוּ לְעוֹלָם וָעֶד.
צוּר חַיֵּינוּ, מָגֵן יִשְׁעֵנוּ
אַתָּה הוּא לְדוֹר וָדוֹר.
נוֹדֶה לְּךָ וּנְסַפֵּר תְּהִלָּתֶךָ
עַל חַיֵּינוּ הַמְּסוּרִים בְּיָדֶךָ
וְעַל נִשְׁמוֹתֵינוּ הַפְּקוּדוֹת לָךְ
וְעַל נִסֶּיךָ שֶׁבְּכָל יוֹם עִמָּנוּ
וְעַל נִפְלְאוֹתֶיךָ וְטוֹבוֹתֶיךָ
שֶׁבְּכָל עֵת, עֶרֶב וָבֹקֶר וְצָהֳרָיִם.
הַטּוֹב, כִּי לֹא כָלוּ רַחֲמֶיךָ
וְהַמְרַחֵם, כִּי לֹא תַמּוּ חֲסָדֶיךָ
מֵעוֹלָם קִוִּינוּ לָךְ.

During חזרת הש״ץ, the קהל says quietly:

מוֹדִים אֲנַחְנוּ לָךְ
שָׁאַתָּה הוּא יהוה אֱלֹהֵינוּ
וֵאלֹהֵי אֲבוֹתֵינוּ
אֱלֹהֵי כָל בָּשָׂר
יוֹצְרֵנוּ, יוֹצֵר בְּרֵאשִׁית.
בְּרָכוֹת וְהוֹדָאוֹת
לְשִׁמְךָ הַגָּדוֹל וְהַקָּדוֹשׁ
עַל שֶׁהֶחֱיִיתָנוּ וְקִיַּמְתָּנוּ.
כֵּן תְּחַיֵּנוּ וּתְקַיְּמֵנוּ
וְתֶאֱסוֹף גָּלֻיּוֹתֵינוּ
לְחַצְרוֹת קָדְשֶׁךָ
לִשְׁמוֹר חֻקֶּיךָ וְלַעֲשׂוֹת רְצוֹנֶךָ
וּלְעָבְדְּךָ בְּלֵבָב שָׁלֵם
עַל שֶׁאֲנַחְנוּ מוֹדִים לָךְ.
בָּרוּךְ אֵל הַהוֹדָאוֹת.

וְעַל כֻּלָּם For all these things may Your name be blessed and
exalted, our King, continually, for ever and all time.
Let all that lives thank You, Selah! and praise Your name in truth,
God, our Savior and Help, Selah!
ᵛBlessed are You, LORD, whose name is "the Good"
and to whom thanks are due.

> *The Kohanim do not bless the congregation during the repetition of the Amida.*

PEACE

שִׂים שָׁלוֹם Grant peace, goodness and blessing,
grace, loving-kindness and compassion to us
and all Israel Your people.
Bless us, our Father, all as one, with the light of Your face,
for by the light of Your face You have given us, LORD our God,
the Torah of life and love of kindness,
righteousness, blessing, compassion, life and peace.
May it be good in Your eyes to bless Your people Israel
at every time, in every hour, with Your peace.
Blessed are You, LORD,
who blesses His people Israel with peace.

The following verse concludes the Leader's repetition of the Amida.
Some also say it here as part of the silent Amida.

May the words of my mouth and the meditation of my heart   *Ps. 19*
find favor before You, LORD, my Rock and Redeemer.

אֱלֹהַי My God,   *Berakhot 17a*
guard my tongue from evil and my lips from deceitful speech.
To those who curse me, let my soul be silent;
may my soul be to all like the dust.
Open my heart to Your Torah and let my soul
pursue Your commandments.
As for all who plan evil against me,
swiftly thwart their counsel and frustrate their plans.

וְעַל כֻּלָּם יִתְבָּרַךְ וְיִתְרוֹמַם שִׁמְךָ מַלְכֵּנוּ תָּמִיד לְעוֹלָם וָעֶד.
וְכֹל הַחַיִּים יוֹדוּךָ סֶּלָה, וִיהַלְלוּ אֶת שִׁמְךָ בֶּאֱמֶת
הָאֵל יְשׁוּעָתֵנוּ וְעֶזְרָתֵנוּ סֶלָה.
בָּרוּךְ אַתָּה יהוה, הַטּוֹב שִׁמְךָ וּלְךָ נָאֶה לְהוֹדוֹת.

ברכת כהנים is not said during חזרת הש״ץ.

שלום

שִׂים שָׁלוֹם טוֹבָה וּבְרָכָה
חֵן וָחֶסֶד וְרַחֲמִים עָלֵינוּ וְעַל כָּל יִשְׂרָאֵל עַמֶּךָ.
בָּרְכֵנוּ אָבִינוּ כֻּלָּנוּ כְּאֶחָד בְּאוֹר פָּנֶיךָ
כִּי בְאוֹר פָּנֶיךָ נָתַתָּ לָּנוּ יהוה אֱלֹהֵינוּ
תּוֹרַת חַיִּים וְאַהֲבַת חֶסֶד
וּצְדָקָה וּבְרָכָה וְרַחֲמִים וְחַיִּים וְשָׁלוֹם.
וְטוֹב בְּעֵינֶיךָ לְבָרֵךְ אֶת עַמְּךָ יִשְׂרָאֵל
בְּכָל עֵת וּבְכָל שָׁעָה בִּשְׁלוֹמֶךָ.
בָּרוּךְ אַתָּה יהוה, הַמְבָרֵךְ אֶת עַמּוֹ יִשְׂרָאֵל בַּשָּׁלוֹם.

The following verse concludes the חזרת הש״ץ.
Some also say it here as part of the silent עמידה.

תהלים יט

יִהְיוּ לְרָצוֹן אִמְרֵי־פִי וְהֶגְיוֹן לִבִּי לְפָנֶיךָ, יהוה צוּרִי וְגֹאֲלִי:

ברכות יז.

אֱלֹהַי
נְצֹר לְשׁוֹנִי מֵרָע וּשְׂפָתַי מִדַּבֵּר מִרְמָה
וְלִמְקַלְלַי נַפְשִׁי תִדֹּם, וְנַפְשִׁי כֶּעָפָר לַכֹּל תִּהְיֶה.
פְּתַח לִבִּי בְּתוֹרָתֶךָ, וּבְמִצְוֹתֶיךָ תִּרְדֹּף נַפְשִׁי.
וְכָל הַחוֹשְׁבִים עָלַי רָעָה
מְהֵרָה הָפֵר עֲצָתָם וְקַלְקֵל מַחֲשַׁבְתָּם.

Act for the sake of Your name; act for the sake of Your right hand;
act for the sake of Your holiness; act for the sake of Your Torah.
That Your beloved ones may be delivered, *Ps. 60*
save with Your right hand and answer me.
May the words of my mouth and the meditation of my heart *Ps. 19*
find favor before You, LORD, my Rock and Redeemer.

Bow, take three steps back, then bow, first left, then right, then center, while saying:

May He who makes peace in His high places,
make peace for us and all Israel – and say: Amen.

יְהִי רָצוֹן May it be Your will, LORD our God and God of our ancestors,
that the Temple be rebuilt speedily in our days,
and grant us a share in Your Torah. And there we will serve You
with reverence, as in the days of old and as in former years.
Then the offering of Judah and Jerusalem will be pleasing to the LORD *Mal. 3*
as in the days of old and as in former years.

When praying with a minyan, the Amida is repeated aloud by the Leader.

HALF KADDISH

Leader: יִתְגַּדַּל Magnified and sanctified
may His great name be,
in the world He created by His will.
May He establish His kingdom
in your lifetime and in your days,
and in the lifetime of all the house of Israel,
swiftly and soon – and say: Amen.

All: May His great name be blessed for ever and all time.

Leader: Blessed and praised, glorified and exalted,
raised and honored, uplifted and lauded
be the name of the Holy One,
blessed be He,
beyond any blessing,
song, praise and consolation
uttered in the world – and say: Amen.

עֲשֵׂה לְמַעַן שְׁמֶךָ, עֲשֵׂה לְמַעַן יְמִינֶךָ,
עֲשֵׂה לְמַעַן קְדֻשָּׁתֶךָ, עֲשֵׂה לְמַעַן תּוֹרָתֶךָ.
לְמַעַן יֵחָלְצוּן יְדִידֶיךָ, הוֹשִׁיעָה יְמִינְךָ וַעֲנֵנִי:
יִהְיוּ לְרָצוֹן אִמְרֵי־פִי וְהֶגְיוֹן לִבִּי לְפָנֶיךָ, יהוה צוּרִי וְגֹאֲלִי:

תהלים ס

תהלים יט

Bow, take three steps back, then bow, first left, then right, then center, while saying:

עֹשֶׂה שָׁלוֹם בִּמְרוֹמָיו
הוּא יַעֲשֶׂה שָׁלוֹם עָלֵינוּ וְעַל כָּל יִשְׂרָאֵל, וְאִמְרוּ אָמֵן.

יְהִי רָצוֹן מִלְּפָנֶיךָ יהוה אֱלֹהֵינוּ וֵאלֹהֵי אֲבוֹתֵינוּ
שֶׁיִּבָּנֶה בֵּית הַמִּקְדָּשׁ בִּמְהֵרָה בְיָמֵינוּ, וְתֵן חֶלְקֵנוּ בְּתוֹרָתֶךָ
וְשָׁם נַעֲבָדְךָ בְּיִרְאָה כִּימֵי עוֹלָם וּכְשָׁנִים קַדְמֹנִיּוֹת.
וְעָרְבָה לַיהוה מִנְחַת יְהוּדָה וִירוּשָׁלָ͏ִם כִּימֵי עוֹלָם וּכְשָׁנִים קַדְמֹנִיּוֹת:

מלאכי ג

When praying with a מנין, the עמידה is repeated aloud by the שליח ציבור.

חצי קדיש

ש״ץ: יִתְגַּדַּל וְיִתְקַדַּשׁ שְׁמֵהּ רַבָּא (קהל: אָמֵן)
בְּעָלְמָא דִּי בְרָא כִרְעוּתֵהּ, וְיַמְלִיךְ מַלְכוּתֵהּ
בְּחַיֵּיכוֹן וּבְיוֹמֵיכוֹן וּבְחַיֵּי דְכָל בֵּית יִשְׂרָאֵל
בַּעֲגָלָא וּבִזְמַן קָרִיב, וְאִמְרוּ אָמֵן. (קהל: אָמֵן)

קהל
וש״ץ: יְהֵא שְׁמֵהּ רַבָּא מְבָרַךְ לְעָלַם וּלְעָלְמֵי עָלְמַיָּא.

ש״ץ: יִתְבָּרַךְ וְיִשְׁתַּבַּח וְיִתְפָּאַר וְיִתְרוֹמַם וְיִתְנַשֵּׂא
וְיִתְהַדָּר וְיִתְעַלֶּה וְיִתְהַלָּל
שְׁמֵהּ דְּקֻדְשָׁא בְּרִיךְ הוּא (קהל: בְּרִיךְ הוּא)
לְעֵלָּא מִן כָּל בִּרְכָתָא וְשִׁירָתָא, תֻּשְׁבְּחָתָא וְנֶחֱמָתָא
דַּאֲמִירָן בְּעָלְמָא
וְאִמְרוּ אָמֵן. (קהל: אָמֵן)

REMOVING THE TORAH FROM THE ARK

The Ark is opened and the congregation stands. All say:

וַיְהִי בִּנְסֹעַ Whenever the Ark set out, Moses would say, "Arise, LORD, and may Your enemies be scattered. May those who hate You flee before You." For the Torah shall come forth from Zion, and the word of the LORD from Jerusalem. Blessed is He who in His holiness gave the Torah to His people Israel. *Num. 10 / Is. 2*

Blessed is the name of the Master of the Universe. Blessed is Your crown and Your place. May Your favor always be with Your people Israel. Show Your people the salvation of Your right hand in Your Temple. Grant us the gift of Your good light, and accept our prayers in mercy. May it be Your will to prolong our life in goodness. May I be counted among the righteous, so that You will have compassion on me and protect me and all that is mine and all that is Your people Israel's. You feed all; You sustain all; You rule over all; You rule over kings, for sovereignty is Yours. I am a servant of the Holy One, blessed be He, before whom and before whose glorious Torah I bow at all times. Not in man do I trust, nor on any angel do I rely, but on the God of heaven who is the God of truth, whose Torah is truth, whose prophets speak truth, and who abounds in acts of love and truth. ▸ In Him I trust, and to His holy and glorious name I offer praises. May it be Your will to open my heart to the Torah, and to fulfill the wishes of my heart and of the hearts of all Your people Israel for good, for life, and for peace. *Zohar, Parashat Vayak-hel*

The Leader takes the Torah scroll in his right arm, bows toward the Ark and says:

Magnify the LORD with me, and let us exalt His name together. *Ps. 34*

The Ark is closed. The Leader carries the Torah scroll to the bima and the congregation says:

לְךָ Yours, LORD, are the greatness and the power, the glory and the majesty and splendor, for everything in heaven and earth is Yours. Yours, LORD, is the kingdom; You are exalted as head over all. *1 Chr. 29*

רוֹמְמוּ Exalt the LORD our God and bow to His footstool; He is holy. Exalt the LORD our God, and bow at His holy mountain, for holy is the LORD our God. *Ps. 99*

אַב הָרַחֲמִים May the Father of compassion have compassion on the people borne by Him. May He remember the covenant with the mighty [patriarchs], and deliver us from evil times. May He reproach the evil instinct in the people carried by Him, and graciously grant that we be an everlasting remnant. May He fulfill in good measure our requests for salvation and compassion.

הוצאת ספר תורה

The ארון קודש is opened and the קהל stands. All say:

וַיְהִי בִּנְסֹעַ הָאָרֹן וַיֹּאמֶר מֹשֶׁה, קוּמָה יהוה וְיָפֻצוּ אֹיְבֶיךָ וְיָנֻסוּ מְשַׂנְאֶיךָ מִפָּנֶיךָ: כִּי מִצִּיּוֹן תֵּצֵא תוֹרָה וּדְבַר־יהוה מִירוּשָׁלָיִם: בָּרוּךְ שֶׁנָּתַן תּוֹרָה לְעַמּוֹ יִשְׂרָאֵל בִּקְדֻשָּׁתוֹ.

במדבר י

ישעיה ב

בְּרִיךְ שְׁמֵהּ דְּמָרֵא עָלְמָא, בְּרִיךְ כִּתְרָךְ וְאַתְרָךְ. יְהֵא רְעוּתָךְ עִם עַמָּךְ יִשְׂרָאֵל לְעָלַם, וּפֻרְקַן יְמִינָךְ אַחֲזֵי לְעַמָּךְ בְּבֵית מַקְדְּשָׁךְ, וּלְאַמְטוֹיֵי לָנָא מִטּוּב נְהוֹרָךְ, וּלְקַבֵּל צְלוֹתָנָא בְּרַחֲמִין. יְהֵא רַעֲוָא קֳדָמָךְ דְּתוֹרִיךְ לָן חַיִּין בְּטִיבוּ, וְלֶהֱוֵי אֲנָא פְקִידָא בְּגוֹ צַדִּיקַיָּא, לְמִרְחַם עֲלַי וּלְמִנְטַר יָתִי וְיָת כָּל דִּי לִי וְדִי לְעַמָּךְ יִשְׂרָאֵל. אַנְתְּ הוּא זָן לְכֹלָּא וּמְפַרְנֵס לְכֹלָּא, אַנְתְּ הוּא שַׁלִּיט עַל כֹּלָּא, אַנְתְּ הוּא דְשַׁלִּיט עַל מַלְכַיָּא, וּמַלְכוּתָא דִּילָךְ הִיא. אֲנָא עַבְדָּא דְקֻדְשָׁא בְּרִיךְ הוּא, דְּסָגִדְנָא קַמֵּהּ וּמִקַּמֵּי דִּיקַר אוֹרַיְתֵהּ בְּכָל עִדָּן וְעִדָּן. לָא עַל אֱנָשׁ רָחִיצְנָא וְלָא עַל בַּר אֱלָהִין סָמִיכְנָא, אֶלָּא בֵּאלָהָא דִשְׁמַיָּא, דְּהוּא אֱלָהָא קְשׁוֹט, וְאוֹרַיְתֵהּ קְשׁוֹט, וּנְבִיאוֹהִי קְשׁוֹט, וּמַסְגֵּא לְמֶעְבַּד טָבְוָן וּקְשׁוֹט. ‹ בֵּהּ אֲנָא רָחִיץ, וְלִשְׁמֵהּ קַדִּישָׁא יַקִּירָא אֲנָא אֵמַר תֻּשְׁבְּחָן. יְהֵא רַעֲוָא קֳדָמָךְ דְּתִפְתַּח לִבַּאי בְּאוֹרַיְתָא, וְתַשְׁלִים מִשְׁאֲלִין דְּלִבַּאי וְלִבָּא דְכָל עַמָּךְ יִשְׂרָאֵל לְטַב וּלְחַיִּין וְלִשְׁלָם.

זוהר ויקהל

The שליח ציבור takes the ספר תורה in his right arm, bows toward the ארון קודש and says:

גַּדְּלוּ לַיהוה אִתִּי וּנְרוֹמְמָה שְׁמוֹ יַחְדָּו:

תהלים לד

The ארון קודש is closed. The שליח ציבור carries the ספר תורה to the בימה and the קהל says:

לְךָ יהוה הַגְּדֻלָּה וְהַגְּבוּרָה וְהַתִּפְאֶרֶת וְהַנֵּצַח וְהַהוֹד, כִּי־כֹל בַּשָּׁמַיִם וּבָאָרֶץ, לְךָ יהוה הַמַּמְלָכָה וְהַמִּתְנַשֵּׂא לְכֹל לְרֹאשׁ:

דברי הימים א, כט

רוֹמְמוּ יהוה אֱלֹהֵינוּ וְהִשְׁתַּחֲווּ לַהֲדֹם רַגְלָיו, קָדוֹשׁ הוּא: רוֹמְמוּ יהוה אֱלֹהֵינוּ וְהִשְׁתַּחֲווּ לְהַר קָדְשׁוֹ, כִּי־קָדוֹשׁ יהוה אֱלֹהֵינוּ:

תהילים צט

אַב הָרַחֲמִים הוּא יְרַחֵם עַם עֲמוּסִים, וְיִזְכֹּר בְּרִית אֵיתָנִים, וְיַצִּיל נַפְשׁוֹתֵינוּ מִן הַשָּׁעוֹת הָרָעוֹת, וְיִגְעַר בְּיֵצֶר הָרָע מִן הַנְּשׂוּאִים, וְיָחֹן אוֹתָנוּ לִפְלֵיטַת עוֹלָמִים, וִימַלֵּא מִשְׁאֲלוֹתֵינוּ בְּמִדָּה טוֹבָה יְשׁוּעָה וְרַחֲמִים.

SHAHARIT FOR TISHA B'AV

The Torah scroll is placed on the bima and the Gabbai calls a Kohen to the Torah.

May His kingship over us be soon revealed and made manifest. May He be gracious to our surviving remnant, the remnant of His people the house of Israel in grace, loving-kindness, compassion and favor, and let us say Amen. Let us all render greatness to our God and give honor to the Torah. *Let the Kohen come forward. Arise (*name* son of *father's name*), the Kohen.

*If no Kohen is present, a Levi or Yisrael is called up as follows:

/As there is no Kohen, arise (*name* son of *father's name*) in place of a Kohen./

Blessed is He who, in His holiness, gave the Torah to His people Israel.

Congregation followed by the Gabbai:

You who cling to the LORD your God are all alive today.   *Deut. 4*

The Reader shows the oleh the section to be read. The oleh touches the scroll at that place with the belt or mantle of the Torah, which he then kisses. Holding the handles of the scroll, he says:

Oleh: Bless the LORD, the blessed One.

Cong: Bless the LORD, the blessed One, for ever and all time.

Oleh: Bless the LORD, the blessed One, for ever and all time.

    Blessed are You, LORD our God, King of the Universe,
    who has chosen us from all peoples and has given us His Torah.
    Blessed are You, LORD, Giver of the Torah.

After the reading, the oleh says:

Oleh: Blessed are You, LORD our God, King of the Universe,
    who has given us the Torah of truth,
    planting everlasting life in our midst.
    Blessed are You, LORD, Giver of the Torah.

The ספר תורה is placed on the שולחן and the גבאי calls a כהן to the תורה.

וְתִגָּלֶה וְתֵרָאֶה מַלְכוּתוֹ עָלֵינוּ בִּזְמַן קָרוֹב, וְיָחֹן פְּלֵיטָתֵנוּ וּפְלֵיטַת עַמּוֹ בֵּית יִשְׂרָאֵל לְחֵן וּלְחֶסֶד וּלְרַחֲמִים וּלְרָצוֹן וְנֹאמַר אָמֵן. הַכֹּל הָבוּ גֹדֶל לֵאלֹהֵינוּ וּתְנוּ כָבוֹד לַתּוֹרָה. *כֹּהֵן קְרַב, יַעֲמֹד (פלוני בֶּן פלוני) הַכֹּהֵן.

*If no כהן is present, a לוי or ישראל is called up as follows:

/אֵין כָּאן כֹּהֵן, יַעֲמֹד (פלוני בֶּן פלוני) בִּמְקוֹם כֹּהֵן./

בָּרוּךְ שֶׁנָּתַן תּוֹרָה לְעַמּוֹ יִשְׂרָאֵל בִּקְדֻשָּׁתוֹ.

גבאי: followed by the קהל:

דברים ד

וְאַתֶּם הַדְּבֵקִים בַּיהוה אֱלֹהֵיכֶם חַיִּים כֻּלְּכֶם הַיּוֹם:

The קורא shows the עולה the section to be read. The עולה touches the ספר תורה at that place with the belt or mantle of the תורה, which he then kisses. Holding the handles of the ספר תורה, he says:

עולה: בָּרְכוּ אֶת יהוה הַמְבֹרָךְ.

קהל: בָּרוּךְ יהוה הַמְבֹרָךְ לְעוֹלָם וָעֶד.

עולה: בָּרוּךְ יהוה הַמְבֹרָךְ לְעוֹלָם וָעֶד.

בָּרוּךְ אַתָּה יהוה, אֱלֹהֵינוּ מֶלֶךְ הָעוֹלָם אֲשֶׁר בָּחַר בָּנוּ מִכָּל הָעַמִּים וְנָתַן לָנוּ אֶת תּוֹרָתוֹ. בָּרוּךְ אַתָּה יהוה, נוֹתֵן הַתּוֹרָה.

After the קריאת התורה (on the next page) the עולה says:

עולה: בָּרוּךְ אַתָּה יהוה אֱלֹהֵינוּ מֶלֶךְ הָעוֹלָם אֲשֶׁר נָתַן לָנוּ תּוֹרַת אֱמֶת וְחַיֵּי עוֹלָם נָטַע בְּתוֹכֵנוּ. בָּרוּךְ אַתָּה יהוה, נוֹתֵן הַתּוֹרָה.

TORAH READING

When you shall beget children, and children's children, and you shall have remained long in the land, and shall deal corruptly, and make a carved idol, the likeness of anything, and shall do evil in the sight of the Lord your God, to provoke Him to anger: I call heaven and earth to witness against you this day, that you shall soon utterly perish from the land into which you go over the Jordan to possess it; you shall not prolong your days upon it, but shall utterly be destroyed. And the Lord shall scatter you among the nations, and you shall be left few in number among the nations, where the Lord shall lead you. And there you shall serve gods, the work of men's hands, wood and stone, which neither see, nor hear, nor eat, nor smell. But if from there you shall seek the Lord your God, you shall find Him, if you seek Him with all your heart and with all your soul. *When you are in distress, and all these things are come upon you, in the latter days, if you turn to the Lord your God, and are obedient to His voice; (for the Lord your God is a merciful God;) He will not forsake you, nor will He destroy you, nor forget the covenant of your fathers which He swore to them. For ask now of the days that are past, which were before you, since the day that God created man upon the earth, and from the one side of heaven to the other, whether there has been any such thing as this great thing is, or whether aught has been heard like it? Did ever people hear the voice of God speaking out of the midst of the fire, as you have heard, and live? Or has God ventured to go and take Him a nation from the midst of another nation, by trials, by signs, and by wonders, and by war, and by a mighty hand, and by an outstretched arm, and by great terrors, according to all that the Lord your God did for you in Egypt before your eyes? To you it was shown, that you might know that the Lord, He is God; there is none else beside Him. *Out of heaven He made you hear His voice, that He might instruct you: and upon earth He showed you His great fire; and you did hear His words out of the midst of the fire. And because He loved your fathers, therefore, He chose their seed after them, and brought you out, He Himself being present, with His mighty power, out of Egypt; to drive

Deut. 4:25–40

Levi

Yisrael (Maftir)

קריאת התורה

דברים
ד,כה-מ

כִּי־תוֹלִיד בָּנִים וּבְנֵי בָנִים וְנוֹשַׁנְתֶּם בָּאָרֶץ וְהִשְׁחַתֶּם וַעֲשִׂיתֶם פֶּסֶל תְּמוּנַת כֹּל וַעֲשִׂיתֶם הָרַע בְּעֵינֵי־יְהוָה־אֱלֹהֶיךָ לְהַכְעִיסוֹ: הַעִידֹתִי בָכֶם הַיּוֹם אֶת־הַשָּׁמַיִם וְאֶת־הָאָרֶץ כִּי־אָבֹד תֹּאבֵדוּן מַהֵר מֵעַל הָאָרֶץ אֲשֶׁר אַתֶּם עֹבְרִים אֶת־הַיַּרְדֵּן שָׁמָּה לְרִשְׁתָּהּ לֹא־תַאֲרִיכֻן יָמִים עָלֶיהָ כִּי הִשָּׁמֵד תִּשָּׁמֵדוּן: וְהֵפִיץ יְהוָה אֶתְכֶם בָּעַמִּים וְנִשְׁאַרְתֶּם מְתֵי מִסְפָּר בַּגּוֹיִם אֲשֶׁר יְנַהֵג יְהוָה אֶתְכֶם שָׁמָּה: וַעֲבַדְתֶּם־שָׁם אֱלֹהִים מַעֲשֵׂה יְדֵי אָדָם עֵץ וָאֶבֶן אֲשֶׁר לֹא־יִרְאוּן וְלֹא יִשְׁמְעוּן וְלֹא יֹאכְלוּן וְלֹא יְרִיחֻן: וּבִקַּשְׁתֶּם מִשָּׁם אֶת־יְהוָה אֱלֹהֶיךָ וּמָצָאתָ כִּי תִדְרְשֶׁנּוּ בְּכָל־לְבָבְךָ וּבְכָל־נַפְשֶׁךָ:

לוי

*בַּצַּר לְךָ וּמְצָאוּךָ כֹּל הַדְּבָרִים הָאֵלֶּה בְּאַחֲרִית הַיָּמִים וְשַׁבְתָּ עַד־יְהוָה אֱלֹהֶיךָ וְשָׁמַעְתָּ בְּקֹלוֹ: כִּי אֵל רַחוּם יְהוָה אֱלֹהֶיךָ לֹא יַרְפְּךָ וְלֹא יַשְׁחִיתֶךָ וְלֹא יִשְׁכַּח אֶת־בְּרִית אֲבֹתֶיךָ אֲשֶׁר נִשְׁבַּע לָהֶם: כִּי שְׁאַל־נָא לְיָמִים רִאשֹׁנִים אֲשֶׁר־הָיוּ לְפָנֶיךָ לְמִן־הַיּוֹם אֲשֶׁר בָּרָא אֱלֹהִים ׀ אָדָם עַל־הָאָרֶץ וּלְמִקְצֵה הַשָּׁמַיִם וְעַד־קְצֵה הַשָּׁמָיִם הֲנִהְיָה כַּדָּבָר הַגָּדוֹל הַזֶּה אוֹ הֲנִשְׁמַע כָּמֹהוּ: הֲשָׁמַע עָם קוֹל אֱלֹהִים מְדַבֵּר מִתּוֹךְ־הָאֵשׁ כַּאֲשֶׁר־שָׁמַעְתָּ אַתָּה וַיֶּחִי: אוֹ ׀ הֲנִסָּה אֱלֹהִים לָבוֹא לָקַחַת לוֹ גוֹי מִקֶּרֶב גּוֹי בְּמַסֹּת בְּאֹתֹת וּבְמוֹפְתִים וּבְמִלְחָמָה וּבְיָד חֲזָקָה וּבִזְרוֹעַ נְטוּיָה וּבְמוֹרָאִים גְּדֹלִים כְּכֹל אֲשֶׁר־עָשָׂה לָכֶם יְהוָה אֱלֹהֵיכֶם בְּמִצְרַיִם לְעֵינֶיךָ: אַתָּה הָרְאֵתָ לָדַעַת כִּי יְהוָה הוּא הָאֱלֹהִים אֵין עוֹד מִלְּבַדּוֹ:

ישראל
(מפטיר)

*מִן־הַשָּׁמַיִם הִשְׁמִיעֲךָ אֶת־קֹלוֹ לְיַסְּרֶךָּ וְעַל־הָאָרֶץ הֶרְאֲךָ אֶת־אִשּׁוֹ הַגְּדוֹלָה וּדְבָרָיו שָׁמַעְתָּ מִתּוֹךְ הָאֵשׁ: וְתַחַת כִּי אָהַב אֶת־אֲבֹתֶיךָ וַיִּבְחַר בְּזַרְעוֹ אַחֲרָיו וַיּוֹצִאֲךָ בְּפָנָיו בְּכֹחוֹ הַגָּדֹל מִמִּצְרָיִם: לְהוֹרִישׁ גּוֹיִם גְּדֹלִים וַעֲצֻמִים מִמְּךָ

out nations from before you greater and mightier than you are, to bring you in, to give you their land for an inheritance, as it is this day. Know therefore this day, and consider it in your heare, that the Lord He is God in heaven above, and upon the earth beneath: there is no other. You shall keep therefore His statutes, and His commandments, which I command you this day, that it may go well with you, and with your children after you, and that you may prolong your days upon the earth, which the Lord your God gives you, for ever.

HALF KADDISH

After the Reading of the Torah, the Reader says Half Kaddish:

Reader: יִתְגַּדֵּל Magnified and sanctified
may His great name be,
in the world He created by His will.
May He establish His kingdom
in your lifetime and in your days,
and in the lifetime of all the house of Israel,
swiftly and soon –
and say: Amen.

All: May His great name be blessed for ever and all time.

Reader: Blessed and praised, glorified and exalted,
raised and honored, uplifted and lauded
be the name of the Holy One, blessed be He,
beyond any blessing,
song, praise and consolation
uttered in the world –
and say: Amen.

מִפָּנֶיךָ לַהֲבִיאֲךָ לָתֶת־לְךָ אֶת־אַרְצָם נַחֲלָה כַּיּוֹם הַזֶּה: וְיָדַעְתָּ הַיּוֹם וַהֲשֵׁבֹתָ אֶל־לְבָבֶךָ כִּי יהוה הוּא הָאֱלֹהִים בַּשָּׁמַיִם מִמַּעַל וְעַל־הָאָרֶץ מִתָּחַת אֵין עוֹד: וְשָׁמַרְתָּ אֶת־חֻקָּיו וְאֶת־מִצְוֺתָיו אֲשֶׁר אָנֹכִי מְצַוְּךָ הַיּוֹם אֲשֶׁר יִיטַב לְךָ וּלְבָנֶיךָ אַחֲרֶיךָ וּלְמַעַן תַּאֲרִיךְ יָמִים עַל־הָאֲדָמָה אֲשֶׁר יהוה אֱלֹהֶיךָ נֹתֵן לְךָ כָּל־הַיָּמִים:

חצי קדיש

חצי קדיש: קורא says קריאת התורה, the After the

קורא: יִתְגַּדַּל וְיִתְקַדַּשׁ שְׁמֵהּ רַבָּא (קהל: אָמֵן)
בְּעָלְמָא דִּי בְרָא כִרְעוּתֵהּ
וְיַמְלִיךְ מַלְכוּתֵהּ
בְּחַיֵּיכוֹן וּבְיוֹמֵיכוֹן וּבְחַיֵּי דְּכָל בֵּית יִשְׂרָאֵל
בַּעֲגָלָא וּבִזְמַן קָרִיב
וְאִמְרוּ אָמֵן. (קהל: אָמֵן)

קורא וקהל: יְהֵא שְׁמֵהּ רַבָּא מְבָרַךְ לְעָלַם וּלְעָלְמֵי עָלְמַיָּא.

קורא: יִתְבָּרַךְ וְיִשְׁתַּבַּח וְיִתְפָּאַר וְיִתְרוֹמַם וְיִתְנַשֵּׂא
וְיִתְהַדָּר וְיִתְעַלֶּה וְיִתְהַלָּל
שְׁמֵהּ דְּקֻדְשָׁא בְּרִיךְ הוּא (קהל: בְּרִיךְ הוּא)
לְעֵלָּא מִן כָּל בִּרְכָתָא וְשִׁירָתָא, תֻּשְׁבְּחָתָא וְנֶחֱמָתָא
דַּאֲמִירָן בְּעָלְמָא
וְאִמְרוּ אָמֵן. (קהל: אָמֵן)

SHAHARIT FOR TISHA B'AV

HAGBAHA AND GELILA

The Torah scroll is lifted and the congregation says:

וְזֹאת הַתּוֹרָה This is the Torah *Deut. 4*
that Moses placed before the children of Israel,
at the Lord's commandment, by the hand of Moses. *Num. 9*

Some add:

It is a tree of life to those who grasp it, and those who uphold it are happy. *Prov. 3*
Its ways are ways of pleasantness, and all its paths are peace.
Long life is at its right hand; at its left, riches and honor.
It pleased the Lord for the sake of [Israel's] righteousness, *Is. 42*
to make the Torah great and glorious.

BLESSINGS BEFORE READING THE HAFTARA

Before reading the Haftara, the person called up for Maftir says:

בָּרוּךְ Blessed are You, Lord our God, King of the Universe, who chose good prophets and was pleased with their words, spoken in truth. Blessed are You, Lord, who chose the Torah, His servant Moses, His people Israel, and the prophets of truth and righteousness.

HAFTARA

I will surely consume them, says the Lord: There shall be no grapes on *Jer. 8:13–9:23* the vine, nor figs on the fig tree, and the leaf shall fade; the things that I have given them shall pass away from them. Why do we sit still? Assemble yourselves, and let us enter into the fortified cities, and let us be cut off there: for the Lord our God has cut us off, and given us water of gall to drink, because we have sinned against the Lord. We looked for peace, but no good came; and for a time of health, and behold terror! The snorting of his horses is heard from Dan: the whole land trembles at the sound of the neighing of his strong ones; for they are come, and have devoured the land, and all that is in it; the city, and those who dwell therein. For, behold, I will send venomous serpents among you, which will not be charmed, and they shall bite you, says the Lord. When I would comfort myself against sorrow, my heart is faint in me. Behold the voice of the cry of the daughter of my people coming from a far country: Is not the Lord in Zion? Is not her king in her? Why have they provoked me to anger with their carved idols, and with foreign vanities? The harvest is past, the summer is ended, and we are not saved. For the hurt of the daughter of my people, I am broken; I am thrown into gloom: astonishment has taken

הגבהה וגלילה

The ספר תורה is lifted and the קהל says:

דברים ד
וְזֹאת הַתּוֹרָה אֲשֶׁר־שָׂם מֹשֶׁה לִפְנֵי בְּנֵי יִשְׂרָאֵל:
במדבר ט
עַל־פִּי יהוה בְּיַד־מֹשֶׁה:

Some add:

משלי ג
עֵץ־חַיִּים הִיא לַמַּחֲזִיקִים בָּהּ וְתֹמְכֶיהָ מְאֻשָּׁר:
דְּרָכֶיהָ דַרְכֵי־נֹעַם וְכָל־נְתִיבוֹתֶיהָ שָׁלוֹם:
אֹרֶךְ יָמִים בִּימִינָהּ, בִּשְׂמֹאולָהּ עֹשֶׁר וְכָבוֹד:
ישעיה מב
יהוה חָפֵץ לְמַעַן צִדְקוֹ יַגְדִּיל תּוֹרָה וְיַאְדִּיר:

ברכות ההפטרה

Before reading the הפטרה, the person called up for מפטיר says:

בָּרוּךְ אַתָּה יהוה אֱלֹהֵינוּ מֶלֶךְ הָעוֹלָם אֲשֶׁר בָּחַר בִּנְבִיאִים טוֹבִים, וְרָצָה בְדִבְרֵיהֶם הַנֶּאֱמָרִים בֶּאֱמֶת. בָּרוּךְ אַתָּה יהוה, הַבּוֹחֵר בַּתּוֹרָה וּבְמֹשֶׁה עַבְדּוֹ וּבְיִשְׂרָאֵל עַמּוֹ וּבִנְבִיאֵי הָאֱמֶת וָצֶדֶק.

הפטרה

ירמיהו
ח, יג-ט, כג

אָסֹף אֲסִיפֵם נְאֻם־יהוה אֵין עֲנָבִים בַּגֶּפֶן וְאֵין תְּאֵנִים בַּתְּאֵנָה וְהֶעָלֶה נָבֵל וָאֶתֵּן לָהֶם יַעַבְרוּם: עַל־מָה אֲנַחְנוּ יֹשְׁבִים הֵאָסְפוּ וְנָבוֹא אֶל־עָרֵי הַמִּבְצָר וְנִדְּמָה־שָּׁם כִּי יהוה אֱלֹהֵינוּ הֲדִמָּנוּ וַיַּשְׁקֵנוּ מֵי־רֹאשׁ כִּי חָטָאנוּ לַיהוה: קַוֵּה לְשָׁלוֹם וְאֵין טוֹב לְעֵת מַרְפֵּה וְהִנֵּה בְעָתָה: מִדָּן נִשְׁמַע נַחְרַת סוּסָיו מִקּוֹל מִצְהֲלוֹת אַבִּירָיו רָעֲשָׁה כָּל־הָאָרֶץ וַיָּבוֹאוּ וַיֹּאכְלוּ אֶרֶץ וּמְלוֹאָהּ עִיר וְיֹשְׁבֵי בָהּ: כִּי הִנְנִי מְשַׁלֵּחַ בָּכֶם נְחָשִׁים צִפְעֹנִים אֲשֶׁר אֵין־לָהֶם לָחַשׁ וְנִשְּׁכוּ אֶתְכֶם נְאֻם־יהוה: מַבְלִיגִיתִי עֲלֵי יָגוֹן עָלַי לִבִּי דַוָּי: הִנֵּה־קוֹל שַׁוְעַת בַּת־עַמִּי מֵאֶרֶץ מַרְחַקִּים הַיהוה אֵין בְּצִיּוֹן אִם־מַלְכָּהּ אֵין בָּהּ מַדּוּעַ הִכְעִסוּנִי בִּפְסִלֵיהֶם בְּהַבְלֵי נֵכָר: עָבַר קָצִיר כָּלָה קָיִץ וַאֲנַחְנוּ לוֹא נוֹשָׁעְנוּ: עַל־שֶׁבֶר בַּת־עַמִּי הָשְׁבָּרְתִּי קָדַרְתִּי שַׁמָּה הֶחֱזִקָתְנִי: הַצֳרִי אֵין בְּגִלְעָד אִם־רֹפֵא אֵין שָׁם כִּי מַדּוּעַ לֹא עָלְתָה

hold of me. Is there no balm in Gilead? Is there no physician there? Why then is not the health of the daughter of my people recovered? Oh, that my head were waters, and my eyes a fountain of tears, that I might weep day and night for the slain of the daughter of my people! Oh, that I were in the wilderness, in a lodging place of wayfaring men; that I might leave my people, and go from them! for they are all adulterers, an assembly of treacherous men. And they bend their tongues, their bow of falsehood: but they are not valiant for the truth upon the earth; for they proceed from evil to evil, and they know Me not, says the LORD. Take heed everyone of his neighbor, and trust not in any brother: For every brother acts deceitfully, and every neighbor goes about with slanders. And they deceive everyone his neighbor, and do not speak the truth: they have taught their tongue to speak lies, and weary themselves to commit iniquity. Your habitation is in the midst of deceit; through deceit they refuse to know Me, says the LORD.   Therefore thus says the LORD of hosts, Behold, I will smelt them, and try them; for how else shall I do for the daughter of My people? Their tongue is a sharpened arrow; it speaks deceit: one speaks peaceably to his neighbor with his mouth, but in heart he lies in wait for him. Shall I not punish them for these things? says the LORD: shall not My soul be avenged on such a nation as this?   For the mountains will I take up a weeping and wailing, and for the pastures of the wilderness a lamentation, because they are burned up, so that none can pass through them; neither can men hear the sound of the cattle; both the birds of the heavens and the beasts are fled; they are gone. And I will make Jerusalem heaps, a den of jackals; and I will make the cities of Judah desolate, without inhabitant.   Who is the wise man, that may understand this? And who is he to whom the mouth of the LORD has spoken, that he may declare it? Why does the land perish, and is burned up like a wilderness, that none passes through?   And the LORD says, Because they have forsaken My Torah which I set before them, and have not obeyed My voice, nor walked therein; but have walked after the stubbornness of their own heart, and after the idol worshipers, as their fathers taught them: Therefore thus says the LORD of hosts, the God of Israel; Behold, I will feed them, this people, with wormwood, and give them water of gall to drink. I will scatter them also among the nations, whom neither they nor their fathers have known: and I will send a sword after them, till I have consumed them.   Thus says the LORD of

אֹרְכַת בַּת־עַמִּֽי: מִֽי־יִתֵּ֤ן רֹאשִׁי֙ מַ֔יִם וְעֵינִ֖י מְק֣וֹר דִּמְעָ֑ה וְאֶבְכֶּה֙ יוֹמָ֣ם וָלַ֔יְלָה אֵ֖ת חַֽלְלֵ֥י בַת־עַמִּֽי: מִֽי־יִתְּנֵ֣נִי בַמִּדְבָּ֗ר מְלוֹן֙ אֹֽרְחִ֔ים וְאֶֽעֶזְבָה֙ אֶת־עַמִּ֔י וְאֵלְכָ֖ה מֵֽאִתָּ֑ם כִּ֤י כֻלָּם֙ מְנָ֣אֲפִ֔ים עֲצֶ֖רֶת בֹּֽגְדִֽים: וַֽיַּדְרְכ֤וּ אֶת־לְשׁוֹנָם֙ קַשְׁתָּ֣ם שֶׁ֔קֶר וְלֹ֥א לֶאֱמוּנָ֖ה גָּבְר֣וּ בָאָ֑רֶץ כִּי֩ מֵרָעָ֨ה אֶל־רָעָ֧ה ׀ יָצָ֛אוּ וְאֹתִ֥י לֹֽא־יָדָ֖עוּ נְאֻם־יְהוָֽה: אִ֤ישׁ מֵרֵעֵ֙הוּ֙ הִשָּׁמֵ֔רוּ וְעַל־כָּל־אָ֖ח אַל־תִּבְטָ֑חוּ כִּ֤י כָל־אָח֙ עָק֣וֹב יַעְקֹ֔ב וְכָל־רֵ֖עַ רָכִ֥יל יַהֲלֹֽךְ: וְאִ֤ישׁ בְּרֵעֵ֙הוּ֙ יְהָתֵ֔לּוּ וֶאֱמֶ֖ת לֹ֣א יְדַבֵּ֑רוּ לִמְּד֧וּ לְשׁוֹנָ֛ם דַּבֶּר־שֶׁ֖קֶר הַעֲוֵ֥ה נִלְאֽוּ: שִׁבְתְּךָ֖ בְּת֣וֹךְ מִרְמָ֑ה בְּמִרְמָ֛ה מֵאֲנ֥וּ דַֽעַת־אוֹתִ֖י נְאֻם־יְהוָֽה: לָכֵ֗ן כֹּ֤ה אָמַר֙ יְהוָ֣ה צְבָא֔וֹת הִנְנִ֥י צוֹרְפָ֖ם וּבְחַנְתִּ֑ים כִּֽי־אֵ֣יךְ אֶעֱשֶׂ֔ה מִפְּנֵ֖י בַּת־עַמִּֽי: חֵ֥ץ שׁוֹחֵ֛ט לְשׁוֹנָ֖ם שָׁח֑וּט מִרְמָ֣ה דִבֵּ֑ר בְּפִ֗יו שָׁל֤וֹם אֶת־רֵעֵ֙הוּ֙ יְדַבֵּ֔ר וּבְקִרְבּ֖וֹ יָשִׂ֥ים אָרְבּֽוֹ: הַעַל־אֵ֥לֶּה לֹֽא־אֶפְקָד־בָּ֖ם נְאֻם־יְהוָ֑ה אִ֚ם בְּג֣וֹי אֲשֶׁר־כָּזֶ֔ה לֹ֥א תִתְנַקֵּ֖ם נַפְשִֽׁי: עַל־הֶ֨הָרִ֜ים אֶשָּׂ֧א בְכִ֣י וָנֶ֗הִי וְעַל־נְא֤וֹת מִדְבָּר֙ קִינָ֔ה כִּ֤י נִצְּתוּ֙ מִבְּלִי־אִ֣ישׁ עֹבֵ֔ר וְלֹ֥א שָׁמְע֖וּ ק֣וֹל מִקְנֶ֑ה מֵע֤וֹף הַשָּׁמַ֙יִם֙ וְעַד־בְּהֵמָ֔ה נָדְד֖וּ הָלָֽכוּ: וְנָתַתִּ֧י אֶת־יְרוּשָׁלִַ֛ם לְגַלִּ֖ים מְע֣וֹן תַּנִּ֑ים וְאֶת־עָרֵ֧י יְהוּדָ֛ה אֶתֵּ֥ן שְׁמָמָ֖ה מִבְּלִ֥י יוֹשֵֽׁב: מִֽי־הָאִ֤ישׁ הֶֽחָכָם֙ וְיָבֵ֣ן אֶת־זֹ֔את וַאֲשֶׁ֨ר דִּבֶּ֧ר פִּֽי־יְהוָ֛ה אֵלָ֖יו וְיַגִּדָ֑הּ עַל־מָה֙ אָבְדָ֣ה הָאָ֔רֶץ נִצְּתָ֥ה כַמִּדְבָּ֖ר מִבְּלִ֥י עֹבֵֽר: וַיֹּ֣אמֶר יְהוָ֔ה עַל־עָזְבָם֙ אֶת־תּ֣וֹרָתִ֔י אֲשֶׁ֥ר נָתַ֖תִּי לִפְנֵיהֶ֑ם וְלֹֽא־שָׁמְע֥וּ בְקוֹלִ֖י וְלֹא־הָ֥לְכוּ בָֽהּ: וַיֵּ֣לְכ֔וּ אַחֲרֵ֖י שְׁרִר֣וּת לִבָּ֑ם וְאַחֲרֵי֙ הַבְּעָלִ֔ים אֲשֶׁ֥ר לִמְּד֖וּם אֲבוֹתָֽם: לָכֵ֗ן כֹּֽה־אָמַ֞ר יְהוָ֤ה צְבָאוֹת֙ אֱלֹהֵ֣י יִשְׂרָאֵ֔ל הִנְנִ֧י מַאֲכִילָ֛ם אֶת־הָעָ֥ם הַזֶּ֖ה לַעֲנָ֑ה וְהִשְׁקִיתִ֖ים מֵי־רֹֽאשׁ: וַהֲפִֽצוֹתִים֙ בַּגּוֹיִ֔ם אֲשֶׁר֙ לֹ֣א יָֽדְע֔וּ הֵ֖מָּה וַאֲבוֹתָ֑ם וְשִׁלַּחְתִּ֤י אַֽחֲרֵיהֶם֙ אֶת־הַחֶ֔רֶב עַ֥ד כַּלּוֹתִ֖י אוֹתָֽם: כֹּ֤ה אָמַר֙ יְהוָ֣ה צְבָא֔וֹת הִתְבּֽוֹנְנ֛וּ וְקִרְא֥וּ לַמְקוֹנְנ֖וֹת וּתְבוֹאֶ֑ינָה וְאֶל־הַחֲכָמ֥וֹת שִׁלְח֖וּ

hosts, Consider, and call for the mourning women, that they may come; and send for the skillful women, that they may come: and let them make haste, and take up a wailing for us, that our eyes may run down with tears, and our eyelids gush out with waters. For a voice of wailing is heard out of Zion, How are we ruined! we are greatly confounded, because we have forsaken the land, because our dwellings have cast us out. Yet hear the word of the Lord, O you women, and let your ear receive the word of His mouth, and teach your daughters wailing, and every one her neighbor lamentation. For death is come up into our windows, and is entered into our palaces, to cut off the children from the streets and the young men from the broad places. Speak, Thus says the Lord, And the carcasses of men shall fall as dung upon the open field, and as the handful after the harvester, and none shall gather them. Thus says the Lord, Let not the wise man glory in his wisdom, neither let the mighty man glory in his might, let not the rich man glory in his riches: but let him that glories glory in this, that he understands and knows Me, that I am the Lord who exercises faithful love, justice, and righteousness, in the earth: for in these things I delight, says the Lord.

BLESSINGS AFTER READING THE HAFTARA

After the Haftara, the person called up for Maftir says the following blessings:

בָּרוּךְ Blessed are You, Lord our God, King of the Universe, Rock of all worlds, righteous for all generations, the faithful God who says and does, speaks and fulfills, all of whose words are truth and righteousness. You are faithful, Lord our God, and faithful are Your words, not one of which returns unfulfilled, for You, God, are a faithful (and compassionate) King. Blessed are You, Lord, faithful in all His words.

רַחֵם Have compassion on Zion for it is the source of our life, and save the one grieved in spirit swiftly in our days. Blessed are You, Lord, who makes Zion rejoice in her children.

שַׂמְּחֵנוּ Grant us joy, Lord our God, through Elijah the prophet Your servant, and through the kingdom of the house of David Your anointed – may he soon come and make our hearts glad. May no stranger sit on his throne, and may others not continue to inherit his glory, for You promised him by Your holy name that his light would never be extinguished. Blessed are You, Lord, Shield of David.

וְתָבוֹאֶנָה: וּתְמַהֵרְנָה וְתִשֶּׂנָה עָלֵינוּ נֶהִי וְתֵרַדְנָה עֵינֵינוּ דִּמְעָה וְעַפְעַפֵּינוּ יִזְּלוּ־מָיִם: כִּי קוֹל נְהִי נִשְׁמַע מִצִּיּוֹן אֵיךְ שֻׁדָּדְנוּ בֹּשְׁנוּ מְאֹד כִּי־עָזַבְנוּ אָרֶץ כִּי הִשְׁלִיכוּ מִשְׁכְּנוֹתֵינוּ: כִּי־שְׁמַעְנָה נָשִׁים דְּבַר־יְהֹוָה וְתִקַּח אָזְנְכֶם דְּבַר־פִּיו וְלַמֵּדְנָה בְנוֹתֵיכֶם נֶהִי וְאִשָּׁה רְעוּתָהּ קִינָה: כִּי־עָלָה מָוֶת בְּחַלּוֹנֵינוּ בָּא בְּאַרְמְנוֹתֵינוּ לְהַכְרִית עוֹלָל מִחוּץ בַּחוּרִים מֵרְחֹבוֹת: דַּבֵּר כֹּה נְאֻם־יְהֹוָה וְנָפְלָה נִבְלַת הָאָדָם כְּדֹמֶן עַל־פְּנֵי הַשָּׂדֶה וּכְעָמִיר מֵאַחֲרֵי הַקֹּצֵר וְאֵין מְאַסֵּף: כֹּה ׀ אָמַר יְהֹוָה אַל־יִתְהַלֵּל חָכָם בְּחָכְמָתוֹ וְאַל־יִתְהַלֵּל הַגִּבּוֹר בִּגְבוּרָתוֹ אַל־יִתְהַלֵּל עָשִׁיר בְּעָשְׁרוֹ: כִּי אִם־בְּזֹאת יִתְהַלֵּל הַמִּתְהַלֵּל הַשְׂכֵּל וְיָדֹעַ אוֹתִי כִּי אֲנִי יְהֹוָה עֹשֶׂה חֶסֶד מִשְׁפָּט וּצְדָקָה בָּאָרֶץ כִּי־בְאֵלֶּה חָפַצְתִּי נְאֻם־יְהֹוָה:

ברכות לאחר ההפטרה

After the הפטרה, the person called up for מפטיר says the following blessings:

בָּרוּךְ אַתָּה יְהֹוָה אֱלֹהֵינוּ מֶלֶךְ הָעוֹלָם, צוּר כָּל הָעוֹלָמִים, צַדִּיק בְּכָל הַדּוֹרוֹת, הָאֵל הַנֶּאֱמָן, הָאוֹמֵר וְעוֹשֶׂה, הַמְדַבֵּר וּמְקַיֵּם, שֶׁכָּל דְּבָרָיו אֱמֶת וָצֶדֶק. נֶאֱמָן אַתָּה הוּא יְהֹוָה אֱלֹהֵינוּ וְנֶאֱמָנִים דְּבָרֶיךָ, וְדָבָר אֶחָד מִדְּבָרֶיךָ אָחוֹר לֹא יָשׁוּב רֵיקָם, כִּי אֵל מֶלֶךְ נֶאֱמָן (וְרַחֲמָן) אָתָּה. בָּרוּךְ אַתָּה יְהֹוָה, הָאֵל הַנֶּאֱמָן בְּכָל דְּבָרָיו.

רַחֵם עַל צִיּוֹן כִּי הִיא בֵּית חַיֵּינוּ, וְלַעֲלוּבַת נֶפֶשׁ תּוֹשִׁיעַ בִּמְהֵרָה בְיָמֵינוּ. בָּרוּךְ אַתָּה יְהֹוָה, מְשַׂמֵּחַ צִיּוֹן בְּבָנֶיהָ.

שַׂמְּחֵנוּ יְהֹוָה אֱלֹהֵינוּ בְּאֵלִיָּהוּ הַנָּבִיא עַבְדֶּךָ, וּבְמַלְכוּת בֵּית דָּוִד מְשִׁיחֶךָ, בִּמְהֵרָה יָבֹא וְיָגֵל לִבֵּנוּ. עַל כִּסְאוֹ לֹא יֵשֶׁב זָר, וְלֹא יִנְחֲלוּ עוֹד אֲחֵרִים אֶת כְּבוֹדוֹ, כִּי בְשֵׁם קָדְשְׁךָ נִשְׁבַּעְתָּ לּוֹ שֶׁלֹּא יִכְבֶּה נֵרוֹ לְעוֹלָם וָעֶד. בָּרוּךְ אַתָּה יְהֹוָה, מָגֵן דָּוִד.

RETURNING THE TORAH TO THE ARK

The Ark is opened. The Leader takes the Torah scroll and says:

יְהַלְלוּ Let them praise the name of the Lord, *Ps. 148*
for His name alone is sublime.

The congregation responds:

הוֹדוֹ His majesty is above earth and heaven.
He has raised the horn of His people,
for the glory of all His devoted ones,
the children of Israel, the people close to Him.
Halleluya!

As the Torah scroll is returned to the Ark, say:

לְדָוִד מִזְמוֹר A psalm of David. The earth is the Lord's and all it contains, *Ps. 24*
the world and all who live in it. For He founded it on the seas and established it on the streams. Who may climb the mountain of the Lord? Who may stand in His holy place? He who has clean hands and a pure heart, who has not taken My name in vain, or sworn deceitfully. He shall receive blessing from the Lord, and just reward from God, his salvation. This is a generation of those who seek Him, the descendants of Jacob who seek Your presence, Selah! Lift up your heads, O gates; be uplifted, eternal doors, so that the King of glory may enter. Who is the King of glory? It is the Lord, strong and mighty, the Lord mighty in battle. ▸ Lift up your heads, O gates; be uplifted, eternal doors, so that the King of glory may enter. Who is He, the King of glory? The Lord of hosts, He is the King of glory, Selah!

As the Torah scroll is placed into the Ark, say:

וּבְנֻחֹה יֹאמַר When the Ark came to rest, Moses would say: "Return, *Num. 10*
O Lord, to the myriad thousands of Israel." Advance, Lord, to Your *Ps. 132*
resting place, You and Your mighty Ark. Your priests are clothed in righteousness, and Your devoted ones sing in joy. For the sake of Your servant David, do not reject Your anointed one. For I give you good *Prov. 4*
instruction; do not forsake My Torah. It is a tree of life to those who *Prov. 3*
grasp it, and those who uphold it are happy. Its ways are ways of pleas- *Prov. 3*
antness, and all its paths are peace. ▸ Turn us back, O Lord, to You, and *Lam. 5*
we will return. Renew our days as of old.

The Ark is closed.

הכנסת ספר תורה

The ארון קודש is opened. The שליח ציבור takes the ספר תורה and says:

יְהַלְלוּ אֶת־שֵׁם יהוה, כִּי־נִשְׂגָּב שְׁמוֹ, לְבַדּוֹ

תהלים קמח

The קהל responds:

הוֹדוֹ עַל־אֶרֶץ וְשָׁמָיִם:
וַיָּרֶם קֶרֶן לְעַמּוֹ
תְּהִלָּה לְכָל־חֲסִידָיו
לִבְנֵי יִשְׂרָאֵל עַם קְרֹבוֹ, הַלְלוּיָהּ:

As the ספר תורה is returned to the ארון קודש, say:

לְדָוִד מִזְמוֹר, לַיהוה הָאָרֶץ וּמְלוֹאָהּ, תֵּבֵל וְיֹשְׁבֵי בָהּ: כִּי־הוּא עַל־יַמִּים יְסָדָהּ, וְעַל־נְהָרוֹת יְכוֹנְנֶהָ: מִי־יַעֲלֶה בְהַר־יהוה, וּמִי־יָקוּם בִּמְקוֹם קָדְשׁוֹ: נְקִי כַפַּיִם וּבַר־לֵבָב, אֲשֶׁר לֹא־נָשָׂא לַשָּׁוְא נַפְשִׁי וְלֹא נִשְׁבַּע לְמִרְמָה: יִשָּׂא בְרָכָה מֵאֵת יהוה, וּצְדָקָה מֵאֱלֹהֵי יִשְׁעוֹ: זֶה דּוֹר דֹּרְשָׁו, מְבַקְשֵׁי פָנֶיךָ, יַעֲקֹב, סֶלָה: שְׂאוּ שְׁעָרִים רָאשֵׁיכֶם, וְהִנָּשְׂאוּ פִּתְחֵי עוֹלָם, וְיָבוֹא מֶלֶךְ הַכָּבוֹד: מִי זֶה מֶלֶךְ הַכָּבוֹד: יהוה עִזּוּז וְגִבּוֹר, יהוה גִּבּוֹר מִלְחָמָה: ‹ שְׂאוּ שְׁעָרִים רָאשֵׁיכֶם, וּשְׂאוּ פִּתְחֵי עוֹלָם, וְיָבֹא מֶלֶךְ הַכָּבוֹד: מִי הוּא זֶה מֶלֶךְ הַכָּבוֹד, יהוה צְבָאוֹת הוּא מֶלֶךְ הַכָּבוֹד, סֶלָה:

תהלים כד

As the ספר תורה is placed into the ארון קודש, say:

וּבְנֻחֹה יֹאמַר, שׁוּבָה יהוה רִבְבוֹת אַלְפֵי יִשְׂרָאֵל: קוּמָה יהוה לִמְנוּחָתֶךָ, אַתָּה וַאֲרוֹן עֻזֶּךָ: כֹּהֲנֶיךָ יִלְבְּשׁוּ־צֶדֶק, וַחֲסִידֶיךָ יְרַנֵּנוּ: בַּעֲבוּר דָּוִד עַבְדֶּךָ אַל־תָּשֵׁב פְּנֵי מְשִׁיחֶךָ: כִּי לֶקַח טוֹב נָתַתִּי לָכֶם, תּוֹרָתִי אַל־תַּעֲזֹבוּ: עֵץ־חַיִּים הִיא לַמַּחֲזִיקִים בָּהּ, וְתֹמְכֶיהָ מְאֻשָּׁר: דְּרָכֶיהָ דַרְכֵי־נֹעַם וְכָל־נְתִיבוֹתֶיהָ שָׁלוֹם: ‹ הֲשִׁיבֵנוּ יהוה אֵלֶיךָ וְנָשׁוּבָה, חַדֵּשׁ יָמֵינוּ כְּקֶדֶם:

במדברי
תהלים קלב

משלי ד

משלי ג

משלי ג
איכה ה

The ארון קודש is closed.

קינות ליום

KINOT &
COMMENTARY
FOR THE DAY
OF TISHA B'AV

After the Torah scroll is returned to the Ark,
the congregation sits on the floor and recites kinot.

6

fourth stichs begin with the opening words of verses in Eikha chapter 3 (arranged in a triple alphabetical format – three lines beginning with the same letter). The fifth stich opens with the first word of the corresponding verse in Eikha chapter 2, while the closing stich paraphrases the opening of the corresponding verse in Eikha chapter 1. The nine stanzas take us, in this way, through the last nine letters in the alphabetic arrangement of Eikha. The final stanza is an acrostic of the poet's name, אלעזר*, and connects to the next kina by closing with the refrain of Kina 7. Despite this highly constrained form, the kina is poignant and rich with meaning. Commentary for this kina begins on page 198.*

שָׁבַת [Our joy] ceased! And our detractors said, "Get away from me!"
They called me dirty and repulsive, worse than all my peers.
You spread a canopy over heaven to cover my Temple;
You concealed Yourself and vanquished my strongmen.
My foes applauded while my limbs drooped,
                                      as they trampled upon my heroes.

נָפְלָה She has fallen to the depths and there she remains.
My eyes await [Zechariah] Ben Berekhia's prophecy,
hoping for the miraculous wonders of Gilgal.
My tear-stained face is marred by the mire of Greek sophistry.
He acted first and later regretted, calling others to tears,
                                     as He Himself exclaimed, "I cry for them!"

עַל The [acid] waters of the Euphrates punctured the innards of the pious;
they remembered the [sweet] waters of the Sea of Reeds
    while the enemies razed the Temple foundations.
Fear for Shiloh's sin seized all her advisors.
[The enemy, likened to] wild boars exclaimed,
   "What merit do they have?!"
and they proceeded to force depravity upon the exiles.
                                      Zion spread her hands helplessly.

עַל My opponent's troops ambushed me on the mountain;
they flooded the heads of Zion as a raging river.
The murderous sin of Nob was held fast against me;
You set the snare, inciting my enemies.
My people shrieked in the days of the rebel Ben Dinai:
                                        "God is the Righteous One!"

After the סֵפֶר תּוֹרָה is returned to the אָרוֹן, the קָהָל sits on the floor and recites קִינוֹת.

6

The next fifteen kinot were written by Rabbi Elazar HaKalir (see page 198), and are characterized by their technical virtuosity and multiple references to the Tanakh and midrashim. This first kina exemplifies this virtuosity. Each of its nine stanzas consists of six stichs. In each stanza, the first word of the first stich is the first word of a verse in Eikha chapter 5, while the second word is taken from the beginning of the corresponding verse in Eikha chapter 4. The second, third and

שָׁבַת, סוּרוּ מֶנִּי שִׁמְעוּנִי עוֹכְרַי
סָחִי וּמָאוֹס הֱשִׂימוּנִי בְּעֶדְרֵי חֲבֵרַי
סַכּוֹתָה מִשְׁכַּן מִסְכּוֹת דְּבִירַי
סַכּוֹתָה וְהִבְלֶיגוּ גִבּוֹרַי
סָפְקוּ כַף וּמָעֲדוּ אֵבָרַי.
כָּסְלָה כָל־אַבִּירַי:

נָפְלָה עוֹדֵינוּ בְּצוּל דְּכוּיָה
עֵינֵי חִכְּתָה לַחֲזוֹן בֶּן בְּרֵכְיָה
עַד פִּלְאֵי גַלְגַּל חֲבוּיָה
עֵינֵי מְעוֹלֶלֶת בְּיוֹנִית נְכוּיָה
עָשָׂה וְנִחַם, וַיִּקְרָא לַבְּכִיָּה.
וְנָם, עַל־אֵלֶּה אֲנִי בוֹכִיָּה:

עַל פְּנֵי פְרָת נֻפְּצוּ חֲסִידֶיהָ
פַּלְגֵי סוּף זָכְרָה כְּעָרוּ יְסוֹדֶיהָ
פַּחַד חֵטְא שִׁילֹה, תָּכַף סוֹדֶיהָ
פָּצוּ חַזִּירֵי יַעַר, אַיֵּה חֲסִידֶיהָ
פָּצוּ מַעֲשֵׂה עֶרְוָה לִנְדִידֶיהָ.
פֵּרְשָׂה צִיּוֹן בְּיָדֶיהָ:

עַל הַר צָדוּ שְׁאוֹנֵי מְדָנַי
צָפוּ עַל רָאשֵׁי זֵדוֹנַי
צָמְתוּ בִּנְוֵה לַעֲמֹד זְדוֹנַי
צוּד נָצְרָה לְעוֹרֵר מְדָנַי
צָעַק עַמִּי בִּימֵי בֶן דִּינַי.
צַדִּיק הוּא יהוה:

אַתָּה You lifted up the lowly [Babylon], who stripped me of my glory;
You enabled him to approach me swiftly and ravage me.
I called upon Gibeon our ally, but they, too, betrayed me.
I felt compelled to call upon my Arab kin for help,
but they teased me and disastrously deceived me.
                        I called upon my lovers, but they fooled me.

לָמָּה Why did they lie in wait to slaughter the "breath of our life"?
You saw that my skin glowed like an oven.
You saw that they wrought malice in Your treasured Temple.
Ezekiel foretold that You would take revenge.
See, they wish to exterminate us as a nation.   *Ps. 83:5*
               See, O Lord, my distress; my intestines are shriveled.

הֲשִׁיבֵנוּ May those who exiled me hear that their joy is but temporary;
May You treat their dwellings as they have trampled mine,   *Is. 1:12*
they who silenced the singers of the Temple to torture me.
You heard that they schemed to sweep me away with "switches of wrath."
We dug holes in the earth in which to cook,
   and thus broke our teeth on stones.
                         They heard my desperate sighs!

כִּי You engraved Jacob's image into Your celestial throne.
Repay them, as when You showed Your face to us.
Drive them into the nether world;
   they scheme against Your sheltered ones.
Cast them into hell-fire, they smashed Your pearls.
Summon them to sip Your secret cup of poison.
                    Let all their wickedness come before You.

תָּבֹא Come upon the enemy who has annihilated us,
led us away to the entrance of Hamath,
expelled us to Halah and Habor,
and dragged off in chains, old and young alike.
Look down from on high; we are all Your faithful people!   *Is. 64:8*
                Remember, God, what has happened to us!

Kina 7 starts on page 216.

אַתָּה קַלִּים הִכְבַּדְתָּ, וּמֵעֲדָיִי עֵרְמוּנִי
קָרַבְתָּ בּוֹא אֵלַי, וַיַּחֲרִימוּנִי
קָרָאתִי לְיוֹשְׁבֵי גִבְעוֹן, עוֹד הֵם זֵרְמוּנִי
קוֹלִי לְהַשְׁמִיעַ בָּעֶרֶב הִגְרִימוּנִי
קוּמִי עִבְרִי, בְּהָתֵל הֶעֱרִימוּנִי.

קָרָאתִי לַמְאַהֲבַי, הֵמָּה רִמּוּנִי:

לָמָּה רוּחַ אַפֵּינוּ, לְטֶבַח שָׁמְרוּ
רָאִיתָ, כִּי כְתַנּוּר עוֹרֵנוּ כָּמָרוּ
רָאִיתָ, כִּי עָמָל וָכַעַס בְּאוֹיְבֶיךָ גָּמְרוּ
רַבַּת בְּיַד יְחֶזְקֵאל לְנָקָם, כְּמוֹ מָרוּ
רְאֵה, וְנִכְחִידֵם מִגּוֹי, אָמְרוּ.

תהלים פג, ה

רְאֵה יהוה כִּי־צַר־לִי, מֵעַי חֳמַרְמָרוּ:

הֲשִׁיבֵנוּ, שִׁישִׁי שְׁמַע, לְגוֹי צֹאנִי
שְׁבָתָם, רְמוֹס חֲצֵרַי, לְהַדְבִּיאֵנִי
שִׂפְתֵי מְשׁוֹרְרֵי דְּבִיר דּוּמָמוּ, לְהַדְאֵנִי
שָׁמַעַתְּ, זְמוֹרוֹת אַף הֵכִין לְטַאטְאֵנִי. שָׁכְבוּ וְנָדוּ
חֵץ לְהַבְרִיאֵנִי.

ישעיה א, יב

שִׁמְעוּ כִּי נֶאֱנָחָה אָנִי:

כִּי תָם חֻקַּת בְּכֵס אוֹפַנֶּיךָ
תָּשִׁיב לָהֶם גְּמוּל, כְּאָז חֲזוֹת פָּנֶיךָ
תִּרְדֹּף לְצַלְמוֹן, יוֹעֲצֵי רַע עַל צְפוּנֶיךָ
תִּתֵּן לְהַבְהֹב נוֹתְצֵי פְּנִינֶיךָ
תִּקְרָא לְשַׁכְּרָם כּוֹס, כָּמוּס בְּפָנֶיךָ.

תָּבֹא כָּל־רָעָתָם לְפָנֶיךָ:

תָּבֹא אֶל צַר אֲשֶׁר כִּלָּנוּ
לִמְבוֹא חֲמָת, בְּחֵמָה נְהָלָנוּ
עַד לַחֲלָח וְחָבוֹר הִגְלָנוּ
זָקֵן וּבָחוּר וּבְתוּלָה כִּבְּלָנוּ
רָם הַבֵּט נָא, עַמְּךָ כֻּלָּנוּ.

ישעיה סד, ח

זְכֹר יהוה מֶה־הָיָה לָנוּ:

Kina 7 starts on page 217.

COMMENTARY ON KINA 6

This *kina* was composed by Rabbi Elazar HaKalir, who was the author of the first group of *kinot* recited on the day of Tisha B'Av. There is a degree of uncertainty as to when Rabbi Elazar HaKalir lived. According to many *Rishonim*, Torah scholars of the early Middle Ages, including *Tosafot* (*Ḥagiga* 13a, s.v. *veraglei haḥayyot*), HaKalir was the *tanna* (Mishnaic scholar) Rabbi Elazar the Great, who lived in the second century of the common era. There are indications from the other *kinot*, however, that he may have lived in the tenth or eleventh century, nine hundred years after the destruction of the Temple, or that he may have lived during the sixth or seventh century.

שָׁבַת, סוּרוּ מֶנִּי [*Our joy*] *ceased!... "Get away from me!"* Our sages emphasized that while the word *shavat* means to cease, it also contains a connotation that the cessation occurred suddenly or unexpectedly. It implies that *suddenly* something important has changed. This is illustrated by the commentary of our sages on the verse concerning Shabbat, "וּבַיּוֹם הַשְּׁבִיעִי שָׁבַת וַיִּנָּפַשׁ, And on the seventh day He ceased from work and rested" (Exodus 31:17). Our sages comment that the act of *shavat*, of God's ceasing work, occurred instantaneously in the course of a fraction of a second. During the first part of that second, God was at work, and then, with the other part of the second, Shabbat commenced and God was at rest (*Bereshit Raba* 10:9; see also *Midrash Tanḥuma, Lekh Lekha* 9).

Sometimes, people realize, intuitively or intellectually, that a disaster will occur. As a result, when the disaster does occur, it is not experienced as something new, but as something that was expected. At other times, however, disaster strikes suddenly, and this sudden disaster is emotionally and psychologically more devastating than an anticipated disaster. Given this aspect of human nature, Rabbi Elazar HaKalir is expressing the thought that the major tragedy of the Ḥurban, the destruction, was not just that it occurred, but *shavat*, that it occurred suddenly. Although the people were told that the Ḥurban would occur, they did not really believe the warnings and did not expect that it would ever happen. But then the people arose in the morning and, lo and behold, contrary to everyone's expectations, the Temple, the *Beit HaMikdash*, was gone, Jerusalem was in ruin and the people were in captivity. The realization that the Ḥurban had occurred struck suddenly. It had the emotional and psychological impact of a sudden disaster.

Even Jeremiah the Prophet experienced *shavat*, the suddenness of the

destruction. God instructed Jeremiah to leave Jerusalem and go to the city of Anatot to buy a field from his uncle (Jeremiah 32:6–27). When Jeremiah left, the Temple was still standing, and the Kohanim, the priests, were performing the Temple service as if no threat existed. But when Jeremiah returned, the Temple was gone. Jeremiah realized that the Temple was gone when he was returning from Anatot and he did not see from afar the column of smoke rising from the altar that had always miraculously risen straight to the heavens without being dispersed by the winds (*Avot* 5:5).

Jeremiah was the prophet of the destruction. God told him many times that Jerusalem would be destroyed and the *Beit HaMikdash* consumed by flames. He often beheld a vision of the *Ḥurban*, and he was God's messenger who delivered the prophecy of the *Ḥurban* to the people. Yet even *he* did not realize that the *Ḥurban* would happen so soon. When he left Jerusalem, he had every intention of returning to the *Beit HaMikdash*. But when he returned from Anatot after a day and approached Jerusalem, the reality of the *Ḥurban* suddenly struck him.

The theme of *shavat*, the sudden and unexpected occurrence of the destruction, is also reflected in the story recounted by our sages of the city of Tur Malka (*Gittin* 57a). Half the inhabitants of Tur Malka were celebrating while the other half were already in the midst of destruction. Those who were celebrating did not know and could not comprehend what was happening. They thought the *Ḥurban* could never occur.

Each stanza of this *kina* begins with a word from Lamentations. The word *shavat* is from the verse "שָׁבַת מְשׂוֹשׂ לִבֵּנוּ, The joy of our heart has ceased" (Lamentations 5:15). With the destruction of the Temple, suddenly the joy in our hearts stopped; the Jewish people were not able to find joy anymore. Of course, after the *Ḥurban*, and through the present time, people continued to lead normal lives. Merchants continued to buy and sell, scholars were busy studying the Torah, and workers were occupied with their labor. But inwardly, in the depths of his heart, the Jew cried. There was no joy left in his life.

שִׁמְעוּנִי עוֹכְרַי *Our detractors said*. The word *okherai* refers to someone who does not gain anything from a particular act. He enjoys the suffering and misery of others without deriving any other benefit. Many people rejoiced when Jerusalem was destroyed, and they continue to do so even now. They gain no benefit from the downfall of Jerusalem, but they rejoice over its suffering.

בְּעֶדְרֵי חֲבֵרַי *All my peers*. The phrase is reminiscent of the verse in Song of Songs (1:7), "Tell me, you whom my soul loves, where you feed your flock,

where you make your flock rest at noon, for why should I be as one that veils herself beside עֶדְרֵי חֲבֵרֶיךָ, the flocks of your companions?" Rashi's commentary on this verse (ibid. s.v. *hagida li*) is, "How can you take care of your flock among those wolves in whose midst they live, when the sun is blazing, in times of persecution during this *galut*, when the sheep have no shelter and no shade and are exposed to merciless heat, when the *Knesset Yisrael*, the Jewish people, is completely isolated?"

The common theme shared by Song of Songs and Lamentations is the extreme loyalty of the Jewish people to God, and that is why HaKalir related this *kina* to Song of Songs. The focus of Song of Songs is on the Jewish people's commitment and loyalty to God in spite of the many attempts on the part of others to alienate them from Him. The verse says, "Return, return, O Shulammite; return, return that we may look upon you" (Song of Songs 7:1). The Midrash (*Pesikta Rabati* 21:11) states that the nations of the world said to the Jews, "Leave and desert your people, and we will raise you to the rank of nobility." But the Jewish people resisted all offers and bribes. Similarly, the *kina* refers to the עֶדְרֵי חֲבֵרַי, the allies who advised the Jews many times to leave God. And had they deserted Him perhaps they would not have experienced *sehi uma'os*, such disaster and catastrophe. But the Jewish people were steadfast and refused.

סְחִי וּמָאוֹס הֱשִׂימוּנִי בְּעֶדְרֵי חֲבֵרַי *They called me dirty and repulsive, worse than all my peers.* The *paytan* is not mourning physical destruction in this phrase, but rather *Ḥilul Kevod Yisrael*, the desecration of the honor of Israel, which is parallel to *Ḥilul Hashem*, the desecration of God's name. What has made the nineteen hundred years of exile so terrible is that the exile constitutes *Ḥilul Hashem*, and redemption is so important because it represents the opposite of *Ḥilul Hashem*. Redemption presupposes *Kavod Yisrael*, the honor of Israel and thus the honor of God's name. In effect, God says to the Jewish people, "I will bring you back to the land of Israel, rebuild the *Beit HaMikdash* and restore your former glory, for one reason – not that *you* are deserving, but because *My* name has been desecrated."

In reality, the name of God cannot be desecrated by human beings regardless of how powerful they may be. His name could not be profaned by Rome, or Babylonia, or by any other power in the world. His name is profaned only by the fact that Israel is in exile. Ezekiel says (37:27–28) that one of the reasons that the Messiah will come is not because Israel is worthy, but because while Israel is in exile, the holy name of God is in exile as well, and it is desecrated, profaned and treated with contempt.

The tragedy of the Ḥurban was that it slowed the realization of that great promise that God made to Abraham. The verse in Ezekiel states, "When I have brought them back…and am sanctified in them in the sight of many nations" (Ezekiel 39:27). God will be sanctified when it can be demonstrated that the words of the prophets are correct and true and relate only to the Jewish people and to no others.

At times of catastrophe, the element of *Ḥilul Hashem* becomes insufferable. During the Holocaust years, Christian clergymen argued that God had abandoned the Jews and allowed the complete destruction of the Jewish people, thus fulfilling the words of their bible. I was confronted by these arguments, and I used to cry not only for the Ḥurban, but for the terrible desecration of God's name that these arguments represented. The significance, among other things, of the establishment of the State of Israel was that it put a stop to these arguments.

There is another element of the desecration of God's name that does not relate to God directly, but rather to the Jewish people, and the phrase in the *kina*, "They called me dirty and repulsive, worse than all my peers" epitomizes this element. The Ḥurban led to the contempt and disdain held among the nations for the Jewish people, which also constitutes the desecration of God's name. The enemies of the Jewish people are the enemies of God. This is the reason that there are two variant readings in the blessing of *Velamalshinim*, "For the slanderers," in the *Shemoneh Esreh*. One version of the blessing is, "May all Your people's enemies swiftly be cut down," and the other version is, "May all of Your enemies swiftly be cut down." In truth, both variant readings have essentially the same meaning because the enemies of Israel are also the enemies of God. The reason for this equivalence is that the enemies of Israel want not only to persecute and kill the Jews, but also to deny the extra quality of *beḥira*, of chosenness, that God imparted to the Jews.

The word *hesimuni*, in the singular rather than the plural, is key in interpreting the Ḥurban not only as an event that happened nineteen hundred years ago, but as an event which is meant to be re-experienced in the present. Rabbi Elazar HaKalir is telling us that the Ḥurban is not just to be understood in terms of history, but in terms of each of our own individual experiences. In the first chapter of Lamentations, Zion is addressed in the third person. But the third chapter begins, "אֲנִי הַגֶּבֶר, I am the man that has seen affliction" (Lamentations 3:1). We speak of ourselves, in the first person. The intent is not only to speak of ourselves as a community, but ourselves in terms of *myself*. While the Ḥurban was a communal catastrophe, we do not experience

a communal catastrophe unless it relates directly to ourselves. The *individual* needs to be affected. The importance of the individual experience is the message of the third chapter of Lamentations. There is no discussion of Zion or the Jewish people as a community. Rather, the focus is on each individual.

סַכּוֹתָה מִשְׁכַּן מִסְכוֹת דְּבִירִי *You spread a canopy over heaven to cover my Temple.* The *paytan* laments that God has enveloped and covered both the *Mishkan* (the Tabernacle) and the *Beit HaMikdash* in a cloud in order to prevent the words of the *paytan* from reaching Him. God has completely alienated and separated Himself from His people. There is a similar verse in Lamentations, "סַכּוֹתָה בֶעָנָן לָךְ מֵעֲבוֹר תְּפִלָּה, You have covered Yourself with a cloud, so that no prayer can pass through" (3:44). The term *sakota* represents a complete termination of the relationship between God and the Jewish people, to the extent that prayer is rejected and does not even reach God. God has enveloped not only the *Beit HaMikdash*, but any place of prayer, in a cloud which rejects the prayers of the Jewish people. This is the menacing fulfillment of the verse in Lamentations, "Although I cry out and call for help, סָתַם תְּפִלָּתִי, He shuts out my prayer" (3:8). Access to God is denied.

סַכּוֹתָה וְהִבְלַגְתָּ גִּבּוֹרַי *You concealed Yourself and vanquished my strongmen.* The previous phrase stated that God enveloped His Sanctuary so that prayer could not penetrate. Now, the *paytan* says that God Himself is enveloped in a cloud, and as a result, the heroes of the Jewish people were defeated and overwhelmed.

This is a manifestation of the Kabbalistic concept of *hester panim*, God's deliberate concealment of His countenance. *Hester panim* is mentioned only once in the Torah, "Then My anger shall be kindled against them ... and I will hide My face from them, and they shall be consumed ... And I will surely hide My face on that day for all the evil which they shall have done" (Deuteronomy 31:17–18). The consequence of *hester panim* is וְהָיָה לֶאֱכֹל, that the Jews will be consumed. The Gemara elaborates (*Bava Kama* 60a) and notes that when God does not distinguish between the righteous and the evildoers, a period of *hester panim* prevails. Certainly the Holocaust was a period of *hester panim*. God turned His back on His people.

"*Vayeda Elokim*, and God knew" (Exodus 2:25), is the opposite of *hester panim*. When the Torah states "*vayeda Elokim*," it is an indication that God has removed the *hester panim*. And the moment that *hester panim* is removed is the *athalta dege'ula*, the beginning of the redemption.

In the phrase in Lamentations, "You have covered Yourself with a cloud, so

that no prayer can pass through" (3:44), the cloud is symbolic of *hester panim*, which is a fate that is even worse than the destruction of the *Beit HaMikdash*. It is interesting that "cloud" has conflicting connotations in Tanakh. In many instances, the cloud is symbolic of the closeness of the relationship between God and the Jewish people, as, for example, when the Torah describes God's revelation to Moses with the thirteen attributes of mercy, "And the LORD descended in the cloud" (Exodus 34:5). In times of intimate relationship between God and His people, the cloud is the abode in which God resides. The cloud is symbolic of the presence of God within the community. At times of destruction however, the same cloud signifies God's complete alienation and departure from the community.

סָפְקוּ כַף וּמָעֲדוּ אֵבְרַי *My foes applauded while my limbs drooped.* The *paytan* tells God that as a result of His enveloping Himself in a cloud, all of our heroes and warriors perished; the enemies of the Jews clapped their hands while the limbs of the Jews were faltering.

The root of this tragedy is found in the word *sakota*, which is repeated because of its importance and which represents *hester panim*. *Sakota mishkan*, God's dwelling place was surrounded and enveloped by a cloud, and there could be no communication between the Jewish people and God.

נָפְלָה עוֹדֵינוּ בְּצוּל דְּכוּיָה / עֵינֵי חִכְּתָה לַחֲזוֹן בֶּן בֶּרֶכְיָה *She has fallen to the depths and there she remains. My eyes await [Zechariah] Ben Berekhia's prophecy.* The use of the word עוֹדֵינוּ is an allusion to the verse in Lamentations, "עוֹדֵינוּ תִּכְלֶינָה עֵינֵינוּ, As for us, our eyes yet fail watching for our vain help, in our hoping and watching for a nation that would not save us" (4:17). In spite of the Ḥurban and in spite of the Jewish people's descent into a bottomless abyss, nevertheless, עֵינֵי חִכְּתָה, they have never given up hope, and they are still waiting for the realization of the prophecy of Zechariah that Jerusalem will once again be populated, "There shall yet dwell old men and old women in the streets of Jerusalem" (Zechariah 8:4).

It is noteworthy that HaKalir refers to the prophecy of Zechariah rather than the many other prophecies of consolation that are found in the Tanakh. The reason is that Rabbi Akiva chose this prophecy of Zechariah as the representative prophecy of redemption, as recounted in Tractate *Makkot* (24b). In that selection, the Gemara tells of Rabbi Akiva, Rabban Gamliel, Rabbi Elazar ben Azaria and Rabbi Yehoshua who were walking near the Temple Mount. They saw a fox prowling on the site of the Holy of Holies, and they all began to weep, with the exception of Rabbi Akiva, who rejoiced. They

asked Rabbi Akiva why he was rejoicing, and he in turn asked them why they were weeping. They responded, "It is written about the Holy of Holies that one who is not a priest and enters shall be put to death, and now that we see foxes prowling there, how shall we not weep?" Rabbi Akiva responded that it was precisely for that reason that he was rejoicing, and he quoted for them the verse from Isaiah, "I will bring two trustworthy witnesses, Uriah the Priest and Zechariah ben Yeverekhyahu" (Isaiah 8:2). Rabbi Akiva, in effect, was telling them that we learn from this verse in Isaiah that God made the fulfillment of the prophecy of Zechariah dependent on the fulfillment of the prophecy of Uriah the Priest. Uriah's prophecy was that, because of the sins of the Jewish people, Zion, the Temple Mount, would be destroyed and plowed under like a field (Micah 3:12). In contrast, Zechariah's prophecy was that old men and old women shall yet dwell in the streets of Jerusalem. Rabbi Akiva interpreted the verse in Isaiah to mean that the implementation of the prophecy of Uriah is the guarantee of the fulfillment of the prophecy of Zechariah. Rabbi Akiva told the other rabbis that the fox prowling the site of the Holy of Holies was the fulfillment of Uriah's prophecy, and once he saw the fulfillment of Uriah's prophecy, he was certain that the prophecy of Zechariah would also be fulfilled. The rabbis were persuaded by Rabbi Akiva's argument and said, "Akiva you have comforted us, Akiva you have comforted us."

When the *paytan* writes "נָפְלָה עוֹדֵינוּ בְּצוּל דְּכוּיָה, She has fallen to the depths and there she remains," his intent is that the very fact that the Jews are בְּצוּל דְּכוּיָה, in the bottomless depths, is the reason that עֵינֵי חִכְּתָה לַחֲזוֹן בֶּן בֶּרֶכְיָה, that we have hope that the prophecy of consolation will also be fulfilled. The fact that the Ḥurban was so disastrous is proof that the redemption will be as great.

עַד פִּלְאֵי גִּלְגָּל חֲבוּיָה *Hoping for the miraculous wonders of Gilgal.* The word *Gilgal* in this phrase is not meant to refer only to the place that carries the name Gilgal, but to all of the miracles which transpired during the seven years of Joshua's conquest of the land of Israel, and the ensuing seven years which were devoted to allocating the land among the Tribes of Israel. Gilgal is thus representative of a period of Israel's vigor, might and conquest. HaKalir writes that the Jews expected all of the miracles of Gilgal, which represent the opposite of Ḥurban. Instead, however, the period of Gilgal is *ḥavuya*, concealed.

HaKalir is expressing the idea that the Jewish people thought that the initial sanctity of the land of Israel effected by Joshua's conquest would be

eternal. They thought that the miracles that transpired during the period of conquest would be repeated and that Israel would never be conquered. However, when Nebuchadnezzar invaded, the *kedusha*, sanctity of the land of Israel was extinguished. This is consistent with Maimonides' view (*Mishneh Torah*, Hil. Beit HaBeḥira 6:15–16) with respect to all of Israel other than Jerusalem, that the initial sanctification of the land was temporary and did not sanctify the land for the future.

עֵינַי מְעוֹלֶלֶת בְּיָוָנִית נְבוּיָה *My tear-stained face is marred by the mire of Greek sophistry.* The word *biyevanit* can be understood as a reference to *Yavan*, Greece, and there are various interpretations as to the relationship of Greece to the Ḥurban. One interpretation is that this reference in the *kina* is an allusion to the statement in Tractate *Sofrim* (1:7) that the day the Torah was translated into Greek was as difficult for the Jewish people as the day that the golden calf was made. The translation of the Torah into Greek is further associated with the fast of the tenth day of Tevet, which is directly related to the Ḥurban. Although not mentioned in the Gemara, one of the *seliḥot* recited on the tenth day of Tevet (*Ezkera Matzok*), states that the eighth day of Tevet was established as a fast day because that is the day the Torah was translated into Greek. Even though this event did not occur on Tisha B'Av, it is mentioned in the Tisha B'Av *kinot* because Tisha B'Av is an all-inclusive day of mourning and lamentations for any and all tragedies that befell the Jewish people, without regard to the date of the tragedy. This quality of Tisha B'Av as a comprehensive day of mourning is a recurring theme in the *kinot*.

Another reason for the reference to *Yavan* in the *kina* is that Greece, not Rome, was the source of anti-Semitism. Pre-modern, theoretical anti-Semitism and anti-Semitic literature originated in Greece. Initially, Rome did not persecute the Jews and was quite tolerant of Jewish religious practices for a period of time, which is noted in greater detail in connection with some of the *kinot* below. Rather, it was the Greeks who were the most intolerant. The Hellenizers considered themselves to be aristocrats and the rest of the world barbarians, and they were intolerant, cruel and full of contempt for anyone who was not Greek. During the Second Temple period, anti-Semitism was concentrated in Alexandria in Egypt, which was culturally a Greek city. The notorious Apion, who said that the Jews worshiped the head of an ass (see Flavius Josephus, *Contra Apion* II:10) was from Alexandria. The story of Ḥanukka is further evidence of Greek anti-Semitism. In *Al HaNissim*, the special prayer for Ḥanukka inserted in the Amida and *Birkat HaMazon*,

we recite, "In the days of Mattathias...when the evil Greek kingdom arose against Your people Israel." Although King Antiochus and his followers were, in fact, Syrian, culturally, they were Greek. Syria was one of the sovereign provinces of Alexander the Great's empire, and the leaders were heirs of the Greek culture. Systematic religious persecution of the Jews began with the Greeks in the pre-Maccabean period, and was unknown in Jewish history before this period. The Greeks were responsible for the origin of intellectual anti-Semitism, perhaps not as a people or a race, but as a culture, philosophy and attitude. Greek culture, philosophy and literature permeated the ancient world, including Rome, and the Greek agenda of anti-Semitism was adopted along with Greek culture. The Romans may have resented the staunch political and military resistance of the Jews, but intellectual hatred of the Jews was a Greek creation.

The role of Nazi Germany in modern anti-Semitism is analogous to the influence of the Greeks in the ancient world. Nazi Germany is the parent of modern theoretical, intellectual anti-Semitism. Anti-Semitism may be popular in many countries, and *practical* anti-Semitism may be possible in any country, but the *philosophy* emanated from Germany. Germany's tradition of anti-Semitism permeated not only German philosophy, but the German view of the sciences, their interpretation of history and even their study of anthropology, and this pervasive intellectual anti-Semitism resulted ultimately in Hitler's murderous doctrines.

עָשָׂה וְנִחַם, וַיִּקְרָא לַבְּכִיָּה / וְנָם, עַל־אֵלֶּה אֲנִי בוֹכִיָּה *He acted first and later regretted, calling others to tears, as He Himself exclaimed, "I cry for them!"* The traditional Christian argument against the Jews has been that the destruction of the *Beit HaMikdash* would not have occurred unless God wanted it to happen. Therefore, the destruction of the *Beit HaMikdash* and the exile of the Jewish people are conclusive evidence that God has rejected the Jews. A logical conclusion of this argument is that the Jews should never be permitted to rebuild Jerusalem, as they have been rejected by God.

The answer of the Jews to this argument is contained in this phrase of the *kina*. It is true that God permitted the Ḥurban, but that does not signify God's rejection. In fact, God regretted, as it were, the Ḥurban. The word *niḥam* used in this phrase in the *kina* is similar to the verse, "וַיִּנָּחֶם יהוה כִּי־עָשָׂה אֶת־הָאָדָם, And the Lord regretted that He had made man" (Genesis 6:6). If God had truly rejected Jerusalem, he would not have told the Jews to mourn its destruction. He would simply have obliterated the city and then ignored

it, allowing the city to disappear into oblivion. The *kina* states, "וַיִּקְרָא לַבְּכִיָּה, Calling others to tears," which means that the Jews are required to mourn and lament for Jerusalem every Tisha B'Av and every time a Jew visits Jerusalem. In fact, God Himself mourns the destruction, as the *kina* describes: "וְנָם, and He Himself says, עַל־אֵלֶּה אֲנִי בוֹכִיָּה, on all of this I Myself am weeping" (Lamentations 1:16).

There is another interpretation of this phrase in the *kina*. The word *asa* means that God created and chose the Jewish people, and He built the *Beit HaMikdash*. The Jews may have done the physical work of building, but God was the true builder. As is written in Psalms, "אִם יהוה לֹא יִבְנֶה בַיִת שָׁוְא עָמְלוּ בוֹנָיו בּוֹ" (Psalms 127:1), which, in effect, means that if God does not build, the human architect accomplishes very little. God regretted having built the *Beit HaMikdash*, and He sealed its destiny and condemned it to destruction. He then summoned the people to mourn for it while He also participated in the mourning, lamentation and sorrow for the Ḥurban.

Thus, the destruction of the *Beit HaMikdash* does not demonstrate God's rejection of the Jews. They remain His chosen people and continue to be commanded to rebuild Jerusalem. Furthermore, the destruction of the *Beit HaMikdash* does not mean that sanctity has been removed from the site of the Temple. That location remains holy even though God visited His wrath upon it. "God sanctified it temporarily and eternally for the future, as well" (*Megilla* 10a–b, *Shavuot* 16a).

עַל פְּנֵי פְרָת נִפְצוּ חֲסִידֶיהָ *The [acid] waters of the Euphrates punctured the innards of the pious*. The *Midrash* states (*Midrash Tehillim* [Buber], *Mizmor* 137, s.v. *sham yashavnu*; *Pesikta Rabati* [Ish Shalom] 28, s.v. *davar aḥer al*) that the waters of the Euphrates were polluted, and when the Jews that were exiled to Babylonia drank the waters, they died of a plague. The number of Jews killed by the waters of the Euphrates surpassed the number killed by Nebuchadnezzar.

Until this point, Rabbi Elazar HaKalir has been describing the destruction of the Second Temple, but with this phrase, he shifts focus and refers to the Assyrian exile and the crossing of the Euphrates. Similarly, the phrase at the end of the *kina*, "לִמְבוֹא חֲמָת, בַּחֲמָה נְהָלָנוּ / עַד לַחְלַח וְחָבוֹר הִגְלָנוּ, Led us away to the entrance of Hamath, expelled us to Halah and Habor," refers to locations related to the exile of the Ten Tribes (See I Chronicles 5:26 and II Kings 17:6).

The *paytan* does not distinguish between the *galut* of the Ten Tribes by

Sennacherib, the *galut* of the First Temple by Nebuchadnezzar, or the *galut* of the Second Temple by Rome. The *kina* is not interested in classifying the events chronologically. It deliberately moves from event to event and from period to period, spreading an identity of events and destiny over thousands of years. The personae may change: Titus in one era, Nebuchadnezzar in another, and the mysterious foe who wrestled with Jacob (Genesis 32:25) in yet another – they are all basically one person and one philosophy.

It is noteworthy that the *paytan* uses the word *nuptzu* in referring to the death of the righteous. The difference between *lenapetz* and the similar word *leshaber*, which the *paytan* could have used, is that *lenapetz* means to shatter into small fragments to the extent that the object cannot be reconstructed. With regard to the destruction of the Temples, even though they were tragic events, they can be reconstructed; all is not lost, and all is not hopeless. But the loss of the righteous is different. As our sages say (*Shir HaShirim Raba* 6:12; *Kohelet Raba* 5:16), "If a great scholar dies, who will bring us his replacement?" If a Jewish scholar dies, his loss cannot be reconstructed. There is no substitute.

פְּלְגֵי סוּף זָכְרָה כְּעֵרוּ יְסוֹדֶיהָ *They remembered the [sweet] waters of the Sea of Reeds while the enemies razed the Temple foundations.* One interpretation of this phrase is that at the time of the destruction of the Temple, the Jewish people recalled the glorious chapter in their history of the splitting of the Red Sea. The juxtaposition of the two events, one a source of joy and fulfillment, and the other a source of desolation, sadness and distress, heightens the sense of grief. The splitting of the Red Sea was one of the most exalted moments in Jewish history. It was a *giluy Shekhina*, revelation of God's presence, accessible to everyone, and remembering it at the moment of Ḥurban sharpens and intensifies the feeling of grief.

פַּחַד חֵטְא שִׁילֹה, תָּכַף סוֹדֶיהָ *Fear for Shiloh's sin seized all her advisors.* The word *sodeha* means not only its advisors, but more broadly, its counselors, scholars, leaders and prophets. The fear of the sin of Shiloh, attacked and overpowered the counselors and scholars. What was the sin of Shiloh? The *kina* is referring to the sin of the sons of Eli the Priest. Our sages tell us (*Shabbat* 55b; *Yoma* 9a) that once, when a woman wanted to bring a sacrifice at the end of the day, the sons of Eli told her they were tired and that she would have to wait until morning. It is important to bear in mind the context of their misdeed. As priests in the *Mishkan*, the sons of Eli worked hard. Priests, for example, were not permitted to sit in the sacred area (*Yoma* 25a, 69b), nor were they permitted to wear shoes (*Berakhot* 54a; *Yevamot* 102b). At the end of a long day

when they were ready to close, the woman came in to offer a sacrifice of two birds. One might think that the sons of Eli were justified in asking her to wait until the next morning, especially since she would be provided with lodging. However, because of their misdeed, Shiloh was destroyed! They should have realized that perhaps the woman had young children, and they were taking her away from her family for a night. They should have been sufficiently sensitive to understand that she may have felt humiliated, and thought to herself that if she were the wife of a wealthy and prominent person, the priests would not have delayed her sacrifice. The message of the *kina* is that what is considered a sin is often proportionate to the person who commits it. Great leaders need to have a sense of responsibility and realize that they are held to a higher standard than ordinary people. Similarly, Moses' act in striking the rock instead of speaking to it was but a minor violation and would not have been considered a sin if it had been committed by an ordinary person. But in view of Moses' elevated status and sanctity, even the slightest departure from God's word was considered sinful. God has one scale of values for the average person, and another scale of values for the great leader. However slight it might have been, the consequences of the minor violation by the sons of Eli in the *Mishkan* at Shiloh were *takaf sodeha*, they overpowered the great Torah scholars, because ultimately, who can be sure that they themselves did not ever commit such a sin.

Another interpretation of "פַּחַד חֵטְא שִׁילֹה, תָּכַף סוֹדֶיהָ" is that the counselors of the nation, the leaders, the Torah scholars and prophets, feared that if Israel would not repent, then the *Beit HaMikdash* would suffer the same fate as the Sanctuary at Shiloh. It would be completely forgotten and fall into oblivion. Even more terrible than the curse of destruction is the curse of oblivion after the destruction. This is God's threat that Jeremiah conveys to the children of Israel, "Go now to My place which was in Shiloh, where I caused My name to dwell at first, and see what I did to it because of the evil of My people Israel" (Jeremiah 7:12). The verse in Lamentations states, "They sit upon the ground in silence, the elders of the daughter of Zion" (2:10). The elders, the counselors, were silent because of fright. They suddenly remembered that there existed another kind of Ḥurban, the Ḥurban of Shiloh: not only physical destruction, but spiritual oblivion as well, complete obliteration from the memory of the people. They were frightened that God may have intended the same fate for Jerusalem as He decreed for Shiloh. Jerusalem is part of Jewish consciousness and our national collective memory. Although it is true that on Rosh HaShana, we read the story of Shiloh and the birth

of Samuel, and although Shiloh was a *Beit HaMikdash* for 369 years, neither Shiloh nor those years are an integral part of our history. The memory which embraces Jerusalem does not embrace Shiloh.

The ultimate Ḥurban of the *Beit HaMikdash* would have been the curse of oblivion. In fact, this is what our enemies attempted to accomplish. After the Bar Kokhba insurrection, they changed the name of Jerusalem and plowed it under to erase all physical evidence of the *Beit HaMikdash*. But they did not succeed. The Temple may have been destroyed, but we continue to remember it, and Jerusalem is still a living city in our consciousness.

פָּצוּ חֲזִירֵי יָעַר [*The enemy, likened to*] *wild boars exclaimed.* The word *ḥazir* also means swine, and this phrase can be understood as referring to the swine that was offered as a sacrifice in the Temple by a Jewish Hellenist in the time of the Maccabees. This act led to the rebellion by Mattathias the High Priest against the Syrian-Greek regime. Once again, we see that we mourn on Tisha B'Av not only for the destruction of the Temples but for other Jewish tragedies throughout the ages.

אַיֵּה חֲסִידֶיהָ "*What merit do they have?!*" Our enemies taunt us and ask, "Where are your great, pious, powerful men who should protect you from being completely destroyed on the Day of Judgment?" HaKalir is emphasizing the blasphemy that emerged as a result of the Ḥurban. We know that this blasphemy was expressed during the Holocaust as well, when the enemies of the Jews said, "Let your God help you. Let Him save you."

פָּצוּ מַעֲשֵׂה עֶרְוָה לִנְדֵּיהָ *And they proceeded to force depravity upon the exiles.* Another way of understanding this phrase is that it refers to the incident during the Ḥurban when the Ammonites and Moabites took the cherubs on the Holy Ark, which were entwined in an embrace, and displayed them in the streets of Jerusalem as evidence that the Jews worshiped idols. This is another example of the desecration of Israel's name and honor.

אַתָּה קַלִּים הִכְבַּדְתָּ, וּמֵעֲדָיִי עֵרְמוּנִי *You lifted up the lowly* [*Babylon*], *who stripped me of my glory.* This phrase can be interpreted as an allusion to the account (*Shabbat* 88a) that when the Jewish people said "*na'aseh*, we will observe the commandments," before they said "*nishma*, we will listen to what the commandments entail," six hundred thousand angels presented each Jew with two crowns. One crown was inscribed with *na'aseh* and the other with *nishma*. Then, when the Jewish people transgressed with the golden calf, the wicked

angels descended and stripped each Jew of the two crowns. We remember and lament this tragedy as well on Tisha B'Av.

קָרָאתִי לְיוֹשְׁבֵי גִבְעוֹן, עוֹד הֵם זֵרְמוּנִי *I called upon Gibeon our ally, but they, too, betrayed me.* This is an allusion to the treaty which the Jews had entered into with the inhabitants of Gibeon dating back to the days of Joshua, and to the violation of their treaty by the Gibeonites and their betrayal of the Jewish people. HaKalir is lamenting that the Jews have no friends. We are a lonely people because all others have betrayed us.

קוֹלִי לְהַשְׁמִיעַ בַּעֲרָב הִגְרִימוּנִי *I felt compelled to call upon my Arab kin for help.* This refers to the story in the Midrash (*Eikha Raba* 2:4) of how the Jewish exiles were maltreated by the descendants of Ishmael in the land of Arabia. First they gave the starving Jews exceedingly salty and spicy food. Then they gave the Jews containers, but the containers were filled with stagnant air, not water. This betrayal is also remembered on Tisha B'Av.

קָרָאתִי לַמְאַהֲבַי, הֵמָּה רִמּוּנִי *I called upon my lovers, but they fooled me.* This phrase corresponds to the verse in Lamentations (1:19) that all of the allies of the Jewish people betrayed their covenants and promises and joined the enemy.

לָמָּה רוּחַ אַפֵּינוּ, לָטֶבַח שְׁמָרוּ *Why did they lie in wait to slaughter the "breath of our life"?* This phrase is a eulogy for King Josiah who was killed in a battle with the Egyptians. The *kina* mentions him at this point deliberately. In the midst of the lament for the national catastrophes, the destruction of the two Temples, the extermination and exile of hundreds of thousands, and the enemy's attempt to destroy the Jewish people in its entirety, the *kina* pauses to remember the tragedy of the individual. This is typical of Judaism – the collective tragedy does not cause us to forget the individual tragedy. The eulogy for the individual is just as important as the eulogy for all of Israel.

שִׂפְתֵי מְשׁוֹרְרֵי דְבִיר דּוֹמְמוּ, לְהַדְאֲנִי *They who silenced the singers of the Temple to torture me.* This is an allusion to the Gemara (*Ta'anit* 29a) which recounts that when the *Beit HaMikdash* was being invaded, the Levites remained at their stations and continued singing. They were singing the verse (Psalms 94:23), "And He has brought upon them their own iniquity, and will cut them off in their own evil, the LORD our God will cut them off," and before they could finish "the LORD our God will cut them off," the pagans stormed in and captured them. The enemy thought that when they entered the courtyard the Levites would stop singing, but the Levites did not stop. They wanted to

show the enemy that in spite of their temporary success, the singing in the *Beit HaMikdash* will go on.

There is another possible interpretation of this phrase in which the word *Devir* does not refer to the Temple in general, but to the Holy of Holies. In this interpretation, the "singers" could not be the Levites as they did not enter the Holy of Holies. Rather, it refers to the celestial angels. This is based on a *derasha* from my uncle, Rabbi Menachem Krakovsky. He quoted the *Zohar* in *Aḥarei Mot* which states that in the time of the First Temple, when the High Priest completed the Temple service on Yom Kippur, he would not leave the Holy of Holies until he heard the singing of the angels.

כִּי תָם חַקְתָּ בְּכֵס אוֹפַנֶּיךָ *You engraved Jacob's image into Your celestial throne.* With this phrase, HaKalir begins the words of consolation.

This phrase is a reference to the statements in the Gemara and Midrash (*Ḥullin* 91b; Rashi ad loc. s.v. *b'dyukno*; *Yalkut Shimoni, Vayetzeh* 119; *Bereshit Raba* 68:12) that the likeness of Jacob was engraved on the Throne of Glory. The reason that the likeness of Jacob was engraved and not that of the other patriarchs, is because the name Jacob also connotes the collective Jewish people as an entity. There are many examples of this, such as "None has beheld iniquity in Jacob, nor seen perverseness in Israel" (Numbers 23:21) and "Fear not, Jacob, My servant" (Isaiah 44:2). God engraved the likeness of Jacob on His throne because the name Jacob connotes the Jewish people as an eternal covenantal community.

Engraving the image of Jacob demonstrates that the covenant between God and *Knesset Yisrael* is a permanent one. Whatever is engraved on the Throne of Glory is eternal, as written in Psalms: "Your throne stands firm from of old; You exist eternally" (93:2). The covenant is not merely a transient one that was to be abandoned once the Jews sinned and were exiled from the land. Had Jacob been destined to remain in exile forever, his likeness would not have been engraved on the Throne of Glory. Therefore, the *kina* poses the question: Since You wanted to perpetuate the bond between You and Jacob, why do You not punish the persecutors? What is the benefit of keeping the Jewish people in exile?

The motif that our relationship with God is timeless and immutable is also found in Lamentations. We may alienate God for a brief period, but there is no question that we will ultimately return to Him. This is the point of the verses in Lamentations, "Why do You forget us for such a long time, abandon us for so long? Bring us back to You, O Lord, and we will return, renew our

days as of old" (5:20–21). We cannot ever contemplate the complete severance of the relationship because it would be an impossibility. We know that, at some point in time, You will reconcile Yourself with us, and we will be reconciled with You and we will be close to each other. So why do You wait so long? After all, You have engraved Jacob on the celestial throne.

Rabbi Yosef Ber Soloveitchik *zt"l*, the author of the *Beit HaLevi*, interprets the last several verses of the book of Lamentations as a demonstration of the eternal bond between God and the Jewish people. The desolation of Jerusalem described at the conclusion of Lamentations, "For Mount Zion which is desolate, foxes prowl upon it. You, O Lord, are enthroned forever, Your throne is from generation to generation. Why do You forget us for such a long time, abandon us for so long? Bring us back to You, O Lord, and we will return, renew our days as of old" (5:18–21), is proof that the land is promised to Israel. The fact that "Mount Zion…is desolate," that the site of the *Beit HaMikdash* has remained desolate and that the land of Israel has remained unpopulated and in ruins for millennia, and that no other peoples have successfully resettled and rebuilt it, is itself proof that "You, O Lord, are enthroned forever, Your throne is from generation to generation." The desolation itself is proof of the presence of the *Shekhina* and that the Temple Mount is still saturated with holiness.

The *Beit HaLevi* bases his interpretation on the commentary of the Midrash (*Sifra Beḥukkotai* 2:6; *Yalkut Shimoni Beḥukkotai* 675, s.v. *venatati*) on the verse, "And I will make the land desolate, and your enemies that dwell in it will be astonished" (Leviticus 26:32). The Midrash says, "This is a noble trait of the land of Israel, that it grants from its fruits only to its children." The Midrash understands the second half of the verse, "וְשָׁמְמוּ עָלֶיהָ אֹיְבֵיכֶם הַיֹּשְׁבִים בָּהּ," to mean that the enemies who exile the Jews and take their place in the land of Israel will reside in a desolate land. They will starve because the land will not give of itself to them. There is a sense of loyalty on the part of the land; she will never betray her people; she will never offer anything of herself to strangers or conquerors. The fact that "Mount Zion…is desolate" is proof that the sanctity with which the land was endowed by Joshua and Ezra is still in effect; it was sanctified on a temporary basis, and it was sanctified eternally for the future.

תָּשִׁיב לָהֶם גְּמוּל, כְּאָז חֲזוֹת פָּנֶיךָ *Repay them, as when You showed Your face to us.* The Jewish people should be permitted to return to Israel because God should repay them as dictated by the relationship of *ke'az ḥazot panekha*, when Jacob

beheld the face of God. God cannot forget the Jews because of the covenant with Jacob. When Jacob awoke in Beit El, he was ḥazot panekha, he beheld the face of God when he said, "This is none other than the House of God and this is the gate of heaven" (Genesis 28:17). The *paytan* declares to God that He can never depart from that site, no matter how desolate it may be.

Another interpretation of this phrase is that whoever inflicts harm upon a Jew is treated as if he inflicted harm upon God. The previous phrase stated that the likeness of Jacob, representing all of Israel, is engraved on the Throne of Glory, which reflects the unity of the destiny of the Jewish people with God. Thus, whenever a Jew feels hurt, abused or humiliated, God experiences the same feeling. Therefore, the *paytan* beseeches God to punish our enemies so that we may be able to see His face.

תִּקְרָא לְשַׁבְּרָם כּוֹס, כָּמוּס בְּפָנֶיךָ *Summon them to sip Your secret cup of poison.* HaKalir is asking for revenge. He asks that God repay the enemies of Israel with the cup of bitterness that He has hidden.

תָּבֹא אֶל צָר אֲשֶׁר כִּלָּנוּ *Come upon the enemy who has annihilated us.* The enemy was not successful, and we were not annihilated, but that was certainly their intent.

לִמְבוֹא חֲמָת, בְּחֶמְמָה נְהַלָּנוּ / עַד לַחֲלַח וְחָבוֹר הִגְלָנוּ *Led us away to the entrance of Hamath, expelled us to Halah and Habor.* These places are referred to in connection with the Assyrian exile of the Ten Tribes (II Kings 17:6; Chronicles 5:26). We mourn this exile as well.

רָם הַבֵּט נָא, עַמְּךָ כֻּלָּנוּ *Look down from on high; we are all Your faithful people.* The *paytan* declares, *Ram*, Almighty, in spite of the fact that we have sinned and have been alienated from You for so long, we have still not abandoned hope for our continued relationship. Even now, in spite of all our suffering, *habet na*, look at us, because *amkha kulanu*, we are Your people. True, we are scattered all over the world and we comprise many communities, languages and mores. A Jew from Halah and Habor, and a Canadian or American Jew do not look alike. But in spite of all the differences within the Jewish community, despite the differences of ability and incommensurate historical paths, there is something that unites all of us. What unites the Jews is Your Torah, and since we belong to You, You cannot rid Yourself of us. We belong to You, and You belong to us.

זְכֹר יהוה מֶה־הָיָה לָנוּ **Remember, God, what has happened to us.** One could ask why it is necessary for the *paytan* to speak of remembrance. After all, it is a reality for the Jews that Nebuchadnezzar invaded Israel, destroyed the Temple and slew hundreds of thousands of Jews. Why is memory necessary? The reference, however, is not to the Jewish people, but to God. God should remember what He has promised us because He should look at *meh haya lanu*, what has befallen us.

7

alphabetical alliterative rhyme structure, repeating odd-numbered letters five times, and even-numbered letters six times. The last stanza is probably a later addition, ending with the first phrase of the next kina. Commentary for this kina begins on page 220.

אֵיכָה How could You rush Your wrath,
    ruining Your loyal people at the hand of Rome,
and not remember Your covenant with Abraham,
    who met the challenge of Your trials?
And so, we exclaim,
              Remember, God, what has happened to us!

אֵיכָה How could You scorn us with Your scorn,
exiling at the hand of the haughty, those You freed from Egypt,
and not remember the rapid road You once opened for the
    banner-bearing tribes?
And so, we speak,
               Remember, God, what has happened to us!

אֵיכָה How could You pronounce such words,
thrusting Your masses into wanton hands,
and not remember the assembly place You designated for Your followers?
And so, we lament,
               Remember, God, what has happened to us!

אֵיכָה How could You abandon Your Sanctuary in Your rage,
allowing strangers to defile it,
and not remember the wedding vows at Horeb,
    which You etched in stone for Your dear ones?
And so, we state,
               Remember, God, what has happened to us!

אֵיכָה How could You so diligently toil
to allow brutes to tear Your lambs to pieces,
and not remember the precious friendship
    with those whom You singled out to receive the Torah?
And so, we ululate,
               Remember, God, what has happened to us!

7

Six of the kinot by HaKalir start with the word "Eikha." This kina has eleven three-line stanzas of a recurring form: The first line starts with "Eikha," and speaks of the horrors of the present, the second yearns for the glory of old, and the third line is an expression of mourning, and a repeated plea, "Remember, God, what has happened to us! וְכֹר יהוה מֶה־הָיָה לָנוּ *(Lam. 5:1). The paytan uses an*

אֵיכָה אַצְתָּ בְּאַפֶּךָ, לְאַבֵּד בְּיַד אֲדוֹמִים אֱמוּנֶיךָ.
וְלֹא זָכַרְתָּ בְּרִית בֵּין בְּתָרִים אֲשֶׁר בֵּרַרְתָּ לִבְחוּנֶיךָ.
וּבְכֵן בְּטֻיֵּנוּ.   זְכֹר יהוה מֶה־הָיָה לָנוּ:

אֵיכָה גָּעַרְתָּ בְּגַעֲרָתְךָ, לַגָלוֹת בְּיַד גֵּאִים גְּאוּלֶיךָ.
וְלֹא זָכַרְתָּ דְּלִיגַת דִּלּוּג דֶּרֶךְ, אֲשֶׁר דִּלַגְתָּ לְדִגְלֶיךָ.
וּבְכֵן דֻּבַּרְנוּ.   זְכֹר יהוה מֶה־הָיָה לָנוּ:

אֵיכָה הַגְתָּ בְּהֶגְיֶךָ, לַהֲדֹף בְּיַד הוֹלְלִים הֲמוֹנֶיךָ.
וְלֹא זָכַרְתָּ וְעוּד וֶתֶק וֶסֶת, אֲשֶׁר וְעַדְתָּ לְוֹעוּדֶיךָ.
וּבְכֵן וְקוֹנֵנוּ.   זְכֹר יהוה מֶה־הָיָה לָנוּ:

אֵיכָה זָנַחְתָּ בְּזַעֲמֶךָ, לְזַלְזֵל בְּיַד זָרִים זְבוּלֶיךָ.
וְלֹא זָכַרְתָּ חִתּוּן חֻקֵּי חוֹרֵב, אֲשֶׁר חָקַקְתָּ לַחֲמוּלֶיךָ.
וּבְכֵן חֻוִּינוּ.   זְכֹר יהוה מֶה־הָיָה לָנוּ:

אֵיכָה טָרַחְתָּ בְּטָרְחֲךָ, לִטְרֹף בְּיַד טְמֵאִים טְלָאֶיךָ.
וְלֹא זָכַרְתָּ יְקַר יְדִידוּת יֹשֶׁר, אֲשֶׁר יִחַדְתָּ לְיוֹדְעֶיךָ.
וּבְכֵן יִלַּלְנוּ.   זְכֹר יהוה מֶה־הָיָה לָנוּ:

אֵיכָה How could You aim Your anger,
enabling sinners to despoil Your vineyard,
and not remember the lesson You taught to the ones
    You took to Yourself, not to abandon them?
And so, we howl,
                        Remember, God, what has happened to us!

אֵיכָה How could You reject us,
permitting oppressors to exterminate those who exalt You,
and not remember how You carried us on the wings of eagles?
And so, we moan,
                        Remember, God, what has happened to us!

אֵיכָה How could You condemn us in Your fury,
imprisoning Your faith-witnesses in the hands of fiends,
and not remember the glorious crowns with which
    You bedecked Your servants?
And so, we answer,
                        Remember, God, what has happened to us!

אֵיכָה How could You utter in Your frightening anger,
defiling Your wonderful ones at the hands of the lewd,
and not remember the beautiful Temple songs so special to Your people?
And so, we shout,
                        Remember, God, what has happened to us!

אֵיכָה How could You issue a declaration,
selling Your special servants to slave masters,
and not remember the thousands of angels present at Sinai?
And so, we sigh,
                        Remember, God, what has happened to us!

אֵיכָה How could You open Your mouth and long for
the looting of Your loyal ones at the hands of pirates,
and not remember the resplendent curls of hair which
    You arranged for Your innocents?
And so, we cry,
                        Remember, God, what has happened to us!

תָּאַנְנוּ We cry in anguish, pouring out our hearts like water.
Why, on this day, have we fallen captive twice?
How well do I remember dwelling tranquilly in Jerusalem!
I grieve, and now I [let my laments] soar to heaven!

Kina 8 starts on page 236.

אֵיכָה כּוּנַּנְתָּ בְּכַעְסְךָ, לְכַלּוֹת בְּיַד כּוֹשְׁלִים כַּרְמֶךָ.
וְלֹא זָכַרְתָּ לֹא לְוֻנַּח לְעוֹלָם, אֲשֶׁר לִמַּדְתָּ לְלִקּוּחֶיךָ.
וּבְכֵן לְהַגְּנוּ.   זְכֹר יהוה מֶה־הָיָה לָנוּ:

אֵיכָה מִלֵּלְתָּ בְּמַאַסְךָ, לִמְחוֹת בְּיַד מוֹנִים מְנַשְּׂאֶיךָ.
וְלֹא זָכַרְתָּ נְשִׂיאַת נוֹצַת נֶשֶׁר, אֲשֶׁר נָשָׂאתָ לִנְשׂוּאֶיךָ.
וּבְכֵן נְהִינוּ.   זְכֹר יהוה מֶה־הָיָה לָנוּ:

אֵיכָה סַחְתָּ בְּסַעְרְךָ, לִסְגֹּר בְּיַד סְעִפִים סְהָדֶיךָ.
וְלֹא זָכַרְתָּ עֹז עֲדִי עֲדָיִים, אֲשֶׁר עִטַּרְתָּ לַעֲבָדֶיךָ.
וּבְכֵן עָנִינוּ.   זְכֹר יהוה מֶה־הָיָה לָנוּ:

אֵיכָה פָּצְתָּ בְּפַחְדְּךָ, לִפְגֹּר בְּיַד פָּרִיצִים פְּלָאֶיךָ.
וְלֹא זָכַרְתָּ צַהֲלַת צְבִי צֶדֶק, אֲשֶׁר צִפַּנְתָּ לִצְבָאֶיךָ.
וּבְכֵן צָעַקְנוּ.   זְכֹר יהוה מֶה־הָיָה לָנוּ:

אֵיכָה קָרָאתָ בִקְרִיאָתְךָ, לַקְנוֹת בְּיַד קָמִים קְרוּאֶיךָ.
וְלֹא זָכַרְתָּ רֶגֶשׁ רֶכֶב רִבֹּתַיִם, אֲשֶׁר רִצִּיתָ לְרֵעֶיךָ.
וּבְכֵן רַגְּנוּ.   זְכֹר יהוה מֶה־הָיָה לָנוּ:

אֵיכָה שָׁאַפְתָּ בְּשַׁאְפְּךָ, לִשְׁלוֹת בְּיַד שׁוֹלְלִים שְׁלֵמֶיךָ.
וְלֹא זָכַרְתָּ תְּקֹף תַּלְתַּלֵּי תֹאַר, אֲשֶׁר תִּכַּנְתָּ לִתְמִימֶיךָ.
וּבְכֵן תָּאַנְנוּ.   זְכֹר יהוה מֶה־הָיָה לָנוּ:

תָּאַנְנוּ לִשְׁפֹּךְ כַּמַּיִם / עַל מַה בְּיוֹם זֶה נִשְׁבֵּינוּ פַּעֲמַיִם / זִכְרִי בִּהְיוֹתִי
יוֹשֶׁבֶת בְּשַׁלְוָה בִּירוּשָׁלַיִם / רָגַנְתִּי, וְעַתָּה אֲאַדֶּה עַד חוּג שָׁמַיִם:

Kina 8 starts on page 237.

COMMENTARY ON KINA 7

This *kina* is the first in a series of *kinot* by Rabbi Elazar HaKalir, each beginning with the word *eikha*. The word *eikha* is the main motif of Tisha B'Av and the quintessential question presented by Tisha B'Av: "How is it possible? I do not understand."

אֵיכָה אַצְתָּ בְאַפֶּךָ *How could You rush Your wrath*. One could ask what right we have to pose such a question to the Almighty. Normally, the halakha does not permit us to ask this type of question; rather it prescribes that we unquestioningly accept the judgment of God. We are guided by the concept that a person is required to bless God for bad times, for tragedy and misfortune, just as he blesses God for good times (*Berakhot* 54a). When confronted with tragedy, we do not argue with God; rather we say, "Blessed is the true Judge." We do not understand misfortune because we have no right to expect that we will understand.

The case of *kinot* on Tisha B'Av, however, is an exception to the general rule. We are permitted to ask *eikha*, because we are following the precedent of Jeremiah the Prophet who posed the question *eikha* in the book of Lamentations. And Jeremiah posed this question only because he was given a *heter*, special permission, by God Himself, who instructed him to write *"Eikha yashva vadad,"* the first sentence of the book of Lamentations. In effect, God granted a unique privilege to Jeremiah to address himself to God with these otherwise impermissible questions and to write *kinot*, lamentations, in the form of the book of Lamentations. The reason that God granted permission to express these otherwise inappropriate questions is that Jeremiah was expressing mourning for the destruction of the Temple, and this tragedy was so overwhelming that the prophet, and anyone else, was granted unlimited freedom to pose questions that would have been inappropriate under any other circumstance. Thus, Rabbi Elazar HaKalir is permitted to address the question *eikha* to God, only because that question was already posed to God by Jeremiah in Lamentations.

The book of Lamentations consists of three sections. The first section is comprised of Chapters 1 and 2 which essentially are *kinot* in which the prophet asks the question *eikha*. Thus, in these two chapters, Lamentations asserts that it is appropriate to pose the question *eikha*.

The next section of the book is Chapter 3: "I am the man who has seen the affliction by the rod of His anger" (3:1). This chapter records the answer re-

ceived by Jeremiah from God to the questions posed in the first two chapters. The answer is *tzidduk hadin*, the acknowledgment of the justness of God's ways, and the fact that human beings are endowed with free will. With the beginning of this third chapter, the permission to ask *eikha* has been revoked. According to our sages (*Eikha Raba, Petiḥta* 28 and 3:1), the book of Lamentations originally consisted of only the first two chapters, both of which pose questions. When the book was destroyed and rewritten (Jeremiah, ch. 36), God ordained that it be extended to include the additional chapters, as well.

The last section of Lamentations consists of chapters 4 and 5, which commence with the eulogy that Jeremiah delivered in honor of King Josiah, the subject of an entire *kina*, "וַיְקוֹנֵן יִרְמְיָהוּ עַל־יֹאשִׁיָּהוּ".

לְאַבֵּד בְּיַד אֲדוֹמִים אֱמוּנֶיךָ *Ruining Your loyal people at the hand of Rome.* The simple interpretation is that *Adomim* refers to the Romans, who were responsible for the destruction of the Second Temple. Rome is identified with Edom in the Torah's recounting of the lineage of Esau, who is referred to as Edom: "The chief of Magdiel, the chief of Iram, these are the chiefs of Edom" (Genesis 36:43), and Rashi comments (ad loc.) that Magdiel is Rome.

The reference to Rome, however, should not be taken literally, but should be seen as a symbol for the most powerful of the nations of the world. Historically, the nation that opposed the Jews was always the most powerful nation of its time. In the days of Jeremiah, the Babylonian Empire was the most powerful nation. Five hundred years later, at the time of the Second Temple, this position was occupied by the Roman Empire.

Edom also refers to Amalek, the grandson of Esau (Genesis 36:12). Amalek is not a racial or ethnic concept. Rather, it is the enemy, regardless of race or historical era, that seeks to destroy the Jews, that seeks to destroy the uniqueness and the individual identity and spiritual personality of the Jew. The final *galut*, the final exile, which will be terminated by the arrival of the Messiah, is the *galut* caused by Amalek, as Rashi says, "God's name and His throne will not be complete until the name of Amalek is erased" (Rashi, Exodus 17:16, s.v. *ki yad*).

וְלֹא זָכַרְתָּ בְּרִית בֵּין בְּתָרִים *And not remember Your covenant with Abraham.* The *kina* mentions all of the covenants with God, from Abraham to the time of the destruction of the Temple, and laments that in spite of all of the covenants and promises, the Ḥurban took place.

The *paytan* implies that there is a link between Edom and the *Berit bein*

HaBetarim, the "Covenant between the Pieces," that God entered into with Abraham. The link is found in the statement in the *Berit bein HaBetarim* that the land of Israel is promised to Abraham's descendants (Genesis 15:18). Subsequently, God promises Abraham, "For in Isaac [*beYitzḥak*] shall you have descendants" (Genesis 21:12). Our sages focus on the word *beYitzḥak*, and interpret it as meaning "from Yitzḥak, but not all of Yitzḥak" (*Nedarim* 31a; *Sanhedrin* 59b), that is, not all of Isaac's children will be considered Abraham's descendants. There was a specific promise that Esau, the son of Isaac, would *not* share in the *Berit bein HaBetarim*, nor in the later prophecies and revelations in which Abraham encountered God. And now, the *kina* laments, this same Esau who was excluded from the covenant is the very one, in the person of Titus, who desecrated the Holy of Holies. "How is this turn of events possible?" is the implied challenge posed by the *kina*.

אֲשֶׁר בֵּרַרְתָּ לִבְחוּנֶיךָ *Who met the challenge of Your trials.* The literal meaning of this phrase can be rendered as "the covenant that You clarified to those whom You tested." What God clarified was that from that time forward, He and the Jewish people were partners. Whatever is done to a Jew is considered as if it were done to God. The Torah states, "Rise up, O Lord, and may Your enemies be scattered" (Numbers 10:35). The Midrash (*Sifrei Beha'alotekha*, Piska 26; see also Rashi, ad loc., s.v. *misanekha*) comments, "And does the Almighty have enemies? What the Torah is telling us, is that whoever is an enemy of Israel is considered as though he is an enemy of the Almighty." This concept was established by the *Berit bein HaBetarim*.

The word *liveḥunekha* refers to those who were tested by God and passed the test, such as Abraham. This alludes to the statement of our sages (*Midrash Zuta, Shir HaShirim* [Buber] 1:15), that Esau was also given the option to participate in the divine covenant. If he had not sold the right of the firstborn, he would have been entitled to the same destiny which God bestowed upon Jacob. Our sages say (*Bereshit Raba* 82:13) that "Esau did not want to comply with the contract." The intent is that Esau did not want to enter into a legally binding arrangement which contained, as one of its provisions, "Your descendants will be strangers in a land that is not theirs" (Genesis 15:13).

אֵיכָה גָּעַרְתָּ בְגַעֲרָתָךְ ... וְלֹא זָכַרְתָּ דְּלִיעַת דִּלּוּג דֶּרֶךְ, אֲשֶׁר דִּלַּגְתָּ לְדְגָלֶיךָ *How could You scorn us with Your scorn ... and not remember the rapid road You once opened for the banner-bearing tribes.* The *kina* continues to express the theme that God has been directly involved in Jewish tragedies. When traveling in the desert, God did not guide the Jewish people from the distance of His transcendent

abode. "The LORD went before them by day in a pillar of cloud" (Exodus 13:21). The Almighty Himself traveled with the Jewish people because He Himself was in slavery with them and was liberated with them.

The *kina* is making another point with the use of the phrase "*deligat dilug derekh.*" This phrase refers to *kefitzat derekh*, the supernatural shortening of the time of travel that God may implement. When the Jews left Egypt, the journey from Mount Sinai, which normally takes eleven days, was accomplished in three days (Deuteronomy 1:2; and see Rashi, ad loc.). It is true that the people sinned and their arrival was delayed for thirty-eight years, but, the *kina* stresses, God was initially in haste to bring the Jews to Israel because of the essential link of the Jew to the land of Israel. God, however, has forgotten this eagerness and has exiled His people, and the *kina* poses the challenge, "Why have You wrought this separation between the land and its people?"

There are other possible interpretations of the phrase *dilug derekh*. It may refer to the entire forty-year sojourn of the Jewish people in the desert because God conducted the travels of the Jewish people throughout this period in a miraculous fashion, as described by Moses (Deuteronomy 8:4). Alternatively, *dilug derekh* may be an allusion to the midrash (*Mekhilta, Bo* 14, s.v. *vayisu*) that says that on the night of Pesaḥ, the Jewish people were transported on the wings of the *Shekhina* from the land of Goshen to Egypt's capital city.

Finally, the *paytan* is referring to another aspect of the exodus. When the Jews were redeemed from Egypt and traveled through the desert, it was not only a great miracle, but it was also a testament to the faith of the Jewish people, as the prophet says, "Thus says the LORD: I remember for you the righteousness of your youth…your following after Me in the desert" (Jeremiah 2:2). God told Jeremiah that He will always remember the complete faith and trust which the Jewish people demonstrated when He told them to leave the civilized country of Egypt and venture into the wilderness. The *paytan* argues in the *kina* that the faith of Israel during the exodus should have protected her from the Babylonian and Roman exiles.

The word *lidegalekha* again sounds the theme of God's direct involvement in Israel's tragedies. The banners were not only the banners of the Jews, they were *degalekha, Your* banners, as well. *You* were with us in our travels, *You* were in bondage with us in Egypt, and now *You* are in exile with us.

זְכֹר יהוה מֶה־הָיָה לָנוּ *Remember, God, what has happened to us.* The word *lanu*, "us," does not mean only the Jewish people. Rather, it means "You and us," for God, too, is in exile.

COMMENTARY ON KINA 7

לַהֲדֹף בְּיַד הוֹלְלִים הֲמוֹנֶךְ *Thrusting Your masses into wanton hands.* The distinguishing feature of the *hollelim*, "wanton hands," is that they have no moral standards. They have no code of behavior or sense of discipline and do whatever gives them pleasure. Juxtaposed to the *hollelim*, is the *hamon*, the crowd. But this crowd is not unruly or undisciplined. It is the *Knesset Yisrael*, and the larger the gathering, the more conspicuous is the presence of the *Shekhina*. This principle is expressly articulated in connection with *Birkat HaMazon*, the Grace after Meals. The Mishna says in the name of Rabbi Yose HaGalili (*Berakhot* 49b) that if ten people are present, the one who introduces *Birkat HaMazon* says, "נְבָרֵךְ אֱלֹהֵינוּ" (let us bless our God), if one hundred are present he says, "נְבָרֵךְ יהוה אֱלֹהֵינוּ" (let us bless the LORD our God), if one thousand are present he says, "נְבָרֵךְ לַיהוה אֱלֹהֵינוּ אֱלֹהֵי יִשְׂרָאֵל" (let us bless the LORD our God, the God of Israel), and if ten thousand are present he says "נְבָרֵךְ לַיהוה אֱלֹהֵינוּ אֱלֹהֵי יִשְׂרָאֵל אֱלֹהֵי צְבָאוֹת יוֹשֵׁב הַכְּרוּבִים עַל הַמָּזוֹן שֶׁאָכַלְנוּ" (let us bless the LORD our God, the God of Israel, the God of hosts, enthroned upon the Cherubs, for the food that we have eaten). The more numerous the multitude, the higher is the level on which the Jew finds himself. This is the opposite of the conventional wisdom. Customarily, the crowd lowers the common level of intellect. Judaism, however, has a different dynamic. The Torah wants the assemblage to *raise* the common level of intellect and enable activities that the individual cannot perform such as the recitation of Kaddish, *Kedusha* and *Barekhu*. The Jew becomes exalted and his mind enhanced by joining the multitude.

וְלֹא זָכַרְתָּ וְעוֹד וְתֵק וְסֵת, אֲשֶׁר וְעַדְתָּ לְוֹעוּדֶיךָ *And not remember the assembly place You designated for Your followers.* The *paytan* challenges God that He did not remember the old rendezvous that He had from time to time with His people, the appointments that He granted to those who were worthy of them. The word *vi'udekha* refers to one who is involved with God, one who is tied by an appointment to Him. The *paytan* poses the challenge that if God had an appointment with the Jews, it was clearly to take place in Israel, and if that is the case, why, asks the *paytan*, did You exile the Jews and render it impossible for the appointment to take place?

The word *vi'ud* means a "rendezvous," and the concept of the rendezvous with God is of fundamental importance in Judaism. The *Ohel Mo'ed*, which comes from the same root as the word *vi'ud*, was the meeting place for Moses and God, as the Torah says, "וְנוֹעַדְתִּי לְךָ שָׁם", And there I will meet with you, and I will speak with you from above the cover of the Ark from between the

two cherubs which are upon the Ark of the Testimony" (Exodus 25:22), and "בְּאֹהֶל מוֹעֵד אֲשֶׁר אִוָּעֵד לְךָ שָׁמָּה, in the Tent of Meeting where I will meet with you" (Exodus 30:36). The *Mikdash*, however, was not only the place where God met with Moses, it was also the place אֲשֶׁר וְעַדְתִּי לְועֲדֶיךָ, the place for meetings between God and the entire *Knesset Yisrael*. God declares that He will have a rendezvous with all of *Knesset Yisrael*, as described in the Torah, "It shall be a continual burnt-offering throughout your generations at the door of the *Ohel Mo'ed*, אֲשֶׁר אִוָּעֵד לָכֶם שָׁמָּה, where I will meet with you…וְנֹעַדְתִּי שָׁמָּה לִבְנֵי יִשְׂרָאֵל, And there I will meet with the children of Israel" (Exodus 29:42–43). God will meet not only with Moses, but with all of Israel, and God will keep His rendezvous.

It is God's promise that every Jew has a rendezvous from time to time with Him. Every Jew, no matter how plain or simple, will be able to rise to the level of spiritual greatness that results from God, from time to time, bestowing His greatness upon a person. The definition of a Jew is a person who experiences this periodic rendezvous with God. There can be no delay in the rendezvous. The Jew does not say that he feels like postponing Tisha B'Av for a day. The essence of Judaism is *vi'ud*, the immutable rendezvous. This is what the Torah requires of the Jew.

The Torah introduced the novel concept of *vi'ud* between the Almighty and vast multitudes. There cannot be a rendezvous between a horde, on the one hand, and an individual, on the other. A rendezvous implies the element of confidentiality, privacy and intimacy. This encounter between God and *Knesset Yisrael* can still be called a rendezvous because *Knesset Yisrael* is not merely a crowd of many people, but it can appear as an individual: "My sister, my bride" (Song of Songs 4:9).

The word *veset* means a regular precise time, an appointment that one cannot ignore. It also has the connotation of repetitiveness, an established pattern or way of life. Yom Tov is a *veset*, a special time which is endowed with *kedushat hayom*, the sanctity of the day. The nature of the *veset* on Yom Tov is that, "Three times in the year all your males shall appear before the Lord God" (Exodus 23:17). The mitzva of appearing before God at the *Beit HaMikdash* is separate and apart from the mitzva to bring a sacrifice. It is, rather, a rendezvous with God. The *paytan* is saying that God did not remember the old rendezvous He kept from time to time when *Knesset Yisrael* met with Him on the festivals.

The word *veset* has another connotation. It implies a stable relationship, so that when the regular recurring events are slow in coming, one becomes

anxious and concerned. The Jewish people and God are so intimate with each other that when He omits a visit, they become anxious. In the absence of a meeting with God, *Knesset Yisrael* develops symptoms just as a woman reacts to the absence of her regular menstrual period, which is also referred to as *veset*. The Jewish people must see God periodically and maintain a relationship with Him.

There is a subtle distinction between *veset* and *vi'ud*. *Veset* implies a meeting when there is an appointment, and *vi'ud* can mean a meeting without an appointment. The Jews have the benefit of both. They are assured that, from time to time, God will meet with them, such as on Yom Tov. At other times, they know that even without a planned meeting, there can instantly be a time when they find themselves confronted by God. An example of the sudden meeting with God, without preparation or preliminaries, is Moses' encounter with God at the burning bush (Exodus 3:3). Sometimes God meets man unexpectedly, by surprise, and sometimes He asks man to join Him by extending an invitation. *Veset* means precision as far as time is concerned, and in this regard *veset* is not just a word, but it encapsulates our entire philosophy. Judaism has a unique sensitivity to time which is perhaps the most central idea of the world view of the Jew. For example, if the latest time for reciting *Keriat Shema* is 8:45 in the morning, and one recites it at 8:48, the time for *Keriat Shema* has passed and one has not fulfilled the mitzva of reciting *Keriat Shema*. It is hard for the non-Jewish world to understand what is so important to the Jew about a few minutes. *Veset* represents the sensitivity to time, and the Jew's readiness to live in accordance with the obligations of those times.

אֵיכָה זָנַחְתָּ בְזַעְמְךָ, לְזַלְזֵל בְּיַד זָרִים זְבוּלֶיךָ *How could You abandon Your Sanctuary in Your rage, allowing strangers to defile it.* The first three stanzas of this *kina* addressed God's allowing the Romans to kill the Jews. The *kina* now shifts focus to the destruction of the Temple.

The word *zar*, "stranger," was chosen deliberately. The *zar* cannot claim he has a share in our life. No one can argue that Titus and the Roman legionnaires have anything in common with our family or God. The *zevul*, the Holy of Holies, was prepared exclusively for God and the Jewish people. The *kina* is expressing two laments. First, the destruction of the Temple was, itself, a terrible experience. But, beyond that, the fact that the *Beit HaMikdash* was defiled by strangers is incomprehensible. Sometimes a stranger is permitted to enter the house, but not this House. There was an intimate encounter between the High Priest and the Almighty in the *zevul* on Yom Kippur. "And there shall be no man in the Tent of Meeting when he goes in to make atone-

ment in the holy place" (Exodus 16:17). The *paytan* asks plaintively, "How could Titus invade that exclusive and most intimate hiding place? How is it possible?"

Zevul refers to the innermost place in a house. There are other rooms called *ma'on*, which are public rooms for socializing and entertainment. But the *zevul* is the most intimate, private and exclusive part of the home. It is the private domain of a married couple, associated with the intimacy of family life. In the Midrash, *zevul* is often used to refer to the Holy of Holies because it was the most private site in the Temple, the symbol of the intimate relationship between God and the Jewish people. Titus not only destroyed the Temple, but he desecrated and defiled it. He entered the Holy of Holies while grasping a harlot (*Gittin* 56b). This too is part of the *kina*'s complaint.

וְלֹא זָכַרְתָּ חִתּוּן חֻקֵּי חוֹרֵב, אֲשֶׁר חָקַקְתָּ *And not remember the wedding vows at Horeb, which You etched in stone.* This phrase refers to the revelation at Mount Sinai, which constituted a wedding ceremony between God and the Jewish people. God does not remember that the giving of the Torah at Mount Sinai represented not merely an agreement between Him and the Jewish people, but represented also a betrothal and marriage. The *paytan* says to God, "You give the impression to the world that You have abandoned us completely. But this cannot be true. After all, we are married to one another!" One of the obligations prescribed by the *ketuba* (marriage contract) is that a husband is required to redeem his wife if she is held captive, and yet God has not redeemed His captive wife, the Jewish people.

The Jewish marriage has two components, *erusin*, the betrothal, and *nesu'in*, the wedding. *Erusin* is the performance of a legal act, consisting of the man taking an object of monetary value, such as a ring, and giving it to the woman and stating, "You are hereby betrothed to me with this ring." *Erusin* is the entering into of a contract. *Nesu'in*, in contrast, is not a contract. It is a marriage of destinies, of hopes. The intimacy of married life is the result of *nesu'in*. *Nesu'in* comes to full expression with children and grandchildren. It is a new community; it is something metaphysical, not simply juridical. The event at Mount Sinai was *nesu'in*, not *erusin*. The relationship between God and His people is not a juridical, formalistic one, but is a metaphysical, personal relationship. The symbol for this intimacy between God and *Knesset Yisrael* is the *Beit HaMikdash*, the home that every intimate couple needs. The notion of intimacy is the defining characteristic of *zevul*, the hidden, secret place. It is more than merely a house that provides shade and protection. When a Jew enters the *Beit HaMikdash*, he feels intimate with God, and he says things he

would not say in public. The concept of the intimate relationship with God is manifested in Jewish prayer, as well. Many of our prayers are recited silently, as Hannah exemplified, "And Hannah spoke in her heart...and her voice could not be heard" (1 Samuel 1:13). Sometimes prayer is said aloud and is a public performance, like the repetition of the Amida. But sometimes it is an intimate expression, as the silent Amida.

Rabbi Elazar HaKalir protests and says, in effect, that if God has an intimate home, He should invite only His spouse to enter. Instead, He permitted the hated enemy, Titus, to enter the most intimate chamber of His home, the Holy of Holies. He permitted the intimate *zevul* to be violated by *zarim*, and, "You did not remember the intimacy that You promised the Jewish people and for which the *ḥukei Ḥorev*, the laws of Sinai, were responsible."

Consistent with the view that the experience at Mount Sinai represents the marriage ceremony between God and the Jewish people, the Midrash (*Shemot Raba* 43:1; 46:1) explains why Moses shattered the Tablets. At the marriage ceremony of Mount Sinai, the Tablets of the Law served as the *kesef kiddushin*, the monetary marriage consideration, which God was to give to His bride, *Knesset Yisrael*. The *kiddushin*, the betrothal of Israel by God at Mount Sinai was a *kiddushin al yedei shaliaḥ*, a betrothal by an agent. Moses was the agent of God, charged with the mission of delivering the *kesef kiddushin*, the Tablets, to the bride, the Jewish people. It is a halakhic principle that, before the *kesef kiddushin* is delivered, the *mekadesh*, the husband-to-be, may change his mind and refrain from delivering the *kesef kiddushin*, and the woman will not be betrothed. Consequently, if the woman were to have relations with another man at that point, it would not be considered adultery as she would not have the status of a betrothed woman. It is for this reason that Moses shattered the Tablets. If he had delivered them, *Knesset Yisrael* would have been married to God, and would have been fully responsible for the sin of the golden calf. Moses wanted the *kiddushin* to be null and void, so he destroyed the *kesef kiddushin*.

לַחֲמוּלֶיךָ *Your dear ones.* There are two words in Hebrew for the general concept of mercy: sympathy and compassion *ḥemla* and *raḥamim*. *Raḥamim*, however, has the additional connotation of love. When we say that God has *raḥamim* for us, it means not only that He has compassion for us, but also that He loves us. *Targum Onkelos* often translates *ahava*, love, as *raḥmanuta* (see, for example, his translation of "וְאָהַבְתָּ אֵת יהוה אֱלֹהֶיךָ," Deuteronomy 6:5). The love connoted by *raḥamim* is a conscious act, a deliberate value judgment. I love a person because I consider him to be worthy of my love. *Ḥemla*, on the

other hand, does not involve any value judgment, but is an automatic compulsive reaction on the part of a human being. If I am walking in the street and see someone in pain, I feel compassion for him whether I know him or not, whether he is worthy of my compassion or not. I cannot help myself. The *paytan*'s argument to God is that He has *ḥemla* for the Jewish people. He must love them even if He wants to reject them because they are sinful. He cannot help Himself. He *must* have compassion and love for *Knesset Yisrael*. "If so," says the *paytan*, "why do You punish us so much?"

וּבְכֵן חִוִּינוּ *And so, we state.* The word *hivinu* has the connotation of an authoritative statement which carries significant weight, such as the pronouncement of an opinion by a judge. The Jewish nation is declaring its authoritative opinion as a judge that God is legally obligated to redeem them. God is their husband, and a husband is legally obligated to redeem his wife from captivity.

אֵיכָה טָרַחְתָּ בְּטָרְחָךְ *How could You so diligently toil.* This phrase is another expression of the theme that when the Jewish people are in crisis, God suffers with them. It requires a painful effort by God to punish His people. In fact, it is distressing to Him to punish people in general, even evildoers (*Sanhedrin* 46a). The *paytan*'s argument is: "If it is so painful to You to send the Jewish people into exile, why did You do so?"

לִטְרֹף בְּיַד טְמֵאִים טְלָאֶיךָ *To allow brutes to tear Your lambs to pieces.* Rabbi Elazar HaKalir alludes to the requirement of *ma'aser behema*, bringing a tithe of one's animals, for sacrifice in the Temple. The Mishna (*Bekhorot* 58b) describes the process of selecting the *ma'aser*. One gathers his sheep into a pen and lets them out through a narrow passageway. As they pass, he counts them one by one, and for each of the first nine, he says, "*ḥullin*, not sacred." As the tenth sheep passes, he marks it with red dye and says, "*harei zeh ma'aser*, this one is *ma'aser*." The tenth sheep is sacred and will be taken to Jerusalem and offered as a sacrifice at the Temple.

What is the status of the first nine sheep? Of course they are *ḥullin*. But if not for the fact that one counts the first nine, there would not have been a tenth to be *kodesh*. Only because there were nine sheep that were *ḥullin*, is the tenth considered *kodesh*. The first nine may not be *kodesh*, but they share in the *kedusha* of the tenth. So, too, in this phrase of the *kina*, even the disregarded sheep are *tela'ekha*, Your sheep. They also belong to God. The entire Jewish community is *tela'ekha*. Every Jew has inherent *kedusha*. The entire *Knesset Yisrael*, good or bad, righteous or sinner, is holy.

וְלֹא זָכַרְתָּ יְקַר יְדִידוּת יֶשֶׁר *And not remember the precious friendship.* God failed to regard every Jew as His *yedid*, dear friend. The relationship between God and the Jewish people is not merely one of collegiality or acquaintance, but of *yedidut*. The principal criterion of a *yedid* is that one will defend a *yedid* even if he knows that the *yedid* made mistakes or acted foolishly. Similarly, the *kedusha* of the Jews is ever-present. "A Jew, even though he sinned, is still a Jew" (*Sanhedrin* 44a).

אֲשֶׁר יִחַדְתָּ *Those whom You singled out.* The friendship between God and the Jewish people is a unique one. Earlier, the *paytan* appealed to the marriage union between God and *Knesset Yisrael*. He now emphasizes the aspect of *beḥira*, the quality of the Jews as the chosen people. God loves the Jewish people because He singled them out from all the other nations.

לְיוֹדְעֶיךָ *To receive the Torah.* The literal meaning of *yodekha* is "those who know You." Maimonides recounts the history of the formation of the Jewish people from Abraham through Jacob and his children (*Mishneh Torah*, Hil. Avoda Zara 1:3) until a nation was formed "that knows God." Maimonides designates the Jews as *yodei Hashem*, those who know God.

The Jewish people know God, and perhaps they love Him because they know Him. The word *yodekha* means not only "those who know You," but also "those who love You," as in the verse, "וַיֵּדַע אָדָם עוֹד אֶת־אִשְׁתּוֹ, And Adam knew his wife again" (Genesis 4:25). Similarly, in the verse, "Get men who are wise and understanding and *yedu'im* to your tribes" (Deuteronomy 1:13), one of the interpretations of the phrase *"yedu'im leshivteikhem"* is "beloved to your tribes." The *paytan* says that the Jews are the ones who truly love God in spite of the fact that they sometimes make mistakes. The *paytan* emphasizes that the guarantee for redemption is based on the fact that the love of the Jews for God will never be extinguished.

לְכַלּוֹת בְּיַד בּוֹשְׁלִים כַּרְמֶךָ *Enabling sinners to despoil Your vineyard.* The word *kerem* refers to Israel and also refers to the *Beit HaMikdash*. Our sages comment (*Eruvin* 21b) on the passage in Song of Songs, "*nashkima lakeramim*, Let us go early to the vineyards" (7:13), that the word *keramim* means the houses of prayer and houses of study. This phrase of the *kina* laments the destruction of the centers of Torah, spirituality and sanctity, the vineyards of God.

וְלֹא זָכַרְתָּ לֹא לִזְנֹחַ לְעוֹלָם *And not remember … not to abandon them.* This phrase is an allusion to the passage from Lamentations, "כִּי לֹא יִזְנַח לְעוֹלָם, For He will not reject forever" (3:31–32). In this passage, God promises never to forget or

forsake the Torah. This promise is further expressed in Isaiah: "And My words that I have put in your mouth will not depart from your mouth, nor from the mouth of your descendants, nor from the mouth of your descendants' descendants, says the LORD, from now and forever" (59:21). The *paytan* argues that God has forgotten His promise that the Torah would be the permanent possession of the Jew, and the *paytan* poses the challenge: How is it possible to fulfill that promise when You destroy the centers of Torah – the *yeshivot*, academies, study halls and synagogues?

אֲשֶׁר לִמַּדְתָּ לִלְקוּחֶיךָ *The lesson You taught to the ones You took to Yourself.* In this stanza the Jewish people are referred to as *likuḥekha*, while in the previous stanza they were referred to as *yodekha*. The distinction is that *yodekha* connotes that the Jewish people have chosen God, while *likuḥekha* connotes that God has chosen the Jewish people, as in the verse, "וְלָקַחְתִּי אֶתְכֶם לִי לְעָם, And I will take you to Me for a people, and I will be your God" (Exodus 6:7). God will take the Jews as His people, whether they agree or not.

נָשָׂאתָ לִנְשׂוּאֶיךָ *How You carried us.* The meaning of *nesu'ekha* is "those whom You carry, support or bear." The concept that God carries or supports the Jewish people is the same as Nahmanides' view, expressed repeatedly in his commentary on the Torah (for example, Leviticus 18:25; Deuteronomy 4:15; 29:25), that God bestows a unique type of *hashgaḥa*, divine providence, on the Jewish people. *Hashgaḥa* with regard to other peoples is entrusted to the angels, but *hashgaḥa* over the Jewish people is exclusively by the Almighty. The Jew has a direct relationship with God without the intercession of any intermediary.

Maimonides expresses a similar view in his formulation of the elements of prayer (*Mishneh Torah*, Hil. Tefilla 4:16; see also Maimonides' *Commentary on the Mishna, Sanhedrin* 10:1, Fifth Principle). Maimonides provides that prayer must be directed only to God, and one is not even permitted to ask for some other agent to mediate between the one who prays and the Almighty. The relationship between God and *Knesset Yisrael* is direct. Based on this principle, many question the propriety of the prayer in *Seliḥot*, "מַכְנִיסֵי רַחֲמִים, Those who usher in our prayers" and the prayer in the *Seliḥot* of *Ne'ila*, "מִדַּת הָרַחֲמִים, The attribute of mercy…plead for mercy for your people." After all, one may not ask an angel or other intermediary to present one's prayers.

לְסַגֵּר בְּיַד סְעִפִים סַהֲדֶיךָ *Imprisoning Your faith-witnesses in the hands of fiends.* The Jews are described as witnesses. They bear witness to creation, to God's

providence, to the fundamentals of our faith. The Jew bears witness not only by reciting the *Ani Ma'amin* prayer every day, but by living a life which is dedicated to that message. Whatever activity the Jew engages in, he bears witness that he is a member of a committed community. The Jew testifies to this commitment not only by the twice daily recitation of *Shema Yisrael*; every act, every movement of a muscle, every word should be a testimony to his commitment to God. Whenever the Jew acts, in public or private, he should be *mekadesh Hashem*, sanctifying God. *Sahadekha* are those who bear witness to God's truth in every action.

This *kina* uses many synonyms for the Jewish people, and each one represents an emotional relationship, a commitment or an obligation between God and *Knesset Yisrael*. The single unifying premise of the entire *kina* is that the relationship between God and *Knesset Yisrael* is a deep, intimate relationship that no human being can destroy or even weaken.

Relationships between man and man, between man and woman, between child and parent, are relative, not absolute. Sometimes there is an element of distrust between husband and wife; sometimes there is an element of shyness between parent and child. The relationship between God and *Knesset Yisrael*, however, is all-embracing, all-inclusive and without limitation. There is an absolute relationship of love between man and God. Nothing can change it; nothing can cool it.

The question posed by the *kina* is: How could the Ḥurban, such a total destruction, take place after so many years of the relationship of boundless love between God and *Knesset Yisrael*?

עֹז עֲדִי עֲדָיִים, אֲשֶׁר עִטַּרְתָּ לַעֲבָדֶיךָ *The glorious crowns with which You bedecked Your servants*. This phrase refers to the *tefillin shel rosh*, the phylacteries worn upon the head. The *tefillin shel rosh* are the most conspicuous and unequivocal testimony that a Jew belongs to God. The verse says, "And all the peoples of the earth shall see that the name of the LORD is proclaimed upon you" (Deuteronomy 28:10), and the Gemara comments, "Rabbi Eliezer the Great says, 'This refers to *tefillin* of the head'" (*Berakhot* 6a). It is a manifestation of our being Jewish and a testimony that, in spite of our travail and persecution, we belong to God.

The *tefillin* are a crown upon our head, and they teach us that there is a power above us. The Torah teaches that the King of Israel is to wear a crown, but this crown is not a symbol that the king is an absolute sovereign. Rather, it is a symbol that there is an authority above the king. Modern political phi-

losophy speaks in terms of the "sovereign state," which means that the state has the power to formulate its own policies, ethics and morality. Sovereignty means that the source of authority is within the state, and there is no authority which rises above the state. But from the Jewish perspective, this philosophy is idolatrous because the only source of power is God. Even the state, even the absolute monarch, is committed to a higher power, and that higher power is symbolized by the *tefillin shel rosh*. Every Jew wears a crown, not because he is powerful, but, on the contrary, because he is committed. A crown does not enhance the power of the king; it limits the power of the king.

וְלֹא זָכַרְתָּ צַהֲלַת צְבִי צֶדֶק, אֲשֶׁר צָפַנְתָּ לִצְבָאֶיךָ *And not remember the beautiful Temple songs so special to Your people.* This phrase is an allusion to the verse, "From the furthest part of the earth we heard singing, '*Tzevi latzaddik*, Glory to the righteous!'" (Isaiah 24:16). The Gemara tells us (*Sanhedrin* 94a) that God wanted to make King Hezekiah the Messiah, but He did not implement this plan because Hezekiah did not engage in praise or song after the sudden death of the enemy's army. Then the earth came and said, "I will sing praise in his stead, as it is said, 'From the furthest part of the earth we heard singing, 'Glory to the righteous.'" The intent of this Gemara is that, in the days of the Messiah, nature will also engage in singing hymns to God.

לַקְנוֹת בְּיַד קָמִים קְרוּאֶיךָ *Selling Your special servants to slave masters.* The word *keru'ekha* refers to the Jewish people whom God invited to receive the Torah. By extending this invitation, God placed *Knesset Yisrael* on a status higher than the angels. According to the Gemara (*Shabbat* 88b) and the Midrash (*Yalkut Shimoni, Koraḥ* 752), the angels argued that they should receive the Torah rather than human beings as they were superior to human beings. But Moses argued that mortal man, with all his weaknesses and frailties, is superior to the angels because man has free will. If he observes the Torah, it is his accomplishment. And, indeed, God rejected the claim of the angels and gave the Torah to Moses and the Jewish people. Not only did He reject the angels' claim, He insisted that they be present at the giving of the Torah to the Jews.

The position of Nahmanides (Commentary on the Torah, Genesis 24:1) and all of the Kabbalistic scholars is that the Jews are superior to the angels. The conclusive proof for Nahmanides is that the angels descended to Mount Sinai not to receive the Torah but to witness the Torah being given to the Jews. Indeed, the Gemara (*Ḥullin* 91b) indicates the superiority of the Jews over the angels, because the Jews are able to recite *shira*, songs of praise to God, while the angels are not.

וְלֹא זָכַרְתָּ רֶגֶשׁ רֶכֶב רִבֹּתַיִם, אֲשֶׁר רָצִיתָ לְרֵעֶיךָ *And not remember the thousands of angels present at Sinai.* This is an allusion to the midrash (*Bemidbar Raba* 2:3) that God descended on Mount Sinai to give the Torah accompanied by twenty-two thousand angels. The *paytan* complains that God does not remember when He was present at Mount Sinai for the giving of the Torah and publicly demonstrated the superiority of man to His friends.

וְלֹא זָכַרְתָּ תְּקֶף תַּלְתַּלֵּי תֹאַר, אֲשֶׁר תִּכַּנְתָּ לִתְמִימֶיךָ *And not remember the resplendent curls of hair which You arranged for Your innocents.* The Midrash (*Shir HaShirim Raba* 5, s.v. *patar R. Yehuda*) defines the *taltalei to'ar* as the great Torah scholars.

עַל מַה בְּיוֹם זֶה נִשְׁבִּינוּ פַעֲמַיִם *Why, On This Day, Have We Fallen Captive Twice?* This historical fact has halakhic significance. The Gemara States (*Rosh HaShana* 18b) that the fast of Tisha B'av must be observed even if peace prevails in the world because "*hukhpulu bo tzarot*," because both Ḥurbanot occurred on that day. According to Maimonides (Commentary on the Mishna, *Rosh HaShana* 1:3), Tisha B'av was observed during the period that the Second Temple was in existence.

The theme of this *kina* is that we demand justice from God because of *berit avot*, the covenant with the patriarchs. We are obligated to Him, and He is obligated to us. Although the *zekhut avot*, the merit of the patriarchs, may have terminated, the *berit avot* is eternal. God is obligated, and He must do His share.

8

letter of the fourth stich follows the reverse alphabetic order, from tav ת to mem מ, introducing a verse from Tanakh. The last stanza ends with the first line of the next kina. Commentary for this kina begins on page 240.

אֶאֱדֶה I [let my laments] soar to heaven,
inviting heaven itself to join my lament.
I curse this day that twice destroyed me,
                and grieve, "Would that my head were water!" *Jer. 8:23*

אַבְחִין I will tearfully contemplate the desert's wail,
comparing that night of yore to this night, and that desert to this desert.
I will urge those who came out of that desert to cry.
                I will shout, "Would that I could be in the desert!" *Jer. 9:1*

אָגוּעַ I was severed like olives from their tree.
I will provoke the angels to ally themselves with me.
I will goad the Master of the House to say,
        "Let them [my enemies] be reduced to thorns and thistles." *Is. 27:4*

אֲדֻוָה With a troubled heart, I will seek Him.
I will learn the words by which to encourage Him.
I will anxiously ask, "Where is my Shepherd," but I will not find Him.
                I will sadly say, "Would that I knew how to reach Him!" *Job 23:3*

אֲהַפְּכָה I will whirl my words like a wheel, searching out the right words.
I will express my complaints to Him face-to-face.
The sun and the moon will convey their woe by ceasing to shine.
      I will exclaim, "Would that my words were written into the record!" *Job 19:23*

אֹרַח Those who smuggled their first-fruit offerings past the enemy,
I will deem their stealth sinful.
The heavenly constellation suffered when the [High Priest's]
   tunic was torn.
              I will groan, "Would that I had someone to give me a hearing! *Job 31:35*

8

In this kina, the paytan describes himself lamenting the Ḥurban. Each stich of the twelve stanzas begins with the letter alef, א, usually describing the speaker's own actions. The second letter of the first three stichs of each stanza carry a triple alphabetic acrostic from alef א to lamed ל; the second

אֲאַדֶּה עַד חוּג שָׁמַיִם
אֲאַלֶּה אִתִּי שָׁמַיִם
אָאֹר יוֹם מַחֲרִיבִי פַּעֲמַיִם.
אֶתְאוֹנֵן, מִי־יִתֵּן רֹאשִׁי מַיִם: ירמיה ח, כג

אַבְחִין בִּבְכִי יְלֵל מִדְבָּר
אֲבַחֲנָה לֵיל מֵלִיל, וּמִדְבָּר מִמִּדְבָּר
אֲבַכֶּה אִתִּי עוֹלַת מִדְבָּר.
אֶשְׁאַג, מִי־יִתְּנֵנִי בַמִּדְבָּר: ירמיה ט, א

אֶגְוַע וְאֶנָּשֵׁל כְּנֹקֶף זַיִת
אָגוּרָה בִּי כָּל בְּנֵי בַיִת
אֶגְרֹם שֶׁיֹּאמַר בַּעַל הַבָּיִת.
אֶרְשָׁה, מִי יִתְּנֵנִי שָׁמִיר שָׁיִת: ישעיה כז, ד

אֶדְוֶה בְּכָל לֵב לְהַמְצֵאֵהוּ
אֵדְעָה מִלִּין בָּם לְאַמְּצֵהוּ
אֶדְאַג רוֹעֶה וְלֹא אֶמְצָאֵהוּ.
אֲקוֹנֵן, מִי־יִתֵּן יָדַעְתִּי וְאֶמְצָאֵהוּ: איוב כג, ג

אֶהְפְּכָה וְאֶתְהַפְּכָה כְּאוֹפָן בְּמִלָּי
אֶהְגֶּה פָּנִים בְּפָנִים לְתַנּוֹת עֲמָלִי
אָהַהּ חֶרֶס וְסַהַר, מִלְּהַגִּיהַּ לְמוּלִי.
אֶצְרַח, מִי־יִתֵּן אֵפוֹ וְיִכָּתְבוּן מִלָּי: איוב יט, כג

אֹרַח מִשְׁפָּטֵי גּוֹנְבֵי עָלַי
אוֹדִיעַ בְּבִצְעִי וּמַעֲלַי
אִמְלְלוּ מַזָּלוֹת בִּקְרָעֵי מְעִילִי.
אֲפוּנָה, מִי יִתֶּן־לִי שֹׁמֵעַ לִי: איוב לא, לה

אָזְדָה She fled because the merits of the patriarchs were depleted.
I remember when we were bride and groom.
Like streams flowing down from a pool, I will cry.
> I will shriek, "Would that I had the wings of a dove!" *Ps. 55:7*

אָח Brethren were driven from their secure city to distant Tyre. *Prov. 18:19*
The wells were dry, because God withheld the rain.
The enemy mowed them down like stalks of grain.
> I will murmur, "Would that I could be brought to the bastion!" *Ps. 60:11*

אֶטַּע It would be best to pitch my tent in death's shadow,
and fly away and settle myself in a graveyard;
busy myself; await death as relief.
> I will whine, "What man can live and not see death?" *Ps. 89:49*

אֱיָלוּתִי My Lord, I searched so for Your help. *Ps. 22:20*
Every year, my people hope that this is the year [of redemption].
When that day comes, I will inform them all, *Is. 12:5*
> "That the hand of the Lord has done this!" *Job 12:9*

אָכֹף I bow my head to You, my Lord, my strength.
I bend my knees to You to heal my ills.
I will crown You with a song from among the songs of my timbrel.
> I will devoutly pray, "If only You could be with us as a brother!" *Song. 8:1*

אַל Do not forget the Temple's cries,
and rejoin Judah and Israel to her.
The thousands of guardian angels You appointed, *Ps. 68:18*
> will all say, "Would that the deliverance *Ps. 53:7*
> of Israel will come from Zion!"

יִשְׂרָאֵל [God responds:] Israel, ever since it stopped walking in My ways, / abandoned Me, so I abandoned them and turned My face away. / I grieved, and I mourned, and My innards and heart spilled out. / How they have hurled My glorious crown from My head!

Kina 9 starts on page 254.

אָזְדָה כְּהוּפְרָה הָאֶבְיוֹנָה
אֶזְכְּרָה בִּהְיוֹתִי מְחֻתָּנָה
אָזִיל פְּלָגִים כַּבְּרֵכָה הָעֶלְיוֹנָה.
אֲעֶנֶה, מִי־יִתֶּן־לִי אֵבֶר כַּיּוֹנָה: תהלים נה, ז

אָח נִפְשָׁע מִקִּרְיַת עֹז אֶל צוּר משלי יח, יט
אָחוּ בְּלִי מַיִם בְּאַף לַעֲצֹר
אָחַז קָמוֹת לִקְצֹר, וְעוֹלֵלוֹת לִבְצֹר.
אָשִׂיחָה, מִי יוֹבִלֵנִי עִיר מָצוֹר: תהלים ס, יא

אֶטַּע אָהֳלֵי אַפַּדְנִי בְּצַלְמָוֶת
אָטוּסָה וְאֶשְׁכְּוֹנָה עַד חֲצַר מָוֶת
אֲטַפֵּל אֶת הַמְחַכִּים לַמָּוֶת.
אֶנֶהּ, מִי גֶבֶר יִחְיֶה, וְלֹא יִרְאֶה־מָּוֶת: תהלים פט, מט

אֱיָלוּתִי לְעֶזְרָתִי תֵּרְדִּי לַחֲזוֹת תהלים כב, כ
אֵימָתַי, בְּכָל שָׁנָה אוֹמֶרֶת, הִיא הַשָּׁנָה הַזֹּאת
אֵידַע לַכֹּל כִּי מוּדַעַת זֹאת. ישעיה יב, ה
אִם לֹא כִּי יַד־יהוה עָשְׂתָה זֹּאת: איוב יב, ט

אָכֹף לְךָ רֹאשׁ, חֵילִי
אֶכְרַע לְךָ בֶּרֶךְ, לְחַתֵּל מַחֲלִי
אֶכְתִּירְךָ בְּשִׁיר מִשִּׁירֵי מְחוֹלִי.
אֲכַוֵּן, מִי יִתֶּנְךָ כְּאָח לִי: שיר השירים ח, א

אַל תִּשְׁכַּח צַעֲקַת אֲרִיאֵל
אֵלָיו לֶאֱגֹר יְהוּדָה וְיִשְׂרָאֵל
אַלְפֵי שִׁנְאָן אֲשֶׁר מָסַר אֵל. תהלים סה, יח
לֵאמֹר, מִי יִתֵּן מִצִּיּוֹן יְשׁוּעוֹת יִשְׂרָאֵל: תהלים נג, ז

יִשְׂרָאֵל מֵעֵת בִּדְרָכַי לֹא הָלְכוּ / עֲזָבוּנִי וַעֲזָבְתִּים, וּפָנַי מֵהֶם נֶהְפָּכוּ /
רָגַנְתִּי וְהֵילַלְתִּי, וּמֵעַי וְלִבִּי נִשְׁפָּכוּ / אֵיכָה תִּפְאַרְתִּי מֵרָאשׁוֹתַי הִשְׁלִיכוּ.

Kina 9 starts on page 255.

COMMENTARY ON KINA 8

The underlying theme of this *kina* is that the Ḥurban was not only a historical event that affected the Jewish people. It was also a cosmic catastrophe. All of nature was affected, and the entire world was somehow changed by the Ḥurban. The very cosmos became immoral and corrupt, and nature itself became indifferent and cynical. Therefore, says the *paytan*, the entire cosmos mourns with him for the Ḥurban.

אֲאַדֶּה עַד חוּג שָׁמַיִם *I [let my laments] soar to heaven.* The *paytan* says that the destruction of the *Beit HaMikdash* was not only a historical event that was catastrophic for one nation. It was a cosmic catastrophe, and the entire cosmos mourns.

Various statements of our sages tell us that the Ḥurban was of metaphysical proportions. Our sages say that nature itself changed, as in the passage, "From the time the Temple was destroyed, fruits lost their flavor" (*Sotah* 48a). Similarly, the *kina*, עַד אָנָה בְּכִיָּה בְצִיּוֹן, וּמִסְפֵּד בִּירוּשָׁלָיִם, which is recited on the night of Tisha B'Av, enumerates the twelve *mazalot* or constellations, and describes how each mourns for the Ḥurban. The stars, too, were affected by the Ḥurban, and that is why the *paytan* wants the heavens to cry with him.

אַאֲלֶה אִתִּי שָׁמַיִם *Inviting heaven itself to join my lament.* The unusual word *a'aleh* derives from the root *alah*, meaning an oath. The *paytan* is saying that he will compel the heavens, the entire universe, to take an oath that they will intercede on behalf of the Jewish people and demand from God the restoration of Jerusalem. The welfare of the cosmos is at stake because the restoration of Jerusalem and the final redemption will spell salvation for the entire universe as well.

אָאֹר יוֹם מַחֲרִיבִי פַעֲמַיִם *I curse this day that twice destroyed me.* It is as though the *paytan* is saying that the day of Tisha B'Av itself has destroyed us. An awareness of the Jewish concept of time is essential for an understanding of the *paytan's* point. When the Mishna (*Ta'anit* 26a) remarks that five events befell our ancestors on Tisha B'Av, it is saying that there is something inherent in the day of Tisha B'Av which is responsible for these tragedies. And, in fact, there are additional tragic events that occurred on Tisha B'Av subsequent to the time of the Mishna, such as the expulsion of the Jews from Spain in 1492. As far as Jewish history is concerned, Tisha B'Av is *the* day of tragedy, as though the day itself had somehow been responsible. There is a fatal quality to the day of Tisha B'Av – the day itself destroyed us.

The Jewish view of time is quite different from the view held by Kant and other philosophers. For them, a day has no substance of its own. It is nothing more than a frame of reference, part of a coordinate system, in which events can be located, but one cannot speak of a "bad time" or a "lonely time," a "profane time" or a "blessed time." For us, however, time itself is substantive and has attributes. There is such a thing as "good time," as in a Yom Tov. The concept of *kedushat hayom*, the sanctity of the day of Shabbat and the festivals illustrates the Jewish concept of time. It indicates that there is substance to the day which can be filled with *kedusha*. The kabbalists, based on the Gemara (*Shabbat* 119a), say the day of Shabbat is personified by the Sabbath Queen because the day is not just a mathematical construct; it is a creation in and of itself. Based on this Jewish concept of time, we can understand how Job can curse the day of his birth (Job 3:2). There is a *yom ḥol*, an ordinary day, and there is a *yom kadosh*, a day which is distinct and distinguished from others. And there can be a day filled with curses and profanity.

Tisha B'Av is a day which is saturated with bitterness. In fact, it is not a date; it is a destiny. In correspondence between rabbis, Tisha B'Av is often referred to as *yom hamar vehanimhar*, the day which is *mar* and *nimhar*. Both *mar* and *nimhar* mean "bitter," but *nimhar* is in the passive. I would suggest that the phrase be translated as "the bitter day which is saturated and endowed with bitterness."

אֶתְאוֹנֵן, מִי־יִתֵּן רֹאשִׁי מַיִם *And grieve, "Would that my head were water!"* This phrase is consistent with the view of Nahmanides (*Torat HaAdam* [Chavel edition] p. 242) that there is no *bal tosif*, no halakhic limit, as to the lamentations and mourning for Jerusalem and the Temple. The *paytan* is saying that no amount of tears is enough; he will cause the entire cosmos to weep with him.

אֲבְחֲנָה לֵיל מֵלֵיל, וּמִדְבָּר מִמִּדְבָּר *Comparing that night of yore to this night, and that desert to this desert.* There is one *leil midbar*, night in the desert, that is responsible for the Ḥurban and for all the other calamities that befell the Jewish people on that night. It was the reaction of the Jewish people to the report of the spies, "And the people cried on that night" (Numbers 14:1). Our sages tell us that this was the night of Tisha B'Av (Ta'anit 29a). The *paytan* says that he is mourning not only for the night of the Ḥurban, but also for the night of crying in the desert for the sin of the *meraglim*.

But the word *evḥana* indicates that there is a distinction between the night of the Ḥurban and that other night in the desert. The *paytan* recognizes that

the night of the Ḥurban is a result of the night of crying in the desert. The *paytan* also understands the difference between the two deserts, the desert of Sinai and the desert of exile in which the Jews now find themselves.

Another interpretation is that the two nights which are being contrasted are the night of Tisha B'Av in the desert and the *leil shimurim*, the night of vigil, on which the Jewish people left Egypt and went into the desert. The *leil shimurim* represents faith and absolute trust in God, the opposite of the night of Tisha B'Av in the desert.

אֲבַכֶּה אִתִּי עוֹלַת מִדְבָּר *I will urge those who came out of that desert to cry.* The phrase *olat midbar* refers to the Jewish people. The language is similar to the verse in Song of Songs which describes *Knesset Yisrael* with the phrase "*mi zot ola min hamidbar,* Who is this who comes up from the wilderness, leaning upon her beloved" (8:5).

אֶשְׁאַג, מִי־יִתְּנֵנִי בַמִּדְבָּר *I will shout, "Would that I could be in the desert!"* This phrase is reminiscent of the passage, "מִי־יִתְּנֵנִי בַמִּדְבָּר מְלוֹן אֹרְחִים, Oh that I were in the wilderness, in a lodging place of wayfarers" (Jeremiah 9:1). Maimonides (*Mishneh Torah,* Hil. De'ot 6:1) expresses the view that if humanity is corrupt, one should depart from civilized life and populated areas, pitch one's tent in the desert and lead a solitary life.

אֱגָרֶה בִּי כָּל בְּנֵי בַיִת *I will provoke the angels to ally themselves with me.* The literal meaning of the term *benei vayit* is "members of the household," and this line of the *kina* can be understood as an allusion to an aspect of the Tisha B'Av observance that is expressed in the dynamics of the household. Just as it is a mitzva on Yom Tov to encourage everyone in one's household to be happy and rejoice (Maimonides, *Mishneh Torah,* Hil. Yom Tov 6:17–18), so too on Tisha B'Av, it is important for the head of the family to engender in the members of the household a sense of mourning. When one rejoices, one must try to share one's joy with others, as reflected in the verse describing the festivals, "And you shall rejoice…you and your son and your daughter" (Deuteronomy 16:14). It is the responsibility of the head of the household to explain to the family what happened on that day. So, too, when one is grieving, one should share such feelings with others, as well.

Just as there is a mitzva of *sipur yetziat Mitzrayim,* the recounting of the story of the exodus from Egypt, so too is there a requirement of *sipur ḥurban Yerushalayim,* the recounting of the narrative of the destruction of Jerusalem. While the *sipur ḥurban Yerushalayim* is not a biblical obligation, the story

should be told in the same manner as the story of the exodus from Egypt. In each case, the story should be related in a way that is consistent with the intelligence and understanding of the child to whom it is being told.

אֶדְוֶה בְּכָל לֵב לְהַמְצִיאוֹ *With a troubled heart, I will seek Him.* The *paytan*'s heart is full of longing and nostalgia for God. The *paytan* aches with all his heart to find Him, to make Him reveal Himself. Life is empty and bleak without Him. The word *edveh* comes from the root *dava*, meaning pain, as in "*al eres davai*, on the bed of misery" (Psalms 41:4). Similarly, the Torah refers to a woman who is ill and in pain as *isha dava* (Leviticus 20:18).

This phrase in the *kina* alludes to the verses in Deuteronomy which are part of the Torah reading for the morning of Tisha B'Av, "וּבִקַּשְׁתֶּם מִשָּׁם אֶת־יהוה אֱלֹהֶיךָ וּמָצָאתָ, and from there you will seek the Lord your God, and you will find Him if you search for Him with all your heart and all your soul. In your distress, when all these things will come upon you, in the end of days, you will return to the LORD your God" (Deuteronomy 4:29–30). This selection sounds the theme of *teshuva*, which is one of the themes of Tisha B'Av. The Gemara (*Megilla* 31b) suggests that other sections of the Torah be read on Tisha B'Av, such as the portion pertaining to the *meraglim*, since, from a theological point of view, the spies were the ones responsible for the Ḥurban. But the Gemara insists that the portion from Deuteronomy is the appropriate text to read on Tisha B'Av since that portion is the source in the Torah for *teshuva*.

When one thinks of the passage וּבִקַּשְׁתֶּם מִשָּׁם אֶת־יהוה, one must also consider the selection from *Seliḥot*, "הִמָּצֵא לָנוּ בְּבַקָּשָׁתֵנוּ כְּמָה שֶׁכָּתוּב וּבִקַּשְׁתֶּם מִשָּׁם אֶת־יהוה אֱלֹהֶיךָ, make Your presence known to us when we are searching for You, as it is written, 'And from there you will seek the LORD your God, and you will find Him if you search for Him with all your heart and all your soul.'" The word *bakashatenu* does not mean "our request"; it means "our search." We plead with God to answer us, but what *are* we searching for? We are searching to be close to God. Every person wants to feel the touch of the hand of God on his shoulder. In our ceaseless quest for God, we plead that He permit Himself to be found. We pray that it should be easy to find God. The recitation of *Seliḥot* is not complete without the statement of הִמָּצֵא לָנוּ בְּבַקָּשָׁתֵנוּ. It is the last plea before we stand for the solemn prayer of *Shema Kolenu*, and it is the purpose, objective and ultimate end of *all* prayers. We pray that God should establish a relationship with us; that He should not be transcendent beyond man's reach and that man should not flee from Him.

Moses, too, asks God to make His presence known when he says, "*hareni na et kevodekha*, show me, I pray, Your glory" (Exodus 33:18). In response to Moses' request, God says, "And while My glory passes by, and I will put you in a cleft in the rock... and you will see My back, but My face shall not be seen" (Exodus 33:22–23). Commenting on these verses, the Ḥatam Sofer explains that many times an event will occur, and we do not recognize the hand of God. On the contrary, we express doubt and we question how God could have permitted the event to occur. And then, years later, in retrospect, we understand. Man is "in the rock" and does not see God. The vision of God is shut out by the rock, by the inflexible laws of nature, and we do not recognize Him or feel His presence. Only later, perhaps years later, we "see His back" and we have a glimmer of understanding.

We have several other prayers for the revelation of God's presence, aside from the prayer הִמָּצֵא לָנוּ בְּבַקָּשָׁתֵנוּ. In the Amida for the High Holy Days, for example, we recite "מְלֹךְ עַל כָּל הָעוֹלָם כֻּלּוֹ בִּכְבוֹדֶךָ, reign upon the entire world with Your glory." This is essentially a prayer for *giluy Shekhina*. We want the Almighty to reveal Himself to the entire world, to all of creation. In addition, each individual prays for *giluy Shekhina* in his personal life, for if a person lacks *giluy Shekhina*, he lacks everything. There are times that a person undergoes an ecstatic experience which makes him believe that he has met God and that He is present. This is the great experience of *giluy Shekhina*, and each individual Jew is entitled to it. This is what we beseech God to grant us when we say הִמָּצֵא לָנוּ בְּבַקָּשָׁתֵנוּ.

We ask God to reveal Himself because we do not want to be alone. He has left us, however, because of our sins. The real punishment for sin is God's absenting Himself from us. When Adam was first created, God's intention was *ikar Shekhina betaḥtonim*, the essence of the *Shekhina* was to be located in the human world below (*Bereshit Raba* 19:70). God and man would have interacted frequently; God would have been immediately accessible to man. But Adam sinned, and *Shekhina nistalka limeromim*, the *Shekhina* left and joined the transcendent infinity. God had wanted to live in harmony with man, but man's sin caused His departure. Adam lacked the courage to repent and say to God, "Please do not leave me alone." Instead, he defended his actions. He said to God, "It is not my fault; it is Your fault. You were the marriage broker. Had I not married her, I would not have eaten from the Tree of Knowledge." And so, man lost God.

There was another time that God was very close to us, and we lost Him because we simply did not know how to keep Him. Immediately after the

giving of the Torah, God was in the midst of the community. But the people then sinned with the golden calf. If not for the golden calf, God would have stayed with the Jewish people forever, and Jewish history would have been different. But the people did not understand. They made the golden calf, and the *Shekhina* departed. When Moses says, "show me, I pray, Your glory," God declines, as if to say, "Before the sin of the golden calf, perhaps; but not now." The Gemara says (*Berakhot* 7a) that God responded, "When I wanted to, you did not want to. Now that you want to, I do not want to." Why does God now not want to reveal Himself? Because of the sin of the golden calf.

אֶדְעָה מִלִּין בָּם לְאַמְּצֵהוּ *I will learn the words by which to encourage Him.* In modern Hebrew, the word *le'ametz* means to adopt a child, and it has the connotation of holding fast to someone. The *paytan* is saying that if we meet God again, we will know the appropriate words to keep Him and make Him stay with us forever. The next time He reveals Himself to us, we will not lose Him as we have done in the past.

One of the main motifs of the *kinot* is the quest to encounter God. Once we find Him, we will not repeat our past mistakes. We will not let Him go, and He will stay with us forever. For centuries, the story of Jewish history has been that the Jewish people repeatedly found God, but lost Him each time. The patriarchs found God many times, but *Knesset Yisrael* lost Him. Each time the Jewish people searched for Him and found Him, they lost Him again. After the giving of the Torah, the sin of the golden calf was perpetrated. The Jews were ready to enter the land of Israel, and then the episode of the *meraglim* transpired. God tried many times to keep company with *Knesset Yisrael*, but each time they transgressed, and they lost Him.

In writing this phrase of the *kina*, Rabbi Elazar HaKalir had in mind the description in Song of Songs of the longing for God. The beloved, the metaphor for the Jewish people, searches for God, but does not find Him. And then, God knocks on her door, "Hark! My beloved knocks: Open to me, my sister, my love, my dove, my undefiled; For my head is filled with dew, my locks with the drops of the night" (Song of Songs 5:2). The beloved, *Knesset Yisrael*, is wet and cold. She yearns to see Him. She is on the verge of fainting. And, at the very moment that she pines to see God, He knocks on her door. He is ready, but she is not ready. Instead, she says, "I have taken off my robe; how shall I put it on? I have washed my feet; how shall I soil them?" (Song of Songs 5:3).

The concept expressed by Song of Songs, and which HaKalir adopts in this *kina*, is a simple one. The Jew often has the opportunity to seize hold of God.

He often knocks upon the door of the Jew and wants to share his abode. But somehow, the Jew misses the opportunity. He does not have the fortitude to get out of bed and open the door. By the time he finally arises and opens the door, it is too late, and He is gone. Once He is gone, it is a difficult challenge to get Him to knock on the door again. That is why the exile has lasted so long. In this phrase of the *kina*, Rabbi Elazar HaKalir is saying that the next time we find God it will be different, and we will not repeat the mistakes of the past. Now we know how to accomplish our goal "*le'amtzehu*," to hold fast to Him forever when we find Him. We know the methods of repentance and good deeds that we need to employ to please the Almighty. If we hear that knock on the door, no matter how faint, we will open it immediately, and once He enters our house, we will not allow Him to depart.

אֶדְאַג רוֹעֶה וְלֹא אֶמְצָאֵהוּ *I will anxiously ask, "Where is my Shepherd?" but I will not find Him.* In spite of his search, the *paytan* cannot find God. God is the shepherd, and without the shepherd, the flock cannot exist.

Similar to the prior phrase of the *kina*, this phrase, as well, is reminiscent of a verse in Song of Songs, "הַגִּידָה לִּי שֶׁאָהֲבָה נַפְשִׁי אֵיכָה תִרְעֶה, Tell me, you whom I love so well; where do you pasture your sheep? Where do you make them rest at noon? Let me be not as the veiled one who wanders beside the flocks of your fellows" (1:7). As Maimonides writes (*Mishneh Torah*, Hil. Teshuva 10:3), all of Song of Songs is a metaphor for the longing of man for God. In this verse, God is the shepherd, and His beloved is full of longing for Him. His beloved asks where she can find Him. She needs protection and shelter, and He is the only one who can help her. She asks, "Where do You keep Your flock in the scorching noon sun?" When the burning sun is above the Jewish people, they seek the shade and protection of God. The sheep should be with the shepherd, but strangely, although the shepherd, God, is tall and visible, and not far from His people, He disappears when His flock approaches. Why, asks *Knesset Yisrael*, should she be like the *otya*, the wandering widow who has no one to show her any compassion?

אֲקוֹנֵן, מִי־יִתֵּן יְדַעְתִּי וְאֶמְצָאֵהוּ *I will sadly say, "Would that I knew how to reach Him!"* The *paytan* expresses the fear that God is not coming to him, and he will have to approach God. But he laments that he does not know the way, and he pleads for someone to show him the criteria with which he can identify God. The *paytan* realizes that if he knew the path leading to God, he would have found Him.

This stanza of the *kina*, beginning with אֶדְוֶה בְּכָל לֵב, expresses the longing

of the Jew for God. It is noteworthy that this concept is incorporated in the *kinot* because it demonstrates that regardless of how bleak and bitter the day of Tisha B'Av is, the longing for God is not being suppressed. In fact, this is the central theme of Yom Kippur, as well. The essence of the *kedushat hayom* of Yom Kippur is expressed in the idea of *lifnei Hashem*, being in the presence of God. As Rabbi Akiva said, "You are fortunate, O Israel, for before whom do you purify yourselves? Before your Father in heaven" (*Yoma* 85b). The essence of Yom Kippur is not forgiveness and atonement. Rather, these are consequences of achieving the status of *lifnei Hashem*. It is significant that Rabbi Elazar HaKalir introduces this theme into the *kinot*, as well.

אֹרַח מִשְׁפְּטֵי גוֹנְבֵי עֱלִי *Those who smuggled their first-fruit offerings past the enemy.* This is an allusion to the account in the Gemara (*Ta'anit* 28a) of the *gonvei eli*, literally, "those who deceived by using pestles." The Gemara recounts that the authorities, in all likelihood the Romans, issued an edict prohibiting the bringing of *bikkurim*, the first fruits, to Jerusalem, and posted guards to enforce the edict. The Jews deceived the guards by hiding the *bikkurim* in large pestle-shaped containers filled with dried figs. This episode describes the travail of Jewish life under non-Jewish domination, whether during the Roman times, the Crusades or the Inquisition. The authorities constantly issued edicts forbidding observance of the Torah, and the Jew always had to resort to the tactics of the *gonvei eli*. He had to deceive, go undercover, hide in the basements and the forests.

אוֹדִיעַ בְּבִצְעִי וּמַעֲלִי *I will deem their stealth sinful.* The *paytan* will proclaim the methods which the *gonvei eli* employed in order to bring the *bikkurim* to Jerusalem. In effect, the Jew concedes that, indeed, there were times when he *did* use dishonest methods and immoral means to reach his goals. While there were times he may have used cunning in order to sin, there were other times that he used cunning in order to accomplish good.

אֶטַּע אָהֳלֵי אַפַּדְנִי בְּצַלְמָוֶת *It would be best to pitch my tent in death's shadow.* The *paytan* has reached the point of utter despair, the nadir of sadness and distress, and declares that he will join those who wait for death. Since man is going to die, nothing makes any difference, and the *paytan* decides that he will simply act like a dead person. This stanza is reminiscent of Job's first oration in the third chapter of the book of Job, and it is similar to the expression of Job's hopelessness when he says that he would rather be dead than alive (Job 3:11–13).

אֲטַפֵּל אֶת הַמְחַכִּים לַמָּוֶת *Busy myself; await death as relief.* Those whom the *paytan* wants to join are waiting for death because they derive no enjoyment from life. For them, life is equated with suffering. Without the *Beit HaMikdash*, life has lost its value and significance. They have reached the point of complete despair.

מִי גֶבֶר יִחְיֶה, וְלֹא יִרְאֶה־מָּוֶת *"What man can live and not see death?"* Once again, the *paytan* expresses the depths of despair. What possible words of solace can there be? Man is so vulnerable. It is as though the *paytan* is saying that man will die anyway, so it makes no difference whether he dies sooner or later. Nothing matters at all.

These are the words and thoughts of one who has lost all hope and faith. These ideas are not consistent with the Jewish view of the world. The Jew does not say, "You have to die anyway, so what difference does it make?" The Jewish view is to fight for each moment of life, especially by prayer. The Jewish view is, "Even if the sharp blade of the sword is resting on a person's throat, he should not lose hope of God's mercy" (*Berakhot* 10a). The *paytan*, however, is in despair because without the *Beit HaMikdash* and without reconciliation with God, life is meaningless, and his tent might just as well have been pitched in the graveyard.

אֱיָלוּתִי לְעֶזְרָתִי תַּרְתִּי לַחֲזוֹת *My Lord, I searched so for Your help.* Immediately following the despair of the previous stanza, there is a sudden shift in mood. He may be full of despair, but he is also full of hope. There *is* hope; he *does* believe in God's salvation.

אֵימָתִי, בְּכָל שָׁנָה אוֹמֶרֶת, הִיא הַשָּׁנָה הַזֹּאת *Every year, my people hope that this is the year [of redemption].* Every year we say that this will be the last year of exile. Next year, instead of reciting *kinot*, we will study the laws of the festivals, because Tisha B'Av will be transformed into a Yom Tov, a great holiday, as written in Zechariah, "Thus says the Lord, the fast of the fourth month and the fast of the fifth month ... shall be for the house of Judah joy and gladness" (8:19). This verse from Zechariah which prophesies that Tisha B'Av will be transformed into a day of joy ends with the phrase, "*ha'emet vehashalom ehavu,* truth and peace shall you love." The relationship between this phrase and the transformation of Tisha B'Av into a day of joy is that there is an inherent conflict between *shalom* and *emet,* and the phrase *ha'emet vehashalom ehavu* is a prophecy that, at the time of the ultimate redemption with the coming of the Messiah, this conflict will be resolved.

This conflict was present as early as the dawn of creation. The Midrash recounts (*Bereshit Raba* 8:5) that when God consulted, as it were, with the angels as to whether He should create man, there was a disagreement in the heavenly court. The angels of *ḥesed*, kindness, said that man should be created because his character is kindly and altruistic. The angels of *emet*, truth, however, said that man should not be created because he is replete with falsehood. *Tzedek*, the angels of righteousness, argued that man should be created because he performs deeds of righteousness and charity, while *shalom*, angels of peace, countered that man should not be created because he is quarrelsome and violent. Thus, *ḥesed* and *tzedek* were in favor of man's creation, and *emet* and *shalom* were opposed. My father *zt"l* suggested a reason for the opposition of *emet* and *shalom* to man's creation. It is because a man can be either a perfect man of truth or a perfect man of peace, but he cannot be both. The man of truth does not know the secret of compromise; absolute truth is more important to him than reconciliation. Similarly, the man of peace may agree with another person's opinion not because he genuinely believes that the other person is correct, but because he is willing to concede if the disagreement is not particularly serious. For the man of peace, peace and harmony are more important than absolute truth.

In this world, the world of reality, there is an inherent conflict between *emet* and *shalom*. The *Shulḥan Arukh* (*Ḥoshen Mishpat, siman* 12) recognizes this conflict and clarifies when one should opt for *emet* and when one should opt for *shalom*. But in the era of the Messiah, the conflict will be resolved. Man will not have to sacrifice either *emet* or *shalom* to be a complete person, but will be able to act in accordance with both. Man will be able to act this way because there is no conflict between *emet* and *shalom* for God. This is the meaning of the well-known phrase, "*oseh shalom bimeromav*, He makes peace in His heavens" (Job 25:2).

Our sages are referring to this conflict between *emet* and *shalom* when they speak of "peace between the angels Gabriel and Michael" (see, for example, *Bereshit Raba* 12:8; *Devarim Raba* 5:12). Gabriel is the angel of fire, which represents *emet* and *din*, strict judgment. Michael is the angel of water, which represents *shalom* and *raḥamim*, mercy. God reconciles both *emet* with *shalom*, and *din* with *raḥamim*. Tisha B'Av will become the holiest, most sacred Yom Tov when this reconciliation is realized.

אֲיַדַּע לַכֹּל כִּי מוּדַעַת זֹאת *When that day comes, I will inform them all.* He will announce to all that his salvation will arrive and that the last Tisha B'Av has

occurred because he is absolutely certain. He has no fear that he will be mistaken.

אֶכּף לְךָ רֹאשׁ, חֵילִי *I bow my head to You, my* LORD, *my strength.* In the preceding stanza, when the *paytan* declared that this will be the last Tisha B'Av, he was addressing *Knesset Yisrael.* Now he turns to address God, and his expression of faith and contrition that he will bow before God stands in stark contrast to his despairing lament of two stanzas earlier, "It would be best to pitch my tent in death's shadow." The *paytan* concedes that, in spite of all his questions, notwithstanding all the challenges of *eikha*, he will bow before God and accept His will. After all the questions comes the *tzidduk hadin*, the acknowledgment of God's righteousness.

In fact, the structure of the book of Lamentations is similar. The first chapter begins with the question of *eikha* and continues with the lament of suffering. The second chapter, building on the first, proceeds with the theme of suffering and despair, to the point of asserting that God acted as though He were the enemy of the Jewish people. We are permitted to pose these challenges only because of the special *heter*, permission, granted to us on Tisha B'Av to recite the book of Lamentations. But then the third chapter, after reaching the depths of despair, acknowledges that, despite all the questions represented by *eikha*, and all the challenges to God that His behavior to His people cannot be understood, God is indeed the righteous King. God's judgment is just, and His will is correct. It is up to man to exercise his free will, and God will listen to man's prayers. He will accept man when man approaches Him with humility, prayer and confession.

אַכְתִּירְךָ בְּשִׁיר מִשִּׁירֵי מְחוֹלִי *I will crown You with a song from among the songs of my timbrel.* The word *meḥoli* also has the connotation of "dance." The songs which the *paytan* will sing in honor of God will be from the songs which he sings when he dances; songs to the tune of the eternal dance. It is significant that the *paytan* uses the word *maḥol* rather than *rikud*, which also means dance. The word *maḥol* is used to describe the dance that will take place in the time of the redemption. Jeremiah, for example, in his description of the redemption, prophesies "אָז תִּשְׂמַח בְּתוּלָה בְּמָחוֹל, then shall the maiden dance with joy" (Jeremiah 31:12). And the Gemara, also predicting the joy of the redemption, says, "עָתִיד הַקָּדוֹשׁ בָּרוּךְ הוּא לַעֲשׂוֹת מָחוֹל לַצַּדִּיקִים, it will surely come to pass that God will arrange a dance for the righteous" (*Ta'anit* 31a). There is a distinction between *rikud* and *maḥol*. *Rikud* is a dance in which the dancers

dance opposite each other and move away from each other. *Maḥol*, by contrast, refers to a dance in a circle in which someone is in the middle. In the *maḥol*, the beginning is never estranged from the end because the beginning and the end are linked to one another. The *paytan* is referring to the great dance in which the *tzaddikim* will dance around God. The first dancer will join the last in an eternal circle of dance around God.

אֲכַוֵּן, מִי יִתֶּנְךָ כְּאָח לִי *I will devoutly pray, "If only You could be with us as a brother!"* The *paytan* wants to embrace God, and he loves God as if He were his brother. He has faith that the redemption will finally come, and then he will sing to God. The *paytan* has experienced a complete transformation from despair and mourning into hope, solace and consolation. At this point in the *kina*, the consolation reaches its apex. The *paytan* has reached the level of Rabbi Akiva, who interpreted the verse, "And you shall love the LORD your God with all your heart, and with all your soul and with all your might" (Deuteronomy 6:5), as requiring one to love God with all one's soul, even at the time of death when God takes back possession of the soul (*Berakhot* 54a, 61b).

אַל תִּשְׁכַּח צַעֲקַת אֲרִיאֵל *Do not forget the Temple's cries.* After the stanza of *tzidduk hadin*, the *paytan* is able to turn to God in prayer and says, "Since I accept Your will, bend my knee before You and dance about You, I hope that You will never forget the crying of *ariel*, the altar in the Temple." The word *ariel* can be interpreted as referring specifically to the altar in the Temple.

אֵלָיו לֶאֱגֹר יְהוּדָה וְיִשְׂרָאֵל *And rejoin Judah and Israel to her.* The altar in the Temple is central to both Judea as well as the ten northern tribes of Samaria which were exiled. Jerusalem should be the capital of both Judea and Samaria, and the *paytan* is yearning for the ingathering of all the exiles.

אַלְפֵי שִׁנְאָן אֲשֶׁר מָסַר אֵל *The thousands of guardian angels You appointed.* This refers to the thousands of angels that God has appointed to guard the *Beit HaMikdash* and *Knesset Yisrael* (*Yalkut Shimoni, Zekh.* 569). God has entrusted the mission of the redemption to these multitudes of angels.

יִשְׂרָאֵל מֵעֵת בִּדְרָכַי לֹא הָלְכוּ [*God responds:*] *Israel, ever since it stopped walking in My ways.* After the series of questions posed to Him, God gives His response. The construction of the *kina* is puzzling. The *paytan* first laments with distress, grief and utter despair. Then he expresses hope, faith and expectation of God's salvation with words of solace and expressions of

thanks. He then declares *tzidduk hadin* in which he surrenders to God. At that point, the *paytan* senses redemption. Only then, after grieving over the destruction of the Temple and expressing the hope that it will be rebuilt, does the *paytan* introduce God's response that from the time Israel turned away from Him, He turned away from them. One would have expected the *paytan* to present the response of God several stanzas earlier, immediately after the expression of utter despair that he wishes to associate with those who wait for death. And *then*, after God's response that from the time Israel turned away from Him, He turned away from them, the *paytan* would be in a position to express the hope and expectation that each year they say "this will be the year of redemption."

Perhaps this strange structure instructs us that God does not provide a response unless and until the one who laments, complains, and challenges, has declared his faith in God that no matter how devastating the Ḥurban is, salvation will be forthcoming.

9

out as a dialogue between God and Israel, with alternating refrains expressing first God's claim against Israel, and then the people's claim against God and their hope for a reconciliation. The kina is followed by a short connecting stanza, which is a recent (seventeenth century) addition; older editions have a stanza connecting to Kina 15 "How His quiver is like an open grave" אֵיכָה אַשְׁפָּתוֹ פָּתוּחַ כְּקֶבֶר, *which follows this one in some ancient manuscripts. Commentary for this kina begins on page 264.*

א How they have hurled My glorious crown from My head,
and erected an idol in the Throne of Honor's stead.
Because they abrogated the conditions counseled by My prophets,
for He said: "If you follow My laws."

    Why do you call Me to account? You have spoken harsh
    words against Me! You have done this to yourselves!

Jer. 2:29
Mal. 3:13

ב He devoured my judges, first distorting their judgment.
He hid His face from them when He beheld their wickedness.
He transformed rain to dust to astonish them,
instead of: "I will grant your rain in their season!"

    He has made me filth and refuse! In His anger,
    He persecuted me! May His consolation soon delight me!

ג He cut down their pride and severed their youth,
and besieged their gates with a murderous sword.
In the midst of the harvest, He swelled them with hunger,
instead of: "Your threshing shall overtake the vintage!"

    Why do you call Me to account? You have spoken harsh
    words against Me! You have done this to yourselves!

ד He drew His bow, aiming at total war.
Like iron, He hardened the heavens.
He allowed the enemy to breach me thirteen times,
instead of: "I will grant peace in the land!"

    He has made me filth and refuse! In His anger,
    He persecuted me! May His consolation soon delight me!

9

In this kina, each stanza begins with the first word of the corresponding verse in Eikha chapter 2, comparing it to the covenant laid out at the beginning of Leviticus chapter 26. In the first eleven stanzas, the last stich recalls the promises of reward for keeping the mitzvot (Lev. 26:3–13), and in the latter eleven stanzas, the last stich is based on the first eleven verses of punishment (the Tokhaḥa, or Rebuke) for breaking the covenant (ibid. 14–24). The kina is laid

אֵיכָה תִּפְאַרְתִּי מֵרָאֲשׁוֹתַי הִשְׁלִיכוּ
וּכְנֶגֶד כִּסֵּא הַכָּבוֹד, צֶלֶם הִמְלִיכוּ
בְּחַלְלֵי תְנַאי אֲשֶׁר חוֹזֶי נִמְלְכוּ.
וְנַם, אִם־בְּחֻקֹּתַי תֵּלֵכוּ:

לָמָּה תָרִיבוּ אֵלַי כֻּלְּכֶם / חִזְקוּ עָלַי דִּבְרֵיכֶם / מִיֶּדְכֶם הָיְתָה זֹּאת לָכֶם: ירמיה ב, כט
מלאכי ג, יג

בִּלַּע שׁוֹפְטַי, בְּמוֹעֲצוֹת עוּתָּם
וּפָנִים הִסְתִּיר מֵהֶם, כַּאֲשֶׁר עִוְּתָם
וַיֹּאמֶר לְאָבָק מָטָר לְהַבְעִיתָם.
חֵלֶף וְנָתַתִּי גִשְׁמֵיכֶם בְּעִתָּם:

סְחִי וּמָאוֹס שָׂמֵנִי / כִּלָּה בְאַפּוֹ וַיִּשְׂטְמֵנִי / נִחוּמָיו מְהֵרָה יְשַׁעְשְׁעוּנִי:

גָּדַע רוּם קַרְנָם, וַעֲלוּמָם הִקְצִיר
וּבְאַבְחַת חֶרֶב, שְׂעָרֵיהֶם הִצִּיר
מְזֵי רָעָב עָשׁ בַּקָּצִיר.
תְּמוּר וְהִשִּׂיג לָכֶם דַּיִשׁ אֶת־בָּצִיר:

לָמָּה תָרִיבוּ אֵלַי כֻּלְּכֶם / חִזְקוּ עָלַי דִּבְרֵיכֶם / מִיֶּדְכֶם הָיְתָה זֹּאת לָכֶם:

דָּרַךְ קַשְׁתּוֹ, וְכִלָּה בְחָרֶץ
וְכַבַּרְזֶל עִפֵּל שְׁמֵי אֶרֶץ
פִּרְצֵי שְׁלֹשׁ עֶשְׂרֵה פָּרֶץ.
תַּחַת וְנָתַתִּי שָׁלוֹם בָּאָרֶץ:

סְחִי וּמָאוֹס שָׂמֵנִי / כִּלָּה בְאַפּוֹ וַיִּשְׂטְמֵנִי / נִחוּמָיו מְהֵרָה יְשַׁעְשְׁעוּנִי:

ה He was your Rock, your Strength, your Fortress,
   but He has turned cruel and wages war with you.
   Your Protector has left you; your Lover now abhors you.
   What has become of His promise: "You shall give chase to your
      enemies!"?
   > Why do you call Me to account? You have spoken harsh
   > words against Me! You have done this to yourselves!

ו He has waylaid the dear city, once full of justice,
   because in her secret chambers, He discovered all manner
      of things profane.
   Those who once honored her now treat her as a menstruant woman.
   Quite the opposite of: "Five of you shall give chase to a hundred!"
   > He has made me filth and refuse! In His anger,
   > He persecuted me! May His consolation soon delight me!

ז He has abandoned the city of your festive assembly
   and laid waste to the ramparts where your guards stood.
   Who asked you to speak, pretending to be pious?
      I felt compelled to exile you
   and be done with, "I will look with favor upon you!"
   > Why do you call Me to account? You have spoken harsh
   > words against Me! You have done this to yourselves!

ח He thought to scorn His people, likened to a rose,
   and force them to feed on the flesh of their young.
   The smoke from their bridal canopy rose like from a furnace,
   and they begged for bread, denied the blessing:
      "And you shall eat old grain, long stored!"
   > He has made me filth and refuse! In His anger,
   > He persecuted me! May His consolation soon delight me!

ט Sunk and slaughtered are those who once sung upon My platform;
   in the valley of Hamath were the High Priests butchered.
   For long years now, the foundations of My Temple lie exposed.
   Gone is the promise: "I will establish My abode [in your midst]!"
   > Why do you call Me to account? You have spoken harsh
   > words against Me! You have done this to yourselves!

הָיָה צוּרְכֶם וּמָעֻזְּכֶם וּמִשְׂגַּבְּכֶם
הֶהָפֵךְ לְאַכְזָר וְנִלְחַם בָּכֶם
הַנּוֹצַרְכֶם רִחֲקָכֶם, חוֹשְׁקָכֶם תִּעֲבְכֶם.
וְאַיֵּה הַבִּטָּחַת, וּרְדַפְתֶּם אֶת־אֹיְבֵיכֶם:
לָמָּה תָרִיבוּ אֵלַי כֻּלְּכֶם / חִזְקוּ עָלַי דִּבְרֵיכֶם / מִיֶּדְכֶם הָיְתָה זֹּאת לָכֶם:

וַיַּחְמֹס פִּנַּת צֶדֶק מְלֵאָה
כִּי בְמַשְׂכִּיתָהּ מָצָא כָל טֻמְאָה
וּמְכַבְּדֶיהָ הִזִּילוּהָ כְּדָוָה מְטֻמָּאָה.
בְּשִׁנּוּי וְרָדְפוּ מִכֶּם חֲמִשָּׁה מֵאָה:
סְחִי וּמָאוֹס שָׂמַנִי / כִּלָּה בְאַפּוֹ וַיִּשְׁטְמֵנִי / נִחוּמָיו מְהֵרָה יְשַׁעֲשְׁעוּנִי:

זָנַח עֶלְיוֹן קִרְיַת מוֹעֲדֵיכֶם
וְהֶאֱבִיל שַׁעֲרֵי חַיִל, עֲמִידַת רַגְלֵיכֶם
מִי בִקֵּשׁ זֹאת פָּץ, וְהִגְלְכֶם.
וְגָמַר אָמַר, וּפָנַיְתִי אֲלֵיכֶם:
לָמָּה תָרִיבוּ אֵלַי כֻּלְּכֶם / חִזְקוּ עָלַי דִּבְרֵיכֶם / מִיֶּדְכֶם הָיְתָה זֹּאת לָכֶם:

חָשַׁב שָׂנוּא אִם לֶקֶט כְּשׁוֹשָׁן
וּמֵחֵלֶב עוֹלֵלֶיהָ, אוֹתָהּ דִּשֵּׁן
קִיטוֹר חֲפָתָהּ הֶעֱלָה כַּכִּבְשָׁן.
וְשָׁאֲלוּ אַיֵּה דָגָן, תְּמוֹר וַאֲכָלְתֶם יָשָׁן נוֹשָׁן:
סְחִי וּמָאוֹס שָׂמַנִי / כִּלָּה בְאַפּוֹ וַיִּשְׁטְמֵנִי / נִחוּמָיו מְהֵרָה יְשַׁעֲשְׁעוּנִי:

טָבְעוּ נִכְסוּ רִבְדֵי דּוּכָנִי
בְּגֵיא חֲמַת כְּנִקְטַל מְכַהֲנִי
הֲרֵי כַמָּה שָׁנִים, גֻּלָּה יְסוֹד מְכוֹנִי.
וְסַע מִתּוֹכִי אָמַר, וְנָתַתִּי מִשְׁכָּנִי:
לָמָּה תָרִיבוּ אֵלַי כֻּלְּכֶם / חִזְקוּ עָלַי דִּבְרֵיכֶם / מִיֶּדְכֶם הָיְתָה זֹּאת לָכֶם:

י They sat and cried as your dying men moaned.
To the four deathly punishments, He condemned you:
sword, famine, wild beasts, and plague ravaged you.
Gone was the Protector who once promised:
  "I will walk among you!"
> He has made me filth and refuse! In His anger,
> He persecuted me! May His consolation soon delight me!

כ Instead your tent was reduced to plunder,
and your enemies mocked you in their oaths.
Your babes expired in your laps,
because you detested the words: "I am the LORD, your God!"
> Why do you call Me to account? You have spoken harsh
> words against Me! You have done this to yourselves!

ל Children pleaded with their mothers for food,
and God said to the protesting angels, "Get away from Me!"
I brought you to the fertile Carmel for your pleasure,
but you despised those who warned: "But if you do not obey!"
> He has made me filth and refuse! In His anger,
> He persecuted me! May His consolation soon delight me!

מ To what other nation can I compare you,
your old and your young together trampled?
Confident that you could flee on horseback, you fled!
I could no longer bear your heavy burden. *Is. 1:14*
I warned you when I said: "If you reject My laws."
> Why do you call Me to account? You have spoken harsh
> words against Me! You have done this to yourselves!

נ Your false prophets misled you with vain visions.
I sought to forgive you [by sending you true prophets whom you
  ignored], so why should I forgive? *Jer. 5:7*
I persisted and sent others, to whom you replied brazenly as well.
I angrily said: "I in turn will do this to you!"
> He has made me filth and refuse! In His anger,
> He persecuted me! May His consolation soon delight me!

יֵשְׁבוּ מְבַכִּים מְנַאֵק מֵתֵיכֶם
בְּאַרְבַּע מִיתוֹת הִפִּיל מְתֵיכֶם
חֶרֶב וְרָעָב וְחַיָּה וְדֶבֶר שְׁחֵתָם.
בְּסַר צֵל פָּץ, וְהִתְהַלַּכְתִּי בְתוֹכֲכֶם:
סְחִי וּמָאוֹס שָׂמֵנִי / כָּלָה בְאַפּוֹ וַיִּשְׁטְמֵנִי / נִחוּמָיו מְהֵרָה יְשַׁעְשְׁעוּנִי:

כְּלוּ לְשַׁד בְּרֶגַע אָהֳלֵיכֶם
וּבָכֶם נִשְׁבְּעוּ מְהוֹלְלֵיכֶם
לְחֵיקְכֶם שָׁפְכוּ נַפְשׁוֹת עוֹלְלֵיכֶם.
בְּמָאָסְכֶם שִׂיחַ, אֲנִי יהוה אֱלֹהֵיכֶם:
לָמָּה תָרִיבוּ אֵלַי כֻּלְּכֶם / חִזְקוּ עָלַי דִּבְרֵיכֶם / מִידְכֶם הָיְתָה זֹּאת לָכֶם:

לְאֻמִּתָם, בְּלִבּוּל אָנָה, שָׁוְעוּ
וְצוּר לְמַלְאָכָיו שָׂח, מֶנִּי שָׁעוּ
אֶרֶץ הַכַּרְמֶל הֵבֵאתִים וְשָׂדָיו.
וְשָׂנְאוּ מוֹכִיחַ, וְאִם־לֹא תִשְׁמָעוּ:
סְחִי וּמָאוֹס שָׂמֵנִי / כָּלָה בְאַפּוֹ וַיִּשְׁטְמֵנִי / נִחוּמָיו מְהֵרָה יְשַׁעְשְׁעוּנִי:

מָה אֲעִידֵךְ, יְשִׁישַׁיִךְ עִם גּוּרַיִךְ בּוֹסְסוּ
אוֹמְרִים עַל סוּס נָנוּס, עַל כֵּן נָסוּ
נִלְאֵיתִי נְשֹׂא עֲווֹנֹתֵיכֶם כְּהַעְמָסוּ.
וָאֲיַסְּרֶכֶם כִּנֻמָּתִי, אִם־בְּחֻקֹּתַי תִּמְאָסוּ:   ישעיה א, יד
לָמָּה תָרִיבוּ אֵלַי כֻּלְּכֶם / חִזְקוּ עָלַי דִּבְרֵיכֶם / מִידְכֶם הָיְתָה זֹּאת לָכֶם:

נְבִיאַיִךְ טָעוּ, תַּרְמִית שָׁוְא חָזוּת
וָאֶדְרֹשׁ לִסְלוֹחַ, וּפָצְתִי אֵי לָזֹאת   ירמיה ה, ז
פְּתָיִים, וּכְנֶגְדִּי הֵשִׁיבוּ עַזוּת.
וָאֶנָּפְתִּי וְשָׂחִתִּי, אַף־אֲנִי אֶעֱשֶׂה־זֹּאת:
סְחִי וּמָאוֹס שָׂמֵנִי / כָּלָה בְאַפּוֹ וַיִּשְׁטְמֵנִי / נִחוּמָיו מְהֵרָה יְשַׁעְשְׁעוּנִי:

ס My detractors were puzzled and confounded by my plight.
From enemies within and enemies without, were my people attacked.
The wicked profaned my inner sanctum.
Bad, not good, did He imply when He said:
> "I will set My face [against you]!"
>> Why do you call Me to account? You have spoken harsh
>> words against Me! You have done this to yourselves!

פ The foe teased us: "To whom do you pray?"
You sinned mightily, so God is weary of listening.
Hope no longer for signs and wonders.
In anger, He deserted you and said:
> "And if, for all that [you do not obey Me]!"
>> He has made me filth and refuse! In His anger,
>> He persecuted me! May His consolation soon delight me!

ע He has raised our enemies high, like the waves of the sea,
but made me drink my own blood in the vale of thirst.
Year after year, He adds to my agony and pain;
He angrily said: "I will break your proud glory!"
>> Why do you call Me to account? You have spoken harsh
>> words against Me! You have done this to yourselves!

צ He cried, "Woe! Woe!" even as He emptied His quiver.
From all directions, He rallied swift pursuers.
In a circle enveloping me, they gritted their teeth derisively.
My strength waned with the words:
> "Your strength shall be spent to no purpose!"
>> He has made me filth and refuse! In His anger,
>> He persecuted me! May His consolation soon delight me!

ק Rise! Knock! Scream! Be not silent!
Even pray in the voice of a ghost from the grave.
I have suffered so that I am almost mute.
My path was darkened by the words:
> "And if you remain hostile toward Me."
>> Why do you call Me to account? You have spoken harsh
>> words against Me! You have done this to yourselves!

סָפְקוּ חָרְקוּ שָׁרְקוּ מוֹנַי
מִבִּפְנִים וּמִבַּחוּץ לְהַצְמִית אֱמוּנַי
כִּי בְנֵי זֵדִים חִלְּלוּ סְפוּנַי.
לְרָעָה וְלֹא לְטוֹבָה נָם, וְנָתַתִּי פָנַי:
לָמָּה תָרִיבוּ אֵלַי כֻּלְּכֶם / חִזְקוּ עָלַי דִּבְרֵיכֶם / מִיֶּדְכֶם הָיְתָה זֹּאת לָכֶם:

פָּצוּ זֵדִים, לִפְנֵי מִי תְּחִלָּה
עָם כֶּבֶד עָוֹן, פָּקַד וַיִּלְאֶה
לֹא תֵחָבוּ עוֹד לְמוֹפֵת וָפֶלֶא.
נָסַב וְנָסַע וְנָם, וְאִם־עַד־אֵלֶּה:
סְחִי וּמָאוֹס שָׂמֵנִי / כָּלָה בְאַפּוֹ וַיִּשְׁטְמֵנִי / נְחוּמָיו מְהֵרָה יְשַׁעְשְׁעוּנִי:

עָשָׂה וַיָּרֶם קָדְקֹד בְּנֵי שָׁאוֹן
וְדָמִי שְׁכָרַנִי בְּגֵיא צִמָּאוֹן
וּבְכָל שָׁנָה וְשָׁנָה הוֹסִיף יָגוֹן עַל אוֹן.
מֵעַט כָּעַס וְנָם, וְשָׁבַרְתִּי אֶת־גְּאוֹן:
לָמָּה תָרִיבוּ אֵלַי כֻּלְּכֶם / חִזְקוּ עָלַי דִּבְרֵיכֶם / מִיֶּדְכֶם הָיְתָה זֹּאת לָכֶם:

צָעַק הוֹי הוֹי, וְאַשְׁפָּתוֹ הֵרִיק
מַפָּה וּמִפָּה, הֵבִיא עָלַי מַעֲרִיק
וּבְלַעֲגֵי מָעוֹג, שִׁנֵּי צָר הֶחֱרִיק.
וְכָלָה כֹחִי בְּנָאַם, וְתַם לָרִיק:
סְחִי וּמָאוֹס שָׂמֵנִי / כָּלָה בְאַפּוֹ וַיִּשְׁטְמֵנִי / נְחוּמָיו מְהֵרָה יְשַׁעְשְׁעוּנִי:

קוּמִי דִפְקִי, שַׁוְּעִי, אַל דֳּמִי
וּתְנִי כְאוֹב מֵאֶרֶץ קוֹלֵךְ, וְדֹמִּי
מִי רֹאשׁ הִשְׁקַנִי וְהִדְמִי.
וְחָשַׁךְ הֹלוּכִי בְּנָאַם, וְאִם־תֵּלְכוּ עִמִּי:
לָמָּה תָרִיבוּ אֵלַי כֻּלְּכֶם / חִזְקוּ עָלַי דִּבְרֵיכֶם / מִיֶּדְכֶם הָיְתָה זֹּאת לָכֶם:

ר See the land You apportioned by lottery to
Your people, now barren!
And how I am likened to a desert-owl!
Taunted as an exile and shamefully disdained.
I heard: "I will loose wild beasts upon you!"
> He has made me filth and refuse! In His anger,
> He persecuted me! May His consolation soon delight me!

ש They lolled in a swoon, as if caught in a net, with no rescue;
full with God's rage, with no cure in sight.
For so many years, have they eaten away at me to finish me off.
We despair and stand accused: "And if these things
   [fail to discipline you]."
> Why do you call Me to account? You have spoken harsh
> words against Me! You have done this to yourselves!

ת May the day come when You will dispose of Edom.
Let him perish and be torn asunder, seven times my suffering!
Confound my enemies with a visionary voice,
   echoing from my Temple,
as I was confounded with the curse:
   "I too will remain [hostile to you]."
> He has made me filth and refuse! In His anger,
> He persecuted me! May His consolation soon delight me!

אֲנִי I, too, was trapped like a staggering drunkard.
Joy was dispelled, thwarted by His anger.
I will sit on the ground and sob from my throat:
"How the Rose of Sharon now sits alone!" *Song. 2:1*

Kina 10 starts on page 268.

רְאֵה גּוֹרָל אִוִּיתָ, הוּשַׂם לְעַיִט
וְלִקְאַת מִדְבָּר, הָיִיתִי דְמוּיָת
גּוֹלָה גְנוּיָה וּסְרוּרָה כְּנוּיָה.
בְּשִׁמְעִי, וְהִשְׁלַחְתִּי בָכֶם אֶת־חַיַּת:
סְחִי וּמָאוֹס שָׂמַנִי / כִּלָּה בְאַפּוֹ וַיִּשְׂטְמֵנִי / נִחוּמָיו מְהֵרָה יְשַׁעְשְׁעוּנִי:

שָׁכְבוּ בְעִלּוּף כְּתוֹא, וְאֵין דּוֹלֶה
הַמְלֵאִים גַּעַר, וְאֵין מַרְפֵּא עוֹלֶה
הֲרֵי כַּמָּה שָׁנִים הֲמַמְנִי לְהִתְכַּלֶּה.
אֲנוּשִׁים בְּוִכּוּחַ, וְאִם־בְּאֵלֶּה:
לָמָּה תָרִיבוּ אֵלַי כֻּלְּכֶם / חֲזָקוּ עָלַי דִּבְרֵיכֶם / מִיֶּדְכֶם הָיְתָה זֹּאת לָכֶם:

תִּקְרָא אֵיד עוֹלֶלֶת עַל אַדְמוֹנִי
לְסַחֲפוֹ וּלְשַׁסְּפוֹ שִׁבְעָתַיִם כְּאוֹנִי
תָּהֹם צָרַי בְּצֵאת קוֹל מֵאַרְמוֹנִי.
כְּנֶהֱמָתִי בָרִיב, וְהָלַכְתִּי אַף־אָנִי:
סְחִי וּמָאוֹס שָׂמַנִי / כִּלָּה בְאַפּוֹ וַיִּשְׂטְמֵנִי / נִחוּמָיו מְהֵרָה יְשַׁעְשְׁעוּנִי:

אַף אֲנִי לְכָד בִּקֵּשׁ שִׁבְרוֹן
עָרְבָה שִׂמְחָה וְהִשְׁבִּית חָרוֹן
לָאָרֶץ אֵשֵׁב וְאֶהְגֶּה בְגָרוֹן
אֵיכָה יָשְׁבָה חֲבַצֶּלֶת הַשָּׁרוֹן:

שיר השירים ב, א

Kina 10 starts on page 269.

COMMENTARY ON KINA 9

אֵיכָה תִּפְאַרְתִּי *How... My glorious crown.* The word *eikha* occurs in three places in Tanakh: "אֵיכָה יָשְׁבָה בָדָד, How does the city sit solitary" (Lamentations 1:1); "אֵיכָה הָיְתָה לְזוֹנָה קִרְיָה נֶאֱמָנָה, How has the faithful city become a harlot" (Isaiah 1:21); and "אֵיכָה אֶשָּׂא לְבַדִּי טָרְחֲכֶם וּמַשַּׂאֲכֶם וְרִיבְכֶם, How can I alone bear your cumbrance, and your burden and your strife?" (Deuteronomy 1:12). The question *"eikha?"* implies that there is no logical explanation. When one asks *"eikha,* how is it possible?" the question itself implies that it is impossible. The question *"eikha"* posed by the book of Lamentations, represents so much despair, such a complete lack of understanding, that we do not begin to know how the Ḥurban could have been possible.

מִיֶּדְכֶם הָיְתָה זֹּאת *"You have done this to yourselves!"* In the first stanza, the one speaking is God. He is saying that *we* are responsible for the catastrophe. This is the concept of *tzidduk hadin – we* are at fault.

בִּלַּע שׁוֹפְטַי, בְּמוֹעֲצוֹת עֻוְּתָם *He devoured my judges, first distorting their judgment.* While the previous stanza consisted of God's statement, this stanza contains the words of the *mekonen*, the one who laments and mourns.

This phrase can be understood as referring to the transgression of *ivut hadin*, corruption among the judges. This type of corruption consists of fraud and theft in business and is described in the first chapter of Isaiah, which is read as the *Haftara* on the Shabbat preceding Tisha B'Av, "Your silver has become dross; your wine is mixed with water" (1:22). This was one of the transgressions which was responsible for the destruction of Jerusalem.

סְחִי וּמָאוֹס... נְחוּמָיו... יְשַׁעְשְׁעוּנִי *Filth and refuse... His consolation... delight me.* In these two lines, *Knesset Yisrael* is speaking.

גָּדַע רוּם קַרְנָם *He cut down their pride.* This stanza constitutes the response of God.

פְּרָצַנִי שָׁלֹשׁ עֶשְׂרֵה פֶּרֶץ *He allowed the enemy to breach me thirteen times.* This is a reference to thirteen cracks in the wall of the *Beit HaMikdash* made by the Greeks (Mishna *Middot* 2:3, 35a). Apparently, in commemoration of this event, the cracks were left in an unrepaired state.

הָיָה צוּרְכֶם וּמָעֻזְּכֶם וּמִשְׂגַּבְּכֶם *He was your Rock, your Strength, your Fortress.* The enemies of the Jewish people are speaking, and this stanza was and still is their principal argument against the Jews. They assert that the Jewish people once

did have a covenant with God, but, because of their sins, He annulled it, and now they have no claim to Him or the land of Israel.

וְהֶאֱבִיל שַׁעֲרֵי חֵיל, עֲמִידַת רַגְלֵיכֶם *And laid waste to the ramparts where your guards stood.* The *ḥeil*, a rampart, was a portion of the structure of the Temple compound (*Pesaḥim* 64b), and was the point beyond which non-Jews were prohibited from entering (Mishna *Kelim* 1:8). The intent of this phrase is that God has made the gates of the *ḥeil* desolate, and He no longer visits that site.

דּוּכָנִי *My platform.* This is a reference to the platform on which the Levites stood when they sang in the *Beit HaMikdash*.

כְּסָר צֵל פֵּץ, וְהִתְהַלַּכְתִּי בְּתוֹכֲכֶם *Gone was the Protector who once promised, "I will walk among you!"* This phrase can be interpreted to mean that the shadow of God's promise, "And I shall walk among you" (Leviticus 26:12), was removed. Not only was the promise itself removed, but even the shadow of the promise was taken away. This represents complete *hester panim*, the hiding by God of His presence. Everything that He promised as a reward was reversed and transformed into a curse.

לְאִמּוֹתָם, כְּלִבּוּל אָנָה, שִׁוְּעוּ *Children pleaded with their mothers for food.* This is a paraphrase of the passage from Lamentations, "They say to their mothers, 'Where is grain and wine?'" (2:12).

וְצוּר לְמַלְאָכָיו שָׂח, מֶנִּי שְׁעוּ *And God said to the protesting angels, "Get away from Me!"* The angels approached God begging for mercy, and He said, "*meni she'u*, Get away from Me; I do not want to have mercy on them."

In this phrase, the word *malakhav* could very well be interpreted to refer to the prophets, as in וַיִּשְׁלַח מַלְאָךְ (Numbers 20:16). God is telling the prophets to depart from Him because they will no longer have any contact with Him. This constitutes the extinguishment of prophecy.

וְשָׂנְאוּ מוֹכִיחַ *But you despised those who warned.* Instead of expressing gratitude for the pleasant land which God gave them, the Jewish people displayed ingratitude by venting hatred against the prophets who rebuked them. That is why prophecy was extinguished.

אוֹמְרִים עַל סוּס נָנוּס *Confident that you could flee on horseback.* This is an allusion to the treaty that the Jews entered into with Egypt under which the Jews believed that the Egyptians would protect them from the Babylonians (Jeremiah 37:7; Ezekiel 17:15). The prophets were unhappy with this treaty

and said, "אַשּׁוּר לֹא יוֹשִׁיעֵנוּ עַל־סוּס לֹא נִרְכָּב, Assyria shall not save us; we will not ride upon horses" (Hosea 14:4). The horse represents Egypt, and the prophet's criticism is that the Jews placed too much reliance on the horse, that is, on Egypt.

Every great power has its ultimate weapon of war. For the Egyptians, it was the horse, as the Torah says in describing the Egyptian disaster at the Red Sea, "the horse and its rider, He has thrown into the sea" (Exodus 15:1). Rome developed the weaponry to demolish the walls of fortresses. The United States introduced nuclear weapons in World War II. When the prophet says, "we will not ride upon horses," the intent is that the Jewish people should not concentrate their reliance on any "invincible" weapon because it is ultimately unreliable.

נָסַב וְנָסַע וְנָם, וְאִם־עַד־אֵלֶּה *In anger, He deserted you and said, "And if, for all that [you do not obey Me]*". The *zedim*, the enemies of the Jews, say that there is no more hope for the Jews and that Jewish history has come to an end. They deny that the covenant between God and the Jewish people still exists. As noted above, the argument that there is no longer any special relationship between God and the Jewish people is still marshaled against us even in our own times. This argument forms the basis of their theological argument that the Jewish people are not entitled to the land of Israel.

It is blasphemy to assert that the covenant between God and *Knesset Yisrael* no longer exists. It is blasphemy against God because it accuses Him of not keeping His word. Moses, as well, was concerned with this blasphemy when he said, "Why should the Egyptians speak, saying: For it was with an evil intent that He brought them out, to kill them in the mountains" (Exodus 32:12). Moses is arguing that God should be concerned with the reaction of the Egyptians because their reaction will be blasphemy against Him.

קוּמִי דְּפָקִי, שַׁוְּעִי, אַל דָּמִי *Rise! Knock! Scream! Be not silent!* The *paytan* exhorts *Knesset Yisrael*, "Do not listen to the other nations. Pound on the portals of heaven through prayer. Do not be silent." This phrase alludes to the verse in Lamentations, "קוּמִי רֹנִּי בַלַּיְלָה, Arise, cry out in the night, at the beginning of the watches; pour out your heart like water before the face of the LORD" (2:19). In spite of the disaster, the Jew continues to pray that salvation will come.

תִּקְרָא אֵיד עוֹלֵלֶת עַל אֲדֹמוֹנִי *May the day come when You will dispose of Edom.* The *paytan* is pleading for a heavenly voice to ordain that disaster befall Edom.

Edom initially referred to Rome, but it was later understood to refer to the Catholic Church.

The verse in Job states, "God understands the ways thereof [i.e., the Torah], and He knows the place thereof [i.e., the Torah]" (28:23). The Gemara interprets this verse to mean that "God understood the Jewish people and knew that they would not be able to withstand the edicts of the Romans, so he exiled them to Babylonia" (*Gittin* 17a); that is, He realized that it would be impossible for the Jews to study Torah under the Romans, meaning the Byzantine Christians, so He exiled the Jews to Babylonia, a pagan country, since the pagans were more tolerant than the Christians.

10

א How the Rose of Sharon sat alone,   *Song. 2:1*
   and the song of the Ark bearers, silenced.
      The priests, sons of Aaron, were removed from their terms of service,
         as the Temple was given away during [the watch of]
         those who would rebel [the family of Yehoyariv].

ב The five books of Moses cried and cried
   when the priest and prophet [Zechariah the son of Yehoyada]
      was murdered on Yom Kippur,
   for which budding priests were slaughtered like sacrificial goats;
      and dispersed like birds were the priests of [the watch of] Sepphoris.

ג The beautiful bride is exiled from her land
   because of the sin of failing to tithe and keep the Sabbatical year.
   Punished fourfold [plague, sword, famine, captivity];
      stripped of her raiment was the watch of Mifshata.

ד The Temple's paths fell silent when its walls were breached,
   and when the priestly tunic [with its bells around its hem] was torn!
      Cast down, lowered from its mound, and uprooted from its grove
      were the priests of [the watch of] Ayata-Lo.

ה They derided the Torah scholars,
   who denied breaking bread with the poor,   *Is. 58:7*
   and so hungered for bread and thirsted for water,
      as the two sacrificial breads [brought on Shavuot]
      were no longer offered by [the watch of] Bethlehem.

ו Departed is that nation's beauty, once covered with silver,
   now covered instead by a layer of ash.
   Its candles dim, its Menora inverted.
      Because they denied bread to the poor,
      was [the watch of] Yodfat ensnared.

10

In this kina, each stanza begins with the first word of the corresponding verse in Eikha chapter 1, and laments the loss of one of the twenty-four Mishmarot Kehuna, the priestly families. The Mishmarot Kehuna are often mentioned in piyutim by HaKalir, and modern scholars have even attempted to reconstruct the list of Mishmarot based on his piyutim. Commentary for this kina begins on page 276.

אֵיכָה יָשְׁבָה חֲבַצֶּלֶת הַשָּׁרוֹן
וְדָמַם רֹן מִפִּי נוֹשְׂאֵי אָרוֹן
וְנָעוּ מִמִּשְׁמְרוֹתָם כֹּהֲנִים בְּנֵי אַהֲרֹן.
כְּנִמְסַר הַבַּיִת בִּמְסָרְבֵי מָרוֹן:

שיר השירים
ב, א

בָּכוֹ תִבְכֶּה מֵחֲמֶשֶׁת סְפָרִים
כְּנֶהֱרַג כֹּהֵן וְנָבִיא בְּיוֹם הַכִּפּוּרִים
וְעַל דָּמוֹ נִשְׁחֲטוּ פְּרָחִים כִּצְפִירִים.
וְנָדוּ כִצְפֳּרִים, כֹּהֲנֵי צִפּוֹרִים:

גָּלְתָה מֵאַרְצָהּ כַּלָּה מְקֻשָּׁטָה
בַּעֲוֹן מַעְשְׂרוֹת וּשְׁמִטָּה
וּבְאַרְבַּעַת שְׁפָטִים הֻשְׁפְּטָה.
וּמַעֲדָיהּ הֻפְשְׁטָה, מִשְׁמֶרֶת מַפְשְׁטָה:

דַּרְכֵי הֵיכָל דָּמְמוּ, כְּנִפְרַץ כָּתְלוֹ
וְהַמְּעִיל כְּנִקְרַע פְּתִילוֹ
וְהֻתַּךְ וְהֻשְׁפַּל מַתְלוֹ.
וְנָע מַשְׁתִּילוֹ, כֹּהֵן עִיתָה לוֹ:

הָיוּ מַלְעִיבִים בְּלוֹחֲמֵי לֶחֶם
כְּבִטְּלוּ הֲלוֹא פָרֹס לָרָעֵב לֶחֶם
וְרָעֲבוּ וְצָמְאוּ מִמַּיִם וּמִלֶּחֶם.
כְּבִטְּלוּ שְׁתֵּי הַלֶּחֶם, מִבֵּית לֶחֶם:

ישעיה נח, ז

וַיֵּצֵא הָדָר אֹם בַּכֶּסֶף נֶחְפָּת
וְתִמּוּרוֹ אֵפֶר רֹאשָׁהּ חָפָת
וְנֵרוֹת נִכְבּוּ וּמְנוֹרָה נִכְפָּת.
כְּפָשְׁעוּ בְּלֶחֶם וָפַת, נִלְכְּדָה יוֹדְפַת:

ז She remembered the time when they proclaimed: *Ex. 24:7*
"We will do! We will hear,"
   but now refuse to answer "Amen" [to the prophet's rebuke].
      They are now sated and stuffed with noxious herbs.
      Isolated and mocked were the priests of [the watch of] Eilevu.

ח She sinned when she said of the idol: "This is my God!"
   And she taunted and teased God's visionaries.
      Therefore, revenge was taken upon her by those who anger God,
         and gone from God's abode was [the watch of] Kefar Uziel.

ט Her profanity contaminated the land
   so that the divine Captain left and ascended.
   A cloud of dust at His feet like a mourner;
      no longer clothed in priestly garments were the priests of
      [the watch of] Arbel.

י The enemy stretched his hand against the Temple,
   for we deserved extinction no less than the generation of the Flood.
   The foe slurred God's throne with obscenities;
      bound in chains were the priests of [the watch of] Cabul.

כ The entire nation expressed lament,
   acknowledging that they had angered the zealous god
   who took revenge against them using a nation of knaves.
      Set to flight from her nest was the watch of Kana.

ל [Israel] did not look heavenward,
   but covered her clay vessels with false walls of silver.
   As suffering strengthened, the people weakened;
      broken and faint were the priests of [the watch of] Safed.

מ From on high, He let it be heard that He could tolerate it no longer,
   and He struck me with blindness and madness.
   He recalled against me the sins of Nob and Gibeon.
      Removed from the Temple was the watch of the priests of Beit Ma'on.

שמות כד, ז

זָכְרָה זְמָן, אֲשֶׁר נַעֲשֶׂה וְנִשְׁמַע הֵשִׁיבוּ
וְעַתָּה עֲנוֹת אָמֵן לֹא אָבוּ
לַעֲנָה וָרֹאשׁ שָׂבְעוּ וְרָווּ.
וְהִקְצוּ וְהִלְעִיבוּ, כֹּהֲנֵי עֵילָבוּ׃

חֵטְא חָטְאָה, וְאָמְרָה לָאֱלִיל זֶה אֵל
וְהִלְעִיגָה וְתִתְעַתְּעָה בַחוֹזֵי אֵל
עֲבוּר כֵּן הַקִּנְאָה בְמַרְגִּיזֵי אֵל.
וַיֵּצֵא מִמָּעוֹן אֵל, כְּפַר עֻזִּיאֵל׃

טֻמְאָתָהּ הֶחֱנִיפָה תֵבֵל
וְנַעֲלָה רַב הַחוֹבֵל
וְעָנָן אֲבַק רַגְלָיו כְּאָבֵל.
וְאֵין מִתְכַּרְבֵּל, בְּכֹהֲנֵי אַרְבֵּל׃

יָדוֹ פָּרַשׂ צָר בְּבֵית זְבוּל
כִּי כְלָיָה חִיַּבְתִּי כְּדוֹר הַמַּבּוּל
כִּסְאוֹ הֵשִׁית לְחִבּוּל וְנִבּוּל.
וְיָצָא בְכֶבֶל כָּבוּל, כֹּהֵן כָּבוּל׃

כָּל עַמָּהּ קוֹנְנוּ קִינָה
כִּי הִכְעִיסוּ לְאֵל קַנָּא
בְּגוֹי נָבָל, אוֹתָם קִנֵּא.
וְנָדְדָה מִקְנֶה, מִשְׁמֶרֶת קָנָה׃

לֹא לַמָּרוֹם עֵין צָפַת
וְכֶסֶף עַל חֶרֶשׂ חֻפַּת
וּבְחִזּוּק מוּסַר הֻרְפַּת.
וְנֶהֱרַס וְנִלְפַּת, כֹּהֵן צְפַת׃

מִמָּרוֹם הַשְׁמִיעַ, נִלְאֵיתִי טְעוֹן
וְהִכַּנִי בְעִוָּרוֹן וּבְשִׁגָּעוֹן
וּפָקַד עָלַי עֲוֹן נֹב וְגִבְעוֹן.
וְנָעָה מִמָּעוֹן, מִשְׁמֶרֶת בֵּית מָעוֹן׃

נ The burden of my sins was bound to me painfully,
   as I was rendered bereft, fatherless.
   Silenced from chanting with flute and pipe,
      they issued forth lamentation, the watch of Jeshebeab.

ס He shattered all my heroes, teachers of Torah,
   and did not remember the binding of Isaac on Mount Moriah.
   Because of their great revolt and rebellion,
      He stripped and denuded the watch of Ma'araya.

ע Plowmen plowed across my back, making long furrows.
   They unsheathed against me sword and spear;
   increased my fasts and days of abstinence.
      Expelled from the well-designed Temple was [the watch of] Yevanit.

פ Hands spread in prayer, but no hand was extended to help.
   They did not heed the prophet who was sent to them daily.
   Done were the [Eternal] Salt Covenant and the perfumed sacred oil
      from the head of [the watch of] Mamlaḥ.

צ The LORD is in the right, for I disobeyed Him.
   "Strip her, strip her to her very foundation," and indeed she was stripped.
   Instead of songs of triumph, dirges were inscribed,   *Ex. 15:2*
      and to the ends of the earth was scattered the watch of Nazareth.

ק I called out to my Rock, but He found my voice unpleasant.
   I lodged in the brush, in the woods.
   Extinguished was the light of the westernmost candle.
      The incense was no longer fragrant for [the watch of] Akhala-Arav.

ר Look! I am like a storm-tossed ship,
   mourning and moaning!   *Lam. 2:5*
   My people are like sheep led to slaughter.
      Expelled from Ḥanuya was [the watch of] Migdal Nunia.

נִשְׁקַד עַל עָוֹן, וְנִכְאָב
כְּהוּשַׁבְתִּי אֲנוּנָה, מִבְּלִי אָב
וְדוֹמַמְתִּי מִלְּצַפְצֵף בְּמָנִים וְעָגָב.
וְנָשְׂאָה עָלַי קִינָה, מִשְׁמֶרֶת יְשֶׁבְאָב:

סָלָה כָל אַבִּירַי, מוֹרֵי הוֹרָיָה
וְלֹא נִכַּר לִי עֲקֵדַת מוֹרִיָּה
מֵרֹב מֶרֶד וּמְרִיָה.
הִצִּיגָה עֵרוֹם וְעֶרְיָה, מִשְׁמֶרֶת מַעַרְיָה:

עַל גַּבִּי חָרְשׁוּ חָרָשִׁים, וְהֶאֱרִיכוּ מַעֲנִית
וְהֵרִיקוּ עָלַי חֶרֶב וַחֲנִית
וְהִרְבֵּיתִי צוֹמוֹת וְתַעֲנִית.
וּמְצוּרַת תָּכְנִית, יָצְאָה יָוָנִית:

פֵּרְשָׂה וְאֵין יָד שׁוֹלֵחַ
כִּי לֹא הֶאֱמִינָה בְּהַשְׁכֵּם וְשַׁלּוֹחַ
וְהֻשְׁבְּתָה בְּרִית מֶלַח.
וְאֵין שֶׁמֶן מִמְלָח, בְּרֹאשׁ מַמְלָח:

צַדִּיק הוּא יהוה, כִּי פִיהוּ מָרָת
וְעָרוּ עָרוּ עַד הַיְסוֹד בָּהּ, הָעָרַת הָדָךְ
וּתְמוּר עֻזִּי וְזִמְרָת, קִינִים עָלֶיהָ נֶחֱרָת.
וּבְקַצְוֵי אֶרֶץ נָזְרַת, מִשְׁמֶרֶת נָצְרַת:

שמות טו, ב

קָרָאתִי בַצַּר לִי, וְלֹא קָרֵב
וְקוֹנַנְתִּי בַּיַּעַר בָּעֶרֶב
וְכָבָה נֵר הַדּוֹלֵק בְּמַעֲרָב.
וְרֵיחַ לֹא עָרֵב, מַאֲכָלָהּ עָרֵב:

רְאֵה כִּי הִסְעַרְתִּי כָּאֳנִיָּה
בְּתַאֲנִיָּה וַאֲנִיָּה
וַעֲדָתִי כַּצֹּאן לְטֶבַח מְנוּיָה.
וְנָעָה מֵחֲנוּיָה, מִגְדַּל נוּנִיָּה:

איכה ב, ה

ש My enemies heard that I was stained with filthy sin
and that my prayers were shut out;
He gave me neither mercy nor pity.
    Gone from Kiryat Ḥana [Jerusalem] was
    [the watch residing in] Kefar Yoḥana.

ש The enemy learned that I had gone to captivity,
and that Torah, given from on high, was consumed by fire.
I was condemned to desolation and disorder,
    and banished from the secret sanctum was [the watch of] Beit Ḥovia.

ת Let the evil of those who hacked me to pieces
and laid waste to my gates [be judged by God].
But He withdrew His right hand,
    and for their idolatry, expelled [the watch of] Ginton-Tzalmin.

בְּאֹתָ May the healing balm arrive,
  may my darkness finally shine.
May my bones blossom like grass,
    may my sacrificial offerings once again be fragrant.
And once again, may Your Table host the priests of
    [the watch of] Ḥamat-Ariaḥ.

Kina 11 starts on page 288.

שִׁמְעוּ כִּי נֶהֱמָתִי בְּצַחֲנָה
וְסָתַם מִנִּי תְּחִנָּה
וְלֹא נָתַן לִי רַחֲמִים וַחֲנִינָה.
וּמִקְרִיַּת חָנָה, נָעָה כִּפָר יוֹחֲנָה:

שִׁמְעוּ כִּי יָצָאתִי בַּשִּׁבְיָה
וְנִשְׂרְפָה דָּת, מָרוֹם שְׁבוּיָה
וְהוּשַׁתִּי לְשַׁמָּה וְעַרְבוּבְיָה.
וּמֵהַסְתֵּר חֲבוּיָה, גָּלְתָה בֵּית חוֹבִיָּה:

תָּבֹא רָעַת שָׁמּוּנֵי הַדָּמִין
וְשָׁתוּ שַׁעֲרֵי שׁוֹמְמִין
וְהֵשִׁיב אָחוֹר יָמִין.
וּבַעֲוֹן צַלְמִין, נָעָה גִּנְתוֹן צַלְמִין:

תָּבֹא תַּמְרִיחַ, וְחָשְׁכִּי תָּזְרִיחַ
וְכַדְשָׁא, עַצְמוֹתֵינוּ תַפְרִיחַ
וְרֵיחַ נִיחוֹחֵינוּ, כְּקֶדֶם תָּרִיחַ.
וּמִשִּׁלְחָנְךָ תָּאֲרִיחַ, שׁוּלֵי חֲמַת אָרִיחַ:

Kina 11 starts on page 289.

COMMENTARY ON KINA 10

Up to this point, the *kinot* have dealt with the Ḥurban Beit HaMikdash. The *paytan* now turns to the destruction of the priesthood, because the Kohanim were the guardians of the *Mikdash*.

The Kohanim were divided into twenty-four *mishmarot*, watches or groups. Based on a rotation system, each priestly group would come to Jerusalem for one week at a time to perform the service in the *Mikdash* (*Ta'anit* 27a). Since each priestly group was in Jerusalem for only two weeks during the year, they did not reside in Jerusalem. Rather, each priestly group had its own settlement in which it lived, and there were twenty-four cities of Kohanim, one for each group. These settlements consisted either entirely of Kohanim (*Yerushalmi, Gittin* 5:9; *Berakhot* 5:4) or had a mixed population of Kohanim and others (*Berakhot* 12b and Rashi ad loc, s.v. *vehukne'um*; *Sanhedrin* 95a and elsewhere).

In the course of the *kina*, the *paytan* refers to the names of all twenty-four priestly groups and the cities in which they lived, and this *kina* is the only source that we have for some of these cities' names. Several of the names are mentioned in other sources, such as Yehoyariv (*Ta'anit* 29a; *Bava Kamma* 110a), Yedaya (*Bava Kamma* 110a), Jeshebeab (*Sukka* 56b) and Anatot (Jeremiah 1:1). Rabbi Elazar HaKalir apparently had a source which is no longer available to us which included all the names.

In this *kina*, the *paytan* is telling us that the Kohanim were exiled from their settlements, and each priestly group experienced its own exile. The implied message of the *kina* is that we grieve and mourn not only for the destruction of Jerusalem, but for the destruction of all the cities of Israel, as well, and particularly for the cities of the Kohanim.

The *kina* contains an additional message. The Romans understood that the Kohanim were the intellectuals and the leaders of the rebellion and therefore singled them out for extermination. The cities of the Kohanim fought valiantly, and the Romans were cruel and ruthless when they conquered these cities, systematically destroying each of them. As for Jerusalem itself, the Midrash tells us that the Kohanim were the ones who fought to defend the *Beit HaMikdash* (*Eikha Raba, Petiḥta* 23; *Yalkut Shimoni* Eccl. 989). It is important to keep in mind the geography of Jerusalem. We know that the outer wall of the city was breached by the Romans on the seventeenth day of Tammuz (*Ta'anit* 26b). The *Beit HaMikdash* was not destroyed until three weeks later, on Tisha B'Av. It took the best troops of the powerful Roman legions, the

greatest military force of the ancient world, three weeks to cover the short distance between the city wall and the *Beit HaMikdash*! It was the Kohanim, fighting without food, ammunition or protection, who defended each stone. When the Romans finally conquered the city, they showed the Kohanim no mercy. Yet, despite the efforts of the Romans, the Kohanim survived and the institution of the *Kehuna* survived. The three-part structure of *kedushat Kehuna*, *kedushat Leviya* and *kedushat Yisrael* is an inherent requirement for the continued existence of *kedushat Knesset Yisrael*, the sanctity of the Jewish people. The Romans failed in their attempt to extinguish the *kedushat Kehuna*, without which *kedushat Knesset Yisrael* could not have continued to exist.

וְדָמַם רֹן מִפִּי נוֹשְׂאֵי אָרוֹן *And the song of the Ark bearers, silenced.* The *paytan* appears to be referring to the Levi'im (Levites), whose song in the Temple was silenced by the invaders. As the Gemara recounts (*Ta'anit* 29a), the Levi'im were in the midst of their song when the enemy burst in, overpowered them and silenced them.

In this phrase of the *kina*, Rabbi Elazar HaKalir states that those who performed the singing in the *Mikdash*, the Levi'im, were the same as those who carried the Ark. The issue of who carried the Ark is, in fact, the subject of a disagreement between Nahmanides and Maimonides. Nahmanides' view (*Sefer HaMitzvot, shoresh* 3, s.v., *vekhen*) is that the Levi'im carried the Ark not only in the desert, but continued to do so in the land of Israel as well. In this *kina*, HaKalir's view appears to be consistent with that of Nahmanides.

Maimonides' view (*Sefer HaMitzvot, Mitzvot Aseh* No. 34), on the other hand, is that the initial assignment to the Levi'im of carrying the Ark was of a temporary nature only. It was limited to Israel's sojourn in the desert, and when the Jewish people crossed the Jordan River and entered the land of Israel, the responsibility of carrying the Ark was turned over to the Kohanim. Therefore, according to Maimonides, those who were the *nosei aron* (i.e., the Kohanim), were not the same as those who were engaged in *ron* (i.e., the Levi'im).

Notwithstanding the foregoing, since the entire *kina* is dedicated to the Kohanim, it would seem logical that this phrase in the *kina* refers to the Kohanim, as well, and not to the Levi'im. It is possible to interpret this phrase of the *kina* in a manner consistent with Maimonides' view that the Kohanim carried the Ark, and also to understand the phrase as describing that the singing was also performed by the Kohanim. The notion that the Kohanim performed singing in the *Mikdash* could be based on a statement in the

Midrash (*Yalkut Shimoni* Deut. 915), that at the beginning of Ezra's return to Jerusalem, he appointed the Kohanim to perform the singing in the *Mikdash* because there were no Levi'im to do so. Ezra found authority to permit the Kohanim to perform the singing in the verse, "לֹא יִהְיֶה לַכֹּהֲנִים הַלְוִיִּם כָּל־שֵׁבֶט לֵוִי חֵלֶק וְנַחֲלָה, The priests the Levites, even all the tribe of Levi, shall have no portion nor inheritance with Israel" (Deuteronomy 18:1). Based on the phrase "Kohanim HaLevi'im," Ezra reasoned that the Kohanim also possess attributes of the Levi'im. Perhaps Rabbi Elazar HaKalir is referring to this appointment by Ezra of the Kohanim to perform the singing in the *Mikdash*.

כְּנִמְסַר הַבַּיִת בְּמִסָרְבֵי מָרוֹן *As the Temple was given away during* [*the watch of*] *those who would rebel.* At the end of each stanza there is a reference to the name of the *mishmar* or to the city in which the *mishmar* resided. This phrase refers to the priestly group of Yehoyariv. The root of the name Yehoyariv is *yariv*, which means "will quarrel." The *paytan* instead refers to the group as *mesarvei*, which means "those who are disobedient." It has a connotation that is similar to Yehoyariv, as meaning those who refuse to comply with the will of God.

בָּכוֹ תִבְכֶּה מְחֻמֶּשֶׁת סְפָרִים *The five Books of Moses cried and cried.* This phrase could be interpreted as referring either to the Jewish people, who were the recipients of the Five Books of Moses, or to the Torah itself.

כְּנֶהֱרַג כֹּהֵן וְנָבִיא בְּיוֹם הַכִּפּוּרִים *When the priest and prophet* [*Zechariah the son of Yehoyada*] *was murdered on Yom Kippur.* Zechariah the son of Yehoyada HaKohen, was murdered by the Jewish people in the Temple courtyard during the time of the First Temple. As a sign of this injustice, Zechariah's blood seethed continuously on the Temple floor and could not be quieted. At the time of the Ḥurban, Nevuzaradan, the Babylonian general, found Zechariah's seething blood and began to slaughter countless Jews, elders as well as children, in order to quiet the seething. When he threatened to kill all, God finally permitted the seething to cease.

Rabbi Yehuda HaLevi wrote an entire *kina*, "יוֹם אֲכַפִּי הִכְבַּדְתִּי," concerning this episode.

וְנָדוּ כִּצְפָּרִים, כֹּהֲנֵי צִפּוֹרִים *And dispersed like birds were the priests of* [*the watch of*] *Sepphoris.* It is noteworthy that the *paytan* combines an event concerning the Ḥurban of the First Temple, the death of Zechariah the Prophet, with an event concerning the Ḥurban of the Second Temple, the destruction of Sepphoris.

וְהַמְעִיל כְּנִקְרַע פְּתִילוֹ *And when the priestly tunic [with its bells around its hem] was torn.* The *kina* describes the Roman's tearing the cloak of the High Priest. The *paytan* focuses on this because the Torah contains a specific prohibition against tearing the cloak of the High Priest (Exodus 28:32).

כְּבִטְּלוּ הֲלוֹא פָּרֹס לָרָעֵב לֶחֶם *Who denied breaking bread with the poor.* The *kina* mentions that one of the transgressions that was responsible for the Ḥurban was that the Jews refrained from giving *tzedaka*; they were not generous.

מִבֵּית לֶחֶם *by [the watch of] Bethlehem.* This *kina* is our only source that identifies Bethlehem as one of the twenty-four cities of Kohanim.

כְּפָשְׁעוּ בְּלֶחֶם וּפַת *Because they denied bread to the poor.* Once again, the *kina* stresses that they failed to give bread to the poor and hungry. *Tzedaka*, generosity, is a characteristic Jewish trait, but the *paytan* indicts the Jewish people on the grounds that the destruction of the Temple was due to their failure to give sufficient *tzedaka*.

נִלְכְּדָה יוֹדְפַת *was [the watch of] Yodfat... ensnared.* Yodfat was a well-fortified city in the Galilee. It was the stronghold of the Jewish defenses in that region, and it controlled the road to Judea and Jerusalem. Yodfat was under the command of Yosef ben Gurion, also known as Josephus, who was the high commander of all the Jewish military forces in the Galilee. Apparently, Yodfat, the city of Kohanim, was his native city.

The Roman struggle to conquer Yodfat was long and difficult. The Jews under Josephus' command fought heroically, but gradually the garrison of defenders was isolated and decimated by hunger. With no hope left, the warriors under Josephus' command entered into a suicide pact rather than surrendering and falling into enemy hands. They drew lots and killed themselves one by one. Rather than committing suicide, however, Josephus surrendered to the Romans. He was taken prisoner and ultimately became a Roman citizen and was close with the Roman imperial family.

I would not say that Josephus lacked the courage to commit suicide. From a halakhic point of view, Josephus may not have been permitted to do so. The Midrash clearly says (*Bereshit Raba* 34:13) that committing suicide is an act of murder. The case of King Saul causing himself to be killed is explained by some as an exception to this prohibition because Saul realized that the enemy would kill him imminently in any event. Therefore, if Josephus realized that he was not in imminent danger of being killed by the Romans, he would not have been halakhically permitted to kill himself. Nonetheless, one could

argue that even though *halakha* may not have required Josephus to commit suicide, under *halakha*, one *may* commit suicide to avoid surrendering to the enemy. If so, such discretion would have been available to Josephus as well. In summary, I am not certain that Josephus committed an act of betrayal. He may have been acting in accordance with the prohibition against suicide.

It is interesting that Josephus is not mentioned at all in the Gemara, although Rashi does refer to him (*Bava Batra* 3b, s.v., *hekhi*). Our sages make no mention of the incident despite their extensive discussion of the events of the Second Temple period. It is hard to know what the attitude of our sages was, but I suspect that while they disapproved of what Josephus did, they felt that they did not have the right to condemn him. As a result, they ignored him. The Gemara would have mentioned him if it considered him a traitor.

With the fall of Yodfat, the entire Galilee was lost to the Romans, who inexorably made their way through Samaria and Judea to Jerusalem. The Roman conquest of the Galilee occurred several years before Jerusalem was destroyed, but it is interesting that no fast day was proclaimed to commemorate the destruction of Yodfat or any of the other cities of Kohanim. The only date we note is Tisha B'Av, when we embrace not only the *Ḥurban Beit HaMikdash*, but all the *Ḥurbanot* prior to it and the catastrophes and disasters that occurred subsequently during our lengthy nineteen hundred years of exile. Tisha B'Av is the day to remember them all.

וְעַתָּה עֲנוֹת אָמֵן לֹא אָבוּ   *But now refuse to answer "Amen"* [*to the prophet's rebuke*]. It is interesting that Rabbi Elazar HaKalir lists the failure to answer *amen* as one of the reasons for the *Ḥurban*. The idea that the Jewish people refused to answer *amen* finds expression in the Midrash, as well (*Sifrei, Devarim* 320): Rabbi Dustai ben Yehuda says, "Do not read the verse as, '*lo* **emun** *bam*, there is no faithfulness in them' (Deuteronomy 32:20); rather, the verse should be read as, '*lo* **amen** *bam*, there is no amen in them.' They did not wish to respond *amen* to the prophets when the prophets were blessing them, as it is said (Jeremiah 11:5): 'That I may establish the oath which I swore to their fathers, to give them a land flowing with milk and honey, as at this day' and not one of the people opened his mouth and said *amen* until Jeremiah came and answered *amen*, as it is said: 'and I answered and I said *amen*, O Lord' (ibid.)."

Note the language of this phrase in the *kina*. It says "*anot amen lo avu*." The phrase *lo avu* means they deliberately *refused* to answer *amen*, not that they simply failed to answer *amen* or missed the opportunity to do so. This active refusal demonstrates that they refused to accept the basic principles of our

faith and to surrender to God. Recitation of *amen* constitutes *ha'amanat devarim*, a declaration that "the words are true" (*Shavu'ot* 36a). They lacked the quality of "וַיַּאֲמִינוּ בַּיהוה וּבְמֹשֶׁה עַבְדּוֹ, and they believed in the Lord and in Moses His servant" (Exodus 14:31). In effect, by refusing to answer *amen*, one is guilty of the transgression of *avoda zara*.

In general, people should recognize the importance of *amen* during the repetition of the Amida. When the *shaliaḥ tzibbur* recites a *berakha*, and one fails to answer *amen*, there is an element of implication that one is not in full agreement with the words of the *shaliaḥ tzibbur*. In fact, according to Maimonides, during the repetition of the Amida, the *berakhot* cannot be related to the congregation without the recitation of *amen* (*Mishneh Torah*, Hil. Tefila 8:9).

חָטָא חֲטָאָה, וְאָמְרָה לֶאֱלִיל זֶה אֵל *She sinned when she said of the idol: "This is my God!"* God responds to the Jewish people that they are being punished for the most terrible sin of all, engaging in actual *avoda zara*. This statement in the *kina* is somewhat puzzling because the priestly groups are listed in accordance with the practice during the Second Temple, but *avoda zara* was rampant during the First Temple period only, not the Second Temple (*Yoma* 9b).

וְהִלְעִיגָה וְתִעְתְּעָה בְּחוֹזֵי אֵל *And she taunted and teased God's visionaries.* As with the prior phrase, this too is anachronistic. It was only during the First Temple period that the people ridiculed the prophets. Prophecy no longer existed during the period of the Second Temple.

There is a difference of opinion between Rashi and Maimonides as to the nature of the prohibition against disregarding the words of a prophet. According to Rashi (*Sanhedrin* 89a, s.v. *vehamevater*), the prohibition consists of disregarding the prophet and also ridiculing him. Maimonides, on the other hand (*Mishneh Torah*, Hil. Yesodei HaTorah 9:2), speaks only in terms of "one who does not act in accordance with the words of the prophet." For Maimonides, ridiculing the prophet is not an element of the prohibition. Rabbi Elazar HaKalir appears to agree with Rashi's view. Otherwise, this phrase of the *kina* would have been, "She did not listen to God's visionaries."

טֻמְאָתָהּ הֶחֱנִיפָה תֵבֵל *Her profanity contaminated the land.* Usually, the word *tevel* means the entire universe, as in "*tevel umelo'a*, the world and all that it holds" (Psalms 50:12). In this phrase, however, it is hard to interpret *tevel* in this fashion, as the phrase would then mean that Israel's impurity contaminated the entire universe, which is inconceivable. In this phrase, therefore, *tevel*

should be interpreted more narrowly, as referring to the land of Israel, and the intent of the phrase is that Israel's sins have contaminated the land of Israel.

וְנַעֲלָה רַב הַחוֹבֵל *So that the divine Captain left and ascended.* The underlying meaning is that sin causes the departure of the Divine Presence.

יָדוֹ פָּרַשׂ צָר בְּבֵית זְבוּל *The enemy stretched his hand against the Temple.* There is a similar verse in Lamentations, "יָדוֹ פָּרַשׂ צָר עַל כָּל מַחֲמַדֶּיהָ, The enemy has spread his hand on all her treasures" (1:10). There is a distinction between *beit zevul* and *maḥamadeha*. *Beit zevul* refers to the Holy of Holies, and this phrase in the *kina* alludes to the Gemara's recounting (*Gittin* 56b) that when Titus entered the Holy of Holies, he ripped the *parokhet* and committed an act of defilement in that very place. *Maḥamadeha*, on the other hand, refers to the utensils used in the Temple service, which were taken to Rome in captivity.

כִּי כְלָיָה חִיַּבְתִּי כְּדוֹר הַמַּבּוּל *For we deserved extinction no less than the generation of the Flood.* This passage sounds the recurring theme found in the *kinot* that the *Beit HaMikdash* served as a substitute, as collateral, for the Jewish people, and the physical structure of the *Beit HaMikdash* suffered the destruction that rightfully should have been visited upon the entire nation. The *kina* says that the Jewish people are responsible and are deserving of punishment; *we* are guilty, and *we* should have been destroyed as was the generation of the Flood. God, however, in His mercy and grace, subjected His throne, the *Beit HaMikdash*, rather than the Jewish people, to disgrace, abuse and destruction. It is for this reason that Tisha B'Av contains an element of *mo'ed*, a festival – God rendered His decision on Tisha B'Av that *Knesset Yisrael* is an eternal people and will continue to exist. The *Beit HaMikdash* was humiliated, profaned and destroyed in order to save the people.

This concept is expressed halakhically in the character of Tisha B'Av afternoon. The second half of the day has a contradictory nature in *halakha*. On the one hand, the *avelut*, the mourning, is intensified because the actual burning of the *Beit HaMikdash* commenced in the late afternoon of the ninth day of Av, and the flames continued throughout the tenth (*Ta'anit* 29a). On the other hand, *Naḥem*, the prayer of consolation, is recited in the Amida for Minḥa in the afternoon, and not in Shaḥarit of Tisha B'Av morning or Ma'ariv of the preceding evening (*Shulḥan Arukh, Oraḥ Ḥayyim,* Rama 557:1). Similarly, tefillin are put on in the afternoon, not the morning (*Shulḥan Arukh, Oraḥ Ḥayyim* 555:1), and sitting on chairs rather than on the ground is permitted in the afternoon, not the morning (*Shulḥan Arukh, Oraḥ Ḥayyim* 559:3).

In Minḥa, one re-inserts in Kaddish the phrase "תִּתְקַבֵּל צְלוֹתְהוֹן וּבָעוּתְהוֹן, accept our prayers and entreaties" (see *Beit Yosef, Tur Oraḥ Ḥayyim* 559 s.v. *ve'omer kaddish belo titkabal*, with respect to the recitation of *Titkabal* in Shaḥarit). This phrase is removed from Kaddish earlier on Tisha B'Av because the assertion that "*satam tefillati*, my prayer is rejected" (Lamentations 3:8) which prevails on Tisha B'Av, comes to an end at midday. Paradoxically, the moment the *Beit HaMikdash* was set ablaze was a moment of relief. At that moment, it became clear that God decided to take the collateral, the *Beit HaMikdash*, instead of pursuing the real debtor, the Jewish people. Paradoxically, once He took away the *Beit HaMikdash* in the afternoon of Tisha B'Av, the *neḥama*, the consolation, could begin. Tisha B'Av is a day of limitless despair and boundless hope and faith.

כִּי הִכְעִיסוּ לְאֵל קַנָּא *Acknowledging that they had angered the zealous God.* According to *halakha*, there are two types of *mumar*, apostate. A *mumar lete'avon* is one who is an apostate in order to satisfy his appetites; a *mumar lehakhis*, an apostate because he is simply indifferent (*Avoda Zara* 26b, Rashi s.v. *letei'avon*). An example of a *mumar lehakhis* is one who has no sacrilegious motive but buys non-kosher meat even though both kosher and non-kosher meat are available at the same price. In this phrase of the *kina*, the *paytan* describes the Jews as falling into the category of *mumar lehakhis*, not *mumar letei'avon*.

לֹא לַמָּרוֹם עַיִן צָפַת [Israel] *did not look heavenward.* This alludes to "אֶשָּׂא עֵינַי אֶל הֶהָרִים, I will lift my eyes to the mountains" (Psalms 121:1). The transgression that the *paytan* describes is placing one's trust and confidence in human beings rather than relying on God. The people do not lift their eyes toward the heavens; there is no prayer to God.

וְכֶסֶף עַל חֶרֶשׂ חִפָּת *But covered her clay vessels with false walls of silver.* They perpetrated a fraud by passing off fragments of earthenware as pure silver even though the fragments were only silver plated. This phrase, however, may refer not only to fraud in general, but specifically to hypocrisy. Deliberately trying to convey a misleading impression, such as disguising oneself as a righteous person, is a serious transgression. The source for the prohibition against this type of hypocrisy is found in the verse, "וְלֹא תַחֲנִיפוּ אֶת הָאָרֶץ" (Numbers 35:33), which means that the land of Israel should not attempt to convey or project an image that does not correspond to reality.

It is interesting that Maimonides has a different source for the prohibition against hypocrisy. He attributes it to the verse in Isaiah (66:17), הַמִּתְקַדְּשִׁים

וְהַמִּטַּהֲרִים אֶל־הַגַּנּוֹת, those who, in public places disguise themselves as pious and moral, אַחַר אַחַת בַּתָּוֶךְ, in the midst of the community they appear differently than they actually are, because in private they are אֹכְלֵי בְּשַׂר הַחֲזִיר וְהַשֶּׁקֶץ וְהָעַכְבָּר, they eat swine and other detestable things; and for this they are subjected to the curse of the prophet, יַחְדָּו יָסֻפוּ נְאֻם־יהוה, they shall be consumed together.

וּבְשִׁגָּעוֹן *Madness.* We consider our experience of exile as an experience of insanity.

וּפָקַד עָלַי עֲוֹן נֹב וְגִבְעוֹן *He recalled against me the sins of Nob and Gibeon.* The transgression of Nob was committed by King Saul when he killed the Kohanim of the city of Nob because they aided David (I Samuel 21–22). The transgression of Gibeon, also committed by King Saul, was the murder of the Gibeonites in violation of the treaty which Joshua had entered into with them (II Samuel 21).

Including these transgressions in the *kina* among the causes of the *Ḥurban*, demonstrates that the *Ḥurban* was not only a consequence of sins committed immediately prior to it, but was the result of an accumulation of sins throughout Jewish history. When there is such an accumulation, God does not distinguish between sins which appear more serious and those which appear less so, as reflected in *Pirkei Avot* that human beings do not know the true reward or punishment for their respective mitzvot and *aveirot* (*Avot* 2:1). The punishments for the sins of Nob and Gibeon were meted out hundreds of years after the commission of the sins, and they are manifestations of *poked avon avot al banim*, God's "visiting the guilt of the parents upon the children" (Exodus 20:5; 34:7).

וְדוֹמַמְתִּי מִלְּצַפְצֵף בְּמִנִּים וְעֻגָּב *Silenced from chanting with flute and pipe.* There were two types of music in the *Beit HaMikdash*, vocal and instrumental. Earlier in the *kina*, the *paytan* referred to the silencing of vocal music with the phrase, "וְדָמַם רֹן מִפִּי נוֹשְׂאֵי אָרוֹן." Now he refers to the cessation of instrumental music.

וּמִצּוּרַת תָּכְנִית, יָצְאָה יְוָנִית *Expelled from the well-designed Temple was [the watch of] Yevanit.* We are not certain whether the *paytan* intends the word *Yevanit* to have the connotation of "Greek" or to refer to Yavnit, a town in Israel populated by Kohanim. Since the spelling of the word is *Yevanit*, it would appear that the intent is to refer to Greek, and that the phrase should be interpreted as follows: *umitzurat tokhnit*, in the *Beit HaMikdash*, *yatza Yevanit*, people would

teach Greek wisdom. This is similar to the description by our sages (Ḥagiga 15b) of Elisha ben Avuya, known as Aḥer, the Other, who disseminated Greek literature ridiculing Judaism when he came to the *Beit HaMikdash*.

בְּרִית מֶלַח *The [Eternal] Salt Covenant.* The intent is that the eternal covenant between God and the *kehuna* was discontinued or ceased. This can be viewed as a transgression of the Kohanim in that they failed to observe the commandment of "with all your *korbanot*, offerings, you shall offer salt" (Leviticus 2:13). The Kohanim were not scrupulous in the ritual of salting the *korbanot*. Alternatively, this phrase in the *kina* can be understood not as referring to a sin itself, but to a *consequence* of sin. The *korbanot* ceased as a result of the sins of the Kohanim.

וְאֵין שֶׁמֶן מְמֻלָּח, בְּרֹאשׁ מַמְלָח *The perfumed sacred oil from the head of [the watch of] Mamlaḥ.* In a play on words, the *paytan* refers to Mamlaḥ, which was a city of Kohanim, but also means the captain of a ship, and refers here to the High Priest.

There are two methods of consecrating the High Priest. One is by anointing with *shemen hamishḥa*, the oil of anointment, in the same manner that a king is coronated. The other method is *ribuy begadim*, multiplicity of garments, which required dressing the High Priest in the eight specified priestly garments for seven days in succession. During the period of the First Temple, the High Priest was consecrated to his position by anointment. The special *shemen hamishḥa*, however, was one of the five objects hidden by King Josiah, and the location was not disclosed to Ezra (*Yoma* 52b). Therefore, commencing with the time of Ezra and throughout the period of the Second Temple, the High Priest was consecrated by the method of *ribuy begadim* rather than anointment with *shemen hamishḥa*, as reflected in this phrase of *kina*. There are halakhic differences between the two types of consecration in that there are certain *halakhot* that apply to a High Priest who was anointed and that do not apply to a High Priest who assumed his position by *ribuy begadim* (*Megilla* 9b; *Horayot* 11b).

וְכָבָה נֵר הַדּוֹלֵק בְּמַעֲרָב *Extinguished was the light of the westernmost candle.* This is a reference to the *ner tamid* in the Second Temple, the eternal lamp that miraculously burned continuously. The *paytan* refers to it as the candle "in the west" because the Gemara states (*Shabbat* 22b) that *ner ma'aravi*, the western candle, bears witness to the presence of God in the midst of Israel. Consequently, the western candle was never extinguished in the *Beit*

HaMikdash (*Torat Kohanim Emor* 13). Therefore, the statement in the *kina* that the western candle was extinguished means that the *Shekhina* absented itself from Israel.

The extinguishing of the western candle did not begin with the Ḥurban but with the death of Shimon HaTzaddik at least two hundred and fifty years earlier. The Gemara tells us (*Yoma* 39a; *Tosefta Sota* 13:7) that after he died, sometimes it burned and sometimes it was found unlit. This phenomenon itself was a sign that the destruction had already commenced.

רְאֵה כִּי הִסְעָרֹתִי כָּאֲנִיָּה בְּתַאֲנִיָּה וַאֲנִיָּה *Look! I am like a storm-tossed ship, mourning and moaning!* The *paytan* juxtaposes his own actions with the actions of Jonah. When Jonah was confronted with a similar crisis, he repented and prayed to God to save him (Jonah 2:2–10). The *paytan*, however, engaged only in *ta'aniya va'aniya*, he suffered and cried, but did not engage in repentance or prayer.

וְסָתַם מֶנִּי תְחִנָּה *And that my prayers were shut out.* The gates of prayer were closed. God decreed, "*satam tefillati*, my prayer is rejected" (see *Berakhot* 32b and *Bava Metzia* 59a, based on Lamentations 3:8).

וְנִשְׂרְפָה דָּת, מָרוֹם שְׁבוּיָה *And that Torah, given from on high, was consumed by fire.* This phrase appears to refer to the tragic episode in the Gemara (*Ta'anit* 26b) of the burning of the Torah by Apostomus. We do not know whether Apostomus was a Jew or a non-Jew, but we do know that this event occurred during the Second Temple prior to the Hasmonean period. The Gemara also tells us that this incident took place not on Tisha B'Av, but rather was one of the five infamous events that occurred on the seventeenth day of Tammuz (*Ta'anit* 26a–b).

The reference to the Torah as *shvuya*, in captivity, is an allusion to the Gemara (*Shabbat* 88b) which recounts how the angels argued that the Torah should not be given to the world of human beings. Moses countered their arguments, and thus captured the Torah and seized it from the angels. The phrase is also an allusion to the statement of our sages (*Shemot Raba* 43:1; *Midrash Tanḥuma, Ekev* 11) that both God and Moses held on to the Tablets of the Law, and Moses wrested them from His hands, as it were, by force.

From another perspective, this phrase in the *kina* expresses the idea that if one wants to know the Torah, one must actively pursue the Torah and acquire it by force. One does not receive an invitation to know the Torah.

וּמִשְׁלְחָנְךָ תַּאֲרִיחַ *May Your Table host.* The *paytan* invites God to resume His role of being the generous host and allowing others to eat at the *shulḥan gavoha*, the table of God. It is true that God is still a generous host as far as the entire world is concerned, as stated in Psalms, "You satisfy every living thing with favor" (145:16). But God's hospitality is limited after the Ḥurban. Because there is no longer a *shulḥan gavoha*, the specific relationship of God's hospitality connected to the *kehuna* has been terminated.

שׁוּלֵי חֲמַת אֲרִיחַ *The priests of [the watch of] Ḥamat-Ariaḥ.* The word *shulei* derives from the word *shulya debei nagri* (*Pesaḥim* 108a and Rashi s.v. *beshulya*), and in that selection from Gemara it means a student, a young apprentice, one who is in training with a carpenter. In this phrase of the *kina*, it refers to the young students of the Kohanim of the town of Ariaḥ. God will be hospitable to these young people.

11

וַיְקוֹנֵן "Jeremiah composed laments for Josiah."   *II Chr. 35:25*

א How a wail and a lament issued forth from the mighty leaders,
for [Josiah], who, at the age of eight, began to search
for God on his own.

ב The sons of Ham [Egypt] passed through
[the land of Israel] and encamped there.
The merit of his many good deeds was to no avail.

ג Among all the kings of Israel who sought to mend the breach [of
idolatry], none surpassed him since the days of Avigdor [Moses].

ד But the sin of his hypocritical generation stuck to him;
those who concealed idolatrous images on the interior of their doors.

ה Consumers of the Nile's vegetation [Egyptians],
discolored his golden visage so that it became blacker than coal.

ו The people's many sins caused God to withhold His redeeming right
arm and no longer intercede on their behalf.

ז [Josiah's] promise to uphold the Law was sincere. He rent his clothing
when he learned that those who fail to enforce the Torah are cursed.   *Deut. 27:26*

ח His face became darkened with soot, as the enemy, once distant, now
threatened, all because of the sin of those who rejected statutes and law.

ט The would-be ally [king of Egypt] sent a messenger, assuring peace:
"There is no enmity between us to justify waging war with you!

י Why cause my soldiers to spill much blood? Why should you bear the
blame for my divinely ordained [war against Assyria]?"

כ [Josiah, stubbornly denying Egypt passage,] caused so many to fall at
the battle in distant Aram, near the Euphrates, just so that "no sword"
should, in any way, trespass the land of Ephraim.

ל He ignored [Jeremiah's] instructions not to oppose Egypt's passage,
for Egypt was doomed to self-destruction [and Israel's opposition
thus not needed].

11

In this kina, each line begins with the first word of the corresponding verse in Eikha chapter 4, which according to tradition was the eulogy Jeremiah the prophet said after the death of King Josiah (Rashi, Lam. 4:1). Commentary for this kina begins on page 292.

דברי הימים ב
לה, כה

וַיְקוֹנֵן יִרְמְיָהוּ עַל־יֹאשִׁיָּהוּ:

אֵיכָה אֵלִי, קוֹנְנוּ מֵאֵלָיו
בֶּן שְׁמוֹנֶה שָׁנָה הֵחֵל לִדְרוֹשׁ מֵאֵלָיו.
בְּנֵי חָם בְּעָבְרָם, חָנוּ עָלָיו
וְלֹא הִזְכִּיר לוֹ שׁגּוּי מִפְעָלָיו:

גַּם בְּכָל הַמְּלָכִים אֲשֶׁר קָמוּ לִגְדּוֹר
לֹא קָם כָּמוֹהוּ, מִימוֹת אֲבִיגְדּוֹר.
דָּבַק בּוֹ עֲוֹן לֵיצָנֵי הַדּוֹר
אֲשֶׁר אַחַר הַדֶּלֶת, קָמוּ לְסַדֵּר:

הָאוֹכְלִים זֶרַע שָׁחוֹר
כְּתָמוֹ הַטּוֹב, פָּחֲמוּ מִשָּׁחוֹר.
וַיִּגְדַּל עָוֹן, וְהֵשִׁיב יָמִין אָחוֹר
וְעוֹד לֹא שָׁלַח יָדוֹ מִן הַחוֹר:

זַכּוּ אֲמָרָיו, כְּנָם דָּת לְהָקִים
בְּצַע אֲמָרְתוֹ, בְּאָרוּר אֲשֶׁר לֹא־יָקִים:

דברים כז, כו

חָשַׁךְ תָּאֳרוֹ כְּנַאֲצוּ רְחוּקִים
בְּבֶצַע מוֹאֲסֵי דָת וְחֻקִּים:

טוֹבִים רֵעִים נִקְרְאוּ, כְּשָׁלְחוּ מַלְאָךְ
מַה לִּי וָלָךְ הַיּוֹם, לְתַלְאָךְ.
יְדֵי עַם הָאָרֶץ, דָּמִים בְּמַלְאָךְ
תֵּעָנֵשׁ, בְּבִצְעִי אֶת פְּנֵי פְלָאָךְ:

כִּלָּה הֲמוֹנִי, לָלֶכֶת אֲרָם נַהֲרַיִם
לְמַעַן לֹא יַעֲבֹר חֶרֶב כָּל שֶׁהוּא בְּאֶפְרַיִם.
לֹא שָׁמַע לַחוֹזֶה, לָשׁוּב אֲחוֹרַיִם
כִּי גְזֵרָה נִגְזְרָה לְסַכְסֵךְ מִצְרַיִם בְּמִצְרָיִם:

מ Because they worshiped idols behind closed doors
and scorned the vision of the prophet from Anatot,
נ the Anamites [Egyptians] advanced
and ravaged their bodies;
[Josiah] persisted to do battle, and for that we lament.

ס "Turn back," [the prophets] pleaded, "before disaster strikes!"
But they refused to turn back, thus shaking the earth's foundation.
פ [Josiah] continued to do battle, but his prayers were to no avail;
the arrows of archers pierced Josiah.

II Chr. 35:23

ע His eyes already closed, they continued to pound his body,
shooting forcefully dart after dart.
צ They ambushed him and made him their target,
pelting him with three hundred arrows.

ק Swiftly, they drew near to hear his last words.
His deeds remained beautiful even as he expired.
ר With his last gasp, he mumbled,
"The LORD is righteous; it is I who defied His word!"

ש Rejoice, Nof [Egypt], for He has vent His wrath
to punish that crowd who sinned through theft.
ת Gone because of their sin is the finest gold [King Josiah],
For whom [Jeremiah] composed, "Alas! The gold is dulled!"

Lam. 4:1

ת He met the same fate [as King Ahab],
drinking the bitter cup of Megiddo,
in the post-Sabbatical year, at the time the people would gather.
ת For another twenty-two years, He postponed shattering the Temple's
foundations, corresponding to the twenty-two letters [of the alphabet]
with which the dirge in [Josiah's] honor was composed [by Jeremiah].

אוֹתוֹת My joy was transmuted into letters of lament /
at the time I forgot my Creator.
זְמוֹתִי I had thought that He would shelter me forever, / but I acted
wickedly, was expelled, and my shelter [the Temple] is now forsaken.

Kina 12 starts on page 300.

מַחְטֹאת סְתִירַת מְזוּזוֹת
חֲזוֹן עֲנָתוֹתִי הֶחֱלוּ לְבַזּוֹת.
נָעוּ עֲנָמִים לָחְמוּ לְהַבְזוֹת
וְלֹא הֵסֵב פָּנָיו, וְסָפְדוּ עַל זֹאת:

סוּרוּ הֵעִידוּ, עַד לֹא שָׁאֲיָה
וַיְמָאֲנוּ סוּר, וּמָט יְסוֹד נְשִׁיָּה.
פְּנֵי קְרָב קָרַב, וְלֹא עָלְתָה לּוֹ שְׁעִיָּה
וַיּוֹרוּ הַיּוֹרִים לַמֶּלֶךְ יֹאשִׁיָּהוּ:

דברי הימים ב
לה, כג

עוֹדֶנּוּ עוֹצֵם עֵינָיו, בְּגֵוִיוֹ נוֹחֲצִים
חֵץ אַחַר חֵץ, מוֹרִים וְלוֹחֲצִים.
צָדוּ וְשָׂמוּהוּ כַּמַּטָּרָה לַחִצִּים
וַיִּזְרְקוּ בוֹ שְׁלֹשׁ מֵאוֹת חִצִּים:

קַלִּים צָדְתוּ אַחֲרָיו, אֱזוּן מוֹצָא פִּיהוּ
וְעַד מְצוּי נֶפֶשׁ, מַעֲשָׂיו הֵפִיהוּ.
רוּחַ שְׂפָתָיו הִפְצָה מִפִּיהוּ
צַדִּיק הוּא יהוה, כִּי מָרִיתִי פִּיהוּ:

שִׁישִׁי נוֹף, כִּי קַנּוֹא זָעַם
לְשַׁלֵּם שְׁאוֹנָם בַּעֲוֹן בְּצָעָם.
תָּם כֶּתֶם הַטּוֹב, עִם זוּ בְּפִשְׁעָם
וַיְקוֹנֵן עָלָיו כָּל אֵיכָה יוּעַם זָהָב:

איכה, ד, א

תָּם בְּמִקְרֶה אֶחָד כּוֹס מְגִדּוֹ לִשְׁתּוֹת
בְּמוֹעֵד שְׁנַת הַשְּׁמִטָּה, כְּגַע הַקָּהֵל לֵאָתוֹת.
תָּלָה עֶשְׂרִים וּשְׁתַּיִם, מֵהֲרֹס שָׁתוֹת
כִּי סָפְדוּ לוֹ אֵיכָה, בְּעֶשְׂרִים וּשְׁתַּיִם אוֹתוֹת:

אוֹתוֹת קִינוֹת לְבָטָה מְחוֹלִי / עֵת כִּי שָׁכַחְתִּי מְחוֹלְלִי
זָמוֹתִי כִּי לָעַד יַאֲהִילִי / רָשַׁעְתִּי וְנָסַעְתִּי, וְנִטַּשׁ אָהֳלִי:

Kina 12 starts on page 301.

COMMENTARY ON KINA 11

This *kina* is the eulogy which Jeremiah delivered in memory of King Josiah who was killed at Meggido. King Josiah was one of the greatest and most righteous kings of Israel, and there was none like him other than King David. When Pharaoh Necho of Egypt wanted to traverse the land of Israel in order to attack Babylonia, he asked King Josiah for permission to do so. Jeremiah the Prophet advised him to grant Pharaoh Necho the permission he requested, but King Josiah was opposed, and he ignored Jeremiah's advice. This led to King Josiah's waging war with Egypt, and he was killed at the battle of Megiddo (II Chronicles 35:20–24).

This *kina* is part of the shift in focus from the physical destruction of the Temple. In fact, this transition began with the previous *kina* which, although it dealt with *ḥurban*, described the destruction of the *kehuna*, the priesthood, rather than physical destruction. This *kina* now turns to a eulogy for a great *yaḥid*, an individual, King Josiah. The underlying theme of this *kina* is that when we lose a great leader, it is comparable to losing the *Beit HaMikdash*.

וַיְקוֹנֵן יִרְמְיָהוּ עַל־יֹאשִׁיָּהוּ *Jeremiah composed laments for Josiah.* The verse in Chronicles states, "And Jeremiah lamented for Josiah ... and, behold, they are written *al hakinot*, in the lamentations" (II Chronicles 35:25). Chronicles does not indicate which "book of *kinot*" is being referred to, but in the opinion of our sages (*Eikha Raba* 4:1), the entire fourth chapter of the book of Lamentations is the actual eulogy which Jeremiah delivered for King Josiah (see also Rashi, Lamentations 4:1, s.v. *Eikha yu'am zahav*). The description in Chronicles continues, "and all the male singers and the female singers spoke of King Josiah in their lamentations to this day." The significance of this verse is that not only Jeremiah mourned, but every important prominent person did as well.

Why is it necessary to designate a special *kina* to commemorate the death of one individual when we are so involved in retelling the destruction of the *Beit HaMikdash*, the loss of our independence, and the desolation of our entire country? Why was it that the *ru'aḥ hakodesh*, the divine spirit, told Jeremiah that the book of Lamentations would not be complete if it did not include a eulogy for King Josiah? The reason is that on Tisha B'Av we mourn not only for the physical *Ḥurban* of the *Beit HaMikdash*, but for the *Ḥurban* of a great man, which is as tragic as the *Ḥurban* of the *Beit HaMikdash*. The book of Lamentations would not have been complete if it contained a eulogy

only for Zion, but not for King Josiah. As the Gemara states, "שְׁקוּלָה מִיתָתָן שֶׁל צַדִּיקִים כִּשְׂרֵיפַת בֵּית אֱלֹהֵינוּ, the death of righteous individuals is equivalent to the burning of the House of our God" (*Rosh HaShana* 18b). When we lose a great scholar or leader, it is tantamount to losing the *Beit HaMikdash*.

The phrase, שְׁקוּלָה מִיתָתָן שֶׁל צַדִּיקִים כִּשְׂרֵיפַת בֵּית אֱלֹהֵינוּ, can be interpreted in two ways. First, the loss of a great person is just as tragic as the loss of the *Beit HaMikdash*. Second, the tragedy of the loss of a great person is the *cause* of ḥurban. In fact, both explanations are correct and can be merged into one. The loss of a great person is just as tragic a disaster as the loss of the *Beit HaMikdash*, and it is only the prelude to ḥurban. Thus the murder of Gedalia ben Aḥikam, commemorated by the fast day of *Tzom Gedalia*, was the prelude to the destruction of the land of Israel. Had he lived, the land of Israel would have been populated by Jews, and while there would have been a *galut* in the political sense, there would not have been a *galut* in the geographical sense.

Similarly, if King Josiah had not been killed, the *Beit HaMikdash* may well not have been destroyed. If Josiah had lived and continued to reign, Joachim would not have had a chance to engage in abominable practices and to convert Judah into a pagan country (see II Kings 23:37; II Chronicles 36:5). Josiah inspired the people to do *teshuva*, and if this movement or revival and return had continued, the Ḥurban would never have taken place. Thus Josiah's death was the indirect cause of the Ḥurban.

Thus, there are three reasons why Jeremiah's eulogy of Josiah was incorporated into biblical canon via the book of Lamentations. First, it teaches us that what happens to the individual is important, as the Gemara states, "Whoever saves one Jewish soul, God credits him as though he had saved an entire world" (*Sanhedrin* 37a). Second, Josiah was not just an ordinary individual, but he was a leader and teacher. As the Gemara says with regard to Moses, the epitome of the leader and teacher, "Moses is equal to all of Israel" (*Midrash Tanḥuma, Beshallaḥ* 10). And finally, Josiah's death was the beginning of the Ḥurban. That the *Beit HaMikdash* still physically existed on the Temple Mount is not important; spiritually, its destruction had begun.

בֶּן שְׁמוֹנֶה שָׁנָה הֵחֵל לִדְרוֹשׁ מֵאֵילָיו *For [Josiah], who, at the age of eight, began to search for God on his own.* Josiah was crowned as king as an eight year old boy (II Chronicles 34:1). The initiative to seek God was his alone, notwithstanding his tender age. He was brought to God by himself, *me'eilav*, by inner inspiration, by a spontaneous drive within himself. No one prompted him or guided him. Recall also that Josiah's father, Amon, was not righteous, as

our sages note, "Menashe repented, Amon did not repent" (see *Sanhedrin* 90a, 102b–103a, 104a).

בְּנֵי חָם בְּעָבְרָם *The sons of Ham [Egypt] passed through [the land of Israel].* Pharaoh Necho of Egypt was at war with the King of Assyria, and Pharaoh Necho requested permission to cross the land of Israel on his way to fight Assyria. *Be'avram* – they merely wanted to traverse the land. Jeremiah advised Josiah to grant the permission, but Josiah disagreed. When Josiah attempted to stop the Egyptians at the battle of Megiddo, God did not come to his aid, and he was killed.

לֹא קָם כָּמוֹהוּ, מִימוֹת אֲבִיגְדוֹר *None surpassed him since the days of Avigdor [Moses].* Moses was the king, the High Priest, and also the teacher, par excellence, the head of the *mesora*. Joshua too had a double role, serving as a king and teacher. Joshua was in fact greater than Josiah in the second capacity, as he received the *mesora* directly from Moses. But with regard to kingship, Josiah surpassed Joshua and was like Moses.

Also, Josiah completely destroyed idolatry in the land of Israel, and in this capacity, he was the greatest since Moses. Moses destroyed the golden calf, and since that time, no one did as much for the purification of the land of Israel as did Josiah. David did not have to fight against pagans and idol worshipers, as idolatry began only later, with Ahab.

דָּבַק בּוֹ עֲוֹן לֵיצָנֵי הַדּוֹר אֲשֶׁר אַחַר הַדֶּלֶת *But the sin of his hypocritical generation stuck to him; those who concealed idolatrous images on the interior of their doors.* The implicit question posed is: Why was Josiah, such a great man, killed? The answer is that he was punished not for his own sins but for the sins of the *letzanei hador*, the evildoers of his generation. Josiah is the sacrifice demanded by God for the sins committed by his contemporaries. In spite of all his accomplishments, the Midrash says (*Eikha Raba* 1:53) that the people of his generation could not be completely torn away from idolatry. They worshiped surreptitiously, *ahar hadelet*, behind closed doors, *kamu lisdor*, they arranged it (see Isaiah 57:8; *Eikha Raba, Petihta* 22).

Josiah was responsible for idol worship unknown to him because the king of Israel is responsible for the sin of his people even if the sin is not known to him. Even if the people committed transgressions surreptitiously, the king of Israel *should* have known. As the Torah says, "If the anointed priest shall sin so as to bring guilt upon the people" (Leviticus 4:3), the leader is responsible not only for transgressions done in public, which he can eliminate or change,

but even those done in secret. Here one sees how enormous and frightening the responsibility is on the part of the Jewish leader. Sometimes the leader, the righteous person, is the sacrifice that God demands from the generation. This is the principle of *mitat tzaddikim mekhaperet* (*Midrash Tanḥuma* [Buber], *Aḥarei Mot* 10), the death of the righteous serves as an atonement.

Responsibility is always measured by the greatness of the person. The ordinary person does not have the same level of responsibility as the great person. An ordinary person would not be responsible for the sins of others done in secret, but the King of Israel is responsible. Similarly, God told Moses to address the rock, and he hit it (Rashi, Numbers 20:11). For the ordinary person, this would have not been a sin at all, or even if it had been considered a sin, the ordinary person would not have been punished the way Moses was punished. Because Moses was the the leader, however, he should have been more careful.

הָאוֹכְלִים זֶרַע שִׁיחוֹר *Consumers of the Nile's vegetation [Egyptians]*. *Zera shiḥor* refers to the Nile River (based on Joshua 13:3, Jeremiah 2:18 and 1 Chronicles 13:5). They had eaten something which silver oxidizes when it comes into contact with it. It had a glittery feel, like gold, while they were eating, and it was covered with a thin layer of black carbon. Apparently this was due to some chemical reaction.

כְּתֻמּוֹ הַטּוֹב, פֶּחָמוּ מִשְּׁחוֹר *Discolored his golden visage so that it became blacker than coal*. They covered Josiah's beautiful glitter with coal. When he was killed by the Egyptians, his beautiful countenance became black. "How has the gold become dim" (Lamentations 4:1).

The Egyptians could not do much to Josiah. He was as beautiful and handsome as before, but there was a thin black veil which covered his beauty and the pure glitter of his personality. The intent is that he was not really guilty of sin, but the fact that there were idol worshipers during his reign was a negative reflection upon him.

וְעוֹד לֹא שָׁלַח יָדוֹ מִן הַחוֹר *And no longer intercede on their behalf*. One interpretation of this phrase is that Josiah could not stop those who worshiped idols clandestinely. Another interpretation is that God will just knock softly, His finger lightly tapping at the door. The *giluy Shekhina* will come gradually, and at first not many people will understand that God is calling us to return. It will be a very private, subdued experience, not immediate and obvious. Only those who have sensitive ears will realize that the hour has struck and that

He is ready to receive us back, and the rest will be sleeping, insensitive to the presence of God (see Song of Songs 5:2–6; v. 4, "דּוֹדִי שָׁלַח יָדוֹ מִן־הַחוֹר").

בְּצַע אֶמְרָתוֹ, בְּאָרוּר אֲשֶׁר לֹא־יָקִים *He rent his clothing when he learned that those who fail to enforce the Torah are cursed.* This is an allusion to the story (*Midrash HaGadol* Deut. 27) of how, during the time of Josiah, a *Sefer Torah* was found in the Holy of Holies rolled up to the verse, "Cursed be he that does not confirm the words of this Torah to do them" (Deuteronomy 27:26). Josiah felt that this rebuke applied to him because the people were worshiping idols, and he did not prevent them from doing so (see II Kings 22:11–13). Even though he had no knowledge of their activity he felt that, as the king, he should have known. Jeremiah told him that he was wrong and that he is not responsible (see II Kings 22:11–13).

The *Talmud Yerushalmi* states (*Sota* 7:4) "On this matter Josiah called out and declared *'alai lehakim,'* it is my responsibility to observe." Josiah felt it was his responsibility to introduce the Torah in the land of Israel after he successfully removed the idolatry, because he was the king and therefore capable of doing so. Our sages tell us (*Sanhedrin* 94b) that Hezekiah spread scholarship throughout Israel and not a single woman or child could be found who was not acquainted with the laws of ritual purity and impurity. But after Hezekiah came the sinful Menashe, and then Josiah resumed the thread. The phrase *bitza emrato* can be understood to mean that Josiah implemented the verse, "אָרוּר אֲשֶׁר לֹא יָקִים אֶת דִּבְרֵי הַתּוֹרָה הַזֹּאת", cursed is he who will not uphold the words of this Torah."

כִּלָּה הֲמוֹנַי...לְמַעַן לֹא תַעֲבֹר חֶרֶב כָּל שֶׁהוּא בְּאֶפְרַיִם *Josiah... caused so many to fall... just so that "no sword" should, in any way, trespass the land of Ephraim.* As was noted above, the Egyptians did not intend to wage war with Israel. They merely wanted to traverse the land on their way to do battle with Assyria. According to the Midrash (*Eikha Raba* 1:53; see also *Ta'anit* 22a–b and *Tosefta Ta'anit* 2:10), there was a disagreement between Jeremiah and Josiah as to the meaning of the verse "and the sword shall not go through your land" (Leviticus 26:6). Jeremiah interpreted the verse to apply only to an enemy in time of war. Since Egypt was friendly towards Israel, Jeremiah's position was that Israel should permit them passage. Furthermore, Jeremiah felt that Egypt would neutralize the young, aggressive and well-equipped Assyria. We do not know whether Jeremiah was saying this as a message from God, or was simply expressing his own opinion as a member of the Sanhedrin. Josiah, on the other hand, interpreted the verse to refer to any sword, even a sword of

peace. It was his view that the sword of even a neutral or friendly nation was forbidden to pass through the land. Josiah wanted to be on friendly terms with Assyria and apparently expected that by preventing Egypt from crossing the land of Israel, he would gain the sympathy of the Assyrian Empire. But he was mistaken. Not only did he not gain Assyria's sympathy, he succeeded in alienating Egypt. The result was Josiah's death in the battle of Megiddo.

מֵחֲטֹאת סְתִירַת מְזוּזוֹת *Because they worshiped idols behind closed doors.* Josiah died because of clandestine idol worship taking place behind the *mezuzot*, behind closed doors, even though he had no knowledge of this activity.

חֲזוֹן עֲנָתוֹתִי הֵחֵלּוּ לְבַזּוֹת *And scorned the vision of the prophet from Anatot.* They did not pay attention to the words of Jeremiah, the priest and prophet from Anatot (Jeremiah 1:1). They treated him with contempt because he gave them the advice not to start the war with Egypt.

וַיִּזְרְקוּ בוֹ שְׁלֹשׁ מֵאוֹת חִצִּים *Pelting him with three hundred arrows.* Our sages tell us (*Eikha Raba* 1:53; *Ta'anit* 22b) that Josiah's body was punctured like a sieve. There is an added significance to Josiah's death. It is not just that he was killed in a war; his death is to be seen as a *korban*, a sacrifice, and that is why his martyrdom reached the highest level and is mentioned here. The *halakha* is that a *korban olah* is burned totally, even the bones (*Zevaḥim* 85b), with nothing left over. The same thing happened to Josiah. He was punctured like a sieve; he was a *korban olah*.

קַלִּים צָתְתוּ אַחֲרָיו, אֱזוּן מוֹצָא פִּיהוּ *Swiftly, they drew near to hear his last words.* Apparently Josiah was moving his lips while in the throes of death, and the young boys, his subordinates, tried to overhear what he was whispering to himself.

וְרוּחַ שְׂפָתָיו...צַדִּיק הוּא יהוה, כִּי מָרִיתִי פִּיהוּ *With his last gasp, he mumbled, "The* Lord *is righteous; it is I who defied His word!"* When Josiah was in the throes of death he accepted the judgment of God and said "The Lord is righteous; for I have rebelled against His word" (Lamentations 1:18). This constitutes *tzidduk hadin*, and before he died, he said *viduy*, the confession (*Eikha Raba* 1:53; *Ta'anit* 22b). HaKalir describes Josiah's death the way the Gemara describes the death of Rabbi Akiva (*Berakhot* 61b), as sanctifying the name of God.

עַם זוּ בְּפִשְׁעָם *Gone because of their sin.* Josiah met his end not because of *his* sin, but because of *their* sin.

בְּמוֹעֵד שְׁנַת הַשְּׁמִטָּה, כְּגַע הַקְהֵל לֵאֱתוֹת *In the post-Sabbatical year at the time the*

people would gather. It is noteworthy that HaKalir writes that this occurred immediately following the end of the *shemitta* year, the Sabbatical year. It happened when Josiah read the *Sefer Torah* at the *Hak'hel* ceremony on the holiday of Sukkot at which the king reads the Torah (Deuteronomy 31:10–13; *Sota* 41a). Josiah himself was ready to be the *ba'al koreh*, the reader of the Torah.

תָּלָה עֶשְׂרִים וּשְׁתַּיִם, מֵהֲרוֹס שָׁתוֹת כִּי סָפְדוּ לוֹ...בְּעֶשְׂרִים וּשְׁתַּיִם אוֹתִיּוֹת *For another twenty-two years, He postponed shattering the Temple's foundations, corresponding to the twenty-two letters with which the dirge…was composed.* The people understood the greatness of Josiah and therefore understood the magnitude of the tragedy when he was killed, and Jeremiah expressed this appreciation by delivering a eulogy for Josiah in the fourth chapter of Lamentations. This eulogy "consisted of twenty-two letters," that is, consisted of twenty-two alphabetically arranged verses. Because Jeremiah's eulogy was based on the twenty-two letter Hebrew alphabet, God postponed the destruction of the *Beit HaMikdash* for twenty-two years after Josiah's death. In contrast, our sages tell us (*Shabbat* 105a; *Yalkut Shimoni* Hos. 35) that after the death of Joshua, a violent earthquake occurred that could have wiped out the Jewish people because they did not eulogize Joshua properly. Fulfilling the mitzva of eulogizing a Torah scholar is tantamount to mourning for the destruction of Jerusalem. "The death of the righteous is equivalent to the burning of the House of our God" (*Rosh HaShana* 18b). That is why, after the eulogy for Josiah, there was no need to destroy the *Beit HaMikdash* immediately, and the destruction could be postponed for twenty-two years.

Another interpretation is that King Josiah protected the Torah, which is written with an alphabet of twenty-two letters. Jeremiah therefore dedicated to him a chapter in Lamentations which is arranged in the alphabetical order of these same twenty-two letters.

Why is the use of alphabetical order so significant, and why was the use of this literary device in a eulogy a factor in delaying the Ḥurban? It is because the use of alphabetical order demonstrates the humility of those who express the eulogy, and God rewarded this humility. God is beyond human understanding, and when we follow the alphabetical order in our praise, we express the fact that we know that language cannot possibly be adequate to praise Him. We humbly acknowledge that we have exhausted the totality of our vocabulary, we have exploited our alphabet to the maximum, and we are still not through praising Him because He is infinite.

The same is true in Lamentations as well. It was arranged alphabetically by

ru'aḥ hakodesh, by the divine spirit, to show that the catastrophe was so great that even if we should use our entire vocabulary, we would not succeed in expressing the fullness of our despondence, grief and distress.

And it is for precisely the same reason that God appreciated that the male and female singers eulogized Josiah alphabetically (II Chronicles 35:25, as interpreted by *Eikha Raba* 4:1). It meant that they felt that whatever they could say about Josiah was not adequate, and that the pain and distress of the people could not possibly be expressed. And in their merit, God postponed the *Ḥurban* for twenty-two years.

אוֹתוֹת קִינוֹת לְבָטָה מְחוֹלִי *My joy was transmuted into letters of lament.* The word *otot* can be interpreted as *otiyot*, letters, and the intent of this phrase is that the letters of the *kinot*, that is the eulogy delivered by Jeremiah for Josiah which comprises Chapter 4 of Lamentations, temporarily reconciled the relationship between Israel and *"meḥoli,"* which refers to God, and the *Ḥurban* was postponed for twenty-two years.

רָשַׁעְתִּי וְנִסַּעְתִּי *But I acted wickedly, was expelled, and my shelter [the Temple] is now forsaken.* I do not know why this *kina* does not conclude with *neḥama*, consolation.

12

phrases carries a reverse alphabetic acrostic, while the closing stich refers to a verse from Tanakh. The last stanza connects this kina to Eikha chapter 2, which describes the horrors of the Ḥurban. Commentary for this kina begins on page 304.

אָהֳלִי My Tent [the Temple], which You planned, even before Creation,
   to join with Your Throne of Glory:
  Why is it forever plundered by pirates?   *Lam. 5:20*
  You have become like a shepherd in a mourner's veil,
   storming and protesting: "What have I here now?"   *Is. 52:5*

אָהֳלִי My Tent, which You elevated for the powerful [patriarchs]
   long ago when Isaac trembled:
  Why is it forever firmly gripped by the hands of the foe?
  You have become like a solitary bird,   *Ps. 102:8*
   shrieking bitterly from the rooftop:
 "What are you doing here, My friend
   [Abraham, coming to mourn the destroyed Temple]?"

אָהֳלִי My Tent, regarding which You exclaimed to the envoy [Moses]:
  "Now stand with Me here":
  Why is it forever pillaged by pagans?
  You have become like an enemy, an opponent.
  What has become of Your desire to dwell here?

אָהֳלִי My Tent, toward which, in clouds of glory,
   You guided us all, present and as yet unborn:
  Why is it forever disgraced by the defiant?
  You have become as if helpless,   *Jer. 14:9*
  [While the defiant taunt,] "What have You here,
   and whom have You here?"   *Is. 22:16*

אָהֳלִי My Tent, which You established as Your seat
   from which to spread Your protecting canopy:
  Why is it forever swept away by the hands of the haughty?
  You have become like a drifter in space.
  Gone is the prophet, yet You murmur, "Is there none here?"   *1 Kings 22:7*

12

This kina displays HaKalir's technical artistry. The first line of every stanza begins, "My Tent" (referring to a former glory); the second, "Why is it forever" (conveying a sense of abandonment); and the third, "You have become" (comparing God to a hidden shepherd, a solitary bird, a lonely drifter, etc.). The first letter after each of these three introductory

אָהֳלִי אֲשֶׁר תָּאַבְתָּ עַד לֹא בְרֵאשִׁית, עִם כִּסֵּא כָבוֹד לְצָרְפוֹ.
לָמָה לָנֶצַח שֻׁדַּד בְּיַד שֵׁדִים, וְנִהְיֵיתָ כְּרוֹעֶה כְּעֶטְיָה
וְרָעֲשָׁה וְרָגְנָה, וְעַתָּה מַה־לִּי־פֹה:

איכה ה, כ
ישעיה נב, ה

אָהֳלִי אֲשֶׁר קוֹמֲמַתּ לְאֵיתָנֵי קֶדֶם, בְּחֶרְדַּת מִי אֵפוֹא.
לָמָה לָנֶצַח צָמַת בְּיַד צָרִים, וְנִהְיֵיתָ כְּצִפּוֹר בּוֹדֵד עַל גָּג
מַר צוֹרֵחַ, מֶה לִידִידִי פֹה:

תהלים קב, ה

אָהֳלִי אֲשֶׁר פָּצַתְ לְמַעֲנוֹ לָצִיר, וְאַתָּה עָמַד עִמָּדִי פֹה.
לָמָה לָנֶצַח עַרְעֵר בְּיַד עֲרֵלִים, וְנִהְיֵיתָ כְּשׂוֹנֵא וְצַר
וְאַיֵּה אִוּוּי מוֹשָׁב פֹה:

אָהֳלִי אֲשֶׁר נָחִיתָ בַּעֲנַנֵי הוֹד, לְאֵת אֲשֶׁר יֶשְׁנוֹ פֹה וְאֵינֶנּוּ פֹה.
לָמָה לָנֶצַח מָאַס בְּיַד מוֹרְדִים, וְנִהְיֵיתָ כְּלֹא יוּכַל לְהוֹשִׁיעַ
מַה־לְּךָ פֹה וּמִי לְךָ פֹה:

ירמיה יד, ט
ישעיה כב, טז

אָהֳלִי אֲשֶׁר כּוּנַּתְ מָכוֹן לְשִׁבְתְּךָ, לְחוֹפֵף לְחָפּוֹ.
לָמָה לָנֶצַח יָעָה בְּיַד יְהִירִים, וְנִהְיֵיתָ כְּטָס בְּחָלָל
וְאֵין עוֹד נָבִיא, וְנִמְּתָה, הַאֵין פֹּה:

מלכים א כב, ז

אָהֳלִי My Tent, in whose parallel chambers You once dwelled:
: Why is it forever abandoned to the hands of strangers?
You have become like a long-standing resident who has emigrated,
never to pass this way again.

אָהֳלִי My Tent, which You predestined for lots to be cast before You
  [to foretell the future]:
Why has it been flung into the hands of the Dumim [Edomites]?
You have become like a stranger in the land,
muttering, "Nothing will change until he [the Messiah] comes!"

1 Sam. 16:11

אָהֳלִי My Tent, whose luminous stars were dimmed by my selfish sin:
Why is it forever darkened by the hands of the accursed?
You have become like a wayfarer in search of lodging.
"Whom else have you here?"

Gen. 19:12

אָחוֹר Before and behind, from here and from there, / each generation [not
  having achieved the rebuilding of the Temple] has known His wrath.
Why, of all nations, has He pressed His hand on me? / This much is clear:
  "Defeat" is engraved on His palm.
I am confident of my cure, for "His wrath is but a moment." / Neverthe-
  less, I persist: "Alas, the LORD in His wrath has shamed [fair Zion]!"

Ps. 30:6
Lam. 2:1

Kina 13 starts on page 314.

אָהֳלִי אֲשֶׁר חָנִיתָ מֵאָז בְּתָאֲיו, מִפֹּה וּמִפֹּה.
לָמָה לָנֶצַח זְנַח בְּיַד זָרִים, וְנִהְיֵיתָ כְּוָתִיק יוֹצֵא חוּצָה
וְלֹא עָבַר פֹּה:

אָהֳלִי אֲשֶׁר הֲכִנְתָּ, לְהַשְׁלִיךְ בּוֹ לְפָנֶיךָ גּוֹרַל פֹּה.
לָמָה לָנֶצַח דָּחָה בְּיַד דּוֹמִים, וְנִהְיֵיתָ כְּגֵר בָּאָרֶץ
וְנֵמַתָּ, כִּי לֹא־נָסַב עַד־בֹּאוֹ פֹה:

שמואל א טז, יא

אָהֳלִי אֲשֶׁר בַּעֲוֹן בִּצְעִי, חָשְׁכוּ כּוֹכְבֵי נִשְׁפּוֹ.
לָמָה לָנֶצַח אֹפֶל בְּיַד אֲרוּרִים, וְנִהְיֵיתָ כְּאוֹרֵחַ בְּמָלוֹן
וְעוֹד מִי־לְךָ פֹה:

בראשית יט, יב

אָחוֹר וָקֶדֶם מִפֹּה וּמִפֹּה / לְכָל דּוֹר וָדוֹר נוֹדַע קִצְפּוֹ וְחֻפּוֹ
עַל מֶה מִכָּל אֵם, שָׁת עָלַי כַּפּוֹ / זֹאת לַבְּעָלִיל, כִּי פִיד חֲקוּק בְּכַפּוֹ
רָפִיתִי בְּטוּחָה, כִּי רֶגַע בְּאַפּוֹ / וְעַד עַתָּה, אֵיכָה יָעִיב בְּאַפּוֹ:

תהלים ל, ו
איכה ב, א

Kina 13 starts on page 315.

COMMENTARY ON KINA 12

This *kina* is based upon the dictum in the Gemara (*Nedarim* 39b) that seven things were created before the creation of the world: Torah, repentance, the Garden of Eden, Gehinnom, the *Kiseh HaKavod* (the Throne of Glory), the *Beit HaMikdash*, and the name of the Messiah. The underlying concept of this *kina* is that the *Beit HaMikdash* was already a reality before the world came into existence. The first *Beit HaMikdash* that was built was not the Tabernacle in the desert, but the entire universe which was created during the six days of Creation. This was the *Beit HaMikdash* where God dwelled, but it was lost as a result of Adam's sin. The *kedushat Beit HaMikdash*, the sanctity of the *Beit HaMikdash*, however, reappeared. The tents of the patriarchs and matriarchs were imbued with *kedushat Beit HaMikdash*, the homes of the great sages of Israel were *Batei Mikdash*, and the home of every God-fearing Jew is a *Beit HaMikdash*. The *kedushat Beit HaMikdash* is not limited to the *Beit HaMikdash* on the Temple Mount, but expands almost limitlessly throughout the generations. The motif of this *kina* is that the essence of the *Shekhina* should reside in this world, not in the heavenly realm, and the recurring challenge posed by the *kina* is that if the *Beit HaMikdash* was built and ready before the Creation and destined to be a home for God's presence in this world, why was it destroyed?

אָהֳלִי אֲשֶׁר תָּאַבְתָּ עַד לֹא בְרֵאשִׁית, עִם כִּסֵּא כָבוֹד לְצָרְפוֹ *My Tent* [*the Temple*], *which You planned, even before Creation, to join with Your Throne of Glory.* The meaning of this phrase is that, like the *Kiseh HaKavod*, the *Beit HaMikdash* was constructed, or at least planned, before the creation of the world. Consequently, the argument posed is that the *Beit HaMikdash*, which was planned before the Creation, should not have been destroyed.

The *kina*'s linking of the *Beit HaMikdash* to the *Kiseh HaKavod* expresses another dimension of how we should understand the *Beit HaMikdash*. This is the concept that the entire world will be His Sanctuary, as the verse states, "Even heaven and the heaven of heavens cannot contain You" (I Kings 8:27). The *Beit HaMikdash*, as the site of the holy Ark, is the *Kiseh HaKavod* of God. God wanted the entire universe to be proclaimed as the *Beit HaMikdash*, the dwelling place of God, on the first Shabbat after the Creation, but this was thwarted by Adam's sin. If Adam had not sinned there would have been no need for a physical *Beit HaMikdash*. Rather, the totality of creation, the entirety of the universe, would have been the *Beit HaMikdash*. In the Messianic era, the entire universe will be His sanctuary as He originally intended. At

that time, the *Beit HaMikdash* that was planned before Creation will extend throughout the universe.

לָמָה לָנֶצַח שֻׁדַּד בְּיַד שׁדְדִים *Why is it forever plundered by pirates?* The word *lanetzaḥ*, usually translated as "forever," has, in this phrase, a connotation of "for an extended period of time," as in "Why have You forgotten us *lanetzaḥ*" (Lamentations 5:20).

וְנִהְיֵיתָ כְּרוֹעֶה כְּעֹטְיָה *You have become like a shepherd in a mourner's veil.* The word *otya* means "veil" (see Song of Songs 1:7), and refers to someone who is secret, veiled, invisible. The *paytan* is saying to God, "You make Yourself invisible to Your flock. You hide Yourself because the people do not want Your presence, and if they knew You were there, they would force You to depart. As a consequence You have no home." But, after all, God *does* belong in this world, because the essence of the *Shekhina* is to reside in the human world below, not the transcendental heavens above (*Bereshit Raba* 19:7; *Tanḥuma, Pekudei* 6). And once again, the *kina* poses the implied challenge: If You built a home before the world was created, why was this home destroyed with the result that You are now invisible to Your flock?

וְעַתָּה מַה-לִּי-פֹה *What have I here now?* The *kina* asks, "Where is the real *Beit HaMikdash*? After all, the First Temple and the Second Temple merely reflect the original *Beit HaMikdash* that was created in conjunction with the creation of the world."

אֳהָלִי אֲשֶׁר קוֹמַמְתָּ לְאֵיתָנֵי קֶדֶם *My Tent, which You elevated for the powerful [patriarchs] long ago.* The term *eitanei kedem*, refers to the patriarchs. We know that *Eitan HaEzraḥi* is a reference to Abraham (*Bava Batra* 15a). The High Holiday liturgy similarly reflects this concept in the phrase, "May our Master remember for our benefit the love of *Eitan*, the mighty [Abraham]."

The first *Beit HaMikdash* was the one prior to Creation. The second *Beit HaMikdash* consisted of the tents of the patriarchs and matriarchs. When God postponed His plan to consecrate the entire world as the *Beit HaMikdash* and instead to establish a covenant with a few individuals, He established a *Beit HaMikdash* in the tents of those individuals. The *Beit HaMikdash* was established wherever they pitched their tent. The *Shekhina* dwelled together with the patriarchs, wandering with them from place to place.

The *Beit HaMikdash* for the patriarchs was not a structure built as a *Beit HaMikdash*, per se. Rather, there was a *hashra'at Shekhina*, a bestowal of the

Divine Presence. If the *Shekhina* resides in a place, that place is a *Beit HaMikdash*, wherever it may happen to be located. And the Divine Presence was a reality in the *ohel*, the tent, of Abraham, Isaac and Jacob.

The verse "And he removed from there to the mountain on the east of Bethel and pitched his tent... and he built there an altar to the LORD" (Genesis 12:8) means that Abraham built a *Beit HaMikdash*.

Similarly, the tent of Sarah and Rebecca had the qualities of the *Beit HaMikdash*. Referring to Rebecca, the Torah states, "Isaac brought her into the tent of his mother Sarah" (Genesis 24:67). Rashi notes (based on *Bereshit Raba* 60:16) that the *ohel* of Sarah was distinguished by three traits: the dough rose successfully, the candle burned from one Shabbat eve to the next, and *anan kashur*, a cloud, enveloped it. All of these traits are characteristics of the *Beit HaMikdash*, of *giluy Shekhina*. For example, *anan kashur* alludes to "for I appear in the *anan*, the cloud upon the cover of the Ark" (Leviticus 16:2). It was Sarah who was responsible for the *ohel* of Abraham. Isaac realized that Rebecca was worthy of being in the *Beit HaMikdash* that Sarah had established, and Rebecca continued to preserve it in the same manner.

Jacob's *ohel* was also endowed with holiness. Jacob exclaims, "this is none other than the House of God, and that is the gate of heaven" (Genesis 28:17). Wherever Jacob was, the *Beit HaMikdash* was there as well.

Isaac's relationship with the *Beit HaMikdash* was manifested through the *Akeda*. The designation of the site of the *Beit HaMikdash* was realized at the *Akeda* because the *Akeda* was the first sacrifice that was brought on the *Har HaBayit*, the Temple Mount.

בְּחֶרְדַּת מִי אֵפוֹא *When Isaac trembled*. The Torah states, "Isaac trembled very violently. '*Mi eifoh* ("who was it, then"),' he demanded, '*hatzad tzayid* ("that hunted game") and brought it to me?'" (Genesis 27:33). Why was Isaac so frightened (or, as in the alternative explanation of Rashi, so surprised)? It was because Isaac understood for the first time that Esau had no right to enter the *ohel* of Abraham, Sarah and Rebecca. The *ohel* had *kedushat Beit HaMikdash*, and the hunting of game and *Beit HaMikdash* are mutually exclusive concepts. Esau's home was the antithesis of his mother's home. He was an *ish sadeh*, a man of the field, not an *ish ohalim*, a man of the tents, and he had no use for the *ohel*. As a result, when Esau came in, the entire *ohel* began to tremble.

When Esau came in to Isaac's tent, it was a desecration of the *Mikdash*. Over the centuries, the homes, the *ohalim*, of the Jews that were permeated with *kedushat Mikdash* have been defiled by the same Esau that frightened

Isaac. It was Titus, *saro shel Esav*, the angel of Esau, who defiled the Holy of Holies. Six million Jews were destroyed in the Holocaust, but each Jew, rich or poor, had a home, and each home with its own tradition and *kedusha* was a *Beit HaMikdash*. They who destroyed those homes – *hatzad tzayid* – those who killed them now live in their homes.

I see an image – an image of a carpenter. He was called Elya *der Stolier*. He was a plain Jew, a simple carpenter, and not particularly learned. However, he knew Psalms by heart, and he used to recite certain verses at particular times. When he finished a table, he would recite the last verse of the Book of Psalms "Let every thing that breathes praise the LORD" (150:6); he would recite a different verse when he started work on a project. My father used to say that Elya *der Stolier* was one of the *lamed-vav nistarim*, one of the thirty-six hidden righteous ones. Surely his home was a *Beit HaMikdash*, and there were thousands and thousands of Jews like him.

Tisha B'Av, the day of *avelut*, is the day we should tell the story of the most significant experience of our lives in the last two thousand years. But the focus should not be limited to the destruction of the Holy of Holies. The focus should be every Jewish home that was destroyed, each of which constituted a *Beit HaMikdash*.

וָנִהְיֵיתָ כְּצִפּוֹר בּוֹדֵד עַל גָּג *You have become like a solitary bird.* Until this point the *kina* has described the exile of Israel. Now it turns to the exile of the *Shekhina*. It is as though God is a wanderer. The *Shekhina* has been driven out of Her home and is like a lonely bird without a nest. It is not only the Jew who is barred from entering the *Beit HaMikdash*, but even God is turned away. The only place the *Shekhina* finds shelter is alone, high on the roof of a house which does not belong to Her, hiding from sight to avoid being chased away. Many Holocaust survivors tell of the sense of emptiness which overtook them when they visited the towns and cities of old where they had been raised. They think of what the Vilna *shulhoif*, the neighborhood where the synagogues were located, was like on Yom Kippur with its thousands of Jews, and then suddenly there remains only an abandoned cat or solitary bird, a *tzippor boded*.

אָהֳלִי אֲשֶׁר פָּצַתָ לְמַעֲנוֹ לְצִיר, וְאַתָּה עֲמֹד עִמָּדִי פֹּה *My Tent, regarding which You exclaimed to the envoy [Moses], "Now stand with Me here."* The phrase, "Now stand with Me here," (see Deuteronomy 5:28) is an allusion to Moses. The first *Beit HaMikdash* was created before the world came into existence, the second was in existence when the patriarchs were alive, and the third is the

ohel of Moses. According to Nahmanides, Moses' *ohel* was also a *Beit HaMikdash*. Rabbi Elazar HaKalir here confirms Nahmanides' statement (Exodus 25:2, s.v. *ka'asher*) that the revelation of God's presence in the *Beit HaMikdash* was not a separate or isolated phenomenon, but a continuation of the revelation at Sinai. For Nahmanides, the *Beit HaMikdash* started with the giving of the Torah, and the *ohel* of Moses was a substitute for the *Mishkan*.

The walls and materials, the bricks and stones, are irrelevant to the *Beit HaMikdash*. What is relevant is a public *hashra'at Shekhina*, which everyone can understand and experience. This *hashra'at Shekhina* began at Sinai.

Once the *Shekhina* revealed itself to Moses, it never parted from Israel. During the interim period between the giving of the Torah and the construction of the *Mishkan*, God resided in the *ohel* of Moses, which possessed all the properties of the *Beit HaMikdash*. The *aron kodesh*, the holy Ark, and the *luḥot*, the Tablets of the Covenant, were in the *ohel* of Moses during the construction of the *Mishkan*, and Moses' *ohel* was surrounded with a cloud (Exodus 33:9). The *Mishkan* was an extension of Moses' *ohel*, and Moses' *ohel* was an extension of the giving of the Torah on Mount Sinai.

וְאַיֵּה אִוּוּי מוֹשָׁב פֹּה *What has become of Your desire to dwell here?* This is an allusion to the verse in Psalms (132:14), "Here I will dwell, for I have desired it." The *kina* poses the question, where is the *moshav*, the dwelling place, on Mount Zion, the chosen Temple that is so desired by God?

אָהֳלִי אֲשֶׁר נָחִיתָ בְּעַנְנֵי הוֹד *My Tent, toward which, in clouds of glory, You guided us all.* The *Mishkan*, according to HaKalir, is the fourth *Beit HaMikdash*. The verse, "and the cloud, *the anan*, covered it for six days" (Exodus 24:16) refers to Sinai and the *Mishkan*. When God reveals Himself, this rendezvous always requires *meḥitzot*, separations and privacy. God's revelation is hidden and intimate. The revelation at Sinai was possible because the clouds were the *meḥitzot*.

Another interpretation is that the fourth *Beit HaMikdash* is *Knesset Yisrael*, the entire Jewish people, and the *Mishkan* is the fifth *Beit HaMikdash* referred to in the next stanza. The "clouds of glory" referred to in the *kina* are an allusion to the clouds of glory which marched at the head of the Jewish people on their journey through the desert. Since the clouds of glory surrounded all of *Knesset Yisrael*, the entire Jewish community was transformed into one large *Beit HaMikdash*.

Yet another possible interpretation is that HaKalir may have had Aaron the priest in mind, as the presence of the clouds was a result of Aaron's status

(*Ta'anit* 9a). According to this view, the fourth *Beit HaMikdash* is Aaron, and the *Mishkan*, in the next stanza, is the fifth.

לְאֵת אֲשֶׁר יֶשְׁנוֹ פֹּה וְאֵינֶנּוּ פֹּה *Present and as yet unborn.* This phrase is a response to the possible assertion by God that His promise to have the *Shekhina* reside in the midst of Israel was a promise made only to the generation of Moses and not to future generations. Our response is that God specified that the covenant with the Jewish people is "with him that stands here with us this day... and also with him that is not here with us this day" (Deuteronomy 29:14), with those who are present and with future generations until eternity. The covenant will not be terminated even in the future. Our obligation to God, and His obligation to us, is eternal. If so, why was the *Beit HaMikdash* detroyed?

אָהֳלִי אֲשֶׁר כּוֹנַנְתָּ מָכוֹן לְשִׁבְתֶּךָ *My Tent, which You established as Your seat.* This phrase refers to the verse "You bring them in, and plant them in the mountain of Your inheritance, *makhon leshivtekha*, the place You have made for Yourself to dwell in, O Lord, the Sanctuary, O Lord, which Your hands established" (Exodus 15:17). The interpretation of the preceding stanza of the *kina* determines the meaning of this stanza. If the previous stanza refers to the *Mishkan*, then *"makhon leshivtekha"* in this stanza refers to Jerusalem and the *Beit HaMikdash*. If the previous stanza refers to *Knesset Yisrael* or Aaron the priest, this stanza and *"makhon leshivtekha"* refer to the *Mishkan*.

According to the *Mekhilta* (*Beshalaḥ, Mesikhta deShira* 10), "*makhon leshivtekha*" refers to the *Beit HaMikdash shel ma'ala*, the celestial *Beit HaMikdash*, which is juxtaposed to the *Beit HaMikdash shel mata*, the earthly *Beit HaMikdash* (*Shir HaShirim Raba* 4:6; *Midrash Tanḥuma* [Buber], *Vayera* 45).

וְנִהְיֵיתָ כְּטָס בֶּחָלָל *You have become like a drifter in space.* The *ohel* has been taken away, and it is as if God is flying through a void, completely dislocated and displaced. This again sounds the theme of the loneliness and homelessness of God.

וְאֵין עוֹד נָבִיא *Gone is the prophet.* God asks, "Is there nobody with whom I can communicate?" God communicates with the *navi*, the prophet, and so as long as there is prophecy, God is not lonely. But the destruction of the *Beit HaMikdash* brought about the termination of prophecy, and only the rebuilding of the *Beit HaMikdash* can repair His loneliness.

אָהֳלִי אֲשֶׁר חֲנִית מֵאָז בְּתָאָיו *My Tent, in whose... chambers You once dwelled.* This stanza refers to the *Beit HaMikdash* in Jerusalem, and "*ta'av*," to the "*ta'im*"

of the Temple. The word *ta'im* means rooms or chambers, or, in the context of the *Beit HaMikdash*, it refers to a *meḥitza*, a partition of *kedusha*. The *kedusha* of the physical *Beit HaMikdash* in Jerusalem consists of the *kedusha* of *meḥitzot*, the holiness of separations (*Tosafot, Shavuot* 16a, s.v. *dekhuleh; Yevamot* 82b, s.v. *yerusha*; Maimonides, *Mishneh Torah*, Hil. Beit HaBeḥira 6:14–15). The *Beit HaMikdash* had many compartments, and therefore many *kedushot*, and this concept is referred to as *kedushat hata'im*, the holiness of the compartments. These included the Temple Mount, the rampart, the women's section, the priests' section, the Temple court and the Holy of Holies (Mishna, *Kelim* 1:8–9).

The numerous chambers of the *Beit HaMikdash* demonstrate the intimate relationship between God and the Jewish people. A house with many chambers fosters an intimate relationship. One goes to the innermost chamber, to the chamber surrounded on all sides by other chambers, for the intimate rendezvous. That is the private place to which the eye of the stranger cannot penetrate, and it is there that one converses with his beloved. Song of Songs (1:4) states, "the king has brought me into his chambers."

The first *Beit HaMikdash*, the *Beit HaMikdash* of Creation, represents the *hitpashtut* (the outspreading) of the *Ein Sof* (the Kabbalistic concept of the infinite and eternal nature of God). There are no limitations or boundaries, and it spreads and expands through the finite universe and infinitely beyond as well. "The LORD your God, He is God in heaven above and on earth below" (Joshua 2:11); "Behold, heaven and the heaven of heavens cannot contain You" (I Kings 8:27). But the *Beit HaMikdash* physically constructed in Jerusalem was, on the contrary, an expression of *midat hatzimtzum*, the divine quality of contraction. The *Beit HaMikdash* of *hitpashtut* has no rooms, boundaries or *meḥitzot* because, "the whole earth is full of His glory!" (Isaiah 6:3). However, in the physical *Beit HaMikdash* in Jerusalem, the *Beit HaMikdash* of *tzimtzum* which represents God contracting Himself, the holiness is the *kedushat tzimtzum*. This holiness is not infinite; it is compressed.

The *Batei Mikdash* of the patriarchs, of Moses and of *Knesset Yisrael*, did not have any specific requirements as to construction. The *kedushat HaMikdash* of Abraham's *Beit HaMikdash*, for example, was not *kedushat meḥitzot*. It was simply that wherever Abraham was present, a *mikdash* was established. But the *Beit HaMikdash* in Jerusalem had architectural and structural requirements. The *Beit HaMikdash* that we mourn on Tisha B'Av, the *Beit HaMikdash* of the *ta'im*, was not a *Mikdash* established by the human personality but rather by physical construction.

Ultimately, the *Beit HaMikdash* will be the limitless *Beit HaMikdash* of Creation. On Shabbat Rosh Ḥodesh, the *Haftara* begins with, "The heaven is My throne and the earth is My footstool" (Isaiah 66:1). This is because Rosh Ḥodesh is the day on which the entire creation will be redeemed, and sin will be removed from the earth. Then the original plan of God, that the entire world will be the *Beit HaMikdash*, will be implemented.

מִפֹּה וּמִפֹּה *Parallel chambers.* Throughout the *ta'im*, the chambers of the *Beit HaMikdash*, there are different aspects and levels of *kedusha*. Here, there is a *kedusha ḥamura*, a more stringent holiness; there, a *kedusha kalla*, a less stringent holiness.

וְנִהְיֵיתָ כְּוָתִיק יוֹצֵא חוּצָה *You have become like a long-standing resident who has emigrated.* A *vatik* can also be understood to mean a regular visitor to an inn. But now he does not stop at his usual inn. So too, God has abandoned the *Beit HaMikdash*, the inn He visited so many times, and the inn has been destroyed.

אָהֳלִי אֲשֶׁר הֲכִנֹּתָ, לְהַשְׁלִיךְ בּוֹ לְפָנֶיךָ גּוֹרָל פֹּה *My Tent, which You predestined for lots to be cast before You.* This can be understood to refer to the apportionment of the land of Israel among the tribes that was done by lots "before the Lord at Shiloh at the entrance of *Ohel Mo'ed*" (Joshua 19:51). When God declared, "Nevertheless, the land shall be divided by lot" (Numbers 26:55) this referred not only to the determination of the portions which the tribes acquired, but also to Jerusalem, the portion that was assigned to God. The Gemara states (*Yoma* 12a; *Megilla* 26a) that Jerusalem was not apportioned to the tribes because it was acquired by God Himself. Thus the author of the *kina* is saying, "You Yourself told us to assign You a place in *Eretz Yisrael*, where You could reside, so why do You now reject this place? After all, You participated in the *ḥalukat Eretz Yisrael*, the apportionment of the land, like the rest of us. The *goral*, the lottery, applies to You too!"

There is another aspect of the *ḥalukat ha'aretz* which pertains to the significance of the *Beit HaMikdash*. The *ḥalukat ha'aretz* was done via the *urim vetummim* (the breastplate of the High Priest) *"lifnei Hashem"* ("before the Lord") (Numbers 18:6). Consequently, the existence of the *Beit HaMikdash* makes the *ḥalukat ha'aretz* possible. This is significant because there is no specific promise on the part of God that there will always be a *Beit HaMikdash* or that it will always belong to the Jewish people. There is a promise only that *Eretz Yisrael* will always belong to the Jewish people. But now we see that the promise of *Eretz Yisrael* implies that there is also a promise of

the *Beit HaMikdash*, because without the *Beit HaMikdash* there could be no apportionment of the land, and thus *Eretz Yisrael* would not exist.

דֹּחָה בְּיַד דּוּמִים *Flung into the hands of the Dumim [Edomites]*. This is an allusion to Rome (see Rashi, Joshua 21:11, s.v. *duma*), indicating that the term "My Tent" in this stanza refers to the second *Beit HaMikdash*.

וְנִהְיֵיתָ כְּגֵר בָּאָרֶץ *You have become like a stranger in the land.* As a result of the destruction of the Temple, God has become homeless. The *hashra'at Shekhina* exists in Israel because קְדֻשָּׁה לִשְׁעָתָהּ קְדֻשָּׁה לֶעָתִיד לָבוֹא, the initial sanctification of the land of Israel was effective to sanctify the land eternally for the future. However, the *hashra'at Shekhina* is hidden, like the *ger*, the stranger, who has no right of asylum and stays hidden to protect himself. Our desire is for the *hashra'at Shekhina* to be public and recognized by all.

אָהֳלִי אֲשֶׁר בַּעֲוֹן בִּצְעִי *My Tent... by my selfish sin.* This alludes to the concept of the *Beit HaMikdash* as a *mashkon*, as collateral, a recurring theme in the *kinot*. The *Beit HaMikdash*, per se, is not responsible for having done anything wrong. *We* are the sinners, and the destruction is due to *our* desire for *betza*, for selfish gain.

חָשְׁכוּ כּוֹכְבֵי נִשְׁפּוֹ *Whose luminous stars were dimmed.* The stars were dimmed because of *my* iniquities, and I was spared. This is an allusion to the menora, the candelabrum, in the *Beit HaMikdash* having been extinguished.

The central motif of this *kina* is embodied in the word *po*. When God created the world, it was His intention that His permanent presence be *here*, in this universe, and not in the transcendent celestial world where we have no access to Him. "They heard the voice of the LORD God walking about in the garden" (Genesis 3:8); "the essential aspect of *Shekhina* is in the world below" (*Bereshit Raba* 19:7; *Tanḥuma Pekudei* 6). Adam's sin, however, drove Him out of this world to the transcendent realm. The presence of God returned with Abraham and Moses (*Bereshit Raba* 19:7), but with the sin of the golden calf, God once again absented Himself. The destruction of the *Beit HaMikdash* put an end to the presence of God in this world.

The purpose of the *Beit HaMikdash* is to bring God back into our midst so that He is not distant in the upper realm but close to us and immanent in this world. The *po*, the "here," is the ideal for Judaism, and the final promise is that the *Shekhina* will once again reside in this world. This is the recurrent message of each phrase with *po* – after all, from the very beginning You did desire to dwell among us.

13

אַיֵּה Where is the promise of "So shall your offspring be,"   *Gen. 15:5*
    which You assured to father [Abraham]
  at the time of the "Covenant between the Pieces," as an eternal promise?
וְהֵן And now, my bones are murderously devoured.
  "Why, O God, do You forever reject us?"   *Ps. 74:1*

אַיֵּה Where is the promise to [Isaac,] the one who did not shirk becoming a
    sacrificial lamb in order to obey You?
  They [Abraham and Isaac] seductively said [to their companions],   *Gen. 22:5*
    "We will go up there," heeding Your command.
וְהֵן And now, Your beloved is hacked asunder.
  "Why do You fume in anger at the flock that You tend?"   *Ps. 74:1*

אַיֵּה Where is the promise of [Jacob's] dream of the "streaked and speckled,"   *Gen. 31:10*
    when You hurried to abet him [Jacob] in spite of [Laban's] haggling,
    "If this, then that..."?
וְהֵן And now You have punished an entire clamorous city [Jerusalem].
  "Bestir Yourself, and pound those who wrought such   *Ps. 74:3*
    everlasting destruction."

אַיֵּה Where is the promise to [Moses], who intentionally killed the Egyptian
    by pronouncing Your holy name, shielded by a discrete garden?
  He looked this way and that, confident that the mouths of his holy   *Ex. 2:12*
    compatriots were sealed.
וְהֵן And now, this month [Av] has consumed all their possessions.
  "All the outrages of the enemy in the Sanctuary."   *Ps. 74:3*

אַיֵּה Where is the promise to that good man [Moses],
    sent to redeem Your servants?   *Ex. 3:14*
  [Whom You instructed,] "Thus shall you say,"
    to release a people to serve You.
וְהֵן And now, Your treacherous enemies sit in Your House of Assembly.
  "Your foes roar inside Your meeting place."   *Ps. 74:4*

13

In this kina, HaKalir follows the Midrash (Yalkut Shimoni 1000) which reads the word "Eikha" as a composite of "Ei Ko." Each stanza is constructed of two lines, the first recalling the glorious highlights of our history, and the second, beginning "And now," bewailing present sufferings. The last stich quotes Psalm 74, which Radak (ad loc. 1) read as referring to the Exile. Commentary for this kina begins on page 318.

בראשית טו, ה	אֵי כֹּה אָמַר, כֹּרַת לְאָב בְּפֶצַח
	בִּבְרִית בֵּין הַבְּתָרִים, כֹּה יִהְיֶה לָנֶצַח.
	וְהֵן עַתָּה בִּלְעוּ עֲצָמַי בְּרֶצַח
תהלים עד, א	לָמָה אֱלֹהִים זָנַחְתָּ לָנֶצַח:
בראשית כב, ה	אֵי כֹּה גָּשׁ כְּשֶׂה לְעוֹלָה, לִרְצוֹתֶךָ
	נֵלְכָה עַד כֹּה, פִּתּוֹ בְּעֵדוּתֶיךָ.
	וְהֵן עַתָּה דָּקְרוּ כְּפֶלַח, רַעְיָתֶךָ
תהלים עד, א	יֶעְשַׁן אַפְּךָ בְּצֹאן מַרְעִיתֶךָ:
בראשית לא, י	אֵי כֹּה הַבְטָחַת עֲקֻדִּים נְקֻדִּים, בְּמַשְׂאוֹת
	אִם כֹּה יֹאמַר, כֹּה יוּחַשׁ אוֹת.
	וְהֵן עַתָּה וּכְחַת עִיר מְלֵאָה תְּשֻׁאוֹת
תהלים עד, ג	הָרִימָה פְעָמֶיךָ לְמַשֻּׁאוֹת:
	אֵי כֹּה זָם וְהָרַג מִצְרִי, בְּגַן נָעוּל בַּקֹּדֶשׁ
שמות ב, יב	וַיִּפֶן כֹּה וָכֹה, חָתַם עֵדוּת קֹדֶשׁ.
	וְהֵן עַתָּה חֶלְקָם אָכַל חָדָשׁ
תהלים עד, ג	כָּל־הֵרַע אוֹיֵב בַּקֹּדֶשׁ:
	אֵי כֹּה טוֹב כִּשְׁלַח גְּאוֹל עֲבָדֶיךָ
שמות ג, יד	כֹּה תֹאמַר לְשַׁלַּח עַם לְעָבְדֶךָ.
	וְהֵן עַתָּה יָשְׁבוּ בוֹגְדֶיךָ בְּבֵית וְעוּדֶיךָ
תהלים עד, ד	שָׁאֲגוּ צֹרְרֶיךָ בְּקֶרֶב מוֹעֲדֶךָ:

אֵי Where is the promise to those who newly entered the covenant
    [performing circumcision at the time of the exodus]
        with the words "Thus says the Lord, 'toward midnight,'"
            and with wondrous signs?
וְהֵן And now, they come [to sacred sites] in throngs, with their shoes on.
    "They take their signs for true signs." *Ps. 74:4*

אֵי Where is the promise heard when Moses ascended
    to "thus address" the lofty spouse [the Jewish people]? *Ex. 19:3*
וְהֵן And now she is disgraced by knaves.
    "It is like men wielding axes." *Ps. 74:5*

אֵי Where is the promise of the sixty letters of the ancient priestly blessing?
    "Thus shall You bless," comparable to sixty strong guards. *Num. 6:23*
וְהֵן And now, they are worn and weary,
    "Hatcheted like a gnarled tree." *Ps. 74:5*

אֵי Where is the promise of when [Balaam] tried to curse, but instead
    blessed Your holy people?
        His intended curse was converted to blessing when You said,
            "Return [to Balak] and speak thus." *Num. 23:5*
וְהֵן And now, they besiege Your holy city.
    "They set fire to Your Sanctuary." *Ps. 74:7*

אֵי Where is the promise given to the loyal Levites
    when You selected them?
        "This is what you should do to them to cleanse them" *Num. 8:7*
            for Your eternal abode.
וְהֵן And now, they storm and shake the heavens.
    "They brought low in dishonor the dwelling place of Your Presence." *Ps. 74:7*

אֵי Where is the promise of the seven divinely specified rams' horns?
    "Do this in six days" to collapse the walls. *Josh. 6:3*
וְהֵן And now, our gates have sunk into the ground.
    "They burned all of God's Tabernacles." *Ps. 74:8*

אֵי Where is the promise of the hidden blessed treasures,
    which were assured by the prophets who said, "Thus says [the Lord]"?
וְהֵן And now my budding youths lie swollen with hunger in the courtyards.
    "Till when, O God, will the foe blaspheme?" *Ps. 74:10*

Kina 14 starts on page 328.

אֵי כֹּה כְּרִיתוּת חֲדָשׁוֹת בְּרִיתוֹת
בְּכֹה אָמַר כַּחֲצוֹת לַיְלָה, בְּמוֹפְתֵי אוֹתוֹת.
וְהֵן עַתָּה לָהֵקוּ בְּנַעֲלֵיהֶם לְאֵתוֹת
שָׂמוּ אוֹתֹתָם אֹתוֹת: — תהלים עד, ד

אֵי כֹּה מִשְׁמַע וּמֹשֶׁה עָלָה
כֹּה תֹאמַר לִנְוַת בַּיִת מְעֻלָּה. — שמות יט, ג
וְהֵן עַתָּה נֶאֶצְוָה בְּנֵי עוֹלָה
יוּדַע, כְּמֵבִיא לְמָעְלָה: — תהלים עד, ה

אֵי כֹּה שִׂיחַ שְׂשִׂים אוֹתִיּוֹת הַקְדוּמוֹת
כֹּה תְבָרְכוּ, לְשִׁשִּׁים גִּבּוֹרִים דּוֹמוֹת. — במדבר ו, כג
וְהֵן עַתָּה עַתְּקוּ רְדוּמוֹת
בְּסׇבְךְ־עֵץ קַרְדֻּמּוֹת: — תהלים עד, ה

אֵי כֹּה פָּץ לָקֹב, וּבֵרַךְ עַם קְדוֹשֶׁךָ
בְּשׁוּב וְכֹה תְדַבֵּר, הוּמַר לִקְדוֹשֶׁיךָ. — במדבר כג, ה
וְהֵן עַתָּה צָרוּ עַל עִיר קָדְשֶׁךָ
שִׁלְּחוּ בָאֵשׁ מִקְדָּשֶׁךָ: — תהלים עד, ז

אֵי כֹּה קִיחַת לְוִיִּים שְׁלֵמֶיךָ
כֹּה תַעֲשֶׂה לָהֶם, לְטַהֲרָם לְבֵית עוֹלָמֶיךָ. — במדבר ח, ז
וְהֵן עַתָּה רָעֲשׁוּ וְהִרְעִישׁוּ שָׁמֶיךָ
לָאָרֶץ חִלְּלוּ מִשְׁכַּן־שְׁמֶךָ: — תהלים עד, ז

אֵי כֹּה שִׁבְעַת שׁוֹפְרוֹת עָרֶץ
כֹּה תַעֲשֶׂה שֵׁשֶׁת יָמִים, לְהַפִּיל חוֹמָה לָאָרֶץ. — יהושע ו, ג
וְהֵן עַתָּה שְׁעָרִים טָבְעוּ בָאָרֶץ
שָׂרְפוּ כׇל־מוֹעֲדֵי־אֵל בָּאָרֶץ: — תהלים עד, ח

אֵי כֹּה תְּשׁוּעַת אֲסָמַי אוֹצָר
בְּכֹה אָמַר, אֲשֶׁר לַחוֹזִים נָצַר.
וְהֵן עַתָּה תִּפְּחוּ פְרָחַי בֶּחָצֵר
עַד־מָתַי אֱלֹהִים יְחָרֶף צָר: — תהלים עד, י

Kina 14 starts on page 329.

COMMENTARY ON KINA 13

In this *kina*, Rabbi Elazar HaKalir treats the word *eikha* as though it were a composite word consisting of two separate words, *ei* and *ko*, and therefore, the meaning of the word is not "how?" but rather "where is the *ko*, the 'so'"? Where are the promises that God made to the Jewish people using the word *ko*? HaKalir compares the actual reality of Jewish travail, on the one hand, to the promises made by God using the word *ko*, on the other, and he asks why the promises were not fulfilled. In addition to posing this plaint to God, the *kina* also implicitly leads us to consider the conceptual significance of *ko*. In perusing the various instances that *ko* is used, we find that *ko* serves as a symbol of Jewish uniqueness and the paradoxical historical experience of the Jew.

אֵי כֹּה אָמַר...בִּבְרִית בֵּין הַבְּתָרִים, כֹּה יִהְיֶה לָנֶצַח Where is the promise of "So shall your offspring be"... at the time of the "Covenant between the Pieces" as an eternal promise. The word *ko*, when used with a promise, usually represents something extraordinary, a great blessing, a symbol of success in the future. It represents a promise that cannot be rescinded. We see this in the use of the word *ko* in the *Berit bein HaBetarim*, the "Covenant between the Pieces," in which God told Abraham that his descendants would be as numerous as the stars, and declared, "*ko*, so shall your offspring be" (Genesis 15:5).

וְהֵן עַתָּה בִּלְעוּ עֲצָמַי בְּרֶצַח And now, my bones are murderously devoured. God promised Abraham that his descendants would be as numerous as the stars, but the enemies of Israel want to accomplish the opposite and exterminate the Jewish people. Thus the question posed here by the *kina* is: You made a promise with the word *ko* to Abraham that cannot be rescinded. Why did You not implement that *ko*? The reality is in conflict with the promise.

אֵי כֹּה גָּשׁ כְּשֶׂה לְעוֹלָה...נֵלְכָה עַד כֹּה Where is the promise to [Isaac,] the one who did not shirk becoming a sacrificial lamb... "We will go up there." This stanza is a reference to the *Akeda*, when Abraham says to the two young men, "Abide here with the ass, and I and the lad will go *ad ko*, yonder, and we will worship, and come back to you" (Genesis 22:5).

The *ko* used in this stanza does not represent a promise by God. Rather, it is *Abraham* who uses the word. Nevertheless, this *ko* is particularly significant. It represents absolute obedience and *emuna,* faith, because when Abraham used the word *ko*, he was announcing to the entire world for the first time that he was a man of absolute faith and that if God demands his son, he will

not deny Him the request. In this sense, *ko* is actually the word by which the *Knesset Yisrael* was created. If one looks closely at the narrative of the *Akeda*, it is apparent that throughout most of the story, which culminates in the actual binding of Isaac, we have no explicit knowledge if Abraham decided to comply with God's order or not. It is true that the Torah states, "And Abraham rose early in the morning, and saddled his ass, and took two of his young men with him" (Genesis 22:3), but we do not know what Abraham's intention was. Even the Torah's narrative, "and he cleaved the wood for the burnt-offering" (Genesis 22:3), could be understood to mean that Abraham intended to offer an animal as a sacrifice. He may have thought that God would forgive him if he did not live up to His instructions and an animal was offered instead of Isaac. The first real proof we have of Abraham's commitment is when Abraham declared, "Abide here with the ass, and I and the lad will go *ad ko*, yonder" (Genesis 22:5). If Abraham had intended to offer an animal as a sacrifice, the two lads, Eliezer and Ishmael, and the ass, could have accompanied Abraham and Isaac. By asking them to stay behind, Abraham was, for the first time, indicating that he was about to do something they would not understand.

In view of the fundamental significance of *ko* as used in the *Akeda*, the argument posed by the *kina* is that this word *ko*, which represents unlimited *emuna*, and sometimes *emuna* which is not understandable, merits that God should treat Abraham's children differently than they have been treated until now.

It is a struggle to identify the common denominator, the unifying motif, that Rabbi Elazar HaKalir found which unifies all the instances of the use of the word *ko* he employs in this *kina*. On reflection and analysis, the unifying theme is the understanding of *ko* as representing the unique destination of the Jewish people, which is the unique commitment and unlimited *emuna* of the Jewish people. The message of "I and the lad will go *ad ko*" is perhaps the most significant message in Jewish history, as this statement sealed the destiny of the Jewish people to be different and separate from the rest of the world. The *ko* represents the gap between the committed Abraham and Isaac, on the one hand, and the rest of the world, on the other. The *ko* represents the unique destination that Abraham took upon himself on that day when he parted from the lads.

There is an additional element to the unique destination of the Jew represented by *ko*. The Torah says, "I and the lad will go *ad ko, venishtaḥaveh.*" *Nishtaḥaveh* means to bow, to surrender. The Jew sometimes has to give

up pride. Other times the Jew has to forgo pleasure and comfort. The Jew may have to fight for causes that are unpopular and at other times oppose causes which others cherish. The Jew will be different, singular, unique. "*Venishtaḥaveh*" represents the singularity of the Jew.

The significance of *ko* as representing the unique commitment of the Jewish people and its singularity, is the unifying theme of the various uses of *ko* in this *kina*. For example, in the *ko* of *Berit bein HaBetarim*, "your descendants will be *ko*, as the stars," the intent is that Abraham's children will be different from all others. Similarly, the *kina's* allusion to the incident with Laban, "*Im ko yomar*, if he, Laban, said *ko*, thus: The speckled shall be your wages" (Genesis 31:8), Jacob is saying that he cannot agree with Laban because Laban does not understand the *ko* which Jacob understands. Laban has a different *ko*, and that is why there are always disagreements, negotiations and changes in the original contract. The same theme underlies the *kina's* reference to the incident of Moses killing the Egyptian, and the verse "And he looked *ko vakho*" (Exodus 2:12). The *paytan* does not interpret *"ko vakho"* as "in this direction and in the other direction," but that Moses examined this event from the viewpoint of Jewish destiny – should he defend this Jew or not? Our sages interpreted it as: will killing the Egyptian be consistent with Abraham's *"ko"* ("we will go *ad ko*") or be contrary to it? Will it damage the great cause or not? And after this searching inquiry, *vayifen ko vakho*, Moses decided to go ahead. (see *Shemot Raba* 1:29 and *Midrash Tehillim* [Buber] 24:7.)

Although the phrase, אֵי כֹּה גָּשׁ כְּשֶׂה לְעוֹלָה, לְרַצּוֹתֶךָ pertains to the *Akeda*, the phrase also contains an allusion to a completely different subject, which adds a further layer of meaning to the phrase. In Biblical Hebrew, a *kohen*, a priest, approaching the altar to offer a sacrifice is referred to as נִגַּשׁ אֶל הַמִּזְבֵּחַ, as in "וַיִּגַּשׁ אֵלִיָּהוּ" (1 Kings 18:36). The *kina* paints a picturesque image of the *kohen* approaching the altar with a sacrifice, and the *kina* poses the question, where is the *"ko"* of גָּשׁ שֶׂה לְרַצּוֹתֶךָ, the way the *kohen* walks up to the altar in order to offer the sacrifice.

בְּעֵדוֹתֶיךָ *Your command*. The literal meaning of the word *edotekha* is "Your testimonies." The significance of "testimonies" is that it is the *edut*, or testimony, of the patriarchs that the Jew will go far, *ad ko*, even when the life of Isaac is at stake.

וְהֵן עַתָּה דְּקָרוּ כְּפֶלַח רַעְיָתֶךָ *And now, Your beloved is hacked asunder*. The argument posed by the *kina* is: Given the the merit of the *Akeda*, why did You destroy the *Beit HaMikdash*? Where is the covenant with the patriarchs,

which was concluded at the *Akeda* when Abraham was prepared to offer Isaac as a sacrifice and said, "We will go *ad ko*".

אֵי כֹּה הַבְטָחַת עֲקֻדִּים *Where is the promise of… the "streaked and speckled"?* This stanza refers to the word *ko* used in the transaction between Jacob and Laban regarding the different types of animals in the flock, the *akudim* (speckled) and *verudim* (streaked): "*Im ko yomar*, If he said thus: The speckled shall be your wages" (Genesis 31:8).

It is somewhat difficult to understand what we are to derive from this particular *ko* and why it constitutes an argument that we bring on Tisha B'Av. We understand the *zekhut*, the merit, which arises from the use of *ko* in connection with Abraham and the *Akeda*. נֵלְכָה עַד־כֹּה וְנִשְׁתַּחֲוֶה וְנָשׁוּבָה אֲלֵיכֶם (Genesis 22:5) is a cogent argument for the redemption to take place as soon as possible, because Abraham fulfilled what he was required to do. Since one party has met all the requirements, we now expect the other party, God, to fulfill His promise as well. But it is not readily apparent what the *zekhut* is in connection with the use of *ko* in the transaction between Jacob and Laban.

Perhaps Jacob is referring to the fact that God protected him, and if not for His protection, he would have lost to Laban long ago. Consequently, the argument of the *kina* is: Then, at the time of Jacob, the protection was visible; now it is no longer visible. Alternatively, the intent of the *kina* may be that Jacob was very careful to observe all the terms of the agreement even though Laban took advantage of him. The Gemara notes (*Bava Metzia* 93b) that the type of *shemira*, supervision and safekeeping, that Jacob provided for Laban, transcended the applicable legal requirement. And this is what we demand from God, that He should fulfill *His* promise, which is part of the *berit avot*, the covenant with the patriarchs.

בְּמַשָּׂאוֹת [*Jacob's*] *dream.* Jacob recounts his dream, "and I saw *baḥalom*, in a dream, and, behold, the he-goats which leaped upon the flock were streaked, speckled and grizzled" (Genesis 31:10). It was during this dream that God told Jacob to return to the land of Israel (Genesis 31:13), and that prophecy was fulfilled immediately.

אִם כֹּה יֹאמַר, כֹּה יוֹחַשׁ אוֹת *When You hurried to abet him* [*Jacob*] *in spite of* [*Laban's*] *haggling.* When God promised Jacob, "and return to the land of your nativity" (Genesis 31:13), the promise was fulfilled immediately. In the era of the patriarchs, when God made a promise, it was fulfilled immediately.

וְהֵן עַתָּה *And now.* The *paytan* poses the question: Why does it take so long

for God to fulfill His promises? Why was the salvation in the time of the patriarchs fulfilled immediately, and now, when the destiny of *Knesset Yisrael* is at stake, the redemption comes slowly? Why do You not act now and fulfill the promises You have given us?

וַיִּפֶן כֹּה וָכֹה *He looked this way and that.* This is a quote of the Torah's description of Moses' actions before smiting the Egyptian (Exodus 2:12). This phrase is significant in several different ways. From one perspective, the phrase *"vayifen ko vakho"* represents the importance in Judaism of carefully considering the consequences in the future before taking action in the present. *Midrash Shoḥar Tov* comments, "Moses looked this way and that way, and saw that no good person is destined to be a descendant of this person" (*Midrash Shoḥar Tov* 24:7). Before killing the Egyptian, Moses had a vision of the future. It was important for Moses to ascertain that the Egyptian was not destined for great things, and that none of his descendants, hundreds or thousands of years later, would be converted to Judaism and become a leader among the Jewish people. Similarly, the Gemara states (*Kiddushin* 76a) that when one is betrothed to a woman he is required to investigate her background through four generations to insure that there is no non-Jew in her lineage. Moses' *zekhut* was his caution to investigate what will happen before taking any action.

Another interpretation of *"vayifen ko vakho""* is that Moses defended the sanctity of the Jewish woman, because the Egyptian would have desecrated a Jewess had Moses not killed him. In the exile, the sanctity of the Jewish woman was exposed to desecration countless times. And the argument of the *kina* here is that God should protect the Jewish people as Moses protected Jewish womanhood.

From yet another perspective, *"vayifen ko vakho"* represents the important lesson that Judaism sometimes requires one to act on the spur of the moment without regard to carefully laid plans. The *paytan* poses the plaint to God: If Moses did it, why do *You* not do it? Moses' spontaneity of action becomes apparent if one considers carefully the event of the killing of the Egyptian. Moses saw "an Egyptian smiting a Hebrew" (Exodus 2:12). The Torah does not say that the Egyptian wanted to kill the Jew; it says that the Egyptian merely hit him. And yet Moses still felt compelled to act. Bear in mind that Moses had plans about how to help the Jews. Little by little, by introducing reforms for the treatment of slaves, Moses was hoping to give the Jews a better life. For example, our sages tell us (*Shemot Raba* 1:28) that Moses asked

Pharaoh to allow the Jews to have Shabbat as a day of rest in order to preserve their productivity. Moses knew that the destiny of the Jewish people was at stake, and that his continued presence in Egypt would be of great help to them. Moses knew that killing the Egyptian would start a host of troubles for him, that he would be become a persona non grata with Pharaoh and be forced to leave Egypt. He knew that his careful plans for reforms would not be implemented. Hundreds of thousands of Jews could have been helped if Moses had stayed in Egypt. Moses could have let the Jew defend himself, but instead, Moses acted immediately and energetically to save the individual. Moses felt compelled to act and to sacrifice the good of the community for the sake of this one individual. This is an essential lesson of Judaism: you must help the individual immediately, even though by helping the individual, you may jeopardize your own destiny or the destiny of the people you wish to help. When an individual is tortured, ignore the *klal*, and save the *yaḥid*. You will save the *klal* when you have another opportunity.

The importance of taking action immediately is paramount. This can be seen as well in the book of Esther. Mordekhai spoke with Esther before Pesaḥ, and the extermination was to take place some eleven months later (Rashi on Esther 4:17; *Ta'anit* 15a). Esther wrote to Mordekhai that Ahasuerus would surely summon her to appear before him during that period of time, and she would then have the opportunity to beg him to save the Jews from death. However, if she were to listen to Mordekhai and appear unbidden before Ahasuerus, she would be endangering her own destiny; she may be executed and would not be helping to save the Jewish people from the edict of extermination (Rashi, Esther 4:17; *Ester Raba* 8:6). But Mordekhai was angered by Esther's hesitancy and responded, "Do not postpone" (Esther 4:14). Logically, Mordekhai knew that Esther was right, but Judaism says, "Do not postpone."

Similarly, if Moses had considered the incident of the Egyptian striking the Jew in logical terms, he would not have attacked the Egyptian, because by doing so he undid all his plans. But sometimes *Yahadut* requires a different response.

אֵי כֹּה טוֹב כְּשֻׁלַּח גְּאוּל עֲבָדֶיךָ *Where is the promise to that good man [Moses], sent to redeem Your servants.* Moses was referred to as "*ki tov*" when he was born: "and...she saw *ki tov hu*, he was a goodly child" (Exodus 2:2). The phrase in the *kina*, "*ko tov*," is referring to the "*ki tov*" in the Torah. The intent of the *kina* is to pose the question: Why is it that when the redeemer among Your

servants named *ki tov* was sent to Pharaoh, the action was prompt and quick, but now the action is slow?

כֹּה תֹאמַר לְשַׁלַּח עַם לְעָבְדֶךָ [*Whom You instructed,*] *"Thus shall you say,"* to *release a people to serve You.* When God entrusted the mission of redemption to Moses, Moses said, "Thus says the LORD: Let my people go" (Exodus 8:16). Moses was not afraid to deliver the message of redemption exactly the way God wanted him to deliver it. This represented a complete sacrifice on the part of Moses to the cause of redemption.

יָשְׁבוּ בּוֹגְדֶיךָ בְּבֵית וְעוּדֶיךָ *Your treacherous enemies sit in Your House of Assembly.* They came in without an appointment. When Titus entered the *Beit HaMikdash* and cut the *parokhet* into two pieces, he had no appointment.

אֵי כֹּה כְּרִיתוּת חֲדָשׁוֹת בְּרִיתוֹת *Where is the promise to those who newly entered the covenant.* The message of this stanza, a recurring theme in the *Kinot*, is that *halakha* is very sensitive about time, and *halakha* depends upon precision of time. When God gave the commandments to the Jews in Egypt, the *beritot ḥadashot*, the first ones He gave included the mitzva of *korban Pesaḥ*, the Pesaḥ lamb (Exodus 12:1–13). This mitzva is based upon a time-awareness of several factors. If the *korban Pesaḥ* is slaughtered before *ḥatzot*, midday on Erev Pesaḥ, it is *pasul*, disqualified, but after *ḥatzot*, it is *kasher* (*Pesaḥim* 61a). From the time of *sheki'at haḥama*, sunset, the blood of the *korban Pesaḥ* is disqualified (*Zevaḥim* 56a). According to Rabbi Elazar ben Azaria (*Pesaḥim* 120b), after midnight on the first night of *Pesaḥ*, the *korban Pesaḥ* is *notar*, beyond the permissible time deadline for consumption. And even with regard to *notar*, the remaining portion may not be burned on the next day, but only on the day after the next day (*Pesaḥim* 83b; *Temura* 4b).

In order to be a good Jew, one has to be a disciplined Jew. And in order to be a disciplined Jew, one has to develop a disciplined time-awareness.

כַּחֲצוֹת לַיְלָה *"Toward midnight."* The phrase *kaḥatzot halaila* can also have the connotation of an approximation of midnight. This is an allusion to the verse, "And Moses said: Thus says the LORD: *kaḥatzot halaila, about* midnight, will I go out into the midst of Egypt" (Exodus 11:4). God Himself, however, said *"baḥatzot halaila,"* at *precisely* midnight (*Berakhot* 3b). Our sages say that it was exactly at *ḥatzot*, not an infinitesimal time element before or after (*Mekhilta, Mesikhta DePisḥa* (*Parashat Bo*) 13; *Tanḥuma, Bo* 13). *"Ko"* means utter precision, without approximation or deviation. God wants us to respond to this

demand for precision and to have the discipline of complete precision. And when a Jew is precise, he keeps his appointment with God.

וְהֵן עַתָּה לְהָקוּ בְנַעֲלֵיהֶם לָאֵתוֹת *And now, they come [to sacred sites] in throngs, with their shoes on.* God insisted in Egypt that the Jews should adopt the character trait of *ko*, of eating the *korban Pesaḥ* at the exact time He designated. The *kina* poses the question to God: Why do You not apply this same trait to Yourself and redeem the Jewish people immediately? Of course we will wait, and we believe that all the promises will come true: "Even though the Messiah tarries, I wait for him every day." But You are slow in coming and sometimes it is hard to wait.

כֹּה תֹאמַר לִנְוַת בֵּית מְעֻלָּה *To "thus address" the lofty spouse [the Jewish people].* This alludes to the verse in the Torah, "*ko tomar*, Thus shall you say to the house of Jacob, and tell the children of Israel" (Exodus 19:3). The verse is interpreted to mean that God told Moses to be very gentle with the women, but the enemies of the Jewish people are not so gentle.

The *ko* in the verse "*ko tomar*" alludes to the Jewish people's acceptance of not only the mitzvot, but also of the element of precision and detail in which the mitzvot must be performed. On this verse in the Torah, Rashi comments that the *ko* means "in this language and in this order." Rabbi Ḥayyim Volozhiner compares this to someone who has an idea for a *shiddukh* between two wonderful families, and he asks the *shadkhan* to suggest the match to the father of the bride and the father of the groom. But he tells the *shadkhan* to propose the match exactly as he is presenting it, not to add anything and not to get too excited or enthusiastic, or else the *shadkhan* would spoil the potential match. So too, Moses had a wonderful opportunity to bring the Jewish people together with God at this time before the giving of the Torah. He could have delivered a long oration to the Jewish people about how wonderful it is to join with God and how wonderful the Torah is. But God told Moses, "*ko tomar*, say and repeat *only* the words that I am telling you to say." The Torah continues with, "These are the words which you shall speak to the children of Israel" (Exodus 19:6), and Rashi comments (s.v. *eleh hadevarim*), "not less and not more." God was telling the Jewish people that the Torah which He is giving is the same as what He was saying to Moses, and it is not permissible to reduce or increase the number of mitzvot. The people answered immediately, "*na'aseh venishma*, we will do and we will listen" (Exodus 24:7). The element of discipline that every mitzva requires is called

zerizut. *Zerizut bemitzvot* means the quality of not only fulfilling the mitzva, but also being disciplined in fulfilling the mitzva with precision and attention to detail. The people's response of *"na'aseh venishma"* meant that they agreed to be disciplined in the fulfillment of mitzvot.

The *ko* refers to this element of discipline, and the *kina*'s intent is that not only have we fulfilled the mitzvot, but we have fulfilled them without any doubts, with attention to the element of discipline and precision. But, the *kina* poses the implied question: The Jewish people do not see reciprocity, and do not see this element of precision being applied with regard to their condition. The reality is that the Jewish people are in captivity and are suffering.

שִׁשִּׁים אוֹתִיּוֹת *The sixty letters.* This refers to the *Birkat Kohanim*, the Priestly Blessing, which contains sixty letters. The intent of this stanza is that the substance of the Priestly Blessing, "The LORD bless you and keep you" (Numbers 6:24), should be implemented immediately and not be so long in being realized.

אֵי כֹּה פָּץ לָקֹב, וּבֵרַךְ עַם קְדוֹשֶׁךָ *Where is the promise of when* [*Balaam*] *tried to curse, but instead blessed, Your holy people?* This stanza refers to Balaam and his desire to curse the Jewish people, a curse which God converted to a blessing. The *paytan* asserts that then God acted quickly to give instructions to Balaam, "Return to Balak, *vekho tedaber*, and thus you shall speak" (Numbers 23:5, 16), and poses the question to God, "Why do You not act now with our enemies the same way and do to them what You did to Balaam?"

כֹּה תַעֲשֶׂה לָהֶם, לְטַהֲרָם *"This is what You should do to them to cleanse them."* This verse describes the selection of the Levites and their consecration for sacred service. The argument of this stanza is that the *tahara*, the purification, referred to in this verse was intended by God to be a permanent purification, but if the *Beit HaMikdash* is destroyed and there is no priesthood, of what use is the purification of the Levites? After all, the *Beit HaMikdash* itself is *tameh*, in a state of ritual impurity.

אֵי כֹּה שִׁבְעַת שׁוֹפְרוֹת עָרֶץ *Where is the promise of the seven divinely specified rams' horns?* This is a reference to the *shofarot* that were sounded as the Jews circled Jericho.

כֹּה תַעֲשֶׂה שֵׁשֶׁת יָמִים *"Do this in six days."* The challenge posed by this stanza is that in the time of Joshua and the conquest of Jericho, there was a revelation

of the Divine Presence, and within a week after the promise was made, the fulfillment was accomplished and the promise became a reality, while in our own day it takes so much time for the promise to be realized.

בְּכֹה אָמַר, אֲשֶׁר לַחוֹזִים נָצַר *Which were assured by the prophets who said, "Thus says [the* LORD*]."* This "*ko*" is a reference to the verse, "*Ko amar Hashem*, thus says the LORD: I return to Jerusalem with compassion: My House shall be built in it" (Zechariah 1:16). It is noteworthy that the *kinot* for the night of Tisha B'Av end with this verse from Zechariah rather than with any of the numerous consolations that can be found in Isaiah, Jeremiah and Ezekiel. The reason is because this verse is a response to the question posed by *Eikha*. *Eikha* means *Ei ko* – where is Your promise which commences with the word *ko*? God responds and says, "Do not worry, the *ko* will be realized; sooner or later there will be no need to ask *Eikha*."

14

third stanza is an acrostic of the author's name, "אלעזר בירבי," completed with "קליר" hidden in the initial letters of the final four stichs of the kina (not including the word "hayekarim," carried over from the previous line.) The form was so elaborate, it seems, that not all the copyists of the ancient manuscripts identified it. The last stich reprises the idea of Kina 13, separating the word "Eikha" into "Ei Ko." Commentary for this kina begins on page 338.

א How that which was already decreed [at the time of Creation]   *Eccl. 2:12*
is now demanded of me, holding me to account!
Even before the heavens were stretched, my fate was signaled
   in the words: "The earth was unformed and void!"   *Gen. 1:2*

ב Buried in the message of evening and morning,
the Exalted One foretold the end from the beginning: *Is. 46:10*
built, destroyed, and finally rebuilt again.
With foreknowledge of my sins, He etched its ruin.

> He etched it in the primeval darkness
> so that the earliest men glimpsed it crumble,
> and leaders of generations gone knew it would be crushed.
> Even before its cornicles were erected, they were cut down.

ג He cut down to size the great height of the man He fashioned;
revealed [to Adam] the book of future generations,
the shape of human destiny, disclosed in full detail.
Even the unborn passed in review before him.

ד [Adam] was ejected from the treasure house [of Eden].
He was shown that the couch is too short for stretching.
His heart was pained when he saw the enemy's advance.
He lamented the tragedy with the words, "Where are you,"
   suggesting, "How desolate she sits."

> He formed for him and showed him that which would be.
> That the leaning wall, the tottering fence, was smashed.
> He taught his descendents to wail, to sob, and to bemoan
> the terrible breach that was.

14

This kina alludes to the prophecies warning of the future Ḥurban. Its form is highly complex, comprising eleven groups of three stanzas each. In the first two stanzas, the first line begins with the first word of the corresponding verse in Eikha chapter 2, and the second line begins with the same letter of the alphabet. The third stanza of each group begins with the last word of the preceding line, and ends with the first word of the following one. The second line of every

קהלת ב, יב	אֵיכָה אֵת אֲשֶׁר כְּבָר עָשׂוּהוּ
	תָּבַע מֶנִּי לְגַבּוֹת נִשְׁיֵהוּ.
	אֲשֶׁר עַד לֹא שְׁחָקִים נִמְתָּחוּ
בראשית א, ב	בִּשְׁלֵי רָמַז, וְהָאָרֶץ הָיְתָה תֹהוּ:
	בִּלַּע בָּאוֹת עַרְבִית וְשַׁחֲרִית
ישעיה מו, י	גֵּאֶה מַגִּיד מֵרֵאשִׁית אַחֲרִית.
	בָּנוּי וְחָרֵב וּבָנוּי בְּאַחֲרִית
	וּמֵחוֹבֵי קַלְקָלָתוֹ הֶחֱרִית:

אַחֲרִית אִישׁוֹן וְחֹשֶׁךְ מְיֻדָּע / וְקַדְמוֹנִים חָזוּהוּ מְגֻדָּע.
אָז לְרָאשֵׁי דוֹרוֹת, נִתּוּצוֹ נוֹדָע / עַד לֹא עָשׂוּי, קַרְנוֹתָיו גָּדַע:

גָּדַע גֹּבַהּ קוֹמַת יְצִיר צָר
זֶה סֵפֶר, לְפָנָיו הַבְצָר.
גָּלְמִי רָאוּ עֵינֶיךָ הַפְצֵר
כְּהַעֲבִיר לְפָנָיו כָּל נֶעֱצָר:

דָּרַךְ דּוֹחֵף מִבֵּית הָאוֹצָר
וְהֶרְאָהוּ כִּי הַמַּצָּע קָצָר.
דָּוָה לִבּוֹ, כְּבַט בִּיאַת צָר
וַיְקוֹנֵן עָלָיו אֵיכָה, בְּעֵת צָר:

צָר לוֹ, הֶרְאָה בַּמֶּה שֶׁהָיָה / נִתַּץ קִיר נָטוּי, גָּדֵר הַדְּחוּיָה.
לְדוֹרוֹת לִמֵּד נְהוֹת נְהִי וְנִהְיָה / עַל שֶׁבֶר אֲשֶׁר הָיָה:

ה [Abraham,] who arose from the east,
whose light shone [at the covenant] "between the pieces,"
he too was shown the Four Kingdoms while he slumbered,
    and he shrieked
as the eastern gate sunk into the earth.

ו [God] violently removed [Israel's] crown.
[Abraham] witnessed [Israel's] glory cast to the ground,
and, possessed with fright, dispersed.
[Abraham] yielded to God's harsh judgment when he saw…

> He saw them "naked and bare," and he wept.   *Ezek. 16:7*
> He revealed this secret [knowledge of the future] to his "bound one" [Isaac].
> His eyes dimmed because of his grief; he could not rest,
> seeing his descendants bereft of all good.

ז "The perfect one" [Jacob] despaired of the glorious vision
    [of Israel's ascent],
for he did not believe in that assurance.
His eyes absorbed [God's revelation] in that place.
He sang of its desolation and wailed, "This cannot be!"

ח He was skeptical when he saw that the angels ascended,
    but also descended.
He understood that ascent meant dominion [over Israel].
Why would his descendants need to tremble at [God's] judgment,
and be held responsible for the Temple's destruction by rebels?

> The rebels laid bare the Temple and its secret treasures;
> the spikes of their armored boots stamped on its floor.
> Why am I deprived of the magnificent gates,
> sunk now into the depths of the earth?

ט The insistent [sons of Jacob] demanded knowledge of the time
    [of the final redemption].
Their father was about to disclose it to them.
But the Benevolent One, after divulging that date to him,
took it back, withdrew it, and kept it secret.

הָיָה הַנּוֹעַר מִמִּזְרָח
בֵּין הַבְּתָרִים אוֹרוֹ כְּזָרַח.
הֶרְאָהוּ אַרְבַּע מַלְכִיּוֹת בְּרֶדֶם, וְצָרַח
כִּי טָבַע שַׁעַר הַמִּזְרָח:

וַיֶּחֱמַס וַיִּנָּצֵל זֵרָה
וַיִּרְא הַשְׁלֶכֶת נִזְרָהּ.
וּבְאֵימָה נוֹפֶלֶת בְּזֹרָהּ
וְצָדַק מִדַּת הַדִּין, כְּאָז רָאָה:
רָאָה עֵרֹם וְעֶרְיָה, וְנֶאֱנַח / וְלְעֲקוּדוֹ, סוֹד זֶה פָּנַח.
עָשְׂתָה מִכַּעַס עֵינוֹ, וְלֹא נָח / מֵרְאוֹת גֹּזְעוֹ טוֹב זָנַח:

יחזקאל טז, ז

זָנַח זֹהַר תָּם בַּמַּחֲזֶה
כִּי לֹא הֶאֱמִין בְּנֹאָם זֶה.
זָן עֵינוֹ בַּמָּקוֹם הַזֶּה
וְשָׁר שְׁמוּמוֹ, וַיִּקוֹנֵן אֵין זֶה:

חָשַׁב חָשׁוֹשׁ בְּעוֹלִים וְיוֹרְדִים
וַיָּבֶן כִּי בּוֹ יֵהוּ רוֹדִים.
חֲנִיטָיו עַל מָה בְּדִינוֹ חֲרֵדִים
מֵהֶם נִטְבַּע זְבוּל בַּמּוֹרְדִים:
מוֹרְדִים זְבוּל וּמַצְפּוּנָיו נָבְעוּ / וּמַסְמְרוֹת נַעֲלֵימוֹ בְּקַרְקָעִיתוֹ קָבְעוּ.
זִיו שְׁעָרָיו מֵעֵי מַה נִּטְבָּעוּ / וְהִנָּם טְמוּנִים בָּאָרֶץ כִּי טָבְעוּ:

טָבְעוּ טוֹרְדִים לֵידַע זְמָן
כִּי לְגַלּוֹת קֵץ אָב זָמַן.
טוֹב מְשֻׁגֶּלָה לוֹ קֵץ מְזֻמָּן
הַשַּׁע וְהַבְלִיג, וְקֵץ כָּמַן:

י They persisted and asked their father for the answer:
"When will be the end of these awful things?
When can we hope for salvation?" But it remains unknown
until its time, when it will quickly become apparent.

> The secret will become apparent to the nation which gazed upon You;
> remaining hidden, they could not truly know it.
> Your dear ones are undone by their zeal for Your House;
> their lives are spent in agony.

כ The envoy [Moses] felt faint when he was first designated,
and pleaded that [God] send anyone else. *Ex. 4:13*
For of what benefit is it that I begin this mission,
When those of Gilad [Elijah] will complete it?

ל Infants in the Sea of Reeds asked plaintively of their mothers,
"When will be that long awaited-day?"
Their hearts prepared to sing from the reeds:
"The LORD will reign with His bared arm!"

> He will bare His triumphant arm
> and reveal His exalted right hand.
> His sons now see a torrent of wrath
> and, in the valley of Edom, wearily ask, "What for?"

מ What fault have you found with Me
that you have betrayed Me so?
Then, in the wilderness, you replaced Me.
Even now, you have no faith in Me.

נ Your prophets, disciples of Avigdor [Moses],
despaired of repairing your fallen walls.
I revealed to them My plan for "the day of vengeance,"
but the lawless of that generation were not deserving.

> Generations delved urgently to ascertain the mystery of the end of time,
> but the oath I required of them silenced them.
> When they heard this, their hearts melted,
> and they clapped their hands in despair.

יֵשְׁבוּ יִשְׁאֲלוּ לְאָב לֵידַע
קֵץ הַפְּלָאוֹת מָתַי יוּדַע.
יְקַו לְיוֹם יְשׁוּעָה, וְלֹא נוֹדַע
עַד כִּי בְעִתּוֹ, יוּחַשׁ וְיִתְוָדַע:
יִתְוַדַּע רָז לְעָם, בְּךָ נִסְתַּכְּלוּ / וְנִכְסְפָה מֵהֶם, וְלֹא יוּכָלוּ.
רֵעֶיךָ, מִקִּנְאַת בֵּיתְךָ נֶאֶכְלוּ / וּבִיגוֹן חַיֵּימוֹ כָלוּ:

כָּלוּ כְסָלַי צִיר כְּשָׁלַח
וְנָם, שְׁלַח־נָא בְּיַד־תִּשְׁלָח:
כִּי מַה בֶּצַע לִי לְהִשְׁתַּלַּח
וְאַחֲרֵי גִלְעָדִי יִשְׁלַח:

שמות ד, יג

לְאַמְּתָם לִבְּבוּ עוֹלְלֵי סוּף
אֵי זֶה יוֹם הַכָּסוּף.
לְבָם הֵכִין לְשׁוֹרֵר מָסוֹף
יהוה יִמְלֹךְ בִּזְרוֹעַ חָשׂוּף:
חָשׂוּף בְּיָד רָמָה / נִגְלָה בִּימִין רוֹמֵמָה.
בָּנִים כְּשָׁרוּ חֵמָה זְרוּמָה / קָצְרָה נַפְשָׁם בְּגֵיא אֲדוֹם, דַּעַת עַל מָה:

מַה מָּצְאָת עַוְלָתָה בִּי
כִּי בָגוֹד בָּגַדְתָּ בִּי.
מִמִּדְבָּר, הֱמַרְתְּ בִּי
וְעַד עַתָּה, לֹא הֶאֱמַנְתְּ בִּי:

נְבִיאַיִךְ, נִטְעֵי אֲבִיגְדוֹר
נִשְׁתַּבְּרוּ, פְּרָצוֹת לַגְדֹר.
נִגְלֵיתִי יוֹם נָקָם לְסַדֵּר
וְלֹא קִדְּשׁוּ פְּרִיצֵי הַדּוֹר:
הַדּוֹר יָזְמוּ דַעַת סוֹד, וְדָפְקוּ / הִשְׁבַּעְתִּי אֶתְכֶם שִׁמְעוּ, וּפָקְקוּ.
יַחַד כְּשָׁמְעָם זֹאת נִתְמַקְמְקוּ / וְעַל כַּפַּיִם סָפְקוּ:

ס They clapped their hands in joy, those who entered the land,
as the land's king fell into their hands.
They were confident that their success could endure,
and that they would build "the joy of the world."

פ They exclaimed, "The feast of the LORD is being held at Shiloh,"
thinking that He would rule there forever.
But when they acted treacherously, He removed
   [the Tabernacle] from there,
until the day that Shiloh [the Messiah] will arrive.

Gen. 49:10

> He favored Shiloh, as the ḥalla [the first] offering from the dough,
> but He was disgusted by what transpired there.
> Look what sin does
> to the Omnipotent God!

ע He showed me signs of His favor,
but hurried to react to my stubbornness.
I swooned as if from the desert's heat,
until the LORD will appear from Zion.

Is. 25:5

צ Zion shouted, "How could He permit
that I be attacked by a mighty nation,
who joyously trampled the doorsill
and struck terror everywhere?"

> Struck with fear were the nations, when He who formed me led me
>   [to the land of Israel].
> I assumed that I would stand there forever.
> I am humiliated and ashamed to have erected the idol Bel,
> and now am angrily told, "Get up [and depart]!"

Jer. 31:18

ק I heard "Get up" as an utter rejection.
Get up and depart, for this is no resting place.
I am disgusted with my life because of my grief.
I brought an offering, but it was not found pleasing.

Gen. 27:46

סִפְקוּ, שָׂשׂוּ, בָּאֵי הָאָרֶץ
כִּנָפְלוּ בְיָדָם מַלְכֵי אָרֶץ.
סָבְרוּ כִּי יִשְׁעָם יָרָץ
וְעַל יָדָם יִתְכּוֹנֵן מְשׂוֹשׂ כָּל הָאָרֶץ:

פְּצוּ, חַג לַיהוה בְּשִׁלוֹ
דְּמוּ כִּי לָעַד יִהְיֶה שָׁם מוֹשְׁלוֹ.
פָּעֲלוּ שֶׁקֶר וְהִשִּׁילוֹ
עַד כִּי־יָבֹא שִׁילֹה: בראשית מט, י

שִׁילֹה רָצָה, כְּחַלָּה מֵעִסָּה / וְנִמְאַס, כַּאֲשֶׁר בּוֹ נַעֲשָׂה.
רְאוּ מַה עֲבֵרָה עוֹשָׂה / לְכֹל אֲשֶׁר חָפֵץ עָשָׂה:

עָשָׂה עַמִּי אוֹת בְּצִבְיוֹן
וּלְעֶתוֹ חָשׁ עֲלֵי קִשָּׁיוֹן.
עֻלְּפָתִי כְּחֹרֶב בְּצִיּוֹן
עַד אֲשֶׁר יוֹפִיעַ אֱלֹהִים מִצִּיּוֹן: ישעיה כה, ה

צָעַק, צִיּוֹן אֵיךְ נָתַן
לָשׂוּם עָלַי גּוֹי אֵיתָן.
צָהַל וְרָקַע עַל הַמִּפְתָּן
וּבַחֲמָתוֹ, חִתִּיתוֹ נָתַן:

נָתַן בְּעֵוְתוֹ, עֵת הוֹבִילָנִי רוֹקְמִי / תָּרַתִּי לָעַד, בָּהּ לְקוֹמְמִי.
בּוֹשְׁתִּי וְגַם נִכְלַמְתִּי, בַּל בַּהֲקִימִי / וּבַחֲרִי אַף, נָס לִי קוּמִי: ירמיה לא, יח

קוּמִי קָשַׁבְתִּי בְּהַזְנָחָה
קוּמִי וּלְכִי, כִּי לֹא זֹאת הַמְּנוּחָה.
קַצְתִּי בְחַיַּי מֵאֲנָחָה
וְהִגַּשְׁתִּי, וְלֹא עָרְבָה מִנְחָה: בראשית כז, מו

ר Behold, my gloomy soul, bereft
of peace, of tranquility, of respite.
Stumbling in the hills of darkness,
and finding no rest, even there.

> His hand rested on them, scorching them.
> Men rode over their heads.
> They were tired as they tarried by the rivers of Babylon. Ps. 137:1
> They were punished for their own deeds, and lay in the streets.

ש They lay, their captors piercing their bodies,
taking advantage of them with bestial acts.
They were wounded, blood flowing, Lam. 4:9
and the waters of the Euphrates pierced their innards.

ת Unleash upon them a mighty slaughter,
    and have them drink from a poisoned cup,
those who dare revel over the walls they tore down.
Every nation, every tongue, gazes upon [our downfall],
and the precious children of Zion lament all this. Lam. 4:2

> These precious ones, let the sound of their cry be heard from the heights.
> Why, for what reason, has this happened to us?
> This one says for that, and the other says for this.
> Bitterly, they exchange the phrase, "How terrible!" for the words,
>   "Where are [His promises]?"

Kina 15 starts on page 346.

רְאֵה רֹעַ נַפְשִׁי זְנוּחָה
מִשָּׁלוֹם וּמִשַּׁלְוָה וּמֵהַנָחָה.
רְטוּשָׁה בְּהַרְרֵי נֶשֶׁף, אֲנוּחָה
גַּם שָׁם לֹא נָחָה:

נָחָה יָדוֹ בָּם, וּבָהּ נְכְווּ / אֱנוּשִׁים עַל רֹאשָׁם כִּרְכְּבוּ.
יָגְעוּ עַל נַהֲרוֹת בָּבֶל, כִּנְתְעַכְּבוּ / וּכְעוֹלְלוּ עוֹלֲלוּ, וְחוּצָה שָׁכָבוּ: תהלים קלו, א

שָׁכְבוּ, שׁוֹבִים גּוֹיִם מַדְקִירִים
מִתְעוֹלְלִים בָּמוֹ, כְּמוֹ בְּקָרִים.
שָׁם יָזְבוּ מְדֻקָּרִים איכה ד, ט
וּמֵי פְרָת קָרֵבֵימוֹ דּוֹקְרִים:

תִּקְרָא תְקֶף, טֶבַח וּמֶסֶךְ מַבְקִירִים
קִיר עָרָה, מְקַרְקְרִים.
וְכָל עַם וְלָשׁוֹן, בָּם סוֹקְרִים
וַעֲלֵיהֶם מְקוֹנְנִים, בְּנֵי צִיּוֹן הַיְקָרִים: איכה ד, ב

הַיְקָרִים, קוֹל בְּרָמָה הִשְׁמִיעוּ לִבְכֹּה / לָמָה זֶה וְעַל מַה זֶּה, הַקְרֵנוּ כֹּה
יַחַד, זֶה אוֹמֵר בְּכֹה, וְזֶה אוֹמֵר בְּכֹה / רָגְנוּ לְהָמִיר לָשׁוֹן אֵיכָה, בִּלְשׁוֹן
אֵי כֹּה:

Kina 15 starts on page 347.

COMMENTARY ON KINA 14

The theme of this *kina* is the idea that the destruction of the Temple, the exile and the redemption were known to the patriarchs, Moses and all the prophets. When Jacob assembled his children and told them, "Gather yourselves together, that I may tell you that which shall befall you in the end of days" (Genesis 49:1), he wanted to tell them the exact date of the redemption (see Rashi, s.v. *ve'agida*, citing *Bereshit Raba* 99:5). Moses wanted to do the same in *Parashat Vezot HaBerakha* and so did all the prophets, but God prevented them from doing so, and the time of the redemption remains a mystery. *Knesset Yisrael* know that there will be a final redemption, that evil will be completely defeated and eliminated, but they do not know when. Similarly, they knew that the Ḥurban would take place, but the exact date eluded them.

בָּנוּי וְחָרֵב וּבָנוּי בָּאַחֲרִית *Built, destroyed, and finally rebuilt again.* This is an allusion to the famous dictum of the sages on the verse, "In the mount where the LORD is seen" (Genesis 21:14) that "this verse teaches that God showed him the *Beit HaMikdash* built, destroyed and built" (*Bereshit Raba* 56:10).

גֻּדַּע גֹּבַהּ קוֹמַת יְצִיר צָר *He cut down to size the great height of the man He fashioned.* With this phrase, the *paytan* begins the history from Adam down through the destruction of the *Beit HaMikdash*.

זֶה סֵפֶר, לְפָנָיו הֻבְצַר. גָּלְמִי רָאוּ עֵינֶיךָ הֻפְצַר *Revealed [to Adam] the book of future generations, the shape of human destiny, disclosed in full detail.* God showed Adam all that the mysterious future holds in store for us. Whatever was still in concept, Adam saw and apprehended. This phrase in the *kina* is an allusion to the Midrash (*Bereshit Raba* 56:10) that "until Adam was rendered a *golem*, a mindless automaton, before the Creator, He showed Adam each generation and its scholars, each generation and its wise men, each generation and its scribes, and each generation and its leaders, as it is said 'גָּלְמִי רָאוּ עֵינֶיךָ, Your eyes did see my unformed substance' (Psalms 139:16)."

כְּהַעֲבִיר לְפָנָיו כָּל נֶעֱצָר *Even the unborn passed in review before him.* This phrase can also be understood to mean that He let pass before Adam whatever is mysterious and hidden.

וְהֶרְאָהוּ כִּי הַמַּצָּע קָצָר *He was shown that the couch is too short for stretching.* God showed Adam that King Menashe will bring an idol in to the Holy of Holies (see *Tanḥuma* [Buber] *Beḥukotai* 5, based on Isaiah 28:20).

דָּוָה לִבּוֹ, כְּבָט בִּיאַת צָר *His heart was pained when he saw the enemy's advance.* Adam was very dejected when God showed him the destruction of the Beit HaMikdash.

וַיְקוֹנֵן עָלָיו אֵיכָה, בְּאֵיכָה בְּעֵת צָר *He lamented the tragedy with the words, "Where are you," suggesting, "How desolate she sits."* Because God asked Adam *"ayeka, where are you"* (Genesis 3:9), and Adam did not confess to his sin, there will always be Ḥurban accompanied by *eikha*. "The voice of the Lord God walking in the garden" (Genesis 3:9), the call from God, has a significance that is not limited to the episode of Adam's sin. A call from God comes quite frequently, through history or through events in one's private life, and often man ignores the call. If man does not answer the *ayeka*, the call, he will be destined to say *eikha*, to mourn.

הֶרְאָהוּ אַרְבַּע מַלְכִיּוֹת בְּרָדַם, וְצָרַח *He too was shown the Four Kingdoms while he slumbered, and he shrieked.* We know from the Midrash that Abraham beheld a vision of the Ḥurban. On the verse, "and a dread, great darkness, fell upon him" (Genesis 15:12), the Midrash says, "This teaches that God showed [Abraham] the exile of the four kingdoms," that is, the Ḥurban (see *Bereshit Raba* 44:17; *Vayikra Raba* 13:5).

וַיֵּרָא הַשְׁלָכַת נֶזְרָהּ *[Abraham] witnessed [Israel's] glory cast to the ground.* Abraham witnessed and experienced the Ḥurban.

וְלַעֲקוּדוֹ, סוֹד זֶה פְּעָנַח *He revealed this secret [knowledge of the future] to his "bound one" [Isaac].* Abraham transmitted the secret of the Ḥurban to Isaac. The essence of this secret is that the destiny of Israel is inseparably intertwined with *ḥurban* and suffering, and that without suffering, Israel will not be able to fulfill its mission. Abraham's moral command to Isaac was that Isaac should carry on the heritage of his tradition and fight for all the principles which Abraham formulated. Abraham chose a way of life that isolated him from the crowd. He was Abraham *HaIvri*, "The entire world is on one side, *me'ever eḥad*, and he [Abraham] is on the other side, *me'ever eḥad*" (*Bereshit Raba* 42:8). "You should know, Isaac," Abraham said, "that if you assume this responsibility, you will have to experience this isolation as well. Of course, ultimately you will be victorious, but do not expect victory immediately. There will be successive cycles of building and destruction until God finally redeems us."

נָח זֹהַר תָּם בַּמַּחֲזֶה *"The perfect one" [Jacob] despaired of the glorious vision [of*

Israel's ascent]. When Jacob slept on a pillow of stones and beheld the vision of the ladder (Genesis 28:11–12), he saw the splendor of redemption. Jacob saw the entirety of Jewish history, a history that would prove to be strange and mysterious, until the day when it would ultimately be consummated.

In fact, every prophet saw the entirety of Jewish history. Each prophet knew the purpose of our suffering, understood the impact of the Ḥurban, and knew what *ge'ula* would mean to the Jewish people and the entire world. The vision of history will be consummated with *bayom hahu*, the final day, when "the LORD will be One and His name will be One" (Zechariah 14:9). But no dates were ever revealed. One question remained throughout history, the question of "when?"

כִּי לֹא הֶאֱמִין בִּנְאֻם זֶה *For he did not believe in that assurance.* Jacob did not believe the pronouncement because when he beheld the great vision of "the angels of God ascending and descending" (Genesis 28:12), he saw not only a vision of victory and triumph, but of Ḥurban as well. The Midrash states (*Tanḥuma Vayetzeh* 2) that Jacob saw one angel ascending the ladder and not coming down, and he inquired about that angel. Jacob received the response, "This is Edom, Rome. It will be a long, long journey. For centuries, that angel will be on the top of the ladder, and he will control you." And now, nineteen hundred years later, the angel of Edom is still on the top of the ladder.

זָן עֵינוֹ בַּמָּקוֹם הַזֶּה *His eyes absorbed* [*God's revelation*] *in that place.* The intent of this phrase is that Jacob feasted with his eyes on the splendor of *ge'ula*.

וְשָׁר שְׁמוֹמוֹ, וַיְקוֹנֵן אֵין זֶה *He sang of its desolation and wailed, "This cannot be!"* This is an allusion to Jacob's saying, "אֵין זֶה כִּי אִם־בֵּית אֱלֹהִים, this is none other than the House of God" (Genesis 28:17).

חָשַׁב חָשׁוֹשׁ בְּעוֹלִים וְיוֹרְדִים *He was skeptical when he saw that the angels ascended, but also descended.* Jacob thought, "when will the *Knesset Yisrael* be among the *olim*, those that are ascending?"

This phrase expresses the central motif of this *kina*, the juxtaposition of those that are ascending and those that are descending, of *ge'ula* and *ḥurban*, and the mystery of when these will occur. This juxtaposition is expressed in the calendar as well, which prescribes that each year the first day of Pesaḥ falls on the same day of the week as Tisha B'Av. Pesaḥ represents the ultimate redemption of the Jewish people, and Tisha B'Av represents the destruction and devastation of the *Beit HaMikdash*, the people and the land. God described to all the prophets the day of the destruction and the holiday celebrating

the redemption, but He did not reveal when these events would occur. Even Moses was not able to penetrate this mystery. The juxtaposition of *ḥurban* and *ge'ula* is expressed as well in the difference between the words *Po* and *Ko*. *Po* means *ḥurban*, and *Ko* means the full realization of Jewish destiny, as in "נֵלְכָה עַד־כֹּה, We will go to that place" (Genesis 22:5).

טוֹב מִשֶּׁגִּלָּה לוֹ קֵץ מִזְמָן *But the Benevolent One, after divulging that date to him.* Their father, Jacob, was prepared to tell them when the final redemption will occur. After God revealed this secret to Jacob, however, He concealed it. At first Jacob knew, but then the secret eluded him. The Torah says, "And Jacob called his sons, and said, 'Gather yourselves together that I may tell you that which shall befall you in the end of days. Assemble yourselves and hear, sons of Jacob; and hearken unto Israel your father'" (Genesis 49:1–2). According to our sages (*Bereshit Raba* 99:5) these verses mean that Jacob wanted to tell his sons the secret of *ge'ula*, when the messianic era will take place. But, as our sages said, the Divine Presence left Jacob, and he could not tell them. Jacob beheld a vision, but it was a vision of *ḥurban*, not *ge'ula*.

יָשְׁבוּ יִשְׁאֲלוּ לְאָב לֵידַע *They persisted and asked their father for the answer.* They asked, "when will the end be known?" The answer is that one has to hope for it and expect it every day, "I will await the coming of the Messiah every day."

וְנָם, שְׁלַח נָא בְּיַד תִּשְׁלָח *And pleaded that [God] send anyone else.* According to the Midrash (*Pirkei DeRabbi Eliezer* 40), Moses was referring to the prophet Elijah, as it is written in Malachi, "הִנֵּה אָנֹכִי שֹׁלֵחַ לָכֶם אֵת אֵלִיָּה הַנָּבִיא, Behold, I will send you Elijah the prophet before the coming of the great and terrible day of the Lord" (3:23).

כִּי מַה בֶּצַע לִי לְהִשְׁתַּלֵּחַ וְאַחֲרַי גִּלְעָדִי יִשְׁלַח *For of what benefit is it that I begin this mission, when those of Gilad [Elijah] will complete it.* The reason Moses was reluctant to go to Pharaoh was not because he was afraid. Rather, it was because he foresaw that his mission would not be the final mission of *ge'ula*, and that after a period of freedom, there would be a *Ḥurban*, and that the ultimate message of *ge'ula* would be delivered by Elijah the prophet. Moses' argument to God was that He should just send Elijah now with the message of the final *ge'ula*.

Moses was intimating to God that he did not want a partial assignment, limited to the *shliḥut* of the redemption from Egypt, if Elijah had the role and privilege of being the messenger of the final *ge'ula* and the *Melekh HaMashiaḥ*.

Actually, God had promised the crown of *Melekh HaMashiaḥ* to Moses, and he would have received it if not for the sin of the spies. Immediately after the giving of the Torah, God told Moses that he and the people should depart from Mount Horeb and enter the land of Israel (Deuteronomy 1:6–8; Numbers 10:33). But at that critical moment, the evil inclination emerged and the people asked to send the spies. And so the entire destiny of the Jewish people changed. Had they not sent the spies, the Jewish people would have entered the land of Israel and settled it, and Moses would have sanctified the land. There would have been no *Ḥurban* after Moses, and Moses would have been the *Melekh HaMashiaḥ*.

בִּזְרוֹעַ חָשׂוּף *"The Lord will reign with His bared arm!"* The intent of this phrase is that everyone will recognize the sovereignty of God, as reflected in the High Holiday Amida, "וּבְכֵן תֵּן פַּחְדְּךָ, And so too, Lord our God, instill Your awe upon all Your works, and Your dread upon all that You have created." But they knew that this era had not yet begun.

בָּנִים כְּשָׁרוּ חֵמָה וְרוּגְמָה *His sons now see a torrent of wrath.* This phrase refers to those who sang the hymn at the splitting of the sea.

קָצְרָה נַפְשָׁם בְּגֵיא אֱדוֹם *And, in the valley of Edom, wearily ask.* This is an allusion to the verse "And they journeyed from Mount Hor...to compass the land of Edom; וַתִּקְצַר נֶפֶשׁ־הָעָם בַּדָּרֶךְ, and the soul of the people became impatient because of the journey" (Numbers 21:4). The fact that God instructed Moses not to attack Edom meant that the Jewish people were compelled to circle around Edom for thirty-eight years, and the Torah here recounts how they tired of doing so. Moses had dispatched the spies in the second year after the redemption from Egypt, and when they came back with their report, the decree was issued that the entire generation should die in the desert.

דֵּעַת עַל מָה *"What for?"* The Jewish people lost their patience and their sense of perseverance. They could not understand why it was taking so long. As the Torah says, "We compassed Mount Seir many days" (Deuteronomy 2:1). They were hoping and waiting, the way the Jewish people has been hoping and waiting for nineteen hundred years, for *ge'ula*.

נְטִיעֵי אֲבִיגְדוֹר נִשְׁתַּבְּרוּ, פְּרָצוֹת לִגְדּוֹר *Disciples of Avigdor [Moses], despaired of repairing your fallen walls.* The disciples of Moses almost gave up hope of witnessing the final *ge'ula*.

הִשְׁבַּעְתִּי אֶתְכֶם שָׁמְעוּ, וּפָקְקוּ *But the oath I required of them silenced them.* This

phrase is an allusion to the verse in Song of Songs, "הִשְׁבַּעְתִּי אֶתְכֶם בְּנוֹת יְרוּשָׁלָ͏ִם, I adjure you, O daughters of Jerusalem... that you awaken not, nor stir up love, until it please" (2:7; 3:5). It is an exhortation not to accelerate the *ge'ula*, as it will come at the proper time. The concept of not accelerating the *ge'ula* is referred to in the Talmud in the context of the three oaths which the Talmud recounts were administered by God to the Jewish people and the nations of the world (*Ketubot* 111a).

סָפְקוּ, שָׂשׂוּ, בָּאֵי הָאָרֶץ   *They clapped their hands in joy, those who entered the land.* This is a reference to Joshua's conquest of the land of Israel.

סָבְרוּ כִּי יִשְׁעָם יֶרֶץ וְעַל יָדָם יִתְכּוֹנֵן מְשׂוֹשׂ כָּל הָאָרֶץ, *They were confident that their success could endure and that they would build "the joy of the world."* They hoped that salvation would be permanent and that there would be no exile or destruction any more.

פָּצוּ...בְּשִׁלֹה   *They exclaimed... at Shiloh.* Shiloh is the name of the *Melekh HaMashiah* (*Sanhedrin* 98b; *Eikha Raba* 1:51). This is based on the verse, "*Ad ki yavo Shiloh*" (Genesis 49:10).

דִּמּוּ כִּי לָעַד יִהְיֶה שָׁם מוֹשְׁלוֹ   *Thinking that He would rule there forever.* They thought that Shiloh would be the final *Beit HaMikdash*, and it could have been if not for the sins they committed. As a result, we now have to wait *ad ki yavo Shiloh*, for the Messiah.

שִׁילֹה רָצָה, כְּחַלָּה מֵעִסָּה / וְנִמְאַס, כַּאֲשֶׁר בּוֹ נַעֲשָׂה, *He favored Shiloh, as the Halla [the first] offering from the dough, but He was disgusted by what transpired there.* Initially, God accepted Shiloh in the same manner one takes *halla* from dough. God originally established Shiloh as *kodesh*, as permanent, but He rejected Shiloh later because of what happened there. God told the Jewish people, "It is up to you. If you want, Shiloh will be the final place. Redemption will be complete and there will be no exile or *Hurban*."

רְאוּ מַה עֲבֵרָה עוֹשָׂה   *Look what sin does.* This is a reference to the priests who were the sons of Eli. "Why was Shiloh destroyed? Because of the desecration of the sacrifices that took place there" (*Tosefta, Menahot* 13:22).

The historical background is important. The *Mishkan* was the first sanctuary that the Jews had. It functioned only as long as the Jews moved from place to place in the desert. Once the Jews crossed the Jordan River and conquered and apportioned the land of Israel, the *Mishkan* ceased to function. After the fourteen years of conquest and apportionment of the land, the Jews brought

the Holy Ark and the sacred vessels to Gilgal. Gilgal was not actually a *mekom HaMikdash*, a location of the *Mikdash*. Rather, it was a transition stage from the *Mishkan* in the desert to the stage of the *Beit HaMikdash* described by the Torah.

The Holy Ark resided in Gilgal for fourteen years and then it was removed to Shiloh. There was no *ḥurban* of Gilgal. The Ark then remained in Shiloh for 369 years until the destruction of Shiloh in the days of Eli the priest. The Ark was then moved to Nob where the Jews attempted to establish a *Beit HaMikdash*, but they realized that Jerusalem was the only place that would be accepted by God. Jerusalem, however, was selected only after Shiloh was at first selected and then rejected.

An element of permanence is required for a site to be considered a *Beit HaMikdash*. The commandment to establish the *Beit HaMikdash* has two components. One is to actually build the *Mikdash* (Exodus 25:8). But there is an additional component which is that the *Mikdash* must be established forever, never to be changed or destroyed. The *Mishkan* in the desert had no permanent walls or roof, but rather had tapestries which served these purposes. The structure in Gilgal was the same. Although Shiloh had tapestries for its roof, its walls were stone. Thus it had the attributes of both a *bayit*, a permanent house, and an *ohel*, a non-permanent tent. This dual nature of Shiloh is consistent with the Gemara (*Zevaḥim* 118a) which notes that some verses in the Torah refer to the *Beit HaMikdash* as a *bayit* and some as an *ohel*. The *Beit HaMikdash* in Jerusalem also possessed this dual quality. Its permanent fortress-like walls gave it the quality of a *bayit*. But it also had the quality of an *ohel* through the altar, which was not covered by a roof. It could not be under a roof because the smoke of the sacrifices, one of the altar's most important features, rose unobstructed. Thus the *kedusha* of the *Beit HaMikdash* is based on two contradictory characteristics: *bayit*, the permanent dwelling, and *ohel*, the temporary resting place. This double motif of *bayit* and *ohel* is central to the *kinot*, and in the *kinot* we mourn for both the *bayit* and the *ohel*.

Psalms, as well, identifies this dual character of the *Beit HaMikdash* and describes the requirement for building both an *ohel* and a *bayit*. King David, who was responsible for identifying the site of the *Beit HaMikdash*, said that he would not rest until he found an appropriate location, as he says, "We heard of it being in Efrata, we found it in the field of the forest" (Psalms 132:6). This verse is more suggestive of an *ohel* than a *bayit*. In the same chapter, however,

King David says, "For the Lord has chosen Zion; He has desired it for His habitation: *zot menuḥati adei ad*, This is My resting place forever; here I will dwell, for I have desired it" (Psalms 132:13–14). The phrase *"zot menuḥati adei ad"* surely connotes the permanence of a *bayit*.

15

of the alphabet. and the third stich of each line is a quotation; the first three in each stanza are the openings of verses from Eikha 3, while the concluding stich of each stanza quotes the Tokhaḥa, "the Rebuke" (Lev. 26:25–46), continuing from those verses quoted in Kina 9. Commentary for this kina begins on page 358.

א How His quiver is like an open grave! / He added wings to my furious pursuers! / "I am the man [who has witnessed this]."

א "How can I bear their sins," He proclaimed, / so that my prayers are muzzled. / "He drove me on."

א How He rushed to pour forth His wrath, / pouring it forth, because He could no longer contain it. / "On none but me, He brings down [His hand]."

> He remembers my circling [the golden calf] in the desert heat.
> He insists [that He will never forget] even as the shadows
>   of evening grow long.   *Jer. 6:4*
> "I will bring a sword against you."

ב She wept bitterly, now that I am in total want. / Punished, because I left the path. / "He has worn away my flesh and skin."

ב He has swallowed the Temple, erect and tall, / and hacked away thickets with iron. / "All around me, He has built [misery]."

ב He threatened me that I would eat the fruits of my womb, / and He turned me about in retreat from my foe. / "He has made me dwell in darkness."

> As our heritage was abandoned to the enemy's land,
> He spoke, "I will have neither mercy nor compassion!"
> "When I will break your staff of bread."

ג Exiled is she who radiantly wore her crown / from bridal canopy to exile, predestined. / "He walled me in."

ג He severed the pride of prince and nobleman. / He withdrew His right hand, so as not to save. / "When I cry and plead [He shuts out my prayer]!"

ג He reinforced the power of my slave masters. / To my groans, He shut His windows. / "He has walled in my ways."

> Orphans driven from their inheritance.
> He has not yet turned back His anger
> but has said, "If, despite this [you disobey Me]."

15

This kina is made up of twenty-two stanzas, each divided into four lines of three rhyming stichs. The first word of each line is the first word of a corresponding verse of Eikha – the first word of the first line in each stanza comes from chapter 1, that of the second line from chapter 2, followed by chapter 4 and chapter 5. The second word of each line begins with the corresponding letter

אֵיכָה אַשְׁפָּתוֹ פָּתוּחַ כְּקֶבֶר / וּלְוִדּוּי בְּאַף, הוֹסִיף אֵבֶר / אֲנִי הַגֶּבֶר:
אֵיכָה אֶשָּׂא עֲוֹן הָג, / וְחֻסַּם פִּי מִפַּלֵּל לַהָג / אוֹתִי נָהָג:
אֵיכָה אֶרֶץ זַעְמוֹ לִשְׁפֹּךְ / הָכִיל נִלְאֵיתִי, וְנָס שְׁפֹךְ / אַךְ בִּי יָשֻׁב יַהֲפֹךְ:
זְכֹר אֲפִיפְתִי בַּשֶּׁרֶב / וְנָס, כִּי־יִנָּטוּ צִלְלֵי־עָרֶב: / וַהֲבֵאתִי עֲלֵיכֶם חָרֶב: ירמיה ו, ד

בָּכוֹ תִבְכֶּה, בְּעֵת כָּל חֲסָרַי / וּכְעָזְבִי אֹרַח יְשָׁרַי / בִּלָּה בְשָׂרִי וְעוֹרִי:
בִּלַּע בַּיִת, לָרוּם מְזֻקָּף / וּבְבַרְזֶל סְבָכוֹ נָקָף / בָּנָה עָלַי וַיַּקַּף:
בְּנֵי בִטְנִי לֶאֱכֹל הִקְשִׁיבַנִי / מִנִּי צָר, אָחוֹר הֱשִׁיבַנִי / בְּמַחֲשַׁכִּים הוֹשִׁיבַנִי:
נַחֲלָתֵנוּ נֶהֶפְכָה בְּיַד לוֹחֵם / נָם לֹא אָחוּס וְלֹא אֲרַחֵם / בְּשִׁבְרִי לָכֶם מַטֵּה־לָחֶם:

גָּלְתָה גְּהוּצָה לַעֲנֹד עֶדְיִי / מֶחְפָּה לְגָלוּת בְּהִתְעַתְּדִי / גָּדַר בַּעֲדִי:
גָּדַע גָּאוֹן נָדִיב וָשׁוֹעַ / וְהֵשִׁיב אָחוֹר יָמִין מִלְּהוֹשִׁיעַ / גַּם כִּי אֶזְעַק וַאֲשַׁוֵּעַ:
גַּם גֶּבֶר עָלַי פּוֹרְכִי / וּבְנָאֳקִי, סָתַם חֲרַכַּי / גָּדַר דְּרָכָי:
יְתוֹמִים גְּרוּשִׁים מֵאֲחֻזּוֹת / וְלֹא שָׁב אַפּוֹ בְּכָל זֹאת / וְאָמַר וְאִם־בְּזֹאת:

ד He hedged the happy roads with thorns, making me mournful, / and led me to exile in Babylon. / "He is like a lurking bear to me."

ד The oppressor trod upon my neck, dominating me. / "Let me be," I wept bitterly. / "He has forced me off my way."

ד My pursuer has overtaken me and grips me in his snare / to sharpen his plowshare upon me. / "He has bent his bow."

> He muddied our waters and vowed, "I will destroy you!
> I will cast you into the valley of exile to humiliate you!"
> "I will act against you."

ה With the sound, "Hoah," I cried that day, / the scars of my fiery burns, / "He shot into my kidneys."

ה He who expelled me and scorned me, walked / and gave me to taste my blood as if it was sweet wine. / "I have become a laughing stock to all my people."

ה Those who ate of the Pesaḥ lamb on that special night, / were fed, in their hunger, heads of donkeys. / "He has filled me with bitterness."

> He has fastened a heavy load to my neck
> and vowed to remember my transgressions.
> "You shall eat the flesh of your sons."

ו He went out and bared and smashed their heads, / and tightened my bonds because I was guilty of mockery. / "He has broken [my teeth] on gravel."

ו He pillaged and stripped me of my crown, grinding it to dust. / From the heights, He threw me down to the muddy depths. / "My life was bereft of peace."

ו He magnified and intensified the screams of my murdered ones. / My screams resounded above my head. / "I said that my strength was lost."

> He vowed to return [Israel] to Egypt and Kush
> and judge them for their evil schemes.
> "I will destroy your idolatrous altars."

ז She remembered well how I spoiled my fragrance / and exclaimed to the bride [Israel], "Remove your glory!" / "Recall my distress and my misery."

ז He abandoned, raged, and turned His heart away / when He was wrathful with the anointed. / "When I remembered, I bowed low."

ז My righteous ancestors and their deeds, will I bring to bear, / since He has breached my path. / "This, do I call to mind."

> Our patriarchs cried out, but their prayers were futile
> because of our slanderous behavior.
> [The Lord] spoke only of our many sins.
> "I will lay your cities to ruin."

דַּרְכֵי דִיץ, שָׁךְ לְהַאֲבִילִי / וְגָלוּת לְשֶׁשֶׁךְ הוֹבִילִי / דֹּב אֹרֵב הוּא לִי:
דָּרַךְ דּוֹחֵק עַל בָּמוֹת, לְהִשְׁתָּרֵר / שְׂעוּ מֶנִּי, בִּבְכִי אֲמָרֵר / דְּרָכַי סוֹרֵר:
דָּבַק דּוֹלְקִי וְצָדַנִי בְּרִשְׁתּוֹ / עָלַי לִלְטֹשׁ מַחֲרַשְׁתּוֹ / דָּרַךְ קַשְׁתּוֹ:

מֵימֵינוּ דָלַח, וְנָם אֲשִׂמְכֶם / גֵּיא גָלוּת אַטִּילְכֶם לְהַכְלִימְכֶם / וְהָלַכְתִּי עִמָּכֶם:

הָיוּ הָהּ לְיוֹם בְּכִיּוֹתַי / וְצֹרֶבֶת אֵשׁ, כְּוִיּוֹתַי / הֵבִיא בְכִלְיוֹתָי:
הָיָה הוֹלֵךְ מִפָּנַי וּמַזְעִימִי / וְכָעַסִים, דָּמַי הִטְעִימִי / הָיִיתִי שְׂחֹק
לְכָל-עַמִּי:
הָאֹכְלִים הַקֹּדֶשׁ פֶּסַח בְּלֵיל שִׁמֻּרִים / הֶאֱכִילָם בְּכָפָן, רָאשֵׁי חֲמוֹרִים /
הִשְׂבִּיעַנִי בַמְּרוֹרִים:

עַל צַוָּארֵנוּ הִשְׂרִיג, וְחִלֵּל שֵׁכֶם / וְנָם אֶפְקֹד עַל עֲוֺנוֹתֵיכֶם / וַאֲכַלְתֶּם בְּשַׂר בְּנֵיכֶם:

וַיֵּצֵא וְקָדְקֹד שֵׂפָח וְרָצַץ / וְחִזֵּק מוֹסְרַי, כִּי אֶתְלוֹצֵץ / וַיָּגֶרֶס בֶּחָצָץ:
וַיַּחְמֹס וַיְנַצֵּל מֵעָדַיי לְהַכְפִּישֵׁי / וּמִגַּבְהָה לַתְּהוֹם הִרְפִּישִׁי / וַתִּזְנַח מִשָּׁלוֹם
נַפְשִׁי:

וַיִּגְדַּל וְכָבַד, נַאַק רְצָחַי / וּבְקָדְקֳדִי עָלָה צוֹחִי / וְאָמַר אָבַד נִצְחִי:

מִצְרַיִם וְכוּשׁ, שָׂח אֲשִׁיבְכֶם / וְאֶשְׁפַּטְכֶם כְּזִמַּתְכֶם / וְהִשְׁמַדְתִּי אֶת-בָּמֹתֵיכֶם:

זָכְרָה זֹאת כִּי נִבְאַשׁ נֵרְדִּי / וּלְכַלָּה פָּץ, מִכְּבוֹד רֵדִי / זְכָר-עָנְיִי וּמְרוּדִי:
זָנַח זַעַם, וְלֵב הִקְשִׁיחַ / וּבְהִתְעַבְּרוֹ עִם מָשִׁיחַ / זָכוֹר תִּזְכּוֹר וְתָשׁוּחַ:
זַכּוּ זְקֵנַי, וּפָעֳלָם אָבִיא / כִּי בְכֵן פֶּרֶץ נְתִיבִי / זֹאת אָשִׁיב אֶל-לִבִּי:

אֲבוֹתֵינוּ זָעֲקוּ וְכֻלּוֹ מִדִּבָּה / וְשָׂח עַל רָעָתֵנוּ כִּי רַבָּה / וְנָתַתִּי אֶת-עָרֵיכֶם חָרְבָּה:

ח He saw our transgressions, for we were stained with sin. / He exacted payment for the stench with which we were dirtied. / "The kindness of the Lord has not ended."

ח Those who plowed over me, planned to demolish the precious. / The observing [angels] wept bitterly over my wound. / "They are renewed every morning."

ח Darkened is the vision of those who offered my sacrifices. / I now grope like a blind man along the wall, / [and yet,] "'The Lord is my portion,' I say with a full heart."

> Lowly slaves prevent me from repairing the breach.
> Bitter self-reproof was expressed decisively.
> "I will make the land desolate!"

ט Her uncleanness clung to her so that He drew the line [of retribution], / but did not retreat from those who trust in Him. / "The Lord is good to those who trust in Him."

ט My gates sank, I was grievously silenced. / Every passerby hissed and was appalled. / "It is good to wait patiently."

ט Innocent babes expired as I continued to act treacherously. / Equal to my evil actions, He invoked His wrath. / "It is good for a man to bear a yoke."

> Risking our lives, we grubbed for food.
> Just as we used shovel and fan,
> So He vowed, "I will scatter you."

י His hand hurled fire at me as with Sodom, / and in addition, Edom oppressed me. / "Let him sit alone and be silent."

י They sit in agony over the protective canopy [of the Temple], / hard pressed by His wrath. / "Let him put his mouth in the dust."

י My tormentor inflicted wounds upon me. / I heard my enemy say, "Bow down!" / "Let him offer his cheek to the smiter."

> Our skin has been scarred and dulled like a shard,
> our bodies laid low to the ground.
> "Then shall the land make up [for its Sabbath years]."

כ All of our radiance has been obscured, / yet all of His ways are compassionate. / "For He does not reject forever."

כ [The Jewish nation] has almost disappeared, for He wages war against us, / though He renounces punishment. / "He first afflicts, then pardons."

כ His fury spent, He ignited His fire, / allowing the six [coals He entrusted to the angel Gabriel] to cool. / "For He does not willingly bring grief."

> Weakened like shamed women sitting desolate,
> recalling their guilt year after year.
> "Throughout the time that it is desolate."

חֵטְא חָז, כִּי עָוֹן נִכְתַּמְנוּ / תָּמוּר כִּי בְצִחְיוֹן נֶחֱמַנּוּ /חַסְדֵי יהוה כִּי לֹא־תָמְנוּ:

חָשַׁב חוֹרְשִׁי לְקַרְקַר יְקָרִים / וּמַר יְבַכְּיוּן, מַכְּתִי סוֹקְרִים / חֲדָשִׁים לַבְּקָרִים:

חָשַׁךְ חָזוֹן מַגִּישֵׁי אִשַּׁי / קִיר כְּעִוֵּר לְגַשֵּׁשִׁי / חֶלְקִי יהוה, אָמְרָה נַפְשִׁי:

עֲבָדִים חֲסָמוּנוּ מִלְּגַדֵּר פֶּרֶץ / וְתוֹכָחוֹת קָשׁוֹת פָּץ בְּחֶרֶץ /וַהֲשִׁמֹּתִי אֲנִי אֶת־הָאָרֶץ:

טֻמְאָתָהּ טָפְלָה, וְנָטָה קָו / וְלֹא נָסוֹג אָחוֹר מִקַוִּיו / טוֹב יהוה לְקֹוָו:

טָבְעוּ טִירוֹתַי וּפִי צַר דָּמַם / וְכֹל עֹבֵר עָלַי, שָׁרַק וְשָׁמַם / טוֹב וְיָחִיל וְדוּמָם:

טוֹבִים טַפִּים נִבְלוּ בְּהוֹסִיפִי לְמַעַל / וּכְמַעֲלָלַי, חָרָה בִי לִפְעַל / טוֹב לַגֶּבֶר כִּי־יִשָּׂא עֹל:

בְּנַפְשֵׁנוּ טֶרֶף אֵפֶר נִבְרָה / כִּי כְּמוֹ בָרַחַת וּבַמִּזְרֶה / גַּם וְאַתְּכֶם אֱזָרֶה: ישעיה ל, כד

יָדוֹ יָרָה בִי אוֹר כִּסְדוֹם / וְעַל כָּל אֵלֶּה, הוֹנַתְנִי בַּת אֱדוֹם / יֵשֵׁב בָּדָד וְיִדֹּם:

יֵשְׁבוּ יְגוֹנִים, בָּנַי עָלַי חוֹפְּהוּ / כִּי כָבֵד עָלַי אַפֵּהוּ / יִתֵּן בֶּעָפָר פִּיהוּ:

יְדֵי יוֹסְרַי שָׁתוּ בִי מֶחִי / וְקַשַּׁבְתִּי מִפִּי צַר, שְׁחִי / יִתֵּן לְמַכֵּהוּ לֶחִי:

עוֹרְנוּ יוּעַם כְּחֶרֶשׂ בַּקֶּרֶץ / וְגֵוֵנוּ שַׂמְנוּ כָאָרֶץ / אָז תִּרְצֶה הָאָרֶץ:

כָּל כְּבוֹד תָּאֲרֵנוּ הָכְלָם / וְצוּר, אֲרֻחוֹתָיו חָסֵד כֻּלָּם / כִּי לֹא יִזְנַח לְעוֹלָם:

כָּלוּ כִמְעַט, כִּי בִי נִלְחָם / וְעַל הָרָעָה, הוּא נִחָם / כִּי אִם־הוֹגָה וְרִחַם:

כָּלָה כַעְסוֹ, וְהִצִּית לֶהָבוֹ / וּבְתַכְלִית שִׁשָּׁה, מְאוֹרֵי כְבוֹ / כִּי לֹא עָנָה מִלִּבּוֹ:

נָשִׁים כִּפְרוּעוֹת יוֹשְׁבוֹת שָׁמָּה / בְּכָל שָׁנָה וְשָׁנָה מַזְכִּירוֹת אַשְׁמָה / כָּל־יְמֵי הַשַּׁמָּה:

ל Not for you [the enemy], who have stamped out [Israel's] joy, / and overwhelmed His children with ocean waves, / "And crushed them underfoot."

ל For their mouths, to their mothers, they pined for bread, / punished for engulfing others in throats like open graves, / "To deny a man his rights."

ל He averred never to eradicate His dear people. / Why did He draw His sword from its scabbard? / "To wrong a man in his cause."

> Trapped princes were pulled from the gates [of Jerusalem],
> Rendered like loathsome figs,
> Their "remnants" gleaned.

מ From on high, He wrote a tragic scroll, / filled with lamentation, sorrow and woe. / "Whose decree was even fulfilled?"

מ To what other nation can I compare you, to console you? / None other has suffered strife and contention. / "Not at the word of the Lord on high."

מ I will bemoan the sins of the deceptive prophets. / My Consoler, [like a warrior] shaking off His wine. / "Of what should one complain?"

> Young men, tossed about with much stumbling,
> the Divine Presence departing from their midst.
> "They shall stumble over one another as before the sword."

נ Their crumbling yoke was heavy upon us. / He despised the offerings of our priests. / "Let us search our ways."

נ Your prophets dared wink their eyes deceptively, / so that they turn His divine forbearance into cruelty. / "Let us lift up our hearts with our hands."

נ Shaken heads, cast into pits. / Wicked men, caught in nets. / "We have transgressed and rebelled."

> Aged and very young, thriving multitudes,
> devoured, and made a mockery by the nations,
> As He said, "You shall perish among the nations."

ס Crushed were they who produced fragrant incense. / I opened my mouth and gasped. / "You covered Yourself with anger."

ס My enemies clapped their hands, and I was lacerated. / I cried, "Violence," and grieved. / "You blocked Yourself with a cloud."

ס Our assailants exclaimed, "Away, you unclean ones," / as the heavens were like iron. / "You have made us dirt and filth."

> Silenced are the joyful singers.
> My pursuers are swifter than eagles,
> to destroy "the survivors."

לוֹא אֲלֵיכֶם, לוֹחֲצֵי גִילַי, / עַל בָּנָיו הֶעֱבִיר גַּלָּיו / לְדַכֵּא תַּחַת רַגְלָיו:
לְאַמְּתָם, לְעֵת כַּמְהוּ מַשְׁבֵּר / יַעַן כִּי גָרוֹן פָּתְחוּ כַקֶּבֶר / לְהַטּוֹת מִשְׁפַּט־גָּבֶר:
לֹא לִמְחוֹת פֶּץ לְעַם קְרוֹבוֹ / וְאֵיךְ מִתָּעַר הוֹצִיא חַרְבּוֹ / לְעַוֵּת אָדָם בְּרִיבוֹ:

שָׂרִים לְכוּדִים הוֹצִיא מִשְׁעָרִים / תֵּת כַּתְּאֵנִים הַשֹּׁעָרִים / לְעוֹלֵל הַנִּשְׁאָרִים:

מִמָּרוֹם, מְגִלָּה כָּתַב בְּנֶהִי / קִינִים וָהֶגֶה וָהִי / מִי זֶה אָמַר וַתֶּהִי:
מָה אֲעִידֵךְ, מְאוּסָה מִלְּהֵרָצָה / נְתוּנָה בְּיַד מֵרִיב וּמְנַצֶּה / מִפִּי עֶלְיוֹן לֹא תֵצֵא:
מֵחַטֹּאת מַדִּיחַי אֱקוֹנֵן / מְנַחֲמַי כְּמַיִן מִתְרוֹנֵן / מַה־יִּתְאוֹנֵן:

בַּחוּרִים מוֹטְטוּ כוֹשֵׁל בִּי לְהָרַב / וּשְׁכִינָה הֶעֱלָה מִקֶּרֶב / וְכָשְׁלוּ אִישׁ־בְּאָחִיו כְּמִפְּנֵי־חָרֶב:

נִשְׁקַד נֵטֶל עַל פּוֹרְכֵינוּ / וַיִּתְעַב שַׁי עוֹרְכֵינוּ / נֶחְפְּשָׂה דְרָכֵינוּ:
נְבִיאַיִךְ נָאֲצוּ לַקֶּרֶץ עַפְעַפַּיִם / וְאִכְזְרוּ עָלֵינוּ אֶרֶךְ אַפַּיִם / נִשָּׂא לְבָבֵנוּ אֶל־כַּפָּיִם:
נָעוּ נָדוּ רֹאשׁ בְּמַהֲמוֹרֵינוּ / רְשָׁעִים מַפִּילִים בְּמַכְמוֹרֵינוּ / נַחְנוּ פָשַׁעְנוּ וּמָרִינוּ:

זְקֵנִים נִינִים לְרֹב שָׁגִים / אֲכָלוּם וַהֲשִׁיתוּם מָשָׁל בַּגּוֹיִם / כִּנָּם וַאֲבַדְתֶּם בַּגּוֹיִם:

סָלָה שָׁמַי קְטוֹרָה בְאַף / וָאֶפְעַר פִּי וָאֶשְׁאָף / סַכּוֹתָה בָאָף:
סָפְקוּ שׁוֹטְנַי כַּף וָאֶשְׁתּוֹנֵן / וָאֶזְעַק חָמָס וָאֶתְאוֹנֵן / סַכּוֹתָה בֶעָנָן:
סוּרוּ טָמֵא שָׂחוּ מַאֲשִׁימֵינוּ / בְּהִנָּתֵן כַּבַּרְזֶל שָׁמֵינוּ / סְחִי וּמָאוֹס תְּשִׂימֵנוּ:

שָׁבַת מְשׂוֹשׂ שֶׁמַח מְשׁוֹרְרִים / וְרוֹדְפֵי קָלּוּ מִנְּשָׁרִים / לְאַבֵּד הַנִּשְׁאָרִים:

ע Over and above all this, they tortured me with their scandalous talk, / and multiplied their blasphemous harangues. / "They shouted against us."
פ Their mouths gaped wider than the wellsprings of the netherworld. / They engulfed me with harsh reproof! / "Panic and pitfalls!"
פ The glorious face of my canopied abode, / withered with the rise of my oppressor. / "My eyes shed torrents of water."

> Fallen is the crown of strength, their support,
> as the enemy pained them along seven paths.
> "They confessed their sins."

פ With outspread hands, she exclaimed, "Oh! I am surrounded," / no longer girded with strength. / "My eyes shall flow."
ע He struck in wrath and is still angry, / and hacked at those who provoked quarrel. / "Until the LORD looks down and sees."
ע Divine glory has departed, flown away to heaven, / ten elevations high. / "My eyes have brought me grief."

> For this was the beauty of their pleasantness ended.
> Yet, He promised He would not abandon them to the hands of the foe.
> "Yes, I will walk with them."

צ The Righteous One once took account of my every step, / but when I perverted rectitude and denied [Him], / "They snared me like a bird."
צ My Rock shouted and denied passage [to my prayers]. / Because of my violations, He planned to shatter me. / "They chained me in a dungeon."
צ My trail was ambushed, and my Benefactor left me, / and as they rose like the sea to drive me away, / "Water flooded above my head."

> On Mount Zion, they assembled to cut me down.
> The Rock spoke, "I will have pity on My remnant."
> "I will remember My covenant."

ק I cried out, "Listen to my oppressors blaspheme!" / They strike my children on their cheeks. / "I have called Your name, LORD."
ק Stand and pray, for He will not put your prayers to shame. / He will more than repay those that anger me. / "Hear my plea, do not ignore."
ק Inferiors scalded me, yet You refuse to see. / Strike Your fear against the nations. / "You drew near when I called upon You."

> You, O LORD, do not delay the set time.
> Until when must I be like a forsaken forest?
> "And the land was forsaken."

עַל אֵלֶּה עֲשָׁקוּנוּ בְּחֵרוּפֵיהֶם / וְהִגְדִּילוּ שְׁאוֹן גְּדוּפֵיהֶם / פָּצוּ עָלֵינוּ פִּיהֶם:

פָּצוּ פָּעֲרוּ פֶה מִבְּאֵר שַׁחַת / וְאָטְרוּ עָלַי בְּתוֹכַחַת / פַּחַד וָפָחַת:
פְּנֵי פְאֵר חֻפַּת מְעוֹנִי / הִקְמִיל וְהֵקִים מְעַנִּי / פַּלְגֵי־מַיִם תֵּרַד עֵינִי:
נָפְלָה עֲטֶרֶת עֹז מִשְׁעֵנָם / וְצַר בְּשִׁבְעָה דְרָכִים עִנָּם / וְהִתְוַדּוּ אֶת־עֲוֹנָם:

פָּרְשָׂה פוֹצְצָה, אוֹי כִּי סָגְרָה / תְּמוּר מַתְנֶיהָ בְּעֹז חָגְרָה / עֵינִי נִגְּרָה:
עָשָׂה עֶבְרָתוֹ וַיֶּחֱרָה / וְעֹרֶף אֶת מָדוֹן מִגְּרָה / עַד־יַשְׁקִיף וְיֵרֶא:
עוֹדֵינוּ עָף כָּבוֹד, וְעָלָה / וְעֶשֶׂר מַסָּעוֹת נַעֲלָה / עֵינִי עוֹלְלָה:
עַל זֶה פָּסַק גּוֹי נָעֳמָם / וְצוּר שָׁח, לֹא אֶעֱזְבֵם בְּכַף זוֹעֲמָם / אַף־אֲנִי אֵלֵךְ עִמָּם:

צַדִּיק צַר צְעָדַי לִסְפֹּר / וּבְעָקְלָתִי יִשָּׁר, וְאֶכְפֹּר / צוֹד צָדוּנִי כַּצִּפּוֹר:
צָעַק צוּרִי, וְסִכֵּךְ מֵעֲבוֹר / וּבְחַלְלֵי עָרֶךְ לִשְׁבֹּר / צָמְתוּ בַבּוֹר:
צָדוּ צְעָדַי, וְסָע דּוֹרְשִׁי / וְכַעֲלוֹתָם עָלַי כַּיָּם לְגָרְשִׁי / צָפוּ־מַיִם עַל־רֹאשִׁי:
עַל הַר צִיּוֹן צָבְאוּ לְהַכְרִיתִי / וְצוּר שָׁח, אֶחְמוֹל עַל שְׁאֵרִיתִי / וְזָכַרְתִּי אֶת־בְּרִיתִי:

קְרָאתִי, קְשֹׁב חֶרְפַּת מוֹנַי / עַל הַלֶּחִי, מַכִּים בָּנַי / קָרָאתִי שִׁמְךָ יהוה:
קוּמִי קְרָאִי, כִּי לֹא יְכַלֵּם / עַל יֶתֶר לַמַּקְנִיאַי יְשַׁלֵּם / קוֹלִי שָׁמָעְתָּ אַל־תַּעְלֵם:
קָלִים קְדָחוּנִי, וְעָלַמְתָּ מֵרְאֵךְ / הָשֵׁת בַּגּוֹיִם מוֹרָאֵךְ / קָרַבְתָּ בְּיוֹם אֶקְרָאֶךָּ:

אַתָּה יהוה קֵץ אַל תִּכְזָב / עַד מָתַי, כַּחֶרֶשׁ אֵעָזֵב / וְהָאָרֶץ תֵּעָזֵב:

ר Behold the rage of my severe wound. / I presume that, although He abandoned me to oblivion, / "You have championed my life's cause."
ר Behold, my many terrors. / You have devastated my entire people. / "You have seen the wrong done to me."
ר The spirit in me is weakened, because I fear them. / Their wrath surges up to engulf me. / "You have seen their vengefulness."

> Why do You stand at a distance when they speak so brazenly?
> You vowed to render the desolate [city] as one without walls,
> "Yet, even then."

ש They heard that I succumbed to their assault. / Their darkness rose like a swarm of locusts. / "You heard their taunts."
ש My sons lay prostrate in their agony, / and their captors were haughty with arrogance. / "The lips of my adversaries, and their insults."
ש Rejoice, you who have savaged me, for my hand has fallen, / lowered to the netherworld below. / "Behold them as they sit and as they stand."

> Return us [to Jerusalem], and compensate us for those years,
> and assure us that You will redeem us from that tumult.
> "And I will remember the covenant with the earlier generations."

ת Come and see my persecutors who cut me down. / They have triumphed, and Your cherished place lies in ruins. / "Pay them back [with revenge]."
ת Proclaim and reveal that day, hidden in Your heart, / and for those who plan evil with malice, / "Give them anguish of heart."
ת End their dominion, bring about their defeat. / May they fall, never to rise. / "Pursue them in wrath, and destroy them."

> They constantly poke at us and mock us,
> but we are never distant from Your Torah.
> Take us back, and teach us "these laws."

Kina 16 starts on page 360.

רְאֵה רְגַז מַכַּת אֱנוּשִׁי / וְאֹמַר, בְּהִנָּטְשִׁי בַּנֶּשִׁי / רַבְתָּ אֲדֹנָי רִיבֵי נַפְשִׁי:
רְאֵה רֹב בַּעֲתָתִי / הֲשַׁמּוֹת כָּל עֲדָתִי / רָאִיתָה יהוה עַוָּתָתִי:
רְוַח רָפְתָה בִּי מֵאֵימָתָם / לְבַלְעִי, הֶעֱלוּ חֲמָתָם / רָאִיתָה כָּל־נִקְמָתָם:

לָמָּה רָחוֹק תַּעֲמֹד בְּדַבְּרָם עַזּוּת / נֵמֵת, הַנְּשָׁמָה אוֹשִׁיב פְּרָזוֹת / וְאַף גַּם־זֹאת:

שִׁמְעוּ שֶׁנּוּקַשְׁתִּי בִּדְחִיפָתָם / וְכִלֵּק עָלָה עֵיפָתָם / שָׁמַעְתָּ חֶרְפָּתָם:
שָׁכְבוּ שׁוֹחֲחִים, בְּנֵי מִיגוֹנָם / וְשׂוֹבְעֵיהֶם, גָּאָה מְאֹד גְּאוֹנָם / שִׂפְתֵי קָמַי וְהֶגְיוֹנָם:
שִׁישִׁי שׂוֹשַׂתִּי, כִּי בִּי יָד מָטָה / מֻשְׁפֶּלֶת עַד שְׁאוֹל מַטָּה / שִׁבְתָּם וְקִימָתָם הַבִּיטָה:

הֲשִׁיבֵנוּ שָׁלֵם, שְׁלוֹם שָׁנִים / וְתֹאמַר, אֶפְדֵּם מִשְּׁאוֹנִים / וְזָכַרְתִּי לָהֶם בְּרִית רִאשֹׁנִים:

תָּבֹא, תָּשׁוּר מְעַנֵּי לָמוּל / הֵם שָׁגְבוּ חַיִל, וְאַוֵּיךָ אָמוּל / תָּשִׁיב לָהֶם גְּמוּל:
תִּקְרָא, תְּגַלֶּה יוֹם כָּמוּס בְּלֵב / וּמְחַפְּשֵׂי עוֹלוֹת, לִפְעֹל מִלֵּב / תִּתֵּן לָהֶם מְגִנַּת־לֵב:
תָּם תַּכְלִית תָּקְפָּם לְלָכְדָם / יִפְּלוּ, בְּלִי לְהַעֲמִידָם / תִּרְדֹּף בְּאַף וְתַשְׁמִידֵם:

כִּי תָמִיד דּוֹקְרִים וְשׂוֹחֲקִים / וּמִתּוֹרָתְךָ אָנוּ לֹא רוֹחֲקִים / הֲשִׁיבֵנוּ וְהוֹרֵנוּ אֵלֶּה הַחֻקִּים:

Kina 16 starts on page 361.

COMMENTARY ON KINA 15

הִשְׂבִּיעַנִי בַּמְּרוֹרִים "He has filled me with bitterness." This phrase is a direct quote from the verse in Lamentations, "He has filled me with bitterness, He has sated me with wormwood" (3:15). The intent of the phrase in the *kina* is that in the midst of their hunger on the first night of Pesaḥ, they *did* have *maror* and they ate the *maror* without the *korban Pesaḥ*. Rabbi Elazar HaKalir is alluding to the Midrash (*Eikha Raba* 3:15) which states, "הִשְׂבִּיעַנִי בַּמְּרוֹרִים refers to to the first night of Pesaḥ... הִרְוַנִי לַעֲנָה, on the night of Tisha B'Av."

This interpretation accords well with the view of Maimonides, who takes the position (*Mishneh Torah*, Hil. Ḥametz U'Matza 7:12) that eating *maror* on the night of Pesaḥ is not an independent mitzva, but rather "is dependent on the eating of the *korban Pesaḥ*, because it is one integrated mitzva to eat the meat of the *korban Pesaḥ* with *matza* and *maror*." Eating the *maror* without the *korban Pesaḥ* is not a mitzva and is meaningless.

וּבְהִתְעַבְּרוֹ עִם מָשִׁיחַ *When He was wrathful with the anointed.* The word *Mashiaḥ* refers to Moses, and this phrase is an allusion to God's anger with Moses and His refusal to let Moses cross into the land of Israel. Had Moses crossed the Jordan River, he would have been the *Melekh HaMashiaḥ*, but Moses sinned, and God refused to listen to his entreaties. God, in His wrath, prevented Moses from becoming the *Melekh HaMashiaḥ*, "וַיִּתְעַבֵּר יהוה בִּי לְמַעַנְכֶם, But the LORD was wrathful with me on your account and would not listen to me" (Deuteronomy 3:26). Had Moses' prayer been accepted, Jewish history would have been very different.

16

Titus defiled the Holy of Holies before it was burnt; and the tragedy of the four hundred captive children, who, as related in Gittin 57b, drowned themselves while being taken as captives to Rome. Commentary for this kina begins on page 364.

זְכֹר Remember what the foe [Titus] did within the [Temple] precincts.
   He drew forth his sword and entered the Holy of Holies.
   He shocked our heritage when he profaned the show bread,
   and pierced the curtain, embroidered on both sides.

יְתוֹמִים The orphaned [nation], he disgraced with his bloodstained shield.
   He drew a line in reddish color.
   He dirtied our waters, and his arrows were glutted with blood,
   as he left the Temple with a bloodied sword.

עַל [We mourn] because this mortal schemed evil schemes
   and raised his hand against God, as if to defeat Him, saying:
   "He could defeat Egypt and all other nations.
   But I, inside His precious [Temple], will run against Him boldly."   *Job 15:26*

אֲבוֹתֵינוּ In the time of our forefathers, when the sons [of Aaron]
   brought in alien offerings, they were consumed by fire.   *Ps. 78:63*
   Yet, he dared to bring in a harlot and was not singed by fire.
   Slavish men raked His Tabernacle with flames of fire.
   Why, to the House of [sacrificial] fire,
   did He send down a fire from on high?   *Lam. 1:13*

בְּנַפְשֵׁנוּ Our spirits sank as he took out the Temple vessels,
   and placed them on ships to use them for himself.
   Our skin rotted as the High Priest awoke,
   and could not find the ninety-three Temple vessels.

נָשִׁים Women stared at the approaching tyrant,
   scarring the floor of the Temple with his boots.
   Princes panicked with the general's arrival.
   He dared spray the Holy of Holies with his filth.

16

The first word of each line (the first of each stanza for the last two stanzas), corresponds to the first word of a verse in Eikha chapter 5. Included in this kina are allusions to two descriptions found in the fifth chapter of Tractate Gittin: the account in Gittin 56b, which describes how the conquering

זְכֹר אֵת אֲשֶׁר עָשָׂה צַר בִּפְנִים
שָׁלַף חַרְבּוֹ, וּבָא לִפְנַי וְלִפְנִים.
נִחַלְתָּנוּ בִּעֵת, כְּטִמֵּא לֶחֶם הַפָּנִים
וְגֶדֶר פָּרְכֶת בַּעֲלַת שְׁתֵּי פָנִים:

יְתוֹמִים גֹּעַל בְּמָגֵן מְאָדָּם
וַיְמַדֵּד קָו בְּמַרְאֶה אֲדַמְדָּם.
מֵימֵינוּ דָלַח, וְהִשְׁכִּיר חִצָּיו מִדָּם
כְּיָצָא מִן הַבַּיִת, וְחַרְבּוֹ מְלֵאָה דָם:

עַל הֲגוֹתוֹ הַוּוֹת גֶּבֶר
וְנָטָה אֶל אֵל יָדוֹ, לִמְלֹאוֹ לְהִתְגַּבֵּר.
מִצְרַיִם וְכָל לְאֹם, אֲשֶׁר בָּם גֶּבֶר
וַאֲנִי בְתוֹךְ אַוִּיו, אָרוּץ אֵלָיו בְּצַוָּאר: איוב טו, כו

אֲבוֹתֵינוּ, זָרָה כְּהִכְנִיסוּ בַּחוּרָיו אָכְלָה אֵשׁ
וְזֶה צוֹעָה זוֹנָה הִכְנִיס, וְלֹא נִכְוָה בָּאֵשׁ.
עֲבָדִים חִתּוּ בְסִכּוֹ, לַבַּת אֵשׁ   תהלים עח, סג
וְעַל מָה בְּבֵית אֵשׁ, מִמָּרוֹם שָׁלַח אֵשׁ:   איכה א, יג

בְּנַפְשֵׁנוּ טָבַעְנוּ, כְּהוֹצִיא כְּלֵי שָׁרֵת
וְשָׂמָם בָּאֳנִי שַׁיִט בָּם לְהִשָּׁרֵת.
עוֹרֵנוּ נָמַק כְּהִשְׁכִּים מְשָׁרֵת
וְלֹא מָצָא תִּשְׁעִים וּשְׁלֹשָׁה כְּלֵי שָׁרֵת:

נָשִׁים כִּשָּׁרוּ כִּי בָא עָרִיץ
בְּקַרְקַע הַבַּיִת נֶעֱלָיו הֶחֱרִיץ.
שָׂרִים לְפָתוּ בְּבוֹא פָּרִיץ
בְּבֵית קֹדֶשׁ הַקֳּדָשִׁים, צַחֲנָתוֹ הִשְׁרִיץ:

בַּחוּרִים The young men stood strong at the exterior walls,
   imagining that [the enemy] would be repulsed
      by six hundred thousand demons.
   But the elders trembled, knowing [the enemy]
      was empowered by Heaven,
   to have his way while He restrained Himself, as if in chains.

שָׁבַת Gone is Nebuchadnezzar, but Rome has taken his place,
   encircling the walls and frightening the masses.
   Wrath has befallen the descendants of Jacob
   to the extent that Heaven has abandoned the palace.

עַל He started to approach the Temple Mount's gate,
   ordering the four chiefs of his legion to destroy it.
   He spared the western wall, leaving it as a remembrance.
   [The Almighty] stood behind our wall but did not defend His cause.

אַתָּה You were enraged and allowed the evacuation.
   Children without blemish were expelled from there. *Dan. 1:4*
   Why do the nations storm, while You do not heed Israel's meal-offerings? *Ps. 2:1*
   They carried off [lads and maidens]
      to the distant land [of Utz] in three ships.

הֲשִׁיבֵנוּ They pleaded, "Bring us back," as they sailed the ocean's recesses,
   and joined together to cast themselves into the sea.
   They sang songs of praise as if they were at the Sea of Reeds.
   For Your sake, we are slain upon the depths of the sea. *Ps. 44:23*

כִּי They were overcome by the ocean deep.
   "All this has come upon us, and we have not forgotten You," *Ps. 44:18*
      they implored Him whose reality they sensed.
   They placed their hope in Him, who will retrieve even from Bashan,
   and a heavenly echo resounded, "Awake! Why do you sleep?" *Ps. 44:24*

Kina 17 starts on page 374.

בַּחוּרִים מִבַּחוּץ צַגּוּ מְחֻזָּקִים
וְתָרוּ, כִּי יָזַק בְּשִׁשִּׁים רִבּוֹא מַזִּיקִים.
זְקֵנִים נִבְעֲתוּ כְּהִרְשׁוּהוּ מְשַׂחֲקִים
עֲשׂוֹת רְצוֹנוֹ, וְהוּא אָסוּר בָּאזִקִּים:

שָׁבַת סוֹטֵן, וַיָּבוֹא אַדְמוֹן
וַיְסַבֵּב חוֹמָה, וַיְעַוֵּת הָמוֹן.
נָפְלָה עֲבָרָה, עַל נִינֵי פִּצֵּל לַח לוּז וְעַרְמוֹן
עַד כִּי נֻטַּשׁ מִדֹּק אַרְמוֹן:

עַל פֶּתַח הַר הַבַּיִת הֵחֵל לָבוֹא
בְּיַד אַרְבָּעָה רָאשֵׁי טַפְסְרָיו, לְהַחֲרִיבוֹ.
עַל צַד מַעֲרָבִי לְזֵכֶר, הִשְׁרִיד בּוֹ
וְצָג אַחַר כָּתְלֵנוּ, וְלֹא רָב רִיבוֹ:

אַתָּה קָצַפְתָּ וְהִרְשֵׁיתָ לְפָנוֹת
יְלָדִים אֲשֶׁר אֵין בָּהֶם כָּל מְאוּם, מִשָּׁם לְהִפָּנוֹת. דניאל א, ד
לָמָּה רָגְשׁוּ גוֹיִם, וְלֹא שָׁעִיתָ אֶל הַמִּנְחָה פְּנוֹת. תהלים ב, א
וְשִׁלְּחוּם לְאֶרֶץ עוּץ, בְּשָׁלֹשׁ סְפִינוֹת:

הֲשִׁיבֵנוּ שִׁוְּעוּ, כְּבָאוּ בְּנִבְכֵי יָם
וְשָׁתְפוּ עַצְמָם יַחַד, לִנְפֹּל בַּיָּם.
שִׁיר וְתִשְׁבָּחוֹת שׁוֹרְרוּ, כְּעַל יָם
כִּי עָלֶיךָ הֹרַגְנוּ בִּמְצוּלוֹת יָם: תהלים מד, כג

כִּי תְהוֹמוֹת בָּאוּ עַד נַפְשָׁן
כָּל זֹאת בָּאַתְנוּ וְלֹא שְׁכַחֲנוּךָ, חִלּוּ לְמַמְשָׁן. תהלים מד, יח
תִּקְוָתָם נָתְנוּ לְמֵשִׁיב מִבָּשָׁן
וּבַת קוֹל נִשְׁמְעָה, עוּרָה, לָמָּה תִישָׁן: תהלים מד, כד

Kina 17 starts on page 375.

COMMENTARY ON KINA 16

This *kina*, written by Rabbi Elazar HaKalir, is based on the sayings of our sages as to atrocities which the Roman legionnaires committed against the *Beit HaMikdash* and the Jews in Jerusalem. It is also based on the Midrash (*Tanḥuma* [Warsaw] *Aḥarei Mot*, 4; see also *Vayikra Raba* 20:5) which asks why the two sons of Aaron, who entered the *Mishkan* with improper incense, were punished immediately even though they had good intentions, while Titus, who entered the *Beit HaMikdash* with blasphemy and arrogance, emerged unharmed.

כְּטַמֵּא לֶחֶם הַפָּנִים *When he profaned the show bread.* The contamination by Titus of the *leḥem hapanim*, the show bread, is not mentioned in Gemara *Gittin*, and we do not have any other source for this in the writings of our sages. Apparently HaKalir had a source, unknown to us, that Titus committed this act.

וְגָדַר פָּרֹכֶת *And pierced the curtain.* This story is recounted in the Gemara (*Gittin* 56b) and the Midrash (*Bereshit Raba* 10:7). When Titus entered the Holy of Holies, he cut through the *parokhet*, the curtain, with his sword. The *parokhet* began to bleed, and Titus thought that he had inflicted an injury on God, God forbid.

בַּעֲלַת שְׁתֵּי פָנִים *Embroidered on both sides.* In his commentary on *kinot*, Daniel Goldschmidt correctly comments that this refers to the passage in the Jerusalem Talmud (*Shekalim* 8:4) which describes the *parokhet* as having two *panim*, different figures on each side. It was *ma'aseh rokem*, the work of the weaver, on one side and *ma'aseh ḥoshev*, the work of the skillful artisan, on the other.

וַיְמַדֵּד קָו בְּמַרְאֶה אֲדַמְדָּם *He drew a line in reddish color.* Some interpret this phrase as meaning that Titus rendered a verdict to kill all the Jews, but this is incorrect. Rather, it alludes to the Gemara (*Gittin* 56b), referred to above, which recounts that when Titus pierced the *parokhet*, blood began to flow in that spot, and he thought that he had injured the *Shekhina*, God forbid. In order to highlight that spot, which was red from blood, Titus drew a circle around it. Similarly, the phrase וְנָטִיתִי עַל יְרוּשָׁלַיִם אֶת קָו (II Kings 21:13) means that Jerusalem will be encircled.

עַל הֲגוֹתוֹ הַוּוֹת גֶּבֶר / וְנָטָה אֶל אֵל יָדוֹ, לְמוּלוֹ לְהִתְגַּבֵּר *Because this mortal schemed evil schemes and raised his hand against God, as if to defeat Him.* In this phrase, the word *havot* means blasphemy which a person utters. This stanza is a con-

tinuation of the description of Titus' blasphemous and sacrilegious attitude toward God. When Titus emerged from the Holy of Holies, he moved his hand toward God, which was a gesture of contempt. The Gemara tells us (*Gittin* 56b) that Titus used the verse "Where are their gods, the rock in whom they trusted" (Deuteronomy 32:37) to say, "Where is their God to whom they sacrifice so many sacrifices?"

מִצְרַיִם וְכָל לְאֹם, אֲשֶׁר בָּם גָּבַר *He could defeat Egypt and all other nations.* This phrase can be understood to refer to Titus and his military prowess. The fact that Titus defeated Egypt and so many other peoples, gave him the confidence that he could destroy Israel as well. In fact, it was not initially Rome's intention to destroy the Jews physically. At the beginning, Rome had political objectives. It wanted to subdue Judea and insure that Judea took its orders from Rome, but not to destroy it. Until the Bar Kokhba insurrection, Rome did not engage in religious persecution. The Roman view was that once a people was subdued politically, then its culture, creativity and spiritual identity would gradually disappear, as well. In fact, Rome was very successful in "Romanizing" the ancient world. Latin became the language of the world, and Roman culture and Roman law exist to this day. The only exception was the Jewish people. Consistent with Roman policy, Titus thought that when he conquered Jerusalem he would not only conquer the physical structure of the *Beit HaMikdash*, but וְנָטָה אֶל אֵל יָדוֹ, לְמוּלוֹ לְהִתְגַּבֵּר, that he would conquer the people spiritually and religiously, as well. Although they might still have their religious leaders and scholars, gradually the Jews would completely assimilate into Roman society, and the Jews' spiritual identity would evaporate. But the Bar Kokhba rebellion proved otherwise. By the time of the Bar Kokhba rebellion, some sixty-five years after the Ḥurban, the Jews should have stopped thinking about the *Beit HaMikdash* and the unique way of life it represented. It was only then that Rome realized that the Jews have a very strange identity which is different from their political identity. Even without a state or a king, the Jews' spiritual identity was difficult to conquer. It was only when Rome realized that the Jews had a different identity, that Rome turned against the Jewish religion and commenced its religious persecution.

וַאֲנִי בְּתוֹךְ אוּיּוֹ, אָרוּץ אֵלָיו בְּצַוָּאר *But I, inside His precious [Temple], will run against Him boldly.* One could interpret this phrase not as Titus' challenge to God, but as the Jews' response to Titus. The answer to Titus' proud statement, that he will conquer not only the political existence of the Jew but his spirit as well, is וַאֲנִי בְּתוֹךְ אוּיּוֹ אָרוּץ אֵלָיו בְּצַוָּאר, that in spite of Titus' desire, I, the Jew,

will appear before him with pride and defy him. My neck will be straight. This was the answer given to Rome by Bar Kokhba and his insurrection.

Titus' mistake was to reduce the Jew's identity to his political identity. While political identity is important, the Jew's identity is spiritual, not political.

אֲבוֹתֵינוּ, זָרָה כְּהִכְנִיסוּ בַּחוּרָיו אָכְלָה אֵשׁ *In the time of our forefathers, when the sons [of Aaron] brought in alien offerings, they were consumed by fire.* When Nadab and Abihu entered the *Mishkan* humbly, they had good intentions but God punished them immediately, and they were consumed by fire because they brought a *ketoret zara*, an incense which they were not commanded to bring. God consumed the two sons of Aaron by fire for a minor infraction (*Vayikra Raba* 20:8).

וְזֶה צוֹעָה זוֹנָה הִכְנִיס, וְלֹא נִכְוָה בָאֵשׁ *Yet, he dared to bring in a harlot and was not singed by fire.* The *paytan* poses the question asked by the Midrash (*Vayikra Raba* 20:5): Why was it that Nadab and Abihu, the chosen ones among the people, were punished immediately for their infraction of bringing in alien fire, while Titus, who profaned and defiled the Holy of Holies by bringing in a harlot, was not punished immediately?

עֲבָדִים חִתּוּ בְסֻכּוֹ, לַבַּת אֵשׁ *Slavish men raked His Tabernacle with flames of fire.* This is a reference to *"Avdei Hashem,"* those who serve the LORD, the High Priests, who used to bring the pan with burning coals into the Holy of Holies on Yom Kippur (Mishna *Yoma* 5:1).

וְעַל מֶה בְּבֵית אֵשׁ, מִמָּרוֹם שָׁלַח אֵשׁ *Why, to the House of [sacrificial] fire, did He send down a fire from on high?* It is a mystery how the *Beit HaMikdash*, called the House of fire, was consumed by fire. The *kina* is posing a rhetorical question: How is it possible that fire can consume fire?

בְּנַפְשֵׁנוּ טָבַעְנוּ, כְּהוֹצִיא כְּלֵי שָׁרֵת *Our spirits sank as he took out the Temple vessels.* This is a reference to the Romans' preparation of the *klei sharet*, the sacred vessels, accessories and utensils used in the Temple service, to be taken to Rome (*Yalkut Shimoni, Kohelet* 978). It also refers to Nebuchadnezzar who similarly took the sacred vessels of the *Beit HaMikdash* to Babylonia.

The *kina* contains several earlier references to the sacred vessels before this stanza. "כְּטַמֵּא לֶחֶם הַפָּנִים, he profaned the show bread," refers to one of the sacred vessels. Similarly, "וְגָדַר פָּרֹכֶת, and pierced the curtain," and "יְתוֹמִים גִּעֵל בְּמָגֵן מְאָדָם וַיְמַדֵּד קָו בְּמַרְאֶה אֲדַמְדָּם, The orphaned [nation], he disgraced with his bloodstained shield. He drew a line in reddish color," refer to the desecration

of the *parokhet*, another of the sacred accessories. The Romans found many *klei sharet* which they defiled.

וְשָׂמָם בָּאֳנִי שַׁיִט בָּם לְהִשָּׁרֵת And placed them on ships to use them for himself. This is an allusion to the statement in the Midrash (*Yalkut Shimoni Kohelet* 978) that Titus took all the sacred vessels, accessories and utensils, including the *parokhet*, to Rome in order to use them for idolatrous service.

עוֹרֵנוּ נָמַק כְּהַשְׁכִּים מְשָׁרֵת וְלֹא מָצָא תִּשְׁעִים וּשְׁלֹשָׁה כְּלֵי שָׁרֵת, Our skin rotted as the High Priest awoke, and could not find the ninety-three Temple vessels. The Mishna says that the priests used ninety-three sacred gold and silver vessels for each *tamid* sacrifice in the *Beit HaMikdash* (*Tamid* 3:4), and that they used to arrange them the night before so that they would be ready to be taken out of the utensil repository the following morning. The import of this phrase is that our skin rotted when the High Priest arose the next day and wanted to take out the ninety-three vessels from the chamber where they were kept, and he could not find them because they were removed from the *Beit HaMikdash* under Titus' orders.

The picture painted here by Rabbi Elazar HaKalir is puzzling. He describes the High Priest as though he did not know what Titus had done. He arose in the morning, walked into the *Beit HaMikdash* to commence the service and told the other priests to take out the sacred vessels, but to his surprise, they did not find the vessels because Titus had removed them. This is a strange description because the High Priest surely knew the previous night that Titus was emptying the treasury of the *Beit HaMikdash*.

בְּקַרְקַע הַבַּיִת נְעָלָיו הֶחֱרִיץ Scarring the floor of the Temple with his boots. The *Beit HaMikdash* was stripped bare to such an extent that the nails in the soles of Titus' boots left marks on the floor. Titus' disregard of the prohibition against wearing shoes on the Temple Mount (for example, *Berakhot* 54a and 62b), is yet another example of his arrogance.

צַחֲנָתוֹ הִשְׁרִיץ He dared spray... with his filth. This is an allusion to the story cited earlier that Titus brought a harlot into the Holy of Holies.

בַּחוּרִים מִבַּחוּץ צְגוּ מְחֻזָּקִים / וְתֵרוּ, כִּי יֻזַּק בְּשִׁשִּׁים רִבּוֹא מַזִּיקִים The young men stood strong at the exterior walls, imagining that [the enemy] would be repulsed by six hundred thousand demons. According to our sages (*Devarim Raba* 1:17), when the Romans approached the *Beit HaMikdash*, there were six hundred thousand *mazikim*, destructive angels, ready to defend it and repel the Roman

legions. Therefore the *baḥurim*, the young warriors who defended the *Beit HaMikdash*, felt encouraged. *Tzagu meḥuzakim*, they made a show of strength, *vetaru*, and they hoped and visualized the downfall of the enemy at the hands of the *mazikim*. But when the enemy appeared, the *Shekhina* was silent. The moment that the *mazikim* saw that the *Shekhina* was quiet and passive, they ceased their defense and left the *Beit HaMikdash* to Titus.

זְקֵנִים נִבְעֲתוּ כְּהִרְשׁוּהוּ מְשַׂחֲקִים *But the elders trembled, knowing [the enemy] was empowered by Heaven.* Unlike the young warriors, the elders, the Torah scholars, the members of the Sanhedrin, were frightened, כְּהִרְשׁוּהוּ מְשַׂחֲקִים, because they felt that the Almighty had given Titus free reign to do whatever he wanted, with no hope of help from Heaven. They knew that Titus was sent by God, and that the *mazikim* would not engage in battle.

עֲשׂוֹת רְצוֹנוֹ, וְהוּא אָסוּר בָּאזִקִּים *To have his way while He restrained Himself, as if in chains.* In this phrase, the word *retzono*, which literally means "his will," should be interpreted as "His will," the will of God. Similarly, the literal translation of "וְהוּא אָסוּר בָּאזִקִּים," is "He is bound in chains," and this phrase should also be understood to refer to God. On this phrase, the Midrash (*Eikha Raba, Petiḥta* 34) comments succinctly, "כִּבְיָכוֹל הוּא הוּא," meaning that, as it were, God Himself is in chains. This phrase in the *kina* thus expresses a paradox. On the one hand, Titus and the Roman enemy fulfilled the will of God in destroying the *Beit HaMikdash*. And yet, on the other hand, God was in chains and had no power. In effect, God chained Himself; He chained and arrested the *midat haraḥamim*, the attribute of mercy, and let the *midat hadin*, the attribute of judgment, prevail. The concept of God being chained is similar to the kabbalistic notion of *Shekhinta begaluta*, the Divine Presence in exile. This is what the kabbalistic scholars mean when they speak of "מֶלֶךְ אָסוּר בָּרְהָטִים, The king is held captive in the tresses" (Song of Songs 7:6).

נָפְלָה עֶבְרָה, עַל נִינֵי פִּצֵּל לַח לוּז וְעַרְמוֹן *Wrath has befallen the descendants of Jacob.* This is an allusion to the verse pertaining to Jacob "וַיִּקַּח־לוֹ יַעֲקֹב מַקַּל לִבְנֶה לַח וְלוּז וְעַרְמוֹן, And Jacob took rods of fresh poplar, and of the almond and of the plane tree" (Genesis 30:37).

עַל פֶּתַח הַר הַבַּיִת הֵחֵל לָבוֹא / בְּיַד אַרְבָּעָה רָאשֵׁי טַפְסְרָיו, לְהַחֲרִיבוֹ *He started to approach the Temple Mount's gate, ordering the four chiefs of his legion to destroy it.* The Midrash states (*Eikha Raba* 1:31) that Titus, as commander-in-chief, appointed four commanders to conquer Jerusalem. Each of his commanders, *tafserav*, was assigned the task of leading a force to conquer one side of the city.

Before setting fire to the *Beit HaMikdash*, Titus consulted with his commanders. According to Josephus, Titus himself voted against destroying the *Beit HaMikdash*. It was the soldiers who started the fire without any orders from him, and Titus tried to protect the *Beit HaMikdash*. But Josephus' account is clearly false. Titus himself suggested to the four commanders that the *Beit HaMikdash* be destroyed (*Devarim Raba* 21; *Gittin* 56b). In Titus' opinion, the Jews would seek political independence as long as the *Beit HaMikdash* was intact. The only way to subdue the people and make them abandon the idea of political independence was to destroy their spiritual center.

In its account of the four commanders, the Midrash demonstrates how much attention the Romans paid to Jerusalem. After all, Jerusalem had been conquered, and the Temple Mount was surrounded. Consequently, there was no need to appoint four commanders to conquer the *Beit HaMikdash*. However, Rome saw in Judea a major foe. Rome's perception was that either Judea will be conquered and Rome will survive, or if Judea survives, Rome will disappear. Titus, the non-Jew, understood the significance of the Temple Mount to the Jew, and he knew that the Jew would defend it to the last drop of blood. Therefore, he appointed four commanders to conquer it.

עַל צַד מַעֲרָבִי לְזֵכֶר, הִשְׁרִיד בּוֹ *He spared the western wall, leaving it as a remembrance.* Three of Titus' four commanders carried out their orders fully in accordance with Titus' instructions and destroyed the walls of the *Beit HaMikdash*. The one commander who failed was the one who was assigned to conquer the western side. This attack was not successful, and the *kotel hama'aravi*, the Western Wall, survived. Had the Temple Mount been completely destroyed, God would have departed, but because He left a remnant, the *Shekhina* has not departed from the Temple Mount. The *Shekhina* was always found in the west; the Holy of Holies was in the western section of the *Beit HaMikdash*. Since the *Shekhina* resided at the Western Wall even during the time of the *Ḥurban*, the wall remained.

וְצָג אַחַר כָּתְלֵנוּ [*The Almighty*] *stood behind our wall.* God allowed the Western Wall to survive intact, and He remains behind it. He chose the western side of the Temple Mount as His home, and therefore He did not allow Titus to attack it successfully. He is still behind the Western Wall. As long as the *Shekhina* abides in a place, that place cannot be destroyed. *Ḥurban* is possible only when there is the departure of the *Shekhina* from the *Beit HaMikdash*. Our sages say "קִימְחָא טְחִינָא טְחִינַת, you didn't grind wheat, you ground flour which had already been ground" (*Sanhedrin* 96b; *Eikha Raba* 1:41). The

meaning of this statement is that the *Beit HaMikdash* without the presence of the *Shekhina*, is merely a structure consisting of stones and wood, devoid of significance. The Temple Mount is significant only as long as the *Shekhina* resides there.

It is an interesting observation that Rabbi Elazar HaKalir combines the fact that the *Shekhina* never departed, with the idea that the Western Wall could not be destroyed.

It is noteworthy that the Western Wall is not referred to at all in the Babylonian Talmud or the Jerusalem Talmud and is hardly mentioned in the *Rishonim*. For example, Maimonides' letter describing his arrival in Jerusalem does not mention anything about the Western Wall. There is a reference to the Western Wall in the Midrash on the verse from Song of Songs, "Behold, he stands *aḥar kotlenu*, behind our wall, He looks in through the windows, He peers through the lattice" (2:9). The Midrash says (*Shemot Raba* 2:2) that this refers to the Western Wall and that the *Shekhina* is behind the Western Wall, in its shadow. I have always been somewhat skeptical of the authenticity of the midrashic references to the Western Wall, and I suspect they may be of a later period, because the classical Talmudic sources make no mention of the Western Wall. In my view, this *kina* of Rabbi Elazar HaKalir is one of the earliest documents in which the Western Wall is mentioned.

The concept underlying the phrase "עַל צַד מַעֲרָבִי לְזֵכֶר, הִשְׂרִיד בּוֹ וְצָג אַחַר כָּתְלֵנוּ, וְלֹא רָב רִיבוֹ," that the *Shekhina* resides behind the Western Wall, appears in Maimonides' *Mishneh Torah*. Maimonides distinguishes (*Mishneh Torah*, Hil. Beit HaBeḥira 6:14–16) between *kedushat ha'aretz*, the sanctity of the land of Israel, and *kedushat HaMikdash*, the sanctity of the *Beit HaMikdash*, maintaining that the former was suspended with the destruction of the *Beit HaMikdash* by Nebuchadnezzar and the latter was not suspended. Maimonides' view is that in the case of the *Beit HaMikdash*, קִדְּשָׁה לְשַׁעְתָּהּ קִדְּשָׁה לֶעָתִיד לָבוֹא, it was sanctified initially on a temporary basis, and its sanctity continues eternally for the future; but Joshua's conquest of the land of Israel, on the other hand, had the status only of קִדְּשָׁה לְשַׁעְתָּהּ וְלֹא לֶעָתִיד לָבוֹא, it was sanctitified initially on a temporary basis, and its sanctity does not continue for the future. Maimonides explains the distinction as follows. In the case of Joshua's conquest of the land of Israel, the *kedushat ha'aretz* was dependent on physical might. The Jews were powerful and conquered the land, and therefore the land was endowed with *kedusha*. Subsequently, Nebuchadnezzar was more powerful and drove the Jews out of the land of Israel, and therefore the *kedusha* was terminated; whoever is more powerful

annuls the conquest of the predecessor. But, Maimonides continues, "the sanctity of the *Mikdash* and Jerusalem is dependent upon the *Shekhina,* and the *Shekhina* is always present; it is not annulled … and the sages said, 'Even though they [the Temple and Jerusalem] are desolate and destroyed, they remain in their state of *kedusha*.'" Maimonides' view is based on the concept that the *Shekhina* never departed from the Temple Mount; the *Shekhina* is present behind the Western Wall. The concept of the *Shekhina* not departing from the Temple Mount results in the important halakhic conclusion that *kedushat HaMikdash* is presently in full force. Consequently, if we had the opportunity, we could build the altar and offer sacrifices in our own day because this depends on the same *kedushat HaMikdash,* which continues in effect.

וְלֹא רָב רִיבוֹ *But did not defend His cause.* One interpretation of this phrase is that it refers to Titus, who did not insist that his commander carry out the assignment to destroy the Western Wall.

Another, more likely, interpretation is that this phrase refers to God; that in collecting what was due to Him, He did not resort to the Western Wall. This interpretation is based on the concept expressed by our sages that the *Beit HaMikdash* is collateral for the obligations of the Jewish people, which is a recurring theme in the *kinot*. If the Jewish people are indebted to God and do not pay their debts, He will collect payment from the collateral, the *Beit HaMikdash*. The entire Temple Mount was condemned to destruction as payment for the debt of the Jewish people, but God freed the Western Wall from the indebtedness and permitted it to remain standing. Since the immediately preceding phrase, "*vetzag aḥar kotlenu,*" clearly refers to God, this phrase, "*velo rav rivo,*" in all likelihood refers to Him, as well.

אַתָּה קָצַפְתָּ…בִּשְׁלֹשׁ סְפִינוֹת *You were enraged … in three ships.* This stanza, as well as the rest of the *kina,* refers to the incident recounted in the Gemara (*Gittin* 57b) of four hundred boys and girls who were captured by the Romans and sent by ship to Rome to be used for immoral purposes. The children realized what their fate would be and while on the high seas, asked the oldest and most knowledgeable among them whether they will have a share in the World to Come if they jump into the sea and commit suicide. In response, the young boy quoted the verse, "The Lord said: 'I will bring back from Bashan, I will bring them back from the depths of the sea'" (Psalms 68:23). He told them that they will have a share in the World to Come regardless of the manner in which they die, even those who die in the depths of the sea. Having heard this response, all the children threw themselves into the sea.

According to Maimonides' view, there is a question as to whether the girls were required to commit suicide (*Mishneh Torah*, Hil. Yesodei HaTorah 5:2). The conclusion that the girls would not have been required to commit suicide would be based on the halakhic principle that a woman is not required to sacrifice her life to avoid coerced prohibited sexual relations because she is merely *karka olam*, a completely passive participant. However, it is quite possible that the purpose of shipping the boys and girls to Rome was not for purposes of the Romans satisfying their physical desire, but for religious conversion. If that was the Romans' intent, then the girls as well as the boys were required to sacrifice their lives.

The martyrdom recorded in this *kina* involved four hundred children who were taken to Rome to be dishonored. This type of event occurred with greater frequency in the Middle Ages and during the Holocaust, as well. There is a story of a group of religious young women in Warsaw who were selected by the Germans for immoral purposes and who committed suicide rather than submit to immorality. As with many of the calamities described in the *kinot*, the story of the four hundred children should not be seen just as an event which occurred nineteen hundred years ago, but as an event that has been repeated over the years and which happened in our own time, as well.

שִׁיר וְתִשְׁבָּחוֹת שׁוֹרְרוּ, כְּעַל יָם / כִּי עָלֶיךָ הֹרַגְנוּ בִּמְצוּלוֹת יָם *They sang songs of praise as if they were at the Sea of Reeds. For Your sake, we are slain upon the depths of the sea.* They said *shira*, a song of praise, when they leapt into the sea, the same way Moses said *shira* at the splitting of the Red Sea. The *shira* said by the children was כִּי עָלֶיךָ הֹרַגְנוּ בִּמְצוּלוֹת יָם, which is an allusion to the verse, "כִּי־עָלֶיךָ הֹרַגְנוּ כָל־הַיּוֹם, for Your sake are we killed all the day" (Psalms 44:23).

17

done evil, woe is me!" The last stanza also hints at the source in Eikha, with God reminding the people of their own sins, which were the cause of the calamity. Commentary for this kina begins on page 378.

אָ As I recall,

אָ women eating their own fruit, their coddled babes,
>   Woe is me!

אָ the compassionate cooking their own children,
>   once preciously measured ounce by ounce,
>   Woe is me!

אָ the braids of their head torn from them,
>   after being tied to racing horses,
>   Woe is me!

אָ the tongues of infants, stuck to their palates, parched with thirst,
>   Woe is me!

אָ women wailing to each other, "Come, let us cook our squealing children,"
>   Woe is me!

אָ the two encountering each other, saying, "Give me your child,"
>   [the child] hidden, already cut into sections,
>   Woe is me!

אָ children encountering their parents' flesh in caves and pits,
>   Woe is me!

אָ condemned maidens, upon their mother's laps, swollen with hunger,
>   Woe is me!

אָ the souls of babes expiring in the village streets, swollen with hunger,
>   Woe is me!

אָ burdened with miscarriage and shriveled breasts,
>   a mother collapsed over her children,
>   Woe is me!

אָ eight hundred shield-bearers, humbled and exiled to
>   Arabia to be executed,
>   Woe is me!

17

This kina by HaKalir is based on Eikha 2:20, and describes the horrors experienced at the time of the siege and the subsequent pillaging of the city. It is arranged in alphabetical order, each line opening with the feminine verb form and ending with "Woe is me!" echoing Job 10:15: "If I have

אִם־תֹּאכַלְנָה נָשִׁים פִּרְיָם, עֹלְלֵי טִפֻּחִים.
אַלְלַי לִי:

אִם תְּבַשֵּׁלְנָה רַחֲמָנִיּוֹת יַלְדֵיהֶן, הַמְּדוּדִים טְפָחִים טְפָחִים.
אַלְלַי לִי:

אִם תְּגוֹזְנָה פְּאַת רֹאשָׁם, וְתִקְשַׁרְנָה לְסוּסִים פּוֹרְחִים.
אַלְלַי לִי:

אִם תִּדְבַּק לָשׁוֹן יוֹנֵק לְחֵךְ, בְּצִמְאוֹן צְחִיחִים.
אַלְלַי לִי:

אִם תֶּהְמֶנָה זוֹ לְעֻמַּת זוֹ, בּוֹאִי וּנְבַשֵּׁל אֶת בָּנֵינוּ צוֹרְחִים.
אַלְלַי לִי:

אִם תִּוָּעַדְנָה זוֹ לָזוֹ, תְּנִי בְנֵךְ, וְהוּא חָבוּי מְנַתַּח נְתָחִים נְתָחִים.
אַלְלַי לִי:

אִם תְּזַמֵּנָה בְּשַׂר אָבוֹת לַבָּנִים, בִּמְעָרוֹת וְשִׂיחִים.
אַלְלַי לִי:

אִם תְּחַיְּבֶנָה בָּנוֹת, אֶל חֵיק אִמּוֹתָם נְתָפָּחִים.
אַלְלַי לִי:

אִם תְּטַסְּנָה רוּחוֹת עוֹלְלִים בִּרְחוֹבוֹת קִרְיָה תְּפוּחִים.
אַלְלַי לִי:

אִם תִּיקַרְנָה בְּשִׁכּוּל רֶחֶם וְצִמּוּק שָׁדַיִם, וְאִם עַל בָּנִים שָׁחִים.
אַלְלַי לִי:

אִם תְּכַשֵּׁלְנָה שְׁמוֹנֶה מֵאוֹת מָגִנִּים, בַּעֲרָב אֱלוּחִים.
אַלְלַי לִי:

אִם their spirits enflamed by salty food and empty swollen flasks,
> Woe is me!

אִם reduced from a thousand to a hundred, from a hundred to ten, and then to a sorrowful single one,
> Woe is me!

אִם eighty thousand budding priests, fleeing behind the Temple's curtains,
> Woe is me!

אִם to be burned alive like cut kindling wood,
> Woe is me!

אִם eighty thousand murdered priests, hacked to death on account of the death of an innocent one,
> Woe is me!

אִם those who breathed their last, punctured by the odor of the fruits of the field,
> Woe is me!

אִם heaped on one stone, nine large measures of crushed children's brains,
> Woe is me!

אִם three hundred infants, hung and strung on one long tree branch,
> Woe is me!

אִם gentle and delicate damsels, led away in chains by the chief executioner,
> Woe is me!

אִם elegant princesses, violated by the roadside,
> Woe is me!

אִם young lads and lasses, faint with parching thirst,
> Woe is me!

וְרוּחַ The Holy Spirit thunders against them.
Woe to the wicked of the Jewish people!
They inform others about what has befallen them,
but do not inform others about what they have done.
They give voice to the fact that women eat their children,
but, to the fact that they killed a prophet and a priest in the Temple,
they do not give voice.

Kina 18 starts on page 382.

אִם תְּלַהֲטֶנָּה רוּחָם בְּמִינֵי מְלוּחִים וְנֹאדוֹת נְפוּחִים.
אַלְלַי לִי:

אִם תְּמַעֲטֶנָּה מֵאֶלֶף מֵאָה, וּמִמֵּאָה עֲשָׂרָה, עַד אֶחָד לְמַפָּחִים.
אַלְלַי לִי:

אִם תְּנַסְּנָה לְמָסַךְ הֵיכָל, שְׁמוֹנִים אֶלֶף כֹּהֲנִים פְּרָחִים.
אַלְלַי לִי:

אִם תִּשְׂרְפֶנָּה שָׁם כָּל אוֹתָן הַנְּפָשׁוֹת, בְּקוֹצִים כְּסוּחִים.
אַלְלַי לִי:

אִם תְּעָרְפֶנָּה עַל דַּם נָקִי, שְׁמוֹנִים אֶלֶף כֹּהֲנִים נִרְצָחִים.
אַלְלַי לִי:

אִם תְּפַחֲנָה נְפָשׁוֹת מְדֻקָּרִים, מֵרֵיחַ תְּנוּבוֹת שִׂיחִים.
אַלְלַי לִי:

אִם תִּצְבְּרֶנָּה עַל אֶבֶן אַחַת, תִּשְׁעָה קַבִּין מוֹחֵי יְלָדִים מֻנָּחִים.
אַלְלַי לִי:

אִם תִּקְעָנָה שְׁלֹשׁ מֵאוֹת יוֹנְקִים, עַל שׂוֹכָה אַחַת מְתוּחִים.
אַלְלַי לִי:

אִם תֵּרָאֶינָה רַבּוֹת וַעֲנֻגוֹת, כְּבוּלוֹת עַל יַד רַב הַטַּבָּחִים.
אַלְלַי לִי:

אִם תִּשְׁכַּבְנָה בֵּין שְׁפַתַּיִם, בְּנוֹת מְלָכִים מְשֻׁבָּחִים.
אַלְלַי לִי:

אִם תִּתְעַלְּפֶנָּה הַבְּתוּלוֹת וְהַבַּחוּרִים, בְּצִמְאוֹן צְחִיחִים.
אַלְלַי לִי:

וְרוּחַ הַקֹּדֶשׁ לְמוּלָם מַרְעִים / הוֹי עַל כָּל שְׁכֵנַי הָרָעִים
מַה שֶּׁהִקְרָאָם מוֹדִיעִים / וְאֵת אֲשֶׁר עָשׂוּ לֹא מוֹדִיעִים
אִם־תֹּאכַלְנָה נָשִׁים פִּרְיָם, מַשְׁמִיעִים
אִם־יֵהָרֵג בְּמִקְדַּשׁ אֲדֹנָי כֹּהֵן וְנָבִיא, לֹא מַשְׁמִיעִים:

Kina 18 starts on page 383.

COMMENTARY ON KINA 17

This *kina* is another composition of Rabbi Elazar HaKalir. None of the images recorded in this *kina* is a creation of Rabbi Elazar HaKalir's imagination, but all are based on statements in the Midrash or other *aggadot* of the sages found in the Gemara.

אִם תְּבַשֵּׁלְנָה רַחֲמָנִיּוֹת יַלְדֵיהֶן, הַמְדוּדִים טְפָחִים טְפָחִים *The compassionate cooking their own children, once preciously measured ounce by ounce.* The Gemara (*Yoma* 38b) tells of a wealthy woman who measured her child's growth every day, and for each *tefaḥ* (a measurement equal to the width of a fist) that he grew, she would contribute a gold coin to the *Beit HaMikdash*. When Jerusalem was under siege, however, the hunger drove her to kill her beloved child and consume his flesh.

וְתִקָּשְׁרֶנָה לְסוּסִים פּוֹרְחִים *After being tied to racing horses.* This phrase is an allusion to the story told by the Midrash about Miriam bat Baytos (*Eikha Raba* 1:47). She was bound to the tail of a horse, and when the horse began to gallop she was killed. This atrocity was perpetrated not only nineteen hundred years ago, but in our own time as well, during the Holocaust. In fact, it happened to a cousin of mine, Yeshayahu Glikson, whose father was Rabbi Hirsch Glikson and whose mother was the daughter of Rav Ḥayyim Brisk. I knew Yeshayahu, who was slightly younger than I, very well. He was a righteous person and a great scholar. When the Nazis conquered Warsaw and found him and his wife, it was the first week after their wedding. The Nazis tied him to one automobile and his wife to another, and then drove off at high speed, which, of course, resulted in their gruesome deaths. This is precisely the same story as related by the *kina*.

אִם תֶּהֱמֶנָה זוֹ לְעֻמַּת זוֹ *Women wailing to each other.* Two women would conspire and establish a partnership. One day they would kill the child of one of them and feed themselves on the flesh of the child, and the next day they would kill the child of the other woman.

וְהוּא חָבוּי מְנֻתָּח נְתָחִים נְתָחִים *[The child] hidden, already cut into sections.* The intent is to describe a complete dehumanization.

אִם תְּלַהֲטֶנָה רוּחָם בְּמִינֵי מְלוּחִים *Their spirits enflamed by salty food.* Some fugitives from Israel fled to Arabia. When thirsty, they asked the Arabs for water. In response the Arabs first gave the Jews *minei meluḥim*, spicy and salty foods, which precipitated a terrible thirst.

וְנֹאדוֹת נְפוּחִים *And empty swollen flasks.* The Arabs refused to give the Jews water, and instead gave them bags inflated with air.

שְׁמוֹנִים אֶלֶף כֹּהֲנִים פְּרָחִים *Eighty thousand budding priests.* This refers to a story that eighty thousand young *kohanim* hid themselves in the *heikhal*, the sanctuary of the Temple, because they believed that it would be safe from fire. But they were consumed in the conflagration of the *Beit HaMikdash*. The ultimate goal of Nebuchadnezzar and Titus was to destroy the scholars and the intellectual elite among the Jews, but the *kohanim* were the first victims.

אִם תֵּעָרְפָה עַל דַּם נָקִי *Hacked to death on account of the death of an innocent one.* This alludes to the story of Nebuzaradan (*Gittin* 57b) who found the seething blood of Zechariah the prophet. In response to his insistence on knowing the source of this phenomenon, Nebuzaradan was told that this was the blood of the sacrifices, but he was not satisfied with this explanation. In order to quiet the blood of Zechariah, Nebuzaradan embarked on a frenzy of killing.

שְׁמוֹנִים אֶלֶף כֹּהֲנִים נִרְצָחִים *Eighty thousand murdered priests.* These numbers indicate that many more people were killed than we are aware of.

תִּשְׁעָה קַבִּין מוֹחֵי יְלָדִים מֻנָּחִים *Nine large measures of crushed children's brains.* They killed babies by swinging the baby by his legs and dashing his skull against the wall. This happened, as well, during the Nazi regime. Whatever atrocities are related in connection with the Ḥurban Beit HaMikdash happened with more cruelty and on a larger scale during the Nazi period. There is not a single detail which Rabbi Elazar HaKalir records from the midrashim of our sages which did not occur in the 1940s in Lithuania, Russia, Poland, Hungary and Romania.

אִם תִּצְבְּרֶנָה...אִם תִּקְעֶנָה *Heaped ... Hung and strung.* The urge to kill children was more compelling than the desire to kill adults. From the viewpoint of the psychopath, this type of killing satisfies his psychopathic urge to a greater degree. The murderer sees the future of the people in the children, and he wants to destroy the future. Once the children are killed, the future is destroyed.

A similar nefarious strategy was implemented during the Holocaust. The children were taken away immediately, even before the liquidation of the ghettos. There were not many children left by the time the adults were sent off to Treblinka, Auschwitz and Buchenwald. The children had already been exterminated by the time the Nazis started to liquidate the middle aged and elderly. This psychopathic desire to kill the children is identical to what happened

during the Ḥurban Beit HaMikdash. They first killed the children and the intellectuals. They killed the intellectuals among all the nations, but the killing of children was a special "privilege" that was bestowed upon the Jewish people alone.

וְרוּחַ הַקֹּדֶשׁ לְמוּלָם מַרְעִים *The Holy Spirit thunders against them.* The *kina* is not just the Jewish people speaking. In fact, it is a dialogue.

מַה שֶּׁהִקְרָאָם מוֹדִיעִים / וְאֵת אֲשֶׁר עָשׂוּ לֹא מוֹדִיעִים *They inform others about what has befallen them, but do not inform others about what they have done.* They announce and publicize what has happened to them, but they do not disclose to anybody the misdeed they have committed. The *kina* here highlights the protracted refusal of the Jewish people to repent for the murder of the prophet Zechariah. Repentance took place only after Nebuzaradan killed so many innocents in order to quiet the seething blood of Zechariah (*Gittin* 57b).

אִם־תֹּאכַלְנָה נָשִׁים פִּרְיָם...אִם־יֵהָרֵג בְּמִקְדַּשׁ אֲדֹנָי *That women eat their children... that they killed... in the Temple.* The *kina* is quoting the verse in Lamentations, "Shall the women eat their own fruit, the children that are dandled in the hands? Shall the priest and the prophet be slain in the Sanctuary of the Lord?" (2:20). According to the literal meaning of the text, the Jewish people are asserting one unified challenge, posing one combined complaint: how can You allow the merciful mothers to kill their own babies, the fruit of their womb, and how is it possible that You allowed a *kohen venavi*, Zechariah, to be killed by our people in the *Beit HaMikdash* on Yom Kippur?

Another possible interpretation is that both phrases are an indictment of *Knesset Yisrael*. First of all, the mothers became cannibals, and second, a *kohen* and *navi* was killed in the *Beit HaMikdash*.

In each of the foregoing interpretations of the verse from Lamentations, the dual challenge or indictment is posed by one speaker. HaKalir, however, does not view the verse from Lamentations this way, and interprets the two phrases differently. The Jewish people ask, "אִם־תֹּאכַלְנָה נָשִׁים פִּרְיָם, how could You have permitted the mothers to eat their children," and the answer that comes forth from God is, "אִם־יֵהָרֵג בְּמִקְדַּשׁ אֲדֹנָי כֹּהֵן וְנָבִיא, how could you have murdered a *kohen* and *navi* in the *Beit HaMikdash*?" God says to the Jewish people, "All of you have questions as far as *I* am concerned, but you do not answer any questions as far as *you* are concerned."

18

line with וְלָמָּה, "Why, then?" The last stanza breaks with the alphabetical order and form of the preceding stanzas and lays the blame for the Ḥurban at the feet of the Jewish people. Commentary for this kina begins on page 386.

א You assured us, "I will be exceedingly good to you,"   *Gen. 32:13*
    and that, "Your people and I will be distinguished."
ב Why, then, do knaves profane Your name,
    and do You not pour forth Your wrath on them?

ג You raised and elevated children to nurture them,
    as a nursemaid rears a suckling child.   *Num. 11:12*
ד Why, then, have the Dodanim suffocated them with thirst,
    and the lion strangled to provide for his cubs?

ה You fed them honey from the rock
    and extracted flowing water from the rock.
ו Why, then, have their judges slipped upon the rock,
    and were their babes smashed against the rock?

ז You eliminated and rejected every other nation,
    and took for Yourself one nation from another's midst.
ח Why, then, has a nation rushed to attack my land
    and said, "Let us wipe them out as a nation!"?   *Ps. 83:5*

ט You swept sixty, and then eighty,
    to bring forth a nation, keeping the faith.   *Is. 26:2*
י Why, then, have Moabites and Ammonites schemed
    against this people, as numerous as the stars?

כ You prepared a dwelling place for Your glory.
    You acquired this mountain with Your right hand.   *Ps. 78:54*
ל Why, then, have You retracted Your majestic right hand
    and dishonored the throne of Your glory?

18

In this kina, HaKalir repeats the theme of Kina 12, contrasting the ancient mutual love between God and His people, with the apparent turning away by God of the present. The first line of each stanza is addressed to God directly with the word אַתָּה, "You," and the third

וְאַתָּה אָמַרְתָּ, הֵיטֵב אֵיטִיב עִמָּךְ: — בראשית לב, יג
וְנִפְלִינוּ אֲנִי וְעַמָּךְ.
וְלָמָּה בְּנֵי בְלִיַּעַל חִלְּלוּ שְׁמָךְ
וְלֹא שָׁפַכְתָּ עֲלֵיהֶם זַעְמָךְ:

אַתָּה גִדַּלְתָּ וְרוֹמַמְתָּ בָנִים לְהָנֵק
כַּאֲשֶׁר יִשָּׂא הָאֹמֵן אֶת הַיֹּנֵק. — במדבר יא, יב
וְלָמָּה דּוֹדָנִים צְחוּם לְשַׁנֵּק
וְאַרְיֵה בְּדֵי גוֹרוֹתָיו מְחַנֵּק:

אַתָּה הֵינַקְתָּ דְּבַשׁ מִסֶּלַע
וְתוֹצִיא נוֹזְלִים מִסָּלַע.
וְלָמָּה וְשׁוֹפְטֵיהֶם נִשְׁמְטוּ בִּידֵי סֶלַע
וְעוֹלְלֵיהֶם נֻפְּצוּ אֶל הַסָּלַע:

אַתָּה זָנַחְתָּ וַתִּמְאַס כָּל גּוֹי
לָקַחַת לְךָ גּוֹי מִקֶּרֶב גּוֹי.
וְלָמָּה חָשׁ וְעָלָה עַל אַרְצִי גוֹי
וְאָמְרוּ לְכוּ וְנַכְחִידֵם מִגּוֹי: — תהלים פג, ה

אַתָּה טֵאטֵאת שָׂשִׂים וּשְׂמֵנִים
לְהָבִיא גּוֹי שֹׁמֵר אֱמֻנִים. — ישעיה כו, ב
וְלָמָּה יָזְמוּ מוֹאָבִים וְעַמּוֹנִים
לְעַם זוּ כַּכּוֹכָבִים נִמְנִים:

אַתָּה כּוֹנַנְתָּ לְשֶׁבֶת הוֹדְךָ
הַר זֶה קָנְתָה יְמִינְךָ וְיָדְךָ. — תהלים עח, נד
וְלָמָּה לְאָחוֹר הֵשַׁבְתָּ יְמִין הוֹדְךָ
וַתְּנַבֵּל כִּסֵּא כְבוֹדֶךָ:

מ You are supreme in the world from the beginning.
You established an exalted Temple from the beginning.
נ Why, then, has the wicked one scorned with mouth and tongue,
until the foe touched the pupil of the eye?

ס You rejoiced for the good upon them, *Ex. 15:17*
and vowed that You would bring them and plant them.
ע Why, then, has the tyrant blasphemed, saying, "Where is their God *Deut. 32:37*
who consumes the fat of their sacrifices?"

פ You broke the sea with Your might, *Ps. 74:13*
and contained the sea with doors.
צ Why, then, have I descended to the ocean's depths,
and my breach is as wide as the ocean?

ק You are holy, enthroned by the praises of the holy,
by the council of sainted elders.
ר Why, then, do profane nations agitate
and lay waste to the House of the Holy of Holies?

ש You have heard that we have become an ignominy,
and that Your Tabernacle was consumed by fire.
ת Why, then, have You devoured the canopied possession?
Let healing sprout and shelter us.

צ You are right with regard to all that has happened. *Neh. 9:33*
With You, O Lord, is the right, and we affirm this lovingly. *Dan. 9:7*
נ Why, then, do we complain and lament,
when all this has befallen us because of our sins?

Kina 19 starts on page 392.

אַתָּה מָרוֹם לְעוֹלָם רִאשׁוֹן
כּוֹנַנְתָּ מָרוֹם מֵרִאשׁוֹן.
וְלָמָּה נִאֵץ רָשָׁע בְּפֶה וְלָשׁוֹן
עַד כִּי נָגַע צַר בָּאִישׁוֹן:

אַתָּה שַׁתָּ לְטוֹב עָלֵימוֹ
בְּשִׂיחַ תְּבִיאֵמוֹ וְתִטָּעֵמוֹ. שמות טו, יז
וְלָמָּה עָרִיץ חֵרֵף וְאָמַר אֵי אֱלֹהֵימוֹ דברים לב, לז
אֲשֶׁר יֹאכַל חֵלֶב זְבָחֵימוֹ:

אַתָּה פוֹרַרְתָּ בְעָזְּךָ יָם תהלים עד, יג
וַתָּסֶךְ בִּדְלָתַיִם יָם.
וְלָמָּה צָלַלְתִּי עַד נִבְכֵי יָם
וַיְגַדֵּל שִׁבְרִי כַיָּם:

אַתָּה קָדוֹשׁ, יוֹשֵׁב תְּהִלּוֹת קְדוֹשִׁים
בְּסוֹד יְשִׁישִׁים מְקֻדָּשִׁים.
וְלָמָּה רָגְשׁוּ גוֹיִם קְדֵשִׁים
וְהֵשִׁימוּ בֵּית קֹדֶשׁ הַקֳּדָשִׁים:

אַתָּה שָׁמַעְתָּ כִּי הָיִינוּ חֶרְפָּה
וְסִכַּתְךָ בָּאֵשׁ נִשְׂרְפָה.
וְלָמָּה תִּבְלַע נַחֲלַת חֻפָּה
תַּצְמִיחַ תְּרוּפָה וְעָלֵינוּ חוּפָפָה:

אַתָּה צַדִּיק עַל כָּל הַבָּא נחמיה ט, לג
לְךָ יהוה הַצְּדָקָה וְנִצְדַּיְקָךְ בְּחִבָּה. דניאל ט, ז
וְלָמָּה נָהִינוּ וְלָנוּ הַדִּבָּה
כִּי כָל זֹאת בָּאַתְנוּ בְּחוֹבָה:

Kina 19 starts on page 393.

COMMENTARY ON KINA 18

The guiding motif of this *kina* is *berit avot*, the covenant with the patriarchs, as opposed to *zekhut avot*, the merit of the patriarchs. *Zekhut avot*, which was based on God's feelings of love for the patriarchs, has ceased to exist because we are different from the patriarchs. But the *berit avot* is an eternal obligation of God not to desert the Jewish people and ultimately to redeem them. The underlying concept of this *kina* is that God confirmed that He is concerned with the Jewish people. Otherwise, He would not have established a covenant with Abraham and taken the Jews out of Egypt. He would not have fed them the manna in the desert and given them water from the rock. If that is the case, the *kina* asks, why did God destroy the *Beit HaMikdash* and send the Jewish people into exile? The *kina* expresses our inability to understand the contradiction between the events of the past and those of the present. In the past, God did everything for us, but now He is punishing us.

At this point, it would be useful to make some general observations about Rabbi Elazar HaKalir and the the style of his *piyutim*, his religious poetry. The *piyutim* of Rabbi Elazar HaKalir, including his *kinot*, serve two purposes. The first is *limmud*, learning. Every sentence of the *piyut* quotes *ma'amarei Ḥazal*, teachings of the sages. The second purpose is *tokhaḥa*, rebuking the people for their misdeeds and instructing them in the proper way to act. These *piyutim* deal with reproach, repentance, petition and acknowledgment of God's justice. The *shali'aḥ tzibbur* was not merely a *ḥazan*, a cantor, but was one of the great scholars of the generation who was the principal *mokhiaḥ*, moral critic of the people. This *kina* is an example of the second type of HaKalir's *piyutim*.

Rabbi Elazar HaKalir was a master of the Hebrew language and very creative in his use of Hebrew. If not for him, modern Hebrew could not have come into existence. Before HaKalir, the Hebrew language was very rigid. For example, the nouns and verbs were fixed in their form. It was difficult to transform a verb into a noun or a noun into a verb, a simple matter in other languages. The gender of words was also inflexible. For example, in the Bible the word *"shoshana"* (perhaps a rose or lily, although we are not precisely certain of the meaning) is always in the feminine, as in *"ani ḥavatzelet hasharon shoshanat ha'amakim"* (Song of Songs 2:1). But Rabbi Elazar HaKalir, in his *piyut* for Musaf of Yom Kippur, states *"shoshan emek,"* in the masculine. His linguistic style was very complex and often obscure, and he therefore had many critics. Ibn Ezra, for example, in his commentary on Ecclesiastes 5:1,

rails against HaKalir. But HaKalir made a critical contribution to the development of the Hebrew language by endowing the language with flexibility, thereby paving the way for the development of modern Hebrew. There were other early *paytanim*, composers of *piyut*, such as Yose ben Yose, but they were not as radical in their literary style as HaKalir. HaKalir was the the father of the *paytanim*, and he dared to do more than any other *paytan*.

It is true that at times he writes so obscurely that it is almost impossible to decode the meaning. The *kinot* composed by HaKalir which appear earlier in the Tisha B'Av service are extremely difficult to understand because they were written for scholars. But, the *kinot* by HaKalir which appear at this later point in the service demonstrate that he could write in simpler Hebrew. In fact, HaKalir's language in his *kinot* is generally simpler and more understandable than in any of his other *piyutim*. One could think that these *kinot* by HaKalir which appear later in the service were composed by Rabbi Yehuda HaLevi, Ibn Ezra, Kalonymos, or the *paytanim* of Germany and France. Apparently, HaKalir deliberately composed the *kinot* in language that was more readily intelligible to the general population. Had he not done so, these *piyutim* could not have effectively served the function of *kinot*.

As noted above, Rabbi Elazar HaKalir's *piyutim* served two purposes: *limmud*, study, and *tokhaḥa*, rebuke. As for the element of study, one of the dimensions of HaKalir's *piyutim* is that they are compilations of statements of the sages. Most of us, who are expert in neither Hebrew nor *aggadot Ḥazal*, find HaKalir's corpus of *piyutim* boring. But it is not boring at all; it is like a gold mine. His *piyutim* for Yom Tov explain the essence of the Yom Tov. The midrashim concerning Sukkot are replete with information about the *sukka*, *etrog* and *lulav*, and all the explanations in the Midrash, all the *ta'amei sukka*, the reasons for the *sukka*, all of the *ma'amarei Ḥazal*, are brought together in HaKalir's *piyutim* for the first day of Sukkot. Similarly, his *piyutim* for Rosh HaShana and Yom Kippur include all the homiletical literature concerning the statement in the Midrash, "On Rosh HaShana, Sarah, Rachel and Hannah were remembered" (*Bereshit Raba* 73:1). If one were to study carefully and thoroughly the *piyutim* of Rabbi Elazar HaKalir for Rosh HaShana, Yom Kippur, Sukkot and Pesaḥ, one would find many applicable halakhot and the entire pertinent Midrash, including many midrashim that are unknown to us from any other source.

It is quite possible that during the time of Roman and Byzantine rule in the land of Israel, the ruling authorities prohibited *shiurim* and afternoon

lectures by Torah scholars and sent officers to the synagogues on Yom Tov afternoon to prevent the people from studying. Consequently, the rabbis introduced the study of Torah into the prayer service via *piyutim*, a subterfuge that eluded the authorities. The *piyutim* were deliberately written in a fashion that would make them difficult to understand, lest the officers recognize their true function and forbid their recitation. As previously noted, we do not know with certainty when Rabbi Elazar HaKalir lived. According to *Tosafot* (*Ḥagiga* 13a, s.v. *veraglei haḥayyot*), he was the *tanna*, Rabbi Elazar HaGadol, who lived in the second century, but according to other *Rishonim*, he was either an *amora* or one of the early liturgical poets, from the sixth or seventh century. But his *piyutim* could certainly have served the purpose of integrating Torah study into the prayers in a way that would not have been obvious to the non-Jewish authorities.

וְלָמָּה בְּנֵי בְלִיַּעַל חִלְּלוּ שְׁמָךְ *Why, then, do knaves profane Your name.* Why do You tolerate the sinners? "*Lama*, why," is tantamount to "*eikha*," the recurring question. But the answer is provided in the very next *kina*, "*Lekha Hashem hatzedaka*, Yours, O Lord, is the righteousness."

כַּאֲשֶׁר יִשָּׂא הָאֹמֵן אֶת הַיֹּנֵק *As a nursemaid rears a suckling child.* This phrase is a quote from *Parashat Beha'alotekha* (Numbers 11:12), and note that the verse refers to a *yonek*, a nursing infant, not to a *yeled*, a child. This is because for a child, the burden on the parent is not total. Although a *yeled* still needs supervision, he can walk, eat, and take care of his basic needs on his own. But in the case of a *yonek*, the mother must provide for all of the the baby's needs. Similarly, God is like an *omen* with regard to *Yisrael*, like the mother who does everything for the infant.

אַתָּה טֵאטֵאתָ שִׁשִּׁים וּשְׁמוֹנִים *You swept sixty, and then eighty.* This phrase is an allusion to the verse in Song of Songs, "There are sixty queens and eighty concubines" (6:8). The Midrash on Song of Songs comments (6:4) that the concubines represent the nations of the world. God swept away all the nations of the world and chose Israel.

וְלָמָּה זָמְמוּ מוֹאָבִים וְעַמּוֹנִים *Why, then, have Moabites and Ammonites schemed.* This phrase is an allusion to the verse in Lamentations, "For she has seen that heathens are entered into her Sanctuary, concerning whom You did command that they should not enter into Your congregation" (1:10) and to the comment of *Ḥazal* that this refers to Ammon and Moab (Midrash *Eikha Petiḥta* 9; 1:4).

כּוֹנַנְתָּ מָרוֹם מֵרִאשׁוֹן *You established an exalted Temple from the beginning.* You established the *Beit HaMikdash* prior to the creation of the world.

וְלָמָה נִאֵץ רָשָׁע *Why, then, has the wicked one scorned.* How did You tolerate the blasphemy of Titus?

עַד כִּי נָגַע צַר בְּאִישׁוֹן *Until the foe touched the pupil of the eye.* Titus cut through the *parokhet* and it began to bleed (*Gittin* 56b). When blood began to flow, he thought that he, God forbid, had touched the pupil of the eye of God and injured Him.

וְאָמַר אֵי אֱלֹהֵימוֹ *Saying, "Where is their God."* Titus was the one who uttered this (*Gittin* 56b).

אַתָּה קָדוֹשׁ, יוֹשֵׁב תְּהִלּוֹת קְדוֹשִׁים / בְּסוֹד יְשִׁישִׁים מְקֻדָּשִׁים *You are holy, enthroned by the praises of the holy, by the council of sainted elders.* This appears to be in accordance with a strange custom on Tisha B'Av mentioned in *Masekhet Sofrim* (18:10) that *Barekhu*, Kaddish and *Kedusha* are not recited on Tisha B'Av until Minḥa when, for the first time on Tisha B'Av, we say the *Kedusha* of Ve'ata kadosh yoshev tehillot Yisrael. This custom was known in the time of the Geonim, as well. Nahmanides, however, declares, "We do not follow this custom" (*Sefer Torat HaAdam*, [Chavel edition], page 259). The *Shulḥan Arukh* follows Nahmanides' position.

יְשִׁישִׁים מְקֻדָּשִׁים *Sainted elders.* This is a reference to the Great Sanhedrin.

וְלָמָה רָגְשׁוּ גוֹיִם קְדֵשִׁים *Why, then, do profane nations agitate.* The word *kedeshim* is juxtaposed to the word *kedoshim* in the previous phrase. They are similar phonetically but they differ in orthography. *Kadosh*, the root of *kedoshim*, means holy, sacred. *Kadesh*, the root of *kedeshim*, means a perverted or immoral person, which is how the pagans are referred to in this phrase.

וְלָמָה תְבַלַּע *Why, then, have You devoured.* This is a petition to God: Why do You destroy?

תַּצְמִיחַ תְּרוּפָה וְעָלֵינוּ חוּפָּה *Let healing sprout and shelter us.* This is a plea to God to heal us and protect us.

אַתָּה צַדִּיק עַל כָּל הַבָּא *You are right with regard to all that has happened.* This phrase represents *tzidduk hadin*, the acknowledgment that God is righteous despite all of the unanswerable questions that are posed.

Kinot is replete with questions: "*Eikha*? How is it possible? We do not

understand." Throughout the year we do not ask any questions. But on Tisha B'Av, it is permissible to ask questions because of the precedent of *Sefer Eikha*. The fact that Jeremiah (who spoke *beru'ah hakodesh*,) posed the question of *eikha*, confirms that one may ask questions.

But the *kina* does not prolong the questioning. Immediately after asking the question, we receive the answer. And the answer, beginning with the phrase "*ata tzaddik al kol haba*" and continuing in the next *kina*, is *tzidduk hadin*. We are quick to acknowledge that it is our fault and our responsibility. We are sinful and God is just; He is charitable; He is compassionate. In fact, *tzidduk hadin* is found within the book of Lamentations: "The LORD is righteous; For I have rebelled against His word" (1:18), and "Wherefore does a living man complain, a strong man because of his sins? Let us search and examine our ways and return to the LORD. Let us lift up our heart with our hands to God in the heavens. We have transgressed and rebelled; You have not pardoned." (3:39–42).

וְלָמָּה נָהִינוּ וְלָנוּ הַדִּבָּה *Why, then, do we complain and lament.* The intent of this phrase is that we are simply gossipers. What we have said until this point is nothing but gossip.

כִּי כָל זֹאת בָּאַתְנוּ בְּחוֹבָה *When all this has befallen us because of our sins.* This phrase is Rabbi Elazar HaKalir's *tzidduk hadin*. We deserve whatever happened to us because we are responsible. Until this point, all was *eikha*, and now comes *tzidduk hadin* and *teshuva*. The Gemara concludes (*Shabbat* 55a) that in the days of the prophet Ezekiel, *zekhut avot*, the merit of the patriarchs ceased to exist. Rabbeinu Tam (*Tosafot* s.v. *uShmuel*) asks, "How can one say that *zekhut avot* has terminated? After all, in the Amida we say 'God of Abraham, God of Isaac and God of Jacob.' If *zekhut avot* has ceased to exist, the Amida would have to be changed." Rabbeinu Tam responds that there are two different catagories, *zekhut avot* and *berit avot*, the covenant with the patriarchs. *Zekhut avot* has terminated, but *berit avot* has not.

The fact that God loved Abraham, Isaac and Jacob does not mean that He has to continue to give that love to us. We did not act like the patriarchs. Our image and likeness have changed. We have sinned and defiled ourselves. The emotions He had for the patriarchs, the *zekhut avot*, lasted to the time of the destruction of the First Temple and the time of Ezekiel, but not beyond.

Berit avot, however, is different. *Berit avot* is not based on emotions. It is a contract, a covenant. The Jewish people obligates itself to God, and God, as

it were, obligates Himself to the Jewish people. Thus Rabbeinu Tam's view is that when one says "*Elokei Avraham, Elokei Yitzḥak, ve'Elokei Ya'akov*" in the Amida, the intent is not that God should love us because He loved Abraham. Rather, the intent is that He signed an agreement with Abraham that is valid and binding for us as well. The covenantal community is an eternal one. Proof of Rabbeinu Tam's view that *berit avot* is everlasting is from the verse, "Then will I remember My covenant with Jacob, and also My covenant with Isaac, and also My covenant with Abraham will I remember" (Leviticus 26:42). The Torah does not specify any time limit to the *berit avot*.

Berit avot is the motif of this *kina*. From the perspective of *zekhut avot*, this *kina* is meaningless because we are not like our ancestors, and God's love for us has died. But from the perspective of *berit avot*, "וְאַתָּה אָמַרְתָּ הֵיטֵב אֵיטִיב עִמָּךְ" means not just that God promised, but rather, God, as it were, has incurred a legally binding contractual obligation, because for God, *amira*, the process of saying something, as it were, constitutes *hitḥayvut*, the incurrence of an obligation. Thus, the entire argument of this *kina* is *keritut berit*, the entering into of a covenant; that it is an obligation on the part of God to redeem us and not to desert us. Each of the statements in the *kina*, "אַתָּה גִדַּלְתָּ וְרוֹמַמְתָּ בָנִים", "אַתָּה זָנַחְתָּ וַתִּמְאַס כָּל גּוֹי" and "אַתָּה הֵינַקְתָּ דְּבַשׁ מִסֶּלַע", constitutes a *keritut berit*. The same concept of *berit avot* is found in *Seliḥot* as well. We say, "*zekhor lanu berit avot ka'asher amarta*, remember the *berit avot* as You have said," not "*zekhor lanu zekhut avot*." The *berit avot* is eternal.

19

לְךָ With You, O Lᴏʀᴅ, is the right:
with the wondrous signs You performed then and now.
And the shame is on us:
for the trials by which You tested us, that we failed,
    so that You rejected us.

לְךָ With You, O Lᴏʀᴅ, is the right:
You took a nation from the midst of a nation, with miracles.   *Deut. 4:34*
And the shame is on us:
Treacherously, we were found to have emulated their ways.

לְךָ With You, O Lᴏʀᴅ, is the right:
when God Himself redeemed a nation for Himself.   *II Sam. 7:23*
And the shame is on us:
for we rebelled at the Sea of Reeds, a nation sinning against its God.

לְךָ With You, O Lᴏʀᴅ, is the right:
when we remember that You designated us witnesses to Your divinity.
And the shame is on us:
when we blasphemed at Sinai, saying to Aaron, "Come, make us a god!"   *Ex. 32:1*

לְךָ With You, O Lᴏʀᴅ, is the right:
for You allowed us to taste the honey-sweet biscuits.   *Ex. 16:31*
And the shame is on us:
when we offered fine flour, oil, and honey to the idol.

לְךָ With You, O Lᴏʀᴅ, is the right:
when You sustained us with manna, and the well,
    and the pillar of cloud.
And the shame is on us:
when our forefathers complained in their tents
    about the miserable food.

לְךָ With You, O Lᴏʀᴅ, is the right:
we lacked nothing in the wilderness.
And the shame is on us:
for the disgraceful way in which we despised the manna,
    rebelled along with Korah, and sinned, surfeited with gold,
    before the golden calf, all as is written.

19

This kina is based on Daniel 9:7, the verse which also begins the Seliḥot service in the Ashkenazic tradition. The first line of each stanza starts with "With You, O LORD, *is the right" "לְךָ יהוה הַצְּדָקָה...," and the second with "And the shame is on us" "...וְלָנוּ בֹּשֶׁת הַפָּנִים בְּ," with each subsequent word following the alphabet. Commentary for this kina begins on page 396.*

לְךָ יהוה הַצְּדָקָה, בְּאוֹתוֹת אֲשֶׁר הִפְלֵאתָ, מֵאָז וְעַד עָתָּה.
וְלָנוּ בֹּשֶׁת הַפָּנִים, בִּבְחִינָה אֲשֶׁר נִצְרַפְנוּ, וְאוֹתָנוּ תִּעֵבְתָּ:

דברים ד, לד
לְךָ יהוה הַצְּדָקָה, בְּגוֹי מִקֶּרֶב גּוֹי לָקַחְתָּ בְּמַסּוֹת.
וְלָנוּ בֹּשֶׁת הַפָּנִים, בְּדֳפִי אֲשֶׁר נִמְצָא בָנוּ, כְּמַעֲשֵׂיהֶם עָשׂוֹת:

שמואל ב ז, כג
לְךָ יהוה הַצְּדָקָה, בְּהָלְכוּ אֱלֹהִים לִפְדּוֹת לוֹ לְעָם.
וְלָנוּ בֹּשֶׁת הַפָּנִים, בְּוַיַּמְרוּ עַל יַם סוּף, גּוֹי בֵּאלֹהָיו בְּפִשְׁעָם:

לְךָ יהוה הַצְּדָקָה, בְּזֵכֶר וְאַתֶּם עֵדַי וַאֲנִי אֱלֹהִים.
שמות לב, א
וְלָנוּ בֹּשֶׁת הַפָּנִים, בְּחָרְפֵנוּ בְּסִין, קוּם עֲשֵׂה לָנוּ אֱלֹהִים:

שמות טז, לא
לְךָ יהוה הַצְּדָקָה, בְּטַעַם שֶׁהִטְעַמְתָּנוּ כְּצַפִּיחַת בִּדְבָשׁ.
וְלָנוּ בֹּשֶׁת הַפָּנִים, בְּיוֹם הִקְרַבְנוּ לְפָנָיו, סֹלֶת וָשֶׁמֶן וּדְבָשׁ:

לְךָ יהוה הַצְּדָקָה, בְּכַלְכּוּל מָן וּבְאֵר וְעַמּוּד עָנָן.
וְלָנוּ בֹּשֶׁת הַפָּנִים, בְּלֶחֶם הַקְּלֹקֵל, אֲבוֹתֵינוּ בְּאָהֳלֵיהֶם בְּרָגְנָן:

לְךָ יהוה הַצְּדָקָה, בַּמִּדְבָּר לֹא חָסַרְנוּ דָּבָר.
וְלָנוּ בֹּשֶׁת הַפָּנִים, בִּנְאָצוֹת לָבָן וַחֲצֵרוֹת וְדִי זָהָב, כְּמִדְבָּר:

לְךָ With You, O Lord, is the right:
against Sihon, Og, and the kingdom of Canaan.
And the shame is on us:
for Achan, who took for himself from the booty for no good reason.

לְךָ With You, O Lord, is the right:
for You wrought fourteen saviors [the Judges].
And the shame is on us:
for we sinned with the idol of Micah.

לְךָ With You, O Lord, is the right:
for erecting Shiloh, Nob, Gibeon, and the eternal abode [of Jerusalem].
And the shame is on us:
for the wickedness within us, destroying them, to our embarrassment.

לְךָ With You, O Lord, is the right:
for we survived, despite the two destructions caused by our greed.
And the shame is on us:
as we return to You wholeheartedly,
    hoping that You will return to us in mercy.

לְךָ With You, O Lord, is the right:
for the nine hundred years during which You
    suppressed hatred for our sins.
And the shame is on us:
as Daniel implored, "Incline Your ear, my God, and hear." *Dan. 9:18*

Kina 20 starts on page 406.

לְךָ יהוה הַצְּדָקָה, בְּסִיחוֹן וְעוֹג וְכֹל מַמְלְכוֹת כְּנָעַן.
וְלָנוּ בְּשֶׁת הַפָּנִים, בְּעָכָן אֲשֶׁר מָעַל בַּחֵרֶם, בְּלִי מָצָא מַעַן:

לְךָ יהוה הַצְּדָקָה, בְּפֹעַל אֲשֶׁר פָּעַלְתָּ, בְּאַרְבָּעָה עָשָׂר מוֹשִׁיעִים.
וְלָנוּ בְּשֶׁת הַפָּנִים, בְּצֶלֶם מִיכָה בּוֹ אֲנַחְנוּ פּוֹשְׁעִים:

לְךָ יהוה הַצְּדָקָה, בְּקִימַת שִׁילֹה וְנוֹב וְגִבְעוֹן וּבֵית עוֹלָמִים.
וְלָנוּ בְּשֶׁת הַפָּנִים, בְּרֶשַׁע שֶׁנִּמְצָא בָּנוּ שֶׁחָרְבוּ, וּבָם אָנוּ נִכְלָמִים:

לְךָ יהוה הַצְּדָקָה, בִּשְׁנֵי חָרְבָנוֹת שֶׁחָרְבוּ בְּבִצְעֵנוּ, וְאָנוּ קַיָּמִים.
וְלָנוּ בְּשֶׁת הַפָּנִים, בְּשׁוּבֵנוּ אֵלֶיךָ בְּכָל לֵב, שֶׁתָּשׁוּב אֵלֵינוּ בְּרַחֲמִים:

לְךָ יהוה הַצְּדָקָה, בִּתְשַׁע מֵאוֹת שָׁנָה, שֶׁהָיְתָה שְׂנָאָה כְּבוּשָׁה מִלְהַשְׁמֵעַ.
וְלָנוּ בְּשֶׁת הַפָּנִים, כִּטְבַע אִישׁ חֲמוּדוֹת, וְשׁוּעַ, הַטֵּה אֱלֹהַי אָזְנְךָ וּשֲׁמָע: דניאל ט, יח

Kina 20 starts on page 407.

COMMENTARY ON KINA 19

The previous *kina* posed eleven questions, and this *kina* responds immediately with twelve answers, each with the phrase *lekha Hashem hatzedaka*.

לְךָ יהוה הַצְּדָקָה...וְלָנוּ בֹּשֶׁת הַפָּנִים *With You, O* LORD, *is the right… And the shame is on us.* This phrase constitutes acknowledgment of God's justice, which is the ultimate answer to the question posed by "*eikha*." This response is what the Gemara seeks of people in times of crisis, the acknowledgment "בָּרוּךְ דַּיַּן אֱמֶת, Blessed be the true Judge" (*Berakhot* 54a). The destruction of the *Beit HaMikdash* was due to the accumulated sinful history of the Jewish people dating back to the complaints of the Jews at the Red Sea where, upon seeing the Egyptians in pursuit, they said, "What have You done to us, to take us out of Egypt?" (Exodus 14:11). The *kina* begins with this complaint, and mentions all the sins throughout Jewish history until the time of the Ḥurban.

לְךָ יהוה הַצְּדָקָה, בְּאוֹתוֹת אֲשֶׁר הִפְלֵאתָ *With You, O* LORD, *is the right: with the wondrous signs You performed.* This phrase refers to the bestowal of God's grace upon the Jewish people and the performance of miracles for them.

וְלָנוּ בֹּשֶׁת הַפָּנִים, בְּדֹפִי *And the shame is on us: Treacherously….* The Jewish people were guilty of ingratitude.

כְּמַעֲשֵׂיהֶם עָשׂוֹת *Emulated their ways.* The Jewish people imitated the despicable behavior of the Egyptians. Hence, they should not be treated any differently than the Egyptians. The *boshet hapanim*, shame, being described by the *kina* is not just that God bestowed kindness and *later* the people sinned. The idea the *paytan* wants to convey is that the Jewish people were thankless *at the very time* that God was expressing kindness to them. At the very time of the exodus from Egypt, לָנוּ בֹּשֶׁת הַפָּנִים... כְּמַעֲשֵׂיהֶם עָשׂוֹת, many of the Jews imitated the Egyptians.

לְךָ יהוה הַצְּדָקָה, בְּהָלְכוּ אֱלֹהִים לִפְדּוֹת *With You, O* LORD, *is the right: when God Himself redeemed.* God Himself descended into Egypt, and He redeemed the people by splitting the Red Sea.

בַּיַּמְרוּ עַל יָם סוּף *For we rebelled at the Sea of Reeds.* The Midrash (*Shemot Raba* 24, s.v. *vayasa Moshe*) comments that this refers to the Jews taking the idol of Micah with them across the Red Sea. But the simple interpretation is that the Jewish people did not want to go to the land of Israel, as the Torah recounts, "And the children of Israel cried out to the LORD. And they said to Moses:

'Because there were no graves in Egypt have you taken us away to die in the wilderness?'" (Exodus 14:10–11).

It is noteworthy that the Jews said this at the time when every one of them, even the simplest person, experienced the revelation of the *Shekhina* as the Midrash states, "At the sea, the maidservant saw that which Ezekiel the prophet was not able to see even through a prophetic vision" (*Mekhilta, Beshallaḥ* 3, s.v. *zeh Keli*). The *giluy Shekhina* was present at the Red Sea, and one could actually point to it and say, "This is my God, and I will glorify Him" (Exodus 15:2). And yet, in spite of the *giluy Shekhina*, they complained and said, "Let us make a leader and let us return to Egypt" (Numbers 14:4). The *kina* again points out that the people turned against God at the very moment that He was performing *ḥesed* for them.

לְךָ יהוה הַצְּדָקָה, בְּזָכֵר וְאַתָּם עֵדַי *With You, O Lord, is the right: when we remember that You designated us witnesses.* This occurred at the time of the giving of the Torah.

וְלָנוּ בֹּשֶׁת הַפָּנִים...קוּם עֲשֵׂה לָנוּ אֱלֹהִים *And the shame is on us… "Come, make us a god!"* This is a reference to the golden calf. Simultaneously with the giving of the Torah, the people deserted God and worshiped the golden calf.

בְּיוֹם הִקְרַבְנוּ לְפָנָיו, סֹלֶת וָשֶׁמֶן וּדְבַשׁ *When we offered fine flour, oil, and honey to the idol.* The word לְפָנָיו refers to the golden calf. It is interesting that HaKalir describes מִנְחַת נְסָכִים (an accompanying meal and libation offering), while the Torah refers to זְבָחִים (animal sacrifices) being offered to the golden calf: "and they offered *olot* (burnt-offerings) and brought *shelamim* (peace-offerings)" (Exodus 32:6). One possible explanation is that since a *minḥa* offering generally accompanies a *zevaḥ*, the Jews offered a מִנְחַת נְסָכִים to the golden calf as well. In all likelihood, however, HaKalir's source is from Ezekiel's description of idol worship, "You also took your beautiful things of My gold and My silver, which I had given you, and you made for yourself images of men … and you took your richly woven garments and covered them, and you set My oil and My incense before them. My bread also which I gave you, fine flour, oil and honey which I fed you, you even set it before them for a sweet savor, and thus it was; declares the Lord God" (Ezekiel 16:17–19). Actually, the way this phrase in the *kina* is written is misleading, and I would change it to "בְּיוֹם הִקְרַבְנוּ לִפְנֵי עֲבוֹדָה זָרָה סֹלֶת וָשֶׁמֶן וּדְבַשׁ."

One might also suggest that the word לְפָנָיו refers to God, and that the transgression being described violates the Torah's prohibition, "For you shall not

COMMENTARY ON KINA 19

turn into smoke any leaven or honey, as an offering made by fire to the LORD" (Leviticus 2:11). The problem with this interpretation is that we do not find any evidence in scripture that the Jews did this, and we therefore do not know any source that Rabbi Elazar HaKalir might have had for this statement.

לְךָ יהוה הַצְּדָקָה, בְּכַלְכּוּל מָן וּבְאֵר וְעַמּוּד עָנָן *With You, O LORD, is the right: when You sustained us with manna, and the well, and the pillar of cloud.* According to the Gemara (*Ta'anit* 9a), this is a reference to Moses (the manna), Aaron (the pillar of cloud) and Miriam (the well).

If one interprets מָן as a literal reference to the manna, this appears to be repetitious because the *kina* has already referred to God's *ḥesed* in giving the manna with the phrase, "בְּטַעַם שֶׁהִטְעַמְתָּנוּ כְּצַפִּיחִת בִּדְבָשׁ, For You allowed us to taste the honey-sweet biscuits." However, this earlier reference to the manna expresses God's separate *ḥesed* that, miraculously, according to Ḥazal, the manna could taste like anything one desired (*Sifrei Bemidbar* 87). In this second phrase, however, the emphasis is simply on the fact that He sustained us, as כַּלְכּוּל means sustenance.

אֲבוֹתֵינוּ בְּאָהֳלֵיהֶם בְּרָגְנָן *When our forefathers complained in their tents.* This phrase refers to the verse "And the people were as *mitonenim*, murmurers" (Numbers 11:1). Essentially, this verse in the Torah is the starting point of the episode of the *meraglim*, spies, which we commemorate on Tisha B'Av. If not for the *mitonenim*, the incident of the *meraglim* would never have taken place, and the entire history of the Jews would have been different. Immediately before the *mitonenim*, Moses was ready to enter the land of Israel, as he said to Jethro, "come with us and we will do you good; for the LORD has spoken good concerning Israel" (Numbers 10:29). However, the *mitonenim* came, and the entry to Israel was postponed. In the meantime the idea of the *meraglim* arose, and that changed the entire destiny of *Klal Yisrael*. Therefore, "בְּאָהֳלֵיהֶם בְּרָגְנָן" is indirectly responsible for Tisha B'Av.

לְךָ יהוה הַצְּדָקָה, בַּמִּדְבָּר לֹא חָסַרְנוּ דָבָר. וְלָנוּ בֹּשֶׁת הַפָּנִים, בְּנָאֲצוּת לָבָן וַחֲצֵרוֹת וְדִי זָהָב *With You, O LORD, is the right: we lacked nothing in the wilderness. And the shame is on us: for the disgraceful way in which we despised the manna, rebelled along with Korah, and sinned, surfeited with gold, before the golden calf.* Again the *kina* emphasizes that the Jewish people did not appreciate the kindnesses of God at the very time He was bestowing them. "לֹא חָסַרְנוּ דָבָר" is an allusion to the verse, "לֹא חָסַרְתָּ דָּבָר, You have lacked nothing" (Deuteronomy 2:7).

כְּמִדְבָּר *As is written.* The word כְּמִדְבָּר means "the way these words were in-

terpreted in the Midrash." דִּי זָהָב, חֲצֵרוֹת and לָבָן were interpreted to refer not to names of geographic locations, but to historical events, actual episodes of transgressions that Moses was mentioning, such as the golden calf and the spies. The one who composed the cantillation for the Torah had the same interpretation. The *te'amim*, the cantillation, on these words are *pazer, telisha gedola, kadma ve'azla* and *darga tevir*. The solemn sounds of the *te'amim* indicate that what is involved is not simple place names, but episodes that changed the course of Jewish history.

In accordance with the interpretation that these words refer to events in Jewish history rather than geographical locations, our sages say that דִּי זָהָב means "too much gold" and refers to the sin of the golden calf. This relates to a statement in the Gemara (*Berakhot* 32a) which HaKalir apparently had in mind even though the reference is not explicit. The Gemara states that Moses' defense of the Jewish people at the time of the golden calf was: "Master of the Universe, it is because of the silver and gold that You granted the Jews in abundance until they said 'enough,' that they made the golden calf." In effect, Moses was saying that God granted the Jews too much prosperity. As the saying goes, a lion roars not when one feeds him with straw, but when one feeds him with meat. The Jews made the golden calf because they had too much gold, and if God had given them less gold, they would not have made the golden calf. This same idea also applies to the verses from Ezekiel cited above in the context of the offering of *shemen* and *devash*. God is saying, "I gave you the *devash*, I gave you the *shemen*, I gave you the wine, I gave you the fancy clothes, and you turned them all over to *avoda zara*."

לְךָ יהוה הַצְּדָקָה, בְּסִיחוֹן וְעוֹג וְכֹל מַמְלְכוֹת כְּנָעַן. וְלָנוּ בֹּשֶׁת הַפָּנִים, בְּעָכָן אֲשֶׁר מָעַל בַּחֵרֶם *With You, O* Lord, *is the right: against Sihon, Og, and the kingdom of Canaan. And the shame is on us: for Achan, who took for himself from the booty*. An understanding of the conceptual connection between Sihon, Og and the kings of Canaan on the one hand, and the story of Achan on the other, clarifies the intent of the *paytan* in this stanza. The halakha was that in the battles against the seven Canaanite nations, the Jewish soldiers were permitted to take from the booty, including even forbidden foods (*Ḥulin* 17a). The only exception to this rule was the booty from Jericho, on which Joshua placed a total prohibition, a *ḥerem*, because he consecrated it to God. Achan, therefore, could have assembled a vast quantity of wealth, including jewelry, gold and garments, in a permissible fashion. He could have eaten forbidden foods to his heart's content had he wanted to. But Achan wanted to "have it all" – the

permissible booty, and also the prohibited booty of Jericho. The intent of the *paytan* in this stanza is, לְךָ יהוה הַצְּדָקָה, in permitting the Jews to enjoy the booty, and וְלָנוּ בֹּשֶׁת הַפָּנִים, we are embarrassed by Achan who could have had almost everything, but that was not enough for him.

The transgression of Adam was analogous. God told Adam, "Of every tree of the garden you may freely eat, but of the tree of knowledge of good and evil, you shall not eat of it" (Genesis 2:16–17). In effect, God was saying to Adam, "Do not complain later. Do not defend yourself and say that you had to eat from the tree of knowledge because you were hungry. After all, 'of every tree of the garden you may freely eat.' I issued a prohibition as to just one tree. As a result there cannot possibly be any emergency that would justify your action or mitigate your sin should you eat from the tree of knowledge." But Adam had boundless desire, and he could not tolerate that of the hundreds of trees, one was not available to him. He wanted *all* the trees to be his.

בְּעָכָן אֲשֶׁר מָעַל בַּחֵרֶם *For Achan, who took for himself from the booty.* There is *tzidduk hadin* not only for collective transgressions, but for the transgressions of an individual, as well. Achan's transgression was committed by an individual, but the community was responsible because of the principle *kol yisrael arevim zeh bazeh*, all Jews are responsible one for the other (*Shavuot* 39a; *Sanhedrin* 27b).

בְּלִי מְצֹא מַעַן *For no good reason.* Achan could not explain his actions or apologize. God was offended that Achan did not try to justify himself.

בְּאַרְבָּעָה עָשָׂר מוֹשִׁיעִים *Fourteen saviors.* This is a reference to the fourteen *shoftim*, judges, during the period from Joshua to Samuel.

בְּצֶלֶם מִיכָה *With the idol of Micah.* Only one individual was responsible for the idol of Micah, but, as with Achan, the entire community accepts responsibility for the transgressions of the individual.

בּוֹ אֲנַחְנוּ פּוֹשְׁעִים *For we sinned.* The literal translation of this phrase is, "For we are sinning." The present tense is difficult to understand because those alive today are not the ones responsible for the transgression of *pesel Mikha*. The *paytan* should have used the past tense.

בְּקִימַת שִׁילֹה וְנוֹב וְגִבְעוֹן וּבֵית עוֹלָמִים *For erecting Shiloh, Nob, Gibeon, and the eternal abode [of Jerusalem].* The *Mikdash* stood in Gilgal for fourteen years, in Shiloh for three hundred and sixty-nine years and in Nob and Gibeon for fifty-two years. The *kina* does not mention Gilgal, however, because Gilgal

was not destroyed and did not experience Ḥurban. In fact, as a conceptual matter, Gilgal did not have the status of an independent site of the *Mikdash*. It was simply an extension of the wandering of the *Mishkan* in the desert when the Holy Ark was taken from place to place. During the fourteen years of conquest and division of the land of Israel, the *Mikdash* of Gilgal was identical to the *Mishkan* in the desert. After this period came to an end, Joshua was instructed to move the Holy Ark to Shiloh, which, unlike Gilgal, had the status of a separate site of the *Mikdash*. Subsequently, Shiloh was destroyed by the Philistines, and Nob was destroyed by Saul. Gibeon apparently also was destroyed, but not Gilgal.

Another reason that Gilgal is not mentioned here is that the root of the word בְּקִימַת means "erected," and Gilgal was not erected. The site of the *Mikdash* at Shiloh was constructed, and, apparently, at Nob and Gibeon, as well. No construction, however, took place at Gilgal. The *Mishkan* was simply placed there the way it was in the desert.

וְלָנוּ בֹּשֶׁת הַפָּנִים, בְּרֶשַׁע שֶׁנִּמְצָא בָנוּ שֶׁחָרְבוּ, וּבָם אָנוּ נִכְלָמִים *And the shame is on us: for the wickedness within us, destroying them, to our embarrassment.* The intent of this stanza is to highlight that it was not only our ancestors who sinned and were punished with the Ḥurban of the *Beit HaMikdash*, but we too are sinners in this regard. The *kina* refers to the evil that is found within *us*. Every day that the *Beit HaMikdash* lies in ruins, *we* are responsible for it. "Every generation in whose time the *Beit HaMikdash* is not rebuilt, is as though the *Beit HaMikdash* was destroyed in its time" (Talmud Yerushalmi, *Yoma* 5:1). The *Beit HaMikdash* should have been rebuilt many years ago, but has not been rebuilt because *we* are not deserving. The text of the *kina* should read "וּבָם אָנוּ עֲדַיִן נִכְלָמִים, we are *still* embarrassed," because the continuation of the Ḥurban is an indictment of *our* generation, not only the generation of our ancestors.

בִּשְׁנֵי חָרְבָנוֹת שֶׁחָרְבוּ בְּבִצְעֵנוּ, וְאָנוּ קַיָּמִים *For we survived, despite the two destructions caused by our greed.* The שְׁנֵי חָרְבָּנוֹת, the destructions of the First and Second Temples, are distinguished from Shiloh, Nob and Gibeon. Of course, these other Ḥurbanot were tragedies as well, but they were just temporary phenomena which were forgotten and dismissed from the collective national memory of the Jewish people. The destruction of Shiloh, Nob and Gibeon did not precipitate any *avelut*, mourning. But the שְׁנֵי חָרְבָּנוֹת affected the whole unfolding of Jewish history. Unlike the destruction of Shiloh, Nob and Gibeon, the שְׁנֵי חָרְבָּנוֹת have been integrated and assimilated into the memory of the Jewish people as real and eternal experiences.

The *kina* refers to two destructions because our sages tell us (*Yalkut Shimoni* 1:469, s.v. *vetaval*) that the Second Temple was not equivalent to the First Temple. The verse says (Ezra 3:12) that those who witnessed the First Temple wept at the dedication ceremonies for the Second Temple, because it neither compared to, nor was it a substitute for, the First Temple. Furthermore, by the time of the Second Temple, it is probable that the major part of the Jewish people lived outside the land of Israel. The situation at the time of the Second Temple was vastly different from what it had been during the First Temple.

Each phrase that begins with לְךָ יהוה הַצְּדָקָה recounts an instance of kindness, of *ḥesed*, that God bestowed upon the Jewish people. This phrase of "לְךָ יהוה הַצְּדָקָה בִּשְׁנֵי חָרְבָּנוֹת" expresses *tzidduk hadin*, the concept that God is just in that He destroyed both Temples. However, this particular לְךָ יהוה הַצְּדָקָה also expresses an element of thanks, in that although the two Temples were destroyed, still וְאָנוּ קַיָּמִים, the Jewish people continue to exist. This thought is echoed in the saying of our sages (*Eikha Raba* 4, s.v. *kala Hashem*): "The psalm says 'מִזְמוֹר לְאָסָף', a praise of Asaf' [Psalms 79], but shouldn't it say 'קִינָה לְאָסָף', a lamentation of Asaf'? However, it is because He wrought His anger on wood and stones." Essentially, the Jewish people deserved to be destroyed, but instead of destroying the people, God destroyed the *Beit HaMikdash*. Thus, paradoxically, the *Ḥurban* turns out to be an expression of the *ḥesed* of God for the Jewish people.

This concept of the *Beit HaMikdash* serving as the collateral for the Jewish people, which is a recurring theme in the *kinot*, explains why the mourning on Tisha B'Av subsides in the afternoon, and the *neḥama*, the consolation, commences. Our sages say (*Ta'anit* 29a) that it was late on the afternoon of Tisha B'Av that the enemy set fire to the *Beit HaMikdash*. One would have thought that at this point the level of mourning should increase rather than subside. Apparently, however, until that point during the course of the day of Tisha B'Av, God had not decided whether or not to destroy the Jewish people, and after Minḥa, He finally decided to take the collateral, the *Beit HaMikdash*, and permit the people to survive. Thus, once the *Beit HaMikdash* was set ablaze, there was no longer any threat to the existence of the Jewish people.

וְלָנוּ בֹּשֶׁת הַפָּנִים, בְּשׁוּבֵנוּ אֵלֶיךָ בְּכָל לֵב, שֶׁתָּשׁוּב אֵלֵינוּ בְּרַחֲמִים *And the shame is on us: as we return to You wholeheartedly, hoping that You will return to us in mercy.* The standard interpretation is that we are embarrassed that we have missed many opportunities to come back to God, although He is ready to accept

and embrace us at any time. This is consistent with the recurring theme in the *kina* of וְלָנוּ בֹּשֶׁת הַפָּנִים, that we are ungrateful and do not understand God's kindness. However, the real meaning of this instance of וְלָנוּ בֹּשֶׁת הַפָּנִים is different from its previous uses in this *kina*. Here it is to be understood in a positive sense. It refers to the *busha*, the embarrassment, which is an element of *teshuva*. *Teshuva* requires that one regret the act of transgression to such an extent that one feels a sense of shame. Maimonides mentions this aspect of *teshuva* in his requirement that the individual recite, "And I regret and am ashamed of my actions" (*Mishneh Torah*, Hil. Teshuva 1:1). Thus, this penultimate וְלָנוּ בֹּשֶׁת הַפָּנִים expresses the positive idea of the Jewish people declaring that they are ashamed and embarrassed בְּשׁוּבֵנוּ אֵלֶיךָ, that they feel the way God wants them to feel when they do *teshuva*, שֶׁתָּשׁוּב אֵלֵינוּ בְּרַחֲמִים, so that God will return to them.

בְּתִשַׁע מֵאוֹת שָׁנָה *For the nine hundred years.* Although some are of the opinion that Rabbi Elazar HaKalir lived in the sixth or seventh century, one could infer from this phrase that he lived in the tenth century, nine hundred years after the Ḥurban. The reference to nine hundred years is also found earlier in the *kinot* of HaKalir, in his *piyut*, or *kerova*, to be said as part of the *Shemoneh Esreh* in Shaḥarit for the morning of Tisha B'Av. In the stanza for the letter *alef*, he writes "אֲאַבִּין תְּשַׁע מֵאוֹת, I ponder that nine hundred years have passed, and the Messiah has not yet appeared." This selection is further evidence that HaKalir may have lived in the tenth century.

Alternatively, nine hundred years could refer to the period from the time the Jews entered the land of Israel until the destruction of the First Temple.

שֶׁהָיִיתָ שׂנְאָה כְּבוּשָׁה מִלְּהַשְׁמַע *During which You suppressed hatred for our sins.* Yet another interpretation of the nine-hundred-year period is that it refers to the period from King Solomon to the destruction of the Second Temple. The four hundred and ten years of the First Temple, plus the seventy years between the two Temples, plus the four hundred and twenty years of the Second Temple, equal nine hundred years (*Seder Olam Raba*, ch. 27–30). The Gemara in *Sanhedrin* states (21b; see also *Bemidbar Raba* 10:4) that, strictly speaking, the *Beit HaMikdash* should have been destroyed the very moment King Solomon married the daughter of Pharaoh. When King Solomon completed the *Beit HaMikdash*, God told him that if he will observe His laws, He will reside in the House that Solomon built for Him (1 Kings 9:3–9). But Solomon sinned with his marriage to the daughter of Pharaoh. The sages say that the keys to the *Beit HaMikdash* were entrusted to Solomon, but he

overslept the day after he married the daughter of Pharaoh, and the priests were unable to bring the daily sacrifice on time. Thus the *Beit HaMikdash* was doomed from that day. Nevertheless, God granted a reprieve through an act of *ḥesed* and extended the existence of the *Beit HaMikdash*. The phrase in the *kina* is an allusion to the Midrash (*Vayikra Raba* 7:1), "קָרוֹב לִתְשַׁע מֵאוֹת שָׁנָה הַשִּׂנְאָה כְּבוּשָׁה בֵּין יִשְׂרָאֵל וּבֵין אֲבִיהֶם שֶׁבַּשָּׁמַיִם, for close to nine hundred years, the acrimony between Israel and their Father in heaven was restrained."

The phrase לְךָ יהוה הַצְּדָקָה in this stanza refers not only to the kindness of God in extending the existence of the *Beit HaMikdash*. It also expresses our acknowledgment that the persecution and deep-seated hatred by the non-Jews for nine hundred years is not an indication of our righteousness. *We were not right, You were right.*

Although the literal translation of the word שִׂנְאָה is "hatred," its intent in this phrase is different. Rather, it has the same sense as "כִּי שְׂנוּאָה לֵאָה" (Genesis 29:31), which does not mean that Jacob hated Leah, rather that he did not love Leah the way he loved Rachel. It means limited or restricted love, a love which was "כְּבוּשָׁה מִלְּהִשָּׁמַע," which literally means "was hidden from being pronounced." In this phrase in the *kina*, שִׂנְאָה refers to His *midat hadin*, the attribute of strict judgment. Even though there was good reason to condemn the *Beit HaMikdash* to immediate destruction, God suppressed His *midat hadin* and did not pronounce judgment. And because God controlled his *midat hadin*, the *Beit HaMikdash* stood, with an interruption of seventy years, for nine hundred years.

הַטֵּה אֱלֹהַי אָזְנְךָ וּשְׁמָע "Incline Your ear, my God, and hear." This phrase is included in the daily *Taḥanun* prayer, and it continues with "כִּי לֹא עַל־צִדְקֹתֵינוּ, For it is not based on our righteousness that we cast down before You our petitions, but rather based on Your abundant mercy." This corroborates the interpretation mentioned above that "וְלָנוּ בֹּשֶׁת הַפָּנִים" here is not to be understood in a negative sense, as an accusation against the Jewish people. On the contrary, it means that even though the Jewish people are sinners, nevertheless they are embarrassed and ashamed. They are in utter despair and want to come back.

40

10:1 Incline Your ear, my God, to the earth, and lift up Your eyes
       Which rest in the Heavens:
    And hear the shouting of Your adversaries crying,
    Risen is Israel, down to the foundations of the gates of heaven.

10:2 Incline Your ear, my God, to the crown which grew
       about the Righteous One with corruption.
    And hear the victorious shouts of Rome
       shouting their own downfall.

10:3 Incline Your ear, my God, to the envoy who was sent and said:
       Let her rise up against Israel's pride,
    And it is the stories in a house who so that the gate has come
       to defend it with him in His House.

10:4 Incline Your ear, my God, to those who, so disposed, had
       plotted to do the impossible,
    And hear the conversation of those with counsel together
       and plans to line up against You.

10:5 Incline Your ear, my God, to those who, in sacrilege
       unto the truth the massacre's temple,
    And hear those who revile You and silence their singing
       and the sound of songs.

10:6 Incline Your ears, my God, to the soul that cries to You
    And hear the pleas that they have flung at You
       and cause Your faith to fall upon them.

20

הַטֵּה Incline Your ear, my God, to the fearful and scandalous cry,
    "Whom need I fear in heaven?" *Ps. 73:25*
  And hear the shouting of Your adversaries saying,
    "Raze it, raze it down to the foundations" of the gates of heaven. *Ps. 137:7*

הַטֵּה Incline Your ear, my God, to the crowd which speaks
    about the Righteous One with contempt.
  And hear the clamorous sounds of Rome,
    silencing their outpour of wrath.

הַטֵּה Incline Your ear, my God, to the envoy who was sent and said,
    "Up! Let us rise up against her in battle!" *Ob. 1:1*
  And hear the horror of those who say that the time has come
    to do battle with Him in His House.

הַטֵּה Incline Your ear, my God, to those who schemed and
    plotted to do the impossible.
  And hear the conversation of those who counsel together, *Ps. 83:6*
    intending to rise up against You.

הַטֵּה Incline Your ear, my God, to those who, in sacrilege,
    put to the torch the awesome Temple.
  And hear those who revile You and silence thanksgiving
    and the sound of song. *Is. 51:3*

הַטֵּה Incline Your ear, my God, to the scoffers eager to scoff. *Prov. 1:22*
  And hear the abuse that they have flung at You *Ps. 79:12*
    and cause Your fear to fall upon them.

20

This kina, the last of a sequence of fifteen kinot by HaKalir, is based on Daniel 9:18, the culmination of Daniel's prayer. The first line of each stanza starts with "Incline Your ear, my God" "...הַטֵּה אֱלֹהַי אָזְנְךָ לְ," and the second with "And hear" "וּשְׁמַע," with each subsequent word following the alphabet in reverse. Commentary for this kina begins on page 410.

הַטֵּה אֱלֹהַי אָזְנְךָ, לְתִפְלֶצֶת מְנֹאֶצֶת, מִי לִי בַשָּׁמָיִם. תהלים עג, כה
וּשְׁמַע שַׁאֲגַת צוֹרְרֶיךָ, הָאוֹמְרִים עָרוּ עָרוּ עַד הַיְסוֹד, שַׁעַר הַשָּׁמָיִם: תהלים קלז, ז

הַטֵּה אֱלֹהַי אָזְנְךָ, לְרָגְשַׁת הַדּוֹבֶרֶת עַל צַדִּיק עָתָק.
וּשְׁמַע קוֹל שָׁאוֹן מֵעִיר, בְּחֵמָה שְׁפוּכָה לְשַׁתֵּק:

הַטֵּה אֱלֹהַי אָזְנְךָ, לְצִיר שָׁלַח, וְגַם קוּמוּ וְנָקוּמָה עָלֶיהָ לַמִּלְחָמָה. עובדיה א, א
וּשְׁמַע פְּלַצּוּת הוֹמִים, בָּא הָעֵת, אִתּוֹ בְּבֵיתוֹ לְהִלָּחֲמָה:

הַטֵּה אֱלֹהַי אָזְנְךָ, לְעֵצוּ עֵצָה וְחָשְׁבוּ מְזִמָּה, בַּל יוּכָלוּ.
וּשְׁמַע שִׂיחַת נוֹעֲצוּ לֵב יַחְדָּו, עָלֶיךָ עֵלוֹת נִסְתַּכָּלוּ: תהלים פג, ו

הַטֵּה אֱלֹהַי אָזְנְךָ, לְנִאֲצוּ וְשִׁלְּחוּ בָאֵשׁ מִקְדַּשׁ הַמּוֹרָא.
וּשְׁמַע מְחָרְפֶיךָ, מַדְמִימֵי תוֹדָה וְקוֹל זִמְרָה: ישעיה נא, ג

הַטֵּה אֱלֹהַי אָזְנְךָ, לְלֵצִים לָצוֹן חָמְדוּ לָהֶם. משלי א, כב
וּשְׁמַע כָּל חֶרְפָּתָם אֲשֶׁר חֵרְפוּךָ, וְהַפֵּל אֵימָתְךָ עֲלֵיהֶם: תהלים עט, יב

הַטֵּה Incline Your ear, my God, to those who arrogantly put the
   Cherubim on display in the streets.
  And hear the irksome defilement as they offered
   swine upon Your altar.

הַטֵּה Incline Your ear, my God, to those who have profaned
   and dirtied the House of the Holy of Holies.
  And hear the knaves who fling up to You the circumcised
   parts of the sainted ones.

הַטֵּה Incline Your ear, my God, to the brazen aliens who say,
   "Let us wage war with Him in His House."
  And hear those who derisively say that the *Prov. 7:19*
   Man is not in His home.

הַטֵּה Incline Your ear, my God, to he who proclaims,
   "I am, and there is none but me." *Is. 47:8*
  And hear the heresy and blasphemy of those who boast
   even against Your throne.

הַטֵּה Incline Your ear, my God, to those who taunt and mock,
   "Why hope for what will never be rebuilt?"
  And hear the tears of those who grieve, rend their clothes,
   and await its rebuilding.

הַטֵּה Incline Your ear, my God, to those who say it is forsaken,
   forgotten, abandoned, and forever desolate.
  And hear our cries, be zealous for our cause, and shine
   Your countenance upon Your desolate Sanctuary. *Dan. 9:17*

Kina 21 starts on page 414.

הַטֵּה אֱלֹהַי אָזְנְךָ, לְיָהֲרוּ וְהוֹצִיאוּ הַכְּרוּבִים בִּרְחוֹבוֹת מַחֲזִירִים.
וּשְׁמַע טְרָחוֹת טְנוּפָם, כְּהֶעֱלוּ עַל מִזְבַּחֲךָ חֲזִירִים:

הַטֵּה אֱלֹהַי אָזְנְךָ, לְחִלְּלוּ וְטִנְּפוּ בֵּית קֹדֶשׁ הַקֳּדָשִׁים.
וּשְׁמַע זֵדִים מְזָרְקִים לְמוּלְךָ מִילוֹת קְדוֹשִׁים:

הַטֵּה אֱלֹהַי אָזְנְךָ, לְוֹעֲזִים מְעִיזִים מֵצַח, לְכוּ וְנִלָּחֲמָה אִתּוֹ בְּבֵיתוֹ.
וּשְׁמַע הַוּוֹת הוֹלְלִים מְהַלְלִים, כִּי אֵין הָאִישׁ בְּבֵיתוֹ: משלי ז, יט

הַטֵּה אֱלֹהַי אָזְנְךָ, לְדוֹבֶרֶת אֲנִי וְאַפְסִי עוֹד. ישעיה מז, ח
וּשְׁמַע גִּדּוּפֶיהָ וְחֵרוּפֶיהָ, מִשְׁתַּחֲצֶת עַד כִּסְאֲךָ עוֹד:

הַטֵּה אֱלֹהַי אָזְנְךָ, לְבוּזָה וּמֻלְעֶגֶת, מַה תּוֹחִילִי וְאֵינוּ נִבְנֶה.
וּשְׁמַע בְּכִית מַסְפִּידִים וְקוֹרְעִים, וּמְחַכִּים מָתַי יִבָּנֶה:

הַטֵּה אֱלֹהַי אָזְנְךָ, לְאוֹמְרִים עָזַב וְשָׁכַח וְנָטַשׁ, וְלָעַד שׁוֹמֵם.
וּשְׁמַע אֶנְקָתֵנוּ, וְקַנֵּא קִנְאָתֵנוּ, וְהָאֵר פָּנֶיךָ עַל מִקְדָּשְׁךָ הַשָּׁמֵם: דניאל ט, יז

Kina 21 starts on page 415.

COMMENTARY ON KINA 20

This *kina* by Rabbi Elazar HaKalir is directed against Christian Rome and the Church, not ancient Rome, and concerns *Ḥilul Shem Shamayim*, the desecration of God's name, and *Ḥilul Knesset Yisrael*, the desecration of the Jewish people. Perhaps the main motif of this *kina* can be characterized as חִלּוּל שֵׁם הַגָּדוֹל שֶׁל הַקָּדוֹשׁ בָּרוּךְ הוּא בַּגּוֹיִם, the desecration of the great name of God among the nations of the world, and that this desecration can only be brought to an end and transformed to קִדּוּשׁ שְׁמוֹ הַגָּדוֹל, the sanctification of His great name, by the rebuilding of Jerusalem and the *Beit HaMikdash*.

עָלֶיךָ עֲלוֹת נִסְתַּכְּלוּ *Intending to rise up against You.* The thrust of the *paytan*'s thought is that it is not a war of the enemy against Israel, but of the enemy against God.

מִדַּמְּמֵי תוֹדָה וְקוֹל זִמְרָה *And silence thanksgiving and the sound of song.* They silenced the *Kedusha* prayer, the *toda*, the thanksgiving, and the voice of *zimra*, of song. This clearly refers to the prohibition by Byzantium against the recitation of *Keriat Shema* and *Kedusha* during the regular prayers. This is the reason that *Keriat Shema* was later introduced into the *Kedusha* of Musaf on Shabbat and why *Kedusha* is repeated in the *Kedusha deSidra* of *Uva Letzion* (see *Minhagei Yeshurun* 64).

וְהוֹצִיאוּ הַכְּרוּבִים בִּרְחוֹבוֹת מְחַזְרִים *Who arrogantly put the Cherubim on display in the streets.* This describes an event that occurred during the destruction of the First Temple. As noted above in connection with the *kina* "וְאַתָּה אָמַרְתָּ הֵיטֵב אֵיטִיב," our sages say (*Yalkut Shimoni* 1:474 s.v. *anokhi*) that during the destruction, soldiers of Ammon and Moab removed the cherubs from the Holy of Holies, displayed them and said, "This is the people which takes pride in the fact that their God is not visible, and yet look at their God. They too were idol-worshipers."

כְּהֶעֱלוּ עַל מִזְבַּחֲךָ חֲזִירִים *As they offered swine upon Your altar.* In fact, there is no record in the *Aggada* that the Romans attempted to sacrifice swine on the altar. We do know, however, from the book of Maccabees (1:1:50) that during the period of the Hellenists, it was precisely this act of offering swine on the altar that precipitated the rebellion of the Maccabees and the killing of Holofernes by Judith. One could interpret this reference in the *kina* as an allusion to the story of the Maccabean period. Alternatively, one does not have to view the Maccabean revolt as separate from the war with the Romans or from

any other struggle of the Jewish people for survival. Rather, each of these battles is part of one long war, beginning with the attack of Amalek (Exodus 17:8) down to the time of Hitler and the Arab attempt to obliterate Israel.

וְשָׁמַע זֵדִים מְזָרְקִים לְמוּלְךָ מִילוֹת קְדוֹשִׁים *And hear the knaves who fling up to You the circumcised parts of the sainted ones.* This is an allusion to the Midrash (*Tanḥuma Ki Tetzeh* 14) on the verse, "All the stragglers in your rear" (Deuteronomy 25:18), which describes the attack of Amalek. The Midrash comments, "This teaches that they took the circumcised organs of the Jews and threw them toward the heavens." Although Amalek is equivalent to Edom, and Edom is equivalent to Rome, we have no source that similar mutilation occurred during the destruction of the Temple. Apparently HaKalir did have a source for this.

כִּי אֵין הָאִישׁ בְּבֵיתוֹ *That the Man is not in His home.* They denied the presence of God, as if He had disappeared and absented Himself from the midst of *Knesset Yisrael*.

לְדוֹבֵרֶת אֲנִי וְאַפְסִי עוֹד...עַל מִקְדָּשְׁךָ הַשָּׁמֵם *To he who proclaims, "I am, and there is none but me"... upon Your desolate Sanctuary.* These concluding stanzas of the *kina* constitute a rendition of the blasphemy of the Church vis-à-vis the Jews. This *kina* addresses Christian Rome, not ancient Rome.

מִשְׁתַּחֲצֶת עַד כִּסְאֲךָ עוֹד *Those who boast even against Your throne.* The intent here is that the Church is insolent. The *kina* refers to the theme that God has abandoned the Jews, which was first developed by Justin Martyr in the second century and became a permanent motif of Christian theology. It is the common argument of the Christians against the Jews.

הַטֵּה אֱלֹהַי אָזְנְךָ, לְבוֹזָה וּמַלְעֶגֶת *Incline Your ear, my God, to those who taunt and mock.* Note the sarcasm here. This refers to those who treat the Jewish people with contempt, and ridicule their expectations and hopes.

מַה תּוֹחִילִי *"Why hope...."* Rabbi Elazar HaKalir recounts how the enemies of the Jews used to ridicule the Jews and say, "What are you hoping for?"

וְאֵינוֹ נִבְנֶה *"For what will never be rebuilt?"* This portrays the arrogant Christian argument that the *Beit HaMikdash* will never be restored, that God has left the Jews and is now with the Christians.

The basic opposition of the Christians to the State of Israel and to the fact that the Jews have returned to Israel is not based on anti-Semitism. The reason for such opposition is that the existence of the State of Israel and the

Jewish presence in the land of Israel contradict the essential Christian dogma that the Jew has lost his right to the land. This dogma was developed by Justin Martyr and remains central to the theology of the Catholic Church to this day. The fact that Jews control any portion, no matter how small, of the land of Israel is contrary to basic Christian theology.

וּמְחַכִּים מָתַי יִבָּנֶה *And await its rebuilding.* In spite of the ridicule and contempt of the blasphemers, we wait every day for the rebuilding of the *Beit HaMikdash*.

הַטֵּה אֱלֹהַי אָזְנְךָ, לְאוֹמְרִים עָזֻב וְשָׁכֻחַ וְנָטֻשׁ, וְלָעַד שׁוֹמֵם *Incline Your ear, my God, to those who say it is forsaken, forgotten, abandoned, and forever desolate.* Once again, this expresses the theology of the Catholic Church, that the Temple will remain forever abandoned, that all the promises made to the prophets are forfeited, that the Jews have lost their privilege, and that God will never restore His relationship with the Jewish people. The truth is, however, that although the *Beit HaMikdash* has not yet been rebuilt, Jerusalem is being rebuilt – and conceptually, Jerusalem is not merely a city, it is an integral part of the *Beit HaMikdash*. The "עָזֻב וְשָׁכֻחַ וְנָטֻשׁ וְלָעַד שׁוֹמֵם" is not true.

Rabbi Elazar HaKalir could not have portrayed the attitude of the Church toward the land of Israel more accurately than he did with this phrase of "עָזֻב וְשָׁכֻחַ וְנָטֻשׁ וְלָעַד שׁוֹמֵם." We do not know with certainty where Rabbi Elazar HaKalir lived. One view is that he lived in Israel as evidenced by the fact that he composed no *piyutim* for the second day of Rosh HaShana and apparently did not observe it. This is one of the proofs brought by the Rishonim (Rabbi Asher, *Berakhot* 5:21) that in the time of HaKalir, Rosh HaShana was observed for only one day in Israel. In any event, perhaps in Israel he became exposed to Byzantine theology, and this was his source of knowledge of the basic tenets of Christianity.

21

lines form an acrostic, first of the alphabet, and then of the author's name, "מאיר בן יחיאל חזק ואמץ, יחיה בן יחיאל," *identifying him as Rabbi Meir ben Yeḥiel, an Ashkenazic rabbi of the early thirteenth century. Commentary for this kina begins on page 418.*

א Cedars of Lebanon, masters of Torah,
ב shield bearers in Mishna and Gemara,
ג powerful heroes, toiling in purity:
ד Their blood is spilled like water, and their strength, sapped.
ה They are ten holy ones, martyred by the kingdom.
ו For them, I cry, and my eyes flow with tears.

ז When I remember this, I cry a great and bitter cry.
ח Israel's delight, holy vessels, a wreath and a crown,
ט pure of heart, holiest of holy, slaughtered in horrible death.

י They cast lots to determine who would first be chosen for the sword.
כ When the lot fell upon Rabban Shimon [ben Gamliel],
he stretched his neck and cried, accepting the decree.
ל The executioner turned to Rabban Shimon,
killing him with pent-up fury.

מ The descendant of Aaron [Rabbi Yishma'el]
begged to be allowed to grieve for the prince.
נ [Rabbi Yishma'el] took [Rabban Shimon's]
head and placed it upon his knees, as if it were a pure Menora.
ש Placing his eyes upon his eyes, and his mouth upon his
mouth with sincere love,
ע he proclaimed, "A mouth, vigorous with Torah,
פ suddenly condemned to a horrible and freakish death!"

צ [The prelate] ordered to flay his head with a sharpened razor.
ק He fulfilled with his skin the saying,
"Get down, that we may walk over you!"   *Is. 51:23*
ר The villain did the flaying, and as he reached the place of the special commandment of tefillin,
ש [Rabbi Yishma'el] let out a scream, causing the world
to shake and the earth to tremble.
ת "His merit will stand for all generations,"
said the voice of God in His glory.

21

This kina describes the martyrdom of the Aseret Harugei Malkhut, the ten sages who were martyred by the Romans in the middle of the second century CE. The theme was a common one among paytanim, appearing as early as the tenth century (Seder Rav Sa'adia Gaon). The

אַרְזֵי הַלְּבָנוֹן, אַדִּירֵי הַתּוֹרָה.
בַּעֲלֵי תְרִיסִין בְּמִשְׁנָה וּבִגְמָרָא.
גִּבּוֹרֵי כֹחַ, עֲמֵלֶיהָ בְּטָהֳרָה.
דָּמָם נִשְׁפַּךְ כַּמַּיִם, וְנַשְׁתָּה גְּבוּרָה.
הֵם קְדוֹשֵׁי הֲרוּגֵי מַלְכוּת, עֲשָׂרָה.
וְעַל אֵלֶּה אֲנִי בוֹכִיָּה, וְעֵינִי נִגְּרָה:

זֹאת בְּזָכְרִי, אֶזְעַק זְעָקָה גְּדוֹלָה וּמָרָה.
חֶמְדַּת יִשְׂרָאֵל, כְּלֵי הַקֹּדֶשׁ, נֵר וַעֲטָרָה.
טְהוֹרֵי לֵב, קָדְשֵׁי קָדָשִׁים, שְׁחִיטָתָן בְּמִיתָה חֲמוּרָה:

יַדּוּ גוֹרָל, מִי רִאשׁוֹן לַחֶרֶב בְּרוּרָה.
כְּנָפַל גּוֹרָל עַל רַבָּן שִׁמְעוֹן, פָּשַׁט צַוָּארוֹ וּבָכָה כִּנְגֻזְרָה גְּזֵרָה.
לְרַבָּן שִׁמְעוֹן חָזַר הַהֶגְמוֹן, לְהָרְגוֹ בְּנֶפֶשׁ נְצוּרָה:

מִזֶּרַע אַהֲרֹן שָׁאַל בְּבַקָּשָׁה לִבְכּוֹת עַל בֶּן הַגְּבִירָה.
נָטַל אֶת רֹאשׁוֹ, וּנְתָנוֹ עַל אַרְכֻּבּוֹתָיו, מְנוֹרָה הַטְּהוֹרָה.
שָׂם עֵינָיו עַל עֵינָיו, וּפִיו עַל פִּיו בְּאַהֲבָה גְּמוּרָה.
עָנָה וְאָמַר, פֶּה הַמִּתְגַּבֵּר בַּתּוֹרָה.
פִּתְאוֹם נִקְנְסָה עָלָיו מִיתָה מִשְׁנֶה וַחֲמוּרָה:

צִוָּה לְהַפְשִׁיט אֶת רֹאשׁוֹ הַמֶּלֶךְ, בְּתַעַר הַשְּׂכִירָה.
קָם בְּעָוְרוֹ, אָמְרוּ לְנַפְשֵׁךְ, שְׁחִי וְנַעֲבֹרָה.
רָשָׁע הַפּוֹשֵׁט, עֵת הִגִּיעַ לִמְקוֹם תְּפִלִּין, מִצְוָה בָּרָה.
שָׁמַע צְעָקָה, וְנִזְדַּעְזְעוּ עוֹלָם, וְאֶרֶץ הִתְפּוֹרְרָה.
תַּעֲמֹד זְכוּתוֹ לְדוֹרוֹת, קוֹל יהוה בֶּהָדָר:

ישעיה נא, כג

מֵאַחֲרָיו Afterwards, they brought Rabbi Akiva, uprooter of mountains, who ground one against the other with his intellect. / They combed his flesh with an iron comb to break it. / His soul departed with the word "One," and a heavenly voice said, / "Rabbi Akiva, you are fortunate; your body is pure in every manner of purity."

בֶּן Rabbi Yehuda ben Bava, they brought in with a broken heart and a warning, / killed at age seventy by the cursed evil kingdom. / He fasted frequently, was clean and pious, and was diligent in his work.

חֲנַנְיָא After him was Rabbi Ḥananya ben Teradyon, assembler of great crowds at Zion's gate. / Sitting and teaching, a Torah scroll at his side, they enveloped him with bundles of twigs / and set them afire, winding the Torah scroll around him and lighting a bonfire. / They attached moistened bits of wool to his heart to prolong his agony.

חָסִיד The pious Rabbi Yeshevav the Scribe was killed by this nation of Gomorrah. / They cast him, threw him to the dogs, so that he was never properly buried. / A heavenly voice declared that there was nothing in the Torah of Moses that he did not observe.

אֶת Rabbi Ḥanina ben Ḥakhinai, and after him, Rabbi Ḥutzpit, on that wrathful day. / Birds flying overhead were singed as if torched by the breath of his mouth.

צַדִּיק The righteous Rabbi Elazar ben Shamua was killed with a chisel. / It was Sabbath eve, the time for Kiddush, and as he recited it, / they drew the sword upon him, not permitting him to live to finish it. / His soul departed at the words "God created," the Creator and Sculptor of forms. *Gen. 2:3*

הִנֵּה On and on, these villains tortured and threatened. / Stoning, burning, killing, and choking; who can assess [this calamity]? / Of the remnants, lions consumed those scattered sheep! / Eaten in a sacred place like the sin-offering and guilt-offering leaving no trace, / the special offerings of breast and thigh, lion and cub devoured. / May it be good in the eyes of God to never again punish us. / Make firm the tottering knees, O Jacob's Portion, *Jer. 10:16* and Deliverer in troubled times.

לְצֶדֶק "The King shall reign in righteousness." / "Your days of mourning shall *Is. 32:1* cease." / By His light, we shall journey forward. *Is. 60:20*

Kina 22 starts on page 424.

מֵאַחֲרָיו הֵבִיאוּ אֶת רַבִּי עֲקִיבָא, עוֹקֵר הָרִים וְטוֹחֲנָן זוֹ בָּזוֹ בְּסִבְרָה.
אֶת בְּשָׂרוֹ מְסָרְקִין, בְּמַסְרֵק הַבַּרְזֶל לְהִשְׁתַּבְּרָה.
יָצְתָה נִשְׁמָתוֹ בְּאֶחָד, וּבַת קוֹל אָמְרָה.
רַבִּי עֲקִיבָא, אַשְׁרֶיךָ, גּוּפְךָ טָהוֹר בְּכָל מִינֵי טָהֳרָה:

בֶּן בָּבָא רַבִּי יְהוּדָה אַחֲרָיו הֵבִיאוּ, בְּשִׁבְרוֹן לֵב וְאַזְהָרָה.
נֶהֱרַג בֶּן שִׁבְעִים שָׁנָה, בִּידֵי רְשָׁעָה אֲרוּרָה.
יוֹשֵׁב בְּתַעֲנִית הָיָה, נָקִי וְחָסִיד בִּמְלַאכְתּוֹ לְמַהֲרָה:

חֲנַנְיָא בֶּן תְּרַדְיוֹן אַחֲרָיו, מַקְהִיל קְהִלּוֹת בְּצִיּוּן שְׂעָרָה.
יוֹשֵׁב וְדוֹרֵשׁ, וְסֵפֶר תּוֹרָה עִמּוֹ, וְהִקִּיפוּהוּ בַּחֲבִילֵי זְמוֹרָה.
אֶת הָאוּר הִצִּיתוּ בָהֶם, וְכָרְכוּהוּ בְּסֵפֶר תּוֹרָה, וּבָעֲרוּ בוֹ הַבְּעֵרָה.
לְלִבּוֹ סְפוֹגִין שֶׁל צֶמֶר הִנִּיחוּ, שֶׁלֹּא יָמוּת מְהֵרָה:

חָסִיד רַבִּי יְשֵׁבָב הַסּוֹפֵר, הֲרָגוּהוּ עִם עֲמוֹרָה.
זְקָפוּהוּ וְהִשְׁלִיכוּהוּ לַכְּלָבִים, וְלֹא הַקֶּבֶר בִּקְבוּרָה.
קוֹל בַּת יָצְאָה עָלָיו, שֶׁלֹּא הִנִּיחַ כְּלוּם מִתּוֹרַת מֹשֶׁה לְשָׁמְרָה:

אֶת רַבִּי חֲנִינָא בֶּן חֲכִינַאי, וְאַחֲרָיו רַבִּי חֲצָפִית, בְּיוֹם עֶבְרָה.
מִיַּד עוֹף הַפּוֹרֵחַ, בַּהֶבֶל פִּיו נִשְׂרַף כְּבַמְּדוּרָה:

צַדִּיק, רַבִּי אֶלְעָזָר בֶּן שַׁמּוּעַ, בָּאַחֲרוֹנָה נֶהֱרַג בַּמְּדוּקְרָה.
יוֹם עֶרֶב שַׁבָּת הָיָה, זְמַן קִדּוּשׁ, וַיְקַדֵּשׁ וַיִּקְרָא.
חֶרֶב שָׁלְפוּ עָלָיו, וְלֹא הִנִּיחוּהוּ בַּחַיִּים, לְסַיֵּם וְלִגְמֹרָה.
יָצְתָה נִשְׁמָתוֹ בְּבָרָא אֱלֹהִים, יוֹצֵר וְצָר צוּרָה: <small>בראשית ב, ג</small>

הִנֵּה כַּהֲנָא וְכַהֲנָה, הוֹסִיפוּ בְּנֵי עַוְלָה לְעַנּוֹת בִּגְעָרָה.
בִּסְקִילָה, שְׂרֵפָה, הֶרֶג וָחֶנֶק, מִי יוּכַל לְשַׁעֲרָה.
נוֹתֶרֶת מִמֶּנָּה יֹאכְלוּ אֲרָיוֹת, שֶׂה פְזוּרָה.
יֹאכְלוּהָ בְּמָקוֹם קָדוֹשׁ, כַּחַטָּאת וְכָאָשָׁם, לְאַבֵּד זִכְרָהּ.
חֲזֵה הַתְּנוּפָה וְשׁוֹק הַתְּרוּמָה, טָרְפוּ אַרְיֵה וְהַכְּפִירָה.
יִיטַב בְּעֵינֵי יהוה, וְלֹא יוֹסִיף עוֹד לְיִסְּרָה.
אַמֵּץ בִּרְכַּיִם כּוֹשְׁלוֹת, חֵלֶק יַעֲקֹב, וּמוֹשִׁיעַ בְּעֵת צָרָה: <small>ירמיה י, טז</small>

לְצֶדֶק יִמְלָךְ מֶלֶךְ / וְשָׁלְמוּ יְמֵי אֶבְלֵךְ / לְאוֹרוֹ נֵסַע וְנֵלֵךְ: <small>ישעיה לב, א
ישעיה ס, כ</small>

Kina 22 starts on page 425.

COMMENTARY ON KINA 21

This *kina* was written by an Ashkenazi, Rabbi Meir ben Yeḥiel, who was, in all likelihood, one of the German Tosafists. It is not explicitly about the destruction of the *Beit HaMikdash*, but rather about the עֲשָׂרָה הֲרוּגֵי מַלְכוּת, the ten great Torah scholars who were martyred by the Romans. Until this point in the Tisha B'Av service, the *kinot* have dealt primarily with the destruction of Jerusalem and the *Beit HaMikdash*. Now the topic of the *kinot* shifts to the martyrdom of Torah scholars, righteous individuals and communities. This group of *kinot* begins with the story of the Ten Martyrs and continues with accounts of the death and destruction during the Crusades in Germany. As was noted above in connection with the *kina* "וַיִּקוֹנֵן יִרְמְיָהוּ עַל יֹאשִׁיָּהוּ", this martyrdom is just as tragic as the destruction of the Temple, "שְׁקוּלָה מִיתָתָן שֶׁל צַדִּיקִים כִּשְׂרֵיפַת בֵּית אֱלֹהֵינוּ, the death of the righteous is comparable to the burning of the House of our God" (*Rosh HaShana* 18b).

The brutal execution of the Ten Martyrs must be seen against the backdrop of Rome's policy toward the Jews at the time of the Ḥurban and thereafter. As described above in the commentary on the *kina* "זְכֹר אֵת אֲשֶׁר עָשָׂה צַר בִּפְנִים", initially Rome did not institute any religious persecution. Rome had thought that once the *Beit HaMikdash* was destroyed, the Jewish people would assimilate into the general population. With the Bar Kokhba rebellion, however, they realized that even though they had destroyed the *Beit HaMikdash*, the Jewish community still remained loyal to God. They realized that the strength of the Jew was not dependent on the *Beit HaMikdash*, but that the Torah and the observance of mitzvot were the cohesive forces that united the Jews and made them carry on even under the worst of circumstances. A wave of persecution in the form of restrictive decrees inundated the Jewish community, and it was at that time that the first of the Ten Martyrs was killed.

The story of the Ten Martyrs is recounted twice each year, once on Tisha B'Av in this *kina* of "אַרְזֵי הַלְּבָנוֹן," and once on Yom Kippur in the *piyut* "אֵלֶּה אֶזְכְּרָה," following the *Avoda*, the description of the Temple service on Yom Kippur. Each has a different style and vocabulary. The *piyut* for Yom Kippur was written as a *seliḥa*, a penitential prayer, while the *piyut* for Tisha B'Av was written as a *kina*. In addition, the purposes and objectives for the recital of the story on Tisha B'Av and Yom Kippur are different. On Yom Kippur, the story of the Ten Martyrs is recited because our sages tell us (*Mo'ed Katan* 28a) that the death of the righteous serves as a *kapara*, an atonement, as did the sacrifices in the *Beit HaMikdash*.

It is noteworthy that the story of the Ten Martyrs is included in the Yom Kippur liturgy as part of the *Avoda*. The *Avoda* describes all the sacrifices that were brought on Yom Kippur. First there is the description of the sacrifices brought by the High Priest as part of the service in the Temple. Then, the liturgy focuses on the martyrdom of the righteous as another type of sacrifice that God considers as an atonement. Although there were thousands of these sacrifices over the years, we describe only the ten most outstanding examples. The atonement is granted to *us* because *they* made the supreme sacrifice.

Yom Kippur's theme as a day of forgiveness may be the underlying reason that the story of the Ten Martyrs recited on Yom Kippur includes a reference to the sale of Joseph by his brothers. On Yom Kippur, the day of forgiveness, one is required to articulate the transgression for which he seeks atonement. Since the sale of Joseph by his brothers was the shameful deed that set in motion the chain of events that culminated in the tragedy of the Ten Martyrs, it is explicitly mentioned in the story of the Ten Martyrs recited on Yom Kippur.

Tisha B'Av, by contrast, is not a day of atonement, but a day of mourning. If the destruction of the *Beit HaMikdash* requires mourning, it is incumbent on the Jewish people to recount on Tisha B'Av all the major catastrophes and disasters that have befallen them. The story of the Ten Martyrs is incorporated in the *kinot* as an expression of the theme of mourning.

In addition, our sages say, "The death of the righteous is equivalent to the burning of the House of our God" (*Rosh HaShana* 18b). There is a relationship between the death of the righteous and the *Hurban*. The obligation to mourn for the destruction of the *Beit HaMikdash* includes the idea that one should mourn for and mention the saintly individuals who suffered martyrdom, as well. The death of the righteous gives rise to a general *ḥiyuv avelut*, a religious obligation of mourning. And, in fact, the murder of ten of the sages of Israel is a greater catastrophe for the Jewish people than the destruction of the *Beit HaMikdash*. The *Beit HaMikdash* was built of stones. It is true that the stones were endowed with *kedusha*, holiness, but a stone remains a stone. When they killed Rabbi Akiva, however, their goal was to uproot *Knesset Yisrael*.

The formulation, emphasis, and length of the story differs between Yom Kippur and Tisha B'Av because the motifs of the two days are completely different. The version recited on Yom Kippur is longer, more elaborate and more detailed than the version recited on Tisha B'Av. As mentioned above, the theme on Tisha B'Av is mourning, not atonement. The focus is on the

catastrophic dimension of the Ḥurban and on commemorating the disaster that took away the greatest of our people. The many details which are important for the aspect of atonement on Yom Kippur are not included in the Tisha B'Av version.

אַרְזֵי הַלְּבָנוֹן, אַדִּירֵי הַתּוֹרָה *Cedars of Lebanon, masters of Torah.* The Martyrs are referred to as cedars of Lebanon because the verse in Psalms, "he shall grow like a cedar in Lebanon" (92:13), is a description of the righteous.

בַּעֲלֵי תְרִיסִין *Shield bearers.* These great scholars are described as shield bearers because they engage in the combat of Torah. Torah study involves combat because it consists of arguments and a variety of opinions; it consists of proving and disproving, confirming and rejecting. When two rabbis debate in the Gemara, they reject each other's arguments the way a shield deflects an arrow.

The story is told that Rabbi Yisrael Salanter once visited Reb Abbele Preslover, who was possessed of tremendous erudition. After they exchanged pleasantries, Reb Abbele took Rabbi Yisrael by the hand, told him to sit down, opened Tractate *Sota* and directed his attention to a particular line. Then Rabbi Yisrael opened Tractate *Nedarim* and showed Reb Abbele a line. Reb Abbele then opened Tractate *Shavuot* and showed Rabbi Yisrael a line, and Rabbi Yisrael showed him another tractate. Not a single word was exchanged. They were engaged in a struggle about a particular point of Torah study, and they simply referred each other to the printed text without explicating the importance or relevance of the texts to the question at hand. Although this story may well not be true, it is an illustration of the meaning of shield bearers in the context of Torah study. When one attacks the other, the attack is parried immediately by deploying a shield. The defender opens a Gemara and shows the attacker a line in the Gemara or a *Tosafot*, and the argument is over.

גִּבּוֹרֵי כֹחַ *Powerful heroes.* This is an allusion to the verse in Psalms, "גִּבּוֹרֵי כֹחַ עֹשֵׂי דְבָרוֹ, You mighty in strength, that fulfill His word" (103:20). The Gemara states (*Shabbat* 88a), "At the time that the Jewish people said '*Na'aseh*' before '*Nishma*' a heavenly voice emerged and said to them: 'Who disclosed to My children this secret which the angels make use of?' As it is said, 'Bless the Lord, you angels of His, you mighty in strength that fulfill His word, hearkening to the voice of His word.' First, they fulfill His word, and then they hearken."

וְעַל אֵלֶּה אֲנִי בוֹכִיָּה *For them, I cry.* This phrase is contained in a verse from Lamentations (1:16), and our sages say (*Gittin* 58a) that Jeremiah said this verse about Rabbi Yishma'el's son and daughter, who committed suicide rather than be exposed to a life of immorality. Therefore, in the context of the Ten Martyrs, the *paytan* incorporates the expression which Jeremiah used in relation to the death of the righteous.

אֶזְעַק וְזַעֲקָה גְדוֹלָה וּמָרָה *I cry a great and bitter cry.* This phrase is an allusion to the verse in Esther (4:1), "וַיִּזְעַק זְעָקָה גְדוֹלָה וּמָרָה, and he cried with a loud and bitter cry." Mordekhai cried out bitterly because the Jewish people were on the brink of disaster. And here we cry because the great scholars of Israel were destroyed.

חֶמְדַּת יִשְׂרָאֵל *Israel's delight.* As the most precious beings, the Ten Martyrs were more precious than the *Beit HaMikdash* and the holy vessels used in the *Beit HaMikdash*; more precious than the priestly garments.

כְּלֵי הַקֹּדֶשׁ, נֵזֶר וַעֲטָרָה *Holy vessels, a wreath and a crown.* The great Torah scholars are referred to as *klei sharet*, the sacred vessels used in the *Beit HaMikdash*. One of the characteristics of the *klei sharet* is that they impart *kedusha* (*Mishneh Torah*, Hil. Pesulei HaMukdashin 3:18). Thus, once ordinary oil is poured into a *kli sharet*, the oil becomes sanctified from the mere contact with the sacred vessel. Similarly, the great Torah scholars are not only saintly in their own right, but also impart sanctity to anyone who comes into contact with them. Some may become totally sanctified. Some may not respond immediately and do not change, but the impact of contact with great Torah scholars is left upon everyone who experiences it. As the Torah says "whatever touches the altar shall be holy" (Exodus 29:37).

נָטַל אֶת רֹאשׁוֹ, וּנְתָנוֹ עַל אַרְכֻּבּוֹתָיו [*Rabbi Yishma'el*] *took* [*Rabban Shimon's*] *head and placed it upon his knees.* This raises the halakhic question of how Rabbi Yishma'el, who was a *kohen*, could come into contact with the dead body of Rabban Shimon ben Gamliel, as this would result in ritual impurity. Perhaps the explanation is since Rabban Shimon ben Gamliel was the *nasi*, the prince, he had the status of a *met mitzva*, a deceased person with whom even a *kohen* is permitted to have contact. This is corroborated by the Jerusalem Talmud in *Nazir* (7:1), which says "When Rabbi Yehuda HaNasi died Rabbi Yannai announced, 'There is no *kehuna* today.'" All could have contact with his body because when a *nasi* dies, it is as though all are his relatives be-

מֵאַחֲרָיו הֵבִיאוּ אֶת רַבִּי עֲקִיבָא *Afterwards, they brought Rabbi Akiva.* The intent is that this did not happen contemporaneously, but at a later time.

עוֹף הַפּוֹרֵחַ, בַּהֶבֶל פִּיו נִשְׂרָף כִּבְמְדוּרָה *Birds flying overhead were singed as if torched by the breath of his mouth.* The Gemara (*Sukka* 28a) uses this image to describe Yonatan ben Uziel, who was the principal disciple of Hillel the Elder. But here, the *paytan* applies the description to Rabbi Ḥutzpit HaMeturgeman. All we know from the Gemara (*Kiddushin* 39b) about Rabbi Ḥutzpit HaMeturgeman is that "Aḥer," the infamous Rabbi Elisha ben Avuya, saw the tongue of the deceased Rabbi Ḥutzpit covered with dust and said, "the tongue that produced pearls licks the dust." Apparently, the *paytan* considered Yonatan ben Uziel and Ḥutzpit HaMeturgeman to be of equal stature.

יוֹם עֶרֶב שַׁבָּת הָיָה, זְמַן קִדּוּשׁ, וַיְקַדֵּשׁ וַיִּקְרָא...יָצְתָה נִשְׁמָתוֹ בְּבָרָא אֱלֹהִים *It was Sabbath eve, the time for Kiddush, and as he recited it... His soul departed at the words "God created."* The word וַיִּקְרָא refers to the customary practice of reciting the paragraph of וַיְכֻלּוּ (Genesis 2:1–3) as the first part of Kiddush on Friday night, and the phrase "יָצְתָה נִשְׁמָתוֹ בְּבָרָא אֱלֹהִים" in this *kina* is the source for "the widespread custom" mentioned by Maimonides, of reciting the paragraph of וַיְכֻלּוּ before Kiddush (*Mishneh Torah*, Hil. Shabbat 29:7). The Gemara does refer to reciting וַיְכֻלּוּ on Shabbat but not in the context of Kiddush (*Shabbat* 119b). Based on this *kina*, it appears that this paragraph was recited as part of Kiddush in the time of the Mishna. Presumably the *paytan* had a source for this.

יוֹצֵר וְצָר צוּרָה *The Creator and Sculptor of forms.* With the exception of Rabbi Elazar ben Dama, who was killed for wearing tefillin, the *paytan* does not record the specific violation of which any of the Martyrs was accused. It would appear that most of them were killed for the same reason as Rabbi Ḥanania ben Teradyon, propagation of Torah among the people.

הִנֵּה כָּהֵנָּה *On and on.* In general, we mortals do not have the right to question God's permitting evil to befall the righteous (*Menaḥot* 29b). We are, however, permitted to express these arguments on Tisha B'Av because of the precedent of Jeremiah who was permitted to say *"eikha"* on Tisha B'Av.

נוֹתֶרֶת מִמֶּנָּה יֹאכְלוּ אֲרָיוֹת, שֶׂה פְזוּרָה *Of the remnants, lions consumed those scattered sheep.* Just as sheep that are dispersed are easily devoured by lions, so too are the dispersed Jews vulnerable.

There is another dimension of interpretation embodied in this phrase. The death of the righteous is here considered as an offering of *kodshei kodoshim*, the most holy offerings. There are two *mekhaprim*, two elements of atonement, associated with *kodshei kodoshim*. The primary one is the *hakrava*, the bringing of the sacrifice, the *zerikat hadam*, the spilling of the blood on the altar. A second element, however, is *akhila*, the act of the priests eating the sacrifice, as the Gemara says, "This teaches us that the priests eat, and the owners receive atonement" (*Yevamot* 90a). The intent of this phrase is that God should consider the נוֹתֶרֶת מִמֶּנָּה יֹאכְלוּ אֲרָיוֹת שֶׂה פְזוּרָה, these devoured remnants, as if יֹאכְלוּהָ בְּמָקוֹם קָדוֹשׁ כַּחַטָּאת וְכָאָשָׁם, as if they were eaten in a sacred place as a sin-offering and a guilt-offering (Mishna *Zevaḥim* 14:8). Thus the plea of the *kina* is that Jewish people should attain both elements of atonement, the atonement of *hakrava* as well as the atonement of *akhila*.

22

הַחֲרִישׁוּ Be quiet, allow me to speak, come what may. / I will shout to You who dwells in heaven, "Violence! Pillage!" / My spirit is oppressed, and I cannot be silent. / I will scream and moan and gasp like a woman in labor. / I will compose a bitter eulogy and lament with a sigh. / The words of my roar will pour out like the sea. / I bemoan my people who have been delivered to desolation.

    I will sob as I tell my tale, and moan, / and raise my voice in distress.

אֵיךְ Happiness has ceased, and joy is gone; / every face ashen, and every head bare; / every beard shorn, and every heart pained; / ever since a brazen nation arose to dig my grave. / Cut down are my heroes who contemplate Your mighty stronghold [Torah]. / My young maidens and lads are torn to bits, / their corpses strewn like rubbish on every street corner. / My infants and babes are like lambs led to slaughter. / I will wail about this, tears upon cheek. / Join me, dejected ones of the outcast flock, / to intensify the cry and lift up the shouting. / Let the heavens wail and the earth scream! *Lam. 2:19*

    I will sob as I tell my tale, and moan, / and raise my voice in distress.

אֶרְאֶלִּים Angels! Go out and rant bitterly. / Join together in anguished lament. / The sound of a woman in labor, suffering as she delivers her firstborn. / Bemoan that people, scattered sheep; / upon them has been declared a decree / of wrath and rage and anger. / They assembled, pious and pure, / to sanctify the holy, fearful name, / encouraging the other, supportively, / to cleave in pure awe, / and not submit to alien gods. / They pitied neither lad nor lass, / nor the radiant little children. / But drawing upon superior strength, / they severed heads and sliced through spines, / and told them this message: / "We were not privileged to rear you in accordance with Torah, / so we offer you as a sacrifice, a burnt-offering. / And together with you, we will experience that light, / mysterious and hidden from every eye!"

    I will sob as I tell my tale, and moan, / and raise my voice in distress.

22

This kina describes the mass suicides which some European communities committed rather than submit to forced conversion to Christianity. The kina is comprised of five stanzas of varying length. Each stanza ends with a refrain, the first stich of which is a quote from Psalms 55:3, and the second, a paraphrasing of Jeremiah 31:14. Commentary for this kina begins on page 430.

הֶחֱרִישׁוּ מִמֶּנִּי וַאֲדַבֵּרָה, וְיַעֲבֹר עָלַי מָה.
חָמָס אֶזְעַק וָשֹׁד, לְךָ שׁוֹכֵן שָׁמַיְמָה / הֱצִיקַתְנִי רוּחִי, וְלֹא אוּכַל אֲדָמָה.
כְּיוֹלֵדָה אֶפְעֶה, אֶשְׁאַף וְאֶשֹּׁמָה / מִסְפֵּד מַר אֶעֱשֶׂה, וַאֲקוֹנֵן בְּנֵהִימָה.
דִּבְרֵי שַׁאֲגוֹתַי יִתְכוּ כַיָּמָּה / סִפְדִי עַל עֲדָתִי אֲשֶׁר נִתְּנָה לְשַׁמָּה.
אָרִיד בְּשִׂיחִי וְאָהִימָה / וְקוֹל נְהִי אָרִימָה:

אֵיךְ שָׁבַת מָשׂוֹשׂ, וְעָרְבָה שִׂמְחָה / כָּל פָּנִים פָּארוּר, וְכָל רֹאשׁ קָרְחָה.
וְכָל זָקָן גְּרוּעָה, וְעַל כָּל לֵב אֲנָחָה / מֵאָז נִתְעוֹרֵר גּוֹי עַז, כּוֹרָה שׁוּחָה.
סִלָּה אַבִּירַי, הוֹגֵי עֹז מִבְטָחָה / בְּתוּלוֹתַי וּבַחוּרַי נֻסַּח בְּנָסִיחָה.
בְּרֹאשׁ כָּל חוּצוֹת נִבְלָתָם כַּסּוּחָה / עוֹלָלַי וְטַפַּי נֶחְשְׁבוּ כְּצֹאן טִבְחָה.   איכה ב, יט
אֵילֵילָה עַל זֹאת, וְדִמְעָתִי עַל לֶחָה / הֵאָסְפוּ אֵלַי, דְּוָיֵי צֹאן נִדָּחָה.
לְהַרְבּוֹת הַבְּכִי וּלְהָרִים הַצְּוָחָה / הֵילִילוּ שָׁמַיִם וְזַעֲקִי אֲדָמָה:
אָרִיד בְּשִׂיחִי וְאָהִימָה / וְקוֹל נְהִי אָרִימָה:

אֶרְאֶלִּים צָאוּ, וְצַעֲקוּ מָרָה / סְפֹד תַּמְרוּר, הָאָגְדוּ בַחֲבוּרָה.
קוֹל כְּחוֹלָה, צָרָה כְּמַבְכִּירָה / הִתְאוֹנְנוּ עַל עֲדַת שֶׂה פְזוּרָה.
עֲלֵימוֹ כִּי נִגְזְרָה גְּזֵרָה / בָּחֳרִי אַף וָזַעַם וְעֶבְרָה.
וְנִתְוַעֲדוּ בִּפְרִישׁוּת וּבְטָהֳרָה / לְקַדֵּשׁ שֵׁם הַגָּדוֹל וְהַנּוֹרָא.
וְאִישׁ אֶת אָחִיו חִזְּקוּ בְעֶזְרָה / לְהִדָּבֵק בְּיִרְאָה טְהוֹרָה / בְּלִי לִכְרֹעַ לַעֲבוֹדָה זָרָה.

וְלֹא חָסוּ עַל גֶּבֶר וּגְבִירָה / עַל בָּנִים צְפִירַת תִּפְאָרָה.
אֲבָל אָזְרוּ גְּבוּרָה יְתֵרָה / לַהֲלֹם רֹאשׁ, וְלִקְרֹעַ שִׁזְרָה.
וְאֵלֵימוֹ דִּבְּרוּ בַּאֲמִירָה / לֹא זָכִינוּ לְגַדֶּלְכֶם לְתוֹרָה / נַקְרִיבְכֶם כְּעוֹלָה וְהַקְטָרָה.
וְנִזְכֶּה עִמָּכֶם לָאוֹרָה / הַצְּפוּנָה מֵעֵין כֹּל, וַעֲלוּמָה:
אָרִיד בְּשִׂיחִי וְאָהִימָה / וְקוֹל נְהִי אָרִימָה:

אָז The great and the small all consented / to lovingly accept the judgment of the One who dwells on high. / The elders, full of vigor and vitality, / were the first to be condemned. / The brazen ones came upon them, / and masses, masses, were massacred, / innards and entrails intermingled. / And fathers, once compassionate, / turned cruel like ostriches, / and cast lots over fathers and sons. / And the one fated to be first / was slaughtered with daggers and knives. / And young lads, reared on silk, / licked the dust like snakes. / And brides, bedecked in scarlet, / swooned in the arms of grooms, / hacked by swords and spears. / Remember this, sage people, / and do not refrain from amplifying lamentation, / and mourn the pious and the just / who sank into the seething waters. / Remembering this, my soul is aggrieved.

I will sob as I tell my tale, and moan, / and raise my voice in distress.

תּוֹרָה Torah, Torah, wrap yourself in sackcloth, and wallow in the dust! / Mourn, *Jer. 6:26* as if for an only child, a bitter lament / for those who gripped your oars and spread your nets; / sailors and mariners on mighty waters. / Those who arranged your arrangements and straightened that which was twisted, / uncovered your secrets and revealed your mysteries. / Who will level the hills, and who will hew down the mountains? / Who will solve puzzles, and who will repair breaches? / Who will articulate Nazirite vows, and who will assess the value of your pledges? / Who will plow your fields, now that the farmers are gone? / Who will wage your wars and return to the gates? / The weapons are lost, the heroes have fallen. / Fortunate are they, wise and radiant like the sky; / in peaceful repose, rest the righteous. / Woe and alas, plunder and blunder, to the survivors! / Disillusionment, pangs, and pain. / Disappointment, death, and chaos. / In the evening, they say, "Would that it were dawn," / and in the morning, they await the removal of light, / because of the picture that their eyes have seen. / Outside, the sword slays, and indoors, there is terror.

אָז הִסְכִּימוּ גְדוֹלִים וּקְטַנִּים / לְקַבֵּל בְּאַהֲבָה, דִּין שׁוֹכֵן מְעוֹנִים.
וּזְקֵנִים דְּשֵׁנִים וְרַעֲנַנִּים / הֵם הָיוּ תְּחִלָּה נְדוֹנִים.
וְיָצְאוּ לִקְרָאתָם עַזֵּי פָנִים / וְנֶהֶרְגוּ הֲמוֹנִים הֲמוֹנִים / וְנִתְעָרְבוּ פְּדָרִים עִם פַּרְשְׁדוֹנִים.
וְהָאָבוֹת, אֲשֶׁר הָיוּ רַחֲמָנִים / נֶהְפְּכוּ לְאַכְזָר כַּיְעֵנִים / וְהֵפִיסוּ עַל אָבוֹת וְעַל בָּנִים.
וּמִי שֶׁגּוֹרָל עָלָה לוֹ רִאשׁוֹנִים / הוּא נִשְׁחַט בַּחֲלָפוֹת וְסַכִּינִים.
וּבַחוּרִים, עֲלֵי תוֹלָע אֱמוּנִים / הֵם לָחֲכוּ עָפָר כְּתַנִּינִים.
וְהַכַּלּוֹת לְבוּשׁוֹת שָׁנִים / מְעֻלָּפוֹת בִּזְרוֹעוֹת חֲתָנִים / מְנֻתָּחוֹת בְּחֶרֶב וְכִידוֹנִים.
זִכְרוּ זֹאת, קְהַל עֲדַת נְבוֹנִים / וְאַל תֶּחֱשׁוּ מֵהַרְבּוֹת קִינִים.
וְהַסְפִּידוּ עַל חֲסִידִים וַהֲגוּנִים / אֲשֶׁר צָלְלוּ בַּמַּיִם הַזֵּידוֹנִים.
לְזֵכֶר זֹאת, נַפְשִׁי עֲגוּמָה.
אָרִיד בְּשִׂיחִי וְאָהִימָה / וְקוֹל נְהִי אָרִימָה:

תּוֹרָה תּוֹרָה חִגְרִי שַׂק, וְהִתְפַּלְּשִׁי בָּאֵפֶר / אֵבֶל יָחִיד עֲשִׂי לָךְ, מִסְפַּד תַּמְרוּרִים.   ירמיה ו, כו

עַל תּוֹפְשֵׂי מְשׁוֹטַיִךְ וּפוֹרְשֵׂי מִכְמוֹרִים / מַלָּחַיִךְ וְחֹבְלַיִךְ בְּמַיִם אַדִּירִים.
עוֹרְבֵי מַעֲרָבֵךְ, מְיַשְּׁרֵי הַדּוּרִים / מְפַעַנְחֵי צְפוּנַיִךְ וּמְגַלֵּי מִסְתּוֹרִים.
מִי יָקְצֶה בִּגְבָעוֹת, וּמִי יְסַתֵּת בֶּהָרִים / מִי יְפָרֵק הֲוָיוֹת, וּמִי יְתָרֵץ שְׁבָרִים.
מִי יַפְלִיא נְזִירוֹת, וּמִי יַעֲרֹךְ נְדָרִים / מִי יְשַׂדֵּד מַעֲמַקַּיִךְ, וְחַתּוּ אַפְרִים.
וּמִי יִלְחַם מִלְחַמְתֵּךְ וְיָשׁוּב לַשְּׁעָרִים / כְּלֵי מִלְחָמָה אָבָדוּ, וְנָפְלוּ גִבּוֹרִים:
אַשְׁרֵיהֶם מַשְׂכִּילִים, כָּרָקִיעַ זוֹהֲרִים / בִּמְנוּחוֹת שָׁלוֹם נָחוּ יְשָׁרִים.
אוֹי וַאֲבוֹי, שֹׁד וָשֶׁבֶר, לַנּוֹתָרִים.
לִמְדִיבַת נֶפֶשׁ, וַחֲבָלִים וְצִירִים / לְכִלְיוֹן עֵינַיִם, צַלְמָוֶת וְלֹא סְדָרִים.
עֶרֶב אוֹמְרִים, מִי יִתֵּן צָפְרַיִם / וּבֹקֶר מְצַפִּים, מִי יְגַלֶּה אוֹרִים.
מִמַּרְאֶה עֵינֵימוֹ אֲשֶׁר הֵמָּה שָׂרִים / מִחוּץ שִׁכְּלָה חֶרֶב, וְאֵימָה מֵחֲדָרִים:

How long will You look on, He who sees all that is hidden? / Be zealous for Your Torah, flushed away by rivers. / They have roasted it, rent it, ripped it into fragments. / Fueled by tangled thorns, they fed the flames. / After all this, can You restrain Yourself, Master of all creations? / Avenge blood spilled like streaming waters. / From the pillage of the poor, from the cries of those beset by storms, / a people turning back from sin, exasperated and embittered; / rise up and rise above the attacking foe! / Raise Your footsteps, destroying them!   *Is. 64:11*

I will sob as I tell my tale, and moan, / and raise my voice in distress.

Kina 23 starts on page 438.

עַד מָתַי תַּבִּיט, רוֹאֶה כָּל סְתָרִים / קַנֵּא לְתוֹרָתְךָ, אֲשֶׁר בָּאוּ נָכְרִים.
קְלָאוּהָ, פְּרָעוּהָ, קָרְעוּהָ לִגְזָרִים / כְּסִירִים סְבוּכִים הִגְדִּילוּ הַמְּדוּרִים.
הַעַל אֵלֶּה תִּתְאַפָּק, אֲדוֹן כָּל יְצוּרִים.

ישעיה סד, יא

תִּנְקֹם דָּם הַנִּשְׁפָּךְ כַּמַּיִם הַמֻּגָּרִים / מְשׁוֹד עֲנִיִּים, מֵאַנְקַת סְעוּרִים.
עַם שָׁבֵי פֶשַׁע, לְעֵינַיִם וּמְרוּרִים / קוּמָה, וְהִנָּשֵׂא עַל צָרִים הַצּוֹרְרִים.
פְּעָמֶיךָ לְמַשֻּׁאוֹת הָרִימָה.

אָרִיד בְּשִׂיחִי וְאָהִימָה / וְקוֹל נְהִי אָרִימָה:

Kina 23 starts on page 439.

COMMENTARY ON KINA 22

As the previous *kina*, this *kina*, as well, was composed by Rabbi Meir ben Yeḥiel.

After shifting from *kinot* for the Ḥurban Beit HaMikdash to a *kina* for the Ten Martyrs, there is now a further shift in the subject matter of the *kinot*. This *kina* is the first of several commemorating the massacres in Speyer, Mainz and Worms, and other related tragedies during the Crusades in Germany at the end of the eleventh century. These *kinot* recount the Ḥurban Batei Mikdash of the Ḥakhmei Ashkenaz, the slaughter of the Torah scholars and the destruction of the Jewish communities.

In a sense, however, this *kina* is a continuation of the *kina* "אַרְזֵי הַלְּבָנוֹן". In both *kinot*, the deaths that are described represent a double catastrophe. Thousands of Jews were killed during the Crusades. But the tragedy was not just the murder of ten people during the Roman times or the myriads during the Crusades. The tragedy was also the fact that the greatest scholars of the Jewish people were killed. In this *kina*, the mourning that is expressed is not just for the inhuman act of the massacre. Rather, the principal emphasis is on the destruction of the Torah centers in Germany.

The dates of these massacres are known to us. The Crusaders generally started out on their journey in the spring, and the massacres took place in the months of Iyar and Sivan, around the time of Shavuot. Even though these events did not occur on Tisha B'Av, they are included in the *kinot* and are commemorated on Tisha B'Av because of the principle, already noted in connection with other *kinot*, that the death of the righteous is equivalent to the burning of the Beit HaMikdash. If the Beit HaMikdash was sacred, how much more sacred were entire Jewish communities which consisted of thousands of scholars. These communities were also, collectively, a Beit HaMikdash in the spiritual sense. If the *kinot* speak about the Ḥurban Beit HaMikdash in the material sense, they also mourn the Ḥurban Beit HaMikdash in the sprirítual sense, the destruction of centers of Torah and the killing of great Torah scholars. In fact, sometimes the death of the righteous is even a greater catastrophe than the destruction of the physical Beit HaMikdash.

There is an additional reason for including these *kinot* dealing with the massacres in Germany in the Tisha B'Av service. Ḥurban Beit HaMikdash is an all-inclusive concept. All disasters, tragedies and sufferings that befell the Jewish people should be mentioned on Tisha B'Av. Rashi says (II Chronicles 35:25, s.v. *vayitnum leḥok*) that when one has to mourn for an event, it should

be done on Tisha B'Av. When these *kinot* relating to the Crusades are recited, one should remember that the tragedies being described happened not only in 1096 but in the 1940s as well. These *kinot* are not only a eulogy for those murdered in Mainz, Speyer and Worms, but also for those murdered in Warsaw and Vilna and in the hundreds and thousands of towns and villages where Jews lived a sacred and committed life. The *kinot* are a eulogy not only for the Ten Martyrs and those killed in the Crusades, but for the martyrdom of millions of Jews throughout Jewish history.

The historical background is important. The center of Torah in Europe, and the school of the Tosafists commenced in Germany, not France. The Torah scholars in Germany were more numerous than the Tosafists in France. Speyer, Mainz and Worms were densely populated with *Gedolei Yisrael*. Yet, we hardly know many of them. All of the Torah scholars of Germany perished, and many of their writings were destroyed.

It is a miracle that *Torah shebe'al peh* continued, in spite of the fact that the center of Torah at that time in Germany was destroyed. *Torah shebe'al peh* was able to survive because, by then, centers of Torah had already begun to be established in France. Rabbeinu Tam and the Ri (Rabbi Yitzḥak) were French scholars, not German. Rashi was the one who turned France into a center of Torah. When Rashi was born in France, there was limited Torah scholarship there. As a young boy, before the Crusades, Rashi had no place to study in France, and he had to travel to the Torah centers which were in Germany. Rashi came to Worms to study with Rabbi Yaakov ben Yakar and Rabbi Yitzḥak ben Eliezer HaLevi. He returned to France well trained by the German Torah scholars, and upon his return, he established France as a center of Torah scholarship. In time, France became the center of Jewish wisdom. Instead of traveling from France to Germany as Rashi did, the generation after Rashi traveled to France to study in the academies of Rabbeinu Tam and Rabbi Yeḥiel of Paris. All of the *Tosafot* glosses in the Talmud are from the French Torah scholars, and none from the German Torah scholars because they were slain during the Crusades. While French Jewry was affected by the Crusades, and many Jews in France were killed in the Second Crusade in 1146, the situation in France was not nearly as dire as in Germany. There was no total destruction of Torah scholarship in France. Total destruction is a German performance.

Our *Torah shebe'al peh* is based on Rashi and the Tosafists. If Jewish history had not included Maimonides, the Jewish world would have missed a great deal. Maimonides enriched our thinking and world view tremendously, but

the *Torah shebe'al peh* would have survived without him. However, without Rashi and the Tosafists, there would not have been any *mesora*, any chain of tradition; we could not teach *Torah shebe'al peh* today. Take as a simple example, the Jerusalem Talmud. Many *Rishonim*, the early Medieval scholars, speak about the Jerusalem Talmud, and certain parts were interpreted and explained, but without commentaries of Rashi and the Tosafists, it is a sealed book.

סִפְדִי עַל עֲדָתִי *I bemoan my people.* Initially, the *paytan* does not mention Torah scholars who perished. Rather he refers to congregations that were destroyed. These congregations are not yet explicitly named. They will be identified in a subsequent *kina*.

וְקוֹל נְהִי אָרִימָה *And raise my voice in distress.* The *kina* is describing heroic martyrdom. During the Crusades, the martyrdom was not limited to the great scholars and leaders; rather, everyone offered his or her life, including young children. The enemies had a simple demand: all the Jew had to do was kiss the cross. The Jews could have saved their lives, but they would not agree to become apostates.

וְכָל רֹאשׁ קָרְחָה וְכָל זָקָן גְּרוּעָה *And every head bare; every beard shorn.* The *kina* describes the same methods practiced by the Nazis and the Poles during the Holocaust, which consisted of ridiculing and abusing the Jews and then killing them. For example, they would cut off half of a Jew's beard or would cut off one side-lock and leave the other one on.

מֵאָז נִתְעוֹרֵר גּוֹי עַז *Ever since a brazen nation arose.* This is a reference to Germany. The word *az* can be translated as "cruel," and it is interesting that the *paytan* refers to Germany as a cruel nation.

סֻלָּה אַבִּירַי... בְּתוּלוֹתַי וּבַחוּרַי *Cut down are my heroes... My young maidens and lads.* The enemy destroyed my heroes, the scholars, the *gedolei Yisrael*. But not only did he destroy the scholars, but also the young girls and boys, as well.

בְּרֹאשׁ כָּל חוּצוֹת נִבְלָתָם כְּסוּחָה *Their corpses strewn like rubbish on every street corner.* During the Crusades there was no burial for the martyrs, as in the case of the Ten Martyrs during the Roman era.

סְפֹד תַּמְרוּר, הָאָגְדוּ בַּחֲבוּרָה *Join together in anguished lament.* The mourning of Tisha B'Av is communal, unlike the individual mourning due to the death of a member of one's household. The verse in Jeremiah says, "Make for yourself

evel yaḥid" (6:26). The connotation is that the mourning is individual, alone. This is in contrast to the mourning for the destruction of the *Beit HaMikdash* (*Yevamot* 43b), which is an *avelut hatzibbur*, involving the entire community together. On Tisha B'Av, *kinot* and the *Naḥem* and *Anenu* prayers are recited by us not as individuals but as a community.

בְּלִי לִכְרֹעַ לַעֲבוֹדָה זָרָה **And not submit to alien gods.** *Tosafot* raise the question (*Sanhedrin* 74b, s.v. *veha Ester*) that it is not clear why the Jews felt obligated to kill themselves and each other in the circumstance of forced baptism. After all, if they were physically taken and baptized completely by force without any action of their own, they were not committing any transgression of their own volition and should not have been obligated to kill themselves. The answer is that, in fact, they were not obligated to do so, but they considered any gesture to idolatry, even an involuntary one, as requiring them to suffer death rather than submit.

There is a dispute among the *Rishonim* whether parents have the right to sacrifice their small children in order to prevent them from being converted to Christianity. The author of this *kina* apparently approved of this practice. Other *Rishonim*, however, did not approve (see, for example, *Responsa Ba'alei HaTosafot* 101).

There were two justifications for committing suicide and killing the children. First, as in the case of King Saul, they knew that when the enemy would capture them they would be tortured. The Midrash says (*Bereshit Raba* 34:13) that Saul asked the Amalekite to kill him because he was afraid of torture. Our sages say (Rabbi Asher, *Mo'ed Katan* 3:94) that under these circumstances, if it is certain that one will fall into the hands of the enemy, one is permitted to kill one's children and commit suicide. Second, the Jews did not trust themselves that they would be able to withstand the pressure of converting to Christianity under threat of death.

The *paytan* describes not only the collective tragedy, but also the individual tragedies of people who performed acts of *Kiddush Hashem* and committed suicide in order not to be forced to worship *avoda zara*.

נַקְרִיבְכֶם כְּעוֹלָה וְהַקְטָרָה **So we offer you as a sacrifice, a burnt-offering.** The parents were particularly concerned with the children. They were afraid that when they themselves would be killed, the Crusaders would take the children, baptize them and raise them as Christians. The parents tried to influence the older children to remain faithful, but could not accomplish this with the younger children. Therefore, the parents killed the younger children first.

COMMENTARY ON KINA 22

הֵם הָיוּ תְּחִלָּה נִדּוֹנִים *Were the first to be condemned.* The older people came out to the enemy and were killed first. It is noteworthy that the elderly did not commit suicide. They went out to resist the enemy and were killed in battle.

תּוֹרָה תּוֹרָה חִגְרִי שָׂק *Torah, Torah, wrap yourself in sackcloth.* With this stanza, the actual eulogy begins, and the *paytan* portrays the devastation and spiritual destruction in the centers of Torah. By depicting the Torah itself as dressed in sackcloth, the *paytan* emphasizes that we mourn not only for those who were killed, but also for the diminution of Torah.

עַל תּוֹפְשֵׂי מָשׁוֹטַיִךְ וּפוֹרְשֵׂי מִכְמוֹרִים *For those who gripped your oars and spread your nets.* The Torah scholars of Germany are referred to metaphorically as the crew of a ship.

עוֹרְבֵי מַעֲרָבֵךְ, מְיַשְּׁרֵי הַדּוּרִים *Those who arranged your arrangements and straightened that which was twisted.* This is a beautiful description of the role of the Tosafists, which was to blaze the trail in the Gemara, to reconcile contradictions and to "straighten" the difficulties in the text.

מְפַעְנְחֵי צְפוּנַיִךְ *Uncovered your secrets.* The *paytan* addresses himself to the Torah, and says that you, the Torah, should mourn more than anyone else the loss of the Torah scholars.

וּמִי יְסַתֵּת בֶּהָרִים *And who will hew down the mountains?* This phrase is reminiscent of the description by our sages regarding Resh Lakish (*Sanhedrin* 24a), that he uprooted mountains from their places and crushed them. The intent is that his mind was powerful and precise.

The same image is employed to describe what the Tosafists accomplished. When one studies the Tosafists, one has the impression that they came into a territory that was uneven and difficult. There were hills, valleys and jungles. The Tosafists evened out the terrain, blazed a trail and made a highway for the study of Torah.

וּמִי יְתָרֵץ שְׁבָרִים *And who will repair breaches?* One interpretation is, "Who will explain something that is broken, obscure?" It may also mean, "Who will correct the corrupt text?"

מִי יַפְלִיא נְזִירוֹת, וּמִי יַעֲרֹךְ נְדָרִים *Who will articulate Nazirite vows, and who will assess the value of your pledges?* It may seem strange that the *kina* refers to *nezirot*, Nazirite vows, and *nedarim*, pledges and oaths, which on the face of it, are not subjects of pressing practical importance. The intent is to allude to a particular

set of circumstances that pertain to two tractates of the Talmud in which these topics are discussed. We do not have an authentic commentary of Rashi on the tractates of *Nazir* and *Nedarim*. Although the Gemara texts do have a commentary printed on the page which purports to be Rashi's commentary, it is, in fact, not by Rashi, and it is very difficult to understand. Therefore, the Tosafists here were to have assumed Rashi's traditional role and interpret the text in these two tractates. Normally, the Tosafists do not interpret. Customarily, Rashi is the interpreter, and the Tosafists compare and resolve problems. Indeed, the *Tosafot* glosses in *Nazir* serve as a commentary, and do not play the Tosafists' usual role of posing questions and marshaling responses. Since the German Tosafists were killed, we are left without the analysis that they normally would have provided, and the *kina* mourns, and says, "Who will fully interpret the tractate of *Nazir* and who will interpret the tractate of *Nedarim*?"

In fact, *Nedarim* and *Nazir* are two very difficult tractates. If the massacres in Speyer and Mainz had not taken place, there would have been a *gadol* who would have written an exhaustive commentary. But the German Torah scholars were killed, and there was no one to write the commentary, and to this day we have trouble studying these two tractates. I once attempted to study Tractate *Nedarim* with my father using the pseudo-Rashi's commentary, but we were not successful. We were able to proceed only by using the commentary of the Ran, Rabbeinu Nissim, who lived in the fourteenth century, considerably later than the period described by the *kina*. The Ran gave us both the interpretation, usually provided by Rashi, and the analysis, usually provided by the Tosafists.

It is interesting to note that there is evidence that even as early as the days of the Geonim the tractate of *Nedarim* was not studied regularly. A question was posed to Rabbi Hai Gaon concerning an issue in Tractate *Nedarim*, to which the Gaon responded, "we have not studied the tractate of *Nedarim* in the yeshiva for over one hundred years, for Rabbi Yehudai Gaon instructed us not to study it" (*Teshuvot HaGeonim HaHadashot* 58:780). In fact, the Geonim did study *Nedarim*, but they did not study it in depth, which is why the Gaon declined to answer the question.

אַשְׁרֵיהֶם מַשְׂכִּילִים, כִּרְקִיעַ זוֹהֲרִים *Fortunate are they, wise and radiant like the sky.* Since they enjoy the bliss of the World to Come, the *paytan* does not mourn the death of the martyrs. Instead, he mourns the destiny of the survivors because they remain without teachers and leaders, lonely, hopeless and full of despair.

עֶרֶב אוֹמְרִים, מִי יִתֵּן צְפָרִים *In the evening, they say, "Would that it were dawn."* This is an allusion to the verse, "And at evening you shall say: 'Would it were morning!'" (Deuteronomy 28:67), which appears in the *tokhaḥa*, the description of the ultimate divine punishment to be visited upon the Jewish people if they transgress. This is a description of the mood of the Jew in the Middle Ages, and it reflects the precarious political situation and fate of the Jew at that time.

קְלָאוּהָ, פְּרָעוּהָ, קְרָעוּהָ לִגְזָרִים *They have roasted it, rent it, ripped it into fragments.* It is noteworthy that there is a special prayer here for *kevod sefer Torah*, for the honor of the parchment on which the Torah was written. After killing the Jews, the Crusaders would open the Ark and defile the Torah scrolls by tearing them into pieces.

הַעַל אֵלֶּה תִּתְאַפַּק, אֲדוֹן כָּל יְצוּרִים *After all this, can You restrain Yourself, Master of all creations?* Similar to this *kina*, the *Av HaRaḥamim* prayer, recited in the Shabbat Musaf service, emerged from the Crusades. As the first sentence of that prayer states, "Father of compassion, who dwells on high, with His powerful compassion, may He recall with compassion the righteous, the upright, and the perfect ones, the holy congregations who gave their lives for *Kiddush Hashem*, the sanctification of the name."

The Crusades effected a permanent change in the collective temperament of the Jewish people by injecting an indelible mark of sadness. According to the Taz (*Shulḥan Arukh, Oraḥ Ḥayyim* 493:2), the mourning during the period of the counting of the Omer is not due to the death of the students of Rabbi Akiva, but to the massacres of the Crusades.

85) My Temple - on was destroyed in
Like my tears stream down my cheeks
On this day I will shave my worn eye
And I mourn from year to year.

86) With an aggrieved heart, impossible to console
of all injuries, my pain is no equal.
over the son and daughter of R[abbi] Yishmael the High Priest
their blood in my veins like a fire in my heart
And I mourn from year to year.

87) I Had captive in the possess yet two different masters
who disrobed on a by, and attach
and as they discussed various millions,
one raised "1A pious lepraves
I purchased, [a maid] clothed in satire,
blu-ish, smooth in stature and beauty,
and in appearance like Rachel and Jemima,
And I mourn from year to year.

88) The tempter responded with double the price
Jason, visited Jerusalem's captives,
and purchased a slave boy with beautiful eyes
like the sun in full force at dawn,
and like the moon in its fullness
And I mourn from year to year.

23

וְאֵת My Temple – my sins destroyed it!
   I let my tears stream down my cheeks.
   On this day, I will raise a woeful cry.
      And I mourn from year to year.

אֲבֵל With an aggrieved heart, impossible to console,
   of all injuries, my pain is unique,
   over the son and daughter of Rabbi Yishma'el, the High Priest.
   Their memory is like a fire in my heart.
      And I mourn from year to year.

עֵת Held captive in the possession of two different masters
   who dwelled nearby one another,
   and as they discussed various matters,
   one related, "Of Zion's captives,
   I purchased a maid, clothed in scarlet,
   like the moon in radiance and beauty,
   and in appearance like Keziah and Jemima.
      And I mourn from year to year.

רֵעֵהוּ His comrade responded with double the praise.
   "I, too, visited Jerusalem's captives,
   and purchased a slave-boy with beautiful eyes
   like the sun in full force, at noon,
   and like the moon in its fullness.
      And I mourn from year to year.

23

This kina, of uncertain authorship, is based on a story in Gittin 58a, and is found (with slight variations) in both Ashkenazic and Oriental liturgy. Commentary for this kina begins on page 442.

וְאֶת נָוִי, חָטָאתִי הַשָּׁמֵיְמָה
וְדִמְעָתִי, עַל לֶחָיִ אֲזֵרֵימָה.
וּבְיוֹם זֶה, נְהִי נִהְיָה אָרִימָה.
וְאָהֵימָה מִיָּמִים יָמֵימָה:

אֲבֶל לֵב, וְנִחוּם חָדַל חָדוֹל
וּמִכָּל כְּאֵב, צִירִי נִבְדַּל בָּדוֹל.
עַל בֵּן וּבַת רַבִּי יִשְׁמָעֵאל כֹּהֵן גָּדוֹל
זִכְרָם, יְקוֹד בְּלִבָּבִי אָשִׂימָה.
וְאָהֵימָה מִיָּמִים יָמֵימָה:

עֵת נִשְׁבּוּ, וְנָפְלוּ לִשְׁנֵי אֲדוֹנִים
וְהֵם שְׁכֵנִים, זֶה לְעֻמַּת זֶה חוֹנִים.
וַיְסַפְּרוּ זֶה לָזֶה עִנְיָנִים
זֶה אָמַר, מַשְׁבִּית צִיּוֹנִים.
שָׁבִיתִי שִׁפְחָה לְבוּשַׁת שָׁנִים
כַּלְּבָנָה בְזִיו וְקִלַּסְתֵּר פָּנִים.
וּבְתֹאַר, כִּקְצִיעָה וִימִימָה.
וְאָהֵימָה מִיָּמִים יָמֵימָה:

רֵעֵהוּ סִפֵּר לוֹ בִּכְפֻלַיִם
הֵן אֲנִי בָא מִשְּׁבִי יְרוּשָׁלָיִם.
שָׁבִיתִי עֶבֶד יְפֵה עֵינַיִם
כַּשֶּׁמֶשׁ, בְּתָקְפּוֹ עֵת צָהֳרָיִם.
וְסַהַר, עֵת זְמַנָּהּ הַשְּׁלֵימָה.
וְאָהֵימָה מִיָּמִים יָמֵימָה:

בֹּא "Let us mate them and evenly split
   the offspring, sure to be like stars in the sky."
   Hearing this makes one's ears ring!
   Recalling this, I rend my garments.
      And I mourn from year to year.

כְּהַסְכִּימוּ Together, they both agreed to this,
   and that night, coupled them into one room.
   The slave-masters stood outside with identical intention,
   while the slaves cried, embittered, and frightened.
   Until dawn, their crying did not abate.
      And I mourn from year to year.

זֶה One lamented with a feverish and melted heart,
   "How will a grandson of Aaron marry a slave-girl?"
   And she, too, wailed, "Because of a villain's transaction,
   will a daughter of Yokheved marry a slave?"
   Woe that He, who does what He says, has thus decreed!
   Over this, the celestial constellations weep!
      And I mourn from year to year.

אוֹר With the break of dawn, they recognized one another
   and overpowered each other, crying, "Oh, brother!" "Oh, sister!"
   They embraced and clung to each other
   until their souls departed with one last breath.
      And I mourn from year to year.

לְזֹאת For this, Jeremiah lamented in horror.
   This horrid decree, I will forever bemoan.
   In my heart burns a fire, a scorching flame.
   For the son and daughter, I will deliver a powerful lament!
      And I mourn from year to year.

Kina 24 starts on page 446.

בֹּא וּנְזוּגֵם, וְנַחְלְקָה בְּנֻתַּיִם
בּוֹלְדוֹת, כְּמוֹ כּוֹכְבֵי שָׁמַיִם.
לִשְׁמֹעַ זֹאת, תִּצַּלְנָה אָזְנַיִם
לִזְכֹּר זֹאת, אֶת מַדַּי אַפְרִימָה.
וְאָהִימָה מִיָּמִים יָמִימָה:

כְּהִסְכִּימוּ עַל זֹאת שְׁנֵיהֶם יַחַד
לָעֶרֶב זוּגִים בְּחֶדֶר אֶחָד.
וְהָאֲדוֹנִים בַּחוּץ, לְכֻלָּם כְּאֶחָד
וְהֵם בּוֹכִים בְּמַר נֶפֶשׁ, וָפָחַד.
עַד בֹּקֶר, בִּכְיָתָם לֹא הִדְמִימָה.
וְאָהִימָה מִיָּמִים יָמִימָה:

זֶה יִסְפֹּד, בִּיקוֹד לֵבָב יְמַסֶּה
נִין אַהֲרֹן, אֵיךְ לְשִׁפְחָה יְהִי נוֹשֵׂא.
וְהִיא גַם הִיא, תְּיַלֵּל בְּתִגְרַת שׁוֹסֶה
בַּת יוֹכֶבֶד, אֵיךְ לְעֶבֶד תִּנָּשֵׂא.
אוֹי כִּי זֹאת גָּזַר אוֹמֵר וְעוֹשֶׂה
לְזֹאת יִבְכּוּ עָשׁ, כְּסִיל וְכִימָה.
וְאָהִימָה מִיָּמִים יָמִימָה:

אוֹר בֹּקֶר, זֶה אֶת זֶה כְּהִכִּירוּ.
הוֹי אָחִי, וְהוֹי אָחוֹת, הִגְבִּירוּ.
וְנִתְחַבְּקוּ יַחַד וְנִתְחַבְּרוּ
עַד יָצְאָה נִשְׁמָתָם בִּנְשִׁימָה.
וְאָהִימָה מִיָּמִים יָמִימָה:

לְזֹאת יְקוֹנֵן יִרְמְיָה בִּשְׁאִיָּה
גְּזֵרָה זוֹ, תָּמִיד אֲנִי בוֹכִיָּה.
וּבְלִבָּבִי יְקַד יְקוֹד וּכְוִיָּה
עַל בֵּן וּבַת מִסְפַּד רַב אֲנַהִימָה.
וְאָהִימָה מִיָּמִים יָמִימָה:

Kina 24 starts on page 447.

COMMENTARY ON KINA 23

The name of the author of this beautifully written *kina* is Yeḥiel. We do not know who he was, but he was clearly Ashkenazic. He may have been Rabbi Yeḥiel of Paris.

This *kina* is based on the tragic story (*Gittin* 58a; *Eikha Raba* 1:22) of the son and daughter of Rabbi Yishma'el, each of whom was taken captive by a different Roman slave owner. Because the son was very handsome and the daughter very beautiful, the two slave owners decided to marry their two slaves to each other with the expectation that the union would produce beautiful and talented children who could then fetch a high price on the slave market. The son and daughter were told they would be married the next day, she to a slave, and he to a slave-girl. They were locked together for the night in a dark room, and neither could see the other. She cried all night, "How can the daughter of the High Priest be married to a slave?" He cried all night, "How can the son of the High Priest take a maid-servant for a wife?" As the morning dawned, they recognized each other and, distraught at their fate, died in an embrace.

The placement of this *kina* in the sequence of the *kinot* initially appears odd. The order of "הַחֲרִישׁוּ מִמֶּנִּי" following "אַרְזֵי הַלְּבָנוֹן" is logical and proper. However, one would have expected that the the *kina* following "הַחֲרִישׁוּ מִמֶּנִּי," which commemorates the martyrs of German Jewry, would have been "מִי יִתֵּן רֹאשִׁי מַיִם," the second *kina* pertaining to the Crusades in which Speyer, Worms and Mainz are mentioned by name and the dates of their destruction are recorded. Instead, the story of the death of Rabbi Yishma'el's son and daughter is interjected, interrupting the series of *kinot* about the destruction of the Jewish communities in Germany. To compound the question, one could also ask why it is necessary to interrupt the description in the *kinot* of major national catastrophes with a story of a young man and woman who suffered as a result of the Ḥurban of Jerusalem, but whose deaths did not change the course of Jewish history or the routine of daily Jewish life. The narrative flow of the *kinot* mourns the destruction of the state, the land and the *Beit HaMikdash* – all of which changed Jewish history – then the martyrdom of the ten greatest scholars of the Talmud, and then the massacre of thousands of people and the destruction of the most important communities in the Middle Ages, both spiritually and numerically. In the midst of this national commemoration of the tragedies that befell the community, the sequence of *kinot* is interrupted with the story of the death of two individuals.

The answer is that Judaism has a different understanding of and approach to the individual. We mourn for the individual even if he or she was not a significant person. Rabbi Yishma'el, the father of these youngsters was already killed, and they were orphans. In light of the major calamities, who is responsible to remember a story about an individual young man and woman who were taken captive by some slave merchants? The answer is that *we* are. We have a special *kina* dedicated just to them, as if one hundred thousand people were involved, not just two individuals. Their life and their death may not have changed Jewish history, but we suffer and remember. We do not forget the faceless, nameless individual even in the midst of national disaster and upheaval, even when telling the story of the greatest of all the disasters in our history, the destruction of the *Beit HaMikdash*. In this *kina* we mourn not for the Jews of Worms or Mainz, not for the Ḥurban Yerushalayim, and not for the *Beit HaMikdash*. We mourn for a boy and a girl who were not leaders or scholars and who did not play any major public role. They are as important as the greatest leaders. Sometimes we become so engrossed in the national tragedy that we forget the individual, and the sequence of the *kinot* is interrupted to highlight the worth of the individual.

There is an additional, pedagogical, reason that the description of the overwhelming national tragedy is interrupted with the story of the personal tragedy of two individuals. People respond to the story of an individual personal tragedy more readily than to a national tragedy on a large scale. The Midrash on *Parashat Noaḥ* (*Gen. Raba* 33:5) recounts that Rabbi Akiva came to the city of Ginzak to collect money for charity. He expounded on the story of the flood when all of humanity was drowned. The people did not cry; they were not touched; they did not respond emotionally. Then Rabbi Akiva told them the story of Job, and they immediately broke out in tears and complied generously with Rabbi Akiva's request. It is easier to move someone when they are told of a personal tragedy that befell a specific individual rather than telling them of the death of hundreds of thousands.

זִכְרָם, יְקוֹד בְּלִבָּבִי אֲשִׂימָה *Their memory is like a fire in my heart.* The *paytan* will not forget them even though they are merely individuals, not a community.

שִׁפְחָה לְבוּשַׁת שָׁנִים *A maid, clothed in scarlet.* He recognized from her dress that she came from a prominent aristocratic family.

וּבְתֹאַר, כִּקְצִיעָה וִימִימָה *And in appearance like Keziah and Jemima.* These are the names of the daughters of Job (Job 42:14), who were very beautiful.

לְזֵכֶר זֹאת, אֶת מַדַּי אַפְרִימָה *Recalling this, I rend my garments.* The *paytan* writes of *keria*, the ritual tearing of clothes by mourning family members at a funeral, to mourn the deaths of the son and daughter of Rabbi Yishma'el. The question can be posed: why is there a general obligation to tear *keria* in this situation? For example, there is an obligation on all to tear *keria* upon the death of the *Av Beit Din*, the leader of the Sanhedrin, of a prince of Israel or a great Torah scholar (*Shulḥan Arukh, Yoreh De'ah* 340:7, 8, 17). But why was it necessary to tear *keria* for the son and daughter of Rabbi Yishma'el? In my opinion, the laws regarding which decedent generates a general obligation on all Jews to tear *keria* apply only in the case of decedents who died under ordinary circumstances. However, in the case of those who died in the sanctification of God's name, we do not analyze whether the person was a scholar, a prince or an *Av Beit Din*. If an ordinary Jew sacrificed his or her life in order to maintain the principles of the Torah, then all are obligated to tear *keria* for, and eulogize, that person.

אֵיךְ לְשִׁפְחָה יְהִי נוֹשֵׂא *"How will… marry a slave-girl?"* There is a separate prohibition for a kohen to marry a maid-servant (*Mishneh Torah*, Hil. Isurei Bi'ah 21:17).

בַּת יוֹכֶבֶד, אֵיךְ לְעֶבֶד תִּנָּשֵׂא *"Will a daughter of Yokheved marry a slave?"* Although the literal meaning of the word *eved* is "slave," the word *eved* here does not refer to a Canaanite slave. Rather, it means a non-Jew.

לְזֹאת יִבְכּוּ עָשׁ, כְּסִיל *Over this, the celestial constellations weep!* The intent in referring to the constellations weeping is that the entire universe cries for these individuals, not only for the multitudes.

עַד יָצְאָה נִשְׁמָתָם בִּנְשִׁימָה *Until their souls departed with one last breath.* They committed suicide.

לְזֹאת יְקוֹנֵן יִרְמְיָה בִּשְׁאִיָּה *For this, Jeremiah lamented in horror.* This incident occurred in the aftermath of the destruction of the Second Temple. Jeremiah, who lived at the time of the First Temple, apparently foresaw this tragedy and prophesied about it. He lamented for each individual who perished during the destruction of the First Temple and the Second Temple.

24

the reading of Megillat Eikha; and the Eastern Ashkenazic tradition, followed nowadays, which places it here, at the opening of the second group of kinot by HaKalir. The kina consists of twenty-two stanzas of three stichs each, in receding alphabetical order. Commentary for this kina begins on page 452.

עַל־אֵלֶּה For these things do I weep, my eyes flow with tears.   Lam. 1:16

עַל Upon the destruction of the Temple,
torn down and trampled,
I will lament a new lament every year,
upon the sacred and upon the Sanctuary.

תִּסָּתֵר You hid Yourself, silencing the angels' song,
when You shook the world in anger,
as the fire burned between the Ark's two poles.

שְׁנֵי The two Temples, earthly and celestial,
one upon the other, darkened in gloom.
And You responded, "I will be silent, I will restrain Myself,   Is. 42:14
    I will look on."

רָאשֵׁי The Ark's poles were buried [no longer protruding
    from the curtains].
Four fiery coals made their way down to the Temple
and incinerated the forty foundations down to the depths.

קֹדֶשׁ As the holy band [of angels] abandoned the Holy of Holies,
You proclaimed and cried that Your Tent was ravaged.
You said, "I will clap hand against hand," and You roared with a shout!

צְפִירַת When Your crown of glory was delivered to the foe,
and the precious Temple vessels [transported] with other treasures,
You had power and might, but they exclaimed, "He is impotent!"

פְּנֵי The throne's face darkened,
Heaven's heights were lowered into gloom.
The Temple's two pillars crumbled and fell.

24

This kina, by Rabbi Elazar HaKalir, describes the actual destruction of the Temple. It has a prefatory stanza calling for mourning, which is an opening to the whole of the kinot – as it is indeed in the Western Ashkenazic tradition, which has it as the very first kina said at night after

איכה א, טז

עַל־אֵלֶּה אֲנִי בוֹכִיָּה, עֵינִי עֵינִי יֹרְדָה מָּיִם:

עַל חֻרְבַּן בֵּית הַמִּקְדָּשׁ
כִּי הֹרַס, וְכִי הוּדָשׁ
אֶסְפֹּד בְּכָל שָׁנָה, מִסְפֵּד חָדָשׁ
עַל הַקֹּדֶשׁ וְעַל הַמִּקְדָּשׁ:

תִּסָּתֵר לְאֵלֶּם תַּרְשִׁישִׁים מֵרֹן
כְּזַעֲזַעַת עוֹלָם מִפְּנֵי חָרוֹן
כְּלַהֲטָה אֵשׁ בֵּין בַּדֵּי אָרוֹן:

שְׁנֵי מִקְדָּשִׁים, אֲשֶׁר בְּמַעְלָה וּבְמַטָּה
זֶה עַל גַּבֵּי זֶה, הָאָפְלוּ בְּעֶלְטָה
וְנָמַתִּי, אַחֲרִישׁ, אֶתְאַפַּק וְאַבִּיטָה:

ישעיה מב, יד

רָאשֵׁי הַבַּדִּים, כְּנִגְנְזוּ מִבֵּין הַפָּרוֹכוֹת
וְאַרְבַּע גְּחָלִים, בַּדְּבִיר מְהַלְּכוֹת
וְאַרְבָּעִים יְסוֹד, עַד תְּהוֹם מְלֻחָכוֹת:

קֹדֶשׁ הַקֳּדָשִׁים, מִכִּתֵּי קֹדֶשׁ כְּנִבְדָּד
סָחַת וְהֵילֵלַת, אָהֳלִי שֻׁדַּד
וְנָמַתִּי, אַכֶּה כַף אֶל כָּף, וְשַׁאֲגַת, הֵידָד:

צְפִירַת תִּפְאַרְתְּךָ, כְּנִתְּנָה בְּיַד צָר
וְכָל כְּלִי חֶמְדָּה, אֲוּוּי עִם הָאוֹצָר
וּלְךָ הַכֹּחַ וְהַגְּבוּרָה, וְנָמוּ עָצַר:

פְּנֵי הַכִּסֵּא, אָז אָפְלוּ
וְגָבְהֵי שָׁמַיִם, לַקַּדְרוּת הֻשְׁפְּלוּ
יָכִין וּבֹעַז לְהִשְׁתַּבֵּר, כְּנָפְלוּ:

עֲשָׂרָה The ten tables were then looted,
and they taunted the priests saying, "Where is their Master?"
Delivered to the storage rooms of Shinar [Babylon] for lewd purpose.

שְׂרָפִים The Seraphim departed from their stations
when the bronze stands were torn from the Temple.
The villains called for annihilation.

נְחֹשֶׁת The brass basin and ten fountains,
surrendered to the god of Babylon, broken.
The sun and the moon both are since darkened.

מַעֲשֵׂה The wheels of the celestial chariot
lowered to the earth, the glow of the heavens dimmed,
as the vanquisher of nations [Nebuchadnezzar]
    entered the Cherubim's domain.

לֻיוֹת From the time the Cherubim, hammered [in bronze],
    were cast down,
the blessed dew ceased to fall.
[Instead,] mad dogs flew on the tips of the clouds.

כָּל All the vessels, golden and silver,
were torn out and plundered from the flaming Temple.
As the glory departed, even the entourage of the mighty was humbled.

יוֹם On that day of tumult and confusion,
bands of angels were as bewildered as a woman in labor.
He spoke, and [the angels] responded, "Alas! [Lonely sits the city]!"

טָס The Ammonites and Moabites hastened to pull out the Cherubim,
and circulated them in a crate,
insisting that Judah was no better than other nations.

חֵיל The army of holy Seraphim was demoted from its eminence,
and God, exalted is His name, refused to hear His praise.
His House of Prayer had been reduced to rubble.

עֲשָׂרָה שֻׁלְחָנוֹת, אָז שׁוֹלְלוּ
וּלְעוֹרְכֵיהֶם נָמוּ, אַיֵּה אָדוֹן אֵלּוּ
לְאוֹצְרוֹת שִׁנְעָר, לִקְדֵשִׁים כְּהִנְחִלוּ:

שְׂרָפִים עוֹמְדִים, נָעוּ מִמַּעֲמָד
כְּנֶהֶרְסוּ מְכוֹנוֹת מִתּוֹךְ מַחֲמָד
זָרִים קָרְאוּ יְמֵי הַשְׁמָד:

נְחֹשֶׁת יָם, וַעֲשָׂרָה כִּיּוֹרוֹת
כְּנִמְסְרוּ לַבֶּל, וְהִנָּם שְׁבוּרוֹת
וּשְׁנֵי הַמְּאוֹרוֹת מֵאָז קְדוּרוֹת:

מַעֲשֵׂה הָאוֹפַנִּים אֲשֶׁר בַּמֶּרְכָּבָה
כְּהוּרְדוּ לָאָרֶץ, זֹהַר הָרָקִיעַ כָּבָה
חוֹלֵשׁ עַל גּוֹיִם, לִפְנֵי כְרוּבִים בָּא:

לְוָיוֹת הַמּוֹרָד, מֵעֵת הוּרְדוּ
הַטְּלָלִים עוֹד לִבְרָכָה לֹא יָרְדוּ
כְּלָבִים רָעִים עַל בָּמֳתֵי עָב דָּדוּ:

כָּל כְּלֵי הַכֶּסֶף וּכְלֵי הַזָּהָב
קִצְּצוּ וְשָׁסּוּ מִבֵּית הַלַּהַב
בְּצֵאת הֶהָדָר, שָׁחֲחוּ עוֹרְיֵ רַהַב:

יוֹם אֲשֶׁר נִקְרָא מְהוּמָה וּמְבוּכָה
לַהֲקַת מַלְאָכִים, כְּאִשָּׁה מְצֵרָה נְבוֹכָה
דִּבּוּר פָּתַח, וְעָנוּ אַחֲרָיו אֵיכָה:

טָס עַמּוֹנִי וּמוֹאָבִי, וְהוֹצִיאוּ הַכְּרוּבִים
וּבְכְלִיבָה, הָיוּ בָם מְסוֹבְבִים
הִנֵּה כְּכָל הַגּוֹיִם, בֵּית יְהוּדָה חֲשׁוּבִים:

חֵיל שָׂרְפֵי מַעְלָה חִלֵּף מִגְדַּלְתּוֹ
וְאֵל, אַדִּיר שְׁמוֹ, לֹא אָבָה תְהִלָּתוֹ
לְגִלּוּלִים כְּהוּשַׁם בֵּית תִּפְאַרְתּוֹ:

זִמְרֵי The celestial singers were silenced from song,
and He said, "Why bother, there is no good reason [to sing].
How can you laud the King in His moment of fury?"

וְהַכֹּהֲנִים Priests and Levites, butchered at their stations,
their positions overrun by legions of warriors,
asking, "Where is the King, committed to the people of Israel?"

הַכֵּלִים Vessels and their bearers, gone to captivity.
Princes and viceroys dragged away in chains.
The angels exchanged their linen raiment for sackcloth.

דָּץ The lion [Nebuchadnezzar] pranced and opened his eyes
to see the angel Michael guiding him,
his armies witnessing princes [angels] servile as slaves.

גַּאֲוָה He draped himself in arrogance and snuffed out the Menora,
stretching out his hand against mighty God,
and extinguished the light of He who is wrapped in light.

בִּשְׁאֲגוֹ When this idol worshiper roared in the Holy of Holies,
my beloved [people] departed as the one who mourns the dead,
and He rejected those who entrust their souls to Him each night.

אָמַר He told the demons that He had spent His wrath,
and delivered His beloved to the hands of her enemies.
"I abandoned My House and deserted My inheritance."

Kina 25 starts on page 454.

זִמְרֵי שַׁחַק הֶחֱשׁוּ מִנֹּעַם
וְנָם, מַה לָּכֶם פֹּה, אֵין הַיּוֹם טַעַם
מַה תְּקַלְּסוּן לַמֶּלֶךְ בִּשְׁעַת הַזַּעַם:

וְהַכֹּהֲנִים וְהַלְוִיִּם, עַל מִשְׁמְרוֹתָם נִשְׁחָטִים
וְעַל מַחְלְקוֹתָם, שַׁעֲטַת אִסְטְרַדְיוֹטִים
וְנָמוּ, אַיֵּה מֶלֶךְ אָסוּר בָּרְהָטִים:

הַכֵּלִים וְהַמְשַׁמְּשִׁים, בַּשְּׁבִי הוֹלְכִים
הַשָּׂרִים וְהַסְּגָנִים, בְּכֶבֶל מְשׁוּכִים
וּתְמוּר בַּדִּים, שַׂק חָגְרוּ מַלְאָכִים:

דָּץ לָבִיא, וּפָקַח עֵינָיו
וְהִנֵּה מִיכָאֵל מְהַלֵּךְ לְפָנָיו
וְשָׂרִים הוֹלְכִים כַּעֲבָדִים, חֲזוּ הֲמוֹנָיו:

גַּאֲוָה עָטָה, וְכִבָּה אֶת הַמְּנוֹרָה
וְנָטָה יָדוֹ אֶל אֵל הַמּוֹרָא
וַיַּחְשִׁיךְ, אוֹר עוֹטֶה אוֹרָה:

בְּשַׁאֲגוֹ כַאֲרִי, בִּדְבִיר בֵּל
בָּרַח דּוֹדִי, כְּעַל מֵת מִתְאַבֵּל
פִּקְדוֹן הָרוּחוֹת, בּוֹ בַּלַּיְלָה לֹא קִבֵּל:

אָמַר לַמַּשְׁחִיתִים, חֲמָתִי הִתַּכְתִּי
אֶת יְדִידוּת נַפְשִׁי, בְּכַף אוֹיְבֶיהָ נָתַתִּי
עָזַבְתִּי אֶת בֵּיתִי, וְנָחֲלָתִי נָטָשְׁתִּי:

Kina 25 starts on page 455.

COMMENTARY ON KINA 24

The very last line of this *kina* by Rabbi Elazar HaKalir highlights a fundamental principle of the Ḥurban. "I abandoned My House and deserted My inheritance" expresses the concept that God is directly involved in the tragedy. It was *His* House that was destroyed.

It is important to note that the role of God in connection with the destruction of the Temple is not merely that of a judge, but also that of a litigant; He Himself is a party to the legal proceedings. The source for this concept is found in the *Berit bein HaBetarim*, the "Covenant between the Pieces." In this covenant, God promises Abraham, "And also that nation to which they will be enslaved, *dan anokhi*" (Genesis 15:14). The words *dan anokhi* are customarily translated as "I will judge." Rav Ḥayyim Brisk, however, points out that if the covenant was providing for God's promise to judge the Egyptians, the words should have been "*adin anokhi*." This would be the proper term to refer to a judge who decides between two litigants. The term *dan anokhi*, however, has a different connotation. It refers to one who is in litigation with another. God is the universal Judge who always sits in judgment and resolves every situation in accordance with the dictates of justice. He is the Judge of the entire world (Genesis 18:25). One does not need a special covenant to ensure that God performs His role as judge of the Egyptians. Rav Ḥayyim points out that in the *Berit bein HaBetarim* God promises much more. He promises not only to be the judge, but to be one of the litigants. Says God, "*I* will be a party to the litigation. *I* will quarrel with the Egyptians. I will treat them as if they enslaved *Me*; as if they snatched *My* children and drowned them in the Nile." The power of the *Berit bein HaBetarim* is that it promises the special relationship between God and *Knesset Yisrael*. If harm is inflicted on the Jewish people it is as though harm has been inflicted on God. If one humiliates the Jew or holds him in contempt, it is as though the same has been done to God.

Similarly, the role of God with respect to the destruction of the Temple is one of a litigant. It is not only a tragedy for the Jewish people, but an affront to God. Furthermore, God views the tragedy as the destruction of *His* House. *He* is directly involved. The direct involvement of God in the Ḥurban, and the greater impact of the Ḥurban on Him than on the Jewish people may be apparent by viewing the Ḥurban from a different perspective. I will tell you frankly, that studying the Gemara in Tractate *Zevaḥim*, which deals with sacrifices, brings me greater pleasure than the pleasure I would receive from

bringing sacrifices in the *Beit HaMikdash*. Through the *Torah shebe'al peh*, one can actually replace the Temple sacrifice with an idea, with a thought, with a penetrating analysis of the sections of the Gemara dealing with the Temple service. From this perspective, the destruction of the Temple is less devastating.

Similarly, if the *Beit HaMikdash* existed, I would certainly bring the *korban Pesaḥ*. The true enjoyment of this experience for me, however, would be from the study of the relevant portions of *Torah shebe'al peh*. I know what would happen. I would bring the *korban Pesaḥ*, have the *seder* and, as Hillel says, I would combine the meat of the *korban Pesaḥ* with *matza* and *maror*. This would be wonderful. The *seder* would continue, and about one o'clock in the morning I would take a look at Nahmanides' discussion of the four cups of wine in the *Milḥamot*, which is difficult. I would then invite one of the family members to study along with me in analyzing Nahmanides' words, and finally we would arrive at the true explanation. My pleasure from this study of Nahmanides would be greater than my pleasure from the *korban Pesaḥ*! I find that I have more joy when I study about the mitzva than when I actually perform the mitzva. Therefore, from a certain perspective, one might say that when we pray for the rebuilding of the *Beit HaMikdash*, it is for *His* sake because as long as the Jews are in exile, a *Ḥilul Hashem*, a desecration of God's name, exists. When one ponders Rav Ḥayyim's observation that God is directly involved in the *Ḥurban* as one of the litigants, the *Beit HaMikdash* is more important to God than it is to us.

25

community only, with the stanzas about Worms and Mainz being written by other paytanim (similar stanzas were written about the martyrs of Cologne and Frankfurt). Commentary for this kina begins on page 460.

מִי Would that my head were water, and my eyes a fountain of tears, / and I would cry all my days and nights / for the corpses of my babes and infants, and the aged of my community. / I ask you to respond, "Oh! Woe! Alas!" / And weep a weeping, much weeping. *Jer. 8:23*

        For the house of Israel and the people of the Lord who have fallen by sword.

וְדָמֹעַ My eyes flow with tears, and I will betake myself to the fields to weep, / and ask others stunned and embittered to join in my wailing / for the beautiful maidens and delicate lads, / wrapped in their schoolbooks and led to slaughter. / Their bodies, rosier than rubies, sapphire, or turquoise, / were slung and trampled like mud in the streets. / "Stay away! They are unclean," shouted the enemy about them. *Jer. 13:17* *Lam. 4:7* *Lam. 4:15*

        For the house of Israel and the people of the Lord who have fallen by sword.

וְתֵרַד Let my eyes flow with tears, I will wail and shake my head. / I will eulogize [the Torah] with weeping and with sackcloth. / She is more dear than fine gold, more precious than gold, / her glory inward, the glory of all precious vessels. / I have seen her torn, bereaved, and desolate. / Torah, Scripture, Mishna, and Aggada: / raise your voice, lament, and tell this tale. / Where are Torah, Talmud, and students? / The place is in ruin, no one there! *Jer. 13:17* *Is. 49:21*

        For the house of Israel and the people of the Lord who have fallen by sword.

וְעַפְעַפַּי My eyelids flow with water, dripping tears. / I weep bitterly for the murdered of Speyer. / It happened on the eighth day of the second month [Iyar] on the day of rest. / "Rest" was transposed to "tempest" destructive. / Handsome youths and dignified elders were killed. / They assembled, all agreeing to be martyred, / testifying to the unity of God's name, courageously. / Mighty men, who do His bidding speedily. / My priests and my young men, all ten expired. *Ezek. 23:12* *Ps. 103:20*

        For the house of Israel and the people of the Lord who have fallen by sword.

25

This kina, by Rabbi Kalonymos ben Yehuda of Speyer, laments the massacres perpetrated by the Crusaders in 1096, which destroyed the most prominent Jewish communities of the Rhineland. Some have suggested that Rabbi Kalonymos wrote a kina eulogizing the martyrs of his own

מִי יִתֵּן רֹאשִׁי מַיִם, וְעֵינִי מְקוֹר נוֹזְלִי.   — ירמיה ח, כג

וְאֶבְכֶּה כָּל יְמוֹתַי וְלֵילִי / אֶת חַלְלֵי טַפַּי וְעוֹלָלַי, וִישִׁישֵׁי קְהָלִי.
וְאֶתֵּם עֶנוּ אֲבוֹי, אוֹי וַאֲלֲלַי / וּבְכוּ בְכֶה רַב, וָהֶרֶב.
עַל בֵּית יִשְׂרָאֵל וְעַל עַם יהוה, כִּי נָפְלוּ בֶחָרֶב:

וְדִמְעַוֹת תֵּרַד עֵינִי, וְאֵלְכָה לִי שָׂדֶה בּוֹכִים / וַאֲבַכֶּה עַמִּי מָרֵי לֵבָב הַנְּבוֹכִים. — ירמיה יג, יז

עַל בְּתוּלוֹת הַיָּפוֹת, וִילָדִים הָרַכִּים / בְּסִפְרֵיהֶם נִכְרָכִים, וְלַטֶּבַח נִמְשָׁכִים.
אָדְמוּ עֶצֶם מִפְּנִינִים, סַפִּירִים וּנְפָכִים / כְּמוֹ טִיט חוּצוֹת, נִדָּשִׁים וְנִשְׁלָכִים. — איכה ד, ז
סוּרוּ טָמֵא, קָרְאוּ לָמוֹ מִלְּקָרֵב. — איכה ד, טו
עַל בֵּית יִשְׂרָאֵל וְעַל עַם יהוה, כִּי נָפְלוּ בֶחָרֶב:

וְתֵרַד עֵינִי דִמְעָה, וְאֵילִילָה וְאֶנוּדָה / וְלִבְכִי וְלַחֲגֹר שַׂק, אֶקְרָא לְהַסְפִּידָהּ. — ירמיה יג, יז
מִפָּז יְקָרָה, וּמִזָּהָב חֲמוּדָה / פְּנִימָה כְּבוּדָה, כְּבוֹד כָּל כְּלִי חֶמְדָּה.
רְאִיָּתָהּ קְרוּעָה, שְׂכוּלָה וְגַלְמוּדָה / הַתּוֹרָה וְהַמִּקְרָא וְהַמִּשְׁנָה וְהָאַגָּדָה. — ישעיה מט, כא
עֲנוּ וְקוֹנְנוּ זֹאת לְהַגִּידָהּ / אֵי תּוֹרָה וְתַלְמוּד וְהַלּוֹמְדָהּ.
הֲלֹא הַמָּקוֹם מֵאֵין יוֹשֵׁב חָרֵב.
עַל בֵּית יִשְׂרָאֵל וְעַל עַם יהוה, כִּי נָפְלוּ בֶחָרֶב:

וְעַפְעַפַּי יִזְּלוּ מַיִם, דֶּמַע לְהַגִּירָה / וַאֲקוֹנֵן מַר, עַל הֲרוּגֵי אַשְׁפִּירָא.
בַּשֵּׁנִי בִּשְׁמוֹנָה בוֹ, בְּיוֹם מַרְגּוֹעַ, הַקָּרָה / מַרְגּוֹעַי לִרְגוֹעַי, נֶחְלְפוּ לְהַבְעִירָה.
נֶהֶרְגוּ בַּחוּרֵי חֶמֶד, וִישִׁישֵׁי הֲדָרָה / נֶאֶסְפוּ יַחַד, נַפְשָׁם הִשְׁלִימוּ בְּמוֹרָא. — יחזקאל כג, יב
עַל יִחוּד שֵׁם הַמְיֻחָד, יִחֲדוּ בִּגְבוּרָה / גִּבּוֹרֵי כֹחַ, עֹשֵׂי דְבָרוֹ לְמַהֲרָה. — תהלים קג, כ
וְכֹהֲנֵי וַעֲלָמַי נִגּוֹעוּ, כֻּלָּהֶם עֲשָׂרָה.
עַל בֵּית יִשְׂרָאֵל וְעַל עַם יהוה, כִּי נָפְלוּ בֶחָרֶב:

וּבְמַר In my bitter agony and grief, I will compose a dirge. / Holy congregations! / Their massacre I remember today. / The community of Worms, special and unique. / Giants of the earth, innocent and pure! / Twice, they sanctified the One Name in awe, / cleansed once on the twenty-third of the month Ziv [Iyar], / And on [the first day of] the third month [Sivan], as they chanted Hallel, / they made a pact to be martyred for the love [of God]. / I will moan for them with a torrent of tears of woe, / all deserving to be endowed with majestic crowns!

1 Kings 6:1

> For the house of Israel and the people
> of the LORD who have fallen by sword.

וְעַל And upon the great of the wonderful community of Mainz, / swifter than eagles and stronger than lions, / they too consented in unison to sanctify the awesome One Name. / For them, I will scream a piercing scream with bitter soul, / as if for the destruction of both Temples, razed today, / and for the destruction of minor temples [synagogues] and study halls of Torah!

> For the house of Israel and the people
> of the LORD who have fallen by sword.

בַּחֹדֶשׁ On the third day of the third month [Sivan], these were added to my sorrow and curse. / That month was transformed into one of agony and trouble / on the day the Law was given, when I hoped to be spared in her merit. / On the very day she was given, she departed. / Gone back on high to her original home, / with her "containers" and her "pouches," those who searched her and studied her. / Her disciples and her students in darkness as in light!

> For the house of Israel and the people
> of the LORD who have fallen by sword.

שִׂימוּ Take this to heart, and compose a bitter eulogy. / Their murder is worthy of mourning and placing ash, / equal to the burning of the House of our God, the porch and the Palace, / because it is improper to add a day of breach and conflagration, / and wrong to advance the date; rather, to postpone it. / Therefore, today [Tisha B'Av], I will arouse my grief / and lament, and wail, and cry with bitter soul, / with sighs weighing heavily from dawn to dusk,

> For the house of Israel and the people
> of the LORD who have fallen by sword.

וּבְמַר יְגוֹנִי וְעָצְבִּי, יְלֵל אַחְבִּירָה / קְהִלּוֹת הַקֹּדֶשׁ, הֲרִיגָתָם הַיּוֹם בְּזָכְרָה.
קְהַל וֽוֹרְמַיְזָא, בְּחוּנָה וּבְחוּרָה / גְּאוֹנֵי אֶרֶץ, וּנְקִיֵּי טָהֳרָה.
פַּעֲמַיִם, קִדְּשׁוּ שֵׁם הַמְיֻחָד בְּמוֹרָא / בְּעֶשְׂרִים וּשְׁלֹשָׁה בְּחֹדֶשׁ זִיו, מלכים א ו, א
לְטָהֳרָה / וּבַחֹדֶשׁ הַשְּׁלִישִׁי, בִּקְרִיאַת הַלֵּל לְשׁוּרָה.
הִשְׁלִימוּ נַפְשָׁם בְּאַהֲבָה קְשׁוּרָה / אָהֵימָה עֲלֵיהֶם בִּבְכִי יְלֵל לְהַשְׁרָה.
כְּלוּלֵי כֶתֶר, עַל רֹאשָׁם לַעֲטָרָה.
עַל בֵּית יִשְׂרָאֵל וְעַל עַם יהוה, כִּי נָפְלוּ בֶחָרֶב:

וְעַל אַדִּירֵי קְהַל מַגֶּנְצָא הַהֲדוּרָה / מְנֻשָּׁרִים קַלּוּ, מֵאֲרָיוֹת לְהִתְגַּבְּרָה.
הִשְׁלִימוּ נַפְשָׁם עַל יִחוּד שֵׁם הַנּוֹרָא / וַעֲלֵיהֶם זַעֲקַת שֶׁבֶר אֶזְעַק, בְּנֶפֶשׁ מָרָה.
עַל שְׁנֵי מִקְדָּשַׁי, יְסוֹדָם כְּהַיּוֹם עֹרְעָרָה / וְעַל חָרְבוֹת מְעַט מִקְדָּשַׁי, וּמִדְרְשֵׁי הַתּוֹרָה.
עַל בֵּית יִשְׂרָאֵל וְעַל עַם יהוה, כִּי נָפְלוּ בֶחָרֶב:

בַּחֹדֶשׁ הַשְּׁלִישִׁי בַּשְּׁלִישִׁי, נוֹסָף לְדָאֲבוֹן וּמְאֵרָה / הַחֹדֶשׁ אֲשֶׁר נֶהְפַּךְ לְיָגוֹן וְצָרָה.
בְּיוֹם מַתַּן דָּת, שְׁבַרְתִּי לְהִתְאַשְּׁרָה / וּבְיוֹם נְתִינָתָהּ, כְּמוֹ כֵן אָז חָזְרָה.
עָלְתָה לָּהּ לַמָּרוֹם, לַמָּקוֹם מְדוֹרָה / עִם תִּיקָהּ וְנַרְתִּקָהּ, וְהַדּוֹרְשָׁהּ וְחוֹקְרָהּ.
לוֹמְדֶיהָ וְשׁוֹנֶיהָ בָּאִישׁוֹן, כְּמוֹ אוֹרָה.
עַל בֵּית יִשְׂרָאֵל וְעַל עַם יהוה, כִּי נָפְלוּ בֶחָרֶב:

שִׂימוּ נָא עַל לְבַבְכֶם, מִסְפֵּד מַר לְקָשְׁרָה / כִּי שְׁקוּלָה הֲרִיגָתָם, לְהִתְאַבֵּל וּלְהִתְעַפְּרָה / כִּשְׂרֵפַת בֵּית אֱלֹהֵינוּ, הָאוּלָם וְהַבִּירָה.
וְכִי אֵין לְהוֹסִיף מוֹעֵד שֶׁבֶר וְתַבְעֵרָה / וְאֵין לְהַקְדִּים, זוּלָתִי לְאַחֲרָה.
תַּחַת כֵּן, הַיּוֹם לִוְיָתִי אֲעוֹרְרָה / וְאֶסְפְּדָה וְאֵילִילָה, וְאֶבְכֶּה בְּנֶפֶשׁ מָרָה.
וְאֶנְחָתִי כָבְדָה, מִבֹּקֶר וְעַד עֶרֶב.
עַל בֵּית יִשְׂרָאֵל וְעַל עַם יהוה, כִּי נָפְלוּ בֶחָרֶב:

עַל For these, I cry and moan moans, / and summon the lamenters and wise women. / "Alas," and "Alack," they all murmur. / Does any wound compare to my wound? / Outside, the sword murders, and indoors, there is terror! / My corpses, killed by the sword, lie strewn, nude and naked. / Bodies lying like refuse for wild beasts and animals. / Nursing child and aged man, lads and lasses / were teased by my oppressors and endured great shame. / "Where is their God? The Rock they trusted in" until death? / Let Him come and rescue and resurrect their souls! / Mighty God, who like You forgives bundles of sins? / You are silent and restrained; why do You not gird Yourself with fury? / When my mockers say to me, "If He is a God, let Him do battle!" *Lam. 1:16*

Is. 5:25
Deut. 32:25
Deut. 32:37

Judges 6:31

> For the house of Israel and the people
> of the LORD who have fallen by sword.

עֵינִי My eyes, my eyes, flow with tears. Our singing has turned into mourning. / My flute accompanies mourners, without respite and never abating. / Who will approach me consolingly, and who will encourage me to awaken? / Wrath issues forth, and a tempest arrives. / The attacking foe devours me and panics me, / breaks my bones, strews them and scatters them. / He has hacked down my great ones, the navel and nucleus. / My wound is fatal, none to heal or cure. / That is why I say, "Let me be, I will weep bitterly." / Shedding tears until my cheeks shrivel, *Lam. 1:16*
Lam. 5:15
Job 30:31
Jer. 30:23
Num. 10:9
Lam. 3:4
Lam. 1:15
Jer. 15:18
Is. 22:4

> For the house of Israel and the people
> of the LORD who have fallen by sword.

Kina 26 starts on page 468.

איכה א, טז	עַל אֵלֶּה אֲנִי בוֹכִיָּה, וְלִבִּי נוֹהֵם נְהִימוֹת / וְאֶקְרָא לַמְקוֹנְנוֹת, וְאֶל הַחֲכָמוֹת.
	אֵלִי וְאֶלְיָה, כֻּלָּם הוּמוֹת / הֲיֵשׁ מַכְאוֹב לְמַכְאוֹבִי לְדַמּוֹת.
	מִחוּץ תְּשַׁכֶּל חֶרֶב, וּמֵחֲדָרִים אֵימוֹת / חַלָלַי, חַלְלֵי חֶרֶב, מוּטָלִים עֲרֻמִּים וַעֲרֻמּוֹת.
ישעיה ה, כה דברים לב, כה	נִבְלָתָם כַּסּוּחָה, לְחַיַּת אֶרֶץ וְלִבְהֵמוֹת / יוֹנֵק עִם אִישׁ שֵׂיבָה, עֲלָמִים וַעֲלָמוֹת.
דברים לב, לז	מִתְעַתְּעִים בְּמוֹ מוֹנֵי, וּמְרַבִּים כְּלִמּוֹת / אֵי אֱלֹהֵימוֹ אָמְרוּ, צוּר חָסָיוּ בוֹ עַד מוֹת / יָבוֹא וְיוֹשִׁיעַ, וְיַחֲזִיר נְשָׁמוֹת.
	חֲסִין יָהּ, מִי כָמְוֹךָ, נוֹשֵׂא בָּאֱלָמוֹת / תֶּחֱשֶׁה וְתִתְאַפַּק, וְלֹא תַחְגֹּר חֵמוֹת.
שופטים ו, לא	בֶּאֱמוֹר אֵלַי מַלְעִיגַי, אִם אֱלֹהִים הוּא, יָרֵב.
	עַל בֵּית יִשְׂרָאֵל וְעַל עַם יהוה, כִּי נָפְלוּ בֶּחָרֶב:
איכה א, טז איכה ה, טו איוב ל, לא	עֵינִי עֵינִי יֹרְדָה מַּיִם, כִּי נֶהְפַּךְ לְאֵבֶל מְשׂוֹרֵר / וְעֻגָבִי לְקוֹל בּוֹכִים, מִלְּהָפֵג וּלְקָרֵר.
ירמיה ל, כג	מִי יָנוּד לִי, וְאֵין מַחֲזִיק לְהִתְעוֹרֵר / חֵמָה בִּי יָצְאָה, וְסַעַר מִתְגּוֹרֵר.
במדבר י, ט איכה ג, ד איכה א, טו	אֲכָלָנִי, הֲמָמָנִי, הַצַּר הַצּוֹרֵר / שִׁבֵּר עַצְמוֹתַי, זוֹרֵר וּמְפָרֵר / סָלָה כָל אַבִּירַי, הַטַּבּוּר וְהַשְׁדֵּרָה.
ירמיה טו, יח	מַכָּתִי אֲנוּשָׁה, בְּאֵין מַתְעִיל וּמְזוֹרֵר / רְטִיָּה וּמָזוֹר אֵין לְבָרֵר.
ישעיה כב, ד	עַל כֵּן אָמַרְתִּי, שְׁעוּ מֶנִּי, אֲמָרֵר / בַּבֶּכִי, דִּמְעָתִי עַל לֶחָיַי לְצָרֵר.
	עַל בֵּית יִשְׂרָאֵל וְעַל עַם יהוה, כִּי נָפְלוּ בֶּחָרֶב:

Kina 26 starts on page 469.

COMMENTARY ON KINA 25

With this *kina*, we return to a description of the massacres in Germany during the Crusades. In the previous *kina* concerning the Crusades ("הֶחֱרִישׁוּ מִמֶּנִּי וַאֲדַבֵּרָה"), the names of the communities were not mentioned. In this *kina*, the names of specific communities, as well as dates of the massacres, are identified.

The author of this *kina* is the famous Kalonymos ben Yehuda, a member of an Italian family of *paytanim* that settled in Germany. Rashi mentions a Rabbi Kalonymos (*Betzah* 24b, s.v. *ule'erev*), and the author of this *kina* was a descendant of that Rabbi Kalonymos.

The main motif of this *kina*, a motif found in some of the prior *kinot*, is that the death of the righteous is equivalent to the burning of the *Beit HaMikdash*. If we are to mourn for the *Beit HaMikdash*, we must also mourn the death of the great Torah scholars. Since the tragedy of the destruction of the Torah centers in Germany is equivalent to the Ḥurban Beit HaMikdash, we are justified in thinking that a special fast day should have been established to mourn for the martyrs of those massacres. However, the *kina* declares, we are not to add any fast day beyond Tisha B'Av to commemorate any other catastrophe, massacre or destruction.

It is interesting that a fast day was instituted on the twentieth day of Sivan by Rabbeinu Tam to commemorate an attack against the Jews, unrelated to the Crusades (*Emek HaBakha* of Rabbi Yosef HaKohen; *Magen Avraham, Oraḥ Ḥayyim* 580:9; *Sha'arei Teshuva* ibid., 9). Centuries later, when the Khmelnitsky pogroms occurred in 1648, the twentieth day of Sivan was proclaimed to be a fast day for both the persecutions against the German Jews and the Khmelnitsky persecutions. There are *seliḥot*, penitential prayers, composed for that day. Notwithstanding the tradition of observing the twentieth day of Sivan, this *kina* declares that Tisha B'Av is the exclusive fast day that commemorates all of the tragedies that befell the Jewish people, and that no other fast day should be instituted for this purpose.

I do not know why there are no *kinot* recited on Tisha B'Av which commemorate the Khmelnitsky persecutions. The *kinot* that were composed to commemorate the Khmelnitsky persecutions and which are recited on the twentieth of Sivan are not said on Tisha B'Av.

טַפַּי וְעוֹלָלַי, וִישִׁישֵׁי קְהָלִי *My babes and infants and the aged of my community.* We mourn not only for the Torah scholars, but for all Jews, infants and the elderly, children and great scholars.

וְאִתֶּם עֲנוּ אֲבוֹי, אוֹי וְאַלְלַי *I ask you to respond, "Oh! Woe! Alas!"* This is the classic formulation of a *kina*. The Gemara states (*Mo'ed Katan* 28b) that a *kina* consists of a responsive cry, "One says and the others respond."

וַאֲבַכֶּה עִמִּי מָרֵי לֵבָב הַנְּבוּכִים *And ask others stunned and embittered to join in my wailing.* The term *"marei lev"* means those who are stunned or confused. When a catastrophe occurs in Jewish life, the first reaction of the people is confusion. They ask, "How could it happen? Why did it happen?" Times of Ḥurban are times of "נְבֻכִים הֵם בָּאָרֶץ, *They are wandering astray in the land*" (Exodus 14:3).

Many Jews were perplexed during the Holocaust era. In those years, I traveled between Boston and New York by train, and people used to sit next to me and ask me questions many of which were influenced by missionary literature. Many of those questions have been answered by the establishment of the State of Israel, and the confusion subsided. The emergence of the State was a *hashgaḥa*, an act of Divine Providence.

כְּמוֹ טִיט חוּצוֹת, נִדָּשִׁים וְנִשְׁלָכִים *Were slung and trampled like mud in the streets.* Apparently, they did not permit the Jews to bury their dead. The Nazis did the same during the Holocaust.

בְּכוֹד כָּל כְּלֵי חֶמְדָּה *The glory of all precious vessels.* This is a eulogy for the physical *Sefer Torah*, for the obliteration of the parchment and the ink.

רְאִיתִיהָ קְרוּעָה, שְׁכוּלָה וְגַלְמוּדָה *I have seen her torn, bereaved, and desolate.* The Torah is described as a forlorn mother: *keru'a*, she is dressed in rags, *shekhula*, she has lost her children, *vegalmuda*, she is alone.

הַתּוֹרָה וְהַמִּקְרָא וְהַמִּשְׁנָה וְהָאַגָּדָה *Torah, Scripture, Mishna, and Aggada.* This refers to the *Torah shebikhtav*, the written law, as well as the *Torah shebe'al peh*, the Oral Law.

אֵי תוֹרָה וְתַלְמוּד וְהַלּוֹמְדָהּ *Where are Torah, Talmud, and students?* Some versions of this phrase have *"talmud,"* but the proper version contains the word *"talmid."* The version with the word *talmud* does not seem to me to be correct. There is a difference between *talmid* and *lomda*, even though both words mean "a student." *Talmid* refers to a *talmid ḥaham*, a great scholar, one who accomplishes a great deal in his study. *Lomda* refers to anyone who is engaged in Torah study, whether or not he accomplishes much. The message of this phrase of the *kina* is that it is important to mourn not only for the great scholars but for the ordinary Jews as well. One does not have to be a genius or a great teacher of Torah. All one has to do is study, at any level. This

itself is part of *mesora*, the chain of tradition. Our *mesora* consists not only of brilliant scholars, but also of simple Jews who study even if they do not understand what they study.

The phrase "אֵי תוֹרָה וְתַלְמוּד וְהַלּוֹמְדָהּ" was the phrase used by a Holocaust survivor to describe to me his feelings at visiting Vilna on *Kol Nidrei* night in 1945. Shortly after he was liberated, he returned to Vilna where he had lived before the War, for the High Holidays. It is difficult to describe what Vilna looked like on Rosh HaShana and Yom Kippur before the War. In one neighborhood there were eight or nine synagogues, including the *Beit Knesset HaGra* and a synagogue that dated back to the Middle Ages. This person remembered what the Vilna *shulhoif*, the neighborhood where the synagogues were located, was like on *Kol Nidrei* night when tens of thousands of Jews would congregate. On that *Kol Nidrei* night in 1945, he returned to the synagogue where his mother used to pray, and it was deserted. He used the phrase from this *kina* to describe his feelings, "Where is the Torah and those who study it? Her place is desolate, with none to dwell therein."

This survivor continued with a haunting story. His mother was a pious Jewess and of course attended shul on Yom Kippur. When it came time for *Maftir Yonah*, she used to leave the shul for half an hour and feed her cat at home. The cat would wait for her, and after feeding the cat she would return to shul. This man, who knew the cat, spent Yom Kippur of 1945 at the home where his parents had lived, and at 4:30 in the afternoon, there was a scratching at the door. It was the same cat waiting for him to feed her the way his mother had. This visit had a traumatic effect on him. At that moment, he felt the full magnitude of the Holocaust. Indescribable despair and bleakness overwhelmed him.

This story also illustrates how accurately Lamentations captures the devastation of the Ḥurban. When a place is desolate and devoid of human beings, it is tragic; but when animals prowl there, the pain is almost unbearable. As the verse in Lamentations (5:18) says, "For Mount Zion is desolate." It is tragic that Mount Zion is desolate and deserted; but, not only are people absent, the verse continues, "foxes prowl over it." The fox and the cat walk around. All he saw was the ruins of the synagogues and the cat prowling amidst the ruins. The only link between the past and present was the cat.

This is the same picture painted by Kalonymos, the author of this *kina*. He certainly was familiar with Speyer, Mainz and Worms when there was vibrant Torah study, liveliness and enthusiasm in the *yeshivot* and noise and bustle

in the streets. And now, he visits the same places, and all he sees is "the cat" and he asks, "Where are the Torah scholars? Behold, her place is desolate."

עַל הֲרוּגֵי אַשְׁפִּירָא *For the murdered of Speyer.* Speyer is the first of the three communities described in this *kina*: Speyer, Mainz and Worms. Each of these communities was a major center of Torah study. Rabbeinu Gershom had lived in Mainz, and Rashi in Worms, and many of the Tosafists lived in Speyer.

נֶהֶרְגוּ בַּחוּרֵי חֶמֶד, וִישִׁישֵׁי הֲדָרָה *Handsome youths and dignified elders were killed.* From this phrase it appears that the yeshiva in Speyer was destroyed.

כֻּלָּהֶם עֲשָׂרָה *All ten expired.* Speyer was attacked twice. The first time, only ten people, *talmidei ḥakhamim*, were killed. The bishop of the city protected the Jews. But the Crusaders then returned several days later, and the bishop abandoned the Jews. The Crusaders destroyed the entire community. The *paytan* combines these two incidents in his description. This phrase, which recounts the murder of the ten leaders and youths, refers to the initial massacre, and the phrase several lines above, נֶהֶרְגוּ בַּחוּרֵי חֶמֶד, refers to the total destruction of the community.

הֲרִיגָתָם הַיּוֹם בְּזִכְרָה *Their massacre I remember today.* The emphasis is on "*hayom*," on *this* day. They are remembered on Tisha B'Av, not on the day of their *yahrzeit*. The proper day of mourning, fasting and *kinot* for all Jewish tragedies is Tisha B'Av.

בִּקְרִיאַת הַלֵּל לְשׁוֹרְרָה *As they chanted Hallel.* The community in Worms was also attacked twice. The second massacre took place on Rosh Ḥodesh Sivan, while they were reciting Hallel. It is possible to interpret this phrase as referring to the holiday of Shavuot, but the Ra'avan in his responsa (*Sefer Rokeaḥ* 212; *Beit Yosef, Oraḥ Ḥayyim* 579:2) confirms that the attack took place on Rosh Ḥodesh Sivan.

וְעַל חָרְבוֹת מְעַט מִקְדָּשַׁי *And for the destruction of minor temples.* The Gemara in *Megilla* states (*Megilla* 29a) that the synagogues and study houses are *mikdeshei me'at*, miniature versions of the *Beit HaMikdash*. We mourn for the miniature *Batei Mikdash* that were destroyed in these communities as much as we mourn for the destruction of the two Temples in Jerusalem.

בַּחֹדֶשׁ הַשְּׁלִישִׁי בַּשְּׁלִישִׁי *On the third day of the third month.* The Crusades always began in the spring because the armies did not march in the winter.

The *kinot* identify only the cities of Speyer, Mainz and Worms. However,

there were numerous smaller towns and villages as well that were set upon by the Crusaders and in which the Jewish communities were destroyed. The *kinot* name only the major centers because one cannot mention all of the destroyed communities. Similarly, when we refer to the Ḥurban Yerushalayim, the intent is not to refer to Jerusalem exclusively, but to the destruction of the hundreds of towns and villages that was perpetrated as well.

וּבְיוֹם נְתִינָתָהּ, כְּמוֹ כֵן אָז חָזְרָה *On the very day she was given, she departed.* On Shavuot, the day of the massacre, great Torah scholars were murdered. Thus on the anniversary of the very day on which the Torah was given, it was returned to God.

עִם תֵּיקָהּ וְנַרְתֵּקָהּ *With her "containers" and her "pouches."* The *kina* refers here to the burning of *sifrei Torah* and the Talmud which occurred on Shavuot. A similar event of the burning of the Talmud also occurred many years later, and this is commemorated in a separate *kina*, "שַׁאֲלִי, שְׂרוּפָה בָאֵשׁ," composed by the Maharam of Rothenburg, the teacher of Rabbeinu Asher. There were instances when the Pope would suddenly issue an order that all *sifrei kodesh*, books of Jewish learning, should be burned, throughout Germany, France, Italy, Spain or elsewhere. It is important to bear in mind that these events occurred before the invention of printing, and it was very difficult and expensive to copy a Talmud or, for example, the Code of Maimonides. The Jews remained without *sifrei kodesh* and simply had to know all of the subject matter by heart. Otherwise, they could not continue learning.

One should note that this *kina* records several different tragedies. First, the pogroms in Speyer, Worms and Mainz in which thousands of people were killed, among whom were the greatest scholars. Second, the destruction of houses of study and synagogues, which constituted persecution aimed against the study of Torah. And third, the physical destruction of *sifrei Torah* and books of the Talmud.

וְהַדּוֹרְשָׁהּ וְחוֹקְרָהּ *Those who searched her and studied her.* The *kina* uses a metaphor. The Torah is dressed beautifully, with its cover and its crowns. The Torah is leaving and returning to heaven, and she has invited those who study her and know her, to accompany her.

כִּי שְׁקוּלָה הֲרִיגָתָם...כִּשְׂרֵפַת בֵּית אֱלֹהֵינוּ... וְכִי אֵין לְהוֹסִיף מוֹעֵד שֶׁבֶר וְתַבְעֵרָה *Their murder is...equal to the burning of the House of our God...because it is improper to add a day of breach and conflagration.* As noted above, this is the main motif of this *kina*. The death and destruction of Speyer, Worms and Mainz are as

tragic as the destruction of the *Beit HaMikdash*. Tisha B'Av, however, must remain the exclusive fast day on which we mourn all Jewish tragedies.

וְאֵין לְהַקְדִּים, זוּלָתִי לְאַחֲרָה *And wrong to advance the date; rather, to postpone it.* The language of this phrase is difficult to understand, and we are not certain what it means. If the intent of the *paytan* is that no day of mourning other than Tisha B'Av should be designated, the language should have been "וְאֵין לְהַקְדִּים וְאֵין לְאַחֲרָה, One should not have a day of mourning before Tisha B'Av, nor should one postpone it." According to the language of this phrase, the word *zulati* means that one *may* delay or postpone, and this seems to imply that one may designate a separate day of mourning after Tisha B'Av. *Zulati* is a strange word, and a scribal or printing error may have occurred in the text.

Perhaps this phrase can be interpreted in light of the statement in the Gemara (*Megilla* 5a) regarding the fast of the seventeenth day of Tammuz that "אַקְדּוּמֵי פּוּרְעָנוּת לָא מַקְדְּמִים, One should not advance the day of mourning." With the exception of the Fast of Esther, we do not observe a fast day earlier than its calendar date. This rule is based on the operative principle that we delay the observance of *puranut,* of mourning and travail, rather than accelerating it. Consequently, when a fast day falls on Shabbat, the observance is delayed until Sunday, rather than predated to Thursday. Similarly, we cannot observe a day of mourning earlier in the calendar than the seventeenth of Tammuz. Thus, if one wanted to introduce a new day of mourning, it would have to be after the seventeenth of Tammuz, and it would make sense to delay it as much as possible, and in that case it would fall in the calendar after Tisha B'Av. If that were to be done, Tisha B'Av would not be the final day of mourning, but only one among other days of mourning. Since the *paytan* wants to avoid that result, the commemoration must take place on Tisha B'Av itself.

Perhaps another way of approaching this phrase is to interpret it not as relating to time, but rather as relating to the worth or appreciation of Tisha B'Av. The intent of the phrase is that if one proclaims a separate fast day for some event, it is an indication that that person does not appreciate the power of Tisha B'Av and does not consider Tisha B'Av sufficiently worthy to cover that event as well.

מִי כָמוֹךָ, נוֹשֵׂא בַּאֲלֻמּוֹת *Who like You forgives bundles of sins?* Another way of translating this phrase is, "Who is as mute as You are?" In an ironic twist, the *paytan* has taken the word *eilim* ("mighty") from the phrase "מִי כָמֹכָה

בָּאֵלִם יהוה, Who is like You, O Lord, among the mighty?" (Exodus 15:11), and rendered it as "*alumot*, mute."

בֶּאֱמוֹר אֵלַי מַלְעִיגַי, אִם אֱלֹהִים הוּא, יָרֵב *When my mockers say to me: "If He is a God, let Him do battle!"* It is interesting that toward the end of the *kina*, the *paytan* places the emphasis upon the blasphemy and ridicule which the Crusaders perpetrated.

26

א Then, Jeremiah went to the graves of the patriarchs
and said, "Dear departed ones,
why do you lie dormant?
ב Your children are exiled, and your homes destroyed!
Where is the merit of their forefathers, earned in the wilderness?"
> If they, mortal men, transgressed the covenant, where is the
> merit of those who accepted the covenant [the patriarchs]?

ג They all cried out in lament
over the absent children.
ד They prayed for mercy from the One who dwells on high:
"Where is the promise, 'I will remember the covenant with the ancients'?" *Lev. 26:45*
> What can I do for you, My children? This is My decree!

ה [God responded,] "They exchanged My honor for naught.
They had no fear and no remorse.
ו I turned My eyes from them, but they did not repent or show distress.
How can I restrain Myself when they deny Me?"
> If they, mortal men, transgressed the covenant, where is the
> merit of those who accepted the covenant [the patriarchs]?

ז The father of the multitude [Abraham] shouted in their defense,
and pleaded with the exalted God:
ח "Is it in vain that I suffered ten trials?
Now I see their collapse.
Where is the promise, 'Fear not, Abraham!'?" *Gen. 15:1*
> What can I do for you, My children? This is My decree!

ט [God responded,] "They erred and estranged themselves
by worshiping idols.
י They intended to hew cisterns, broken cisterns.
How can I restrain Myself when they have annulled the
Ten Commandments?"
> If they, mortal men, transgressed the covenant, where is the
> merit of those who accepted the covenant [the patriarchs]?

26

In this kina, HaKalir uses a similar structure to that of Kina 9, namely an imagined dialogue between God and the mourning nation, with alternating refrains reflecting the two voices. The kina is based on the Midrash (Eikha Raba, Petiḥta 24) which describes the prophet Jeremiah calling upon the patriarchs to beg for mercy for their exiled children. Commentary for this kina begins on page 472.

אָז בַּהֲלֹךְ יִרְמְיָהוּ אֶל קִבְרֵי אָבוֹת / וְנָם, עֲצָמוֹת חֲבִיבוֹת, מָה אַתֶּם שׁוֹכְבוֹת.

בְּנֵיכֶם גָּלוּ, וּבָתֵּיכֶם חֲרֵבוֹת / וְאַיֵּה זְכוּת אָבוֹת, בְּאֶרֶץ תַּלְאוּבוֹת:

אִם כְּאָדָם עָבְרוּ בְרִית / אַיֵּה זְכוּת כְּרוּתֵי בְרִית.

גָּעוּ כֻלָּם בִּבְכִיִּים / עַל חֶסְרוֹן בָּנִים

דּוֹבְבוּ בְּקוֹל תַּחֲנוּנִים / פְּנֵי שׁוֹכֵן מְעוֹנִים.

וְאַיֵּה הַבְטָחַת, וְזָכַרְתִּי לָהֶם בְּרִית רִאשֹׁנִים:

ויקרא כו, מה

מָה אֶעֱשֶׂה לָכֶם בָּנַי / גְּזֵרָה הִיא מִלְּפָנַי.

הֵם הֵמִירוּ כְבוֹדִי בְּתֹהוּ / וְלֹא פָחֲדוּ וְלֹא רָהוּ.

וָאַעֲלִים עֵינַי מֵהֶם, וְלֹא שָׁבוּ וְלֹא נָהוּ.

וְאֵיךְ אֶתְאַפַּק עַל אֲמִירַת לֹא הוּא:

אִם כְּאָדָם עָבְרוּ בְרִית / אַיֵּה זְכוּת כְּרוּתֵי בְרִית.

זָעַק אָב הֲמוֹן בַּעֲבוּרָם / וְחִנֵּן פְּנֵי אֵל רָם.

חִנָּם נִסֵּיתִי עֶשֶׂר בְּחִינוֹת עֲבוּרָם / וְהֵן חָזִיתִי שִׁבְרָם.

בראשית טו, א

וְאַיֵּה הַבְטָחַת, אַל תִּירָא אַבְרָם:

מָה אֶעֱשֶׂה לָכֶם בָּנַי / גְּזֵרָה הִיא מִלְּפָנַי.

טָעוּ לְהָזְרוֹת / בַּעֲבוֹדוֹת זָרוֹת.

יָעֲצוּ לַחְצֹב בֵּארוֹת / בֹּארֹת נִשְׁבָּרוֹת.

וְאֵיךְ אֶתְאַפַּק עַל בִּטּוּל עֲשֶׂרֶת הַדִּבְּרוֹת:

אִם כְּאָדָם עָבְרוּ בְרִית / אַיֵּה זְכוּת כְּרוּתֵי בְרִית.

כ So Isaac screamed to the One who dwells on high,
ל "Was it in vain that I was inscribed to be slaughtered?
Now my descendants are crushed and obliterated.
Where is the promise, 'My covenant, I will maintain with Isaac!'?" *Gen 17:21*
        What can I do for you, My children? This is My decree!

מ [God responded,] "They rebelled against Jeremiah
and profaned Mount Moriah.
נ I tire of hearing the cry *Is. 1:14*
that rises up from oblivion.
How can I restrain Myself over the murder of Zechariah?"
        If they, mortal men, transgressed the covenant, where is the
        merit of those who accepted the covenant [the patriarchs]?

ס [Jacob,] who was born to study, spoke up,
shedding tears like a crocodile,
ע "The children I raised with such travail,
how they have been shorn from me and are gone.
And I have been punished a thousand-fold for the blood they shed."
        What can I do for you, My children? This is My decree!

פ The faithful shepherd [Moses] uttered,
ground into ash and dirtied,
צ "The sheep I nurtured in my lap
are prematurely shorn!
Where is the promise, '[Israel] is not bereft!'?" *Jer. 51:5*
        If they, mortal men, transgressed the covenant, where is the
        merit of those who accepted the covenant [the patriarchs]?

ק The sound of Leah's wail, pounds upon her heart;
ר her sister Rachel bemoans her children;
Zilpah, slaps her face;
Bilhah, laments with both hands!
        What can I do for you, My children? This is My decree!

ש [God's final response:] "Return, perfect ones, to your place of rest.
I will indeed fulfill your requests.
ש I was sent to Babylon because of you,
and will return your children from exile."

Kina 27 starts on page 478.

כֹּה צָוַח יִצְחָק / פְּנֵי שׁוֹכֵן שְׁחַק.
לָשָׁוְא בִּי טֶבַח הוּחַק / וְהֵן זַרְעִי נִשְׁחַק וְנִמְחַק.
וְאַיֵּה הַבְטָחַת, וְאֶת־בְּרִיתִי אָקִים אֶת־יִצְחָק: בראשית יז, כא
מָה אֶעֱשֶׂה לָכֶם בָּנַי / גְּזֵרָה הִיא מִלְּפָנַי.

מָרוּ בְיִרְמְיָה / וְטִמְּאוּ הַר הַמּוֹרִיָּה.
נִלְאֵיתִי נְשֹׂא גֵעְיָה / עוֹלָה לִי מִנְּשִׁיָּה. ישעיה א, יד
וְאֵיךְ אֶתְאַפַּק עַל הֲרִיגַת זְכַרְיָה:
אִם כְּאָדָם עָבְרוּ בְרִית / אַיֵּה זְכוּת כְּרוּתֵי בְרִית.

סָח יֶלֶד בְּתֶלֶף / דְּמָעוֹת כְּתַנִּין זוֹלֵף.
עוֹלָלַי אֲשֶׁר טִפַּחְתִּי בְעֶלֶף / אֵיךְ גֻּוַּז מֶנִּי בְחֶלֶף.
וְאֵיךְ הָפְרַע מֶנִּי, דָּמִים בְּדָמִים כַּמָּה אָלֶף:
מָה אֶעֱשֶׂה לָכֶם בָּנַי / גְּזֵרָה הִיא מִלְּפָנַי.

פָּץ רוֹעֶה נֶאֱמָן / כָּפוּשׁ בָּאֵפֶר, וּמְדַמָּן.
צֹאן אֲשֶׁר בְּחֵיקִי הָאֱמַן / אֵיךְ גֻּוַּז בְּלֹא זְמָן.
וְאַיֵּה הַבְטָחַת, כִּי לֹא־אַלְמָן: ירמיה נא, ה
אִם כְּאָדָם עָבְרוּ בְרִית / אַיֵּה זְכוּת כְּרוּתֵי בְרִית.

קוֹל בִּכִי לֵאָה, מִתְוַפֶּפֶת עַל לְבָבֶיהָ.
רָחֵל אֲחוֹתָהּ, מְבַכָּה עַל בָּנֶיהָ.
זִלְפָּה מַכָּה פָנֶיהָ / בִּלְהָה מְקוֹנֶנֶת בִּשְׁתֵּי יָדֶיהָ:
שׁוּבוּ תְמִימִים לִמְנוּחַתְכֶם / מַלֵּא אֲמַלֵּא כָּל מִשְׁאֲלוֹתֵיכֶם.
שְׁלַחְתִּי בַבָּלָה לְמַעַנְכֶם / הִנְנִי מְשׁוֹבֵב גָּלוּת בְּנֵיכֶם:

Kina 27 starts on page 479.

COMMENTARY ON KINA 26

This *kina*, composed by Rabbi Elazar HaKalir, is based on the Midrash (*Eikha Raba*, *Petiḥta* 24) that at the time that the *Beit HaMikdash* was being destroyed, God told Jeremiah to go to the Cave of Makhpela and awaken the patriarchs and Moses and tell them to appear before the celestial throne to plead for the redemption of their descendants. The three patriarchs and Moses interceded on behalf of the Jewish people, but were not successful in arousing God's mercy. Then the matriarch Rachel offered her petition, and God responded, "Refrain your voice from weeping and your eyes from tears; for your work shall be rewarded ... and your children shall return to their own border" (Jeremiah 31:16–17).

אָז בַּהֲלֹךְ יִרְמְיָהוּ אֶל קִבְרֵי אָבוֹת *Then, Jeremiah went to the graves of the patriarchs.* Jeremiah went to fulfill the decree of God and visit the graves of the patriarchs. What follows is a dialogue between God and the patriarchs in which He tells them why He was so harsh on their descendants.

וְאַיֵּה זְכוּת אָבוֹת, בְּאֶרֶץ תַּלְאוּבוֹת *Where is the merit of their forefathers, earned in the wilderness?* The implication is that the patriarchs should demand that God comply with the *berit avot*, the covenant with the patriarchs.

אִם כְּאָדָם עָבְרוּ בְרִית / אַיֵּה זְכוּת כְּרוּתֵי בְרִית *If they, mortal men, transgressed the covenant, where is the merit of those who accepted the covenant?* If the Jewish people violated the covenant with God because of human frailty, then the covenant between God and the patriarchs should have been a mitigating factor.

וְזָכַרְתִּי לָהֶם בְּרִית רִאשֹׁנִים *I will remember the covenant with the ancients.* This verse from Leviticus (26:45) refers to the covenant with the Jews who were redeemed from Egypt. It is difficult to understand why Rabbi Elazar HaKalir uses this phrase, when it is clear from the context that his intent is to refer to the covenant with the patriarchs, and not to the covenant with the Jews who left Egypt. The question is compounded by the existence of another verse which HaKalir could have used which does refer specifically to the *berit avot*: "then I will remember My covenant with Jacob, and also My covenant with Isaac, and also My covenant with Abraham will I remember, and I will remember the land" (Leviticus 26:42).

מָה אֶעֱשֶׂה לָכֶם בָּנַי / גְּזֵרָה הִיא מִלְּפָנַי *What can I do for you, My children? This is My decree!* When the Gemara speaks about something incomprehensible that

can be understood only within the infinite mind of God but not within the finite minds of human beings, it uses the term *gezera*. There are many things that a human being cannot understand, no matter how exalted his or her intellectual talent – these matters are referred to as *gezerot*.

עַל אֲמִירַת לֹא הוּא **When they deny Me.** This is an allusion to the verse in Jeremiah, "And they have been false to the Lord and said: It is not He" (5:12).

זָעַק אַב הֲמוֹן **The father of the multitude [Abraham] shouted.** With this stanza, the *kina* introduces the individual arguments of each patriarch. This stanza contains the plea of Abraham.

טָעוּ לִהְזָרוֹת / בַּעֲבוֹדוֹת זָרוֹת **They erred and estranged themselves by worshiping idols.** God's response to Abraham's plea is: Why are you, of all people, interceding on their behalf? You are the one who destroyed *avoda zara* and introduced monotheism into the world, and they engaged in the very idolatry that you destroyed.

יָעֲצוּ לַחְצֹב בֹּארוֹת / בֹּארֹת נִשְׁבָּרוֹת **They intended to hew cisterns, broken cisterns.** God continues His response to Abraham: You are the one who dug wells, which, according to our sages (see *Torah Shelema* to Genesis 26:15), were not ordinary wells, but wells of knowledge and enlightenment. And what did they do? They dug wells with polluted water. They were guilty not only of worshiping *avoda zara*, but of other transgressions as well. The phrase "to hew" is an allusion to the similar phrase in Jeremiah (2:13) in which Israel is rebuked for forsaking the Almighty's source of living water, for the shattered cisterns that will not hold water.

וְאַיֵּה הַבְטָחַת, וְאֶת־בְּרִיתִי אָקִים אֶת־יִצְחָק **Where is the promise, 'My covenant, I will maintain with Isaac!'?** In this stanza, Isaac asserts the argument that God should remember His promise to fulfill His covenant with him. This raises a question: The verse in Leviticus (26:42) refers to God's covenant with Jacob, His covenant with Isaac and His covenant with Abraham. Yet in this *kina*, only the covenant with Isaac is mentioned. The stanzas in which Abraham and Jacob make their pleas to God make no mention of God's covenant with either of them. The answer is that Isaac's covenant with God is superior to the covenant of Abraham and the covenant of Jacob. This can be seen from the verse in Leviticus, "I will remember My covenant with Jacob, and also My covenant with Isaac, and also My covenant with Abraham I will remember." Note that the verse does not contain a form of the word remembrance with

respect to Isaac. Our sages say (quoted in Rashi, ibid. s.v. *vezakharti*) that there was no need for remembrance with respect to the covenant with Isaac; there was no need to remind God, as it were, of the covenant with Isaac because "the ashes of Isaac appear before Me, gathered and lying on the altar" (*Vayikra Raba* 36:5). The altar on which Isaac was brought is constantly in front of the Throne of Glory. God looks upon *Akedat Yitzḥak* as a contemporaneous event; as if, just a short while ago, Isaac lay down on the altar and was ready to accept death. For the covenants with Abraham and Jacob, remembrance of a past event is necessary, but not for the covenant with Isaac. In effect, the covenant with Isaac recurs every day and in every epoch.

וְטִמְאוּ הַר הַמּוֹרִיָּה *And profaned Mount Moriah.* God's response to Isaac is: The Jews have defiled Mount Moriah, and you, Isaac, should be particularly concerned with Mount Moriah because you sanctified and hallowed it with your sacrifice.

סָח יֻלַּד בְּתֶלֶף [*Jacob,*] *who was born to study, spoke up.* The word *betelef* is similar in meaning to *aluf bina* (wisdom), and the phrase *yulad betelef* means one who was raised (not literally born) in the place of instruction, in the *beit midrash*. The Gemara states (*Shabbat* 104a), "*alef beit, alef bina*, study and acquire knowledge." Jacob, who sat and studied, the *yoshev ohalim* (Genesis 25:27), learned Torah in the *beit midrash* of Shem and Ever (Rashi on Genesis 25:27 and 28:9).

עוֹלָלַי אֲשֶׁר טִפַּחְתִּי בְּעֶלֶף *The children I raised with such travail.* The word *be'elef* has the same meaning as *hitalef* (fainting). Jacob is saying that he raised his children with hardship, suffering and great effort. Jacob experienced *tza'ar gidul banim*, the travails of rearing children, with Reuben, Simeon and Levi in connection with the incident of Shekhem, and above all, with the pain of losing Joseph.

דָּמִים בְּדָמִים כַּמָּה אֶלֶף *Punished a thousand-fold for the blood they shed.* This is an allusion to Nebuzaradan's killing of thousands of people because of the killing of just one person, Zechariah the Prophet. Jacob's plea is: If Zechariah was killed, why did so many others have to perish on his account?

It is noteworthy that, while the *kina* contains answers from God to Abraham's plea and Isaac's plea, it does not contain an answer from God to Jacob's plea.

פָּץ רוֹעֶה נֶאֱמָן *The faithful shepherd* [*Moses*] *uttered.* As with Jacob, the *kina* does not contain a response from God to Moses' plea.

קוֹל בְּכִי לֵאָה *The sound of Leah's wail.* In this stanza, Leah, Rachel, Bilhah and Zilpah appear and present their plea.

The *kina* varies from the Midrash on which the *kina* is based. The Midrash mentions only Rachel, and her intercession was the most effective one. In the Midrash, there is no mention of Leah, Bilhah or Zilpah. God rejected the arguments of the patriarchs and Moses, and accepted the argument of Rachel and said, "Because of you, I will forgive." The Midrash recounts Rachel's argument: When Jacob was about to marry Rachel, he expected Laban to trick him into first marrying Leah, the older unmarried daughter. In order to thwart Laban, Jacob and Rachel decided on a secret password so that Jacob would be sure of Rachel's identity. Laban did, in fact, substitute Leah for Rachel on the wedding night. Rachel, however, could not bear the thought of her sister's humiliation upon the discovery of Laban's trickery, and Rachel divulged the password to Leah. The message of the Midrash is that the arguments of Moses were not sufficient to persuade God; the arguments of Isaac, who was prepared to be sacrificed on the altar, were not sufficient; the arguments of Abraham, who had to undergo the ten trials and who was prepared to sacrifice all for God, were not sufficient. The sole argument that was persuasive to God was that of Rachel who shared in the suffering and despair of her sister on a single occasion.

The version of the story in this *kina*, however, is different from the Midrash. As noted above, the *kina* includes Leah, Bilhah and Zilpah, in addition to Rachel. Furthermore, In the *kina*, Rachel is not singled out as the successful petitioner. Rather, God accepted all of the pleas, and His response is directed collectively to all of the petitioners. The patriarchs and matriarchs and Moses, in a joint effort, prevailed in the debate with God, and He promises all of them that ultimately the Jews will be redeemed and brought back.

שָׁלַחְתִּי בָּבֶלָה לְמַעַנְכֶם *I was sent to Babylon because of you.* God's final answer is that He will fulfill all of the petitions, and the Jewish people ultimately will be redeemed. And if the petitioners were to ask: How do we know that He will fulfill this promise? His answer is "שָׁלַחְתִּי בָּבֶלָה לְמַעַנְכֶם, I guarantee that I will fulfill My promise because I Myself am in exile. *I* am in *galut* together with My children. *I* am in captivity just as you are. In order to secure your return, I, Myself, share in the suffering of the *galut*." The best assurance and guarantee that God can give to the patriarchs and matriarchs is that since He will have to liberate Himself from captivity, He will liberate the Jewish people as well.

The concept that God is Himself in *galut* and that this is the guarantee for

redemption is alluded to in the Torah, as well. In the verse "וְשָׁב יהוה אֱלֹהֶיךָ אֶת־שְׁבוּתְךָ... מִכָּל־הָעַמִּים אֲשֶׁר הֱפִיצְךָ" (Deuteronomy 30:3), the word *veshav* is not a transitive verb. Rather it means, "He will return" and the word *et* means "with." Thus the sentence means that God, who Himself is in captivity, will return together with the other captives, the Jewish people. And since He cannot be held captive indefinitely, there is an implied promise that the liberation of all those in exile will soon be implemented.

The *Hoshana* prayer "כְּהוֹשַׁעְתָּ אֵלִים בְּלוּד" similarly expresses the theme that God is in exile, and that this constitutes the guarantee for the redemption. The initial phrase, כְּהוֹשַׁעְתָּ אֵלִים בְּלוּד עִמָּךְ בְּצֵאתְךָ לְיֵשַׁע עַמָּךְ כֵּן הוֹשַׁע נָא means "Just as You helped the Jewish people in Egypt when You came out of Your hiding, so should You help *us*." The next phrase, גּוֹי וֵאלֹהִים דְּרוּשִׁים לְיֵשַׁע אֱלֹהִים means "Not only the *goy*, the nation, requires salvation, but God, Himself, as well." The phrase "מַאֲמַר וְהוֹצֵאתִי אֶתְכֶם נָקוּב וְהוּצֵאתִי אִתְּכֶם" means: Although it is pronounced "I have taken you out" (Exodus 6:6), the phrase could also be read to mean "I Myself have been taken out with you." The message of this *Hoshana* prayer is that God Himself is in exile, and God's exile is the guarantee, the collateral, for the redemption of the Jewish people.

27

א Then, when the measure of the sins of she [Israel] who is as beautiful as
Tirzah, had reached its fill, the Arielites [angels] cried out aloud. *Is. 33:7*
ב [Jeremiah,] the son of Hilkiyahu came upon, leaving the Temple,
a once beautiful woman, now disheveled.

ג [He said,] "I insist in the name of God and man,
[that you tell me] whether you are a demon among demons,
or a mortal human.
ד For you are as comely as one of flesh and blood,
but you are as awesome and frightening as only an angel can be."

ה [She responded,] "I am neither a demon nor something of little value.
I once knew stillness and quiet.
ו I am of the stock of three and seventy-one,
and twelve, and sixty, and one.

ז "One was father Abraham,
and I am a child of the triad of three patriarchs.
ח The number twelve refers to the tribes of the Lord,
and sixty ten-thousands [the six hundred thousand Jews who left Egypt],
and the seventy-one members of the holy Sanhedrin."

ט [Jeremiah responded,] "Heed my counsel and repent,
because you are indeed of great consequence.
י Laughter and joy, they behoove you;
no longer should you be called 'wayward daughter'!"

כ [She responded,] "How can I rejoice and raise my voice proudly?
My babes are given over to the foe!
ל My prophets are stricken, their blood flowing!
My kings are exiled, and my priests, in chains!

27

In this kina the prophet Jeremiah meets a woman of unearthly beauty, a personification of Knesset Yisrael. Commentary for this kina begins on page 482.

אָז בִּמְלֹאת סֶפֶק, יָפָה כְּתִרְצָה
הֵן אֶרְאֶלָּם, צָעֲקוּ חֻצָה.
בְּן־חֶלְקִיָּהוּ מֵאַרְמוֹן כְּיָצָא
אִשָּׁה יְפַת תֹּאַר מְנֻוֶּלֶת, מָצָא:

גּוֹזְרַנִי עָלַיִךְ, בְּשֵׁם אֱלֹהִים וְאָדָם
אִם שֵׁד לַשֵּׁדִים אַתְּ, אוֹ לִבְנֵי אָדָם.
דְּמוּת יָפְיֵךְ כְּבָשָׂר וָדָם
פַּחְדֵּךְ וְיִרְאָתֵךְ, כְּמַלְאָכִים לְבַדָּם:

הֵן לֹא שֵׁד אֲנִי, וְלֹא גֹּלֶם פָּחַת
יְדוּעָה הָיִיתִי בְּשׁוּבָה וָנַחַת.
וְהֵן, לְשָׁלֹשׁ אֲנִי, וְלְשִׁבְעִים וְאֶחָד
וְלִשְׁנֵים עָשָׂר, וְשִׁשִּׁים, וְאֶחָד:

זֶה הָאֶחָד אַבְרָהָם הָיָה
וּבֶן הַשְּׁלֹשָׁה, אָבוֹת שְׁלִישִׁיָּה.
חֹק שְׁנֵים עָשָׂר, הֵן הֵן שִׁבְטֵי יָהּ
וְשִׁשִּׁים רִבּוֹא, וְשִׁבְעִים וְאֶחָד סַנְהֶדְרֵי יָהּ:

טַעֲמִי הַקְשִׁיבִי, וַעֲשִׂי תְּשׁוּבָה
יַעַן הֱיוֹתֵךְ כָּל כָּךְ חֲשׁוּבָה.
יָפָה לִיךְ בְּאֶרֶץ, וְלִשְׂמֹחַ בְּטוֹבָה
וְלֹא לְקָרֵא עוֹד בַּת הַשּׁוֹבֵבָה:

כִּי אֵיךְ אֶשְׂמַח, וְקוֹלִי מָה אָרִים
הֵן עוֹלָלַי נִתְּנוּ בְּיַד צָרִים.
לֻקְּחוּ נְבִיאַי, וְדָמָם מְגֻרִים
גָּלוּ מְלָכַי וְשָׂרַי, וְכֹהֲנַי בְּקוֹלָרִים:

ישעיה לג, ז

מ "My holy Temple wanders because of my sins.
My Beloved of yore has fled and flown away.
נ My pleasant abode has been plundered against my will.
How she, who once was filled with people, is now all alone!"

ס The woman entreated the prophet Jeremiah, "Speak to your God
on behalf of the tempest-torn, afflicted people,
ע so that He will answer and say, 'Enough,'
and save me from sword and captivity."

פ [Jeremiah] prayed, entreating his Maker,
"Most compassionate One, have pity as a father would for his son."
צ [God] shouted, "Woe to the father who expelled his son,
and woe, too, to the son who is gone from his father's table!

ק "Rise, Jeremiah! Why be silent?
Go summon the patriarchs, Aaron, and Moses.
ר Let the shepherds come and express lament.
Wolves of the wilderness have attacked the sheep."

ש Jeremiah the prophet roared,
howling like a lion, in the cave of the patriarchs,
ת "Give voice to your tears, ye fathers of the gazelle [Israel]!
Your children have lost their way; they are in captivity!

שָׁמֵם "The Temple lies desolate with no one gathering for festivals,   *Lam. 1:4*
because its comrades have fallen and faltered.
May He who supports and sustains bring them back as before.
Have mercy upon Zion; its time has come."

Kina 28 starts on page 488.

מְלוֹן מִקְדָּשִׁי, בַּעֲוֹנִי נָדַד
דּוֹדִי מֵאָז בָּרַח וַיִּדַּד.
נָעַם אָהֳלִי, בְּעַל כָּרְחִי שֻׁדַּד
רַבָּתִי עָם, אֵיכָה יָשְׁבָה בָדָד:

סָחָה הָאִשָּׁה לַנָּבִיא יִרְמְיָה
שָׂח לֵאלֹהֶיךָ, בְּעַד סוֹעֲרָה מַכַּת עֲנִיָּה.
עַד יַעֲנֶה אֵל, וְיֹאמַר דַּיָּה
וְיַצִּילֵנִי מֵחֶרֶב וְשִׁבְיָה:

פִּלֵּל תְּחִנָּה לִפְנֵי קוֹנוֹ
מָלֵא רַחֲמִים, רַחֵם כְּאָב עַל בְּנוֹ.
צָעַק, אוֹי לָאָב שֶׁהִגְלָה נִינוֹ
וְגַם אוֹי לַבֵּן, שֶׁבִּשְׁלָחַן אָב אֵינוֹ:

קוּם לֵךְ יִרְמְיָה, לָמָּה תֶּחֱשֶׁה
לֵךְ קְרָא לְאָבוֹת, וְאַהֲרֹן וּמֹשֶׁה.
רוֹעִים יָבוֹאוּ, קִינָה לְהַנְשֵׂא
כִּי זְאֵבֵי עֶרֶב טָרְפוּ אֶת הַשֶּׂה:

שׁוֹאֵג הָיָה יִרְמְיָה הַנָּבִיא
עַל מַכְפֵּלָה, נוֹהֵם כְּלָבִיא.
תְּנוּ קוֹל בִּבְכִי, אֲבוֹת הַצְּבִי
תְּעוּ בְנֵיכֶם, הֲרֵי הֵן בַּשֶּׁבִי:

שָׁמֵם מִקְדָּשׁ מִבְּלִי בָּאֵי מוֹעֵד
עַל כִּי יְדִידִים נִתְּנוּ לְהַמְעֵד.
תְּשִׁיבֵם כְּמֵאָז, סוֹמֵךְ וְסוֹעֵד
תְּרַחֵם צִיּוֹן, כִּי בָא מוֹעֵד:

איכה א, ד

Kina 28 starts on page 489.

COMMENTARY ON KINA 27

This *kina* by Rabbi Elazar HaKalir tells the story of *Knesset Yisrael* appearing to the prophet Jeremiah in the guise of an elderly woman. She presents herself with traces of aristocracy and of past glory and beauty, but now she is poor and disheveled. The motif of this *kina* is that *Knesset Yisrael* is internally beautiful. Sometimes, however, she becomes externally defiled and corrupt because of difficult circumstances. It is these difficulties which lead her to sin even though it is against her nature to do so.

אָז בִּמְלֹאת סֵפֶק *Then, when the measure of the sins... had reached its fill.* This phrase refers to the time when the Jews suffered enough, when they reached the apex of distress and the height of Ḥurban.

אִשָּׁה יְפַת תֹּאַר מְנֻוֶּלֶת *A once beautiful woman, now disheveled.* The woman that appeared to Jeremiah was in a strange condition. She was simultaneously *yefat to'ar*, beautiful, and *menuvelet*, repulsive and disheveled. The woman symbolizes *Knesset Yisrael*, which is by nature an *isha yefat to'ar*, beautiful, honest, sincere and possessed of great talent and potential. However, somehow circumstances have transformed her into a *menuvelet*, and she has become ugly and corrupted and forced into a world of evil.

The Mishna (*Nedarim* 66a) recounts the story of a man who was afraid that he would be pressured by family members to marry a certain woman whom he considered unattractive. In order to forestall such pressure, he took a vow not to wed the woman. Later this woman was taken in and she was washed, cleansed and dressed properly, and as a result, her appearance changed. When the man who had taken the vow saw her, he thought she was a different woman. He had thought she was unattractive, but in fact she was not, and he regretted the vow not to marry her. Rabbi Yishma'el was able to undo the restriction of the vow when he asked the man, "Is it regarding this woman that you took your vow?" and the man responded, "No." Rabbi Yishma'el then wept and said, "Jewish daughters are always beautiful, but poverty makes them appear to be ugly."

Rabbi Yishma'el was not referring to Jewish women and their physical beauty. He was referring to *Knesset Yisrael* as a whole and to the abasement of the Jew. Intrinsically, *Knesset Yisrael* is noble, good, holy and beautiful. If the Jews become corrupted, the corruption is never internal; it never becomes part of the personality of *Knesset Yisrael*. Their innermost personality is *"yafot hena*, beautiful and good," but *"ha'aniyut menavlatan,"* a long exile of nineteen

hundred years is responsible for the ugliness they sometimes display. Persecution, homelessness, deportations, ridicule and hostile environs are all factors in the aspects of ugliness that Jews sometimes exhibit.

The possibility of *teshuva*, repentance, is based on this concept. A person cannot raise himself or herself if he or she is corrupt and completely defiled. *Teshuva* can only be accomplished because there is something internal within the person that is beautiful and that can never be extinguished. The corruption is only external.

פַּחְדֵּךְ וְיִרְאָתֵךְ, כְּמַלְאָכִים לְבַדָּם *But you are as awesome and frightening as only an angel can be.* Although the literal meaning of the word *paḥdekh* is "fear," in this context it refers rather to awe and reverence. The woman aroused in Jeremiah a sense of awe and reverence, as though she were a transcendental being, an angel, and not an ordinary human.

יְדוּעָה הָיִיתִי *I once knew.* The mysterious woman in effect replies to Jeremiah, "I am known to you from a happier time. I was prominent, and people knew me." And then, she identifies herself as the *Knesset Yisrael*, the daughter of the patriarchs.

וְשִׁשִּׁים רִבּוֹא, וְשִׁבְעִים וְאֶחָד סַנְהֶדְרֵי יָהּ *And sixty ten-thousands* [*the six hundred thousand Jews who left Egypt*], *and the seventy-one members of the holy Sanhedrin.* The way that the mysterious woman identifies herself teaches us the proper way for a Jew to do so. The response should be: "I am the grandson of the patriarchs, a member of the Twelve Tribes, one of the six hundred thousand, and my teachers and judges are the seventy-one members of the Sanhedrin."

Jeremiah is frightened by this strange woman and thinks she is an apparition. He thinks that she is so alienated that she does not remember any of her past. But when he asks her identity, she identifies herself as a daughter of Abraham, Isaac and Jacob. She declares, "I am a *menuvelet*, obnoxious, now; I have alienated myself from God, but I still remember Abraham, Isaac and Jacob and the Twelve Tribes. I know of the great Sanhedrin and the six hundred thousand. I am still related to my past. I will never forget my past." Once again, the *kina* makes the point that even if *Knesset Yisrael* has sunk into an abyss of corruption and sin, she remains beautiful.

טַעֲמִי הַקְשִׁיבִי, וַעֲשִׂי תְשׁוּבָה *Heed my counsel and repent.* Jeremiah realizes that the mysterious woman represents *Knesset Yisrael* and reproaches her: "If, in fact, what you say is true, you are capable of doing *teshuva*. It is not too late;

you have not lost what you possessed. You are intrinsically good and beautiful, but dirt has accumulated on you because of the persecution and suffering that you have experienced. All you have to do is shake off the dirt and you will be elevated to the beauty you always were, before you sinned. Deep in your heart you never believed in the idols you worshiped. You did it only under pressure. Your inner desire was always to be close to God."

יַעַן הֱיוֹתֵךְ כָּל כָּךְ חֲשׁוּבָה *Because you are indeed of great consequence.* Jeremiah encourages her: "You are still an aristocrat, full of dignity. You are important and prominent even though you are not aware of it. If you had lost your dignity, I would not be appealing to you now. You have the potential to achieve great heights." Jeremiah tells her precisely what we read in God's promise, *uvikashtem misham,* "And from there you shall seek the LORD your God; and you shall find Him, if you search after Him with all your heart and all your soul. In your distress…" (Deuteronomy 4:29–30). Even when one is in distress, *batzar lekha,* and when one has lost courage and does not believe in oneself and has no faith that *teshuva* is a possibility, nevertheless one should search and will surely find Him. There is only one *conditio sine qua non*: that the quest must be "with all your heart and all your soul."

יָפֶה לִיךְ בְּעֵלֶץ, וְלִשְׂמֹחַ בְּטוֹבָה *Laughter and joy, they behoove you.* Jeremiah continues and says, "Why do you prefer to live in filth and mourning, in desolation and despair when you can live in joy and luxury? Is it not better to enjoy life and the blessings of God?"

It is noteworthy that HaKalir expresses the thought that the sinner is not happy and does not enjoy himself.

וְלֹא לְקָרֵא עוֹד בַּת הַשּׁוֹבֵבָה *No longer should you be called "wayward daughter."* Jeremiah tells her that the epithet *bat hashoveva,* "the disobedient daughter," does not fit her.

Jeremiah is expressing the principle of free will, when he tells her, "If you are the *Knesset Yisrael,* you certainly have the choice to come back and re-establish the old relationship between yourself and God." Jeremiah tells her that *teshuva* is the remedy for her troubles, and that she should have the courage to do *teshuva* and return to God.

גָּלוּ מְלָכַי וְשָׂרַי, וְכֹהֲנַי בְּקוֹלָרִים *My kings are exiled, and my priests, in chains!* She tells Jeremiah that she does not have the community or society that would encourage her. The best were killed or exiled. She is overwhelmed with suffering and responds to him saying, "The suffering and punishment meted out

to me are crushing. I was robbed of my human dignity and of all hope." She is telling Jeremiah that when a person experiences disaster, it is hard for him to do *teshuva*. When a person is overwhelmed by tragedy, when a person is depressed, he loses courage and faith in himself and cannot repent. In order to do *teshuva*, one must have courage. In order to inspire *teshuva*, God should free man from disaster. *Teshuva* should always be performed with a feeling of joy and delight.

מְלוֹן מִקְדָּשִׁי, בַּעֲוֹנִי נָדָד *My holy Temple wanders because of my sins.* She tells Jeremiah that she cannot rejoice because the *Beit HaMikdash* is desolate as a result of her sins. Her intent is that sometimes the environment can change a person, and if the *Beit HaMikdash* had still been in existence she would enter it. But it is destroyed, and God has departed from her.

דּוֹדִי מֵאָז בָּרַח וַיִּדַּד *My Beloved of yore has fled and flown away.* Knesset Yisrael says that God has absented Himself from her. She feels alone and does not feel the presence of God. On the contrary, she feels very distant from Him, as though He were beyond a thick cloud. There is no sign that God is waiting for her or wants her back. She feels that there is no hope for her, and she is full of resignation and despair.

רַבָּתִי עָם, אֵיכָה יָשְׁבָה בָדָד *How she, who once was filled with people, is now all alone!* She continues her response to Jeremiah and tells him that it is this question of "*eikha yashva vadad*" that prevents her doing *teshuva*. In effect, her response is that *teshuva* requires a degree of happiness and a spark of hope. If one is punished and completely bitter, one has no hope.

The great scholars of the *Musar* movement stated that *teshuva* requires two elements. The first is *hakarat haḥet*, recognition of the sin. The person must understand that he is absolutely, ultimately and unconditionally guilty and that there are no defenses to his behavior. If he tries to find mitigating or extenuating circumstances, he will never do *teshuva*. The second element is that the declaration of guilt should not interfere with the hope that he has the capacity to change himself; that from the bottomless pit of sin, crime and corruption, he can rise to great heights. It is true that one needs despair and real regret for *teshuva*, but one also has to have faith in God and in the power of *teshuva*. In this *kina*, the woman's response to Jeremiah is that she cannot do *teshuva* because she has given up all hope; she has suffered too much to come back.

The concept that adverse circumstances affect a person's ability to come

close to God is reflected in a statement by Maimonides, "By maintaining the body in health and vigor, one walks in the ways of God, as it is impossible to have any understanding or knowledge of the Creator when one is ill" (*Mishneh Torah*, Hil. De'ot 4:1). It is impossible for a person to dedicate himself to God if he is sick and hungry. Too much suffering cuts off the road that leads to God. When a person is ill, he cannot serve God with all his heart and all his soul, because his mind is distracted.

Ultimately, however, the argument of *Knesset Yisrael* that *teshuva* can arise only from happiness is not completely true. On the contrary, there is also the concept in Judaism that troubles and afflictions generate a *ḥiyuv tefilla*, an obligation to pray. As noted above, the Torah states, "But from there you will seek the LORD your God…In your distress, when all these things have come upon you, in the end of days, you will return to the LORD your God" (Deuteronomy 4:29–30). Essentially, if one has strength of character and is conscious of his mission, he can accomplish *teshuva* in circumstances of distress as well.

סָחָה הָאִשָּׁה לַנָּבִיא יִרְמְיָה / שַׂח לֵאלֹהֶיךָ, בְּעַד סוֹעֲרָה מֻכַּת עֲנִיָּה *The woman entreated the prophet Jeremiah, "Speak to your God on behalf of the tempest-torn, afflicted people."* The woman pleads with Jeremiah to communicate with God on her behalf and says, "I have no faith. I am broken in spirit and body. My prayers are without avail, but if you want to help me, *you* start reciting the prayer. I appoint you to pray on behalf of one who is incapable of doing so by herself. *You* plead with God. *You* pray for me to give me courage to repent."

וְיַצִּילֵנִי מֵחֶרֶב וְשִׁבְיָה *And save me from sword and captivity.* The woman tells Jeremiah that if his prayers are accepted, *then* she will do *teshuva*. Her desire that God take the initiative is reflected in the Midrash (*Eikha Raba* 5:21), which recounts a dispute between God and *Knesset Yisrael*. God says, "שׁוּבוּ אֵלַי וְאָשׁוּבָה אֲלֵיכֶם, Return to Me, and I will accept you; I will meet you halfway" (Malachi 3:7). But *Knesset Yisrael* says the opposite, "Return to us, and we will return to You; *You* take the initiative" (Lamentations 5:21).

פִּלֵּל תְּחִנָּה [*Jeremiah*] *prayed.* Jeremiah complied with her request and pleaded with God on her behalf.

צָעַק, אוֹי לָאָב שֶׁהִגְלָה נִינוֹ / וְגַם אוֹי לַבֵּן [*God*] *shouted, "Woe to the father who expelled his son, and woe, too, to the son."* This phrase can be interpreted as God's passionate response to Jeremiah. It can also be understood as Jeremiah's entreaty to God. Jeremiah prayed to God for two reasons. First, because

Israel suffers, and second because God suffers as well. This phrase in the *kina* refers to the concept that the *Shekhina* is in exile as well as the Jewish people. It is painful for the *Shekhina* to be alone and separated from *Knesset Yisrael*.

לֵךְ קְרָא לָאָבוֹת *Go summon the patriarchs.* Although this is often understood as God's response, it can also be interpreted as the woman's reaction. After Jeremiah finished praying on behalf of the woman, she said to him, "If you are not successful with God, perhaps the patriarchs will be."

זְאֵבֵי עֶרֶב *Wolves of the wilderness.* This is an allusion to the nations of the world.

28

א How dare you offer me empty consolation,   *Job 21:34*
    when my lyre has turned to grief?
In the land of my heritage, a heavy yoke weighs heavy upon me.
    How can I be consoled?

ב On this day, every year, time changes for me.
I feel gloomy and woebegone for more than a thousand years.
    How can I be consoled?

ג Fury has triumphed. The Ark is interred,
repeatedly stricken, because of those who spitefully rebelled.
    How can I be consoled?

ד My dwellings are ruined, my flock carried off,
and the populous Jerusalem now sits alone.
    How can I be consoled?

ה The lion [Nebuchadnezzar] lurched from its lair
upon Ariel [the Temple], to strangle it.
He expelled from His Tabernacle His meal-offering and libation.
    How can I be consoled?

ו He slaughtered throngs of those anointed with sacred oil.
Young budding priests, eighty thousand.
    How can I be consoled?

ז He cut them down as would a snake, causing blood to flow
in the courtyard of the Temple.
Aryokh [Nebuzaradan], like a lion, [avenged]
the blood of the high priest and prophet [Zechariah].
    How can I be consoled?

28

This kina is last of the kinot by HaKalir. It details the sufferings of the Jewish people throughout the generations. Each of the first twenty-two stanzas is built of four rhyming stichs, and ends with the note of despair "How can I be consoled?" However, the last stanza ends with a note of hope – that these prayers have been heard, and that redemption and consolation are soon to come. Commentary for this kina begins on page 494.

איוב כא, לד

אֵיךְ תְּנַחֲמוּנִי הֶבֶל / וְכִנּוֹרִי נֶהְפַּךְ לְאֵבֶל.
בְּנַחֲלַת חֶבֶל / כָּבַד עָלַי עַל סֵבֶל.
וְאֵיךְ אֶנָּחֵם:

בָּזֶה יוֹם בְּכָל שָׁנָה / עִדָּן עָלַי שָׁנָה.
וְהִנְנִי עֲגוּמָה וַעֲגוּנָה / יוֹתֵר מֵאֶלֶף שָׁנָה.
וְאֵיךְ אֶנָּחֵם:

גֶּבֶר חָרוֹן / וְנִגְנַז אָרוֹן.
בְּמִשְׁנֵה שִׁבְרוֹן / בְּמִסְרְבֵי מָרוֹן.
וְאֵיךְ אֶנָּחֵם:

דִּירָתִי חָרְבָה / וְעֶדְרִי נִשְׁבָּה.
וְרַבַּת אֲהָלִיבָה / בָּדָד יָשְׁבָה.
וְאֵיךְ אֶנָּחֵם:

הוֹעַל אַרְיֵה מִסֻּבְּכוֹ / עַל אֲרִיאֵל, וְהִסְבִּיכוֹ.
וְהִגְלָה מִסֻּכּוֹ / מִנְחָתוֹ וְנִסְכּוֹ.
וְאֵיךְ אֶנָּחֵם:

וְהָרַג הֲמוֹנִים / מְשׁוּחֵי שְׁמָנִים.
פִּרְחֵי כֹהֲנִים / אֲלָפִים שְׁמוֹנִים.
וְאֵיךְ אֶנָּחֵם:

זִנְּבָם כְּחִוִּי וְהַדְּבִיא / בְּעֶזְרַת הַמַּלְבִּיא.
אָרִיוֹךְ כְּמוֹ לָבִיא / עַל דַּם כֹּהֵן וְנָבִיא.
וְאֵיךְ אֶנָּחֵם:

ה He plowed into a wasteland, that city, once so tumultuous,
with houses for scribes and scholars, numbering more
> than four hundred.
>> How can I be consoled?

ט Media [Persia] hastened to destroy my dear ones.
She dominated my precious Temple as I tore my garments.
>> How can I be consoled?

י She schemed to strangle the sons of the prancing cubs [the tribe of Dan].
Together, they agreed to choke elder, aged, and infant.
>> How can I be consoled?

כ The third [kingdom, Greece,] weighed heavily upon
> His sacred firstborn.
With silent fury, he laid waste to him.
>> How can I be consoled?

ל [Greece] pressed hard to divide [the sons of Jacob from their God,]
the sons of the smooth-skinned one from He whose portion
> they are, [saying,]
"You have no share in the fiery living God."
>> How can I be consoled?

מ Edom [the fourth kingdom, Rome,] rebelled, she of the red lentil stew,
and cruelly rushed to destroy throne and footstool.
>> How can I be consoled?

נ Joined with Edom were Moab and Ammon,
to abrogate the Torah and demolish the Palace.
>> How can I be consoled?

ס Downtrodden are the mighty ones and the flocks of my comrades. *Lam. 1:15*
Defeated are my heroes in the presence of all who pass me by.
>> How can I be consoled?

חָרַשׁ לְמַשּׁוּאוֹת / עִיר מְלֵאָה תְשׁוּאוֹת.
בָּתֵּי סוֹפְרִים וּמִשְׁנָאוֹת / יוֹתֵר מֵאַרְבַּע מֵאוֹת.
וְאֵיךְ אֲנַחֵם:

טָסָה מָדַי / לְאַבֵּד חֲמוּדַי.
וּמָשְׁלָה בְּמַחֲמַדַּי / בְּקָרְעִי מַדַּי.
וְאֵיךְ אֲנַחֵם:

יָעֲצָה לְחַנֵּק / בְּנֵי גּוּר מְזֻנָּק.
בְּפֶה אֶחָד לְשַׁנֵּק / זָקֵן וְיָשִׁישׁ וְיוֹנֵק.
וְאֵיךְ אֲנַחֵם:

כָּבְדָה שְׁלִישִׁית / עַל קֹדֶשׁ רֵאשִׁית.
בְּשֶׁצֶף חֲרִישִׁית / בָּתָה לְהָשִׁית.
וְאֵיךְ אֲנַחֵם:

לָחֲצָה לְחַלֵּק / בְּנֵי חָלָק וְחוֹלֵק.
אֵין לָכֶם חֵלֶק / בְּשֵׁם אֵל דּוֹלֵק.
וְאֵיךְ אֲנַחֵם:

מָרְדָה אֱדוֹם / עֲדוּשַׁת אָדֹם.
וְאָצָה בְזָדוֹן / לְאַבֵּד כֵּס וַהֲדוֹם.
וְאֵיךְ אֲנַחֵם:

נוֹעֲדוּ עִם אַדְמוֹן / מוֹאָב וְעַמּוֹן.
לְהַשְׁבִּית אָמוֹן / וּלְהַחֲרִיב אַרְמוֹן.
וְאֵיךְ אֲנַחֵם:

סִלָּה כָל אַבִּירַי / וְעֶדְרֵי חֲבֵרַי.
וְהִבְלִיגוּ גִבּוֹרַי / לְעֵין כָּל עוֹבְרַי.
וְאֵיךְ אֲנַחֵם:

איכה א, טו

ע I feel faint before the killers, because of the number of victims *Jer. 4:31*
crying like hinds, slaughtered for Your name.
>How can I be consoled?

פ Trembling on the day of battle in the east and in the west,
their blood intermingled, a great mass of people! *Ezek. 26:7*
>How can I be consoled?

צ Woe upon woe, each worse than the one before!
Great and mighty! Of long, not short, duration!
>How can I be consoled?

ק They fastened their shields, girded their spears,
gathered their troops, and made long furrows. *Ps. 129:3*
>How can I be consoled?

ר Many are my moans, mighty are my laments;
my groans increase, and You, O Lord, how long? *Ps. 6:4*
>How can I be consoled?

ש You heard their mockery; how they insulted me with their words.
Sitting or standing, I was the butt of their gibes.
>How can I be consoled?

ת "Where is your hope? What have you here?
He is angry with you, and there is no one to heal you!"
>How can I be consoled?

ת "Of your replies, only perfidy remains," say those pagans tauntingly.
Until the Lord looks down from heaven, casts down into the grave *1 Sam. 2:6*
and raises up.
>Then will I be consoled.

Kina 29 starts on page 496.

עָיְפָה נַפְשִׁי לְהוֹרְגִים / לְמִסְפַּר הַהֲרוּגִים.　　ירמיה ד, לא
כְּאַיָּל עוֹרְגִים / וְעָלֶיךָ נֶהֱרָגִים.
וְאֵיךְ אֶנָּחֵם:

פָּלְצוּ בְּיוֹם קְרָב / בְּמִזְרָח וּבְמַעֲרָב.
דָּמָם מְעֹרָב / קָהָל וְעַם רָב.　　יחזקאל כו, ז
וְאֵיךְ אֶנָּחֵם:

צָרוֹת עַל צָרוֹת / זוּ מִזּוֹ מְצֵרוֹת.
גְּדוֹלוֹת וּבְצוּרוֹת / אֲרֻכּוֹת וְלֹא קְצָרוֹת.
וְאֵיךְ אֶנָּחֵם:

קָשְׁרוּ צִנָּתָם / וְחָגְרוּ חֲנִיתָם.
וְאָסְפוּ מַחֲנוֹתָם / וְהֶאֱרִיכוּ לְמַעֲנִיתָם.　　תהלים קכט, ג
וְאֵיךְ אֶנָּחֵם:

רַבּוֹת אַנְחוֹתַי / וַעֲצוּמוֹת קִינוֹתַי.
רַבּוּ נְהָמוֹתַי / וְאַתָּה יהוה עַד מָתַי.　　תהלים ו, ד
וְאֵיךְ אֶנָּחֵם:

שָׁמְעוּ חֶרְפָּתָם / חֵרְפוּנִי בְּשִׂפְתָם.
שִׁבְתָּם וְקִימָתָם / אֲנִי מַנְגִּינָתָם.
וְאֵיךְ אֶנָּחֵם:

תִּקְוַתְכֶם אֵפוֹא / מַה לָּכֶם פֹּה.
חָרָה אַפּוֹ / וְאֵין עוֹד לִרְפֹּא.
וְאֵיךְ אֶנָּחֵם:

תְּשׁוּבוֹתֵיכֶם נִשְׁאַר מָעַל / הוֹנוּנִי עוֹבְדֵי הַבָּעַל.
עַד יַשְׁקִיף וְיֵרֶא מִמַּעַל / מוֹרִיד שְׁאוֹל וַיָּעַל.　　שמואל א ב, ו
וְאָז אֶנָּחֵם:

Kina 29 starts on page 497.

COMMENTARY ON KINA 28

This *kina* by Rabbi Elazar HaKalir contains a litany of the persecutions and exiles that the Jewish people have suffered over the centuries at the hands of Babylonia, Media, Greece, Rome, Moab and Ammon. He despairs of finding true consolation.

The *kinot* of Rabbi Elazar HaKalir, in general, contain a multiplicity of events and chronologies. The message of this varied focus embodies two components. First, mentioning all of these tragedies on one day teaches that the tragedy of every Jew deserves to be remembered, whether it befell the Ten Tribes, the inhabitants of Judea or the Jews in the medieval German communities. Second, all the evil decrees, persecutions and exiles merge into one and our enemy ultimately is the same. Sometimes the enemy takes the guise of the King of Babylonia, and sometimes he appears in a different era, in a different place with a different language, and his name is Edom, but he is the same. Our enemy is still alive, and he has not reconciled himself to the existence of the Jewish people. When Jacob struggled with the mysterious stranger, the Torah tells us that Jacob asked his name (Genesis 32:30). Our sages say that Jacob asked this question because he could not determine what nature of person the stranger was. On the one hand, he gave Jacob the impression he was a great Torah scholar (*Ḥulin* 91a). On the other hand, he gave the impression of being a poor shepherd (*Midrash Tanḥuma* [Buber], *Vayishlaḥ* 7). When Jacob asked his name, the stranger replied, in effect, "It makes no difference who I am. Whoever I am, I have one mission, and that is to defy you. My mission is to oppose your return to the land of Israel and the development of a people in Israel." Similarly, the Gemara often will begin a story about the First Temple and conclude by discussing the Second Temple. Our sages were well aware of the correct sequence, and their intermingling of chronologies was deliberate. The depiction of multiple events without regard to chronology is an expression of the drama of Jewish history in which events repeat themselves. The names, the dates and the places may change, but it is all one continuing drama. This is the story of Jewish destiny.

The deliberate imprecision of the chronological sequence contains an additional message. It is an expression of *avelut*, mourning. As long as one's memory of time functions properly, mourning has not reached its height. When one lives through a fateful period, when one is in despair, one cannot be too concerned with the calendar. One *has* to make a mistake. The

chronology is deliberately imprecise because the *avelut* should attain a level of complete confusion, a loss of perspective as far as time is concerned. This principle is illustrated by the following discussion of one of the chronological details of the Ḥurban. The Gemara (*Ta'anit* 28b) asks why we say that the walls of Jerusalem were breached on the seventeenth day of Tammuz if the prophet says that this occurred on the ninth day of the month (Jeremiah 52:6). *Tosafot* (*Rosh HaShana* 18b, s.v. *zeh tisha beTammuz*) quotes the Jerusalem Talmud which answers, *kilkul ḥeshbonot yesh kan*, there is a mistake as to the chronology. The walls were actually breached on the seventeenth of Tammuz. But the people were so bitter and full of despair that they were confused as to the correct date. God instructed Jeremiah to perpetuate this mistake by recording the wrong date because one of the manifestations of *avelut* is the failure to remember the precise chronology of the event. Maximum *avelut* is the goal that God wanted to achieve.

29

א I said, "Let me be, I will weep bitterly
with my embittered soul, calming myself
in the companionship of those who are destined to rouse lament."

ב Weep for your agony [as Moab wept] for Yazer [her capital].
Daughter of my people, roll in the dust for yourself.
Do not stop; do not let your eyes be still.   *Lam. 2:18*

ג Shriek tearfully, you whom we once bedecked with joy
in days of old, but are now plundered.
How did this terrible thing happen?   *Judges 20:3*

ד Do not be silent, surviving remnant,
but lift your voice and shout bitterly,
disaster overtakes disaster!   *Jer. 4:20*

ה Indeed, the nations are now assembled.
Living One, they wish to band together against You!
They plot craftily against Your people and scheme.   *Ps. 83:4*

ו They planned wickedly to cause me to falter,
to follow false gods and tremble before them.
They say, "Let us wipe them out as a nation;
Israel's name will be mentioned no more."   *Ps. 83:5*

ז But those whom He called [Israel] responded,
"Even if He slays me, I will trust in Him and exalt His wonders."
The Lord has prepared a sacrificial feast and summoned His guests.   *Zeph. 1:7*

ח The number of victims mounted, and the best were killed.
My enemies and opponents afflicted me sorely.
I was beaten by those who pretended they were my friends.

29

Rabbi Kalonymos ben Yehuda (who also composed Kina 25), signed this kina acrostically with the name קלונימוס הקטן. Like Kina 25, this lament describes the atrocities suffered by the Jews at the time of the first Crusade. The kina consists of thirty-four stanzas in triplet form (a structure common in Ashkenazic liturgy), with the third stich usually a biblical quote. Commentary for this kina begins on page 504.

אָמַרְתִּי שְׁעוּ מִנִּי, בְּבִכְי אֲמָרֵר
מַר נַפְשִׁי וְרוּחִי אֲקָרֵר
עִם לִוְיָתָן הָעֲתִידִים עוֹרֵר:

בִּבְכִי יַעֲזָר עֲלֵי יְגוֹנֵךְ
בַּת עַמִּי, הִתְאַבְּכִי בִּגִינֵךְ
אַל־תִּתְּנִי פוּגַת לָךְ, אַל־תִּדֹּם בַּת־עֵינֵךְ:   איכה ב, יח

גְּעִי בִּבְכִיָּה, מְעֻטֶּרֶת בַּעֲלִיזוֹת
הָיִית מִקֶּדֶם, וְהִנָּךְ לְבִזּוֹת
אֵיכָה נִהְיְתָה הָרָעָה הַזֹּאת: שופטים כ, ג

דָּמִי אַל תִּתְּנִי, פְּלֵטָה הַנִּשְׁאָרָה
הָרִימִי קוֹל וְזַעֲקִי מָרָה
כִּי שֶׁבֶר עַל־שֶׁבֶר נִקְרָא: ירמיה ד, כ

הֵן לְאֻמִּים עֵת נִקְבָּצוּ
חַי, עָלֶיךָ כְּרֹת בְּרִית כְּחָפָצוּ
עַל־עַמְּךָ יַעֲרִימוּ סוֹד, וְיִתְיָעֲצוּ:   תהלים פג, ד

וְנִכְלוּ מְזִמּוֹת נְטוֹת, אַשּׁוּרֵי לְמֵעַד
אַחֲרֵי הַהֶבֶל לְהַהְבִּיל, וּמִפָּנָיו לִרְעַד
אָמְרוּ, לְכוּ וְנַכְחִידֵם מִגּוֹי, וְלֹא־יִזָּכֵר שֵׁם־יִשְׂרָאֵל עוֹד: תהלים פג, ה

זֹאת הִשְׁמִיעוּ בְּנֵי מִקְרָאָיו
לוּ נִחֵל אִם יִקְטְלֵנוּ, נַעֲרִיץ לְמוֹרָאָיו
הֵכִין יהוה זֶבַח, הִקְדִּישׁ קְרֻאָיו: צפניה א, ז

חֲלָלַי אָז הֵרַבּוּ, וְהָרְגוּ טוֹבַי
יִסְּרוּנִי קָשׁוֹת, צָרַי וְאוֹיְבַי
הַמַּכּוֹת הָאֵלֶּה, הֻכֵּיתִי בֵּית מְאַהֲבָי:

ט I refused to join them in their stinking filth.
   They smashed all my heroes in one swift stroke.
   Every choice piece, thigh and shoulder. *Ez. 24:4*

י Together, they were led to slaughter like lambs and goats;
   maidens well formed, crowned decoratively,
   newly weaned from milk, just taken away from the breast. *Is. 28:9*

כ The father suppressed his compassion at the massacre,
   offering his children like sheep to the knife,
   preparing his children for the slaughtering block.

ל To their mothers, they said, "We are being slaughtered and massacred,"
   as they were being slain and delivered to the sword.
   Women [eat their] own fruit, the children they have raised. *Lam. 2:20*

מ Who can listen and not shed tears,
   as the son is slain, the father recites Shema?
   Who ever witnessed such, who ever heard? *Is. 66:8*

נ Beautiful housewife, virginal daughter of Judah,
   stretched out her neck, whetted and sharpened the knife.
   His eye observed this and testified!

ס The mother was tortured, her spirit spent.
   She surrendered to the slaughter as if to a festive meal,
   happy mother of children. *Ps. 113:9*

ע They rejoiced, both the married and the betrothed,
   yielding to the sword willingly and happily,
   their blood on the bare rock, uncovered.

פ The father took his turn wailing and sighing,
   fell upon the sword, stabbing himself,
   drenched in blood in the middle of the road. *II Sam. 20:12*

טָנֵף צַחֲנָתָם, מֵאַנְתִּי בָם לְהִשְׁתַּתֵּף
הִשְׁמִידוּ גִבּוֹרַי כֻּלָּם בְּחֶתֶף
כָּל־נֵתַח טוֹב, יָרֵךְ וְכָתֵף: יחזקאל כד, ד

יַחַד לַטֶּבַח הוּבָלוּ, כִּטְלָאִים וּגְדָיִים
בָּנוֹת מְחֻטָּבוֹת מְשֻׁבָּצוֹת עֲדִי עֶדְיַיִם
גְּמוּלֵי מֵחָלָב, עַתִּיקֵי מִשָּׁדַיִם: ישעיה כח, ט

כָּבַשׁ הָאָב רַחֲמָיו לִזְבֹּחַ
יְלָדִים הִשְׁלִים כְּכָרִים לִטְבֹּחַ
הֵכִין לְבָנָיו מַטְבֵּחַ:

לְאִמּוֹתָם נוֹאֲמִים, הִנְנוּ נִשְׁחָטִים וְנִטְבָּחִים
כְּהִקְדִּישׁוּם לַטֶּבַח וְהִתִּיקוּם לַאֲבָחִים
נָשִׁים פִּרְיָם עֹלֲלֵי טִפֻּחִים: איכה ב, כ

מִי יִשְׁמַע וְלֹא יֵדְמַע
הַבֵּן נִשְׁחָט, וְהָאָב קוֹרֵא אֶת שְׁמַע
מִי רָאָה כָזֹאת, מִי שָׁמַע: ישעיה סו, ח

נְוֵה בֵית הַיָּפָה, בְּתוּלַת בַּת יְהוּדָה
צַוָּארָהּ פָּשְׁטָה, וּמַאֲכֶלֶת הַשְּׁחִיזָה וְחִדְּדָה
עַיִן רָאֲתָה וַתְּעִידָהּ:

סָגְפָה הָאֵם, וּפָרְחָה רוּחָהּ
וְנַפְשָׁהּ הַשְּׁלֵמָה לַטֶּבַח, אֲרוּחָה כַּאֲרֻחָה
אֵם־הַבָּנִים שְׂמֵחָה: תהלים קיג, ט

עָלְצוּ הַבָּנוֹת, כְּנוּסוֹת וַאֲרוּשׂוֹת
לִאֲבֹחַת חֶרֶב לְקַדֵּם, דָּצוֹת וְשָׂשׂוֹת
דָּמָם עַל־צְחִיחַ סֶלַע, לְבִלְתִּי הִכָּסוֹת:

פּוֹנֶה הָאָב בִּבְכִי וִילָלָה
עַצְמוֹ עַל חַרְבּוֹ, לְדָקְרוֹ וּלְהַפִּילָה
וְהוּא מִתְגֹּלֵל בַּדָּם, בְּתוֹךְ הַמְסִלָּה: שמואל ב כ, יב

צ The fruitful vine accepted judgment as she offered her boughs
   [as a sacrifice],
   and received blood in her skirts, rather than in a temple vessel,
   panting, stretching out her hands! — *Jer. 4:31*

ק Plunder and disaster beset me; who can approach me [comfortingly]?
   The delight of my eyes has been surrendered to mayhem and murder.
   Did he suffer such slaughter as did his slayers? — *Is. 27:7*

ר My thoughts are confounded; I am seized by terror and panic.
   In the merit of but one good deed was [Aviya the son of Jeroboam]
      assured the hope that he alone, of Jeroboam's family,
      shall be brought to burial. — *1 Kings 14:13*

ש But he, perfect in all his deeds, surrendered
   to slaughter out of fear of his Maker.
   He was not even accorded a burial! — *Eccl. 6:3*

ת I focused my heart, striving for the meaning of all this.
   I am convinced that His judgments are righteous and fair.
   It will be well with those who revere God since they revere Him. — *Eccl. 8:12*

ק He trusts not even His saints,
   but holds them accountable for sins thin as a thread of hair.
   It is a good omen for a person who is neither eulogized
      nor buried befittingly.
   He need not fear the frightful Judgment Day!

ל For this, my heart trembles and leaps from its place with a shudder.
   My mighty ones were crushed and submitted to degradation,
   fallen before treacherous men! — *II Sam. 3:34*

ו How long will You be like a helpless hero?
   Make it known that You will avenge the blood of Your servants!
   God of revenge, LORD, God of revenge, appear! — *Ps. 94:1*

נ Take revenge against my oppressors.
   It is a time for vengeance, to judge my case.
   The LORD is a passionate, avenging God! — *Nah. 1:2*

צְדָקָה דִינָהּ פּוֹרִיָּה, בְּהַקְרִיבָהּ עֲנָפֶיהָ
וְתָמוּר מִזְרָק, דָּם קִבְּלָה בִּכְנָפֶיהָ
תִּתְיַפֵּחַ, תְּפָרֵשׂ כַּפֶּיהָ: ירמיה ד, לא

קוֹרְוֹתַי מִי יָנוּד, שֹׁד וָשֶׁבֶר יִשְׂתָּרֵג
מַחֲמַד עֵינַי כְּנִמְסַר לַחֲרָם וְלַהֲרֹג
אִם־כַּהֶרֶג הֲרֻגָיו הֹרָג: ישעיה כז, ז

רַעְיוֹנַי נִבְהָלוּ, וַאֲחָזַתְנִי פַּלָּצוּת וָשֶׁבֶר
בְּאַחַת נִמְצָא, הַכָּתוּב בּוֹ תִקְוָה וְסֵבֶר
כִּי־זֶה לְבַדּוֹ, יָבֹא לְיָרָבְעָם אֶל־קָבֶר: מלכים א יד, יג

שָׁלֵם נִמְצָא בְּכָל פָּעֳלוֹ
נַפְשׁוֹ לַטֶּבַח הִשְׁלִים, מִפַּחַד חֵילוֹ
וְגַם־קְבוּרָה לֹא־הָיְתָה לּוֹ: קהלת ו, ג

תִּתִּי לִבִּי, מָצֹא תֹכֶן עִנְיָנָיו
יָדַעְתִּי אָנִי, צֶדֶק וְיֹשֶׁר דִּינָיו
יְהְיֶה־טּוֹב לְיִרְאֵי הָאֱלֹהִים, אֲשֶׁר יִירְאוּ מִלְּפָנָיו: קהלת ח, יב

קְדוֹשָׁיו לֹא יַאֲמִין, הִשְׁלִים עֲוֹנוֹתָם לְשַׁעֲרָה
סִימָן טוֹב לְאָדָם, בְּלֹא נִסְפַּד וְנִקְבַּר כַּשּׁוּרָה
בְּיוֹם עֶבְרָה לֹא יִירָא:

לְזֹאת יֶחֱרַד לִבִּי, יֶתֶר בְּחַלְחָלָה
גִּבּוֹרַי נִרְעֲצוּ וְנִכְנְעוּ לְהַשְׁפִּילָה
כִּנְפוֹל לִפְנֵי בְנֵי־עַוְלָה: שמואל ב ג, לד

וְעַד מָתַי תִּהְיֶה כְּגִבּוֹר לֹא יוּכַל לְהוֹשִׁיעַ
לְעֵינֵינוּ בַגּוֹיִם, נִקְמַת דַּם עֲבָדֶיךָ תּוֹדִיעַ
אֵל־נְקָמוֹת יְהוָה, אֵל נְקָמוֹת הוֹפִיעַ: תהלים צד, א

נָקֹם נִקְמָתִי מֵאֵת מְעַנַּי
עֵת נְקָמָה הִיא לָדוּן דִּינַי
אֵל קַנּוֹא וְנֹקֵם יְהוָה: נחום א, ב

| י | Lord, go forth like a warrior; repay Your debt.
Record full payment, and tear up the deed of indebtedness.
Break the power of the wicked and evil man! | *Ps. 10:15* |

| מ | From above, as fire consumed the timbers of the Temple's roof,
a wall of flame enveloped its enclosures and dwellings.
He who started the fire must make restitution. | *Zech. 2:9*
Ex. 22:5 |

| ו | He will pay them their just deserts,
quickly bring about their downfall and vanquish them,
for the Lord is a God of requital; He deals retribution. | *Jer. 51:56* |

| ש | He will annihilate my enemies,
    forcing them to drink the bowl of poison.
Those who died at his hand will be avenged.
Shall I not bring retribution upon a nation such as this? | *Jer. 5:9* |

| ה | It is for this that You are known as a warrior,
to defeat Your enemies and take revenge upon them.
The Lord is vengeful and fierce in wrath. | *Ex. 15:3*

Nah. 1:2 |

| ק | Be zealous, Almighty, for Your name's sake,
and for the spilled blood of Your servants,
    and for the ruins of the Temple.
Avenge the sons of Israel! | *Num. 31:2* |

| ט | The drops of my blood are counted one by one.
The bloodstains will be spattered all over Your cloak.
He judges the nations, heaping up bodies. | *Ps. 110:6* |

| נ | I am too weary to bear all this burden.
Hasten the redemption, and hurry the vision.
I plan a day of vengeance, and My year of redemption has arrived. | *Is. 63:4* |

Kina 30 starts on page 508.

יהוה כַּגִּבּוֹר צֵא, יְדֵי חוֹבְךָ פְּרַע
שׁוֹבֵר כְּתָב, שְׁטַר חוֹב תִּקְרַע
שְׁבֹר זְרוֹעַ רָשָׁע וָרָע:　　　תהלים י, טו

מִמָּרוֹם כְּהִסִּיק אֵשׁ, בְּמַעֲזִיבָה וְתִקְרָה
חוֹמַת אֵשׁ סָבִיב, שׁוֹמְרָה וּבֵית דִּירָה　　　זכריה ב, ט
שַׁלֵּם יְשַׁלֵּם הַמַּבְעִר אֶת־הַבְּעֵרָה:　　　שמות כב, ה

וּכְעַל גְּמוּלוֹת נָא שַׁלֵּם
אוֹיְבִי תַּפִּיל מְהֵרָה וּתְכַלֵּם
כִּי אֵל גְּמֻלוֹת יהוה, שַׁלֵּם יְשַׁלֵּם:　　　ירמיה נא, נו

שׂוֹנְאַי תַּצְמִית, סַף רַעַל תַּשְׁקֵם
הֲמֵת תַּחַת יָדוֹ, נָקֹם יִנָּקֵם
אִם בְּגוֹי אֲשֶׁר כָּזֶה לֹא תִתְנַקֵּם:　　　ירמיה ה, ט

הֲעַל כֵּן נִקְרֵאתָ אִישׁ מִלְחָמָה　　　שמות טו, ג
צָרֶיךָ לְכַלּוֹת וּבָהֶם לְהִנָּקְמָה
נֹקֵם יהוה וּבַעַל חֵמָה:　　　נחום א, ב

קַנֵּא לְשִׁמְךָ עֲבוּרְךָ הָאֵל
וּלְדַם עֲבָדֶיךָ הַשָּׁפוּךְ, וּלְחָרְבוֹת אֲרִיאֵל
נְקֹם נִקְמַת בְּנֵי יִשְׂרָאֵל:　　　במדבר לא, ב

טִפֵּי דָמַי, אַחַת לְאַחַת מְנוּיוֹת
וְיֵז נִצְחָם עַל בְּגָדֶיךָ, בְּפַרְפּוּרְךָ הֱיוֹת
יָדִין בַּגּוֹיִם מָלֵא גְוִיּוֹת:　　　תהלים קי, ו

נִלְאֵיתִי נְשֹׂא אֶת כָּל הַתְּלָאָה
מַהֵר גְּאָלְתִּי וְתָחִישׁ הַמַּרְאָה
כִּי יוֹם נָקָם בְּלִבִּי, וּשְׁנַת גְּאוּלַי בָּאָה:　　　ישעיה סג, ד

Kina 30 starts on page 509.

COMMENTARY ON KINA 29

This *kina* was composed by Rabbi Kalonymos ben Yehuda and is the third *kina* which pertains to the Crusades.

עַל־עַמְּךָ יַעֲרִימוּ סוֹד, וְיִתְיָעֲצוּ *They plot craftily against Your people and scheme.* The Crusaders conspired against Your people and said, "Before we conquer the Muslims, let us dispose of the Jews."

אָמְרוּ, לְכוּ וְנַכְחִידֵם מִגּוֹי, וְלֹא־יִזָּכֵר שֵׁם־יִשְׂרָאֵל עוֹד *They say, let us wipe them out as a nation; Israel's name will be mentioned no more.* The Crusaders had two goals. Their primary goal was to reach the Holy Land and "liberate" Jerusalem. Second, they wanted to destroy the Jewish people. "Why should we only liberate the land?" they said. "Let us also kill all those who deny Christianity." This phrase in the *kina* is a quote from Psalms (83:5), and could just as well have been written in the 1940s, as nine hundred years ago. Physical annihilation and total extermination of the Jews was precisely the goal decided upon at the infamous Wannsee Conference attended by the Nazi hierarchy.

זֹאת הִשְׁמִיעוּ בְּנֵי מִקְרָאָיו / לוֹ נְיַחֵל אִם יִקְטְלֵנוּ *But those whom He called [Israel] responded, "Even if He slays me, I will trust in Him."* When the Jews were given the choice of baptism or death, they answered, *"Lo neyaḥel,"* our hopes are pinned on Him. We trust in Him even if we have to give up our lives for Him." The *kina* then proceeds to describe what ensued after the Jews gave their response.

כָּל־נֵתַח טוֹב, יָרֵךְ וְכָתֵף *Every choice piece, thigh and shoulder.* This is a metaphor for the elite of the people.

יַחַד לַטֶּבַח הוּבָלוּ *Together, they were led to slaughter.* The *kina* does not stress that the Crusaders killed the Jews. Rather, the focus of the *kina* is that the Jews took their own lives so as not to fall into the hands of the enemy and be forced to accept Christianity.

צִדְקָה דִינָה פּוֹרִיָּה *The fruitful vine accepted judgment.* In this phrase, the word *"poria*, the fruitful vine," is a synonym for *Knesset Yisrael* and is the subject of the sentence. The intent of the phrase is that the Jews pronounced the *Tzidduk HaDin* prayer, accepting the divine judgment as they died.

בְּהַקְרִיבָהּ עֲנָפֶיהָ *As she offered her boughs.* The mother offers her branches, her children.

אִם־כַּהֶרֶג הֲרוּגָיו הֹרָג *Did he suffer such slaughter as did his slayers?* One of the

great *Rishonim* (*Responsa Ba'alei HaTosafot* 101) tells the story of a righteous Jew who was faced with the Crusaders approaching the house where he and his family were hiding. He killed his wife and three children and was going to kill himself as well, but suddenly a group of soldiers came and drove the Crusaders away. The disconsolate survivor then asked whether he is required to do *teshuva* or not.

בְּאַחַת נִמְצָא, הַכָּתוּב בּוֹ תִּקְוָה וְסֵבֶר / כִּי־זֶה לְבַדּוֹ, יָבֹא לְיָרָבְעָם אֶל־קָבֶר *In the merit of but one good deed was* [Aviya the son of Jeroboam] *assured the hope that he alone, of Jeroboam's family, shall be brought to burial.* Because he performed one good deed, Aviya, the son of King Jeroboam was permitted to have a proper burial, as opposed to the rest of his wicked family who were cursed by the prophet Ahiya (I Kings 14:13). King Jeroboam had prohibited the people from traveling to Jerusalem for the festival pilgrimage and had posted guards to prevent the people from crossing the border between the kingdoms of Samaria and Judea. Aviya intervened with his father, who revoked the prohibition (*Mo'ed Katan* 28b; see also *Zohar Ḥadash* 20a).

שָׁלֵם נִמְצָא בְּכָל פָּעֳלוֹ *But he, perfect in all his deeds.* The Jews of Speyer and Mainz were perfect.

וְגַם־קְבוּרָה לֹא־הָיְתָה לּוֹ *He was not even accorded a burial!* Aviya the son of Jeroboam merited to be buried for his one accomplishment, yet people who consecrated their lives to Torah were not buried.

תַּתִּי לִבִּי, מָצֹא תֹכֶן עִנְיָנָיו *I focused my heart, striving for the meaning of all this.* The *paytan* has tried very hard to understand God's logic and to comprehend His will.

יָדַעְתִּי אֲנִי, צֶדֶק וְיֹשֶׁר דִּינָיו *I am convinced that His judgments are righteous and fair.* The *paytan* wants to understand, not because he doubts that God is just, but, to the contrary, because he acknowledges that God's laws are just and righteous.

קְדוֹשָׁיו לֹא יַאֲמִין, הַשְׁלִים עֲוֹנוֹתָם לְשַׂעֲרָה *He trusts not even His saints, but holds them accountable for sins thin as a thread of hair.* God is very precise and meticulous in the way He treats His holy ones. Again, the intent here is that the *paytan* is seeking to understand the judgment. He knows that what he has described is *tzidduk hadin,* but he does not understand it.

טִפֵּי דָמַי, אַחַת לְאַחַת מְנוּיוֹת...עַל בְּגָדֶיךָ, בְּפֻרְפּוּרְךָ הֱיוֹת *The drops of my blood are counted one by one... all over Your cloak.* This is an allusion to the story, also found in the Midrash (*Midrash Tehillim* 9:13), that God gathered all the drops of blood that the Jews had shed over thousands of years, He counted them all, and each drop of blood found its place on the mantle of God. *"Befurpurkha"* refers to the robe or mantle worn by a judge.

יָדִין בַּגּוֹיִם מָלֵא גְוִיּוֹת *He judges the nations, heaping up bodies.* When He sits in judgment, God wraps Himself in the *purpur*, the judicial robe.

30

emphasis and its technique of gathering seemingly disconnected sources that include the same word motif. The author has signed his name at the beginning of the stanzas, repeating each letter of his first name twice. Commentary for this kina begins on page 512.

מְעוֹנֵי The chambers of the highest heavens are Your abode.
   They are full of Your glory and cannot contain You.
      How much less so, this House. — *1 Kings 8:27*

מַה How pleasant and delightful it is that You dwelled with companions — *Ps. 133:1*
   among the sculptured cherubs! You wanted to build a House! — *II Chr. 6:8*

נָאוֹר Resplendent, You showed Your love to Your people,
   for they are Your portion.
   They will know that Your name is attached to this House. — *1 Kings 8:43*

נָכְרִים Other nations came there, and other people prayed at that mountain — *Deut. 33:19*
   and saw Your signs, so that they would be awestruck
      by the glory of the LORD on the House. — *II Chr. 7:3*

חֲטָאַי As my sins increased, I was consumed by His wrath,
   and the foe razed its foundations, despoiling me.
   The House shall be torn down. — *Lev. 14:45*

חֲמוּדֵי The precious treasures, they took to their temples, filling their bellies.
   The priest shall order the House cleared. — *Lev. 14:36*

מַדּוּעַ Why has such wrath been poured, uncalmed?
   Why did the LORD do thus to this land and to this House? — *II Chr. 7:21*

מְקוֹם The places where my priests approached and were hallowed there,
   are now trampled by an unruly throng of nations,
      gathered about the House. — *Gen. 19:4*

בַּת A heavenly echo responds, "Why do you wonder about this calamity?
   You erected a provocative idol!"
   Something like a plague appeared in My House. — *Lev. 14:35*

30

This kina, written by Rabbi Menahem ben Yaakov of Worms (twelfth century) is devoted to the subject of the Temple. It is written in a combination of two styles: the technically elegant Sephardic style, with its careful meter and rhyming; and the style of HaKalir, with its thematic

מְעוֹנֵי שָׁמַיִם, שְׁחָקִים יְזַבְּלוּךָ.
מְלֵאִים מֵהוֹדְךָ. וְהֵם לֹא יְכַלְכְּלוּךָ, אַף כִּי־הַבָּיִת: מלכים א ח, כז

מַה טוֹב וּמַה נָּעִים. שִׁבְתְּךָ עִם רֵעִים.   תהלים קלג, א
בְּכַנְפֵי צַעֲצֻעִים. יַעַן הָיָה עִם־לְבָבְךָ לִבְנוֹת בָּיִת: דברי הימים ב ג, י

נָאוֹר, אַהֲבָתְךָ הֶרְאֵיתָ לְעַמֶּךָ.
כִּי הֵם נַחֲלָתְךָ. וְלֵידַע כִּי־שִׁמְךָ נִקְרָא עַל־הַבָּיִת: מלכים א ח, מג

נָכְרִים שָׁם בָּאוּ. וְעַמִּים הַר יִקְרָאוּ.   דברים לג, יט
וְאוֹתוֹתֵיוּ רָאוּ, לְמַעַן יִירָאוּ. וּכְבוֹד יהוה עַל־הַבָּיִת: דברי הימים ב ז, ג

חֲטָאַי כִּי עָצְמוּ, אֲכָלַתְנִי קִנְאָה.
וְעֵרָה צָר הַיְסוֹד, שָׁמֵנִי שׁוֹאָה. וְנָתַץ אֶת־הַבָּיִת: ויקרא יד, מה

חֲמוּדֵי אוֹצָר הֵן הֱבִיאוּם בְּהֵיכְלֵיהֶן.
מִלְּאוּ כְרֵסֵיהֶן. וְצִוָּה הַכֹּהֵן, וּפִנּוּ אֶת־הַבָּיִת: ויקרא יד, לו

מַדּוּעַ נִתְּכָה. חֵמָה לֹא שָׁכְכָה.
עַל מַה זֶּה עָשָׂה צוּרֵנוּ כָּכָה, לָאָרֶץ הַזֹּאת וְלַבָּיִת: דברי הימים ב ז, כא

מְקוֹם כֹּהֲנֵי נִגְּשׁוּ, וְשָׁם יִתְקַדָּשׁוּ.
וְהֵם כָּעֵת רָפְסוּ. הֲמוֹן גּוֹיִם רַגְשׁוּ. נָסַבּוּ עַל־הַבָּיִת: בראשית יט, ד

בַּת קוֹל הִיא עוֹנָה. מַה תִּתְמְהוּ פֶּגַע.
סֵמֶל הַקִּנְאָה הֱבֵאתֶם, וּכְנֶגַע נִרְאָה לִי בַּבָּיִת: ויקרא יד, לה

רְבִיצַת He, whose dwelling place is infinite,
    chose to confine His presence to His Temple.
      Do you dare make a rival for Him?
        No one blind or lame can enter the House!   *II Sam. 5:8*

יַעַן Because you debased yourselves, these catastrophes have befallen you.
    The Sanctuary is defiled. He provided recesses
      around the outside of the House.   *I Kings 6:6*

קָדוֹשׁ The Holy One will forgive, but we will be truly ashamed.   *Dan. 9:7*
    He will send a healing balm and not hold us to account for our sins,
      and He will cleanse the House.   *Lev. 14:52*

בִּמְקוֹר With an open fountain overflowing its brim,
    watering fruits which will flourish each month,
    whose very leaves will be curative,
      from below the platform of the House.   *Ezek. 47:1, 12*

חֲמֹל Have mercy on the destroyed city,
    and instead of the flaming fire,
    encircle it with a protective wall of fire,
    and be a glory inside it,
      in the shrine of the House.   *I Kings 8:6*

זָרֵה Cast out and remove defilement
    from Your House, my King!
    May You obliterate the idol completely,
      and may You proclaim, "I have cleaned out the House!"   *Gen. 24:31*

קַדֵּשׁ Sanctify the House of my abode,
    and return to my dwelling place,
    and may my legions gather and behold;
      the presence of the LORD entered the House!   *Ezek. 43:4*

Kina 31 starts on page 514.

רְבִיצַת עוֹלָם מָלֵא. שׁוֹכֵן בְּהֵיכָלוֹ.
הִתְעַשּׁוּ צָרָה לוֹ. עִוֵּר וּפִסֵּחַ לֹא יָבוֹא אֶל־הַבָּיִת: שמואל ב ה, ח

יַעַן הִשְׁחַתֶּם, מַצְאוּנְכֶם רָעוֹת.
חֲלַל הַמִּקְדָּשׁ, וְהִנֵּה מִגְרָעוֹת נָתַן לַבָּיִת: מלכים א ו, ו

קָדוֹשׁ יִתְעַשֵּׁת. אֱמֶת לָנוּ בֹּשֶׁת.
יִשְׁלַח תַּחְבֹּשֶׁת. וְחָטָאת אֵל יָשֵׁת. וְחִטֵּא אֶת־הַבָּיִת: ויקרא יד, נב

בִּמְקוֹר הַנִּפְתָּח. וּמַעֲלֶה עַל שָׂפָה.
מְבַכֵּר לָחֳדָשָׁיו, וְעָלֵהוּ לִתְרוּפָה. מִתַּחַת מִפְתַּן הַבָּיִת: יחזקאל מז, א, יב

חֲמֹל עִיר הַחֲרֵבָה. תְּמוּר מוֹקֵד שְׁבִיבָהּ.
חוֹמַת אֵשׁ סוֹבְבָהּ. לְכָבוֹד תִּהְיֶה בָהּ. אֶל־דְּבִיר הַבָּיִת: מלכים א ח, ו

זָרָה וְהַעֲבֵר טֻמְאָה מִבֵּיתְךָ, מַלְכִּי.
אֱלִיל כָּלִיל תַּחֲלֹף, וְתִקְרָא אָנֹכִי פְּנִיתִי הַבָּיִת: בראשית כד, לא

קַדֵּשׁ בֵּית מְעוֹנִי. וְתָשׁוּב לִמְלוֹנִי.
וְנִקְבְּצוּ לְגִיוֹנַי. וְהִנֵּה כְּבוֹד יהוה בָּא אֶל־הַבָּיִת: יחזקאל מג, ד

Kina 31 starts on page 515.

COMMENTARY ON KINA 30

A theme of this *kina* is that the physical destruction of the edifice of the *Beit HaMikdash* symbolizes the more tragic destruction of the unique covenantal relationship between God and the Jewish people.

וְהֵם לֹא יְכַלְכְּלוּךָ, אַף כִּי־הַבַּיִת *They... cannot contain You. How much less so, this House.* The *kina* commences with an allusion to the prayer of King Solomon at the time of the dedication of the First Temple (1 Kings 8:27), which expresses the thought that the Almighty cannot be contained in any house. He is infinite; not even the cosmos can contain Him, and certainly not the *Beit HaMikdash*. The implied question posed by the *kina* is: If God fills the entire universe, why do we mourn the destruction of the *Beit HaMikdash*?

יַעַן הָיָה עִם־לְבָבְךָ לִבְנוֹת בַּיִת *You wanted to build a House!* It was necessary to build the *Beit HaMikdash* as a symbol of the unique relationship between the Jewish people and God. The Jewish people enjoy a dual relationship with God. On one level, there is the relationship that prevails between God and all humanity, and on another level, there is the special covenantal relationship that exists only between God and the Jewish people. The *Beit HaMikdash* symbolizes this special covenantal relationship.

כִּי שִׁמְךָ נִקְרָא עַל־הַבַּיִת *That Your name is attached to this House.* God's relationship with other peoples is a universal, cosmic relationship, for God resides everywhere. However, there is an intimate relationship between God and the Jewish people, and that is symbolized by the *Beit HaMikdash*.

נָכְרִים שָׁם בָּאוּ *Other nations came there.* This is a further allusion to King Solomon's prayer, in which he said, "Moreover, concerning the stranger that is not of Your people Israel, when he shall come from a far country... when he shall come and pray toward this House" (1 Kings 8:41–42).

וְאוֹתוֹתָיו רָאוּ *And saw Your signs.* When those who came to the *Beit HaMikdash* saw miracles, they experienced the presence of God. The *Beit HaMikdash* was not built for God, it was built for us. If we want to come close to Him, we should come to the *Beit HaMikdash*.

חֲמוּדֵי אוֹצָר *The precious treasures.* The Ḥurban Beit HaMikdash was not just the destruction of a physical edifice. Such destruction, in and of itself, would not have been so devastating. However, the destruction of the edifice symbol-

izes the severing of the unique relationship between God and Israel. All that remains is the cosmic, universal relationship between all humanity and God.

וְצִוָּה הַכֹּהֵן, וּפִנּוּ אֶת־הַבַּיִת *The priest shall order the House cleared.* This is an allusion to the verse in Leviticus (14:36) which concerns a house in which one finds a blemish. If this occurs, one is required to remove all of the furnishings and utensils from the house. The intent of this phrase in the *kina* is that once the unique relationship between God and the Jewish people was disturbed, the *Beit HaMikdash* served no purpose.

וּכְנֶגַע נִרְאָה לִי בַּבַּיִת *Something like a plague appeared in My House.* Based on the verse in Leviticus (14:35), the intent of the phrase is that the *Bayit* has lost its spirituality.

חֻלַּל הַמִּקְדָּשׁ *The Sanctuary is defiled.* When the *kedusha* is gone, the *Bayit* no longer has any significance. Our sages say (*Sanhedrin* 96b) that when Nebuzaradan set fire to the *Beit HaMikdash*, he thought that he accomplished a great feat. However, a heavenly voice said, "You are grinding flour which has already been ground." The meaning is that by the time Nebuzaradan ignited the fire, the *Bayit* no longer had any significance, as the *kedusha* had departed and the glory was gone. The unique relationship between God and His people had vanished.

וְתִקְרָא אָנֹכִי פִּנִּיתִי הַבַּיִת *And may You proclaim, "I have cleaned out the House!"* The implication is that the *paytan* declares that he cannot remove *avoda zara* from the world, and pleads to God, "You do it."

31

the first line emphasizes the close bond between God and His people, the second gives a sense of separation, with a joyous coda of return to Jerusalem. Commentary for this kina begins on page 520.

א A fire burns within me as I recall,
    When I left Egypt.
I will invoke lamentations so that I will remember,
    When I left Jerusalem.

א Then Moses sang an unforgettable song,   *Ex. 15:1*
    When I left Egypt.
Whereas Jeremiah lamented and wailed a woeful wail,   *Mic. 2:4*
    When I left Jerusalem.

ב My House was founded and the divine cloud dwelled there,
    When I left Egypt.
But God's wrath descended upon me like a cloud,
    When I left Jerusalem.

ג The waves of the sea raised themselves and stood erect like a wall,
    When I left Egypt.
The foe flooded me, overflowing my head,
    When I left Jerusalem.

ד A heavenly harvest and water from a rock,
    When I left Egypt.
Bitter grass and wormwood and bitter waters,
    When I left Jerusalem.

ה Morning and evening roundabout Mount Horeb,
    When I left Egypt.
Summoned to mourning by the rivers of Babylon,   *Ps. 137:1*
    When I left Jerusalem.

ו A vision of God's glory like a consuming fire before me,   *Ex. 24:17*
    When I left Egypt.
A sharpened sword let loose to slaughter,
    When I left Jerusalem.

ז Sacrificial offerings and meal-offerings and the anointing oil,
    When I left Egypt.
God's treasure led away like lambs to the slaughter,
    When I left Jerusalem.

31

This kina, its author unknown, is also written in the Sephardic style. With short, succinct phrases, it contrasts the glorious euphoria of the exodus from Egypt with the tragedy and destruction of the exile from Jerusalem. Each of the twenty-three alphabetic stanzas is made of two internally rhyming lines. In each stanza, the second line echoes and contrasts the detail of the first. While

אֵשׁ תּוּקַד בְּקִרְבִּי / בְּהַעֲלוֹתִי עַל לִבִּי. ‎ בְּצֵאתִי מִמִּצְרָיִם:
וְקִינִים אָעִירָה / לְמַעַן אַזְכִּירָה. ‎ בְּצֵאתִי מִירוּשָׁלָיִם:

אָז יָשִׁיר מֹשֶׁה / שִׁיר לֹא יִנָּשֶׂה. ‎ בְּצֵאתִי מִמִּצְרָיִם: שמות טו, א
וַיְקוֹנֵן יִרְמְיָה / וְנָהָה נְהִי נִהְיָה. ‎ בְּצֵאתִי מִירוּשָׁלָיִם: מיכה ב, ד

בֵּיתִי הִתְכּוֹנָן / וְשָׁכַן הֶעָנָן. ‎ בְּצֵאתִי מִמִּצְרָיִם:
וַחֲמַת אֵל שָׁכְנָה / עָלַי כַּעֲנָנָה. ‎ בְּצֵאתִי מִירוּשָׁלָיִם:

גַּלֵּי יָם רָמוּ / וְכַחוֹמָה קָמוּ. ‎ בְּצֵאתִי מִמִּצְרָיִם:
זֵידוֹנִים שָׁטָפוּ / וְעַל רֹאשִׁי צָפוּ. ‎ בְּצֵאתִי מִירוּשָׁלָיִם:

דְּגַן שָׁמַיִם / וּמְצוּר מַיִם. ‎ בְּצֵאתִי מִמִּצְרָיִם:
לַעֲנָה וּמְרוֹרִים / וּמַיִם הַמָּרִים. ‎ בְּצֵאתִי מִירוּשָׁלָיִם:

הִשְׁכֵּם וְהַעֲרֵב / סְבִיבוֹת הַר חוֹרֵב. ‎ בְּצֵאתִי מִמִּצְרָיִם:
קוֹרֵא אֶל אֵבֶל / עַל נַהֲרוֹת בָּבֶל. ‎ בְּצֵאתִי מִירוּשָׁלָיִם: תהלים קלז, י

וּמַרְאֵה כְּבוֹד יהוה / כְּאֵשׁ אוֹכֶלֶת לְפָנַי. ‎ בְּצֵאתִי מִמִּצְרָיִם: שמות כד, יז
וְחֶרֶב לְטוּשָׁה / וּלְטֶבַח נְטוּשָׁה. ‎ בְּצֵאתִי מִירוּשָׁלָיִם:

זֶבַח וּמִנְחָה / וְשֶׁמֶן הַמִּשְׁחָה. ‎ בְּצֵאתִי מִמִּצְרָיִם:
סְגֻלַּת אֵל לְקוּחָה / כַּצֹּאן לַטִּבְחָה. ‎ בְּצֵאתִי מִירוּשָׁלָיִם:

ה Festivals and Sabbaths and signs and wonders,
  When I left Egypt.
  Fast days and mourning and vain pursuits,
  When I left Jerusalem.

ט Wondrous tents around four banners,
  When I left Egypt.
  Tents of Ishmaelites and encampments of the uncircumcised,
  When I left Jerusalem.

י Jubilee and Sabbatical year and a tranquil land,
  When I left Egypt.
  Sold beyond reclaim, forever severed,
  When I left Jerusalem.

כ The Ark and its cover and gemstones of remembrance,
  When I left Egypt.
  Slingstones and tools of destruction,
  When I left Jerusalem.

ל Levites and Aaron's kin and seventy elders,
  When I left Egypt.
  Oppressors and persecutors, slave merchants and purchasers,
  When I left Jerusalem.

מ Moses cared for us and Aaron guided us,
  When I left Egypt.
  Nebuchadnezzar and the Emperor Hadrian,
  When I left Jerusalem.

נ We waged war and God was there,
  When I left Egypt.
  Distant from us and utterly absent,
  When I left Jerusalem.

ס The folds of the Tabernacle curtain
  and the rows of bread on the Tabernacle Table,
  When I left Egypt.
  Fury vented, enveloping me,
  When I left Jerusalem.

ע Burnt-offerings and peace-offerings and fragrant fiery sacrifices,
  When I left Egypt.
  Stabbed by the sword were the precious sons of Zion,
  When I left Jerusalem.

Lam. 4:2

חַגִּים וְשַׁבָּתוֹת / וּמוֹפְתִים וְאוֹתוֹת. בְּצֵאתִי מִמִּצְרָיִם:
תַּעֲנִית וָאֵבֶל / וּרְדֹף הַהֶבֶל. בְּצֵאתִי מִירוּשָׁלָיִם:

טוּבוּ אֹהָלִים / לְאַרְבָּעָה דְגָלִים. בְּצֵאתִי מִמִּצְרָיִם:
אָהֳלֵי יִשְׁמְעֵאלִים / וּמַחֲנוֹת עֲרֵלִים. בְּצֵאתִי מִירוּשָׁלָיִם:

יוֹבֵל וּשְׁמִטָּה / וְאֶרֶץ שׁוֹקְטָה. בְּצֵאתִי מִמִּצְרָיִם:
מָכוּר לִצְמִיתוּת / וְכָרוּת לִכְרִיתוּת. בְּצֵאתִי מִירוּשָׁלָיִם:

כַּפֹּרֶת וְאָרוֹן / וְאַבְנֵי זִכָּרוֹן. בְּצֵאתִי מִמִּצְרָיִם:
וְאַבְנֵי הַקֶּלַע / וּכְלֵי הַבֶּלַע. בְּצֵאתִי מִירוּשָׁלָיִם:

לְוִיִּם וְאַהֲרוֹנִים / וְשִׁבְעִים זְקֵנִים. בְּצֵאתִי מִמִּצְרָיִם:
נוֹגְשִׂים וּמוֹנִים / וּמוֹכְרִים וְקוֹנִים. בְּצֵאתִי מִירוּשָׁלָיִם:

מֹשֶׁה יִרְעֵנוּ / וְאַהֲרֹן יַנְחֵנוּ. בְּצֵאתִי מִמִּצְרָיִם:
נְבוּכַדְנֶאצַּר / וְאַדְרִיאָנוּס קֵיסָר. בְּצֵאתִי מִירוּשָׁלָיִם:

נַעֲרֹךְ מִלְחָמָה / וַיהוה שָׁמָּה. בְּצֵאתִי מִמִּצְרָיִם:
רָחַק מִמֶּנּוּ / וְהִנֵּה אֵינֶנּוּ. בְּצֵאתִי מִירוּשָׁלָיִם:

סִתְרֵי פָרֹכֶת / וְסִדְרֵי מַעֲרֶכֶת. בְּצֵאתִי מִמִּצְרָיִם:
חֵמָה נִתֶּכֶת / עָלַי סוֹכֶכֶת. בְּצֵאתִי מִירוּשָׁלָיִם:

עוֹלוֹת וּזְבָחִים / וְאִשֵּׁי נִיחוֹחִים. בְּצֵאתִי מִמִּצְרָיִם:
בַּחֶרֶב מְדֻקָּרִים / בְּנֵי צִיּוֹן הַיְקָרִים. בְּצֵאתִי מִירוּשָׁלָיִם: איכה ד, ב

פ Decorated turbans fastened in reverence,
    When I left Egypt.
  Shrieking and blaring trumpets and cries of horror,
    When I left Jerusalem.

צ The gold frontlet and power and pride,
    When I left Egypt.
  The crown is cast down and assistance gone,
    When I left Jerusalem.

ק Holiness and prophecy and God's glory visible,
    When I left Egypt.
  Defiled and polluted and the spirit of profanity,
    When I left Jerusalem.

ר Song and salvation and trumpets sounding blasts,
    When I left Egypt.
  The screaming of babes and the gasping of corpses,
    When I left Jerusalem.

ש The Table and the Menora, burnt-offerings and incense,
    When I left Egypt.
  Idol and abomination, graven images and pagan monuments,
    When I left Jerusalem.

ת The Torah and its message and precious vessels,
    When I left Egypt.
  Happiness and joy; gone are sorrow and sighing,
    When I return to Jerusalem.

Kina 32 starts on page 524.

פַּאֲרֵי מִגְבָּעוֹת / לְכָבוֹד נִקְבָּעוֹת.	בְּצֵאתִי מִמִּצְרָיִם:
שְׁרִיקוֹת וּתְרוּעוֹת / לְקָלוֹן וּזְוָעוֹת.	בְּצֵאתִי מִירוּשָׁלָיִם:
צִיץ הַזָּהָב / וְהַמְשֵׁל וָרָהַב.	בְּצֵאתִי מִמִּצְרָיִם:
הֻשְׁלַךְ הַנֵּזֶר / וְאָפֵס הָעֵזֶר.	בְּצֵאתִי מִירוּשָׁלָיִם:
קְדֻשָּׁה וּנְבוּאָה / וּכְבוֹד יהוה נִרְאָה.	בְּצֵאתִי מִמִּצְרָיִם:
נְגָאֲלָה וּמוֹרָאָה / וְרוּחַ הַטֻּמְאָה.	בְּצֵאתִי מִירוּשָׁלָיִם:
רִנָּה וִישׁוּעָה / וַחֲצוֹצְרוֹת הַתְּרוּעָה.	בְּצֵאתִי מִמִּצְרָיִם:
זַעֲקַת עוֹלָל / וְנַאֲקַת חָלָל.	בְּצֵאתִי מִירוּשָׁלָיִם:
שֻׁלְחָן וּמְנוֹרָה / וְכָלִיל וּקְטֹרָה.	בְּצֵאתִי מִמִּצְרָיִם:
אֱלִיל וְתוֹעֵבָה / וּפֶסֶל וּמַצֵּבָה.	בְּצֵאתִי מִירוּשָׁלָיִם:
תּוֹרָה וּתְעוּדָה / וּכְלֵי הַחֶמְדָּה.	בְּצֵאתִי מִמִּצְרָיִם:
שָׂשׂוֹן וְשִׂמְחָה / וְנָס יָגוֹן וַאֲנָחָה.	בְּשׁוּבִי לִירוּשָׁלָיִם:

Kina 32 starts on page 525.

COMMENTARY ON KINA 31

The authorship of this *kina* is unknown, but it is fairly certain that the author was a *Rishon*. The theme of this *kina* is the comparison between *yetziat Mitzrayim*, the exodus from Egypt, and *yetziat Yerushalayim*, the exile from Jerusalem. It describes the beauty and the glory that each Jew experienced in the desert, when God was so close to him. Each individual saw and experienced the presence of God in the midst of His people. Contrasted to this is the mood of the people when they left Jerusalem, exiled by Nebuchadnezzar and Titus. Everything was gone. The Jew was lonely. Contempt and disdain were his lot.

שִׁיר לֹא יִנָּשֶׁה *An unforgettable song.* This is an allusion to Rashi's quoting (Exodus 15:1) of the Midrash (*Sanhedrin* 91b; *Mekhilta Beshallaḥ, Masekhet Shira*) which makes the observation that *"Az yashir Moshe"* (Exodus 15:1) is in the future tense, that Moses will sing in the future. Rashi did not mean that Moses did not sing the song at the Red Sea, but rather that the song was not meant to be sung only once. It will also be the song for the redemption of the Messiah. That is why it is referred to as *"shir lo yinasheh,* the unforgettable song."

בֵּיתִי הִתְכּוֹנָן *My House was founded.* This refers to the establishment of the *Mishkan* and the *Beit HaMikdash*.

וְשָׁכַן הֶעָנָן *And the divine cloud dwelled there.* The *Mishkan* was enveloped by a cloud. This represents *giluy Shekhina*.

וַחֲמַת אֵל שָׁכְנָה / עָלַי כַּעֲנָנָה *But God's wrath descended upon me like a cloud.* The cloud separated the Jews from God.

It is noteworthy that at certain times the cloud is the symbol of God's protection of the Jews and of *giluy Shekhina*. The Torah says, "And the LORD descended in the cloud (*anan*)" (Exodus 34:5). Also, "And the LORD went before them by day in a pillar of *anan*" (Exodus 13:21). In these verses, *anan* is a manifestation of revelation. When God joins Israel, He descends in a pillar of cloud, and this is a sign of His glory, of *hashra'at Shekhina*. At other times, however, the *anana*, the cloud, is the symbol of the *absence* of God and the separation of man from God. It is the symbol of alienated man and darkness.

It is interesting that the *paytan* distinguishes between the feminine and masculine forms of the word *anan*. *Anan* in the masculine form is the symbol of glory and the nearness of God to Israel. "And the LORD descended in *anan*"

means that He came down and wanted to be close to Moses. But *anana* in the feminine form means separation and alienation. *Anana* represents the wall which separates man from God.

גַּלֵּי יָם רָמוּ / וְכַחוֹמָה קָמוּ *The waves of the sea raised themselves and stood erect like a wall.* This is a reference to the splitting of the Red Sea.

וּמַיִם הַמָּרִים *And bitter waters.* This is an allusion to the bitter water drunk by the *sota*, the suspected adulteress (Numbers 5:18, 24). Israel had the status of a *sota*, and in fact Israel's guilt was proven. *Avoda zara* is often referred to in the Bible as betrayal or adultery.

סְגֻלַּת אֵל לְקוּחָה *God's treasure led away.* The uniqueness of the Jewish people has been taken away from them. They are no longer a treasure.

אָהֳלֵי יִשְׁמְעֵאלִים / וּמַחֲנוֹת עֲרֵלִים *Tents of Ishmaelites and encampments of the uncircumcised.* The word *Yishme'elim* refers to Arabs, and from this phrase it is apparent that the Roman forces included mercenaries from many other countries.

וְאַבְנֵי זִכָּרוֹן *And gemstones of remembrance.* This refers to the stones on the breastplate of the High Priest.

לְוִיִּם וְאַהֲרוֹנִים *Levites and Aaron's kin.* The word *aharonim*, which refers to the kohanim, is not grammatically correct as the word *aharon* does not appear in the plural form. However, this is an example of the literary license which the *paytanim* allowed themselves when using the Hebrew language.

וְאַדְרִיָאנוּס קֵיסָר. בְּצֵאתִי מִירוּשָׁלַיִם *And the Emperor Hadrian, When I left Jerusalem.* This phrase refers to Hadrian, but it was Vespasian, not Hadrian, who was the Roman Caesar at the time of the destruction of the Temple. Our sages referred to Hadrian because he was the Caesar at the time of the defeat of the Bar Kokhba rebellion and perpetrated the massacre at Beitar, which transcended the tragedy of the destruction of the Temple. In addition, Hadrian was responsible for the deaths of the Ten Martyrs. Thus our sages viewed Hadrian, and not Vespasian, as the prototypic evildoer. It is Hadrian's name, not Vespasian's, to which our sages attached the epithet, "*sheḥik atzamot*, may his bones be ground" (for example, *Eikha Raba* 1:16, 3:23).

שָׂשׂוֹן וְשִׂמְחָה / וְנָס יָגוֹן וַאֲנָחָה. בְּשׁוּבִי לִירוּשָׁלַיִם *Happiness and joy; gone are sorrow and sighing, When I return to Jerusalem.* This phrase is an allusion to the Gemara (*Rosh HaShana* 18b) which states that if there is peace in the world, then

there will be *sasson vesimḥa*. Peace in the world, in turn, prevails when the *Beit HaMikdash* exists. This is in accordance with the opinion of Nahmanides (*Torat HaAdam* [Chavel edition], page 243; *Beit Yosef Oraḥ Ḥayyim* 550:1; cf. Rashi ad loc.).

In the *kina* "שָׁבַת, סוּרוּ מֶנִּי," Rabbi Elazar HaKalir writes that the Jewish people remembered the splitting of the Red Sea at the time of the Ḥurban ("*palgu suf zakhru*"). As this *kina*, "אֵשׁ תּוּקַד בְּקִרְבִּי," emphasizes, the recollection was one of contrasts. The Jewish people contrasted their plight at the time of the Ḥurban with their elation at the time of the exodus from Egypt. They remembered the glorious miracle of the Red Sea, when they were innocent of sin and when a beautiful relationship existed between God and the Jewish people. They recalled that image of the exodus when Titus entered the Temple and publicly defiled it. Now, instead of the closeness that existed during the exodus from Egypt, the relationship with God is alien; it is a relationship of *din*, not *ḥesed*.

Another interpretation is that the recollection of the splitting of the Red Sea was not a remembrance of the contrast, but of a common element in the two events. The Midrash says (*Yalkut Shimoni Beshallaḥ* 241; see also *Vayikra Raba* 23:2) that on the night of the seventh day of Pesaḥ, preceding the drowning of the Egyptians in the Red Sea, there was a debate between Uzah, the *sar* (celestial representative), of Egypt, and God. Uzah argued that the Jewish people were no better than the Egyptians. After all, they too worshiped idolatry, dressed like the Egyptians and behaved like the Egyptians. Therefore, he argued, God had no justification to punish the Egyptians. God then motioned to the angel Gabriel, who brought a brick soaked with the blood of a Jewish child, and that ended the debate. It is noteworthy that the Midrash does not say that God completely rejected Uzah's claim. True, the Egyptians deserved punishment, but the Jewish people deserved punishment as well. They were equally as sinful as the Egyptians, and on that night of *din*, which the Torah describes as "*vehamayim lahem ḥoma*, and the water was like a wall" (Exodus 14:22), the water was poised and ready to destroy both the Jews and the Egyptians. "אַל תִּקְרֵי חוֹמָה אֶלָּא חֵמָה, Do not read the word *ḥoma*, wall, but rather *ḥema*, anger" (*Yalkut Shimoni Beshallaḥ* 238). God did not deny that *Knesset Yisrael* were very far from perfect, and according to the *midat hadin*, the strict standard of judgment, they should have been punished as the Egyptians were. But God applied the *midat haḥesed*, the standard of mercy and grace, to *Knesset Yisrael* and ignored Uzah's arguments.

If that was the case, the Jewish people had an old debt to pay to God. The *paytan* is reminding us that we should not be asking "*eikha*, why?" in connec-

tion with the destruction of the Temple. We should know the reason for our misfortune. We were still obligated on the debt to God, when He saved us at the Red Sea because He embraced exclusively the *midat haḥesed*. At the time of the Ḥurban, we remembered that we were not as guiltless as we had imagined, and that we had not repaid God for saving us at the Red Sea. God tried to collect the debt through the exhortations of the prophets, but the Jews were lazy and forgetful. Throughout Jewish history, they ignored the debt that was owed. Then the Ḥurban took place, and the Jews understood why. The failure of the Jewish people to have awareness of *hakarat hatov* (gratitude) may have been the reason for the Ḥurban.

32

א My fingers are lowered, and my foundations, fallen.
    Oh!
  Children of Zion are exiled, and all of my enemies are at peace.
    Oh! What has become of us!

ב The Temple and its courtyards have been spilled out on the day of wrath.
    Oh!
  The faces of princes and princesses are blackened like the bottoms of skillets.
    Oh! What has become of us!

ג The crowning globe is smashed like an earthen jug.
    Oh!
  The glorious diadem is dragged to the ground.
    Oh! What has become of us!

ד The city's roads are in mourning; all sounds have ceased.   *Ex. 9:33*
    Oh!
  Well-traveled highways are dark and dim.
    Oh! What has become of us!

ה The Temple and its walls; my innards yearn for it.   *Song. 5:4*
    Oh!
  And for the Table and its utensils, and for the robe and its hem.
    Oh! What has become of us!

ו The hooks of the posts are in the hands of the sons of slaves.   *Ex. 27:10*
    Oh!
  And the platforms, roundabout, many and revered.
    Oh! What has become of us!

ז Burnt-offerings and meal-offerings, wasted and deserted.
    Oh!
  The splendor of the altars, in agony and sorrow.
    Oh! What has become of us!

ח The fenced areas about the Temple, to destruction and to slaughter!
    Oh!
  The woven structure, crumpled by the threshing board.
    Oh! What has become of us!

32

A kina by the Tosafist Rabbi Barukh ben Shmuel of Mainz (early thirteenth century), the author of the now lost Sefer HaḤokhma, which was often quoted by the late Rishonim of Ashkenaz. It echoes Kina 1 (with the refrains "Oh!" and "Oh! What has become of us!"), but each stanza shows Sephardic influence in the meter and internal rhyme. The acrostic includes the alphabet, followed by ברוך חזק.

אֶצְבְּעוֹתַי שָׁפְלוּ / וַאֲשִׁיּוֹתַי נָפְלוּ, אוֹיָה.
בְּנֵי צִיּוֹן גָּלוּ / וְכָל אוֹיְבַי שָׁלוּ. אוֹי מֶה הָיָה לָנוּ:

בַּיִת וַעֲזָרוֹת / בְּיוֹם אַף נִגְרָרוֹת, אוֹיָה.
פְּנֵי שָׂרִים וְשָׂרוֹת / כְּמוֹ שׁוּלֵי קְדֵרוֹת. אוֹי מֶה הָיָה לָנוּ:

גֻּלַּת הַכּוֹתֶרֶת / כְּנֵבֶל נִשְׁבֶּרֶת, אוֹיָה.
עֲטֶרֶת תִּפְאֶרֶת / לָאָרֶץ נִגְרֶרֶת. אוֹי מֶה הָיָה לָנוּ:

דַּרְכֵי עִיר אֲבֵלוֹת / וַיַּחְדְּלוּ הַקְּלוֹת, אוֹיָה.   *שמות ט, לג*
אָרְחוֹת הַסְּלוּלוֹת / חֲשֵׁכוֹת וַאֲפֵלוֹת. אוֹי מֶה הָיָה לָנוּ:

הֵיכָל וּכְתָלָיו / מֵעַי הָמוּ עָלָיו, אוֹיָה.   *שיר השירים ה, ד*
וְעַל שֻׁלְחָן וְכֵלָיו / וּמְעִיל עַל שׁוּלָיו. אוֹי מֶה הָיָה לָנוּ:

וָוֵי הָעַמּוּדִים / בְּיַד בְּנֵי עֲבָדִים, אוֹיָה.   *שמות כו, י*
וְהֶקֵּף רוֹבְדִים / רַבִּים וְנִכְבָּדִים. אוֹי מֶה הָיָה לָנוּ:

זְבָחִים וּמְנָחוֹת / לְמַשּׂוּאוֹת מַדּוּחוֹת, אוֹיָה.
הֲדַר מִזְבְּחוֹת / בְּיָגוֹן וַאֲנָחוֹת. אוֹי מֶה הָיָה לָנוּ:

חֵל זֶה וְהַסּוּרֵג / לַחֲרָם וְלַהֲרֹג, אוֹיָה.
בִּנְיַן הַנֶּאֱרָג / נִדָּשׁ בְּמוֹרָג. אוֹי מֶה הָיָה לָנוּ:

ט Lambs, free of blemish, are now lacking from me.
   Oh!
  The rings, arranged in rows, and the handsome platforms.
   Oh! What has become of us!

י The beauty [Jerusalem] with its ponds, how it is overturned!
   Oh!
  The golden vine and the curtain, and the well-soaked meal-offering.
   Oh! What has become of us!

כ The laver and its copper stand, you see it, then it's gone.
   Oh!
  The candle and its oil, taken from its platform.
   Oh! What has become of us!

ל The show bread, raise a lament for it.
   Oh!
  And the rows of decorative pomegranates are trampled underfoot.
   Oh! What has become of us!

מ The pure Menora, gone is its light!
   Oh!
  The music of the precious organ is taken and is missing.
   Oh! What has become of us!

נ The luster of the copper basin is now for those who worship shame! — *II Kings 25:13*
   Oh!
  The mesh handiwork, and the loaves baked in a pan.
   Oh! What has become of us!

ס The flour and the wine are denied us.
   Oh!
  And the two Temple pillars are thrown to the ground.
   Oh! What has become of us!

ע Over the goblets and fire pans did the foe gnash his teeth.
   Oh!
  He discarded basket and flask and polished his sword until it glistened.
   Oh! What has become of us!

פ Doorways and gates are dragged to the earth.
   Oh!
  The Thummim and Urim, where are they hidden?
   Oh! What has become of us!

אוֹיָה.	טְלָאִים מְבֻקָּרִים / מִנִּי נֶעְדָּרִים,
אוֹי מֶה הָיָה לָנוּ:	וְטַבָּעוֹת סְדוּרִים / וְנַסִּין הַהֲדוּרִים.
אוֹיָה.	יָפְיִי נִבְרֶכֶת / אֵיכָה נֶהְפֶּכֶת,
אוֹי מֶה הָיָה לָנוּ:	וְגֶפֶן וּפֹרֶכֶת / וּמִנְחָה מְרֻבֶּכֶת.
אוֹיָה.	כִּיּוֹר עִם כַּנּוֹ / הֶעְתָּיף בּוֹ וְאֵינוֹ,
אוֹי מֶה הָיָה לָנוּ:	הַנֵּר עִם שַׁמְנוֹ / לָקַח מִמְּכוֹנוֹ.
אוֹיָה.	לֶחֶם הַפָּנִים / שָׂאוּ עָלָיו קִינִים,
אוֹי מֶה הָיָה לָנוּ:	וְטוּרֵי רִמּוֹנִים / לְמִרְמָס נְתוּנִים.
אוֹיָה.	מְנוֹרָה הַטְּהוֹרָה / אוֹרָהּ נֶעְדָּרָה,
אוֹי מֶה הָיָה לָנוּ:	וּמַגְרֵפָה יְקָרָה / נְטוּלָה וַחֲסֵרָה.
אוֹיָה.	נוֹי יָם הַנְּחֹשֶׁת / לְעוֹבְדִים לַבֹּשֶׁת,
אוֹי מֶה הָיָה לָנוּ:	וּמַעֲשֵׂה הָרֶשֶׁת / וְחַלּוֹת מַרְחֶשֶׁת.
אוֹיָה.	סְלָתוֹת וּנְסָכִים / מֶנּוּ נֶחְשָׂכִים,
אוֹי מֶה הָיָה לָנוּ:	וּבְעֹז גַּם יָכִין / לָאָרֶץ נִשְׁלָכִים.
אוֹיָה.	עַל מַחְתָּה וּמִזְרָק / אוֹיֵב שֵׁן חָרַק.
אוֹי מֶה הָיָה לָנוּ:	טְנֵי גַּם כּוֹז זָרַק / וְאֶת חַרְבּוֹ הֵבְרִיק.
אוֹיָה.	פִּשְׁפְּשִׁים וּשְׁעָרִים / אַרְצָה נִגְרָרִים,
אוֹי מֶה הָיָה לָנוּ:	הַתַּמִּים וְהָאוּרִים / אֵיכָה נִסְתָּרִים.

מלכים ב כה, יג

KINA 32

צ The priestly headpieces were hatefully struck.
>Oh!
>>The beautiful chambers, and the storeroom for knives.
>>>Oh! What has become of us!

ק [The enemy city] Kir bared its shield and howled in the hills.
>Oh!
>>They instilled bitter fear and burned the Palace.
>>>Oh! What has become of us!

ר The chieftains of the priestly watches, entangled in troubles.
>Oh!
>>And the princes of groups of ten, in the hands of those who beat them.
>>>Oh! What has become of us!

ש The gate through which multitudes passed *Song. 7:5*
is now for the wolves of the wilderness.
>Oh!
>>They took the cherubs, the drums, and the flutes.
>>>Oh! What has become of us!

ת The pretty chambers to despicable youths.
>Oh!
>>Children as comely as gold now resemble weasels of the woods.
>>>Oh! What has become of us!

ב Dear children, stabbed by swords.
>Oh!
>>Singing Levites, and priests bringing offerings.
>>>Oh! What has become of us!

ר Blossoming lads, to arrows and daggers.
>Oh!
>>First born and coddled babes, sighing in agony.
>>>Oh! What has become of us!

ו They threw the keys heavenward when they saw that they were smitten.
>Oh!
>>Wasted by sin, hands wrenched in pain.
>>>Oh! What has become of us!

כ Ladles and incense cups Are gone from me.
>Oh!
>>And my sons are choking in a distant land.
>>>Oh! What has become of us!

צְפִירַת מַעֲטָפוֹת / בְּאֵיבָה נֶהְדָּפוֹת,	אוֹיָה.
לְשָׁכוֹת הַיָּפוֹת / וּבֵית הַחֲלִיפוֹת.	אוֹי מֶה הָיָה לָנוּ:
קִיר מָגֵן עֵרָה / וְקִרְקֵר הַהֲרָה,	אוֹיָה.
וְזָרְקוּ הַמָּרָה / וְשָׂרְפוּ הַבִּירָה.	אוֹי מֶה הָיָה לָנוּ:
רָאשֵׁי מִשְׁמָרוֹת / סְבוּכִים בַּצָּרוֹת,	אוֹיָה.
וְשָׂרֵי הָעֲשָׂרוֹת / בְּיַד בַּעֲלֵי חֲטָרוֹת.	אוֹי מֶה הָיָה לָנוּ:
שַׁעַר בַּת רַבִּים / לְאֹיְבֵי עֲרָבִים,	אוֹיָה.
לָקְחוּ הַכְּרוּבִים / תֻּפִּים וַאֲבוּבִים.	אוֹי מֶה הָיָה לָנוּ:
תְּאָמִים הַנָּאִים / לַבָּנִים הַשְּׁנוּאִים,	אוֹיָה.
בַּפָּז מְסֻלָּאִים / לְחֻלְדוֹת הַסְּנָאִים.	אוֹי מֶה הָיָה לָנוּ:
בָּנִים הַיְקָרִים / בַּחֲרָבוֹת נִדְקָרִים,	אוֹיָה.
לְוִיִּם הַמְשׁוֹרְרִים / וְכֹהֲנִים מַקְטִירִים.	אוֹי מֶה הָיָה לָנוּ:
רוֹבִים וּפָרְחִים / לְחִצִּים וּשְׁלָחִים,	אוֹיָה.
בְּכוֹרוֹת וּטְפוּחִים / בְּיָגוֹן נֶאֱנָחִים.	אוֹי מֶה הָיָה לָנוּ:
וּמַפְתְּחוֹת זָרְקוּ / בְּשׁוּרָם כִּי לָקוּ,	אוֹיָה.
בְּעוֹן נָמֹקּוּ / וְכַפַּיִם סָפְקוּ.	אוֹי מֶה הָיָה לָנוּ:
כַּפּוֹת וּבְזִכִּים / מִנִּי נִפְסָקִים,	אוֹיָה.
וּבָנַי נֶאֱנָקִים / בְּאֶרֶץ מֶרְחַקִּים.	אוֹי מֶה הָיָה לָנוּ:

שיר השירים
ז, ה

ח The living [God] has demanded His debt,
   and the frontlet of pure gold has been captured.
      Oh!
   The westernmost candle is extinguished
   along with the joy of the water-fetching celebration.
      Oh! What has become of us!

ט Knaves, the descendants of the pampered one [Babylon],
   dominated the numberless [people of Israel].
      Oh!
   The glorious priestly garments are given over to their hands.
      Oh! What has become of us!

ק The fragrant incense is absent along with the Ark and its cover.
      Oh!
   [God], who gauged the heavens with a span, gather the scattered,
   and triumph will swiftly be ours!

Kina 33 starts on page 532.

חַי חוֹבוֹ גָּבָה / וְצִיץ טָהוֹר נִשְׁבָּה, אוֹיָה.
נֵר מַעֲרָב כָּבָה / וְשִׂמְחַת בֵּית הַשּׁוֹאֵבָה. אוֹי מֶה הָיָה לָנוּ:

זֵדִים בְּנֵי עֲדִינָה / עַל בְּנֵי מִי מָנָה, אוֹיָה.
פְּאֵר בִּגְדֵי כְהֻנָּה / בִּידָם נִתָּנָה. אוֹי מֶה הָיָה לָנוּ:

קְטֹרֶת נֶעֱדֶרֶת / וְאָרוֹן וְכַפֹּרֶת, אוֹיָה.
תָּבֵן בַּצֶּרֶת / תְּקַבֵּץ נִפְזֶרֶת. עֹז מְהֵרָה יִהְיֶה לָנוּ:

Kina 33 starts on page 533.

33

of Mainz, who were involved in many halakhic disputes with Rashi in the late eleventh century. Rabbi Menaḥem was a survivor of the 1096 Crusade, which he laments in this kina. Despite witnessing these traumatic events, Rabbi Menaḥem had faith in the ultimate redemption (as expressed in the concluding stanza), and went on to found the great Torah centre of Regensburg (Ratisbon in Bavaria). Commentary for this kina begins on page 538.

א I will arouse grief, I will continue in mourning!
    Woe is me!

ב I will weep bitterly because of the wrathful foe
  who has strewn my path with thorns. *Lam. 3:11*
    Wail for me!

ג He has extended my exile and weakened my heart.
    Woe is me!

ד He has tread and crushed.
  He has driven me to Edom and roasted his prey.
    Wail for me!

ה Did my enemies do but a little? They destroyed my holy Temple!
    Woe is me!

ו They plundered my sacred objects.
  They began with my Sanctuary and humiliated my saints!
    Wail for me!

ז In the year 4856 [1096 C.E.], the eleventh year of the 256th cycle,
    Woe is me!

ח They armed their hordes, left their homes,
  and were numbered like locusts!
    Wail for me!

ט They searched for their mistaken faith and made my yoke heavy.
    Woe is me!

י They rattled their religious objects and tapped their crucifixes,
  and they charged me with false faith.
    Wail for me!

כ They rejected ransom; they wanted our souls!
    Woe is me!

33

This kina, like the previous one, shows a similar combination of styles. Each stanza is divided into two internally rhyming lines, with alternating refrains. However, the lines themselves are not identical in form – the first line of each stanza has two stichs, while the second has three. The alphabetic acrostic is followed by אנכי מנחם העלוב ברבי מכיר *("I am Menaḥem the lowly, son of Rabbi Makhir"), identifying the author as a member of the aristocratic Benei Makhir family*

אֵבֶל אֲעוֹרֵר / אֲנִינוּת אֶגְרֹר.
אוֹיָה לִי:

בְּבִכְיִ אֹמַר / בַּחֲמַת צוֹרֵר / דְּרָכַי סוֹרֵר.   איכה ג, יא
אֲלָלַי לִי:

גָּלוּת אָרַךְ / וְלִבִּי הֵרַךְ.
אוֹיָה לִי:

דָּרַךְ וּפָרַךְ / נָחֲנִי נַח שָׁרַךְ / וְצֵידוֹ חָרַךְ.
אֲלָלַי לִי:

הַמְעַט מַבְאִישַׁי / חִלְּלוּ מִקְדָּשַׁי.
אוֹיָה לִי:

וְהֵם בָּזוּ קָדָשַׁי / הֶחֱלוּ מִמִּקְדָּשַׁי. וְזִלְזְלוּ קְדוֹשַׁי.
אֲלָלַי לִי:

זְמַן שְׁנַת תתנ"ו / בִּי"א לַמַּחֲזוֹר רנ"ו.
אוֹיָה לִי:

חֵילוֹת זֵינוּ / מְקוֹמָם פִּנּוּ / כָּאַרְבֶּה נִמְנוּ.
אֲלָלַי לִי:

טָעוּת בִּקְּשׁוּ / וְעָלַי הִקְשׁוּ.
אוֹיָה לִי:

יְרָאָתָם קִשְׁקְשׁוּ / וְאוֹתוֹת הִקִּישׁוּ / וְאוֹתִי עִקְּשׁוּ.
אֲלָלַי לִי:

כֹּפֶר מָאָסוּ / נְפָשׁוֹת חָמָסוּ.
אוֹיָה לִי:

ל My Levites, they trampled; my priests, they pulverized;
my modest ones, they raped!
    Wail for me!

מ Victims of the sword, hacked to pieces! Undeserving of death!
    Woe is me!

נ The corpses of the innocent, free of all blemish, are laid waste!
    Wail for me!

ס Dragged out and left lying, stripped naked to be dirtied!   *Jer. 22:19*
    Woe is me!

ע Worshiper of Molekh!
An army to do battle with the [divine] King,
dominating the entire region!
    Wail for me!

פ Keep your hair unshaven and your garments torn
for the perfect Torah!
    Woe is me!

צ The foe, with upraised hand and choice wood [for his crucifix],   *Is. 40:20*
promised to abrogate [the Torah]!
    Wail for me!

ק The cries of the synagogues and houses of study.
    Woe is me!

ר Merciful mothers with innocent hands [slaughtered their children],
as sacrifices of visitation [to the Temple]!
    Wail for me!

ש As peace-offerings and burnt-offerings, were grooms and brides!
    Woe is me!

ת Like thanksgiving-offerings and offerings of meal mixed with oil,
were lads and lasses and elders of the community.
    Wail for me!

אַחִים Brothers united, their blood spilled as one!
    Woe is me!

בֵּן So too, sisters, out of fear and reverence for the One God,
were slaughtered together.
    Wail for me!

לְוִיַּי בּוֹסְסוּ / כֹּהֲנַי בּוֹשְׁשׁוּ / צְנוּעַי אָנְסוּ.
אֲלָלַי לִי:

מֵתֵי חֶרֶב מְהֻדָּמִים / בְּאֶפֶס דָּמִים.
אוֹיָה לִי:

נִבְלַת תְּמִימִים / בְּלִי מוּמִים / הָיוּ שׁוֹמֵמִים.
אֲלָלַי לִי:

סָחוֹב וְהַשְׁלֵךְ / עָרוֹם לְלַכְלֵךְ. ירמיה כב, יט
אוֹיָה לִי:

עוֹבְדֵי לַמֶּלֶךְ / חֵיל יָרֵב מֶלֶךְ / וְרָדוּ בְפֶלֶךְ.
אֲלָלַי לִי:

פְּרִיעָה וּפְרִימָה / עַל תּוֹרָה תְמִימָה.
אוֹיָה לִי:

צָר בְּיָד רָמָה / הַמִּשְׁכָּן תְּרוּמָה / נָם לְהַחֲרִימָה. ישעיה מ, ב
אֲלָלַי לִי:

קוֹל בָּתֵּי כְנֵסִיּוֹת / וּבָתֵּי תוּשִׁיּוֹת.
אוֹיָה לִי:

רַחֲמָנִיּוֹת / בִּידֵיהֶן נְקִיּוֹת / זִבְחֵי רְאִיּוֹת.
אֲלָלַי לִי:

שְׁלָמִים וְעוֹלוֹת / חֲתָנִים וְכַלּוֹת.
אוֹיָה לִי:

תּוֹדוֹת וּבְלִילוֹת / בַּחוּרִים וּבְתוּלוֹת / וְטוֹבֵי קְהִלּוֹת.
אֲלָלַי לִי:

אַחִים גַּם יַחַד / נִשְׁפַּךְ דָּמָם כְּאֶחָד.
אוֹיָה לִי:

כֵּן אֲחָיוֹת בְּפַחַד / יִרְאַת שֵׁם הַמְיֻחָד / לַטֶּבַח לְהֵאָחַד.
אֲלָלַי לִי:

מְלַמְּדֵי Students of holy books, morning and night!
> Woe is me!

חֵךְ Mouths, which expressed lovely sayings, now filled with pebbles and ash. Where is one who could count or measure?
> Wail for me!

הֲהָיְתָה Has this ever happened before, that such a ruthless nation should arise –
> Woe is me!

לְהַשְׁמִיד To brazenly exterminate, and assemble a barbarous folk of scoundrels and foreigners? *Is. 33:19*
> Wail for me!

בִּקֵּשׁ He sought alien allies, just to decimate and uproot!
> Woe is me!

בְּקַו With a false, idolatrous creed, the Aramean [Christian] sought to eradicate, and not leave a single bone, until dawn!
> Wail for me!

מְקַיֵּם He who keeps the covenant, had He not spared a remnant in this deep Diaspora,
> Woe is me!

כְּשָׂר When He observed the horrible plight of His Jewish beloved, He showed compassion, so as not to annihilate them, and there is now hope for the future!

לוֹבֵשׁ He who clothes Himself in vengeance, rise and stand!
Stand up against the tall ones!
Do justice for the corpses yet unborn, and let the Divine Presence stand in Her rightful place!

Kina 34 starts on page 540.

מְלַמְּדֵי סֵפֶר / נֶשֶׁף וָצֶפֶר.
אוֹיָה לִי:

חֵךְ אִמְרֵי שֶׁפֶר / מָלֵא חָצָץ וָאֵפֶר / וְאַיֵּה שׁוֹקֵל וְסוֹפֵר.
אֲלְלַי לִי:

הֲהָיְתָה זֹאת מֵאָז / עָלָה גּוֹי עַז.
אוֹיָה לִי:

לְהַשְׁמִיד הוּעַז / וְאָסַף עַם נוֹעַז / בְּנֵי נָבָל וְלוֹעֵז.   ישעיה לג, יט
אֲלְלַי לִי:

בִּקֵּשׁ עֵקֶר / רַק לַעֲקֹר וּלְעַקֵּר.
אוֹיָה לִי:

בְּקוֹ אֲרַמַּאי מְשַׁקֵּר / יָזֵם אֲרַמִּי לְעַקֵּר / וְלֹא לְגֶרֶם בָּקָר.
אֲלְלַי לִי:

מְקַיֵּם הַבְּרִית / לוּלֵי הוֹתִיר שְׁאֵרִית / בְּגֵיא נָכְרִית.
אוֹיָה לִי:

כְּשָׂר שַׁעֲרוּרִית / יְדִידַת עִבְרִית / רַחֲמָם מֵהַכְרִית / וְיֵשׁ תִּקְוָה וְאַחֲרִית:

לוֹבֵשׁ נְקָמָה / עוּרָה וְקוּמָה / לְהִתְקוֹמְמָה / בְּרָמֵי קוֹמָה / יָדִין גְּוִיּוֹת
רְקָמָה / וּשְׁכִינָה קָמָה עַל מְקוֹמָהּ:

Kina 34 starts on page 541.

COMMENTARY ON KINA 33

This is the fourth *kina* concerning the destruction of the German Jewish communities during the First Crusade. It is noteworthy that there are four *kinot* describing the Crusades, but only one *kina*, "אֲרְזֵי הַלְּבָנוֹן," for the Ten Martyrs.

וְרָדוּ בְּפֶלֶךְ *Dominating the entire region.* They took over the entire district of Worms and Speyer.

פְּרִיעָה וּפְרִימָה / עַל תּוֹרָה תְּמִימָה *Keep your hair unshaven and your garments torn for the perfect Torah!* This phrase is an allusion to the tearing of the Torah scrolls.

כְּשָׂר שַׁעֲרוּרִית / יְדִידַת עִבְרִית *When He observed the horrible plight of His Jewish beloved.* When God saw the massacre, He reminded Himself of His friendship for the Jewish people, and God did not allow the enemy to carry out their intentions in full.

34

Sanhedrin 96b) describes the massacre as a retribution for the murder of the Priest Zechariah in the time of King Yeho'ash, two and a half centuries before (Chronicles II 24:20–22). Commentary for this kina begins on page 544.

יוֹם The day of my oppression weighed heavily upon me,
    and my sins doubled,
as I sent my hand against the life of a prophet in the very courtyard
    of God's Temple.
And the earth did not cover it until the arrival of my tormentor's sword,
And it was not silenced until [the blood of the prophet
    Zechariah was] avenged, and ghastly acts performed.
        He has increased, in Judah's daughter, agony and mourning!   *Lam. 2:5*

הָיָה [The blood] continued to seethe until the arrival of the chief
    executioner [Nebuzaradan],
who came to God's Sanctuary and discovered the boiling blood.
He inquired about this of the priests offering sacrifices.
They responded that it was nothing more than the blood
    of sacrificial animals.
        He, too, slaughtered [animals] to further
        investigate what this was and why,
        and I said to myself, "This is your sin, and this is its fruit!"

וּבְכָל [The blood] was still not silenced but persisted like a storming sea.
The matter was researched, and it was explicitly discovered
that [it was] the blood of a man of God who had done no injustice   *Is. 53:9*
    but was uprooted.
Nebuzaradan said, "Now comes the reckoning for his blood!
        Gather the priests unto me, and remove them from God's House.
        I will not be silent until silenced is the
        blood of the prophet Zechariah!"

דָּקַר He stabbed aged men by the hundreds,
    and youths by tens of thousands.
He massacred the priests of the LORD of hosts,
and school children before the eyes of their fathers,
Yet the blood of the prophet was not silent! A sign and a wonder!
        The enemy's sword avenging; the entire city in an uproar!
        Nonetheless, his wrath did not subside, and
        his hand remained outstretched.

34

A kina by Rabbi Yehuda HaLevi (c. 1075–1141), the great poet of Jewish Sepharad, and the author of Sefer HaKuzari, who has signed the stanzas with the letters of his name. It is based on the story brought in the Talmud about the murders committed by Nebuzaradan, the Babylonian official in charge of the actual destroying of the Temple (Kings II 25:8). The Talmud (Gittin 57b;

יוֹם אָכְפִּי הִכְבַּדְתִּי, וַיִּכָּפְלוּ עֲוֹנַי
בְּשָׁלְחִי יָד בְּדַם נָבִיא, בַּחֲצַר מִקְדַּשׁ יהוה
וְלֹא כִסַּתְהוּ אֲדָמָה, עַד בּוֹא חֶרֶב מוֹנַי
וְלֹא שָׁקַט עֲדֵי הֵקַם, וְגַם הִפְלִיא פְּלִילִיָּה
וַיֶּרֶב בְּבַת יְהוּדָה תַּאֲנִיָּה וַאֲנִיָּה:

איכה ב, ה

הָיָה הוֹלֵךְ וְסוֹעֵר, עַד בּוֹא רַב טַבָּחִים
וּבָא אֶל מִקְדַּשׁ יהוה, וּמָצָא דָּמִים רוֹתְחִים
וַיִּשְׁאַל לַבַּעֲבוּר זֶה, לַכֹּהֲנִים הַזּוֹבְחִים
וַיַּעֲנוּהוּ, אֵין זֶה כִּי אִם דַּם הַזְּבָחִים
גַּם הוּא זֶבַח לַחֲקֹר, מַה זֶּה וְעַל מֶה הָיָה:
וַיֹּאמֶר לְנַפְשִׁי, זֶה חַטָּאתֵךְ וְזֶה פִּרְיָהּ:

וּבְכָל זֹאת לֹא שָׁקַט, וְעוֹדוֹ כַּיָּם נִגְרָשׁ
וַיְבַקֵּשׁ הַדָּבָר, וַיִּמָּצֵא מְפֹרָשׁ
כִּי דַּם אִישׁ הָאֱלֹהִים, עַל לֹא חָמָס שֹׁרָשׁ
וַיֹּאמֶר נְבוּזַרְאֲדָן, וְגַם דָּמוֹ הִנֵּה נִדְרָשׁ
אִסְפוּ לִי הַכֹּהֲנִים, וְהוֹצִיאוּם מִבֵּית יָהּ
וְלֹא אֶשְׁקוֹט, עַד יִשְׁקוֹט דַּם הַנָּבִיא זְכַרְיָה:

ישעיה נג, ט

דָּקַר יְשִׁישִׁים לְמֵאוֹת, וּבַחוּרִים לִרְבוֹאוֹת
וַיּוֹרֶד לַטֶּבַח כֹּהֲנֵי יהוה צְבָאוֹת
וְתִינוֹקוֹת שֶׁל בֵּית רַב, וְעֵינֵי אָבוֹת רוֹאוֹת
וְאֵין שֶׁקֶט לְדַם נָבִיא, וַיְהִי לְמוֹפֵת וּלְאוֹת
וְחֶרֶב צָר נוֹקֶמֶת וְהַקִּרְיָה הוֹמִיָּה
בְּכָל זֹאת לֹא שָׁב אַפּוֹ, וְעוֹד יָדוֹ נְטוּיָה:

הוֹסִיף He continued to kill women with nursing infants,
blood rising among them like the blood of the River Nile,
until Nebuzaradan lifted his eyes heavenward
and said, "Is this not enough, the blood of Jerusalem's daughters?
>> Will You eradicate completely the remnants of the captivity?"
>> Then the innocent blood quieted, and the
>> sword of vengeance had its fill.

לְךָ To You, LORD, we sinned, did wrong, transgressed!
We killed Your prophet and knew we did evil!
May Your compassion nevertheless console us,
> for we cry out from the grave!
And from the fruits of our deeds, we have fully suffered.
>> Still unpitied is the storm-tossed unfortunate one;
>> her eyes, she raises to You, hopeful for Your help!

Kina 35 starts on page 548.

הוֹסִיף לַהֲרֹג נָשִׁים עִם יוֹנְקֵי שָׁדַיִם
וְדָם עוֹלֶה בֵּינֵיהֶם, כְּדַם יְאוֹר מִצְרַיִם
עֲדֵי נָשָׂא נְבוּזַרְאֲדָן עֵינָיו לַשָּׁמַיִם
וַיֹּאמֶר, הַאֵין דַּי לְדָם בִּבְנוֹת יְרוּשָׁלַיִם
הֲכָלָה אַתָּה עֹשֶׂה אֶת שְׁאֵרִית הַשְּׁבִיָּה
וְאָז שָׁקַט דָּם נָקִי, וְחֶרֶב נָקָם רְוָיָה:

[לְךָ חָטָאנוּ אֱלֹהִים, הֶעֱוִינוּ וְהִרְשַׁעְנוּ
וְהָרַגְנוּ נְבִיאֶיךָ, וְרָשַׁעְנוּ יָדָעְנוּ
יְהִי חַסְדְּךָ לְנַחֲמֵנוּ, כִּי מִשְּׁאוֹל שִׁוַּעְנוּ
וּמִפְּרִי מַעֲלָלֵינוּ, זֶה כַּמָּה שָׂבַעְנוּ
רַחֵם לֹא רֻחָמָה, הַסּוֹעֲרָה הָעֲנִיָּה
עֵינֶיהָ לְךָ תִשָּׂא, וְעֶזְרָתְךָ צוֹפִיָּה:]

Kina 35 starts on page 549.

COMMENTARY ON KINA 34

This *kina* was composed by Rabbi Yehuda HaLevi and is the second *kina* which revolves around an individual (the first being "וַיְקוֹנֵן יִרְמְיָהוּ עַל יֹאשִׁיָּהוּ," which pertained to King Josiah). It is based on the disturbing story recounted by our sages and recorded in several sources (*Gittin* 57b; *Sanhedrin* 96b, and others), about the murder of the prophet Zechariah in the courtyard of the First Temple. The murder took place on Yom Kippur which fell that year on Shabbat. In addition to being a prophet, Zechariah was also the High Priest. He had rebuked the Jews for bringing an idol into the Temple, but they rejected his reprimands, turned on him and murdered him. After the murder, Zechariah's blood was not absorbed, but continued to bubble and seethe ceaselessly on the ground. His murder had to be avenged.

This story is analogous to the story of Cain's murder of Abel. God's accusation to Cain, "the voice of your brother's blood cries to Me from the ground" (Genesis 4:10), similarly expresses the idea that the innocent blood that was shed demands justice. As long as the blood of Abel was not at peace, God could not forgive Cain.

Zechariah's blood continued to seethe for years until Nebuzaradan, who was the Babylonian chief executioner, entered the Temple courtyard at the time of the destruction of the First Temple. He saw the pool of blood seething on the floor and demanded to know the source of this phenomenon. At first he was told that it was merely blood of animals that were sacrificed on the nearby altar. He discovered, however, what the true source was, and he undertook to silence the seething. A veritable struggle ensued between Nebuzaradan, who attempted to silence the blood, and the blood, which continued to seethe and boil in protest. He first slaughtered numerous animals that qualified as sacrifices, but Zechariah's blood was not silenced. Nebuzaradan then began to kill people, and he executed thousands of kohanim, young and old, as well as members of the Sanhedrin and the aristocracy of Israel, but the blood continued to seethe. Finally, the rampant slaughter and bloodletting was so abhorrent that even Nebuzaradan could no longer tolerate it, and he turned heavenward and called to God, "Is it not enough? Do You want more sacrifices? Do You want me to destroy Your world? If Zechariah's blood will stop seething, I will stop the killing." Finally Zechariah's blood quieted.

Then, in a very strange statement, our sages say that Nebuzaradan repented. He realized the depraved immorality of his behavior, left his position of royal power and converted to Judaism (*Gittin* 57b).

Why is this story incorporated into the *kinot*? Because, as we draw close to

the end of the *kinot*, our sages wanted to leave us with the concept that no matter how evil and corrupt a person is, he still has within him the potential to do good. They wanted to show the power of *teshuva*. Even Nebuzaradan, the chief executioner, who slaughtered men, women and children by the thousands and who personified cruelty, was accepted by God when he did *teshuva* sincerely.

It might perhaps be more appropriate to recite this *kina* on Yom Kippur. Tisha B'Av, however, is also a day of *teshuva*. The principle of free will, which is the foundation of human freedom, is clearly expressed in Lamentations. The verse, "Out of the mouth of the Most High proceeds not evil and good" (Lamentations 3:38), is interpreted by Maimonides to mean that moral decisions are not coerced by God, but are made by the person himself or herself (*Mishneh Torah*, Hil. Teshuva 5:2). (Note that Maimonides interprets this verse as an affirmative statement rather than giving it the traditional interpretation of a rhetorical question.) Similarly, the verse, "Why does a living man complain, a strong man because of his sins?" (Lamentations 3:39), in effect is saying, "Man should not complain. The result is up to the person himself. He is always capable of choosing the alternative." The verse, "We have transgressed and have rebelled; You have not pardoned" (Lamentations 3:42), strikes a similar theme. It states that *we* are responsible because free will is the key to responsibility. Finally, the verse, "Let us search and try our ways, and return to the Lord" (Lamentations 3:40), expresses the essence of soul-searching and *teshuva*. In addition to these citations from Lamentations, the Torah reading for the morning of Tisha B'Av also expresses the concept of *teshuva*: "In your distress, when all these things have come upon you, וְשַׁבְתָּ עַד־יהוה אֱלֹהֶיךָ, you will return to the Lord your God" (Deuteronomy 4:30). Thus Tisha B'Av is not only a day of mourning, but is also a day of *teshuva*.

As noted in the *kina* "אֵיכָה אָצְתָּ בְּאַפְּךָ," the book of Lamentations consists of three sections. The first section is comprised of chapters 1 and 2, which essentially are *kinot* in which the prophet asks the question "*eikha*?" Thus, in these two chapters, the book of Lamentations asserts that it is appropriate to pose the question "*eikha*?" The next section of the book is chapter 3, "*Ani hagever*, I am the man who has seen the affliction by the rod of His anger" (3:1). This chapter records the answer given by God to the prophet, to the questions posed in the first two chapters. The answer is *tzidduk hadin*, the acknowledgment of the justness of God's ways, and the fact that human beings are endowed with free will. With the beginning of this third chapter, the permission to ask "*eikha*" has been revoked. According to our sages (*Eikha Raba*, Petiḥta 28 and 3:1), originally the book of Lamentations consisted of only the first two chapters, both of which pose questions. When the book was

destroyed and rewritten (Jeremiah ch. 36), God ordained that it be extended to include the additional chapters, as well.

The last section of the book of Lamentations consists of chapters 4 and 5, which commence with the eulogy that Jeremiah delivered in honor of King Josiah, the subject of an entire *kina*, "וַיְקוֹנֵן יִרְמְיָהוּ עַל יֹאשִׁיָּהוּ".

As noted above, Maimonides views the third chapter of the book of Lamentations as containing verses which declare the principle of free will and man's responsibility for his actions. It is noteworthy that, from a literary point of view, the third chapter of Lamentations is distinctive. The sentence structure is quite different in that the sentences are very short in contrast to those of the prior chapters. Furthermore, in some traditions, such as in the Ukraine, the third chapter of Lamentations is chanted with its own unique melody that is not the same as the traditional *Eikha* melody. The distinctiveness of the third chapter marks a substantive shift. In the first two chapters of Lamentations, Jeremiah beseeches God to explain why His providence led to the destruction of the *Beit HaMikdash*. The answer, which is presented in the third chapter, is that human beings are endowed with free will, and it is our wrongdoing which is responsible for our predicament. Furthermore, just as a person had responsibility before the sin, the person continues to have responsibility after the sin, and this is the responsibility to do *teshuva*.

Teshuva is a positive force even for the most evil person. As Maimonides stated, "There is nothing that can stand in the way of *teshuva*" (*Mishneh Torah*, Hil. Teshuva 3:14). The example of King Manasseh is instructive. We are told about him: "Moreover, Manasseh shed the blood of so many innocent persons" (II Kings 21:16). The Gemara (*Sanhedrin* 101b, 103a) recounts that when Manasseh was taken captive, he was tortured, and he began to pray to the Almighty in order to repent. The angels, however, closed all the gates of heaven to prevent Manasseh's prayers from reaching God. But God opened a small space beneath the celestial Throne of Glory, and the prayers of Manasseh were able to reach Him in an unconventional manner. The lesson of this story is that even a person who, based on logic, should never be granted the privilege of *teshuva*, does have the opportunity. Manasseh did *teshuva* only after he was captured and tortured. As long as he was triumphant and prosperous, he did not repent. Logically, such *teshuva* should have been rejected, but there are occasions on which God acts in a manner that is contrary to human logic and beyond the understanding of the angels.

וְלֹא כִסַּתְהוּ *And the earth did not cover it.* Understood literally, this phrase means that the ground did not absorb the blood of Zechariah. On a meta-

phorical level, as well, there are other examples (*Sanhedrin* 37b) of crimes that are so terrible that the earth refuses to cover the blood which has been shed.

וְלֹא שָׁקַט *And it was not silenced.* This could refer either to Nebuzaradan and his sword, which would not rest, or to the blood of Zechariah, which refused to cease its seething.

וָאֹמַר לְנַפְשִׁי, זֶה חַטָּאתֵךְ וְזֶה פִּרְיָהּ *And I said to myself, "This is your sin, and this is its fruit!"* I tell myself that *Knesset Yisrael* is guilty of the murder of Zechariah.

וְגַם דָּמוֹ הִנֵּה נִדְרָשׁ *Now comes the reckoning for his blood!* Nebuzaradan declared that he had the status of *go'el hadam*, the family member who is permitted to avenge one's death.

הוֹסִיף לַהֲרֹג נָשִׁים עִם יוֹנְקֵי שָׁדָיִם *He continued to kill women with nursing infants.* Initially, Nebuzaradan executed the elders and the priests, people who could have been responsible for the murder of Zechariah. But then in a bloodthirsty rage, he killed women, children and babies, who could not possibly have been responsible for Zechariah's death.

עֲדֵי נָשָׂא נְבוּזַרְאֲדָן עֵינָיו לַשָּׁמַיִם *Until Nebuzaradan lifted his eyes heavenward.* This does not mean that Nebuzaradan physically looked toward heaven. Rather, the intent is to refer to the movement of a sinner who wants to return to God. Nebuzaradan regretted his actions and repented with a contrite heart.

לְךָ חָטָאנוּ אֱלֹהִים *To You, Lord, we sinned.* This final stanza is a statement of *teshuva*. When the congregation comes to the story of Nebuzaradan, they recite this stanza which represents their declaration that no matter how sinful they were, the path to *teshuva* has not been closed. They accept the sovereignty of God and do *teshuva* for their transgressions.

The reason that this story of Nebuzaradan and the blood of Zechariah is included in the *kinot* is based on an observation that has been noted at several points above. The concept of the *Ḥurban Beit HaMikdash* contains within it not only the destruction of the physical structure of the *Beit HaMikdash*, but also all of the tragedies that have befallen the Jewish people that are also expressions of *Ḥurban*. The same thought is true of the story of Nebuzaradan and the blood of Zechariah. Even though the story itself has little direct relevance to the physical destruction of the Temple, it is included in the *kinot* because it recounts the killing by Nebuzaradan of hundreds of thousands of Jews, a tragic event that merits mention at the same time we recall the physical destruction of the Temple.

35

שִׁכֻּרַת You, who are drunk, but not with wine, discard your timbrels.
Shear off your hair, make yourself bald, and maim your face.
Take up a lament on the heights, and roam endlessly.
Cry out to God about your destroyed portals.
       For the sake of your children's lives, lift up your hands to Him!

אֵיכָה How the foe, the enemy, did come upon the royal city! *Lam. 4:12*
How the foot of the knave did trample the magnificent earth!
When they came, they discovered priests guarding the altar,
standing at their station, not forsaking their mission,
until their blood poured forth like a deluge of water.
And every uncircumcised and unclean person infiltrated the curtain,
that place where the High Priest feared to go.
They destroyed your wooden frames and your latticed windows.
Cry out to God about your destroyed portals.
       For the sake of your children's lives, lift up your hands to Him!

קוֹל The sound of Zion's daughter's wail is heard from afar.
She cried an outcry like [the city of] Heshbon
and wept the weeping of [the city of] Mephaath.
Alas, I have drunk from the cup of wrath and even sucked its dregs.
The teeth of lions have devoured me with sharpened fangs:
Babylon the predator, and evil Edom [Rome].
How can you complain, Zion? Your sin is evident.
Your people were exiled because of your many transgressions and neglect, *Jer. 30:14*
because you abandoned your seers and obeyed the voice of your idols!
Cry out to God about your destroyed portals.
       For the sake of your children's lives, lift up your hands to Him!

35

A kina by Shlomo ben Yitzḥak of Gerona in Spain (13th century), in which the paytan addresses Knesset Yisrael, calling her "one who is drunk, but not with wine" but with misery, based on Isaiah 51:21. Commentary for this kina begins on page 552.

שְׁכֻרַת וְלֹא מִיַּיִן, הַשְׁלִיכִי תָפַּיִךְ
קָרְחִי נָא וָגֹזִּי, וְהַשְׁחִיתִי אַפַּיִךְ
שְׂאִי עַל שְׁפָיִם קִינָה, וְסֹבִּי כָל אֲגַפַּיִךְ
וְצַעֲקִי לִפְנֵי יהוה, עַל חֹרֶב סִפֵּךְ / עַל־נֶפֶשׁ עוֹלָלַיִךְ, שְׂאִי אֵלָיו כַּפַּיִךְ.

איכה ד, יב

אֵיכָה בָא צַר וְאוֹיֵב, בְּצִיּוֹן עִיר מַמְלֶכֶת
אֵיכָה רֶגֶל זֵדִים, אַדְמַת צְבִי דּוֹרֶכֶת
בְּבוֹאָם מָצְאוּ כֹהֲנִים, שׁוֹמְרֵי הַמַּעֲרֶכֶת
וְעַל מִשְׁמְרוֹתָם עָמְדוּ, וְלֹא עָזְבוּ הַמְּלָאכֶת
עַד אֲשֶׁר שָׁפַךְ דָּמָם, כְּמֵימֵי הַמַּהְפֶּכֶת
וּבָא כָּל עָרֵל וְטָמֵא, מִבֵּית לַפָּרֹכֶת
מְקוֹם אֲשֶׁר כֹּהֵן גָּדוֹל, יָרֵא שָׁם לָלֶכֶת
וְהֶחֱרִיבוּ שְׂחִיפַיִךְ וְחַלּוֹנֵי שְׁקוּפַיִךְ
וְצַעֲקִי לִפְנֵי יהוה, עַל חֹרֶב סִפֵּךְ / עַל־נֶפֶשׁ עוֹלָלַיִךְ, שְׂאִי אֵלָיו כַּפַּיִךְ.

קוֹל יְלָלַת בַּת צִיּוֹן, מֵרָחוֹק נִשְׁמַעַת
תִּזְעַק זַעֲקַת חֶשְׁבּוֹן, תִּבְכֶּה בְכִי מֵיפָעַת
אֲהָהּ כִּי כוֹס שָׁתִיתִי, וּמְצִיתִי קֻבַּעַת
אֲכָלוּנִי שְׁנֵי אֲרָיוֹת חִדּוּדֵי מַלְתָּעַת
בַּת בָּבֶל הַשְּׁדוּדָה, וּבַת אֱדוֹם הַמְּרֻשַּׁעַת
מַה תִּתְאוֹנְנִי צִיּוֹן, וְחֶטְאָתֵךְ נוֹדַעַת

ירמיה ל, יד

עַל רֹב עֲווֹנֵךְ, גָּלָה עַמֵּךְ מִבְּלִי דָעַת
עַל עָזְבֵךְ צוֹפַיִךְ, וְשָׁמְעֵךְ קוֹל תְּרָפַיִךְ
וְצַעֲקִי לִפְנֵי יהוה, עַל חֹרֶב סִפֵּךְ / עַל־נֶפֶשׁ עוֹלָלַיִךְ, שְׂאִי אֵלָיו כַּפַּיִךְ.

אַל Do not rejoice over me, my enemy, because of the ruin which has befallen me! *Mic. 7:8*
Though I have fallen, I will rise again, and God will help me. *Mic. 7:8 / Ps. 118:13*
He will bring me back, the God who dispersed me,
and He, my Rock who sold me, will redeem me from you!
Over you too will pass the cup which passed over me.
Then, against your jutting rocks, I will smash your children!
Cry out to God about your destroyed portals.
        For the sake of your children's lives, lift up your hands to Him!

Kina 36 starts on page 554.

| מיכה ז, ח |
| מיכה ז, ח |
| תהלים קיח, יג |

אַל תִּשְׂמְחִי אוֹיַבְתִּי, עַל כִּי שֶׁבֶר קַרְנִי
כִּי נָפַלְתִּי קָמְתִּי, וַיהוה עֲזָרָנִי
הִנֵּה יַאַסְפֵנִי, אֵלִי אֲשֶׁר פִּזְּרָנִי
וְיִגְאָלֵנִי מִמֶּךְ, צוּרִי אֲשֶׁר מְכָרָנִי
גַּם עָלַיִךְ יַעֲבֹר, כּוֹס אֲשֶׁר עֲבָרָנִי
וְאָז בְּסַלְעֵי סְעִיפַיִךְ אֲנַגֵּץ אֶת טַפָּיִךְ.

וְצַעֲקִי לִפְנֵי יהוה, עַל חֹרֶב סִפֵּךְ / עַל־נֶפֶשׁ עוֹלָלַיִךְ, שְׂאִי אֵלָיו כַּפָּיִךְ.

Kina 36 starts on page 555.

COMMENTARY ON KINA 35

וְעַל מִשְׁמְרוֹתָם עָמְדוּ, וְלֹא עָזְבוּ הַמְּלֶאכֶת עַד אֲשֶׁר שָׁפַךְ דָּמָם, כְּמֵימֵי הַמַּהְפֵּכֶת *Standing at their station, not forsaking their mission, until their blood poured forth like a deluge of water.* The Gemara (*Ta'anit* 29a; see also *Seder Olam Raba* 30, s.v. *haya Rabbi Yose*) recounts that during the destruction of the First Temple, the Levites were singing Psalms in the *Beit HaMikdash* when the enemy entered and ordered them to cease. They refused and fell to the enemy in the midst of singing and performing the *avoda*, the Temple service.

One could ask why it was necessary for the Levites to accept a martyr's death rather than cease singing. Apparently, this circumstance was considered to have occurred during a period in which royal edicts persecuting the Jews had been decreed. During such a period, a Jew is prohibited by halakha, on pain of death, from complying with a demand made by the oppressor even if it seems insignificant, such as altering the way one fastens one's shoes (*Sanhedrin* 74b).

36

has widely been considered more authentic, often quoted in Torah and academic circles, and is therefore printed here, in a departure from the otherwise Ashkenazic presentation of the kinot. Commentary for this kina begins on page 558.

צִיּוֹן Zion, surely you will inquire after the well-being of your imprisoned ones, those who seek your well-being and are the remnant of your flock. / From west, east, north, and south, promote the well-being of the distant and the close, from every direction. / As well as the well-being of those bound by longing, shedding tears like the dew on Mount Hermon, wishing to shed them on your mountains. *Ps. 133:3*

לִבְכּוֹת Like a jackal, I cry for your anguish, and when I dream of the return of your captives, I am a harp for your songs. / My heart is to Bethel and yearns excessively for Peniel and for Maḥanayim, and all the places where your pure ones pray. / There the Divine Presence resides close by, and there your Creator opened up the gates of heaven opposite your gates. / And the glory of God alone was your light, and not the sun, the moon, or starlight. / I choose to pour out my soul at that place where God's spirit is poured upon your chosen ones. / You are the royal palace and God's throne, and how do slaves now sit on the thrones of your noblemen? / Would that I could wander among the places where God was revealed to your seers and envoys. / Who can make wings for me so that I can roam afar and move my ruptured heart to your ruptured hills? *Ps. 55:8*

אֶפּוֹל I will fall to my face upon your land and treasure your stones and cherish your soil. / I will even stand near the graves of my forefathers and be transfixed in Hebron at the site of your prestigious graves. / I will pass through your forest and your Carmel, and I will stand at your Gilead, and I will be awestruck at your Mount Abarim. / Mount Abarim and Mount Hor, where there lie the two great lights; your luminaries and your teachers. / Your souls come alive [from] the air of your land, and from the flowing myrrh of the dust of your soil, and the dripping honey of your rivers.

יִנְעַם It would be pleasant for me to walk naked and barefoot upon the desolate ruins that were once your shrines. / In the place of your Ark, now buried, and in the place of the cherubs who once dwelled in your innermost chambers. / I will shear myself, cast off my crown of glory, and curse the day that your saints were defiled in a profane land. / How can I enjoy eating and drinking when I behold dogs dragging your young lions? / Or how can the daylight be sweet to my eyes when I still see, in the mouths of ravens, the corpses of your eaglets? / The cup of agony, slow down! Let up a bit, for already my innards are full and my soul, embittered. / When I remember Ohola [Samaria], I absorb your poison, and I remember Oholiva [Jerusalem] and suck dry your dregs. *Is. 20:2*

36

This famous piyut by Rabbi Yehuda HaLevi, was widely copied and emulated throughout the ages, and seen as the ultimate expression of the Jewish people's longing for their homeland. There are several notable differences between the Ashkenazic and Sephardic versions. The Sephardic tradition

צִיּוֹן, הֲלֹא תִשְׁאֲלִי לִשְׁלוֹם אֲסִירַיִךְ, דּוֹרְשֵׁי שְׁלוֹמֵךְ, וְהֵם יֶתֶר עֲדָרָיִךְ:
מִיָּם וּמִזְרָח וּמִצָּפוֹן וְתֵימָן, שְׁלוֹם רָחוֹק וְקָרוֹב, שְׂאִי מִכֹּל עֲבָרָיִךְ:
וּשְׁלוֹם אֲסִיר תַּאֲוָה, נוֹתֵן דְּמָעָיו כְּטַל חֶרְמוֹן, וְנִכְסָף לְרִדְתָּם עַל הֲרָרָיִךְ: תהלים קלג, ג

לִבְכּוֹת עֱנוּתֵךְ אֲנִי תַנִּים, וְעֵת אֶחֱלֹם שִׁיבַת שְׁבוּתֵךְ, אֲנִי כִנּוֹר לְשִׁירָיִךְ:
לִבִּי לְבֵית אֵל, וְלִפְנִיאֵל מְאֹד יֶהֱמֶה, וּלְמַחֲנַיִם, וְכָל פִּגְעֵי טְהוֹרָיִךְ:
שָׁם הַשְּׁכִינָה שְׁכֵנָה לָךְ, וְהַיּוֹצְרֵךְ פָּתַח לְמוּל שַׁעֲרֵי שַׁחַק, שְׁעָרָיִךְ:
וּכְבוֹד יהוה לְבַד הָיָה מְאוֹרֵךְ, וְאֵין שֶׁמֶשׁ וְסַהַר וְכוֹכָבִים מְאִירָיִךְ:
אֶבְחַר לְנַפְשִׁי לְהִשְׁתַּפֵּךְ, בְּמָקוֹם אֲשֶׁר רוּחַ אֱלֹהִים שְׁפוּכָה, עַל בְּחִירָיִךְ:
אַתְּ בֵּית מְלוּכָה, וְאַתְּ כִּסֵּא יהוה, וְאֵיךְ יָשְׁבוּ עֲבָדִים עֲלֵי כִסְאוֹת גְּבִירָיִךְ:
מִי יִתְּנֵנִי מְשׁוֹטֵט, בַּמְּקוֹמוֹת אֲשֶׁר נִגְלוּ אֱלֹהִים לְחוֹזַיִךְ וְצִירָיִךְ:
מִי יַעֲשֶׂה לִי כְנָפַיִם וְאַרְחִיק נְדֹד, אָנִיד לְבִתְרֵי לְבָבִי בֵּין בְּתָרָיִךְ: תהלים נה, ח

אֶפֹּל לְאַפַּי עֲלֵי אַרְצֵךְ, וְאֶרְצֶה אֲבָנַיִךְ מְאֹד, וַאֲחֹנֵן אֶת עֲפָרָיִךְ:
אַף כִּי בְעָמְדִי עֲלֵי קִבְרוֹת אֲבוֹתַי, וְאֶשְׁתּוֹמֵם בְּחֶבְרוֹן עֲלֵי מִבְחַר קְבָרָיִךְ:
אֶעֱבֹר בְּיַעְרֵךְ וְכַרְמִלֵּךְ, וְאֶעֱמֹד בְּגִלְעָדֵךְ וְאֶשְׁתּוֹמֲמָה אֶל הַר עֲבָרָיִךְ:
הַר הָעֲבָרִים וְהֹר הָהָר, אֲשֶׁר שָׁם שְׁנֵי אוֹרִים גְּדוֹלִים, מְאִירַיִךְ וּמוֹרַיִךְ:
חַיֵּי נְשָׁמוֹת אֲוִיר אַרְצֵךְ, וּמִמָּר דְּרוֹר אַבְקַת עֲפָרֵךְ, וְנֹפֶת צוּף נְהָרָיִךְ:

יִנְעַם לְנַפְשִׁי, הֲלֹךְ עָרֹם וְיָחֵף, עֲלֵי חָרְבוֹת שְׁמָמָה, אֲשֶׁר הָיוּ דְּבִירָיִךְ: ישעיה כ, ב
בִּמְקוֹם אֲרוֹנֵךְ אֲשֶׁר נִגְנַז, וּבִמְקוֹם כְּרוּבַיִךְ, אֲשֶׁר שָׁכְנוּ חַדְרֵי חֲדָרָיִךְ:
אָגֹז וְאַשְׁלִיךְ פְּאֵר נִזְרִי, וְאֶקֹּב זְמָן, חִלֵּל בְּאֶרֶץ טְמֵאָה אֶת נְזִירָיִךְ:
אֵיךְ יֶעֱרַב לִי אֲכֹל וּשְׁתוֹת, בְּעֵת אֶחֱזֶה כִּי יִסְחֲבוּ הַכְּלָבִים אֶת כְּפִירָיִךְ:
אוֹ אֵיךְ מְאוֹר יוֹם יְהִי מָתוֹק לְעֵינַי, בְּעוֹד אֶרְאֶה בְּפִי עוֹרְבִים פִּגְרֵי נְשָׁרָיִךְ:
כּוֹס הַיְגוֹנִים, לְאַט. הַרְפִּי מְעַט, כִּי כְבָר מָלְאוּ כְסָלַי וְנַפְשִׁי מַמְּרוֹרָיִךְ:
עֵת אֶזְכְּרָה אָהֳלָה אֶשְׁתֶּה חֲמָתֵךְ, וְאֶזְכֹּר אָהֳלִיבָה וְאֶמְצָה אֶת שְׁמָרָיִךְ:

צִיּוֹן Zion, perfectly beautiful, with love and grace you were bound long ago, and bound to you are the souls of your comrades. / Those are the ones who rejoice in your tranquility, and who are anguished by your ruin, and who weep for your tragedy. / From the prisoner's dungeon, they yearn for you and bow, each one of them from his place, toward your gates. / The flocks of your multitudes, which have been exiled and dispersed from mountain to hill, have not forgotten your walls. / They hold fast to your skirts and struggle to rise and grasp the branches of your palm tree. / Shinar [Babylon] and Pathros [Egypt], can their greatness compare to yours? And can their vain faith be likened to your perfect faith and light? / To whom can they compare your anointed one? And to whom, your prophets? And to whom, your Levites and singers? / They will fade and totally vanish, these pagan kingdoms, but your power is forever, and your crowns for all generations. *Lam. 2:15*

אוֹדֵךְ Your God has preferred you as an abode, and happy is the man who will choose to draw near and dwell in your courtyards. / Happy is he who waits and is privileged to witness the rising of your light, and upon whom your dawn will break, / To witness the success of your chosen ones, and to delight in your joy, when you return to your past youth.

Kina 37 starts on page 570.

איכה ב, טו

צִיּוֹן כְּלִילַת יֳפִי, אַהֲבָה וָחֵן תִּקְשְׁרִי מֵאָז, וּבָךְ נִקְשְׁרוּ נַפְשׁוֹת חֲבֵרָיִךְ:
הֵם הַשְּׂמֵחִים לְשַׁלְוָתֵךְ, וְהַכּוֹאֲבִים עַל שׁוֹמֵמוּתֵךְ, וּבוֹכִים עַל שְׁבָרָיִךְ:
מִבּוֹר שְׁבִי שׁוֹאֲפִים נֶגְדֵּךְ, וּמִשְׁתַּחֲוִים אִישׁ מִמְּקוֹמוֹ אֱלֵי נֹכַח שְׁעָרָיִךְ:
עֶדְרֵי הֲמוֹנֵךְ, אֲשֶׁר גָּלוּ וְנִתְפַּזְּרוּ מֵהַר לְגִבְעָה, וְלֹא שָׁכְחוּ גְדֵרָיִךְ:
הַמַּחֲזִיקִים בְּשׁוּלָיִךְ, וּמִתְאַמְּצִים לַעֲלוֹת וְלֶאֱחֹז בְּסַנְסִנֵּי תְמָרָיִךְ:
שִׁנְעָר וּפַתְרוֹס הֲיַעַרְכוּךְ בְּגָדְלָם, וְאִם הֶבֶל הֵם יְדַמּוּ לְתֻמַּיִךְ וְאוּרָיִךְ:
אֶל מִי יְדַמּוּ מְשִׁיחַיִךְ, וְאֶל מִי נְבִיאַיִךְ, וְאֶל מִי לְוִיַּיִךְ וְשָׁרָיִךְ:
יִשְׁנֶה וְיַחֲלֹף כְּלִיל, כָּל־מַמְלְכוֹת הָאֱלִיל, חָסְנֵךְ לְעוֹלָם, לְדוֹר וָדוֹר נְזָרָיִךְ:

אִוָּךְ לְמוֹשָׁב אֱלֹהָיִךְ. וְאַשְׁרֵי אֱנוֹשׁ, יִבְחַר יְקָרֵב וְיִשְׁכֹּן בַּחֲצֵרָיִךְ:
אַשְׁרֵי מְחַכֶּה, וְיַגִּיעַ וְיִרְאֶה עֲלוֹת אוֹרֵךְ, וְיִבָּקְעוּ עָלָיו שְׁחָרָיִךְ:
לִרְאוֹת בְּטוֹבַת בְּחִירַיִךְ, וְלַעֲלֹז בְּשִׂמְחָתֵךְ, בְּשׁוּבֵךְ אֱלֵי קַדְמַת נְעוּרָיִךְ:

Kina 37 starts on page 571.

COMMENTARY ON KINA 36

The *kinot* conclude with a group of ten *piyutim* known as the *Tziyon* (Zion) *Kinot*. All of them (with one exception) begin with the word *Tziyon* and have a characteristic literary style and form. They are all concerned with one topic, the fact that Israel was selected as the Chosen Land. The first of the *Tziyon Kinot* is "צִיּוֹן הֲלֹא תִשְׁאֲלִי" by Rabbi Yehuda HaLevi, and the others are by *paytanim* who imitated his style and form, with varying degrees of success. The *kina* composed by the Maharam of Rothenburg, "שַׁאֲלִי שְׂרוּפָה בָאֵשׁ" is also considered a part of the *Tziyon Kinot* because of its style and form, although its subject is the burning of the Talmud and destruction of the Torah rather than the destruction of the land of Israel.

The meaning of the word *Tziyon* is somewhat unclear. As a literary matter, it may refer to any or all of the land of Israel, Jerusalem, the *Beit HaMikdash*, or the Holy of Holies. The precise definition of *Tziyon* is a signpost on a road, as in "Set up *tziyunim* (signposts)" (Jeremiah 31:20).

Tziyon, however, has another definition. It means a tall mountain or bold rock, and it has the connotation of something which is difficult to conquer. Initially, even before King David's conquest of Jerusalem, *Tziyon* was the name of the region of the Jebusites. It had this name because it was well fortified, strategically located and difficult to conquer. When the prophets and the author of Psalms referred to *Tziyon* and Jerusalem, their intent was to emphasize to the enemies of the Jews all over the world that Zion is difficult to overcome. In addition, *Tziyon* in the prophetic books began to take on the connotation of some spiritual, transcendental beauty or something out of the ordinary. The prophets speak about *Tziyon* not only in terms of a mighty city but also in terms of uniqueness.

This *kina*, "צִיּוֹן הֲלֹא תִשְׁאֲלִי," reflects the principle in Rabbi Yehuda HaLevi's important philosophical work, the *Kuzari*, that the land of Israel is unique not only in a metaphysical sense, but in a natural sense, as well. The air is clearer and charged with *ruaḥ hakodesh*, the divine spirit. Nature is more beautiful and magnificent in *Tziyon* than elsewhere. The rain, the soil, the stones, are all physically different in the land of Israel. When the Torah describes the land of Israel as "a land flowing with milk and honey" (Deuteronomy 26:9), the intent is that there is a unique quality in the nature of the land itself.

Rabbi Yehuda HaLevi was in love with the land of Israel. While there were many pilgrims who traveled to Israel, none expressed their love for Israel as passionately as he. Maimonides, for example, mentions the land

of Israel only once in his *Guide for the Perplexed* in a discussion of Israel as the promised land (II:29). Rabbeinu Baḥya's *Duties of the Heart* does not mention the land of Israel at all. Although Nahmanides was a lover of Zion, Rabbi Yehuda HaLevi was perhaps the most "Zionist" of the Torah scholars of the Middle Ages. Nahmanides expressed his love for Israel in halakhic terms which are familiar to us. Rabbi Yehuda HaLevi, however, expressed his passion somewhat differently.

Rabbi Yehuda lived a comfortable existence in Muslim Spain where he was well connected with the caliphate government and was held in high regard. He yearned, however, to go to the land of Israel, which in that era was an arduous and dangerous undertaking. Legend has it (first recorded in Rabbi Gedalia ibn Yahya's *Shalshelet HaKabbala* [1586, Venice edition], page 92) that when Rabbi Yehuda finally arrived in the land of Israel, he prostrated himself on the ground, and at that moment a Bedouin horseman rode past and killed him.

The *Tziyon Kinot* highlight an important aspect of Tisha B'Av. There are two elements to the observance of Tisha B'Av and the recitation of the *kinot*. One is to remember *Tziyon* in its state of destruction. The second is to remember *Tziyon* in its magnificence prior to the destruction. Up to this point, the book of Lamentations and the *kinot* have focused on the first element, on the bloodshed and destruction and the exile and persecution of the *Ḥurban*. With this *kina*, the focus shifts to remembering Jerusalem *before* the *Ḥurban*. The verse in Lamentations states, "Jerusalem remembers in the days of her affliction and her anguish all her treasures that she had from the days of old" (1:7). The *kinot* have already remembered the affliction and anguish of the *Ḥurban*, and now they turn to the beautiful life of Jerusalem before the destruction. The *Tziyon Kinot* all describe in glorious terms the beauty and holiness of Jerusalem and the wisdom of her people. This second element is necessary because, in order to appreciate the magnitude of the *Ḥurban* and what was lost, we have to be familiar with the beauty of the *Beit HaMikdash* and Jerusalem *before* the disaster occurred.

This second element of the *kinot* is reflected in halakha as well. Rabbi Yoḥanan ben Zakkai instituted that "the *lulav* should be taken in the provinces all seven days as a remembrance of the *Mikdash*" (*Sukka* 41a). Rabbi Yoḥanan ben Zakkai's goal was to cultivate the emotion of joy and happiness, and to remember the beauty of the *Beit HaMikdash*. This demonstrates that certain types of *zikhron haMikdash*, remembrance of the Temple, arouse *simḥa* and not *avelut*, joy and not mourning. Rabbi Yoḥanan ben Zakkai's goal was to perpetuate an experience *zekher leMikdash*, not *zekher leḤurban*.

צִיּוֹן, הֲלֹא תִשְׁאֲלִי לִשְׁלוֹם אֲסִירָיִךְ *Zion, surely you will inquire after the well-being of your imprisoned ones.* The *paytan* asks whether Zion is concerned with the well-being of her captives. It is noteworthy that they are described as the captives of Zion, not as the captives of the Romans or Babylonians. Indeed, the Jewish people are prisoners of the land. They love the land, are loyal to the land, and never want to be separated from the land. They are *asirayikh*, *your* captives. *You*, the land, have imprisoned them. No matter how difficult it will be for them, they will always try to return to you.

Perhaps with a touch of irony, the *paytan* directs his question to the land: "Are you interested in the welfare of your captives? They are concerned with you. Are you concerned with them?"

דּוֹרְשֵׁי שְׁלוֹמֵךְ *Those who seek your well-being.* The Jews constantly inquire about Zion and send greetings to Zion at every opportunity.

מִיָּם וּמִזְרָח וּמִצָּפוֹן וְתֵימָן *From west, east, north, and south.* The *paytan* has greetings for Zion from all directions.

שְׁלוֹם רָחוֹק וְקָרוֹב *The well-being of the distant and the close.* One way of interpreting this phrase is that Zion should be concerned with the well-being of those near and far. From another perspective, this phrase can be viewed as the *paytan* declaring that there are greetings to Zion from those who are very distant, and also from those who are very close, emotionally, to Zion.

שְׂאִי מִכָּל עֲבָרַיִךְ *Promote … from every direction.* Rabbi Yehuda HaLevi is saying, in effect, that the Jewish people will never desert Zion. Even though they are *asurim*, exiles taken away against their will, they are still *dorshei shlomekh*, they still send Zion greetings day after day. No matter how dispersed Jews are around the globe, they are committed to finding their way back to Zion.

The *paytan* is emphasizing the eternal bond between the Jewish people and Zion. He describes the beautiful relationship between the people and the land. The land inquires about the people and sends regards to them, and the people send their regards to the land. It is comparable to the bond between a mother and her child who, because of grave circumstances, are separated from each other. They have not seen each other for a very long time, but they continue to cry for, and convey their fervent feelings to each other.

The Jewish people have remained loyal to Zion for nineteen hundred years and have not betrayed or deserted her. One could ask whether Zion, for her part, has been loyal to the Jewish people. The answer provided by the

Midrash is clearly affirmative. On the verse, "And I will make the land desolate, and your enemies that dwell in it will be astonished" (Leviticus 26:32), the Midrash (*Sifra Beḥukkotai* 2:65) says, "This is a noble trait of the land of Israel, that it grants from its fruits only to its children." The Midrash understands the second half of the verse, "and your enemies that dwell in it will be astonished (*veshamemu*)," to mean that the enemies who exile the Jews and take their place in the land of Israel will reside in a desolate land (*shemama*). They will starve because the land will not give of itself to them. In effect, it was a promise that the land would keep all of its bounty for the Jewish people.

Our enemies drove us out of Jerusalem and destroyed the site of the *Beit HaMikdash*, but no other nation succeeded in colonizing the land. The land was occupied by many powers, Rome, Byzantium, the Muslims, the Crusaders, and then the Muslims again. But no one developed the land of Israel agriculturally, industrially or scientifically. Shortly before World War I, Germany established settlements in Israel, and some were successful, but England defeated Germany and assumed dominion of the land of Israel, and the German effort failed. During the eighteenth and nineteenth centuries, entire continents were colonized and settled by the British, yet these same British could not colonize the land of Israel. Contrast this to the Jewish *yishuv*! See what the Jews have accomplished in Israel in such a short period of time! There is a sense of loyalty on the part of the land; she will never betray her people; she will never offer anything of herself to strangers or conquerors. The fact that "Mount Zion ... is desolate" is proof that the sanctity with which the land was endowed by Joshua and Ezra is still in effect; it was sanctified on a temporary basis, and it was sanctified eternally for the future.

Thus, Zion has kept faith with Israel, as Israel has kept faith with Zion.

וּשְׁלוֹם אֲסִיר תַּאֲוָה *As well as the well-being of those bound by longing.* There is a different version of the text which reads "*asir tikva*, bound by hope," which I believe is the correct version. "*Ta'ava*" means that the person has a desire to return to the land. "*Asir tikva*," however, means that one can never surrender. No matter how bleak the situation and no matter how long the exile, one cannot give up hope. The prisoner of hope has faith that Zion will be rebuilt and that God will finally redeem Israel.

Implicit in this phrase is the idea that Rabbi Yehuda HaLevi himself is the *asir tikva* who is inquiring after the welfare of the land of Israel. The intent is that the *paytan* is speaking about himself and is saying to Zion, "Accept my own greetings. I am sending you greetings from a prisoner of hope, and my hope is that I will return to you."

נוֹתֵן דְּמָעָיו כְּטַל חֶרְמוֹן *Shedding tears like the dew on Mount Hermon.* The image of the dew of Mount Hermon is an allusion to the verse: "Like the dew of Hermon, that comes down upon the mountains of Zion" (Psalms 133:3). Just as the dew of Hermon reaches Zion, the *paytan* is shedding tears on the hills of Zion.

לִבִּי לְבֵית אֵל *My heart is to Bethel.* On one specific level, this phrase expresses the emotion that the *paytan*'s heart's desire is the House of God, the place where God meets man. The *paytan* yearns for the *Beit HaMikdash*.

On a more general and conceptual level, this phrase is the commencement of the *kina*'s explanation of why the land of Israel is unique and why the *paytan* is so attached to it. The ideas presented in this *kina* are a quintessence of Rabbi Yehuda HaLevi's philosophy which is developed in greater detail in the *Kuzari*. One of those ideas is that prophecy in the land of Israel is a natural condition (*Kuzari* II:12–14). In Israel, prophecy is a stream that descends from heaven in the same manner that rain and dew descend. The quality of the atmosphere in the land of Israel is imbued with prophecy and *ruaḥ hakodesh*, the holy spirit. In fact, in Israel, prophecy can be received by anyone who desires it. The only reason that no prophets exist today is because there is no worthy recipient. The people are thirsty and want the rain, but they do not have the vessel to draw water from the stream, and therefore remain thirsty. But when the worthy person will come, he will have the proper vessels and will fill them immediately with *ruaḥ hakodesh*.

וְלִפְנִיאֵל מְאֹד יֶהֱמֶה *And yearns excessively for Peniel.* This is an allusion to the verse, "And Jacob called the name of the place Peniel: 'for I have seen God face to face, and my life has been saved'" (Genesis 32:31). Again the *paytan* refers to a meeting place between God and man.

There is another version of this text which reads, "וְלִפְנֵי אֵל מְאֹד יֶהֱמֶה, and before God, I am in great longing." This version of the text conveys that Rabbi Yehuda HaLevi's longing for Zion is not for the land but for the *Shekhina*, the Divine Presence which dwells in the land. He explains in the *Kuzari* (II:22–24) that the *Shekhina* has never departed from the land of Israel and is still present. This entire *kina* is devoted to the motif that the *Shekhina* is still present in the land. The *paytan* is longing for God and knows he will find Him in the land of Israel.

וּלְמַחֲנַיִם *And for Maḥanayim.* This is an allusion to the place which Jacob named Maḥanayim because that is where he met the angels of God (Genesis 32:3).

Maḥanayim should be understood as the place where God, either Himself or through His angels, has a rendezvous with man. In fact, Rabbi Yehuda HaLevi's view is that the entire land of Israel should be referred to as Maḥanayim. According to Rabbi Yehuda HaLevi, God's angels are always present in the land of Israel. The only reason that we do not meet them is because, apparently, we do not *want* to meet them. Had we wanted to, we would have met them.

שָׁם הַשְּׁכִינָה שְׁכֵנָה לָךְ *There the Divine Presence resides close by.* Here the *paytan* declares explicitly what he has been hinting at, that in the land of Israel, the *Shekhina* is one's neighbor. The *Shekhina* resides there even now.

Depending upon how broadly one interprets this phrase of the *kina*, Rabbi Yehuda HaLevi's statement may be in conflict with the position of Maimonides. As previously noted, Maimonides' view (*Mishneh Torah*, Hil. Beit HaBeḥira 6:16–17) is that the initial sanctification of the land of Israel by Joshua was annulled by Nebuchadnezzar's conquest. The reason is that the initial sanctification was based on conquest, which was terminated by Nebuchadnezzar's superior forces. But the sanctification which was bestowed upon the Temple by King Solomon was not terminated, and continues to exist because the status of *kedushat haMikdash*, the sanctity of the Temple, is completely independent of conquest. Rather, it stems from the presence of the *Shekhina*, and the *Shekhina* is never annulled. If Rabbi Yehuda HaLevi's statement that "the *Shekhina* is your neighbor" refers to the *Beit HaMikdash* as being close to the *Shekhina*, his statement is consistent with Maimonides' view. If, however, his intent is that all of the land of Israel is endowed with the holiness of the *Shekhina*, then there is an element of contradiction between his position and that of Maimonides.

פָּתַח לְמוּל שַׁעֲרֵי שַׁחַק, שְׁעָרָיִךְ *And there your Creator opened up the gates of heaven opposite your gates.* From one perspective, the meaning of this phrase is that the gates of heaven are open to Zion. Any influence which emerges from the gates of heaven, descends to Zion. This is similar to the concept that there are special windows in heaven that are open only to the land of Israel, as reflected in the verse, "the eyes of the Lord your God are always upon [the land], from the beginning of the year to the end of the year" (Deuteronomy 11:12).

From another perspective, Rabbi Yehuda HaLevi's intent with this phrase is to reflect the halakhic aspect of prayer (*Berakhot* 3a; I Kings 8:48), that one who prays must pray via the land of Israel; that the gates of prayer are open only in Israel. This refers to the *aggada* (*Midrash Tehillim* 91:7; Rashi

on Genesis 28:17) that prayers do not rise directly to the heavens from where one prays. Rather, they travel first to the Temple Mount and rise from there to heaven. The שַׁעֲרֵי שַׁחַק, the gates of Heaven, are open only opposite שְׁעָרֶיךָ, the gates of the *Beit HaMikdash*.

Alternatively, this phrase reflects Rabbi Yehuda HaLevi's philosophy and his understanding of the land of Israel. For him, *hashra'at Shekhina* is part of the climate of the land of Israel. Just as it is natural to arise in the morning and see the sun shining or hear the rain falling, so, too, it is natural in the land of Israel to arise in the morning and find the *Shekhina*. Thus in Israel, when one opens the astronomical gates and sees the sun, one also automatically opens the metaphysical gates of heaven, the *sha'arei Shekhina* through which God speaks to the Jew if he is willing to respond and enter into a dialogue with Him.

No one emphasizes this quality of the land of Israel in quite the same manner as Rabbi Yehuda HaLevi. For him, *giluy Shekhina* is not just a transcendental event. The *Shekhina* is part of the person's environment, just as the sunlight is part of a person's environment. For Rabbi Yehuda HaLevi, the fact that God spoke with a prophet at a particular location has the effect that that place absorbs holiness or achieves a certain metaphysical quality. These locations are still endowed with this potential of *hashra'at Shekhina* for anyone who finds them. This is a quality that only the land of Israel possesses. In this regard, Rabbi Yehuda HaLevi is reminiscent of the students of the Ba'al Shem Tov.

וּכְבוֹד יהוה לְבַד הָיָה מְאוֹרֵךְ *And the glory of God alone was your light.* The idea that the *Shekhina* radiates light, is found in the verses, "Arise, shine, for your light has come, and the glory of the LORD has shone upon you. Behold, darkness shall cover the earth, and thick clouds the nations; but upon you the LORD will shine, and His glory will be seen upon you" (Isaiah 60:1–2).

וְאֵין שֶׁמֶשׁ וְסַהַר וְכוֹכָבִים מְאִירָיִךְ *And not the sun, the moon, or starlight.* One does not need the sun, the moon or the stars, nor the *sha'arei shaḥak*. All that one needs are the gates of the *Shekhina*, which, according to Rabbi Yehuda HaLevi, are available every morning.

אֶבְחַר לְנַפְשִׁי לְהִשְׁתַּפֵּךְ, בְּמָקוֹם אֲשֶׁר רוּחַ אֱלֹהִים שְׁפוּכָה, עַל בְּחִירֶיךָ *I choose to pour out my soul at that place where God's spirit is poured upon your chosen ones.* Prayer in the land of Israel is different from prayer in any other location. The *paytan* wants his soul to extend to those places that God chose for the

purpose of saturating His chosen ones with the divine spirit, and those places are only in the land of Israel.

This is again an expression of Rabbi Yehuda HaLevi's philosophy that *hashra'at Shekhina* and prophecy in Israel are similar to natural phenomena. They are *shefukha*, they simply pour forth like the rain. Rabbi Yehuda HaLevi emphasizes the principle that the *Shekhina* resides only in the land of Israel (*Kuzari* 11:14), and there is no prophecy outside Israel.

It is noteworthy that Maimonides' approach is quite different from that of Rabbi Yehuda HaLevi. For Maimonides, if one wants to achieve the stage of experiencing *hashra'at Shekhina*, one must do considerably more than open a window. Maimonides' view is that attaining such a stage depends upon intellectual achievement and prowess (*Mishneh Torah,* Hil. Yesodei HaTorah 7:1).

אַתְּ בֵּית מְלוּכָה, וְאַתְּ כִּסֵּא יהוה *You are the royal palace and God's throne.* This is an allusion to the dictum of our sages that God's throne of glory and the celestial *Beit HaMikdash* correspond to the *Beit HaMikdash* located on earth.

A more literal interpretation for the concept that Zion is considered to be the "royal palace and God's throne," is based on verses in the High Holy Day Amida: "And then You, Lord, will reign over all Your works, on Mount Zion, resting place of Your glory, and in Jerusalem, Your holy city, as it is written in Your sacred writings: The Lord shall reign forever. He is your God, O Zion, from generation to generation. Halleluya!"

מִי יִתְּנֵנִי מְשׁוֹטֵט, בַּמְּקוֹמוֹת אֲשֶׁר נִגְלוּ אֱלֹהִים לְחוֹזַיִךְ וְצִירַיִךְ *Would that I could wander among the places where God was revealed to your seers and envoys.* Rabbi Yehuda HaLevi yearned for the experience of exploring the places in the land of Israel where a prophet spoke with God. As noted above, he considered every location where God revealed Himself to a prophet to be endowed with holiness. This is a novel concept from a halakhic point of view.

מִי יַעֲשֶׂה לִי כְנָפַיִם *Who can make wings for me.* Rabbi Yehuda HaLevi clearly wrote this *kina* while still in Spain before he traveled to Israel.

אָנִיד לְבִתְרֵי לְבָבִי בֵּין בְּתָרָיִךְ *And move my ruptured heart to your ruptured hills.* The *paytan's* heart is already in Israel, as he wrote in one of his most well-known poems, "My heart is in the east, and I am in the most distant west." Spiritually, he is already in Israel. If he travels, he will be going to find his heart.

With the phrase *bitrei levavi*, the *paytan* expresses the link between the

ruptured "pieces" of his heart and that of the "pieces" of the *Berit bein HaBetarim*, the "Covenant between the Pieces." In effect, he means that his heart was united with the heart of Abraham, the father of the Jewish nation, into one common heart, and he is striving to reach the place which actually witnessed the Covenant. "One heart" means that the Jew's desire is to be in the land of Israel, and that the Jewish people cannot separate themselves from the land.

אֶפּוֹל לְאַפַּי עֲלֵי אַרְצֵךְ *I will fall to my face upon your land.* If God will grant his request and provide him with wings, then the very moment he arrives, he will remember the heart which he and God jointly consecrated, and he will go directly to the place where so many years ago, Abraham and God joined in the covenant.

וְאֶרְצֶה אֲבָנַיִךְ מְאֹד *And treasure your stones.* Even the stones of the land of Israel are endowed with desirable qualities. There is a reference in the Gemara that it was Rabbi Abba's custom to kiss the stones of Acre (*Yalkut Shimoni* 11:855, s.v. *ki ratzu*).

As soon as the *paytan* arrives in the land of Israel, he will embrace the rocks. His intent is that his love of Israel will be so deep and beautiful that the stones themselves will become living beings which will help restore the old love between him and God.

וַאֲחוֹנֵן אֶת עֲפָרֶיךָ *And cherish your soil.* The progression of these few lines of the *kina* is noteworthy. The *paytan* started with the heart, then moved on to stones, and now lauds the earth. He will cherish not only the stones of Israel, but even the earth itself. He declares his love for the earth because the patriarchs are buried in the earth of the land of Israel.

וְאֶשְׁתּוֹמֵם בְּחֶבְרוֹן *And be transfixed in Hebron.* He will be completely confused by the magnetic attraction he feels for Hebron.

The *paytan* here introduces the principle that the sanctity of the land of Israel arises also from the fact that the graves of our ancestors are there. This principle is enunciated in the book of Nehemiah. The land of Israel and Jerusalem were desolate, and Nehemiah came before the king of Persia to request permission to go to Jerusalem. When the king asked him why he appeared dejected, Nehemiah responded, "Why should my countenance not be sad, when the city, the place of my forefathers' graves, lies in ruins?" (Nehemiah 2:3).

הַר הָעֲבָרִים וְהֹר הָהָר *Mount Abarim and Mount Hor.* These two mountains are the final resting places of Moses and Aaron. The *paytan* cherishes not only the gravesite of Hebron, but *all* of the graves found in Israel.

חַיֵּי נְשָׁמוֹת אֲוִיר אַרְצֵךְ *Your souls come alive [from] the air of your land.* The air of your land, Israel, is not only ordinary air which benefits the body, but rather is of a spiritual nature which benefits the soul.

The idea that the air in the land of Israel sustains the soul is developed by Rabbi Yehuda HaLevi in great detail in the *Kuzari*. Just as the body requires oxygen, the soul, as well, requires a delicate and fine spiritual air. In the land of Israel, when one breathes, one inhales not only physical oxygen, but also a substance which is spiritually potent and invigorating; the very air is different from the air outside of Israel. The atmosphere in Israel is infused with *ruaḥ hakodesh*, a quality which is not present elsewhere. This concept is consistent with Rabbi Yehuda HaLevi's philosophy noted above, that *giluy Shekhina* is a continuous process in Israel. Just as one who walks in the rain will inevitably get wet, and one who walks in the sunshine will inevitably feel warm, so, too, one who lives in the land of Israel will inevitably feel and absorb the *ruaḥ hakodesh* and be saturated with the glory of God. All one needs to do is open oneself to the abundant glory that is like the dew that descends from heaven.

וּמִמֹּר דְּרוֹר אַבְקַת עֲפָרֵךְ *And from the flowing myrrh of the dust of your soil.* Myrrh was a costly spice used in Spain, imported from India. The earth of Israel is sweeter and more delightful than the finest spices of the Orient. Another interpretation is that the earth of Israel is redolent with the beautiful fragrance of spices which arouses feelings of longing for God.

וְנֹפֶת צוּף נְהָרָיִךְ *And the dripping honey of your rivers.* The rivers of Israel taste different from the rivers of any other land, another example of God's special providence over the land of Israel.

יִנְעַם לְנַפְשִׁי, הֲלֹךְ עָרֹם וְיָחֵף, עֲלֵי חָרְבוֹת שְׁמָמָה *It would be pleasant for me to walk naked and barefoot upon the desolate ruins.* He would far prefer to walk barefoot in the land of Israel near the desolate graves and ruins, than to walk in Spain in the finest shoes.

אֲשֶׁר הָיוּ דְּבִירָיִךְ *That were once your shrines.* These lines are the quintessential expression of the idea that to be present in the land of Israel is to be overladen with pervasive memories of the past. But for Rabbi Yehuda HaLevi, they are

not memories, they are a reality. The cumulative message of these images is, once again, the essence of Rabbi Yehuda HaLevi's philosophy that it is impossible to be in Israel and not be permeated with *ruaḥ hakodesh*.

כִּי יִסְחֲבוּ הַכְּלָבִים אֶת כְּפִירָיִךְ *Dogs dragging your young lions*. It is not natural for the lowly dog to conquer the regal lion and drag away its remains. Similarly, the destruction of the *Beit HaMikdash* was an unnatural phenomenon.

בְּעוֹד אֶרְאֶה בְּפִי עוֹרְבִים פִּגְרֵי נְשָׁרָיִךְ *When I still see, in the mouths of ravens, the corpses of your eaglets*. Similar in concept to the previous phrase, it is unnatural for the raven to kill the eagle.

וּבָךְ נִקְשְׁרוּ נַפְשׁוֹת חֲבֵרָיִךְ *And bound to you were the souls of your comrades*. The *paytan* is conveying regards to Zion on behalf of its friends. If one tells a person that someone has inquired after him, that makes the person feel better. So too, Zion should feel gratified. There is no separation between the people and Zion. All the people are bound up with Zion and are totally devoted to her. They continually ask after Zion and inquire as to her welfare.

הֵם הַשְּׂמֵחִים לְשַׁלְוָתֵךְ, וְהַכּוֹאֲבִים עַל שׁוֹמְמוּתֵךְ *Those are the ones who rejoice in your tranquility, and who are anguished by your ruin*. Zion should not think that she has lost all her friends. "On the contrary," the *paytan* tells Zion, "you have good friends. They enthusiastically rejoice when you feel better, and when you are lonely and sick, they suffer with you." Every Jew is concerned with the destiny of Israel, and every Jew shares the pain of a crisis in Israel.

וּבוֹכִים עַל שְׁבָרָיִךְ *And who weep for your tragedy*. The *paytan* continues addressing Zion: "When you feel hurt, the people cry out with you. In spite of your weakness and your sickness, you are still our leader and we need your leadership."

From a psychological point of view, Rabbi Yehuda HaLevi is saying to Zion precisely what one should say to a friend who is ill or who is in difficult circumstances, in order to make him feel better. "It is lonely without you. When are you coming back? Never mind that I am healthy and you are ill, that I am younger and you are older. No matter how prosperous we may be, we cannot go on without you. Get up!"

וּמִשְׁתַּחֲוִים אִישׁ מִמְּקוֹמוֹ אֱלֵי נֹכַח שְׁעָרָיִךְ *And bow, each one of them from his place, toward your gates*. This phrase reflects the halakhic dictum that when praying, one should face in the direction of Jerusalem (*Berakhot* 30a).

Why should one face Jerusalem when praying? Because it demonstrates that one who prays has not forgotten Jerusalem. In effect, it is as though Zion is an elderly mother with many children dispersed in distant locations, and the *paytan* is telling her, "Remember one thing. No matter how far from you they may be, they are still your children."

שִׁנְעָר וּפַתְרוֹס הֲיַעַרְכוּךְ בְּגָדְלָם, וְאִם הֲבָלָם יִדְמוּ לְתָמַּיִךְ וְאוּרָיִךְ Shinar and Pathros; can their greatness compare to yours? Can the two greatest civilizations of antiquity, Mesopotamia and Egypt, compare to Zion?

אֶל מִי יִדְמוּ מְשִׁיחַיִךְ, וְאֶל מִי נְבִיאַיִךְ To whom can they compare your anointed one? And to whom, your prophets? In this phrase, Rabbi Yehuda HaLevi has in mind Christianity and Islam and declares that they cannot compare with our saintly sages and great leaders.

יִשְׁנֶה וְיַחֲלוֹף כָּלִיל, כָּל־מַמְלְכוֹת הָאֱלִיל They will fade and totally vanish, these pagan kingdoms. Zion is identified with faith in God, and all the enemies of Israel with idolatry.

37

Jewish people, in their system of government, and particularly in their knowledge of astronomy, accurately calculating the seasons and regulating leap years. Commentary for this kina begins on page 574.

צִיּוֹן Zion, take all the balm of Gilead for your travail. It will not suffice, because your calamity is as great as the ocean. / You are designated as the most beautiful of all nations, for from Eden, the site of all that is precious, do your rivers flow! / And this is proof: Naaman bathed his flesh in the waters of the Jordan and was healed; so much more so, your pure ones! / The soil of your land cannot be measured with the finest gold. Precious as a diamond is that which is hewn from your mountains. / Even your unique fruits are delicious and not sour to the tooth. Your bitter herbs are also sweet as honey. / Your fruits heal, and every leaf is indeed a cure. Like hives of honey are your forests. / Your people have a covenant with serpents, and no one comes to harm. Indeed, the lions have made peace with them! / Your animals and fowl are intelligent; like the donkey which once belonged to [Rabbi Pineḥas] Ben Yair are your donkeys! / God Himself guides you, none other, and you are famous, for you have made God's name famous with your songs.

מַה How wonderful and pleasant it is when all the tribes of Jacob come to your gates three times each year. / You have the secret of good counsel and the secret of wisdom so that people from the Orient, and the wise of Sheba come to copy your books. / Your king is in your midst along with well-armed generals. Triumphant over all nations are your heroes. / Officers along the entire border; judges in every city. Truthful elders are they, and there are no teachers like your teachers. / In youth, they were chosen by God as a holy people, and your young lads, as prophets and sons of the Living God. / By you were the seasons accurately measured, and the generations adjusted by the additional month of Adar. / The first sign of the new moon is in accordance with your longitude, and it is first seen in your latitude, and thus you demonstrated your esoteric knowledge. / The southern constellation rises in Tammuz in your land and ordains the climates of all the months in your region.

1 Kings 5:10

Deut. 32:7

אַיֵּה Where is your shrine, the location of the Ark, and where is the beauty of the Temple and the altars? Where are your courtyards? / Where is the anointed one to bring atonement for your people? And what has happened to the sons of Kehat [the Levites]? Where are your Nazirites? / Where are the prophets, the sons of the One Above? All your counselors are lost, and gone into captivity are your kings and princes!

37

One of the oldest of the Tziyon Kinot, and the thematic and stylistic "descendant" of Rabbi Yehuda HaLevi's צִיּוֹן הֲלֹא תִשְׁאֲלִי, *this kina was written by Rabbi Avraham HaḤozeh ("the Seer") of Tiberias, whom some identify as Rabbi Avraham ibn Ezra. It praises the land of Israel: its very soil, its produce and animals; and also praises the wisdom of its inhabitants, the*

צִיּוֹן, קְחִי כָּל צֳרִי גִלְעָד לְצִירַיִךְ. אֵין דַּי, לְמַעַן כִּיָּם גָּדְלוּ שְׁבָרָיִךְ:
אֶרֶץ צְבִי, אַתְּ בְּתוֹךְ גּוֹיִם נְתוּנָה. וּמִן עֵדֶן מְקוֹם כָּל יָקָר, יָצְאוּ נְהָרָיִךְ:
וִיהִי לְאוֹת, נַעֲמָן רָחַץ בְּשָׂרוֹ בְּמֵי יַרְדֵּן, אֲזַי נֶאֱסַף. אַף כִּי טְהוֹרָיִךְ:
אַף לֹא יְסֻלֶּה עֲפַר אַרְצֵךְ בְּזָהָב וּפָז, יָקָר כְּמוֹ יַהֲלוֹם מַחֲצַב הֲרָרָיִךְ:
כָּל תַּעֲנוּגִים בְּבוֹא בָסֹרֶךְ, וְלֹא קָהֲתָה הַשֵּׁן. וְאוּלָם כְּצוּף מָתְקוּ מְרוֹרָיִךְ:
פִּרְיֵךְ לְמַרְפֵּא, וְכָל עָלֶה תְּעָלָה. הֲלֹא וְכִוֲרַת הַדְּבַשׁ הָיוּ יְעָרָיִךְ:
עִם הַפְּתָנִים בְּרִית כָּרַתּוּ מֵתַיִךְ. וְאֵין שָׂטָן, אֲבָל הַשְׁלִמוּ לָהֶם כְּפִירָיִךְ:
בָּךְ כָּל בְּהֵמָה וְעוֹף חָכְמוּ. עֲדֵי כַחֲמוֹר הָיָה לִפְנֵי לָבָן יָאִיר חֲמוֹרָיִךְ:
בָּךְ אֵל לְבַדּוֹ וְאֵין בִּלְתּוֹ. וַיֵּצֵא שְׁמֵךְ, כִּי שֵׁם אֱלֹהֵי אֱמֶת נוֹדַע בְּשָׁרַיִךְ:

מַה טּוֹב וְנָעִים, בְּבוֹא שִׁבְטֵי בְנֵי יַעֲקֹב שָׁלֹשׁ פְּעָמִים בְּכָל שָׁנָה, שְׁעָרַיִךְ:
בָּךְ סוֹד תְּעוּדָה וְסוֹד חָכְמוֹת, וּבָאוּ בְנֵי קֶדֶם וְחַכְמֵי שְׁבָא לִכְתֹּב סְפָרָיִךְ: מלכים א ה, י
מַלְכֵּךְ בְּקִרְבֵּךְ, וּבָךְ שָׂרֵי חֲיָלִים בְּכָל נֶשֶׁק, וְעַל כָּל לְאֹם גָּבְרוּ גִבּוֹרָיִךְ:
שׁוֹטְרִים בְּכָל הַגְּבוּל, שׁוֹפְטִים בְּכָל עִיר וָעִיר. זִקְנֵי אֱמֶת הֵם, וְאֵין מוֹרֶה כְּמוֹרָיִךְ:
בִּימֵי בְחוּרוֹת, הֱיוֹת קֹדֶשׁ לְאֵל נִבְחָרוּ. וּבְנֵי נְבִיאִים בְּנֵי אֵל חַי, נְעָרָיִךְ:
בָּךְ הַתְּקוּפָה, עֲלֵי קַו הָאֱמֶת נִשְׁקָלָה. תְּכֹן שְׁנוֹת דּוֹר וָדוֹר, בִּשְׁנֵי אֲדָרָיִךְ: דברים לב, ז
מוֹלַד הַלְּבָנָה כְּפִי אָרְכֵּךְ, וְהַמַּחֲזֵה שׂוּמָה לְרָחְבֵּךְ. וּבָהּ הֵרָאִית סְתָרָיִךְ:
נִרְאָה בְּתַמּוּז כְּסִיל, בָּךְ יַעֲלֶה. כִּי שְׁאָר כָּל הֶחֳדָשִׁים לְבַד זֶה, בַּחֲדָרָיִךְ:

אַיֵּה דְבִירֵךְ מְקוֹם אָרוֹן, וְאַיֵּה הֲדַר הֵיכָל וְהַמִּזְבְּחוֹת, אַיֵּה חֲצֵרָיִךְ:
אַיֵּה מְשִׁיחֵךְ, בְּעַד עַמֵּךְ יְכַפֵּר. וּמֶה הָיָה לְיַלְדֵי קְהָת, אַיֵּה נְזִירָיִךְ:
אֵיפֹה נְבִיאִים בְּנֵי עֶלְיוֹן, וְכָל יוֹעֲצֵךְ. אָבְדוּ וְהָלְכוּ שְׁבִי מַלְכֵּךְ וְשָׂרָיִךְ:

הָיִית Your landscape was once the prettiest in all the world, your pines so high! Ps. 48:3
Your sins spoiled you and cut down your harvest. / The land forsook you, and alien waters washed you away, and every wind scattered you, and fire consumed your cities. / You rebelled against your Protector, who guarded you from foe, and then strangers ruined you, but you caused your own ruin. / God elevated you, dubbing you "Ariel." How, then, did the lion invade your home, devouring your flock?

שׁוּבִי Return to God, your Master. Do not be silent until His glory returns and until He rebuilds your walls. / I greatly long to see your shining beauty. Peace unto you and much peace to your supporters!

Kina 38 starts on page 576.

תהלים מח,ג

הָיִית יְפֵה נוֹף לְרֹאשׁ תֵּבֵל, בְּרוֹשֵׁךְ לְנֵס. חֲטָאֵךְ בְּאַף סְעָפֵךְ, קָצַר קְצִירֵךְ:
אֶרֶץ מְאָסֵךְ, וּמֵי נָכְרִים שְׁטָפוּךְ, וְכָל רוּחַ הֱפִיצֵךְ. וְאֵשׁ בָּעֲרָה בְּעָרֵיךְ:
מָרִית בְּצוּרֵךְ אֲשֶׁר מִצַּר נְצָרֵךְ. וְאָז זָרִים עֲבָרוּךְ, וְאַתְּ הָיִית בְּעוֹכְרֵיךְ:
אֵל הֶאֱמִירֵךְ עֲדֵי נִקְרֵאת אֲרִיאֵל, וְאֵיךְ עָבַר בָּנֵךְ אֲרִי טוֹרֵף עֲדָרֵיךְ:

שׁוּבִי לְאֵל בּוֹעֲלֵךְ, אַל תִּתְּנִי לוֹ דֳמִי. עַד שׁוּב כְּבוֹדוֹ, וְעַד יִבְנֶה גְדֵרֵיךְ:
נַפְשִׁי מְאֹד נִכְסְפָה, לִרְאוֹת בְּזִיו זָהֳרֵךְ. שָׁלוֹם יְהִי לָךְ, וְרֹב שָׁלוֹם לְעוֹזְרֵיךְ:

Kina 38 starts on page 577.

COMMENTARY ON KINA 37

עִם הַפְּתָנִים בְּרִית כָּרְתוּ מֵתֶיךָ *Your people have a covenant with serpents.* This is an allusion to the Mishna in *Avot* (5:5) which states that no snake or scorpion ever inflicted an injury in Jerusalem.

וּבָאוּ בְנֵי קֶדֶם וְחַכְמֵי שְׁבָא לִכְתֹּב סְפָרֶיךָ *So that people from the Orient and the wise of Sheba come to copy your books.* This phrase is reminiscent of the statement of Rabbi Yehuda HaLevi (*Kuzari* 1:63; 11:66) that the Greeks, Babylonians and Assyrians copied Jewish books of wisdom, and that all Greek science, astronomy, mathematics and philosophy was copied from Jewish sources. It is interesting that there is a source for the statement by Plato (see Clement of Alexandria, *Stromata*, Book 1, chapter 1) that he met Hebrew scholars and learned from them as much as he could, although there are those who question the veracity of this source. Along similar lines, Maimonides refers to the descendants of the Tribe of Issachar having written many books on astronomy which are no longer extant (*Mishneh Torah*, Hil. Kiddush HaHodesh 17:24).

בִּימֵי בַחוּרוֹת, הֱיוֹת קֹדֶשׁ לָאֵל נִבְחֲרוּ *In youth, they were chosen by God as a holy people.* This is a reference to Samuel, who was chosen as a young boy to be dedicated and committed to God.

בָּךְ הַתְּקוּפָה, עֲלֵי קַו הָאֱמֶת נִשְׁקְלָה *By you were the seasons accurately measured.* This refers to the institution of sanctifying the new moon and determining leap years.

אַיֵּה מְשִׁיחֶךָ *Where is the anointed one.* This is reference to the High Priest.

38

צִיּוֹן Zion, you were a crown of glory, a joy to your throng. Peace, like a river, take for your LORD! / Celestial angels, who guard your walls and ramparts; night and day, they solicit peace for your encampments. / Even those scattered to the earth's four extremities seek your welfare; they are your daughters and sons. / Residents of the grave await and anticipate the day of your salvation, for the dead shall blossom and live. / As for me, when I inquire after your well-being, I cry aloud from the mountaintops and am like a bird upon your flourishing [forests].

שָׁלוֹם Peace to Zion, the abode of righteousness, and peace to your ramparts and walls, your precious pearl stones. / Peace to the fair land, peace to the entire territory of Gilead and Samaria and all the other neighbors. / Zion, your appearance was once so beautiful! How did your face and features turn black?! / Once you wore the finery of princesses, but now you gird sackcloth upon your hips and loins. / Sighing becomes my bread when you substitute ash for glory, and agony is my drink when you are anguished. / Rise, and let us raise a cry, and shed a sea of tears which will flow like rivers from my eyes to yours. / For your widowhood, your lover has gone, and He has ruined His shrine and all your hidden treasures. / When I behold your beauty, I summon singers to song; when I see your affliction, I summon your mourners. / I would prefer that owls and vultures dwell in your place. But, woe is me, Edom [Rome] and Arabia occupy your nest. *Jer. 50:7*

עִיר As David and Solomon's royal city were you built, and they were your early foundations. / You were a temple for God; you were a repose for the Rock. You were the one into whose gardens He descended daily. / There were the Table, the Menora, and the Ark of the Covenant. God, between your loving breasts, dwelled in your lodgings. / Upon your altar stood priests offering sacrifices and burnt-offerings to atone for your sins. / The High Priest, upon whom eight precious garments were fastened; from the hem of his gown, the sound of bells was heard. / Once a year, he entered the inner sanctum and brought a fistful of incense, and your handful. / Cassia and cane and all sorts of spice; the scent of your oils reached until the city of palms [Jericho]! / The Levites too, who guarded your gates and even sang songs by mouth, along with your many melodies. / Standing opposite them were those who manned the prayer

38

Composed by Elazar ben Moshe of Wurzburg, this poem recasts some of the themes of Rabbi Yehuda HaLevi's צִיּוֹן, הֲלֹא תִשְׁאֲלִי לִשְׁלוֹם אֲסִירַיִךְ. *Commentary for this kina begins on page 580.*

צִיּוֹן עֲטֶרֶת צְבִי, שִׂמְחַת הֲמוֹנַיִךְ. שָׁלוֹם כְּנָהָר קְחִי מֵאֵת אֲדוֹנָיִךְ:
אֱלֵי שְׁחָקִים אֲשֶׁר שׁוֹמְרִים לְחוֹמוֹת וְחֵל, לַיְלָה וְיוֹם יִדְרְשׁוּן שָׁלוֹם לְמַחֲנָיִךְ:
גַּם הַנְּפוֹצִים בְּכָל אַרְבַּע קְצָווֹת, וְהֵם דּוֹרְשֵׁי שְׁלוֹמֵךְ, בְּנוֹתַיִךְ וּבָנָיִךְ:
שׁוֹכְנֵי קְבָרִים, מְחַכִּים וּמְצַפִּים לְיוֹם יִשְׁעֵךְ, וְאָז יִצְמְחוּ יִחְיוּ יְשֵׁנָיִךְ:
וַאֲנִי בְּשָׁאֳלִי שְׁלוֹמֵךְ, אֶקְרָא קוֹל בְּרֹאשׁ הָרִים, וְאַדְמָה לְעוֹף עַל רַעֲנָנָיִךְ:

ירמיה ג, א

שָׁלוֹם לְצִיּוֹן נְוֵה צֶדֶק, וְשָׁלוֹם עֲלֵי חֵלֵךְ וְחוֹמוֹת, יָקָר אַבְנֵי פִנָּיִךְ:
שָׁלוֹם לְאֶרֶץ צְבִי, שָׁלוֹם לְכָל הַגְּבוּל, גִּלְעָד וְשׁוֹמְרוֹן, וְכָל יֶתֶר שְׁכֵנָיִךְ:
צִיּוֹן, לְפָנִים הֲלֹא הָיִית יְפַת מַרְאֶה, אֵיךְ נֶהֶפְכוּ לִשְׁחוֹר תֹּאֲרֵךְ וּפָנָיִךְ:
כִּבְנוֹת מְלָכִים, יָקָר עָטִית תְּחִלָּה, וְאֵיךְ שַׂק תַּחְגְּרִי עַל חֲלָצַיִךְ וּמָתְנָיִךְ:
לַחְמִי אֲנָחָה, בְּעֵת תֶּעְדִּי לְתַחַת פְּאֵר אֵפֶר, וְאִשְׁתֶּה יָגוֹן עַל יְגוֹנָיִךְ:
קוּמִי וְנַשְׂאִי נְהִי, נִבְכֵּה דְּמָעוֹת כְּיָם, יִזְּלוּ נְהָרוֹת לְמִן עֵינֵי לְעֵינָיִךְ:
עַל אַלְמְנוּתֵךְ, אֲשֶׁר הָלַךְ יְדִידֵךְ. וְהוּא הֶחֱרִיב דְּבִירוֹ, וְכָל סִתְרֵי צְפוּנָיִךְ:
עֵת אֶרְאֶה יָפְיֵךְ, אֶקְרָא מְשׁוֹרְרִים בְּשִׁיר. עֵת אֶחֱזֶה עָנְיֵךְ, אֶקְרָא מְקוֹנְנָיִךְ:
אֶבְחַר לְקָאַת וְקִפּוֹד יִשְׁכְּנוּ בָךְ. וְאוֹי לִי, אִם אֱדוֹם וַעֲרָב קִנְּנוּ בְקִנָּיִךְ:

עִיר הַמְּלוּכָה לְדָוִד וּשְׁלֹמֹה בְנוֹ הָיִית בְּנוּיָה, וְהֵם קֶדֶם מְכוֹנָיִךְ:
אַתְּ הִיא לְמִקְדַּשׁ לָאֵל, אַתְּ הִיא מְנוּחָה לַצּוּר. אַתְּ הִיא, אֲשֶׁר יוֹם בְּיוֹם יָרַד לְגַנָּיִךְ:

שָׁם שֻׁלְחָן וּמְנוֹרָה וַאֲרוֹן הַבְּרִית. אֵל בֵּין שְׁדֵי אַהֲבָה, לָן בִּמְלוֹנָיִךְ:
עַל מִזְבְּחֵךְ, כֹּהֲנִים עָמְדוּ מְשָׁרְתִים, בָּמוֹ זֶבַח וְעוֹלָה, לְכַפֵּר עַל עֲווֹנָיִךְ:
רֹאשׁ הַכְּהֻנָּה, אֲשֶׁר אֵפוֹד לְבוּשֵׁי יָקָר. נִשְׁמַע בְּשׁוּלֵי מְעִיל, קוֹל פַּעֲמוֹנָיִךְ:
אַחַת בְּשָׁנָה, פְּנִים הָלַךְ לְחַדְרֵי דְבִיר. הֵבִיא קְטֹרֶת מְלֹא קָמְצוֹ וְחָפְנָיִךְ:
קִדָּה וְקָנֶה וְכָל רָאשֵׁי בְשָׂמִים, עֲדֵי עִיר הַתְּמָרִים, בְּבוֹא רֵיחַ שְׁמָנָיִךְ:
אַף הַלְוִיִּם אֲשֶׁר שׁוֹמְרִים שְׁעָרִים, וְגַם הַמְשׁוֹרְרִים שִׁיר בְּפֶה, עִם כָּל רְנָנָיִךְ:

stations, and there ascended your multitudes for your festive occasions. / Within you were the prophets, included in God's counsel, and within you were those wise in knowledge and your seventy elders. / Your land is laden with ten layers of holiness, and with your tithes and your choice grain offerings. / All this is now desolate, bereft of sons and daughters. And where are your king, your prophets, Levites, and priests?

מָתַי When will they return and again enter your tent, those who yearn to dwell under your clouds of glory? / Would that I could witness the time you gave birth to children, as Shifra and Puah delivered at the birth stools? / Would that I be granted the time I wish for, the day your Bridegroom will arrive, and you, the bride, exult in your gorgeous garments. / My heart longs to hold in my arms the earth of your land, and I desire to kiss your stones with my mouth. / Would that I could see you rebuilt with precious gemstones, and your majestic glory visible to the north and to the sea. / I long for and strongly desire the consolation of hearing the words of the herald resonating in my ears and yours. / Stand up and welcome your Beloved, and shake off the dust, as He returns to your abode!

Kina 39 starts on page 582.

נֶגְדָּם בְּנֵי מַעֲמָד עוֹרְכִים תְּפִלָּה. וְלָךְ יַעֲלֶה הֶמוֹנֵךְ, בְּכָל פַּעֲמֵי זְמַנֵּךְ:
בָּךְ הַנְּבִיאִים כְּבָר הָיוּ בְּסוֹד אֵל. וּבָךְ חַכְמֵי תְבוּנָה, וּבָךְ שְׁבָעִים זְקֵנֶךְ:
אַרְצֵךְ מְלֵאָה בְּמוֹ עֶשֶׂר קְדֻשּׁוֹת, וְכָל מַעְשַׂר תְּרוּמָה, וְגַם מִבְחַר דְּגָנֵךְ:
עַתָּה שְׁמָמָה בְּלִי בָנִים וּבָנוֹת. וְאָן מַלְכֵּךְ, נְבִיאֵךְ, לְוִיֵּךְ וְכֹהֲנָיֵךְ:

מָתַי יָשׁוּבוּן וְיָבוֹאוּ בְּתוֹךְ אָהֳלֵךְ, הַמִּתְאַוִּים שְׁכֹן תַּחַת עֲנָנֵךְ:
מִי יִתְּנֵנִי לְעֵת תֵּלְדִי יְלָדִים, כְּמוֹ שִׁפְרָה וּפוּעָה, מְיַלֶּדֶת בְּאָבְנֵךְ:
מִי יִתְּנֵנִי לְעֵת אֶתְאָו, לְיוֹם יָבוֹא חֲתָנֵךְ. וְאַתְּ כַּלָּה, וְהִתְפָּאֲרִי בַּעֲדִי עֶדְנֵךְ:
לִבִּי יְאַוֶּה לְחַבֵּק בִּזְרוֹעוֹת עֲפַר אַרְצֵךְ, וְאֶחְשֹׁק בְּפִי נַשֵּׁק אֲבָנָיֵךְ:
לוּ אֶרְאֵךְ, בִּהְיוֹת נְבִיּוֹת בְּנוֹפֵךְ וּפוּךְ, יִרְאוּ לְצָפוֹן וָיָם, גְּבַהּ קַרְנֵךְ:
אֶכְסֹף וְאֶחְמֹד לְנֶחָמָה וְתִשָּׁמַעְנָה, דִּבְרֵי מְבַשֵּׂר בְּקוֹל אָזְנִי וְאָזְנֵךְ:
הִתְעוֹרְרִי לִקְרַאת דּוֹדֵךְ, וְהִתְנַעֲרִי מִן הָאֲדָמָה, בְּשׁוּבוֹ אֶל מְעוֹנֵךְ:

Kina 39 starts on page 583.

COMMENTARY ON KINA 38

אֵלֵי שְׁחָקִים אֲשֶׁר שׁוֹמְרִים לְחוֹמוֹת וָחֵל *Celestial angels, who guard your walls and ramparts.* Even though Zion is desolate and deserted, the angels continue to guard her.

שׁוֹכְנֵי קְבָרִים, מְחַכִּים וּמְצַפִּים *Residents of the grave await and anticipate.* Not only the living, but also the deceased await Zion's salvation.

גִּלְעָד וְשׁוֹמְרוֹן *Gilead and Samaria.* Gilead is located in what is today known as Jordan. Apparently the *paytan* considered Jordan to be part of the land of Israel.

אֲשֶׁר יוֹם בְּיוֹם יָרַד לְגַנֶּיךָ *Into whose gardens He descended daily.* This phrase is an allusion to the verse in Song of Songs, "My beloved has gone down to his garden" (6:2). In Song of Songs, the *Beit HaMikdash* is referred to metaphorically as a garden.

הֵבִיא קְטֹרֶת מְלֹא קֻמְצוֹ וְחָפְנֶיךָ *And brought a fistful of incense, and your handful.* The use of the word *kumtzo* here is incorrect. *Kometz* means a measure equal to one fistful of incense, and *ḥafanim* means a measure equal to two fistfuls. The *kometz* was offered only as part of the *minḥa* sacrifice, not as part of the Yom Kippur service (Leviticus 2:1–3; 16:12).

עֲדֵי עִיר הַתְּמָרִים, בְּבוֹא רֵיחַ שְׁמָנֶיךָ *The scent of your oils reached until the city of palms [Jericho].* The identification of עִיר הַתְּמָרִים with Jericho is found in Deuteronomy 34:3. This phrase of the *kina* is an allusion to the Gemara (*Yoma* 39b; *Tamid* 30b) and the Jerusalem Talmud (*Sukka* 5:3) which relate that the fragrance of the *ketoret*, the incense, was so powerful that it extended as far away from Jerusalem as Jericho.

הַמְשׁוֹרְרִים שִׁיר בְּפֶה, עִם כָּל רְנָנֶיךָ *Sang songs by mouth, along with your many melodies.* The Gemara in *Sukka* (50b–51a) deals with the issue of whether the essence of music in the Temple was vocal or instrumental. This phrase therefore mentions both modes of musical rendition.

שִׁבְעִים זְקֵנֶיךָ *Your seventy elders.* This refers to the Great Sanhedrin.

אַרְצֵךְ מְלֵאָה בְּמוֹ עֶשֶׂר קְדֻשּׁוֹת *Your land is laden with ten layers of holiness.* This is an allusion to the dictum of our sages (*Kelim* 1:6) that the land of Israel is imbued with ten levels of sanctity.

39

צִיּוֹן Zion, lament for your House which is burned. Shriek bitterly for the desolation of your vines. / Zion, wail like a widow who has become subservient to every passerby because of your sins. / Upon the hilltops, raise a lament and a bitter complaint, and also moan aloud, for your multitudes have been smitten. / How Zion's sons have been angrily mortified in spite of your greatness; summon your mourners! / Zion, raise wailing and lament with bitterness and woe. Weep, as if stunned, for the ruins of your House. / Lament, be not silent. Cry aloud! For pestilence and sword have been let loose upon your encampments. / Trapped like a bird with no one to help, for they have spread snares to expose your shame. / He has cast down Israel's glory and has not remembered the oath He established with your ancestors. / Raise your voices like the grunts of the crocodile, precious habitations of Jacob! Raise up a lament and a weeping for your many offenses. / Shear your locks, and cast your head down to the ground. Fasten sackcloth, and bind it to your loins. / Lament guiltily, without respite. Take up a lament upon the heights about your many oppressors. / Fairest of all lands, bring a lament and wail to the heights, in place of your joy! / May all kings lament and all chieftains wail, along with all the east and all the west, over your great subjection. / Shed your cloak, and cast it to the ground. Gird your sackcloth, and whimper under your bed covers. / Young and old, babes and infants, raise up a soulful cry in the presence of all your elders.

Lam. 1:1

Lam. 2:2
Jer. 7:29

Jer. 3:19

צִיּוֹן Zion, your joy has vanished like thorns upon your water; it has been overturned because of your many transgressions. / Dimmed are the luminaries, and also the heavens; and every road, very dark and barricaded before you. / The heavens have become estranged and have withdrawn their light from the entire populace, adding to your agony.

צִיּוֹן Zion, sound the shofar on every visible hill and mountain. Scream with bitterness and tears over the death of your rulers. / They have set fire to your treasure! Zion is trampled! Behold! Your gates have sunk! The silver sockets, buried in the earth! / Behold! Judah's daughter has been trampled, and there is no one to revive her; and so too, the wasted precious oils.

צִיּוֹן Zion, weep bitterly without the Comforter who has distanced Himself exceedingly from extending consolation to your chosen ones. / [Raise] your voice like the sea, the jackal, and the ostrich; moans and tears for those who are under your thorns.

39

In this kina, the paytan, Rabbi Asher HaKohen (c. fifteenth century), addresses Zion herself, demanding that she should mourn for the suffering of her people.

צִיּוֹן תְּקוֹנְנִי עֲלֵי בֵיתֵךְ אֲשֶׁר נִשְׂרָף, צְרָחִי בְמֵרֶר עֲלֵי שׁוֹמֵמוֹת גְּפָנָיִךְ:

איכה א, א — צִיּוֹן תְּעוֹרְרִי כְּאַלְמָנָה, אֲשֶׁר הָיְתָה לָמַס לְכָל עוֹבְרִים, מֵרֹב עֲווֹנָיִךְ:

עַל הַגְּבָעוֹת שְׂאִי קִינָה וְתַמְרוּר, וְגַם נְהִי בְּקוֹל רָם, אֲשֶׁר הֵכּוּ הַמּוֹנָיִךְ:

אֵיכָה לְמוֹאָב בְּנֵי צִיּוֹן, בְּאַף חוֹלְלוּ עַל רֹב גְּאוֹנֵךְ. וְקִרְאִי אֶל מְקוֹנְנָיִךְ:

הֵילֵל וְקִינָה שְׂאִי צִיּוֹן, בְּמַר וּנְהִי, וּבְכִי שְׁמָמוֹת עֲלֵי שׁוֹמֵמוֹת מְעוֹנָיִךְ:

קוֹנְנִי וְאַל תִּדְמִי, קוֹלֵךְ בְּבִכְיֵי שָׂאִי. דֶּבֶר וְחֶרֶב אֲשֶׁר שָׁלַח לְמַחֲנָיִךְ:

צָדוּ כַצִּפּוֹר, וְאֵין עוֹזֵר לְנֶגְדּוֹ. אֲשֶׁר פֵּרְשׂוּ רְשָׁתוֹת לְגַלּוֹת אֶת קְלוֹנָיִךְ:

אֵיךְ הִשְׁלִיךְ תִּפְאֶרֶת יִשְׂרָאֵל, וְלֹא זָכַר שְׁבוּעָה אֲשֶׁר כָּרַת לְאוֹמְנָיִךְ:

איכה ב, ב — קוֹלֵךְ כְּקוֹל נֶהֱמַת תַּנִּים, נְאוֹת יַעֲקֹב. בְּכִי וְקִינָה שְׂאִי, עַל רֹב תְּלוּנָיִךְ:

ירמיה ו, כט — גָּזִי נִזְרֵךְ, וְהַשְׁלִיכִי לְרֹאשֵׁךְ עֲלֵי אָרֶץ. וְשַׂק תִּקְשְׁרִי עֶצְרֵי בְמָתְנָיִךְ:

קוֹנְנִי בְפֶשַׁע, וְאַל תִּתְּנִי מְנוּחָה. וְקִינָה עַל שְׁפָיִים שְׂאִי, מֵרֹב מְעַנָּיִךְ:

ירמיה ג, יט — אֶרֶץ צְבִי צְבָאוֹת, קִינָה וָנֶהִי תְּעוֹרְרִי אֶל שְׁפָיִים, הֲלֹא תַחַת שְׁשׁוֹנָיִךְ:

קוֹנְנוּ מְלָכִים וְהֵילִילוּ קְצִינִים, וְכָל מִזְרָח וְכָל מַעֲרָב, עַל שִׂמְלוֹנָיִךְ:

פִּשְׁטִי מְעִילֵךְ וְהַשְׁלִיכִי לָאָרֶץ, וְחִגְרִי שָׂק, וְגַם תְּהֹמִי תַּחַת סְדִינָיִךְ:

בָּחוּר וָזָקֵן, וְגַם עוֹלֵל וְיוֹנֵק, שְׂאוּ תַמְרוּר לְנֶפֶשׁ, לְעֵינֵי כָּל זְקֵנָיִךְ:

צִיּוֹן, שְׂשׂוֹנֵךְ הֲלֹא עָבַר כְּקוֹצִים עֲלֵי מָיִם, וְנֶהְפְּכוּ מֵרֹב זְדוֹנָיִךְ:

חָשְׁכוּ מְאוֹרוֹת, וְגַם כָּל הַשְּׁחָקִים, וְכָל דֶּרֶךְ מְאֹד נֶחְשַׁךְ, סָתוּם לְפָנָיִךְ:

כִּי הַשְּׁחָקִים מְאֹד זֹרוּ, וְאָסְפוּ לְאוֹרָם לִפְנֵי כָּל שָׁאוֹן, עַל רֹב יְגוֹנָיִךְ:

צִיּוֹן בְּשׁוֹפָר תִּקְעִי, עַל הַר וְגֶבַע רְאִי, צְרָחִי בְמַר וּבְכִי, עַל מוֹת סְרָנָיִךְ:

שִׁלְחוּ שְׁלָלֵךְ בָּאֵשׁ, צִיּוֹן לְמִרְמָס. הֲלֹא טָבְעוּ שְׁעָרַיִךְ בְּתוֹךְ אֶרֶץ אֲדָנָיִךְ:

הִנֵּה לְמִרְמָס נְתוּנָה בַת יְהוּדָה, וְאֵין מֵשִׁיב לְנַפְשָׁהּ, עֲלֵי שׁוֹמֵמוֹת שְׁמָנָיִךְ:

צִיּוֹן, בְּמַר תִּבְכִּי מֵאֵין מְנַחֵם, אֲשֶׁר רָחַק מְאֹד מִקָּרוֹב, נַחֵם בְּחוּנָיִךְ:

קוֹלֵךְ כְּקוֹל יָם, וְגַם תָּפִין וְיֵעָנֶה, וְקוֹל נְהִי וּבְכִי, אֲשֶׁר תַּחַת סֻלּוֹנָיִךְ:

צִיּוֹן Zion, lift your eyes heavenward, and see and eulogize and wail, for your Advocate has abandoned you. / Zion, cry out to your forefathers, and request the establishment of your House, and also your succor and the authority of your rulers. / Go to the cave [of the patriarchs], and scream with bitterness and tears; they have tortured your sons, your daughters, your descendants. / Sarah, when she hears your voice, will also cry for children captured by all who surround you. / Rachel and Leah, cry! Bilhah and Zilpah, also lament, and cry out loud, tear at your face! / For God is eternal and will not forsake. There is hope; great peace will come for your children!

Kina 40 starts on page 586.

צִיּוֹן, לַמָּרוֹם שְׂאִי עֵינַיִךְ. וְגַם תִּרְאִי, סִפְדִי וְהֵילִילִי, עֲלֵי עָזְבֵךְ תּוֹאֲנָךְ:
צִיּוֹן, תְּקוֹנְנִי עֲלֵי אָבוֹת, וְשַׁאֲלִי מָכוֹן בֵּיתָךְ. וְגַם עֶזְרָךְ, חֹסֶן קְצִינַיִךְ:
אֶל הַמְּעָרָה לְכִי, צָרְחִי בְמַר וּבְכִי. עֲנוּ בָנַיִךְ וּבְנוֹתַיִךְ וְנִינַיִךְ:
שָׂרָה כְשָׁמְעָה לְקוֹלֵךְ, גַּם מְבַכָּה עֲלֵי בָנִים, אֲשֶׁר נִשְׁבּוּ אֶל כָּל שְׁכֵנָיִךְ:
רָחֵל וְלֵאָה בָכוּ, בִּלְהָה וְזִלְפָּה הֲלֹא קוֹנְנוּ. וְקִרְאוּ בְקוֹל, מְחִי בְּפָנָיִךְ:
כִּי הָאֱלֹהִים הֲלֹא לָנֶצַח, וְלֹא יָזְנַח. כִּי תִקְוָה הִיא, וְרֹב שָׁלוֹם לְבָנָיִךְ:

Kina 40 starts on page 587.

40

צִיּוֹן Zion, beloved, youngest comrade in your company of noblemen, you dwelled between his shoulders in your great majestic humility. / Zion, most resplendent of all bed chambers and all lovers' couches, your dear One would enter your most intimate chambers. / Zion, you are blessed with a divine blessing over your head. Your gates are carved so that they face you. / Zion, the inheritance of the wolf of the evening [Benjamin]! Your beauty was enhanced by gorgeous decoration; your crown stood out prominently.

יְפַת Beautiful with great treasure and grace, indeed with great wisdom as well, more intelligent than Egypt's sages are your young lads! / You were of perfect beauty, pretty beyond praise. You grew and took possession of the bounty of all neighboring kingdoms. / Within you, all had room to sleep without sin. Within you, your daily sacrifices atoned for all. / You were founded in Iyar, in glory. You were destroyed in Av, in wrath. I desire to fetch from your bitter waters. / Visible in your city were the children of the Master of the face of the encampment; the favor of the dweller in the fiery bush is in your two courtyards. / Those who did your work by the thread [in every detail], became rich with fortune; every precious treasure was possessed by your wealthy ones. / Your place was chosen by God, who also chose the nation that chose Him. He chose the one who founded you [David], and [He chose] your choice priests. / Within you dwelled the glorious One in great joy; your mighty One in every generation. Your full worth will be attained when you will tend the entire flock of your companions. / Your boundary extended to the abode of Zela and Jebus and not to Ein Eitam [a high place], so that the slopes of Your shrine would not be excessively high! / God called your name after the names of two priests [Abraham and Melchizedek]. David discovered you in the region of your forest fields [Benjamin's territory]. / His son built your Abode and dedicated it in the name of his father who preceded him, and eternalized it in your Psalms.

וּבְמַחְשְׁבוֹת You arose in the thoughts of your Creator, before the creation of the universe, the heavens, and your earth. / During the Great Flood, God's anger, your land was pure, and it did not rain there when your creatures were eradicated. / Rain came down to your land in its proper time; at night, it came as a blessing, and the dew descended at your harvest. / You were the center of earth's foundation. From you came forth counsel, and the procedure of sanctifying the new moon at the testimony of witnesses; your judges

40

This kina was first published, anonymously, in the sixteenth century.

צִיּוֹן, יְדִידוּת יָדִיד צָעִיר לְשָׂרָיִךְ. שָׁכַנְתְּ כִּתְפָיו בְּרֹב עֲנוֹת הֲדָרָיִךְ:
צִיּוֹן, הֲדַר כֹּל חֶדֶר מִטּוֹת, וְכָל מִשְׁכַּב דּוֹדִים. יָדֵךְ בְּבוֹא חַדְרֵי חֲדָרָיִךְ:
צִיּוֹן, בְּרוּכָה בְּרָכָה עֶלְיוֹנָה עֲלֵי רֹאשֵׁךְ, לְמוֹלֵךְ מַחְטָבִים שְׁעָרָיִךְ:
צִיּוֹן, יָרְשַׁת זְאֵב עֶרֶב, שְׂבִי פְאֵרֵךְ בַּעֲדִי עֲדָנִים, עֲדִי עָלוּ כֻתָּרָיִךְ:

יָפִית בְּרֹב הוֹן, וְחֵן רָבִית בְּדֵעוֹת, וְהֵן מִזְקְנֵי צוֹעֲנִים חָכְמוּ נְעָרָיִךְ:
הָיִית יְפִי מִכְלָל, נָאוָה בְּכֹל מַהֲלָל, עָלִית וְשָׁבִית שְׁלַל מַלְכֵי מְגוּרָיִךְ:
בָּךְ בִּרְוָחָה, אֱנוֹשׁ לָן מִבְּלִי חֵטְא. וּבָךְ כִּפֶּר, בְּקָרְבַּן תְּמִידִין חֵטְא מְכַפְּרָיִךְ:
יְסַדְתְּ בְּזִיו לַפֵּאֵר, חָרַבְתְּ בְּתוֹךְ אָב בְּאַף, אֲשֶׁאַף לָזֹאת אֶשְׁאַב מֵימֵי תַּמְרוּרָיִךְ:

נִרְאוּ בְּעִירֵךְ בְּנֵי קוֹנֵהּ פְּנֵי מַחֲנֶה, רָצוֹן לְשֹׁכְנֵי סְנֶה, בִּשְׁנֵי חֲצֵרָיִךְ:
עוֹשֵׂי מְלַאכְתֵּךְ בְּחוּט הִתְעַשְּׁרוּ בִּרְכוּשׁ, כָּל הוֹן יָקָר נִמְצָא לִקְהַל עֲשִׁירָיִךְ:
נִבְחַר מְקוֹמֵךְ לַצּוּר, בָּחַר בְּאָם בּוֹחֲרָיו, בָּחַר בְּמוֹצָאֵךְ וּבַכֹּהֲנִים בְּחִירָיִךְ:
בָּךְ דָּר בְּגִיל נֶהְדָּר, אֲדָרֵךְ בְּכָל דּוֹר וָדוֹר, עָרְכֵךְ בְּבוֹא לַעֲדֹר עֶדְרֵי חֲבֵרָיִךְ:

עָלָה גְבוּלֵךְ דְּבִיר, צֶלַע יָבוֹס. לֹא לְעֵין עֵיטָם, לְבִלְתִּי שְׂאֵת כַּתְּפוֹת דְּבִירָיִךְ:
קָרָא יהוה שְׁמֵךְ עַל שֵׁם שְׁנֵי כֹהֲנִים. דָּוִד מְצָאֵךְ בְּחַיִל, בִּשְׂדֵי יְעָרָיִךְ:
בָּנָה מְעוֹנֵךְ בְּנוֹ, וַיְחַנְּכֵךְ שֵׁם בְּשֵׁם אָבִיו אֲשֶׁר קִדְּמוֹ, נֶחְתָּם בְּשִׁירָיִךְ:

וּבְמַחְשָׁבוֹת בּוֹרְאֵךְ עָלִית, בְּטֶרֶם בָּרָא תֵבֵל וָעוֹלָם, עַל עֲפָרָיִךְ:
וּבִימֵי מְרִיבָה בְּיוֹם זַעַם, אֱוֵי טָהֳרָה אָרְצֵךְ, וְלֹא גְשָׁמָה בְּכַלּוֹת יְצוּרָיִךְ:
יָרַד בְּעִתּוֹ מְטַר אַרְצֵךְ, זְמַן לַיְלָה בָּא לִבְרָכָה, וְטַל לָן בִּקְצִירָיִךְ:
הָיִית לְשִׁית חוּג יְסוֹד, מִמֶּךְ תְּעוּדָה. וְסוֹד קָדוֹשׁ יְרַחֵךְ, לְפִי עֵדִים מְעַבְּרָיִךְ:

determined the length of each month. / Dear boys and girls shouted and played in the streets, dashed about and joined the throngs journeying to you. / During the Pesaḥ holiday, they were wondrous, more precious than gold, full of the dew of light and grace. How virtuous were your pious ones!

אֵיךְ How can I again rejoice in the festivals? How can I again be gleeful on Purim? Only when days of joy will once again be your lot! / Your land, so desirable, was yet not desired by others when your precious sons went up to the House in which you desired to dwell. / A cloud of incense would rise, originating from the place of your Sanctuary. In its place is the smoke of fire from your nostrils! / As the enemy approached the city, they sent cattle to devour your vineyards. They razed, and they dislodged the Divine Presence from your cities. / There was no sound of metal when you were built. Yet now, swords of flint are thrust at you by your foes. / For this, the Hebrews don sackcloth, although they are confident they will again rejoice after your enemies are dismembered. / A heart pained and aggrieved because of its yearning is in deep slumber until your dawn will shine again. / Wail too, to the cry of my voice, how can you restrain yourself? For the companion of your youth has called for sackcloth and weeping.

אָקוּם I will arise at midnight at [the time of] the watches of the dark, awaiting the light which comes at morning for those who wait! / Then you will find the honeycomb and will not lament with bitter herbs, for your mountain will soar above all mountain tops. / The honor of Lebanon will come your way, and you will be whitened as lambs, all your borders beautiful. / Wake up, and shake it off like one shakes off dead leaves in the woods. A lad who can barely count will be able to record the remaining pigs [your surviving enemies] in the forest. / Rise and shine for those who anticipate your light but now walk in darkness, awaiting your lights to glow again.

Prov. 16:24

צִיּוֹן Zion, you will once again be a sign of strength and a banner to all nations, and prominent will be the footsteps of your heralds. / Shed the garments of poverty and wear raiment of silk. Bedeck yourself in a bride's gown and decorations. / Do not tell me that you are too old to be with a man! You will once again be proud to bare your breast to your babes. / You will give birth to playful children at a youthful time. You will renew your youth, as do your eagles! / He will direct your will to the good. Your Creator will protect you! You will be well guarded like a united city for your teachers! / He will redeem with might from captivity, to rescue the deer from the hand of the boar, to become a crown of glory for the remnant of your flock!

Kina 41 starts on page 590.

בָּנִים וּבְנוֹת תְּשׁוּקָה, בַּשּׁוּק שׁוֹקְקוּ, שָׂחֲקוּ וְהִשְׁתַּקְשְׁקוּ בְּסָךְ עֲבָרֶיךָ:
בְּחַג פֶּסַח נִפְלְאוּ, בַּפָּז סֻלָּאוּ, טַל אוֹר וְחֵן נִמְלְאוּ, זַכּוּ נְזִירֶיךָ:

אֵיךְ אֶשְׂמְחָה עוֹד בְּחַג, אֵיךְ אֶעֱלֶה עוֹד בְּפוּר, עַד כִּי יָבוֹאוּן יְמֵי שָׂשׂוֹן לְפוּרֶיךָ:
אַרְצֵךְ חֲמוּדָה מְאֹד, לֹא נֶחֱמָדָה. בַּעֲלוֹת בָּנִים חֲמוּדִים, לְבֵית מַחְמַד מְגוּרֶיךָ:

נַעֲלָה עֲנַן הַקְּטֹרֶת מִמְּקוֹם מִקְדָּשֵׁךְ, יָצָא מְקוֹמוֹ עֲשַׁן אֵשׁ מִנְחִירֶיךָ:
בְּקֶרֶב מְרֵעִים בָּעִיר, שִׁלְּחוּ בְכַרְמֵךְ בָּעִיר. עֲרוּ וְעוֹרְרוּ בָּעִיר וְקַדִּישׁ בְּעָרֶיךָ:

בַּרְזֶל בְּלִי נִשְׁמַע קוֹלוֹ בְּעֵת נִבְנֵית. אֵיךְ חָרְבוֹת צוּר, בָּךְ תָּקְעוּ מְצֵרֶיךָ:
עַל זֹאת בְּשַׂק עוֹבְרִים עִבְרִים, אֲבָל בּוֹטְחִים כִּי יִשְׂמְחוּ אַחֲרֵי חִתּוּךְ בְּתָרֶיךָ:
לֵב מַדְוֶה יֶחֱלֶה, לַתַּאֲוָה יִכְלֶה. יִישַׁן עֲדֵי יַעֲלֶה עַמּוּד שְׁחָרֶיךָ:
בִּילֵּל לְקוֹלִי אֵלִי, אֵיךְ תִּתְאַפַּק?י. הֲלֹא קָרָא לְשַׂק וּבְכִי, אַלּוּף נְעוּרֶיךָ:

אָקוּם חֲצוֹת לַיְלָה עַל מִשְׁמָרוֹת מַאֲפֵל, לִשְׁמוֹר לָאוֹר, יֶאֱתֶה בֹּקֶר לְשׁוֹמְרֶיךָ:

אָז תִּמְצָאִי צוּף דְּבַשׁ, אָז לֹא תִקּוֹנְנִי בָרֹאשׁ, כִּי תִתְכּוֹנְנִי בְּרֹאשׁ הָרֵי הֲרָרֶיךָ: משלי ט, כד

יָבוֹא כְבוֹד הַלְּבָנוֹן לָךְ, וְתִתְלַבְּנִי כִּבְנֵי עֲדָרִים, בְּנֵי אֶדֶר גְּדֵרֶיךָ:
עוּרִי וְהִתְנַעֲרִי, עֶרֶךְ יַעַר נוֹעָרִים. נַעַר יָתוֹ אוֹת, לְעֵץ יַעַר חֲזִירֶיךָ:
קוּמִי וָאוֹרִי לְכָל חוֹשְׁקֵי מְאוֹרֵךְ, וְהֵם הַהוֹלְכִים בַּחֹשֶׁךְ, עֲדֵי אוֹרוּ מְאוֹרֶיךָ:

צִיּוֹן לְצִיּוּן וָאוֹת, עֹז עוֹד תְּהִי, וְלָנֵס עַמִּים. וְתִגְבַּהְנָה רַגְלֵי מְבַשְּׂרָיִךְ:
נַצְּלִי עֲדִי הֶעָנִי, וְתִנִי לִבוּשֵׁךְ שְׁנִי תוֹלָע, כְּכַלָּה עֲדִי לִקְשֹׁר קִשּׁוּרָיִךְ:
אַל תֹּאמְרִי לִי, אֲשֶׁר זָקַנְתְּ הֱיוֹתֵךְ לְאִישׁ. עוֹד תִּתְעַדְּנִי, חֲלֹץ הַשַּׁד לְגוּרָיִךְ:
תֵּלְדִי בְּנֵי שַׁעֲשׁוּעַיִךְ בְּעֵת עֶדְנָה, תִּתְחַדְּשִׁי בִנְעוּרִים כִּנְשָׁרָיִךְ:
יָפֶה לְטוֹב יִצְרֵךְ, צוּר יוֹצְרֵךְ יְצָרֵךְ. תְּהִי נְצוּרָה, כְּעִיר חֻבְּרָה לִמְאוֹרָיִךְ:
יִגְאַל בְּעֹז מַשְׂבִּי, לְהָשִׁיב מִיַּד חֲזִיר הַצְּבִי. וִיהִי עֲטֶרֶת צְבִי, לִשְׁאָר עֲדָרָיִךְ:

Kina 41 starts on page 591.

41

שַׁאֲלִי Inquire, consumed in fire, after the well-being of your mourners, who so strongly desire to reside in your dwellings, / who yearn for the earth of the land [Israel], and who are pained and shocked by the conflagration of your scrolls. / They walk in darkness, unillumined, but hope for the light of day to shine upon them and upon you; / and inquire, too, of the welfare of that sighing man, crying with a broken heart, constantly bemoaning your pangs of torment! / Who wails like jackals and ostriches, and calls for a bitter eulogy on your behalf. *Amos 2:7* *Is. 50:10* *Amos 2:7*

אֵיכָה How can that which was given in a [divine] consuming fire, be consumed by a fire kindled by mortals? And [how can] those intruders not be scorched by your embers? / Until when, O pampered one [Rome], will you dwell in great tranquility, while the faces of my flowers are covered by thorns? / [How long] will you sit in arrogance, judging the sons of God with such harsh judgments and presenting them to your tribunals, / and decree to burn the fiery Law and statutes [Torah and Talmud]? Happy is He who will repay you in kind!

צוּרִי Did my Protector present you in the presence of torches and fire, so that, at your end, you would be set on fire from below? / Sinai! Is this why you were chosen by God, higher mountains rejected, and your borders favored? / Were you to be an omen that the Torah would be reduced and lowered from its glory? Can I make such a comparison? / A comparison to a king who cried at his son's wedding feast, knowing that his son would die; is that what you [Sinai] stand for? / Instead of a noble gown, Sinai, cover yourself in a garment of sackcloth, wear a widow's clothes, change your dress!

אוֹרִיד I will shed enough tears for a river to reach the graves of your two noble princes, / Moses, and Aaron on Mount Hor, and will ask them, "Has a new Torah been given? Is that why the [old] scrolls were burned?" / In [Sivan] the third month [was the Torah given], and the connected fourth month [Tammuz] already saw the destruction of your treasure and all your beautiful wreaths. / The tablets shattered [in Tammuz], and the wrong-doing redoubled with the fiery destruction of the radiant Torah. Is this how you were doubly compensated?

אֶתְמַהּ I wondered how my palate could ever again savor food, after I witnessed how all of your treasured possessions were gathered / in the open square like an apostate town, and [how] the divine treasure was burned by those who were banned from entering your community. / I cannot find a clear path; turned to grief are those straight paths of yours! / It is sweeter to my mouth than honey, to dilute my drink with tears, and to chain my feet in your chains.

41

This elegy addresses the Torah rather than Zion or the Jewish people. It was written by the Maharam of Rothenburg (1215–1293) to commemorate the burning of the Talmud in Paris in 1242. Commentary for this kina begins on page 594.

שַׁאֲלִי, שְׂרוּפָה בָאֵשׁ, לִשְׁלוֹם אֲבֵלָיִךְ. הַמִּתְאַוִּים שְׁכֹן בַּחֲצַר זְבוּלָיִךְ:

הַשּׁוֹאֲפִים בַּעֲפַר אֶרֶץ, וְהַכּוֹאֲבִים הַמִּשְׁתּוֹמְמִים עֲלֵי מוֹקַד גְּוִילָיִךְ: עמוס ב, ז

הוֹלְכִים חֲשֵׁכִים וְאֵין נֹגַהּ, וְקַוִּים לְאוֹר יוֹמָם, עֲלֵיהֶם אֲשֶׁר יִזְרַח וְעָלָיִךְ: ישעיה נ, י

וּשְׁלוֹם אֱנוֹשׁ נֶאֱנָח, בּוֹכֶה בְּלֵב נִשְׁבָּר, תָּמִיד מְקוֹנֵן עֲלֵי צִירֵי חֲבָלָיִךְ:

וְיִתְאוֹנֵן כְּתַנִּים וּבְנוֹת יַעֲנָה, וְיִקְרָא מִסְפֵּד מַר בִּגְלָלָיִךְ:

אֵיכָה נְתוּנָה בָאֵשׁ אוֹכְלָה, תֵּאָכֵל בְּאֵשׁ בָּשָׂר, וְלֹא נִכְווּ זָרִים בְּגַחֲלָיִךְ:

עַד אָן עֲדִינָה, תְּהִי שׁוֹכְנָה בְּרֹב הַשְׁקֵט, וּפְנֵי פְרָחַי הֲלֹא כָסּוּ חֲרֻלָּיִךְ:

תֵּשֵׁב בְּרֹב גַּאֲוָה לִשְׁפֹּט בְּנֵי אֵל בְּכָל הַמִּשְׁפָּטִים, וְתָבִיא בִּפְלִילָיִךְ:

עוֹד תִּגְזֹר לִשְׂרֹף דָּת אֵשׁ וְחֻקִּים, וְלָכֵן אַשְׁרֵי שֶׁיְשַׁלֶּם לָךְ גְּמוּלָיִךְ:

צוּרִי, בְּלַפִּיד וְאֵשׁ הַלְבַעֲבוּר זֶה נְתָנֵךְ, כִּי בְאַחֲרִיתֵךְ תְּלַהֵט אֵשׁ בְּשׁוּלָיִךְ:

סִינַי, הֲעַל כֵּן בָּךְ בָּחַר אֱלֹהִים, וּמָאַס בִּגְדוֹלִים וְיָרַח בִּגְבוּלָיִךְ:

לִהְיוֹת לְמוֹפֵת, לְדָת כִּי תִתְמַעֵט וְתֵרֵד מִכְּבוֹדָהּ. וְהֵן אֶמְשֹׁל מְשָׁלָיִךְ:

מָשָׁל לְמֶלֶךְ אֲשֶׁר בָּכָה לְמִשְׁתֵּה בְנוֹ, צָפָה אֲשֶׁר יִגְוָע. כֵּן אַתְּ בְּמִלָּלָיִךְ:

תַּחַת מְעִיל, תִּתְכַּס סִינַי לְבוּשֵׁךְ בְּשַׂק, תַּעֲטֶה לְבוּשׁ אַלְמָנוּת, תַּחֲלִיף שְׂמָלָיִךְ:

אוֹרִיד דְּמָעוֹת, עֲדֵי יִהְיוּ כְנָחַל, וְיַגִּיעוּ לְקִבְרוֹת שְׁנֵי שָׂרֵי אֲצִילָיִךְ:

מֹשֶׁה וְאַהֲרֹן בְּהֹר הָהָר. וְאֶשְׁאַל, הֲיֵשׁ תּוֹרָה חֲדָשָׁה, בְּכֵן נִשְׂרְפוּ גְלִילָיִךְ:

חֹדֶשׁ שְׁלִישִׁי, וְהַקֶּשֶׁר הָרְבִיעִי לְהַשְׁחִית חֲמֻדָּתֵךְ, וְכָל יֳפִי כְלִילָיִךְ:

גֶּדַע לַלּוּחוֹת, וְעוֹד שָׁנָה בְּאִוַּלְתּוֹ, לִשְׂרֹף בְּאֵשׁ דָּת. הֲזֶה תַשְׁלוּם כְּפָלָיִךְ:

אֶתְמַהּ לְנַפְשִׁי. וְאֵיךְ יֶעֱרַב לְחִכִּי אֲכֹל, אַחֲרֵי רְאוֹתִי אֲשֶׁר אָסְפוּ שְׁלָלָיִךְ:

אֶל תּוֹךְ רְחוֹבָהּ כִּנְדָּחַת, וְשָׂרְפוּ שְׁלַל עֶלְיוֹן, אֲשֶׁר תִּמְאַס לָבוֹא קְהָלָיִךְ:

לֹא אֵדְעָה לִמְצֹא דֶרֶךְ סְלוּלָה, הֲכִי הָיוּ אֲבֵלוֹת נְתִיב יֹשֶׁר מְסִלָּיִךְ:

יִמְתַּק בְּפִי מִדְּבַשׁ, לְמֶסֶךְ בְּמַשְׁקֶה דְמָעוֹת. וּלְרַגְלִי, הֱיוֹת כָּבוּל כְּבַלָּיִךְ:

I find it pleasing to fetch all my tears until they are gone, for all those who cling to the hem of your robes. / But my tears dry up as they run down my cheeks, for my compassion is in a fever over the departure of your Master! / He took His pouch of silver and went on a distant journey, and with Him fled your [protective] shadows! / And I, bereaved and forlorn, remained alone without them, like a mast atop the mountains of your towers. / No longer will I listen to the voices of your singers, for severed are the strings of your timbrels and flutes. / I will dress and cover myself with sackcloth, for very precious to me, greater and more numerous than sand, are the souls of your victims. / I am very puzzled by the light of day which shines upon all, but remains dark for me and for you.

זַעֲקִי Cry in a bitter voice to your Rock about your breach and your illness. Perhaps He will remember the love of your betrothed! / Gird yourself in a sack garment because of the fire which tore you to shreds and flattened your hills! / For as long as your suffering lasted will your Rock console you. And He will bring back from captivity the tribes of Jeshurun and will lift up your lowly ones! / You will again adorn yourself in scarlet and take up the timbrel, march in a circle, and rejoice in your dances! / My heart will be uplifted when my Rock is again a light for you, when He will illuminate your darkness and dispel your gloom! *Jer. 31:3*

Kina 42 starts on page 598.

יֶעֱרַב לְעֵינַי, שְׂאָב מֵימֵי דְמָעַי, עֲדֵי כָלוּ לְכָל מַחֲזִיק בִּכְנַף מְעִילָיִךְ:
אַךְ יֶחֱרוּ בְרִדְתָּם עַל לְחָיַי, עֲבוּר כִּי נִכְמְרוּ רַחֲמַי לְנִדֹּד בְּעָלָיִךְ:
לָקַח צְרוֹר כַּסְפּוֹ, הָלַךְ בְּדֶרֶךְ לְמֵרָחוֹק, וְעַמּוֹ הֲלֹא נָסוּ צְלָלָיִךְ:
וַאֲנִי כְשָׁכוּל וְגַלְמוּד נִשְׁאַרְתִּי לְבַד מֵהֶם, כַּתֹּרֶן בְּרֹאשׁ הַר מִגְדָּלָיִךְ:
לֹא אֶשְׁמַע עוֹד לְקוֹל שָׁרִים וְשָׁרוֹת, עֲלֵי כִּי נִתְּקוּ מֵיתְרֵי תֻפֵּי חֲלִילָיִךְ:
אֶלְבַּשׁ וְאֶתְכַּס בְּשַׂק, כִּי לִי מְאֹד יָקְרוּ. עַצְמוֹ כְחוֹל יִרְבְּיוּן נַפְשׁוֹת חֲלָלָיִךְ:
אֶתְמַהּ מְאֹד עַל מְאוֹר הַיּוֹם, אֲשֶׁר יִזְרַח אֶל כֹּל, אֲבָל יֶחְשַׁךְ אֵלַי וְאֵלָיִךְ:

זַעֲקִי בְקוֹל מַר לְצוּר, עַל שִׁבְרוֹנֵךְ וְעַל חָלְיֵךְ. וְלוּ יִזְכֹּר אַהֲבַת כְּלוּלָיִךְ:
חִגְרִי לְבוּשׁ שָׂק, עֲלֵי הַהַבְעָרָה אֲשֶׁר יָצְאָה לַחֲלֹק, וְסָפְתָה אֶת תְּלוּלָיִךְ:
כְּימוֹת עֱנוּתֵךְ יְנַחֲמֵךְ צוּר, וְיָשִׁיב שְׁבוּת שִׁבְטֵי יְשֻׁרוּן, וְיָרִים אֶת שְׁפָלָיִךְ:
עוֹד תַּעְדִּי בַעֲדִי שָׁנִי, וְתֹף תִּקְחִי, תֵּלְכִי בְמָחוֹל וְצַהֲלִי בִמְחוֹלָיִךְ:
יָרוּם לְבָבִי, בְּעֵת צוּרִי לְאוֹר לָךְ, וְיִגַּהּ לַחֲשֵׁכֵךְ וְיָאִירוּ אֲפֵלָיִךְ:

ירמיה ל״א, ג

593 — שחרית לתשעה באב • קינות

Kina 42 starts on page 599.

COMMENTARY ON KINA 41

The author of this *kina* is the Maharam of Rothenburg, who was the teacher of the Rosh (Rabbeinu Asher). The Maharam was the last of the Tosafists, and many of the customs quoted by Rabbi Moses Isserles derive from the Rosh, who, in turn, received them from the Maharam of Rothenburg. The style and form of this *kina* follow that of Rabbi Yehuda HaLevi's "צִיּוֹן הֲלֹא תִשְׁאֲלִי לִשְׁלוֹם אֲסִירָיִךְ" and it is therefore included in the group of *Tziyon Kinot*, even though its lament is not for the land of Israel.

The subject of this *kina* is the burning of the Talmud, along with many other books of Jewish learning and scholarship, in Paris in 1242. This event was not merely a capricious act on the part of the Catholic Church. Rather, it was the culmination of a systematic and organized plan to collect books of the Oral Law (*Torah shebe'al peh*) from all over Europe and gather them to be burned in Paris, in the central square of the city. The burning of these books was a great catastrophe for the Jewish community, since before the invention of printing, all books were written by hand, an exceedingly time-consuming and expensive process. We have only one manuscript of the Talmud from that era that survived the edict, the Munich Manuscript, quoted in the *Dikdukei Sofrim* which published the variants between this manuscript and our standard edition of the Talmud. All other manuscripts were burned. In fact, the Maharam of Rothenburg was afraid that, as a result of the burning of the books, the Oral Law would be totally forgotten or, at best, limited to a small group, and that the Jewish community would be compelled to return to the days when Torah was taught orally, by word of mouth only. One can sense that the *kina* was composed in a mood of pessimism and gloom. However, in one of the great miracles of Jewish history, *Torah shebe'al peh* was not forgotten. On the contrary, the tragic burning of the Talmud motivated the Jews to renewed commitment and dedication, and they devoted their financial resources and efforts to recopying the lost manuscripts.

לִשְׁלוֹם אֲבֵלַיִךְ *After the well-being of your mourners.* A reference to the Torah scholars.

הַשּׁוֹאֲפִים בַּעֲפַר אֶרֶץ *Who yearn for the earth of the land.* The Jewish people yearn to dwell in the Promised Land.

It is interesting that although this *kina* is devoted to the description of a catastrophe that occurred in the thirteenth century in Paris, the *paytan* refers here to Zion. He addresses himself to Zion and tells her the story of the tragedy that occurred.

וְהַכּוֹאֲבִים הַמִּשְׁתּוֹמְמִים עֲלֵי מוֹקֵד גְּוִילָיִךְ *And who are pained and shocked by the conflagration of your scrolls.* The Jewish people experienced two emotional reactions to the catastrophe. First, they were in mourning and in pain because of the raging bonfire which consumed the Torah parchments. Second, they were confused and perplexed.

הוֹלְכִים חֲשֵׁכִים *They walk in darkness.* Metaphorically, the Jews are in darkness. They no longer have the resources to ascertain the halakhot because all the books have been burned. Take the Gemara away from the Jew, and he does not know what to do.

אֵיכָה נְתוּנָה בְּאֵשׁ אוֹכְלָה, תֵּאָכֵל בְּאֵשׁ בָּשָׂר *How can that which was given in a [divine] consuming fire be consumed by a fire kindled by mortals.* The phrase וְאֵשׁ אוֹכְלָה is an allusion to the verse in Deuteronomy, "For the Lord your God is אֵשׁ אוֹכְלָה, a devouring fire" (4:24). The *paytan* asks, "How is it possible that the Torah which was given by the fire of God can be consumed by the fire ignited by a human being?"

עַד אָן עֲדִינָה *Until when, O pampered one.* The *paytan* addresses himself to the Catholic Church, which was responsible for the burning of the Talmud.

עוֹד תִּגְזֹר *And decree.* This is a challenge to the Catholic Church and poses the more general question, "What right does the Church have to tell the world what to do and what not to do?"

צוּרִי, בְּלַפִּיד וְאֵשׁ הַלְבַעֲבוּר זֶה נְתָנֵךְ *Did My Protector present you.* The *paytan* now refers to the giving of the Torah by God on Mount Sinai and speaks to the Torah directly.

הַלְבַעֲבוּר זֶה נְתָנֵךְ, כִּי בְאַחֲרִיתֵךְ תְּלַהֵט אֵשׁ בְּשׁוּלָיִךְ *So that, at your end, you would be set on fire from below.* This phrase can be understood as a statement rather than a question. The experience of the giving of the Torah on Mount Sinai which was described and defined by the phrase, "you heard His words out of the midst of the fire" (Deuteronomy 4:36) was symbolic of the destiny of the *Torah shebe'al peh* to be consumed by fire.

וּמָאַס בִּגְדוֹלִים *Higher mountains rejected.* This phrase alludes to the story recounted by our sages (*Midrash Tehillim* 68:9) that Mount Carmel, Mount Tabor, and all of the other high mountains beseeched God to give the Torah on one of them. The modest and humble Mount Sinai, much smaller than the other mountains, did not presume to ask for this honor. God rejected the pleas of the higher mountains because they were arrogant, and instead chose the lowly Mount Sinai.

לִהְיוֹת לְמוֹפֵת, לָדַת כִּי תִתְמַעֵט וְתֵרֵד מִכְּבוֹדָהּ *Were you to be an omen that the Torah would be reduced and lowered from its glory?* The selection by God of the low instead of the high mountains was an indication that He foresaw that the glory of the Torah is destined to be belittled, and that the Torah will be abandoned, desecrated and destroyed.

An alternate interpretation is to view this phrase as a question: Did God choose the lowest mountain in order to portend that the glory of the Torah will be diminished and that Sinai will lose its glory? Surely, the *paytan* implies, this is an impossibility.

תַּחֲלִיף שְׂמָלַיִךְ *Change your dress.* Sinai was enshrouded in clouds because the destiny of the Torah to be burned thousands of years later was already known. Sinai was mourning the burning of the Talmud, and it was enveloped in clouds as a sign of mourning and an expression of grief.

וְאֶשְׁאַל, הֲיֵשׁ תּוֹרָה חֲדָשָׁה, בְּכֵן נִשְׂרְפוּ גְלִילָיִךְ *And will ask them, "Has a new Torah been given? Is that why the [old] scrolls were burned?"* The *paytan* addresses Moses and Aaron and says, "I will ask you a simple question. Is the Almighty ready to give a new Torah? Is that why the parchment of the old Torah was burned? Surely this cannot be!"

חֹדֶשׁ שְׁלִישִׁי, וְהָקְשַׁר הָרְבִיעִי *In the third month, and the connected fourth month.* The burning of the Talmud commenced in the month of Sivan and continued into the beginning of the month of Tammuz.

הֲזֶה תַשְׁלוּם כְּפֵלַיִךְ *Is this how you were doubly compensated?* Another tragic event occurred during the month of Tammuz: the shattering of the Tablets of the Law (*Ta'anit* 26b; 28b). Now, there has been a repetition of this event, with the burning of the *Torah shebe'al peh.*

וְאֵיךְ יֶעֱרַב לְחִכִּי אֱכֹל, אַחֲרֵי רְאוֹתִי אֲשֶׁר אָסְפוּ שְׁלָלָיִךְ *How my palate could ever again savor food after I witnessed how all of your treasured possessions were gathered.* How can I eat? How can I enjoy life when I see that they assembled your treasures for destruction?

אֶל תּוֹךְ רְחוֹבָהּ כְּנִדַּחַת *In the open square like an apostate town.* They assembled all of the books in the center of town like the contents of an *ir hanidaḥat*, a city of apostates. The mitzva concerning *ir hanidaḥat* is that all of the booty is to be assembled in the center of the city and burned (Deuteronomy 13:17).

וְשָׂרְפוּ שְׁלַל עֶלְיוֹן *And [how] the divine treasure was burned.* One of the halakhot pertaining to *ir hanidaḥat* is that the destruction of the contents of the city is

limited to שְׁלָלָהּ וְלֹא שְׁלַל שָׁמַיִם, to the booty of the city, but not booty which belongs to heaven (*Sanhedrin* 111b–112a; *Temura* 8a). *Shelal shamayim*, or *shelal elyon*, is not required to be destroyed. And yet, the *paytan* mourns, in Paris they burned the Torah even though it belongs to the category of *shelal elyon* and surely should have been exempt from destruction.

לָקַח צְרוֹר כַּסְפּוֹ *He took His pouch of silver.* God absented Himself and left nothing behind. Sometimes one deserts his wife, but leaves money to enable her to support herself. But in this case, God deserted the Jewish people and took away the צְרוֹר כַּסְפּוֹ, the purse of money, His Torah, which supports and guides the people in times of loneliness and desolation.

הֲלֹא נָסוּ צְלָלֶיךָ *Fled your [protective] shadows.* The protective shade of God and His Torah are gone.

From another perspective, this phrase alludes to the idea that a person without a shadow has no strength. If God has absented Himself, the Jewish people have no shadow. The Torah quotes Joshua, who argues with the *meraglim*, the spies, and says that the inhabitants of Canaan are defenseless and that, "their *tzel*, shadow, has departed from them" (Numbers 14:9). Nahmanides comments (ad loc.) that a person who does not cast a shadow is weak and condemned to death. This concept is related to the custom which the Rama quotes (*Oraḥ Ḥayyim* 664:1) that on the night of Hoshana Raba, people go outdoors to see if their shadow is complete.

כַּתֹּרֶן בְּרֹאשׁ הַר מִגְדְּלַיִךְ *Like a mast atop the mountains of your towers.* This phrase alludes to a verse in Isaiah (30:17). Sometimes people set up camp on the top of a hill and raise a flag or a banner as a symbol of pride. Then they fold up their tents and move on but leave the flag behind. Sometimes there is a busy harbor, full of activity, with a flag flying over it, which symbolizes energy, commerce and industry. And then, suddenly, ships stop coming and the harbor becomes desolate. It is quiet, but the flag remains. The flag is transformed to a symbol of loneliness and desolation.

Now that God and His Torah have departed, the Jewish people are like the "*toren*," the flag on the top of the mountain after the people have moved away, the banner over the harbor when it has become deserted.

לֹא אֶשְׁמַע עוֹד לְקוֹל שָׁרִים וְשָׁרוֹת *No longer will I listen to the voices of your singers.* The *paytan* expresses the fear that the singers, the Torah scholars, will disappear and Torah will be forgotten. The Torah is referred to as a song in the verse "Now, write this song for yourselves and teach it to the children of Israel" (Deuteronomy 31:19). Thus the Torah scholars are referred to as singers.

42

צִיּוֹן Zion, glorious crown, joy to your faithful,
raise your voice on high on behalf of your victims.
א Direct your prayers to the intact celestial Temple.
Ask that peace be granted to you and to your chosen ones.
ב The Master who chose you and loved you so,
has now become a stranger to you and to your armies.
ג As long as He was engraved and carved into your heart,
you were still, secure, at peace, tranquil with your beloved.
ד Speak directly to your comrades [the angels]
to intercede on your behalf, and even utter aloud your own splendid prayers.
ה Bring your lover back to your bed, to sleep in your shadow
and to stroll in your fenced-in rose garden.
ו [Israel] is designated as yours by dowry, betrothal,
and marriage document; for you, to assist you, destined to be your lot.
ז You gave birth to such finely sculpted children for your husband.
How bereft you are now of your pious ones!
ח Vanished, gone, shorn from you [is God],
and you were not expelled; you have not received your bill of divorce!
ט You stand accused of having spurned Him rebelliously;
therefore, you have become a mockery, debased is your beloved nation.
י You sit alone, your skirts shamefully stripped, exposed, your honor diminished.
כ All who supported your crown have now abandoned
you hurriedly, in a panic. They were once your loyal ones.
ל My heart feels hollow, unceasingly, for your sweet fruits have turned bitter. *Lam. 3:49*
מ Full of tears, flowing like a flood of water; my cheeks full of tears,
as are the eyes of all your princes!
נ My soul swoons as I recall your fire, now extinguished
so that your fine flour offerings cannot be baked.
ס Your libations of wine are diluted with water, *Is. 1:22*
and gone from the pens are the cattle once sacrificed by your worshipers.
ע Your foundation is shoveled and plowed into an empty,
furrowed field. The fire of your own torch has devoured and consumed you.
פ I am overcome by trembling and fever when I see my
tormentors at peace, they who trapped your followers.
צ I summon the lamenters to weep for you, to scream and wail bitterly,
 "Woe!" because of your collapse.
ק My own suffering dims when I behold your suffering;
the guards have found you and carried off your mantle.

42

This kina was composed by Rabbi Me'ir ben Elazar, the Darshan of Lombardy (c. 1200). It combines the style of Rabbi Yehuda HaLevi, with an alphabetic acrostic appearing in both the first and last word of each line, and ending with מאיר חזק, "Me'ir: may he be strong." Similar to the first chapter of Eikha, it compares Zion to a bereaved woman, forsaken by her husband and bereft of her children.

צִיּוֹן צְפִירַת פְּאֵר, חֶדְוַת אֲגוּדַיִךְ, וְעַקִּי בְרָמָה בְּקוֹלֵךְ עַל אֲבוּדַיִךְ:

אֶל הַבְּנוּיָה, לְבַקֵּשׁ וּלְחַנֵּן לָאֵל. שְׁלוֹם שְׁפֹת לָךְ, וְגַם לִבְנֵי בְחִירַיִךְ:

בַּעַל בְּחִירֵךְ, אֲשֶׁר לָךְ אַהֲבָתוֹ, לָזָר נֶהְפַּךְ לְנֶגְדֵּךְ, וְגַם נֶגֶד גְּדוּדַיִךְ:

גָּלַף וּפָתַח בְּלוּחַ לֵב, אֲזַי נִשְׁקֶטֶת בֶּטַח בְּשַׁלְוָה, שְׁדוּכָה עַל דּוֹדַיִךְ:

דִּבְרֵי נְכוֹחוֹת לְרֵעַיִךְ לְהָלִיץ עֲבוּרֵךְ, אַף תִּצְפְּצְפִי לְהָרִים קוֹל הֲדָרַיִךְ:

הָשֵׁב יָדֵךְ לְמַטָּתֵךְ, וְלָלוּן בְּצִלֵּךְ, וּלְטַיֵּל בְּסִגַּת גַּן וְרָדַיִךְ:

וְעַד בְּמֹהַר וְקִדּוּשִׁין וְגַם בִּכְתֻבָּה לָךְ לְעָזְרֵךְ, וְהֵם בְּרוּר זְבָדַיִךְ:

זֶרַע וּבָנִים מְחֻטָּבִים, לְאִישֵׁךְ הֲלֹא יָלָדְתְּ. וְאֵיךְ נִשְׁכַּלְתְּ מִכָּל חֲסִידַיִךְ:

חָמַק וְעָבַר וְגַז מִמֵּךְ, וְלֹא נִשְׁלַחַת, לֹא בָא בְיָדֵךְ שְׁטַר סֵפֶר טֵרוּדַיִךְ:

טוֹעֵן בְּטַעֲנַת מְמָאֶנֶת בְּמֶרֶד, עָלַי כֵּן נִתְקַלַּסְתְּ, וְהָשְׁפַּל עִם יְדִידַיִךְ:

יוֹשֶׁבֶת בְּדוּדָה דְּמוּיָה, כִּי חֲשׂוּפָה קָלוֹן שׁוּלַיִךְ, וְנִגְלֵית וְנִדַּלְלוּ כְּבוֹדַיִךְ:

כָּל מַחֲזִיקִים בְּנוּרֵךְ, הֵם יָצְאוּךְ דְּחוּפִים וּבְהוּלִים, וְהֵם הָיוּ לְבוּדַיִךְ:

לִבִּי הֲלֹא נֶחְלַל מֵאֵין הֲפוּגוֹת, אֲשֶׁר הוּמַר וְנֶחֱלַף לְמַר, מֶתֶק מְגָדַיִךְ:

איכה ג, מט

מָלֵא דְמָעוֹת כְּמַיִם נִשְׁטָפוּ, נִמְלְאוּ דִמְעוֹת לֶחָיַי, וְכָל עֵינֵי נְגִידַיִךְ:

נַפְשִׁי עֲטוּפָה, בְּעֵת זָכְרִי לְאִישֵׁךְ. הֲלֹא נִכְבָּה, וְלֹא יָכְלוּ לְאַפּוֹת סְמִידַיִךְ:

סָמֶךְ אֲשִׁישֵׁי עֵנָב מָהוּל בְּמָיִם, וּפַס מִן הָרְפָתִים בְּקַר זִבְחֵי עוֹבְדַיִךְ:

ישעיה א, כב

עֵדֶר וְנֶחֱרַשׁ יְסוֹדֵךְ לְשָׂדֶה בּוּר וְנִיר, לַחֲכָה וְאָכְלָה סְבִיבֵךְ אֵשׁ פְּלָדַיִךְ:

פֶּלֶץ וְשֶׁבֶץ לְבָשׁוּנִי, בְּעֵת אֶחֱזֶה מוֹנֵי שְׁקֵטִים, וְהֵם צָדוּ צְעָדַיִךְ:

צוֹעֵק אֲנִי לַמְקוֹנְנוֹת לִבְכּוֹת, וּבְמַר לִזְעֹק נְהִי נִהְיָה הוֹי, עַל קְפָדַיִךְ:

קָלוּ יְמֵי עָנְיִי, עֵת אֶחֱזֶה עָנְיֵךְ. שׁוֹמְרִים מְצָאוּךְ, וְהֵם נָשְׂאוּ רְדִידַיִךְ:

ר My limbs shiver for the precious children who were burned
like limestone, your remnant firebrands consumed in fire.
ש My antagonists diligently burned my scrolls of Law.
Oh! How apt is the comparison of your Torah to a hammer's flying sparks!
ת My heart is astounded that an unclean land has the benefit
of that wine which accompanied your daily offerings!

ציון Zion, how long will your mouth be restrained by your hand from expressing wonder at how your noblemen fell into the hands of your enemies? / Your children, more precious than gold, have disappeared. This deserves a bitter cry, a wail for your sorrows. / How the date for you to give birth has been postponed! How long will you be held fast by the birth pangs which have seized you? / Nine months is the term for all women to give birth; why have you carried your children for so many years? / Pray to the One who protects the gazelle in her labor, and He will loosen your birth pangs upon your embroidered couch. / He calculates precisely the time for the mountain goat to deliver its young, but He has not yet calculated the time to remove your terror. / The keys to open four sealed chambers are in His hands only; He will surely also open your treasured Temple. / He will let a voice be heard, gathering the faithful, and those He entrusted with your keys will open His doors.

ציון Zion, those who are tormented by your pain, will be enthused by your beauty when the sun shines upon your ruins. / Zion, they will bring gifts to appease your wrath, and those who have terrorized you will bow at your feet. / Zion, adorn yourself with your brocaded garments. And with courage and strength, wear your glorious and precious clothing. *Is. 51:9*

Kina 43 starts on page 602.

רָחֲפוּ עֲצָמַי עֲלֵי בָנִים יְקָרִים, אֲשֶׁר כַּסִּיד שְׂרוּפִים, בְּאוּר אוּדֵי שְׂרִידָיִךְ:
שָׁקְדוּ וְיָקְדוּ גְּוִילֵי דָת, מִשַּׂנְאַי. וְאוֹי, אֵיךְ נִמְשְׁלַתְּ לַפַּטִּישׁ, תְּעוּדָיִךְ:
תּוֹחֶה לְבָבִי, אֲשֶׁר נִרְצָה בְּאֶרֶץ טֻמְאָה לְנִדָּבָה, לִנְסוּךְ יֵין תְּמִידָיִךְ:

צִיּוֹן, עֲדִי אָן מַשִּׂימָה אַתְּ לְפֶה אֶת יָדֵךְ, אֵיכָה בְּיַד אוֹיְבֵךְ נָפְלוּ נְגִידָיִךְ:
מִמֵּךְ אֲבוּדִים יְלָדַיִךְ, חֲמוּדִים כַּפּוּ. עַל זֹאת בְּמֶרֶר בְּכִי, יְלָלַת מְרוּדָיִךְ:
אֵיכָה מְעֻכָּב זְמַן לְדָתֵךְ, וְעַד אָן תְּהִי אַתְּ נִקְשֶׁרֶת בְּחֵיל צִירֵי אֲחוּדָיִךְ:
יוֹלְדוֹת לְתִשְׁעָה יְרָחִים, עֵת נָשֵׁי כֹל. וְאֵיךְ רַבּוּ שְׁנוֹתֵךְ, אֲשֶׁר הָרִית יְלָדָיִךְ:
רַנִּי לְשׁוֹמֵר לָאַיֶּלֶת חֲבָלִים, וְהוּא יַתִּיר לְצִיְּרֵךְ עֲלֵי רֶבֶד רְפִידָיִךְ:
חוֹשֵׁב זְמַן יַעֲלֵי סֶלַע לְהַתִּיר. וְלֹא חָשַׁב זְמַנֵּךְ, לְהָסִיר כָּל חֲרָדָיִךְ:
זְמַן בְּיָדוֹ פָּתַח אַרְבַּע נְעוּלִים, וְגַם כֵּן יִפְתַּח גִּנְזֵי אוֹצַר זְבוּלָיִךְ:
קוֹל יַשְׁמִיעַ לְקַבֵּץ הָאֱמוּנִים. וְאָז דְּלָתָיו פָּתוֹחַ, יַפְקִידֵם עַל קָלִידָיִךְ:

צִיּוֹן, מַעֲשִׂים בְּצָעֳרֵךְ, וּבְיָפְיֵךְ מְעֻשָּׁתִים, אֲשֶׁר יִזְרַח חֶרֶס חֲדוּדָיִךְ:
צִיּוֹן בְּמִנְחָה יְכַפְּרוּן אֶת פְּנֵי זַעְמֵךְ. אָז יִשְׁתַּחֲווּ לְכַף רַגְלֵךְ חֲרֵדָיִךְ:
צִיּוֹן, עֲדִי עֶדְיֵךְ רִקְמַת בְּגָדַיִךְ, עֹז וּזְרוֹעַ וּפְאֵר, בִּגְדֵי חֲמוּדָיִךְ:

ישעיה נא, ט

43

צִיּוֹן Zion, pursue justice against those sorcerers
who so falsely misled you and did not disclose your sins to you.

א Indeed, vile men have oppressed you and possessed you.
You once were the abode of righteousness to all your neighbors. *Jer. 31:22*

ב You disgraced the One who coronated you,
and disobeyed the One who guided you well,
when you yet dwelled in your land and your holy One was in your lodging.

ג You exposed your shame, and your filth was on your skirt.
You also poured forth your brazenness and greatly increased your infidelities.

ד You walked in the way of your sister; you strayed as she strayed,
and you led astray your own daughters and sons.

ה You have been beaten and struck with no cure; you have been thrown into the *Ps. 18:43*
mud of the streets! Behold, you are the laughingstock of your oppressors.

ו You have become a song of derision in the mouths of those cursed knaves who
said to you, "Get down, so that we may smash your teeth!" *Is. 51:23*

ז Remember, poor victim, with a broken heart, and cry aloud for your wound
and against your tormentor who cut down your might.

ח Wait in truth for God who formed and created you,
and trust only in your King, for He is your Master.

ט Purify your heart and your hands, and return to your Husband,
your holy One, and offer Him many songs of prayer.

י All day and night, give voice to a bitter cry for the royal city
and the mound upon which your palace stood.

כ Glory and splendor and great beauty were once in your midst; behold, the face
of your holy One has been discovered, and is now given over to your oppressors.

ל Why [has the Temple turned] to rubble and a den of jackals, and to the nest of *Jer. 9:10*
the owl and the jackdaw? And even your fountains are now mere pools of water!

מ You refused to listen to the lessons of those who rebuked you,
and, therefore, you drank and sucked dry your oils and your dregs!

נ Toward the One above, pour out your heart like a river's waters;
give your eyes no respite! *Lam. 2:18*

ס Go about and clamor in the town, call forth the mourners and all the wailing
women. Let all your lamenters cry a great cry.

ע For your royal turban, until when will it be trampled? Until when will your
princes, your nobility, be held in the hand of the enemy?

פ The Temple gates opened, those very gates which sank into the ground
without a trace, so that there is no lodging for your priests.

43

This kina was written by Rabbi Yosef ben Ḥayyim HaKohen (c. sixteenth century). Like the previous kina, this too follows an alphabetic order in the first twenty-three lines. All the lines of the last stanza begin with the word "Tziyon," with subsequent words on these lines forming the acrostic, יוסף בר חיים הכהן "Yosef bar Ḥayyim HaKohen."

צִיּוֹן בְּמִשְׁפָּט לְכִי לָךְ עִם מְעוֹנָיִךְ. הִתְעוֹךְ בְּכָזָב, וְלֹא גִלּוּ עֲווֹנָיִךְ:

אֶבֶן בְּנֵי עוֹלָה עֲנוּךְ וִירְשׁוּךְ. נְוֵה צֶדֶק הָיִית אֶל כָּל שְׁכֵנָיִךְ:

בָּזִית מַמְלִיכֵךְ, וְלֹא הִקְשַׁבְתְּ לְמוֹרֵךְ לְטוֹב, בִּשְׁכֹן בְּאַרְצֵךְ קְדוֹשֵׁךְ בִּמְלוֹנָיִךְ:

גָּלִית קְלוֹנֵךְ וְטֻמְאָתֵךְ בְּשׁוּלָיִךְ, וְגַם שָׁפַכְתְּ נְחֻשְׁתֵּךְ. מְאֹד הִרְבֵּית זְנוּנָיִךְ:

דֶּרֶךְ אֲחוֹתֵךְ הֲלֹא הָלָכְתְּ, וְזָנִית בְּתַזְנוּתָהּ, וְהִזְנֵית בְּנוֹתַיִךְ וּבָנָיִךְ:

תהלים יח, מג

הַבֵּית וְנִגְפַּת לְאֵין מַרְפֵּא, וְהִשְׁלַכְתְּ כְּטִיט חוּצוֹת, וְהִנָּךְ שְׂחוֹק לִבְנֵי מְעַנָּיִךְ:

ישעיה נא, כג

וַתְּהִי נְגִינָה בְּפִי זֵדִים אֲרוּרִים, אֲשֶׁר אָמְרוּ לְנַפְשֵׁךְ שְׁחִי, הָרוּס לְשָׁנָיִךְ:

זִכְרִי עָנְיָהּ בְּלֵב נִשְׁבָּר, וְזַעֲקִי עֲלֵי מַכֵּךְ וְנוֹגְשֵׂךְ, אֲשֶׁר גָּדַע קַרְנָיִךְ:

חַכִּי בֶּאֱמֶת לְאֵל צוּרֵךְ וּבוֹרְאֵךְ, וְהוֹחִילִי לְמַלְכֵּךְ לְבַד, כִּי הוּא אֲדוֹנָיִךְ:

טַהֲרִי לְבָבֵךְ וְכַפַּיִךְ, וְשׁוּבִי עֲדֵי אִישֵׁךְ קְדוֹשֵׁךְ, וְלוֹ הַרְבִּי רְנָנָיִךְ:

יוֹמָם וָלַיְלָה תְּנִי קוֹל בִּבְכִי מַר, עֲלֵי קִרְיַת מְלוּכָה, וְעַל תֵּל אַרְמוֹנָיִךְ:

כָּבוֹד וְהָדָר וְרֹב יְפִי בְּתוֹכֵךְ, הֲלֹא נִמְצָא פְּנֵי קְדוֹשֵׁךְ, וְהֵן נָתַן לְעֵינָיִךְ:

ירמיה ט, י

לָמָּה לְגַלִּים מְעוֹן תַּנִּים, וּמוֹרַשׁ קָאַת וְקִפּוֹד, וְגַם אַגְמֵי מַיִם מַעֲנָיִךְ:

מֵאַנְתְּ שְׁמֹעַ לְקוֹל מוּסָר מְיַסְּרֵךְ, בְּכֵן שָׁתִית וּמָצִית שְׁמָנַיִךְ שְׁמָרָיִךְ:

איכה ב, יח

נֹכַח פְּנֵי עֶלְיוֹן, שִׁפְכִי לְבָבֵךְ כְּמֵי נָהָר. וְאַל תִּתְּנִי פוּגַת לְעֵינָיִךְ:

סֹבִי וְהֹמִי בָעִיר, קִרְאִי מְקוֹנְנוֹת וְכָל נָשִׁים מְבַכּוֹת, בִּבְכִי גָדוֹל מְקוֹנְנָיִךְ:

עֲלֵי צְנִיף מַלְכֵּךְ, עַד אָן לְמִרְמָס יְהִי. עַד מָה בְּיַד צָר, בְּנֵי שָׂרִים, סְגָנָיִךְ:

פְּתַח לְבָנוֹן שְׁעָרֶיךָ, אֲשֶׁר טָבְעוּ בְאֶרֶץ נְשִׁיָּה, וְאֵין מָלוֹן לְכֹהֲנָיִךְ:

צ Zion, weep for them, and do not be silent. *Mic. 2:4*
Gather and assemble your old women and old men.
ק Shear off your hair. Make yourself bald like an eagle *Mic. 1:16*
for your delightful children and for all your leaders and lords.
ר Higher and mightier than the waves in the heart of the sea were your sufferings,
on that night when your rows of gemstones were pillaged.
ש Pillaged were your abode and all your precious treasures!
No Urim and Thummim to reveal your secrets.
ת Mount Tabor and Mount Carmel will be like Mount Gilboa,
with neither dew nor rain, without the light of your clouds.

ציון Zion, forget your agony! Cleanse yourself, and prepare yourself. Put on precious
garments and fragrant oils. / Zion, your days of mourning have ended in joy and in *Is. 60:20*
glee. Your sins are over and done with, as are your two great catastrophes. / Zion,
a treasure for kings and nations shall you be! Gentle waters will yet flow from your *Ps. 23:2*
fountain! / Zion, hope for your redemption. You will again be called a crown of *Is. 28:5*
glory by the upright and by your musicians! / Zion, blessing and life are with you, *Gen. 49:24*
for the LORD of Jacob has ordered this forever, and they will yet proclaim this to
your ears! / Zion, a multitude of priests will serve you, and God Himself will again
secure your commanders.

Kina 44 starts on page 606.

צִיּוֹן עֲלֵיהֶם נְהִי נִהְיָה, וְלֹא תֶחֱשִׁי, אִסְפִי וְקַבְּצִי זְקֵנוֹת וּזְקֵנֶיךְ:   מיכה ב, ד

קָרְחִי וָגֹזִּי כַּנֶּשֶׁר עַל בְּנֵי תַעֲנוּגַיִךְ, וְעַל כָּל נְשִׂיאַיִךְ וְרוֹזְנָיִךְ:   מיכה א, טז

רָמוּ וְגָדְלוּ כְּמוֹ גַלִּים בְּלֵב יָם מְזוֹרָיִךְ, בְּלֵיל שֻׁדְּדוּ טוּרֵי אֲבָנָיִךְ:

שֻׁדַּד מְלוֹנֵךְ וְכָל מַחְמַד יָקָרֵךְ, בְּאֵין אוּרִים וְתֻמִּים אֲשֶׁר גְּלוּ צְפוּנָיִךְ:

תָּבוֹר וְכַרְמֶל כְּהָרֵי גִלְבֹּעַ, בְּלִי טַלֵּךְ וּמִטְרֵךְ, וְלֹא אוֹר עֲנָנָיִךְ:

צִיּוֹן יְגוֹנֵךְ נָשִׁי, טַהֲרִי וְהִתְקַדְּשִׁי, עֲדִי יְקָר לִבְשִׁי, תַּמְרוּק שְׁמָנָיִךְ:

צִיּוֹן, וְשָׁלְמוּ יְמֵי אֶבְלֵךְ בְּשָׂשׂוֹן וָגִיל, כִּי תַם עֲוֹנֵךְ וּמִשְׁנֶה שִׁבְרוֹנָיִךְ:   ישעיה ס, כ

צִיּוֹן, סְגֻלַּת מְלָכִים וּמְדִינוֹת תְּהִי, עוֹד יִזְלוּ מֵי מְנוּחוֹת מַעְיָנָיִךְ:   תהלים כג, ב

צִיּוֹן, פְּדוּתֵךְ צְפִי. עוֹד יִקְרָאוּךְ צְפִירַת תִּפְאֶרֶת, בְּפִי יְשָׁרִים וְנוֹגְנָיִךְ:   ישעיה כח, ה

צִיּוֹן, בְּרָכָה וְחַיִּים בָּךְ אֲבִיר יַעֲקֹב צִוָּה לְעוֹלָם, וְעוֹד יֹאמְרוּ בְאָזְנָיִךְ:   בראשית מט, כד

צִיּוֹן, הֲמוֹן כֹּהֲנִים הֵמָּה יְשָׁרְתוּנֵךְ, וְגַם יוֹסִיף יְהֹוָה קְנוֹת שֵׁנִית קְצִינָיִךְ:

Kina 44 starts on page 607.

44

צִיּוֹן Zion, once you were mistress over the kingdom that now oppresses you; accept the many calls of greeting of your exiled prisoners. / My heart is numbed by the sounds emitted by those arrogant sons of Seir and Moab in the center of your Temple's shrine. / Stained are my anointed ones by blood; the scalps of my nobles are ripped; the elegant and elite, trampled; my nation, your chosen ones! / Fortified cities, seized; a tower built, a mound cast. Cedars of Lebanon cut from the trees of your forests. / The visions of your prophets were delusions; they foretold peace for the holy city. Your wounds were not healed. / My heart leaps from its place because of the Ark, and Tabernacle, and golden frontlet, and tunic, and the holy name you concealed within them. / Distant isles told of the mysteries and wonders that could mend your breach. Weep for your double calamity! / The sun and all the stars of the sky were stilled in the valley. Raise your voice on the heights. Raise the voice of your embitterment. / The moon and all the constellations wept for this, that the brightness of your morning stars was withdrawn. / The staff of the wicked, *Is. 14:5* when it was raised to hang princes by their hands; your happiness is ended, your joy and the instruments of your song. / In mourning is Lebanon [the Temple], and Mount Carmel's glee is not heard. Shamed were the nobles when the foe entered your gates. / The wisdom of the sages was lost on that day, and your officers were imprisoned. And your dear children of Zion were debased. / Royal raiment, the garb of heathen women, gorgeous coral and crystal, and *Job 28:18* even your hewn sapphires! / Streams shriveled in the once joyful city. Where *Is. 18:7* there was limitless treasure, they shattered your fences! / High hill and verdant *Is. 22:2* tree and every leafy oak, were places of idol worship, full of your slain corpses. / My innards rumble like the sea, my tears flow like the waters of Nimrim, on *Is. 15:6* that day when lions ripped apart your cubs. / My heart rages like a tempest, a storm, like chaff whirled away from the threshing floor, because of the sins of your idolatrous priests. / My flesh creeps on that day when the Holy One of Jacob disdained His Temple and altar, no longer entering your courtyards. / A choice vine, a noble planting, you were! And one morning, as flower and bud began to bloom, your thorns sprouted.

44

This is another anonymous kina, which appears in manuscripts dating from the sixteenth century. The paytan recounts the horrors of the Destruction, and turns to Zion, pleading with her to return to God.

צִיּוֹן, גְּבֶרֶת לְמַמְלָכוֹת מִצִּירַיִךְ, רַבֵּי שְׁלוֹמִים שְׂאִי מֵאֵת אֲסִירַיִךְ:
יֶחֱמַץ לְבָבִי, לְקוֹל נָתְנוּ רְאֵמִים, בְּנֵי שֵׂעִיר וּמוֹאָב, בְּתוֹךְ הֵיכַל דְּבִירַיִךְ:
לְבִסֵּס מְשִׁיחַי בְּדָם קָדְקֹד סְגָנִים, טְרֹף שׁוֹעַ וְקֹוֹעַ, רְמֹס עַמִּי בְּחִירַיִךְ:
עָרִים בְּצוּרוֹת תִּפֹּשׂ, דַּיֵּק וְסוֹלְלָה שְׁפֹךְ, אַרְזֵי לְבָנוֹן כְּרֹת מֵעֲצֵי יְעָרַיִךְ:
חָזוּ נְבִיאִים בַּשָּׁוְא, דַּבֵּר בְּשֵׁם עִיר קָדוֹשׁ יַעֲקֹב, לְשָׁלוֹם. וְלֹא חֻבְּשׁוּ מְזוֹרַיִךְ:
יֻתַּר לְבָבִי עֲלֵי אָרוֹן וּמִשְׁכָּן, וְצִיץ זָהָב וְאֵפוֹד, וְשֵׁם קֹדֶשׁ סְתָרַיִךְ:
אִיִּים יַחֲוּוּ לְךָ אוֹת וּמוֹפֵת, עָלַי שַׁבְּרֵךְ יְרַפְּאוּ, אֱלֵי מִשְׁנֶה שְׁבָרַיִךְ:
שֶׁמֶשׁ וְכָל כּוֹכְבֵי שַׁחַק, בְּעֵמֶק דִּמּוּ. קוֹלֵךְ בְּרָמָה שְׂאִי, קוֹל תַּמְרוּרַיִךְ:
סַהַר וְכִימָה וָעָשׁ וּכְסִיל לְזֹאת יִבְכּוּ, נָגְהָם אֲשֶׁר אָסְפוּ, כּוֹכְבֵי שְׁחָרַיִךְ:
מַטֵּה רְשָׁעִים בְּקָם, שָׂרִים בְּיָדָם תְּלוּוֹת, שָׁבַת מְשׂוֹשֵׂךְ, גִּיל וּכְלִי זְמָרַיִךְ:   *ישעיה יד, ה*
אָבַל לְבָנוֹן, וְגִיל כַּרְמֶל בְּלִי נִשְׁמַע. חָפְרוּ סְגָנִים, בְּבוֹא צַר בִּשְׁעָרַיִךְ:
חָכְמַת נְבוֹנִים בְּיוֹם אָבְדָה, וְאָסְרוּ קְצִינַיִךְ, וְשָׁחוּ בְּנֵי צִיּוֹן יְקָרָיִךְ:
מִכְלוֹל מְלָכִים, לְבוּשׁ בְּנוֹת עֲרָלוֹת. פְּאֵר רָאמוֹת וְגָבִישׁ, וְאַף סַפִּיר גִּזְרָיִךְ:   *איוב כח, יח*
בְּזָאוּ נְהָרִים בְּתוֹךְ קִרְיָה עֲלִיזָה, לְאֵין קֵץ לַתְּבוּנָה וָסוֹף, פָּרְצוּ גְדֵרָיִךְ:   *ישעיה יד, ז*
  ישעיה כב, ב
גִּבְעָה וְעֵץ רַעֲנָן, אֵלָה עֲבֻתָּה, מְקוֹם פִּגּוּל. מְלֵאִים מְחַלֵּל פְּגָרָיִךְ:
יֶהֱמוּ קְרָבַי כַּיָּם, יִזְּלוּ דְמָעַי כְּמֵי נְמֵרִים, לַבָּאִים בְּיוֹם טָרְפוּ כְּפִירָיִךְ:   *ישעיה טו, ו*
יִסְעַר לְבָבִי כְּמוֹ סוּפָה וָסַעַר, כְּמֹץ גֹּרֶן יִסָּעַר, עָלַי אַשְׁמוֹת כְּמָרַיִךְ:
סָמַר בְּשָׂרִי, לְיוֹם נֹאַר קְדוֹשׁ יַעֲקֹב, מִקְדָּשׁ וּמִזְבֵּחַ, בְּלִי בוֹא בַּחֲצֵרָיִךְ:
שׁוֹרֵק נֶטַע נַעֲמָן הָיִיתְ, וּבַקֵּר כְּצִץ פֶּרַח וְנִצָּה, תְּשַׂגְשְׂגִי זְמוֹרָיִךְ:

שׁוּבִי Return, O fawn, to the God who fashioned you and upheld you. In your midst the husband of your youth shall dwell, from generation to generation! / The lion will never again find his way up to your pasture; no mighty ships or vessels will sail through your rivers. / My soul seeks to desire your well-being. Like clear heat upon the grass, like a cloud of dew on a warm day, is your heaping harvest. / I will rejoice, I will be happy, on the day I will hear it announced aloud, "Seek peace and tranquility and the welfare of your prisoners." *Is. 18:4*

Kina 45 starts on page 610.

שׁוּבִי צְבִיָּה, לָאֵל יוֹצְרֵךְ יְכוֹנְנֵךְ. לְדוֹר וָדוֹר בְּתוֹכֵךְ שְׁכֹן בַּעַל נְעוּרָיִךְ:
אַרְיֵה בָּנֵךְ, לְבַל יַעֲלֶה מְסִלּוֹת. וְצִי אַדִּיר וְשַׁיִט, לְבַל יַעֲבֹר יְאוֹרָיִךְ:
נַפְשִׁי שְׁלוֹמֵךְ דְּרֹשׁ, אִוְּתָה כְחֹם צַח עֲלֵי אוֹרוֹת. כְּעָב טַל בְּחֹם יוֹם, ישעיה יח, ד
נֵד קְצִירָיִךְ:
אֶשְׂמַח וְאָשִׂישׂ, בְּיוֹם אֶשְׁמַע מְבַשֵּׂר בְּקוֹל. שָׁלוֹם מְנוּחָה דְּרֹשׁ, וְשָׁלוֹם אֲסִירָיִךְ:

Kina 45 starts on page 611.

45

אֱלִי Lament, Zion and her cities, like a woman in her labor pains,
like a maiden girt in sackcloth for the husband of her youth.   *Joel 1:8*

עֲלֵי For the palace now deserted because
  of the sin of the sheep of her flocks,
and for the intrusion of God's blasphemers
  into the chambers of her sanctuary.

עֲלֵי For the exile of God's servants, the sweet singers of her songs,
and for their blood which has been spilled like the waters of her rivers.

עֲלֵי For the lyrics of her dances, now silenced in her cities,
and for the council now devastated, and the abolition of her high courts.

עֲלֵי For her daily sacrifices and the redemption of her first born,
and for the defilement of the Temple vessels and the altar of her incense.

עֲלֵי For the little children of her kings, the sons of David, her princes,
and for their beauty which was darkened
  when she was divested of her crowns.

עֲלֵי For the glory that was dispelled at the time her shrines were destroyed,
and for the oppressor who tormented
  and placed sackcloth around her waist.

עֲלֵי For the wounds and many blows with which her sainted ones were struck,
and for the smashing upon the rock of her babes, her young ones.

עֲלֵי For the joy of her enemy rejoicing over her downfall,
and for the torture of those once free, her noblemen, her pious ones.

At this point, many congregations say one or more of the kinot in memory of the victims of the Holocaust (page 620).
The following kina is said standing and recited responsively with the Leader.

45

This elegy, the only one which is chanted to a melody, closes the kinot. The first stanza, often repeated as a refrain, calls upon Zion to weep, comparing her to woman in the pangs of childbirth, and to a young wife bereaved of her husband. The eleven subsequent stanzas follow a fixed form: rhyming couplets which include an alphabetic acrostic, with each stich detailing one of the calamities of the Destruction. Commentary for this kina begins on page 614.

אֱלִי צִיּוֹן וְעָרֶיהָ / כְּמוֹ אִשָּׁה בְּצִירֶיהָ.
וְכִבְתוּלָה חֲגוּרַת שַׂק / עַל בַּעַל נְעוּרֶיהָ:

יואל א, ח

עֲלֵי אַרְמוֹן אֲשֶׁר נֻטַּשׁ / בְּאַשְׁמַת צֹאן עֲדָרֶיהָ.
וְעַל בִּיאַת מְחָרְפֵי אֵל / בְּתוֹךְ מִקְדַּשׁ חֲדָרֶיהָ:

עֲלֵי גָלוּת מְשָׁרְתֵי אֵל / מַנְעִימֵי שִׁיר זְמָרֶיהָ.
וְעַל דָּמָם אֲשֶׁר שֻׁפַּךְ / כְּמוֹ מֵימֵי יְאוֹרֶיהָ:

עֲלֵי הֶגְיוֹן מְחוֹלֶיהָ / אֲשֶׁר דָּמַם בְּעָרֶיהָ.
וְעַל וַעַד אֲשֶׁר שָׁמֵם / וּבִטּוּל סַנְהֶדְרֶיהָ:

עֲלֵי זִבְחֵי תְמִידֶיהָ / וּפִדְיוֹנֵי בְכוֹרֶיהָ.
וְעַל חִלּוּל כְּלֵי הֵיכָל / וּמִזְבַּח קְטוֹרֶיהָ:

עֲלֵי טַפֵּי מְלָכֶיהָ / בְּנֵי דָוִד גְּבִירֶיהָ.
וְעַל יָפְיָם אֲשֶׁר חָשַׁךְ / בְּעֵת סָרוּ כְתָרֶיהָ:

עֲלֵי כָבוֹד אֲשֶׁר גָּלָה / בְּעֵת חָרְבַּן דְּבִירֶיהָ.
וְעַל לוֹחֵץ אֲשֶׁר לָחַץ / וְשָׂם שַׂקִּים חֲגוֹרֶיהָ:

עֲלֵי מַחַץ וְרֹב מַכּוֹת / אֲשֶׁר הֻכּוּ נְזִירֶיהָ.
וְעַל נִפּוּץ אֱלֵי סֶלַע / עוֹלָלֶיהָ נְעָרֶיהָ:

עֲלֵי שִׂמְחַת אוֹיְבֶיהָ / בְּשָׂחֳקָם עַל שְׁבָרֶיהָ.
וְעַל עִנּוּי בְּנֵי חוֹרִין / נְדִיבֶיהָ טְהוֹרֶיהָ:

עֲלֵי For the sin which diverted her footsteps from the cleared path,
and for her numerous communities, tarnished and charred.

עֲלֵי For the voices of those who mocked her as her corpses mounted,
and to the scoffing mob in the very midst of her Temple courtyards.

עֲלֵי For Your name which is desecrated in the mouth
   of those who stand against her,
and for the prayer which they shout to You, "Hear and heed her words!"

אֱלִי Lament, Zion and her cities, like a woman in her labor pains,
like a maiden girt in sackcloth for the husband of her youth.

Kina 46 starts on page 616.

עֲלֵי פֶשַׁע אֲשֶׁר עָוְתָה / סָלַל דֶּרֶךְ אֲשׁוּרֶיהָ:
וְעַל צִבְאוֹת קְהָלֶיהָ / שְׁזוּפֶיהָ שְׁחֹרֶיהָ:

עֲלֵי קוֹלוֹת מְחָרְפֶיהָ / בְּעֵת רַבּוּ פְגָרֶיהָ.
וְעַל רִגְשַׁת מְגַדְּפֶיהָ / בְּתוֹךְ מִשְׁכַּן חֲצֵרֶיהָ:

עֲלֵי שִׁמְךָ אֲשֶׁר חִלֵּל / בְּפִי קָמֵי מְצֵרֶיהָ.
וְעַל תַּחַן יְצַוְּחוּ לָךְ / קְשָׁב וּשְׁמַע אֲמָרֶיהָ:

אֱלֵי צִיּוֹן וְעָרֶיהָ / כְּמוֹ אִשָּׁה בְּצִירֶיהָ.
וְכִבְתוּלָה חֲגוּרַת שַׂק / עַל בַּעַל נְעוּרֶיהָ:

Kina 46 starts on page 617.

COMMENTARY ON KINA 45

This *kina*, recited while standing, has traditionally been the last of the *kinot* recited on the morning of Tisha B'Av. With this *kina*, we close the formal recitation of the *kinot*. It is not known with certainty who composed "אֱלִי צִיּוֹן," although some have suggested that the author was Rabbi Yehuda HaLevi. The motif of this *kina*, and the reason that it is the closing *kina*, is that no matter how much we have cried and grieved with the recitation of the *kinot*, it is not sufficient, and we must continue to mourn for the *Beit HaMikdash*.

אֱלִי צִיּוֹן *Lament, Zion.* The word אֱלִי, which means to mourn or lament, comes from the root א-ל-ה. The same root is used in the phrase "אֲאַלֶּה אִתִּי שָׁמַיִם" in the *kina*, "אֲאַדֶּה עַד חוּג שָׁמַיִם" which can be interpreted as, "I will make the heavens mourn with me."

The intent of the phrase "אֱלִי צִיּוֹן וְעָרֶיהָ" is that we should continue to mourn. At the point that we are ready to close the book of *kinot* and depart, we say, "No. *Kinot* can never be finished until the *Beit HaMikdash* is rebuilt." Although we have recited so many *kinot*, we are compelled to continue. If a person actually grieves and mourns for the destruction of the *Beit HaMikdash* and the losses the Jewish people have sustained, can one really believe that by reciting the *kinot* he has discharged his duty? The inescapable conclusion is that one can never mourn sufficiently for Jerusalem.

כְּמוֹ אִשָּׁה בְּצִירֶיהָ *Like a woman in her labor pains.* Just as a woman who suffers the excruciating pain of childbirth has no choice but to cry out, so, too, we cannot cease crying as long as the *Beit HaMikdash* is in ruins. The need to continue mourning is part of our human nature, just as it is human nature for the woman in labor to cry out in pain. It would be futile to tell a woman in labor not to cry. Similarly, it would be utter foolishness to tell the Jewish people to stop weeping for Jerusalem.

וְכִבְתוּלָה חֲגוּרַת שַׂק / עַל בַּעַל נְעוּרֶיהָ *Like a maiden girt in sackcloth for the husband of her youth.* Just as it would be foolish to tell a woman in labor not to cry, so, too, it would be the height of insensitivity to tell a newly-wed bride whose young husband has just died, to stop shedding tears. So, too, let Zion continue to mourn over the *Ḥurban*, and do not tell her to stop.

The concept of continued, unending mourning is a special, unique aspect of *avelut yeshana*, mourning for a tragedy that occurred long ago, as opposed to *avelut ḥadasha*, mourning for the recent bereavement. In the case of *avelut*

ḥadasha, there *are* limits, and Maimonides says (*Mishneh Torah*, Hil. Avel 13:11) that one who mourns "too much" is acting foolishly. But with respect to *avelut yeshana* for the Ḥurban, the concept of "too much" does not apply.

The message of this *kina* is that the *kinot* for Jerusalem have no end. It is for this reason that certain prayers are sung to the unique somber melody of "אֵלִי צִיּוֹן." We use this haunting melody when we want to express the intensity of our loneliness and longing for the *Beit HaMikdash* and the strength of our faith that the redemption will come. Thus on Friday night of *Shabbat Ḥazon*, the Shabbat immediately preceding Tisha B'Av, *Lekha Dodi* is sung to this melody. The phrase "Enter in peace, O crown of her husband, even in gladness and good cheer," not only refers to the coming of Shabbat, but also alludes to the rebuilding of the *Beit HaMikdash*. Similarly, we use this melody for the phrase in the Yom Tov Musaf Amida, "Rebuild Your House as it was in the beginning." Our waiting for the arrival of the Messiah and rebuilding of the *Beit HaMikdash* has no limit. We will never be satisfied with any gift God bestows upon us if the *Beit HaMikdash* remains in ruins. May it be rebuilt and restored soon, in our day.

46

שׁוֹמְרוֹן Samaria [the ten tribes of Israel, "Ohola"] proclaimed,
"My sins have caught up with me! My children have left me for another land!"
    And Oholiva [Jerusalem, Judah] screamed in response,
        "My palaces are in flames!" And Zion said, "The Lord has forsaken me." *Is. 49:14*

לֹא [Samaria answered,] "You cannot equate your plight to mine!
Can your downfall compare to my collapse?
I, Ohola, acted with spite and treachery;
my betrayal opposed me, and my rebellion accused me.
In a few short days, I paid my debt, and the Assyrian king devoured my fruits.
He stripped me bare of my treasures and jewels,
and carried off my captives to Halah and Habor.
So be still, Oholiva, don't cry as I do;
your years endured, but my years did not!"
    And Oholiva screamed in response, "My palaces are in flames!"
    "The Lord has forsaken me."

מְשִׁיבָה Oholiva responded, "I, too, was perverse
and betrayed the Companion of my Youth just as you did.
So be still, Ohola, as I recall my anguish.
You wandered but once; while I, many times.
I was entrapped by Chaldean hands
and descended to Babylon as a destitute prisoner.
The Temple of which I was so proud was burned.
After seventy years in Babylon, I was remembered
and returned to Zion to found my Temple yet again.
But this time, too, I was not long entrenched
before Rome snatched me, and I was almost no more,
for my multitudes were scattered to distant lands."
    And Oholiva screamed in response, "My palaces are in flames!"
    "The Lord has forsaken me."

הַחוֹמֵל He who pities the poor, take pity on their plight!
See their desolation and lengthy exile.
Do not be implacably angry, but remember their lowliness.
Remember not their foolish iniquities forever.
Mend their fissures, soothe their grief, for You are their Hope and their Hero.
Renew our days like the days long gone,
as You have spoken, "The Lord rebuilds Jerusalem." *Ps. 147:2*

46

This kina was written by Rabbi Solomon ibn Gabirol (Spain, 1021–1058). In Ezekiel chapter 23, the kingdoms of Israel and Judea are depicted as two unfaithful wives, Ohola and Oholiva. This kina is written as a conversation between them, and concludes with a prayer to God to have mercy on them. Commentary for this kina begins on page 618.

שׁוֹמְרוֹן קוֹל תִּתֵּן, מְצָאוּנִי עֲוֹנַי / לְאֶרֶץ אַחֶרֶת יְצָאוּנִי בָּנָי.
וְאָהֳלִיבָה תִּזְעַק נִשְׂרְפוּ אַרְמוֹנַי / וַתֹּאמֶר צִיּוֹן עֲזָבַנִי יהוה: ישעיה מט, יד

לֹא לָךְ אָהֳלִיבָה, חֲשׁוֹב עֲוֹנֵךְ כְּעֲוֹנִי / הֲתַמְשִׁילִי שִׁבְרֵךְ לְשִׁבְרִי וּלְחָלְיִי.
אֲנִי אָהֳלָה, סוּרָה בָּגַדְתִּי בְּקַשְׁיִי / וְקָם עָלַי כַּחֲשִׁי, וְעָנָה בִי מֶרְיִי.
וּלְמִקְצָת הַיָּמִים שָׁלַמְתִּי נִשְׁיִי / וְתִגְלַת פִּלְאֶסֶר אָכַל אֶת פִּרְיִי.
חֲמוּדוֹתַי הִפְשִׁיט, וְהִצִּיל אֶת עֶדְיִי / וְלַחֲלַח וְחָבוֹר נָשָׂא אֶת שִׁבְיִי.
דְּמִי אָהֳלִיבָה, וְאַל תִּבְכִּי כְּבִכְיִי / שְׁנוֹתַיִךְ אָרְכוּ, וְלֹא אָרְכוּ שָׁנַי:
וְאָהֳלִיבָה תִּזְעַק נִשְׂרְפוּ אַרְמוֹנַי / וַתֹּאמֶר צִיּוֹן עֲזָבַנִי יהוה:

מְשִׁיבָה אָהֳלִיבָה, אֲנִי כֵן נְעֶקַשְׁתִּי / וּבְאַלּוּף נְעוּרַי כְּאָהֳלָה בָּגַדְתִּי.
דְּמִי אָהֳלָה, כִּי יְגוֹנִי זָכַרְתִּי / נָדַדְתְּ אַתְּ אַחַת, וְרַבּוֹת נָדַדְתִּי.
הִנֵּה בְּיַד כַּשְׂדִּים פַּעֲמַיִם נִלְכַּדְתִּי / וּשְׁבִיָּה עֲנִיָּה לְבָבֶל יָרַדְתִּי.
וְנִשְׂרַף הַהֵיכָל אֲשֶׁר בּוֹ נִכְבַּדְתִּי / וּלְשִׁבְעִים שָׁנָה בְּבָבֶל נִפְקַדְתִּי.
וְשַׁבְתִּי לְצִיּוֹן עוֹד, וְהֵיכָל יָסַדְתִּי / גַּם זֹאת הַפַּעַם, מְעַט לֹא עָמַדְתִּי.
עַד לְקָחַנִי אֱדוֹם, וְכִמְעַט אֲבַדְתִּי / וְעַל כָּל הָאֲרָצוֹת נָפוֹצוּ הֲמוֹנַי:
וְאָהֳלִיבָה תִּזְעַק נִשְׂרְפוּ אַרְמוֹנַי / וַתֹּאמֶר צִיּוֹן עֲזָבַנִי יהוה:

הַחוֹמֵל עַל דַּל, חֲמוֹל עַל דַּלּוּתָם / וּרְאֵה שׁוֹמְמוֹתָם וְאוֹרֶךְ גָּלוּתָם.
וְאַל תִּקְצֹף עַד מְאֹד, וּרְאֵה שִׁפְלוּתָם / וְאַל לָעַד תִּזְכֹּר עֲוֹנָם וְסִכְלוּתָם.
רְפָא נָא אֶת שִׁבְרָם, וְנַחֵם אֲבֵלוּתָם / כִּי אַתָּה סִבְרָם וְאַתָּה אֱיָלוּתָם.
חַדֵּשׁ יָמֵינוּ כִּימֵי קַדְמוֹנִי / כְּנָאֱמָךְ: בּוֹנֵה יְרוּשָׁלַיִם יהוה: תהלים קמז, ב

At the conclusion of the kinot, the congregation says the following:

עַד How long must Zion cry and Jerusalem mourn?
    Pity Zion, rebuild the walls of Jerusalem! *Ps. 102:14*

תְּרַחֵם Pity Zion as You have spoken.
    Make her firm as You gave Your word.
תְּמַהֵר Hasten salvation, hurry redemption.
    And return to Jerusalem with great compassion.

כַּכָּתוּב As is written by the hand of Your prophet: "Therefore, thus says the LORD: I have returned to Jerusalem with mercies, My House shall be rebuilt in it, says the LORD of hosts, and a line shall be stretched forth over Jerusalem." And it is said: "Proclaim further, saying, Thus says the LORD of hosts: My cities shall again overflow with prosperity; and the LORD shall yet comfort Zion, and shall yet choose Jerusalem." And it is said: "For the LORD shall comfort Zion: He will comfort all her waste places; and He will make her wilderness like Eden, and her desert like the garden of the LORD; joy and gladness shall be found in it, thanksgiving, and the voice of melody." *Zech. 1:16–17* *Is. 51:3*

COMMENTARY ON KINA 46

This *kina*, composed by Solomon ibn Gabirol, consists of a debate between Oholiva (which represents Judea, Hebron and Jerusalem), and Ohola (Samaria and the Ten Tribes), as to which of them suffered more over the years. Samaria addresses Judea, asserting that Judea cannot compare its suffering to Samaria's, and asks rhetorically, "Can you compare your sickness and disease with mine?" Samaria continues, enumerating its tragedies, and declares, "וְתִגְלַת פִּלְאֶסֶר אָכַל אֶת פִּרְיִי, and Tiglat Pileser [who is identified with Sennacherib] consumed my offspring," which refers to the exile of the Ten Tribes by the Assyrian invaders. Judea responds, "No, my misfortune is worse,

At the conclusion of the קינות, *the* קהל *says the following:*

עַד אָנָה בְּכִיָּה בְצִיּוֹן, וּמִסְפֵּד בִּירוּשָׁלָיִם.
תְּרַחֵם צִיּוֹן וְתִבְנֶה חוֹמוֹת יְרוּשָׁלָיִם:

תהלים
קב, יד

תְּרַחֵם צִיּוֹן כַּאֲשֶׁר אָמַרְתָּ / וּתְכוֹנְנֶהָ כַּאֲשֶׁר דִּבַּרְתָּ /
תְּמַהֵר יְשׁוּעָה וְתָחִישׁ גְּאֻלָּה / וְתָשׁוּב לִירוּשָׁלַיִם בְּרַחֲמִים רַבִּים:

כַּכָּתוּב עַל יַד נְבִיאֶךָ: לָכֵן כֹּה־אָמַר יהוה, שַׁבְתִּי לִירוּשָׁלַם בְּרַחֲמִים, בֵּיתִי יִבָּנֶה בָּהּ, נְאֻם יהוה צְבָאוֹת, וְקָו יִנָּטֶה עַל־יְרוּשָׁלָיִם: וְנֶאֱמַר: עוֹד קְרָא לֵאמֹר, כֹּה אָמַר יהוה צְבָאוֹת, עוֹד תְּפוּצֶנָה עָרַי מִטּוֹב, וְנִחַם יהוה עוֹד אֶת־צִיּוֹן, וּבָחַר עוֹד בִּירוּשָׁלָיִם: וְנֶאֱמַר: כִּי־נִחַם יהוה צִיּוֹן, נִחַם כָּל־חָרְבֹתֶיהָ, וַיָּשֶׂם מִדְבָּרָהּ כְּעֵדֶן, וְעַרְבָתָהּ כְּגַן־יהוה, שָׂשׂוֹן וְשִׂמְחָה יִמָּצֵא בָהּ, תּוֹדָה וְקוֹל זִמְרָה:

זכריה א,
טז–יז

ישעיה נא, ג

---

my suffering more profound. You were exiled just once, but I was captured twice and was taken captive to Babylon… I returned again to Zion… until Edom seized me."

This *kina* commemorates the exile of the Ten Tribes even though that catastrophe did not occur on Tisha B'Av. The Mishna tells us (*Ta'anit* 26a–b) that five tragic events occurred on Tisha B'Av: the sin of the spies, the destructions of the First Temple and the Second Temple, the fall of Beitar, and the plowing under of Jerusalem. The events that occurred on Tisha B'Av as well as other events that did not occur on that day are all commemorated on Tisha B'Av, the universal day of mourning for all tragedies that befell the Jewish people.

KINOT IN COMMEMORATION OF THE HOLOCAUST

47

Elegy on the Ḥurban
by Rabbi Shimon Schwab

הַזּוֹכֵר He, mindful of those who are mindful of Him,
  each generation and its sainted martyrs,
  ever since first He chose us;
  may He remember the fate that befell the last generation.
  Woe! What has befallen us!
  All who were swept away in the deluge of blood,
  whose lives were lost, drowned in the valleys of tears –
  may God remember them in the lands of eternal life.
  May their memory be a blessing.

שְׂאוּ Lift up your hands to Him – alas, O ye heavens!
  Alas for the best among Yisrael's tribes,
  communities, congregations, towns and districts,
  brotherhoods, institutions, houses of God!
  Would that streams could flow from my eyes,
  joining the torrents of tears
  already shed for the millions of dead
  consumed in the fires of terror and ruin.

וְעַל For the princes of Torah, pillars of tradition,
  for the flower of priestly youth,
  for the scholars, the teachers, men and women,
  and for the precious young in the houses of study.
  The pious daughters, grandfathers, grandmothers,
  and their progeny, infants newborn,
  all of them – thousands upon thousands,
  beloved in life, in death not divided.

אֶת Search Thou for their blood!
  Remember each driven leaf,
  each life wiped out in the Holocaust –
  six million struck dead by lightning,
  in the storm that felled fully one-third
  of the precious stock from the vineyard so dearly beloved by Thee.
  O Avenger of innocent blood, erase not the tale of their pain
  from the record Thou hast inscribed.

קינות על קדושי השואה
47
קינה על החורבן האחרון
מאת הרב שמעון שוואב, אב״ד דקהל עדת ישורון, ניו יורק

הַזוֹכֵר מַזְכִּירָיו, דוֹר דוֹר וּקְדוֹשָׁיו, מֵעֵת אֲשֶׁר אָז בְּחַרְתָּנוּ
יִזְכּוֹר דְּרָאוֹן, שֶׁל דּוֹר אַחֲרוֹן, אוֹיָה מֶה הָיָה לָנוּ
שְׁטוּפֵי מַבּוּל דָּם, שֶׁמָּסְרוּ נַפְשׁוֹתָם, כָּל שְׁקוּעֵי עִמְקֵי הַבָּכָא
יִפְקְדֵם אֱלֹהִים, בְּאַרְצוֹת הַחַיִּים, וַעֲדֵי עַד זִכְרָם לִבְרָכָה.

שְׂאוּ אֵלָיו כַּפַּיִם, אֲהָהּ אֵי שָׁמַיִם, הוֹי עַל מֵיטַב שִׁבְטֵי יִשְׂרָאֵל
עֵדוֹת וּקְהִלּוֹת, עָרִים וּגְלִילוֹת, חֲבוּרוֹת, מוֹסָדוֹת, כָּל מוֹעֲדֵי אֵל
מִי יִתֵּן פַּלְגֵי מַיִם, תֵּרַדְנָה עֵינַיִם, אֶל אֲשְׁדוֹת נַחֲלֵי הַדְּמָעוֹת
עֲלֵי אַלְפֵי אֲלָפִים, גּוּפִים נִשְׂרָפִים, בְּמוֹ אֵשׁ הַחֻרְבָּן וּזְוָעוֹת.

וְעַל שָׂרֵי הַתּוֹרָה, וּמַחֲזִיקֵי מְסוֹרָה, וְעַל פִּרְחֵי הַכְּהֻנָּה הַצְּעִירִים
וְעַל חוֹבְשֵׁי מִדְרָשׁוֹת, מוֹרִים וּמוֹרוֹת, תִּינוֹקוֹת בֵּית רַבָּן יַקִּירִים
עַל בָּנוֹת בּוֹטְחוֹת, סָבִים וְסָבוֹת, וְעַל זֶרַע וְטַפָּם שֶׁיִּלְדוּ
וְגַם לְרִבּוֹת, וּרְבָבוֹת, נֶאֱהָבִים בַּחַיִּים, בְּמוֹתָם לֹא נִפְרָדוּ.

אֶת דָּמָם דְּרשׁ, כִּי תִשָּׂא אֶת ראשׁ, שֶׁל כָּל נִדָּף לְעָלִים הַטְּרוּפִים
כָּל נַפְשׁוֹת מֵת, בִּימֵי שֶׁבֶר וָשֵׁאת, שִׁשָּׁה אַלְפֵי פְּעָמִים אֲלָפִים
שְׁלִישִׁיָּה לַבְּעֵר, בִּבְרַק זַעַם סוֹעֵר, מִכַּרְמֵי הַחֶמֶד אֲהַבְתָּ
גּוֹאֵל הַדָּם, נָא זְכֹר צַעֲרָם, אַל תִּמְחֶה מִסְפַּר כְּתֻבַּת.

זְכֹר Remember each moan, each heart-rending scream
as they went to the slaughter;
rivers of blood, tear-drenched faces – let them not be forgotten!
The shrieks, the groans, the piercing cries
as wild dogs tore into soft flesh –
Remember them! Count them! Gather them up in Thy bond
until the day of Thy vengeance
for the shame of downtrodden.

בְּמַחֲנוֹת Camps of barbarians: pain and disease,
anguish of ravaged souls,
insults and sneers, spittle and shame,
searing wounds from merciless whips;
hunger, thirst, madness, torture –
the stumbling of the faint whose strength was gone;
death-rattle of each life draining away in agony –
far be it from Thee ever to forget!

וְתִימָרוֹת The chimneys – thick smoke from the furnaces,
bones and limbs piled high, halls of poison –
moans and screams of multitudes
choking in gas chambers; the stench of corpses;
dead bundles of skin and bones,
food for the soil of the hangmen;
how the tormentors turned human fat into soap,
and skin into ornaments for their women!

וּקְרִיצַת Flicks of the fingers of brutal taskmasters:
To the right – slave labor! To the left – the shadow of death!
Shots of the savage marksmen
felling the hapless who dug their own graves,
to be buried, bodies still twitching in final agony.
Our sisters raped, our daughters made barren;
draughts of poison from evil physicians,
fugitives hiding in holes and bunkers,
their children abandoned in soul-snatchers' homes!

שֶׂה Lambs without blemish –
blood of our captive children offered upon the great altar –
Alas, Thy loving servants' lifeless flesh!
Who could count the saintly flock?
May their light be unfailing, for they have stood Thy test;

זְכֹר הַנְּאָקוֹת, וְרַעַשׁ צְעָקוֹת, אָז יוּבְלוּ לָרֶצַח
יְאוֹרֵי דְמֵיהֶם, וְדִמְעוֹת פְּנֵיהֶם, לֹא תִשָּׁכַחְנָה לָנֶצַח
כָּל חִיל וּגְנִיחָה, וּנְהִי צְרִיחָה, מִשַּׁדּוּדֵי לַהֲקוֹת הַכְּלָבִים
זְכֹר וּסְפֹר, בְּנֹאדְךָ צְרֹר, עַד עֵת נְקֹם עֶלְבּוֹן עֲלוּבִים.

בְּמַחֲנוֹת הַפְּרָאִים, כְּאֵב וּנְגָעִים, וּפַחֵי נְפָשׁוֹת עֲגוּמוֹת
חֲרָפוֹת וּצְחוֹק, כַּלְמוֹת וָרֹק, פִּצְעֵי הֲכָאוֹת אֲיֻמּוֹת
וּרְעָבוֹן, צִמָּאוֹן, שִׁגָּעוֹן, עִצָּבוֹן, וְכִשָּׁלוֹן נֶחֱלָשִׁים בְּלִי כֹחַ
וְכָל נַאֲקוֹת חָלָל, מִכָּל יָחִיד אֻמְלָל, חָלִילָה לְךָ מִלִּשְׁכֹּחַ.

וְתִימְרוֹת עָשָׁן, וְקִיטּוֹר מִכִּבְשָׁן, תִּלֵּי תִלִּים עֲצָמוֹת וְגִידִים
וְחַדְרֵי הָרַעַל, קוֹל שְׁאָגוֹת מִקָּהָל, הַנֶּחְנָקִים תּוֹךְ תָּאֵי הָאֵדִים
וְסִרְחוֹן גּוּפוֹת, וּגְוִיּוֹת סְגוּפוֹת, גַּלַּל דְּמֵן אַדְמַת נוֹאָצִים
אֵיךְ הָפְכוּ טוֹרְפֵיהֶם, לְבוֹרִית חֶלְבֵּיהֶם, וְעוֹר אִישׁ לְקִשּׁוּטֵי הַנָּשִׁים.

וּקְרִיעַת אֶצְבָּעוֹת, שֶׁל רָאשֵׁי הַפְּרָעוֹת, לְיָמִין שֶׁעֲבוּד פֶּרֶךְ, צַלְמָוֶת לִשְׂמֹאל
וְאֵיךְ יָרוּ יְרִיּוֹת, עַל חוֹפְרֵי הַבּוֹרוֹת, בְּיִסּוּרֵי חִבּוּט קֶבֶר הוֹרִידוּם שְׁאוֹל
אֵיךְ עִנּוּ אֲחִיּוֹתֵינוּ, וְסֵרְסוּ בְּנוֹתֵינוּ, כּוֹסוֹת תַּרְעֵלָה מִידֵי רוֹפְאִים אַכְזָרִים
וּפְלִיטֵי הַשְּׂרִידִים, בִּמְחִלּוֹת וּסְתָרִים, וְטִמְיוֹן יְלָדִים בְּבָתֵּי שְׁמָד כְּמָרִים.

שֶׂה תָמִים לְעוֹלָה, דַּם בְּנֵי הַגּוֹלָה, הוֹי אֲרִיאֵל מְנֻבֶּלֶת חֲסִידֶיךָ
צֹאן קָדָשִׁים מִי יִמְנֶה, אֲשֶׁר אִשָּׁם לֹא תִכְבֶּה, בְּחוּנֶיךָ הָיוּ מְקַדְּשֵׁי שְׁמֶךָ

They hallowed thy Name; proclaiming, "Shema Yisrael!"
They gave up their lives for God
so that He might gather them in.
Believing in His justice until the last,
singing Ani Ma'amin, proud hymn of eternal faith.

וּבְכֵן We are still here: a people bereft, bewildered like orphans,
no graves at which to pray;
no tombstones at which to shed the tears from our seared hearts.
The blood of their sacrifice their only memorial,
blood which will seethe forever, never to be forgotten;
the mountains of ashes their last offering –
the ash-heaps at the altars
their tribute for all time to come.

מִי Who could retell Yisrael's pain – minds dazed with grief,
shattered remnants of former glory;
its greatness crushed –
O living, merciful God!
Comfort Thy flock which yearns for Thee.
Cause a new light to shine,
rays of new glory,
and may the spirit of God rest upon us once more.

Kina 48 starts on page 626.

בְּקוֹל שְׁמַע יִשְׂרָאֵל, מָסְרוּ נֶפֶשׁ לָאֵל, שֶׁהוּא יְאַסְּפֵם, וְעַד יוֹם אַחֲרוֹן
הַצְדִּיקוּ דִין, וְאַף אֲנִי מַאֲמִין עָנָו, וְשָׁרוּ שִׁירַת בִּטָּחוֹן.

וּבְכֵן נִשְׁאַר עָם, כְּיַתּוֹם נִדְהָם, בְּלִי קְבָרִים לְהִשְׁתַּטֵּחַ
וְלֹא מַצֵּבוֹת, אֵיפֹה לִבְכּוֹת, יְבָבוֹת לֵבָב רוֹתֵחַ
רַק נִסְכֵי הַדָּם, אַזְכָּרוֹתָם, תּוֹסְסִים בְּלִי שׁוֹכֵחַ
וַהֲרֵי אֶפְרֵי עֲקֵדָתָם, תְּרוּמוֹת דִּשְׁנֵי מִזְבֵּחַ.

מִי יְמַלֵּל, צַעַר יִשְׂרָאֵל, אֲשֶׁר דַּעְתּוֹ מִכְּאֵב נִטְרֶפֶת
וּשְׁאֵרִית הַפְּאֵר, כִּמְעַט מִזְעֵיר, וְאֵיךְ קוֹמָתָהּ הַיּוֹם נִכְפֶּפֶת
אֵל חַי מְרַחֵם, עֲדָתְךָ נַחֵם, אֲשֶׁר לְךָ מְאֹד נִכְסֶפֶת
אוֹר חָדָשׁ תָּזְרִיחַ, קַרְנֵי הוֹד תַּצְמִיחַ, וְרוּחַ אֱלֹהִים מְרַחֶפֶת.

Kina 48 starts on page 627.

48

*In Memory of the Martyrs of the European Ḥurban
by Rabbi Shlomo Halberstam, the Bobover Rebbe*

זִכְרוּ Always remember, and mourn all of Israel,
    let your voices be heard on high.
  For Germany has destroyed our nation in the furious days of the war,
  with cruel and unusual deaths, by hunger and thirst;
  do not forget for all generations, until we merit consolation.

צַעֲקָתָם Their shouts and their cries, crowded into cattle cars
  like sheep to the slaughter, led to the crematoria.
  Let the sound of their pleas forever reverberate
    before the One who dwells on high,
  as they shouted out "Shema Yisrael" and martyred themselves for the
    Master of all Masters.

רָאשֵׁי Revered teachers of Yeshivot and their prize students, and the multitudes
    of the nation,
  were enslaved, inhumanly tortured, and murdered with no compunction.
  The blood of young children cries out to You from the ground;
  avenge the infants and the women! Spare no soul among Your enemies.

עַל For the burning of countless houses of study and prayer,
  tens of thousands of Torah scrolls and Torah scholars,
  we will eulogize with songs of desolation.
  They set fire to sanctuaries of God, set the pyres as we looked on.
  The arsonists must pay for their arson!
    He will pass judgment on the nations so full of corpses.

זַעֲקוּ Cry out, Heaven and Earth, for the thousands of towns,
    fortresses of Torah,
  each European country and its communities,
    observers of our sacred tradition,
  for the righteous, the elders, the devout who clung to their pure faith.
  From the day we were exiled from our homeland we have not experienced
    such catastrophe.

רַחֵם Have mercy on the remnants of our nation. Look down from heaven
  upon the holy camps, ten times the number of those
    redeemed from Egypt.
  Re-establish our Holy Sanctuary, redouble our solace:
  Lift us up, and bring us to Zion and Jerusalem.

Kina 49 starts on page 628.

48

קינה לזכרון הקדושים של חורבן יהודי אירופה
מאת הרב שלמה הלברשטם, האדמו"ר מבובוב

זִכְרוּ נָא וְקוֹנְנוּ כָּל יִשְׂרָאֵל, קוֹלְכֶם יִשָּׁמַע בָּרָמָה
כִּי הִשְׁמִידָה גֶּרְמַנְיָה אֶת עַמֵּנוּ בִּימֵי זַעַם הַמִּלְחָמָה
בְּמִיתוֹת מְשֻׁנּוֹת אַכְזָרִיּוֹת, בְּרָעָב וּבַצָּמָא
אַל תִּשָּׁכְחוּ בְּכָל הַדּוֹרוֹת, עֲדֵי תִּזְכּוּ לִרְאוֹת בַּנֶּחָמָה

צַעֲקָתָם וּבְכִיּוֹתֵיהֶם, צְפוּפִים וּסְגוּרִים בַּקְרוֹנִים
כַּצֹּאן לַטֶּבַח יוּבְלוּ לִשְׂרֵפָה בַּכִּבְשׁוֹנִים
קוֹל שַׁוְעָם יִזָּכֵר תָּמִיד לִפְנֵי שׁוֹכֵן מְעוֹנִים
בְּקָרְאָם שְׁמַע יִשְׂרָאֵל, מָסְרוּ נַפְשָׁם לַאֲדוֹנֵי הָאֲדוֹנִים

רָאשֵׁי יְשִׁיבוֹת וְתַלְמִידֵיהֶם, וַהֲמוֹנֵי עַמְּךָ שָׁמָּה
הֶעֱבִידוּם בְּעִנּוּיִים קָשִׁים, וַהֲרָגוּם בְּיָד רָמָה
דְּמֵי יְלָדִים רַכִּים צוֹעֲקִים אֵלֶיךָ מִן הָאֲדָמָה
נְקֹם נִקְמַת טַף וְנָשִׁים, לֹא תְחַיֶּה כָּל נְשָׁמָה

עַל שְׂרֵפַת אַלְפֵי מִדְרָשׁוֹת וּבָתֵּי כְנֵסִיּוֹת
רִבְבוֹת סִפְרֵי תוֹרָה וְלוֹמְדֶיהָ, נְקוֹנֵן בִּשְׁאִיּוֹת
שָׁלְחוּ בָאֵשׁ מִקְדְּשֵׁי אֵל, הִצִּיתוּ וְעֵינֵינוּ צוֹפִיּוֹת
יְשַׁלֵּם הַמַּבְעִיר אֶת הַבְּעֵרָה, יָדִין בַּגּוֹיִם מָלֵא גְוִיּוֹת

זָעֲקוּ שָׁמַיִם וַאֲדָמָה עַל אַלְפֵי עֲיָרוֹת מִבְצָרֵי תוֹרָה
אַרְצוֹת אֵירוֹפָּה וּקְהִלּוֹתֶיהָ, נוֹחֲלֵי וּמְקִימֵי מְסוֹרָה
צַדִּיקִים זְקֵנִים וַחֲסִידִים, דְּבֵקֵי אֱמוּנָה טְהוֹרָה
מִיּוֹם גָּלִינוּ מֵאַרְצֵנוּ, לֹא הָיָה כָזֶה כִּלָּיוֹן נוֹרָא

רַחֵם עַל שְׁאֵרִיתֵנוּ, הַבֶּט נָא מִשָּׁמַיִם
לְמַחֲנוֹת הַקְּדוֹשִׁים, פִּי עֶשֶׂר כְּיוֹצְאֵי מִצְרַיִם
קוֹמֵם בֵּית קָדְשֵׁנוּ, וְנַחֲמֵנוּ בְּכִפְלַיִם
רוֹמְמֵנוּ, וַהֲבִיאֵנוּ לְצִיּוֹן וִירוּשָׁלָיִם.

49

Eli, Eli
(Lament, Lament)
by Yehuda Leib Bialer

אֱלִי Lament, lament, my soul; cry out
and mourn, O Daughter of Israel,
in eulogy, in howls of grief,
for the flames have consumed Israel.

עַל For the genocide, so carefully planned;
O pangs of grief for the cascades of blood –
none were spared, not old, not young;
all were sacrificed – holy and pure.

עַל For the newborn babes, for the nursing infants,
crushed and dismembered against the cruel stones.
For their blood that flowed in the apathetic streets,
as helpless parents looked on in defeat.

עַל For the holy communities, wiped away;
for the houses of prayer and study,
consumed in flames, in burning pyres,
majestic centers of Jewish life.

עֲלֵי For the generations that were cut down,
blood of the fathers with blood of the sons.
In the killing fields of Auschwitz they were expunged,
in the furnaces of the crematoria.

עֲלֵי For the imprisoned, O God, clothed only in rags,
expiring in droves, in multitudes;
in Treblinka and Majdanek,
their bones were scattered, left to rot.

49

"אֵלִי, אֵלִי"
מאת יהודה לייב ביאלר

אֵלִי, אֵלִי, נַפְשִׁי, בְּכִי
וְזַעֲקִי, בַּת יִשְׂרָאֵל
מִסְפֵּד שְׂאִי וְהִתְיַפְּחִי
אָכְלָה הָאֵשׁ בְּיִשְׂרָאֵל.

עַל טֶבַח עַם, אֲשֶׁר הוּכַן
יִסּוּרֵי שְׁכוֹל, אַשְׁדּוֹת דָּמִים
זָקֵן גַּם טַף לֹא רֻחַם
עַל עֲקֵדָה קָרְבָּן תָּמִים.

עַל עוֹלָלִים, גְּמוּלֵי חָלָב
הַמְרֻטָּשִׁים לְפִי צוּרִים
וְעַל דָּמָם, אֲשֶׁר זָב
בְּרֹאשׁ חוּצוֹת לְעֵין הוֹרִים.

עַל הַקְּהִלּוֹת הַשּׁוֹמֵמוֹת
וְעַל חֻרְבַּן מִקְדְּשֵׁי אֵל
יְקוֹדֵי לַהַב שַׁלְהָבוֹת
עָרֵי פְּאֵר בְּיִשְׂרָאֵל.

עֲלֵי דוֹרוֹת אֲשֶׁר נִגְדְּעוּ
דְּמֵי אָבוֹת עַל דְּמֵי בָנִים
בְּגֵיא אוֹשְׁוִיץ תַּמּוּ גָּוְעוּ
עֲלֵי מוֹקְדוֹת הַכִּבְשָׁנִים

עֲלֵי כְלוּאִים, חֲגוּרֵי שַׂק
הַנִּמְקִים בְּרִבְבוֹתֵיהֶם
בְּטְרֶבְּלִינְקִי וּמַיְדָנֶק
וְאֵין מְלַקֵּט עַצְמוֹתֵיהֶם.

עָלַי For the cattle cars, crammed with human cargo
   that were cushioned with nothing but tar and chalk.
   Bleached by thirst, their souls parched and dry,
   they called for water; no hand reached out.

עָלַי For the young girls whose strength gave out,
   young wives who took their own lives.
   The ninety-three pure souls who acted as one,
   preferred a pure death to a life of shame.

עָלַי For those frozen in fields of snow,
   young children in their mothers' arms.
   For the martyrs whose wailing could be heard,
   buried alive in the communal graves.

עָלַי For the sacred scrolls defiled and torn,
   stained by the Nazi hands – those profaners of God.
   They lay in tatters, disgraced and abused;
   none came to protect their dignity.

עָלַי For the righteous ones, the humblest ones,
   the noble ones, immersed in Torah.
   In the poisoned chambers their voices were stilled;
   all is dark, even the sacred Menora.

עָלַי For the cadets, the nation's youth,
   the front lines of battle, lions of rebellion:
   In the face of the wicked, the spillers of their blood,
   they breathed fire, poured out their wrath.

עַל By the rivers of blood and tears,
   vengeance yet burned in their hearts.
   In the battle of the ghetto, fearless and true,
   their courage shone through, a beacon of valor.

עֲלֵי קְרוֹנוֹת, צְפוּפֵי אָדָם
אֲשֶׁר רֻפְּדוּ גָפְרִית וָסִיד
צְחֵי צָמָא, כִּכְלוֹת נַפְשָׁם
צָעֲקוּ מַיִם וְאֵין מוֹשִׁיט.

עֲלֵי בָנוֹת, אֲשֶׁר עֻלְּפוּ
רְעָיוֹת בְּנַפְשָׁן שָׁלְחוּ יָדָן
צ"ג הַטְּהוֹרוֹת יַחְדָּו נִסְפּוּ
וְלֹא חֻלַּל תֹּם כְּבוֹדָן.

עֲלֵי קְפוּאִים בִּשְׂדוֹת שְׁלָגִים
יְלָדִים רַכִּים בְּחֵיק אִמָּהוֹת
וְעַל קְדוֹשִׁים הַשּׁוֹאֲגִים
קְבוּרֵי חַיִּים מִתּוֹךְ בּוֹרוֹת.

עֲלֵי גְוִילִים הַמְחֻלָּלִים
בִּידֵי נָאֲצִים מְנַאֲצֵי אֵל
טְרוּפִים, קְרוּעִים וּמְגֹאָלִים
בֵּין אַשְׁפַּתּוֹת וְאֵין גּוֹאֵל.

עַל צַדִּיקִים, עַנְוֵי עוֹלָם
נְדִיבֵי עָם, הוֹגֵי תוֹרָה
בְּתָאֵי רַעַל נֶחֱנַק קוֹלָם
נָפְלָה, כָּבְתָה הַמְּנוֹרָה.

עֲלֵי נֹעַר פִּרְחֵי הָעָם
חֲלוּצֵי קְרָב, כְּפִירֵי מְרִי
מוּל זְדוֹנִים שׁוֹפְכֵי הַדָּם
הִשְׁתַּלְהֲבוּ רִשְׁפֵּי חֳרִי.

עַל נַהֲרוֹת דָּם וּבְכִי
נִקְמַת בְּרִית בַּלֵּב שְׁמוּרָה
בִּקְרָב גֶּטוֹ לְלֹא רְהִי
נֶחְשַׂף הָעֹז טְמִיר גְּבוּרָה.

עָלַי For the sanctity of God and Nation,
  in the name of the blood of the innocent,
  they steeled themselves, and gave their lives,
  they fought and fell, a heroic death.

עֲלֵה Arise, Hero, on an eternal mount,
  as the everlasting light of the new dawn,
  each drop of blood, each sacrifice,
  will be remembered for all time.

עַל For the decimation of a nation we raise a dirge,
  bound up in sorrow, cloaked in destruction.
  Will hatred's shadow forever reign?
  Will the struggle never end?

רְאֵה See, O God, how my skin has shriveled;
  my heart is broken as my enemies rise up.
  Hear my plea, provide a haven;
  Save my soul from the murderous mob.

אֱלִי Lament, lament, my soul; cry out
  and mourn, O Daughter of Israel,
  in eulogy, in howls of grief,
  for the flames have consumed Israel.

Kina 50 starts on page 634.

עֲלֵי קְדוֹשׁ הַשֵּׁם וָעָם
וְעַל נִקְמַת דַּם טְהוֹרִים
בְּתַעֲצוּמוֹת מָסְרוּ נַפְשָׁם
לָחֲמוּ, נָפְלוּ הַגִּבּוֹרִים.

עֲלֵה גִבּוֹר עַל בָּמֳתֵי עַד
כְּנֵר תָּמִיד בְּהוֹד זַרְחִים
כָּל נֵטֶף דָּם, קָרְבָּן לְשַׁד
נִזְכֹּר עַד נֵצַח נְצָחִים.

עַל שֶׁבֶר עַם נָשָׂא קִינָה
כְּבוּלֵי יָגוֹן, עֲטוּיֵי שׁוֹאָה
הֲלָנֶצַח תַּאֲפִיל שִׂנְאָה
וְלֹא תִפְרֹשׂ הַנְגָהָה?

רְאֵה, אֱלֹהִים, עוֹרִי צָפַד
נָפַל לִבִּי, שׂוֹנְאַי קָמִים
הַקְשִׁיבָה שַׁוְעִי, חִישָׁה מִפְלָט
הַצִּילָה נַפְשִׁי מֵאַנְשֵׁי דָמִים.

אֵלִי, אֵלִי, נַפְשִׁי, בְּכִי
וְזַעֲקִי, בַּת יִשְׂרָאֵל
מִסְפֵּד שְׂאִי וְהִתְיַפְּחִי
אָכְלָה הָאֵשׁ בְּיִשְׂרָאֵל.

Kina 50 starts on page 635.

50

*In Memory of Our Six Million Martyrs Who Perished during 1939–1945
by Rabbi Abraham Rosenfeld*

א Alas, how You have cast down the glory from our heads.
א Alas, how You have kept Your face hidden from us.
א Alas, how You have grown angry and refused to show compassion.

ב With a broken, heavy heart, on a day of fasting and commemoration,
ב we have come before You to eulogize and shed tears,
  in elegies and wailing,
ב as we recall the martyrs of the Holocaust, 1939–1945.

ג You have smashed the glory of Jacob that You once loved.
ג You have cut down those men of stature and
  laid low those who were once high.
ג You rendered our vines desolate and left our figs trees to be ravaged.

ד Our bones stuck to our skin and flesh.
ד You abased our lives into the dirt.
ד Our souls have given out from sorrow and groaning.

ה The beloved ones, the pleasing ones, the honest and the innocent
ה were loaded up into cattle cars like sheep.
ה The heat was stifling and the doorways were sealed.

ו Pious individuals sat silent on the ground
ו asking what their sin was,
ו and why judgment was passed without any pity.

ז Recall the screams of the humble,
ז the shouts of the orphans, the lonely and abandoned,
ז the mocking of the wise, and their beloved students.

ח Soldiers, mighty heads of households,
ח murdered and pierced, they fell by the millions,
ח bringing shame and desolation upon the nations.

50

קינה לשש מאות ריבוא קדושי שואת תרצ״ט-תש״ה
מאת הרב אברהם רוזנפלד

אֵיכָה תִּפְאַרְתֵּנוּ מֵרָאשֵׁינוּ הִשְׁלַכְתָּ
אֵיכָה פָּנֶיךָ מִמֶּנּוּ הִסְתַּרְתָּ
אֵיכָה קָצַפְתָּ וְלֹא חָמַלְתָּ:

בְּלֵב נִשְׁבָּר וְנִדְכֶּה, בְּיוֹם צוֹם וַעֲצָרָה
בָּאנוּ לְפָנֶיךָ לִסְפֹּד וְלִבְכּוֹת בְּקִינָה וּבִילָלָה
בְּזָכְרֵנוּ אֶת קְדוֹשֵׁי הַשּׁוֹאָה תרצ״ט-תש״ה:

גְּאוֹן יַעֲקֹב אֲשֶׁר אָהַבְתָּ שִׁבַּרְתָּ.
גָּדַעְתָּ רָמֵי הַקּוֹמָה, וְהַגְּבֹהִים הִשְׁפַּלְתָּ
גִּפְּנֵנוּ לְשַׁמָּה וּתְאֵנָתֵנוּ לִקְצָפָה שַׂמְתָּ:

דָּבְקוּ עַצְמֵינוּ לְעוֹרֵנוּ וּבְשָׂרֵנוּ
דָּכֹה דֻּכָּה דְּבֵית לָאָרֶץ חַיֵּינוּ
דָּלְפָה מִתּוּגָה וַאֲנָחָה נַפְשֵׁנוּ:

הַנֶּאֱהָבִים וְהַנְּעִימִים, הַיְשָׁרִים וְהַתְּמִימִים
הִטְעֲנוּ בַּקְּרוֹנוֹת כִּכְבָשִׂים וּבְקָרִים
הַחֹם מַחֲנָק, וְהַפְּתָחִים חֲתוּמִים:

וַתִּיקִים יוֹשְׁבִים עַל הָאָרֶץ דּוֹמְמִים
וּמֶה הָיְתָה חַטָּאתָם, הֵם שׁוֹאֲלִים
וְלָמָּה נִגְזַר הַדִּין בְּלִי רַחֲמִים:

זְכוֹר תִּזְכֹּר אֶת צַעֲקַת הָעֲנִיִּים
זַעֲקַת הַיְתוֹמִים הַגַּלְמוּדִים וְהַנֶּעֱזָבִים
זִלְזוּל חֲכָמִים, וְתַלְמִידֵיהֶם הָאֲהוּבִים:

חֲיָלִים רָאשֵׁי בֵּית אָבוֹת גִּבּוֹרִים
חֲלָלִים וּמְדֻקָּרִים נָפְלוּ מִלְּיוֹנִים
חֶרְפָּה וּמְשַׁמָּה הָיְתָה לַגּוֹיִם:

ט We nurtured and multiplied, but the cruel one destroyed them.
ט They tore our young like wolves to spill their blood.
ט Whoever plotted the slaughter of six million?

י Life has been lowered into the afterlife,
to the sounds of "Shema Yisrael" and "Ani Ma'amin."
י Their souls gave out as they were adorned with tallit and tefillin.
י May the murderers be shamed and embarrassed
and become non-existent.

כ Our remnants and hearts have given out over the ruin of our lot.
כ We all raise our voices in lament as half our nation was lost.
כ For the Holocaust was equal to the burning of the House of our God.

ל To Auschwitz, Buchenwald, Bergen-Belsen, Dachau,
Majdanek and Treblinka,
ל they were taken away and pressed into gas chambers,
and burnt in the flames of the furnaces in shame.
ל The holy martyrs fought and fell as heroes in the Warsaw Ghetto.

מ From every corner their dried blood screams.
מ When shall an end be put to these mortal dangers?
מ Till when must we eulogize the holy martyrs in bitter lamentations?

נ The Nazis disgraced our covenant and Torah.
נ Those who shame You, fell upon us, and we cry our hearts out in fasting.
נ The crown of our heads has fallen, woe is our heritage.

ס The Torah scrolls were torn to pieces and defiled in their hands.
ס They scraped the flesh off our remnants,
and turned their skin into adornments.
ס Lament and don sackcloth, sing the praises of the martyrs
and their children.

ע Our eyes run with the blood of tears,
ע for the burning of the synagogues,
ע and the destruction of the schools and study halls.

פ They smashed our congregations and destroyed our communities.
פ Fear and trembling took hold of us.
פ Our faces were covered with shame in our time of trouble.

טִפְּחָנוּ וְרִבִּינוּ, הָאַכְזָר כֻּלָּם וַהֲשַׁמָּם
טָרוֹף טָרְפוּ כִּזְאֵבִים לִשְׁפֹּךְ דָּמָם
טֶבַח שֵׁשׁ מֵאוֹת רִבּוֹא מִי זָמָם:

יָרְדוּ חַיִּים שְׁאוֹלָה, בִּשְׁמַע יִשְׂרָאֵל וּבַאֲנִי מַאֲמִין
יָצְאוּ נִשְׁמוֹתֵיהֶם מְעֻטָּרִין בְּטַלִּית וּתְפִלִּין
יֻבְּשׁוּ וַיִּכָּלְמוּ וְיִהְיוּ כְּאַיִן הָרוֹצְחִין:

כָּלָה שְׁאֵרֵנוּ וּלְבָבֵנוּ עַל שֶׁבֶר חֶלְקֵנוּ
כֻּלָּנוּ נוֹשְׂאִים קִינָה בְּאָבְדָן חֲצִי עַמֵּנוּ
כִּי שְׁקוּלָה הַשּׁוֹאָה כִּשְׂרֵפַת בֵּית אֱלֹהֵינוּ:

לְאוֹשְׁוִיץ בּוּכֶנְוַולְד, בֶּרְגֶן־בֶּלְזֶן, דַּאכָאוּ, מַידַּנֶק וּטְרֶבְּלִינְקָה
לֻקְּחוּ וְהֻדְחֲקוּ בְּחַדְרֵי גַז, וְנִשְׂרְפוּ בְּמוֹקְדוֹת הַכִּבְשָׁנִים בְּחֶרְפָּה
לָחֲמוּ הַקְּדוֹשִׁים הַטְּהוֹרִים, וְנָפְלוּ כְּגִבּוֹרִים בְּגִיטוֹ וַרְשָׁה:

מִכָּל פִּנָּה זוֹעֲקִים דְּמֵיהֶם הַקְּרוּשִׁים
מָתַי יָבוֹא קֵץ לַפְּגָעִים הָאֲנוּשִׁים
מִסְפֵּד מַר וְקִינָה שְׂאוּ עַל הַקְּדוֹשִׁים:

נִאֲצוּ הַנּוֹאָצִים אֶת הַבְּרִית וְאֶת תּוֹרָתֵנוּ
נָפְלוּ עָלֵינוּ מְחָרְפֶיךָ, וַנִּבְכֶּה בַצּוֹם נַפְשֵׁנוּ
נָפְלָה עֲטֶרֶת רֹאשֵׁנוּ, אוֹי נָא לְנַחֲלָתֵנוּ:

סִפְרֵי תוֹרָה לִגְזָרִים קָרְעוּ וְטִמְּאוּ בִּידֵיהֶם
סָרְקוּ בְּשַׂר שְׁאֵרֵינוּ, וְעוֹרָם הָפְכוּ לְקִשּׁוּטֵיהֶם
סָפְדוּ וְחָגְרוּ שַׂק, וְהֵילִילוּ עֲלֵיהֶם וְעַל טַפֵּיהֶם:

עֵינֵינוּ זוֹלְגוֹת דַּם דְּמָעוֹת
עַל שְׂרֵפַת בָּתֵּי כְנֵסִיּוֹת
עַל הֲרִיסַת יְשִׁיבוֹת וּבָתֵּי מִדְרָשׁוֹת:

פָּרְצוּ קְהִלּוֹתֵינוּ וְהָרְסוּ עֲדָתֵנוּ
פַּחַד קְרָאָנוּ וּרְעָדָה אֲחָזַתְנוּ
פָּנֵינוּ כִּסְּתָה כְלִמָּה בְּצָרוֹתֵינוּ:

- צ They escaped to the wilderness in a time of want and famine.
- צ Those modest by nature tried their hand,
- צ but their voices were heard like the screams by the Sea of Reeds.

- ק Relatives, friends, beloved ones, the pious and honest,
- ק the holy and pure, they shine with the brilliance of heaven.
- ק Receive them and hide them in the folds of Your wings forever.

- ר O compassionate One, recall the remnants of Your heritage with pity.
- ר Master of the universe, remove all worry and sorrow
from the heart of Your nation.
- ר In Your anger, uproot the evil of the nations of the world
and those who hate Israel.

- ש Free the captives and break open the prison for those who are bound.
- ש Anoint us with joyous ointment in place of mourning.
- ש Bring peace and calm to us and our land.

- ת Raise up our glory and hasten our redemption in our days.
- ת May the plains of Jordan rejoice and may our
State of Israel bloom like a desert rose.
- ת Bless us by the grace of Abraham, Isaac and Jacob, our forefathers.

צִיָּה עָרְקוּ בְּחֶסֶר וּבְכָפָן
צְנוּעוֹת בְּנַפְשָׁן שָׁלְחוּ יָדָן
צְעָקָה בְּיָם סוּף נִשְׁמַע קוֹלָן:

קְרוֹבִים וִידִידִים חֲבִיבִים, חֲסִידִים וִישָׁרִים
קְדוֹשִׁים וּטְהוֹרִים, כְּזֹהַר הָרָקִיעַ מַזְהִירִים
קַבְּלֵם וְהַסְתִּירֵם בְּסֵתֶר כְּנָפֶיךָ לְעוֹלָמִים:

רַחוּם, זְכֹר בְּרַחֲמֶיךָ אֶת שְׁרִידֵי נַחֲלָתֶךָ
רִבּוֹן הָעוֹלָמִים, הָסֵר דְּאָגָה וְתוּגָה מֵעַמֶּךָ
רִשְׁעַת הַגּוֹיִם וְשׂוֹנְאֵי יִשְׂרָאֵל תַּעֲקֹר בְּזַעֲמֶךָ:

שְׁבוּיִם הַדְּרוֹר, וּפְקַח קוֹחַ לַאֲסוּרֵנוּ
שֶׁמֶן שָׂשׂוֹן תַּחַת אֵבֶל תַּעְטְרֵנוּ
שָׁלוֹם וְשַׁלְוָה תָּשִׂים לָנוּ וּלְאַרְצֵנוּ:

תָּרִים קַרְנֵנוּ וְתָחִישׁ גְּאֻלָּתֵנוּ בִּמְהֵרָה בְיָמֵינוּ
תָּגֵל עֲרָבָה וְתִפְרַח כַּחֲבַצֶּלֶת יִשְׂרָאֵל מְדִינָתֵנוּ
תְּבָרְכֵנוּ בְּבִרְכַּת אַבְרָהָם יִצְחָק וְיַעֲקֹב אֲבוֹתֵינוּ:

CONCLUSION OF THE SERVICE

אַשְׁרֵי Happy are those who dwell in Your House;   *Ps. 84*
they shall continue to praise You, Selah!
Happy are the people for whom this is so;   *Ps. 144*
happy are the people whose God is the LORD.
A song of praise by David.   *Ps. 145*

> I will exalt You, my God, the King, and bless Your name for ever and all time. Every day I will bless You, and praise Your name for ever and all time. God is great and greatly to be praised; His greatness is unfathomable. One generation will praise Your works to the next, and tell of Your mighty deeds. On the glorious splendor of Your majesty I will meditate, and on the acts of Your wonders. They shall talk of the power of Your awesome deeds, and I will tell of Your greatness. They shall recite the record of Your great goodness, and sing with joy of Your righteousness. The LORD is gracious and compassionate, slow to anger and great in loving-kindness. The LORD is good to all, and His compassion extends to all His works. All Your works shall thank You, LORD, and Your devoted ones shall bless You. They shall talk of the glory of Your kingship, and speak of Your might. To make known to mankind His mighty deeds and the glorious majesty of His kingship. Your kingdom is an everlasting kingdom, and Your reign is for all generations. The LORD supports all who fall, and raises all who are bowed down. All raise their eyes to You in hope, and You give them their food in due season. You open Your hand, and satisfy every living thing with Your favor. The LORD is righteous in all His ways, and kind in all He does. The LORD is close to all who call on Him, to all who call on Him in truth. He fulfills the will of those who revere Him; He hears their cry and saves them. The LORD guards all who love Him, but all the wicked He will destroy.
> ‣ My mouth shall speak the praise of the LORD, and all creatures shall bless His holy name for ever and all time.

We will bless the LORD now and for ever. Halleluya!   *Ps. 115*

סיום התפילה

אַשְׁרֵי יוֹשְׁבֵי בֵיתֶךָ, עוֹד יְהַלְלוּךָ סֶּלָה:
אַשְׁרֵי הָעָם שֶׁכָּכָה לּוֹ, אַשְׁרֵי הָעָם שֶׁיהוה אֱלֹהָיו:
תְּהִלָּה לְדָוִד
אֲרוֹמִמְךָ אֱלוֹהַי הַמֶּלֶךְ, וַאֲבָרְכָה שִׁמְךָ לְעוֹלָם וָעֶד:
בְּכָל־יוֹם אֲבָרְכֶךָּ, וַאֲהַלְלָה שִׁמְךָ לְעוֹלָם וָעֶד:
גָּדוֹל יהוה וּמְהֻלָּל מְאֹד, וְלִגְדֻלָּתוֹ אֵין חֵקֶר:
דּוֹר לְדוֹר יְשַׁבַּח מַעֲשֶׂיךָ, וּגְבוּרֹתֶיךָ יַגִּידוּ:
הֲדַר כְּבוֹד הוֹדֶךָ, וְדִבְרֵי נִפְלְאוֹתֶיךָ אָשִׂיחָה:
וֶעֱזוּז נוֹרְאוֹתֶיךָ יֹאמֵרוּ, וּגְדֻלָּתְךָ אֲסַפְּרֶנָּה:
זֵכֶר רַב־טוּבְךָ יַבִּיעוּ, וְצִדְקָתְךָ יְרַנֵּנוּ:
חַנּוּן וְרַחוּם יהוה, אֶרֶךְ אַפַּיִם וּגְדָל־חָסֶד:
טוֹב־יהוה לַכֹּל, וְרַחֲמָיו עַל־כָּל־מַעֲשָׂיו:
יוֹדוּךָ יהוה כָּל־מַעֲשֶׂיךָ, וַחֲסִידֶיךָ יְבָרְכוּכָה:
כְּבוֹד מַלְכוּתְךָ יֹאמֵרוּ, וּגְבוּרָתְךָ יְדַבֵּרוּ:
לְהוֹדִיעַ לִבְנֵי הָאָדָם גְּבוּרֹתָיו, וּכְבוֹד הֲדַר מַלְכוּתוֹ:
מַלְכוּתְךָ מַלְכוּת כָּל־עֹלָמִים, וּמֶמְשַׁלְתְּךָ בְּכָל־דּוֹר וָדֹר:
סוֹמֵךְ יהוה לְכָל־הַנֹּפְלִים, וְזוֹקֵף לְכָל־הַכְּפוּפִים:
עֵינֵי־כֹל אֵלֶיךָ יְשַׂבֵּרוּ, וְאַתָּה נוֹתֵן־לָהֶם אֶת־אָכְלָם בְּעִתּוֹ:
פּוֹתֵחַ אֶת־יָדֶךָ, וּמַשְׂבִּיעַ לְכָל־חַי רָצוֹן:
צַדִּיק יהוה בְּכָל־דְּרָכָיו, וְחָסִיד בְּכָל־מַעֲשָׂיו:
קָרוֹב יהוה לְכָל־קֹרְאָיו, לְכֹל אֲשֶׁר יִקְרָאֻהוּ בֶאֱמֶת:
רְצוֹן־יְרֵאָיו יַעֲשֶׂה, וְאֶת־שַׁוְעָתָם יִשְׁמַע, וְיוֹשִׁיעֵם:
שׁוֹמֵר יהוה אֶת־כָּל־אֹהֲבָיו, וְאֵת כָּל־הָרְשָׁעִים יַשְׁמִיד:
תְּהִלַּת יהוה יְדַבֶּר פִּי, וִיבָרֵךְ כָּל־בָּשָׂר שֵׁם קָדְשׁוֹ לְעוֹלָם וָעֶד:
וַאֲנַחְנוּ נְבָרֵךְ יָהּ מֵעַתָּה וְעַד־עוֹלָם, הַלְלוּיָהּ:

*On Tisha B'Av the verse beginning "As for Me," customarily
included in the following, is omitted.*

וּבָא לְצִיּוֹן גּוֹאֵל "A redeemer will come to Zion,   *Is. 59*
to those in Jacob who repent of their sins," declares the LORD.

▸ You are the Holy One, enthroned on the praises of Israel.   *Ps. 22*
And (the angels) call to one another, saying, "Holy, holy, holy   *Is. 6*
is the LORD of hosts. The whole earth is full of His glory."

And they receive permission from one another, saying: *Targum Yonatan*
"Holy in the highest heavens, home of His Presence; holy on earth,   *Is. 6*
the work of His strength; holy for ever and all time is the LORD of hosts; the
whole earth is full of His radiant glory."

▸ Then a wind lifted me up and I heard behind me the sound of a great   *Ezek. 3*
noise, saying, "Blessed is the LORD's glory from His place."

Then a wind lifted me up and I heard behind me   *Targum Yonatan*
the sound of a great tempest of those who uttered praise, saying,   *Ezek. 3*
"Blessed is the LORD's glory from the place of the home of His Presence."

The LORD shall reign for ever and all time.   *Ex. 15*
The LORD's kingdom is established for ever and all time.   *Targum Onkelos Ex. 15*

יהוה LORD, God of Abraham, Isaac and Yisrael, our ancestors, may You   *1 Chr. 29*
keep this for ever so that it forms the thoughts in Your people's heart, and
directs their heart toward You. He is compassionate. He forgives iniquity   *Ps. 78*
and does not destroy. Repeatedly He suppresses His anger, not rousing
His full wrath. For You, my LORD, are good and forgiving, abundantly   *Ps. 86*
kind to all who call on You. Your righteousness is eternally righteous, and   *Ps. 119*
Your Torah is truth. Grant truth to Jacob, loving-kindness to Abraham, as   *Mic. 7*
You promised our ancestors in ancient times. Blessed is my LORD for day   *Ps. 68*
after day He burdens us [with His blessings]; God is our salvation, Selah!
The LORD of hosts is with us; the God of Jacob is our refuge, Selah! LORD   *Ps. 46*
of hosts, happy is the one who trusts in You. LORD, save! May the King   *Ps. 84*
answer us on the day we call.   *Ps. 20*

בָּרוּךְ Blessed is He, our God, who created us for His glory, separating
us from those who go astray; who gave us the Torah of truth, planting
within us eternal life. May He open our heart to His Torah, imbuing our
heart with the love and awe of Him, that we may do His will and serve
Him with a perfect heart, so that we neither toil in vain nor give birth
to confusion.

On תשעה באב the verse beginning וַאֲנִי זֹאת בְּרִיתִי, customarily included in the following, is omitted.

ישעיה נט — וּבָא לְצִיּוֹן גּוֹאֵל, וּלְשָׁבֵי פֶשַׁע בְּיַעֲקֹב, נְאֻם יהוה:

תהלים כב / ישעיה ו — וְאַתָּה קָדוֹשׁ יוֹשֵׁב תְּהִלּוֹת יִשְׂרָאֵל: וְקָרָא זֶה אֶל־זֶה וְאָמַר ־ קָדוֹשׁ, קָדוֹשׁ, קָדוֹשׁ, יהוה צְבָאוֹת, מְלֹא כָל־הָאָרֶץ כְּבוֹדוֹ:

תרגום יונתן ישעיה ו — וּמְקַבְּלִין דֵּין מִן דֵּין וְאָמְרִין, קַדִּישׁ בִּשְׁמֵי מְרוֹמָא עִלָּאָה בֵּית שְׁכִינְתֵהּ קַדִּישׁ עַל אַרְעָא עוֹבַד גְּבוּרְתֵהּ, קַדִּישׁ לְעָלַם וּלְעָלְמֵי עָלְמַיָּא יהוה צְבָאוֹת, מַלְיָא כָל אַרְעָא זִיו יְקָרֵהּ.

יחזקאל ג — ־ וַתִּשָּׂאֵנִי רוּחַ, וָאֶשְׁמַע אַחֲרַי קוֹל רַעַשׁ גָּדוֹל ־ בָּרוּךְ כְּבוֹד־יהוה מִמְּקוֹמוֹ:

תרגום יונתן יחזקאל ג — וּנְטָלַתְנִי רוּחָא, וּשְׁמָעִית בַּתְרַי קָל זִיעַ סַגִּיא, דִּמְשַׁבְּחִין וְאָמְרִין בְּרִיךְ יְקָרָא דַיהוה מֵאֲתַר בֵּית שְׁכִינְתֵהּ.

שמות טו — יהוה יִמְלֹךְ לְעֹלָם וָעֶד:

תרגום אונקלוס שמות טו — יהוה מַלְכוּתֵהּ קָאֵם לְעָלַם וּלְעָלְמֵי עָלְמַיָּא.

דברי הימים א׳ כט — יהוה אֱלֹהֵי אַבְרָהָם יִצְחָק וְיִשְׂרָאֵל אֲבֹתֵינוּ, שָׁמְרָה־זֹּאת לְעוֹלָם לְיֵצֶר מַחְשְׁבוֹת לְבַב עַמֶּךָ, וְהָכֵן לְבָבָם אֵלֶיךָ:
תהלים עח — וְהוּא רַחוּם יְכַפֵּר עָוֹן וְלֹא־יַשְׁחִית, וְהִרְבָּה לְהָשִׁיב אַפּוֹ, וְלֹא־יָעִיר כָּל־חֲמָתוֹ:
תהלים פו — כִּי־אַתָּה אֲדֹנָי טוֹב וְסַלָּח, וְרַב־חֶסֶד לְכָל־קֹרְאֶיךָ:
תהלים קיט — צִדְקָתְךָ צֶדֶק לְעוֹלָם וְתוֹרָתְךָ אֱמֶת:
מיכה ז — תִּתֵּן אֱמֶת לְיַעֲקֹב, חֶסֶד לְאַבְרָהָם, אֲשֶׁר־נִשְׁבַּעְתָּ לַאֲבֹתֵינוּ מִימֵי קֶדֶם:
תהלים סח — בָּרוּךְ אֲדֹנָי יוֹם יוֹם יַעֲמָס־לָנוּ, הָאֵל יְשׁוּעָתֵנוּ סֶלָה:
תהלים מו / תהלים פד — יהוה צְבָאוֹת עִמָּנוּ, מִשְׂגָּב־לָנוּ אֱלֹהֵי יַעֲקֹב סֶלָה: יהוה צְבָאוֹת,
תהלים כ — אַשְׁרֵי אָדָם בֹּטֵחַ בָּךְ: יהוה הוֹשִׁיעָה, הַמֶּלֶךְ יַעֲנֵנוּ בְיוֹם־קָרְאֵנוּ:

בָּרוּךְ הוּא אֱלֹהֵינוּ שֶׁבְּרָאָנוּ לִכְבוֹדוֹ, וְהִבְדִּילָנוּ מִן הַתּוֹעִים, וְנָתַן לָנוּ תּוֹרַת אֱמֶת, וְחַיֵּי עוֹלָם נָטַע בְּתוֹכֵנוּ. הוּא יִפְתַּח לִבֵּנוּ בְּתוֹרָתוֹ, וְיָשֵׂם בְּלִבֵּנוּ אַהֲבָתוֹ וְיִרְאָתוֹ וְלַעֲשׂוֹת רְצוֹנוֹ וּלְעָבְדוֹ בְּלֵבָב שָׁלֵם, לְמַעַן לֹא נִיגַע לָרִיק וְלֹא נֵלֵד לַבֶּהָלָה.

יְהִי רָצוֹן May it be Your will, O Lord our God and God of our ancestors, that we keep Your laws in this world, and thus be worthy to live, see and inherit goodness and blessing in the Messianic Age and in the life of the World to Come. So that my soul may sing to You and not be silent. *Ps. 30* Lord, my God, for ever I will thank You. Blessed is the man who trusts *Jer. 17* in the Lord, whose trust is in the Lord alone. Trust in the Lord for *Is. 26* evermore, for God the Lord is an everlasting Rock. ▸ Those who know *Ps. 9* Your name trust in You, for You, Lord, do not forsake those who seek You. The Lord desired, for the sake of Israel's merit, to make the Torah *Is. 42* great and glorious.

FULL KADDISH

Leader: **יִתְגַּדַּל** Magnified and sanctified may His great name be,
in the world He created by His will.
May He establish His kingdom in your lifetime
and in your days, and in the lifetime of all the house of Israel,
swiftly and soon – and say: Amen.

All: May His great name be blessed for ever and all time.

Leader: Blessed and praised,
glorified and exalted,
raised and honored,
uplifted and lauded be
the name of the Holy One,
blessed be He, beyond any blessing,
song, praise and consolation uttered in the world –
and say: Amen.

The verse "May the prayers and pleas of all Israel" is omitted.

May there be great peace from heaven,
and life for us and all Israel –
and say: Amen.

*Bow, take three steps back, as if taking leave of the Divine Presence,
then bow, first left, then right, then center, while saying:*

May He who makes peace in His high places,
make peace for us and all Israel – and say: Amen.

יְהִי רָצוֹן מִלְּפָנֶיךָ יהוה אֱלֹהֵינוּ וֵאלֹהֵי אֲבוֹתֵינוּ, שֶׁנִּשְׁמֹר חֻקֶּיךָ בָּעוֹלָם הַזֶּה, וְנִזְכֶּה וְנִחְיֶה וְנִרְאֶה וְנִירַשׁ טוֹבָה וּבְרָכָה, לִשְׁנֵי יְמוֹת הַמָּשִׁיחַ וּלְחַיֵּי הָעוֹלָם הַבָּא. לְמַעַן יְזַמֶּרְךָ כָבוֹד וְלֹא יִדֹּם, יהוה אֱלֹהַי, לְעוֹלָם אוֹדֶךָּ: בָּרוּךְ הַגֶּבֶר אֲשֶׁר יִבְטַח בַּיהוה, וְהָיָה יהוה מִבְטַחוֹ: בִּטְחוּ בַיהוה עֲדֵי־עַד, כִּי בְּיָהּ יהוה צוּר עוֹלָמִים: ‣ וְיִבְטְחוּ בְךָ יוֹדְעֵי שְׁמֶךָ, כִּי לֹא־עָזַבְתָּ דֹרְשֶׁיךָ, יהוה: יהוה חָפֵץ לְמַעַן צִדְקוֹ, יַגְדִּיל תּוֹרָה וְיַאְדִּיר:

תהלים ל
ירמיה יז
ישעיה כו
תהלים ט
ישעיה מב

קדיש שלם

ש״ץ: יִתְגַּדַּל וְיִתְקַדַּשׁ שְׁמֵהּ רַבָּא (קהל: אָמֵן)
בְּעָלְמָא דִּי בְרָא כִרְעוּתֵהּ, וְיַמְלִיךְ מַלְכוּתֵהּ
בְּחַיֵּיכוֹן וּבְיוֹמֵיכוֹן וּבְחַיֵּי דְכָל בֵּית יִשְׂרָאֵל
בַּעֲגָלָא וּבִזְמַן קָרִיב, וְאִמְרוּ אָמֵן. (קהל: אָמֵן)

קהל
ויש״ץ: יְהֵא שְׁמֵהּ רַבָּא מְבָרַךְ לְעָלַם וּלְעָלְמֵי עָלְמַיָּא.

ש״ץ: יִתְבָּרַךְ וְיִשְׁתַּבַּח וְיִתְפָּאַר
וְיִתְרוֹמַם וְיִתְנַשֵּׂא וְיִתְהַדָּר וְיִתְעַלֶּה וְיִתְהַלָּל
שְׁמֵהּ דְּקֻדְשָׁא בְּרִיךְ הוּא (קהל: בְּרִיךְ הוּא)
לְעֵלָּא מִן כָּל בִּרְכָתָא וְשִׁירָתָא, תֻּשְׁבְּחָתָא וְנֶחֱמָתָא
דַּאֲמִירָן בְּעָלְמָא, וְאִמְרוּ אָמֵן. (קהל: אָמֵן)

The verse תתקבל is omitted.

יְהֵא שְׁלָמָא רַבָּא מִן שְׁמַיָּא
וְחַיִּים, עָלֵינוּ וְעַל כָּל יִשְׂרָאֵל, וְאִמְרוּ אָמֵן. (קהל: אָמֵן)

Bow, take three steps back, as if taking leave of the Divine Presence, then bow, first left, then right, then center, while saying:

עֹשֶׂה שָׁלוֹם בִּמְרוֹמָיו
הוּא יַעֲשֶׂה שָׁלוֹם עָלֵינוּ וְעַל כָּל יִשְׂרָאֵל, וְאִמְרוּ אָמֵן. (קהל: אָמֵן)

Stand while saying Aleinu. Bow at ˈ.

עָלֵינוּ It is our duty to praise the Master of all,
and ascribe greatness to the Author of creation,
who has not made us like the nations of the lands,
nor placed us like the families of the earth;
who has not made our portion like theirs,
nor our destiny like all their multitudes.
(For they worship vanity and emptiness,
and pray to a god who cannot save.)
ˈBut we bow in worship and thank the Supreme King of kings,
the Holy One, blessed be He,
who extends the heavens and establishes the earth,
whose throne of glory is in the heavens above,
and whose power's Presence is in the highest of heights.
He is our God; there is no other.
Truly He is our King, there is none else,
as it is written in His Torah:
"You shall know and take to heart this day that the Lord is God, *Deut. 4*
in heaven above and on earth below. There is no other."

Therefore, we place our hope in You, Lord our God,
that we may soon see the glory of Your power,
when You will remove abominations from the earth,
and idols will be utterly destroyed,
when the world will be perfected under the sovereignty of the Almighty,
when all humanity will call on Your name,
to turn all the earth's wicked toward You.
All the world's inhabitants will realize and know
that to You every knee must bow and every tongue swear loyalty.
Before You, Lord our God, they will kneel and bow down
and give honor to Your glorious name.
They will all accept the yoke of Your kingdom,
and You will reign over them soon and for ever.
For the kingdom is Yours, and to all eternity You will reign in glory,
as it is written in Your Torah: "The Lord will reign for ever and ever." *Ex. 15*
▸ And it is said: "Then the Lord shall be King over all the earth; *Zech. 14*
on that day the Lord shall be One and His name One."

Bow at ׳. *Stand while saying* עָלֵינוּ.

עָלֵינוּ לְשַׁבֵּחַ לַאֲדוֹן הַכֹּל, לָתֵת גְּדֻלָּה לְיוֹצֵר בְּרֵאשִׁית
שֶׁלֹּא עָשָׂנוּ כְּגוֹיֵי הָאֲרָצוֹת, וְלֹא שָׂמָנוּ כְּמִשְׁפְּחוֹת הָאֲדָמָה
שֶׁלֹּא שָׂם חֶלְקֵנוּ כָּהֶם וְגוֹרָלֵנוּ כְּכָל הֲמוֹנָם.
(שֶׁהֵם מִשְׁתַּחֲוִים לְהֶבֶל וָרִיק וּמִתְפַּלְלִים אֶל אֵל לֹא יוֹשִׁיעַ.)
וַאֲנַחְנוּ כּוֹרְעִים וּמִשְׁתַּחֲוִים וּמוֹדִים
לִפְנֵי מֶלֶךְ מַלְכֵי הַמְּלָכִים, הַקָּדוֹשׁ בָּרוּךְ הוּא
שֶׁהוּא נוֹטֶה שָׁמַיִם וְיוֹסֵד אָרֶץ, וּמוֹשַׁב יְקָרוֹ בַּשָּׁמַיִם מִמַּעַל
וּשְׁכִינַת עֻזּוֹ בְּגָבְהֵי מְרוֹמִים.
הוּא אֱלֹהֵינוּ, אֵין עוֹד.
אֱמֶת מַלְכֵּנוּ, אֶפֶס זוּלָתוֹ
כַּכָּתוּב בְּתוֹרָתוֹ

דברים ד

וְיָדַעְתָּ הַיּוֹם וַהֲשֵׁבֹתָ אֶל־לְבָבֶךָ
כִּי יהוה הוּא הָאֱלֹהִים בַּשָּׁמַיִם מִמַּעַל וְעַל־הָאָרֶץ מִתָּחַת, אֵין עוֹד:

עַל כֵּן נְקַוֶּה לְּךָ יהוה אֱלֹהֵינוּ, לִרְאוֹת מְהֵרָה בְּתִפְאֶרֶת עֻזֶּךָ
לְהַעֲבִיר גִּלּוּלִים מִן הָאָרֶץ, וְהָאֱלִילִים כָּרוֹת יִכָּרֵתוּן
לְתַקֵּן עוֹלָם בְּמַלְכוּת שַׁדַּי.
וְכָל בְּנֵי בָשָׂר יִקְרְאוּ בִשְׁמֶךָ לְהַפְנוֹת אֵלֶיךָ כָּל רִשְׁעֵי אָרֶץ.
יַכִּירוּ וְיֵדְעוּ כָּל יוֹשְׁבֵי תֵבֵל
כִּי לְךָ תִּכְרַע כָּל בֶּרֶךְ, תִּשָּׁבַע כָּל לָשׁוֹן.
לְפָנֶיךָ יהוה אֱלֹהֵינוּ יִכְרְעוּ וְיִפֹּלוּ, וְלִכְבוֹד שִׁמְךָ יְקָר יִתֵּנוּ
וִיקַבְּלוּ כֻלָּם אֶת עֹל מַלְכוּתֶךָ
וְתִמְלֹךְ עֲלֵיהֶם מְהֵרָה לְעוֹלָם וָעֶד.
כִּי הַמַּלְכוּת שֶׁלְּךָ הִיא וּלְעוֹלְמֵי עַד תִּמְלֹךְ בְּכָבוֹד
כַּכָּתוּב בְּתוֹרָתֶךָ, יהוה יִמְלֹךְ לְעֹלָם וָעֶד:

שמות טו

זכריה יד

‹ וְנֶאֱמַר, וְהָיָה יהוה לְמֶלֶךְ עַל־כָּל־הָאָרֶץ
בַּיּוֹם הַהוּא יִהְיֶה יהוה אֶחָד וּשְׁמוֹ אֶחָד:

Some add:

Have no fear of sudden terror or of the ruin when it overtakes the wicked. *Prov. 3*
Devise your strategy, but it will be thwarted; propose your plan, *Is. 8*
but it will not stand, for God is with us. When you grow old, I will still be the same. *Is. 46*
When your hair turns gray, I will still carry you. I made you, I will bear you,
I will carry you, and I will rescue you.

MOURNER'S KADDISH

The following prayer requires the presence of a minyan.
A transliteration can be found on page 792.

Mourner: יִתְגַּדַּל Magnified and sanctified
may His great name be,
in the world He created by His will.
May He establish His kingdom
in your lifetime and in your days,
and in the lifetime of all the house of Israel,
swiftly and soon –
and say: Amen.

All: May His great name be blessed for ever and all time.

Mourner: Blessed and praised, glorified and exalted,
raised and honored, uplifted and lauded
be the name of the Holy One, blessed be He,
beyond any blessing, song, praise and consolation
uttered in the world –
and say: Amen.

May there be great peace from heaven,
and life for us and all Israel –
and say: Amen.

Bow, take three steps back, as if taking leave of the Divine Presence,
then bow, first left, then right, then center, while saying:

May He who makes peace in His high places,
make peace for us and all Israel –
and say: Amen.

The Daily Psalm is said at Minḥa.

Some add:

אַל־תִּירָא מִפַּחַד פִּתְאֹם וּמִשֹּׁאַת רְשָׁעִים כִּי תָבֹא:
עֻצוּ עֵצָה וְתֻפָר, דַּבְּרוּ דָבָר וְלֹא יָקוּם, כִּי עִמָּנוּ אֵל:
וְעַד־זִקְנָה אֲנִי הוּא, וְעַד־שֵׂיבָה אֲנִי אֶסְבֹּל
אֲנִי עָשִׂיתִי וַאֲנִי אֶשָּׂא וַאֲנִי אֶסְבֹּל וַאֲמַלֵּט:

משלי ג
ישעיה ח
ישעיה מו

קדיש יתום

The following prayer requires the presence of a מנין.
A transliteration can be found on page 792.

אבל: יִתְגַּדַּל וְיִתְקַדַּשׁ שְׁמֵהּ רַבָּא (קהל: אָמֵן)
בְּעָלְמָא דִּי בְרָא כִרְעוּתֵהּ, וְיַמְלִיךְ מַלְכוּתֵהּ
בְּחַיֵּיכוֹן וּבְיוֹמֵיכוֹן וּבְחַיֵּי דְּכָל בֵּית יִשְׂרָאֵל
בַּעֲגָלָא וּבִזְמַן קָרִיב, וְאִמְרוּ אָמֵן. (קהל: אָמֵן)

קהל ואבל: יְהֵא שְׁמֵהּ רַבָּא מְבָרַךְ לְעָלַם וּלְעָלְמֵי עָלְמַיָּא.

אבל: יִתְבָּרַךְ וְיִשְׁתַּבַּח וְיִתְפָּאַר
וְיִתְרוֹמַם וְיִתְנַשֵּׂא וְיִתְהַדָּר וְיִתְעַלֶּה וְיִתְהַלָּל
שְׁמֵהּ דְּקֻדְשָׁא בְּרִיךְ הוּא (קהל: בְּרִיךְ הוּא)
לְעֵלָּא מִן כָּל בִּרְכָתָא וְשִׁירָתָא, תֻּשְׁבְּחָתָא וְנֶחֱמָתָא
דַּאֲמִירָן בְּעָלְמָא, וְאִמְרוּ אָמֵן. (קהל: אָמֵן)

יְהֵא שְׁלָמָא רַבָּא מִן שְׁמַיָּא
וְחַיִּים, עָלֵינוּ וְעַל כָּל יִשְׂרָאֵל, וְאִמְרוּ אָמֵן. (קהל: אָמֵן)

*Bow, take three steps back, as if taking leave of the Divine Presence,
then bow, first left, then right, then center, while saying:*

עֹשֶׂה שָׁלוֹם בִּמְרוֹמָיו
הוּא יַעֲשֶׂה שָׁלוֹם עָלֵינוּ וְעַל כָּל יִשְׂרָאֵל, וְאִמְרוּ אָמֵן. (קהל: אָמֵן)

The שיר של יום *is said at* מנחה.

מנחה לתשעה באב

MINḤA FOR
TISHA B'AV

Minḥa for Tisha B'Av

TALLIT

Say the following meditation before putting on the tallit. Meditations before the fulfillment of mitzvot are to ensure that we do so with the requisite intention (kavana). This particularly applies to mitzvot whose purpose is to induce in us certain states of mind, as is the case with tallit and tefillin, both of which are external symbols of inward commitment to the life of observance of the mitzvot.

בָּרְכִי נַפְשִׁי Bless the LORD, my soul. LORD, my God, You are very great, clothed in majesty and splendor, wrapped in a robe of light, spreading out the heavens like a tent. *Ps. 104*

Some say:

For the sake of the unification of the Holy One, blessed be He, and His Divine Presence, in reverence and love, to unify the name *Yod-Heh* with *Vav-Heh* in perfect unity in the name of all Israel.

I am about to wrap myself in this tasseled garment (tallit). So may my soul, my 248 limbs and 365 sinews be wrapped in the light of the tassel (*hatzitzit*) which amounts to 613 [commandments]. And just as I cover myself with a tasseled garment in this world, so may I be worthy of rabbinical dress and a fine garment in the World to Come in the Garden of Eden. Through the commandment of tassels may my life's-breath, spirit, soul and prayer be delivered from external impediments, and may the tallit spread its wings over them like an eagle stirring up its nest, hovering over its young. May the commandment of the tasseled garment be considered before the Holy One, blessed be He, as if I had fulfilled it in all its specifics, details and intentions, as well as the 613 commandments dependent on it, Amen, Selah. *Deut 32*

Before wrapping oneself in the tallit, say:

בָּרוּךְ Blessed are You, LORD our God, King of the Universe,
who has made us holy through His commandments,
and has commanded us to wrap ourselves in the tasseled garment.

According to the Shela (R. Isaiah Horowitz), one should say these verses after wrapping oneself in the tallit:

מַה־יָּקָר How precious is Your loving-kindness, O God, and the children of men find refuge under the shadow of Your wings. They are filled with the rich plenty of Your House. You give them drink from Your river of delights. For with You is the fountain of life; in Your light, we see light. Continue Your loving-kindness to those who know You, and Your righteousness to the upright in heart. *Ps. 36*

מנחה לתשעה באב
עטיפת טלית

Say the following meditation before putting on the טלית. Meditations before the fulfillment of מצוות are to ensure that we do so with the requisite intention (כוונה). This particularly applies to מצוות whose purpose is to induce in us certain states of mind, as is the case with טלית and תפילין, both of which are external symbols of inward commitment to the life of observance of the מצוות.

בָּרְכִי נַפְשִׁי אֶת־יהוה, יהוה אֱלֹהַי גָּדַלְתָּ מְּאֹד, הוֹד וְהָדָר לָבָשְׁתָּ: עֹטֶה־אוֹר כַּשַּׂלְמָה, נוֹטֶה שָׁמַיִם כַּיְרִיעָה: תהלים קד

Some say:

לְשֵׁם יִחוּד קֻדְשָׁא בְּרִיךְ הוּא וּשְׁכִינְתֵּהּ בִּדְחִילוּ וּרְחִימוּ, לְיַחֵד שֵׁם י"ה בו"ה בְּיִחוּדָא שְׁלִים בְּשֵׁם כָּל יִשְׂרָאֵל.

הֲרֵינִי מִתְעַטֵּף בַּצִּיצִית. כֵּן תִּתְעַטֵּף נִשְׁמָתִי וְרַמַ"ח אֵבָרַי וּשְׁסָ"ה גִידַי בְּאוֹר הַצִּיצִית הָעוֹלָה תַּרְיַ"ג. וּכְשֵׁם שֶׁאֲנִי מִתְכַּסֶּה בְּטַלִּית הַזֶּה, כָּךְ אֶזְכֶּה לַחֲלוּקָא דְרַבָּנָן וּלְטַלִּית נָאָה לָעוֹלָם הַבָּא בְּגַן עֵדֶן. וְעַל יְדֵי מִצְוַת צִיצִית תִּנָּצֵל נַפְשִׁי רוּחִי וְנִשְׁמָתִי וּתְפִלָּתִי מִן הַחִיצוֹנִים. וְהַטַּלִּית תִּפְרֹשׂ כְּנָפֶיהָ עֲלֵיהֶם וְתַצִּילֵם, כְּנֶשֶׁר יָעִיר קִנּוֹ עַל גּוֹזָלָיו יְרַחֵף. וּתְהֵא חֲשׁוּבָה מִצְוַת צִיצִית לִפְנֵי הַקָּדוֹשׁ בָּרוּךְ הוּא, כְּאִלּוּ קִיַּמְתִּיהָ בְּכָל פְּרָטֶיהָ וְדִקְדּוּקֶיהָ וְכַוָּנוֹתֶיהָ וְתַרְיַ"ג מִצְוֹת הַתְּלוּיוֹת בָּהּ, אָמֵן סֶלָה.   דברים לב

Before wrapping oneself in the טלית, say:

בָּרוּךְ אַתָּה יהוה אֱלֹהֵינוּ מֶלֶךְ הָעוֹלָם
אֲשֶׁר קִדְּשָׁנוּ בְּמִצְוֹתָיו וְצִוָּנוּ לְהִתְעַטֵּף בַּצִּיצִית.

According to the Shela (R. Isaiah Horowitz), one should say these verses after wrapping oneself in the טלית:

מַה־יָּקָר חַסְדְּךָ אֱלֹהִים, וּבְנֵי אָדָם בְּצֵל כְּנָפֶיךָ יֶחֱסָיוּן: יִרְוְיֻן מִדֶּשֶׁן בֵּיתֶךָ, וְנַחַל עֲדָנֶיךָ תַשְׁקֵם: כִּי־עִמְּךָ מְקוֹר חַיִּים, בְּאוֹרְךָ נִרְאֶה־אוֹר: מְשֹׁךְ חַסְדְּךָ לְיֹדְעֶיךָ, וְצִדְקָתְךָ לְיִשְׁרֵי־לֵב: תהלים לו

TEFILLIN

Some say the following meditation before putting on the tefillin.

For the sake of the unification of the Holy One, blessed be He, and His Divine Presence, in reverence and love, to unify the name *Yod-Heh* with *Vav-Heh* in perfect unity in the name of all Israel.

> By putting on the tefillin I hereby intend to fulfill the commandment of my Creator who commanded us to wear tefillin, as it is written in His Torah: "Bind them as a sign on your hand, and they shall be an emblem on the center of your head." They contain these four sections of the Torah: one beginning with *Shema* [Deut. 6:4–9]; another with *Vehaya im shamoa* [ibid. 11:13–21]; the third with *Kadesh li* [Ex. 13:1–10]; and the fourth with *Vehaya ki yevi'akha* [ibid. 13:11–16]. These proclaim the uniqueness and unity of God, blessed be His name in the world. They also remind us of the miracles and wonders which He did for us when He brought us out of Egypt, and that He has the power and the dominion over the highest and the lowest to deal with them as He pleases. He commanded us to place one of the tefillin on the arm in memory of His "outstretched arm" (of redemption), setting it opposite the heart, to subject the desires and designs of our heart to His service, blessed be His name. The other is to be on the head, opposite the brain, so that my mind, whose seat is in the brain, together with my other senses and faculties, may be subjected to His service, blessed be His name. May the spiritual influence of the commandment of the tefillin be with me so that I may have a long life, a flow of holiness, and sacred thoughts, free from any suggestion of sin or iniquity. May the evil inclination neither incite nor entice us, but leave us to serve the LORD, as it is in our hearts to do.

Deut. 6

And may it be Your will, LORD our God and God of our ancestors, that the commandment of tefillin be considered before You as if I had fulfilled it in all its specifics, details and intentions, as well as the 613 commandments dependent on it, Amen, Selah.

Stand and place the hand-tefillin on the biceps of the left arm (or right arm if you are left-handed), angled toward the heart, and before tightening the strap, say:

בָּרוּךְ Blessed are You, LORD our God,
King of the Universe,
who has made us holy through His commandments,
and has commanded us to put on tefillin.

הנחת תפילין

Some say the following meditation before putting on the תפילין.

לְשֵׁם יִחוּד קֻדְשָׁא בְּרִיךְ הוּא וּשְׁכִינְתֵּהּ בִּדְחִילוּ וּרְחִימוּ, לְיַחֵד שֵׁם י״ה בו״ה בְּיִחוּדָא שְׁלִים בְּשֵׁם כָּל יִשְׂרָאֵל.

הִנְנִי מְכַוֵּן בַּהֲנָחַת תְּפִלִּין לְקַיֵּם מִצְוַת בּוֹרְאִי, שֶׁצִּוָּנוּ לְהָנִיחַ תְּפִלִּין, כַּכָּתוּב בְּתוֹרָתוֹ: וּקְשַׁרְתָּם לְאוֹת עַל־יָדֶךָ, וְהָיוּ לְטֹטָפֹת בֵּין עֵינֶיךָ: וְהֵן אַרְבַּע פָּרָשִׁיּוֹת אֵלּוּ, שְׁמַע, וְהָיָה אִם שָׁמֹעַ, קַדֶּשׁ לִי, וְהָיָה כִּי יְבִאֲךָ, שֶׁיֵּשׁ בָּהֶם יִחוּדוֹ וְאַחְדוּתוֹ יִתְבָּרַךְ שְׁמוֹ בָּעוֹלָם, וְשֶׁנִּזְכֹּר נִסִּים וְנִפְלָאוֹת שֶׁעָשָׂה עִמָּנוּ בְּהוֹצִיאוֹ אוֹתָנוּ מִמִּצְרַיִם, וַאֲשֶׁר לוֹ הַכֹּחַ וְהַמֶּמְשָׁלָה בָּעֶלְיוֹנִים וּבַתַּחְתּוֹנִים לַעֲשׂוֹת בָּהֶם כִּרְצוֹנוֹ. וְצִוָּנוּ לְהָנִיחַ עַל הַיָּד לְזִכָּרוֹן זְרוֹעַ הַנְּטוּיָה, וְשֶׁהִיא נֶגֶד הַלֵּב, לְשַׁעְבֵּד בָּזֶה תַּאֲווֹת וּמַחְשְׁבוֹת לִבֵּנוּ לַעֲבוֹדָתוֹ יִתְבָּרַךְ שְׁמוֹ. וְעַל הָרֹאשׁ נֶגֶד הַמֹּחַ, שֶׁהַנְּשָׁמָה שֶׁבְּמֹחִי עִם שְׁאָר חוּשַׁי וְכֹחוֹתַי כֻּלָּם יִהְיוּ מְשֻׁעְבָּדִים לַעֲבוֹדָתוֹ, יִתְבָּרַךְ שְׁמוֹ. וּמִשֶּׁפַע מִצְוַת תְּפִלִּין יִתְמַשֵּׁךְ עָלַי לִהְיוֹת לִי חַיִּים אֲרוּכִים וְשֶׁפַע קֹדֶשׁ וּמַחֲשָׁבוֹת קְדוֹשׁוֹת בְּלִי הִרְהוּר חֵטְא וְעָוֹן כְּלָל, וְשֶׁלֹּא יְפַתֵּנוּ וְלֹא יִתְגָּרֶה בָּנוּ יֵצֶר הָרָע, וְיַנִּיחֵנוּ לַעֲבֹד אֶת יהוה כַּאֲשֶׁר עִם לְבָבֵנוּ.

דברים ו

וִיהִי רָצוֹן מִלְּפָנֶיךָ, יהוה אֱלֹהֵינוּ וֵאלֹהֵי אֲבוֹתֵינוּ, שֶׁתְּהֵא חֲשׁוּבָה מִצְוַת הֲנָחַת תְּפִלִּין לִפְנֵי הַקָּדוֹשׁ בָּרוּךְ הוּא, כְּאִלּוּ קִיַּמְתִּיהָ בְּכָל פְּרָטֶיהָ וְדִקְדּוּקֶיהָ וְכַוָּנוֹתֶיהָ וְתַרְיַ״ג מִצְוֹת הַתְּלוּיוֹת בָּהּ, אָמֵן סֶלָה.

Stand and place the תפילין של יד *on the biceps of the left arm (or right arm if you are left-handed), angled toward the heart, and before tightening the strap, say:*

בָּרוּךְ אַתָּה יהוה אֱלֹהֵינוּ מֶלֶךְ הָעוֹלָם
אֲשֶׁר קִדְּשָׁנוּ בְּמִצְוֹתָיו
וְצִוָּנוּ לְהָנִיחַ תְּפִלִּין.

Wrap the strap of the hand-tefillin seven times around the arm.
Place the head-tefillin above the hairline, centered between the eyes, and say quietly:

בָּרוּךְ Blessed are You, Lord our God,
King of the Universe,
who has made us holy through His commandments,
and has commanded us about the commandment of tefillin.

Adjust the head-tefillin and say:

בָּרוּךְ Blessed be the name of His glorious kingdom for ever and all time.

> *Some say:*
>
> From Your wisdom, God Most High, grant me [wisdom], and from Your understanding, give me understanding. May Your loving-kindness be greatly upon me, and in Your might may my enemies and those who rise against me be subdued. Pour Your goodly oil on the seven branches of the menora so that Your good flows down upon Your creatures. You open *Ps. 145* Your hand and satisfy every living thing with Your favor.

Wind the strap of the hand-tefillin three times around the middle finger, saying:

וְאֵרַשְׂתִּיךְ I will betroth you to Me for ever; *Hos. 2*
I will betroth you to Me in righteousness and justice,
loving-kindness and compassion;
I will betroth you to Me in faithfulness;
and you shall know the Lord.

After putting on the tefillin, some say the following paragraphs. According to the Ḥazon Ish these paragraphs are said on Tisha B'Av, and according to the Mishna Berura they are not.

וַיְדַבֵּר The Lord spoke to Moses, saying, "Consecrate to Me every firstborn *Ex. 13* male. The first offspring of every womb among the Israelites, whether man or beast, belongs to Me." Then Moses said to the people, "Remember this day on which you left Egypt, the slave-house, when the Lord brought you out of it with a mighty hand. No leaven shall be eaten. You are leaving on this day, in the month of Aviv. When the Lord brings you into the land of the Canaanites, Hittites, Amorites, Hivites and Jebusites, the land He swore to your ancestors to give you, a land flowing with milk and honey, you are to observe this service in this same month. For seven days you shall eat unleavened bread, and make the seventh day a festival to the Lord. Unleavened bread shall be eaten throughout the seven days. No leavened bread may be seen in your possession, and no leaven shall be seen anywhere within your borders. On that day you shall tell your son, 'This is because of what the Lord did for

Wrap the strap of the תפילין של יד seven times around the arm.
Place the תפילין של ראש above the hairline, centered between the eyes, and say quietly:

בָּרוּךְ אַתָּה יהוה אֱלֹהֵינוּ מֶלֶךְ הָעוֹלָם
אֲשֶׁר קִדְּשָׁנוּ בְּמִצְוֹתָיו
וְצִוָּנוּ עַל מִצְוַת תְּפִלִּין.

Adjust the תפילין של ראש and say:

בָּרוּךְ שֵׁם כְּבוֹד מַלְכוּתוֹ לְעוֹלָם וָעֶד.

Some say:

וּמֵחָכְמָתְךָ אֵל עֶלְיוֹן תַּאֲצִיל עָלַי, וּמִבִּינָתְךָ תְּבִינֵנִי, וּבְחַסְדְּךָ תַּגְדִּיל עָלַי, וּבִגְבוּרָתְךָ תַּצְמִית אוֹיְבַי וְקָמַי. וְשֶׁמֶן הַטּוֹב תָּרִיק עַל שִׁבְעָה קְנֵי הַמְּנוֹרָה, לְהַשְׁפִּיעַ טוּבְךָ לִבְרִיּוֹתֶיךָ. פּוֹתֵחַ אֶת־יָדֶךָ וּמַשְׂבִּיעַ לְכָל־חַי רָצוֹן.

תהלים קמה

Wind the strap of the תפילין של יד three times around the middle finger, saying:

וְאֵרַשְׂתִּיךְ לִי לְעוֹלָם
וְאֵרַשְׂתִּיךְ לִי בְּצֶדֶק וּבְמִשְׁפָּט וּבְחֶסֶד וּבְרַחֲמִים:
וְאֵרַשְׂתִּיךְ לִי בֶּאֱמוּנָה, וְיָדַעַתְּ אֶת־יהוה:

הושע ב

After putting on the תפילין, some say the following paragraphs. According to the חזון איש these paragraphs are said on תשעה באב, and according to the משנה ברורה they are not.

וַיְדַבֵּר יהוה אֶל־מֹשֶׁה לֵּאמֹר: קַדֶּשׁ־לִי כָל־בְּכוֹר, פֶּטֶר כָּל־רֶחֶם בִּבְנֵי יִשְׂרָאֵל, בָּאָדָם וּבַבְּהֵמָה, לִי הוּא: וַיֹּאמֶר מֹשֶׁה אֶל־הָעָם, זָכוֹר אֶת־הַיּוֹם הַזֶּה, אֲשֶׁר יְצָאתֶם מִמִּצְרַיִם מִבֵּית עֲבָדִים, כִּי בְּחֹזֶק יָד הוֹצִיא יהוה אֶתְכֶם מִזֶּה, וְלֹא יֵאָכֵל חָמֵץ: הַיּוֹם אַתֶּם יֹצְאִים, בְּחֹדֶשׁ הָאָבִיב: וְהָיָה כִי־יְבִיאֲךָ יהוה אֶל־אֶרֶץ הַכְּנַעֲנִי וְהַחִתִּי וְהָאֱמֹרִי וְהַחִוִּי וְהַיְבוּסִי, אֲשֶׁר נִשְׁבַּע לַאֲבֹתֶיךָ לָתֶת לָךְ, אֶרֶץ זָבַת חָלָב וּדְבָשׁ, וְעָבַדְתָּ אֶת־הָעֲבֹדָה הַזֹּאת בַּחֹדֶשׁ הַזֶּה: שִׁבְעַת יָמִים תֹּאכַל מַצֹּת, וּבַיּוֹם הַשְּׁבִיעִי חַג לַיהוה: מַצּוֹת יֵאָכֵל אֵת שִׁבְעַת הַיָּמִים, וְלֹא־יֵרָאֶה לְךָ חָמֵץ וְלֹא־יֵרָאֶה לְךָ שְׂאֹר, בְּכָל־גְּבֻלֶךָ: וְהִגַּדְתָּ לְבִנְךָ בַּיּוֹם הַהוּא לֵאמֹר, בַּעֲבוּר זֶה עָשָׂה יהוה לִי בְּצֵאתִי מִמִּצְרָיִם: וְהָיָה

שמות יג

me when I left Egypt." [These words] shall also be a sign on your hand, and a reminder above your forehead, so that the Lord's Torah may always be in your mouth, because with a mighty hand the Lord brought you out of Egypt. You shall therefore keep this statute at its appointed time from year to year."

וְהָיָה After the Lord has brought you into the land of the Canaanites, as He swore to you and your ancestors, and He has given it to you, you shall set apart for the Lord the first offspring of every womb. All the firstborn males of your cattle belong to the Lord. Every firstling donkey you shall redeem with a lamb. If you do not redeem it, you must break its neck. Every firstborn among your sons you must redeem. If, in time to come, your son asks you, "What does this mean?" you shall say to him, "With a mighty hand the Lord brought us out of Egypt, out of the slave-house. When Pharaoh stubbornly refused to let us leave, the Lord killed all the firstborn in the land of Egypt, both man and beast. That is why I sacrifice to the Lord the first male offspring of every womb, and redeem all the firstborn of my sons." [These words] shall be a sign on your hand and as an emblem above your forehead, that with a mighty hand the Lord brought us out of Egypt.

THE DAILY PSALM

One of the following psalms is said on the appropriate day of the week as indicated. After the psalm, the Mourner's Kaddish on page 662 is said.

Sunday: Today is the first day of the week,
on which the Levites used to say this psalm in the Temple:

לְדָוִד מִזְמוֹר A psalm of David. The earth is the Lord's and all it contains, the world and all who live in it. For He founded it on the seas and established it on the streams. Who may climb the mountain of the Lord? Who may stand in His holy place? He who has clean hands and a pure heart, who has not taken My name in vain or sworn deceitfully. He shall receive a blessing from the Lord, and just reward from the God of his salvation. This is a generation of those who seek Him, the descendants of Jacob who seek Your presence, Selah! Lift up your heads, O gates; be uplifted, eternal doors, so that the King of glory may enter. Who is the King of glory? It is the Lord, strong and mighty, the Lord mighty in battle. Lift up your heads, O gates; be uplifted, eternal doors, that the King of glory may enter. ▸ Who is He, the King of glory? The Lord of hosts, He is the King of glory, Selah! *Ps. 24*

Mourner's Kaddish (page 662)

לְךָ לְאוֹת עַל־יָדְךָ וּלְזִכָּרוֹן בֵּין עֵינֶיךָ, לְמַעַן תִּהְיֶה תּוֹרַת יהוה בְּפִיךָ, כִּי בְּיָד חֲזָקָה הוֹצִאֲךָ יהוה מִמִּצְרָיִם: וְשָׁמַרְתָּ אֶת־הַחֻקָּה הַזֹּאת לְמוֹעֲדָהּ, מִיָּמִים יָמִימָה:

וְהָיָה כִּי־יְבִאֲךָ יהוה אֶל־אֶרֶץ הַכְּנַעֲנִי כַּאֲשֶׁר נִשְׁבַּע לְךָ וְלַאֲבֹתֶיךָ, וּנְתָנָהּ לָךְ: וְהַעֲבַרְתָּ כָל־פֶּטֶר־רֶחֶם לַיהוה, וְכָל־פֶּטֶר שֶׁגֶר בְּהֵמָה אֲשֶׁר יִהְיֶה לְךָ הַזְּכָרִים, לַיהוה: וְכָל־פֶּטֶר חֲמֹר תִּפְדֶּה בְשֶׂה, וְאִם־לֹא תִפְדֶּה וַעֲרַפְתּוֹ, וְכֹל בְּכוֹר אָדָם בְּבָנֶיךָ תִּפְדֶּה: וְהָיָה כִּי־יִשְׁאָלְךָ בִנְךָ מָחָר, לֵאמֹר מַה־זֹּאת, וְאָמַרְתָּ אֵלָיו, בְּחֹזֶק יָד הוֹצִיאָנוּ יהוה מִמִּצְרַיִם מִבֵּית עֲבָדִים: וַיְהִי כִּי־הִקְשָׁה פַרְעֹה לְשַׁלְּחֵנוּ, וַיַּהֲרֹג יהוה כָּל־בְּכוֹר בְּאֶרֶץ מִצְרַיִם, מִבְּכֹר אָדָם וְעַד־בְּכוֹר בְּהֵמָה, עַל־כֵּן אֲנִי זֹבֵחַ לַיהוה כָּל־פֶּטֶר רֶחֶם הַזְּכָרִים, וְכָל־בְּכוֹר בָּנַי אֶפְדֶּה: וְהָיָה לְאוֹת עַל־יָדְכָה וּלְטוֹטָפֹת בֵּין עֵינֶיךָ, כִּי בְּחֹזֶק יָד הוֹצִיאָנוּ יהוה מִמִּצְרָיִם:

שיר של יום

One of the following psalms is said on the appropriate day of the week as indicated. After the psalm, קדיש יתום *on page 663 is said.*

Sunday הַיּוֹם יוֹם רִאשׁוֹן בְּשַׁבָּת, שֶׁבּוֹ הָיוּ הַלְוִיִּם אוֹמְרִים בְּבֵית הַמִּקְדָּשׁ:

תהלים כד

לְדָוִד מִזְמוֹר, לַיהוה הָאָרֶץ וּמְלוֹאָהּ, תֵּבֵל וְיֹשְׁבֵי בָהּ: כִּי־הוּא עַל־יַמִּים יְסָדָהּ, וְעַל־נְהָרוֹת יְכוֹנְנֶהָ: מִי־יַעֲלֶה בְהַר־יהוה, וּמִי־יָקוּם בִּמְקוֹם קָדְשׁוֹ: נְקִי כַפַּיִם וּבַר־לֵבָב, אֲשֶׁר לֹא־נָשָׂא לַשָּׁוְא נַפְשִׁי, וְלֹא נִשְׁבַּע לְמִרְמָה: יִשָּׂא בְרָכָה מֵאֵת יהוה, וּצְדָקָה מֵאֱלֹהֵי יִשְׁעוֹ: זֶה דּוֹר דֹּרְשָׁיו, מְבַקְשֵׁי פָנֶיךָ יַעֲקֹב סֶלָה: שְׂאוּ שְׁעָרִים רָאשֵׁיכֶם, וְהִנָּשְׂאוּ פִּתְחֵי עוֹלָם, וְיָבוֹא מֶלֶךְ הַכָּבוֹד: מִי זֶה מֶלֶךְ הַכָּבוֹד, יהוה עִזּוּז וְגִבּוֹר, יהוה גִּבּוֹר מִלְחָמָה: שְׂאוּ שְׁעָרִים רָאשֵׁיכֶם, וּשְׂאוּ פִּתְחֵי עוֹלָם, וְיָבֹא מֶלֶךְ הַכָּבוֹד: ◆ מִי הוּא זֶה מֶלֶךְ הַכָּבוֹד, יהוה צְבָאוֹת הוּא מֶלֶךְ הַכָּבוֹד סֶלָה:

קדיש יתום (page 663)

Tuesday: Today is the third day of the week,
on which the Levites used to say this psalm in the Temple:

מִזְמוֹר לְאָסָף A psalm of Asaph. God stands in the divine assembly. Among the judges He delivers judgment. How long will you judge unjustly, showing favor to the wicked? Selah. Do justice to the weak and the orphaned. Vindicate the poor and destitute. Rescue the weak and needy. Save them from the hand of the wicked. They do not know nor do they understand. They walk about in darkness while all the earth's foundations shake. I once said, "You are like gods, all of you are sons of the Most High." But you shall die like mere men, you will fall like any prince. ‣ Arise, O Lord, judge the earth, for all the nations are Your possession. *Ps. 82*

Mourner's Kaddish (page 662)

Thursday: Today is the fifth day of the week,
on which the Levites used to say this psalm in the Temple:

לַמְנַצֵּחַ For the conductor of music. On the Gittit. By Asaph. Sing for joy to God, our strength. Shout aloud to the God of Jacob. Raise a song, beat the drum, play the sweet harp and lyre. Sound the shofar on the new moon, on our feast day when the moon is hidden. For it is a statute for Israel, an ordinance of the God of Jacob. He established it as a testimony for Joseph when He went forth against the land of Egypt, where I heard a language that I did not know. I relieved his shoulder of the burden. His hands were freed from the builder's basket. In distress you called and I rescued you. I answered you from the secret place of thunder; I tested you at the waters of Meribah, Selah! Hear, My people, and I will warn you. Israel, if you would only listen to Me! Let there be no strange god among you. Do not bow down to an alien god. I am the Lord your God who brought you out of the land of Egypt. Open your mouth wide and I will fill it. But My people would not listen to Me. Israel would have none of Me. So I left them to their stubborn hearts, letting them follow their own devices. If only My people would listen to Me, if Israel would walk in My ways, I would soon subdue their enemies, and turn My hand against their foes. Those who hate the Lord would cower before Him and their doom would last for ever. ‣ He would feed Israel with the finest wheat – with honey from the rock I would satisfy you. *Ps. 81*

Mourner's Kaddish (page 662)

Tuesday הַיּוֹם יוֹם שְׁלִישִׁי בְּשַׁבָּת, שֶׁבּוֹ הָיוּ הַלְוִיִּם אוֹמְרִים בְּבֵית הַמִּקְדָּשׁ:

תהלים פב מִזְמוֹר לְאָסָף, אֱלֹהִים נִצָּב בַּעֲדַת־אֵל, בְּקֶרֶב אֱלֹהִים יִשְׁפֹּט: עַד־מָתַי תִּשְׁפְּטוּ־עָוֶל, וּפְנֵי רְשָׁעִים תִּשְׂאוּ־סֶלָה: שִׁפְטוּ־דַל וְיָתוֹם, עָנִי וָרָשׁ הַצְדִּיקוּ: פַּלְּטוּ־דַל וְאֶבְיוֹן, מִיַּד רְשָׁעִים הַצִּילוּ: לֹא יָדְעוּ וְלֹא יָבִינוּ, בַּחֲשֵׁכָה יִתְהַלָּכוּ, יִמּוֹטוּ כָּל־מוֹסְדֵי אָרֶץ: אֲנִי־אָמַרְתִּי אֱלֹהִים אַתֶּם, וּבְנֵי עֶלְיוֹן כֻּלְּכֶם: אָכֵן כְּאָדָם תְּמוּתוּן, וּכְאַחַד הַשָּׂרִים תִּפֹּלוּ: ‏‎•‎‏ קוּמָה אֱלֹהִים שָׁפְטָה הָאָרֶץ, כִּי־אַתָּה תִנְחַל בְּכָל־הַגּוֹיִם:

קדיש יתום (page 663)

Thursday הַיּוֹם יוֹם חֲמִישִׁי בְּשַׁבָּת, שֶׁבּוֹ הָיוּ הַלְוִיִּם אוֹמְרִים בְּבֵית הַמִּקְדָּשׁ:

תהלים פא לַמְנַצֵּחַ עַל־הַגִּתִּית לְאָסָף: הַרְנִינוּ לֵאלֹהִים עוּזֵּנוּ, הָרִיעוּ לֵאלֹהֵי יַעֲקֹב: שְׂאוּ־זִמְרָה וּתְנוּ־תֹף, כִּנּוֹר נָעִים עִם־נָבֶל: תִּקְעוּ בַחֹדֶשׁ שׁוֹפָר, בַּכֶּסֶה לְיוֹם חַגֵּנוּ: כִּי חֹק לְיִשְׂרָאֵל הוּא, מִשְׁפָּט לֵאלֹהֵי יַעֲקֹב: עֵדוּת בִּיהוֹסֵף שָׂמוֹ, בְּצֵאתוֹ עַל־אֶרֶץ מִצְרָיִם, שְׂפַת לֹא־יָדַעְתִּי אֶשְׁמָע: הֲסִירוֹתִי מִסֵּבֶל שִׁכְמוֹ, כַּפָּיו מִדּוּד תַּעֲבֹרְנָה: בַּצָּרָה קָרָאתָ וָאֲחַלְּצֶךָּ, אֶעֶנְךָ בְּסֵתֶר רַעַם, אֶבְחָנְךָ עַל־מֵי מְרִיבָה סֶלָה: שְׁמַע עַמִּי וְאָעִידָה בָּךְ, יִשְׂרָאֵל אִם־תִּשְׁמַע־לִי: לֹא־יִהְיֶה בְךָ אֵל זָר, וְלֹא תִשְׁתַּחֲוֶה לְאֵל נֵכָר: אָנֹכִי יהוה אֱלֹהֶיךָ, הַמַּעַלְךָ מֵאֶרֶץ מִצְרָיִם, הַרְחֶב־פִּיךָ וַאֲמַלְאֵהוּ: וְלֹא־שָׁמַע עַמִּי לְקוֹלִי, וְיִשְׂרָאֵל לֹא־אָבָה לִי: וָאֲשַׁלְּחֵהוּ בִּשְׁרִירוּת לִבָּם, יֵלְכוּ בְּמוֹעֲצוֹתֵיהֶם: לוּ עַמִּי שֹׁמֵעַ לִי, יִשְׂרָאֵל בִּדְרָכַי יְהַלֵּכוּ: כִּמְעַט אוֹיְבֵיהֶם אַכְנִיעַ, וְעַל־צָרֵיהֶם אָשִׁיב יָדִי: מְשַׂנְאֵי יהוה יְכַחֲשׁוּ־לוֹ, וִיהִי עִתָּם לְעוֹלָם: ‏‎•‎‏ וַיַּאֲכִילֵהוּ מֵחֵלֶב חִטָּה, וּמִצּוּר, דְּבַשׁ אַשְׂבִּיעֶךָ:

קדיש יתום (page 663)

MINḤA FOR TISHA B'AV

MOURNER'S KADDISH

The following prayer requires the presence of a minyan.
A transliteration can be found on page 792.

Mourner: יִתְגַּדַּל Magnified and sanctified
may His great name be,
in the world He created by His will.
May He establish His kingdom
in your lifetime and in your days,
and in the lifetime of all the house of Israel,
swiftly and soon –
and say: Amen.

All: May His great name be blessed for ever and all time.

Mourner: Blessed and praised, glorified and exalted,
raised and honored, uplifted and lauded
be the name of the Holy One,
blessed be He,
beyond any blessing, song,
praise and consolation
uttered in the world –
and say: Amen.

May there be great peace from heaven,
and life for us and all Israel –
and say: Amen.

Bow, take three steps back, as if taking leave of the Divine Presence,
then bow, first left, then right, then center, while saying:
May He who makes peace in His high places,
make peace for us and all Israel –
and say: Amen.

קדיש יתום

The following prayer requires the presence of a מנין.
A transliteration can be found on page 792.

אבל יִתְגַּדַּל וְיִתְקַדַּשׁ שְׁמֵהּ רַבָּא (קהל: אָמֵן)
בְּעָלְמָא דִּי בְרָא כִרְעוּתֵהּ
וְיַמְלִיךְ מַלְכוּתֵהּ
בְּחַיֵּיכוֹן וּבְיוֹמֵיכוֹן וּבְחַיֵּי דְכָל בֵּית יִשְׂרָאֵל
בַּעֲגָלָא וּבִזְמַן קָרִיב
וְאִמְרוּ אָמֵן. (קהל: אָמֵן)

קהל ואבל: יְהֵא שְׁמֵהּ רַבָּא מְבָרַךְ לְעָלַם וּלְעָלְמֵי עָלְמַיָּא.

אבל יִתְבָּרַךְ וְיִשְׁתַּבַּח וְיִתְפָּאַר
וְיִתְרוֹמַם וְיִתְנַשֵּׂא וְיִתְהַדָּר וְיִתְעַלֶּה וְיִתְהַלָּל
שְׁמֵהּ דְּקֻדְשָׁא בְּרִיךְ הוּא (קהל: בְּרִיךְ הוּא)
לְעֵלָּא מִן כָּל בִּרְכָתָא וְשִׁירָתָא, תֻּשְׁבְּחָתָא וְנֶחֱמָתָא
דַּאֲמִירָן בְּעָלְמָא
וְאִמְרוּ אָמֵן. (קהל: אָמֵן)

יְהֵא שְׁלָמָא רַבָּא מִן שְׁמַיָּא
וְחַיִּים, עָלֵינוּ וְעַל כָּל יִשְׂרָאֵל
וְאִמְרוּ אָמֵן. (קהל: אָמֵן)

Bow, take three steps back, as if taking leave of the Divine Presence,
then bow, first left, then right, then center, while saying:

עֹשֶׂה שָׁלוֹם בִּמְרוֹמָיו
הוּא יַעֲשֶׂה שָׁלוֹם עָלֵינוּ וְעַל כָּל יִשְׂרָאֵל
וְאִמְרוּ אָמֵן. (קהל: אָמֵן)

Some have the custom to touch the hand-tefillin at° and the head-tefillin at°°.

אַשְׁרֵי Happy are those who dwell in Your House; they shall continue to praise You, Selah! Happy are the people for whom this is so; happy are the people whose God is the LORD.

Ps. 84

Ps. 144

A song of praise by David.

Ps. 145

> I will exalt You, my God, the King, and bless Your name for ever and all time. Every day I will bless You, and praise Your name for ever and all time. God is great and greatly to be praised; His greatness is unfathomable. One generation will praise Your works to the next, and tell of Your mighty deeds. On the glorious splendor of Your majesty I will meditate, and on the acts of Your wonders. They shall talk of the power of Your awesome deeds, and I will tell of Your greatness. They shall recite the record of Your great goodness, and sing with joy of Your righteousness. The LORD is gracious and compassionate, slow to anger and great in loving-kindness. The LORD is good to all, and His compassion extends to all His works. All Your works shall thank You, LORD, and Your devoted ones shall bless You. They shall talk of the glory of Your kingship, and speak of Your might. To make known to mankind His mighty deeds and the glorious majesty of His kingship. Your kingdom is an everlasting kingdom, and Your reign is for all generations. The LORD supports all who fall, and raises all who are bowed down. All raise their eyes to You in hope, and You give them their food in due season.° You open Your hand,°° and satisfy every living thing with Your favor. The LORD is righteous in all His ways, and kind in all He does. The LORD is close to all who call on Him, to all who call on Him in truth. He fulfills the will of those who revere Him; He hears their cry and saves them. The LORD guards all who love Him, but all the wicked He will destroy. ‣ My mouth shall speak the praise of the LORD, and all creatures shall bless His holy name for ever and all time.

We will bless the LORD now and for ever. Halleluya!

Ps. 115

Some have the custom to touch the תפילין של יד at°, and the תפילין של ראש at°°.

אַשְׁרֵי יוֹשְׁבֵי בֵיתֶךָ, עוֹד יְהַלְלוּךָ סֶּלָה:
אַשְׁרֵי הָעָם שֶׁכָּכָה לּוֹ, אַשְׁרֵי הָעָם שֶׁיהוה אֱלֹהָיו:
תְּהִלָּה לְדָוִד
אֲרוֹמִמְךָ אֱלוֹהַי הַמֶּלֶךְ, וַאֲבָרְכָה שִׁמְךָ לְעוֹלָם וָעֶד:
בְּכָל־יוֹם אֲבָרְכֶךָּ, וַאֲהַלְלָה שִׁמְךָ לְעוֹלָם וָעֶד:
גָּדוֹל יהוה וּמְהֻלָּל מְאֹד, וְלִגְדֻלָּתוֹ אֵין חֵקֶר:
דּוֹר לְדוֹר יְשַׁבַּח מַעֲשֶׂיךָ, וּגְבוּרֹתֶיךָ יַגִּידוּ:
הֲדַר כְּבוֹד הוֹדֶךָ, וְדִבְרֵי נִפְלְאֹתֶיךָ אָשִׂיחָה:
וֶעֱזוּז נוֹרְאֹתֶיךָ יֹאמֵרוּ, וּגְדוּלָּתְךָ אֲסַפְּרֶנָּה:
זֵכֶר רַב־טוּבְךָ יַבִּיעוּ, וְצִדְקָתְךָ יְרַנֵּנוּ:
חַנּוּן וְרַחוּם יהוה, אֶרֶךְ אַפַּיִם וּגְדָל־חָסֶד:
טוֹב־יהוה לַכֹּל, וְרַחֲמָיו עַל־כָּל־מַעֲשָׂיו:
יוֹדוּךָ יהוה כָּל־מַעֲשֶׂיךָ, וַחֲסִידֶיךָ יְבָרְכוּכָה:
כְּבוֹד מַלְכוּתְךָ יֹאמֵרוּ, וּגְבוּרָתְךָ יְדַבֵּרוּ:
לְהוֹדִיעַ לִבְנֵי הָאָדָם גְּבוּרֹתָיו, וּכְבוֹד הֲדַר מַלְכוּתוֹ:
מַלְכוּתְךָ מַלְכוּת כָּל־עֹלָמִים, וּמֶמְשַׁלְתְּךָ בְּכָל־דּוֹר וָדֹר:
סוֹמֵךְ יהוה לְכָל־הַנֹּפְלִים, וְזוֹקֵף לְכָל־הַכְּפוּפִים:
עֵינֵי־כֹל אֵלֶיךָ יְשַׂבֵּרוּ, וְאַתָּה נוֹתֵן־לָהֶם אֶת־אָכְלָם בְּעִתּוֹ:
°פּוֹתֵחַ אֶת־יָדֶךָ, °°וּמַשְׂבִּיעַ לְכָל־חַי רָצוֹן:
צַדִּיק יהוה בְּכָל־דְּרָכָיו, וְחָסִיד בְּכָל־מַעֲשָׂיו:
קָרוֹב יהוה לְכָל־קֹרְאָיו, לְכֹל אֲשֶׁר יִקְרָאֻהוּ בֶאֱמֶת:
רְצוֹן־יְרֵאָיו יַעֲשֶׂה, וְאֶת־שַׁוְעָתָם יִשְׁמַע, וְיוֹשִׁיעֵם:
שׁוֹמֵר יהוה אֶת־כָּל־אֹהֲבָיו, וְאֵת כָּל־הָרְשָׁעִים יַשְׁמִיד:
‹ תְּהִלַּת יהוה יְדַבֶּר פִּי, וִיבָרֵךְ כָּל־בָּשָׂר שֵׁם קָדְשׁוֹ לְעוֹלָם וָעֶד:
וַאֲנַחְנוּ נְבָרֵךְ יָהּ מֵעַתָּה וְעַד־עוֹלָם, הַלְלוּיָהּ:

HALF KADDISH

Leader: יִתְגַּדַּל Magnified and sanctified may His great name be,
in the world He created by His will.
May He establish His kingdom
in your lifetime and in your days,
and in the lifetime of all the house of Israel,
swiftly and soon –
and say: Amen.

All: May His great name be blessed for ever and all time.

Leader: Blessed and praised, glorified and exalted,
raised and honored, uplifted and lauded
be the name of the Holy One, blessed be He,
beyond any blessing,
song, praise and consolation
uttered in the world –
and say: Amen.

REMOVING THE TORAH FROM THE ARK

The Ark is opened and the congregation stands. All say:

וַיְהִי בִּנְסֹעַ Whenever the Ark set out, Moses would say, "Arise, Lord, *Num. 10* and may Your enemies be scattered. May those who hate You flee before You." For the Torah shall come forth from Zion, and the word *Is. 2* of the Lord from Jerusalem. Blessed is He who in His holiness gave the Torah to His people Israel.

Blessed is the name of the Master of the Universe. Blessed is Your crown and *Zohar,* Your place. May Your favor always be with Your people Israel. Show Your people *Parashat Vayak-hel* the salvation of Your right hand in Your Temple. Grant us the gift of Your good light, and accept our prayers in mercy. May it be Your will to prolong our life in goodness. May I be counted among the righteous, so that You will have compassion on me and protect me and all that is mine and all that is Your people Israel's. You feed all; You sustain all; You rule over all; You rule over kings, for sovereignty is Yours. I am a servant of the Holy One, blessed be He, before whom

חצי קדיש

ש״ץ: יִתְגַּדַּל וְיִתְקַדַּשׁ שְׁמֵהּ רַבָּא (קהל: אָמֵן)
בְּעָלְמָא דִּי בְרָא כִרְעוּתֵהּ, וְיַמְלִיךְ מַלְכוּתֵהּ
בְּחַיֵּיכוֹן וּבְיוֹמֵיכוֹן וּבְחַיֵּי דְכָל בֵּית יִשְׂרָאֵל
בַּעֲגָלָא וּבִזְמַן קָרִיב, וְאִמְרוּ אָמֵן. (קהל: אָמֵן)

קהל ורש״ץ: יְהֵא שְׁמֵהּ רַבָּא מְבָרַךְ לְעָלַם וּלְעָלְמֵי עָלְמַיָּא.

ש״ץ: יִתְבָּרַךְ וְיִשְׁתַּבַּח וְיִתְפָּאַר וְיִתְרוֹמַם וְיִתְנַשֵּׂא
וְיִתְהַדָּר וְיִתְעַלֶּה וְיִתְהַלָּל
שְׁמֵהּ דְּקֻדְשָׁא בְּרִיךְ הוּא (קהל: בְּרִיךְ הוּא)
לְעֵלָּא מִן כָּל בִּרְכָתָא וְשִׁירָתָא, תֻּשְׁבְּחָתָא וְנֶחֱמָתָא
דַּאֲמִירָן בְּעָלְמָא
וְאִמְרוּ אָמֵן. (קהל: אָמֵן)

הוצאת ספר תורה

The ארון קודש is opened and the קהל stands. All say:

וַיְהִי בִּנְסֹעַ הָאָרֹן וַיֹּאמֶר מֹשֶׁה, קוּמָה יְהוָה וְיָפֻצוּ אֹיְבֶיךָ וְיָנֻסוּ במדבר
מְשַׂנְאֶיךָ מִפָּנֶיךָ: כִּי מִצִּיּוֹן תֵּצֵא תוֹרָה וּדְבַר־יְהוָה מִירוּשָׁלָיִם: ישעיה ב
בָּרוּךְ שֶׁנָּתַן תּוֹרָה לְעַמּוֹ יִשְׂרָאֵל בִּקְדֻשָּׁתוֹ.

בְּרִיךְ שְׁמֵהּ דְּמָרֵא עָלְמָא, בְּרִיךְ כִּתְרָךְ וְאַתְרָךְ. יְהֵא רְעוּתָךְ עִם עַמָּךְ יִשְׂרָאֵל זהר ויקהל
לְעָלַם, וּפֻרְקַן יְמִינָךְ אַחֲזֵי לְעַמָּךְ בְּבֵית מַקְדְּשָׁךְ, וּלְאַמְטוֹיֵי לָנָא מִטּוּב נְהוֹרָךְ,
וּלְקַבֵּל צְלוֹתָנָא בְּרַחֲמִין. יְהֵא רַעֲוָא קֳדָמָךְ דְּתוֹרִיךְ לָן חַיִּין בְּטִיבוּ, וְלֶהֱוֵי אֲנָא
פְקִידָא בְּגוֹ צַדִּיקַיָּא, לְמִרְחַם עֲלַי וּלְמִנְטַר יָתִי וְיָת כָּל דִּי לִי וְדִי לְעַמָּךְ יִשְׂרָאֵל.
אַנְתְּ הוּא זָן לְכֹלָּא וּמְפַרְנֵס לְכֹלָּא, אַנְתְּ הוּא שַׁלִּיט עַל כֹּלָּא, אַנְתְּ הוּא דְשַׁלִּיט
עַל מַלְכַיָּא, וּמַלְכוּתָא דִּילָךְ הִיא. אֲנָא עַבְדָּא דְקֻדְשָׁא בְּרִיךְ הוּא, דְּסָגִדְנָא

and before whose glorious Torah I bow at all times. Not in man do I trust, nor on any angel do I rely, but on the God of heaven who is the God of truth, whose Torah is truth, whose prophets speak truth, and who abounds in acts of love and truth. ▸ In Him I trust, and to His holy and glorious name I offer praises. May it be Your will to open my heart to the Torah, and to fulfill the wishes of my heart and of the hearts of all Your people Israel for good, for life, and for peace.

The Leader takes the Torah scroll in his right arm, bows toward the Ark and says:
Magnify the LORD with me, and let us exalt His name together. *Ps. 34*

The Ark is closed. The Leader carries the Torah scroll to the bima and the congregation says:
לְךָ Yours, LORD, are the greatness and the power, the glory and the majesty and splendor, for everything in heaven and earth is Yours. Yours, LORD, is the kingdom; You are exalted as head over all. *1 Chr. 29*

רוֹמְמוּ Exalt the LORD our God and bow to His footstool; He is holy. Exalt the LORD our God, and bow at His holy mountain, for holy is the LORD our God. *Ps. 99*

אַב הָרַחֲמִים May the Father of compassion have compassion on the people borne by Him. May He remember the covenant with the mighty [patriarchs], and deliver us from evil times. May He reproach the evil instinct in the people carried by Him, and graciously grant that we be an everlasting remnant. May He fulfill in good measure our requests for salvation and compassion.

The Torah scroll is placed on the bima and the Gabbai calls a Kohen to the Torah.
May His kingship over us be soon revealed and made manifest. May He be gracious to our surviving remnant, the remnant of His people the house of Israel in grace, loving-kindness, compassion and favor, and let us say Amen. Let us all render greatness to our God and give honor to the Torah. *Let the Kohen come forward. Arise (*name* son of *father's name*), the Kohen.

**If no Kohen is present, a Levi or Yisrael is called up as follows:*
/As there is no Kohen, arise (*name* son of *father's name*) in place of a Kohen./

Blessed is He who, in His holiness, gave the Torah to His people Israel.

Congregation followed by the Gabbai:
You who cling to the LORD your God are all alive today. *Deut. 4*

קָמֵהּ וּמִקַּמֵּי דִּיקַר אוֹרַיְתֵהּ בְּכָל עִדָּן וְעִדָּן. לָא עַל אֱנָשׁ רָחִיצְנָא וְלָא עַל בַּר אֱלָהִין סָמִיכְנָא, אֶלָּא בֵּאלָהָא דִשְׁמַיָּא, דְּהוּא אֱלָהָא קְשׁוֹט, וְאוֹרַיְתֵהּ קְשׁוֹט, וּנְבִיאוֹהִי קְשׁוֹט, וּמַסְגֵּא לְמֶעְבַּד טַבְוָן וּקְשׁוֹט. ❖ בֵּהּ אֲנָא רָחִיץ, וְלִשְׁמֵהּ קַדִּישָׁא יַקִּירָא אֲנָא אֵמַר תֻּשְׁבְּחָן. יְהֵא רַעֲוָא קֳדָמָךְ דְּתִפְתַּח לִבַּאי בְּאוֹרַיְתָא, וְתַשְׁלִים מִשְׁאֲלִין דְּלִבַּאי וְלִבָּא דְכָל עַמָּךְ יִשְׂרָאֵל לְטַב וּלְחַיִּין וְלִשְׁלָם.

The שליח ציבור takes the ספר תורה in his right arm, bows toward the ארון קודש and says:

גַּדְּלוּ לַיהוה אִתִּי וּנְרוֹמְמָה שְׁמוֹ יַחְדָּו:

תהלים לד

The ארון קודש is closed. The שליח ציבור carries the ספר תורה to the בימה and the קהל says:

לְךָ יהוה הַגְּדֻלָּה וְהַגְּבוּרָה וְהַתִּפְאֶרֶת וְהַנֵּצַח וְהַהוֹד, כִּי־כֹל בַּשָּׁמַיִם וּבָאָרֶץ, לְךָ יהוה הַמַּמְלָכָה וְהַמִּתְנַשֵּׂא לְכֹל לְרֹאשׁ:

דברי הימים א, כט

רוֹמְמוּ יהוה אֱלֹהֵינוּ וְהִשְׁתַּחֲווּ לַהֲדֹם רַגְלָיו, קָדוֹשׁ הוּא: רוֹמְמוּ יהוה אֱלֹהֵינוּ וְהִשְׁתַּחֲווּ לְהַר קָדְשׁוֹ, כִּי־קָדוֹשׁ יהוה אֱלֹהֵינוּ:

תהלים צט

אַב הָרַחֲמִים הוּא יְרַחֵם עַם עֲמוּסִים, וְיִזְכֹּר בְּרִית אֵיתָנִים, וְיַצִּיל נַפְשׁוֹתֵינוּ מִן הַשָּׁעוֹת הָרָעוֹת, וְיִגְעַר בְּיֵצֶר הָרַע מִן הַנְּשׂוּאִים, וְיָחֹן אוֹתָנוּ לִפְלֵיטַת עוֹלָמִים, וִימַלֵּא מִשְׁאֲלוֹתֵינוּ בְּמִדָּה טוֹבָה יְשׁוּעָה וְרַחֲמִים.

The ספר תורה is placed on the שולחן and the גבאי calls a כהן to the תורה.

וְתִגָּלֶה וְתֵרָאֶה מַלְכוּתוֹ עָלֵינוּ בִּזְמַן קָרוֹב, וְיָחֹן פְּלֵיטָתֵנוּ וּפְלֵיטַת עַמּוֹ בֵּית יִשְׂרָאֵל לְחֵן וּלְחֶסֶד וּלְרַחֲמִים וּלְרָצוֹן וְנֹאמַר אָמֵן. הַכֹּל הָבוּ גֹדֶל לֵאלֹהֵינוּ וּתְנוּ כָבוֹד לַתּוֹרָה. *כֹּהֵן קְרָב, יַעֲמֹד, (פלוני בֶּן פלוני) הַכֹּהֵן.

*If no כהן is present, a לוי or ישראל is called up as follows:

/אֵין כַּאן כֹּהֵן, יַעֲמֹד, (פלוני בֶּן פלוני) בִּמְקוֹם כֹּהֵן./

בָּרוּךְ שֶׁנָּתַן תּוֹרָה לְעַמּוֹ יִשְׂרָאֵל בִּקְדֻשָּׁתוֹ.

גבאי, followed by the קהל:

וְאַתֶּם הַדְּבֵקִים בַּיהוה אֱלֹהֵיכֶם חַיִּים כֻּלְּכֶם הַיּוֹם:

דברים ד

The Reader shows the oleh the section to be read. The oleh touches the scroll at that place with the tzitzit of his tallit, which he then kisses. Holding the handles of the scroll, he says:

Oleh: Bless the LORD, the blessed One.

Cong: Bless the LORD, the blessed One, for ever and all time.

Oleh: Bless the LORD, the blessed One, for ever and all time.

> Blessed are You, LORD our God, King of the Universe,
> who has chosen us from all peoples and has given us His Torah.
> Blessed are You, LORD, Giver of the Torah.

After the reading, the oleh says:

Oleh: Blessed are You, LORD our God, King of the Universe, who has given us the Torah of truth, planting everlasting life in our midst. Blessed are You, LORD, Giver of the Torah.

TORAH READING

And Moses besought the LORD his God, and said, LORD, why does Your wrath burn against Your people, whom You have brought forth out of the land of Egypt with great power, and with a mighty hand? Why should Egypt speak, and say, In an evil hour did He bring them out, to slay them in the mountains, and to consume them from the face of the earth? Turn from Your fierce anger, and relent of this evil against Your people. Remember Abraham, Isaac, and Jacob, Your servants, to whom You did swear by Your own self, and did say to them, I will multiply your seed as the stars of heaven, and all this land that I have spoken of will I give to your seed, and they shall inherit it for ever. And the LORD relented of the evil which He thought to do to His people. *Ex. 32:11–14*

And the LORD said to Moses, Hew for yourself two tablets of stone like the first: and I will write upon these tablets the words that were on the first tablets, which You did break. And be ready in the morning, and come up in the morning to Mount Sinai, and present yourself there to Me on the top of the mountain. And no man shall come up with you, neither let any man be seen throughout all the mountain; neither let the flocks nor herds feed before that mountain. *And he hewed two tablets of stone like the first; and Moses rose up early in the morning, and went *Ex. 34:1–10 Levi*

Yisrael (Maftir)

The קורא shows the עולה the section to be read. The עולה touches the
ספר תורה at that place with the belt or mantle of the תורה, which he
then kisses. Holding the handles of the ספר תורה, he says:

עולה: בָּרְכוּ אֶת יהוה הַמְבֹרָךְ.

קהל: בָּרוּךְ יהוה הַמְבֹרָךְ לְעוֹלָם וָעֶד.

עולה: בָּרוּךְ יהוה הַמְבֹרָךְ לְעוֹלָם וָעֶד.

בָּרוּךְ אַתָּה יהוה, אֱלֹהֵינוּ מֶלֶךְ הָעוֹלָם
אֲשֶׁר בָּחַר בָּנוּ מִכָּל הָעַמִּים וְנָתַן לָנוּ אֶת תּוֹרָתוֹ.
בָּרוּךְ אַתָּה יהוה, נוֹתֵן הַתּוֹרָה.

After the קריאת התורה (on the next page) the עולה says:

עולה: בָּרוּךְ אַתָּה יהוה אֱלֹהֵינוּ מֶלֶךְ הָעוֹלָם
אֲשֶׁר נָתַן לָנוּ תּוֹרַת אֱמֶת וְחַיֵּי עוֹלָם נָטַע בְּתוֹכֵנוּ.
בָּרוּךְ אַתָּה יהוה, נוֹתֵן הַתּוֹרָה.

קריאת התורה

שמות לב:
יא-יד

וַיְחַל מֹשֶׁה אֶת־פְּנֵי יהוה אֱלֹהָיו וַיֹּאמֶר לָמָה יהוה יֶחֱרֶה אַפְּךָ
בְּעַמֶּךָ אֲשֶׁר הוֹצֵאתָ מֵאֶרֶץ מִצְרַיִם בְּכֹחַ גָּדוֹל וּבְיָד חֲזָקָה: לָמָּה
יֹאמְרוּ מִצְרַיִם לֵאמֹר בְּרָעָה הוֹצִיאָם לַהֲרֹג אֹתָם בֶּהָרִים וּלְכַלֹּתָם
מֵעַל פְּנֵי הָאֲדָמָה שׁוּב מֵחֲרוֹן אַפֶּךָ וְהִנָּחֵם עַל־הָרָעָה לְעַמֶּךָ: זְכֹר
לְאַבְרָהָם לְיִצְחָק וּלְיִשְׂרָאֵל עֲבָדֶיךָ אֲשֶׁר נִשְׁבַּעְתָּ לָהֶם בָּךְ וַתְּדַבֵּר
אֲלֵהֶם אַרְבֶּה אֶת־זַרְעֲכֶם כְּכוֹכְבֵי הַשָּׁמָיִם וְכָל־הָאָרֶץ הַזֹּאת אֲשֶׁר
אָמַרְתִּי אֶתֵּן לְזַרְעֲכֶם וְנָחֲלוּ לְעֹלָם: וַיִּנָּחֶם יהוה עַל־הָרָעָה אֲשֶׁר
דִּבֶּר לַעֲשׂוֹת לְעַמּוֹ:

שמות לד:א-י
לוי

וַיֹּאמֶר יהוה אֶל־מֹשֶׁה פְּסָל־לְךָ שְׁנֵי־לֻחֹת אֲבָנִים כָּרִאשֹׁנִים וְכָתַבְתִּי
עַל־הַלֻּחֹת אֶת־הַדְּבָרִים אֲשֶׁר הָיוּ עַל־הַלֻּחֹת הָרִאשֹׁנִים אֲשֶׁר
שִׁבַּרְתָּ: וֶהְיֵה נָכוֹן לַבֹּקֶר וְעָלִיתָ בַבֹּקֶר אֶל־הַר סִינַי וְנִצַּבְתָּ לִי שָׁם
עַל־רֹאשׁ הָהָר: וְאִישׁ לֹא־יַעֲלֶה עִמָּךְ וְגַם־אִישׁ אַל־יֵרָא בְּכָל־הָהָר

up to Mount Sinai, as the LORD had commanded him, and took in his hand the two tablets of stone. And the LORD descended in the cloud, and stood with him there, and proclaimed the name of the LORD. And the LORD passed by before him, and proclaimed, The LORD, The LORD, mighty, merciful and gracious, long-suffering, and abundant in love and truth, keeping troth to thousands, forgiving iniquity, and transgression, and sin, but who will by no means clear the guilty; punishing the iniquity of the fathers on the children, and on the children's children, to the third and to the fourth generation. And Moses made haste, and bowed his head toward the earth, and worshiped. And he said, If now I have found favor in Your sight, O LORD, let my LORD, I pray You, go among us; for it is a stiffnecked people; and pardon our iniquity and our sin, and take us for Your inheritance. And He said, Behold, I make a covenant: before all your people I will do marvels, such as have not been done in all the earth, nor in any nation: and all the people among whom you are shall see the work of the LORD that I will do with you, that it is tremendous.

HAGBAHA AND GELILA

The Torah scroll is lifted and the congregation says:

וְזֹאת הַתּוֹרָה This is the Torah
that Moses placed before the children of Israel,
at the LORD's commandment, by the hand of Moses.

Deut. 4

Num. 9

> *Some add:*
> It is a tree of life to those who grasp it, and those who uphold it are happy. *Prov. 3*
> Its ways are ways of pleasantness, and all its paths are peace.
> Long life is at its right hand; at its left, riches and honor.
> It pleased the LORD for the sake of [Israel's] righteousness, *Is. 42*
> to make the Torah great and glorious.

BLESSINGS BEFORE READING THE HAFTARA

Before reading the Haftara, the person called up for Maftir says:

בָּרוּךְ Blessed are You, LORD our God, King of the Universe, who chose good prophets and was pleased with their words, spoken in truth. Blessed are You, LORD, who chose the Torah, His servant Moses, His people Israel, and the prophets of truth and righteousness.

ישראל (מפטיר)

גַּם־הַצֹּאן וְהַבָּקָר אַל־יִרְעוּ אֶל־מוּל הָהָר הַהוּא: ★וַיִּפְסֹל שְׁנֵי־לֻחֹת אֲבָנִים כָּרִאשֹׁנִים וַיַּשְׁכֵּם מֹשֶׁה בַבֹּקֶר וַיַּעַל אֶל־הַר סִינַי כַּאֲשֶׁר צִוָּה יְהֹוָה אֹתוֹ וַיִּקַּח בְּיָדוֹ שְׁנֵי לֻחֹת אֲבָנִים: וַיֵּרֶד יְהֹוָה בֶּעָנָן וַיִּתְיַצֵּב עִמּוֹ שָׁם וַיִּקְרָא בְשֵׁם יְהֹוָה: וַיַּעֲבֹר יְהֹוָה ׀ עַל־פָּנָיו וַיִּקְרָא יְהֹוָה ׀ יְהֹוָה אֵל רַחוּם וְחַנּוּן אֶרֶךְ אַפַּיִם וְרַב־חֶסֶד וֶאֱמֶת: נֹצֵר חֶסֶד לָאֲלָפִים נֹשֵׂא עָוֹן וָפֶשַׁע וְחַטָּאָה וְנַקֵּה לֹא יְנַקֶּה פֹּקֵד ׀ עֲוֹן אָבוֹת עַל־בָּנִים וְעַל־בְּנֵי בָנִים עַל־שִׁלֵּשִׁים וְעַל־רִבֵּעִים: וַיְמַהֵר מֹשֶׁה וַיִּקֹּד אַרְצָה וַיִּשְׁתָּחוּ: וַיֹּאמֶר אִם־נָא מָצָאתִי חֵן בְּעֵינֶיךָ אֲדֹנָי יֵלֶךְ־נָא אֲדֹנָי בְּקִרְבֵּנוּ כִּי עַם־קְשֵׁה־עֹרֶף הוּא וְסָלַחְתָּ לַעֲוֹנֵנוּ וּלְחַטָּאתֵנוּ וּנְחַלְתָּנוּ: וַיֹּאמֶר הִנֵּה אָנֹכִי כֹּרֵת בְּרִית נֶגֶד כָּל־עַמְּךָ אֶעֱשֶׂה נִפְלָאֹת אֲשֶׁר לֹא־נִבְרְאוּ בְכָל־הָאָרֶץ וּבְכָל־הַגּוֹיִם וְרָאָה כָל־הָעָם אֲשֶׁר־אַתָּה בְקִרְבּוֹ אֶת־מַעֲשֵׂה יְהֹוָה כִּי־נוֹרָא הוּא אֲשֶׁר אֲנִי עֹשֶׂה עִמָּךְ:

הגבהה וגלילה

The ספר תורה is lifted and the קהל says:

דברים ד

וְזֹאת הַתּוֹרָה אֲשֶׁר־שָׂם מֹשֶׁה לִפְנֵי בְּנֵי יִשְׂרָאֵל:

במדבר ט

עַל־פִּי יְהֹוָה בְּיַד־מֹשֶׁה:

Some add:

משלי ג

עֵץ־חַיִּים הִיא לַמַּחֲזִיקִים בָּהּ וְתֹמְכֶיהָ מְאֻשָּׁר:
דְּרָכֶיהָ דַרְכֵי־נֹעַם וְכָל־נְתִיבוֹתֶיהָ שָׁלוֹם:
אֹרֶךְ יָמִים בִּימִינָהּ, בִּשְׂמֹאולָהּ עֹשֶׁר וְכָבוֹד:

ישעיה מב

יְהֹוָה חָפֵץ לְמַעַן צִדְקוֹ יַגְדִּיל תּוֹרָה וְיַאְדִּיר:

ברכות ההפטרה

Before reading the הפטרה, the person called up for מפטיר says:

בָּרוּךְ אַתָּה יְהֹוָה אֱלֹהֵינוּ מֶלֶךְ הָעוֹלָם אֲשֶׁר בָּחַר בִּנְבִיאִים טוֹבִים, וְרָצָה בְדִבְרֵיהֶם הַנֶּאֱמָרִים בֶּאֱמֶת. בָּרוּךְ אַתָּה יְהֹוָה, הַבּוֹחֵר בַּתּוֹרָה וּבְמֹשֶׁה עַבְדּוֹ וּבְיִשְׂרָאֵל עַמּוֹ וּבִנְבִיאֵי הָאֱמֶת וָצֶדֶק.

HAFTARA

Seek the Lord while He may be found, call upon Him while He is near: *Is. 55:6–56:8* let the wicked forsake his way, and the unrighteous man his thoughts: and let him return to the Lord, and He will have mercy upon him; and to our God, for He will abundantly pardon. For My thoughts are not Your thoughts, neither are Your ways My ways, says the Lord. For as the heavens are higher than the earth, so are My ways higher than Your ways, and My thoughts than Your thoughts. For as the rain comes down, and the snow from heaven, and returns not there, but waters the earth, and makes it bring forth and bud, that it may give seed to the sower, and bread to the eater: so shall be My word that goes out of My mouth: it shall not return to Me void, but it shall accomplish that which I please, and it shall prosper in that for which I sent it. For you shall go out with joy, and be led forth with peace: the mountains and the hills shall break forth before you into singing, and all the trees of the field shall clap their hands. Instead of the thorn shall the cypress come up, and instead of the nettle shall the myrtle tree come up: and it shall be to the Lord for a name, for an everlasting sign that shall not be cut off. Thus says the Lord, Keep judgment, and do justice: for My salvation is near to come, and My righteousness to be revealed. Happy is the man that does this, and the son of man that lays hold on it; that keeps the Sabbath and does not profane it, and keeps his hand from doing any evil. Neither let the son of the stranger, that has joined himself to the Lord, speak, saying, The Lord shall surely separate me from His people: neither let the eunuch say, Behold, I am a dry tree. For thus says the Lord to the eunuchs that keep My Sabbaths, and choose the things that please Me, and take hold of My covenant; And to them will I give in My house and within My walls a memorial better than sons and daughters: I will give them an everlasting name, that shall not be cut off. Also the sons of the stranger, that join themselves to the Lord, to serve Him, and to love the name of the Lord, to be His servants, every one that keeps the Sabbath and does not profane it, and all that hold fast to My covenant. Even them will I bring to My holy mountain, and make them joyful in My House of prayer: their burnt offerings and their sacrifices shall be accepted on My altar; for My House shall be called a House of prayer for all peoples. The Lord God who gathers the outcasts of Israel says, Yet will I gather others to Him, beside those of Him that are already gathered.

הפטרה

ישעיה
נה:ו-נו:ח

דִּרְשׁוּ יְהוָה בְּהִמָּצְאוֹ קְרָאֻהוּ בִּהְיוֹתוֹ קָרוֹב: יַעֲזֹב רָשָׁע דַּרְכּוֹ וְאִישׁ אָוֶן מַחְשְׁבֹתָיו וְיָשֹׁב אֶל־יְהוָה וִירַחֲמֵהוּ וְאֶל־אֱלֹהֵינוּ כִּי־יַרְבֶּה לִסְלוֹחַ: כִּי לֹא מַחְשְׁבוֹתַי מַחְשְׁבוֹתֵיכֶם וְלֹא דַרְכֵיכֶם דְּרָכָי נְאֻם יְהוָה: כִּי־גָבְהוּ שָׁמַיִם מֵאָרֶץ כֵּן גָּבְהוּ דְרָכַי מִדַּרְכֵיכֶם וּמַחְשְׁבֹתַי מִמַּחְשְׁבֹתֵיכֶם: כִּי כַּאֲשֶׁר יֵרֵד הַגֶּשֶׁם וְהַשֶּׁלֶג מִן־הַשָּׁמַיִם וְשָׁמָּה לֹא יָשׁוּב כִּי אִם־הִרְוָה אֶת־הָאָרֶץ וְהוֹלִידָהּ וְהִצְמִיחָהּ וְנָתַן זֶרַע לַזֹּרֵעַ וְלֶחֶם לָאֹכֵל: כֵּן יִהְיֶה דְבָרִי אֲשֶׁר יֵצֵא מִפִּי לֹא־יָשׁוּב אֵלַי רֵיקָם כִּי אִם־עָשָׂה אֶת־אֲשֶׁר חָפַצְתִּי וְהִצְלִיחַ אֲשֶׁר שְׁלַחְתִּיו: כִּי־בְשִׂמְחָה תֵצֵאוּ וּבְשָׁלוֹם תּוּבָלוּן הֶהָרִים וְהַגְּבָעוֹת יִפְצְחוּ לִפְנֵיכֶם רִנָּה וְכָל־עֲצֵי הַשָּׂדֶה יִמְחֲאוּ־כָף: תַּחַת הַנַּעֲצוּץ יַעֲלֶה בְרוֹשׁ תַּחַת הַסִּרְפַּד יַעֲלֶה הֲדַס וְהָיָה לַיהוָה לְשֵׁם לְאוֹת עוֹלָם לֹא יִכָּרֵת: כֹּה אָמַר יְהוָה שִׁמְרוּ מִשְׁפָּט וַעֲשׂוּ צְדָקָה כִּי־קְרוֹבָה יְשׁוּעָתִי לָבוֹא וְצִדְקָתִי לְהִגָּלוֹת: אַשְׁרֵי אֱנוֹשׁ יַעֲשֶׂה־זֹּאת וּבֶן־אָדָם יַחֲזִיק בָּהּ שֹׁמֵר שַׁבָּת מֵחַלְּלוֹ וְשֹׁמֵר יָדוֹ מֵעֲשׂוֹת כָּל־רָע: וְאַל־יֹאמַר בֶּן־הַנֵּכָר הַנִּלְוָה אֶל־יְהוָה לֵאמֹר הַבְדֵּל יַבְדִּילַנִי יְהוָה מֵעַל עַמּוֹ וְאַל־יֹאמַר הַסָּרִיס הֵן אֲנִי עֵץ יָבֵשׁ: כִּי־כֹה ׀ אָמַר יְהוָה לַסָּרִיסִים אֲשֶׁר יִשְׁמְרוּ אֶת־שַׁבְּתוֹתַי וּבָחֲרוּ בַּאֲשֶׁר חָפָצְתִּי וּמַחֲזִיקִים בִּבְרִיתִי: וְנָתַתִּי לָהֶם בְּבֵיתִי וּבְחוֹמֹתַי יָד וָשֵׁם טוֹב מִבָּנִים וּמִבָּנוֹת שֵׁם עוֹלָם אֶתֶּן־לוֹ אֲשֶׁר לֹא יִכָּרֵת: וּבְנֵי הַנֵּכָר הַנִּלְוִים עַל־יְהוָה לְשָׁרְתוֹ וּלְאַהֲבָה אֶת־שֵׁם יְהוָה לִהְיוֹת לוֹ לַעֲבָדִים כָּל־שֹׁמֵר שַׁבָּת מֵחַלְּלוֹ וּמַחֲזִיקִים בִּבְרִיתִי: וַהֲבִיאוֹתִים אֶל־הַר קָדְשִׁי וְשִׂמַּחְתִּים בְּבֵית תְּפִלָּתִי עוֹלֹתֵיהֶם וְזִבְחֵיהֶם לְרָצוֹן עַל־מִזְבְּחִי כִּי בֵיתִי בֵּית־תְּפִלָּה יִקָּרֵא לְכָל־הָעַמִּים: נְאֻם אֲדֹנָי יֱהוִֹה מְקַבֵּץ נִדְחֵי יִשְׂרָאֵל עוֹד אֲקַבֵּץ עָלָיו לְנִקְבָּצָיו:

BLESSINGS AFTER READING THE HAFTARA

After the Haftara, the person called up for Maftir says the following blessings:

בָּרוּךְ Blessed are You, Lord our God, King of the Universe, Rock of all worlds, righteous for all generations, the faithful God who says and does, speaks and fulfills, all of whose words are truth and righteousness. You are faithful, Lord our God, and faithful are Your words, not one of which returns unfulfilled, for You, God, are a faithful (and compassionate) King. Blessed are You, Lord, faithful in all His words.

רַחֵם Have compassion on Zion for it is the source of our life, and save the one grieved in spirit swiftly in our days. Blessed are You, Lord, who makes Zion rejoice in her children.

שַׂמְּחֵנוּ Grant us joy, Lord our God, through Elijah the prophet Your servant, and through the kingdom of the house of David Your anointed – may he soon come and make our hearts glad. May no stranger sit on his throne, and may others not continue to inherit his glory, for You promised him by Your holy name that his light would never be extinguished. Blessed are You, Lord, Shield of David.

RETURNING THE TORAH TO THE ARK

The Ark is opened. The Leader takes the Torah scroll and says:

יְהַלְלוּ Let them praise the name of the Lord, for His name alone is sublime. *Ps. 148*

The congregation responds:

הוֹדוֹ His majesty is above earth and heaven. He has raised the horn of His people, for the glory of all His devoted ones, the children of Israel, the people close to Him. Halleluya!

As the Torah scroll is returned to the Ark, say:

לְדָוִד מִזְמוֹר A psalm of David. The earth is the Lord's and all it contains, *Ps. 24* the world and all who live in it. For He founded it on the seas and established it on the streams. Who may climb the mountain of the Lord? Who may stand in His holy place? He who has clean hands and a pure heart, who has not taken My name in vain, or sworn deceitfully. He shall receive blessing from the Lord, and just reward from God, his salvation.

ברכות לאחר ההפטרה

After the הפטרה, the person called up for מפטיר says the following blessings:

בָּרוּךְ אַתָּה יהוה אֱלֹהֵינוּ מֶלֶךְ הָעוֹלָם, צוּר כָּל הָעוֹלָמִים, צַדִּיק בְּכָל הַדּוֹרוֹת, הָאֵל הַנֶּאֱמָן, הָאוֹמֵר וְעוֹשֶׂה, הַמְדַבֵּר וּמְקַיֵּם, שֶׁכָּל דְּבָרָיו אֱמֶת וָצֶדֶק. נֶאֱמָן אַתָּה הוּא יהוה אֱלֹהֵינוּ וְנֶאֱמָנִים דְּבָרֶיךָ, וְדָבָר אֶחָד מִדְּבָרֶיךָ אָחוֹר לֹא יָשׁוּב רֵיקָם, כִּי אֵל מֶלֶךְ נֶאֱמָן (וְרַחֲמָן) אָתָּה. בָּרוּךְ אַתָּה יהוה, הָאֵל הַנֶּאֱמָן בְּכָל דְּבָרָיו.

רַחֵם עַל צִיּוֹן כִּי הִיא בֵּית חַיֵּינוּ, וְלַעֲלוּבַת נֶפֶשׁ תּוֹשִׁיעַ בִּמְהֵרָה בְיָמֵינוּ. בָּרוּךְ אַתָּה יהוה, מְשַׂמֵּחַ צִיּוֹן בְּבָנֶיהָ.

שַׂמְּחֵנוּ יהוה אֱלֹהֵינוּ בְּאֵלִיָּהוּ הַנָּבִיא עַבְדֶּךָ, וּבְמַלְכוּת בֵּית דָּוִד מְשִׁיחֶךָ, בִּמְהֵרָה יָבוֹא וְיָגֵל לִבֵּנוּ. עַל כִּסְאוֹ לֹא יֵשֵׁב זָר, וְלֹא יִנְחֲלוּ עוֹד אֲחֵרִים אֶת כְּבוֹדוֹ, כִּי בְשֵׁם קָדְשְׁךָ נִשְׁבַּעְתָּ לּוֹ שֶׁלֹּא יִכְבֶּה נֵרוֹ לְעוֹלָם וָעֶד. בָּרוּךְ אַתָּה יהוה, מָגֵן דָּוִד.

הכנסת ספר תורה

The ארון קודש is opened. The שליח ציבור takes the ספר תורה and says:

יְהַלְלוּ אֶת־שֵׁם יהוה, כִּי־נִשְׂגָּב שְׁמוֹ, לְבַדּוֹ

תהלים קמח

The קהל responds:

הוֹדוֹ עַל־אֶרֶץ וְשָׁמָיִם: וַיָּרֶם קֶרֶן לְעַמּוֹ, תְּהִלָּה לְכָל־חֲסִידָיו, לִבְנֵי יִשְׂרָאֵל עַם קְרֹבוֹ, הַלְלוּיָהּ:

As the ספר תורה is returned to the ארון קודש, say:

לְדָוִד מִזְמוֹר, לַיהוה הָאָרֶץ וּמְלוֹאָהּ, תֵּבֵל וְיֹשְׁבֵי בָהּ: כִּי־הוּא עַל־יַמִּים יְסָדָהּ, וְעַל־נְהָרוֹת יְכוֹנְנֶהָ: מִי־יַעֲלֶה בְהַר־יהוה, וּמִי־יָקוּם בִּמְקוֹם קָדְשׁוֹ: נְקִי כַפַּיִם וּבַר־לֵבָב, אֲשֶׁר לֹא־נָשָׂא לַשָּׁוְא נַפְשִׁי וְלֹא נִשְׁבַּע לְמִרְמָה: יִשָּׂא בְרָכָה מֵאֵת יהוה, וּצְדָקָה מֵאֱלֹהֵי יִשְׁעוֹ: זֶה דּוֹר דֹּרְשָׁיו, מְבַקְשֵׁי פָנֶיךָ, יַעֲקֹב, סֶלָה: שְׂאוּ שְׁעָרִים רָאשֵׁיכֶם,

תהלים כד

This is a generation of those who seek Him, the descendants of Jacob who seek Your presence, Selah! Lift up your heads, O gates; be uplifted, eternal doors, so that the King of glory may enter. Who is the King of glory? It is the Lord, strong and mighty, the Lord mighty in battle. ▸ Lift up your heads, O gates; be uplifted, eternal doors, so that the King of glory may enter. Who is He, the King of glory? The Lord of hosts, He is the King of glory, Selah!

As the Torah scroll is placed into the Ark, say:

וּבְנֻחֹה יֹאמַר When the Ark came to rest, Moses would say: "Return, O Lord, to the myriad thousands of Israel." Advance, Lord, to Your resting place, You and Your mighty Ark. Your priests are clothed in righteousness, and Your devoted ones sing in joy. For the sake of Your servant David, do not reject Your anointed one. For I give you good instruction; do not forsake My Torah. It is a tree of life to those who grasp it, and those who uphold it are happy. Its ways are ways of pleasantness, and all its paths are peace. ▸ Turn us back, O Lord, to You, and we will return. Renew our days as of old.   *Num. 10 / Ps. 132 / Prov. 4 / Prov. 3 / Prov. 3 / Lam. 5*

The Ark is closed.

HALF KADDISH

Leader: יִתְגַּדַּל Magnified and sanctified
may His great name be,
in the world He created by His will.
May He establish His kingdom
in your lifetime and in your days,
and in the lifetime of all the house of Israel,
swiftly and soon – and say: Amen.

All: May His great name be blessed for ever and all time.

Leader: Blessed and praised, glorified and exalted,
raised and honored, uplifted and lauded
be the name of the Holy One, blessed be He,
beyond any blessing, song, praise and consolation
uttered in the world – and say: Amen.

וְהִנָּשְׂאוּ פִּתְחֵי עוֹלָם, וְיָבוֹא מֶלֶךְ הַכָּבוֹד: מִי זֶה מֶלֶךְ הַכָּבוֹד, יהוה עִזּוּז וְגִבּוֹר, יהוה גִּבּוֹר מִלְחָמָה: ◂ שְׂאוּ שְׁעָרִים רָאשֵׁיכֶם, וּשְׂאוּ פִּתְחֵי עוֹלָם, וְיָבֹא מֶלֶךְ הַכָּבוֹד: מִי הוּא זֶה מֶלֶךְ הַכָּבוֹד, יהוה צְבָאוֹת הוּא מֶלֶךְ הַכָּבוֹד, סֶלָה:

As the ספר תורה is placed into the ארון קודש, say:

<small>במדברי
תהלים קלב</small>

וּבְנֻחֹה יֹאמַר, שׁוּבָה יהוה רִבְבוֹת אַלְפֵי יִשְׂרָאֵל: קוּמָה יהוה לִמְנוּחָתֶךָ, אַתָּה וַאֲרוֹן עֻזֶּךָ: כֹּהֲנֶיךָ יִלְבְּשׁוּ־צֶדֶק, וַחֲסִידֶיךָ יְרַנֵּנוּ:

<small>משלי ד</small>

בַּעֲבוּר דָּוִד עַבְדֶּךָ אַל־תָּשֵׁב פְּנֵי מְשִׁיחֶךָ: כִּי לֶקַח טוֹב נָתַתִּי

<small>משלי ג</small>

לָכֶם, תּוֹרָתִי אַל־תַּעֲזֹבוּ: עֵץ־חַיִּים הִיא לַמַּחֲזִיקִים בָּהּ, וְתֹמְכֶיהָ

<small>משלי ג
איכה ה</small>

מְאֻשָּׁר: דְּרָכֶיהָ דַרְכֵי־נֹעַם וְכָל־נְתִיבוֹתֶיהָ שָׁלוֹם: ◂ הֲשִׁיבֵנוּ יהוה אֵלֶיךָ וְנָשׁוּבָה, חַדֵּשׁ יָמֵינוּ כְּקֶדֶם:

The ארון קודש is closed.

חצי קדיש

ש״ץ: יִתְגַּדַּל וְיִתְקַדַּשׁ שְׁמֵהּ רַבָּא (קהל: אָמֵן) בְּעָלְמָא דִּי בְרָא כִרְעוּתֵהּ, וְיַמְלִיךְ מַלְכוּתֵהּ בְּחַיֵּיכוֹן וּבְיוֹמֵיכוֹן וּבְחַיֵּי דְכָל בֵּית יִשְׂרָאֵל בַּעֲגָלָא וּבִזְמַן קָרִיב, וְאִמְרוּ אָמֵן. (קהל: אָמֵן)

קהל
וש״ץ: יְהֵא שְׁמֵהּ רַבָּא מְבָרַךְ לְעָלַם וּלְעָלְמֵי עָלְמַיָּא.

ש״ץ: יִתְבָּרַךְ וְיִשְׁתַּבַּח וְיִתְפָּאַר וְיִתְרוֹמַם וְיִתְנַשֵּׂא וְיִתְהַדָּר וְיִתְעַלֶּה וְיִתְהַלָּל שְׁמֵהּ דְּקֻדְשָׁא בְּרִיךְ הוּא (קהל: בְּרִיךְ הוּא) לְעֵלָּא מִן כָּל בִּרְכָתָא וְשִׁירָתָא, תֻּשְׁבְּחָתָא וְנֶחֱמָתָא דַּאֲמִירָן בְּעָלְמָא, וְאִמְרוּ אָמֵן. (קהל: אָמֵן)

THE AMIDA

The following prayer, until "in former years," on page 698, is said silently, standing with feet together. If there is a minyan, the Amida is repeated aloud by the Leader. Take three steps forward and at the points indicated by ˙, bend the knees at the first word, bow at the second, and stand straight before saying God's name.

When I proclaim the Lord's name, give glory to our God. — *Deut. 32*
O Lord, open my lips, so that my mouth may declare Your praise. — *Ps. 51*

PATRIARCHS

˙בָּרוּךְ Blessed are You, Lord our God and God of our fathers,
God of Abraham, God of Isaac and God of Jacob;
the great, mighty and awesome God,
God Most High,
who bestows acts of loving-kindness
and creates all,
who remembers the loving-kindness of the fathers
and will bring a Redeemer to their children's children
for the sake of His name, in love.
King, Helper, Savior, Shield:
˙Blessed are You, Lord,
Shield of Abraham.

DIVINE MIGHT

אַתָּה גִּבּוֹר You are eternally mighty, Lord.
You give life to the dead
and have great power to save.

In Israel: He causes the dew to fall.

He sustains the living with loving-kindness,
and with great compassion revives the dead.
He supports the fallen, heals the sick,
sets captives free,
and keeps His faith with those who sleep in the dust.

עמידה

The following prayer, until קַדְמֹנִיּוֹת, on page 699, is said silently, standing with feet together. If there is a מנין, the עמידה is repeated aloud by the שליח ציבור. Take three steps forward and at the points indicated by ּ׳, bend the knees at the first word, bow at the second, and stand straight before saying God's name.

דברים לב

כִּי שֵׁם יהוה אֶקְרָא, הָבוּ גְדֶל לֵאלֹהֵינוּ:

תהלים נא

אֲדֹנָי, שְׂפָתַי תִּפְתָּח, וּפִי יַגִּיד תְּהִלָּתֶךָ:

אבות

יבָּרוּךְ אַתָּה יהוה, אֱלֹהֵינוּ וֵאלֹהֵי אֲבוֹתֵינוּ
אֱלֹהֵי אַבְרָהָם, אֱלֹהֵי יִצְחָק, וֵאלֹהֵי יַעֲקֹב
הָאֵל הַגָּדוֹל הַגִּבּוֹר וְהַנּוֹרָא, אֵל עֶלְיוֹן
גּוֹמֵל חֲסָדִים טוֹבִים, וְקֹנֵה הַכֹּל
וְזוֹכֵר חַסְדֵי אָבוֹת
וּמֵבִיא גוֹאֵל לִבְנֵי בְנֵיהֶם
לְמַעַן שְׁמוֹ בְּאַהֲבָה.
מֶלֶךְ עוֹזֵר וּמוֹשִׁיעַ וּמָגֵן.
יבָּרוּךְ אַתָּה יהוה, מָגֵן אַבְרָהָם.

גבורות

אַתָּה גִּבּוֹר לְעוֹלָם, אֲדֹנָי
מְחַיֶּה מֵתִים אַתָּה, רַב לְהוֹשִׁיעַ

בארץ ישראל: מוֹרִיד הַטָּל

מְכַלְכֵּל חַיִּים בְּחֶסֶד, מְחַיֵּה מֵתִים בְּרַחֲמִים רַבִּים
סוֹמֵךְ נוֹפְלִים, וְרוֹפֵא חוֹלִים, וּמַתִּיר אֲסוּרִים
וּמְקַיֵּם אֱמוּנָתוֹ לִישֵׁנֵי עָפָר.

Who is like You, Master of might,
and to whom can You be compared,
O King who brings death and gives life,
and makes salvation grow?
Faithful are You to revive the dead.
Blessed are You, LORD, who revives the dead.

When saying the Amida silently, continue with "You are holy" on the next page.

KEDUSHA

*During the Leader's repetition, the following is said standing
with feet together, rising on the toes at the words indicated by ▲.*

Cong. then Leader:

נְקַדֵּשׁ We will sanctify Your name on earth,
as they sanctify it in the highest heavens,
as is written by Your prophet,
"And they [the angels] call to one another saying: Is. 6

Cong. then Leader:

▲Holy, ▲holy, ▲holy is the LORD of hosts
the whole world is filled with His glory."
Those facing them say "Blessed – "

Cong. then Leader:

"▲Blessed is the LORD's glory from His place."   Ezek. 3
And in Your Holy Writings it is written thus:

Cong. then Leader:

▲The LORD shall reign for ever. He is your God, Zion,   Ps. 146
from generation to generation, Halleluya!"

Leader:

From generation to generation we will declare Your greatness,
and we will proclaim Your holiness for evermore.
Your praise, our God, shall not leave our mouth forever,
for You, God, are a great and holy King. Blessed are You, LORD,
the holy God.

The Leader continues with "You grace humanity" on the next page.

מִי כָמְוֹךָ, בַּעַל גְּבוּרוֹת
וּמִי דּוֹמֶה לָךְ
מֶלֶךְ, מֵמִית וּמְחַיֶּה וּמַצְמִיחַ יְשׁוּעָה.
וְנֶאֱמָן אַתָּה לְהַחֲיוֹת מֵתִים.
בָּרוּךְ אַתָּה יהוה, מְחַיֵּה הַמֵּתִים.

When saying the עמידה silently, continue with אַתָּה קָדוֹשׁ on the next page.

קדושה

During חזרת הש״ץ, the following is said standing
with feet together, rising on the toes at the words indicated by ⸱.

קהל then שליח ציבור:

נְקַדֵּשׁ אֶת שִׁמְךָ בָּעוֹלָם, כְּשֵׁם שֶׁמַּקְדִּישִׁים אוֹתוֹ בִּשְׁמֵי מָרוֹם
כַּכָּתוּב עַל יַד נְבִיאֶךָ, וְקָרָא זֶה אֶל־זֶה וְאָמַר

ישעיהו ו

קהל then שליח ציבור:

⸱קָדוֹשׁ, ⸱קָדוֹשׁ, ⸱קָדוֹשׁ, יהוה צְבָאוֹת, מְלֹא כָל־הָאָרֶץ כְּבוֹדוֹ:
לְעֻמָּתָם בָּרוּךְ יֹאמֵרוּ

קהל then שליח ציבור:

⸱בָּרוּךְ כְּבוֹד־יהוה מִמְּקוֹמוֹ:
וּבְדִבְרֵי קָדְשְׁךָ כָּתוּב לֵאמֹר

יחזקאל ג

קהל then שליח ציבור:

⸱יִמְלֹךְ יהוה לְעוֹלָם, אֱלֹהַיִךְ צִיּוֹן לְדֹר וָדֹר, הַלְלוּיָהּ:

תהלים קמו

שליח ציבור:

לְדוֹר וָדוֹר נַגִּיד גָּדְלֶךָ, וּלְנֵצַח נְצָחִים קְדֻשָּׁתְךָ נַקְדִּישׁ
וְשִׁבְחֲךָ אֱלֹהֵינוּ מִפִּינוּ לֹא יָמוּשׁ לְעוֹלָם וָעֶד
כִּי אֵל מֶלֶךְ גָּדוֹל וְקָדוֹשׁ אָתָּה.
בָּרוּךְ אַתָּה יהוה, הָאֵל הַקָּדוֹשׁ.

The שליח ציבור continues with אַתָּה חוֹנֵן on the next page.

HOLINESS

אַתָּה קָדוֹשׁ You are holy and Your name is holy,
and holy ones praise You daily, Selah!
Blessed are You, LORD, the holy God.

KNOWLEDGE

אַתָּה חוֹנֵן You grace humanity with knowledge
and teach mortals understanding.
Grace us with the knowledge, understanding
and discernment that come from You.
Blessed are You, LORD, who graciously grants knowledge.

REPENTANCE

הֲשִׁיבֵנוּ Bring us back, our Father,
to Your Torah.
Draw us near, our King,
to Your service.
Lead us back to You in perfect repentance.
Blessed are You, LORD, who desires repentance.

FORGIVENESS

Strike the left side of the chest at °.

סְלַח לָנוּ Forgive us, our Father, for we have °sinned.
Pardon us, our King, for we have °transgressed;
for You pardon and forgive.
Blessed are You, LORD,
the gracious One who repeatedly forgives.

REDEMPTION

רְאֵה Look on our affliction, plead our cause,
and redeem us soon for Your name's sake,
for You are a powerful Redeemer.
Blessed are You, LORD, the Redeemer of Israel.

קדושת השם
אַתָּה קָדוֹשׁ וְשִׁמְךָ קָדוֹשׁ
וּקְדוֹשִׁים בְּכָל יוֹם יְהַלְלוּךָ סֶּלָה.
בָּרוּךְ אַתָּה יהוה, הָאֵל הַקָּדוֹשׁ.

דעת
אַתָּה חוֹנֵן לְאָדָם דַּעַת
וּמְלַמֵּד לֶאֱנוֹשׁ בִּינָה.
חָנֵּנוּ מֵאִתְּךָ דֵּעָה בִּינָה וְהַשְׂכֵּל.
בָּרוּךְ אַתָּה יהוה, חוֹנֵן הַדָּעַת.

תשובה
הֲשִׁיבֵנוּ אָבִינוּ לְתוֹרָתֶךָ
וְקָרְבֵנוּ מַלְכֵּנוּ לַעֲבוֹדָתֶךָ
וְהַחֲזִירֵנוּ בִּתְשׁוּבָה שְׁלֵמָה לְפָנֶיךָ.
בָּרוּךְ אַתָּה יהוה, הָרוֹצֶה בִּתְשׁוּבָה.

סליחה
Strike the left side of the chest at °.

סְלַח לָנוּ אָבִינוּ כִּי °חָטָאנוּ
מְחַל לָנוּ מַלְכֵּנוּ כִּי °פָשָׁעְנוּ
כִּי מוֹחֵל וְסוֹלֵחַ אָתָּה.
בָּרוּךְ אַתָּה יהוה, חַנּוּן הַמַּרְבֶּה לִסְלֹחַ.

גאולה
רְאֵה בְעָנְיֵנוּ, וְרִיבָה רִיבֵנוּ
וּגְאָלֵנוּ מְהֵרָה לְמַעַן שְׁמֶךָ
כִּי גּוֹאֵל חָזָק אָתָּה.
בָּרוּךְ אַתָּה יהוה, גּוֹאֵל יִשְׂרָאֵל.

The Leader adds:
עֲנֵנוּ Answer us, LORD, answer us on our Fast Day, for we are in great distress. Look not at our wickedness. Do not hide Your face from us and do not ignore our plea. Be near to our cry; please let Your loving-kindness comfort us. Even before we call to You, answer us, as is said, "Before they call, I will answer. While they are still speaking, I will hear." Is. 65 For You, LORD, are the One who answers in time of distress, redeems and rescues in all times of trouble and anguish. Blessed are You, LORD, who answers in time of distress.

HEALING
רְפָאֵנוּ Heal us, LORD, and we shall be healed.
Save us and we shall be saved,
for You are our praise.
Bring complete recovery for all our ailments,

The following prayer for a sick person may be said here:
May it be Your will, O LORD my God and God of my ancestors, that You speedily send a complete recovery from heaven, a healing of both soul and body, to the patient (*name*), son/daughter of (*mother's name*) among the other afflicted of Israel.

for You, God, King, are a faithful and compassionate Healer.
Blessed are You, LORD, Healer of the sick of His people Israel.

PROSPERITY
בָּרֵךְ Bless this year for us, LORD our God,
and all its types of produce for good.
Grant blessing
on the face of the earth,
and from its goodness satisfy us,
blessing our year as the best of years.
Blessed are You, LORD,
who blesses the years.

שליח ציבור *adds: The*

עֲנֵנוּ יהוה עֲנֵנוּ בְּיוֹם צוֹם תַּעֲנִיתֵנוּ, כִּי בְצָרָה גְדוֹלָה אֲנָחְנוּ. אַל תֵּפֶן אֶל רִשְׁעֵנוּ, וְאַל תַּסְתֵּר פָּנֶיךָ מִמֶּנּוּ, וְאַל תִּתְעַלַּם מִתְּחִנָּתֵנוּ. הֱיֵה נָא קָרוֹב לְשַׁוְעָתֵנוּ, יְהִי נָא חַסְדְּךָ לְנַחֲמֵנוּ, טֶרֶם נִקְרָא אֵלֶיךָ עֲנֵנוּ, כַּדָּבָר שֶׁנֶּאֱמַר: וְהָיָה טֶרֶם יִקְרָאוּ וַאֲנִי אֶעֱנֶה, עוֹד הֵם מְדַבְּרִים וַאֲנִי אֶשְׁמָע: כִּי אַתָּה יהוה הָעוֹנֶה בְּעֵת צָרָה, פּוֹדֶה וּמַצִּיל בְּכָל עֵת צָרָה וְצוּקָה. בָּרוּךְ אַתָּה יהוה, הָעוֹנֶה בְּעֵת צָרָה. ישעיה סה

רפואה

רְפָאֵנוּ יהוה וְנֵרָפֵא
הוֹשִׁיעֵנוּ וְנִוָּשֵׁעָה, כִּי תְהִלָּתֵנוּ אָתָּה
וְהַעֲלֵה רְפוּאָה שְׁלֵמָה לְכָל מַכּוֹתֵינוּ

The following prayer for a sick person may be said here:

יְהִי רָצוֹן מִלְּפָנֶיךָ יהוה אֱלֹהַי וֵאלֹהֵי אֲבוֹתַי, שֶׁתִּשְׁלַח מְהֵרָה רְפוּאָה שְׁלֵמָה מִן הַשָּׁמַיִם רְפוּאַת הַנֶּפֶשׁ וּרְפוּאַת הַגּוּף לַחוֹלֶה/לַחוֹלָה *name of patient* בֶּן/בַּת *mother's name* בְּתוֹךְ שְׁאָר חוֹלֵי יִשְׂרָאֵל.

כִּי אֵל מֶלֶךְ רוֹפֵא נֶאֱמָן וְרַחֲמָן אָתָּה.
בָּרוּךְ אַתָּה יהוה, רוֹפֵא חוֹלֵי עַמּוֹ יִשְׂרָאֵל.

ברכת השנים

בָּרֵךְ עָלֵינוּ יהוה אֱלֹהֵינוּ אֶת הַשָּׁנָה הַזֹּאת
וְאֶת כָּל מִינֵי תְבוּאָתָהּ, לְטוֹבָה
וְתֵן בְּרָכָה עַל פְּנֵי הָאֲדָמָה, וְשַׂבְּעֵנוּ מִטּוּבָהּ
וּבָרֵךְ שְׁנָתֵנוּ כַּשָּׁנִים הַטּוֹבוֹת.
בָּרוּךְ אַתָּה יהוה, מְבָרֵךְ הַשָּׁנִים.

INGATHERING OF EXILES

תְּקַע Sound the great shofar for our freedom,
raise high the banner to gather our exiles,
and gather us together from the four quarters of the earth.
Blessed are You, LORD,
who gathers the dispersed of His people Israel.

JUSTICE

הָשִׁיבָה Restore our judges as at first
and our counselors as at the beginning,
and remove from us sorrow and sighing.
May You alone, LORD,
reign over us with loving-kindness and compassion,
and vindicate us in justice.
Blessed are You, LORD,
the King who loves righteousness and justice.

AGAINST INFORMERS

וְלַמַּלְשִׁינִים For the slanderers let there be no hope,
and may all wickedness perish in an instant.
May all Your people's enemies swiftly be cut down.
May You swiftly uproot, crush, cast down
and humble the arrogant swiftly in our days.
Blessed are You, LORD,
who destroys enemies and humbles the arrogant.

THE RIGHTEOUS

עַל הַצַּדִּיקִים To the righteous, the pious,
the elders of Your people the house of Israel,
the remnant of their scholars, the righteous converts, and to us,
may Your compassion be aroused, LORD our God.
Grant a good reward to all who sincerely trust in Your name.
Set our lot with them,
so that we may never be ashamed, for in You we trust.
Blessed are You, LORD, who is the support and trust of the righteous.

קיבוץ גליות
תְּקַע בְּשׁוֹפָר גָּדוֹל לְחֵרוּתֵנוּ, וְשָׂא נֵס לְקַבֵּץ גָּלֻיּוֹתֵינוּ
וְקַבְּצֵנוּ יַחַד מֵאַרְבַּע כַּנְפוֹת הָאָרֶץ.
בָּרוּךְ אַתָּה יהוה, מְקַבֵּץ נִדְחֵי עַמּוֹ יִשְׂרָאֵל.

משפט
הָשִׁיבָה שׁוֹפְטֵינוּ כְּבָרִאשׁוֹנָה וְיוֹעֲצֵינוּ כְּבַתְּחִלָּה
וְהָסֵר מִמֶּנּוּ יָגוֹן וַאֲנָחָה
וּמְלֹךְ עָלֵינוּ אַתָּה יהוה לְבַדְּךָ בְּחֶסֶד וּבְרַחֲמִים
וְצַדְּקֵנוּ בַּמִּשְׁפָּט.
בָּרוּךְ אַתָּה יהוה, מֶלֶךְ אוֹהֵב צְדָקָה וּמִשְׁפָּט.

ברכת המינים
וְלַמַּלְשִׁינִים אַל תְּהִי תִקְוָה, וְכָל הָרִשְׁעָה כְּרֶגַע תֹּאבֵד
וְכָל אוֹיְבֵי עַמְּךָ מְהֵרָה יִכָּרֵתוּ
וְהַזֵּדִים מְהֵרָה תְעַקֵּר וּתְשַׁבֵּר וּתְמַגֵּר וְתַכְנִיעַ בִּמְהֵרָה בְיָמֵינוּ.
בָּרוּךְ אַתָּה יהוה, שׁוֹבֵר אוֹיְבִים וּמַכְנִיעַ זֵדִים.

על הצדיקים
עַל הַצַּדִּיקִים וְעַל הַחֲסִידִים
וְעַל זִקְנֵי עַמְּךָ בֵּית יִשְׂרָאֵל, וְעַל פְּלֵיטַת סוֹפְרֵיהֶם
וְעַל גֵּרֵי הַצֶּדֶק, וְעָלֵינוּ
יֶהֱמוּ רַחֲמֶיךָ יהוה אֱלֹהֵינוּ
וְתֵן שָׂכָר טוֹב לְכָל הַבּוֹטְחִים בְּשִׁמְךָ בֶּאֱמֶת
וְשִׂים חֶלְקֵנוּ עִמָּהֶם, וּלְעוֹלָם לֹא נֵבוֹשׁ כִּי בְךָ בָּטָחְנוּ.
בָּרוּךְ אַתָּה יהוה, מִשְׁעָן וּמִבְטָח לַצַּדִּיקִים.

REBUILDING JERUSALEM

וְלִירוּשָׁלַיִם To Jerusalem, Your city,
may You return in compassion,
and may You dwell in it as You promised.
May You rebuild it rapidly in our days
as an everlasting structure,
and install within it soon the throne of David.
> Console, O LORD our God,
> the mourners of Zion
> and the mourners of Jerusalem,
> and the city that is in sorrow, laid waste,
> scorned and desolate;
> that grieves for the loss of its children,
> that is laid waste of its dwellings,
> robbed of its glory, desolate without inhabitants.
> She sits with her head covered like a barren childless woman.
> Legions have devoured her;
> idolaters have taken possession of her;
> they have put Your people Israel to the sword
> and deliberately killed
> the devoted followers of the Most High.
> Therefore Zion weeps bitterly,
> and Jerusalem raises her voice.
> My heart, my heart grieves for those they killed;
> I am in anguish, I am in anguish for those they killed.
> For You, O LORD, consumed it with fire,
> and with fire You will rebuild it in the future,
> as is said,
>> "And I Myself will be a wall of fire around it, says the LORD,   *Zech. 2*
>> and I will be its glory within."

Blessed are You, LORD,
who consoles Zion and rebuilds Jerusalem.

בניין ירושלים

וְלִירוּשָׁלַיִם עִירְךָ בְּרַחֲמִים תָּשׁוּב
וְתִשְׁכֹּן בְּתוֹכָהּ כַּאֲשֶׁר דִּבַּרְתָּ
וּבְנֵה אוֹתָהּ בְּקָרוֹב בְּיָמֵינוּ בִּנְיַן עוֹלָם
וְכִסֵּא דָוִד מְהֵרָה לְתוֹכָהּ תָּכִין.
נַחֵם יהוה אֱלֹהֵינוּ אֶת אֲבֵלֵי צִיּוֹן וְאֶת אֲבֵלֵי יְרוּשָׁלָיִם
וְאֶת הָעִיר הָאֲבֵלָה וְהַחֲרֵבָה וְהַבְּזוּיָה וְהַשּׁוֹמֵמָה.
הָאֲבֵלָה מִבְּלִי בָנֶיהָ, וְהַחֲרֵבָה מִמְּעוֹנוֹתֶיהָ
וְהַבְּזוּיָה מִכְּבוֹדָהּ, וְהַשּׁוֹמֵמָה מֵאֵין יוֹשֵׁב.
וְהִיא יוֹשֶׁבֶת וְרֹאשָׁהּ חָפוּי, כְּאִשָּׁה עֲקָרָה שֶׁלֹּא יָלְדָה.
וַיְבַלְּעוּהָ לִגְיוֹנוֹת
וַיִּירָשׁוּהָ עוֹבְדֵי פְסִילִים
וַיַּטִּילוּ אֶת עַמְּךָ יִשְׂרָאֵל לֶחָרֶב
וַיַּהַרְגוּ בְזָדוֹן חֲסִידֵי עֶלְיוֹן.
עַל כֵּן צִיּוֹן בְּמַר תִּבְכֶּה, וִירוּשָׁלַיִם תִּתֵּן קוֹלָהּ.
לִבִּי לִבִּי עַל חַלְלֵיהֶם, מֵעַי מֵעַי עַל חַלְלֵיהֶם
כִּי אַתָּה יהוה בָּאֵשׁ הִצַּתָּהּ
וּבָאֵשׁ אַתָּה עָתִיד לִבְנוֹתָהּ.
כָּאָמוּר:
וַאֲנִי אֶהְיֶה־לָּהּ, נְאֻם־יהוה, חוֹמַת אֵשׁ סָבִיב
וּלְכָבוֹד אֶהְיֶה בְתוֹכָהּ:

זכריה ב

בָּרוּךְ אַתָּה יהוה
מְנַחֵם צִיּוֹן וּבוֹנֵה יְרוּשָׁלָיִם.

KINGDOM OF DAVID

אֶת צֶמַח May the offshoot of Your servant David soon flower,
and may his pride be raised high by Your salvation,
for we wait for Your salvation all day.
Blessed are You, Lord,
who makes the glory of salvation flourish.

RESPONSE TO PRAYER

שְׁמַע קוֹלֵנוּ Listen to our voice, Lord our God.
Spare us and have compassion on us,
and in compassion and favor accept our prayer,
for You, God, listen to prayers and pleas.
Do not turn us away, O our King,
empty-handed from Your presence.

During the silent Amida, the congregation adds the following:

Answer us, Lord,
answer us on our Fast Day,
for we are in great distress.
Look not at our wickedness.
Do not hide Your face from us
and do not ignore our plea.
Be near to our cry;
please let Your loving-kindness comfort us.
Even before we call to You, answer us, as is said,
"Before they call, I will answer.   *Is. 65*
While they are still speaking, I will hear."

For You, Lord, are the One who answers in time of distress,
redeems and rescues in all times of trouble and anguish.
for You listen with compassion
to the prayer of Your people Israel.
Blessed are You, Lord,
who listens to prayer.

מלכות בית דוד
אֶת צֶמַח דָּוִד עַבְדְּךָ מְהֵרָה תַצְמִיחַ
וְקַרְנוֹ תָּרוּם בִּישׁוּעָתֶךָ, כִּי לִישׁוּעָתְךָ קִוִּינוּ כָּל הַיּוֹם.
בָּרוּךְ אַתָּה יהוה, מַצְמִיחַ קֶרֶן יְשׁוּעָה.

שומע תפילה
שְׁמַע קוֹלֵנוּ יהוה אֱלֹהֵינוּ
חוּס וְרַחֵם עָלֵינוּ
וְקַבֵּל בְּרַחֲמִים וּבְרָצוֹן אֶת תְּפִלָּתֵנוּ
כִּי אֵל שׁוֹמֵעַ תְּפִלּוֹת וְתַחֲנוּנִים אָתָּה
וּמִלְּפָנֶיךָ מַלְכֵּנוּ רֵיקָם אַל תְּשִׁיבֵנוּ.

During the silent עמידה, *the* קהל *adds the following:*
עֲנֵנוּ יהוה עֲנֵנוּ בְּיוֹם צוֹם תַּעֲנִיתֵנוּ
כִּי בְצָרָה גְדוֹלָה אֲנָחְנוּ.
אַל תֵּפֶן אֶל רִשְׁעֵנוּ, וְאַל תַּסְתֵּר פָּנֶיךָ מִמֶּנּוּ
וְאַל תִּתְעַלַּם מִתְּחִנָּתֵנוּ.
הֱיֵה נָא קָרוֹב לְשַׁוְעָתֵנוּ, יְהִי נָא חַסְדְּךָ לְנַחֲמֵנוּ
טֶרֶם נִקְרָא אֵלֶיךָ עֲנֵנוּ, כַּדָּבָר שֶׁנֶּאֱמַר:
וְהָיָה טֶרֶם יִקְרָאוּ וַאֲנִי אֶעֱנֶה
עוֹד הֵם מְדַבְּרִים וַאֲנִי אֶשְׁמָע:
כִּי אַתָּה יהוה הָעוֹנֶה בְּעֵת צָרָה
פּוֹדֶה וּמַצִּיל בְּכָל עֵת צָרָה וְצוּקָה.

ישעיה סה

כִּי אַתָּה שׁוֹמֵעַ תְּפִלַּת עַמְּךָ יִשְׂרָאֵל בְּרַחֲמִים.
בָּרוּךְ אַתָּה יהוה, שׁוֹמֵעַ תְּפִלָּה.

TEMPLE SERVICE

רְצֵה Find favor, LORD our God, in Your people Israel and their prayer.
Restore the service to Your most holy House,
and accept in love and favor
the fire-offerings of Israel and their prayer.
May the service of Your people Israel always find favor with You.
And may our eyes witness Your return to Zion in compassion.
Blessed are You, LORD, who restores His Presence to Zion.

THANKSGIVING

Bow at the first nine words.

מוֹדִים We give thanks to You,
for You are the LORD our God
and God of our ancestors
for ever and all time.
You are the Rock of our lives,
Shield of our salvation
from generation to generation.
We will thank You and
declare Your praise for our lives,
which are entrusted into Your hand;
for our souls,
which are placed in Your charge;
for Your miracles
which are with us every day;
and for Your wonders and favors
at all times, evening,
morning and midday.
You are good –
for Your compassion never fails.
You are compassionate –
for Your loving-kindnesses never cease.
We have always
placed our hope in You.

During the Leader's repetition, the congregation says quietly:
מוֹדִים We give thanks to You,
for You are the LORD
our God
and God of our ancestors,
God of all flesh,
who formed us
and formed the universe.
Blessings and thanks are due
to Your great and holy name
for giving us life
and sustaining us.
May You continue
to give us life and sustain us;
and may You gather our exiles
to Your holy courts,
to keep Your decrees,
do Your will and serve You
with a perfect heart,
for it is for us
to give You thanks.
Blessed be God
to whom
thanksgiving is due.

עבודה

רְצֵה יהוה אֱלֹהֵינוּ בְּעַמְּךָ יִשְׂרָאֵל, וּבִתְפִלָּתָם
וְהָשֵׁב אֶת הָעֲבוֹדָה לִדְבִיר בֵּיתֶךָ
וְאִשֵּׁי יִשְׂרָאֵל וּתְפִלָּתָם בְּאַהֲבָה תְקַבֵּל בְּרָצוֹן
וּתְהִי לְרָצוֹן תָּמִיד עֲבוֹדַת יִשְׂרָאֵל עַמֶּךָ.
וְתֶחֱזֶינָה עֵינֵינוּ בְּשׁוּבְךָ לְצִיּוֹן בְּרַחֲמִים.
בָּרוּךְ אַתָּה יהוה, הַמַּחֲזִיר שְׁכִינָתוֹ לְצִיּוֹן.

הודאה

Bow at the first five words.

מוֹדִים אֲנַחְנוּ לָךְ
שָׁאַתָּה הוּא יהוה אֱלֹהֵינוּ
וֵאלֹהֵי אֲבוֹתֵינוּ לְעוֹלָם וָעֶד.
צוּר חַיֵּינוּ, מָגֵן יִשְׁעֵנוּ
אַתָּה הוּא לְדוֹר וָדוֹר.
נוֹדֶה לְּךָ וּנְסַפֵּר תְּהִלָּתֶךָ
עַל חַיֵּינוּ הַמְּסוּרִים בְּיָדֶךָ
וְעַל נִשְׁמוֹתֵינוּ הַפְּקוּדוֹת לָךְ
וְעַל נִסֶּיךָ שֶׁבְּכָל יוֹם עִמָּנוּ
וְעַל נִפְלְאוֹתֶיךָ וְטוֹבוֹתֶיךָ
שֶׁבְּכָל עֵת, עֶרֶב וָבֹקֶר וְצָהֳרָיִם.
הַטּוֹב, כִּי לֹא כָלוּ רַחֲמֶיךָ
וְהַמְרַחֵם, כִּי לֹא תַמּוּ חֲסָדֶיךָ
מֵעוֹלָם קִוִּינוּ לָךְ.

During חזרת הש״ץ,
the קהל says quietly:

מוֹדִים אֲנַחְנוּ לָךְ
שָׁאַתָּה הוּא יהוה אֱלֹהֵינוּ
וֵאלֹהֵי אֲבוֹתֵינוּ
אֱלֹהֵי כָל בָּשָׂר
יוֹצְרֵנוּ, יוֹצֵר בְּרֵאשִׁית.
בְּרָכוֹת וְהוֹדָאוֹת
לְשִׁמְךָ הַגָּדוֹל וְהַקָּדוֹשׁ
עַל שֶׁהֶחֱיִיתָנוּ וְקִיַּמְתָּנוּ.
כֵּן תְּחַיֵּנוּ וּתְקַיְּמֵנוּ
וְתֶאֱסֹף גָּלֻיּוֹתֵינוּ
לְחַצְרוֹת קָדְשֶׁךָ
לִשְׁמֹר חֻקֶּיךָ וְלַעֲשׂוֹת רְצוֹנֶךָ
וּלְעָבְדְּךָ בְּלֵבָב שָׁלֵם
עַל שֶׁאֲנַחְנוּ מוֹדִים לָךְ.
בָּרוּךְ אֵל הַהוֹדָאוֹת.

וְעַל כֻּלָּם For all these things may Your name be blessed and
exalted, our King, continually, for ever and all time.
Let all that lives thank You, Selah! and praise Your name in truth,
God, our Savior and Help, Selah!
▸Blessed are You, LORD, whose name is "the Good"
and to whom thanks are due.

---

*The following is said by the Leader during the repetition of the Amida,
although in some congregations it is omitted. In Israel (and some congregations
outside Israel), if Kohanim bless the congregation turn to page 706.*

Our God and God of our fathers, bless us with the threefold blessing in
the Torah, written by the hand of Moses Your servant and pronounced by
Aaron and his sons the priests, Your holy people, as it is said:

> May the LORD bless you and protect you. *Num. 6*
> *Cong:* May it be Your will.
> May the LORD make His face shine on you and be gracious to you.
> *Cong:* May it be Your will.
> May the LORD turn His face toward you, and grant you peace.
> *Cong:* May it be Your will.

PEACE

שִׂים שָׁלוֹם Grant peace, goodness and blessing,
grace, loving-kindness and compassion to us
and all Israel Your people.
Bless us, our Father, all as one, with the light of Your face,
for by the light of Your face You have given us, LORD our God,
the Torah of life and love of kindness,
righteousness, blessing, compassion, life and peace.
May it be good in Your eyes to bless Your people Israel
at every time, in every hour, with Your peace.
Blessed are You, LORD,
who blesses His people Israel with peace.

*The following verse concludes the Leader's repetition of the Amida.
Some also say it here as part of the silent Amida.*

May the words of my mouth and the meditation of my heart *Ps. 19*
find favor before You, LORD, my Rock and Redeemer.

וְעַל כֻּלָּם יִתְבָּרַךְ וְיִתְרוֹמַם שִׁמְךָ מַלְכֵּנוּ תָּמִיד לְעוֹלָם וָעֶד.
וְכֹל הַחַיִּים יוֹדוּךָ סֶּלָה, וִיהַלְלוּ אֶת שִׁמְךָ בֶּאֱמֶת
הָאֵל יְשׁוּעָתֵנוּ וְעֶזְרָתֵנוּ סֶלָה.
בָּרוּךְ אַתָּה יהוה, הַטּוֹב שִׁמְךָ וּלְךָ נָאֶה לְהוֹדוֹת.

The following is said by the שליח ציבור during the חזרת הש״ץ, although in some congregations it is omitted. In ארץ ישראל (and some congregations outside ארץ ישראל), if ברכת כהנים say כהנים turn to page 707.

אֱלֹהֵינוּ וֵאלֹהֵי אֲבוֹתֵינוּ, בָּרְכֵנוּ בַּבְּרָכָה הַמְשֻׁלֶּשֶׁת בַּתּוֹרָה, הַכְּתוּבָה
עַל יְדֵי מֹשֶׁה עַבְדֶּךָ, הָאֲמוּרָה מִפִּי אַהֲרֹן וּבָנָיו כֹּהֲנִים עַם קְדוֹשֶׁךָ,
כָּאָמוּר

במדברו

יְבָרֶכְךָ יהוה וְיִשְׁמְרֶךָ: קהל: כֵּן יְהִי רָצוֹן
יָאֵר יהוה פָּנָיו אֵלֶיךָ וִיחֻנֶּךָּ: קהל: כֵּן יְהִי רָצוֹן
יִשָּׂא יהוה פָּנָיו אֵלֶיךָ וְיָשֵׂם לְךָ שָׁלוֹם: קהל: כֵּן יְהִי רָצוֹן

ברכת שלום
שִׂים שָׁלוֹם טוֹבָה וּבְרָכָה
חֵן וָחֶסֶד וְרַחֲמִים
עָלֵינוּ וְעַל כָּל יִשְׂרָאֵל עַמֶּךָ.
בָּרְכֵנוּ אָבִינוּ כֻּלָּנוּ כְּאֶחָד בְּאוֹר פָּנֶיךָ
כִּי בְאוֹר פָּנֶיךָ נָתַתָּ לָּנוּ יהוה אֱלֹהֵינוּ
תּוֹרַת חַיִּים וְאַהֲבַת חֶסֶד
וּצְדָקָה וּבְרָכָה וְרַחֲמִים וְחַיִּים וְשָׁלוֹם.
וְטוֹב בְּעֵינֶיךָ לְבָרֵךְ אֶת עַמְּךָ יִשְׂרָאֵל
בְּכָל עֵת וּבְכָל שָׁעָה בִּשְׁלוֹמֶךָ.
בָּרוּךְ אַתָּה יהוה, הַמְבָרֵךְ אֶת עַמּוֹ יִשְׂרָאֵל בַּשָּׁלוֹם.

The following verse concludes the חזרת הש״ץ.
Some also say it here as part of the silent עמידה.

יִהְיוּ לְרָצוֹן אִמְרֵי פִי וְהֶגְיוֹן לִבִּי לְפָנֶיךָ, יהוה צוּרִי וְגֹאֲלִי:

תהלים יט

אֱלֹהַי **My God,**
guard my tongue from evil and my lips from deceitful speech.
To those who curse me, let my soul be silent;
may my soul be to all like the dust.
Open my heart to Your Torah and let my soul
pursue Your commandments. As for all who plan evil against me,
swiftly thwart their counsel and frustrate their plans.
> Act for the sake of Your name; act for the sake of Your right hand;
> act for the sake of Your holiness; act for the sake of Your Torah.

That Your beloved ones may be delivered,
save with Your right hand and answer me.
May the words of my mouth and the meditation of my heart
find favor before You, LORD, my Rock and Redeemer.

Bow, take three steps back, then bow, first left, then right, then center, while saying:

May He who makes peace in His high places,
make peace for us and all Israel – and say: Amen.

יְהִי רָצוֹן **May it be Your will,** LORD our God and God of our ancestors,
that the Temple be rebuilt speedily in our days,
and grant us a share in Your Torah.
And there we will serve You with reverence,
as in the days of old and as in former years.
Then the offering of Judah and Jerusalem will be pleasing to the LORD
as in the days of old and as in former years.

Berakhot 17a

Ps. 60

Ps. 19

Mal. 3

FULL KADDISH

Leader: יִתְגַּדַּל **Magnified and sanctified** may His great name be,
in the world He created by His will.
May He establish His kingdom
in your lifetime and in your days,
and in the lifetime of all the house of Israel,
swiftly and soon – and say: Amen.

All: May His great name be blessed for ever and all time.

אֱלֹהַי

נְצֹר לְשׁוֹנִי מֵרָע וּשְׂפָתַי מִדַּבֵּר מִרְמָה
וְלִמְקַלְלַי נַפְשִׁי תִדֹּם, וְנַפְשִׁי כֶּעָפָר לַכֹּל תִּהְיֶה.
פְּתַח לִבִּי בְּתוֹרָתֶךָ, וּבְמִצְוֹתֶיךָ תִּרְדֹּף נַפְשִׁי.
וְכָל הַחוֹשְׁבִים עָלַי רָעָה
מְהֵרָה הָפֵר עֲצָתָם וְקַלְקֵל מַחֲשַׁבְתָּם.
עֲשֵׂה לְמַעַן שְׁמֶךָ, עֲשֵׂה לְמַעַן יְמִינֶךָ,
עֲשֵׂה לְמַעַן קְדֻשָּׁתֶךָ, עֲשֵׂה לְמַעַן תּוֹרָתֶךָ.
לְמַעַן יֵחָלְצוּן יְדִידֶיךָ, הוֹשִׁיעָה יְמִינְךָ וַעֲנֵנִי:
יִהְיוּ לְרָצוֹן אִמְרֵי־פִי וְהֶגְיוֹן לִבִּי לְפָנֶיךָ, יהוה צוּרִי וְגֹאֲלִי:

Bow, take three steps back, then bow, first left, then right, then center, while saying:

עֹשֶׂה שָׁלוֹם בִּמְרוֹמָיו
הוּא יַעֲשֶׂה שָׁלוֹם עָלֵינוּ וְעַל כָּל יִשְׂרָאֵל, וְאִמְרוּ אָמֵן.

יְהִי רָצוֹן מִלְּפָנֶיךָ יהוה אֱלֹהֵינוּ וֵאלֹהֵי אֲבוֹתֵינוּ
שֶׁיִּבָּנֶה בֵּית הַמִּקְדָּשׁ בִּמְהֵרָה בְיָמֵינוּ, וְתֵן חֶלְקֵנוּ בְּתוֹרָתֶךָ
וְשָׁם נַעֲבָדְךָ בְּיִרְאָה כִּימֵי עוֹלָם וּכְשָׁנִים קַדְמוֹנִיּוֹת.
וְעָרְבָה לַיהוה מִנְחַת יְהוּדָה וִירוּשָׁלָ͏ִם כִּימֵי עוֹלָם וּכְשָׁנִים קַדְמוֹנִיּוֹת:

קדיש שלם

ש״ץ: יִתְגַּדַּל וְיִתְקַדַּשׁ שְׁמֵהּ רַבָּא (קהל: אָמֵן)
בְּעָלְמָא דִּי בְרָא כִרְעוּתֵהּ, וְיַמְלִיךְ מַלְכוּתֵהּ
בְּחַיֵּיכוֹן וּבְיוֹמֵיכוֹן וּבְחַיֵּי דְכָל בֵּית יִשְׂרָאֵל
בַּעֲגָלָא וּבִזְמַן קָרִיב, וְאִמְרוּ אָמֵן. (קהל: אָמֵן)

קהל וש״ץ: יְהֵא שְׁמֵהּ רַבָּא מְבָרַךְ לְעָלַם וּלְעָלְמֵי עָלְמַיָּא

Leader: Blessed and praised,
glorified and exalted, raised and honored,
uplifted and lauded be
the name of the Holy One, blessed be He,
beyond any blessing,
song, praise and consolation uttered in the world –
and say: Amen.

May the prayers and pleas of all Israel
be accepted by their Father in heaven –
and say: Amen.

May there be great peace from heaven,
and life for us and all Israel –
and say: Amen.

*Bow, take three steps back, as if taking leave of the Divine Presence,
then bow, first left, then right, then center, while saying:*

May He who makes peace in His high places,
make peace for us and all Israel –
and say: Amen.

Stand while saying Aleinu. Bow at ˙.

עָלֵינוּ It is our duty to praise the Master of all,
and ascribe greatness to the Author of creation,
who has not made us like the nations of the lands,
nor placed us like the families of the earth;
who has not made our portion like theirs,
nor our destiny like all their multitudes.
(For they worship vanity and emptiness,
and pray to a god who cannot save.)
˙But we bow in worship and thank the Supreme King of kings,
the Holy One, blessed be He,
who extends the heavens and establishes the earth,
whose throne of glory is in the heavens above,
and whose power's Presence is in the highest of heights.

ש"ץ: יִתְבָּרַךְ וְיִשְׁתַּבַּח וְיִתְפָּאַר
וְיִתְרוֹמַם וְיִתְנַשֵּׂא וְיִתְהַדָּר וְיִתְעַלֶּה וְיִתְהַלָּל
שְׁמֵהּ דְּקֻדְשָׁא בְּרִיךְ הוּא (קהל: בְּרִיךְ הוּא)
לְעֵלָּא מִן כָּל בִּרְכָתָא וְשִׁירָתָא, תֻּשְׁבְּחָתָא וְנֶחֱמָתָא
דַּאֲמִירָן בְּעָלְמָא, וְאִמְרוּ אָמֵן. (קהל: אָמֵן)

תִּתְקַבַּל צְלוֹתְהוֹן וּבָעוּתְהוֹן דְּכָל יִשְׂרָאֵל
קֳדָם אֲבוּהוֹן דִּי בִשְׁמַיָּא, וְאִמְרוּ אָמֵן. (קהל: אָמֵן)

יְהֵא שְׁלָמָא רַבָּא מִן שְׁמַיָּא
וְחַיִּים, עָלֵינוּ וְעַל כָּל יִשְׂרָאֵל, וְאִמְרוּ אָמֵן. (קהל: אָמֵן)

Bow, take three steps back, as if taking leave of the Divine Presence,
then bow, first left, then right, then center, while saying:

עֹשֶׂה שָׁלוֹם בִּמְרוֹמָיו
הוּא יַעֲשֶׂה שָׁלוֹם עָלֵינוּ וְעַל כָּל יִשְׂרָאֵל, וְאִמְרוּ אָמֵן. (קהל: אָמֵן)

Stand while saying עָלֵינוּ. Bow at ˚.

עָלֵינוּ לְשַׁבֵּחַ לַאֲדוֹן הַכֹּל, לָתֵת גְּדֻלָּה לְיוֹצֵר בְּרֵאשִׁית
שֶׁלֹּא עָשָׂנוּ כְּגוֹיֵי הָאֲרָצוֹת, וְלֹא שָׂמָנוּ כְּמִשְׁפְּחוֹת הָאֲדָמָה
שֶׁלֹּא שָׂם חֶלְקֵנוּ כָּהֶם וְגוֹרָלֵנוּ כְּכָל הֲמוֹנָם.
(שֶׁהֵם מִשְׁתַּחֲוִים לְהֶבֶל וָרִיק וּמִתְפַּלְלִים אֶל אֵל לֹא יוֹשִׁיעַ.)
˚וַאֲנַחְנוּ כּוֹרְעִים וּמִשְׁתַּחֲוִים וּמוֹדִים
לִפְנֵי מֶלֶךְ מַלְכֵי הַמְּלָכִים, הַקָּדוֹשׁ בָּרוּךְ הוּא
שֶׁהוּא נוֹטֶה שָׁמַיִם וְיוֹסֵד אָרֶץ
וּמוֹשַׁב יְקָרוֹ בַּשָּׁמַיִם מִמַּעַל וּשְׁכִינַת עֻזּוֹ בְּגָבְהֵי מְרוֹמִים.

He is our God; there is no other.
Truly He is our King, there is none else,
as it is written in His Torah:
"You shall know and take to heart this day — *Deut. 4*
that the Lord is God, in heaven above and on earth below.
There is no other."

Therefore, we place our hope in You, Lord our God,
that we may soon see the glory of Your power,
when You will remove abominations from the earth,
and idols will be utterly destroyed,
when the world will be perfected
under the sovereignty of the Almighty,
when all humanity will call on Your name,
to turn all the earth's wicked toward You.
All the world's inhabitants will realize and know
that to You every knee must bow and every tongue swear loyalty.
Before You, Lord our God, they will kneel and bow down
and give honor to Your glorious name.
They will all accept the yoke of Your kingdom,
and You will reign over them soon and for ever.
For the kingdom is Yours,
and to all eternity You will reign in glory,
as it is written in Your Torah:
"The Lord will reign for ever and ever." — *Ex. 15*
▸ And it is said: "Then the Lord shall be King over all the earth; — *Zech. 14*
on that day the Lord shall be One and His name One."

Some add:
Have no fear of sudden terror or of the ruin when it overtakes the wicked. — *Prov. 3*
Devise your strategy, but it will be thwarted; propose your plan, — *Is. 8*
but it will not stand, for God is with us. When you grow old, I will still be the — *Is. 46*
same. When your hair turns gray, I will still carry you.
I made you, I will bear you,
I will carry you, and I will rescue you.

הוּא אֱלֹהֵינוּ, אֵין עוֹד.
אֱמֶת מַלְכֵּנוּ, אֶפֶס זוּלָתוֹ
כַּכָּתוּב בְּתוֹרָתוֹ
וְיָדַעְתָּ הַיּוֹם וַהֲשֵׁבֹתָ אֶל־לְבָבֶךָ   דברים ד
כִּי יהוה הוּא הָאֱלֹהִים בַּשָּׁמַיִם מִמַּעַל וְעַל־הָאָרֶץ מִתָּחַת
אֵין עוֹד:

עַל כֵּן נְקַוֶּה לְךָ יהוה אֱלֹהֵינוּ, לִרְאוֹת מְהֵרָה בְּתִפְאֶרֶת עֻזֶּךָ
לְהַעֲבִיר גִּלּוּלִים מִן הָאָרֶץ, וְהָאֱלִילִים כָּרוֹת יִכָּרֵתוּן
לְתַקֵּן עוֹלָם בְּמַלְכוּת שַׁדַּי.
וְכָל בְּנֵי בָשָׂר יִקְרְאוּ בִשְׁמֶךָ לְהַפְנוֹת אֵלֶיךָ כָּל רִשְׁעֵי אָרֶץ.
יַכִּירוּ וְיֵדְעוּ כָּל יוֹשְׁבֵי תֵבֵל
כִּי לְךָ תִּכְרַע כָּל בֶּרֶךְ, תִּשָּׁבַע כָּל לָשׁוֹן.
לְפָנֶיךָ יהוה אֱלֹהֵינוּ יִכְרְעוּ וְיִפֹּלוּ וְלִכְבוֹד שִׁמְךָ יְקָר יִתֵּנוּ
וִיקַבְּלוּ כֻלָּם אֶת עֹל מַלְכוּתֶךָ
וְתִמְלֹךְ עֲלֵיהֶם מְהֵרָה לְעוֹלָם וָעֶד.
כִּי הַמַּלְכוּת שֶׁלְּךָ הִיא וּלְעוֹלְמֵי עַד תִּמְלֹךְ בְּכָבוֹד
כַּכָּתוּב בְּתוֹרָתֶךָ, יהוה יִמְלֹךְ לְעֹלָם וָעֶד: שמות טו
▸ וְנֶאֱמַר, וְהָיָה יהוה לְמֶלֶךְ עַל־כָּל־הָאָרֶץ   זכריה יד
בַּיּוֹם הַהוּא יִהְיֶה יהוה אֶחָד וּשְׁמוֹ אֶחָד:

Some add:

אַל־תִּירָא מִפַּחַד פִּתְאֹם וּמִשֹּׁאַת רְשָׁעִים כִּי תָבֹא: משלי ג
עֻצוּ עֵצָה וְתֻפָר, דַּבְּרוּ דָבָר וְלֹא יָקוּם, כִּי עִמָּנוּ אֵל: ישעיה ח
וְעַד־זִקְנָה אֲנִי הוּא, וְעַד־שֵׂיבָה אֲנִי אֶסְבֹּל   ישעיה מו
אֲנִי עָשִׂיתִי וַאֲנִי אֶשָּׂא וַאֲנִי אֶסְבֹּל וַאֲמַלֵּט:

MOURNER'S KADDISH

> *The following prayer requires the presence of a minyan.*
> *A transliteration can be found on page 792.*

Mourner: יִתְגַּדֵּל Magnified and sanctified
may His great name be,
in the world He created by His will.
May He establish His kingdom
in your lifetime and in your days,
and in the lifetime of all the house of Israel,
swiftly and soon –
and say: Amen.

All: May His great name be blessed for ever and all time.

Mourner: Blessed and praised,
glorified and exalted,
raised and honored,
uplifted and lauded
be the name of the Holy One,
blessed be He, beyond any blessing,
song, praise and consolation
uttered in the world –
and say: Amen.

May there be great peace from heaven,
and life for us and all Israel –
and say: Amen.

> *Bow, take three steps back, as if taking leave of the Divine Presence,*
> *then bow, first left, then right, then center, while saying:*

May He who makes peace in His high places,
make peace for us and all Israel –
and say: Amen.

קדיש יתום

The following prayer requires the presence of a מנין.
A transliteration can be found on page 792.

אבל: יִתְגַּדַּל וְיִתְקַדַּשׁ שְׁמֵהּ רַבָּא (קהל: אָמֵן)
בְּעָלְמָא דִּי בְרָא כִרְעוּתֵהּ, וְיַמְלִיךְ מַלְכוּתֵהּ
בְּחַיֵּיכוֹן וּבְיוֹמֵיכוֹן וּבְחַיֵּי דְכָל בֵּית יִשְׂרָאֵל
בַּעֲגָלָא וּבִזְמַן קָרִיב
וְאִמְרוּ אָמֵן. (קהל: אָמֵן)

קהל ואבל: יְהֵא שְׁמֵהּ רַבָּא מְבָרַךְ לְעָלַם וּלְעָלְמֵי עָלְמַיָּא.

אבל: יִתְבָּרַךְ וְיִשְׁתַּבַּח וְיִתְפָּאַר
וְיִתְרוֹמַם וְיִתְנַשֵּׂא וְיִתְהַדָּר וְיִתְעַלֶּה וְיִתְהַלָּל
שְׁמֵהּ דְּקֻדְשָׁא בְּרִיךְ הוּא (קהל: בְּרִיךְ הוּא)
לְעֵלָּא מִן כָּל בִּרְכָתָא וְשִׁירָתָא, תֻּשְׁבְּחָתָא וְנֶחֱמָתָא
דַּאֲמִירָן בְּעָלְמָא
וְאִמְרוּ אָמֵן. (קהל: אָמֵן)

יְהֵא שְׁלָמָא רַבָּא מִן שְׁמַיָּא
וְחַיִּים, עָלֵינוּ וְעַל כָּל יִשְׂרָאֵל
וְאִמְרוּ אָמֵן. (קהל: אָמֵן)

Bow, take three steps back, as if taking leave of the Divine Presence,
then bow, first left, then right, then center, while saying:

עֹשֶׂה שָׁלוֹם בִּמְרוֹמָיו
הוּא יַעֲשֶׂה שָׁלוֹם עָלֵינוּ וְעַל כָּל יִשְׂרָאֵל
וְאִמְרוּ אָמֵן. (קהל: אָמֵן)

BIRKAT KOHANIM

In Israel (and some congregations outside Israel), the following is said by the Leader during the repetition of the Amida when the Kohanim bless the congregation. If there is more than one Kohen, a member of the congregation calls:

Kohanim!

The Kohanim respond:

בָּרוּךְ Blessed are You, Lord our God, King of the Universe, who has made us holy with the holiness of Aaron, and has commanded us to bless His people Israel with love.

The Leader calls word by word, followed by the Kohanim:

יְבָרֶכְךָ May the Lord bless you and protect you. (*Cong:* Amen.)   *Num. 6*
May the Lord make His face shine on you and be gracious to you. (*Cong:* Amen.)
May the Lord turn His face toward you, and grant you peace. (*Cong:* Amen.)

The Leader continues with "Grant peace" below.

The congregation says:

אַדִּיר Majestic One on high who dwells in power: You are peace and Your name is peace. May it be Your will to bestow on us and on Your people the house of Israel, life and blessing as a safeguard for peace.

The Kohanim say:

רִבּוֹנוֹ Master of the Universe: we have done what You have decreed for us. So too may You deal with us as You have promised us. Look down from Your holy dwelling place, from heaven, and bless Your people Israel and the land You have given us as You promised on oath to our ancestors, a land flowing with milk and honey.   *Deut. 26*

The Leader continues:

שִׂים שָׁלוֹם Grant peace, goodness and blessing, grace, loving-kindness and compassion to us and all Israel Your people. Bless us, our Father, all as one, with the light of Your face, for by the light of Your face You have given us, Lord our God, the Torah of life and love of kindness, righteousness, blessing, compassion, life and peace. May it be good in Your eyes to bless Your people Israel at every time, in every hour, with Your peace. Blessed are You, Lord, who blesses His people Israel with peace.

The following verse concludes the Leader's repetition of the Amida.
May the words of my mouth and the meditation of my heart   *Ps. 19*
find favor before You, Lord, my Rock and Redeemer.

בִּרְכַּת כֹּהֲנִים

In ארץ ישראל (and some congregations outside ארץ ישראל), the following is said by the שליח ציבור during the חזרת הש״ץ when כהנים say ברכת כהנים. If there is more than one כהן, a member of the קהל calls.

כֹּהֲנִים

The כהנים respond:

בָּרוּךְ אַתָּה יהוה אֱלֹהֵינוּ מֶלֶךְ הָעוֹלָם, אֲשֶׁר קִדְּשָׁנוּ בִּקְדֻשָּׁתוֹ שֶׁל אַהֲרֹן, וְצִוָּנוּ לְבָרֵךְ אֶת עַמּוֹ יִשְׂרָאֵל בְּאַהֲבָה.

The שליח ציבור calls word by word, followed by the כהנים:

יְבָרֶכְךָ יהוה וְיִשְׁמְרֶךָ: קהל: אָמֵן

יָאֵר יהוה פָּנָיו אֵלֶיךָ וִיחֻנֶּךָּ: קהל: אָמֵן

יִשָּׂא יהוה פָּנָיו אֵלֶיךָ וְיָשֵׂם לְךָ שָׁלוֹם: קהל: אָמֵן

במדברו

The שליח ציבור continues with שים שלום below.

The כהנים say:	The קהל says:
רִבּוֹנוֹ שֶׁל עוֹלָם, עָשִׂינוּ מַה שֶּׁגָּזַרְתָּ עָלֵינוּ, אַף אַתָּה עֲשֵׂה עִמָּנוּ כְּמוֹ שֶׁהִבְטַחְתָּנוּ. הַשְׁקִיפָה מִמְּעוֹן קָדְשְׁךָ מִן הַשָּׁמַיִם, וּבָרֵךְ אֶת עַמְּךָ אֶת יִשְׂרָאֵל, וְאֵת הָאֲדָמָה אֲשֶׁר נָתַתָּה לָּנוּ, כַּאֲשֶׁר נִשְׁבַּעְתָּ לַאֲבֹתֵינוּ, אֶרֶץ זָבַת חָלָב וּדְבָשׁ:	אַדִּיר בַּמָּרוֹם שׁוֹכֵן בִּגְבוּרָה, אַתָּה שָׁלוֹם וְשִׁמְךָ שָׁלוֹם. יְהִי רָצוֹן שֶׁתָּשִׂים עָלֵינוּ וְעַל כָּל עַמְּךָ בֵּית יִשְׂרָאֵל חַיִּים וּבְרָכָה לְמִשְׁמֶרֶת שָׁלוֹם.

דברים כו

The שליח ציבור continues:

שִׂים שָׁלוֹם טוֹבָה וּבְרָכָה, חֵן וָחֶסֶד וְרַחֲמִים עָלֵינוּ וְעַל כָּל יִשְׂרָאֵל עַמֶּךָ. בָּרְכֵנוּ אָבִינוּ כֻּלָּנוּ כְּאֶחָד בְּאוֹר פָּנֶיךָ, כִּי בְאוֹר פָּנֶיךָ נָתַתָּ לָּנוּ יהוה אֱלֹהֵינוּ, תּוֹרַת חַיִּים וְאַהֲבַת חֶסֶד, וּצְדָקָה וּבְרָכָה וְרַחֲמִים וְחַיִּים וְשָׁלוֹם. וְטוֹב בְּעֵינֶיךָ לְבָרֵךְ אֶת עַמְּךָ יִשְׂרָאֵל, בְּכָל עֵת וּבְכָל שָׁעָה בִּשְׁלוֹמֶךָ. בָּרוּךְ אַתָּה יהוה, הַמְבָרֵךְ אֶת עַמּוֹ יִשְׂרָאֵל בַּשָּׁלוֹם.

The following verse concludes the חזרת הש״ץ.

יִהְיוּ לְרָצוֹן אִמְרֵי־פִי וְהֶגְיוֹן לִבִּי לְפָנֶיךָ, יהוה צוּרִי וְגֹאֲלִי:

תהלים יט

מעריב למוצאי תשעה באב

MA'ARIV FOR MOTZA'EI TISHA B'AV

Ma'ariv for Motza'ei Tisha B'Av

וְהוּא רַחוּם He is compassionate. *Ps. 78*
He forgives iniquity and does not destroy.
Repeatedly He suppresses His anger, not rousing His full wrath. *Ps. 20*
Lord, save! May the King answer us on the day we call.

BLESSINGS OF THE SHEMA

The Leader says the following, bowing at "Bless," standing straight at "the Lord"; the congregation, followed by the Leader, responds, bowing at "Bless," standing straight at "the Lord":

Leader: # BLESS
the Lord, the blessed One.

Congregation: Bless the Lord, the blessed One,
for ever and all time.

Leader: Bless the Lord, the blessed One,
for ever and all time.

בָּרוּךְ Blessed are You, Lord our God,
King of the Universe,
who by His word brings on evenings,
by His wisdom opens the gates of heaven,
with understanding makes time change
and the seasons rotate,
and by His will orders the stars in their constellations in the sky.

מעריב למוצאי תשעה באב

תהלים עח

וְהוּא רַחוּם, יְכַפֵּר עָוֹן וְלֹא־יַשְׁחִית
וְהִרְבָּה לְהָשִׁיב אַפּוֹ, וְלֹא־יָעִיר כָּל־חֲמָתוֹ:

תהלים כ

יהוה הוֹשִׁיעָה, הַמֶּלֶךְ יַעֲנֵנוּ בְיוֹם־קָרְאֵנוּ:

קריאת שמע וברכותיה

The שליח ציבור *says the following, bowing at* בָּרְכוּ, *standing straight at* ה'; *the* קהל, *followed by the* שליח ציבור, *responds, bowing at* בָּרוּךְ, *standing straight at* ה':

ש״ץ: **בָּרְכוּ**

אֶת יהוה הַמְבֹרָךְ.

קהל: בָּרוּךְ יהוה הַמְבֹרָךְ לְעוֹלָם וָעֶד.

ש״ץ: בָּרוּךְ יהוה הַמְבֹרָךְ לְעוֹלָם וָעֶד.

בָּרוּךְ אַתָּה יהוה אֱלֹהֵינוּ מֶלֶךְ הָעוֹלָם
אֲשֶׁר בִּדְבָרוֹ מַעֲרִיב עֲרָבִים
בְּחָכְמָה פּוֹתֵחַ שְׁעָרִים
וּבִתְבוּנָה מְשַׁנֶּה עִתִּים וּמַחֲלִיף אֶת הַזְּמַנִּים
וּמְסַדֵּר אֶת הַכּוֹכָבִים בְּמִשְׁמְרוֹתֵיהֶם בָּרָקִיעַ כִּרְצוֹנוֹ.

He creates day and night, rolling away the light before the darkness,
and darkness before the light.
▸ He makes the day pass and brings on night,
distinguishing day from night: the Lord of hosts is His name.
May the living and forever enduring God rule over us for all time.
Blessed are You, Lord, who brings on evenings.

אַהֲבַת עוֹלָם With everlasting love
have You loved Your people, the house of Israel.
You have taught us Torah and commandments,
decrees and laws of justice.
Therefore, Lord our God, when we lie down and when we rise up
we will speak of Your decrees, rejoicing in the words of Your Torah
and Your commandments for ever.
▸ For they are our life and the length of our days;
on them will we meditate day and night.
May You never take away Your love from us.
Blessed are You, Lord, who loves His people Israel.

The Shema must be said with intense concentration.
When not with a minyan, say:
God, faithful King!

The following verse should be said aloud, while covering the eyes with the right hand:

Listen, Israel: the Lord is our God, the Lord is One.

Deut. 6

Quietly: Blessed be the name of His glorious kingdom for ever and ever.

וְאָהַבְתָּ Love the Lord your God with all your heart, with all your soul, and with all your might. These words which I command you today shall be on your heart. Teach them repeatedly to your children, speaking of them when you sit at home and when you travel on the way, when you lie down and when you rise. Bind them as a sign on your hand, and they shall be an emblem between your eyes. Write them on the doorposts of your house and gates.

Deut. 6

בּוֹרֵא יוֹם וָלָיְלָה, גּוֹלֵל אוֹר מִפְּנֵי חֹשֶׁךְ וְחֹשֶׁךְ מִפְּנֵי אוֹר
‹ וּמַעֲבִיר יוֹם וּמֵבִיא לָיְלָה
וּמַבְדִּיל בֵּין יוֹם וּבֵין לָיְלָה,
יהוה צְבָאוֹת שְׁמוֹ.
אֵל חַי וְקַיָּם תָּמִיד, יִמְלֹךְ עָלֵינוּ לְעוֹלָם וָעֶד.
בָּרוּךְ אַתָּה יהוה, הַמַּעֲרִיב עֲרָבִים.

אַהֲבַת עוֹלָם בֵּית יִשְׂרָאֵל עַמְּךָ אָהָבְתָּ
תּוֹרָה וּמִצְוֹת, חֻקִּים וּמִשְׁפָּטִים, אוֹתָנוּ לִמַּדְתָּ
עַל כֵּן יהוה אֱלֹהֵינוּ בְּשָׁכְבֵנוּ וּבְקוּמֵנוּ נָשִׂיחַ בְּחֻקֶּיךָ
וְנִשְׂמַח בְּדִבְרֵי תוֹרָתֶךָ וּבְמִצְוֹתֶיךָ לְעוֹלָם וָעֶד
‹ כִּי הֵם חַיֵּינוּ וְאֹרֶךְ יָמֵינוּ, וּבָהֶם נֶהְגֶּה יוֹמָם וָלָיְלָה.
וְאַהֲבָתְךָ אַל תָּסִיר מִמֶּנּוּ לְעוֹלָמִים.
בָּרוּךְ אַתָּה יהוה, אוֹהֵב עַמּוֹ יִשְׂרָאֵל.

The שמע must be said with intense concentration.
When not with a מנין, say:

אֵל מֶלֶךְ נֶאֱמָן

The following verse should be said aloud, while covering the eyes with the right hand:

שְׁמַע יִשְׂרָאֵל, יהוה אֱלֹהֵינוּ, יהוה ׀ אֶחָד: דברים ו

Quietly
בָּרוּךְ שֵׁם כְּבוֹד מַלְכוּתוֹ לְעוֹלָם וָעֶד.

וְאָהַבְתָּ אֵת יהוה אֱלֹהֶיךָ, בְּכָל־לְבָבְךָ וּבְכָל־נַפְשְׁךָ וּבְכָל־מְאֹדֶךָ: דברים ו
וְהָיוּ הַדְּבָרִים הָאֵלֶּה, אֲשֶׁר אָנֹכִי מְצַוְּךָ הַיּוֹם, עַל־לְבָבֶךָ: וְשִׁנַּנְתָּם
לְבָנֶיךָ וְדִבַּרְתָּ בָּם, בְּשִׁבְתְּךָ בְּבֵיתֶךָ וּבְלֶכְתְּךָ בַדֶּרֶךְ, וּבְשָׁכְבְּךָ
וּבְקוּמֶךָ: וּקְשַׁרְתָּם לְאוֹת עַל־יָדֶךָ וְהָיוּ לְטֹטָפֹת בֵּין עֵינֶיךָ:
וּכְתַבְתָּם עַל־מְזֻזוֹת בֵּיתֶךָ וּבִשְׁעָרֶיךָ:

וְהָיָה If you indeed heed My commandments with which I charge you today, to love the Lord your God and worship Him with all your heart and with all your soul, I will give rain in your land in its season, the early and late rain; and you shall gather in your grain, wine and oil. I will give grass in your field for your cattle, and you shall eat and be satisfied. Be careful lest your heart be tempted and you go astray and worship other gods, bowing down to them. Then the Lord's anger will flare against you and He will close the heavens so that there will be no rain. The land will not yield its crops, and you will perish swiftly from the good land that the Lord is giving you. Therefore, set these, My words, on your heart and soul. Bind them as a sign on your hand, and they shall be an emblem between your eyes. Teach them to your children, speaking of them when you sit at home and when you travel on the way, when you lie down and when you rise. Write them on the doorposts of your house and gates, so that you and your children may live long in the land that the Lord swore to your ancestors to give them, for as long as the heavens are above the earth. *Deut. 11*

וַיֹּאמֶר The Lord spoke to Moses, saying: Speak to the Israelites and tell them to make tassels on the corners of their garments for all generations. They shall attach to the tassel at each corner a thread of blue. This shall be your tassel, and you shall see it and remember all of the Lord's commandments and keep them, not straying after your heart and after your eyes, following your own sinful desires. Thus you will be reminded to keep all My commandments, and be holy to your God. I am the Lord your God, who brought you out of the land of Egypt to be your God. I am the Lord your God. *Num. 15*

True –

The Leader repeats:
▸ The Lord your God is true –

דברים יא

וְהָיָ֗ה אִם־שָׁמֹ֤עַ תִּשְׁמְעוּ֙ אֶל־מִצְוֺתַ֔י אֲשֶׁ֧ר אָנֹכִ֛י מְצַוֶּ֥ה אֶתְכֶ֖ם הַיּ֑וֹם, לְאַהֲבָ֞ה אֶת־יְהוָ֤ה אֱלֹֽהֵיכֶם֙ וּלְעָבְד֔וֹ, בְּכָל־לְבַבְכֶ֖ם וּבְכָל־נַפְשְׁכֶֽם: וְנָתַתִּ֧י מְטַֽר־אַרְצְכֶ֛ם בְּעִתּ֖וֹ, יוֹרֶ֣ה וּמַלְק֑וֹשׁ, וְאָסַפְתָּ֣ דְגָנֶ֔ךָ וְתִֽירֹשְׁךָ֖ וְיִצְהָרֶֽךָ: וְנָתַתִּ֛י עֵ֥שֶׂב בְּשָׂדְךָ֖ לִבְהֶמְתֶּ֑ךָ, וְאָכַלְתָּ֖ וְשָׂבָֽעְתָּ: הִשָּֽׁמְר֣וּ לָכֶ֔ם פֶּ֥ן יִפְתֶּ֖ה לְבַבְכֶ֑ם, וְסַרְתֶּ֗ם וַעֲבַדְתֶּם֙ אֱלֹהִ֣ים אֲחֵרִ֔ים וְהִשְׁתַּחֲוִיתֶ֖ם לָהֶֽם: וְחָרָ֨ה אַף־יְהוָ֜ה בָּכֶ֗ם, וְעָצַ֤ר אֶת־הַשָּׁמַ֨יִם֙ וְלֹא־יִהְיֶ֣ה מָטָ֔ר, וְהָ֣אֲדָמָ֔ה לֹ֥א תִתֵּ֖ן אֶת־יְבוּלָ֑הּ, וַאֲבַדְתֶּ֣ם מְהֵרָ֗ה מֵעַל֙ הָאָ֣רֶץ הַטֹּבָ֔ה אֲשֶׁ֥ר יְהוָ֖ה נֹתֵ֥ן לָכֶֽם: וְשַׂמְתֶּם֙ אֶת־דְּבָרַ֣י אֵ֔לֶּה עַל־לְבַבְכֶ֖ם וְעַֽל־נַפְשְׁכֶ֑ם, וּקְשַׁרְתֶּ֨ם אֹתָ֤ם לְאוֹת֙ עַל־יֶדְכֶ֔ם, וְהָי֥וּ לְטוֹטָפֹ֖ת בֵּ֥ין עֵינֵיכֶֽם: וְלִמַּדְתֶּ֥ם אֹתָ֛ם אֶת־בְּנֵיכֶ֖ם לְדַבֵּ֣ר בָּ֑ם, בְּשִׁבְתְּךָ֤ בְּבֵיתֶ֨ךָ֙ וּבְלֶכְתְּךָ֣ בַדֶּ֔רֶךְ וּֽבְשָׁכְבְּךָ֖ וּבְקוּמֶֽךָ: וּכְתַבְתָּ֛ם עַל־מְזוּז֥וֹת בֵּיתֶ֖ךָ וּבִשְׁעָרֶֽיךָ: לְמַ֨עַן יִרְבּ֤וּ יְמֵיכֶם֙ וִימֵ֣י בְנֵיכֶ֔ם עַ֚ל הָֽאֲדָמָ֔ה אֲשֶׁ֨ר נִשְׁבַּ֧ע יְהוָ֛ה לַאֲבֹתֵיכֶ֖ם לָתֵ֣ת לָהֶ֑ם, כִּימֵ֥י הַשָּׁמַ֖יִם עַל־הָאָֽרֶץ:

במדבר טו

וַיֹּ֥אמֶר יְהוָ֖ה אֶל־מֹשֶׁ֥ה לֵּאמֹֽר: דַּבֵּ֞ר אֶל־בְּנֵ֤י יִשְׂרָאֵל֙ וְאָמַרְתָּ֣ אֲלֵהֶ֔ם, וְעָשׂ֨וּ לָהֶ֥ם צִיצִ֛ת עַל־כַּנְפֵ֥י בִגְדֵיהֶ֖ם לְדֹרֹתָ֑ם, וְנָ֥תְנ֛וּ עַל־צִיצִ֥ת הַכָּנָ֖ף פְּתִ֥יל תְּכֵֽלֶת: וְהָיָ֣ה לָכֶם֮ לְצִיצִת֒, וּרְאִיתֶ֣ם אֹת֗וֹ וּזְכַרְתֶּם֙ אֶת־כָּל־מִצְוֺ֣ת יְהוָ֔ה וַעֲשִׂיתֶ֖ם אֹתָ֑ם, וְלֹֽא־תָתֻ֜רוּ אַחֲרֵ֤י לְבַבְכֶם֙ וְאַחֲרֵ֣י עֵֽינֵיכֶ֔ם, אֲשֶׁר־אַתֶּ֥ם זֹנִ֖ים אַחֲרֵיהֶֽם: לְמַ֣עַן תִּזְכְּר֔וּ וַעֲשִׂיתֶ֖ם אֶת־כָּל־מִצְוֺתָ֑י, וִהְיִיתֶ֥ם קְדֹשִׁ֖ים לֵֽאלֹהֵיכֶֽם: אֲנִ֞י יְהוָ֣ה אֱלֹֽהֵיכֶ֗ם, אֲשֶׁ֨ר הוֹצֵ֤אתִי אֶתְכֶם֙ מֵאֶ֣רֶץ מִצְרַ֔יִם, לִהְי֥וֹת לָכֶ֖ם לֵאלֹהִ֑ים, אֲנִ֖י יְהוָ֥ה אֱלֹהֵיכֶֽם:

אֱמֶת

The שליח ציבור *repeats:*

• יהוה אֱלֹהֵיכֶם אֱמֶת

וֶאֱמוּנָה – and faithful is all this,
and firmly established for us
that He is the LORD our God,
and there is none beside Him,
and that we, Israel, are His people.
He is our King,
who redeems us from the hand of kings
and delivers us from the grasp of all tyrants.
He is our God, who on our behalf repays our foes
and brings just retribution on our mortal enemies;
who performs great deeds beyond understanding
and wonders beyond number;
who kept us alive, not letting our foot slip;
who led us on the high places of our enemies,
raising our pride above all our foes;
who did miracles for us
and brought vengeance against Pharaoh;
who performed signs and wonders
in the land of Ham's children;
who smote in His wrath all the firstborn of Egypt,
and brought out His people Israel from their midst
into everlasting freedom;
who led His children through the divided Reed Sea,
plunging their pursuers and enemies into the depths.
When His children saw His might,
they gave praise and thanks to His name,
▸ and willingly accepted His Sovereignty.
Moses and the children of Israel
then sang a song to You with great joy,
and they all exclaimed:

    מִי־כָמֹכָה "Who is like You, LORD, among the mighty? *Ex. 15*
    Who is like You, majestic in holiness,
      awesome in praises, doing wonders?"

וֶאֱמוּנָה כָּל זֹאת וְקַיָּם עָלֵינוּ
כִּי הוּא יהוה אֱלֹהֵינוּ וְאֵין זוּלָתוֹ
וַאֲנַחְנוּ יִשְׂרָאֵל עַמּוֹ.
הַפּוֹדֵנוּ מִיַּד מְלָכִים
מַלְכֵּנוּ הַגּוֹאֲלֵנוּ מִכַּף כָּל הֶעָרִיצִים.
הָאֵל הַנִּפְרָע לָנוּ מִצָּרֵינוּ
וְהַמְשַׁלֵּם גְּמוּל לְכָל אוֹיְבֵי נַפְשֵׁנוּ.
הָעוֹשֶׂה גְדוֹלוֹת עַד אֵין חֵקֶר
וְנִפְלָאוֹת עַד אֵין מִסְפָּר
הַשָּׂם נַפְשֵׁנוּ בַּחַיִּים, וְלֹא נָתַן לַמּוֹט רַגְלֵנוּ
הַמַּדְרִיכֵנוּ עַל בָּמוֹת אוֹיְבֵינוּ
וַיָּרֶם קַרְנֵנוּ עַל כָּל שׂוֹנְאֵינוּ.
הָעוֹשֶׂה לָּנוּ נִסִּים וּנְקָמָה בְּפַרְעֹה
אוֹתוֹת וּמוֹפְתִים בְּאַדְמַת בְּנֵי חָם.
הַמַּכֶּה בְעֶבְרָתוֹ כָּל בְּכוֹרֵי מִצְרָיִם
וַיּוֹצֵא אֶת עַמּוֹ יִשְׂרָאֵל מִתּוֹכָם לְחֵרוּת עוֹלָם.
הַמַּעֲבִיר בָּנָיו בֵּין גִּזְרֵי יַם סוּף
אֶת רוֹדְפֵיהֶם וְאֶת שׂוֹנְאֵיהֶם בִּתְהוֹמוֹת טִבַּע
וְרָאוּ בָנָיו גְּבוּרָתוֹ, שִׁבְּחוּ וְהוֹדוּ לִשְׁמוֹ
‹ וּמַלְכוּתוֹ בְרָצוֹן קִבְּלוּ עֲלֵיהֶם.
מֹשֶׁה וּבְנֵי יִשְׂרָאֵל, לְךָ עָנוּ שִׁירָה בְּשִׂמְחָה רַבָּה
וְאָמְרוּ כֻלָּם

שמות טו

מִי־כָמֹכָה בָּאֵלִם יהוה
מִי כָּמֹכָה נֶאְדָּר בַּקֹּדֶשׁ
נוֹרָא תְהִלֹּת עֹשֵׂה פֶלֶא:

> Your children beheld Your majesty
> as You parted the sea before Moses.
> "This is my God!" they responded, and then said:

> > "The LORD shall reign for ever and ever." *Ex. 15*

> And it is said, "For the LORD has redeemed Jacob *Jer. 31*
> and rescued him from a power stronger than his own."
> Blessed are You, LORD, who redeemed Israel.

הַשְׁכִּיבֵנוּ **Help us lie down**, O LORD our God, in peace,
and rise up, O our King, to life.
Spread over us Your canopy of peace.
Direct us with Your good counsel,
and save us for the sake of Your name.
Shield us and remove from us every enemy,
plague, sword, famine and sorrow.
Remove the adversary from before and behind us.
Shelter us in the shadow of Your wings,
for You, God, are our Guardian and Deliverer;
You, God, are a gracious and compassionate King.

> Guard our going out and our coming in,
> for life and peace, from now and for ever.
> Blessed are You, LORD,
> who guards His people Israel for ever.

In Israel the service continues with Half Kaddish on page 722.

בָּרוּךְ **Blessed** be the LORD for ever. Amen and Amen. *Ps. 89*
Blessed from Zion be the LORD *Ps. 135*
who dwells in Jerusalem. Halleluya.
Blessed be the LORD, God of Israel, *Ps. 72*
who alone does wondrous things.
Blessed be His glorious name for ever,
and may the whole earth be filled with His glory. Amen and Amen.

◂ מַלְכוּתְךָ רָאוּ בָנֶיךָ, בּוֹקֵעַ יָם לִפְנֵי מֹשֶׁה
זֶה אֵלִי עָנוּ, וְאָמְרוּ
שמות טו
יהוה יִמְלֹךְ לְעֹלָם וָעֶד:

◂ וְנֶאֱמַר
כִּי־פָדָה יהוה אֶת־יַעֲקֹב, וּגְאָלוֹ מִיַּד חָזָק מִמֶּנּוּ.
ירמיהו לא
בָּרוּךְ אַתָּה יהוה, גָּאַל יִשְׂרָאֵל.

הַשְׁכִּיבֵנוּ יהוה אֱלֹהֵינוּ לְשָׁלוֹם
וְהַעֲמִידֵנוּ מַלְכֵּנוּ לְחַיִּים
וּפְרֹשׂ עָלֵינוּ סֻכַּת שְׁלוֹמֶךָ
וְתַקְּנֵנוּ בְּעֵצָה טוֹבָה מִלְּפָנֶיךָ
וְהוֹשִׁיעֵנוּ לְמַעַן שְׁמֶךָ.
וְהָגֵן בַּעֲדֵנוּ, וְהָסֵר מֵעָלֵינוּ אוֹיֵב, דֶּבֶר וְחֶרֶב וְרָעָב וְיָגוֹן
וְהָסֵר שָׂטָן מִלְּפָנֵינוּ וּמֵאַחֲרֵינוּ, וּבְצֵל כְּנָפֶיךָ תַּסְתִּירֵנוּ
כִּי אֵל שׁוֹמְרֵנוּ וּמַצִּילֵנוּ אָתָּה
כִּי אֵל מֶלֶךְ חַנּוּן וְרַחוּם אָתָּה.
◂ וּשְׁמֹר צֵאתֵנוּ וּבוֹאֵנוּ לְחַיִּים וּלְשָׁלוֹם מֵעַתָּה וְעַד עוֹלָם.
בָּרוּךְ אַתָּה יהוה, שׁוֹמֵר עַמּוֹ יִשְׂרָאֵל לָעַד.

In ארץ ישראל *the service continues with* חצי קדיש *on page 723.*

בָּרוּךְ יהוה לְעוֹלָם, אָמֵן וְאָמֵן:
תהלים פט
בָּרוּךְ יהוה מִצִּיּוֹן, שֹׁכֵן יְרוּשָׁלָםִ, הַלְלוּיָהּ:
תהלים קלה
בָּרוּךְ יהוה אֱלֹהִים אֱלֹהֵי יִשְׂרָאֵל, עֹשֵׂה נִפְלָאוֹת לְבַדּוֹ:
תהלים עב
וּבָרוּךְ שֵׁם כְּבוֹדוֹ לְעוֹלָם
וְיִמָּלֵא כְבוֹדוֹ אֶת־כָּל־הָאָרֶץ, אָמֵן וְאָמֵן:

Ma'ariv for Motza'ei Tisha B'Av

May the glory of the Lord endure for ever; *Ps. 104*
may the Lord rejoice in His works.
May the name of the Lord be blessed now and for all time. *Ps. 113*
For the sake of His great name, *1 Sam. 12*
the Lord will not abandon His people,
for the Lord vowed to make you a people of His own.
When all the people saw [God's wonders] they fell on their faces *1 Kings 18*
and said: "The Lord, He is God; the Lord, He is God."
Then the Lord shall be King over all the earth; *Zech. 14*
on that day the Lord shall be One and His name One.
May Your love, Lord, be upon us, as we have put our hope in You. *Ps. 33*

הוֹשִׁיעֵנוּ Save us, Lord our God, gather us *Ps. 106*
and deliver us from the nations,
to thank Your holy name, and glory in Your praise.
All the nations You made shall come and bow before You, *Ps. 86*
Lord, and pay honor to Your name,
for You are great and You perform wonders:
You alone are God.
We, Your people, the flock of Your pasture, will praise You for ever. *Ps. 79*
For all generations we will relate Your praise.

בָּרוּךְ Blessed is the Lord by day, blessed is the Lord by night.
Blessed is the Lord when we lie down;
blessed is the Lord when we rise.
For in Your hand are the souls of the living and the dead,
[as it is written:] "In His hand is every living soul, *Job 12*
and the breath of all mankind."
Into Your hand I entrust my spirit: *Ps. 31*
You redeemed me, Lord, God of truth.
Our God in heaven, bring unity to Your name,
establish Your kingdom constantly,
and reign over us for ever and all time.

תהלים קד	יְהִי כְבוֹד יהוה לְעוֹלָם, יִשְׂמַח יהוה בְּמַעֲשָׂיו:
תהלים קיג	יְהִי שֵׁם יהוה מְבֹרָךְ מֵעַתָּה וְעַד־עוֹלָם:
שמואל א, יב	כִּי לֹא־יִטּשׁ יהוה אֶת־עַמּוֹ בַּעֲבוּר שְׁמוֹ הַגָּדוֹל
	כִּי הוֹאִיל יהוה לַעֲשׂוֹת אֶתְכֶם לוֹ לְעָם:
מלכים א, יח	וַיַּרְא כָּל־הָעָם וַיִּפְּלוּ עַל־פְּנֵיהֶם
	וַיֹּאמְרוּ, יהוה הוּא הָאֱלֹהִים, יהוה הוּא הָאֱלֹהִים:
זכריה יד	וְהָיָה יהוה לְמֶלֶךְ עַל־כָּל־הָאָרֶץ
	בַּיּוֹם הַהוּא יִהְיֶה יהוה אֶחָד וּשְׁמוֹ אֶחָד:
תהלים לג	יְהִי־חַסְדְּךָ יהוה עָלֵינוּ, כַּאֲשֶׁר יִחַלְנוּ לָךְ:

תהלים קו	הוֹשִׁיעֵנוּ יהוה אֱלֹהֵינוּ, וְקַבְּצֵנוּ מִן־הַגּוֹיִם
	לְהֹדוֹת לְשֵׁם קָדְשֶׁךָ, לְהִשְׁתַּבֵּחַ בִּתְהִלָּתֶךָ:
תהלים פו	כָּל־גּוֹיִם אֲשֶׁר עָשִׂיתָ, יָבוֹאוּ וְיִשְׁתַּחֲווּ לְפָנֶיךָ, אֲדֹנָי
	וִיכַבְּדוּ לִשְׁמֶךָ:
	כִּי־גָדוֹל אַתָּה וְעֹשֵׂה נִפְלָאוֹת, אַתָּה אֱלֹהִים לְבַדֶּךָ:
תהלים עט	וַאֲנַחְנוּ עַמְּךָ וְצֹאן מַרְעִיתֶךָ, נוֹדֶה לְּךָ לְעוֹלָם
	לְדוֹר וָדֹר נְסַפֵּר תְּהִלָּתֶךָ:

	בָּרוּךְ יהוה בַּיּוֹם, בָּרוּךְ יהוה בַּלָּיְלָה
	בָּרוּךְ יהוה בְּשָׁכְבֵנוּ, בָּרוּךְ יהוה בְּקוּמֵנוּ.
	כִּי בְיָדְךָ נַפְשׁוֹת הַחַיִּים וְהַמֵּתִים.
איוב יב	אֲשֶׁר בְּיָדוֹ נֶפֶשׁ כָּל־חָי, וְרוּחַ כָּל־בְּשַׂר־אִישׁ:
תהלים לא	בְּיָדְךָ אַפְקִיד רוּחִי, פָּדִיתָה אוֹתִי יהוה אֵל אֱמֶת:
	אֱלֹהֵינוּ שֶׁבַּשָּׁמַיִם, יַחֵד שִׁמְךָ וְקַיֵּם מַלְכוּתְךָ תָּמִיד
	וּמְלֹךְ עָלֵינוּ לְעוֹלָם וָעֶד.

יִרְאוּ May our eyes see, our hearts rejoice,
and our souls be glad in Your true salvation,
when Zion is told, "Your God reigns."
The Lord is King, the Lord was King,
the Lord will be King for ever and all time.
▸ For sovereignty is Yours,
and to all eternity You will reign in glory,
for we have no king but You.
Blessed are You, Lord,
the King who in His constant glory will reign over us
and all His creation for ever and all time.

HALF KADDISH

Leader: יִתְגַּדַּל Magnified and sanctified
may His great name be,
in the world He created by His will.
May He establish His kingdom
in your lifetime and in your days,
and in the lifetime of all the house of Israel,
swiftly and soon – and say: Amen.

All: May His great name be blessed for ever and all time.

Leader: Blessed and praised, glorified and exalted,
raised and honored,
uplifted and lauded
be the name of the Holy One,
blessed be He,
beyond any blessing,
song, praise and consolation
uttered in the world –
and say: Amen.

יִרְאוּ עֵינֵינוּ וְיִשְׂמַח לִבֵּנוּ
וְתָגֵל נַפְשֵׁנוּ בִּישׁוּעָתְךָ בֶּאֱמֶת
בֶּאֱמֹר לְצִיּוֹן מָלַךְ אֱלֹהָיִךְ.
יהוה מֶלֶךְ, יהוה מָלָךְ, יהוה יִמְלֹךְ לְעֹלָם וָעֶד.
כִּי הַמַּלְכוּת שֶׁלְּךָ הִיא, וּלְעוֹלְמֵי עַד תִּמְלֹךְ בְּכָבוֹד
כִּי אֵין לָנוּ מֶלֶךְ אֶלָּא אָתָּה.
בָּרוּךְ אַתָּה יהוה
הַמֶּלֶךְ בִּכְבוֹדוֹ תָּמִיד, יִמְלֹךְ עָלֵינוּ לְעוֹלָם וָעֶד
וְעַל כָּל מַעֲשָׂיו.

חצי קדיש

ש״ץ: יִתְגַּדַּל וְיִתְקַדַּשׁ שְׁמֵהּ רַבָּא (קהל: אָמֵן)
בְּעָלְמָא דִּי בְרָא כִרְעוּתֵהּ
וְיַמְלִיךְ מַלְכוּתֵהּ
בְּחַיֵּיכוֹן וּבְיוֹמֵיכוֹן וּבְחַיֵּי דְכָל בֵּית יִשְׂרָאֵל
בַּעֲגָלָא וּבִזְמַן קָרִיב, וְאִמְרוּ אָמֵן. (קהל: אָמֵן)

קהל
 וש״ץ: יְהֵא שְׁמֵהּ רַבָּא מְבָרַךְ לְעָלַם וּלְעָלְמֵי עָלְמַיָּא.

ש״ץ: יִתְבָּרַךְ וְיִשְׁתַּבַּח וְיִתְפָּאַר וְיִתְרוֹמַם וְיִתְנַשֵּׂא
וְיִתְהַדָּר וְיִתְעַלֶּה וְיִתְהַלָּל
שְׁמֵהּ דְּקֻדְשָׁא בְּרִיךְ הוּא (קהל: בְּרִיךְ הוּא)
לְעֵלָּא מִן כָּל בִּרְכָתָא וְשִׁירָתָא, תֻּשְׁבְּחָתָא וְנֶחֱמָתָא
דַּאֲמִירָן בְּעָלְמָא
וְאִמְרוּ אָמֵן. (קהל: אָמֵן)

THE AMIDA

The following prayer, until "in former years," on page 738, is said silently, standing with feet together. Take three steps forward and at the points indicated by ˙, bend the knees at the first word, bow at the second, and stand straight before saying God's name.

O Lord, open my lips,   Ps. 51
so that my mouth may declare Your praise.

PATRIARCHS

˙בָּרוּךְ Blessed are You, Lord our God and God of our fathers,
God of Abraham, God of Isaac and God of Jacob;
the great, mighty and awesome God, God Most High,
who bestows acts of loving-kindness and creates all,
who remembers the loving-kindness of the fathers
and will bring a Redeemer to their children's children
for the sake of His name, in love.
King, Helper, Savior, Shield:
˙Blessed are You, Lord,
Shield of Abraham.

DIVINE MIGHT

אַתָּה גִּבּוֹר You are eternally mighty, Lord.
You give life to the dead
and have great power to save.

     In Israel: He causes the dew to fall.

He sustains the living with loving-kindness,
and with great compassion revives the dead.
He supports the fallen, heals the sick,
sets captives free,
and keeps His faith with those who sleep in the dust.

עמידה

The following prayer, until קַדְמֻנִיּוֹת, *on page 739, is said silently, standing with feet together. Take three steps forward and at the points indicated by ׳, bend the knees at the first word, bow at the second, and stand straight before saying God's name.*

תהלים נא

אֲדֹנָי, שְׂפָתַי תִּפְתָּח, וּפִי יַגִּיד תְּהִלָּתֶךָ:

אבות

׳בָּרוּךְ אַתָּה יהוה, אֱלֹהֵינוּ וֵאלֹהֵי אֲבוֹתֵינוּ
אֱלֹהֵי אַבְרָהָם, אֱלֹהֵי יִצְחָק, וֵאלֹהֵי יַעֲקֹב
הָאֵל הַגָּדוֹל הַגִּבּוֹר וְהַנּוֹרָא, אֵל עֶלְיוֹן
גּוֹמֵל חֲסָדִים טוֹבִים, וְקוֹנֵה הַכֹּל
וְזוֹכֵר חַסְדֵי אָבוֹת
וּמֵבִיא גוֹאֵל לִבְנֵי בְנֵיהֶם, לְמַעַן שְׁמוֹ בְּאַהֲבָה.
מֶלֶךְ עוֹזֵר וּמוֹשִׁיעַ וּמָגֵן.
׳בָּרוּךְ אַתָּה יהוה, מָגֵן אַבְרָהָם.

גבורות

אַתָּה גִּבּוֹר לְעוֹלָם, אֲדֹנָי
מְחַיֵּה מֵתִים אַתָּה, רַב לְהוֹשִׁיעַ

בארץ ישראל: מוֹרִיד הַטָּל

מְכַלְכֵּל חַיִּים בְּחֶסֶד
מְחַיֵּה מֵתִים בְּרַחֲמִים רַבִּים
סוֹמֵךְ נוֹפְלִים, וְרוֹפֵא חוֹלִים, וּמַתִּיר אֲסוּרִים
וּמְקַיֵּם אֱמוּנָתוֹ לִישֵׁנֵי עָפָר.

Who is like You, Master of might,
and to whom can You be compared,
O King who brings death and gives life,
and makes salvation grow?
Faithful are You to revive the dead.
Blessed are You, Lord, who revives the dead.

HOLINESS
אַתָּה קָדוֹשׁ You are holy and Your name is holy,
and holy ones praise You daily, Selah!
Blessed are You, Lord,
the holy God.

KNOWLEDGE
אַתָּה חוֹנֵן You grace humanity with knowledge
and teach mortals understanding.
Grace us with the knowledge, understanding
and discernment that come from You.
Blessed are You, Lord,
who graciously grants knowledge.

REPENTANCE
הֲשִׁיבֵנוּ Bring us back, our Father, to Your Torah.
Draw us near, our King, to Your service.
Lead us back to You in perfect repentance.
Blessed are You, Lord, who desires repentance.

FORGIVENESS
Strike the left side of the chest at °.
סְלַח לָנוּ Forgive us, our Father,
for we have °sinned.
Pardon us, our King,
for we have °transgressed;
for You pardon and forgive.
Blessed are You, Lord, the gracious One who repeatedly forgives.

מִי כָמְוֹךָ, בַּעַל גְּבוּרוֹת
וּמִי דּוֹמֶה לָּךְ
מֶלֶךְ, מֵמִית וּמְחַיֶּה וּמַצְמִיחַ יְשׁוּעָה.
וְנֶאֱמָן אַתָּה לְהַחֲיוֹת מֵתִים.
בָּרוּךְ אַתָּה יהוה, מְחַיֵּה הַמֵּתִים.

קדושת השם

אַתָּה קָדוֹשׁ וְשִׁמְךָ קָדוֹשׁ
וּקְדוֹשִׁים בְּכָל יוֹם יְהַלְלוּךָ סֶּלָה.
בָּרוּךְ אַתָּה יהוה, הָאֵל הַקָּדוֹשׁ.

דעת

אַתָּה חוֹנֵן לְאָדָם דַּעַת, וּמְלַמֵּד לֶאֱנוֹשׁ בִּינָה.
חָנֵּנוּ מֵאִתְּךָ דֵּעָה בִּינָה וְהַשְׂכֵּל.
בָּרוּךְ אַתָּה יהוה, חוֹנֵן הַדָּעַת.

תשובה

הֲשִׁיבֵנוּ אָבִינוּ לְתוֹרָתֶךָ, וְקָרְבֵנוּ מַלְכֵּנוּ לַעֲבוֹדָתֶךָ
וְהַחֲזִירֵנוּ בִּתְשׁוּבָה שְׁלֵמָה לְפָנֶיךָ.
בָּרוּךְ אַתָּה יהוה, הָרוֹצֶה בִּתְשׁוּבָה.

סליחה

Strike the left side of the chest at °.

סְלַח לָנוּ אָבִינוּ כִּי °חָטָאנוּ
מְחַל לָנוּ מַלְכֵּנוּ כִּי °פָשָׁעְנוּ
כִּי מוֹחֵל וְסוֹלֵחַ אָתָּה.
בָּרוּךְ אַתָּה יהוה, חַנּוּן הַמַּרְבֶּה לִסְלֹחַ.

REDEMPTION

רְאֵה Look on our affliction,
plead our cause,
and redeem us soon for Your name's sake,
for You are a powerful Redeemer.
Blessed are You, Lord,
the Redeemer of Israel.

HEALING

רְפָאֵנוּ Heal us, Lord, and we shall be healed.
Save us and we shall be saved,
for You are our praise.
Bring complete recovery for all our ailments,

> *The following prayer for a sick person may be said here:*
> May it be Your will, O Lord my God and God of my ancestors, that You speedily send a complete recovery from heaven, a healing of both soul and body, to the patient (*name*), son/daughter of (*mother's name*) among the other afflicted of Israel.

for You, God, King, are a faithful and compassionate Healer.
Blessed are You, Lord,
Healer of the sick of His people Israel.

PROSPERITY

בָּרֵךְ Bless this year for us, Lord our God,
and all its types of produce for good.
Grant blessing
on the face of the earth,
and from its goodness satisfy us,
blessing our year as the best of years.
Blessed are You, Lord,
who blesses the years.

גאולה

רְאֵה בְעָנְיֵנוּ, וְרִיבָה רִיבֵנוּ
וּגְאָלֵנוּ מְהֵרָה לְמַעַן שְׁמֶךָ
כִּי גּוֹאֵל חָזָק אָתָּה.
בָּרוּךְ אַתָּה יהוה, גּוֹאֵל יִשְׂרָאֵל.

רפואה

רְפָאֵנוּ יהוה וְנֵרָפֵא
הוֹשִׁיעֵנוּ וְנִוָּשֵׁעָה, כִּי תְהִלָּתֵנוּ אָתָּה
וְהַעֲלֵה רְפוּאָה שְׁלֵמָה לְכָל מַכּוֹתֵינוּ

The following prayer for a sick person may be said here:

יְהִי רָצוֹן מִלְּפָנֶיךָ יהוה אֱלֹהַי וֵאלֹהֵי אֲבוֹתַי, שֶׁתִּשְׁלַח מְהֵרָה רְפוּאָה שְׁלֵמָה מִן הַשָּׁמַיִם רְפוּאַת הַנֶּפֶשׁ וּרְפוּאַת הַגּוּף לַחוֹלֶה/לַחוֹלָה *name of patient* בֶּן/בַּת *mother's name* בְּתוֹךְ שְׁאָר חוֹלֵי יִשְׂרָאֵל.

כִּי אֵל מֶלֶךְ רוֹפֵא נֶאֱמָן וְרַחֲמָן אָתָּה.
בָּרוּךְ אַתָּה יהוה, רוֹפֵא חוֹלֵי עַמּוֹ יִשְׂרָאֵל.

ברכת השנים

בָּרֵךְ עָלֵינוּ יהוה אֱלֹהֵינוּ אֶת הַשָּׁנָה הַזֹּאת
וְאֶת כָּל מִינֵי תְבוּאָתָהּ, לְטוֹבָה
וְתֵן בְּרָכָה עַל פְּנֵי הָאֲדָמָה
וְשַׂבְּעֵנוּ מִטּוּבָהּ
וּבָרֵךְ שְׁנָתֵנוּ כַּשָּׁנִים הַטּוֹבוֹת.
בָּרוּךְ אַתָּה יהוה, מְבָרֵךְ הַשָּׁנִים.

INGATHERING OF EXILES

תְּקַע Sound the great shofar for our freedom,
raise high the banner
to gather our exiles,
and gather us together
from the four quarters of the earth.
Blessed are You, LORD,
who gathers the dispersed
of His people Israel.

JUSTICE

הָשִׁיבָה Restore our judges as at first
and our counselors as at the beginning,
and remove from us sorrow and sighing.
May You alone, LORD,
reign over us
with loving-kindness and compassion,
and vindicate us in justice.
Blessed are You, LORD,
the King who loves righteousness and justice.

AGAINST INFORMERS

וְלַמַּלְשִׁינִים For the slanderers let there be no hope,
and may all wickedness perish in an instant.
May all Your people's enemies swiftly be cut down.
May You swiftly uproot, crush, cast down
and humble the arrogant
swiftly in our days.
Blessed are You, LORD,
who destroys enemies
and humbles the arrogant.

קיבוץ גלויות
תְּקַע בְּשׁוֹפָר גָּדוֹל לְחֵרוּתֵנוּ
וְשָׂא נֵס לְקַבֵּץ גָּלֻיּוֹתֵינוּ
וְקַבְּצֵנוּ יַחַד מֵאַרְבַּע כַּנְפוֹת הָאָרֶץ.
בָּרוּךְ אַתָּה יהוה
מְקַבֵּץ נִדְחֵי עַמּוֹ יִשְׂרָאֵל.

השבת המשפט
הָשִׁיבָה שׁוֹפְטֵינוּ כְּבָרִאשׁוֹנָה
וְיוֹעֲצֵינוּ כְּבַתְּחִלָּה
וְהָסֵר מִמֶּנּוּ יָגוֹן וַאֲנָחָה
וּמְלוֹךְ עָלֵינוּ אַתָּה יהוה לְבַדְּךָ בְּחֶסֶד וּבְרַחֲמִים
וְצַדְּקֵנוּ בַּמִּשְׁפָּט.
בָּרוּךְ אַתָּה יהוה
מֶלֶךְ אוֹהֵב צְדָקָה וּמִשְׁפָּט.

ברכת המינים
וְלַמַּלְשִׁינִים אַל תְּהִי תִקְוָה
וְכָל הָרִשְׁעָה כְּרֶגַע תֹּאבֵד
וְכָל אוֹיְבֵי עַמְּךָ מְהֵרָה יִכָּרֵתוּ
וְהַזֵּדִים מְהֵרָה תְעַקֵּר וּתְשַׁבֵּר וּתְמַגֵּר וְתַכְנִיעַ בִּמְהֵרָה בְיָמֵינוּ.
בָּרוּךְ אַתָּה יהוה
שׁוֹבֵר אוֹיְבִים וּמַכְנִיעַ זֵדִים.

THE RIGHTEOUS
עַל הַצַּדִּיקִים To the righteous, the pious,
the elders of Your people the house of Israel,
the remnant of their scholars,
the righteous converts, and to us,
may Your compassion be aroused,
Lord our God.
Grant a good reward to all
who sincerely trust in Your name.
Set our lot with them,
so that we may never be ashamed,
for in You we trust
Blessed are You, Lord,
who is the support and trust of the righteous.

REBUILDING JERUSALEM
וְלִירוּשָׁלַיִם To Jerusalem, Your city,
may You return in compassion,
and may You dwell in it as You promised.
May You rebuild it rapidly in our days
as an everlasting structure,
and install within it soon the throne of David.
Blessed are You, Lord,
who builds Jerusalem.

KINGDOM OF DAVID
אֶת צֶמַח May the offshoot of Your servant David soon flower,
and may his pride be raised high by Your salvation,
for we wait for Your salvation all day.
Blessed are You, Lord,
who makes the glory of salvation flourish.

על הצדיקים

עַל הַצַּדִּיקִים וְעַל הַחֲסִידִים
וְעַל זִקְנֵי עַמְּךָ בֵּית יִשְׂרָאֵל
וְעַל פְּלֵיטַת סוֹפְרֵיהֶם
וְעַל גֵּרֵי הַצֶּדֶק, וְעָלֵינוּ
יֶהֱמוּ רַחֲמֶיךָ יהוה אֱלֹהֵינוּ
וְתֵן שָׂכָר טוֹב לְכָל הַבּוֹטְחִים בְּשִׁמְךָ בֶּאֱמֶת
וְשִׂים חֶלְקֵנוּ עִמָּהֶם
וּלְעוֹלָם לֹא נֵבוֹשׁ כִּי בְךָ בָּטָחְנוּ.
בָּרוּךְ אַתָּה יהוה, מִשְׁעָן וּמִבְטָח לַצַּדִּיקִים.

בניין ירושלים

וְלִירוּשָׁלַיִם עִירְךָ בְּרַחֲמִים תָּשׁוּב
וְתִשְׁכּוֹן בְּתוֹכָהּ כַּאֲשֶׁר דִּבַּרְתָּ
וּבְנֵה אוֹתָהּ בְּקָרוֹב בְּיָמֵינוּ בִּנְיַן עוֹלָם
וְכִסֵּא דָוִד מְהֵרָה לְתוֹכָהּ תָּכִין.
בָּרוּךְ אַתָּה יהוה, בּוֹנֵה יְרוּשָׁלָיִם.

משיח בן דוד

אֶת צֶמַח דָּוִד עַבְדְּךָ מְהֵרָה תַצְמִיחַ
וְקַרְנוֹ תָּרוּם בִּישׁוּעָתֶךָ
כִּי לִישׁוּעָתְךָ קִוִּינוּ כָּל הַיּוֹם.
בָּרוּךְ אַתָּה יהוה, מַצְמִיחַ קֶרֶן יְשׁוּעָה.

MA'ARIV FOR MOTZA'EI TISHA B'AV

RESPONSE TO PRAYER

שְׁמַע קוֹלֵנוּ Listen to our voice, LORD our God.
Spare us and have compassion on us,
and in compassion and favor accept our prayer,
for You, God, listen to prayers and pleas.
Do not turn us away, O our King,
empty-handed from Your presence,
for You listen with compassion
to the prayer of Your people Israel.
Blessed are You, LORD,
who listens to prayer.

TEMPLE SERVICE

רְצֵה Find favor, LORD our God,
in Your people Israel and their prayer.
Restore the service to Your most holy House,
and accept in love and favor,
the fire-offerings of Israel and their prayer.
May the service of Your people Israel always find favor with You.
And may our eyes witness
Your return to Zion in compassion.
Blessed are You, LORD,
who restores His Presence to Zion.

THANKSGIVING

Bow at the first nine words.

מוֹדִים We give thanks to You,
for You are the LORD our God and God of our ancestors
for ever and all time.
You are the Rock of our lives,
Shield of our salvation
from generation to generation.

שומע תפילה
שְׁמַע קוֹלֵנוּ יהוה אֱלֹהֵינוּ
חוּס וְרַחֵם עָלֵינוּ
וְקַבֵּל בְּרַחֲמִים וּבְרָצוֹן אֶת תְּפִלָּתֵנוּ
כִּי אֵל שׁוֹמֵעַ תְּפִלּוֹת וְתַחֲנוּנִים אָתָּה
וּמִלְּפָנֶיךָ מַלְכֵּנוּ רֵיקָם אַל תְּשִׁיבֵנוּ
כִּי אַתָּה שׁוֹמֵעַ תְּפִלַּת עַמְּךָ יִשְׂרָאֵל בְּרַחֲמִים.
בָּרוּךְ אַתָּה יהוה
שׁוֹמֵעַ תְּפִלָּה.

עבודה
רְצֵה יהוה אֱלֹהֵינוּ בְּעַמְּךָ יִשְׂרָאֵל, וּבִתְפִלָּתָם
וְהָשֵׁב אֶת הָעֲבוֹדָה לִדְבִיר בֵּיתֶךָ
וְאִשֵּׁי יִשְׂרָאֵל וּתְפִלָּתָם בְּאַהֲבָה תְקַבֵּל בְּרָצוֹן
וּתְהִי לְרָצוֹן תָּמִיד עֲבוֹדַת יִשְׂרָאֵל עַמֶּךָ.
וְתֶחֱזֶינָה עֵינֵינוּ בְּשׁוּבְךָ לְצִיּוֹן בְּרַחֲמִים.
בָּרוּךְ אַתָּה יהוה
הַמַּחֲזִיר שְׁכִינָתוֹ לְצִיּוֹן.

הודאה

Bow at the first five words.

ᵒמוֹדִים אֲנַחְנוּ לָךְ
שָׁאַתָּה הוּא יהוה אֱלֹהֵינוּ וֵאלֹהֵי אֲבוֹתֵינוּ לְעוֹלָם וָעֶד.
צוּר חַיֵּינוּ, מָגֵן יִשְׁעֵנוּ
אַתָּה הוּא לְדוֹר וָדוֹר.

We will thank You
and declare Your praise for our lives,
which are entrusted into Your hand;
for our souls, which are placed in Your charge;
for Your miracles which are with us every day;
and for Your wonders and favors at all times,
evening, morning and midday.
You are good –
for Your compassion never fails.
You are compassionate –
for Your loving-kindnesses never cease.
We have always placed our hope in You.
For all these things may Your name be blessed and exalted,
our King, continually, for ever and all time.
Let all that lives thank You, Selah!
and praise Your name in truth,
God, our Savior and Help, Selah!
▸Blessed are You, LORD,
whose name is "the Good"
and to whom thanks are due.

PEACE

שָׁלוֹם רָב Grant great peace to Your people Israel for ever,
for You are the sovereign LORD of all peace;
and may it be good in Your eyes
to bless Your people Israel
at every time, at every hour, with Your peace.
Blessed are You, LORD,
who blesses His people Israel with peace.

Some say the following verse:
May the words of my mouth and the meditation of my heart *Ps. 19*
find favor before You, LORD, my Rock and Redeemer.

נוֹדֶה לְּךָ וּנְסַפֵּר תְּהִלָּתֶךָ
עַל חַיֵּינוּ הַמְּסוּרִים בְּיָדֶךָ
וְעַל נִשְׁמוֹתֵינוּ הַפְּקוּדוֹת לָךְ
וְעַל נִסֶּיךָ שֶׁבְּכָל יוֹם עִמָּנוּ
וְעַל נִפְלְאוֹתֶיךָ וְטוֹבוֹתֶיךָ שֶׁבְּכָל עֵת
עֶרֶב וָבֹקֶר וְצָהֳרָיִם.
הַטּוֹב, כִּי לֹא כָלוּ רַחֲמֶיךָ
וְהַמְרַחֵם, כִּי לֹא תַמּוּ חֲסָדֶיךָ
מֵעוֹלָם קִוִּינוּ לָךְ.
וְעַל כֻּלָּם יִתְבָּרַךְ וְיִתְרוֹמַם שִׁמְךָ מַלְכֵּנוּ תָּמִיד לְעוֹלָם וָעֶד
וְכֹל הַחַיִּים יוֹדוּךָ סֶּלָה, וִיהַלְלוּ אֶת שִׁמְךָ בֶּאֱמֶת
הָאֵל יְשׁוּעָתֵנוּ וְעֶזְרָתֵנוּ סֶלָה.
בָּרוּךְ אַתָּה יהוה
הַטּוֹב שִׁמְךָ וּלְךָ נָאֶה לְהוֹדוֹת.

ברכת שלום

שָׁלוֹם רָב עַל יִשְׂרָאֵל עַמְּךָ תָּשִׂים לְעוֹלָם
כִּי אַתָּה הוּא מֶלֶךְ אָדוֹן לְכָל הַשָּׁלוֹם.
וְטוֹב בְּעֵינֶיךָ לְבָרֵךְ אֶת עַמְּךָ יִשְׂרָאֵל
בְּכָל עֵת וּבְכָל שָׁעָה בִּשְׁלוֹמֶךָ.
בָּרוּךְ אַתָּה יהוה
הַמְבָרֵךְ אֶת עַמּוֹ יִשְׂרָאֵל בַּשָּׁלוֹם.

Some say the following verse:

יִהְיוּ לְרָצוֹן אִמְרֵי־פִי וְהֶגְיוֹן לִבִּי לְפָנֶיךָ, יהוה צוּרִי וְגֹאֲלִי:

תהלים יט

MA'ARIV FOR MOTZA'EI TISHA B'AV

אֱלֹהַי **My God,** *Berakhot 17a*
guard my tongue from evil and my lips from deceitful speech.
To those who curse me, let my soul be silent;
may my soul be to all like the dust.
Open my heart to Your Torah
and let my soul pursue Your commandments.
As for all who plan evil against me,
swiftly thwart their counsel and frustrate their plans.
> Act for the sake of Your name; act for the sake of Your right hand;
> act for the sake of Your holiness; act for the sake of Your Torah.

That Your beloved ones may be delivered, *Ps. 60*
save with Your right hand and answer me.
May the words of my mouth *Ps. 19*
and the meditation of my heart find favor before You,
LORD, my Rock and Redeemer.

Bow, take three steps back, then bow, first left, then right, then center, while saying:

May He who makes peace in His high places,
make peace for us and all Israel – and say: Amen.

יְהִי רָצוֹן **May it be Your will,** LORD our God and God of our ancestors,
that the Temple be rebuilt speedily in our days, and grant us a share in Your Torah.
And there we will serve You with reverence,
as in the days of old and as in former years.
Then the offering of Judah and Jerusalem *Mal. 3*
will be pleasing to the LORD as in the days of old and as in former years.

FULL KADDISH

Leader: יִתְגַּדַּל **Magnified and sanctified** may His great name be,
in the world He created by His will.
May He establish His kingdom
in your lifetime and in your days,
and in the lifetime of all the house of Israel,
swiftly and soon –
and say: Amen.

All: May His great name be blessed for ever and all time.

אֱלֹהַי

נְצֹר לְשׁוֹנִי מֵרָע וּשְׂפָתַי מִדַּבֵּר מִרְמָה
וְלִמְקַלְלַי נַפְשִׁי תִדֹּם, וְנַפְשִׁי כֶּעָפָר לַכֹּל תִּהְיֶה.
פְּתַח לִבִּי בְּתוֹרָתֶךָ, וּבְמִצְוֹתֶיךָ תִּרְדּוֹף נַפְשִׁי.
וְכָל הַחוֹשְׁבִים עָלַי רָעָה
מְהֵרָה הָפֵר עֲצָתָם וְקַלְקֵל מַחֲשַׁבְתָּם.
עֲשֵׂה לְמַעַן שְׁמֶךָ, עֲשֵׂה לְמַעַן יְמִינֶךָ
עֲשֵׂה לְמַעַן קְדֻשָּׁתֶךָ, עֲשֵׂה לְמַעַן תּוֹרָתֶךָ.
לְמַעַן יֵחָלְצוּן יְדִידֶיךָ, הוֹשִׁיעָה יְמִינְךָ וַעֲנֵנִי:
יִהְיוּ לְרָצוֹן אִמְרֵי־פִי וְהֶגְיוֹן לִבִּי לְפָנֶיךָ, יהוה צוּרִי וְגֹאֲלִי:

Bow, take three steps back, then bow, first left, then right, then center, while saying:

עֹשֶׂה שָׁלוֹם בִּמְרוֹמָיו
הוּא יַעֲשֶׂה שָׁלוֹם עָלֵינוּ וְעַל כָּל יִשְׂרָאֵל, וְאִמְרוּ אָמֵן.

יְהִי רָצוֹן מִלְּפָנֶיךָ יהוה אֱלֹהֵינוּ וֵאלֹהֵי אֲבוֹתֵינוּ
שֶׁיִּבָּנֶה בֵּית הַמִּקְדָּשׁ בִּמְהֵרָה בְיָמֵינוּ, וְתֵן חֶלְקֵנוּ בְּתוֹרָתֶךָ
וְשָׁם נַעֲבָדְךָ בְּיִרְאָה כִּימֵי עוֹלָם וּכְשָׁנִים קַדְמוֹנִיּוֹת.
וְעָרְבָה לַיהוה מִנְחַת יְהוּדָה וִירוּשָׁלָםִ כִּימֵי עוֹלָם וּכְשָׁנִים קַדְמוֹנִיּוֹת:

קדיש שלם

ש״ץ: יִתְגַּדַּל וְיִתְקַדַּשׁ שְׁמֵהּ רַבָּא (קהל: אָמֵן)
בְּעָלְמָא דִּי בְרָא כִרְעוּתֵהּ
וְיַמְלִיךְ מַלְכוּתֵהּ
בְּחַיֵּיכוֹן וּבְיוֹמֵיכוֹן וּבְחַיֵּי דְכָל בֵּית יִשְׂרָאֵל
בַּעֲגָלָא וּבִזְמַן קָרִיב, וְאִמְרוּ אָמֵן. (קהל: אָמֵן)

קהל וש״ץ: יְהֵא שְׁמֵהּ רַבָּא מְבָרַךְ לְעָלַם וּלְעָלְמֵי עָלְמַיָּא.

Leader: Blessed and praised,
glorified and exalted,
raised and honored,
uplifted and lauded be
the name of the Holy One,
blessed be He, beyond any blessing,
song, praise and consolation
uttered in the world – and say: Amen.

May the prayers and pleas of all Israel
be accepted by their Father in heaven – and say: Amen.

May there be great peace from heaven,
and life for us and all Israel – and say: Amen.

*Bow, take three steps back, as if taking leave of the Divine Presence,
then bow, first left, then right, then center, while saying:*

May He who makes peace in His high places,
make peace for us and all Israel – and say: Amen.

Stand while saying Aleinu. Bow at ˇ.

עָלֵינוּ It is our duty to praise the Master of all,
and ascribe greatness to the Author of creation,
who has not made us like the nations of the lands
nor placed us like the families of the earth;
who has not made our portion like theirs,
nor our destiny like all their multitudes.
(For they worship vanity and emptiness,
and pray to a god who cannot save.)
ˇBut we bow in worship
and thank the Supreme King of kings,
the Holy One, blessed be He,
who extends the heavens and establishes the earth,
whose throne of glory is in the heavens above,
and whose power's Presence is in the highest of heights.

ש״ץ: יִתְבָּרַךְ וְיִשְׁתַּבַּח וְיִתְפָּאַר
וְיִתְרוֹמַם וְיִתְנַשֵּׂא וְיִתְהַדָּר וְיִתְעַלֶּה וְיִתְהַלָּל
שְׁמֵהּ דְּקֻדְשָׁא בְּרִיךְ הוּא (קהל: בְּרִיךְ הוּא)
לְעֵלָּא מִן כָּל בִּרְכָתָא וְשִׁירָתָא, תֻּשְׁבְּחָתָא וְנֶחֱמָתָא
דַּאֲמִירָן בְּעָלְמָא, וְאִמְרוּ אָמֵן. (קהל: אָמֵן)

תִּתְקַבַּל צְלוֹתְהוֹן וּבָעוּתְהוֹן דְּכָל יִשְׂרָאֵל
קֳדָם אֲבוּהוֹן דִּי בִשְׁמַיָּא, וְאִמְרוּ אָמֵן. (קהל: אָמֵן)

יְהֵא שְׁלָמָא רַבָּא מִן שְׁמַיָּא
וְחַיִּים, עָלֵינוּ וְעַל כָּל יִשְׂרָאֵל, וְאִמְרוּ אָמֵן. (קהל: אָמֵן)

Bow, take three steps back, as if taking leave of the Divine Presence,
then bow, first left, then right, then center, while saying:

עֹשֶׂה שָׁלוֹם בִּמְרוֹמָיו
הוּא יַעֲשֶׂה שָׁלוֹם עָלֵינוּ וְעַל כָּל יִשְׂרָאֵל
וְאִמְרוּ אָמֵן. (קהל: אָמֵן)

Stand while saying עָלֵינוּ. *Bow at* ׳.

עָלֵינוּ לְשַׁבֵּחַ לַאֲדוֹן הַכֹּל, לָתֵת גְּדֻלָּה לְיוֹצֵר בְּרֵאשִׁית
שֶׁלֹּא עָשָׂנוּ כְּגוֹיֵי הָאֲרָצוֹת, וְלֹא שָׂמָנוּ כְּמִשְׁפְּחוֹת הָאֲדָמָה
שֶׁלֹּא שָׂם חֶלְקֵנוּ כָּהֶם וְגוֹרָלֵנוּ כְּכָל הֲמוֹנָם.
(שֶׁהֵם מִשְׁתַּחֲוִים לְהֶבֶל וָרִיק וּמִתְפַּלְּלִים אֶל אֵל לֹא יוֹשִׁיעַ.)
׳וַאֲנַחְנוּ כּוֹרְעִים וּמִשְׁתַּחֲוִים וּמוֹדִים
לִפְנֵי מֶלֶךְ מַלְכֵי הַמְּלָכִים, הַקָּדוֹשׁ בָּרוּךְ הוּא
שֶׁהוּא נוֹטֶה שָׁמַיִם וְיוֹסֵד אָרֶץ
וּמוֹשַׁב יְקָרוֹ בַּשָּׁמַיִם מִמַּעַל
וּשְׁכִינַת עֻזּוֹ בְּגָבְהֵי מְרוֹמִים.

He is our God; there is no other.
Truly He is our King, there is none else,
as it is written in His Torah:
"You shall know and take to heart this day — *Deut. 4*
that the Lord is God, in heaven above and on earth below.
There is no other."

Therefore, we place our hope in You, Lord our God,
that we may soon see the glory of Your power,
when You will remove abominations from the earth,
and idols will be utterly destroyed,
when the world will be perfected
under the sovereignty of the Almighty,
when all humanity will call on Your name,
to turn all the earth's wicked toward You.
All the world's inhabitants will realize and know
that to You every knee must bow and every tongue swear loyalty.
Before You, Lord our God, they will kneel and bow down
and give honor to Your glorious name.
They will all accept the yoke of Your kingdom,
and You will reign over them soon and for ever.
For the kingdom is Yours, and to all eternity You will reign in glory,
as it is written in Your Torah:
"The Lord will reign for ever and ever." — *Ex. 15*
▸ And it is said: "Then the Lord shall be King over all the earth; — *Zech. 14*
on that day the Lord shall be One and His name One."

Some add:
Have no fear of sudden terror or of the ruin when it overtakes the wicked. — *Prov. 3*
Devise your strategy, but it will be thwarted; propose your plan, — *Is. 8*
but it will not stand, for God is with us.
When you grow old, I will still be the same. — *Is. 46*
When your hair turns gray, I will still carry you.
I made you, I will bear you,
I will carry you, and I will rescue you.

מעריב למוצאי תשעה באב • סיום התפילה

הוּא אֱלֹהֵינוּ, אֵין עוֹד.
אֱמֶת מַלְכֵּנוּ, אֶפֶס זוּלָתוֹ
כַּכָּתוּב בְּתוֹרָתוֹ

דברים ד
וְיָדַעְתָּ הַיּוֹם וַהֲשֵׁבֹתָ אֶל־לְבָבֶךָ
כִּי יהוה הוּא הָאֱלֹהִים בַּשָּׁמַיִם מִמַּעַל וְעַל־הָאָרֶץ מִתָּחַת
אֵין עוֹד:

עַל כֵּן נְקַוֶּה לְּךָ יהוה אֱלֹהֵינוּ, לִרְאוֹת מְהֵרָה בְּתִפְאֶרֶת עֻזֶּךָ
לְהַעֲבִיר גִּלּוּלִים מִן הָאָרֶץ, וְהָאֱלִילִים כָּרוֹת יִכָּרֵתוּן
לְתַקֵּן עוֹלָם בְּמַלְכוּת שַׁדַּי.
וְכָל בְּנֵי בָשָׂר יִקְרְאוּ בִשְׁמֶךָ לְהַפְנוֹת אֵלֶיךָ כָּל רִשְׁעֵי אָרֶץ.
יַכִּירוּ וְיֵדְעוּ כָּל יוֹשְׁבֵי תֵבֵל
כִּי לְךָ תִּכְרַע כָּל בֶּרֶךְ, תִּשָּׁבַע כָּל לָשׁוֹן.
לְפָנֶיךָ יהוה אֱלֹהֵינוּ יִכְרְעוּ וְיִפֹּלוּ, וְלִכְבוֹד שִׁמְךָ יְקָר יִתֵּנוּ
וִיקַבְּלוּ כֻלָּם אֶת עֹל מַלְכוּתֶךָ
וְתִמְלֹךְ עֲלֵיהֶם מְהֵרָה לְעוֹלָם וָעֶד.
כִּי הַמַּלְכוּת שֶׁלְּךָ הִיא וּלְעוֹלְמֵי עַד תִּמְלֹךְ בְּכָבוֹד

שמות טו
כַּכָּתוּב בְּתוֹרָתֶךָ, יהוה יִמְלֹךְ לְעֹלָם וָעֶד:

זכריה יד
‹ וְנֶאֱמַר, וְהָיָה יהוה לְמֶלֶךְ עַל־כָּל־הָאָרֶץ
בַּיּוֹם הַהוּא יִהְיֶה יהוה אֶחָד וּשְׁמוֹ אֶחָד:

Some add:

משלי ג
אַל־תִּירָא מִפַּחַד פִּתְאֹם וּמִשֹּׁאַת רְשָׁעִים כִּי תָבֹא:

ישעיה ח
עֻצוּ עֵצָה וְתֻפָר, דַּבְּרוּ דָבָר וְלֹא יָקוּם, כִּי עִמָּנוּ אֵל:

ישעיה מו
וְעַד־זִקְנָה אֲנִי הוּא, וְעַד־שֵׂיבָה אֲנִי אֶסְבֹּל
אֲנִי עָשִׂיתִי וַאֲנִי אֶשָּׂא וַאֲנִי אֶסְבֹּל וַאֲמַלֵּט:

MOURNER'S KADDISH

The following prayer requires the presence of a minyan.
A transliteration can be found on page 792.

Mourner: יִתְגַּדַּל Magnified and sanctified may His great name be,
in the world He created by His will.
May He establish His kingdom
in your lifetime and in your days,
and in the lifetime of all the house of Israel,
swiftly and soon – and say: Amen.

All: May His great name be blessed for ever and all time.

Mourner: Blessed and praised, glorified and exalted,
raised and honored, uplifted and lauded
be the name of the Holy One,
blessed be He, beyond any blessing,
song, praise and consolation
uttered in the world – and say: Amen.

May there be great peace from heaven,
and life for us and all Israel – and say: Amen.

Bow, take three steps back, as if taking leave of the Divine Presence,
then bow, first left, then right, then center, while saying:

May He who makes peace in His high places,
make peace for us and all Israel – and say: Amen.

HAVDALA

If Tisha B'Av began on Motza'ei Shabbat, Havdala is said.
The blessings for the spices and flame are omitted.

Take a cup of wine in the right hand and say:

Please pay attention, my masters.

Blessed are You, Lord our God, King of the Universe,
who creates the fruit of the vine.

Blessed are You, Lord our God, King of the Universe, who distinguishes between sacred and secular, between light and darkness, between Israel and the nations, between the seventh day and the six days of work. Blessed are You, Lord, who distinguishes between sacred and secular.

קדיש יתום

The following prayer requires the presence of a מנין.
A transliteration can be found on page 792.

אבל יִתְגַּדַּל וְיִתְקַדַּשׁ שְׁמֵהּ רַבָּא (קהל: אָמֵן)
בְּעָלְמָא דִּי בְרָא כִרְעוּתֵהּ, וְיַמְלִיךְ מַלְכוּתֵהּ
בְּחַיֵּיכוֹן וּבְיוֹמֵיכוֹן וּבְחַיֵּי דְכָל בֵּית יִשְׂרָאֵל
בַּעֲגָלָא וּבִזְמַן קָרִיב, וְאִמְרוּ אָמֵן. (קהל: אָמֵן)

קהל ואבל: יְהֵא שְׁמֵהּ רַבָּא מְבָרַךְ לְעָלַם וּלְעָלְמֵי עָלְמַיָּא.

אבל יִתְבָּרַךְ וְיִשְׁתַּבַּח וְיִתְפָּאַר
וְיִתְרוֹמַם וְיִתְנַשֵּׂא וְיִתְהַדָּר וְיִתְעַלֶּה וְיִתְהַלָּל
שְׁמֵהּ דְּקֻדְשָׁא בְּרִיךְ הוּא (קהל: בְּרִיךְ הוּא)
לְעֵלָּא מִן כָּל בִּרְכָתָא וְשִׁירָתָא, תֻּשְׁבְּחָתָא וְנֶחֱמָתָא
דַּאֲמִירָן בְּעָלְמָא, וְאִמְרוּ אָמֵן. (קהל: אָמֵן)

יְהֵא שְׁלָמָא רַבָּא מִן שְׁמַיָּא
וְחַיִּים, עָלֵינוּ וְעַל כָּל יִשְׂרָאֵל, וְאִמְרוּ אָמֵן. (קהל: אָמֵן)

Bow, take three steps back, as if taking leave of the Divine Presence,
then bow, first left, then right, then center, while saying:

עֹשֶׂה שָׁלוֹם בִּמְרוֹמָיו
הוּא יַעֲשֶׂה שָׁלוֹם עָלֵינוּ וְעַל כָּל יִשְׂרָאֵל, וְאִמְרוּ אָמֵן. (קהל: אָמֵן)

הבדלה

If תשעה באב *began on* מוצאי שבת, הבדלה *is said.*
The blessings for the spices and flame are omitted.

Take a cup of wine in the right hand and say:

סַבְרִי מָרָנָן
בָּרוּךְ אַתָּה יהוה אֱלֹהֵינוּ מֶלֶךְ הָעוֹלָם, בּוֹרֵא פְּרִי הַגָּפֶן.
בָּרוּךְ אַתָּה יהוה אֱלֹהֵינוּ מֶלֶךְ הָעוֹלָם, הַמַּבְדִּיל בֵּין קֹדֶשׁ לְחֹל, בֵּין אוֹר
לְחֹשֶׁךְ, בֵּין יִשְׂרָאֵל לָעַמִּים, בֵּין יוֹם הַשְּׁבִיעִי לְשֵׁשֶׁת יְמֵי הַמַּעֲשֶׂה. בָּרוּךְ
אַתָּה יהוה, הַמַּבְדִּיל בֵּין קֹדֶשׁ לְחֹל.

BLESSING OF THE NEW MOON

One should eat and put on one's shoes before saying the Blessing of the New Moon.

הַלְלוּיָהּ Halleluya! Praise the LORD from the heavens, praise Him in the heights. Praise Him, all His angels; praise Him, all His hosts. Praise Him, sun and moon; praise Him, all shining stars. Praise Him, highest heavens and the waters above the heavens. Let them praise the name of the LORD, for He commanded and they were created. He established them for ever and all time, issuing a decree that will never change. *Ps. 148*

Look at the moon, then say:

כִּי־אֶרְאֶה When I see Your heavens, the work of Your fingers, the moon and the stars which You have set in place: What is man that You are mindful of him, the son of man that You care for him? *Ps. 148*

בָּרוּךְ Blessed are You, LORD our God, King of the Universe who by His word created the heavens, and by His breath all their host. He set for them laws and times, so that they should not deviate from their appointed task. They are joyous and glad to perform the will of their Owner, the Worker of truth whose work is truth. To the moon He said that it should renew itself as a crown of beauty for those He carried from the womb [Israel], for they are destined to be renewed like it, and to praise their Creator for the sake of His glorious majesty. Blessed are You, LORD, who renews the months.

The following five verses are each said three times:

Blessed is He who formed you; blessed is He who made you;
blessed is He who owns you; blessed is He who created you.

The following verse is said rising on the toes.

Just as I leap toward you but cannot touch you,
so may none of my enemies be able to touch me to do me harm.

May fear and dread fall upon them; *Ex. 15*
by the power of Your arm may they be still as stone.

May they be still as stone through the power of Your arm,
when dread and fear fall upon them.

David, king of Israel, lives and endures.

קידוש לבנה

One should eat and put on one's shoes before saying the קידוש לבנה.

הַלְלוּיָהּ, הַלְלוּ אֶת־יהוה מִן־הַשָּׁמַיִם, הַלְלוּהוּ בַּמְּרוֹמִים: הַלְלוּהוּ כָל־מַלְאָכָיו, הַלְלוּהוּ כָּל־צְבָאָו: הַלְלוּהוּ שֶׁמֶשׁ וְיָרֵחַ, הַלְלוּהוּ כָּל־כּוֹכְבֵי אוֹר: הַלְלוּהוּ שְׁמֵי הַשָּׁמָיִם, וְהַמַּיִם אֲשֶׁר מֵעַל הַשָּׁמָיִם: יְהַלְלוּ אֶת־שֵׁם יהוה, כִּי הוּא צִוָּה וְנִבְרָאוּ: וַיַּעֲמִידֵם לָעַד לְעוֹלָם, חָק־נָתַן וְלֹא יַעֲבוֹר:

תהלים קמח

Look at the moon, then say:

כִּי־אֶרְאֶה שָׁמֶיךָ מַעֲשֵׂה אֶצְבְּעֹתֶיךָ, יָרֵחַ וְכוֹכָבִים אֲשֶׁר כּוֹנָנְתָּה: מָה־אֱנוֹשׁ כִּי־תִזְכְּרֶנּוּ, וּבֶן־אָדָם כִּי תִפְקְדֶנּוּ:

תהלים ח

בָּרוּךְ אַתָּה יהוה אֱלֹהֵינוּ מֶלֶךְ הָעוֹלָם, אֲשֶׁר בְּמַאֲמָרוֹ בָּרָא שְׁחָקִים, וּבְרוּחַ פִּיו כָּל צְבָאָם, חֹק וּזְמַן נָתַן לָהֶם שֶׁלֹּא יְשַׁנּוּ אֶת תַּפְקִידָם. שָׂשִׂים וּשְׂמֵחִים לַעֲשׂוֹת רְצוֹן קוֹנָם, פּוֹעֵל אֱמֶת שֶׁפְּעֻלָּתוֹ אֱמֶת. וְלַלְּבָנָה אָמַר שֶׁתִּתְחַדֵּשׁ, עֲטֶרֶת תִּפְאֶרֶת לַעֲמוּסֵי בָטֶן, שֶׁהֵם עֲתִידִים לְהִתְחַדֵּשׁ כְּמוֹתָהּ וּלְפָאֵר לְיוֹצְרָם עַל שֵׁם כְּבוֹד מַלְכוּתוֹ. בָּרוּךְ אַתָּה יהוה, מְחַדֵּשׁ חֳדָשִׁים.

The following five verses are each said three times:

בָּרוּךְ יוֹצְרֵךְ, בָּרוּךְ עוֹשֵׂךְ, בָּרוּךְ קוֹנֵךְ, בָּרוּךְ בּוֹרְאֵךְ.

The following verse is said rising on the toes.

כְּשֵׁם שֶׁאֲנִי רוֹקֵד כְּנֶגְדֵּךְ וְאֵינִי יָכוֹל לִנְגֹּעַ בָּךְ כָּךְ לֹא יוּכְלוּ כָּל אוֹיְבַי לִנְגֹּעַ בִּי לְרָעָה.

תִּפֹּל עֲלֵיהֶם אֵימָתָה וָפַחַד, בִּגְדֹל זְרוֹעֲךָ יִדְּמוּ כָּאָבֶן: כָּאֶבֶן יִדְּמוּ זְרוֹעֲךָ בִּגְדֹל, וָפַחַד אֵימָתָה עֲלֵיהֶם תִּפֹּל.

שמות טו

דָּוִד מֶלֶךְ יִשְׂרָאֵל חַי וְקַיָּם.

Turn to three people and say to each:

Peace upon you.

They respond:

Upon you, peace.

Say three times:

May it be a good sign and a good omen for us and all Israel. Amen.

קוֹל Hark! My beloved! Here he comes, leaping over the mountains, bounding over the hills. My beloved is like a gazelle, like a young deer. There he stands outside our wall, peering in through the windows, gazing through the lattice. *Song. 2*

שִׁיר לַמַּעֲלוֹת A song of ascents. I lift my eyes up to the hills; from where will my help come? My help comes from the LORD, Maker of heaven and earth. He will not let your foot stumble; He who guards you does not slumber. See: the Guardian of Israel neither slumbers nor sleeps. The LORD is your Guardian; the LORD is your Shade at your right hand. The sun will not strike you by day, nor the moon by night. The LORD will guard you from all harm; He will guard your life. The LORD will guard your going and coming, now and for evermore. *Ps. 121*

הַלְלוּיָהּ Halleluya! Praise God in His holy place; praise Him in the heavens of His power. Praise Him for His mighty deeds; praise Him for His surpassing greatness. Praise Him with blasts of the ram's horn; praise Him with the harp and lyre. Praise Him with timbrel and dance; praise Him with strings and flute. Praise Him with clashing cymbals; praise Him with resounding cymbals. Let all that breathes praise the LORD. Halleluya! Let all that breathes praise the LORD. Halleluya! *Ps. 150*

תָּנָא In the academy of Rabbi Yishma'el it was taught: Were the people of Israel privileged to greet the presence of their heavenly Father only once a month, it would have been sufficient for them. Abaye said: Therefore it [the blessing of the moon] should be said standing. Who is this coming up from the desert, leaning on her beloved? *Sanhedrin 42a*

Song. 8

וִיהִי May it be Your will, LORD my God and God of my ancestors, to make good the deficiency of the moon, so that it is no longer in its diminished state. May the light of the moon be like the light of the sun and like the light of the seven days of creation as it was before it was diminished, as it says, "The two great luminaries." And may there be fulfilled for us the verse: "They shall seek the LORD their God, and David their king." Amen. *Gen. 1 / Hos. 3*

Turn to three people and say to each:

שָׁלוֹם עֲלֵיכֶם.

They respond:

עֲלֵיכֶם שָׁלוֹם.

Say three times:

סִימָן טוֹב וּמַזָּל טוֹב יְהֵא לָנוּ וּלְכָל יִשְׂרָאֵל, אָמֵן.

שיר השירים ב
קוֹל דּוֹדִי הִנֵּה־זֶה בָּא, מְדַלֵּג עַל־הֶהָרִים, מְקַפֵּץ עַל־הַגְּבָעוֹת: דּוֹמֶה דוֹדִי לִצְבִי אוֹ לְעֹפֶר הָאַיָּלִים, הִנֵּה־זֶה עוֹמֵד אַחַר כָּתְלֵנוּ, מַשְׁגִּיחַ מִן־הַחֲלֹּנוֹת, מֵצִיץ מִן־הַחֲרַכִּים:

תהלים קכא
שִׁיר לַמַּעֲלוֹת, אֶשָּׂא עֵינַי אֶל־הֶהָרִים, מֵאַיִן יָבֹא עֶזְרִי: עֶזְרִי מֵעִם יְהוָה, עֹשֵׂה שָׁמַיִם וָאָרֶץ: אַל־יִתֵּן לַמּוֹט רַגְלֶךָ, אַל־יָנוּם שֹׁמְרֶךָ: הִנֵּה לֹא־יָנוּם וְלֹא יִישָׁן, שׁוֹמֵר יִשְׂרָאֵל: יְהוָה שֹׁמְרֶךָ, יְהוָה צִלְּךָ עַל־יַד יְמִינֶךָ: יוֹמָם הַשֶּׁמֶשׁ לֹא־יַכֶּכָּה, וְיָרֵחַ בַּלָּיְלָה: יְהוָה יִשְׁמָרְךָ מִכָּל־רָע, יִשְׁמֹר אֶת־נַפְשֶׁךָ: יְהוָה יִשְׁמָר־צֵאתְךָ וּבוֹאֶךָ, מֵעַתָּה וְעַד־עוֹלָם:

תהלים קנ
הַלְלוּיָהּ, הַלְלוּ־אֵל בְּקָדְשׁוֹ, הַלְלוּהוּ בִּרְקִיעַ עֻזּוֹ: הַלְלוּהוּ בִגְבוּרֹתָיו: הַלְלוּהוּ כְּרֹב גֻּדְלוֹ: הַלְלוּהוּ בְּתֵקַע שׁוֹפָר, הַלְלוּהוּ בְּנֵבֶל וְכִנּוֹר: הַלְלוּהוּ בְּתֹף וּמָחוֹל, הַלְלוּהוּ בְּמִנִּים וְעֻגָב: הַלְלוּהוּ בְּצִלְצְלֵי־שָׁמַע, הַלְלוּהוּ בְּצִלְצְלֵי תְרוּעָה: כֹּל הַנְּשָׁמָה תְּהַלֵּל יָהּ, הַלְלוּיָהּ:

סנהדרין מב
תָּנָא דְּבֵי רַבִּי יִשְׁמָעֵאל: אִלְמָלֵי לֹא זָכוּ יִשְׂרָאֵל אֶלָּא לְהַקְבִּיל פְּנֵי אֲבִיהֶם שֶׁבַּשָּׁמַיִם פַּעַם אַחַת בַּחֹדֶשׁ, דַּיָּם. אָמַר אַבַּיֵי: הִלְכָּךְ צָרִיךְ לְמֵימְרָא מְעֻמָּד. מִי זֹאת עֹלָה מִן־הַמִּדְבָּר, מִתְרַפֶּקֶת עַל־דּוֹדָהּ:
שיר השירים ח

וִיהִי רָצוֹן מִלְּפָנֶיךָ יְהוָה אֱלֹהַי וֵאלֹהֵי אֲבוֹתַי, לְמַלֹּאת פְּגִימַת הַלְּבָנָה וְלֹא יִהְיֶה בָּהּ שׁוּם מֵעוּט. וִיהִי אוֹר הַלְּבָנָה כְּאוֹר הַחַמָּה וּכְאוֹר שִׁבְעַת יְמֵי בְרֵאשִׁית, כְּמוֹ שֶׁהָיְתָה קֹדֶם מִעוּטָהּ, שֶׁנֶּאֱמַר: אֶת־שְׁנֵי הַמְּאֹרֹת הַגְּדֹלִים: וְיִתְקַיֵּם בָּנוּ מִקְרָא שֶׁכָּתוּב: וּבִקְשׁוּ אֶת־יְהוָה אֱלֹהֵיהֶם וְאֵת דָּוִיד מַלְכָּם: אָמֵן.
בראשית א
הושע ג

לַמְנַצֵּחַ For the conductor of music. With stringed instruments, a psalm. A *Ps. 67*
song. May God be gracious to us and bless us. May He make His face shine
on us, Selah. Then will Your way be known on earth, Your salvation among
all the nations. Let the peoples praise You, God; let all peoples praise You.
Let nations rejoice and sing for joy, for You judge the peoples with equity,
and guide the nations of the earth, Selah. Let the peoples praise You, God;
let all peoples praise You. The earth has yielded its harvest. May God, our
God, bless us. God will bless us, and all the ends of the earth will fear Him.

Stand while saying Aleinu. Bow at ˙.

עָלֵינוּ It is our duty to praise the Master of all, and ascribe greatness to the
Author of creation, who has not made us like the nations of the lands, nor
placed us like the families of the earth; who has not made our portion like
theirs, nor our destiny like all their multitudes. (For they worship vanity and
emptiness, and pray to a god who cannot save.) ˙But we bow in worship and
thank the Supreme King of kings, the Holy One, blessed be He, who extends
the heavens and establishes the earth, whose throne of glory is in the heavens
above, and whose power's Presence is in the highest of heights. He is our God;
there is no other. Truly He is our King, there is none else, as it is written in
His Torah: "You shall know and take to heart this day that the Lord is God, *Deut. 4*
in heaven above and on earth below. There is no other."

Therefore, we place our hope in You, Lord our God, that we may soon see
the glory of Your power, when You will remove abominations from the earth,
and idols will be utterly destroyed, when the world will be perfected under
the sovereignty of the Almighty, when all humanity will call on Your name, to
turn all the earth's wicked toward You. All the world's inhabitants will realize
and know that to You every knee must bow and every tongue swear loyalty.
Before You, Lord our God, they will kneel and bow down and give honor to
Your glorious name. They will all accept the yoke of Your kingdom, and You
will reign over them soon and for ever. For the kingdom is Yours, and to all
eternity You will reign in glory, as it is written in Your Torah: "The Lord will *Ex. 15*
reign for ever and ever." ▸ And it is said: "Then the Lord shall be King over all *Zech. 14*
the earth; on that day the Lord shall be One and His name One."

Some add:

Have no fear of sudden terror or of the ruin when it overtakes the wicked. Devise *Prov. 3*
your strategy, but it will be thwarted; propose your plan, but it will not stand, for God *Is. 8*
is with us. When you grow old, I will still be the same. When your hair turns gray, I *Is. 46*
will still carry you. I made you, I will bear you, I will carry you, and I will rescue you.

לַמְנַצֵּחַ בִּנְגִינֹת, מִזְמוֹר שִׁיר: אֱלֹהִים יְחָנֵּנוּ וִיבָרְכֵנוּ, יָאֵר פָּנָיו אִתָּנוּ סֶלָה: לָדַעַת בָּאָרֶץ דַּרְכֶּךָ, בְּכָל־גּוֹיִם יְשׁוּעָתֶךָ: יוֹדוּךָ עַמִּים אֱלֹהִים, יוֹדוּךָ עַמִּים כֻּלָּם: יִשְׂמְחוּ וִירַנְּנוּ לְאֻמִּים, כִּי־תִשְׁפֹּט עַמִּים מִישֹׁר, וּלְאֻמִּים בָּאָרֶץ תַּנְחֵם סֶלָה: יוֹדוּךָ עַמִּים אֱלֹהִים, יוֹדוּךָ עַמִּים כֻּלָּם: אֶרֶץ נָתְנָה יְבוּלָהּ, יְבָרְכֵנוּ אֱלֹהִים אֱלֹהֵינוּ: יְבָרְכֵנוּ אֱלֹהִים, וְיִירְאוּ אוֹתוֹ כָּל־אַפְסֵי־אָרֶץ:

Stand while saying עָלֵינוּ. *Bow at* וַ.

עָלֵינוּ לְשַׁבֵּחַ לַאֲדוֹן הַכֹּל, לָתֵת גְּדֻלָּה לְיוֹצֵר בְּרֵאשִׁית, שֶׁלֹּא עָשָׂנוּ כְּגוֹיֵי הָאֲרָצוֹת, וְלֹא שָׂמָנוּ כְּמִשְׁפְּחוֹת הָאֲדָמָה, שֶׁלֹּא שָׂם חֶלְקֵנוּ כָּהֶם וְגוֹרָלֵנוּ כְּכָל הֲמוֹנָם. (שֶׁהֵם מִשְׁתַּחֲוִים לְהֶבֶל וָרִיק וּמִתְפַּלְלִים אֶל אֵל לֹא יוֹשִׁיעַ.) וַאֲנַחְנוּ כּוֹרְעִים וּמִשְׁתַּחֲוִים וּמוֹדִים, לִפְנֵי מֶלֶךְ מַלְכֵי הַמְּלָכִים, הַקָּדוֹשׁ בָּרוּךְ הוּא, שֶׁהוּא נוֹטֶה שָׁמַיִם וְיֹסֵד אָרֶץ, וּמוֹשַׁב יְקָרוֹ בַּשָּׁמַיִם מִמַּעַל, וּשְׁכִינַת עֻזּוֹ בְּגָבְהֵי מְרוֹמִים. הוּא אֱלֹהֵינוּ, אֵין עוֹד. אֱמֶת מַלְכֵּנוּ, אֶפֶס זוּלָתוֹ, כַּכָּתוּב בְּתוֹרָתוֹ, וְיָדַעְתָּ הַיּוֹם וַהֲשֵׁבֹתָ אֶל־לְבָבֶךָ, כִּי יהוה הוּא הָאֱלֹהִים בַּשָּׁמַיִם מִמַּעַל וְעַל־הָאָרֶץ מִתָּחַת, אֵין עוֹד:

עַל כֵּן נְקַוֶּה לְּךָ יהוה אֱלֹהֵינוּ, לִרְאוֹת מְהֵרָה בְּתִפְאֶרֶת עֻזֶּךָ, לְהַעֲבִיר גִּלּוּלִים מִן הָאָרֶץ, וְהָאֱלִילִים כָּרוֹת יִכָּרֵתוּן, לְתַקֵּן עוֹלָם בְּמַלְכוּת שַׁדַּי. וְכָל בְּנֵי בָשָׂר יִקְרְאוּ בִשְׁמֶךָ לְהַפְנוֹת אֵלֶיךָ כָּל רִשְׁעֵי אָרֶץ. יַכִּירוּ וְיֵדְעוּ כָּל יוֹשְׁבֵי תֵבֵל, כִּי לְךָ תִּכְרַע כָּל בֶּרֶךְ, תִּשָּׁבַע כָּל לָשׁוֹן. לְפָנֶיךָ יהוה אֱלֹהֵינוּ יִכְרְעוּ וְיִפֹּלוּ, וְלִכְבוֹד שִׁמְךָ יְקָר יִתֵּנוּ, וִיקַבְּלוּ כֻלָּם אֶת עֹל מַלְכוּתֶךָ וְתִמְלֹךְ עֲלֵיהֶם מְהֵרָה לְעוֹלָם וָעֶד. כִּי הַמַּלְכוּת שֶׁלְּךָ הִיא וּלְעוֹלְמֵי עַד תִּמְלֹךְ בְּכָבוֹד, כַּכָּתוּב בְּתוֹרָתֶךָ, יהוה יִמְלֹךְ לְעֹלָם וָעֶד: וְנֶאֱמַר, וְהָיָה יהוה לְמֶלֶךְ עַל־כָּל־הָאָרֶץ, בַּיּוֹם הַהוּא יִהְיֶה יהוה אֶחָד וּשְׁמוֹ אֶחָד:

Some add:

אַל־תִּירָא מִפַּחַד פִּתְאֹם וּמִשֹּׁאַת רְשָׁעִים כִּי תָבֹא: עֻצוּ עֵצָה וְתֻפָר, דַּבְּרוּ דָבָר וְלֹא יָקוּם, כִּי עִמָּנוּ אֵל: וְעַד־זִקְנָה אֲנִי הוּא, וְעַד־שֵׂיבָה אֲנִי אֶסְבֹּל, אֲנִי עָשִׂיתִי וַאֲנִי אֶשָּׂא וַאֲנִי אֶסְבֹּל וַאֲמַלֵּט:

MOURNER'S KADDISH

The following prayer, said by mourners, requires the presence of a minyan.
A transliteration can be found on page 792.

Mourner: יִתְגַּדַּל Magnified and sanctified may His great name be,
in the world He created by His will.
May He establish His kingdom
in your lifetime and in your days,
and in the lifetime of all the house of Israel,
swiftly and soon – and say: Amen.

All: May His great name be blessed for ever and all time.

Mourner: Blessed and praised,
glorified and exalted,
raised and honored,
uplifted and lauded
be the name of the Holy One,
blessed be He,
beyond any blessing,
song, praise and consolation
uttered in the world –
and say: Amen.

May there be great peace from heaven,
and life for us and all Israel –
and say: Amen.

Bow, take three steps back, as if taking leave of the Divine Presence,
then bow, first left, then right, then center, while saying:
May He who makes peace in His high places,
make peace for us and all Israel –
and say: Amen.

קדיש יתום

The following prayer requires the presence of a מנין.
A transliteration can be found on page 792.

אבל: יִתְגַּדַּל וְיִתְקַדַּשׁ שְׁמֵהּ רַבָּא (קהל: אָמֵן)
בְּעָלְמָא דִּי בְרָא כִרְעוּתֵהּ, וְיַמְלִיךְ מַלְכוּתֵהּ
בְּחַיֵּיכוֹן וּבְיוֹמֵיכוֹן וּבְחַיֵּי דְכָל בֵּית יִשְׂרָאֵל
בַּעֲגָלָא וּבִזְמַן קָרִיב
וְאִמְרוּ אָמֵן. (קהל: אָמֵן)

קהל ואבל: יְהֵא שְׁמֵהּ רַבָּא מְבָרַךְ לְעָלַם וּלְעָלְמֵי עָלְמַיָּא.

אבל: יִתְבָּרַךְ וְיִשְׁתַּבַּח וְיִתְפָּאַר
וְיִתְרוֹמַם וְיִתְנַשֵּׂא וְיִתְהַדָּר וְיִתְעַלֶּה וְיִתְהַלָּל
שְׁמֵהּ דְּקֻדְשָׁא בְּרִיךְ הוּא (קהל: בְּרִיךְ הוּא)
לְעֵלָּא מִן כָּל בִּרְכָתָא וְשִׁירָתָא, תֻּשְׁבְּחָתָא וְנֶחֱמָתָא
דַּאֲמִירָן בְּעָלְמָא
וְאִמְרוּ אָמֵן. (קהל: אָמֵן)

יְהֵא שְׁלָמָא רַבָּא מִן שְׁמַיָּא
וְחַיִּים, עָלֵינוּ וְעַל כָּל יִשְׂרָאֵל
וְאִמְרוּ אָמֵן. (קהל: אָמֵן)

*Bow, take three steps back, as if taking leave of the Divine Presence,
then bow, first left, then right, then center, while saying:*

עֹשֶׂה שָׁלוֹם בִּמְרוֹמָיו
הוּא יַעֲשֶׂה שָׁלוֹם עָלֵינוּ וְעַל כָּל יִשְׂרָאֵל
וְאִמְרוּ אָמֵן. (קהל: אָמֵן)

רשימות

RESHIMOT

RESHIMOT

AVELUT YESHANA AND AVELUT ḤADASHA

A Jew lives with a unique time consciousness. He experiences time not in the standard tripartite division of past, present, and future; rather, all three dimensions converge into a single integrated existence. This unique orientation toward time enables a Jew to pre-experience events of the distant future and to relive occurrences of the ostensibly dead past.

In this vein, the institutions of *avelut yeshana*, mourning for a past tragedy, and *avelut ḥadasha*, grief for a recent loss, are experientially akin to one another. Although the historical moment of loss may divide the two institutions, the quality of the experience of mourning and the penetrating, encompassing sense of loss are, nonetheless, identical in both contexts. A Jew has the unique capacity to relive past tragedies and to experience them anew as if the wounds were still fresh. As a result, the abiding sentiment of grief, the resulting sense of void, and the hopeless feelings of groping in the dark are felt just as powerfully when mourning for past events.

Despite the experiential similarity between *avelut yeshana* and *avelut ḥadasha*, the evolution of the experience of mourning develops in a relatively inverse pattern from one to the other. The moment of death is the critical moment in the context of *avelut ḥadasha*. The loss is felt most palpably and severely at the initial moment, and it slowly ebbs with the passage of time. The period of *shiva* which immediately follows the burial of the deceased, reflects the most intense period of mourning. Gradually, the sense of mourning and the attendant restrictions begin to wane with the passage of *sheloshim* and the twelve months. In the instance of *avelut yeshana*, though, the process of mourning is inverted. The mourning for past events intensifies with the passage of time. The initial period of the Three Weeks is the most relaxed of the three phases of mourning. The process intensifies with the arrival of the Nine Days, and it reaches its pinnacle on Tisha B'Av when the sense of mourning is felt most acutely.

The establishment of *minhagim* (customs) must occur within the framework of pre-existing halakhic categories. The development of mourning rites during the Three Weeks thus finds its roots in the parallel phases of mourning that comprise *avelut ḥadasha*. The observance of the Three Weeks parallels the institution of the twelve months of mourning for the loss of a parent. The Nine Days correspond to the intermediate phase of *sheloshim*. Finally, the laws of Tisha B'Av reflect the rites of *shiva*.

This schematic arrangement produces two novel ramifications with respect to the customs of the Three Weeks. One the one hand, it yields a leniency regarding the practice of refraining from shaving. During the twelve months of mourning for the loss of a parent, an individual is permitted to shave when the growth of his hair reaches the point of "עַד שֶׁיִּגְעֲרוּ בּוֹ חֲבֵרָיו," the stage at which a peer will reprimand the mourner for his unkempt appearance. The parallelism between the Three Weeks of *avelut yeshana* and the twelve month mourning period of *avelut ḥadasha* dictates that the same allowance should apply to the mourning rites of the Three Weeks. Conversely, the twinning of the Three Weeks with the mourning rites of the twelve-months produces an accompanying stringency. The twelve-month mourning period for a parent engenders a restriction of participating in שִׂמְחַת מֵרֵעוּת, joyous gatherings. As a result, during the Three Weeks, the concomitant stage of *avelut yeshana*, similar gatherings of friends must be avoided.

THE DISTINCTION BETWEEN TISHA B'AV AND OTHER FAST DAYS

The Gemara (*Pesaḥim* 54b) states that Tisha B'Av differs from communal fast days that were declared in response to a dire communal emergency, in two primary respects. Unlike communal fast days, Tisha B'Av lacks the additional prayer of *Ne'ila*, and, in addition, engagement in vocational activity is not prohibited, strictly speaking. On a superficial level, the discrepancies between the two categories of fasts strike a note of intrigue as to the underlying source of the differences. On a deeper level, though, the differentiation between the two categories is questionable and problematic.

A cursory reading of Maimonides' presentation of the two categories of fast days, the communal fasts called in response to a current crisis

(*Hilkhot Ta'aniyot* 1:1–4), and the four predetermined fast days that commemorate historical calamities (*Hilkhot Ta'aniyot* 5:1), highlights the common content and goals of both sets of fast days, rather than the differences. Both categories of fast days are marked by a common fulfillment of *ze'aka*, crying out, and *teshuva*, repentance. A fast day declared during a time of crisis engenders a positive commandment to "cry out and sound the trumpets" as a manner of calling attention to the evil ways of the nation. This mandated response serves to embody and impel an expression of national repentance. Similarly, Maimonides describes the function of the four legislated fast days that commemorate national tragedies as intending to "stir the hearts in order to open the pathways of repentance." Moreover, the verses in Zechariah (7:3) introduce the element of *bekhi*, of wailing, as a prominent feature of the day. In light of the striking parallelism that seems to characterize the two categories of fast days, the absences of an additional prayer of *Ne'ila* and a prohibition forbidding vocational activity on Tisha B'Av stand out with greater distinction.

Upon further reflection and investigation, the two types of fast days, despite their surface level similarities, in truth, differ fundamentally in their essence and their means of expression. Communal fast days observed during a crisis situation are fundamentally geared toward serving as a catalyst for repentance. It is for this reason that the elders of the nation would convene on the fast day in order to investigate the spiritual state of the nation (*Hilkhot Ta'aniyot* 1:17). The four predetermined fast days that seek to commemorate calamitous events of our national history, however, are essentially days of mourning. The dimension of repentance exists as an outgrowth of that commemoration, like it does during any observance of mourning (see Rama, *Yoreh De'ah* 403:10). At the same time, the essential fulfillment of the day is one of mourning and a sense of loss.

This fundamental distinction is reflected in the type of *ze'aka*, in the means of expression, that dominates the experience of the respective days. During a time of national crisis, the fitting mode of expression that further enhances our fulfillment of the day's essence is one of prayer. In contrast, the four commemorative fasts find their primary expression through crying, eulogizing, and the observance of the rites of mourning. The mode of *ze'aka* for each category of fast days is patterned after the day's essential character.

The notion that even overlapping phenomena shared by the two categories of fasts adopt a unique color and character due to the context within which they appear, is further underscored by a perplexing *barayta* in *Masekhet Ta'anit* (30a). The *barayta* states that "All observances conducted during *avelut* are likewise conducted on Tisha B'Av. It is forbidden to eat, drink, anoint oneself, to wear leather shoes, to cohabit, and to study Torah." On the surface, the inclusion of eating and drinking as a rite of mourning is incomprehensible since there is no existing ordinance forbidding the mourner from ingesting food and drink. Rashi (ibid. s.v. *assur*) is sensitive to this difficulty, and explains that once the *barayta* began to enumerate the practices of Tisha B'Av that parallel the institution of *avelut*, it also introduced other additional aspects of Tisha B'Av that are extraneous to that relationship. It is conceivable, however, that the *barayta* was seeking to convey the previously developed principle. Even though the prohibition against eating and drinking is shared by Tisha B'Av and other fast days alike, the forbidden nature of those activities differs in the varying contexts. Just as the expression of *ze'aka* on Tisha B'Av reflects the unique mourning character of the day, in a similar manner, the injunction forbidding eating and drinking is colored by its respective context. On Tisha B'Av, even the dimension of fasting further enhances the fulfillment of mourning which comprises the essence of the day.

A refined understanding of the uniqueness of each category of fast days illuminates the presence of the two discrepancies outlined at the start. The additional prayer of *Ne'ila* focuses on the theme of repentance, as we state, "You extend Your hand to those who have sinned, and Your right hand is outstretched to receive those who repent." As such, the prayer's incorporation is particularly appropriate on a fast day whose essential theme is one of repentance, and whose primary mode of expression is through prayer. In that context, the inclusion of an additional prayer whose theme is repentance is apropos. On Tisha B'Av, however, the essential focus is on mourning, not repentance, and the primary mode of expression is crying and eulogizing, not prayer. As such, the additional prayer of *Ne'ila* is omitted on Tisha B'Av unlike the other communal fast days. Moreover, the prospect of instituting additional prayers on Tisha B'Av is not only incongruous with the essential focus of the day, it is, on

some level, antithetical to the day's essence. Tisha B'Av is a day characterized by the spirit of "When I cry and call for help, He shuts out my prayer" (Lamentations 3:8). It is for this reason, that we do not recite *Taḥanun*, *Seliḥot*, or *Kaddish Titkabel* on Tisha B'Av.

The absence of any prohibition forbidding engagement in vocational activity also results from the difference in nature distinguishing the two sets of fast days from one another. The Gemara (*Ta'anit* 12b) derives the prohibition against work on communal fast days from the verse, "Sanctify a fast, call a solemn assembly, gather the elders" (Joel 1:14) which strikes a comparison between a holiday and a fast day. Part of the essential function of prohibiting vocational activity on the fast day, is to help coordinate the gathering of the elders to enable them to investigate and scrutinize the spiritual state of the nation. As such, the restriction against engaging in work is limited to communal fast days declared during times of crisis, whose essential fulfillment is repentance.

It is possible, though, to bridge the gap between the two categories of fast days. The two types of fasts do not differ in their essential function and makeup; rather, one type of fast day is a specific example of the overarching category established by the second type. It is noteworthy that Maimonides first expounds upon the halakhot concerning the communal fast days during a time of crisis (*Hilkhot Ta'aniyot*, ch. 1) prior to enumerating and elaborating upon the four legislated commemorative fast days (*Hilkhot Ta'aniyot*, ch. 5). The communal fast days declared during emergency situations provide the framework through which to understand the four commemorative fast days. The occasions that we commemorate are not historical events of the distant past; instead, they provide the nation with instances of crisis and emergency. The Gemara states that any generation that does not witness the rebuilding of the *Beit HaMikdash* is as if it has witnessed its destruction. Maimonides describes the *tzarot* (tragedies) that we recall, as affecting not only the prior generations, but the current generation as well. As such, the four legislated fast days are mere instances of the general category established in the opening chapter of *Hilkhot Ta'aniyot*. The theme of repentance and revealing the underlying causes of destruction and calamity, comprise the central focus of the four fast days to the same degree that they characterize the communal fast days during times of crisis.

THE PROHIBITION ON WEARING FRESHLY WASHED CLOTHES DURING THE WEEK THAT PRECEDES TISHA B'AV

The Rama (*Shulḥan Arukh, Oraḥ Ḥayyim* 551:1) rules that it is forbidden to wear special Shabbat clothing on Shabbat Ḥazon (the Shabbat that precedes Tisha B'Av). The *Magen Avraham*, commenting on the Rama's ruling, explains that Shabbat clothes are generally pressed and ironed, and such clothes are prohibited in the week that precedes Tisha B'Av. Thus, even if the clothes have been worn several times previously, they are forbidden during the week before Tisha B'Av since the pressing is still apparent. The question can be posed that in the week that precedes Tisha B'Av, wearing freshly washed clothing, even if not pressed, is forbidden, and if so, why does the *Magen Avraham* explain the Rama's ruling based on the prohibition of wearing pressed clothing and not the more basic category of wearing freshly washed clothing?

The answer to this question can be found in the principle that some of the prohibitions of the week preceding Tisha B'Av are modeled after the laws of *shiva*, while others are modeled after the laws of *sheloshim*. In particular, freshly washed clothes are prohibited only during *shiva*, while pressed clothes are prohibited throughout the *sheloshim* period. Moreover, with regard to the general laws of *avelut*, Shabbat suspends the laws of *shiva*, but not of *sheloshim*. For example, shaving and taking haircuts are forbidden during *sheloshim* and remain forbidden even as preparations for Shabbat. Shabbat thus suspends the prohibition of wearing freshly washed clothing because this prohibition is a law rooted in *shiva*, but Shabbat does not cancel the prohibition of wearing pressed clothing which is rooted in *sheloshim*. This explains why the *Magen Avraham* based the Rama's ruling that wearing Shabbat clothes is prohibited on *Shabbat Ḥazon*, not on the prohibition of wearing freshly washed clothing, but rather on the prohibition of wearing pressed clothing.

The Mishna (*Ta'anit* 26) states, "During the week that precedes Tisha B'Av it is forbidden to take a haircut and wash clothes, but on Thursday it is permitted for the honor of Shabbat." The *Hagahot Ashri* explains that the Mishna means that only washing clothing is permitted on Thursday as preparation for Shabbat, but not taking a haircut. The *Magen Avraham* (*Shulḥan Arukh, Oraḥ Ḥayyim* 551:14) explains this distinction between washing clothing and taking haircuts by noting that, as a practical matter,

since people do not generally get a haircut every week before Shabbat, the Rabbis did not make an allowance to get a haircut specifically on the Thursday before Tisha B'Av. However, according to our earlier analysis, the reason for the distinction is obvious. The honor of Shabbat suspends the prohibition of washing clothes which is rooted in *shiva*, but it cannot cancel the prohibition against taking a haircut which is rooted in *sheloshim*.

If the prohibition against wearing freshly washed clothes the week before Tisha B'Av is in fact rooted in the laws of *shiva*, we may ask the following question: Why don't the other prohibitions of *shiva* also apply during the week that precedes Tisha B'Av? For example, wearing leather shoes, learning Torah, and extending greetings are all prohibited during *shiva* and yet they are only prohibited on Tisha B'Av itself and not the during the preceding week. What makes the prohibition of wearing freshly washed clothes unique? The answer is that different prohibitions of *shiva* have different sources and reasons. Specifically, the Rabbis did not extend to the week that precedes Tisha B'Av the laws of *shiva* intended to create a state of discomfort or sadness. The prohibition of washing clothes, however, is based on a different reason. Rashi (*Ta'anit* 29b, s.v. *afilu*) writes that washing clothes is forbidden because "it appears that he is distracting himself by busying himself with washing clothes." Of all the prohibitions of *shiva*, the Rabbis prohibited only washing clothes, an activity which would otherwise disrupt the proper mindset of mourning and concentration on the destruction of the *Beit HaMikdash*.

THE PROHIBITION ON HAIRCUTS AND LAUNDRY DURING THE WEEK PRECEDING TISHA B'AV WHEN THE OBSERVANCE OF TISHA B'AV IS DEFERRED

When Tisha B'Av falls on Shabbat, the fast is deferred to the next day, the tenth of Av. In this situation, the *Shulḥan Arukh* (*Oraḥ Ḥayyim* 551:4) presents a difference of opinion regarding the practice of haircuts and laundry in the week preceding the fast. The first opinion permits laundering and haircutting; the second forbids them.

Many explain that this dispute centers on the nature of the fast when it is deferred. The first opinion believes that originally the fast was to have been on the tenth of Av. This is supported by the Gemara in *Ta'anit* (29a),

which says that while the *Beit HaMikdash* began burning toward the end of the ninth of Av, it continued burning the entire day of the tenth. The Gemara cites the statement of Rabbi Yoḥanan, "Had I lived in the generation that established the fast of Tisha B'Av, I would have established the fast on the tenth of Av because most of the *Heikhal* [Sanctuary] burned that day." The sages, however, chose to establish the fast on the ninth, the day the burning began, because they believed it is more appropriate to commemorate the beginning of the punishment. One can suggest that the sages disagreed with Rabbi Yoḥanan only when it was possible to fast on the ninth. However, when Tisha B'Av falls on Shabbat and it is impossible to fast on the ninth, the sages themselves established the tenth as *yom hata'anit*, the day of the fast. In that case, the week preceding the fast on the tenth is *not* the *shavua shehal bo*, the week in which the fast falls, because the *yom hata'anit* is actually on Sunday of the next week. Therefore, the prohibitions of *shavua shehal bo* are not applicable to the preceding week.

The second opinion, on the other hand, believes that when we fast on the tenth, it is simply *kiyum hata'anit*, the technical fulfillment of the requirement of fasting. Therefore, the week preceding the fast is considered *shavua shehal bo* because the *yom hata'anit* was really meant to be Shabbat.

With this understanding, we can perhaps explain another disagreement between the *Shulḥan Arukh* and the Rama. The *Shulḥan Arukh* (554:19) writes that when Tisha B'Av falls on Shabbat, all of the Tisha B'Av proscriptions are lifted, including the prohibition of marital relations. The Rama, however, maintains that while the public prohibitions (eating, drinking, etc.) are permitted, marital relations are still forbidden because they are observed in private and therefore do not infringe on the Shabbat. It seems that the Rama believes that the *yom hata'anit* is *always* on the ninth, even when the *kiyum hata'anit* is deferred to the tenth as a compensatory fast. Therefore, it is understandable to retain the private prohibitions. However, the *Shulḥan Arukh* believes that when Tisha B'Av falls on Shabbat, the *yom hata'anit* was established on the *tenth* of Av, meaning that the ninth has no association with the fast at all, and there is no reason to retain any prohibitions on Shabbat.

However, this approach is difficult to reconcile with a different halakha.

The *Shulḥan Arukh* (559:9) writes that when Tisha B'Av falls on Shabbat and the fast is deferred to the next day, one who celebrates a *Brit Mila* on Sunday is allowed to eat and drink after Minḥa on Sunday but need not undertake a compensatory fast. The *Magen Avraham* points out that this is true only when the fast has been deferred; however, when the fast is observed on the ninth, the *ba'al brit* must make up the fast. Now, if we maintain that the *Shulḥan Arukh* believes that the *yom hata'anit* is on the tenth when it is impossible to fast on the ninth, why should the fact that the ninth is on Shabbat make any difference? Just as the *ba'al brit* must make up the fast when it is observed on the ninth, so too he should have to make up the fast when it is observed on the tenth.

Therefore, it seems we must explain that the aforementioned dispute between the *Shulḥan Arukh* and the Rama revolves around a different issue. The Rama's opinion can be explained as before, that the ninth is always essentially considered a day of *avelut*, even when it falls on Shabbat. The *avelut* of the day never fully disappears, and the private proscription against cohabitation is preserved to commemorate this *avelut*. The *Shulḥan Arukh*, however, believes this opinion to be untenable simply because the sages never instituted *two* days of Tisha B'Av. Once the *kiyum hata'anit* was transferred to the tenth of Av, it is impossible to say that the *yom hata'anit* was on the ninth of Av, as doing so would in a sense be observing two days of Tisha B'Av.

In a similar vein, perhaps we can explain the first argument presented, the argument of *shavua sheḥal bo*, differently as well. The two opinions in the *Shulḥan Arukh* are not disagreeing about the nature of Tisha B'Av when observed on the tenth, rather they argue about the nature of *shavua sheḥal bo*. The first opinion believes that the prohibitions of *shavua sheḥal bo* are intimately connected to the prohibitions of Tisha B'Av itself. *Shavua sheḥal bo* is essentially an introduction to Tisha B'Av, steadily building up to the ultimate *avelut* observed on the fast day itself. Therefore, when the observance of Tisha B'Av is deferred to the next week, the preceding week can no longer be considered connected to the fast day and it loses the status of *shavua sheḥal bo*. The second opinion, however, believes that *shavua sheḥal bo* is not simply a lead-in to Tisha B'Av; rather, the *avelut* established for *shavua sheḥal bo* is separate and distinct from the *avelut* of Tisha B'Av. Therefore, it does not matter if Tisha B'Av actually falls during

the week of *shavua shehal bo*; the prohibitions of the week preceding the fast – the separate entity called *shavua shehal bo* – apply, even if the fast is observed during the following week.

SE'UDA HAMAFSEKET AND ZIMMUN

The *Shulhan Arukh* (*Orah Hayyim* 552:8) states that during the *Se'uda HaMafseket*, the meal eaten immediately prior to the onset of Tisha B'Av, individuals should not eat together in order to avoid being obligated in *zimmun*. The *Magen Avraham* comments that even if three people ate together, they do not recite the *zimmun*, and the Gaon of Vilna cites, "One should sit alone and be silent" (Lamentations 3:28) as the scriptural source. However, this is difficult to understand in light of the fact that the Gemara in *Berakhot* (18a) explicitly states that even in the first seven days of *shiva*, mourners are still obligated in *zimmun*. Why should the *Se'uda HaMafseket* be any different?

It would appear that the reason that mourners within *shiva* join together for *zimmun* is that while the participants are in a state of mourning, the meal itself is not part of *nihug avelut*, the observance of mourning. However, *Se'uda HaMafseket*, whose very purpose is to serve as an expression of mourning, lacks by this nature the formality to bind individuals together for a *zimmun*. The idea that the *Se'uda HaMafseket* is by its very nature a form of mourning is illustrated by the fact that Rav would dip bread in ash and say, "This is the meal of Tisha B'Av" (Talmud Yerushalmi, cited by *Beit Yosef* 552).

Still, a difficulty remains, as we find that mourners do join together for *zimmun* at a *Se'udat Havra'a*, the first meal the mourner eats after the funeral. An answer may be, while a mourner is not allowed to eat his own food in his first meal, a *Se'udat Havra'a* is not intrinsically related to mourning whereas eating the *Se'uda HaMafseket* is itself an act of mourning.

One might add that since the mourner eats the *Se'udat Havra'a* together with individuals not in mourning, the meal cannot be considered a *nihug avelut*. On the other hand, everyone is in mourning at the *Se'uda HaMafseket*, and the meal is intrinsically linked to mourning; therefore, there cannot be a *zimmun*. It also follows that the obligation in eating the *Se'uda HaMafseket* is beyond simply having the strength to fast all of

Tisha B'Av, but is an integral part of the mourning. Therefore, even if one is not capable of fasting, he or she must still eat the *Se'uda HaMafseket*.

In addition, *Se'udat Havra'a* is not part of *nihug avelut* but *nihum avelim*, a requirement that the mourner not eat alone. Hence, *Se'udat Havra'a* applies also on Hol HaMo'ed, when there is public *nihug avelut*.

THE NATURE OF PROHIBITIONS ON THE NIGHT A FAST DAY COMMENCES

The *Shulḥan Arukh* (*Oraḥ Ḥayyim* 502:2) states that unlike Tisha B'Av, the minor fasts (10th of Tevet, 3rd of Tishrei, 17th of Tammuz) do not have any restrictions on washing or anointing oneself, wearing leather shoes, or having marital relations. Additionally, one need not begin fasting until daybreak. While the *Shulḥan Arukh* implies that the minor fast days do not begin until the morning, various sources indicate otherwise. These sources indicate that the *yom ta'anit* actually begins at nightfall even though the *issur akhila*, the prohibition against eating, begins in the morning.

One source indicating this is the Gemara (*Ta'anit* 12a) which records a tannaitic dispute regarding the starting point of a *ta'anit yaḥid*, a voluntary fast. Rebbe is of the opinion that the fast day begins at sunrise (*alot hashaḥar*), while Rabbi Eliezer bar Shimon holds that the fast day begins at the rooster's crow (*kerot hagever*). The Gemara qualifies this dispute with two traditions in the name of Rava. The first tradition is that the argument exists only in a case where the individual did not formally finish his evening meal, but had he done so, both Rebbe and Rabbi Eliezer Bar Shimon agree, his fast would begin immediately afterwards. The second tradition maintains the argument to exist only where the individual had not gone to sleep, but had he gone to sleep, his fast would begin immediately upon falling asleep. In either case the fast begins at night. How would the Rif, who does not accept the principle of *tosefet ta'anit* (extending the fast), explain Rava's opinion? Apparently, we must distinguish between the *yom ta'anit* and the *issur akhila*. According to Rava, all fast days actually begin prior to daybreak; however, one may eat and drink until one formally finishes his meal (which, according to the second tradition mentioned above, is accomplished by going to sleep).

Another indication that the *yom ta'anit* begins at nightfall is that most

Rishonim actually require the prayer of *Anenu* is to be said at Ma'ariv before daybreak of the fast day. While one may eat until *alot hashaḥar*, the day has already begun from nightfall.

There is a peculiar law regarding voluntary fasts which our distinction seems to illuminate. If the fast begins only at daybreak, why can't one accept the fast at Ma'ariv, which is still prior to the start of the day? Why must the fast be accepted at Minḥa? However, if the *yom ta'anit* begins at nightfall, it is clear that the latest one can accept it upon himself is at Minḥa, before nightfall.

This distinction also seems to explain a seemingly strange practice mentioned by *Torat Shelamim* (*Yoreh De'ah* 185:10). He writes that one should refrain from meat and wine on the nights prior to the 17th of Tammuz, the fast of Gedalia, and the 10th of Tevet, even though one may eat until daybreak. Although the clear rationale is that since these fasts were all instituted to mourn over the destruction of the *Beit HaMikdash*, one should refrain from happiness, why must we refrain even prior to the fast? However, if the *yom ta'anit* begins already at nightfall, the practice becomes quite logical.

As consequence of this principle that the preceding night is integrated into *yom hata'anit*, it would be forbidden to have a wedding the night of the 17th of Tammuz, as the prohibitions of the "three-week period" between the 17th of Tammuz and Tisha B'Av would have begun, even though one may eat until the daybreak of the fast.

THINKING ABOUT TORAH ON TISHA B'AV

The *Shulḥan Arukh* (*Oraḥ Ḥayyim* 554:3) says that "There are those who forbid thinking about Torah." Rav Ḥayyim Brisk pointed out that the language of "there are those who forbid" seems to indicate that there is a dissenting opinion. What would be the logic of saying it is permissible?

The *Magen Avraham* and the Gaon of Vilna explain as follows. The general prohibition to learn Torah on Tisha B'Av is rooted in the fact that Torah "makes the heart glad" (Psalms 19:9), and since even thinking about Torah accomplishes this feat, it too is prohibited. However, the opinion that allows thinking about Torah, understands the general prohibition of learning differently. Since learning Torah gladdens the heart it becomes forbidden as part of the general law forbidding happiness

during mourning. The laws of mourning prohibit *nihug avelut* – that is, *specific actions* such as bathing, getting a haircut, etc. Therefore, there is room to differentiate between active learning, which would fall under the general rules of mourning, and simply thinking about Torah, which does not involve an action.

TORAH STUDY BY CHILDREN ON TISHA B'AV

In its ruling that on Tisha B'Av one may not engage in Torah study, the *Shulḥan Arukh* (*Oraḥ Ḥayyim* 554:1) includes the statement that the "*tinokot shel beit rabban*" (young school children who study with their teachers), as well, are to cease from studying Torah on that day. The reason given by the *Shulḥan Arukh* for the prohibition against Torah study is that the study of Torah "gladdens the heart" (Psalms 19:9), and the *Shulḥan Arukh* further notes that one may read from the book of Job and the melancholy writings of Jeremiah, but one must omit any words of consolation.

The Taz (*Oraḥ Ḥayyim* 554:1) explains that Torah study with children is prohibited on Tisha B'Av even though children are not joyful at the classroom study of Torah, but rather because the study of Torah brings joy to their teacher. Therefore, notes the Taz, it would be permissible for the teacher to study with the children selections from Job or other somber selections of Torah study. Rav Ḥayyim Brisk offered another explanation as to why we do not study Torah with children on Tisha B'Av. Tisha B'Av commemorates more than just the destruction of our Temple. It is also a day to mourn the diminution of Torah. As we say in *Kinot*, "*Torah Torah ḥigri sak*" (Torah, Torah, wrap yourself in sackcloth). Many *kinot* are dedicated to this theme, as we mourn the loss of Torah leaders and Torah scholarship. Most notably we mourn the "*asara harugei malkhut*" (the ten martyrs), the destruction of Torah centers, and the murder of Torah scholars, as well as the burning of the Talmud that was deliberately destroyed and the loss of Torah learning that this caused.

The Gemara (*Mo'ed Katan* 22b) says that when a *talmid ḥakham* (Torah scholar) dies, his *beit midrash* is idled, and when the *Nasi* (a Torah leader) dies, all *batei midrash* are closed. Just as we are required to close a *beit midrash* to conduct a communal mourning for the loss of Torah, so too on Tisha B'Av all *batei midrash* are closed as an expression of national mourning.

At the end of Minḥa on Shabbat we recite the three-sentence paragraph that begins with "צִדְקָתְךָ צֶדֶק לְעוֹלָם, Your righteousness is everlasting." The word *tzidkatekha* is repeated three times in the paragraph to allude to our acceptance of God's justice, since it was at this time, Shabbat afternoon, that three great *tzaddikim* died. The *Eliyahu Raba* comments that the first sentence is in remembrance of Moses, the second is for Joseph, and the third is for King David. The *Tur* (*Oraḥ Ḥayyim* 292) adds that it is therefore customary not to establish a public lecture at this time. The *Magen Avraham* (*Oraḥ Ḥayyim* 292:5) explains that the *Tur*'s dictum is based on the above Gemara (*Mo'ed Katan* 22b) that when a *talmid ḥakham* dies, his *beit midrash* is idled.

According to this reasoning, it would be inappropriate to publicly study with children, even somber and melancholy teachings. Aside from refraining on Tisha B'Av from involving ourselves in joyful activities, there is also a requirement that there be no public display of Torah study, for this too is the way we mourn over our loss of Torah. For this reason, even the *batei midrash* of the *"tinokot shel beit Rabban"* must be closed.

TASTING ON PUBLIC AND PRIVATE FASTS

The Talmud (*Berakhot* 14a) asks the following question: May one who is fasting, taste food (i.e. put food in his mouth then spit it out or ingest a small amount) on the grounds that one who is fasting accepted upon himself only the prohibition of "eating and drinking," and not any other prohibition such as tasting? Or, continues the Talmud, does one who accepts the obligation of fasting, accept not only the prohibition of eating and drinking, but also the prohibition against receiving any benefit from food, such as by tasting? The Talmud concludes that tasting is permitted on a fast day.

Tosafot comment that the language of this selection from the Talmud implies that the question was only asked about a private fast, a fast that a person accepts for himself. On a public fast day, however, even tasting is prohibited. *Tosafot* deduce this from the Talmud's reasoning that the person fasting "accepted" upon himself only the prohibition against eating and drinking. If the discussion was of a public fast no "acceptance" is necessary, because everyone is required to fast.

Tosafot's limitation of the leniency regarding tasting to private fasts

only, needs to be explained. A person who accepts upon himself a private fast is not analogous to one who takes an oath not to eat. One who takes an oath not to eat is creating his own new prohibition and can dictate the extent of what is prohibited. One who accepts upon himself a private fast, however, is accepting a preexisting form of prohibition which follows its own rules. An example of the special nature of the fasting prohibition is that one who accepts a private fast may decide to observe it at a later date if he finds fasting now too difficult. This is in distinction to one who takes an oath not to eat and drink for a day, who may not exchange this day with another day. Therefore, if a person who accepts a fast upon himself is accepting the rules of a preexisting halakhic concept, how can we say that he did not also accept the prohibition against tasting? Just like a public fast, the scope of a private fast should not be dependent on the intention or language of the acceptance.

A clearer understanding of the structure of the laws of fasting will allow us to understand *Tosafot*'s limitation of the leniency regarding tasting to only private fasts. There are two categories of prohibitions on a fast day. The main component of the fast is the prohibition against eating and drinking. This is the most basic element of a fast, and one who eats even once during a fast cannot be said to have fasted. The secondary aspects comprise all the other laws of a fast, such as not wearing leather shoes and not washing. These are not an integral part of the definition of a fast, and even if a person does not observe these secondary aspects he can still be said to have fasted, as long as he did not actually eat. An application of this distinction is that a person who is sick and eats on a fast day is not permitted to read from the Torah portion at Minḥa (*Shulḥan Arukh, Oraḥ Ḥayyim* 566:6). However, if a sick person wears leather shoes on a fast day but does not eat or drink, he would be permitted to read the Torah.

Based on this distinction between the fundamental aspect of a fast – eating and drinking – and all other aspects of a fast, we can understand *Tosafot*'s assertion that the leniency which permits tasting food on a fast day applies only to a private fast. According to this analysis, tasting is included in the category of the secondary aspects of the fast, similar to wearing leather shoes. Consistent with this view, if one tastes a small amount of food on a fast day, but does not otherwise eat or drink, it is analogous to wearing leather shoes on the fast day – he is still considered

to have fasted, because neither the tasting of food nor the wearing of leather shoes contradicts the basic elements of the fast day. Only the basic elements of a fast – eating and drinking – apply to a private fast. Both elements, primary and secondary, apply to a public fast. This is the rationale of *Tosafot*'s statement that it is permissible to taste food on a private fast – tasting a small amount of food is a secondary prohibition, and secondary prohibitions do not apply to a private fast.

The following distinction constitutes a proof that the secondary prohibitions do not apply to a private fast. If one eats during a private fast he is not required to refrain from eating for the rest of the fast day; if one eats on a public fast day, however, he is required to refrain from eating and to complete the fast for the rest of the day. The reason for this distinction is based on the analysis that on the private fast day, once one has eaten, the basic element of the fast day no longer exists, and it is considered as though he has not fasted at all. There is, therefore, no purpose to resuming the fast on the private fast day. If one eats on a public fast day, however, secondary elements of the fast are applicable, and even if one is considered not to have fasted (because he ate), nonetheless he is still required to fulfill the secondary aspects of the fast. The prohibition against eating for the rest of the day after one has eaten on a public fast day would be considered a secondary aspect of the fast, and therefore is a prohibition which should be fulfilled on a public fast day but not a private fast day.

THE CONCEPT OF ḤATZOT ON TISHA B'AV

Tosafot (*Ta'anit* 30a) rule that when Tisha B'Av falls on Thursday, one may launder clothing and cut one's hair after *ḥatzot* (midday) on Tisha B'Av in honor of Shabbat. Generally, these actions are prohibited from the beginning of the month of Av until the tenth of Av, the day after Tisha B'Av. However, in this instance one need not wait until Friday, as he will be busy then with other Shabbat preparations. This leniency needs to be explained. Why does the halakha distinguish between before and after *ḥatzot* on the day of Tisha B'Av?

Indeed, this distinction is reflected in a number of scenarios in halakha. For example, the *Shulḥan Arukh* (*Oraḥ Ḥayyim* 559:3) states that our practice is to sit on the ground on the eve of Tisha B'Av, and in the morning until Minḥa, or after *ḥatzot*, and only after *ḥatzot* is one permitted

to sit on a chair. The Rama (*Oraḥ Ḥayyim* 554:22) also records that the custom of not performing *melakha* (productive work) on Tisha B'Av extends only until *ḥatzot*. Likewise, the *Shulḥan Arukh* (*Oraḥ Ḥayyim* 555:1) rules that one should don his tallit and tefillin at Minḥa and not at Shaḥarit. At Minḥa, we resume saying "*titkabel*," the verse in Kaddish in which we beseech God to accept our prayers (Rama, *Oraḥ Ḥayyim* 559:4), and we add "*Naḥem*," the prayer for consolation, to the Amida at Minḥa only (ibid. 557:1). These distinctions must be explained in order to understand the nature of *ḥatzot* on Tisha B'Av.

There are three approaches to this question. The Vilna Gaon (*Bi'ur HaGra*, *Oraḥ Ḥayyim* 555) writes that our sages permitted the donning of tallit and tefillin at Minḥa, because it was at *ḥatzot* on the day of Tisha B'Av that our enemies set fire to the *Beit HaMikdash*. God's anger was expressed by the destruction of the physical structure of the Temple, and not through the destruction of the Jewish people. In a sense, there is an element of consolation that exists behind this tragedy, and the Rabbis saw fit, consequently, to reduce the practices of mourning to some degree.

This element of consolation is manifested in the text of Psalm 79 when describing the invasion of the *Beit HaMikdash* by our enemies. The psalm begins, "A song of Assaf; God, the nations have invaded Your heritage. They have defiled Your Temple and laid waste to Jerusalem." Despite the depiction of devastation, the author introduces the psalm as a "song," rather than an elegy or lament. The destruction of the *Beit HaMikdash* reflected an encouraging sign of God's mercy. Therefore, certain aspects of mourning are lifted at the time of Minḥa. Specifically, mourning practices that stem from custom alone and not from formal rabbinic decree are not in force after *ḥatzot*. This may also explain why the *Shulḥan Arukh* (*Oraḥ Ḥayyim* 559:10) permits cooking and baking of foods needed after Tisha B'Av, once *ḥatzot* arrives (see *Bi'ur HaGra* ibid., which offers an alternative understanding).

In the words of the Ritva (see *Beit Yosef*, *Oraḥ Ḥayyim* 557), we find a different approach. Halakha treats the period of time before *ḥatzot* as "*meto mutal lefanav*," as if one's relative who has just deceased lies unburied before him. Each individual who is a relative of the unburied decedent has the status of an "*onen*," and it is prohibited for one who is an *onen* to

be distracted by anything unrelated to the mourning. Indeed, it is this recognition by the halakha that an *onen* is totally preoccupied and absorbed by the bereavement, which exempts an *onen* from all commandments until the deceased relative has been buried. Prior to *ḥatzot* on Tisha B'Av, a Jew is an *onen*, as it were, vis-à-vis the tragedy of the destruction of the *Beit HaMikdash*. Therefore, strict rules of mourning apply, including the requirement to sit on the floor, abstaining from *melakha*, and other limitations on comfort and pleasure. Midday, however, signifies the "*stimat hagolel*," the equivalent of the grave being sealed. In the same way that certain stringencies applicable to *aninut* (the period that one is an *onen*) are lifted when burial is completed, so too, some prohibitions of Tisha B'Av are mitigated at *ḥatzot*.

Based on the Ritva's view that the period before *ḥatzot* on Tisha B'Av has the status of *aninut*, the recital of *Kinot* can be viewed as representing a eulogy for the deceased unburied relative, the *Beit HaMikdash*. Since one must devote all of his energies to crying and eulogizing through the *Kinot*, one is enjoined against performing *melakha* and the wearing of tallit and tefillin during that time. This obligation, however, extends only until *ḥatzot* when the state of *aninut* concludes. Likewise, the other leniencies discussed above may only be applied after *ḥatzot* when the obligation to recite *Kinot* and the status of *aninut* are no longer in effect.

The *Magen Avraham* (*Oraḥ Ḥayyim* 554:1) cites the *Otzar HaGeonim* (*Ta'anit* 113) that records a practice of the Jewish community in Egypt allowing one to wear leather shoes after *ḥatzot* on Tisha B'Av. The *Otzar HaGeonim* implies that this leniency is based on the halakhic concept of "*miktzat hayom kekulo*," that a small portion of a day may be treated as tantamount to a complete day. According to this principle, it would be sufficient to observe the prohibition against wearing leather shoes for half of Tisha B'Av, as this would be halakhically equivalent to observing the prohibition for the entire day. This conclusion, however, demands explanation, as *ḥatzot* is irrelevant to the notion of *miktzat hayom kekulo* as it is generally applied by the halakha. When this principle is found in other areas of halakha, it is applied immediately at the beginning of the day, that is, a small segment of time at the beginning of the day is viewed halakhically as equivalent to the passage of the entire day; there is no requirement that half (or more) of the day needs to have elapsed. If so,

what is the significance of *ḥatzot* in the early termination of the prohibition against wearing leather shoes on Tisha B'Av?

The Talmud (*Ta'anit* 27b) states that on the seventh and final day of *shiva*, all *avelut* (mourning) restrictions are terminated when the visitors who come to perform the mitzva of *niḥum avelim*, consoling the family of the deceased, conclude their visit to the house of the mourners. This early termination of the *avelut* restrictions (before the completion of the last day of *shiva*), is based on the concept of *miktzat hayom kekulo*, though the application of this principle is deferred from the beginning of the day until the visit of consolation is complete. Indeed, this is a unique exception to the manner in which the principle *miktzat hayom kekulo* is applied. It seems that this unusual halakha is reflected in the mourning of Tisha B'Av, as well. While there are no actual visitors to console the mourners on Tisha B'Av, there is a form of *niḥum avelim* which first occurs after *ḥatzot*, when we add the *Naḥem* paragraph to the Amida of Minḥa (see *Beit Yosef, Oraḥ Ḥayyim* 557). Therefore, the mitigation of the stringencies of Tisha B'Av after *ḥatzot* parallels the application of the principle of *miktzat hayom kekulo* in situations of *avelut*.

Alternatively, the Mishna (*Ta'anit* 19a) describes the laws of a *Ta'anit Tzibbur*, (a communal fast) in response to a lack of rain. The opinion of Rabbi Elazar is that if rain begins to fall on a day when a fast has already been declared, the observance of the fast day must be completed only if the rain begins to fall after *ḥatzot*. If rain falls before *ḥatzot*, the laws of the *Ta'anit* no longer apply. Perhaps this indicates that halakha views the beginning of the fast day only from *ḥatzot* and on. Likewise, we may suggest that only after *ḥatzot* on Tisha B'Av, also a *Ta'anit Tzibbur*, can the principle of *miktzat hayom kekulo* apply. Halakhically, *ḥatzot* is the true beginning of the day.

Practically, we do not follow the custom of the Egyptian Jewish community. Rabbi Ḥai Gaon explains that we cannot allow leather shoes after *ḥatzot*, because the prohibition on wearing leather shoes is one of the *inuyim*, the specific prohibitions meant to reduce pleasure on Tisha B'Av. *Miktzat hayom kekulo* can be applied only to restrictions due to *avelut*, and these are not included in the category of *inuyim*. In addition, even after *ḥatzot*, the leniencies that do apply relate to prohibitions that stem from *minhag* (custom), such as not sitting on a chair but on the

floor, not wearing tallit and tefillin, etc. The restriction against wearing shoes was instituted by our sages and so it must be observed the entire day. However, the fundamental understanding of *miktzat hayom kekulo* that emerges may still provide a valid explanation for the laws in which we do apply leniencies after *ḥatzot*.

THE CONCEPT OF *MIKTZAT HAYOM KEKULO* ON TISHA B'AV

The Jewish community in Egypt posed a question to Rabbi Hai Gaon concerning the application of the prohibition forbidding the wearing of leather shoes throughout the entire day of Tisha B'Av. On the surface, the injunction against wearing leather shoes should be governed by the rule of *miktzat hayom kekulo*, a halakhic principle which deems the observance of a portion of the day as the halakhic equivalent of the entire day. Just as the general observance of *avelut* is subject to this guiding principle, so too should the practices of Tisha B'Av be. In one response, Rabbi Hai Gaon characterizes the practices of Tisha B'Av as reflecting the self-abnegation of a fast day, and not the mourning character of a *yom avelut*. For this reason, the laws of Tisha B'Av are not governed by the same set of principles which apply to the area of *avelut*. In a second answer, however, Rabbi Hai Gaon cryptically suggests that "it is inconceivable to observe the rites of mourning for only a portion of the day." At first glance, the distinction between Tisha B'Av and the general observance of mourning for a deceased relative is not readily apparent.

A sharpened understanding of the parameters that delimit the application of the principle of *miktzat hayom kekulo* will illuminate Rabbi Hai Gaon's response. The Gemara presents conflicting evidence regarding the appropriate application of *miktzat hayom kekulo*. On the one hand, the Gemara applies the rule of *miktzat hayom kekulo* even to observances that are self-contained within a single day. For example, the Gemara (*Mo'ed Katan* 20b) asserts that *avelut* in a case of a *shemua reḥoka* (an instance in which an individual learns of the passing of a relative, thirty days subsequent to the moment of death), is observed for a single hour of one day. Similarly, the Mishna (*Megilla* 20a) establishes that a woman who obtains the status of a *zava ketana*, the experience of a bodily emission that demands her observance of a single clean day, is permitted to immerse herself moments after sunrise on the clean day. At the same time,

the Gemara (*Mo'ed Katan* 8a) determines that an individual who inters a parent, acts in accordance with the rites of mourning for the entire day until the evening.

Evidently, the application of the principle of *miktzat hayom kekulo* is reserved for institutions of halakha that require counting. Whether the necessary count entails a single day observance, as in the case of a *shemua rehoka* or a *zava ketana*, or it concludes a succession of days, as in a standard situation of *avelut*, the observance of a small component of the day renders the day counted in its entirety. The occasion of interment does not require the day to be counted; rather, the day should be marked by an atmosphere and demeanor of mourning. Since the interment is not marked by any element of counting, the principle of *miktzat hayom kekulo* is inapplicable, thereby necessitating the observance of *avelut* for the complete day.

A halakhic viewpoint of Rabbi Meir of Rothenburg establishes a firm foundation for the distinction between the observances of mourning that are due to the concept of *sefira*, counting, on the one hand, and a period of time which is marked by an atmosphere of *avelut*, on the other, with respect to the principle of *miktzat hayom kekulo*. There is a general debate amongst the *Rishonim* whether the application of *miktzat hayom kekulo* can be triggered by a component of the evening or whether it is reserved for the partial observance of the daytime (see *Tosafot, Mo'ed Katan* 21b, s.v. *afilu*, and Nahmanides, *Torat HaAdam*, pg. 215). Rabbi Meir of Rothenburg offers an intriguing compromise between the two extreme perspectives. An institution of halakha that entails the counting of days, like the observance of *shiva* or *sheloshim*, requires the observance of a portion of the day for the implementation of *miktzat hayom kekulo*; however, the observance of *shemua rehoka*, which in his view does not result from any count, may be fulfilled with a momentary nighttime observance. Rabbi Meir of Rothenburg assumes that the application of *miktzat hayom kekulo* is reserved for an observance of *avelut* which is rooted in *sefira*, and, in those cases, only the daytime hours qualify for the principle's application. The observance of a *shemua rehoka*, however, does not entail any count, and, as a result, is not governed by the principle of *miktzat hayom kekulo*. It is only due to the nature of the initial enactment, which in its theoretical ideal, only demanded a brief momentary observance, that one is able to fulfill the rites of mourning even at nighttime.

Rabbi Hai Gaon's response to the Jewish community in Egypt is sensible in light of the above analysis. The application of the rules of *avelut* throughout the day of Tisha B'Av results from the strict parameters that govern the application of *miktzat hayom kekulo*. Unlike an ordinary situation of *avelut hadasha* due to the loss of a close relative, the mourning character of Tisha B'Av does not entail any dimension of *sefira*. The day as a whole was designated to mourn the loss of the *Beit HaMikdash*, and as such, each moment carries with it an obligation to engage in the rites of mourning.

An additional interpretation of Rabbi Hai Gaon's second answer may be suggested. The concept of *miktzat hayom kekulo* is reserved for institutions of halakha that possess the quality of being a *melot*. The characterization as a *melot* is generally dependent upon the presence of three factors. Most often, a *melot* entails an observance that is sustained over the course of a succession of days. The rites of mourning observed during *shiva*, the seven clean days of a *zav* and *zava*, and, possibly, the weeklong celebration of *sheva berakhot* following a wedding, are all examples of sustained observances. An additional criterion relates to the coincidence of a certain observance on a particular day. The quality of being a *melot* is reserved for experiences and halakhic institutions which are not tied to a specific calendar date; rather, their presence on a specific date is coincidental. Finally, a halakhic observance adopts the character of a *melot* only if there exists a positive, active dimension to the observance, a positive fulfillment, and not merely a series of abstentions, of passive withdrawal from activity. The coalescence of these three conditions results in an institution's characterization as a *melot*, thereby enabling the application of *miktzat hayom kekulo*. The momentary, positive activity on the final day of the *melot* has the capacity of marking the entirety of the day, and creating a positive fulfillment of the final component of a protracted process. Tisha B'Av, however, is an observance of mourning that is tied to a particular calendar date. Moreover, the day's content is comprised of the restrictions of mourning, not the positive fulfillment of a halakhic norm. As such, the day as a whole is invested with significance, preventing the application of *miktzat hayom kekulo*.

THE SIGNIFICANCE OF *NAḤEM*

In the special blessing of *Naḥem*, which is added on Tisha B'Av to the Minḥa Amida, we ask God to comfort the mourners of Jerusalem, the city that is in mourning, ruined, scorned, and deserted. After the Six Day War, when the city of Jerusalem was being repopulated and rebuilt, there was a movement to change the text of this blessing, as people felt that the words were no longer accurate. This view, however, was mistaken on two accounts. First, we, today, do not have the authority to make any change, no matter how slight, in the sacred texts of our sages. Second, the view is based on a misunderstanding of the halakhic status and significance of Jerusalem. The *kedushat Beit HaMikdash*, the sanctity of the Temple, extends over three components, in decreasing order of sanctity – *Maḥaneh Shekhina* (the *Azara*), *Maḥaneh Leviya* (the Levite Camp), and *Maḥaneh Yisrael* (the Israelite Camp). The *azara* of the *Beit HaMikdash* has the status of *Maḥaneh Shekhina*; the Temple Mount (beyond the actual structure of the *Beit HaMikdash*) has the status of *Maḥaneh Leviya*; and the city of Jerusalem (beyond the Temple Mount) has the status of *Maḥaneh Yisrael*. In this sense, the city of Jerusalem constitutes the outer perimeter of the *Beit HaMikdash* and as such is endowed with special sanctity. For example, *kodashim kalim* (sacrifices with a lesser degree of holiness, such as the *korban Pesaḥ*) must be eaten within the walls of the city. In a similar vein, the Mishna (*Sukka* 3:10) states that originally the *lulav* was taken all seven days, only in the *Beit HaMikdash*, while outside of the *Beit HaMikdash* it was taken only on the first day. This is based on the verse, "And you shall celebrate לִפְנֵי יהוה אֱלֹהֵיכֶם, before the Lord your God, seven days" (Leviticus 23:40), since being within the confines of the *Beit HaMikdash* was deemed to be "before God." Yet Maimonides (Commentary on the Mishna) states that this elevated status of being "before God," includes all of Jerusalem. Similarly, although the Mishna (*Rosh HaShana* 4:1) states that the practice was to blow *shofar* on Rosh HaShana that fell on Shabbat in the *Mikdash*, Maimonides (Commentary on the Mishna) explains that the term *Mikdash* is often used to refer to the entire city of Jerusalem. Based on the foregoing, it is apparent that the city of Jerusalem is imbued with a component of the sanctity of the *Beit HaMikdash*. Consequently, as long as the *Beit HaMikdash* is in a state of destruction, we cannot consider the city of Jerusalem to be rebuilt.

WHERE NAḤEM IS RECITED

The Talmud Yerushalmi says that we should say *Naḥem* in the blessing of *Avoda*. *Beit Yosef* (557) quotes the Rif and the Rosh, who say that the tradition is to say it in the blessing of *"Boneh Yerushalayim."* The root of this dispute seems to depend on what loss we are mourning on Tisha B'Av. The Talmud Yerushalmi thinks that the crucial element of the mourning is the cessation of the sacrifices, and therefore we should say *Naḥem* in *Avoda*. However, our tradition focuses on the mourning over the destruction of the Temple and of Jerusalem; therefore, we say *Naḥem* in *"Boneh Yerushalayim."*

NE'ILA ON TISHA B'AV

The Gemara (*Pesaḥim* 54b) states in the name of Rabbi Yoḥanan that Tisha B'Av is unlike all other public fast days. While on other public fast days we recite *Ne'ila*, the *Ne'ila* service is not recited on Tisha B'Av. This calls for an explanation.

The *Ne'ila* prayer is uniquely associated with fast days. It is the additional prayer, not recited on any other day, which requests that all of our other prayers be accepted. Therefore Yom Kippur, the fast day *par excellence*, has *Ne'ila* as its conclusion and climax. We see the association between *Ne'ila* and fasting borne out in the ruling of Rav Ḥayyim Brisk that if a Jew must eat on Yom Kippur, he should not recite *Ne'ila*.

On Tisha B'Av, however, this special prayer which implores God to accept all of our prayers is inappropriate. It is about Tisha B'Av that the prophet Jeremiah declared (Lamentations 3:8) "שָׂתַם תְּפִלָּתִי, He shut out my prayer." On Tisha B'Av, God closes the gates of prayer and is not attentive to our pleas. Tisha B'Av is a day of mourning; it is not a day of prayer. It is for this same reason that on Tisha B'Av, we omit the phrase "תִּתְקַבֵּל צְלוֹתְהוֹן, Let our prayers be accepted," from Kaddish. Similarly, we do not recite *Taḥanun* on Tisha B'Av. Maimonides (*Hilkhot Tefilla* 5:1 and 13) explains that the bowing that one performs during *Taḥanun* is the completing component of *tefilla*. One can well understand why *Taḥanun* is omitted in light of the somber theme of *"satam tefillati"* which characterizes Tisha B'Av.

However, one may question the above explanation as to why *Ne'ila* is not recited on Tisha B'Av. After midday on Tisha B'Av, there is a marked

shift in the character of the day, from one of mourning to one of consolation. In the Minḥa Amida we include the *Naḥem* paragraph, whose theme is consolation, and we resume recitation of the phrase *"titkabel tzelotehon"* in Kaddish. Apparently in the afternoon of Tisha B'Av, we have moved past the period of *"satam tefillati"* to a time for consolation. (Although we do not recite *Taḥanun* at Minḥa on Tisha B'Av, this might be due to the concept, almost paradoxical, that in some sense Tisha B'Av contains an element of *Mo'ed*, a festival.) Why then, do we not recite *Ne'ila*?

Rabbi Moshe Soloveitchik was of the view that if one did not recite the first four prayer services on Yom Kippur (Ma'ariv, Shaḥarit, Musaf and Minḥa) then one may not recite *Ne'ila*. Since *Ne'ila* is the prayer in which we ask that all of our prayers recited on the Fast should be accepted, it is not meaningful unless we have recited the other prayers. Rabbi Moshe was uncertain if one is permitted to recite *Ne'ila* if one missed only one of the prayer services of Yom Kippur but recited the others. Do we say that since *Ne'ila* is a prayer for our other prayers to be accepted, it is a condition for the recitation of *Ne'ila* that *all* the other prayers be said; or is the condition for recitation of *Ne'ila* satisfied if only one or two, but not all, of the prayer services of the day were recited?

If we were to explain that the recitation of *Ne'ila* is contingent on *all of* the prayers of the day being recited, then we can understand why we do not recite *Ne'ila* on Tisha B'Av. Even though Minḥa is recited in the afternoon of Tisha B'Av, when the spirit of consolation begins to emerge, since the first two prayer services of Tisha B'Av (Ma'ariv and Shaḥarit) were offered during the period of *"satam tefillati,"* we cannot ask that they be accepted. Unless we can request that all of the prayers of the day be accepted, we do not recite *Ne'ila*.

הלכות

HALAKHA GUIDE

Abbreviations

A.H. = *Arukh HaShulḥan*
B.H. = *Biur Halakha*
E.Y. = *Even Yisrael (Fischer)*
K.H. = *Kaf HaḤayyim*
K.S.A. = *Kitzur Shulḥan Arukh*
M.B. = *Mishna Berura*
M.H. = *Mipi HaShemua*
N.H. = *Nefesh HaRav*
O.Ḥ. = *Oraḥ Ḥayyim*
S.A. = *Shulḥan Arukh*
S.H. = *Shiurei HaRav, Inyanei Tisha B'Av*
S.S.K. = *Shemirat Shabbat Kehilkhata*
S.T. = *Sha'ar HaTziyun*
S.Te. = *Sha'arei Teshuva*
Y.O. = *Yabia Omer*

DIGEST OF TISHA B'AV LAWS

THREE WEEKS

1. The period of the Three Weeks commences with the evening of (before) the seventeenth of Tammuz and continues through midday after Tisha B'Av (S.H. 2, 31).
2. During the Three Weeks, one is not permitted to (a) take a haircut or shave (Rama, O.Ḥ. 551:4), (b) get married or participate in a wedding (Rama, O.Ḥ. 551:2), (c) listen to music (M.B. 551:16), or (d) recite the *Sheheḥeyanu* blessing (Rama, O.Ḥ. 551:17).
3. One is permitted to sing, dance and recite *Sheheḥeyanu* on Shabbat (M.B. 551:98).

NINE DAYS

4. The Nine Days commence with the evening of (before) Rosh Ḥodesh Av and continue until midday of the tenth of Av (M.B. 551:58).
5. In addition to the restrictions of the Three Weeks, during the Nine Days one is not permitted to (a) eat meat (including fowl) (S.A., O.Ḥ. 551:9–10; M.B. 551:58), (b) drink wine (ibid.), (c) expand one's business (S.A., O.Ḥ. 551:2), (d) build items that bring pleasure or make preparations for joyous events (ibid.), (e) wash or iron clothes, or (f) wear new or newly washed clothes (Rama, O.Ḥ. 551:3).
6. If a *Se'udat Mitzva*, meal in connection with a mitzva, takes place during the Nine Days, such as a *Siyum* or Brit Mila, one may eat meat at that meal (Rama, O.Ḥ. 551:10).
7. One may eat meat and drink wine on Shabbat, but for Havdala, one should give the wine to a child to drink. If one cannot do that, one may use wine (Rama, O.Ḥ. 551:10).

8 Grape juice is included in the prohibition of wine and therefore one may not drink it (E.Y. vol. 9, p. 110).

9 The general custom is to forbid bathing for pleasure during the Nine Days (S.A., O.Ḥ. 551:16).

10 There is a custom to postpone lawsuits against gentiles until after this inauspicious month, or at least until after Tisha B'Av (S.A., O.Ḥ. 551:1; M.B. 551:2).

RESTRICTIONS OF TISHA B'AV

On Tisha B'Av one is not permitted to (1) eat or drink, (2) wash one's body, (3) anoint oneself, (4) wear leather shoes, or (5) engage in marital relations (S.A., O.Ḥ. 554:1).

1. Eating and Drinking

11 One is not permitted to put any food or drink in one's mouth, even if one spits it out without swallowing (S.A., O.Ḥ. 567:1).

12 Someone who is ill and needs to eat, and a woman up to thirty days after childbirth, may eat on Tisha B'Av (S.A., O.Ḥ. 554:6). If Tisha B'Av falls on a Sunday, these individuals should recite Havdala before eating (S.Te. 556:1).

13 If one eats bread on Tisha B'Av, when one recites *Birkat HaMazon* one should begin the third blessing with the word "*Naḥem*" instead of the usual "*Raḥem*" (Rama, O.Ḥ. 557:1; N.H. p. 198).

2. Washing

14 One is not allowed to wash one's hands or even dip one's finger in water (S.A., O.Ḥ. 554:7). However, one may rinse dirt off with water (S.A., O.Ḥ. 554:9).

15 When one awakens in the morning, one should wash one's hands only up to the knuckles (S.A., O.Ḥ. 554:10). The same should be done after one uses the facilities, although if necessary one may wash any dirty area of one's hands even beyond the knuckles (A.H., O.Ḥ. 554:10). If one is allowed to eat and needs to wash his hands for bread, he washes all the way to the wrist (S.S.K. ch. 39, n.101).

16 One may prepare food for children or for after the fast, even if the consequence is that one's hands get wet (M.B. 554:19).

3. Anointing

17 One is allowed to anoint oneself for any purpose that is not pleasurable (S.A., O.Ḥ. 554:15). This includes medical ointments and deodorant (B.H. 554:15).

4. Leather Shoes

18 One may wear any shoe that is not made of leather (S.A., O.Ḥ. 554:16).

19 If one has no other options, one may wear leather shoes but must take them off as soon as possible (S.A., O.Ḥ. 554:17).

Other Restrictions

20 One may not study Torah on Tisha B'Av except for melancholy passages in Torah texts, the laws of mourning and Tisha B'Av, and works of *Musar* (S.A., O.Ḥ. 554:1; Y.O. 2:26).

21 One is not required to omit any Torah passage that is part of the regular daily prayer service (S.A., O.Ḥ. 554:4).

22 One may not greet another person with a verbal greeting such as "Hello" or "Good morning." If someone greets you, you may respond in a serious tone (S.A., O.Ḥ. 554:20).

23 One may not sit on a chair until after midday (taking into account the extra hour of daylight saving time). Until then, one should sit on the floor or a low chair (S.A., O.Ḥ. 559:3; N.H. p. 253).

24 One should not work before midday unless refraining from work will result in a significant and irretrievable loss (S.A., O.Ḥ. 554:22–24).

EREV TISHA B'AV

25 Some have the custom not to learn Torah on the afternoon before Tisha B'Av other than such passages that are permitted on Tisha B'Av, but many authorities are lenient because of the importance of Torah study (A.H., O.Ḥ. 553:4). However, all agree that one should not take a pleasure trip or even an enjoyable stroll on the afternoon before Tisha B'Av (Rama, O.Ḥ. 553:2).

26 The custom is to eat a large meal before Minḥa that will sustain one through the fast (Rama, O.Ḥ. 552:9). This is in addition to the later *Se'uda HaMafseket*.

27 *Taḥanun* (on Shabbat, "*Tzidkatekha*") is omitted from Minḥa (S.A., O.Ḥ. 552:12, 559:1).

28 After Minḥa, one eats the *Se'uda HaMafseket*, the final meal before the fast. At this meal, one may not eat more than one cooked item (S.A., O.Ḥ. 552:1). One should drink less than usual at this meal (Rama, O.Ḥ. 552:1). The custom is to sit on the floor and eat bread and a hard-boiled egg with ashes (Rama, O.Ḥ. 552:5–7).

29 Three adult males should not eat together to avoid having to say *Birkat HaMazon* with a *zimmun* (S.A., O.Ḥ. 552:8).

30 On Shabbat, one eats as usual and does not have to observe any of the restrictions of a *Se'uda HaMafseket* (S.A., O.Ḥ. 552:10). However, one must cease eating by sundown (Rama, O.Ḥ. 552:10).

31 The fast begins at sundown and all restrictions begin at that time (S.A., O.Ḥ. 553:2).

32 If Tisha B'Av falls on Shabbat, the fast is held on Sunday (S.A., O.Ḥ. 550:3). Shabbat is observed as usual except that marital relations are forbidden (Rama, O.Ḥ. 554:19).

MA'ARIV

33 For Ma'ariv, we remove the curtain from the Ark and dim the lighting. After *Barekhu*, one sits on the floor or a low seat (Rama, O.Ḥ., 559:1–3).

34 If Tisha B'Av begins on Motza'ei Shabbat, one may not make any preparations for Tisha B'Av, including bringing *kinot* or alternate shoes to shul, until after Shabbat is over. Many people bring them on Friday, before Shabbat begins. One removes weekday shoes after saying *Barekhu* at Ma'ariv but one should be careful not to dirty one's hands before prayer (Rama, O.Ḥ. 553:2; M.B. 553:6). Alternatively, one may take off one's shoes after saying "*Barukh HaMavdil*" as a form of Havdala, after nightfall but before Ma'ariv (S.S.K. ch. 28, n. 179).

35 Ma'ariv proceeds as usual until after the Kaddish following the Amida. On Motza'ei Shabbat, one recites *Ata Ḥonantanu* in Ma'ariv and then one recites Kaddish immediately after the Amida.

36 On Motza'ei Shabbat, after Kaddish one lights a Havdala candle and recites the "*Boreh Me'orei HaEsh*" blessing. The rest of Havdala is delayed until after Tisha B'Av (S.A., O.Ḥ. 556:1; M.B. 556:1).

37. After Kaddish (or Havdala), the *Shaliaḥ Tzibbur* reads *Eikha* followed by *kinot* (Rama, O.Ḥ. 559:2).
38. Following *kinot*, even on Motza'ei Shabbat, the congregation says *VeAta Kadosh* (omitting the verse *"VaAni Zot Beriti"* – M.B. 559:6), followed by Kaddish without *Titkabal* (Rama, O.Ḥ. 559:4), and Aleinu.

SHAḤARIT

39. Men do not wear tallit and tefillin in the morning, although they put on a *tallit katan* (tzitzit) without a blessing when they get dressed in the morning (S.A., O.Ḥ. 555:1).
40. Shaḥarit proceeds as usual, but without sitting in regular chairs. In the repetition of the Amida, the *Shaliaḥ Tzibbur* adds *Anenu* (M.B. 557:13) and omits *Birkat Kohanim* (K.S.A. 124:3). One does not say *Taḥanun* (S.A., O.Ḥ. 131:7).
41. The appropriate Torah portion for Tisha B'Av is read, followed by Kaddish and Haftara, and the Torah is returned to the Ark.
42. The congregation then recites *kinot*. During the recitation of *kinot*, one may not conduct idle conversations that distract one from the mourning (S.A., O.Ḥ. 559:5).
43. After *kinot*, the congregation recites *Ashrei* and continues to Aleinu, omitting *LaMenatze'aḥ* and the verse *"VaAni Zot Beriti"* from *Uva LeTziyon*. Kaddish is recited without *Titkabal* (Rama, O.Ḥ. 559:4). The psalm of the day is omitted (K.S.A. 124:3).

MINḤA

44. The curtain is returned to the Ark before Minḥa (K.H. 559:19).
45. Before Minḥa, men put on tallit and tefillin with blessings and wear them until after Minḥa (S.A., O.Ḥ. 555:1).
46. The psalm of the day, which was omitted at the end of Shaḥarit, is now recited, followed by *Ashrei* and Kaddish (K.S.A. 124:19). Then the Torah scroll is removed from the Ark, the customary portion for the fast days (*Vayeḥal*) is read, and the Haftara is recited (M.B. 566:3). After the Torah is returned to the Ark, the *Shaliaḥ Tzibbur* recites Kaddish, which is followed by the silent Amida.

47 During the silent Amida, one adds *Naḥem* in the *"Boneh Yerushalayim"* blessing and *Anenu* in the *"Shomei'a Tefilla"* blessing (S.A., O.Ḥ. 557:1). If one is not fasting, then one says *Naḥem* but not *Anenu* (B.H. 565:1). One says *Sim Shalom* instead of the usual *Shalom Rav* (Rama, O.Ḥ. 127:2).

48 If one forgets to say *Naḥem*, one may insert it into the *"HaMaḥazir Shekhinato"* blessing before the word *"Veteḥezena."* In such a case, one concludes the blessing with *"HaMaḥazir"* and not *"Menaḥem Tziyon"* (M.B. 557:2). If one already finished that blessing, one does not insert *Naḥem* at all and just continues praying. If one forgets to say *Anenu*, one may insert it at the end of the Amida, before *Elokai Netzor* (M.B. 119:19).

49 In the repetition of the Amida, the *Shaliaḥ Tzibbur* says *Anenu* after the *"Go'el Yisrael"* blessing, and *Naḥem* in the *"Boneh Yerushalayim"* blessing. He also says *Birkat Kohanim* and *Sim Shalom*.

50 In the event the *Shaliaḥ Tzibbur* forgets to say *Anenu* in the repetition of the Amida, if he has not yet finished the next blessing (*Refa'enu*) then he should say *Anenu* and then begin *Refa'enu* again. If he has finished that blessing, then he should insert *Anenu* into the *"Shomei'a Tefilla"* blessing (Rama, O.Ḥ. 119:4).

THE END OF TISHA B'AV

51 A regular Ma'ariv service is prayed.

52 On Sunday night, one says Havdala over a cup of wine but without the introductory verses and without a flame or spices (S.A., O.Ḥ. 556:1).

53 One should eat and put on one's shoes before reciting *Kiddush Levana* (M.B. 426:11). However, if that is not possible, one may recite *Kiddush Levana* even before eating and putting on shoes (S.T. 426:9).

54 The restrictions of the Nine Days are still in effect until midday on the tenth of Av, the day after Tisha B'Av. Therefore, one may not eat meat, drink wine, wash clothes, bathe in a pleasing way, take a haircut or shave, until midday after Tisha B'Av (S.A., O.Ḥ. 558:1; N.H. 31). However, if Tisha B'Av falls on Thursday, one may wash clothes, bathe, take a haircut and shave in order to prepare for Shabbat (M.B. 558:3). If Tisha B'Av is deferred from Shabbat to Sunday, one need not observe all these restrictions after the fast ends, with the exception of eating meat and drinking wine which are still prohibited the night following the fast (Rama, O.Ḥ. 558:1).

MOURNER'S KADDISH

Mourner: Yitgadal ve-yitkadash shemeh raba. (*Cong:* Amen)
Be-alema di vera khir'uteh, ve-yamlikh malkhuteh,
be-ḥayeikhon, uv-yomeikhon, uv-ḥayei de-khol beit Yisrael,
ba-agala uvi-zman kariv, ve-imru Amen. (*Cong:* Amen)

All: Yeheh shemeh rabba mevarakh le'alam ul-alemei alemaya.

Mourner: Yitbarakh ve-yishtabaḥ ve-yitpa'ar ve-yitromam ve-yitnaseh
ve-yit-hadar ve-yit'aleh ve-yit-hallal
shemeh dekudsha, berikh hu. (*Cong:* Berikh hu)
Le-ela min kol birkhata
ve-shirata tushbeḥata v'neḥemata, da-amiran be-alema,
ve-imru, Amen. (*Cong:* Amen)

Yeheh shelama raba min shemaya
ve-ḥayyim aleinu ve-al kol Yisrael,
ve-imru Amen. (*Cong:* Amen)

*Bow, take three steps back, as if taking leave of the Divine Presence,
then bow, first left, then right, then center, while saying:*

Oseh shalom
bim-romav,
hu ya'aseh shalom aleinu, ve-al kol Yisrael,
ve-imru Amen.

RABBIS' KADDISH

Mourner: Yitgadal ve-yitkadash shemeh raba. (*Cong:* Amen)
Be-alema di vera khir'uteh, ve-yamlikh malkhuteh,
be-hayeikhon, uv-yomeikhon, uv-hayei de-khol beit Yisrael,
ba-agala uvi-zman kariv, ve-imru Amen. (*Cong:* Amen)

All: Yeheh shemeh rabba mevarakh le'alam ul-alemei alemaya.

Mourner: Yitbarakh ve-yishtabah ve-yitpa'ar ve-yitromam ve-yitnaseh
ve-yit-hadar ve-yit'aleh ve-yit-hallal
shemeh dekudsha, berikh hu. (*Cong:* Berikh hu)
Le-ela min kol birkhata
ve-shirata tushbehata v'nehemata, da-amiran be-alema,
ve-imru, Amen. (*Cong:* Amen)

Al Yisrael, ve-al rabanan,
ve-al talmideihon, ve-al kol talmidei talmideihon,
ve-al kol man de-asekin be-oraita
di be-atra (*In Israel:* kadisha) ha-dein ve-di be-khol atar va-atar,
yeheh lehon ul-khon shelama raba,
hina ve-hisda, ve-rahamei,
ve-hayei arichei, um-zonei re-vihei,
u-furkana min kodam avuhon di vish-maya, ve-imru Amen.

Yeheh shelama raba min shemaya
ve-hayyim (tovim) aleinu ve-al kol Yisrael,
ve-imru Amen. (*Cong:* Amen)

*Bow, take three steps back, as if taking leave of the Divine Presence,
then bow, first left, then right, then center, while saying:*

Oseh shalom
bim-romav,
hu ya'aseh ve-rahamav shalom aleinu, ve-al kol Yisrael,
ve-imru Amen.